Yearbook on
International
Communist Affairs
1991

Yearbook on International Communist Affairs

1991

Parties and Revolutionary Movements

EDITOR: Richard F. Staar

MANAGING EDITOR: Margit N. Grigory

AREA EDITORS

Africa	•	Thomas H. Henriksen
The Americas	•	William Ratliff
Asia and the Pacific	•	Ramon H. Myers
Eastern Europe and the	•	Richard F. Staar
Soviet Union		Robert Conquest
The Middle East and	•	James H. Noyes
North Africa		
Western Europe	•	Dennis L. Bark

HOOVER INSTITUTION PRESS
Stanford University, Stanford, California

The text of this work is set in Times Roman;
display headings are in Melior. Typeset by
Harrison Typesetting, Inc., Portland, Oregon.
Printed and bound by Braun-Brumfield, Inc.,
Ann Arbor, Michigan.

Hoover Press Publication 408

International Standard Book Number 0-8179-9161-1
International Standard Serial Number 0084-4101
Library of Congress Catalog Number 67-31024

Contents

ASIA AND THE PACIFIC

EASTERN EUROPE AND THE SOVIET UNION

THE MIDDLE EAST AND NORTH AFRICA

WESTERN EUROPE

Preface

With this volume, we celebrate a quarter century of the *Yearbook* and its 25th consecutive volume. Over the years the *Yearbook* has chronicled the domestic and international activities of nonruling communist parties, national liberation movements, and ruling parties that regard Moscow or Beijing as their guiding lights. This past year we have continued to trace the momentous changes and subsequent metamorphoses of various communist parties into quasi-democratic, self-proclaimed socialist movements or loose federations. Entrenched Marxist parties remain, such as the ruling regimes in North Korea, Cuba, and Albania (although its hard-line facade has developed some cracks) and those that depend on violent guerrilla activities to bring about Marxist or Maoist dominance, such as the Shining Path in Peru and the Communist Party of the Philippines. In many countries, communist parties as such no longer exist; as nearly as we can determine from the scant information available, they are represented only in clandestine or exiled cells, such as those in Thailand, Malaysia, and Burma.

This 1991 volume includes 125 country profiles, three essays on international communist organizations, and an essay on Soviet propaganda themes by a total of 81 authors, as well as several brief biographies following certain essays. A cumulative index of biographies follows the bibliography. Information has been collected throughout the year, primarily from published sources such as domestic and foreign newspapers, communist party publications, journals, and transcripts of broadcasts that are monitored and translated by the U.S. Foreign Broadcast Information Service. Dates without a year in the text refer to 1990, the period under review.

When is a party a communist party at times defies precise definition; we have included parties or governments whose existence may not be acknowledged by Moscow, although they seem to be following the Communist Party of the Soviet Union's line in organization, policies, and rhetoric, as well as participating in activities of communist front organizations. The "vanguard revolutionary democracies" such as Zimbabwe seem to have strong connections to the international communist movement. Less clearly defined cases are discussed in the introduction to this volume.

To the librarians and staff of the Hoover Institution, our thanks for their assistance in checking information and contributing to the bibliography.

Richard F. Staar
Editor in Chief

Margit N. Grigory
Managing Editor

The following abbreviations are used for frequently cited publications and news agencies:

CSM	*Christian Science Monitor*
FBIS-AFR	*Foreign Broadcast Information Service-Africa*
FBIS-CHI	*Foreign Broadcast Information Service-China*
FBIS-EAS	*Foreign Broadcast Information Service-East Asia*
FBIS-EEU	*Foreign Broadcast Information Service-Eastern Europe*
FBIS-LAT	*Foreign Broadcast Information Service-Latin America*
FBIS-NES	*Foreign Broadcast Information Service-Near East and Southern Asia*
FBIS-SOV	*Foreign Broadcast Information Service-Soviet Union*
FBIS-WEU	*Foreign Broadcast Information Service-Western Europe*
FEER	*Far Eastern Economic Review*
HUM	*L'Humanité*
JPRS-EEU	*Joint Publications Research Service-Eastern Europe*
JPRS-LAT	*Joint Publications Research Service-Latin America*
JPRS-WEU	*Joint Publications Research Service-Western Europe*
LAT	*Los Angeles Times*
ND	*Neues Deutschland*
NYT	*New York Times*
UN	*L'Unità*
VS	*Volksstimme*

WMR	*World Marxist Review*	ČTK	Československá Tisková Kancelář
WP	*Washington Post*	DPA	Deutsche Presse Agentur
WSJ	*Wall Street Journal*	EFE	Agencia EFE, Spanish News Agency
YICA	*Yearbook on International Communist Affairs*	KPL	Khaosan Pathet Lao
		MENA	Middle East News Agency
ACAN	Agencia Central Americano Noticias	MTI	Magyar Távirati Iroda
ADN	Allgemeiner Deutscher Nachrichtendienst	NCNA	New China News Agency
AFP	Agence France-Presse	PAP	Polska Agencja Prasowa
ANSA	Agenzia Nazionale Stampa Associata	RFE	Radio Free Europe
AP	Associated Press	RL	Radio Liberty
BBC	British Broadcasting Corporation	TASS	Telegrafnoe Agentstvo Sovetskogo Soiuza
BTA	Bulgarska Telegrafna Agentsiia	UPI	United Press International
CANA	Caribbean News Agency	VNA	Vietnam News Agency

Party Congresses, National Conferences, and Elections

Country	Congress	Date (1990)
Hungary (HSWP)	14th, 2d round	27 January
Austria	27th	19–21 January
Denmark (DKP)	29th Extraordinary	20–21 January and
	30th	14–15 April
Yugoslavia	14th Extraordinary	21 January and
		25 May
Bulgaria (BCP)	14th	30 January–
		2 February
(BSP)	39th (new numbering)	22–25 September
Berlin (SEW)	Extraordinary	17–18 February
(SI)	Founding	28–29 April
Finland (SKP)	22d	23–25 February
Senegal (PIT)	3d	23–25 March
Germany, West (DKP)	10th	26–27 March
Mongolia	20th Extraordinary	10–13 April
San Marino	12th	27–29 April
Finland (Left Alliance, VL)	Founding	29 April
Israel	21st	21–23 May
Portugal	13th Special	18–20 May
Sweden (Left Party)	29th	23–26 May
Ireland	20th (reconvened)	26–27 May
Australia (New Left Party)	Founding	9–11 June
Netherlands	Extraordinary	10 June
Afghanistan	2d	27–28 June
USSR	28th	2–13 July
Japan	19th	9–13 July
Venezuela	8th	25–27 August
Costa Rica (PVP)	17th	14–16 September
Denmark (KF)	1st	29–30 September
Cyprus (AKEL)	17th	3–7 October
(ADISOK)	1st	7–8 July
Canada	28th	5–8 October
Uruguay	22d	5–8 October
Czechoslovakia (KSČ=KSČS)	18th	3–4 November
Luxembourg	26th	10–11 November
Mexico (PRD)	1st	16–20 November
Bolivia (renewal faction)	6th	23–25 November
(majority faction)	6th	December
New Zealand	24th	1–4 December
Congo	4th Extraordinary	3–10 December

Angola (MPLA-PT)	3d	4–9 December
Great Britain	42d Special	9 December
Argentina	17th	13 December
Algeria	1st (legal)	16–17 December
France	27th	18–22 December

Country	*National Conferences*	*Date (1990)*
Chile		May
Spain (PCE)	6th	April
Cambodia	Cadres	5–12 April
Romania (NSF)	1st	7–10 April
Switzerland		19–20 May
Brazil (PT)		June
Guadeloupe		December

1990 ELECTIONS

Country	Type	Date (1990)
Costa Rica	General	15 February
Japan	Parliament	18 February
Nicaragua	General	25 February
Colombia	Parliament	11 March
	Constituent Assembly	7 December
Grenada	Parliament	13 March
Germany, East (GDR)	Parliament	18 March
Australia	General	24 March
Hungary	Parliament	25 March and 8 April
Zimbabwe	President and Parliament	28 March
Greece	Parliament	8–9 April
Peru	President and Parliament	8 April and 10 June
Korea, North	Parliament	22 April
Dominican Republic	General	16 May
Romania	President and Parliament	20, 29 May
Syria	General	22 May
Burma	Parliament	27 May
Czechoslovakia	Parliament	8–9 June
Bulgaria	Parliament and President	10, 17 June
Ecuador	Parliament	17 June
Mongolia	Parliament	26, 29 July
Brazil	Parliament	3 October, 25 November
Austria	Parliament	7 October
New Zealand	Parliament	27 October
Egypt	Parliament	10 November
Guatemala	General	11 November
Poland	President	25 November and 9 December
Germany (united)	Parliament	2 December
Denmark	Parliament	12 December
Haiti	General	16 December

Register of Communist Parties

Status: * ruling   # unrecognized
            + legal   0 proscribed

Country: Party(ies)/Date Founded	Mid-1990 Population (est.) (World Fact Book)	Communist Party Membership (claimed or est.)	Party Leader (general sec.)	Status	Last Congress	Last Election (percentage of vote; seats in legislature)
AFRICA (11)						
Angola Popular Movement for the Liberation of Angola (MPLA), 1956 (MPLA-PT, 1977)	8,534,483	45,000 cl.	José Eduardo dos Santos	*	Third 4–9 Dec. 1990	(1986); all 203 MPLA approved
Benin People's Revolutionary Party of Benin (PRPB), 1975	4,673,964	300 est.	Mathieu Kérékou (chairman, CC)	+	Second 18–24 Nov. 1985	89.6 (1989); all 206 PRPB approved
Congo Congolese Party of Labor (PCT), 1969	2,242,274	10,000 cl. (Nguesso, at 4th congress)	Denis Sassou-Nguesso (chairman)	*	Fifth 3–10 Dec. 1990	95.0 (1984); all 153 PCT approved
Ethiopia Workers' Party of Ethiopia (WPE), 1984	51,666,622	25,000 est.	Mengistu Haile Mariam	*	First (Const.) 6–10 Sept. 1984	85.0 (1987); 835 WPE members
Lesotho Communist Party of Lesotho (CPL), 1962	1,754,664	no data	Jacob M. Kena	0 (tolerated)	Seventh "early 1987"	(1985)

Country: Party(ies)/Date Founded	Mid-1990 Population (est.) (World Fact Book)	Communist Party Membership (claimed or est.)	Party Leader (general sec.)	Status	Last Congress	Last Election (percentage of vote; seats in legislature)
Mozambique Front for the Liberation of Mozambique (FRELIMO), 1962	15,700,000	201,440 cl. (Southscan, Aug. 1989; Horizon, no. 9, 1989)	Joaquim Albert Chissano	*	Fifth 24–30 July 1989	(1986); incomplete
Réunion Réunion Communist Party (PCR), 1959	596,583 (1990 French census, Témoignages, 4 July)	2,000 est.	Paul Vergès	+	Fifth 12–14 July 1980	35.0 (1988); 13 of 44 left coal., 9 for PCR (local assembly), 2 in Paris
Senegal Independence and Labor Party (PIT), 1957	7,713,851	no data	Amath Dansoko	+	Third 23–25 March 1990	0.84 (1988); none
Democratic League/Movement for the Party Labor (LD/MPT)			Abdoulaye Bathily		Third 16–17 Feb. 1990	1988; none
South Africa South African Communist Party (SACP), 1921	39,549,941	no data	Joe Slovo Dan Tloome (chairman)	0/+ + as of 2 Feb.	Seventh June 1989 in Havana (Africa Confidential, 12 Jan.)	n/a
Sudan Sudanese Communist Party (SCP), 1946	24,971,806	9,000 est.	Muhammad Ibrahim Nugud Mansur	0	Fourth (legal) 31 Oct. 1967	1.67 (1986); 5 of 301, 2 in territ., 3 in grad. constituencies
Zimbabwe Zimbabwe African National Union–Patriotic Front (ZANU-PF), 1989	10,392,161	2,125,903 (Pravda, 20 Dec. 1989)	Robert G. Mugabe (president and first secretary)	*	First (united) 18–22 Dec. 1989 (founding)	80.0 (1990); 117 of 120 elected seats (30 are appointed)
TOTAL	167,801,349	2,418,643				

THE AMERICAS (28)

Country / Party	Population		Leadership	Membership	Congress	Elections
Argentina Communist Party of Argentina (PCA), 1918	32,290,066	+	Patricio Echegaray Athos Fava (chairman)	80,000 cl.	Seventeenth 13 Dec. 1990	3.5 (1989); none in United Left coal. (1 for MAS in coal.)
Bolivia Communist Party of Bolivia (PCB), 1950	6,706,854	+	Humberto Ramírez to Dec. Jorge Ibanez from Dec. (majority faction)	500 cl.	Sixth Dec. 1990	7.28 (1989); 12 of 130 are in United Left (IU) coalition (PCB's share of 12 is not known)
(split 1985, minority faction)			Simon Reyes and Marcos Domic (minority faction)			
(split again, 1990, Renewal and Change faction)			Oscar Salas (one of four leaders, Renewal and Change faction)	500 cl.	Sixth 23–25 Nov. 1990	
Brazil Brazilian Communist Party (PCB), 1922	152,505,077	+	Salomão Malina (chairman)	130,000 cl. (*Pravda*, 9 Apr.)	Eighth (called National Meeting of Communists) 17–20 July 1987	(1990); 5 of 586
Canada Communist Party of Canada (CPC), 1921	26,538,229	+	George Hewison William Kashtan (chairman)	3,000 est.	Twenty-eighth 5–8 Oct. 1990	.09 (1988); none
Chile Communist Party of Chile (CPC), 1922	13,082,842	0/+ (legal as of 15 Oct.)	Volodia Teitelboim	48,000 est.	Fifteenth 5–12 May 1989	ca. 6.0 (1989); none; candidates via coalition of Broad Party of Socialist Left (PAIS)

Country: Party(ies)/Date Founded	Mid-1990 Population (est.) (World Fact Book)	Communist Party Membership (claimed or est.)	Party Leader (general sec.)	Status	Last Congress	Last Election (percentage of vote; seats in legislature)
Colombia Communist Party of Colombia (PCC), 1930	33,076,188	18,000 est. (incl. youth org.)	Gilberto Vieira White	+	Fifteenth 12–15 Dec. 1988	1.2 (1990); 7 of 199 as part of Patriotic Union
Costa Rica Popular Vanguard Party (PVP), 1931	3,032,795	7,500 est. (for all left parties)	Humberto Vargas Carbonell	+	Seventeenth 14–16 Sept. 1990	0.8 (1990); 3 of 57
Costa Rican People's Party (PPC), split from PVP, 1984		no data	Lenin Chacón Vargas	+	Fifteenth 23–24 Aug. 1987	(1990); 1 of 57, United People's Coalition
Cuba Cuban Communist Party (PCC), 1965	10,620,099	600,000 est. (*Pravda*, 22 May)	Fidel Castro Ruz	*	Third 4–7 Feb. and 30 Nov.–2 Dec. 1986	(1986); all 499 PCC approved
Dominican Republic Dominican Communist Party (PCD), 1944	7,240,793	700 est.	Narciso Isa Conde	+	Fourth 16–19 Mar. 1989	(1990) boycotted vote
Ecuador Communist Party of Ecuador (PCE), 1928	10,506,668	5,000 est.	René Mauge Mosquera (member of Parliament)	+	Eleventh 21–23 July 1988	3.6 (1990): 2 of 72, Broad Leftist Front, FADI
Popular Democratic Movement (MPD), 1978; successor to Marxist-Leninist Communist Party of Ecuador (PCE-ML), 1972		3,000 est.	José Moreno Ordoñez (national director)	+		3.0 (1990); 1 of 72
El Salvador Communist Party of El Salvador (PCES), 1930 (one of five in FMLN)	5,309,685	1,000 est.	Jorge Shafik Handal	0	Seventh Apr. 1979	(1988)

Country / Party	Population	Membership	Affiliation	Leadership	Last Congress	Legislative/Electoral
Grenada Maurice Bishop Patriotic Movement (MBPM), 1984	84,135	300	+	Terrence Marryshow	Second May 1988	1.0 (1990); none
Guadeloupe Communist Party of Guadeloupe (PCG), 1958	386,000 (French census, *Témoignages*, 4 July)	3,000 est.	+	Christian Céleste	Ninth 12–13 Mar. 1988	(1988); 22 of 42 left coal. (PCG, 10 of 22), local assembly, also 1 of 3 in Paris
Guatemala Guatemalan Party of Labor (PGT), 1949 (legalized, 1952)	9,097,636	250 est.	0 0 0	Carlos González Orellana ("Camarilla" faction) Juan Manuel Diaz/Mario Sánchez "PGT 6 de Enero" faction (formerly National Leadership Nucleus faction) (1988) "Benedicto" Revolutionary October (OR) faction (1987)	Fourth Dec. 1969 First (1988)	(1990)
Guyana People's Progressive Party (PPP), 1950	764,649	300 est. (100 leaders)	+	Cheddi Jagan	Twenty-third 30 July–1 Aug. 1988	16.8 (1985); 8 of 53 elected members
Haiti Unified Party of Haitian Communists (PUCH), 1968	6,142,141	350 est.	+	René Théodore	First 1979	(1990) (PUCH boycotted)
Honduras Communist Party of Honduras (PCH), 1954 (one of six in the Unified National Directorate—Honduran Revolutionary Movement, DNU-MRH, 1982)	5,259,699	100 est.	0	Rigoberto Padilla Rush (in exile) Mario Sosa Navarro	Fourth Jan. 1986 (clandestine)	(1985)

Country: Party(ies)/Date Founded	Mid-1990 Population (est.) (World Fact Book)	Communist Party Membership (claimed or est.)	Party Leader (general sec.)	Status	Last Congress	Last Election (percentage of vote; seats in legislature)
Jamaica	2,441,396					
Workers' Party of Jamaica (WPJ), 1978		100 est.	Trevor Munroe	+	Fourth 11–13 Sept. 1988	(1989) did not contest
Jamaican Communist Party (JCP), 1975		no data	Christopher Lawrence	+	no data	
Martinique	359,800 (French census, *Justice*, 19 July)					
Martinique Communist Party (PCM), 1957		1,000 est.	Armand Nicolas	+	Ninth 12–13 Dec. 1988	(1988); 2 of 45 (local assembly), none in Paris
Mexico	87,870,154					
Mexican Socialist Party (PMS), 1987		merged with PRD in 1989	Gilberto Rincón Gallardo	+	First 14 May 1989	(1988) (presid.)
Democratic Revolution Party (PRD), May 1989		no data	Cuauhtémoc Cardenas (non-communist co-ordinator general)	+	First 16–20 Nov. 1990	(1988)
Nicaragua	3,722,683					
Nicaraguan Socialist Party (PSN), 1937		1,400 est.	Gustavo Tablada	+	Tenth Oct. 1973	(1990); 2 of 92 (part of UNO)
Communist Party of Nicaragua (PCN, as splinter of PSN), 1970		1,600 est.	Eli Altamirano Pérez	+	Second June 1986	(1990); 1 of 92 (part of UNO)
Sandinista Front of National Liberation (FSLN), 1961		60,000 cl. (*Barricada*, 27 Feb.)	Daniel Ortega (coord. of Executive Commission)	*/+	FSLN Assembly 18 Feb., 24 Sept. 1989	40.8 (1990): 38 of 92

Country / Party (founded)	Population	Status	Leader	Members	Last Congress	Last election
Panama People's Party (PDP), 1943	2,425,400	+	Rubén Darío Sousa	3,000 est. (*World Fact Book*, 1990)	Eighth 24–26 Jan. 1986	2.0 (1989); none
Paraguay Paraguayan Communist Party (PCP), 1928	4,660,270	0 (tolerated)	Julio Rojas (acting), died in March Ananias Maidana	4,000 est.	Third 10 Apr. 1971	(1989)
Peru Peruvian Communist Party (PCP), 1930	21,905,605	+	Jorge del Prado Chavez	4,000 est.	Ninth 27–30 May 1987	6.0 (1990); 16 of 180, United Left Coalition
Shining Path (SL) 1980 (active since 1982)		0	Isidorio Santiago N. Garcia	no data	First 1988	
Puerto Rico Puerto Rican Communist Party (PCP), 1934	3,291,207	+	Frank Irrizarry	100 est.	Fourth 1954	(1988); none (did not contest)
United States of America Communist Party USA (CPUSA), 1919	250,410,000	+	Gus Hall	20,000 cl. (4,000–6,000 est.)	Twenty-fourth 13–16 Aug. 1987	(1988); none (did not contest)
Uruguay Communist Party of Uruguay (PCU), 1920	3,036,660	+	Jaime Pérez Gerschuni	50,000 cl. (*Voz*, 25 Oct.)	Twenty-second 6–18 Oct. 1990	34.0 (1989); 22 of 99; Frente Amplio coal. (10% and 11 seats for PCU)
Venezuela Communist Party of Venezuela (PCV), 1931	19,698,104	+	Alonso Ojeda Olaechea to Aug., Trinio Melean from Aug.	4,000 est.	Eighth 25–27 Aug. 1990	2.0 (1988); 1 of 201
TOTAL	722,465,780			1,050,900		

Country: Party(ies)/Date Founded	Mid-1990 Population (est.) (World Fact Book)	Communist Party Membership (claimed or est.)	Party Leader (general sec.)	Status	Last Congress	Last Election (percentage of vote; seats in legislature)
ASIA AND THE PACIFIC (20)						
Australia	16,923,478					
Communist Party of Australia (CPA), 1920		merged into New Left Party	Brian Aarons, et al. (nat'l executive)	+	Thirtieth/special 2–3 Dec. 1989 (voted to dissolve, create New Left Party)	0.3 (1990); none, did not contest
Socialist Party of Australia (SPA), 1971		no data	Peter Dudley Symon Jack McPhillips (pres.)	+	Sixth 3 Oct. 1988	negl. (1990); none
New Left Party (NLP), 1989		1,000 cl.	Di Bolton, et al. leadership group	+	First (founding) 9–11 June 1990	(1990) did not contest
Bangladesh	118,433,062					
Communist Party of Bangladesh (CPB), 1948		50,000 est.	Saifuddin Ahmed Manik Nurul Islam, sec. of CPB (FBIS-NES, 12 May 1989)	+	Fourth 7–11 Apr. 1987	(1988) boycotted
Burma	41,277,389					
Burmese Communist Party (BCP), 1939		200 est.	Bo Kyin Maung (chairman)	0	Third 9 Sept.–2 Oct. 1985	(1990)

Country / Party	Population	Party membership	Secretary general / Leader		Last party congress	Last election
Cambodia Khmer People's Revolutionary Party (KPRP), 1951	6,991,107	10,000 est. (June)	Heng Samrin	*	Fifth 13–16 Oct. 1985 (national conference of cadres, 5–12 Apr. 1990)	99.0 (1981); all 117
Party of Democratic Kampuchea (PDK), or Kampuchean Communist Party (KCP), 1951		no data	Khieu Sampan (chairman)	0	Third 14 Dec. 1975	
China Chinese Communist Party (CCP), 1921	1,133,682,501 (official census)	48,000,000 cl.	Jiang Zemin	*	Thirteenth 25 Oct.–1 Nov. 1987	(1987); all 3,202 CCP approved
India Communist Party of India (CPI), 1928	849,746,001	467,539 cl.	C. Rajeswara Rao (to 20 Apr.) Indrajit Gupta (from 20 Apr.)	+	Fourteenth 6–12 Mar. 1989	(1989); 12 of 545
Communist Party of India-Marxist (CPM), 1964		450,000 cl.	E. M. S. Namboodiripad	+	Thirteenth 26–31 Dec. 1988	(1989); 32 of 545
United Communist Party of India (UCPI), 1989		negligible	Mohit Sen S. A. Dange (chairman)	+	nat'l conf. in Salem, 29 May 1989	negl. (1989)
Indonesia Indonesian Communist Party (PKI), 1920 (split)	190,136,221	1,500 est. ca. 200 exiles	Jusuf Adjitorop (pro-Beijing faction) Thomas Sinuraya (pro-Moscow faction)	0	Seventh Extraordinary Apr. 1962	(1987)
Japan Japanese Communist Party (JCP), 1922	123,642,461	500,000 est. (*WSJ*, 10 June; Tokyo, Kyodo, 5 July; *FBIS-EAS*, 5 July)	Tetsuzo Fuwa (Presidium chairman) Kenji Miyamoto (CC chairman)	+	Nineteenth 8–13 July 1990	7.9 (1990); 16 of 512

Country: Party(ies)/Date Founded	Mid-1990 Population (est.) (World Fact Book)	Communist Party Membership (claimed or est.)	Party Leader (general sec.)	Status	Last Congress	Last Election (percentage of vote; seats in legislature)
Korea (North) Korean Workers' Party (KWP), 1946 (as united party, 1949)	21,292,649	2,000,000 cl.	Kim Il-song	*	Sixth 10–15 Oct. 1980	99.8 (1990); all 687 KWP approved
Laos Lao People's Revolutionary Party (LPRP), 1955	4,023,726	40,000 cl.	Kaysone Phomvihane	*	Fourth 13–15 Nov. 1986	(1989); Supreme People's Assembly (65 of 79 are LPRP members)
Malaysia Communist Party of Malaya (CPM), 1930 (may be active under new party name per agreement of 2 Dec. 1989; renamed Malaysian People's Party, 1990)	17,510,546	1,100 est.	Chin Peng (pseud. of Ong Boo Hwa)	0	1965	(1984)
Communist Party of Malaysia (MCP), 1983		800 est.	Ah Leng	0	unknown	(1984)
Mongolia Mongolian People's Revolutionary Party (MPRP), 1921	2,187,275	100,049 cl. (Montsame, 2 Nov.)	Jambyn Batmonh (resigned 12 March) Gomboyabyn Ochirbat	*	Twentieth Extraordinary 10–13 Apr. 1990	60.0 (1990); 370 of 430
Nepal Nepal Communist Party (NCP), 1949 (factions)	19,145,800	10,000 est. (75% pro-Beijing and neutral)	Man Mohan Adhikary[†]	+	Third 1961 (before split; right wing held its own third in 1968)	(1986) (United Left Front)

Country / Party	Population	Party membership	Leaders	Electoral	Last congress	Last election (% / seats)
New Zealand Communist Party of New Zealand (CPNZ), 1921	3,384,600 (N.Z. Dept. of Stat. *Yearbook*, 1990)	50 est.	Grant Morgan Harold Crook (chairman; ret. in Dec.)	+	Twenty-fourth 1–4 Dec. 1990	(1990); none
Socialist Unity Party (SUP), 1966		60 est.	George H. Jackson (pres.) Marilyn Tucker (sec.) Ken Douglas (chmn.)	+	Eighth 22–24 Oct. 1988	(1987); none
Pakistan Communist Party of Pakistan (CPP), 1948	114,649,406	200 est.	Ali Nazish	+	Third 25–27 May 1989	(1988)
Philippines Philippine Communist Party (PKP), 1930	66,117,284	5,000–8,000 est.	Merlin Magallona Felicismo Macapagal (chmn.)	+	Ninth Dec. 1986	(1987)
Communist Party of the Philippines (CPP), 1968		25,000–35,000 est.	Ricardo Reyes Benito Tiamzon (acting chmn.) Jose Maria Sison (chmn. in absentia)	0	Founding/Reest. 26 Dec. 1968– 7 Jan. 1969	(1987)
Singapore Communist Party of Malaya (CPM), 1930	2,720,915	300 est.	Chin Peng (pseud.)	0	1965 (last known)	(1984)
Sri Lanka Communist Party of Sri Lanka (CPSL), 1943	17,196,436	5,000 est.	Kattorge P. Silva	+	Thirteenth 22–26 March 1987 Extraordinary 9–11 Dec. 1989	2.9 (1989); 3 of 225, as part of United Socialist Alliance

Country: Party(ies)/Date Founded	Mid-1990 Population (est.) (World Fact Book)	Communist Party Membership (claimed or est.)	Party Leader (general sec.)	Status	Last Congress	Last Election (percentage of vote; seats in legislature)
Janatha Vimukthi Peramuna (JVP), 1968		no data	Rohana Wijewwera (leader) Upatissa Gamana-yake (dep.) (both killed Nov. 1989)	+		did not contest
Thailand Communist Party of Thailand (CPT), 1942	56,000,000	250–500 est.	Thong Jaensri (pseudonym?)	0	Fourth Mar.–Apr. 1984 (clandestine)	(1988)
Vietnam Vietnamese Communist Party (VCP), 1930	66,170,889	2,195,824 cl. (*Nhan Dan*, 3 Feb. 1989)	Nguyen Van Linh	*	Sixth 15–18 Dec. 1986	98.8 (1987); 496, all VCP endorsed
TOTAL	2,871,281,746	53,868,997				

EASTERN EUROPE AND USSR (9)

Country: Party(ies)/Date Founded	Mid-1990 Population (est.) (World Fact Book)	Communist Party Membership (claimed or est.)	Party Leader (general sec.)	Status	Last Congress	Last Election (percentage of vote; seats in legislature)
Albania Albanian Party of Labor (APL), 1941	3,237,131	135,000 cl.	Ramiz Alia	*	Ninth 3–8 Nov. 1986	100 (1987); all 250 Democratic Front
Bulgaria Bulgarian Communist Party (BCP), 1903; changed to Bulgarian So-cialist Party (BSP), 3 April 1990	8,933,544	477,000 cl. (number of membership cards distributed) (*Duma*, 6 March 1991; *FBIS-EEU*, 13 March 1991)	Petúr Mladenov to 3 Apr. Alexander Lilov (chairman, Supreme Party Council)	*/+	Fourteenth 30 Jan.–2 Feb. 1990 Thirty-ninth, 22–25 Sept. 1990 (new numbering system)	47.1 (1990); 211 of 400
Bulgarian Communist Party (BCP, 1990; formerly, Party of the Work-ing People), 1990		15,000 cl.	Vladimir Asenov (chairman)			supported BSP

Country / Party	Population	Membership	Leader		Latest congress	Electoral strength
Czechoslovakia						
Communist Party of Czechoslovakia (KSČ), 1921; name changed to Federation of Communist Party of Bohemia and Moravia and Communist Party of Slovakia (Nov. 1990); in brief, Communist Party of Czechoslovakia (KSČS)	15,683,234	700,000 cl.	Vasil Mohorita to Nov. 1990 (first secretary position abolished) Pavel Kanis—Slovak Miroslav Grebeníček—Czech (rotating chairmen)	+	Eighteenth 3–4 Nov. 1990	14.0 (1990); 48 of 300 (lower house: 23 of 150)
Germany						
German Party of Democratic Socialism (PDS), 1990	16,307,170	214,000 cl. (*Pravda*, 28 Jan. 1991)	Gregor Gysi	+	First Congress of Renewal, 24–25 Feb. 1990 (reconvened, 16 Sept. 1990)	16.0 (1990); 65 of 400 (18 March 1990—for GDR Volkskammer); 2.4 (1990) 17 of 662 (2 Dec. 1990—for FRG Bundestag)
Hungary						
Hungarian Socialist Workers' Party (HSWP), 1956; reconstituted	10,568,686	no data	Gyula Thurmer	+	Fourteenth (second session) 27 Jan. 1990	3.68 (1985); none
Hungarian Socialist Party (HSP), split from HSWP, 1989		37,500 cl. (35,000–40,000 est., *Magyar Hirlap*, 9 March 1991)	Gyula Horn	+	Fourteenth (founding) 6–10 October 1989	8.55 (1990); 33 of 386
Poland						
Social Democracy of the Republic of Poland (SDRP; reoriented PZPR), 1990	37,776,725	60,000 cl. (*Radio Warsaw*, 23 Aug.; *Report on Eastern Europe*, 7 Sept.)	Leszek Miller Aleksander Kwaśniewski (chairman)	+	First (founding) 29 Jan. 1990	(1989); 173 of 460
Union of the Social Democracy of the Republic of Poland (USDRP; splinter of SDRP), 1990		5,000 est. (*Dziennik Łódzki*, 17 July; *Report on Eastern Europe*, 7 Sept.)	Tadeusz Fiszbach	+		(1989)

Country: Party(ies)/Date Founded	Mid-1990 Population (est.) (World Fact Book)	Communist Party Membership (claimed or est.)	Party Leader (general sec.)	Status	Last Congress	Last Election (percentage of vote; seats in legislature)
Romania National Salvation Front (NSF), 1989	23,273,285	1,000,000	Ion Iliescu to 5 July Nicolae S. Dumitru and Claudiu Iordache (first deputy chairmen)	+	First nat'l conf. 7–10 Apr. 1990	66.0 (1990); 263 of 396
USSR Communist Party of the Soviet Union (CPSU), 1898	290,938,469	16,900,000 cl. (Literaturnaya gazeta, 30 Jan. 1991)	Mikhail S. Gorbachev	*	Twenty-eighth 2–13 July 1990	(1989); 2,250 (87.6% are CPSU members)
Yugoslavia League of Communists of Yugoslavia (LCY), 1920 (dissolved 20 May 1990)	23,841,608	1,167,203 est. (Report on Eastern Europe, 7 Sept.)	Milan Pančevski to May Miomir Grbović (pres. of Presidium)	*	Fourteenth Extraordinary 21 January 1990; reconvened 25 May 1990	(1986); all 308 LCY approved, Socialist Alliance
League of Communists— Movement for Yugoslavia (LC-MY; self-proclaimed successor to LCY), 1990		140,000 cl. (applications received)	Dragan Atanasovski (president)	+	Founding 24 Dec. 1990	
TOTAL	430,559,852	20,850,703				

MIDDLE EAST (15)

Afghanistan   15,862,293

Country / Party	Population	Membership	Party Leader		Last Congress	Last Election
People's Democratic Party of Afghanistan (PDPA), 1965; re-named Homeland Party (HP), 28 June 1990	25,566,507	200,000 cl. (Radio Kabul, 29 Nov.; *FBIS-NES*, 3 Dec.)	Dr. Mohammed Najibullah	*	Second 27–28 June 1990	38.0 (1988); 69 of 184 elected of 234 total (National Front) (22.6% and 42 for PDPA)
Algeria Algerian Communist Party, 1920; Socialist Vanguard Party (PAGS), 1966		15,000 (French est.)	Sadiq Hadjeres (first secretary)	+	First (legal) 16–17 Dec. 1990	(1982)
Bahrain Bahrain National Liberation Front (NLF/B), 1955	520,186	negligible	Saif ben Ali Yusuf al-Hassan al-Ajajai (chair-man; not noted since 1983)	0	unknown	
Egypt Egyptian Communist Party (ECP), 1921	54,705,764	500 est.	Farid Mujahid (apparently)	0	Second Sept. 1984	(1990)
Iran Communist Party of Iran (Tudeh Party), 1941 (dissolved May 1983)	55,647,001	1,500 est.	Ali Khavari (first sec. of CC, party leader in exile)	0	National Con-ference 1986	(1988)
Iraq Iraqi Communist Party (ICP), 1934	18,781,770	no data	Aziz Muhammad (first secretary)	0	Fourth 10–15 Nov. 1985	(1989)
Israel Palestine Communist Party, 1922; Communist Party of Israel (CPI, RAKAH), 1948	4,409,218 (excl. E. Jerusalem and the West Bank)	2,000 est.	Meir Vilner	+	Twenty-first 21–23 May 1990	3.7 (1988); 4 of 120 (with Dem. Front of Peace and Equality)
Jordan Communist Party of Jordan (CPJ), 1951	3,064,508	no data	Dr. Ya'qub Zayadin	0 (party banned but not political activity)	Second Dec. 1983	(1989); 1 of 80

Country: Party(ies)/Date Founded	Mid-1990 Population (est.) (World Fact Book)	Communist Party Membership (claimed or est.)	Party Leader (general sec.)	Status	Last Congress	Last Election (percentage of vote; seats in legislature)
Lebanon	3,339,331					
Lebanese Communist Party (LCP), 1924		2,500 est. (20,000 cl.)	George Hawi	+	Fifth 3–5 Feb. 1987	(1972); none
Organization of Communist Action in Lebanon (OCAL), 1970		1,500 est.	Muhsin Ibrahim	+	First 1971	
Morocco	25,684,241					
Moroccan Communist Party, 1943; Party of Progress and Socialism (PPS), 1974		4,500 est. (50,000 cl.)	'Ali Yata	+	Fourth 17–19 July 1987	2.3 (1984); 2 of 306
Palestinian Communist Party (PCP), 1982	5,000,000 est. Palestinians (incl. E. Jerusalem, Gaza, Jordan, and the West Bank)		Bashir al-Barghuti (?) Sulayman al-Najib (dep. gen. secretary)	0 (tolerated)	First late 1983	
Saudi Arabia Communist Party of Saudi Arabia (CPSA), 1975	17,115,728	negligible	Mahdi Habib	0	Third Aug. 1989	
Syria Syrian Communist Party (SCP), 1924 (as separate party, 1944)	12,483,440	5,000 est.	Khalid Bakhdash Yusuf Faysal (dep. gen. secretary)	+	Sixth July 1986	(1990); 8 of 250 (newly increased)
Tunisia Tunisian Communist Party (PCT), 1934	8,095,492	2,000 est. (4,000 cl.)	Muhammad Harmel (first secretary; gen. secy. in *WMR*, Jan.)	+	Tenth June 1989	(1989); none
Yemen (PDRY)/Republic of Yemen	9,746,465 (ROY)					

Party	Population	Membership	Leadership		Last Party Congress	Elections; seats
(ROY; 22 May 1990) Yemen Socialist Party (YSP), 1978	(2,585,448 for PDRY and 7,160,981 for YAR)		'Ali Salim al-Bayd (also dep. chmn. of Presidential Council)	*	Fourth 20–21 June 1987	(1986); all 111 YSP approved
TOTAL	260,021,926	234,500				

WESTERN EUROPE (23)

Party	Population	Membership	Leadership		Last Party Congress	Elections; seats
Austria Communist Party of Austria (KPÖ), 1918	7,644,275	11,000–12,000 (congress report)	Walter Silbermayr Susanne Sohn (cochairwoman)	+	Twenty-seventh 19–21 Jan. 1990	0.55 (1990); none
Belgium Belgian Communist Party (PCB/KPB), 1921	9,909,285	4,000 est.	Louis van Geyt (president)	+	Twenty-sixth 18–19 Mar. 1989	0.8 (1987); none
Cyprus Communist Party of Cyprus, 1922; Progressive Party of the Working People (AKEL), 1941	707,776	16,000 cl. (official AKEL cl. Nov. 1990)	Dimitris Christofias	+	Seventeenth 3–7 Oct. 1990	27.4 (1985); 10 of 56 (5 of 15 elected deputies left AKEL to found ADISOK)
Democratic Socialist Renewal Movement (ADISOK, split from AKEL), April 1990		1,200 cl.	Pavlos Dinglis (president)	+	First 7–8 July 1990	(1985) 5 former AKEL representatives of 56
Denmark Communist Party of Denmark (DKP), 1919; disbanded, June 1990	5,195,100	3,000 est. (*Det Fri Aktuelt*, 5–6 Jan.)	Anne-Marie Jørgensen (secretariat leader) Ole Sohn (chairman)	+	Twenty-ninth Extraordinary 20–21 Jan. 1990 Thirtieth 14–15 Apr. 1990	1.9 (1990); none (Unity List Coal. includes DKP)
Communist Forum (KF), 1990		200 est.	Betty Frydensbjerg Carlsson (chairman)	+	First (founding) 29–30 Sept. 1990	

Country: Party(ies)/Date Founded	Mid-1990 Population (est.) (World Fact Book)	Communist Party Membership (claimed or est.)	Party Leader (general sec.)	Status	Last Congress	Last Election (percentage of vote; seats in legislature)
Finland	4,977,325					
Finnish Communist Party (SKP), 1918		terminated pol. activity	Heljä Tammisola to Apr. Asko Mäki from Apr. Jarmo Wahlström (chairman) to Apr. Heljä Tammisola from Apr.	+	Twenty-second 23–25 Feb. 1990	9.4 (1987); 16 of 200 SKDL Front (11 of 16 for SKP; SKDL disbanded 29 Apr.)
Finnish Communist Party—Unity (SKP-Y), 1986		10,000 est.	Yrjö Häkanen to 10 Sept. Arto Viitaniemi from Sept. Esko-Juhani Tennilä (chairman) to 26 July Yrjö Häkanen from July	+	First 5–7 June, 1987	4.3 (1987); 4 of 200 DEVA Front (disbanded 1990)
Communist Workers' Party (KTP), 1988		1,000 est.	Heikki Mannikko Timo Lahdenmaeki (chairman)	+	First 17–18 June 1989 (founding, 23–24 May 1988)	registered part of DEVA Front
Left Alliance (VL), 1990		12,500 cl.	Matti Viialainen Claes Andersson (chairman)		Founding 29 Apr. 1990	20 of 200 (16 former SKDL and 4 DEVA deputies are now VL representatives)

Country / Party	Population / Founded	Membership	Leadership		Congress	Last election
France						
French Communist Party (PCF), 1920	56,358,331; 56,556,000 (census 1990)	200,000 cl. (*FBIS-WEU*, 30 Jan. 1989, p. 13)	Georges Marchais	+	Twenty-seventh 18–22 Dec. 1990	11.3 (1988); 25 of 577 (and 2 from overseas depts.)
Germany: Federal Republic of Germany						
German Communist Party (DKP), 1968	62,168,200 (excl. W. Berlin)	20,000 cl. (10,000 est.)	Heinz Stehr Anne Frohnweiler Helga Rosenberg Rolf Priemer (collective leadership)	+	Tenth 26–27 Mar. 1990	2.4 (1990); 17 of 662 for Peace List/PDS coal. in which DKP participated
Great Britain						
Communist Party of Great Britain (CPGB), 1920	57,365,665	6,000 est. (*Morning Star*, 10 Dec.)	Nina Temple (secretary)	+	Forty-second/ special, 9 Dec. 1990	0.1 (1987); none
Communist Party of Britain, (CPB), 1988 (hard-line *Morning Star* splinter)		no data				
Greece						
Communist Party of Greece (KKE), 1921	10,028,171	50,000 est. (all factions)	Grigoris Farakos Kharilaos Florakis (chairman)	+	Twelfth 12–16 May 1987	10.28 (1990); 19 of 300 (Coalition of the Left and Progress)
Communist Party of Greece—Interior (KKE-I), 1968; split, now Greek Left (E.AR), 1987			Fotis Kouvelis Leonidas Kyrkos (president)	+	24–26 Apr. 1987	
Iceland						
People's Alliance (PA), 1968	251,000	3,000 est.	Olafur Ragnar Grimsson (chairman) Bjorn Sveinsson (party secretary)	+	Biennial 16–20 Nov. 1989	14.4 (1990); 9 of 63

Country: Party(ies)/Date Founded	Mid-1990 Population (est.) (World Fact Book)	Communist Party Membership (claimed or est.)	Party Leader (general sec.)	Status	Last Congress	Last Election (percentage of vote; seats in legislature)
Ireland Communist Party of Ireland (CPI), 1933	3,500,212	500 est.	James Stewart	+	Twentieth 28–29 Oct. 1989; reconvened 26–27 May 1990	(1989); none
Italy Italian Communist Party (PCI), 1921	57,664,405	1,300,000 cl. (at end of 1990)	Achille Ochetto	+	Nineteenth 8–12 March 1990	26.6 (1987); 177 of 630
Luxembourg Communist Party of Luxembourg (CPL), 1921	383,813	500 est.	René Urbany (chairman, died 10 Oct.) Aloyse Bisdorff	+	Twenty-sixth 10–11 Nov. 1990	3.6 (1989); 1 of 64
Malta Communist Party of Malta (CPM), 1969	354,679 (Malta Office of Statistics, Sept.)	100 est.	Anthony Vassallo	+	Fourth 15–17 July 1988	0.08 (1987); none
Netherlands Communist Party of the Netherlands (CPN), 1909	14,936,032	3,000–5,000 est.	Henk Hoekstra (chairman)	+	Extraordinary 10 June 1990 Thirty-first 8–11 April 1989	4.1 (1989); 6 of 150 (with Green Left)
Norway Norwegian Communist Party (NKP), 1923	4,252,806	1,750 est.	Kåre André Nilsen (chairman)	+	Nineteenth 23–26 Apr. 1987	0.84 (1989); none (joint with AKP)
Workers' Communist Party (AKP), 1973		6,000 est.	Siri Jensen (chairman)	+	Fifth Dec. 1988 (secret)	(1989); none (see NKP)

Country / Party	Population	Party membership	Party leader		Last congress	Last election; parliamentary representation
Portugal Portuguese Communist Party (PCP), 1921	10,354,497	200,000 cl. (Apr.)	Álvaro Cunhal	+	Thirteenth (special) 18–20 May 1990	11 (1987); 30 of 250 United Democratic Coalition (25 of 30 for PCP)
San Marino Communist Party of San Marino (PCS), 1921; renamed Progressive Democratic Party of San Marino (PPDS), 1990	23,123	1,100 cl. (*L'Unità*, 23 March; *FBIS-WEU*, 10 May)	Gilberto Ghiotti	+	Twelfth 27–29 Apr. 1990	28.71 (1988); 18 of 60
Spain Spanish Communist Party (PCE), 1920	39,268,715	83,000 cl. (*FBIS-EEU*, 17 Aug. 1989)	Julio Anguita González	+	Twelfth 19–21 Feb. 1988	9.05 (1989); 18 of 350 United Left Coalition
Communist Party of the Peoples of Spain (PCPE), 1984		16,500 est.	Juan Ramos Camarero	+	Third Extra-ordinary March 1989	as above
Spanish Workers' Party—Communist Unity (PTE-UC), 1987		14,000 est.	Adolfo Pinedo Santiago Carrillo (chairman)	+	First 8 Feb. 1987	(1989); none
Sweden Left Party Communists (VPK), 1921; renamed Left Party (V), 1990	8,526,452	17,800 cl.	Lars Werner (chairman)	+	Twenty-ninth 23–26 May 1990	5.8 (1988); 21 of 349
Communist Workers' Party (APK), 1977		5,000 cl.	Rolf Hagel (chairman)	+	Twenty-ninth 4–6 May 1989 (*Pravda*, 4 May 1989)	(1988); no data
Switzerland Swiss Labor Party (PdAS), 1921 (re-established, 1944)	6,742,461	4,500 est.	Jean Spielman	+	Thirteenth 27 Feb.–1 Mar. 1987	0.8 (1987); 1 of 200

Country: Party(ies)/Date Founded	Mid-1990 Population (est.) (World Fact Book)	Communist Party Membership (claimed or est.)	Party Leader (general sec.)	Status	Last Congress	Last Election (percentage of vote; seats in legislature)
Turkey United Communist Party of Turkey (TBKP), 1988	57,163,085	negligible	Nabi Yagci (aka Haydar Kutlu) Nihat Sargin (chairman)	0 (quasi-legal)	First 12–13 Oct. 1988	(1987)
Berlin Socialist Unity Party of West Berlin (SEW), 1949; renamed Socialist Initiative (SI), 1990	3,500,000	1,600 cl.	Dietmar Ahrens (resigned, Feb.)	+	Extraordinary 17–18 Feb. 1990 Founding 28–29 Apr. 1990	(1990) did not contest
TOTAL	421,462,881	1,994,750				
GRAND TOTAL	4,873,593,534	80,418,493				

MAJOR TRADITIONAL INTERNATIONAL FRONT ORGANIZATIONS*

Organization (18)	Year Founded	Headquarters	Claimed Membership#	Affiliates	Countries
Afro-Asian Peoples' Solidarity Organization (AAPSO) (Murad Ghalib, Nuri Abd-al Razzaq Husayn)	1957	Cairo	unknown	87	unknown
Asian Buddhist Conference for Peace (ABCP) (Kharkuu Gaadan, G. Lubsan Tseren)	1970	Ulan Bator	unknown	15	12
Berlin Conference of European Catholics (BCEC) (Ewa Roman-Zukowicz[1], Elia Lazzari[1], Helmut Ridder[1])	1964	East Berlin	unknown	unknown	45
Christian Peace Conference (CPC) (Richard Adriamanjato[2], Kenyon Wright[2])	1958	Prague	unknown	unknown	ca. 80

Organization	Founded	Headquarters	Membership		
Continental Organization of Latin American Students (OCLAE) (Jorge Arias Díaz, Angel Arzuaga Reyes)	1966	Havana	unknown	34	26
International Association of Democratic Lawyers (IADL) (Stefano Rodota[3], Amar Bentoumi)	1946	Brussels	25,000	unknown	101[4]
International Federation of Resistance Movements (FIR) (Arialdo Banfi, Alix Lhote)	1951	Vienna	5,000,000	78	27
International Institute for Peace (IIP) (Erwin Lanc, Max Schmidt)	1957	Vienna	unknown	unknown	unknown
International Organization of Journalists (IOJ) (Armando Rollemberg[5], Gerard Gatonot[5])	1946	Prague	ca. 260,000[6]	101[6]	90[6]
International Radio and Television Organization (OIRT)	1946	Prague	unknown	29	23
International Union of Students (IUS) (Josef Scala, Georgios Michaelides)	1946	Prague	ca. 40,000,000	117	110
Organization of Solidarity of the Peoples of Africa, Asia and Latin America (OSPAAAL) (Susumu Osaki? René Anillo Capote)	1966	Havana	unknown	unknown	unknown
Women's International Democratic Federation (WIDF) (Freda Brown)	1945	East Berlin	200,000,000	142	124
World Federation of Democratic Youth (WFDY) (a South African[7] and a Hungarian[7])	1945	Budapest	150,000,000	ca. 270	123
World Federation of Scientific Workers (WFSW) (Jean-Marie Legay, Stan Davison)	1946	London	1,000,000+	ca. 46	70+
World Federation of Teachers' Unions (FISE) (Lesturuge Ariyawansa, Gérard Montant)	1946	East Berlin	26,000,000	150	79
World Federation of Trade Unions (WFTU) (Ibrahim Zakariya[8], Aleksandr Zharikov[8])	1945	Prague	ca. 214,000,000	92	81
World Peace Council (WPC) (Evangelos Maheras[9], Ray Stewart[9])	1950	Helsinki	unknown	unknown	145

New information is footnoted.

*All those noted as having attended meetings of the "closely coordinating nongovernmental organizations" (YICA, 1990).

#As of 1989. These and the figures on affiliates and countries do not take into consideration East European (and other) defections or 1990 additions because the full extent of either is presently unknown. The exceptions here are the 1990 statistics for IADL and IOJ.

1. Prague, CPC Information, 25 November
2. Prague, CPC Information, 28 June
3. Paris, Est et Ouest, December
4. U.N. ECOSOC, Congo, E/C.2/1991/2 Add. 1, 9 August

5. Harare, SAPA, 30 January 1991; *FBIS-AFR*, 1 February 1991

6. U.N. ECOSOC, Congo, E/C.2/1991/2 Add. 2, 2 September

7. Athens, *Rizospastis*, 12 Dec. The names of the officeholders were not given.

8. Moscow, *Trud*, 21 November

9. Helsinki, *Peace Courier*, no. 3 (March)

---

† Soviet-recognized leader of one faction is Bishnu Bahadur Manandhar; October 1988 (*WMR* describes him without qualification as having been the CPN general secretary since 1977)

Introduction
The Communist World in 1990

For the second consecutive year, no claims were made by the Soviet Union that the global number of communist party (CP) members had increased. The decline, in fact, has been striking, from ca. 90.5 million in early 1989 to an estimated 82 million two years later. Excluded from these figures are the so-called revolutionary-democratic as well as the national-democratic parties, which have also declined, from a high of 28 down to a much smaller number.[1]

Beginning with the November 1989 issue, the official monthly journal of the Communist Party of the Soviet Union (CPSU) Central Committee began publishing biographic sketches of leaders from "communist, workers', revolutionary-democratic and national-democratic parties" throughout the world.[2] These sketches ran in the last two issues for 1989, seven numbers in 1990, and may or may not be continued during calendar year 1991. Among those so honored thus far have been chairmen or general secretaries of movements in Cambodia, Cape Verde, Congo (Brazzaville), Guinea and Cape Verde, Mali, Mozambique, Senegal (Party for Independence and Labour as well as the Democratic League—Movement for a Party of Labour), Zambia, and Zimbabwe.

It will be interesting to see whether those formerly designated as "vanguard revolutionary democratic parties" that are no longer in power (e.g., because of the lost election in Nicaragua or the unification of South Yemen with North Yemen) will remain in that category. Many African regimes are turning away from their imported Soviet political and economic models, which signifies a loss of influence by Moscow in that part of the Third World.

This volume of the *Yearbook on International Communist Affairs* (*YICA*) covers 106 countries or territories. Several of them include self-avowed Marxist-Leninist movements that have not been recognized by the CPSU. All population statistics are dated mid-1990 and come from the same source,[3] with the exception of China, France, Malta, and New Zealand, for which the profile contributors gave indigenous figures. Names of leaders are provided in the "Register of Communist Parties" only for the positions of general secretary and/or chairman, with the latter frequently occupied by a retired former leader. This list also includes the most recent congress or national conference, the movement's legal status, the percentage of votes, and the number of seats won in the legislature during the latest elections. The "Party Congresses" section gives information on 43 congresses (2 each in Berlin, Bulgaria, Denmark, and Yugoslavia) and seven national conferences held during the past calendar year. Elections were conducted in 29 countries throughout the world.

A conference of CP newspaper editors involving only thirteen countries, four of which (Czechoslovakia, [East] Germany, Hungary, and Poland) no longer had ruling movements, was held in Moscow under the auspices of *Pravda*. It is significant that the former sixteen ruling CPs have been reduced by the same four members and are down to an even dozen in this category. Editors from Albania, China, and Romania were absent from the Moscow meeting.[4]

Among the twelve ruling movements, China's claimed 48 million members or well over half the world's total (82 million). The CPSU, in contrast, lost 2.7 million over a fifteen-month period and was down to a membership of 16.5 million as of April 1991, according to *Pravda*. Another source revealed the previous month that more than eighteen million Union of Communist Youth members had left the *Komsomol* over the past two years, which dropped from 42 to 23.6 million. Some 40 percent of the CPSU members had either stopped paying their dues or become inactive, according to Fëdor Burlatskii. This may be one reason the ruling party had a shortfall of 4.7 billion rubles in its annual budget, which sum reportedly will be withdrawn from reserve funds.[5]

Other movements in the ruling category include North Korea's, which admits a one-third loss in membership, from three down to two million members. The National Salvation Front, successor to the Romanian Communist Party (RCP), estimated its membership at around 1.0 million, substantially below the 3.8 million claimed by the RCP. Loss of membership may be occurring in Cuba and Vietnam, although neither regime has admitted it. Bulgaria announced that it has lost more than half its members,[6] whereas Mongolia claimed a 10 percent gain.

Several nonruling parties in Latin America claimed substantial expansion in membership: Chile, Ecuador, Nicaragua (Sandinistas), and Uruguay. Panamanian assertions of 25,600 members conflict with the Central Intelligence Agency *World Fact Book*, which estimates the total as 3,000 at most. The Italian increase by 500,000 to 1.3 million is the most striking in Western Europe.

The status of certain movements has changed over the past year. The South African CP became legal on 2 Febrary 1990, as did the CP in Chile, on 15 October 1990. The United Left Front in Nepal comprises seven communist factions, from radicals to centrists. Not only is this organization legal, but it also served as part of the interim government. The Jordanian CP remains banned. However, political activity is allowed by individual members, one of whom serves as a deputy in parliament.

Ten leadership changes took place for various reasons throughout the world communist movement in the following countries: Uruguay and Luxembourg (both leaders died); New Zealand and Greece (former general secretaries became chairmen); Venezuela (a multicandidate election took place); Philippines (replaced a leader who had fled to the Netherlands); India (retirement of a 76-year-old general secretary); Mongolia (a change in politics); and Bulgaria, Hungary, and Romania (replacement of party leaders).

CP congresses that took place during the year in both Western and East-Central Europe usually resulted in a change of party name and adoption of a non-Stalinist socialism. In Sweden, the Left Party Communist dropped the last word from its title; in Finland, the CP dissolved itself, with some members joining the broad-based Left Alliance. Hardliners established a new Communist Workers' Party in Helsinki and a Democratic Socialist Renewal Movement on Cyprus. A founding congress of the Socialist Initiative in West Berlin superseded the former Socialist (communist) Unity Party that had operated in that part of the city. The old Bulgarian Communist Party changed the middle word to *socialist* in April 1990.

Elections were held by 29 governments (twice in Colombia), including 6 of the 8 countries in East-Central Europe during 1990 (the 2 exceptions were Albania and Yugoslavia). East Germany voted for a new parliament in March and a united all-German *Bundestag* in December. Poland also held presidential elections toward the end of the year that required a runoff. Czechoslovak and Hungarian voters weakened the communist representation even more in their respective national legislatures. Parliamentary as well as presidential elections were held in Romania and Bulgaria, where former communists continued to control the decision-making process.

Highlights of major developments in the geographic regions covered by the *YICA* are discussed below.

Africa. As mentioned above, the Soviet model has been thoroughly discredited throughout most countries in this part of the world. The ruling parties in Angola, Benin, Congo (Brazzaville), Ethiopia, and Mozambique have recognized the need for change in their economies and, to some extent, politics. It is primarily these Marxist-Leninist movements out of power that have continued to espouse a rigid orthodoxy.

In the case of Angola, 1990 passed under the slogan "Year of the MPLA—Labour Party 3rd Congress and for Expansion of Democracy." This gathering in early December reelected José Eduardo dos Santos as leader. It approved proposals for a multiparty political system, an application for full membership in the Socialist International, and the development of a mixed economy. A special congress in April 1991 was scheduled to finalize these proposals, although a law on multiparty democracy was to be adopted before that event. Unitá rebels continued to contest MPLA-PT authority.[7]

Disintegration has affected the Congolese Party of Labor (PCT), which agreed at midyear to allow multiparty elections that would not be held, however, until after its next congress in December 1990. It decided to drop Marxism-Leninism, replacing it with a social-democratic platform.[8] Several prominent PCT leaders defected to opposition parties, and Moroccan troops were requested to replace the Cubans as protection for the regime in power.

Ethiopia's leader, Mengistu Haile Mariam, also abandoned Marxism-Leninism and the destructive program that had forced the rural population into villages. He ended producer cooperatives and allowed free trade as well as midlevel private industries. The communist Workers' Party became the Democratic Unity Party of Ethiopia, which did not save it from disintegrating in the countryside under pressure by guerrilla forces. The two insurgent groups from Eritrea and Tigre have coordinated military operations to defeat troops loyal to Mengistu in several engagements.[9]

The Front for Liberation of Mozambique (FRELIMO) on 30 November 1990 adopted a new constitution, providing for multiparty elections the following year. It also deleted the word *people's* from the name, Republic of Mozambique. This did not disarm or prevent the RENAMO insurgents from occupying much of the countryside, despite a cease-fire agreement.[10]

Benin became the first African country to vote its leader of eighteen years out of office in March 1991. The new president, Nicephore Soglo, is a former World Bank official and prime minister who won by a two to one margin. These elections were held after widespread demonstrations had resulted in destruction of statues to Marx and Lenin.[11]

The Americas. In contrast with other parts of the world, CPs in Latin America held several regional meetings: at Quito early in the year, Havana in the spring, and Mexico City in the winter. The last session appeared to be the most dogmatic in its defense of Marxist-Leninist relevance and validity. Disagreements also surfaced when the Sandinistas claimed *perestroika* as their idea and Cubans called it a Soviet phenomenon not applicable to them.

Fidel Castro announced that Cuba was the last bastion of Marxism-Leninism, despite a bankrupt economy and much less aid from the USSR projected over the next three years. Obviously worried about a potential military coup, the Castro brothers retired 70 percent of the officers in their western army, according to *Radio Rebelde* in Cuba. General Arnaldo Ochoa would have assumed command there, had he not been executed after returning from Angola.[12] A closed conference took place on 24 February 1991 in preparation for the fourth party congress to be held later in the year. Castro rejected any experiment with a multiparty system, and no national elections have been scheduled.

Given a chance to vote in such an election on 25 February 1990, the Nicaraguan opposition won 54.7 percent and ousted the Sandinistas from the power that they had seized more than ten years earlier. Although the armed forces have remained under the former defense minister, Humberto Ortega (brother of Daniel), President Violeta Chamorro de Barrios has been able to maintain herself in office. In neighboring Honduras, the local army on 24 February 1990 intercepted, about three miles north of the border with Nicaragua, a truck loaded with RPG-7 rocket launchers, rockets, bomb detonators, and wire. These arms were destined for the local Cinchonero People's Liberation Movement, always closely aligned with Salvadoran guerrillas. The Sandinistas refused to accept responsibility for smuggling Soviet antiaircraft missiles to rebels in El Salvador.[13]

These weapons were given to the Farabundo Martí National Liberation Front (FMLN) and then used to shoot down a U.S. helicopter. Two of the Americans who survived the crash were murdered. Unable to sabotage national elections on 10 March 1991, the FMLN supported both leftist opposition parties, which received less than 20 percent of the vote. Meanwhile, communist guerrilla commander Joaquín Villalobos announced from Mexico City that his group would no longer be Marxist or pursue armed revolution.[14] It promised, henceforth, to participate as a political movement in a pluralistic and "competitive" democracy.

The National Liberation Army (ELN), originally founded with Cuban support, also laid down its arms during the same month in Colombia after 23 years of guerrilla activity. Two of its two thousand members joined the constituent assembly, meeting to rewrite the constitution. The M-19, another former rebel organization with Cuban and Sandinista ties, emerged as the third-largest political force, winning 27 percent of the vote for that assembly in December. Two more groups remain active, including the traditional CP military organization called Revolutionary Armed Forces (FARC), although a third entered into negotiations with the government. Mass graves holding about four hundred bodies were discovered at the former FARC stronghold in Casa Verde. Many skulls had single bullet holes.[15]

According to a Peruvian government report the *Sendero Luminoso* (Shining Path) guerrillas, espousing a Maoist philosophy, have killed more than twenty thousand persons and damaged nearly $18 billion worth of power plants and other public works property over the past ten years. In a series of raids, police uncovered safe houses in Lima and arrested about twenty Shining Path leaders in addition to confiscating a cache of documents. Within an hour, however, a total of seventeen bombs went off at banks in the nation's capital.[16] A newer and much smaller guerrilla group, the Tupac Amaru Revolutionary Movement, is also communist but with ties to Cuba.

Elsewhere, the communists were less successful. The party received legal status in Chile, although defections and expulsions had left it considerably weakened. The movements in Canada and the United States competed for the title of most insignificant. Gus Hall, national Communist Party of the United States of America chairman, condemned the Bush administration for its alleged support of separatist movements in the USSR. *Pravda* devoted six paragraphs to excerpts from Hall's statement.[17]

Asia and the Pacific. With the exception of Mongolia, communist-ruled governments in this region continued to resist political pluralism and unqualified private enterprise economics. Most of these leaderships purged from their ranks those who even mentioned political reform, holding on to power in true Leninist fashion. Apart from the Philippines, however, communist guerrilla warfare had ended throughout the region.

Among ruling parties, the one in the People's Republic of China (PRC) experienced a power struggle among several leadership factions. The 1989–1990 purge expelled 72,000 CP members and punished 256,000 others considered politically unreliable or corrupt. Compromise, however, remained the order of the day, as reflected in the vague guidelines for the 1991–1995 economic plan, announced at the end of December 1990 under the slogan, "socialism with Chinese characteristics." The PRC also moved toward closer relations with like-minded communist leaders in North Korea, Cuba, Laos, and Romania.[18]

The hard-line regime of North Korea announced on 24 May 1990 that it would adhere to its "own style of socialism." The country had suffered several years of poor harvests and the lowest economic growth rate since 1986. Furthermore, the Soviets announced that as of 1 January 1991 bilateral trade would be transacted for convertible currency only. The USSR also reminded the North Koreans of its assistance during the 1950–1953 war and that it had carried out geological surveys to "uncover their undergound [mineral] wealth."[19] Domestically, the struggle for Kim Il-sung's mantle heated up, with his son Kim Chong-il claiming "blood lineage" as the party's main asset.

Vietnam adhered to policies that blocked political pluralism and allowed only minimal economic reforms. One such reform called for leasing land to peasant families in April 1988 by independent economic units. This experiment apparently has worked well.[20] Foreign investments have been welcomed, with France being the number one investor

and the USSR in eighth place. The attraction includes cheap minerals and inexpensive labor. The year 1991 however, "looks like a disaster," according to one Western banker, as some 140,000 Vietnamese laborers returned home from the USSR and East-Central Europe to look for work.[21]

The CP leadership in Laos arrested a small group of individuals advocating political pluralism. Yet the party insists on the "transformation of the command economy into a market economy," according to Article 14 of the draft constitution and its fifth congress at the end of March 1991. In neighboring Cambodia, the Khmer Rouge continued to attack the Vietnamese-installed government with weapons supplied by China.[22]

The most remarkable developments occurred in the People's Republic of Mongolia, which had been under Soviet control since 1924. After intense public demonstrations, opposition political movements were legalized and free elections permitted. The Mongolian Democratic Union forced the ruling CP to relinquish its monopoly on power and allow a market economy to evolve. The twentieth congress of the communist Mongolian People's Revolutionary Party (MPRP), attended by observers from the USSR and China, took place toward the end of February 1991. Accounts reveal that the MPRP considers itself the guarantor of political stability and will attempt to overcome socioeconomic difficulties.[23]

The banned CP in Thailand has had no success in promoting insurgency because of the country's prosperity. In Burma, the underground movement remains fragmented, and a dozen of the old Burmese CP leaders have returned to China. The New People's Army in the Philippines, which operates through an extensive network of civilian front organizations, continued its military operations, claiming responsibility for the murder of two U.S. servicemen.

Legal movements in Sri Lanka included a pro-Moscow CP, a Trotskyite group, and a radical Maoist organization. The Communist Party of India (CPI) continued to rail against U.S. imperialism. Its new general secretary, Indrajit Gupta, met with national CPSU secretary V. M. Falin in Moscow. The largest of the three CPs in India is CPI-Marxist, which issued a 33-page indictment of changes in the Soviet Union. It controls West Bengal, along with Calcutta, and Kerala. Parliamentary elections were scheduled for May 1991.[24]

Finally, the Japanese CP lost eleven seats after the 1990 elections to parliament. Its nineteenth congress in July of that year elected 35-year-old Kazuo Shii as head of the national secretariat, relegating 82-year-old Kenji Miyamoto to the chairmanship and virtual retirement.

Eastern Europe and the USSR. Most of the former Soviet dependencies throughout East-Central Europe have embarked on the road to political pluralism and elimination of the old communist *nomenklatura* from government as well as from the economy. They also aspire to free market systems, a transition that will require considerable time and help from the West. Poland is at the forefront of this change, followed by Czechoslovakia and then Hungary. Much slower progress has been made in other countries of the region, with Albania at the bottom of the list.

The USSR is no longer looked on as a model. The Warsaw Pact military alliance and the Council for Mutual Economic Assistance now belong to the past. Soviet troops are being withdrawn from Czechoslovakia, the former East Germany, and Hungary. Negotiations with Poland were proceeding in April 1991 toward the same result. All of this is being accomplished within a short period of time.[25]

The USSR. Almost five years to the day after he had been co-opted as general secretary for the CPSU, Mikhail S. Gorbachev became executive president of the country. That same 13 March 1990, the legislature repealed Article 6 of the constitution, which guaranteed the "leading role" of the CPSU. The latter led to the establishment and recognition of other political movements, whereas the former allowed Gorbachev to rule by decree. He also strengthened his position at the 28th CPSU congress in July, when his choice for deputy general secretary won over a "conservative" challenger. The new CPSU politburo,[26] enlarged to some 25 members, became even less important.

An eighteen-member Presidential Council lasted from March to December 1990, when it was superseded by the Security Council of the USSR with a membership of only eight persons: Foreign Minister Aleksandr A. Bessmertnykh, KGB chief Vladimir A. Kriuchkov, Prime Minister Valentin S. Pavlov, Defense Minister Dmitrii T. Iazov, Vice-President Gennadii I. Ianaev, Interior Minister Boris K. Pugo, Middle East expert Evgenii M. Primakov, and former Interior Minister Vadim V. Bakatin, who will deal with domestic issues. Although one of Gorbachev's choices, Valerii I.

Boldin, was not confirmed by the USSR Supreme Soviet,[27] he will be entrusted with organizational matters for the new council.

The CPSU continued its involvement with international communist front organizations, although the monthly *World Marxist Review*, which had claimed a circulation of 500,000 copies at one time, was discontinued in mid-1990. Only the Soviets and Mongolians continued to subsidize it to the bitter end.[28] Several front headquarters in East-Central Europe were to be evicted from Prague and apparently East Berlin as well as Budapest. The new postcommunist governments in that region have stopped sending annual subsidies to the World Peace Council, the preeminent front organization.

Eastern Europe. The transition away from the Soviet model of a command economy and communist monopoly over political power has not encompassed all governments to the same extent. Neither Albania nor Romania had permitted political pluralism to threaten communist rule through the end of 1990. Yugoslavia, much like the USSR, seems to be disintegrating.

Albania. Antigovernment demonstrations started early in the year and escalated to the point where the army had to be called out in December. This forced the regime to recognize independent political organizations, the first one calling itself the Democratic Party. National multiparty elections on 31 March 1991, the first since the communists seized power at the end of World War II, resulted in a majority for the ruling party, which had scheduled its next congress two months after that vote. Communist leader Ramiz Alia lost his seat in parliament, as did his foreign minister.[29]

Bulgaria. Using subterfuge, the ruling movement dropped the word *communist* and became known as the Bulgarian Socialist Party (BSP). It won 211 of the 400 seats in mid-1990 parliamentary elections. The opposition Union of Democratic Forces emerged second, and its leader was elected president of the republic. Communist Prime Minister Andrei Lukanov, born in the USSR, admitted in an interview that he had never become a Bulgarian citizen. At its 39th congress in the fall, the BSP acknowledged "past distortions in every sphere of life," although it refused to apologize for them. The congress did abandon any claim to a monopoly of political power in the government, however. National elections were scheduled for May 1991, after which the BSP may become a minority in the parliament. A new Bulgarian Communist Party/Revolutionary, with only 111 members, claims to be based on genuine Marxism-Leninism.[30]

Czechoslovakia. The former ruling movement also changed its name, although retaining the word *communist.* Several high-level former party members remained in the government: the federal premier, chairman of parliament, and foreign minister. Expropriation of communist property, amassed since the seizure of power in 1948, left the party with about one-tenth of its previous assets. Membership dropped from a claimed 1.7 million to an estimated several hundred thousand. No longer faced with any possibility that the communists would return to power, certain Slovak politicians began demanding independence for that eastern region.[31] With only five million inhabitants, less than one-third of the total population, there would be little basis for self-sufficiency.

East Germany. Today East Germany comprises the five eastern provinces of the Federal Republic and will become the recipient of an estimated $1 trillion over the next decade in reconstruction investment from the Bonn government and private business. The merger had created two CPs in the same country, one in the west and the other in the east. The second congress of the renamed Party of Democratic Socialism (PDS) met in East Berlin toward the end of January 1991. The chairman claimed that his movement had 214,000 members and was based on "democratic socialism." The predecessor Socialist (communist) Unity Party of Germany, when in power, claimed a membership above two million.[32]

Hungary. The former ruling movement changed its name to the Hungarian Socialist Party (HSP), after a split that left only 35,000 to 40,000 (formerly 700,000) members. Spring elections to parliament gave it 10.9 percent of the vote, although about 70 percent of the HSP's five hundred local council chairmen were reelected in the fall. Government thus remained divided between the two levels. Although the USSR has apologized to Czechoslovakia for the 1968 invasion, it refuses to do the same for suppressing Hungarian freedom fighters in 1956. Prime Minister József Antall claims that the Soviets owe his government $2 billion for ecological damages resulting from the "temporary" stationing of their armed forces since that time.[33]

Poland. Polish communists changed their designation to Social Democracy of the Republic of Poland (SDRP), with a smaller rival group carrying a similar name. Neither will play any role in government after the fall 1991 parliamentary elections. The SDRP claims only 60,000 members, a significant drop from the two million in its predecessor organization during mid-1989. Some 95 percent of the former communist movement's assets were nationalized in November 1990, including 1,869 expropriated buildings. Lech Wałęsa succeeded the communist Wojciech Jaruzelski as president of Poland on 9 December 1990. No communists serve in the new cabinet.[34] Elections for parliament will be held on 27 October 1991.

Romania. The National Salvation Front (NSF), claiming about one million members, is the successor to the CP, which had boasted almost four times that many. A former Marxist-Leninist ideology chief under Nicolae Ceauşescu is president of the country. Although other political movements are allowed, no power sharing has taken place. The brutalizing of unarmed civilians and destruction of opposition party offices during mid-1990 resulted in denial of most-favored-nation status by the U.S. government. The NSF convened during 16–17 March 1991 to transform itself into a "center-left party of social democratic orientation" affiliated with the Socialist International, and early the following month President Ion Iliescu signed a new fifteen-year treaty of friendship and cooperation in Moscow.[35] The text has not been released by either party.

Yugoslavia. This country seems the least stable of all the East-Central European states, perhaps an example of what awaits the Soviet Union. The collective presidency almost fell apart in mid-March 1991 when the president resigned and the communist leader of Serbia refused to recognize decisions made by the federation body. The issue involved a resolution on the use of federal troops to put down disorders, which had proliferated. The problem could not be resolved, even after parties to the dispute decided to retain their previous positions. The League of Communists—Movement for Yugoslavia claims a membership of 450,000 (most of them in the armed forces). However, in Bosnia-Hercegovina, Croatia, Slovenia, and Macedonia the former LCY is called the Party of Democratic Change.[36]

The Middle East. Four of the region's wars have involved regimes associated the USSR: Afghanistan, South Yemen, and Iraq (twice). The long Soviet involvement ended in debacle, with the Marxist regimes at Kabul and Aden nearly consumed by civil strife.

In contrast with Lebanon and Jordan, where CPs have at least a fragile base, the Iraqi communist movement maintains only a symbolic presence apart from its former military wing in the Kurdish north. The earlier resettlement, mass killing, and estimated flight of 250,000 Kurds into Iran and Turkey would not seem to have left much opposition to Saddam Husayn before his 2 August 1990 invasion of Kuwait. That impression proved illusory after the Iraqi defeat in "Desert Storm" and forced withdrawal. During much of March 1991, the Kurds in the north and Shiites in the south were fighting against the Baghdad regime. History seemed to repeat itself when both insurgent movements were crushed by Iraqi troops.

Afghanistan is still ruled by a Marxist party, albeit one that most recently changed its name a second time from Democratic Party of the Afghan Masses to Homeland Party in mid-1990. The value of continuing arms deliveries from Moscow has grown from $300 million to $400 million per month, according to Western estimates. Guerrillas control two-fifths of the countryside, about two hundred district capitals, and six province capitals. At the end of March 1991, they captured the garrison town of Khost with four generals and 2,500 government troops.[37]

The new Republic of Yemen merged the two governments in the north and south during May 1990. The former ruling YSP or Yemen Socialist (communist) Party now shares power with the northern military, tribal, and merchant leaders who belong to a thriving capitalist economy. Plans have been announced to consolidate the two armies and disband both security services. If this materializes, it is doubtful that the YSP will gain control over a population five times what it had in the south.

The Communist Party of Jordan (CPJ) benefited in January 1990 from repeal of the 1953 anticommunist law. It joined a leftist National Front in parliament at midyear to oppose the Islamic bloc.[38] The following month, the CPJ became part of a larger National Front to protest foreign intervention in the Persian Gulf. By contrast, the Lebanese Communisst Party (LCP) attempted to become a peacemaker between warring Islamic factions in the south and welcomed the USSR's *perestroika* as a

"real attempt at liberating socialism from mistakes of the past."[39] The Tunisian CP felt a need to support the central government because it prefers a pluralistic regime to an Islamic one.

Soviet foreign policy in the region has again shown that Moscow will sacrifice local communist movements to serve its own national interests. Resumption of natural gas imports from Iran, after a ten-year hiatus, disregarded the physical destruction of local Tudeh (communist) Party leaders.[40] Establishment of diplomatic relations with Saudi Arabia also completely ignored the banned and presumably exiled communist movement of that country.

Western Europe. The most important event, with an impact on the communist movement throughout this region, involved the unification of Germany on 2 December 1990. The communist version of "socialism" had become thoroughly discredited. The only other general election in these thirteen countries took place in Greece. For this reason, a true measure of communist strength could not be taken this past year.

The Communist Party of Great Britain, after 70 years, changed its name to Democratic Left toward the end of March 1991. Membership had declined from ten thousand in 1987 to approximately seven thousand.

The French Communist Party (PCF) claimed approximately 200,000 adherents, although this number may have declined in view of the revolt by a faction calling itself *refondateur* and considered pro-Gorbachev. At its 27th congress, just before the end of 1990, the PCF voted down a proposal to change its name or eliminate the hammer and sickle emblem.[41] Reform party statutes were promised for 1993, at the next congress (i.e., after future national elections).

The Italian communist movement did change its name to Democratic Party of the Left (DPL) at its twentieth and last congress in early February 1991 and also eliminated the hammer and sickle symbol. In contrast to the French neighbors, the DPL welcomes *perestroika* in the Soviet Union. Approximately one-third of the congress delegates opposed dropping the old party name. A second congress was scheduled for early 1991, under the "new look" and presumably before the next parliamentary elections in May 1992 or perhaps earlier.[42]

The largest communist movement in Spain (PCE) has only 83,000 members, due to a previous three-way split. The PCE has refused to change its name, although its leader also serves as coordinator for the United Left Coalition, which is an umbrella organization for electoral purposes. The neighboring Communist Party of Portugal has done the same thing, with a United People's Alliance Coalition of leftist groups. This CP remains the most Stalinist throughout all of Western Europe, even though its leader, Alvaro Cuñhal, received a half-page interview in *Pravda* on his 70th birthday.[43]

A United Communist Party of Turkey (UCPT), resulting from a merger between the communist workers' movements, has remained under an official ban. The two leaders returned from abroad and were immediately jailed. Released from prison, they were subject to legal proceedings during all of 1990. The UCPT attempted to register as did a new Unity Party of the Socialists, which may become a cover organization for the communists, should they be declared illegal once again.

The Communist Party of Greece (KKE) only had about 50,000 members and yet participated in the national government as part of the Coalition of Left and Progress, headed by the KKE chairman. This ended in April 1990, when the coalition's candidates polled just over 10 percent of the vote in national elections. The KKE's thirteenth congress in February 1991 (postponed from the previous November) discussed revised theses under pressure from those who wanted more of a voice in party decisions. The following month, Maria Dhamanaki succeeded Kharilaos Florakis as chairperson of the above-named coalition. The new KKE general secretary is Aleka Papariga.[44]

The (West) German Communist Party (DKP) ceased receiving financial subsidies from its sister movement in the former East Germany. An extraordinary party congress during March 1990 ended in disarray. DKP fielded no candidates during the all-German elections in December, supporting the Left List-PDS (Party for Democratic Socialism) ticket that originated in East Berlin.[45] That organization won only 2.4 percent of the vote, giving it seventeen seats in the all-German *Bundestag*. Next time PDS will have to more than double that showing to receive any representation under the 5 percent rule.

Richard F. Staar
Hoover Institution

NOTES

1. A list of the 28 appears in Richard F. Staar, *Foreign Policies of the Soviet Union* (Stanford: Hoover Institution Press, 1991), Table 1.4, pp. 15–16. See also David E. Albright, *Vanguard Parties & Revolutionary Change in the Third World* (Berkeley: Institute of International Studies, University of California, 1990); note 1, pp. 117–18, names twenty parties in this category during the latter half of the 1970s and identifies what became of many of them.

2. "Kratkie biografii rukovoditelei," *Izvestiia TsK KPSS*, no. 11 (November 1989): 101–7.

3. Central Intelligence Agency, *The World Fact Book 1990* (Washington, D.C.: U.S. Government Printing Office, 1991).

4. M. Tret'iakov, "Do novykh vstrech," *Pravda*, 14 March 1991, p. 5.

5. S. Alekseev, F. Burlatskii, and Stanislav Shatalin, "Alternativa," *Literaturnaia gazeta*, 30 January 1991, p. 5; A. Petrushov, "KPSS: dokhody i raskhody," *Pravda*, 21 February 1991, p. 2; *Argumenty i fakty*, no. 12 (March 1991): 8, for Komsol figures; O. Voznesenskii and I. Podsvirov, "U kommunistov net tain ot gosudarstva," *Pravda*, 12 April 1991, p. 2, for latest CPSU membership.

6. L. Zhmyrev, "Bolgariia: vremia bol'shikh peremen," *Pravda*, 27 March 1991, p. 5

7. V. Tiurkin, "Kilometr zero," *Pravda*, 10 January 1991, p. 5. See also "Round Six of Peace Talks Collapses when MPLA Refuses to Sign Agreement on Principles," *Angola Peace Monitor* (Washington, D.C.) 3, no. 12 (6 March 1991): 1–2.

8. "Congo Party Drops Marxism," *WSJ*, 11 December 1990, p. A-10.

9. Aleksandr Kirov, "Commentary on Eritrean Rebels," Moscow Radio, 8 February 1991; *FBIS-SOV*, 21 February 1991, pp. 21–22. Jane Perlez, "As Rebels Surge in Ethiopia, Government Seems Near End," *NYT*, 23 March 1991, pp. 1 and 3.

10. Kurt Pelda, "Mozambique on the Threshold," *Swiss Review of World Affairs*, January 1991, pp. 26–27.

11. TASS, "Benin," *Pravda*, 26 March 1991, p. 5; Kenneth B. Noble, "Despots Dwindle as Reform Alters Face of Africa," *NYT*, 13 April 1991, pp. A-1 and A-3.

12. *El Nuevo Herald* (Miami), 9 January 1991; cited by *Update on Cuba* (Washington, D.C.), 22 January 1991, p. 1, about military officers. Pedro Prado, "Put' vybrali sami," *Pravda*, 17 April 1991, p. 5.

13. TASS (Managua), "Pokhishcheny rakety," *Pravda*, 3 January 1991, p. 1; Shirley Christian, "Nicaragua Defends Role as Rebel Haven," *NYT*, 15 April 1991, p. A-3.

14. Mark A. Uhlig, "Top Salvador Rebel Alters His Goals," *NYT*, 7 March 1991, p. A-3; V. Listov, "Kogda tretii—ne lishnii," *Pravda*, 27 March 1991, p. 5.

15. Special dispatch (Bogota), "Colombia Rebel Group Quits after 23 Years," *NYT*, 2 March 1991, p. 3; James Brooke, "Mass Graves Linked to Rebels," *NYT*, 7 April 1991, p. 3.

16. Nathaniel C. Nash (Lima), "Peru under Challenge," *NYT*, 27 February 1991, p. A-12; AP dispatch, "Rebels Black Out...," *NYT*, 7 April 1991, p. 4.

17. TASS (New York), "Osuzhdeny popytki razvalit' SSSR," *Pravda*, 21 February 1991, p. 5.

18. Willy Wo-Lap Lam, "Beijing Boosts Ties with Fellow Socialists," *The Australian* (Sydney), 19–20 January 1991, p. 13; reprinted from the *South China Morning Post* (Hong Kong). See also James McGregor, "China's Premier Lists Economic Woes," *WSJ*, 26 March 1991, p. A-19; "Chinese Communists Purged," *WSJ*, 17 April 1991, p. A-12.

19. S. Tikhomirov, "Na okraine Sarivona," *Pravda*, 27 December 1990, p. 5.

20. M. Domogatskikh (Hanoi), "Zemlia ikh voznagradit," *Pravda*, 17 January 1991, p. 5.

21. Cited by Steven Erlanger, "Vietnam Tries to Salvage Its Economy," *NYT*, 17 February 1991, sect. 3, p. 12; Nayan Chanda (Hanoi), "Vietnamese Rejected in East Bloc, Return Home Less Sure of Communism," *WSJ*, 2 April 1991, p. A-20.

22. Petr Tsvetov (Vientiane), "Vyverit' kurs," *Pravda*, 27 March 1991, p. 4; TASS (Vientiane), "Kambodzha," *Pravda*, 4 January 1991, p. 4.

23. "Nuzhny dela, a ne slova," *Pravda*, 26 February 1991, p. 5; V. Sapov (Ulan Bator), "Kurs—ne sdavat' pozitsii," *Pravda*, 28 February 1991, p. 4.

24. TASS, "Tovarishcheskaia vstrecha," *Pravda*, 19 February 1991, p. 5; Barbara Crossette, "India Dissolves Parliament," *NYT*, 14 March 1991, p. A-4; "India's Political Picture," *NYT*, 24 April 1991, p. A-4.

25. Richard F. Staar, ed., *East-Central Europe and the USSR* (New York: St. Martin's Press, 1991), passim.

26. See Table 2.2 for identification of the members in Staar, *Foreign Policies of the Soviet Union*, pp. 29–30.

27. A. Stepovoi and S. Chugaev, "Formiruetsia Sovet bezopasnosti SSSR," *Izvestiia*, 8 March 1991, p. 2.

28. TASS (Prague), "Zhurnal zakryt," *Pravda*, 23 May 1990, p. 7.

29. N. Miroshnik (Rome), "Voz'mite na dovol'stvie," *Pravda*, 12 March 1991, p. 5; E. Fadeev (Tiranë), "Peremeny v 'orlinom gnezde,'" *Pravda*, 30 March 1991, pp. 1 and 6; David Binder (Tiranë), "Communist Party Wins Majority in Albania's First Free Balloting," *NYT*, 2 April 1991, pp. A-1 and A-5.

30. "New Bulgarian Communist Party," RFE/RL *Daily Report*, no. 50 (12 March 1991): 3; "Lukanov Never a Bulgarian Citizen," RFE/RL *Daily Report*, no. 56 (20 March 1991): 2. See also L. Zhmyrev, "Ot diskussii k protivostoianiiu," *Pravda*, 20 March 1991, p. 4.

31. A. Krushinskii, "Raskol tait ugrozu," *Pravda*, 8 March 1991, p. 5; E. Fadeev and A. Krushinskii, "Federatsiia pod ugrozoi," *Pravda*, 13 March 1991, p. 1.

32. Ferdinand Protzman, "Germans Lower Expectations on East's Economic Recovery," *NYT*, 12 February 1991, pp. A-1 and C-2. M. Podkliuchnikov (Berlin), "PDS: Strategiia na zavtra," *Pravda*, 28 January 1991, p. 4; Podkliuchnikov, "Nozhnitsy vse shire," *Pravda*, 9 March 1991, p. 3; and Podkliuchnikov, "Glasnost' ili 'okhota na ved'm?'" *Pravda*, 30 March 1991, p. 6.

33. HSP figures in *Magyar Hirlap* (Budapest), 9 March 1991, p. 7; "MSZP Chairman on Tasks, Party's Struggle," *FBIS-EEU*, 14 March 1991, p. 28. On the anti-Soviet attitude in Hungary, see Vladimir Gerasimov (Budapest), "Imena steret' legko. A pamiat'?" *Pravda* 11 March 1991, p. 5.

34. See interview with the new Wałęsa-appointed prime minister by Anatolii Starukhin (Warsaw), "Khoziain novyi, kurs—prezhnii," *Pravda*, 4 February 1991, p. 5; Starukhin, "Pol'sha: tozhe natsionalnyi vopros?" *Pravda*, 9 March 1991, p. 6; and Starukhin, "Pamiat' nuzhna zhivym," *Pravda*, 23 March 1991, p. 6.

35. "National Salvation Front Convention," RFE/RL *Daily Report*, no. 54 (18 March 1991): 2; "Romania's Iliescu to Moscow" RFE/RL *Daily Report*, no. 64 (3 April 1991): 1–2.

36. E. Fadeev (Belgrade), "V Prezidiume—raskol, v armii—edinstvo," *Pravda*, 20 March 1991, p. 4. George Melloan, "One Yugoslav Crisis Is Over, but More Are Due." *WSJ*, 1 April 1991, p. A-13. For LC-MY members, see *Pobjeda* (Titograd), 3 March 1991, p. 5; "LC-MY Leader Explains Party's Positions," *FBIS-EEU*, 21 March 1991, p. 44.

37. V. Semenov, "Dva goda spustia: Pochemu my pomogaem Kabulu," *Pravda*, 15 February 1991, p. 4; J. Michael Luhan, "Afghan Rebels Revived by a Victory," *NYT*, 16 April 1991, p. A-7.

38. *Jordan Times* (Amman), 20 August 1990, pp. 1–4; "Islamists, Leftists Form 'National Front,'" *FBIS-NES*, 29 August 1990, pp. 38–39.

39. Walid Barakat and Muhammad 'Agl, "Interview with Kamil Muruwwah, Deputy General Secretary of the LCP," *al-Nida* (Beirut), 22 July 1990, p. 4; translation courtesy of Edward Jajko, deputy curator (Middle East) at the Hoover Institution.

40. Radio of the Iranian Toilers (clandestine in Farsi from Kabul), 10 October 1990; "Commentary Previews Tudeh Party Congress," *FBIS-NES*, 22 October 1990, pp. 62–64.

41. See the unusually detailed coverage of the PCF congress in *Pravda*, 20 December 1990, p. 4, 21 December 1990, p. 4, 22 December 1990, p. 1, and 23 December 1990, p. 5.

42. I. Miroshnik and A. Tarakanov, "S'ezd poslednii, s'ezd pervyi," *Pravda*, 1 February 1991, p. 1; "Universal'naia tsennost'," *Pravda*, 2 February 1991, p. 6. See also Clyde Haberman, "Italy's Cabinet Resigns Yet Again; Predictable Uncertainty Returns," *NYT*, 30 March 1991, p. 3.

43. V. Volkov, "Ubezhdennost'," *Pravda*, 6 March 1991, p. 5. See also Cuñhal's speech over Lisbon Radio, 24 March 1991; "PCP Leader Addresses Rally on Party Program," *FBIS-WEU*, 27 March 1991, pp. 21–22.

44. TASS (Athens), "Izbran sostav Politbiuro," *Pravda*, 11 March 1991, p. 6. Athens Radio, 9 March 1991; "New Coalition Chairperson, KKE Bureau Named," *FBIS-WEU*, 11 March 1991, p. 33. See also "Biodata on KKE Political Bureau Members," *Kiriakatiki Elevtherotipia*, 17 February 1991, pp. 12–13; translated in *FBIS-WEU*, 28 March 1991, pp. 38–40.

45. Note the meeting between four top PDS leaders with CPSU national secretary V. M. Falin; TASS (Moscow), "Mezhpartiinye sviazi," *Pravda*, 11 Janaury 1991, p. 4. See also Hamburg radio, 26 March 1991; "PDS Funds Deposited in Trust Agency," *FBIS-WEU*, 27 March 1991, p. 4.

Yearbook on
International
Communist Affairs
1991

AFRICA

Introduction

Communist regimes in Africa reflected to some degree the disintegration of communism or at least the loss of faith in Marxism among East European countries. In 1990 the ruling African communist parties continued to shift away from one-party organizations with centralized economic planning toward more-open systems. Internal opposition to the Marxist-Leninist policies and collapsing Socialist economies necessitated change in such states as Angola, Mozambique, Congo, Benin, and even Ethiopia. Change, however, was not uniform or far-reaching, and communist movements out of power generally adhered to orthodox Marxist-Leninist programs.

Once the most revolutionary African Marxist state, Mozambique during 1990 pursued the political and economic changes it had begun over the past three years. Its ruling party, Front for the Liberation of Mozambique (FRELIMO), debated, passed, and promulgated a new constitution allowing for multiparty elections in 1991. By mid-1990 two opposition parties had formed to challenge FRELIMO. The new constitution guaranteed freedom of the press and workers' right to strike. Symbolically, FRELIMO changed the country's name to the Republic of Mozambique, deleting the communist-inspired *people's* from the title.

Other dramatic shifts away from FRELIMO's previous policies were, first, negotiations with its guerrilla opponent and, second, an agreement between the government and the Mozambique National Resistance (RENAMO). After several talks the two sides entered into a limited agreement concerning the bitter guerrilla war that has plagued the countryside since the mid-1970s. The FRELIMO government and the RENAMO rebels accepted limiting Zimbabwe's troops to two narrow corridors across Mozambique. The two corridors coincide with the Beira and Limpopo rail and road links from the Zimbabwean border to the Mozambican coast.

An ally of FRELIMO, Zimbabwe relies on the two communication routes for import and export.

In the West African country of Benin, a process similar to the one under way in Mozambique has been at work as the People's Republic of Benin moved toward a multiparty system, a diminution of the state's role in the economy, and a change in the country's foreign policy orientation. But the ruling party, the Revolutionary Party of the People of Benin (PRPB), witnessed a fracturing of unity and a breakdown in control as Chairman Mathieu Kérékou (who is also president of the republic) sought to distance himself from the party. The PRPB also experienced criticism from the army, a main buttress of the party's authority since its founding in 1975. But Kerekou retained his power amid a collapsing PRPB because of his position of supreme commander of the army. Party leaders also exerted continued domination over the trade union, youth and women's movements, and the media, as well as the military; otherwise the party was a shell.

Down the West African coast, the Congo's ruling party also experienced a disintegration of control that resembled events a year earlier in Eastern Europe. During the July Central Committee meeting of the Congolese Party of Labor (PCT), it was agreed that a multiparty system be allowed to develop following a party congress scheduled for February 1991. This decision marked a sharp departure from the Leninist form of vanguard party that had dominated the country since a 1968 coup. The same meeting saw the departure of a number of prominent Central Committee leaders.

After the July meeting, the regime's plans to limit and control the process of change became frayed. First, the government arrested opponents for demanding democracy. Then the PCT moved against its own trade union federation when it declared its independence from the party. Rioting erupted in major cities when the unions declared a general strike. Finally, the government gave in to most of the federation's demands. Some churches and university students also confronted the government with demands for an end to Marxism-Leninism.

The most serious challenge to the PCT's domination, however, came from a revolt within its own ranks. Several prominent leaders defected to the opposition parties, which have been officially tolerated since June. Privatization of some government holdings, such as gasoline distributors, took place. The Congo's foreign affairs reflected the domestic changes, as when the PCT asked a contingent of Moroccan troops to replace the Cubans as the regime's main security unit.

Across the continent, Ethiopia's Socialist system underwent a marked deterioration. President Mengistu Haile Mariam announced the abandonment of Marxism-Leninism. Weakened by civil war and economic failures, the government began to move away from past policies, but its ability to control change slipped badly.

Reformers within the Workers' Party of Ethiopia (WPE) achieved far-reaching economic reforms, most significantly in agriculture. The government abandoned the destructive campaign whereby rural residents were forced into villages, allowed free trade in most agricultural commodities, abolished the rigid delivery quota system, and ended producer cooperatives.

Other areas also experienced limited change. Small-scale trade and midlevel private industry expanded in urban sectors to match the increased agricultural production. But the regime's reluctance to follow through with further reforms deprived the economy of greater strides. The WPE also resisted pressure from the World Bank and major aid donors to reduce the size of government and to devalue the currency.

Despite some economic changes, political reform remained stalemated. The president's announced transformation of the WPE into the Democratic Unity Party of Ethiopia went nowhere. But the party structure disintegrated in the countryside, and members left it. The regime appeared isolated when, after a trial, it executed twelve army generals for their role in an attempted coup. This political stalemate was matched by the central government's position in the civil war against secessionists. Government forces managed to regain some early losses by the last quarter of the year, but the long war continued to sap the regime's strength and debilitate the economy.

In Zimbabwe, the collapse of one-party states and of communism in Eastern Europe also had repercussions. These dramatic changes undermined Zimbabwean adherents to Marxist-Leninist politics and economics in the southern African state. A general election, the third since independence, revealed discontent and apathy among the electorate, with the opposition doing well in urban centers. President Robert Mugabe lost Politburo support for his de jure one-party state and dropped plans to legislate for it. He conceded in September to the wishes of the Central Committee, which strove to enjoy the benefits of a de facto one-party state while maintaining a multiparty system in deference to popular demand.

Other policy changes in Zimbabwe during 1990 moved the economy from a Socialist orientation toward a market-driven system. The government also permitted the state of emergency to lapse after 25 years. Although modest in scope, a trade liberalization program and restructuring were put into effect. Foreign investment, long recognized by some as necessary for economic development, was encouraged by generous allowances for repatriation of profits and the government's signing investment protection guarantees. Price controls for most products have been lifted as part of the restructuring, and wage negotiations are to be handled by employer and employee councils. The government announced plans to eliminate or privatize parastatals and to trim the size of the civil service by 25 percent to reduce its deficit.

But government intervention in agricultural production appeared to be strengthened when the Lancaster House agreement, signed at independence to limit Mugabe's distribution of land to peasants, expired. A major peasant grievance during the war against white rule, land redistribution was blocked until 1990 by independence terms negotiated in London. Parliament also amended the constitution in the year under review so that the government may acquire land through compulsion at prices it determines without the present owners' having recourse to the courts to question the price. The government announced plans to acquire half the land in commercial hands and redistribute it to master communal farmers.

Among nonruling communist parties, only one appeared influenced enough by international circumstances and African realities to change its policies and perspective on the world. In Senegal the Independence and Labor Party (PIT) held its Third Congress to usher in a pragmatic approach to the country's problems; the PIT, that West African nation's communist party, accepted not only a market economy but also a liberal democratic system. General Secretary Amath Dansokho declared that "the socialist revolution, as it occurred in October 1917, has exhausted its potential" (*WMR*, February).

Nonruling communist parties, however, tended

to adhere to an orthodox approach to questions of politics, economics, and foreign relations. In the Sudan, for example, the Sudanese Communist Party (SCP) made few changes in its domestic politics. As a small party on the periphery, the SCP is noted for its participation in an opposition coalition to the military regime in power. In foreign policy, it remained a relatively orthodox, Soviet-oriented communist party that endorsed policies leading to the end of the cold war but maintained an anti-imperialist view of the world.

Off the coast of the Indian Ocean on Réunion Island, the Réunion Communist Party (PCR) continued its traditional collaboration with opposition forces to government policies. It remained an advocate of programs to remedy economic and social inequalities, as well as industrial and agricultural underdevelopment. The PCR also fully supported an April general strike, along with numerous smaller strikes across the island.

The African continent's oldest communist organization, the South African Communist Party (SACP), experienced a dramatic change in its legal status. In February it was unbanned by the white government of F. W. de Klerk along with the major antiapartheid movement, the African National Congress (ANC). This resulted in significant internal discussions of and efforts at reorientation and reorganization, as the SACP made the transition from a clandestine, subversive organization into a legitimate party. The SACP established open party organizations, debated the size of an appropriate membership, and sought a new role in South African politics. In December, it moved its publication offices from London to Johannesburg.

The declaration of legality occurred during a time of great soul-searching in communist parties because of the profound transformations of socialism in Eastern Europe and, to a lesser degree, within the Soviet Union. Joe Slovo, the general secretary, early in the year publicly stated that socialism was in the throes of a crisis greater than any since 1917. Although acknowledging the need for self-examination, he defended the future of socialism and "its inherent moral superiority" and would not "dismiss its whole past as an unmitigated failure." But Slovo concluded that past failures had to be recognized and that "its fundamental tenet—socialist democracy—occupies a rightful place in future practice" (*Has Socialism Failed?* pamphlet published by the SACP). Slovo was criticized for his negative assessment of the development of the Soviet Union.

In fact, links between the SACP and the Soviet Union remained close. Slovo met with a Politburo member of the Communist Party of the Soviet Union who reaffirmed the "Soviet Communist Party's invariable solidarity with South African Communists" (*FBIS-SOV*, 21 August). The SACP's connection also remained with the ANC. Appearing almost as an anachronism in light of events in Eastern Europe, SACP demonstrators often carried posters in rallies proclaiming orthodox communist slogans about class struggle, imperialism, and the primacy of the party in politics and the economy.

Thomas H. Henriksen
Hoover Institution

Angola

Population. 8,534,483 (July)
Party. Popular Movement for the Liberation of Angola—Labor Party (Movimento Popular de Libertação—Partido do Trabalho, MPLA-PT)
Founded. December 1956 (renamed December 1977)
Membership. 45,000 (Radio Luanda, 8 December; *FBIS-AFR*, 9 December 1987)
Head of State and Party. José Eduardo dos Santos (since 21 September 1979)
Politburo. 21 members: 17 full, 4 alternate. Full, as of 12 December: José Eduardo dos Santos, Afonso Domingos van Dunem Mbinda, Alberto Correia Neto, Antonio dos Santos Franca Ndalu, Bornito de Sousa Baltazar Diogo, Domingos Manuel Njinga, Fernando Jose Franca van Dunem, Francisco Magalhães Paiva Nvunda, Jacinto Venancio Chipopa, João Manuel Goncalves Lourenco, Juliao Mateus Paulo Dino Matross, Kundi Paihama, Lopo Fortunato Ferreira do Nascimento, Marcolino Jose Carlos Moco, Maria Mambo Cafe, Maria Ruth Neto, and Roberto Antonio Vitor Francisco de Almeida. Alternate: Manuel Pedro Pacavira, Norberto Fernandes dos Santos, Pedro de Castro van Dúnem Loy, and Pedro Mutinde.

Central Committee. 90 members: 75 full, 15 alternate

Status. Ruling party

Last Congress. Third, 4–9 December 1990

Last Election. December 1986 (legislative only); all 203 candidates MPLA-PT approved

Auxiliary Organizations. National Union of Angolan Workers (UNTA), Organization of Angolan Women (OMA), MPLA Youth (JMPLA), Angolan National Peasants' Union (UNACA), People's Defense Organization (ODP), Agostinho Neto Young Pioneer Organization (OPA)

Publication. *Jornal de Angola* (official newspaper, daily); ANGOP is the Angolan news agency.

The government of the People's Republic of Angola termed 1990 the year of the MPLA Labor Party Third Congress for the expansion of democracy. It was also nearly the year of a decisive victory over the National Union for the Total Independence of Angola, UNITA.

Both sides suffered heavy losses when between late December 1989 and May 1990 the MPLA attempted to subdue UNITA by launching an attack on a UNITA base of operation in the Mavinga-Jamba area. The net result was basically a stalemate: MPLA's superior conventional forces inflicted heavy damage on the Mavinga-Jamba area, while UNITA's guerrilla activity spread throughout the nation, causing disruption in power and water lines. UNITA was able to keep the MPLA forces busy without any outside help. After May, the conflict abated and the peace process gained momentum.

The Peace Process. UNITA had previously recognized José Eduardo dos Santos as the Angolan head of state on 1 May. The insurgents urged that "Engineer José Eduardo dos Santos be above political clashes and referee the conflict" (Voice of Resistance of the Black Cockerel, 2 May; *FBIS-AFR*, 2 May).

From June until November representatives of UNITA and MPLA met four times in Portugal. Both sides had grown wary of Joseph Mobutu of Zaire as mediator. Each time the participants discussed arrangements for a cease-fire and recognition of UNITA. UNITA's agenda called for explicit mutual recognition by both parties, a firm and irreversible commitment to multiparty democracy with a timetable set for free and fair elections, a cease-fire monitored by the international community, the formation of a national army, and assurances of

fundamental liberties including freedom of speech, religion, press, and association. MPLA countered with its own proposals: the cease-fire should come first and UNITA would be demilitarized and placed under a special (undefined) regime according to the Angolan constitution.

The two groups made intermittent progress at best until the December MPLA party congress and the subsequent MPLA, UNITA, USSR, United States, and Portugal meeting in Washington (see International Affairs below). The next session between MPLA-UNITA was scheduled for late January 1991 in Portugal, where it was expected that the two sides would sign a cease-fire agreement leading to elections at some future date.

Mass Organizations. In keeping with Angola's trend toward democratization, the MPLA Youth (JMPLA) announced in April that the organization would drop its Marxist-Leninist character. JMPLA assistant secretary Mario Pinto de Andrade said the group must become more democratic, permitting participation by every young person, irrespective of their political beliefs. (Radio Luanda, 21 April; *FBIS-AFR*, 23 April.)

The Organization of Angolan Women (OMA) refused to make their formal presentation to the MPLA-PT Third Congress to protest the small number of women delegates. Ruth Neto, secretary general of OMA, announced from her seat (rather than the podium) that only 59 of 700 delegates to the congress were women. In addition, the Politburo had only one woman, with six on the Central Committee. President dos Santos apologized for the inequity and promised to correct the situation in the future. (Radio Luanda, 6 December; *FBIS-AFR*, 7 December.)

The Angolan National Peasants' Union (UNACA) also presented a report to the Third Congress. UNACA's goal was to promote cooperation among the 300,000 peasants in the peasant associations and agricultural cooperatives. The UNACA delegate stressed, however, that "the weapons must be silenced so that peasants can have multi-faceted development in the villages." (Radio Luanda, 6 December; *FBIS-AFR*, 7 December.)

Party Leadership. President dos Santos, perhaps in expectation of the December Third Party Congress, began to emerge as a more dynamic, decisive leader. At times his pronouncements on reform went well beyond those approved by the more conservative Politburo. On 15 June, dos Santos appointed Boaventura da Silva Cardoso to the powerful position of minister of information. Cardoso, a close political ally of the president, was expected to use the Information and Propaganda Department to create a favorable political climate for the president's policies. (Luanda, ANGOP, 15 June; *FBIS-AFR*, 20 June.) There were some minor administrative changes early in the year. (Luanda, ANGOP, 26 February; *FBIS-AFR*, 1 March.) The president dismissed Carlos Fernandes, minister of transportation and communications, and Eduardo Paulo Bonga, secretary of state for town planning, housing and water, for laziness and nonimplementation of legal directives (Radio Luanda, 5 May; *FBIS-AFR*, 7 May).

President dos Santos continued to encounter difficulties in implementing Angola's economic and financial restructuring program, Saneamento Económico e Financiero (SEF). In an attempt to shake up the SEF bureaucracy, dos Santos fired the finance and planning ministers, Augusto Teixeira de Matos and António Henriques da Silva, on 14 June. Aguinaldo Jaime, previously head of the foreign investment office in the Ministry of Planning, was appointed finance minister, and Fernando José de Franca Van-Dúnem was moved from justice to planning. The president also removed the governor of the National Bank of Angola (BNA), António da Silva Inácio, appointing in his place Pedro da Cunha Neto, previously deputy governor of the bank.

At the swearing-in ceremony, dos Santos said that the changes in personnel should not "be viewed as just another government reshuffle but as a necessary measure." The Angolan head of state said that the government's sluggish approach to implementing SEF had weakened "the authority of government members in implementing defined programs." (Radio Luanda, 18 June; *FBIS-AFR*, 20 June.) The SEF program has lagged because (1) the president and upper echelons of MPLA have been preoccupied with the war and peace negotiations, (2) there has been a shortage of trained economic personnel to draft and implement the reform effort, and (3) key governmental officials continued to ignore or sabotage official SEF directives.

The Council of Ministers of the Angolan government devalued the national currency by 100 percent on 21 September. Another 100 percent devaluation was also predicted. The council abolished the kwanza as the national currency and introduced the new kwanza. Citizens were given seven days to exchange old currency for new. (Radio Luanda,

FBIS-AFR, 21 September.) President dos Santos acknowledged the unpopularity of the devaluation but warned that "there is no other medicine for the serious evils afflicting our economy." UNITA reported protests to the currency conversion. (Kwacha, UNITA Press, 23 October; *FBIS-AFR*, 24 October.) One effect of the new currency was to make UNITA's vast holdings of old kwanzas valueless.

By November, dos Santos had relieved Pedro Neto as governor of the BNA, replacing him with Fernando Alberto da Graca Teixeira. Also, Minister of Trade and Industry Dumilde das Chagas Rangel was replaced on an interim basis by Deputy Trade Minister Antonio de Oliveira Silvestre. (Radio Luanda, 4 November; *FBIS-AFR*, 6 November.) In another appointment, Lopo do Nascimento became special assistant to the president for political affairs. A pragmatist, Nascimento spent the rest of the year negotiating with the UNITA insurgents.

On the military front, dos Santos replaced Southern Front commander Lieutenant General António dos Santos Franca ("Ndalu") in May, transferring him to the Cuanza-Bengo political and military front. The Cuanza-Bengo area is southeast of Luanda and had become heavily infiltrated by UNITA forces heeding Savimbi's order to spread the war nationwide. (Radio Luanda, 7 May; *FBIS-AFR*, 11 May.) Ndalu, an MPLA hard-liner, had argued for an attack on Mavinga to knock UNITA out of the war. Failure to capture the UNITA bases led to his dismissal. (*Africa Confidential*, 9 March.) More ominously, on 7 November, President dos Santos took charge of the Defense Ministry and assumed the post of FAPLA chief of general staff. A communiqué announced the changes "in light of the needs arising from ongoing political change in the country." (Radio Luanda, 7 November; *FBIS-AFR*, 8 November.)

Although the Third Party Congress reaffirmed his leadership, the Angolan president faced a difficult future. On the one hand, he was attempting to create conditions conducive for the installation of a democratic form of government and a free market economy. On the other hand, dos Santos had to protect his policies from hard-liners within the MPLA who feared Jonas Savimbi and UNITA. MPLA cadres were concerned that free and fair elections in a multiparty system would mean the end of their privileges in Angolan society and that negotiations with UNITA suggested defeat. Assuming the role of defense minister and FAPLA chief of staff may have been an attempt by dos Santos to forestall a coup by hard-liners within the military.

Party Affairs. The MPLA Central Committee's Twenty-fourth Ordinary Session met 15–18 January and decided that the party should change its role from "avant-garde of the working class" to "avant-garde of all the working people" but that "the single-party system is the most appropriate at this historic stage and most in line with the political choices governing the People's Republic of Angola" (AFP, 20 January; *FBIS-AFR*, 23 January). Days later, MPLA secretary for ideological affairs Robert de Almeida reiterated the party's position that "elections cannot be held with other parties, because they would cause a great deal of confusion" (*Noticias*, 12 February; *FBIS-AFR*, 23 March). A document from the 24–26 February Special Session of the Central Committee, however, stated that only a single party system "can realistically serve the country's political, economic and social development" but acknowledged that when peace and internal security had been restored, a multiparty system might evolve.

By July, at the Twenty-fifth Ordinary Session, the Central Committee voted to "evolve toward a multiparty system," though adoption of the multiparty system needed approval via a popular referendum. President dos Santos noted that MPLA would have "to grow to earn its place in society on its own merits." (Radio Luanda, 3 July; *FBIS-AFR*, 5 July.) The communiqué issued at the conclusion of the Central Committee meeting warned that intellectuals, managers, students, and administrative officials "deserve special attention because of some ideological confusion being experienced as a result of the changes occurring in Eastern European countries" (*Jornal de Angola*, 4 July; *FBIS-AFR*, 29 August).

At this time the committee agreed to relaunch SEF and accelerate its implementation. The Central Committee, which was scheduled to meet for three days, was in session for eight. The debate was acrimonious; when the meeting adjourned the hardliners of MPLA had been defeated. (Between the February Special Session and the July Ordinary Session of the Central Committee, the FAPLA offensive against Mavinga-Jamba failed.)

President dos Santos convened a Special Session of the Central Committee on 25–26 October that agreed to amend the Angolan constitution to allow for a multiparty system. Dos Santos noted that general elections could only be held three years after the end of the war. (ANGOP, 25 October; *FBIS-AFR*, 26 October.) UNITA welcomed dos Santos's remarks but rejected the three-year date for national elections (Voice of the Resistance of the Black Cockerel, 5 November; *FBIS-AFR*, 8 November).

Another Special Session of the Central Committee met in Luanda from 14 to 16 November to finalize preparations for the Third Party Congress. The committee decided to support a policy of "democratic socialism," move from observer status in the Socialist International to full membership, and develop a mixed economy. (Radio Luanda, 17 November; *FBIS-AFR*, 19 November.)

The MPLA-PT's Third Ordinary Congress began in Luanda on 4 December with the opening speech by President dos Santos. In his remarks, dos Santos told the seven hundred delegates that "this will perhaps be the last MPLA-Labor Party Congress to be held under a one-party system." (Radio Luanda, 4 December; *FBIS-AFR*, 5 December.) The MPLA congress was noteworthy for its openness (although some sessions were closed) and the candor of the speeches and documents. For example, the 134-page Central Committee report stated that in 1988, $1 billion had been spent on defense alone and that the economic crisis exacerbated by the drop in global oil prices had as a root cause "mismanagement, incompetence, corruption and foot dragging." Angola's foreign debt was placed at $6 billion ($4 billion of which was owed to the USSR); since 1986 the deficit had almost doubled. (ANGOP, 5 December; *FBIS-AFR*, 6 December.)

The National Constitutional Revision Committee proposed for either discussion or approval deleting "People's" from the official name of the People's Republic of Angola, renaming the People's Assembly the National Assembly, renaming the army the Angolan Armed Forces, and changing the title of MPLA—Labor Party to MPLA, MPLA—Party of the People, or no change. Recommendations for the National Assembly included five-year terms for deputies, election by direct universal voting on the basis of proportional representation, and having the assembly function year round. (Radio Luanda, 7 December; *FBIS-AFR*, 7 December.)

The Constitutional Revision Committee proposed that a semipresidential system be introduced in Angola. One plan suggested that the president of the republic be elected by direct and secret universal suffrage based on a majority over two election rounds. The president would hold office for seven years and could be reelected once. The alternative plan suggested a five-year term with the possibility of two other terms.

The president would appoint a prime minister and a council of ministers. The chief executive would also have the power to command the armed forces, dissolve the assembly, and take exceptional measures. The minimum age for a presidential candidate would be 35 years. (ANGOP, 6 December; *FBIS-AFR*, 7 December.)

The civil war and the future of UNITA were also discussed but did not dominate the proceedings. The message from the general staff to the congress reiterated FAPLA's determination "to annihilate the agents of armed banditry . . . UNITA." Later, in debating the ongoing peace negotiations, a delegate who was a member of the armed forces accused UNITA of "behaving irresponsibly and in a deceitful manner. Incomprehensibly, UNITA has been increasing its acts of terrorism and sabotage, its murders of defenseless civilians, and its attacks on economic and social targets." (Radio Luanda, 9 December; *FBIS-AFR*, 10 December.) Although not explicitly recognizing UNITA, the congress gave its support to the MPLA-UNITA peace talks.

In his closing speech to the party congress, the Angolan chief executive summarized the highlights of the six-day event: "The MPLA-Labor Party Third Congress ratified the choice of a multiparty political system; a mixed economic system based on market forces; and the transformation of the party's nature and orientation." He went on to remind the delegates, however, that

> it is up to the militants to explain to the people throughout the country the process of democratization and openness. They must report the true objectives of those who want to destroy democracy. . . . Those people want to hamper the building of a democratic and legal state in which each person can freely follow his or her political choice and choose the party that defends his or her interests and rights without being forced to do so at gunpoint. (Radio Luanda, 9 December; *FBIS-AFR*, 10 December.)

Most of these proposals are to be finalized at a special MPLA congress scheduled for April 1991. Reports indicate that the military will resist several of the recommendations. (*CSM*, 18 December.)

After the Third Party Congress, the MPLA Central Committee held its first ordinary meeting 19–20 December. The first order of business was the election of the Politburo. The committee, following decisions made by the congress, transformed the Central Committee Secretariat into the Politburo Secretariat. The committee also re-

affirmed that all political forces in Angola would have to agree on a timetable for elections. (Radio Luanda, 20 December; *FBIS-AFR*, 20 December.)

International Affairs. Close relations with Brazil continued especially in the petroleum exploration field. Agreements signed in late 1989 between the two nations stressed cooperation in prospecting and drilling for oil. Petroleum Minister Zeferino Yombo initialed the documents for Angola. (*Diario de Noticias*, 4 December 1989; *FBIS-AFR*, 17 January.) Other 1990 agreements with Brazil focused on agriculture, mineral extraction, and small business development.

Angola continued to cultivate good relations with the European Community (EC). Spain announced that it would financially assist in rehabilitating Angola's fishing industry. In addition, Angola contracted to purchase eleven coastal patrol vessels. Originally the Soviet Union had supplied the Angolan fleet; the Spanish agreement was thought to be further evidence of the growing separation between Angola and the USSR. (*Insight*, 5 February.) Also in November, Spain granted Angola $10.3 million in credit packages (Radio Luanda, *FBIS-AFR*, 29 November).

French trade with Angola climbed to record levels. In seeking to diversify sources of military hardware, France has become Angola's main source of Western arms. Additionally, French exports to Angola increased by 26 percent. In September, France agreed to finance a national system of satellite programming receivers. (*Insight*, 17 September.) The France-Angola Friendship Association was proclaimed in September to "promote friendly relations" between the two nations.

Great Britain, Belgium, Italy, Germany, and the Netherlands also provided credits, grants, or signed various contracts for construction or rehabilitation projects. Numerous other companies promised assistance when the civil war was resolved.

On 12 April ANGOP began a "full-duplex" link with China's Xinhua news agency. The connection, which began within the sphere of previous agreements, allowed ANGOP to be disseminated throughout Asia. (ANGOP, 12 April; *FBIS-AFR*, 13 April.) In May a Chinese delegation visited places of social, economic, and cultural interest in Angola. The People's Republic of China (PRC) team was repaying a visit an MPLA delegation made to China in 1989. (Radio Luanda, 24 May; *FBIS-AFR*, 25 May.) The PRC deputy culture minister visited Luanda in September to reaffirm his government's desire for strengthened Angola-PRC cultural relations. A signed agreement called for art expositions, cultural teams, and musicians to visit both nations.

PRC ambassador to Angola Hu Lipeng announced that China had granted two loans of $21 million to Angola to buy Chinese products. Dry batteries, toys, bicycles, and tires were among the best-selling Chinese products on the Angolan market. The ambassador noted that bilateral trade was low in comparison to other years but announced that China was prepared for cooperation in tourism and the hotel industry if the Angolan authorities supported it. (Radio Luanda, 27 September; FBIS-AFR, 28 September.)

African National Congress (ANC) leader Nelson Mandela visited Luanda in May. Mandela thanked the government and people of Angola for their support. "The progress we have made in our armed struggle is owed largely to Angola," said the ANC leader. At a ceremony, President dos Santos awarded Mandela the Agostinho Neto Order, Angola's highest decoration. (Radio Luanda, 12 May; FBIS-AFR, 14 May.)

In December, Palestine Liberation Organization (PLO) chairman Yassir Arafat visited Angola. During his short stay, Arafat met with President dos Santos and other Politburo members.

Ties between Cuba and Angola remained firm despite the withdrawal of Cuban troops and the expulsion of an ANGOP journalist from Havana. According to the U.N. monitoring team, 32,800 soldiers had departed Angola by 1 April. (Radio Luanda, 19 April; FBIS-AFR, 19 April.) By year's end, the United Nations had verified the Cuban troop withdrawal to be on schedule. Because of the Cuban withdrawal, only 86 doctors were left in Angola as opposed to 310 in 1988. According to the Health Ministry, doctors from the Soviet Union, Bulgaria, Vietnam, and the United Nations would help alleviate the shortage. (ANGOP, 7 November; FBIS-AFR, 9 November.)

The Angolan Politburo issued a declaration 15 May condemning the broadcast of TV Marti from the United States to Cuba. The statement urged the United States to "abdicate its aggressive stance against the Republic of Cuba."

Angolan-Soviet relations continued on an uneven course. Standing joint commissions continued their labors. In February, the Joint Angolan-USSR Energy Subcommission met to discuss the USSR's participation in constructing Capanda dam, Angola's biggest economic project. The Soviet Union

has provided money and equipment toward completion. The USSR-Angola Friendship Association met in August. The Soviets donated movie cameras, books, games, and other means of recreation and were also financing construction of a sports palace in Luanda.

Soviet foreign minister Eduard Shevardnadze visited Angola 18–19 March. At a press conference, the Soviet foreign minister said,

> I believe that we have an African solution to the problem. The country's clemency policy is the key to this program. . . . However, we fully agree with the measures taken by the government of the People's Republic of Angola, because there can only be a political solution; obviously there cannot be a military solution. (Radio Luanda, 18 March; FBIS-AFR, 19 March.)

In September the Soviet government suggested and Angola accepted the "triple zero" proposal. Under that plan, the USSR would end military aid to MPLA, the United States would cease assistance to UNITA, and both MPLA and UNITA would refrain from seeking armaments from third parties. UNITA and the United States rejected the triple zero strategy. (NYT, 17 September.) As the negotiation process deteriorated for MPLA, Shevardnadze met with Savimbi on 12 December. At the conclusion of the meeting the Soviet foreign minister remarked, "Savimbi made a great impression on me as an educated man with an original turn of mind and an interesting interlocutor." More important, Shevardnadze agreed that early elections were preferable to the three-year timetable advocated by MPLA. (Washington Times, 21 December.)

Angolan relations with the United States continued to be unsatisfactory. The Bush administration refused to abandon UNITA. Secretary of State for African Affairs Herman Cohen arrived in Luanda 24 January. The Angolans told him that the civil war continued "because the United States, its successive governments, have always interfered in Angola's internal affairs." (FBIS-AFR, 25 January.) A scheduled February visit to the United States by President dos Santos was canceled because of "private pressure brought to bear by the Bush Administration." A spokesman for Transafrica, a private U.S. group that lobbies for black American interests said, "The Bush Administration's back-channel pressure violates the cardinal principle of an open society." (WP, 25 January.) Transafrica has consistently refused to meet with UNITA leader Jonas Savimbi despite his many visits to the United States.

Despite uncertain relations, the U.S. petroleum industry maintained close relations with Angola. The Iraqi invasion of Kuwait highlighted the importance of Angola's oil to the United States, which imports 20 percent of its average daily oil demand from Africa. The United States imports more oil from Nigeria and Angola than from Kuwait and Iraq; in fact, Angola sold twice as much oil to the United States as Kuwait did. (*CSM*, 11 December.)

Luanda reacted to the Iraqi invasion of Kuwait with "indignation." The Angolan government "condemns the invasion of Kuwait...and calls on the Iraqi government to unconditionally withdraw its troops." (Radio Luanda, 6 August; *FBIS-AFR*, 7 August.) However, the resultant dramatic increase in oil prices, combined with an increase in the volume of oil production, provided short-term relief to Angola's balance of payments.

Still, the United States refused to abandon UNITA as witness Savimbi's visit to Washington in October. Savimbi met with President Bush, Secretary of State Baker, and key members of Congress. (*Washington Times*, 3 October.) Later in October the House of Representatives refused to end the $60 million aid package to UNITA, although it passed an amendment providing for the suspension of aid if the Angolan government moved toward a peaceful settlement and if the Soviet Union cut off aid to MPLA (*WP*, 23 October). President Bush later vetoed the amendment because he viewed it as unduly restrictive of executive power.

Because of the fifteen-year civil war, the drought, and the indiscriminate laying of mines by both sides, more than 2 million people, or one-fourth of the Angolan population, were threatened with starvation. Under pressure from the United States, the USSR, and world relief organizations, the two warring sides agreed to establish "corridors of peace" to permit safe transportation of foodstuffs. (*NYT*, 3 November.) On 2 November, after months of accusations and uncertainties, a U.N. convoy carrying food and medicine left the port city of Lobito for famine-stricken areas in central Angola.

The UNITA insurgents were concerned that convoys might conceal government troops conducting offensive operations, whereas the Angolan government was suspicious that food shipments would be used to supply UNITA militarily. The relief program finally moved forward because neither MPLA nor UNITA wished to be cast as the villain in the famine tragedy.

The United States and the Soviet Union seemed determined to halt the Angolan civil war. Economically, the Soviet Union could no longer shoulder Angola's military failures. Nor did Moscow seem to possess the ideological fervor to maintain MPLA's commitment to Marxism-Leninism. The Soviet Union was also in no position to object to Washington's requests. Food aid, repeal of Jackson-Vanik, loans, grants and credits were vital to the economic revitalization of the USSR. It appeared that if Washington insisted then Soviet president Gorbachev was prepared to abandon MPLA. The United States was under pressure from the business community to resolve the civil war peacefully. Angola's potential petroleum reserves made it a lucrative market, unlike the rest of Africa. Further, the congressional support forged by Presidents Reagan and Bush was slowly unraveling as Congress began to view the Angolan civil war as an anachronism of the cold war era. Finally, resolving the war in Angola would allow the Bush administration to focus efforts on the disintegrating situation in South Africa.

In December, at the request of Portugal and under the aegis of the USSR and the United States, Jonas Savimbi and Lopo do Nascimento met in Washington. There the two sides agreed to set a date for free elections monitored by the international community, sign a cease-fire guaranteed by international forces, and end outside military assistance on signature of the cease-fire agreement. Lopo do Nascimento left Washington asking for more time to confer with his superiors. (*NYT*, 15 December.)

Most damaging for the MPLA was the Shevardnadze meeting with Savimbi discussed above. Shevardnadze reportedly guaranteed Moscow's support for a peaceful solution to the civil war no matter what the adverse consequences for MPLA might be.

MPLA seemed to have placed great expectations on the FAPLA assault against Mavinga-Jamba. When that effort failed in May, dos Santos used that failure to purge some party hard-liners and replace them with party pragmatists. President dos Santos faced the daunting task of trying to end the civil war while maintaining political support within the Politburo. MPLA hard-liners suffered a number of setbacks but still held prominent positions in both the party and the government.

W. Martin James III
Henderson State University

Benin

Population. 4,673,964
Party. Revolutionary Party of the People of Benin (Parti Révolutionnaire du Peuple du Bénin, PRPB)
Founded. 1975
Membership. No more than a few hundred
Chairman. Mathieu Kérékou (also president of the republic)
Politburo. Kérékou, Martin Dohou Azonhiho, Joseph Deguela, Gado Giriguissou, Roger Imoru Garba, Justin Guidehou, Sanni Mama Gomina, Romain Vilon Guezo, Vincent Guezodje, Idi Abdoulaye Mallam, Simon Ifede Ogouma
Central Committee. 45 members
Status. Uncertain since March
Last Congress. Second (ordinary), November 1985
Last Election. 18 June 1989. All 206 National Assembly members were nominated by the PRPB; all were elected.
Auxiliary Organizations. Organization of the Revolutionary Youth of Benin (PJRB), Organization of the Revolutionary Women of Benin (OFRB), National Federation of Workers' Unions of Benin (UNSTB), Committees for the Defense of the Revolution (CDR)
Publications. *Handoria* (PRPB publication); *Ehuzu* (government-controlled daily); *Bénin-Magazine* (monthly), published by the government-run National Press, Publishing and Printing Office.

Party Affairs. The year 1990 witnessed Benin's continuous transition from the proclaimed "scientific socialism" of the Kérékou regime toward a multiparty, free-for-all system, a diminution of the state's role in the economy, and a reorientation of the country's foreign and security policies. The decomposition of PRPB rule, which had begun at the end of 1989, accelerated rapidly, as did the breakdown of the already tenuous party unity. Although President Kérékou succeeded in retaining some authority, he is becoming increasingly marginalized. Army and party rule have been coterminous in Benin since 1975, and the first clear indication that PRPB rule was collapsing was a 29 January public statement by the Garrison Revolutionary Committee—the military wing of the party. Signed by the group's leader, Warrant Officer Alassane Issifou Yabe, also a PRPB Central Committee member, and Major Philippe Gnamou, Kérékou's military secretary, the statement charged that PRPB rule was based on "influence-peddling and sectarianism" and called for a two-party state, the separation of state and party, the depoliticization of the military, and an economy based on free enterprise (Paris, AFP, 30 January; *FBIS-AFR*, 31 January). The military statement demonstrated that Kérékou's control over his army as a whole had collapsed but did not indicate that the president had lost significant, indeed essential, support. The statement refrained from attacking Kérékou personally, and signs of divisions within the military and the PRPB became clearer after the change of government on 1 March. Hard-line party barons, particularly Martin Dohou Azonhiho, were openly and plausibly accused of plotting a coup (London, BBC, 14 May; *FBIS-AFR*, 17 May); some units have accepted both the reforms and the leadership of the transitional prime minister, Nicephore Soglo, who is also defense minister; and some, the most important ones, remain loyal to Kérékou, if not to the PRPB. Among those loyal to Kérékou are the fifteen hundred members of the Presidential Guard Battalion (BGP) commanded by Jean Thia and made up exclusively of Kérékou's own ethnic group; the BGP is the only military unit with permanent access to ammunition. (Ibid., 27 April; *Africa Confidential*, 10 August.) In addition to the BGP, Kérékou also retains his grip on the security services, particularly the Service de Documentation et d'Information (SDI), led by the former chief of the presidential military cabinet, Capt. Jerome Soglohoun (London, *Africa Confidential*, 6 April; *FBIS-AFR*, 16 May).

Kérékou remained as supreme commander of the army, but the commander in chief, Politburo member Vincent Guezodje, a known hard-liner, had to be stopped from shooting the unarmed demonstrators of December 1989 by Kérékou himself. The outcome of that episode reinforced the popular perception that Kérékou is the PRPB's leading reformer and the only one who can prevent or stop a coup by hard-liners like Azonhiho and Guezodje. That perception also fits with Kérékou's strategy of detaching himself from the sinking PRPB boat while retaining his authority, his job, and a share in policy-making. In light of these realities, Soglo's calls for a complete restructuring of the military remain in the realm of good intentions.

Despite his talent for survival, Kérékou's political future is far from certain, particularly after the July extradition from the Ivory Coast of his former personal adviser, security chief, and widely feared and hated alter ego, Mohamed Amadou Cisse. Accused of embezzling more than $100 million, Cisse could be a dangerous witness against his former boss, the PRPB leadership, and senior military officers. The PRPB as a party, never a particularly credible or coherent organization, virtually collapsed in 1990.

Whatever power the PRPB's top leaders retain is exclusively related to their concomitant military ranks (Kérékou, Guezodje); the party has lost all credibility and no longer dominates trade unions, youth and women's organizations, or the media, making it little more than an empty shell. Nowhere is this clearer than in Kérékou's 19 February speech to the newly convened Conference of the Active Forces of the Nation. Throughout his speech he was defensive, barely mentioning the PRPB but applauding democracy and freedom of expression and calling for open public debate on all national issues. (Cotonou Domestic Service, 19 February; *FBIS-AFR*, 21 February.) Kérékou did, however, warn against "dangerous adventurism of regionalism and tribalism" and a "situation likely to cause disturbances, violence and useless clashes" (ibid.). A poignant symbol of the changes in Benin was the 10 August removal of Lenin's massive statue in Cotonou (later sent to Moscow "for repairs") amid popular jubilation and slogans like "Lenin, it was he who brought famine to Benin!" and "Moscow, we've had our fill of books. We need financial aid, and now!" (Cotonou, *La Gazette du Golfe*, 10 August; *FBIS-AFR*, 9 October.)

Opposition and Reforms. The 19–25 February Conference of the Active Forces of the Nation, presided over by Msgr. Isidore de Souza, chairman of the Beninese Catholic Bishop's Conference, resulted in what could only be described as a peaceful revolution. The PRPB-imposed Constitution was declared void, and all of the former ruling party's organs, illegal; free enterprise and multiparty democracy were declared to be the basic principles of Benin's future economic and political life. The army was to be totally depoliticized, freedom of expression guaranteed, and a new constitution adopted before the 12 April 1991 democratic elections. (Paris, AFP, 25 February; *FBIS-AFR*, 26 February.) A provisional government led by a prime minister—a newly established and important office—was to be installed on 12 March to oversee the transition to free enterprise and democracy. Kérékou, however, was to complete his term, which expires in 1994. To be sure, Kérékou initially opposed both the suspension of the PRPB Constitution because he claimed to see a "civilian coup" behind it and the demands for his own resignation because it amounted to "high treason." (Dakar, PANA, 27 February; *FBIS-AFR*, 1 March.)

Even before the conference ended, and for the first time since 1972, the Beninese media had become one of the freest in Africa, with *L'Opinion and La Gazette du Golfe* the most lively publications in francophone Africa. Exiled "bourgeois" politicians, including former Presidents Emile-Derlin Zinsou and Hubert Maga, returned to Benin and established their own personalistic parties.

The new prime minister, Nicephore Soglo, and his cabinet typify the changes in Benin. Soglo was a finance minister during 1965–1967 and after that, a World Bank official; his cabinet includes apolitical technocrats like Finance Minister Ildephonse Lemon, a former adviser to the Ivory Coast government; career diplomats like Foreign Minister Theophile Nata, a former ambassador to Washington; and human rights activists like Jean-Florentin Feliho, all of whom are former opponents of Kérékou's regime—in fact, Kérékou once sentenced Lemon to death. (*Africa Confidential*, 6 April.) None of the new ministers is a member of Kérékou's last cabinet, and many are known supporters of former President Zinsou.

The most surprising development in Benin during 1990 was the rapid growth, influence, and indeed threat to the coming democracy of the previously outlawed pro-Albanian Communist Party of Dahomey (PCD) and its front umbrella, the People's Convention. Together, the two are the most popular, violent, and rapidly growing opposition groups in Benin. Long the only significant opponent of the PRPB regime, and its most conspicuous victim, the PCD is led by Professor Pascal Fatondji and engineer Jean Zounon. (*Africa Confidential*, 6 April.) The PCD aims toward realizing a "truly" communist regime in Benin as opposed to that of the false prophets of the PRPB. The PCD has no interest in a democracy in Benin, at least inasmuch as democracy means nonviolent competition for popular support. In February a PCD militant student, Maurice Dansou, was killed by the military following violent demonstrations in the northern township of Djacotome. (Ibid., 16 February.) The PCD was the only major opposition party to boycott the convention of February 1990 and to call for strikes and violence against the outgoing Kérékou regime, provoking a violent response. The party, however, rejected accusations of being implicated in banditry in the Djacotome area, while appealing for tax boycotts and "peaceful resistance" against the provisional and democratic Soglo regime to provoke the Soglo government into repression. Although a PCD appeal to military draftees and recruits to join its ranks was partially successful, it brought down the hatred of the armed forces.

Economics and Foreign Affairs. The Soglo government, which inherited a total disaster in the country's economy, decided to depend on the help of the International Monetary Fund (IMF) and the World Bank. Trade unions liberated from PRPB control demanded absurd raises; students demonstrated for impossibly high levels of scholarships; and everyone expected immediate improvements in living standards as a result of the collapse of Marxism-Leninism.

None of those exaggerated expectations came true, and the result was general disappointment with the democratization process, which may explain the success of the PCD. Nor did the promised inquiries into the PRPB finances (the previous regime had left nothing in the national treasury [ibid., 20 June]), properties, and abuses of power lead to any definitive results. The Soglo government, then, had no choice but to apply the Structural Adjustment Program recommended by the IMF.

The foreign policy of the new regime was redirected toward the normal sources of economic aid and alternative security. Thus, relations with France—the privileged aid supplier, according to Soglo—and Morocco, a security ally, were both stressed during the year. (Ibid., 29 June.) Soglo's initial statement on taking office mentioned "our age-long partner" France, the United States, Germany, other European Community members, and then the Soviets, with Brazil and Arab countries given the same importance as the Soviets (ibid., 15 March).

Michael S. Radu
Foreign Policy Research Institute
Philadelphia, Pennsylvania

Congo

Population. 2,242,274
Party. Congolese Party of Labor (Parti Congolais du Travail, PCT)
Founded. December 1969
Membership. 10,000
Politburo. 23 members
President. Gen. Denis Sassou-Nguesso (also president of the Republic)
Secretariat. General secretary: Ambroise Edouard Noumazalaye; permanent secretaries: Fulgence Milandou (organization), Andre Abami-Itou (external relations), Alphonse Gondzia (administration), Jean-Royal Kississou-Boma (education and communications), Elise Therese Gavassa (social affairs and women's affairs)
Central Committee. 249 members
Status. Ruling party
Last Congress. December 3–10, 1990
Last Election. 1984
Publication. *Etumba* (daily, circulation less than 5,000)

Ideology and Party Affairs. Throughout the year the disintegration of Congo's version of communism gained speed. That process in many ways resembled the 1989 events in most of Eastern Europe: the regime's grudging and mostly rhetorical concessions to multiparty democracy and free markets, intended as a managed process of relegitimization, escaped control. Economic and political pressures from below, combined with growing disunity among the ruling PCT's ranks, resulted in massive government concessions.

In his 1989 year-end address—also the twentieth anniversary of the PCT—Congo and PCT president Denis Sassou-Nguesso stated that the country "rejects servile imitations and alienating mimicries," a clear reference to the revolutionary events of 1989 in Eastern Europe (Paris, AFP, 31 December 1989; *FBIS-AFR*, 4 January). Nevertheless, he also rejected complete state control over the economy and civil service jobs as a solution to unemployment (ibid.).

On 4 July, following a PCT Central Committee meeting, the party promised to allow a multiparty system to develop in Congo following a party congress to be held in February 1991. Vague as it was, the decision marked a sharp departure from the one-party, "scientific socialist," Leninist vanguard party that had dominated the country since the 1968 coup of Marien Ngouabi. At the same meeting, a number of prominent PCT Central Committee leaders were purged or forced to resign including Gabriel Oba Opounou, Central Committee secretary of youth; Gen. Norbert Dabira, army political commissar; Jean-Michel Bokamba Yangouma, a top PCT leader and Central Committee secretary in charge of mass and social organizations; and Pierre Moussa, Central Committee secretary in charge of planning the economy and a prominent party leader (Ndjamena Domestic Service, 4 July; *FBIS-AFR*, 5 July). It was initially unclear whether those purged were among the opponents or supporters of the move toward democratization. In fact, it was not clear where Sassou-Nguesso himself stood, for he told the same meeting that "we welcome freedom, but never chaos...greater democracy but never to the detriment of public order." (Brazzaville Domestic Service, 29 July; *FBIS-AFR*, 6 July.)

Immediately after the Central Committee meeting, the regime's plans to limit and control the process of change became unraveled. Thus, after plans were announced in May to build a new jail for important political prisoners in the northern jungle (*Africa Confidential*, 5 June), and the signatories of an open letter to the president that demanded a multiparty democracy were arrested for "subversion" in July (Paris, AFP, 13 July; *FBIS-AFR*, 16 July), the regime suddenly retreated, and on 14 August the president released all political prisoners (*FBIS-AFR*, 17 August).

The June Central Committee meeting did state the party's intention to give more freedom to its auxiliary organizations, including the trade union federation (CSC). However, when on 17 July the CSC declared its independence from the party and reelected Jean-Michel Bokamba-Yangouma, the purged former Politburo member, as its head, the regime reacted strongly. Verbal attacks from the presidential palace, Sassou-Nguesso's attempt to annul the CSC Congress, and his refusal to accept the unions' demands—including the unfreezing of wages—led to an open confrontation. On 13 September the security forces took over the CSC headquarters, and the next day the unions declared a general strike (Paris, AFP, 13 September; *FBIS-AFR*, 14 September). Riots and looting took place in Pointe Noire and Loubomo (the second and third

largest cities, respectively), rail and road transportation came to a standstill, and veiled threats from the president to restore order and prevent "chaos" went unheeded (Brazzaville Domestic Service, 16 September; *FBIS-AFR*, 17 September). Presidential and PCT attempts to convene a new trade union congress under submissive leaders failed, and the country came close to a repetition of the August 1963 events when union militancy brought down the first postindependence government and ushered in the era of Congolese radicalism.

The regime blinked first, and on 17 September a "compromise" was reached, with the government giving in to almost all the CSC demands: the initial trade union congress was allowed to resume, Bokamba-Yangouma was recognized as leader, the National Committee on the Coordination of Trade Union Activities—the PCT's tool of control over the unions—was formally abolished, the government's plans for compulsory retirement at age 50 were shelved, and the issue of promotions was solved in favor of the employees. (Ibid.)

The unions' newly found militancy was closely related to the development of open opposition from the usually acquiescent Congolese churches. On 8 September the Ecumenical Council of Christian Churches of Congo issued a statement "deploring" the PCT policy of unilaterally deciding the speed and nature of the democratization process. (*Libreville Africa*, no. 1 [9 September]; *FBIS-AFR*, 13 September.)

The youth, traditionally the most radical segment of Congolese society, also changed their attitudes dramatically. At the end of October, the students at the Marien Ngouabi University started a strike to change the name of the institution—thus rejecting Marxism-Leninism as the top symbol of the regime—and to remove unqualified faculty and PCT control over their organization. (Paris, AFP, 31 October; *FBIS-AFR*, 2 November.)

Although the sudden independence of the churches and unions was a serious blow to PCT rule, it was the revolt within the party's own ranks that forced the virtual collapse of the regime. At the June Central Committee meeting, two hard-line and corrupt Politburo members, Brazzaville's mayor Jean Jules Okabando and Youth Minister Gabriel Oba-Apounou, were voted out, and their colleagues Jean-Baptiste Tati-Loutard and Pierre-Damien Bousoukou-Boma lost badly in their competition for the post of secretary general (*Jeune Afrique*, 1 January 1991). The CSC itself, at its controversial congress, decided to expel all PCT Central Committee members from the ranks of its leadership. Furthermore, and perhaps more significantly, a growing number of prominent PCT leaders, past and present, openly and sometimes defiantly (see the case of Bokamba-Yangouma) left the party, usually to join the opposition. Among the most important defectors, in addition to Bokamba-Yangouma, were former Politburo members Claude-Ernest Ndalla, Jean-Pierre Thystere Tchikaya, Clement Mierassa, Pierre Nze, Pierre Moussa and former Prime Minister Ange Edouard Poungui (ibid., 4 December). Finally, on 3 December, Prime Minister Alphonse Poaty-Souchlaty formally resigned both from his job and from the PCT itself (ibid.).

The Opposition. Although political opposition parties have been tolerated since June, their existence was formally accepted only after the September meeting of the Central Committee of the PCT. Not surprisingly, some of the newly formed opposition parties are of dubious democratic inclination. The most typical in this respect are the Democratic Forum (yet another echo of Eastern Europe), led by former hard-liner Central Committee chief of propaganda and PCT second-ranking leader Jean-Pierre Thystere Tchikaya and former Foreign Minister and dogmatic ideologue Pierre Nze, and the Social Democratic party, led by former Central Committee member Clement Mierassa. (Ibid., 8 November.) In contrast, the Movement for Democracy and Total Development, led by longtime dissident and regime opponent Bernard Kolelas, is a bona fide, popular, if poorly organized, democratically minded group, while groups like the Bateke Liberation Front are openly tribal in nature.

The Economy. The general drift of the regime from the last remnants of "scientific socialism" and state ownership of the means of production reached a new level with the de facto abandonment of Hydrocongo, the state-owned monopoly of gasoline distribution. Hydrocongo's refining monopoly is now to be shared with ELF and its distribution network with Shell, BP, Amoco, and Chevron (*Africa Confidential*, 26 January). Some seven hundred employees, half of a work force whose cost was more than half the company's expenses, are to be fired (ibid.). The privatization of HUILKA (Huilerie de Nkayi), the state-owned cooking oil monopoly, led to its acquisition by a Lebanese firm, Tabet, which also bought a soap factory owned by Pierre Otto Mbongo, a member of the president's own Mbochi clan and owner of Transafrica Airline. Mbongo is closely linked to business interests in South Africa and Zaire and is one of the Congo's richest men. (*Africa Confidential*, 14 April.)

The government's attempts to trim the numbers and limit the cost of the country's bloated civil service and state payroll, however, failed as a result of the September strikes and the general weakening of the regime.

Foreign Affairs. Perhaps nowhere is the change in Congo's security and foreign policy orientation more dramatic than in the decision to ask for a contingent of Moroccan troops to replace the Cubans as the regime's main security unit (also in charge of presidential security) (*Africa Confidential*, 7 December). Relations with neighboring strongly pro-Western and capitalist-minded Gabon, generally good ever since the early 1970s, became closer still with the 3 January marriage between the Gabonese president, Omar Bongo, and Sassou-Nguesso's daughter, Edith. (Paris, AFP, 4 January; *FBIS-AFR*, 9 January).

Michael S. Radu
Foreign Policy Research Institute
Philadelphia, Pennsylvania

Ethiopia

Population. 51,666,622
Party. Workers' Party of Ethiopia (WPE)
Founded. September 1984
Membership. Ca. 25,000
General Secretary. Mengistu Haile Mariam, 49 (military officer)
Politburo. 11 full members: Mengistu Haile Mariam, Fisseha Desta, Tesfaye Gebre Kidan, Berhanu Bayih, Legesse Asfaw, Haddis Tedla, Hailu Yemenu, Alemu Abebe, Shimelis Mazengia (2 positions vacant); 6 alternate members
Secretariat. 8 members: Fisseha Desta, Legesse Asfaw, Shimelis Mazengia, Fasika Sidelel, Shewandagn Belete, Wubishet Desie, Ashagre Yigletu, Emibel Ayele

Central Committee. 136 full members; 64 alternates

Status. Ruling party

Last Congress. Founding, 6–10 September, 1984; eleventh regular session of WPE Central Committee, 5–8 March 1990

Last Election. June 1987, to Parliament (Shengo): 13.4 million voters elected 835 deputies, all nominally WPE members.

Auxiliary Organizations. Peasant associations, urban dwellers' associations (*kebeles*), All-Ethiopia Trade Union (AETU), Revolutionary Ethiopian Women's Association (REWA), Revolutionary Ethiopian Youth Association (REYA)

Publications. *Ethiopian Herald*, *Addis Zemen*, *Yekatit*, *Negarit Gazeta*, *Meskerem*. All publishing is controlled by the government and subject to censorship.

The year was marked by accelerated deterioration of the Socialist system in Ethiopia. A process of economic reform got under way and has, in part, outrun the regime's ability to control it. The leaders found it extremely difficult to implement political reform, which has lagged far behind the pace in most communist countries. Civil war spread to new areas, and the threat of widespread famine again loomed while regime efforts to negotiate with major insurgent groups made little progress. The regime's relations with major foreign powers remained uneasy, though relations with some states in the region were characterized by slight improvement. Each of these topics will be dealt with separately below.

Economic Reform. Reformers within the regime achieved a major breakthrough when they persuaded President Mengistu to announce far-reaching economic changes in a speech to the WPE Central Committee on 5 March (Addis Ababa Domestic Service, 5 March; *FBIS-AFR*, 12 March). The most significant changes related to agriculture: the rigid delivery quota system was abolished, and the operations of the Agricultural Marketing Corporation were severely curtailed. Free trade in most agricultural commodities was authorized. The hated villagization campaign was abandoned, and producer cooperatives were permitted to dissolve. Private enterprise was permitted in many fields hitherto forbidden, and foreign investment was encouraged by new regulations incorporating tax exemptions and provisions for repatriation of profits. Regulations affecting exports and imports were significantly liberalized. These reforms, despite bureaucratic foot-dragging encouraged by WPE diehards, took effect rapidly. In the countryside, almost all producer cooperatives had been dissolved by the end of the year and most villages were disintegrating, with peasants returning to their former homesites. Helped by good weather in most of the country, agricultural production increased sharply. The Food and Agriculture Organization of the United Nations December 1990 estimates (Addis Ababa, U.S. embassy) indicated increases as great as 14 percent in grain production in all parts of the country except Tigre and Eritrea, where drought persisted. Small-scale trade and small- and medium-level private industry of many kinds mushroomed in most urban areas and small towns, but several major economic problems remained. No significant foreign investment materialized. Local investors remained skeptical about large-scale and long-range ventures because of government failures to follow through reform announcements with detailed regulations. (*CSM*, 7 May.) A large proportion of both foreign and domestic trade continued to take place in unofficial channels, depriving the government of revenue. The regime resisted pressure from the World Bank and major aid donors to devalue the currency and undertake other structural reforms. The black market rate of the birr had fallen to $1/E$7 by the end of the year as against an official rate of $1/E$2.07, unchanged since 1973. With 70 percent of the government's budget going to the military and security forces, domestic expenditures and investment were further curtailed during the course of the year and had a depressing effect on the economy. Major new foreign aid commitments and foreign investments were negatively affected by the continuing civil war in the north and deteriorating security conditions in both western and eastern border areas.

Political Stalemate. President Mengistu's announcement in his 5 March speech of abandoning Marxism-Leninism and transforming the WPE into the Democratic Unity Party of Ethiopia (DUPE) to include all factions in the country remained moot. The DUPE has not been organized. Through the end of the year the WPE continued to function unchanged in Addis Ababa, party brass continued to be referred to in the press as "comrades," and no significant structural changes in the party or government apparatus occurred. In much of the countryside, the party structure disintegrated as opportunists abandoned party membership. The execution in May 1990 of twelve generals implicated in the May 1989 coup attempt after a long trial that generated expectations of leniency had a devastating effect on both governmental and public morale and hastened the de facto suspension of party activity by many government officials and military officers (Addis Ababa Domestic Service, 21 May; *FBIS-AFR*, 22 May). Mengistu revealed in a May Day speech that he had survived nine assassination attempts over an unspecified period of time and that he was deeply depressed about the condition of the regime (Paris, AFP, 1 May; *FBIS-AFR*, 2 May) and prospects for the war against Tigrean and Eritrean insurgents. He appeared to rally a few weeks later when he called for new sacrifices for a total commitment to the "anti-secessionist" struggle before a parliamentary session on 21 June (Addis Ababa Domestic Service, 21 June; *FBIS-AFR*, 25 June). A "general mobilization" was proclaimed on 25 June (Paris, AFP, 25 June; *FBIS-AFR*, 26 June).

Civil War. For the third year running, government forces suffered a severe defeat when the Eritrean Popular Liberation Front (EPLF) captured the port of Mesewa in early February and proceeded to lay siege to the Eritrean capital, Asmara (*Africa Events*, March 1990). In severe fighting during subsequent weeks, government forces succeeded in stabilizing control of Keren, Asmara, and much of the Christian-populated highland area to the south and west, but the rest of Eritrea—some 90 percent—remained in rebel hands. From midsummer onward, the situation remained essentially stalemated, with Asmara supplied by air. Meanwhile, in the region to the south the Tigre Popular Liberation Front (TPLF), in conjunction with Amhara- and Oromo-based organizations supported by it, wrested control of major portions of the provinces of Welo, Gonder, Gojam, and Shewa from the government. During the same period, Oromo Liberation Front (OLF) forces captured the western town of Asosa with EPLF support. The OLF and other insurgent groups opposed to the TPLF and its allies also carried out strikes in parts of Gonder and Gojam and in Harer. During June and July, TPLF-supported rebels approached to within 100 miles of Addis Ababa (Voice of the Broad Masses (clandestine), 25, 29, 31 May; *FBIS-AFR*, 1 June), but a lull in fighting occurred during the final weeks of the summer rainy season. Government forces recaptured Asosa, secured Bahr Dar and the main highway north to Dese (capital of Welo), made other minor gains against the insur-

gents, and maintained a relatively stable situation from September through the end of the year.

The most important insurgent movements—the EPLF and the TPLF—were originally as dogmatically Marxist as the central government itself. During the course of the year, however, both made efforts to project a more liberal political and economic image. The EPLF announced an economic liberalization program on 24 Febrary, and broadcasts of the clandestine radios of both movements stressed measures encouraging trade, industry, and independent peasant agriculture throughout the year. In effect, following Mengistu's reform announcement on 5 March, both the government and the insurgents began to compete for the support of the population by stressing reform. There was mounting evidence that throughout much of the area affected most severely by civil war, the population was relieved at the abandonment of Marxism by all contending parties and increasingly taking management of their affairs into their own hands on a local basis (*Adulis*, EPLF organ, October).

Peace Efforts. The peace process that had begun haltingly during 1989 continued during 1990 with no significant results (Addis Ababa Domestic Service, 19 March; *FBIS-AFR*, 20 March). The central government and the insurgents both reiterated publicly, on several occasions during the year, a commitment to a negotiated settlement of differences. The initiative undertaken by former President Jimmy Carter to bring the government and the EPLF into serious negotiations foundered on procedural issues, however, and efforts by the Italian government to facilitate talks between the government and the TPLF were suspended without significant results. Restoration of diplomatic relations between Ethiopia and Israel at the end of 1989 and the inauguration of a military assistance program by Israel, the exact scope of which remains unclear, contributed to the failure of peace efforts. Mengistu appears to have had exaggerated expectations of the political impact of Israeli assistance, whereas the EPLF and the TPLF were angered by it. The EPLF's capture of Mesewa may have been undertaken as a preemptive measure to forestall government forces' utilization of Israeli support. With the movement of the U.S. government into the situation at the end of the summer, a new stage in the peace process may have begun, though it was too early to tell by the end of the year whether U.S. mediation between the EPLF and government representatives could lead to serious negotiations. With the strong support of the international famine relief community, the U.S. government's mediation initiative initially concentrated on efforts to open the port of Mesewa for food and emergency relief shipments. Both the Ethiopian government and the EPLF announced their willingness in December to cooperate in facilitating the flow of food through Mesewa, but the actual opening of the port depended on potentially difficult talks about concrete transport and cease-fire arrangements.

Famine. The threat of famine loomed over Ethiopia during the entire year. Crop failures in much of Tigre and Eritrea and in parts of Harer complicated the food situation in these regions, though the situation was mitigated to a considerable degree by bumper crops in much of the rest of Ethiopia and resumption of brisk internal trade in grain extending across fighting lines into the two northern provinces. The situation in Eritrea and Tigre continued to be adversely affected by persistence of fighting (*CSM*, 26 March) and complicated by severe crop failure and famine in neighboring areas of Sudan from where refugees began moving back to Ethiopian territory (Eritrean Relief Committee release, 27 November). Governments and nongovernmental organizations administering famine relief have achieved a high degree of efficiency in organizing and coordinating their operations and have maintained an effective working relationship with both Ethiopian central governmental authorities and relief organizations supporting the insurgent movements. Early warning and food stockpiling programs made it possible to avoid major movements of famine victims and deaths despite widespread hardship in areas of fighting during 1990 (*NYT*, 25 November).

International Relations. Soviet relations with the Ethiopian government cooled further during the year, and Soviet press criticism of the regime occurred more frequently. The Soviet government announced that its arms supply agreement would not be renewed after it expired in 1991. Substantial deliveries of Soviet arms and war material continued throughout the year. Ethiopia's close and supportive relations with the former communist regimes in Eastern Europe collapsed with the fall of these regimes, causing serious dislocation and eventual cessation of both military and economic aid arrangements. This led to major losses of support from countries such as Bulgaria and the former German Democratic Republic. Ethiopia's relations with North Korea remained warm. The new relationship with Israel developed less smoothly than

either party had hoped, with serious difficulties arising over the emigration of Falashas to Israel. As a result of both Israeli efforts and U.S. intercession, these appeared to have been solved at the end of the year (*NYT*, 13 July; Tel-Aviv, *Ma'ariv*, 3 October; *FBIS-AFR*, 23 November). Capitalizing on the fortunate accident of Ethiopia's representation on the U.N. Security Council, Mengistu joined the Western effort against Iraqi aggression, giving wholehearted diplomatic support. The Addis Ababa regime's efforts to tar the EPLF with allegations of support for Iraq backfired, however, when forged documents that surfaced in Sweden were quickly exposed by the EPLF as fraudulent (EPLF release, 3 September). Anti-Western rhetoric had largely disappeared from Ethiopian media by the end of the year, but all publications and media remained under tight government control. The government made a considerable effort to improve diplomatic communication with the United States and West European countries but continued to follow highly restrictive policies toward Western journalists (*WP*, 26 December). A visit by Mengistu to Cairo in November marked a warming in relations with Egypt. Yemen had facilitated Addis Ababa–Eritrean talks in April.

Party Affairs. The WPE, never large, atrophied steadily during the course of the year and is believed to retain no more than 25,000 even moderately active members. Auxiliary political organizations such as REWA and REYA likewise suffered serious attrition. Courses in Marxism-Leninism were dropped at Addis Ababa University, and the party's training school was being transformed into a social science research institute at the end of the year.

Paul B. Henze
The Rand Corporation, Washington, D.C.

Lesotho

Population. 1,754,664
Party. Communist Party of Lesotho (CPL)
Founded. 1962
Chairman. R. Mataji
Secretariat. Jacob M. Kena (general secretary), John Motloheloa, Khotso Molekane

Status. Illegal (but tolerated)
Last Congress. Seventh, early 1987
Last Election. September 1985
Auxiliary Organizations. Mine Workers' Union, Writers' Association of Lesotho, Union of Lesotho Journalists, Students' Representative Council, Lesotho Peace and Solidarity Organization

The CPL was distinguished during 1990 chiefly for its absence from public view. Its secretary general, Jacob M. Kena, did not even show up for the November Moscow Twelfth World Trade Union Congress (Twelfth World Trade Union Congress, *List of Participants*). (He attended the Eleventh Congress in East Berlin, four years earlier, in his capacities as secretary general of the Mine Workers' Union and representative of the Lesotho Congress of Free Trade Unions [*YICA*, 1987].) In fact, the only evidence of the CPL's continued existence during the year was its inclusion on the Editorial Council of the Prague-based *World Marxist Review* through its last (May–June) issue; presumably, the representative involved was Sam Moeti, last confirmed in this position by the July 1989 issue.

Similarly, the only coverage of the country during the year by the South African Communist Party's (SACP's) *African Communist*, a London-based quarterly, did not mention the CPL, although it had previously covered that party's activities (*YICA*, 1987). The article in question, which appeared in the second quarter of 1990 issue, was a regurgitation of the December 1988 shooting of an agricultural college student by Military Council chairman Justin M. Lekhanya. General Lekhanya is the chief conservative (pro–South African government/anti–African National Congress [ANC]) force in the country; the occasion for the article was the rather belated inquest into the matter that ended in October 1989 with the general's complete exoneration.

King Moshoshoe II had, to no avail, called for Lekhanya's resignation when the shooting incident became known, for the king had been the chief progressive (anti–South African government/pro-ANC) force in Lesotho before his February house arrest and March exile. These actions had been taken against the king by Lekhanya in the wake of the discovery of an alleged anti–Military Council coup said to have involved, among others, two of the king's cousins (London, BBC, 5 September; *FBIS-AFR*, 10 September; *NYT*, 22 February). The actual trigger for the actions was the king's refusal to acquiesce in Lekhanya's dismissals following the

discovery of the alleged plot (ibid.). As late as mid-September, trade unionists were noted as being detained in connection with allegedly plotting to overthrow the military government (Maseru, *Mirror*, 14 September).

Yet by late September, Lekhanya apparently felt confident enough to receive a delegation led by ANC secretary general Alfred Nzo (Radio Maseru, *FBIS-AFR*, 21 September). (That the SACP-connected ANC had by then been legalized in South Africa and was negotiating with the government there no doubt played a major role in Lekhanya's decision.) By early November the general was sure enough of himself to have the king deposed and his eldest son, Prince Mohato Seeisa, elected his successor by the country's 22 principal chiefs (Johannesburg, SAPA, 8 November, *FBIS-AFR*, 9 November). With apparent stability now obtaining, there is a good chance that the CPL and its auxiliaries may soon be able to operate more freely.

Wallace H. Spaulding
McLean, Virginia

Mozambique

Population. 15,700,000
Party. Front for the Liberation of Mozambique (Frente de Libertação de Moçambique, FRELIMO)
Founded. 1962
Membership. 201,440 (*Southscan*, August 1989; *Horizont*, no. 9 [1989])
President. Joaquim Alberto Chissano
Politburo. 12 members: Joaquim Alberto Chissano, Marcelino dos Santos, Alberto Chipande, Armando Emilio Guebuza, Feliciano Gundana, Mariano de Aráujo Matsinhe, Jacinto Soares Veloso, Mário de Graça Machungo, Rafael Maguni, Pascoal Mocumbi, Eduardo da Silva Nihia, Jorge Rebelo
Secretariat. Joaquim Chissano, Mario Machungo, Julio Carrilho, Pascoal Mocumbi, Eduardo Aaro, José Luís Cabaço, Jorge Rebelo
Status. Ruling party

Last Congress. Fifth, 24–30 July 1989, in Maputo (700 delegates)
Last Election. 1986
Auxiliary Organizations. Organization of Mozambican Women (Organização da Mulher Moçambicana), Mozambique Youth Organization, Mozambique Workers' Organization, National Teachers' Organization, War Veterans' Association
Publications. *Notícias* (daily); *O Tempo* (weekly); *Diário de Moçambique* (daily); *Domingo* (Sunday); *Voz de Revolução* (Central Committee organ); *Economia* (Chamber of Commerce magazine)

Two significant developments took place in Mozambique during 1990. First, Mozambique moved toward a multiparty election system and away from a Socialist one-party state. This dramatic change in policy was in part a response to FRELIMO's armed opposition and the fourteen-year war. Second, FRELIMO agreed to and held a series of direct peace talks with the guerrilla forces fighting in the countryside. A limited agreement resulted from the talks, which called for Zimbabwe's expeditionary forces to be confined within two narrow corridors across the country.

In 1990 FRELIMO's policies, therefore, continued the shift away from Marxism-Leninism that began in previous years. The party's initial changes were set in motion before Samora Machel's death in 1986 in a plane crash. A few reforms were instituted to some degree by the economic rehabilitation program in 1987. Last year's Fifth Party Congress discarded the use of Marxist-Leninist rhetoric in pronouncements and documents. Symbolically, the year under review also witnessed a change in the country's name to the Republic of Mozambique, deleting the communist-inspired "people's" from the title (for background, see *YICA*, 1982).

The party's Central Committee endorsed specific rules in its August meeting for multiparty elections in 1991. This action came after months of national debate on a new draft constitution and after a recommendation by the twelve-member Politburo. The new constitution, which went into effect at the end of November, also abolishes the death penalty, guarantees freedom of the press, recognizes the right to strike, and permits free movement round the country. The successful implementation of these new laws awaits future judgment.

Organization and Leadership. The force for wider political participation than the exclusive

control by FRELIMO in Mozambique stemmed not from a clamor for democracy within the poor and war-ravaged country but from guerrilla war throughout much of the country, according to President Chissano (Jane Perlez, "Mozambique Moving to Democracy," *NYT*, 29 August). Some key changes of the year occurred in the Central Committee's third session, which approved a proposed draft constitution. After nine days of intense debate, the Central Committee authorized the establishment of a multiparty system and established a commission to prepare the final draft of the constitution. It decided that the draft constitution must stipulate the existence of free speech and freedom of the press. The articles in the new constitution for the establishment of new parties were submitted to the final session of the republic's Assembly in November, which also approved it.

Article 29, however, appears to limit the participation of the government's chief rival movement, stating that "all political parties must defend national interests and contribute to the peace and stability of the country" (Maputo, in English, to southern Africa, 20 October; *FBIS-AFR*, 22 October). Article 30 prohibits political parties from resorting to the use of violence "to alter the political and social order of Mozambique" (ibid.). The new constitution, therefore, seems aimed at keeping from power the ruling party's main threat, the Mozambique National Resistance (*Resistência Nacional Moçambicana*, RENAMO, formerly the MNR). RENAMO had battled FRELIMO in the Mozambican bush for fourteen years, but occasionally the war spilled into urban areas, with electrical power outages and bomb attacks.

The Central Committee reaffirmed its choice for a market economy, but by specifying various types of property, notably state owned and cooperative ownership along with private, its guidelines could retard the full development of such an economy. Privatization of land, in fact, was rejected ("FRELIMO Casts off Monopoly of Power," United Kingdom, *Guardian*, 17 August).

During the approval of the new constitution during the fall session of the republic's Assembly, President Chissano proclaimed in his concluding speech that the role of the state was to act as "regulator and promoter of growth and economic as well as social development" (Maputo Domestic Service, 3 November; *FBIS-AFR*, 6 November). Such declarations point to a continued powerful role for the party in the economy rather than reliance on private individuals and companies as the driving force for economic development.

In a continuation of its move away from overt signs of Marxism-Leninism, the Central Committee also approved the deletion of the word *people's* from several of the country's institutions along with the nation's name. For example, the People's Assembly will now be known as the republic's Assembly and the Supreme People's Court will be called simply the Supreme Court (Maputo Domestic Service, 15 August; *FBIS-AFR*, 17 August). Despite these changes, FRELIMO's leadership remained in place, with no significant personnel changes envisioned in the hierarchy at the time of writing.

RENAMO rejected the new constitution. In a statement issued in Portugal, the opposition movement held that the document had been approved by an unconstitutional parliament that lacked a democratic election (Johannesburg Domestic Service, in English, 4 October; *FBIS-AFR*, 5 November).

Mass organizations. Like other communist regimes, FRELIMO, to strengthen its control over the population, secured its participation in various groups. The government formed the Mozambique Youth Organization and the Mozambique Workers' Organization. In 1988 the party set up the War Veterans' Association. Among these government-created organizations, one of the strongest has been the Organization of Mozambican Women, which has criticized FRELIMO for its unresponsiveness to women's concerns.

In 1990 the National Teachers' Organization (ONP) took part in a nationwide strike that closed schools at the beginning of the academic year in February. The government met the teachers' demands for higher wages by suspending the school year, effectively locking out the strikers and closing the schools. When the teachers took to the Maputo streets following a mass meeting, they were met by riot police who injured several strikers and bystanders. In March the government reopened the schools without fully meeting the teachers' demands. The tension caused further confusion by dividing the ONP's loyalties between the teachers and the government that formed it in 1981. ("'Chalk down' in Mozambique," *South African Labour Bulletin* 15, no. 1 [June].)

The Organization of Mozambican Workers (OTM) held its Second National Conference in November. Delegates criticized the high cost of living that resulted from the Economic Rehabilitation Program (PRE), which began in 1987. This program caused price hikes in basic commodities with the devaluation of the currency. Supported by the World Bank and the International Monetary Fund, the PRE seeks to restructure the economy away from central planning toward one based more on market forces than on Marxism. Implementation caused hardship to many sectors of the Mozambican population, which protested the changes.

The delegates, however, were also critical of the OTM for its failure to take action against employees who failed to obey labor laws and health and safety regulations. During this discussion, it was pointed out that the new constitution permits the formation of other trade unions. However, delegates appeared divided on the wisdom of competing trade unions that would reduce the influence of the OTM (Maputo, in English, to southern Africa, *FBIS-AFR*, 15 November).

The war has made enormous claims on Mozambican life and property. An estimated 900,000 deaths have resulted from the civil war, which has also created over a million refugees and put another 5 million people on some form of government or international food relief. Much of the rural infrastructure lies in ruins. Farms and factories no longer function. Schools, hospitals, and civil administrative centers are destroyed or abandoned. Bridges, railways, and roads do not serve commerce. ("Scientific Socialism: Some Lessons from Mozambique," *Southern African Freedom Review* 3, no. 3 [Summer 1990].)

Domestic Affairs. Reacting to widespread dissatisfaction with the police, Chissano addressed a senior group of officers of the newly named Mozambique People's Police (PPM). The president stated that police must respect the rights of citizens. His remarks on Legality Day were directed at the PPM in light of the new constitution. Chissano called upon the PPM "to be above all parties" no matter what its ideological leanings (Maputo Domestic Service, 5 November; *FBIS-AFR*, 6 November).

Two small parties surfaced in Maputo during the year—the Mozambique National Union (UNAMO) and the Liberal and Democratic Party of Mozambique (PALMO). Both these parties are to the political right of the ruling FRELIMO party. PALMO has adopted a pro-African policy. One of the cofounders, Martins Bilal, criticized FRELIMO for granting preferences to Indian traders. The issue of race has been simmering in Mozambique during the past several years. (Julian Borger, "Mozambique's New

Constitution May Help End 15-Year Civil War," *CSM*, 12 December.)

The People's Forces for the Liberation of Mozambique (FPLM). Nearly fifteen years of hit-and-run warfare with RENAMO have left the government's armed forces in a poor state. In widespread disorganization, the 35,000-man army steals food from hungry villages and settles its own scores in a fashion reminiscent of the warlords in China in the 1930s. The war itself has degenerated into a conflict of generalized thuggery and looting, with both sides sharing in the rapine and booty (ibid.; *NYT*, 29 August).

Among the dramatic changes that took place in Mozambique in 1990 were the first direct peace talks between the FRELIMO government and RENAMO to end the war. Zimbabwe and Kenya had tried to mediate an agreement. The first effort failed to materialize in Blantyre, Malawi, in mid-June. Indirect talks started last year in Nairobi with Mozambican church officials representing the FRELIMO government. Pressured by its international backers, FRELIMO agreed in April to hold direct talks with the rebel movement. Chissano announced his willingness to enter into direct discussions with RENAMO in neighboring Malawi. ("Talks for Mozambique Collapse in First Hours," *NYT*, 14 June.)

The second set of talks also collapsed over RENAMO's continuing objections to foreign troops in Mozambique fighting alongside the FPLM. RENAMO put the figure at 30,000 Zimbabwean forces, but other sources list them at between 12,000 and 15,000. A third set of talks during the fall in Rome met with limited success when the two sides agreed to a partial accord on 1 December. Rather than a general cease-fire agreement, the government and rebels accepted a limitation of Zimbabwe's troops to two narrow corridors across Mozambique. These corridors stretch along the Beira and Limpopo rail and road links from the Zimbabwean border to the Mozambican coast. As such, they provide vital outlets for Zimbabwean trade and communication.

By 5 January 1991 the Zimbabwean troops were to be redeployed in the three-kilometer corridors. They are not to move outside these zones; nor are RENAMO forces to attack within the corridors (Maputo Domestic Service, 1 December; *FBIS-AFR*, 3 December). This agreement represents a compromise between the rebels and the government, according to which RENAMO had to concede that Zimbabwe had genuine concerns for the safety of the corridors across Mozambique because they are a cheap and direct route to the sea for the landlocked country. The FRELIMO government had to give up the use of Zimbabwean troops in its war against the guerrillas throughout the country.

International Affairs. The collapse of communist regimes in Eastern Europe during 1989 coupled with the deterioration of the Soviet economy resulted in a serious falling off of aid to Mozambique. The former German Democratic Republic (GDR), Mozambique's staunchest donor in Eastern Europe, has now disappeared from the political map. The GDR had employed about 15,000 Mozambican guest workers throughout its economy, and under a cooperative agreement, part of the workers' salary was repatriated, earning Mozambique valuable foreign exchange. This source of support ended quickly after the absorption of the GDR into West Germany.

Western nations, experiencing "donor fatigue" over the last few years, pledged only $251 million of the requested $383 million in 1989. This past year, they responded to a scaled-down request of $136 million with a mere $46 million in pledges by midyear (Colleen Lowe Morna, "'Aid Fatigue' Threatens Budget Support," *African Business*, September). Mozambican appeals for emergency assistance increasingly met with weariness in the West. Corruption within the FRELIMO government cooled the West's ardor for assisting the southeastern African country as did its centralized control of the economy (ibid.). Because Mozambique depended on foreign aid for 65 percent of its budget, the changed circumstances placed FRELIMO in a difficult position.

The fourth meeting of the World Bank Consultative Group for Mozambique in December promised $1.2 billion a year for the 1991–1993 period. Of this support, $400 million will be earmarked for external debt and $761 million for various programs, including emergency food and rehabilitation of the Nacala railway. The package nevertheless showed the donors' caution and the recipients' desire to avoid a rejection of their request by limiting the amount of aid sought (*Indian Ocean Newsletter*, 15 December).

The year also witnessed Western pressures on the FRELIMO government to negotiate with RENAMO. According to U.S. officials, South Africa halted aid to the rebels in response to Soviet moves. Early in 1990 the Soviet Union withdrew most of its eight hundred military advisers to the government. The Soviet departure also meant diminished rations and munitions for FRELIMO's troops, as Moscow reduced its reported annual $150 million military assistance program to about $100 million (Clifford Krauss, "Mozambique Moves to Start Peace Talks with Rightist Rebels," *NYT*, 12 June).

In addition, countries friendly to Maputo forced the FRELIMO regime to seek talks with its chief antagonist. These countries, which had supplied economic and humanitarian assistance to Mozambique, began to withhold support in light of the endless war and reports of corruption in the government's food distribution system. The United States finally agreed to furnish some $103 million in humanitarian, economic, and regional aid in response to both the desperate Mozambican circumstances and the government's announced reforms (ibid.; *NYT*, 29 August).

Publications. The new constitution guaranteed freedom of the press. How this dramatic policy departure will be implemented remains to be seen because FRELIMO has controlled the media since independence in 1975. Under the former regimen, FRELIMO dominated the daily *Notícias*, the *Diário de Moçambique* in Beira, the Sunday paper *Domingo*, and the national magazine *O Tempo* (for additional background, see *YICA*, 1982). *Voz da Revolução* dealt with Marxist theory and FRELIMO policies. Reflecting the efforts to liberalize the economy over the past few years, the party established *Economia* in 1987 under the Chamber of Commerce.

Thomas H. Henriksen
Hoover Institution

Réunion

Population. 595,583 (*World Fact Book*); according to 1990 census, 596,500 (*Témoignages*, 4 July.)
Party. Réunion Communist Party (Parti communiste réunionnais, PCR)
Founded. 1959
Membership. 7,000–10,000 claimed; 2,000 estimated

General Secretary. Paul Vergès
Politburo. 12 members: Paul Vergès, Julien Ramin; remaining members unknown, although *Témoignages* lists the PCR directorate as including Eli Hoarau, Marcel Soubon, Ary Yee Chong Tchi Kan, Jean-Yves Langenier, Marcel Gironcel, Daniel Jaurés, and Dominique Atchicanon.
Secretariat. 6 members: Paul Vergès, Elie Hoarau, Jean-Baptiste Ponoma, Lucet Langenier, Ary Yee Chong Tchi Kan, remaining member not known.
Status. Legal
Last Congress. Fifth, 12–14 July 1980, in Le Port; there is a plan to hold one in the first half of 1991.
Last Elections. 17 April, 24 April 1988, president of the French Republic; 5 May, 12 May 1988, French National Assembly, 2 of 5 seats, 35 percent of the popular vote; 25 September, 2 October 1988, Réunion General Council, 9 of 44 seats, 27.2 percent of the popular vote; 25 March, partial cantonal elections (St. Denis 2d and 5th); 23 March, 23 September, municipal elections in Ste. Marie and Ste. Suzanne
Auxiliary Organizations. Anticolonialist Front for Réunion Autonomy; Réunion Front of Autonomous Youth; Réunion Peace Committee; Réunion General Confederation of Workers (CGTR), Georges-Marie Lepinay, secretary general; Committee for the Rally of Réunionese Unemployed (CORC); Committee for the Rally of Réunionese Youth (CORJ); Réunion Union of Women (UFR), Huguette Bello, president; Réunion General Union of Workers in France (UGTRF); Réunion General Confederation of Planters and Cattlemen (CGPER)
Publications. *Témoignages* (daily), Elie Hoarau, chief editor; *Travailleur Réunionnais* (semi-monthly), published by CGTR; *Combat Réunionnais*, published by UGTRF. A full-size, 200-page book, *Réunion, Egalité et Développement*, an assessment of the Ripert report with suggestions for implementing the program for economic and social equality in the island was published and actively marketed in October.

The Réunion Communist Party (PCR) is a lively and not inconsequential part of Réunion politics. The family names Hoarau, Vergès, Payet, and Langenier dominate the scene, though, like Socialist André Russel Hoarau, they do not necessarily belong to the PCR. *Témoignages*, the party's organ, is the third-largest daily on the island (circulation, 6,000, compared to the *Journal*'s 26,000 and the

Quotidien's 28,000), with screaming headlines and a lively concern for all events in the small French overseas department. It is the major source of information on the activities of the PCR, once a branch of the French Communist Party. The editor, Elie Hoarau, who is also deputy mayor of St. Pierre and one of the communist deputies to the National Assembly, and General Secretary of the party Paul Vergès, also deputy mayor of St. Paul, counselor general of Le Port, and the other communist deputy in the National Assembly, get, understandably, the lion's share of exposure in the daily.

In addition to the labor unions, the PCR's most frequent coalition partner is the Socialist party. The two parties frequently collaborate on elections, as they did in Ste. Suzanne for the victory of communist mayor Lucet Langenier's third term. In the St. Denis cantonal elections the Communists supported one of the Socialist candidates. The confrontations with the right and with Socialists like Jean-Paul Virapoullé and Jean-Claude Fruteau are drawn out and intense. (*Témoignages*, 22 August, 25, 27, 28 October, 8, 27 November, 3 December.)

Témoignages, in an aggressive quest for identity, is pushing Creole, a phonetic French language, into the forefront as an acceptable means of island communication (ibid., 1 March). It runs opinion pieces on the front page and rubric heads in the rest of the paper in the vernacular, prints regular Creole lessons for its readers, and publicizes the appearance of a Creole dictionary and a linguistic atlas (ibid., 16, 17, 18, 22 May). It even enlisted a native author, Goncourt Prize winner Axel Gauvin, to give credence and support to this venture (ibid., 12 April, 18 September) and sponsored a Creole Week in October (ibid., 26–27 May, 29–30 September).

Although insisting on an identity and a degree of autonomy for the island's population, the party complains of lack of equality in the matter of unemployment compensation (*revenue minimum d'insertion*, RMI), minimum wage rates with metropolitan France, and regulation of the island's communication industry by France as illustrated in the case of a privately owned television station, detailed below. Moreover, the PCR had serious reservations about integration into the Common Market, whose laws and regulations Réunion, as a French department, would also be subject to and that the PCR deems, because of foreign competition, to be detrimental to the island's mainly agricultural economy.

Domestic Concerns. There is a good deal of local preoccupation with a report, prepared by Jean Ripert (*Témoignages*, 9, 10, 11, 12 January) after an extensive study of the overseas departments' (DOM) situation, that consists of 58 proposals to remedy the economic and social inequality between the departments and France. This study determined that Réunion's racially mixed people (white, African, Asian, and admixtures thereof) are undereducated and underemployed, that its industry is underdeveloped, and that its agricultural economy—whose revenues fell by 25–30 percent in 1989 but whose compensation payments from the government have not kept pace with the losses—is unstable. Occasional cyclones, lack of water in the middle highlands and the west, which is separated from the eastern precipitation by a north-south range of tall mountains, keep growers and agricultural workers insecure (ibid., 1, 2, 3, 7 January, 1 March).

The major impact of the report is that economic parity with mainland France for minimum wage rates and unemployment compensation, in periodic increments of 2.1 percent to 2.5 percent, would not be achieved until 1995. The PCR violently objects to such slow progress, and Elie Hoarau in the National Assembly passionately portrayed the misery that such underpayments would bring to the people (*Témoignages*, 3, 13 June). Paul Vergès and militant PCR cells were also vocal about the need to achieve economic and social equality as soon as possible (ibid., 27 March, 31 May, 20 July, 26 September). A massive general strike, "A Day of Action," was called for 26 April to demand that equality (ibid., 24, 25, 26, 27 April). The PCR fully supported and publicized this general strike, demanding a 33 percent increase in wages and compensation (ibid., 26 April). On learning in December that the minimum wage increase will be only 2.1 percent (the same as in France), there was another massive general strike demanding at least a 5 percent increase (ibid., 1–2, 8–9 December).

Directly linked to this economic inequality were the numerous strikes that plagued the island during the year. These were generally supported or directly stage-managed by the PCR and its labor union allies. From January through June, in Le Port, L'Etang Salé and other major towns, postal strikers demanded better wages, better service, and adequate offices (*Témoignages*, 12 January, 15, 22 February, 23, 27, 29, 30 March, 4, 17, 18, 19 April, 7 June). Elie Hoarau fully supported the strikers' demands and to that end sent a telegram to the minister of Intersyndicale to ask for new positions and more facilities to improve service (ibid., 24–25 March).

Public transportation workers also struck but settled, thanks to Elie Hoarau's mediation efforts (*Témoignages*, 4, 21–22, 26 April). Lumberyard workers struck twice (ibid., 1 March, 18 May); growers blocked bridges to protest the high price of water (ibid., 17 May); agricultural workers struck against growers for higher wages (ibid., 19 April, 13, 15 November); oil and gas workers stopped delivery for five days (ibid., 30, 31 October, 2 November); and then gas station owners refused service to protest their profit margin limitation. This last strike crippled transportation, and Prefect Daniel Constantin had to negotiate the settlement (ibid., 26 December). Students demanded better school facilities and teachers (ibid., 20 March, 16 October, 16, 17, 18, 23 November, 5 December); 45 strikers almost put Solpak, a small manufacturing firm in Ste. Suzanne, out of business when their strike stretched from mid-June to late August without settlement (ibid., 28 June, 7, 18–19 August); even lawyers struck, demanding the same perquisites and commissions as their confreres in France (ibid., 5 February).

The Ripert report shaped much of the activity of the PCR and that of its political allies. It was the focal point of press conferences and even of the October *Témoignages* festival. Among labor leaders, Lucien Hoarau, secretary general of Force Ouvrier (FO), demanded that a specific law be passed to right the inequalities (*Témoignages*, 11 January); Georges-Marie Lepinay, secretary general of the CGTR, declared that the government must act quickly and without politics (ibid., 6 February). Paul Vergès proposed that there be, by the year 2000, 33,000 jobs, carefully distributed, on the island (ibid., 7 February). Elie Hoarau in the National Assembly proposed that the details of the plan be worked out by the DOMs; meanwhile, the government should double the rate of increase of wage and compensation payments to make up for the delay (ibid., 11 June). At a press conference on 19 July, Paul Vergès called on officials and people of the island to finally "decolonize the mind," that is, not to depend on France for everything (ibid., 26 September). Vergès and Hoarau severely criticized the timid advances toward parity in the first measures of the Ripert plan, which the minister of DOM, Louis Le Pensec, put before the assembly (ibid., 10–11, 12 November).

Tele-Free-Dom, a television station owned by Camille Sudre, had been broadcasting apparently without a license since the fall of 1989. The government authorities forced it to shut down, but the PCR went to bat for it in the name of freedom of expression. In the streets of St. Denis, after a demonstration march of fervent support that turned bloodily violent, the government granted the station a temporary license (*Témoignages*, 3–4, 6, 7, 8, 9, 10 March). In gratitude, the station gave frequent exposure to PCR leaders. Hoarau was a guest at a call-in program during which he was praised for his honesty and aplomb in handling questions and for his constant efforts to keep his fingers on the public pulse (ibid., 21–22 July). Paul Vergès, in an interview on the eve of the *Témoignages* festival, characterized the party's program as innovative and caring. He announced the appearance of the 200-page book *La Réunion: Egalité et Développement*, edited by the PCR leaders, that assesses and discusses how to implement the Ripert report. Later radio appearances by PCR leaders further discussed and publicized the book (ibid., 11 October).

The *Témoignages* festival, a nine-day period of indoctrination, self-congratulation, camaraderie, and entertainment, has been used by the general secretary as a kind of party congress, the last of which was held ten years ago. Vergès promised during the festival to schedule a congress during the first half of 1991 and declared that he sees no need on that occasion to change the party's name, unlike many East European parties during the past year. The invited guests were two Brazilians—Marxist novelist Jorge Amado and poet Zelia Gattaii—who addressed the young (ibid., 4, 6–7, 8, 9, 10 October).

The two communist deputies proposed to the National Assembly dividing the island into two departments—La Réunion du Vent and La Réunion sous le Vent—using as a boundary the natural geographic division of the mountains, which run roughly north and south. The deputies maintained that the two sections of the island have different needs and would be better served this way. This idea was claimed by the rightists as well; they even accused the PCR of stealing it (*Témoignages*, 1–2 September). Hoarau instituted a series of discussions on the subject; in November, French prime minister Michel Rocard was interested enough to ask for a thorough investigation of the possibility. He may, however, have been simply showing his gratitude for the deputies' no votes on his censure motion in the assembly. Hoarau and Vergès, who voted on party mandate, were part of the narrow margin of five votes that saved Rocard (ibid., 21 November).

There were two cantonal elections in St. Denis and two municipal elections; the one in Ste. Marie was canceled and then rescheduled because of fraud (*Témoignages*, 23 February, 27 March). The one of interest was in Ste. Suzanne, where in July second-term PCR mayor Lucet Langenier and his staff, after nearly a year in office, were recalled by the Council General because incumbents could not stand for election (ibid., 28–29 July, 16 August). Langenier registered for the third term, vowing to fight, and welcomed the special commission set up to monitor the election (ibid., 17 August). A Socialist enemy, Jean-Pierre Virapoullé, deputy mayor of St. André, vigorously campaigned for his protegé against Langenier, even to the extent of having PCR sympathizers roughed up (ibid., 31 July, 22 August); on 23 September, however, Langenier was elected with a comfortable margin: 51.29 percent to his opponent's 43.48 percent (ibid., 24, 25, 29–30 September). His third mayoral installation in eighteen months was indicative of turbulent local politics (ibid., 1 October).

The drought wreaked terrible havoc on sugarcane, vanilla, and other agricultural products of the island (*Témoignages*, 17 July). There were plans for diverting water to the west from the du Mat and du Circque rivers, to which the Société Réunionnaise pour la Protection de l'Environement (SREPEN) objected. Because the water is so desperately needed, those objections were ridiculed by *Témoignages* (9 January). The shortage has reached crisis proportions, especially in the southern and eastern growing areas where the aftermath of the 1989 cyclone Firinga is still visible (ibid., 7 February). Hoarau, in his rounds of visits to various areas of the island, listened to and channeled complaints and requests for aid to the minister of DOM (ibid., 9, 10–12, 14–15, 17, 24 April). On PCR appeal, the western section, where water rationing is in effect (ibid., 28–29 July, 2 November), was declared a disaster area (ibid., 24, 27 April, 26 July). Vergès demanded that the hydroelectric plant capture its spillage into the sea for use elsewhere (ibid., 13 December).

If water resources and conservation were major concerns, so was the environmentally sound development of the island. To balance natural resources, the PCR proposed a six-point scheme to the Regional Forestry Management that included creating special industrial zones, developing the eastern sector, and making new roads north and west through the mountains (*Témoignages*, 8 January). *Témoignages* pledged to participate in Environmental Month with the motto We Have Only One Island (ibid., 16 May) and promised to devote one page each week to environmental concerns (ibid., 25 October).

Unemployment is a serious problem: more than one-third (37 percent) of the population is out of work (*Témoignages*, 3, 4 January, 26 October), and 25 percent of the people live on unemployment compensation (ibid., 1–2, 13, 14 September). Industry representatives blame illiteracy and lack of initiative for unemployment and say that these can be solved only by better education, by the development of entrepreneurial spirit, and by a positive attitude (ibid., 3–4 February). There are training programs: Contrat d'Emploi Solidarité (CES), for unemployed between the ages of 16 and 25 and over 50, and a program of continuing education (Association de Formation des Adultes de la Réunion, (AFPAR), which is rife with misappropriation of funds and other scandals (ibid., 2, 6, 8 November, 6 December). The PCR keeps reminding the Education Ministry that its promises for funds and reforms have not been kept (ibid., 23 October, 2 November).

Housing is another concern, with both Paul Vergès and *Témoignages* fighting for housing aid (*Témoignages*, 7 June, 4 July). During the visit to the island by the minister of housing, Louis Besson, elected officials confronted him with the inadequacy of funds and materials allotted for Réunion. The communist mayor of Ste. Suzanne, Lucet Langenier, emphasized that the important thing is to provide means for proper housing for all people in Réunion (ibid., 12 June). However, Pierre Vergès, communist mayor of Le Port, expelled foreign squatters from public land, saying that he could do nothing else; there simply is no housing, and permitting the squatters to remain would have set an unmanageable precedent he could not permit (ibid., 19–20 May).

Belonging to the European Community and its market via France is worrisome to the islanders (*Témoignages*, 3, 4 January). The elected PCR officials questioned Bruce Miller, head of the European commission in charge of Programme d'Options Spécifiques à L'Eloignement et à l'Insularité des DOM (POSEIDOM), on his four-day visit to Réunion on the matter of subsidies, grants, prices of rum and sugar, transportation allowances, and so forth. He promised that Europe will do nothing against the interests of Réunion. (Ibid., 28 February, 1, 3–4, 6 March.)

Among the interests and goals of the PCR was eliminating racism in Réunion. The PCR reacted strongly when a Socialist candidate, André Russel Hoarau, said to another Socialist candidate, Mookeshchand Beehary, in front of witnesses, "Go home, dirty Maurician, you monkey eater" (*Témoignages*, 28 March), and when Rally for the Republic (RPR, rightist) candidate Michel Chen Liat declared that he is against integration of the races: he is proud of his Chinese roots and wants to preserve them (ibid., 17–18, 29 March). PCR found such statements and other incidents of prejudice unsettling for Réunion's racial harmony (ibid., 4 April, 17, 22 May, 2–4 June).

Women's rights questions and the issue of sexual harassment surfaced during the year, and *Témoignages* fully supported UFR president Huguette Bello's program and activities on the International Day of Women (*Témoignages*, 7, 12, 13 March). When a young woman complained of harassment in a government office, PCR members of the regional council, under the signature of Roger Hoarau, addressed a letter to the president of the regional council demanding a thorough investigation (ibid., 27, 29, 30 March).

International Views and Connections. As to matters abroad, the PCR is concerned about France's supposed racism, not toward Réunionnais people as such but toward blacks and Arabs, and insists that this prejudice radiates to the island. The PCR applauded the PCF proposal to repress racism adopted by the National Assembly (*Témoignages*, 4 May).

The PCR leadership is pleased with Gorbachev's increasing role on the world stage and with his Nobel Prize (ibid., 16 October), although it rues his abandoning his leading role for multipartyism (ibid., 14 March). The PCR leaders, among them Elie Hoarau, dismissed the collapse of the Eastern European communist/Socialist countries as simply those parties' capacity for self-criticism and realignment of goals and ideals with the true aim of communism. As an example, he noted that Ceauşescu's values cannot be equated with those of communism (ibid., 27 March, 21–22 July, 4 October).

The freeing of Nelson Mandela—"an immense victory," said Paul Vergès—(*Témoignages*, 12 February) gave rise to extensive coverage in *Témoignages* (ibid., 3–4, 19, 20 February), which also fully covered the activities of UFR's Huguette Bello, the

only elected communist member of the general council, in her demonstrations against South African apartheid (ibid., 16–17, 19 February, 1, 2 March). On the International Day of Women (8 March), she welcomed Mittah Seperepere, the African National Congress women's representative (ibid., 7, 8, 9, 11–12, 13 March). Elie Hoarau met Nelson Mandela in Paris in June and transmitted the solidarity of Réunion to his cause (ibid., 7 June).

Témoignages (1 August) also rejoiced at the electoral victory of the Mongolian Communist Party and expressed hope for the solid basis of reformation in the former Italian Communist Party, which now includes a broad spectrum of leftists (*Témoignages*, 12 March).

Margit N. Grigory
Hoover Institution

Senegal

Population. 7,713,851
Party. Independence and Labor Party (Parti de l'Indépendance et du Travail, PIT)
Founded. 1957
General Secretary. Amath Dansokho
Politburo. 14 members: Amath Dansokho, Samba Dioulde Thiam, Maguette Thiam, Mady Danfaka, Sadio Camara, Seydou Ndongo, Semou Pathe Gueye, Makthar Mbaye, Bouma Gaye, Mohamed Laye (names of other four not known)
Secretariat. 7 members: Amath Dansokho, Semou Pathe Gueye, Maguette Thiam, Samba Dioulde Thiam, Mady Danfaka, Makhtar Mbaye (name of other member not known)
Central Committee. 55 members (Semou Pathe Gueye, secretary)
Status. Legal
Last Congress. Third, 23–25 March 1990
Last Election. 1988, 0.84 percent, no seats
Auxiliary Organization. Women's Democratic Union
Publications. *Daan Doole*, *Gestu*

The era of *glasnost'* and *perestroika* has arrived in Senegal. The Third Congress of Senegal's Communist Party, PIT (Independence and Labor Party), which was held in March 1990, was marked by a desire for renewal and openness. During three days, the twelve hundred delegates who attended the congress debated 222 theses that had been submitted for discussion. The theses represented a rupture with earlier positions adopted in 1984 during PIT's Second Congress.

As stated in Thesis 200, PIT has now committed itself to a "strategy of reform" favoring the broad unity of patriotic forces. Such unity would bring about the climate necessary for "negotiated political solutions" to Senegal's acute social problems. The unity PIT is calling for, however, does not entail embracing either the governing Socialist Party (PS) or SOPI, the liberal-communist alliance between the Senegalese Democratic Party (PDS) and the Democratic League/Movement for the Party of Labor (LD/MPT). On the contrary, PIT announced a "unilateral break" in its dialogue with the Socialist party and condemned SOPI for its "intolerance and sectarianism" (Dakar, *Sud Hebo*, 22 March; *FBIS-AFR*, 26 June).

At the same time, PIT indicated that it would be willing to reconsider its position if the Socialist party would stop prevaricating. As the secretary of PIT's Central Committee, Semou Pathe Gueye, explained: "We are not ready to resume the dialogue with the PS as long as it has not changed policies. When the PS changes, we shall change our attitude (Dakar, *Wal Fadjri*, 30 March–5 April; *FBIS-AFR*, 18 June). PIT's continuous search for a meaningful dialogue with the PS is based on its realization that reforms will never materialize without the collaboration of the government. Amath Dansokho, in a major article in *World Marxist Review* acknowledged that, although the PS represented "the bureaucratic parasitic bourgeoisie," it remained Senegal's "biggest political force, supported throughout its history by the overwhelming majority of the population" (*WMR*, February). Given this balance of power, a policy of unmitigated opposition to the PS might well lead to bloodshed and chaos. Thus, PIT's leaders realize that at this historical juncture their most reasonable hope is to force the Socialist party into accepting a democratic program that "would draw all [Senegalese] closer together" (ibid.). Not surprisingly, Dansokho affirmed that "we can not only find common ground but also reach agreement with the Social Democrats on many fundamental issues" (ibid.).

An agreement of this kind would not entail a rupture with the existing capitalist order, let alone induce a Socialist revolution. Dansokho acknowledged that "the choice between capitalism and socialism is not on the agenda" (*WMR*, February). Adopting the slogan, "production first, distribution later," the general secretary of PIT made it clear that the party is no longer opposed to capitalism. In fact, Dansokho asserted the PIT was not fighting "against capitalism or even against the policy of adjustment imposed on [Senegal] by the World Bank" (ibid.). The new realities of the world economic order have dictated nonideological policies favoring the rationality of the market and the acceptance of foreign capitalist investments. From Dansokho's perspective, PIT's new pragmatism represents the only viable alternative because, as he puts it, "a proper policy is the art of the possible" (ibid.).

PIT has not only accepted the market economy, it also espouses liberal democracy. According to PIT, the Marxist-Leninist tradition of the single communist party system created uniformity, tyranny, and stagnation. It must be abandoned lest "hypocrisy and cynicism [reign] supreme" (*WMR*, February). In the stark words of Dansokho, "The socialist revolution, as it occurred in October 1917, has exhausted its potential" (ibid.). Progressive forces all over the world have now rejected violent revolution and embraced democracy as "the foremost human value," claims Dansokho (ibid.). PIT's immediate goal, therefore, is to achieve the "broadest possible kind of democracy" and to assure the flourishing of freedom of expression and organization. In Thesis 25, PIT categorically denounced existing Marxist-Leninist states for their "serious restrictions on democracy" and their "dark techniques" of camouflaging human rights abuses as "anti-Soviet and anti-communist" (Dakar, *Sud Hebo*, 22 March; *FBIS-AFR*, 26 June).

Not surprisingly, Dansokho has claimed that "only perestroika can save us all" (*WMR*, February) and that a Senegalese "perestroika" would entail a "national vision, a national consensus" rather than the promotion of any particular class interests (ibid.). Privileging the interests of one class over another would lead to adventurist and dangerous policies of increasing social polarization that might well culminate in civil war. What Senegal needs now, PIT asserts, is responsible political leadership that will preserve and enhance stability—PIT's "foremost concern" (ibid.). This in turn requires a real dialogue with the Socialist party rather than a program of constant harassment of the government. PIT therefore is not prepared to rejoin the PDS-LD/MPT-SOPI alliance unless the alliance abandons its "automatic rejection" of anything proposed by governmental authorities (Dakar, *Sud Hebo*, December 1989; *FBIS-AFR*, 7 March; *WMR*, February).

In contrast to PIT, Senegal's other communist party, the LD/MPT (Democratic League/Movement for the Party of Labor), has committed itself to consolidate the SOPI alliance. During its Third Congress, held 16 and 17 February, the LD/MPT stressed the role of the alliance in providing the basis for a transition government that will replace what it describes as the illegitimate and bankrupt administration of President Abdou Diouf. During the congress, the PDS, the main ally of the LD/MPT, declared through its leader, Abdoulaye Wade, that "[SOPI was] determined to respond in positive fashion to any action designed to overthrow the government" (Dakar, *Sud Hebo*, 22 March; *FBIS-AFR*, 26 June). Moreover, Wade contended that "it would be criminal to let a single day, a single week, pass without pushing the government to the wall" (ibid.).

Not surprisingly, the SOPI alliance has engaged in a series of meetings and marches over the last two years in an attempt to harass the PS regime. Several leaders of the opposition were detained in a November demonstration against what they described as the monopolistic and restrictive media policies of the government (Paris, AFP, 14 November; *FBIS-AFR*, 16 November). Even though the leaders were eventually released, their arrest symbolized Senegal's deteriorating political climate and the increasing polarization between government and opposition.

Public malaise was further exacerbated by the opposition's boycott of the municipal elections in November for which only the governing PS had registered. The opposition denounced the elections as fraudulent, meaningless, and "an abuse of authority" (Paris, AFP, 27 November; *FBIS-AFR*, 3 December), demanding the resignation of President Diouf and the organization of "free and democratic elections" (*Libreville Africa*, no. 1 [11 March]; *FBIS-AFR*, 12 March). In an earlier effort to assuage popular discontent, President Diouf had dismissed Jean Collin, his powerful number two man (London, BBC, 13 April; *FBIS-AFR*, 16 April). Collin, a white Frenchman who had become a Senegalese national, had been the opposition's prime target—a symbol of the neocolonial nature of the Diouf administration (Dakar, *Sud Hebo*, 29 March; *FBIS-AFR*, 14 June). Collin was removed from both the leadership of the PS and from his position as state minister secretary general of the presidency

(Paris, AFP, 13 April; *FBIS-AFR*, 16 April). His departure, however, failed to satisfy the opposition, which maintained its call for "a new electoral code and new elections" (*FBIS-AFR*, 14 June).

Senegal's ongoing political crisis was compounded by persistent economic problems. The Diouf administration was plagued by an external debt of almost $3 billion, high unemployment, and dislocations brought about by the structural adjustment program imposed by the International Monetary Fund and the World Bank. These grim economic circumstances have enhanced the opposition's charges of governmental incompetence and corruption.

Tensions between the government and the opposition have engendered a climate of crisis that has been further exacerbated by the violent campaign of Casamance's separatist movement in southern Senegal. In their struggle for independence, the Casamance Democratic Forces (MFDC) have been waging guerrilla warfare against Senegalese security forces (Dakar Domestic Service, 14 July; London, BBC, 26 July, 18 October; Dakar, PANA, 7 August; Paris, AFP, 6 September; *FBIS-AFR*, 17, 30 July, 9 August, 7 September, 23 October). According to the government, the MFDC has been receiving Iraqi weapons through Mauritania, which had been involved in serious military clashes against Senegal in early January (*Libreville Africa*, no. 1 [11 January]; Dakar, PANA, 18 October; *FBIS-AFR*, 12 January, 18 October). Thus the struggle in Casamance is part and parcel of larger external threats to Senegal's territorial integrity. In addition to confronting Mauritania at Senegal's northern frontier and Casamance's separatist forces from within, the Diouf administration has also had to contend with deteriorating relations with Gambia and Guinea-Bissau (Dakar, PANA, 18 October; *Le Soleil*, 25 July; *FBIS-AFR*, 18, 23 October).

Paradoxically, these internal and external threats to Senegal's nationhood have contributed to what little cooperation exists between the government and opposition. PIT, the SOPI alliance, and numerous other opposition parties have rallied behind the government in the conflicts against Mauritania and Guinea-Bissau (Dakar Domestic Service, 14 July; Dakar, *Wal Fadjri*, 22–28 June; *FBIS-AFR*, 17 July, 31 August). The opposition has firmly rejected the idea of Casamance secession, and it is the Casamance situation that has generated the highest level of cooperation between the Diouf administration and the opposition. Both the PIT and the PDS have actively collaborated with the government to find a peaceful resolution to Casamance's crisis (Dakar, *Wal Fadjri*, 22–28 June, 13–19 July; *FBIS-AFR*, 31 August, 10 September). In July, PDS and PS deputies formed a nonpartisan fact-finding mission to the southern region. As an editorial in the state-owned *Le Soleil* (19 July) put it:

[One] of the lessions of [the] crisis has been that Senegalese who belong to different political groups can nevertheless join forces for the common good. The tour of the deputies' group (PS and PDS) in defense of a common cause is a first in the history of modern Senegal, one that deserves recognition. This "Casamancan perestroyka"...has been warmly welcomed by the people. (*FBIS-AFR*, 10 September.)

The Casamancan *perestroika*, however, is unlikely to extend beyond the issue of Casamance. The opposition's boycott of the November municipal elections and the incidents that marred its demonstrations against the status of the press bode poorly for future cooperative ventures with the Diouf regime.

On the international front, Senegal condemned Iraq's invasion of Kuwait and sent a military contingent to Saudi Arabia to symbolize its full support of operation Desert Shield. In addition, the summit meeting of the Organization of the Islamic Conference, largely sponsored by the exiled Kuwaiti regime, is still scheduled to take place in Dakar in Janaury 1991 (Dakar, *Sud Hebo*, 6 September; *FBIS-AFR*, 25 October). Senegal continues to have excellent relations with the United States, as evidenced by President Diouf's visit to Washington in May (Dakar Domestic Service, 14 May; *FBIS-AFR*, 18 May). In March, the Soviet Union expressed its friendship to PIT on the occasion of its Third Congress.

Robert Fatton, Jr.
University of Virginia

South Africa

Population. 39,549,941
Party. South African Communist Party (SACP)
Founded. 1921
Chairman. Dan Tloome, 73, teacher
General Secretary. Joe Slovo, 64, barrister
Politburo. Chris Hani, chief of staff of the military wing of the African National Congress (ANC); Ray Simons (pen name, R. S. Nyameko), labor theoretician; Mac Maharaj, political strategist, recruitment director in South Africa; Thabo Mbeki, information chief, John Nkadimeng, general secretary of South African Congress of Trade Unions (SACTU); all elected in 1984 at Moscow Congress (*Africa Confidential* 29, no. 17 [1988].)
Interim Leadership Group (ILG). Announced jointly by Joe Slovo of the SACP and Nelson Mandela of the ANC on 29 July, 22 members: Raymond Mhlaba, head; Dan Tloome; Joe Slovo; Brian Bunting, *African Communist* editor; Ray Alexander and John Nkadimeng, both prominent in SACTU; Reg September, active in South African Coloured People's Congress and the ANC; Harry Gwala; Govan Mbeki; Ahmed Kathadra; Billy Nair, Asian trade unionist; Chris Hani, chief of staff of Umkhonto we Sizwe, the military arm of the ANC; Ronnie Kasrils; Mac Maharaj and Sizakele Sigxashe, in ANC intelligence and security work; Essop Pahad, party representative of the now defunct *World Marxist Review* in Prague; Jeremy Cronin, poet; Cheryl Carolus, student leader; Chris Dhlamini, first deputy president of the Congress of South African Trade Unions (COSATU); John Gonomo, shop steward; Moses Mayekiso, general secretary of the National Union of Metal Workers; Sydney Mufamadi, COSATU official
Status. Legal, as of 2 February 1990
Last Congress. Seventh, June 1989
Publications. *African Communist*, quarterly, now published in Johannesburg (earlier abroad), Brian Bunting, editor; *Umsebenzi*, now published openly in South Africa.

After 40 years of illegality and exile, the SACP returned triumphantly to open activity in the Republic of South Africa in the wake of its unbanning on 2 February by President F. W. de Klerk. Retaining its close ties with the simultaneously unbanned ANC, the SACP undertook the transformation to legality amid vigorous internal debates over appropriate strategy, influenced both by the radical changes in the policies of the National party government in South Africa and by the collapse of communist governments in Eastern Europe and continuing turmoil in the international communist movement. By year's end the SACP remained balanced between the familiar clandestine and exile politics of the past four decades and new approaches testing the unfamiliar and uncertain terrain of legality. (For background and history of the SACP, see *YICA*, 1989, 1990.)

It was in late 1989, after his selection as P. W. Botha's successor and his electoral victory in white elections, that newly installed President F. W. de Klerk eased government repression by opening discussions with selected leaders of the black anti-apartheid opposition, freeing Walter Sisulu and all other Rivonia codefendants except Nelson Mandela, and permitting opposition meetings, including a mass rally explicitly for Sisulu and other freed ANC leaders. In a dramatic speech at the opening of Parliament on 2 February, de Klerk confirmed that Nelson Mandela would be freed and promised a new era of reconciliation—legalizing the ANC, SACP, and other banned opposition political organizations, accelerating the repeal of apartheid laws, and offering to negotiate with the ANC and other political opponents to establish a new postapartheid political order. Nine days later, on 11 February, Nelson Mandela was released unconditionally from prison.

Reacting in late 1989 to President de Klerk's initial moves of liberalization, the Central Committee stated that "we must undoubtedly make full use of whatever new space has opened. But in doing so, we must not be trapped into a position which will play into the regime's hands." Specifically, the Central Committee argued that both legal protest and armed challenge, both open organization and clandestine activity must be strengthened to end apartheid.

We stand four-square behind the immediate objectives of the National Democratic Revolution. This will bring about a multi-party, non-racist democracy based on one person one vote, a mixed economy and constitutional safeguards for the social, cultural, linguistic and religious rights of all individuals. The struggle to achieve this calls for the broadest coalition of all class and democratic forces who support these aims and who are not hostile to the ANC and the Mass Democratic Movement. We must also be on guard against the pseudo-revolutionaries who attempt to narrow the base of such a coalition. At the same time the working class and its political and mass organizations must maintain their independence and vigorously spread their ultimate perspective of socialism. If a time ever arrives when the regime is ready to genuinely negotiate the process of moving to democracy as understood by the whole civilized world, it will come as a wonderful surprise. And if the preconditions for talks are met, a dialogue about the process may become possible. Until then there can be no retreat from our policy of mounting even greater pressures on all fronts of struggle, internal and external, legal and illegal. (*African Communist*, no. 120.)

In February, after the unbanning of the ANC and the SACP, the Central Committee continued to voice both hope and skepticism:

Although our Party has been unbanned, the illegitimate apartheid regime remains in power. Highly repressive legislation remains on the South African statute books. FW De Klerk has implemented some important first steps, but his regime is committed to a brutal economic policy that is anti-worker, and indeed against the interests of the majority of South Africans. (*African Communist*, no. 121.)

Organization and Leadership. As the year opened the SACP remained a shadowy body, publicly identifying only a small number of its top leaders in exile who shuttled between major centers of activity in Africa and Europe. At the Seventh Congress of the SACP, held in Havana in June 1989, Dan Tloome (biography, *YICA*, 1988) and Joe Slovo (biography, *YICA*, 1987, 1988) were reelected as chairman and general secretary, respectively; other members of the Central Committee were not identified.

Tloome and Slovo continued an established party tradition of filling top public offices with longtime party members who had joined the legal Communist Party of South Africa (CPSA) in the 1940s, worked underground in the underground successor SACP in the 1950s and early 1960s, and then left the country in the early 1960s under party orders to continue work in Africa and Europe in association with the exiled ANC leadership.

Understandably the SACP revealed neither the membership nor the leadership of the underground party, but the numbers of known committed Communists within the country were augmented in the late 1980s when high-ranking, longtime ANC activists and former CPSA members of the Tloome/Slovo generation were freed from life sentences. In late 1987, Govan Mbeki was released followed by Harry Gwala in late 1988; both unrepentingly articulated their continued loyalties to both the ANC and the SACP. Rivonia trialists Ahmed Kathadra, Raymond Mhlaba, and Elias Motsoaledi joined Mbeki and Gwala to swell the ranks of highly visible avowed Communists when they were released with Walter Sisulu in October 1989.

In response to de Klerk's unbanning of the SACP, the Central Committee immediately declared its intention of taking advantage of the new opportunity to expand the party:

A major objective of the coming months will be the building of a strong, legal SACP rooted among the working masses of our people. A concerted campaign of mobilization and organization will be undertaken, with its focus upon the tens of thousands of militant workers and youth who have, over the past years, openly associated themselves with the traditions and ideals of the South African Communist Party. To this end the SACP is in the process of consulting our underground and other structures, and we shall shortly be announcing a public SACP leadership core within our country. We shall also be despatching Communist Party members into the country to strengthen this core as soon as possible. Our Party is determined to rally all those within our country who are genuinely committed to a socialist future. Now, more than ever, the place of all socialists is within the ranks of the South African Communist Party. In building a powerful, above-board Party let us avoid all forms of sectarianism, elitism and dogmatism. Let us spread and deepen a liberating and democratic socialist culture within our country. (African Communist, no. 121.)

Party discussions recognized that the new situation required new modes of operation and different conceptions of membership. An unidentified party member declared,

There is only a handful of comrades with any experience of existence as a legal party. Generation after generation of communists has been nurtured and has grown to political maturity under conditions of extreme repression. They have developed a style of work which is peculiar to these conditions. . . . It means that the legal communist party will bring into it the best traditions of underground life—traditions of discipline, dedication and unwavering commitment to the cause of socialism. But there is a whole baggage of experience which will have to be shed . . . the style of work that comes with living a totally conspiratorial life. (Work in Progress, May.)

On 19 June, Joe Slovo, flanked by former prisoners Raymond Mhlaba and Mac Maharaj, an Asian who had served a ten-year sentence on Robben Island with Nelson Mandela before leaving the country to work with the ANC in exile and then returned to the internal underground in 1987, held the party's first legal press conference in 40 years. According to the Washington Post,

Slovo said that the Communist Party would work toward complete openness concerning its membership and policies in the future. But because the process of democratization in South Africa was still subject to change, Slovo said that the party would maintain an underground organization and members of its externally based central committee "will not be known politically, not all of it." (WP, 20 June.)

Referring to the secretive Afrikaner Broederbond that has animated the National party for much of its existence, Slovo asserted that

the South African Communist party had never operated with the intention of becoming a Broederbond within any other organization, nor do we intend in the future to act like a Broederbond in any other organization. . . . We intend moving towards a situation where every communist will be proud to acknowledge . . . they are members of the party. (The Star, 20 June.)

He announced that the party leadership would be partially disclosed at a mass rally to be held in Soweto on 29 July, the eve of the 69th anniversary of the CPSA's foundation.

On 29 July, before a crowd estimated by the South African Press Association at more than 60,000 (FBIS-AFR, 30 July) and addressed by both Joe Slovo and Nelson Mandela, party officials announced a 22-member Interim Leadership Group (ILG), headed by 70-year-old Raymond Mhlaba. It included longtime party stalwarts (both freed long-term prisoners and returned exiles) as well as younger members recruited into the underground party in the 1970s and 1980s. Drawn from all the country's population groups, the ILG ranged in age from 30 to 80 years, with an average age of 57. Half the ILG were 60 or older, and most had been members of the legal CPSA. This group of eleven included well-known exiles such as Tloome, Slovo, Brian Bunting (editor of *African Communist*), Ray Alexander, and John Nkadimeng (both prominent in SACTU), and Reg September (active in the South African Coloured People's Congress and the ANC), as well as released long-term prisoners, among them Mhlaba, Gwala, Kathadra, Mbeki, and Billy Nair (an Asian trade union activist who had served twenty years in prison for Umkhonto activities after which he returned to work in the United Democratic Front [UDF]). Five persons in their late 40s or early 50s had often been labeled as SACP members: four who had worked at the center of ANC exile operations in Lusaka—Chris Hani (chief of staff of Umkhonto since 1987), Ronnie Kasrils (head of Umkhonto military intelligence until 1989), Mac Maharaj, and Sizakele Sigxashe (involved in ANC security and intelligence work)—plus Essop Pahad, who had represented the party for fifteen years on the editorial board of the *World Marxist Review* in Prague. Those under 45—including Jeremy Cronin, a poet who had served seven years in prison (1976–1983) for distributing party propaganda, and five UDF and COSATU activists whose party membership was revealed for the first time: Cheryl Carolus (a 33-year-old coloured student leader who had become prominent in the UDF in the Western Cape), Chris Dhlamini (first deputy president of COSATU), John Gomomo (a shop steward and second deputy president of COSATU), Moses Mayekiso (general secretary of the National Union of Metal Workers), and Sydney Mufamadi (a COSATU official and, at 30, the youngest member of the ILG)—had all been recruited to the party internally in the 1970s and 1980s. Together the members of the ILG had served a combined total of 137 years in prison. Twelve of the ILG, none of whom were under 45, were identified as members of the Central Committee.

In assessing the party's immediate prospects for expanded membership, ILG member Chris Dhlamini observed:

As far as actual card-carrying membership goes, if the party simply invited applications for membership, we could expect a really massive party, 20,000–30,000 at least. But we are talking of a party of activists, what [General Secretary Joe] Slovo has called a party of quality and calibre, so we will not necessarily accept just anyone. In the past we have managed this by recruitment and probation. This is going to change as the party becomes more open. But we will have to watch that it does not become a party of paper membership. . . . Administratively, though, there may be problems with the rapid growth of the party. I'm not sure we yet have the resources to immediately build a big party, a mass party. But our ability to do so depends on people actually joining—on our transforming the strong emotional on-the-ground support into organized membership. And to achieve that it is important not to intimidate people with the idea of "quality and calibre." What we mean is a strong, active commitment and participation by members—active participation in party life, in building the ANC, in building COSATU and in building other democratic formations: in other words, active participation in the struggle for democracy. (*Work in Progress*, August.)

Speaking from his perspective as a COSATU member, fellow ILG member Moses Mayekiso asserted his determination to bring his trade union experience to bear in his party work:

I think that my role and that of people like Chris Dhlamini will be informed by our role in building the trade union movement, our role in building the democratic structures in the trade union movement, our role in building the civic structures through the democratic structures, the street and area committees, the shop stewards' councils—all these are structures aimed at encouraging accountability of the leadership of that organization to their constituencies. (*New Nation*, 3–9 August.)

On 1 December the SACP transferred its publication offices from London to new premises in Johannesburg. In other major centers open party organizations also began functioning under the supervision of the ILG. Final authority rests with the Central Committee whose full membership has not yet been announced. Preparations are now being made for the Eighth Congress of the SACP to be held in Johannesburg at the end of July 1991, coinciding with the 70th anniversary of the CPSA. A new central committee will be elected and a new party program discussed.

Domestic Activities and Attitudes. The unexpectedly rapid shift to legality within South Africa coincided with the aftermath of the unexpectedly rapid disintegration of Eastern European communist regimes and continuing rapprochement between the Soviet Union and the United States. Early in the year, General Secretary Slovo received party permission to publish a 28-page discussion paper, "Has Socialism Failed?" in which he sharply criticized past Soviet and East European practice as well as South African party behavior, offering new arguments for the necessity of political pluralism in a postapartheid South Africa:

Socialism is undoubtedly in the throes of a crisis greater than at any time since 1917. The last half of 1989 saw the dramatic collapse of most of the communist party governments of Eastern Europe. Their downfall was brought about through massive upsurges which had the support not only of the majority of the working class but also a large slice of the membership of the ruling parties themselves. *These were popular revolts against unpopular regimes; if socialists are unable to come to terms with this reality, the future of socialism is indeed bleak.* . . . Shockwaves of very necessary self-examination have also been triggered off amongst communists both inside and outside the socialist world. *For our part, we firmly believe in the future of socialism; nor do we dismiss its whole past as an unmitigated failure.* Socialism certainly produced a Stalin and a Ceausescu, but it also produced a Lenin and a Gorbachev. . . . *But it is more vital than ever to subject the past of existing socialism to an unsparing critique in order to draw the necessary lessons. To do so openly is an assertion of justified confidence in the future of socialism and its inherent moral superiority. And we should not allow ourselves to be inhibited merely because an exposure of failures will inevitably provide ammunition to the traditional enemies of socialism: our silence will, in any case, present them with even more powerful ammunition.*

Constituents of what was previously known as the International Communist and Workers' movement [were cautioned against four types of responses:] A: Finding excuses for Stalinism; B: Attributing the crisis to the pace of perestroika; C: Acting as if we have declared a moratorium on socialist criticism of capitalism and imperialism and, worst of all, D: Concluding that socialist theory made the distortions inevitable. [Instead, communists were urged to recognize that] *the fundamental distortions which emerged in the practice of existing socialism cannot be traced to the essential tenets of Marxist revolutionary science. If we are looking for culprits, we must look at ourselves and not at the founders of Marxism* ("Has Socialism Failed?" pp. 25–26, 34.)

Analyzing central Marxist concepts and Soviet experience to determine the appropriate nature of the links between socialism and democracy, Slovo defended Lenin's limitations on democracy under the "dictatorship of the proletariat" as necessary to defend the Bolshevik revolution in its immediate aftermath. But once Socialist power had been won, he argued that there was no justification for the maintenance and "strengthening of the instruments of state suppression and *the narrowing of democracy for the majority of the population, including the working class*" (ibid., p. 39).

He characterized ruling communist parties as

"vanguards" by law and not necessarily by virtue of social endorsement. This was accompanied by negative transformations within the party itself. Under the guise of "democratic centralism" inner-party democracy was almost completely suffocated by centralism. All effective power was concentrated in the hands of a Political Bureau or, in some cases, a single, all-powerful personality. The control of this "leadership" by the party as a whole was purely formal. . . . *The invigorating impact of the contest of ideas in Marxist culture was stifled.* (Ibid., p. 40.)

Focusing on South African Communists, Slovo continued his harsh critique:

The commandist and bureaucratic approaches which took root during Stalin's time affected communist parties throughout the world, including our own. *We cannot disclaim our share of the responsibility for the spread of the personality cult and a mechanical embrace of Soviet domestic and foreign policies, some of which discredited the cause of socialism.* We kept silent for too long after the 1956 Khruschev revelations. It would, of course, be naive to imagine that a movement can, at a stroke, shed all the mental baggage it has carried from the past. And our 7th Congress emphasized the need for on-going vigilance. It noted some isolated reversions to the past, including attempts to engage in intrigue and factional activity in fraternal organizations, sectarian attitudes towards some non-party colleagues, and sloganized dismissals of views which do not completely accord with ours. The implications for socialism of the Stalinist distortions have not yet been evenly understood throughout our ranks. We need to continue the search for a better balance between advancing party policy as a collective and the toleration of on-going debate and even constructive dissent. (Ibid., pp. 44–45.)

Crediting both "the process of perestroika and glasnost which was so courageously unleashed under Gorbachev's inspiration" and "closer to home, the democratic spirit which dominated the re-emerged trade union movement from the early 1970s onward" for contributing to the SACP's changing practices, Slovo contended that "in certain fundamental respects" the party itself had "long ago ceased to be guided by Stalinist concepts" (ibid., p. 45). Referring to a 1970 Central Committee report on organization, Slovo argued that the party's willingness "to safeguard, both in the letter and in the spirit, the independence of the political expressions of other social forces whether economic or national" was exemplified by its "acceptance of the African National Congress as the head of the liberation alliance" (ibid., p. 46).

In a section on "Democracy and the Future," Slovo reiterated the commitment of the 1989 party program

> to a post-apartheid state which will guarantee all citizens the basic rights and freedoms of organization, speech, thought, press, movement, residence, conscience and religion; full trade union rights for all workers including the right to strike, and one person one vote in free and democratic elections. *These freedoms constitute the very essence of our national liberation and socialist objectives and they clearly imply political pluralism....*
>
> The way forward for the whole of humanity lies within a socialist framework guided by genuine socialist humanitarianism and not within a capitalist system which entrenches economic and social inequalities as a way of life. Socialism can undoubtedly be made to work without the negative practices which have distorted many of its key objectives. *But mere faith in the future of socialism is not enough. The lessons of past failures have to be learnt. Above all, we have to ensure that its fundamental tenet—socialist democracy—occupies a rightful place in all future practice.* (Ibid., p. 49.)

Slovo's pamphlet attracted wide attention in the South African press, as did Slovo (and other exiled Communists) on their subsequent return to South Africa. In the glare of publicity—interviews on radio and television, as well as with major South African and foreign newspapers—party officials, led by Slovo, frequently expounded their version of communism to the wider South African public to which they had not had legal access before 2 February. Diverse opinions were expressed by party members ranging from returning exiles to newly freed longtime party members to more recently internally recruited members.

Regularly queried about the SACP's views on economic policy and nationalization, Slovo rejected wholesale nationalization in an interview with the *Washington Post*:

> "We don't go along with the throwing about of this cliche about nationalization," he said. "You had nationalization in socialist countries of various sectors, and people didn't benefit from it." Slovo conceded that capitalism was a superior system for generating wealth, but maintained that it was no good at the task of redistribution. Only the state is capable of achieving a more equitable distribution of wealth than now exists in South Africa, he said. (*WP*, 12 July.)

Not all party members agreed with the formulations put forth by Slovo and others who seemed to accept approaches close to those of Western European Socialists. Party elder Harry Gwala, disagreeing with Slovo's contention that the SACP had correctly abandoned the concept of the "dictatorship of the proletariat," asserted: "It is therefore very clear that, where the majority of the people are made up of working men and women, poor peasants, the petty bourgeoisie and the middle class, the dictatorship of the proletariat cannot be abandoned although it frightens the bourgeoisie out of their sleep" (*African Communist*, no. 123).

In addition to articulating party views both in internal debates and before the broader South African public, visible SACP members also played a prominent public role in ANC activities ranging from cooperative participation in rallies and demonstrations to inclusion in ANC delegations negotiating with the government. At the historic first meeting between a government delegation headed by President F. W. de Klerk and an ANC delegation headed by Nelson Mandela 2–4 May at President de Klerk's Groote Schuur residence, Slovo was among the ten-person delegation, along with Ahmed Kathadra and Cheryl Carolus, who was only later identified as a party member. Subsequently in August, despite government attempts to persuade the ANC to exclude him, Slovo also participated in the Pretoria meetings with President de Klerk in which the five-person ANC delegation agreed to suspend its armed struggle in return for further government moves to meet ANC demands for the release of all political prisoners and further relaxation of security restrictions.

The generally well-informed, London-based *Africa Confidential* characterized the relationship between the SACP and the ANC as one in which "the Party and the ANC have ceased to be two allied organizations and have become one body with two heads. All Party members are also members of the ANC. The Party uses the ANC as a pool in which to recruit the best and the brightest for Party membership." (*Africa Confidential*, 4 May.) Before the SACP partially revealed its leadership in July, *Africa Confidential* estimated that 27 of the 35 members of the National Executive Committee of the ANC were SACP members (ibid.).

When queried about the *Africa Confidential* numbers at the SACP's first news conference, Slovo dismissed them as inaccurate, but "he did not, however, volunteer further information on the strength of the SACP in the ANC's national executive" (*The Star*, 20 June). When Nelson Mandela was asked the same question several weeks later he responded:

> I emphatically deny that the number of members of the South African Communist Party is as you state. I should know better on the question. . . . Although there are far fewer than you state, we don't regard these questions from the point of view of counting heads. We have the confidence that if we declare a policy, it is because that we are convinced that that policy is in the interest of the ANC and the black struggle in this country. At any time, when we feel that an idea is not in the interest of our struggle, we will reject it, no matter from whom it comes. It may come from the National Party, it [may] come from the South African Communist Party, we will reject it. (*FBIS-AFR*, 13 August.)

Both Mandela and SACP spokespersons continued to defend the longtime association of the two organizations. In his 11 February speech in Cape Town on the day of his release from prison, Nelson Mandela saluted the SACP

> for its steady contribution to the struggle for democracy. The memory of great Communists like Moses Kotane, Yusef Dadoo, Bram Fischer, and Moses Mabhida will be cherished for generations to come. I salute the General Secretary Joe Slovo, one of our finest patriots. We are heartened by the fact that the alliance between ourselves and the party remains as strong as it always was. (*NYT*, 12 February.)

At the 29 July rally launching the public SACP, Mandela repeated ANC support of the alliance:

"The Communist Party is and has been a dependable friend who has respected our views and independence. [It] has never sought to transform the ANC into a tool and puppet of the Communist Party." (*WSJ*, 30 July.) He carefully distinguished the ANC from the SACP and forthrightly defended the SACP's right to exist:

> The ANC is not a communist party. But, as a defender of democracy, it has fought and will continue to fight for the right of the Communist Party to exist. As a movement for national liberation, the ANC has no mandate to espouse a Marxist ideology. But as a democratic movement, as a parliament of the people of our country, the ANC has defended and will continue to defend the right of any South African to adhere to the Marxist ideology, if that is their wish. (*Sechaba*, September.)

Speaking from the SACP perspective in a *New York Times* interview, Raymond Mhlaba, chairman of the ILG, said that "dual membership created no conflict of interest. If there is an ANC meeting, I'm going to speak as an ANC member. But if the meeting says they would like to have a Communist speak, then I am a Communist." He went on to describe the ANC as the acknowledged leader in the alliance: "It's accepted as such. Nobody can accuse a Communist of wanting to take over. The Communist Party says that we accept that the ANC is the senior partner." (*NYT*, 11 November.)

The other major partner in the alliance is COSATU, which was formed in 1985 and is still an expanding trade union movement, with a membership of close to 1 million black workers. In February John Nkadimeng, the exiled general secretary of SACTU, the trade union federation allied with the ANC that operated openly in South Africa in the 1950s and early 1960s, indicated that SACTU would dissolve itself and accept COSATU as the dominant trade union organization in South Africa.

In March a 31-person COSATU delegation (headed by Vice-President Chris Dhlamini, subsequently revealed as a party member in July) met a 28-person SACP delegation (headed by Joe Slovo) in Harare, Zimbabwe, to discuss the nature of the relationship between the two organizations. In the view of the *African Communist*, "the role of the principal formations of the working class, the SACP and COSATU, in advancing the national liberation struggle under the leadership of the ANC, and in influencing that struggle in a socialist direction, has taken on a particular strategic importance." Party representatives presented the party's history, including "close attention . . . to certain mistakes and weaknesses in the party's work" that "were discussed openly and frankly." In the discussion of socialist democracy two main points were made:

> First, while a one-party system cannot be ruled out in principle—particular conditions may make it necessary—nevertheless in general the multi-party system provides one of the favorable conditions for democratic participation. Yet, second, a multi-party parliamentary political system is not, on its own, sufficient, it has to be supplemented by strong institutions and mass, independent organizations—women, students, trade unions, civics and so forth—which can participate in the decision-making process. . . . It was agreed that the working class was the major social force in the national liberation struggle and, therefore, had to play a pre-eminent role in the ANC. It was necessary to contribute fully to the reconstruction of the ANC inside the country and to ensure its leading role, not only in the present phase of the struggle, but also after the defeat of apartheid because the national question would not disappear overnight.

In discussing the nature of the independence of trade unions from the party, Slovo "made it plain that all members of the Party in the trade unions and other mass organizations were bound by the discipline and decisions of these organizations. The party would try to influence trade union policy only through a formal, structured relationship." (*African Communist*, no. 122.)

In May, COSATU joined the ANC and the SACP in a tripartite alliance. Jay Naidoo, general secretary of COSATU, characterized the alliance as a reconstruction of the ANC-SACP-SACTU alliance that had emerged in the 1950s and early 1960s: "The ANC is the leader of the alliance, but each organization has its own independence and is under the democratic control of its own constituency." Referring to Eastern Europe he argued that

> one of the weaknesses of socialism there has been the situation where the Party secretary has been the trade union secretary and the local state official. This created problems of making the trade unions and other organizations of civil society a conveyor belt of the Party. This is certainly the situation we want to avoid here. . . . It is clear that the Party will develop a close working relationship with other working class organizations such as trade unions, but we feel that having a mass-based Party and having an independent trade

union movement are indispensable in deepening democracy in a post-apartheid society, ensuring that the political and economic aspirations of the working class are represented. (*New Nation*, 25–31 May.)

In the assessment of the SACP the successful agreement between the ANC and the government at Groote Schuur in May signaled "the beginning of the end of the apartheid system" (*African Communist*, no. 122). "The old center of gravity in South African politics is gone, but in the process of transition to a new South Africa we have entered a period of great instability as the various contending forces struggle for mastery" (ibid.). Despite the detention of ILG members Mac Maharaj and Billy Nair in late July in the wake of government charges of a communist plot to overthrow the government, the party continued to remain cautiously hopeful after the Pretoria agreement in early August:

> The Groote Schuur and Pretoria minutes record appreciable progress on the road to a new South Africa, but the liberation movement cannot afford to be lulled into a false sense of optimism. For all the agreement that has been reached so far, it is clear that the regime and the ANC still have vastly different agendas. . . . However, both parties are agreed that in the present climate conciliation is preferable to confrontation and conflict, and it is to be hoped that in due course some sort of consensus will emerge. (*African Communist*, no. 123.)

International Views and Activities. In editorial comment explaining the decision of the party leadership to publish General Secretary Slovo's pamphlet "Has Socialism Failed?" the *African Communist* asserted that

> the seriousness of the crisis which has overtaken the international Communist movement cannot be overstated. . . . In the immediate postwar period there was a "world socialist system" embracing more than one third of the world's population, ideologically united and constituting a powerful international force for peace and social progress. Today this system is in a state of disarray. (*African Communist*, no. 121.)

It was noted that the communist collapse was benefiting imperialism and drying up sources of support for liberation movements and newly independent countries in the Third World. Specifically, the visit of Foreign Minister Pik Botha to Budapest at the invitation of the Hungarian government was cited as a betrayal of the cause of national liberation. Noting that there was "no easy answer" to the question of why communist regimes collapsed or what was socialism, the editorial stated that "the South African Communist Party is not inclined to succumb to the imperialist ideological offensive seeking to establish that capitalism is superior to socialism, and that the cold war has been won by the West." The party still believed that "no matter what happens to the existing socialist countries, capitalism has failed and will continue to fail to end class struggle and oppression and the fight for socialism will continue." Publication of Slovo's pamphlet as a draft discussion paper by the party was "a contribution to the debate" about the future of socialism and the path to power in South Africa, "the opening shot in a debate to which all interest parties including members of the SACP itself are being asked to contribute." (Ibid.)

In the same issue the full text of a December 1989 speech by Fidel Castro memorializing Cuban "internationalists" who died in Angola and elsewhere was published

> not because we endorse the sharp criticisms made by Castro of policies pursued or advocated in some of the socialist countries, but because we feel that his speech was of such importance at this juncture in international affairs that it demands study by all members of our movement. We believe that what is going on in the international Communist movement today is not a process of demolition but of cleansing. The constitution of the SACP declares that its aim is to establish a socialist republic in South Africa based on the principles of Marxism-Leninism, to promote the ideas of proletarian internationalism and the unity of the workers of South Africa and the world, and to participate in and strengthen the World Communist Movement. Nothing that has happened in Eastern Europe or elsewhere makes us believe that this perspective needs to be altered. (Ibid.)

The responses to Slovo's pamphlet that have been published to date in the *African Communist* (by Harry Gwala of the SACP and by Explo Nani Kofi of the United Revolutionary party of Ghana), have criticized Slovo, particularly for his overly negative assessment of the development of the Soviet Union. As Harry Gwala stated, "I tend to agree with Brezhnev on internationalism. If someone attacks one of us, he attacks us all. We have to defend one another, and I don't see why the imperialists should be given so much latitude to pick us off one by one."

(*African Communist*, no. 120.) In Gwala's view, "the Soviet Union has been a living example of socialism to us, a beacon to our working class" (ibid.), an assessment undoubtedly expressing the sentiments of many in a party that has always closely identified with the Communist Party of the Soviet Union.

Links with the Soviet Union remain close. In mid-July Slovo stated, "The Soviet Union, as other countries and organizations, continues to support our party financially and in many other ways but we have never been dictated to by the Soviet Union...we are an indigenous Communist Party" (*FBIS-AFR*, 20 July). In August, Slovo met in Moscow with Politburo member Gennadi Ianaiev in what TASS described as a "warm and comradely atmosphere." Yanayev "reaffirmed the Soviet Communist Party's invariable solidarity with South African Communists and the African National Congress in their struggle against apartheid and for a nonracial, democratic South Africa" (TASS, 16 August; *FBIS-SOV*, 21 August).

Whereas the Soviet connection continues strong, the SACP has suffered directly from the severing of ties with the German Democratic Republic (GDR).

> A consequence of the removal of the Communists from power has been that the GDR is no longer able to provide the range of solidarity services to liberation movements and independent countries of Asia, Africa and Latin America for which it won the honor and respect of all progressive mankind. ANC students had to be withdrawn from GDR institutions and sent back to Africa.

The *African Communist* was advised to seek new printers after having been printed and distributed without charge to the SACP since mid-1969. Expressing its gratitude for decades of support, the *African Communist* stated:

> We would like to take this opportunity to express our heartfelt thanks to our GDR comrades for the magnificent solidarity service they have rendered to the *African Communist*, the SACP and the whole cause of liberation during the period they exercised power. No matter what the faults for which they were eventually punished by the electorate, our comrades gave us whatever assistance they could in the finest spirit of proletarian internationalism. . . . The contribution of socialist GDR was multi-faceted, consistent and reliable. Perhaps we are only able to appreciate its full

significance now that it has been withdrawn. (*African Communist*, no. 122.)

Publications. For the first time since its creation in 1953, the SACP is publishing legally in South Africa. The previously clandestine journal *Umsebenzi* (the Zulu/Xhosa word for worker and the name of the legal CPSA paper from 1930 to 1936) is now openly printed and distributed. The *African Communist*, the party quarterly, published for two issues in England after the loss of its publication subsidy from the GDR, is now published in Johannesburg. As it has since its first issue in 1959, the *African Communist* characterizes itself as a journal published "in the interest of African solidarity, and as a forum for Marxist-Leninist thought throughout our Continent." Most articles deal with South African affairs, but each issue also carries a section called "Africa Notes and Comment" in which developments elsewhere in the continent are discussed.

Sheridan Johns
Duke University

Sudan

Population. 24,971,806 (July)
Party. Sudanese Communist Party (al-Hizb al-Shuyu'i al-Sudani, SCP)
Founded. 1946
Membership. 9,000 (estimated)
General Secretary. Muhammed Ibrahim Nugud Mansur
Secretariat. Before 30 June 1989: Muhammad Ibrahim Nugud Mansur, Ali al-Tijani al-Tayyib Babikr, Izz al-Din Ali Amir, Abu al-Qasim (Gassim) Muhammad, Sulayman Hamid, al-Gazuli Said Uthman, Muhammad Ahmad Sulayman (Suleiman)
Central Committee. Before 30 June 1989: Sudi Darag, Khidr Nasr, Abd al-Majid Shakak, Hasan Gassim al-Sid, Fatima Ahmad Ibrahim, Ibrahim Zakariya, and the members of the Secretariat
Status. Illegal (after 30 June 1989)

Last Congress. Fourth, 31 October 1967, in Khartoum
Last Election. 1986. 1.67 percent of the total vote in territorial constituencies; 5 seats out of the contested 264 (2 in territorial constituencies and 3 in special ones for "graduates") (Sudan News Agency [SUNA], 25 May 1986)
Auxiliary Organizations. Before 30 June 1989: Democratic Federation of Sudanese Students, Sudanese Youth Union, Sudanese Workers' Trade Union Federation, Sudanese Defenders of Peace and Democracy, Union of Sudanese Women
Publications. *Al-Maydan* (official party newspaper; published clandestinely since July 1989)

The SCP was an active part of the opposition to the military government of Umar al-Bashir during 1990. Since its formation as a party in 1946, the SCP has been a civilian political organization, participating in the nationalist movement and, after independence in 1956, in parliamentary partisan politics. During the periods of military rule in Sudan (1958–1964, 1969–1985, and 1989 to the present), formal civilian parties were banned and the SCP usually joined the other parties in the opposition (see *YICA*, 1990). In the most recent period of parliamentary rule (1986–1989), the SCP had been a vocal part of the legal opposition with a small but visible representation in Parliament.

The military government of Umar al-Bashir, which came to power on 30 June 1989, banned all parties, including the SCP, and arrested their leaders. The SCP and the other parties have operated in exile and as an underground opposition since that time; during 1990 they organized the National Democratic Alliance (NDA) to coordinate the activities of the relatively diverse opposition groups. As a small party, the SCP plays a relatively limited but visible role in this opposition.

Leadership. Because many SCP leaders were arrested in the summer of 1989, SCP affairs were managed by individuals who remained at large or were out of the country. General Secretary Nugud was released in February, but he was immediately put under house arrest following his release (SUNA, 10 February; *FBIS-NES*, 12 February). The SCP leadership was active in the NDA, with Izz al-Din Ali Amir the visible spokesperson for the opposition in exile. The party leadership acted primarily as a part of the opposition coalition rather than independently.

Domestic Issues. Sudanese domestic politics in 1990 involved the efforts of the military government to resolve the problems facing the Sudan. Civil war continued in the southern regions of the country, with the major opposition group, the Sudan People's Liberation Movement (SPLM), gaining strength. The government also faced major financial and economic crises and the possibility of famine. The political stability and strength of the regime were tested by a series of attempted coups. A military opposition group called I Am Sudan, led by a former commander in chief, joined forces with the NDA late in the year (Voice of Sudan [clandestine], 28 September; *FBIS-NES*, 5 October). In responding to these critical situations, the regime became increasingly identified with Islamic revivalist programs, especially as articulated by the National Islamic Front (NIF), and the government acted forcefully to suppress all opposition.

Umar al-Bashir specifically cited the Communists as major agents undermining the peace and stability of the country (*Middle East*, March), and Communists played an important role in professional unions' opposition to the regime and thus were targets for suppression. International attention was drawn to the government's policy by the death of Ali Fadl, a well-known Communist and leader in the Doctors' Union, who reportedly died as a result of torture in prison in April (*Africa Confidential*, 4 May). Despite this attention, however, the SCP was not an important element in the opposition and thus remains a small party on the periphery of the power politics of the Sudan. The party is involved in the major issues of contemporary Sudanese politics through its participation in the opposition coalition and tends not to maintain distinctive positions of its own.

International Positions. The changing global position of communism in 1990 and the development of the gulf crisis following the Iraq invasion of Kuwait in August created complex problems for the SCP. As a relatively orthodox, Soviet-oriented communist party, the SCP supported the policies that ended the cold war but maintained its anti-imperialist position. At the end of 1990 this meant that the party position on the gulf crisis was a difficult one because the Bashir government supported Iraq in the confrontation with the United States.

The year 1990 was not a year of dramatic initiatives in terms of positions on international issues; the primary focus of SCP attention was on domestic affairs within the Sudan. It maintained its support for the Palestine Liberation Organization and its opposition to apartheid in South Africa, but the party did not go beyond its well-established positions of the past.

In general, the SCP in opposition remains a party of intellectuals, students, and organized working groups. It continues to be an important force in professional organizations like the Doctors' Union. There is little indication, however, that the SCP made any progress in 1990 in expanding its base of popular support. In the current world situation, even the intellectual appeal of communism is not as strong as it has been in the past; at present the party remains a visible but small political force in Sudan.

John O. Voll
University of New Hampshire

Zimbabwe

Population. 10,392,161

Party. Zimbabwe African National Union—Patriotic Front (ZANU-PF)

Founded. 19 December 1989

Membership. The united ZANU-PF held its First Congress in Harare 18–22 December 1989. The former Patriotic Front-Zimbabwe African National Union (PF-ZAPU), led by Joshua Nkomo, and ZANU-PF, led by Robert Mugabe, agreed in 1987 to merge their parties. On 19 December 1989, they formally dissolved their central committees and formed the united ZANU-PF. Membership in the united party as of 19 August 1989, according to Vice-President Simon Muzenda, was 2,125,903 (*Herald*, 19 August 1989)

Party Leader. Robert G. Mugabe, 62, president and first secretary. Mugabe is a Zezeru, a large subgrouping of Shona-language speakers.

Leadership Groups. Women's League, Youth League

Politburo. 26 members

Central Committee. 160 members (*Herald*, 23 December 1989)

Opposition Groups. Political parties and their candidates in the 1990 parliamentary elections: Zimbabwe Unity Movement (ZUM), Edgar Tekere; Zimbabwe African National Union (Ndonga), Ndabaningi Sithole; National Democratic Union, Munyamana Gwavu; United African National Congress (UANC), Edward Mazaiwana; National Progressive Alliance, Gregarious Maririmba.

Last Congress. First, 18–22 December 1989

Last Election. 28–30 March 1990. Presidential vote: 78.3 percent, Robert Mugabe; 21.7 percent, Edgar Tekere (Central Intelligence Agency). Parliament: percent of vote by party: ZANU-PF, 80 percent; ZUM, 16 percent. 120 elected seats, 30 appointed. ZANU-PF won 117, ZUM, 2, ZANU (Ndonga), 1 (*Zimbabwe News*, March).

Publications. *Zimbabwe News* (monthly); *The People's Voice*, daily. The major newspapers are government controlled; nongovernment views are expressed through the privately owned *Financial Gazette* (weekly), *Moto* (monthly), and *Parade* (monthly).

The swift and dramatic changes that took place in Eastern Europe, black Africa, and South Africa in 1990 had repercussions in Zimbabwean politics and economics. The collapse of one-party states in Europe and Africa and the failure of Marxist-Leninist economies undermined those who advocated those same policies for Zimbabwe. General elections, the third since independence, revealed popular discontent and apathy. The opposition had a relatively strong showing in urban areas. Voter turnout was low nationwide. This year there were several fundamental policy shifts: the long-discussed trade liberalization program and economic restructuring were finally implemented, albeit cautiously; President Mugabe lost Politburo support for a de jure one-party state and dropped plans to legislate for it; and the government allowed the 25-year-old state of emergency to lapse. In addition, the government amended the constitution to ease restrictions on government acquisition and purchase of land for resettlement, previously restricted by the Lancaster House agreement. Finally, political changes in South Africa brought improved relations between the Zimbabwean and South African governments.

Current Leadership. Political power in Zimbabwe is concentrated in the hands of Robert G. Mugabe, the state president and government leader. Mugabe is president and first secretary of the ruling party, ZANU-PF, and as such he appoints the members of the Politburo. Within the party, his authority is checked only by the need for consensus among

party leaders. Lack of consensus deterred Mugabe from imposing sanctions against South Africa in 1988 and this year from insisting on a legislated one-party state. On a governmental level his authority is checked by the courts, which remain independent, a small but vocal independent press, and opposition cliques within the ruling party.

Domestic Party Affairs. The recent unification of ZANU-PF with Joshua Nkomo's PF-ZAPU has permitted disagreement within the ruling party that would not have been tolerated from ZAPU as an opposition party; former ZAPU members may criticize party and government policies without being branded as dissidents. The Mugabe faction must, however, worry about alliances of former ZAPU members with other elements within ZANU-PF, specifically Eddison Zvobgo and the Karangas from the Midlands. After several years of debate within the party on whether or not to legalize a one-party state, Mugabe found himself increasingly isolated on the issue. A staunch advocate or "apostle of a one party system," as he calls himself (*Sunday Mail*, 8 July), in September, Mugabe conceded to the wishes of the Central Committee, which wanted to maintain the status quo of a multiparty state while enjoying the benefits of a de facto one-party state. The decision by the 160-member Central Committee followed an earlier decision by the Politburo that was overwhelmingly in favor of maintaining a multiparty system. Mugabe lost support of 22 of the 26 Politburo members; the 4 supporters were thought to be himself, Foreign Minister Nathan Shamuyarira, Vice-President Simon Muzenda, and Secretary for Women's Affairs Sally Mugabe (*Financial Gazette*, 10 August), Mugabe's Ghanaian-born wife. Sally has also recently become visible in the media as head of the Child Survival and Development Foundation and become active in the party; she was installed as secretary of Women's Affairs of the Women's League, bypassing the league's choice of Joyce Mujuru, a former combatant.

ZANU-PF is generally not involved in policy decisions (except on ideological issues like land reform and the one-party state). The center for decision making lies in the Cabinet with the technocrats, not the ideologues. The ruling party has become "irrelevant in so many of Zimbabwe's decision-making processes" (Jeffrey Herbst, *State Politics in Zimbabwe* [University of California Press, 1990], p. 260).

The low voter turnout and near upsets in several districts in the March elections may have made party leaders more responsive to the demands for a multiparty system. Politicians, the churches, students, labor leaders, and many public people spoke out against a one-party state, including Canaan Banana, former state president. Former Chief Justice Enock Dumbutshena, a Mugabe appointee and internationally respected jurist, said that "the formation of a one-party state is also a violation of human rights" (*Financial Gazette*, 18 May). Dumbutshena retired in April and was replaced by Anthony Gubbay, a white judge.

During the party primary, several of the old guard, party-backed candidates were defeated. When Community Affairs minister Joyce Mujuru was defeated in the party primary, the election was nullified. She won in a second election because the original winner was banned. In other districts, the Central Committee imposed candidates and declared that no primary would be held. In the general election, ZANU-PF candidates ran unopposed in twelve constituencies. Edgar Tekere's ZUM party ran candidates in 103 of 120 constituencies. (*Herald*, 27 March.) Although winning only two seats in the first-past-the-post system, overall ZUM got about 15 percent of the vote. The voter turnout was low, some 54 percent of the registered voters compared with 90 percent in the 1985 elections. (South Africa *Business Day*, 2 April.)

Intimidation and violence were particularly evident in areas where ZANU-PF/ZUM contests were close. Vice-President Simon Muzenda was in jeopardy of losing his Gweru seat until last-minute gerrymandering deprived the opposition candidate of half his support. The opposition candidate, ZUM member Patrick Kombayi, was seriously injured in a shooting incident with ZANU-PF supporters. Kombayi claimed the shooting was done by members of the Central Intelligence Organization (CIO). (*Financial Gazette*, 6 April.) Opposition parties claimed that they were denied fair access to the mass media. A ZANU-PF advertisement on government-controlled television equated voting for ZUM with dying from AIDS.

With the poor showing in the primaries, party leaders began a massive revitalization program below district level. The Ministry of Political Affairs, originally created to assist with the two-party merger, will now provide administrative services to the party. The government funds the ministry with an annual budget of Z$50 million. (*Financial Gazette*, 18 August.) Appointments to the new Cabinet came

as a surprise. Piqued by the white vote for the Conservative Alliance in the 1985 election, Mugabe had removed all but one white minister from the Cabinet. In a turnabout this year, he appointed three whites to important Cabinet posts: Denis Norman to Transport, Dr. Timothy Stamps to Health, and Chris Andersen to Mines.

After the elections, the Central Committee announced the issues that it would address this year: whether or not to adopt a code of behavior and ethics for the leadership and whether socialism should be the guiding philosophy for the party. When Mugabe addressed the third ordinary session of the Central Committee in the newly opened US$7 million party headquarters, he warned the leadership not to lose their political and ideological bearings and "embark on selfish adventures as you seek for yourselves green pastures in the land of capitalism" (*Sunday Mail*, 23 September). Mugabe has advocated a leadership code since independence; now he says he is waiting for the Central Committee to adopt socialism, saying, "if, however, our Central Committee continued to cherish socialism as our guiding philosophy, then it would remain imperative for us to conclude our long-awaited Leadership Code so our leaders can be bound by a code of behaviour consonant with our socialist ethics and reckoning." Since independence many of the ministers have become large landholders and "highly propertied." (*Financial Gazette*, 13 April.)

Government Coalitions. Unification with PF-ZAPU has not been without problems. Former ZAPU members were disappointed when they did not get a fair proportion of government and party posts. The Constitution of the country was amended to establish a second office of vice-president, which Joshua Nkomo filled. Although room was made on the Politburo for 7 new ZAPU members, only 3 former ZAPU members were appointed out of 30 ministerial posts in the Cabinet (3 of 10 deputy ministers are former ZAPU) (*Financial Gazette*, 12 April). In protest, Dumiso Dabengwa, a former ZAPU military chief known as the Black Russian during the war, delayed accepting the post of deputy minister for Home Affairs.

Domestic Matters. Since the mid-1980s the Zimbabwe government and business community have agreed on the need to increase foreign investment in the country but have debated the pace and extent of the relaxation of controls needed to encourage investment. The conservative Confederation of Zimbabwe Industries found itself allied with Socialist elements in the government who wanted minimal intrusion and competition from foreign concerns. Economic and social pressures on the government prevailed, and the trade liberalization program and restructuring have finally been put into place. The initial program is modest, with just a few goods on an open general import license. Foreign investment is encouraged through generous allowances for repatriation of profits and the government's signing investment protection guarantees. Higher oil prices, however, have limited the foreign currency available to import goods and equipment in the new program. The restructuring of the economy has been much more decisive and will be felt much sooner by the poor and the working class. Price controls for most products have been lifted, and wage negotiations are now conducted by employer and employee councils. To reduce the government's recurrent deficit, Finance Minister Bernard Chidzero announced that the civil service (the largest employer in the country) would reduce its staff by 25 percent (*Herald*, 8 August). Parastatals are to be reorganized, and those considered unnecessary will be eliminated or privatized.

These cutbacks and shifts in the economy from a Socialist orientation toward a market-driven system come at a time when the unemployment level has reached serious proportions. Nearly 200,000 school-leavers come onto the job market each year, whereas the economy creates fewer than 20,000 new jobs annually. One major grievance of the peasants during the liberation war was the inequitable distribution of land. At independence the Lancaster House agreement limited government action in redressing this situation but those restrictions expired this year. Parliament amended the Constitution so that the government may acquire land in Zimbabwe dollars at prices it determines, without the owner having recourse to the courts on the question of price. The government says it intends to buy up nearly half the 11.5 million hectares of farmland currently in commercial use and redistribute it to master communal farmers.

International Views. The loss of East European export and barter markets based on ideology has affected the government's priorities. "Extreme emphasis will be put from now onwards on economic and financial matters in all our diplomatic endeavours around the world. This is no small change in our foreign policy objects," according to

Galilee Jan, an official in the Ministry of Foreign Affairs (*Financial Gazette*, 3 August). One early manifestation of this change was Zimbabwe's quick condemnation of Iraq's invasion of Kuwait and its support of the U.N. Security Council trade ban on Iraq. Iraq and Zimbabwe had been allies during Zimbabwe's war for liberation and had economic, trade, and cooperation agreements. In the interim, Iran has promised to meet all Zimbabwe's oil requirements and agreed to help build an oil refinery in the eastern area, near the border with Mozambique. Over the course of 1990, U.S.-Zimbabwe relations became more cordial. Zimbabwe signed the Overseas Private Investment Corporation agreement, and the two governments agreed on a program that would allow the Peace Corps to operate in the country. Since 1988, when U.S. foreign aid was renewed, that aid has been at the level of US$5 million a year. Soviet foreign minister Eduard Shevardnadze paid an official visit to Zimbabwe on his tour of southern Africa. Soviet military aid has not been forthcoming, with the Soviets "not emphasising confrontation, because the price of this is too high" (South Africa, *Sunday Times*, 25 March). The Soviet airline Aeroflot has begun weekly flights between Moscow and Harare.

Relations with the Chinese government continue to be close. Last year Chinese foreign minister Qian Qichen paid an official visit to give his government's version of the 1989 events in Tiananmen Square. This year a high-ranking Chinese military delegation visited Zimbabwe. China services the MiGs, missiles, and air defense system it sold the Zimbabwe government in 1989.

Following the changes in Eastern Europe, Zimbabwe has maintained good relations with the new Romanian government. East German embassy officials were recalled and the embassy closed; ZANU-PF students receiving training from East Germany's communist party returned home. Cuba continues to provide educational training for more than a thousand Zimbabwe students. In the South African Development Coordination Conference region, Zimbabwe has good relations with the member countries, including Malawi. Ties with Malawi president Hastings Banda have warmed, despite Banda's strong embrace of South Africa in the past. Banda paid a visit to Zimbabwe and was given the keys to Harare.

The release of African National Congress (ANC) leader Nelson Mandela and the South African government's moves to end apartheid have moderated Mugabe's hard-line attitude toward

South Africa and reaffirmed the need to reform the Zimbabwean economy so it can compete with South Africa in regional and European markets. The Zimbabwe government has welcomed South African sports delegations, businesspeople, and members of Parliament to conferences in Harare. Zimbabwe also agreed to sell drought-stricken South Africa 300,000 tons of maize (*Herald*, 9 November), a deal made despite Mugabe's calling for sustained trade boycotts with South Africa.

ANC deputy president Nelson Mandela and ANC president Oliver Tambo were received graciously by the government, although historically ZANU's ties were with the Pan Africanist Congress (PAC). In January, Minister of Home Affairs Moven Mahachi justified the government's renewal of the state of emergency, partly on the strength of the attacks by the Mozambique National Resistance Movement (RENAMO) across Zimbabwe's borders. Just six months later, after South Africa freed Nelson Mandela and lifted bans on the ANC and other political organizations, the Zimbabwe government allowed the 25-year-old state of emergency to expire. Mahachi said in July that activities by RENAMO along the border were under control. Zimbabwe continues its costly military support for the Mozambican government. Zimbabwe has about 10,000 troops guarding the rail and oil pipeline corridors. Estimates for the cost of maintaining those troops range between US$8 million and US$50 million annually (*Financial Gazette*, 7 September).

Zimbabwe also shelters nearly 100,000 Mozambican refugees in camps along the border. In December, as part of an overall accord between the Mozambican government and RENAMO, the Zimbabwe government agreed to confine its troops to six-kilometer-wide strips running along the Limpopo and Beira corridors. Events moved at a quick pace in 1990 both internally and internationally. Partly because of events in Eastern Europe and Africa, where people are demanding multiparty political systems and market-driven economies, Zimbabwe's leaders have opted to become part of the mainstream. How the changes in South Africa will affect Zimbabwe's economy is unknown; however, political stability and an end to destabilizing tactics will give the regional economies the stability they need to attract foreign investment. If the settlement in Mozambique enlarges, Zimbabwe will be one of the major beneficiaries in terms of a reduced military budget and quick and cheap access to Indian Ocean ports. Domestically, the minimum steps for opening the economy have been taken; now Zimbabwe must wait for conflicts beyond its borders—the gulf crisis, the political settlement in South Africa, and the war in Mozambique—to be resolved.

Virginia Knight
Harare, Zimbabwe

THE AMERICAS

Introduction

The ultimate humiliation for Marxist-Leninists in the Americas is having a revolution unfold in their area while they are confusedly carping on the sidelines. But so it is today in much of Latin America. This is not the flaming Leninist "two, three, many Vietnams," anti-imperialist, Socialist revolution Che Guevara called for a quarter century ago in his famous "Message to the Tricontinental" just before he was killed in the Bolivian jungles. Quite the contrary, it is a democratic, free market revolution led by elected officials, businesspeople, and workers. Even though it is not inevitable that this revolution will succeed, one thing is obvious: the Soviet, East European, Cuban, and Nicaraguan models are institutionalized stagnation to which there must be a different alternative.

The Communists held several regional meetings during 1990 to try to understand the political upheavals of the past two years and why they, rather than the capitalists, are suddenly in the dustbin of history. The question underlying these multiparty, as well as most single-party, meetings has been: In view of all that has happened, how they can make people in the hemisphere take their political and economic ideas seriously? Among the major meetings were those of South American parties in Quito, Ecuador, in February; Latin American and Caribbean parties in Havana in March; and Latin American and Caribbean communist and workers' parties in Mexico in November.

A statement from the Havana meeting made the routine charge of a crisis in the world capitalist system but candidly added that there is also an "acute crisis of the bureaucratized socialist models that became highly authoritarian and repressive," something the people attending this meeting had never seemed to notice on their numerous visits over the decades to Soviet-bloc countries. The Mexico City meeting relapsed into the cant of earlier decades, at least in its public statement, for it noted only a crisis in the "model of building socialism" in passing and then dwelt on defending the indefensible, arguing that Marxism-Leninism has demonstrated "its relevance and complete validity" in the world today. Indeed, the Mexico declaration was more defiantly dogmatic than most parties were on their own during the year; the sixteen mostly insignificant groups there seemed set on proving that no miracle of insight has yet restored their sight.

The Mexico declaration came out for "a peaceful, negotiated solution to the crisis in the Middle East and opposition to any military outcomes that would not help check the economic-social crisis in the world and that would endanger world peace." These Western Hemisphere remnants of the former Soviet bloc did not come out in favor of Saddam Husayn, however, as did the Maoist Sendero Luminoso and several other radical groups in the region.

The statements and activities of individual parties and movements were not remarkably different from those of the year before, for they paid some attention to specific domestic affairs but were often distracted by the broader questions of their relevance — raised by members as well as by outsiders — in the contemporary world. Most professed to have learned something from the collapse of the Soviet bloc but argued that their own policies had to be devised according to the needs of their particular countries. Some removed or played down the term *Marxism-Leninism* in their public statements. Most professed their continuing dedication to freedom and progress while trying to distance themselves from once- or currently ruling communist parties in many parts of the world — including Cuba and Nicaragua — arguing that if they were to run their countries they would be nothing like the leaders who had betrayed Socialist and communist ideals in the former Soviet bloc nations. The extremes of reaction to the Soviet bloc reforms were represented by the two largest parties: Fidel Castro said that *perestroika* was a Soviet phenomenon and had nothing to do with Cuba, whereas some of Nicaragua's Sandinistas said *perestroika* was nothing less than their idea in the first place.

By all accounts, including Fidel Castro's, Cubans are now suffering their greatest economic hardships since 1959, when Castro overthrew dictator Fulgencio Batista. But Cuban Communist Party Politburo member Carlos Rafael Rodríguez warned Cubans not to be overly optimistic or to think that things are so bad now they cannot get worse: "The only certainty," he wrote in December, "is that in the immediate future, the situation will worsen." Castro had defiantly rejected almost all the serious democratic and market-oriented reforms accepted in varying degrees by most of the former Soviet bloc—and, indeed, Latin American—countries, proclaiming that Cuba is the last bastion of Marxism-Leninism. His parting verbal shot in all of his speeches now is "socialism or death."

There are a few quiet reforms, such as when the president of the Cuban Chamber of Commerce announced in January 1991 that Cuba would not automatically reject foreign capitalists' offers to make up to 100 percent investments in enterprises on the island; he indicated that the government is considering debt-equity swaps as well. But these openings have been mandated by Cuba's lack of foreign currency reserves at a time when even its former Soviet bloc allies are demanding payment for goods and services in hard currency and do not reflect the general direction, which is toward a more rigidly closed economy with no significant openings in the political system.

Amid much criticism of Castro and this economic waste in the Soviet media and many questions as to why Soviet citizens should keep pumping funds into the black hole of Castro's economy, Moscow is reducing its largesse. The decrease in the level of Soviet aid and subsidies, which stood at about $5–$6 billion annually during most of the 1970s and 1980s, will come over a three-year period, according to the 1991 trade agreement signed at the end of 1990, and will include new formulas for assessing trade costs. The Soviet Union has guaranteed the delivery of some oil and grain for this period as long as conditions in the USSR permit.

Castro's survival strategy is to cut back on reliance on technology, especially petroleum, and play for time, hoping for a resurgence of tyrants like those who until recently ruled in the Soviet bloc and who for decades propped up his petty tyranny.

Economic conditions were no better in Nicaragua than they were in Cuba and indeed little improved under the new non-Sandinista government, which was voted overwhelmingly into office in the elections of 25 February. These elections saw the National Opposition Union (UNO) front headed by Violeta Chamorro de Barrios overwhelmingly defeat the Sandinista front headed by then president Daniel Ortega; Chamorro won the presidency by 54.7 percent to 40.8 percent, with at least 10 percent, Nicaraguans who had fled the country because they detested the Sandinistas, not voting. UNO took 51 of 92 assembly seats and a still larger majority in the more than 100 municipal governments, including the capital of Managua. To many of the thousands of international observers who judged the election fair, including former U.S. president Jimmy Carter, the Sandinistas seemed to have turned over a new democratic leaf.

But there is as yet little evidence of that, despite questions being asked within the Sandinista Front of National Liberation (FSLN)—foremost among them, What happened? Before leaving office, the Sandinistas passed legislation that gave the FSLN and its leaders title to thousands of private houses and state enterprises and passed out many thousands of arms to their loyal supporters. Ortega then said that, after Chamorro's inauguration in April, the FSLN would "govern from below," utilizing their continuing power in the unions and media and their control over the police and army, and that no fundamental changes in the Sandinista revolution would be permitted. "Governing from below" brought Nicaragua several costly strikes, with settlement terms that effectively killed much of UNO's economic reform program.

In addition, because of legislation passed in December 1989 but not made public until September 1990, the head of the military, former Defense Minister Humberto Ortega—left in office by Chamorro as a gesture of reconciliation to the Sandinistas—is a parallel power in the country. Although the size of the military has been substantially reduced, the hard-core Sandinistas remain. Ortega's military faced a major scandal early in 1991 when it was learned that in late 1990 some Sandinista commanders had sent 28 Soviet ground-to-air missiles to the guerrillas in El Salvador. Ortega said the officers were acting on their own, but considering the tight command structure within the military and the strict control over the missile arsenal, it is inconceivable that Ortega did not at the very least give tacit approval to the transfer. The Soviet Union confirmed that Moscow had originally sent at least one of the missiles used in El Salvador to Nicaragua in the mid-1980s, after which the Sandinistas condemned Moscow for playing ball with the U.S. and Salvadoran governments.

At the same time, some Sandinistas have engaged in a degree of self-criticism since their electoral defeat, and a large meeting on the subject of the FSLN's future is scheduled for 1991.

Elsewhere in the hemisphere, nonruling communist parties and movements sought to seize power through armed struggle, to fight while negotiating an end to military conflict, or to compete for power in the democratic systems now found in almost every country.

Among those engaging in simultaneous military and political offensives during the year were the Farabundo Marti National Liberation Front (FMLN) guerrillas in El Salvador. The military conflict in that country escalated in terms of attacks and technology, particularly through ground-to-air missiles received from the Sandinistas over the past year. Part of the military and psychological strategy was executing at least several hundred civilians who opposed their efforts, an action finally condemned openly by the human rights organization Americas' Watch. At the end of the year, in a propaganda fiasco, the guerrillas shot down a U.S. helicopter and executed the two Americans they captured; after an internal investigation the FMLN declared that the deaths had been "mercy killings." Until the killings, the U.S. Congress had held back half of its $42.5 million aid package for the Salvadoran government pending progress in finding the killers of a party of Jesuits during the guerrillas' deadly November 1989 offensive in the capital.

The FMLN also was highly active on the diplomatic front, particularly in the United States, where its criticism was aimed at the Cristiani government for its failure to convict high military officers in the Jesuit case. But the political campaign also involved peace negotiations. In a paid advertisement in the San Salvador paper *La República* on 12 January 1991, the guerrillas proudly proclaimed they were negotiating "with the United Nations as mediator. We have territorial, political, social, and military power recognized even abroad." Meanwhile Washington criticized the U.N. negotiator for being too easy on the FMLN.

In Guatemala, National Revolutionary Unity of Guatemala (URNG) guerrillas stepped up both diplomatic negotiations and military operations, which are increasingly tied to the expanding drug trade in the country. Fighting also increased in Honduras as ties to the FMLN guerrillas increased, with the Salvadoran war spilling evermore over the border. In early 1991 negotiations with some guerrillas reportedly reduced the number of fighters in the field.

Armed conflict also raged in two South American countries. In Colombia, the Revolutionary Armed Forces of Colombia (FARC) and the National Liberation Army (ELN) were the most active groups during 1990. A major offensive by the two in November was followed by another by FARC in January 1991 that left several hundred dead. Still, the year also brought the full entrance of an important former guerrilla group, the M-19, into the political life of the country; the M-19 emerged as the country's third-largest political force in the May presidential election and won 27 percent of the vote in the December elections for the Constituent Assembly.

In Peru, the actions of the Maoist Sendero Luminoso increased during the year. According to Sendero expert Gustavo Gorriti Ellenbogen in Lima's *Expreso* in October, the war against Sendero is going badly; it is a political war more than a military one and is poorly planned and executed on both the political and the military levels. The movement is strongest in Huamachuco, Santiago de Chucho, the Conchucos corridor, the La Libertad mountains, some high provinces in Huanuco, a large part of the Upper Huallaga (known abroad as a primary location of the drug trade), the Ene and Tambo valleys, a good part of Ayacucho, Huancavelica, Apurimac, and some provinces in Puno. A Peruvian Senate committee evaluating the problem of political violence concluded in early 1991 that since the Sendero Luminoso began its armed struggle in 1980 there have been more than 20,000 deaths—40 percent civilians, 45 percent terrorists, and 15 percent policemen—and property damage of nearly $20 billion, equivalent to 90 percent of the country's foreign debt. Some 1,500 people died during the last six months of 1990 under the new Fujimori administration.

Other communist parties participated with varying degrees of success in democratic political systems. The largely social democratic Movement Toward Socialism (MAS) in Venezuela, two decades ago a breakoff from the Communist Party of Venezuela (PCV), is now a major player in Venezuelan politics, whereas the PCV continues to stagnate. In neighboring Guyana, Cheddi Jagan and his People's Progressive party are working for a free election that might bring them back to power for the first time in several decades. On the other end of the continent, the Communist Party of Uruguay has claimed an enormous increase in party membership after taking 10 percent of the vote in the November 1989 elections as a part of the Broad Front. In the Caribbean, communist parties continue to exercise considerable power in the tiny French overseas department governments of Martinique and Guadeloupe.

In Mexico, former officials of the Mexican Communist Party who have joined the Democratic Revolution Party (PRD) of Cuauhtémoc Cárdenas now hold top positions in the PRD, among them editor of the party paper, *6 de Julio*, and secretary for international relations. Cárdenas is expected to be a leading contender in Mexico's next presidential election.

Elsewhere Communists were less influential, either because the parties are small or because recent events have left them in disarray. The party was legalized in Chile after the inauguration of democratically elected President Patricio Aylwin, but a string of defections, resignations, and expulsions, as well as its past mistakes and changing times, have left what was once South America's strongest party a mere shadow of its 1973 self. In Brazil — where the legendary Luis Carlos Prestes, who led the Brazilian Communist Party for 50 years, died — Communists hold several congressional seats, as they do in fronts in Ecuador.

The communist parties of the United States and Canada continue to vie with each other for insignificance.

William Ratliff
Hoover Institution

Argentina

Population. 32,290,966
Party. Communist Party of Argentina (Partido Comunista de la Argentina; PCA)
Founded. 1918
Membership. 80,000 (claimed); 25,000 militants
General Secretary. Patricio Echegaray
Politburo. 12 members; current composition unavailable
Central Committee. 100 members, 15 alternates

Status. Legal
Last Congress. Seventeenth, 13 December 1990
Last Election. 14 May 1989 (presidential, parliamentary). PCA participated as part of the United Left Coalition (IU) with Movement Toward Socialism (MAS) and Broad Liberation Front (FRAL). The IU received 3.5 percent of the vote and 1 congressional deputy (Luis Zamora of MAS).
Auxiliary Organizations. Communist Youth Federation, Union of Argentine Women, local branch of the World Peace Council
Publications. *Nuestra Propuesta* (weekly), *Ideología y política* (theoretical monthly), *Juventud* (biweekly youth magazine)

The year 1990 was a wrenching one for Argentina. The deteriorating economic situation (see *YICA*, 1989) forced President Raúl Alfonsín to leave office in November 1989, seven months early, handing power over to Carlos Saúl Menem, elected the previous May. Although Menem, a traditional Peronist, had campaigned on a populist platform, once in office he reversed himself and adopted economic and foreign policies associated with the conservative Argentine establishment—including orthodox monetary practices, privatization of the overblown network of state enterprises, and rapprochement with both the United States and Great Britain.

The social costs of these policies were quickly felt in diminished purchasing power and growing unemployment. Moreover, Menem's commitment to privatize the national airlines, the railroads, and the national telephone company divided the labor movement. Those syndicates most firmly opposed to privatization (largely drawn from the state enterprises slated for privatization) seceded from the General Confederation of Labor (CGT) to create a "rebel" alternative led by Saúl Ubaldini. The latter convoked 75,000 people in March to protest privatization policies, but the following month Menem's people were able to produce double that number in a counterdemonstration.

Meanwhile, Alfonsín's Radicals, embittered by their sudden plunge from power, immediately shifted leftward and accused Menem of undue subordination to foreign banks, the International Monetary Fund, and (more darkly) the United States. For his part, President Menem characterized his predecessor's policies as "reactionary and conservative" (*Somos*, 14 June; *FBIS*, 19 June), while the more conservative Radical Eduardo Angeloz, defeated by Menem for the presidency, warned that "unless clear signs of [economic] recovery are perceived in time, social upheavals could result, with very grave consequences" (*La Prensa*, 11 June; *FBIS*, 19 June).

There were upheavals in Argentina during 1990, but they were largely the product of military unrest. Menem had attempted to forestall this by promising in advance to study the possibility of a pardon of military leaders imprisoned for their role in the so-called "dirty war" against urban guerrillas (see *YICA*, 1981–1988). Nonetheless, a group of elite troops in the army known as "painted faces" (*caraspintadas*)—troops who use camouflage blacking on their faces during assaults—were known to be conniving at some sort of putsch.

The leader of this group was Colonel Mohammed Ali Seineldín, who, despite his name, considers himself a Catholic nationalist. Indeed, the *caraspintadas* could be described as Catholic, corporatist, syndicalist, militarist, and xenophobic—a sort of original Peronism, circa 1944, preserved in amber. Characteristically, the group had strong ties to Ubaldini's wing of the labor movement, though Radicals often claimed that it was also in touch with elements of the Menem government.

To confuse matters further, former leftist guerrilla leaders Fernando Vaca Narvaja and Roberto Perdía had praised the "painted faces" in May, calling them "a group involved in a debate in the armed forces in the search for a national model of integration" (*Clarín*, 11 May; *FBIS*, 16 May). Meanwhile, however, the two also praised the Menem government, which they insisted they supported.

Rumors of an impending coup circulated in July, with the press reporting that the government possessed a secret document ("Spring Plan") that called for an incident at an army unit followed by a "symbolic seizure" of the army staff headquarters in Buenos Aires with the objective of installing a new army chief of staff. If that failed, the plan contemplated ignoring Menem's authority altogether and moving to a second phase ("radicalization of the crisis"). In this phase the rebels planned to kill key leaders of the Radical party and certain journalists and install civilians to run the country according to rebel directions. (*Noticias Argentinas*, 24 July; *FBIS*, 25 July).

The government almost immediately denied the existence of the plot, seconded in this case by Colonel Seineldín. On 2–3 December, however, a few hours before President George Bush was slated to visit Argentina, a coup following this scenario proceeded far enough to take over one garrison in Buenos Aires and the army headquarters. Within hours President Menem had restored order by deploying loyal troops; the rebellious officers gave themselves up, and Colonel Seineldín (already under house arrest for insubordination) personally accepted responsibility for the affair.

Domestic Party Affairs. The year was no less turbulent for the PCA. Disagreement over the implications of Gorbachev's reforms split the party into three warring factions. At issue was less the question of interparty democracy (though this was discussed) and more the question of the PCA's relationship to other forces on the left. One faction favored the dissolution of the party in favor of a new, broader leftist force; another favored maintenance of the party's identity but greater cooperation with other leftist parties; and yet another, led by Secretary General Patricio Echegaray, argued for strengthening the existing party structure. Although Echegaray was able finally to impose his own line, in November more than a dozen key figures left the party, including Politburo members Eduardo Sigal, Ernesto Salgado, Miguel Ballato, Francisco Alvarez, and Enrique Dratman, as well as longtime militants Jorge Guerra, Marcelo Arbit, Jorge Canells, Unque Ferreyra, Roberto Paez, Jorge Prigoshin, Neto Raceto, and Silvio Shacter.

In an accompanying document the dissidents cited the party leadership's "inability to meet the new challenges and its stubborn refusal to change and to transform the situation." The following month the party's daily newspaper, *Nuevo Sur*, shut down, owing to "grave economic difficulties." Former employees demonstrated outside its offices to protest the fact that their severance pay did not reflect the cost-of-living index. (*Buenos Aires Herald*, 29 December; *FBIS*, 31 December.)

Auxiliary and Front Organizations. The party has territorial organizations in every province, including Tierra del Fuego, and a communist youth federation active in promoting party policy at schools and elsewhere.

The party controls a local chapter of the World Peace Council and also the Argentine Permanent Commission on Human Rights. It has unusually close relations with (such as to suggest covert control of) the Argentine Military Center for Democracy, a group of retired officers and soldiers who purport to favor human rights, democracy, and anti-imperialism—that is, opposition to U.S. military influence in Latin America. It is also the principal component of Broad Liberation Front, an all-purpose political umbrella organization that brings together small leftist political groups and dissidents from the major parties.

International Views, Positions, Activities.
Because the year was so turbulent at home, the PCA was unusually inactive abroad. However, Politburo member and former Secretary General Athos Fava visited Cuba in August.

Relations with the Soviet Union. The important commercial relationship with the Soviet Union declined somewhat in 1990, due largely to Gorbachev's economic crisis and the shortages of foreign currency to purchase Argentine foodstuffs. According to the Argentine-Soviet Chamber of Commerce in Buenos Aires, however, between 1976 and 1989 bilateral trade had produced a trade surplus for the Argentines approaching $14 billion. (DYN, 1 July; *FBIS*, 3 July.)

President Menem visited the Soviet Union in October to discuss a full range of issues, including the Persian Gulf, where—the Argentine president said—President Gorbachev congratulated him for sending two Argentine warships to join the international embargo on Iraq. Menem went on to the People's Republic of China (PRC), returning the May visit of PRC president Yang Shangkun.

Other Leftist Groups. Given the pervasive economic crisis, probably the remarkable thing about 1990 is that the independent left did not make a larger recovery.

The March demonstration against Menem's economic policies included not merely PCA militants and members of the Intransigent party and the MAS but eight human rights groups. It also included the Alfonsín sector of the Radical party and anti-Menem Peronists, represented by the so-called group of eight congressional deputies. This demonstration (billed as a protest against "hunger, repression, and impunity") marks the first time that mainstream leaders of the Radical party openly associated themselves with the left. Whether this presaged the emergence of a genuinely new left-center force in Argentine politics, as some hoped, remains to be seen.

Although Menem claimed in November that there was "no possibility of a subversive resurgence" in Argentina (NA, 7 November; *FBIS*, 8 November), there were two incidents in July. One

involved the kidnapping of a trade union leader's son by a self-styled Ché Guevara Brigade in Buenos Aires; in nearby La Plata, two former members of the disbanded Peoples' Revolutionary Army—objects of an extensive search on charges of looting supermarkets last year—engaged in a shootout with police. Killed was Ricardo Canete; his companion, Gerardo Romero, was seriously wounded. Both were well-armed and, according to police, might be linked to like-minded terrorists who had staged recent incidents in the provincial cities of Córdoba and Rosario.

Mark Falcoff
American Enterprise Institute

Bolivia

Population. 6,706,854

Party. Communist Party of Bolivia (Partido Comunista de Bolivia, PCB) split in August; breakaway group calls itself Renewal and Change Movement.

Founded. 1950. Split 1985 and again 1990.

Membership. Majority faction, 500; minority faction, no data; renewal faction, 500

Leadership. Majority faction: general secretary, Humberto Ramirez until December party congress; Jorge Ibañez thereafter. Minority faction leaders: Simon Reyes and Marcos Domic. Renewal faction leadership group: Oscar Salas Moya, Adalberto Kuajara, Walter Morales, José Luis Nuñez del Prado

Status. Legal

Last Congress. Renewal faction: Sixth, 23–25 November 1990; conservative majority faction: Sixth, December 1990

Last Election. 7 May 1989. The United Left (IU), the coalition in which the PCB participated, gained only 7 percent of the vote and 12 of the 130 seats in the elections and played no role in the congressional vote, which saw Jaime Paz Zamora of the Movement of the Revolutionary Left (MIR) elected president.

Auxiliary Organization. Communist Youth of Bolivia

Publications. Both majority and minority factions of the PCB publish a paper called *Unidad*.

From a political standpoint 1990, the first full year of the Jaime Paz Zamora presidency, was a relatively dull one for Bolivians. In a country where politics becomes the national pastime in the period leading up to presidential elections, day-to-day affairs of governing in nonelection periods are comparatively pedestrian. For those addicted to the Byzantine nature of Bolivian politics, however, the unlikely political marriage of the former radical Paz Zamora and Hugo Banzer, a former military dictator who had jailed Paz Zamora in the 1970s and acted as virtual copresident after he swung the congressional vote to Paz Zamora, remained an interesting spectator sport that did not fail to deliver its share of internecine struggles.

The increasingly testy relations between the U.S. embassy and the Bolivian government spilled over into 1991 and threatened to undo much of the positive accomplishments of the 1990 antidrug war. Within this political milieu the Bolivian Communist Party celebrated its 40th anniversary far from the main political ring.

The Sad Saga of the PCB. The year 1990 was another in a series of bad years for the PCB as it once again failed to be an influential actor on the political stage. The party suffered from internal struggles, small membership, and the worldwide decline of communist parties. Leaders of the PCB were hard-pressed to rationalize to their followers the momentous events of 1989 in Eastern Europe, including the fall of the Berlin Wall, the 1990 unification of the two Germanies, the virtual dissolution of the Warsaw Pact, and the hatred expressed for doctrinaire communist parties in Poland, Hungary, Czechoslovakia, East Germany, and of course the Soviet Union.

The PCB was founded in 1950 as a successor to the Partido Izquierdo Revolucionario (PIR), which had been founded in 1941 in the aftermath of the disastrous Chaco War with Paraguay (1932–1938). The PIR's founders had a profound confidence in Marxism-Leninism as a means of arriving at social equality, but they eventually cooperated with conservative political elements, thus leading to the formation of the PCB by more radical firebrands of the left.

History has now come full circle, for the party is considered an anachronism by young members of the extreme left. In August, the PCB split again.

This second splinter (the first being the minority faction headed by Simon Reyes and Marcos Domic) dubbed itself the Renewal and Change Movement and claimed it was breaking with the "conservative party leadership," because it had illegally suspended the Sixth Congress, which was to have taken place on 25 August, "disregarding the will of the majority and resorting to blackmail" to stay in power. The leader of the miners, Oscar Salas Moya, seemed to be the spokesman; he announced a special Sixth Congress, held 23–25 November, that called for leftist unity and mobilizing the peasants and workers to improve their lot (La Paz, *Presencia*, 26 November; *FBIS-LAT*, 14 December).

On the heels of this congress, on 26 November, the minority faction also began planning its national congress for December (ibid.). The conservative core PBC also held its sixth congress in December, attended by approximately five hundred delegates. Apparently living in a time warp, the party leadership reaffirmed the basic principles of "scientific socialism." Jorge Ibañez was elected first secretary, replacing Humberto Ramirez. (*Hoy*, 15 December.)

The last time the PCB had political influence was during the 1982–1985 government of Hernán Siles Zuazo, when two members of the party occupied important cabinet positions. So poor was the economic performance of the Siles administration that the PCB would have fared better if it had opposed, rather than been part of, that government.

Other elements of the Bolivian extreme left will be discussed below. These parties were marginal political actors at best in 1990, but if the Paz Zamora presidency, with its fate tied to the alliance of the ideologically distinct MIR and the conservative National Democratic Action (ADN) fails to improve the lot of the average Bolivian, then the parties of the left may stage a resurgence in the 1993 elections. The economic problems resulting from the antidrug campaign, and what has been perceived in Bolivia as heavy-handed pressure from the United States to militarize the effort against the cocaine trade, have made the Paz Zamora government vulnerable for a populist attack from the left. But for Bolivia, once known more for coups than cocaine, discussing governmental change in terms of elections rather than violent upheaval is itself a testimony to the growing civic culture of the country and its people.

The Political Landscape in 1990. Paz Zamora, leader of the Movement of the Revolutionary Left (more center left than its name implies) finished third in the May 1989 presidential balloting. Gonzalo Sánchez de Losada, candidate of the incumbent National Revolutionary Movement (MNR) that rescued Bolivia from the economic disaster of 20,000 percent inflation of the Siles Zuazo administration, finished just ahead of the ADN's Banzer. None of the candidates, however, gained the necessary majority.

In the congressional vote for president (Bolivia's election law does not allow for a runoff between the top two vote getters), Banzer threw his support to Paz rather than to Sánchez de Losada, with whom Banzer and his party shared similar political views. Personal animosity between the former president and the MNR candidate apparently caused Banzer to create the strange political union that has since ruled Bolivia.

The year 1990 was dominated by the government's efforts to control coca production, an ongoing dispute between the executive branch and the Supreme Court, efforts to turn over to the private sector most of Bolivia's state-owned enterprises, and an upturn in terrorism and crime for a country heretofore relatively free of such scourges.

The Drug War. On balance, Bolivia got relatively good grades for its efforts to impede the flow of coca leaf into the world's cocaine markets. For the first time there was a net reduction in coca acreage, but Bolivia paid a stiff price: funds generated by illegal cocaine profits have provided a cushion for the debt-ridden country as it seeks to convert to a noncocaine-dependent economy. As efforts move forward to cut illegal coca leaf export, Bolivia, in the words of its ambassador to the United States, Jorge Crespo, may have "become a victim of its own success." (*WP*, 8 December.)

In February, Paz and other Andean presidents met with U.S. president George Bush in Cartagena, Colombia, for the first "drug summit." Bush pledged increased U.S. financial support for the South American countries, and Paz and the other presidents pledged to increase their efforts to wipe out the drug industry. But behind the optimistic communiqués in the aftermath of Cartagena lay a fundamental disagreement between the United States and the South American countries: Washington saw the problem as being at the supply end of the process; Paz Zamora and the other presidents saw it in terms of demand in the "consuming country." Paz and the presidents of Colombia and Peru realized that the draconian efforts necessary to re-

duce the flow of cocaine would have negative impacts on their debt-burdened economies and thus wanted the United States to smooth the way with economic aid that the United States believed was not feasible, given the budgetary woes plaguing Washington.

The concern of Paz and his fellow presidents that the drug war was not, despite the rhetoric from the White House, a high priority for Washington was heightened when it was learned that there would be a 36 percent cut in U.S. economic aid to Latin America to free up funds for greater aid to the newly independent countries of Eastern Europe (*Miami Herald*, 18 February).

The idea behind the U.S.-financed strategy to end the flow of coca leaf from Bolivia to the processing centers in Colombia was to drive the price of coca leaf so low that peasant growers would find it economically feasible to accept the government's offer of $2,000 for every hectare out of which they took coca. By early 1990, thanks more to the efforts of the Colombian government to destroy the Medellin drug cartel than to internal actions in Bolivia, thousands of coca growers in Bolivia decided to accept the government's offer. Demand in Colombia for Bolivian coca leaf had dropped dramatically, resulting in a sharp decline in prices for the leaf. The August 1989 price per 100-pound bale of coca leaf had been $90, but by the spring of 1990 the price had dropped to $11. (*WP*, 30 November.) By the end of 1990, however, due in large measure to greater sophistication in cocaine circles in both Colombia and Bolivia, the price had climbed back to about $30 per hundred pounds (ibid.).

U.S.-Bolivian Relations. Despite the success of the war on drugs in 1990, relations between the two countries became more tense as the year progressed, and this growing animosity spilled over into 1991. The virtual exoneration by a jury of Washington, D.C., mayor Marion Barry on cocaine possession charges was viewed by many in South America, especially in Bolivia and Colombia, as proof that the United States was not serious about fighting a war on drugs. That the U.S. government had put a powerful case together to convict Barry was ignored by these critics, who likewise may not have had a fundamental understanding of the U.S. legal system and the unique circumstances of trying Barry with a jury picked from his own constituents. But because perception can sometimes become reality, the Barry trial reinforced fundamental doubts about U.S. sincerity.

A particular area of contention between the United States and Bolivia during the year was how involved the army should become in the antidrug war. A special 1,200-man national police element, the Rural Mobile Patrol Units (UMOPAR), had been established and trained by agents of the Drug Enforcement Agency and the U.S. military, but Washington wanted a more direct involvement of the Bolivian armed forces. Given Bolivia's history of military coups, and the unmatched record of corruption and brutality by the 1980–82 government of General Luis Garcia Meza, the Bolivian government was understandably reluctant to give the military too direct a role. Even within the military there existed a certain reluctance, despite Washington's sweetening of the pot by allocating $33 million in military aid, because of the unsavory reputation the military had gained during the Garcia Meza years. In a country that has experienced almost two hundred military coups since independence in 1825 and that still has fresh memories of the corruption and human rights abuses of the Garcia Meza military regime, increasing the strength of the army was an extremely touchy matter politically and made worse by what were considered the strong-arm tactics of the U.S. embassy to "militarize" the operations.

The Rico Toro affair. The growing tensions between the United States and Bolivia in 1990 surfaced dramatically in early 1991. The commander of the UMOPAR, Army General Lucio Anez, left the post for health reasons, and Paz Zamora astounded many in his own government, and certainly the U.S. embassy, by naming retired Colonel Faustino Rico Toro to the key position. The U.S. embassy has long suspected Rico Toro of deep involvement in the drug trade, and he had been a key member of the notorious and bloody Garcia Meza government, along with the infamous "minister of cocaine," Colonel Luis Arce Gómez. The United States immediately announced that it would suspend the $100 million in economic and military aid, and Rico Toro, supposedly after a heart-to-heart talk with Hugo Banzer, resigned "so as not to cause any further problems for President Paz Zamora" (*Correo Boliviano*, 11–17 March). Bolivians sensitive to the U.S. tendency to play the role of proconsul charged that the United States was making a serious decision based on rumors. After Rico Toro resigned, the United States pressed the attack on "corruption in high places," specifying the Ministry of the Interior (*WP*, 6 March). A few days later

Interior Minister Capobianco angrily resigned, as did the head of the national police. Both denied that they had engaged in any corrupt practices, and both denounced the U.S. embassy in only slightly veiled terms.

Related to the drug war has been a serious dispute between the Paz Zamora administration and the Supreme Court. In December 1989, former Minister of the Interior Luis Arce Gómez was extradited to the United States to face charges of drug trafficking during the Garcia Meza years.

Lawrence L. Tracy
Washington, D.C.

Brazil

Population. 152,505,077

Parties. Brazilian Communist Party (Partido Comunista Brasileiro; PCB), formerly pro-Soviet; Communist Party of Brazil (Partido Comunista do Brasil; PCdoB), pro-Albanian; Workers' Party (Partido dos Trabalhadores; PT), democratic Socialist with strong Marxist-Leninist and Trotskyist influence

Founded. PCB: 1922; PCdoB: 1961, split from PCB; PT: 1981

Membership. PCB: 130,000; PCdoB: 50,000 claimed, 20,000 estimated; PT: 600,000

Party Leaders. PCB: Salomão Malina, 68, president; PCdoB: João Amazonas, 78, president; PT: Luiz Inácio Lula da Silva, 47, president

Executive Committees. PCB: Roberto Freire (vice-president), Amaro Valentin, Carlos Alberto Torres, Domingos Tódero, Flávio Araújo, Francisco Inácio Almeida, Geraldo Rodríguez dos Santos, Givaldo Siqueira, Jarbas de Hollanda, José Paulo Netto, Luiz Carlos Moura, Paulo Elisiário, Regis Fratti, Sergio Morães, Severino Teodoro Melo. Alternates: Luiz Carlos Azedo, Paulo Fábio Dantas, Byron Sarinho, Raimundo Jinkings; PCdoB: José Duarte, Dyneas Fernández Aguiar, José Renato Rabelo, Roberto D'Olne Lustosa, Ronaldo Cavalcanti Freitas, Elsa de Lima Monnerat, João Batista de Rocha Lemos, Pericles Santos de Souza, Alanir Cardoso, Maria do Socorro Morães Vieira; PT: 19 members, including José Dirceu (general secretary), Luiz Gushiken, Olivio Dutra, José Genoino, Eduardo Jorge, Helio Bicudo, Eduardo Suplicy, Plinio de Arruda Sampaio

Central Committee. PCB: 63 active members, 23 alternates

Last Congress. PCB: Eighth, 17–20 July 1987; PT: National Convention, June 1990

Last Election. State and congressional, 3 October; runoffs, 25 November; PCB and PCdoB: 5 and 3 federal deputies, respectively, of 586; PT: 1 senator of 31 and about 35 federal deputies (*Gazeta Mercantil*, 29 October)

Auxiliary Organizations. The PCB seems to have lost influence in the General Workers' Central (Central Geral dos Trabalhadores; CGT) and the Agricultural Workers Confederation (Confederação Nacional dos Trabalhadores na Agricultura; CONTAG); unions controlled by the PCdoB have joined the PT-dominated Single Labor Central (Central Unica dos Trabalhadores; CUT), which has 14,000 affiliated unions. The PT also has influence in the National Student Union (União Nacional dos Estudantes; UNE), the Basic Christian Communities (Comunidades Eclesiais de Base; CEBs), and the Landless Movement (Movimento dos Sem Terra; MST).

Publications. PCB: *Voz da Unidade*, Luiz Carlos Azedo, director; PCdoB: *Tribuna da Luta Operária*, Pedro de Oliveira, director; Sem Terra publishes a quarterly of the same name.

The radical economic stabilization plan adopted by the new administration of President Fernando Collor de Mello initially brought about drastic reductions in inflation that had reached monthly rates of 80 percent. The success translated into fairly healthy pro-Collor votes in the 3 October first-round elections (ten of eleven new state governors), and a majority in congress were generally favorable to Collor. By the time of the 25 November runoffs, however, inflation that had inched back up to 18 percent a month, and signs of serious recession brought a backlash. Opposition candidates won at least nine of fifteen gubernatorial contests on the second round, including all the major states. With the exception of populist Social Democrat Leonel Brizola, this swing did not benefit the leftist opposition. (Brizola won the governorship of Rio de Janeiro in first-round voting, and candidates of his Democratic Workers' Party [Partido Democrático

dos Trabalhadores; PDT] won the runoffs in Rio Grande do Sul and Espírito Santo.)

PCB. The PCB elected five representatives to the Chamber of Deputies, and PCB candidate Augusto Carvalho was returned to the chamber with the most votes of any candidate in the Federal District. Otherwise, hard work on numerous and varied alliances served to keep a slim PCB presence in state assemblies.

During congressional debate of the economic stabilization plan in April, the PCB, unlike the PT and the PCdoB, considered that some of the measures were positive. In view of the plan's overwhelming support from the moderate majority, all the leftist parties eventually dropped their obstructive tactics in favor of negotiations on amendments that would at least allow them some input. Roberto Freire, a PCB deputy, said that the left had not yet recovered from its defeat in the 1989 presidential election and did not know how to conduct an efficient opposition (*O Estado de São Paulo*, 11 April).

With the PCB's Ninth Congress scheduled for May 1991, most leaders tend to agree with Freire's statement that "communists and social democrats face the challenge of rethinking their course.... The dogmas of the old Communist Party will be discarded and a modern socialist party should arise in its place." (Rede Globo Television, 7 November; *FBIS-LAT*, 13 November.)

Some definitions of the "new party" were considered at a theoretical workshop in Belo Horizonte organized by the PCB and the *World Marxist Review.* An article by Miguel Anacleto Junior of the Pernambuco regional committee contains ideas expressed at the workshop, including hailing *perestroika* as not just a domestic affair of the Soviet Union but a phenomenon that strengthens the international communist movement, permitting it to restore historical ties with major Socialist currents and rallying all democratic forces around the task of attaining world peace. With the fall of repressive regimes in Latin America, revolutionary and democratic forces are working to create new movements to keep up with popular aspirations.

According to the article, when conservatives gained control of the democratic transition in Brazil, the left properly broke away from the democratic front that had been formed earlier; unfortunately, they then concentrated on creating new parties rather than forming a broad opposition bloc. Such a bloc must now be formed around specific political programs not only for electoral results but for rallying all available forces to create a viable alternative on all levels to the present power structure. (*WMR*, February.)

Luis Carlos Prestes, legendary revolutionary of the 1920s and leader of the PCB for nearly 50 years, died in Rio de Janeiro on 7 March. When Prestes returned from exile, he criticized the PCB for straying from Marxist-Leninist dogma; he was removed from office in 1980 and expelled from the party in 1984.

PCdoB. Like the PCB, the PCdoB participated in many electoral alliances and increased its small congressional bloc to three federal deputies. It also had one minor triumph: Lídice da Matta, the PCdoB's only gubernatorial candidate, came in third in Bahia, ahead of the candidates of the PT and the PRN (Partido de Reconstrução Nacional, Collor's party).

Unlike the PCB, the PCdoB will hear nothing of *perestroika*: "a disguise to obscure the return to capitalism. . . . What is happening in Europe is that socialist methods were abandoned a long time ago and now the mask of the imperial militarist state is falling." (*Latin America Weekly Report* [*LAWR*], 15 March.) Earlier the PCdoB hosted the Albanian ambassador, resident in Argentina, on a tour of Brazilian cities. When the ambassador declared at a press conference that "Albania will be the last bastion of socialism," the PCdoB leaders added that criticism of Albania's regime is nothing more than "a press campaign" to discredit the regime (*LAWR*, 15 February).

PT. The party roughly doubled its representation in the Chamber of Deputies and elected its first senator, the aristocratic Eduardo Suplicy of São Paulo. These results would have been better if internal conflicts concerning electoral alliances had been resolved. For example, national leaders who had pledged support to PDT gubernatorial candidates in that party's strongholds of Rio de Janeiro and Rio Grande do Sul were overruled by local directors who insisted on their own candidates, thus losing valuable PDT backing for the PT in other races. Similar disputes occurred in many states at all levels of the campaign; chief protagonists were radical groups, especially the Trotskyist Convergência Socialista, concerned with the ideological purity of the PT. These ultragroups have been an embarrassment to elected PT officials for some time. Luiza Erundina, PT mayor of São Paulo, began purging radicals from appointed posts in

January and has now begun to take on the unions (*O Estado de São Paulo*, 10, 12 January; *LAWR*, 11 October). National leadership gave itself exclusive responsibility for naming the "ministers" in the PT's "parallel cabinet" to limit participation of the ultras.

The problem was addressed by the Seventh National Convention in June. Groups that had operated as parties within the party were ordered to register as PT "tendencies" and give up their separate publications, headquarters, and fund raising. Causa Operária was among the groups that refused and were expelled. *Latinamerica Press* (28 June) ranks the remaining tendencies as follows: Articulação, 60 percent; this is Lula's group and includes union members, intellectuals, church groups, and Social Democrats; Nova Esquerda, defined as Democratic Socialist, represents 15 percent; Vertente Socialista, 12 percent, is Marxist-Leninist; Correntes Trotskistas accounts for 10 percent; and smaller groups make up the remaining 3 percent.

Although the convention endorsed "democratic and pluralistic socialism," it made no formal statement on the collapse of the Eastern European regimes (*LAWR*, 21 June). Da Silva was confirmed as president, and he explained that his decision not to run for any office this year obeyed the need to work on party reorganization. He does not want the PT to become a "one man party" with no one to replace him when he dies (*Latinamerica Press*, 28 June).

Da Silva used this time also to host a meeting of 47 Latin American Socialist parties, including the two Brazilian communist parties, in São Paulo. In the debates, many participants still saw democracy only as a means to bring workers to power, but the closing document stated that "socialism can only support itself on the will of the people" and criticized the Cuban example. It also attacked President Bush's Enterprise for the Americas Initiative as a "neoliberal offensive" intended to destroy national economies. (*Correio Braziliense*, 5 July; *FBIS-LAT*, 28 August.)

Labor opposition has hampered the government's austerity program, which calls for massive layoffs in the public sector, privatization of state-owned firms, and an end to inflation-indexed wages. Indexation was suspended in June by a presidential veto, later declared unconstitutional, and was then ended for one month at a time under the "provisional measures" allowed the president. In mid-December, after attempts to establish a social pact with labor, business, and government failed, Congress voted to restore indexation. Collor is expected to veto the legislation in his continuing struggle to institute free collective bargaining.

The PT-linked CUT led a wave of strikes against the plan during much of the year, but the actions, although numerous and often violent, were inconclusive in the majority. A general strike planned for June failed to materialize. Growing unemployment and labor court warnings that strikes in essential services are abusive probably helped cool enthusiasm. By September CUT president Jair Meneguelli had agreed to join the social pact negotiations, over the protests of CUT's radical elements. The Trotskyists denounced "that old idea of class collaboration" (*LAWR*, 4 October).

Both the CUT and the PT were accused by the Agrarian Reform Ministry of involvement in land invasions, with the PT organizing these in seven states. Da Silva denied the charges, remarking that "land occupations do not depend upon PT organization, not with 15,000 families in road side camps alone" (*O Estado de São Paulo*, 18 July). The Landless Movement (MST), according to the Agrarian Reform Ministry, has been infiltrated by "professional occupiers . . . who incite land invasions for political purposes" (*Latinamerica Press*, 30 August). A list, handed over to the press, of those alleged professionals was headed by PT congressman Virgilio Guimarães. Four landless peasants backed by the MST were elected to Congress in October. The landowners' association, the Rural Democratic Union, also has several representatives in congress.

The MST and the CUT promoted a three-day program of marches and demonstrations for rural workers in July, and thousands of people have participated in the land pilgrimages (*romarias da terra*) sponsored by leftist church groups (ibid.). In December, two ranchers convicted of murdering Chico Mendes, the rubber tapper and Amazon ecological hero, received sentences of nineteen years each. The publicity surrounding this case may have been responsible for a slight reduction in the number of such assassinations this year.

Carole Merten
San Francisco, Calif.

Canada

Population. 26,538,229
Parties. Communist Party of Canada (CPC); Communist Party of Canada (Marxist-Leninist) (CPC-ML); Revolutionary Workers' League (RWL); Trotskyist League (TL); International Socialists (IS)
Founded. CPC: 1921; CPC-ML: 1970; RWL: 1977; TL: 1975
Membership. CPC: 3,000; CPC-ML: 500; RWL: 200 (all estimated)
General Secretaries. CPC: George Hewison; CPC-ML: Hardial Bains; RWL: John Riddell
Central Committee. CPC: 65 members
Status. All legal
Last Congress. CPC: Twenty-eighth, 5–8 October 1990, in Toronto; CPC-ML: Fifth, 28–30 December 1987, in Montreal; RWL: Sixth, 28 July–3 August 1986, in Montreal
Last Federal Election. 21 November 1988; CPC: 52 candidates, average vote 126; no representatives; CPC-ML: no official candidates; RWL: no official candidates
Auxiliary Organizations. CPC: Parti communiste du Québec, Canadian Peace Congress, Conseil québecois de la paix, Association of United Ukrainian Canadians, Congress of Canadian Women, Young Communist League, Workers' Benevolent Association of Canada; CPC-ML: People's Front Against Racist and Fascist Violence, Revolutionary Trade Union Opposition, Democratic Women's Union of Canada, Communist Youth Union of Canada (Marxist-Leninist), Canada-Albania Friendship Association; RWL: Young Socialist Organizing Committee, Comité de la jeunesse révolutionnaire (CJR)
Publications. CPC: *Canadian Tribune* (Tom Morris, editor), *Pacific Tribune, Combat, Communist Viewpoint, Le Communiste, Rebel Youth, Jeunesse militante*; CPC-ML: *Marxist-Leninist, Le Marxiste-Leniniste, Voice of the Youth, Voice of the People, Democratic Women, People's Front Bulletin, Canadian Student, BC Worker*; RWL: *Socialist Voice* (Michael Prairie, editor), *Lutte ouvrière*; TL: *Sparticist Canada*; IS: *Socialist Worker*

The CPC spent 1990 in prolonged and often sharp discussion as to whether it should continue to exist and if so in what form. The party and assorted members continued to come out strongly on domestic and international issues. But overriding attention was focused on preparations for and holding of the 28th convention in Toronto in October.

CPC Internal Affairs. Discussions of the nature of the CPC continued all year, with leaders mouthing some of the old clichés, as party leader George Hewison did in January, sometimes with serious efforts to understand and counter the abject failures of the CPC and the entire world communist movement (*Canadian Tribune*, 22 January). A three-day session of the 65-member Central Committee in March came up with a "manifesto for the 90s," which was released in April as *The Communist Party and the New Decade* (for original text, see *Canadian Tribune*, 16 April). As a *Canadian Tribune* editorial noted on 8 October, the *New Decade* document argued "that socialism is still valid, that it needs to become a viable alternative for the Canadian working class and social movements. It points the way for using Marxist methodology to give socialism a renewed democratic face."

A *Canadian Tribune* editorial (8 October) looking to the convention stated: "Today revolutionary Marxism must be stripped of Stalinism and relinked to its profoundly democratic roots and traditions. If this happens, the working class will be able to forge the necessary alliance, and assert a moral alternative to an exploiting system which threatens the human race as never before." The draft of *New Decade* even proposed conducting a referendum in the coming year on changing the party's name so as to break the public association of "communism" with "authoritarianism" (*Canadian Tribune*, 9 April).

A three-person review commission—Gary Swann (British Columbia), Claire DaSylva (Quebec), and Miguel Figueroa (Nova Scotia)—was set up to tour the country and talk with party members. The commission's report noted: "According to the vast majority of our membership, our main problems relate to the present structures in the party, our style of work with others on the left and in mass movements, our links with the Soviet Union and other socialist countries, and our low ideological level." (*Canadian Tribune*, 3 September.)

In a public withdrawal from the CPC in May—only weeks before he died and after 54 years in the party—Ross Russell of Toronto put basic issues and frustrations before the public:

> I believe the overriding single thing that made possible everything from Stalin's atrocities to present day atrocities and corruption is that we chose to operate the Communist Party by a system called democratic centralism. The words belie the truth. Dictates were brought down from above. . . . The real centralism was a vast bureaucracy built up of party officials, secret police, etc., who ran everything. The people really had no say. Not toeing the line could get you excommunicated or worse. Friends and neighbours suffered. This wasn't the socialism I longed for as a youth.

Russell concluded that "the days of the Communist Party are over in Canada" and that the CPC by any name is "an anachronism." (*Canadian Tribune*, 7 May.) Gerry van Houten, CPC director of education before the October convention, also called bureaucracy the "Achilles heel" of the communist world (ibid., 20 August).

Among the breaks with tradition that occurred at the October convention (see *Canadian Tribune*, 15 October) were the following:

1. After heated debate, an amendment to restore the term *Marxism-Leninism* to *New Decade* was defeated. This was not a rejection of either Marx or Lenin, however, for as the final document said, the party's perspective "arises from and builds upon the theoretical foundations of scientific socialism first elaborated by Marx, Engels, and Lenin." The term *Marxism-Leninism* is associated with Stalinism. (Also see Fred Wilson's comments in the *Canadian Tribune*, 30 July.)

2. A move to delete the term *democratic centralism* from the *New Decade* was successful.

3. Five of the executive officers of the CPC were directly elected by the delegates, rather than all being appointed by the Central Committee, as in the past. The elected members were party leader George Hewison, central organizer John Maclennan, Secretary/Treasurer Lorne Robson, Education Director Tom Morris, and Press/Liaison Officer Kerry McCuaig. (*Canadian Tribune*, 15 October.)

Auxiliary and Other Organizations. The Young Communist League held its 23d Convention in Toronto 18–21 May, for the first time with a few other Canadian leftist youth leaders present. Heated disputes led to a final document that was marked by broad compromises. According to the *Canadian Tribune* (28 May), "reference to democratic centralism was removed from the YCL constitution, but the essence of the concept was retained and strengthened." Reference to the CPC was dropped from the YCL manifesto. Members of the Central Committee will now be elected by local clubs. The YCL agreed to poll the membership to see if the name of the group should be changed.

Substantial CPC support for the Canadian Labour Congress was shaken in November when the CLC provided little institutional support for the National Recall Day "to express popular anger and revulsion for the Tory government" (see *Canadian Tribune*, 4 June, 19 November).

The CPC was pleased by the victory of the New Democratic Party (NDP) in Ontario in September and has pledged to support some NDP candidates in future provincial and federal elections (*Canadian Tribune*, 15 October). In general the party professed support for a more united left in Canada. "Yesterday's clichés and outdated supposition just won't work. A fractured, feuding Left won't win many victories, let alone people's power," a *Canadian Tribune* editorial said on 22 January.

Domestic Affairs. The CPC continued its scathing attacks on the government of Conservative prime minister Brian Mulroney. "They've lied, cheated, sold out and sleazed their way to the lowest depths of public support since records were started back in the 1940s," the *Canadian Tribune* said in a typical editorial on 16 April. What the CPC called the anti-Canada, pro-U.S. Mulroney government promises "a leaner, meaner decade" in the 1990s (*Canadian Tribune*, 8 January). The Canadian market is "being undermined by high unemployment, excessive taxation and high interest rates. As working people are pushed into poverty, social programs are decimated to free up government revenue to further assist the corporations."

The CPC proclaimed that "the unprovoked assault by heavily armed Quebec police on Mohawk ancestral land at Kanesatake on July 11 has brought Canadian-aboriginal relations to a crossroads" and that the "law breakers" at Oka, Kahnawake, and Kanesatake "are not the aboriginal peoples" but the prime minister and his government (*Canadian Tribune*, 23 July, 10 September). The highly controversial Goods and Services Tax (GST) drew special fire and, according to the CPC, "may just be the

vehicle to bring the government down" (*Canadian Tribune*, 12 November).

International Affairs. In general, CPC leaders and statements showed an increasing level of objectivity, as in the *Canadian Tribune* editorial comment on 8 October:

> The CP must move from the intoxicating belief that socialism was winning all down the line, yet avoid going over to the despair that socialism is finished, simply because a certain crude model hit the end of the road. Neither belief is correct. Imperialism is rapidly re-structuring and has the Left on the defensive. Imperialism and reaction is strong and dangerous, but it is not without contradictions and it is not all-powerful. This is a time for creative thinking.

The party weekly noted that "unhitching our country from the U.S. in this area offers a multitude of benefits as the cold war recedes and new challenges arise. An entirely updated and positive foreign and defence policy based on the 1990s and beyond is required." (*Canadian Tribune*, 5 February.)

A central theme in CPC commentary is the Tory government's supposed subservience to Washington. Party editorials condemned Canada's "support for the open-ended U.S. resolution which could unleash a terrible war in the Middle East," attacked Ottawa's involvement in surviving "cold war" games (21 May), and branded Tory support for the U.S. invasion of Panama in December 1989 as "appalling. It is short-sighted toadyism. Mulroney has disgraced our country." (*Canadian Tribune*, 3 December, 21 May, 15 January.)

The Canadian Communists condemned U.S. policy toward Central America (30 April) and Cuba (9 April); Hewison visited Cuba in August and returned with much sympathy for Castro and his "distinctly Cuban 'model' of socialism" (*Canadian Tribune*, 13 August). The PCP welcomed South African Nelson Mandela to Canada in June and argued that "Sanctions must be maintained. Solidarity with the ANC and democratic movements must be expanded."

CPC comments on the Soviet Union ranged from positive to negative. Foreign correspondent Fred Weir noted from Moscow that "no country has set itself a tougher set of goals, nor adopted a higher set of ideals: democratic, humane socialism." Yet when the Soviet Union went along with the "all necessary means" resolution toward Iraq in the U.N. Security Council, the party weekly commented: "We believe that the USSR and China, by not utilizing their vetoes, provided by UN rules precisely to prevent such holocausts, will be dead wrong. They will share responsibility for the looming genocide." (*Canadian Tribune*, 15 January, 3 December.)

Lynn Ratliff
Stanford, California

Chile

Population. 13,082,842 (July)
Party. Communist Party of Chile (Partido Comunista de Chile; PCCh)
Founded. 1922
Membership. 48,000 (estimated)
General Secretary. Volodia Teitelboim
Political Committee. 20 members
Secretariat. 5 members
Central Committee. 55 members, 9 of them publicly identified
Status. Legalized, October 1990
Last Congress. Fifteenth, 5–12 May 1989
Last Election. 14 December 1989. Party presented candidates through leftist alliance created for election and dissolved thereafter. None elected to Senate (38 elected and 9 appointed members) or Chamber of Deputies (120 members).
Publications. *El Siglo*, daily before 1973 coup, clandestine thereafter, weekly since September 1989

In 1990 the Communist Party of Chile attempted to reintegrate itself into the democratic politics of Chile. It achieved legal recognition by conforming to the provisions of the Political Party Law and began to move away from the policy of "popular rebellion of the masses" that it had followed since 1980 and reaffirmed at the 1989 party congress. The party suffered repeated defections, resignations, and expulsions of party leaders and attempted to distance itself from several small terrorist groups that continued to carry out assassinations and bombings after an elected president, Patricio Aylwin, took office in March. The earlier communist alliance with the Socialist party no longer existed,

and the party found itself increasingly isolated on the Chilean political scene.

The creation of a unified Socialist party of Chile on 29 December 1989 meant that the Socialist faction, headed by Clodomiro Almeyda and that had earlier cooperated closely with the Communists, now joined the "renovated" Socialists headed by Jorge Arrate and the former Movement of United Popular Action (MAPU) as part of the governing Coalition (*Concertación*) of Parties for Democracy, abandoning their links to the Communists. The return of democracy to Chile also meant that the communist policy of "popular rebellion of the masses," adopted in 1980, was no longer viable. At the January 1990 celebrations marking the 68th anniversary of the founding of the party, the main speaker formally announced that the policy was no longer applicable under a democratically elected government. The speaker, Gladys Marin, in her first public appearance after seventeen years of exile and clandestine activities, also rejected the dictatorship of the proletariat as a party objective and committed the party to the strengthening of democracy (*FBIS-LAT*, 16 January).

The candidates that the party had presented through the Broad Party of the Socialist Left (PAIS) in the December elections were unsuccessful, and Luis Maira, a PAIS leader, blamed part of the lack of success of the left to a rejection of the earlier communist policy of popular rebellion. The Movement of the Revolutionary Left (MIR), formerly committed to violence, also announced that it would not continue its policy of "armed struggle" under the Aylwin government (*FBIS-LAT*, 29 January). However, two other groups, the Manuel Rodriguez Patriotic Front (FPMR) and the Lautaro Youth Movement (MJL), continued to carry out bombings and assassinations throughout 1990.

The communist party had been instrumental in creating the Manuel Rodriguez Front in 1983 to channel the desires of young people in the shantytowns (*poblaciones*) for direct action against the Pinochet dictatorship. In 1987, however, the front had split over the degree of communist control, and the members of the "autonomous" faction continued to carry out terrorist activities despite communist party insistence that such tactics were no longer appropriate. In March 1990 they seriously wounded retired air force General Gustavo Leigh, a member of the original 1973 junta, and in May they killed a police colonel who had been involved in antisubversive activities. Another guerrilla group, the Lautaro Movement (not related to the Communists), had split off from the left Catholic MAPU movement in 1983 and is believed responsible for the killing of six policemen as well as bomb attacks on banks, party offices, and several Mormon temples (*FBIS-LAT*, 23 May).

At the end of a five-day party conference in May, Communist Party secretary general Teitelboim condemned the murder of the police colonel and called on the Manuel Rodriguez movement to give up violence. He also announced that the party was gathering signatures for legal recognition and studying the changes in its statutes that would be required to conform to the Political Parties Law (*FBIS-LAT*, 6 June). The party had suffered serious internal splits since early in the year. Patricio Hales, one of its chief spokesmen during the Pinochet years, accused it of Stalinism and in April led a group of party leaders out of the party (*FBIS-LAT*, 10 April). In July, Fanny Pollarolo, long the party's leading human rights activist, resigned from the Central Committee. A former communist deputy from Valparaiso and an unsuccessful senatorial candidate in the 1989 elections, Luis Guastavino criticized the party for not admitting that its earlier policy favoring violence was a mistake; he was expelled ("suspended") from the party in August (*APSI*, 15–21 August; *FBIS-LAT*, 21 August). There were also press reports that nearly half the Central Committee of the Communist Youth had left the party, most joining the Socialists (*WSJ*, 21 September).

Nevertheless, the communist party was able to collect more than 60,000 signatures in support of its legalization, nearly double the legal minimum of 33,500, and it was formally recognized on 22 October. It still has a base in the trade unions, especially in the United Workers' Central (CUT) that is the principal representative of organized labor. Its likely electoral strength is estimated at between 3 percent and 5 percent, far below the 17 percent that it received during the Allende period (1970–73). It has finally rejected armed struggle, attempting to play by the rules of democratic electoral politics, but, as in the case of the Spanish Communist Party, it has now been left far behind in the competition for votes of the left by a modernized and effective Socialist party. Its attractiveness to youth, students, and shantytown dwellers has been further undermined by the obvious failures of the Soviet communist party, with which it has been closely tied since its foundation in 1922.

From a broader historical view, the Communist Party of Chile made a number of policy errors in the 1980s: The first was the adoption of armed struggle in 1980, and the second, the creation of the Manuel Rodriguez Front that later escaped its control. Third was the decision—later reversed—to boycott the plebiscite that defeated Pinochet and only belatedly to support the candidacy of Patricio Aylwin in the 1989 elections. Now, as the most dynamic members of the party resign or are expelled and as the Socialist party on its right and the guerrilla groups on its left are more attractive to the new generations, the future looks dim for what was once the dominant party of the Chilean left.

Paul E. Sigmund
Princeton University

Colombia

Population. 33,076,188 (July)
Party. Communist Party of Colombia (Partido Comunista de Colombia; PCC)
Founded. 1930
Membership. 18,000 (estimate, includes Communist Youth Organization)
General Secretary. Gilberto Vieira
Executive Committee. 14 members
Central Committee. 80 members
Status. Legal
Last Congress. Fifteenth, 12–15 December 1988
Last Elections. 1990: congressional, 1.2 percent, 1 of 114 senators, 7 of 199 representatives; 13 deputies to state assemblies; 250 municipal council members
Auxiliary Organizations. United Workers' Confederation (CUT); Federation of Agrarian Syndicates; Communist Youth of Colombia (JUCO), claims 2,000 members
Publications. *Voz* (weekly), 40,000 circulation; *Márgen Izquierda*, political journal, 6,000 circulation; *World Marxist Review*, Colombian edition, 2,000 circulation

Violence attributed to guerrillas, paramilitary groups, death squads, self-defense groups, and bands of assassins organized by drug interests continued to plague Colombia in 1990.

Congressional and presidential elections contributed to political tensions during the first of the year. The assassinations of presidential candidates from the Patriotic Union and the M-19, along with the continued assassinations of lesser political and trade union leaders, dramatically underscored the lack of political guarantees in Colombia, especially for the leftist sectors.

Despite the loss of its most visible national leader, the M-19, in only a few months of campaigning, surpassed the electoral support of the Patriotic Union. The latter's poor showing in the March congressional elections, together with dissension over the issue of armed struggle, led to a split within its leadership and the formation of a new political movement comprised of noncommunist sectors. The PCC, already marginalized in national political life, now finds itself further isolated from the leading progressive forces in the country and in its most weakened position in recent years.

The guerrilla option is no longer seen as viable by significant sectors of the left in Colombia. Guerrilla practices of extortion, blackmail, and kidnapping, which contradict their lip service to peace, have cost the guerrillas much of the political ground and grass roots support that they once had. More important, the M-19's successful transition from a guerrilla movement to a legal political party has restored the legitimacy of dialogue and demonstrates that it is not unthinkable that a combination of military defeats and loss of political ground can persuade the remaining guerrilla forces to abandon the armed option. For the time being, however, Colombia's two largest guerrilla groups, the Revolutionary Armed Forces of Colombia (FARC) and the National Liberation Army (ELN), have rejected peace talks and appear willing to hold out for concessions from the Constituent Assembly scheduled for February 1991.

Although President César Gaviria's successful peace initiatives with the People's Liberation Army (EPL) and several smaller rebel movements promise to reduce further the scope of guerrilla activity, the persistence of paramilitary, criminal, and drug-related violence will continue to represent a serious challenge to Colombia's legal and political institutions.

PCC. A major source of the PCC's influence is its control of the United Workers' Confederation, reportedly Colombia's largest trade union confederation with 800,000 members. Although the party officially disclaims any control over the CUT, it insists on the right to "occupy and exercise any leadership positions that may be assigned to it" (*YICA*, 1989). The CUT's secretary general is Aída Abella. The Executive Committee of the CUT met with the labor minister in August to protest what it called "a publicity offensive seeking to impose labor reform to the detriment of workers' rights" (*Voz*, 23 August). The CUT joined the country's other major labor organizations in staging a "civic strike" on 14 November to protest the rise in the cost of living and to demand a change in the government's economic and social policies, in particular, President Gaviria's proposal to privatize state-owned companies (*El Tiempo*, 15 November).

The PCC's youth organization, the JUCO, plays an active role in promoting party policy among university and secondary school students. According to documents prepared for the PCC's Fifteenth Congress, JUCO continues to be "weak, vulnerable to cyclical leadership, and with little impact on the principal youth concentrations." (*YICA*, 1989.) Although the JUCO plays an active role in student politics at the national level, its middle-level leadership is weak and only marginally involved at the regional and grass roots levels. The JUCO's political role in support of the PCC's electoral and organizational objectives is carried out through the Union of Patriotic Youth.

Guerrilla Warfare. Although not a serious threat to the government, guerrilla warfare has been a feature of Colombian life since the late 1940s; the current wave began in 1964. The three main guerrilla organizations are the FARC, long controlled by the PCC; the pro-Chinese EPL, which is the guerrilla arm of the PCC-ML; and the Castroist ELN. A fourth major guerrilla group, the M-19, signed a peace agreement with the government in March and demobilized to become a political party (see below). Other, smaller guerrilla movements that have emerged in recent years include the Revolutionary Workers' Party (PRT), which is basically concentrated in Sucre and is not known for military or terrorist activities; the Free Fatherland (Patria Libre), which some observers believe to be a spinoff of the EPL; the Trotskyist-oriented Workers' Self-Defense Movement (ADO); and the Quintin Lamé (QL), a pro-Indian group that operates primarily in the Cauca region.

In June, the QL's general commander, Gildardo Fernández, decreed a unilateral cease-fire and spoke about the group's willingness to join the peace process (Radio Cadena Nacional, 18 June; *FBIS-*

LAT, 19 June). On 15 September, the QL and the government agreed to hold regional peace talks in Cauca to determine the means and procedures for the QL's reincorporation into the country's civilian life (*El Tiempo*, 17 September). Discussions beginning in July between government spokesmen and PRT leaders culminated on 28 December with an agreement calling for the PRT to turn over its weapons on 26 January 1991. The government, in turn, pledged to guarantee the group's safety and to allow the PRT to become a legal political party with direct participation in discussions of the Constituent Assembly (Radio Cadena Nacional, 29 December; *FBIS-LAT*, 31 December).

In 1987 leaders from the six principal subversive movements in the country created a revolutionary umbrella group called the Simón Bolívar National Guerrilla Coordinating Board (CNG). By the end of 1990, only the FARC, the ELN, and a dissident faction from the EPL remained active in the CNG. According to Colombian military sources, guerrilla leaders from the three groups agreed at a CNG summit in September to merge and create a single line of command with the authority to order and conduct joint operations (*El Tiempo*, 3 October). Although there are still many areas where guerrilla influence is strong, insurgency in Colombia has been severely weakened through a combination of military offensives and peace agreements.

FARC. According to Colombian military sources, the FARC has a total of 4,900 people (other estimates range as high as 8,000) operating on more than 40 fronts. The FARC expanded its areas of influence in recent years to include portions of the departments of Huila, Caquetá, Tolima, Cauca, Boyacá, Santander, Antioquia, Valle, Meta, Cundinamarca, and the intendance of Arauca. Until December, the FARC's general headquarters was located at La Uribe, Meta. Manuel Marulanda Vélez is the FARC's principal commander. Until his death from heart failure on 10 August, Jacobo Arenas served as Marulanda's second-in-command; other members of the FARC's central staff are Alfonso Caño, Raúl Reyes, and Timoleón Jiménez. Although Marulanda has never confirmed officially that the FARC is the armed wing of the PCC, it is widely believed that the leadership mechanisms and general policy of the FARC are determined by the PCC's bylaws and that political resolutions emitted at party congresses and plenums are transmitted to the fronts through Marulanda's directives.

According to military intelligence, the FARC launched an offensive in January to recover the region of Middle Magdalena from the influence of drug kingpin Gonzalo Rodríguez Gacha (Inravision Television Cadena, *FBIS-LAT*, 12 January). Official sources subsequently reported the discovery of a "war" between the FARC and the Medellín and Cali drug cartels. The FARC reportedly has stopped protecting coca plantations and cocaine production laboratories in the southeastern sector of the country and has even begun to seize the drug to help finance its operations. The cocaine cartels have set up armed self-defense groups to combat the rebels' activities. (AFP, 13 May.)

A rash of FARC kidnappings and attacks in Meta, including the ambush of a military patrol on 28 January that left five soldiers dead and seven wounded, prompted an army offensive. In a letter addressed to former Colombian presidents, the FARC proposed a truce during the congressional and presidential elections. The government minister called the proposal "cynical" and accused the FARC of "extending the olive branch with one hand and brandishing weapons with the other." (*El Tiempo*, 6 March.)

On 23 March, members of the FARC's 8th Front blew up a power substation and attacked a military convoy in southern Cauca to protest the murder of the Patriotic Union's presidential candidate, Bernardo Jaramillo (Radio Cadena Nacional, 23 March; *FBIS-LAT*, 26 March). The government's peace adviser said that the government would be willing to begin talks with the FARC on the conditions that members of the FARC fronts gather in designated areas, as was done with the M-19 in Cauca, and that a viable procedure is agreed on for turning the FARC into a political party (*Semana*, 24 March). Shortly before his death, Jacobo Arenas announced the FARC's willingness to initiate a reconciliation process with the new government of President Gaviria as long as the talks were not conditioned on the demobilization and disarming of all its fronts (EFE, 26 June; *FBIS-LAT*, 28 June).

In early July, army sources reported four soldiers killed and five wounded during military operations directed against FARC training camps in the Perija mountain range in César (Radio Cadena Nacional, 3 July; *FBIS*, 5 July). Several guerrillas were reported killed in clashes between the army and FARC units operating in Boyacá and Santander (*El Tiempo*, 13 July). The Defense Ministry reported an additional 27 guerrillas killed during four days of fighting in Algeciras, Huila (Radio Cadena Nacional, 16 August; *FBIS*, 20 August). One soldier was wounded and four guerrillas killed when a FARC column attacked a combined police and army patrol in El Bordo municipality, Cauca, on 10 September (*El Tiempo*, 11 September).

At ceremonies marking the first month of Jacobo Arenas's death, Marulanda warned about the "dangers" that might result from a possible military offensive waged against the guerrillas on the pretext of forcing them to the bargaining table under conditions of surrender. He reaffirmed that "as long as the problems of national sovereignty, the state of siege, the dismantling of paramilitary groups, land ownership, health, and political freedoms exist, the armed struggle will retain its viability." He added that leaders of the FARC, the ELN, and a faction of the EPL were "seeking a rapprochement that will permit the establishment of a single People's Army." (*Voz*, 20 September.) On 1 October, leaders of the FARC's 12th Front announced their disagreement with the "climate of war," which they claim characterized the CNG's guerrilla summit in mid-September, and added that they would distance themselves from "the whims of comrades in the General Staff who want war" (AFP, 2 October).

In the biggest guerrilla offensive of the year, FARC and ELN units carried out a joint attack on the army base and police station in Taraza, Antioquia, and the neighboring town of Cáceres on 11 November. The attacks, which left sixteen guerrillas and nine soldiers dead, including the commander of the army base, came two days after the guerrillas offered to initiate peace talks with the government and released 22 police hostages as a goodwill gesture. (*NYT*, 12 November.)

On 9 December, troops of the army's 7th Brigade, supported by helicopter gunships, attacked the FARC's general headquarters at La Uribe. Army Commander General Manuel Murillo said the actions, code-named "Operation Centauro," were intended to "liberate" an extensive region of the country that "for more than 25 years has been under the control of the country's largest and oldest armed rebel group." (*El Espectador*, 12 December.) Military spokesmen claimed 40 guerrilla dead, while acknowledging fifteen military casualties. In a televised interview on 13 December, Marulanda called for President Gaviria to order an end to the military operations against the FARC. He admitted that the army had taken over the movement's clandestine radio station and occupied the area where the FARC's main camp was located. Spokesmen for the government do not preclude further dialogue with the FARC, but they insist that talks will only take place if the insurgents prove "with actions" their commitment to peace. (*El Tiempo*, 14 December.)

In a message received by the Bogotá media on 22 December, spokesmen for the FARC and the ELN said they are willing to hold a dialogue with the government "in order to seek political solutions to the confrontation in Colombia" (AFP, 22 December). In an interview on Spanish television, Marulanda confirmed the severity of the military's offensive. He asserted that the army bombed the FARC's headquarters without the government's agreement, claiming that the government was negotiating with the FARC at the time. (Inravision Television Cadena, 28 December; *FBIS-LAT*, 31 December.)

At year's end, Defense Minister General Oscar Botero said that, with the destruction of the FARC's most important center for coordination and control, "armed subversion in Colombia is weakening" (*FBIS-LAT*, 26, 28 December). Military operations continued against FARC satellite command posts at Corinto and in Guaviare, where twenty guerrillas were reported killed during the final days of December (*El Tiempo*, 27 December). On 29 December, Colombia's new government minister said that the government's policy of holding talks with the FARC and the EPL would continue, despite a new round of guerrilla violence launched by the CNG against military installations and towns in various regions throughout the country (Radio Cadena Nacional, 29 December; *FBIS-LAT*, 31 December).

Domestic Attitudes and Activities. The PCC recognizes the experience of the Communist Party of the Soviet Union (CPSU) as an ideological source, but it also takes "maximum account of the national characteristics and revolutionary and democratic traditions of the Colombian people." The practice of combining legitimate, peaceful action and clandestine, armed struggle has been an integral part of the party's strategy for several decades. The documents and declarations approved by the PCC's Fifteenth Congress indicate that the strategy and tactics of the PCC will continue to be a combination of all forms of struggle. According to PCC member José Arizala, the congress reaffirmed that "the communists do not aim at total war: they seek to preserve and consolidate the political ground necessary for launching constitutional action." The PCC proposes the creation of a democratic convergence government as "a step towards a popular, anti-imperialist and democratic revolution which will open the way to socialism." (*YICA*, 1989.)

Much of the PCC's political activity in 1990 concerned its participation in the leadership and activities of the Patriotic Union (UP). The UP was established by the PCC, trade union, and other independent leftist forces in November 1985 to facilitate the transition of FARC guerrillas to legal political life. Since its inception, the UP has counted on the decisive and open participation of the PCC, which assigns members of its political directorate at all levels to participate in the UP's activities.

The PCC does not expect the UP to mechanically reflect the PCC's criteria and objectives in its pronouncements and daily activities. By late 1989, however, the UP's vocal support of the peace process led to increasing friction between the reformist faction, headed by the UP's presidential candidate, Bernardo Jaramillo, and the PCC leadership within the UP, headed by Gilberto Vieira. Under Jaramillo, the UP did not openly support a combination of all the forms of struggle that the PCC defends. In November 1989, Jaramillo insisted that "no party can impose a tactic on UP" and reasserted the UP's support for a political solution to the armed conflict. (*El Tiempo*, 27 November 1989.) After Jaramillo's assassination on 22 March, his successor as UP president, Diego Montaña Cuéllar, continued to clash with his PCC allies over the question of the armed option. On 29 March, twelve of the twenty members of the UP's national coordinating board resigned, among them Montaña and Vice-President Angelino Garzón, leaving only the eight members belonging to the PCC (EFE, *FBIS-LAT*, 30 March). According to sources close to the UP, the reformist faction resigned because it believes that Colombia needs a broad social democratic movement, such as the one advocated by Jaramillo. On 1 April, Montaña announced the formation of a new political movement opposed to armed action and separate from the PCC. (*El Tiempo*, 3 April.)

The PCC convened a plenary session of the UP on 8 April. Representatives from a number of marginal left-wing movements attended, including the Popular Front, To Struggle, the Socialist Workers' party, and the New Independent Liberalism. The reconstituted UP's new president is Oscar Dueñas Ruíz. Urías Oyaga is secretary general. Gilberto Vieira was elected to the revamped national coordinating board. (Radio Cadena Nacional, 8 April; FBIS, 16 April.)

The unprecedented crisis within the UP mirrors an emerging generational conflict within the PCC itself. Angelino Garzón, a member of the PCC for seventeen years, heads a group whose reformist ideas have rankled old guard Marxist-Leninists. His relations with the PCC reached the point of no return on 14 November 1989 when, during a meeting of the PCC Executive Committee, he raised the need to move away from a strict enforcement of democratic centralism as a means of settling internal party differences. The splinter group he represents believes that armed struggle has ceased to be an option and that the party should open a candid debate with the insurgency movement. There remains strong resistance on the part of the old guard headed by Gilberto Vieira, Alvaro Vásquez, and Manuel Cepeda, all of whom, according to Garzón, "say one thing in the open and another internally" (*El Tiempo*, 11 April).

The PCC supports the UP's position that it is a legal movement, unlike the FARC, and can therefore demand guarantees for its followers' lives and its political activities. The year 1990 was marked by continued violence against PCC and UP leaders. In the weeks leading up to the 11 March congressional elections, 74 UP activists, including about 20 leaders, were killed in various parts of the country. Following Jaramillo's assassination, the UP announced its withdrawal from the presidential elections and called for a 48-hour national labor strike. (AFP, 22 March.) In a meeting of opposition groups at the national capitol, Gilberto Vieira condemned the murder and said that the Barco government must be held accountable for the lack of political security in the country (EFE, 23 March; *FBIS-LAT*, 26 March). According to Vieira, the most reactionary Colombian sectors, including the military, have "unleashed a plan to exterminate the PCC, the UP, other leftist organizations, the labor movement, and human rights activists" (*Voz*, 29 March 1989). The majority of UP deaths during the past five years have occurred in the departments of Antioquia, Meta, and Santander, where the party enjoyed strong electoral support during the 1986 presidential and the first-ever mayoral elections in March 1988. With 1,385 of its members murdered, the UP barely has any qualified candidates alive. (*Latin America Weekly Report*, 5 April.)

According to the Fifteenth Party Congress, an essential element in raising the people's consciousness is the struggle against militarism. This means the party's continued opposition to the state of siege, paramilitary actions, disappearance of popular leaders, persecution of the UP, and the national security doctrine adopted by the military in 1965. The party also demands that the army be purged of "fascist elements" and that a civilian be put in charge of the Ministry of Defense. (*YICA*, 1989.) According to Alvaro Mosquera, the national security doctrine emerged from a distorted view of Colombian reality and has left the military politically aligned with and dependent on the United States. The party calls for a new military ideology based on "popular, democratic, independent and anti-imperialist values." (*Voz*, 5 July.)

The PCC celebrated the 60th anniversary of its founding on 17 July. In reviewing the party's accomplishments, Vieira cited the Communists' contribution to the formation of "a conscious need to undertake fundamental changes" in Colombian society. According to Vieira, the party has stimulated among Colombian intellectuals "the seminal task of historical analysis according to Marxist principles" and "opened a decisive breach" in the traditional two-party system, which has been "flooded with a surge of new movements and revolutionary parties." (*Voz*, supplement, 26 July.)

As for PCC strategy and tactics, Vieira said that the leadership recognized early on that armed struggle alone was not sufficient; "thus the party elaborated its historical thesis combining all forms of mass struggle, one that has now come under attack from both extremes of the political spectrum." He reaffirmed the need to defend the basic principles of Marxism-Leninism and insisted that those who believe the historical development of mankind is over are "badly mistaken." According to Vieira, the party's most urgent task is to intensify its efforts to achieve a political solution to the armed conflict by pressuring the government to disarm the paramilitary groups, purge the military, and negotiate directly with the National Guerrilla Coordinating Board. He also stressed the Communists' goal of creating a single party of Marxist-Leninists as part of the broad front needed to achieve a democratic convergence government. (Ibid.)

In discussing parliamentary strategy, Alvaro Vásquez, the UP's lone senator, admitted that the left would have greater difficulty presenting its views in the new Congress as a result of its poor showing in the March elections. He indicated the delegation would adopt primarily a "defensive posture" in support of workers' rights, agrarian and urban reform, and a political opening to the "national crisis." (*Voz*, 26 July.)

On 14 August, the Council of State appointed a representative of the UP to the National Electoral Tribunal, thereby, in the PCC's view, according official third-party status to the UP to the exclusion of the M-19. By law, the National Electoral Tribunal consists of three liberals, three conservatives, and one member from the "third political party." The UP's nominee to the tribunal, Carlos Duíca, said his principal role would be to "protect the parties and movements of the left, including the M-19, in order to neutralize the monopoly of the traditional parties." (*Voz*, 23 August.)

The UP held a national plenum on 7 September to plan strategy and to prepare a joint list for the Constituent Assembly elections on 9 December. In Vieira's opinion, the Communists have no reason to expect that the Constituent Assembly will "achieve the revolution for which we have struggled for 60 years," but they do hope that it will "broaden the present narrow democratic system and put an end to the permanent state of siege." (*Voz*, supplement, 26 July.)

International Views and Positions. The PCC faithfully follows the Soviet line in its international positions. According to Vieira, the party is engaged primarily in the struggle for the emancipation of the Colombian people. The PCC insists, however, that it is impossible to remain neutral in the "great international struggle" between socialism and capitalism. The party therefore "enthusiastically" supports the Socialist countries, particularly the Soviet Union "because it defends genuine socialism, despite its imperfections." (*YICA*, 1989.)

Some party members were critical of the documents prepared for the Fifteenth Party Congress for failing to "reflect properly the transformations underway in the Soviet Union and other socialist countries." In his speech commemorating the PCC's 60th anniversary, Vieira praised *perestroika* in the Soviet Union as "new progress toward a broader democratic socialism and definitive peace in the contemporary world." He warned that imperialism has not "ceased its aggressions," and called for the party to intensify its international solidarity with "all peoples struggling for peace, democracy and humanist socialism." (*Voz*, supplement, 26 July.) At the Central Committee plenum held 23–25 July, the party supported *perestroika* as "an objective reality of contemporary socialism that embodies the need for new political thought, and a new concept of the role of the masses in guiding socialism" (*Voz*, 2 August).

The PCC is consistently internationalist and invariably displays solidarity with the struggles of fraternal parties and peoples. A PCC delegation attended a conference of South American communist parties in Quito in early February. The conference adopted resolutions expressing solidarity with Cuba, Nicaragua, El Salvador, and Guatemala; reaffirming commitment to the "immortal ideas of scientific socialism"; and condemning the "ideological offensive of imperialism" that "distorted" events in the USSR and Eastern Europe trying to "sell the notion that Socialism has died." (*Latin America Weekly Report*, 15 March.) PCC theoretical documents emerging from its July plenum stress the need to develop Latin American unity by drawing more heavily on the legacy of Marxist theorists and continental democratic revolutionary thought (*Voz*, 2 August).

The CPSU Central Committee sent greetings to the PCC on its 60th anniversary, congratulating the party for its "struggle for social justice, democracy, and peace in Colombia" and expressing its gratitude for the PCC's support for "the CPSU's policy of restructuring Soviet society" (*Pravda*, 17 July).

The Maoists. The PCC-ML is firmly pro-Chinese. Its present leadership hierarchy is not clearly known, although until August, Francisco Caraballo was recognized as the movement's first secretary. The PCC-ML has an estimated membership of one thousand. Unlike the PCC, it has not attempted to obtain legal status and its impact on national life is insignificant. Its official news organ is *Revolución*. The Marxist-Leninist League of Colombia publishes the monthly *Nueva Democracia*. PCC-ML statements are sometimes found in Chinese publications and those of pro-Chinese parties in Europe and Latin America.

The PCC-ML's guerrilla arm, the EPL, was the first to attempt a "people's war" in Latin America. According to Colombian intelligence sources, the EPL has an estimated strength of 1,500, making it the third-largest armed group in the country. It is organized in sixteen guerrilla fronts spread throughout the coffee-growing region in the West, the banana-producing area of Urabá in the northwest, the central department of Santander, the southern region of Putumayo, and Amazonia (AFP, 3 April).

On 16 May, a communiqué from the EPL's central command indicated the group's willingness to engage in direct talks with the government (*El Tiempo*, 17 May). Only hours later, Caraballo issued a statement rejecting the possibility that the EPL would follow a policy "similar to the one pursued by M-19." The disagreement brought to light a split between the hard-line led by Caraballo and the more pragmatic position adopted by the EPL's second-in-command, Bernardo Gutiérrez. (*Semana*, 22 May.) On 24 May, the Barco administration announced that it had signed a "letter of intent" with Gutiérrez outlining a timetable for the EPL's disarmament and reincorporation into civilian life (EFE, *FBIS-LAT*, 24 May). The EPL's general staff in Córdoba subsequently announced that it would release its hostages as a gesture of good faith (Radio Cadena Nacional, 9 June; *FBIS-LAT*, 11 June). During June and early July, various EPL fronts operating in Antioquia and Córdoba gathered at a peace camp in Urabá and met with high-ranking government officials to discuss the guerrillas' demobilization. General Nelson Mejía announced that the military was prepared to cooperate in preventing both the camp from being attacked and the rebels from staging any armed attacks. (*El Tiempo*, 15 June.)

At a meeting in mid-July not attended by Caraballo, the EPL warned that the demobilization of its fronts must not be a prerequisite for the continuation of negotiations. According to Gutiérrez, the EPL's decision to begin a dialogue was influenced by what has happened to other guerrilla movements in Latin America. He admitted that differences exist within the PCC-ML over the question of armed struggle: "The newspaper *Revolución* publishes editorials and statements, but it only represents a fraction of the party. . . . We can no longer uphold the old leftist principles. We have to reach a national agreement." (*El Tiempo*, 15 July.)

In August, a communiqué issued by the Central Committee of the PCC-ML and the Central Command of the EPL confirmed the official expulsion of Caraballo from the movement. The PCC-ML's new National Directorate is headed by Gutiérrez, Aníbal Palacio, and José Miguel Restrepo. The EPL's new Central Command consists of Gutiérrez, Jairo Morales, Octavio Hernández, Omar Caicedo, and Marcos Jara. According to Palacio, "with the exception of the three members of the National Directorate appointed by the plenum, no party member has the right to speak on behalf of the PCC/ML." (*El Tiempo*, 27 August.)

On 26 August, representatives of the Gaviria government and the EPL agreed to concentrate all EPL guerrillas in nine camps to be located in Córdoba, Antioquia, Santander, Caldas, and Bolívar.

They also agreed to form four bilateral commissions to study the guerrillas' reincorporation into civilian life. According to presidential peace adviser Jesús Antonio Bejarano, the EPL's full compliance with the agreements will allow it to participate in the Constituent Assembly. (EFE, *FBIS-LAT*, 28 August.) On 2 December, Palacio called for President Gaviria to clarify the government's position regarding the EPL's role in the Constituent Assembly. The EPL has adopted the position that the assembly is the best framework for "a great political and social pact for peace," and it expects the government to encourage proposals to that effect. (Radio Cadena Nacional, 2 December; *FBIS-LAT*, 4 December.)

At year's end, major questions remained to be resolved concerning supervision, pardons, and details governing the reincorporation of EPL guerrillas into civilian life. Until they are, the EPL is unwilling to agree to a specific timetable for demobilization.

The M-19. The M-19, which first appeared in January 1974 as the self-proclaimed armed branch of ANAPO, takes its name from the contested presidential election of 19 April 1970. For most of the period from 1976 through 1988 the M-19 was actively involved in Colombia's guerrilla movement, pursuing "a popular revolution of national liberation toward socialism." The M-19 was the only guerrilla group that welcomed President Barco's peace plan in September 1988. In January 1989 the government agreed to hold direct talks with the M-19 as a first step toward the M-19's demobilization and its incorporation into the country's democratic life.

On 2 November 1989 the government and the M-19 signed a "Political Pact for Peace and Democracy" during a ceremony at the Colombian Congress. The peace accord formalized arrangements for demobilization, general amnesty, and the M-19's participation in the 1990 elections. The final peace agreement was signed on 8 March. At a ceremony at the M-19's camp in Santo Domingo, Cauca, 881 guerrillas turned over their weapons to a special commission of the Socialist International. (*El Tiempo*, 10 March.)

As a legally registered party, the M-19 surprised everyone in the 11 March elections by winning 1 seat in the chamber of representatives, 4 seats in departmental assemblies, 34 positions on local councils, and 3 mayoralities (*NYT*, 14 April). As a last-minute candidate in Bogotá's mayoral election, Carlos Pizarro attracted 8 percent of the vote, while UP candidate Carlos Romero barely managed 1 percent (*Latin America Weekly Report*, 22 March).

Although it was reported that the UP had contacted the M-19 to review a possible alliance and the proclamation of a single presidential candidate, Pizarro was confirmed as the M-19's presidential candidate at the conclusion of the party's convention on 20 March (*El Tiempo*, 21 March). M-19 leaders have not ruled out any type of alliance with other leftist groups; however, their prevailing view is that "communism has no chance in Colombia." According to Pizarro, the difference between the M-19 and the UP is that the latter is "a part of a section of the Communist Party and is deeply attached to the theory that all kinds of struggle can be waged at the same time. . . . This stance seems to be in crisis in Colombia. . . and the UP has paid a high price for its mistaken views." (*YICA*, 1989.) After barely a month of campaigning, Pizarro was assassinated aboard an Avianca jet on April 26. His successor, Antonio Navarro Wolff, said that the M-19 would "continue the struggle for peace." (Radio Cadena Nacional, 29 April; *FBIS-LAT*, 30 April.)

The M-19 unexpectedly emerged as the country's third-largest political force in the 27 May presidential elections. Navarro attracted 12.3 percent of the vote (740,000 votes), twice the share predicted in opinion surveys after the March elections and a record for Colombia's left. In evaluating the election results, President Barco praised the "courage and commitment" of the M-19 for being "the first guerrilla group in Colombia's history to abandon its weapons and participate as a political party in a presidential election." (*El Tiempo*, 29 May.) President-elect Gaviria honored a preelection pledge by subsequently appointing Navarro to his cabinet as minister of health.

In September, the M-19 reshuffled its administrative and political organization. Military commands were eliminated, and a single national leadership was created. Otto Patiño was appointed to head the national party directorate. Other party leaders besides Navarro are Germán Rojas, Libardo Parra, Vera Grave, Eder Bustamante, and Arjaid Arduanduaga. Rósemberg Pabón was selected to head the party's list of candidates for the Constituent Assembly. (Inravision Television Cadena, 13 September; *FBIS-LAT*, 14 September.)

The M-19 was the big winner in the 7 December Constituent Assembly elections, obtaining 27 percent of the votes (950,000) and winning 19 of the 70 seats. In an election characterized by massive abstention, the M-19 was the only party to increase its vote over the presidential election totals. The government will not have a majority in the Constituent Assembly, forcing it to make pacts with either conservative sectors or the M-19 to gain support for constitutional reforms. (*FBIS-LAT*, 11, 14 December.)

According to Navarro, the M-19 is already looking beyond the Constituent Assembly to the formation of a more encompassing political movement: "After the Constituent Assembly the next leap forward must be the creation of a great 19 April social democratic party" (Barcelona, *La Vanguardia*, 8 December; *FBIS*, 21 December).

ELN. The ELN was formed in Santander in 1964 under the inspiration of the Cuban revolution and undertook its first military action in January 1965. Once recognized as the largest and most militant of the guerrilla forces operating in Colombia, the ELN has never recovered from the toll exacted on its leadership and urban networks in the 1970s. The ELN survived a series of internal splits in the early 1980s and reemerged as a significant guerrilla force after reunification in 1983. The ELN was the only major guerrilla movement that did not sign a cease-fire agreement with the government in 1984. Unlike the FARC, the ELN does not accept the doctrine of "combining different forms of struggle" and therefore engages primarily in armed action.

According to Colombian army intelligence, the ELN now has approximately 2,200 combatants organized in 14 rural groups and 5 urban regional committees. Ninety percent of its structure is concentrated in Antioquia, North and South Santander, César, Bolívar, Sucre, and the intendance of Arauca. (*El Tiempo*, 8 July.) Its principal leader is Manuel Pérez Martínez. Other members of the central staff are Nicolás Rodríguez, Milton Hernández, and Gabriel Borja. Because of its revenue from kidnappings, extortion, and bank robberies, the movement is believed to be financially self-supporting. In contrast to the FARC, the ELN has taken a clear public stand against narcotics trafficking and cocaine production and has not been linked to protecting coca plantations, although it opposes extradition of suspected drug traffickers. (*WP*, 28 March.)

The ELN was the most active guerrilla movement in 1990. It started the year by killing fifteen people and wounding three others during operations in Bolívar, Cauca, and Santander (Inravision Television Cadena, 6 January; *FBIS-LAT*, 8 January). On 4 January, the government minister declared "an all-out war" against the ELN, stating that the group "has gone from subversive actions to common crime" (Radio Cadena Nacional, 5 January; *FBIS-LAT*, 8 January). In late January, the army dismantled a large ELN camp in the Middle Magdalena region. Troops intensified search and control operations in the area after repeated ELN threats to disrupt the March municipal and congressional elections. During February and early March, the ELN kidnapped more than 50 public officials and intimidated dozens of candidates in towns near their areas of control into quitting (*WP*, 28 March). In a communiqué sent to media in Bogotá, the ELN declared that all U.S. citizens on Colombian territory, including the U.S. ambassador, were considered "military targets" (EFE, 20 February; *FBIS-LAT*, 21 February). Armed forces reportedly killed twelve guerrillas following an ELN attack in Segovia municipality, Antioquia, on 23 February, during which seven soldiers were killed and twelve captured (Inravision Television Cadena, 25 February; *FBIS-LAT*, 26 February).

In late February, a communiqué issued by the Judicial and Investigative Police Directorate reported a "serious rift" between Manuel Pérez and "the commanders of certain ELN fronts," particularly in North and South Santander. The dissidents, "influenced by the changes which have occurred in the Soviet Union and Eastern Europe," are trying to "abolish the ELN's Marxist-Leninist ideology" and replace it with "an ideology that adapts to current political and social changes" (*El Tiempo*, 27 February).

Through the first half of the year, the ELN carried out 49 attacks on military targets. Takeovers of towns and assaults on military patrols and convoys left 115 officers, enlisted men, and policemen dead. In addition, kidnappings continued to be one of the ELN's main sources of financing and forms of political propaganda, with a reported 217 persons affected in thirteen departments. (Ibid., 8 July.)

The ELN continued its attacks against Colombia's petroleum infrastructure in 1990. In June, Pérez announced that the principal military objective of the ELN's guerrilla policy is to "create a movement for Colombian sovereignty and self-determination regarding natural resources" (EFE, 11 June; *FBIS-LAT*, 13 June). According to Colombian figures, the ELN has dynamited the country's main petroleum pipeline between Caño Limón and Covenas more than 125 times since it began operating in 1986 (*El Tiempo*, 8 July). On 12 May, Colombian authorities declared an ecological emergency in the area of Ciénaga de Zapatosa, César, following an ELN attack on the Caño Limón–Covenas pipeline, which links the eastern plains and the Caribbean coast (EFE, 13 May; *FBIS-LAT*, 14 May). Pérez subsequently admitted that the oil spill resulting from the Zapatosa attack was a "regrettable mistake" and said that the ELN is trying to devise a method "to sabotage Colombia's oil installations without causing ecological damage" (EFE, 11 June; *FBIS-LAT*, 13 June). The ELN did not attack the pipeline between 2 July and 5 September, when it blew up a stretch near the border between North Santander and Arauca.

Manuel Pérez stated at various times during the year that the ELN would never declare a unilateral truce to hold a dialogue with the government or agree to surrender its weapons. In an interview conducted at his camp in La Uribe mountains, he stressed that the ELN intends to go on fighting: "We have never talked about surrendering our arms. . . . We are not on the same track as the M-19 or the EPL regarding negotiations with the government." He endorsed the CNG proposal to "form a single Bolivarist army" by merging the ELN's guerrilla fronts with those of the FARC. He also indicated that the ELN will give priority to the penetration of the cities "because the cities are the life of the country, and we cannot remain satisfied with the countryside." (*Latin America Weekly Report*, 1 November.)

Following the ELN's participation in guerrilla attacks on the towns of Taraza and Cáceres, Antioquia, on 11 November, the Gaviria government ruled out further dialogue with both the FARC and the ELN (Inravision Television Cadena, 11 November; *FBIS-LAT*, 13 November). At year's end, the ELN and the FARC remained actively engaged in guerrilla operations.

Daniel L. Premo
Washington College

Costa Rica

Population. 3,032,795

Parties. Popular Vanguard Party (Partido Vanguardia Popular, PVP). A splinter faction is the Costa Rican People's Party (Partido del Pueblo Costarricense, PPC). Other secondary leftist parties are the Broad Democratic Front (Frente Amplio Democrático, FAD) associated with the PVP and led by Rodrigo Gutiérrez; associated with the PPC are the New Republic Movement (Movimiento de la Nueva República, MNR) led by Sergio Arick Ardón; the Socialist Party of Costa Rica (Partido Socialista Costarricense, PSC) led by Alvaro Mantero Mejia.

Founded. PVP: 1931; PPC: 1984; MNR: 1970 (as the Revolutionary People's Movement, MRP); PSC: 1972

Membership. 5,000–10,000 for all abovementioned groups and parties

General Secretary. PVP: Humberto Vargas Carbonell; PPC: Lenin Chacón Vargas

Central Committee. PVP and PPC: 35 members each, 15 alternates

Status. All legal

Last Congress. PVP: Seventeenth, 14–16 September 1990; PPC: Fifteenth, 23–24 August 1987

Last Election. 1990: United People (Pueblo Unido, PU), including both PVP and PPC, less than 2 percent of the presidential vote; one legislator elected.

Auxiliary Organizations. Unitary Workers' Central (Central Unitaria de Trabajadores, CUT); General Workers' Confederation (Confederación de Trabajadores, CGT); National Peasants' Federation (Federación Campesina Nacional, FCN); Costa Rican Peace and Solidarity Council (umbrella group of approximately 50 unions and solidarity committees)

Publications. PVP: *Adelante* (weekly), Manuel Delgado, director; PPC: *Libertad* (weekly), Rudolfo Ulloas B., director

National elections on 4 February passed uneventfully, with the minority opposition parties failing, as expected, to mount a credible challenge; Pueblo Unido, the leftist coalition, won only a single seat in the Legislative Assembly. In what was essentially a two-party race, the opposition Social Christian Unity Party (PUSC) candidate Rafael Ángel Calderón defeated the ruling National Liberation Party's (PLN's) Carlos Manuel Castillo. The minority parties that fielded presidential candidates garnered less than 2 percent of the total vote in the presidential contest and received only about 12 percent of the vote for deputy seats, managing to wrest only 3 of 57 seats in the Legislative Assembly away from the two main parties. The smaller parties uniformly expressed dissatisfaction with the predominance of the two-party system in Costa Rica, a system that the groups charged is self-perpetuating in that a party must receive at least 5 percent of the vote in the previous election to qualify for government financing. Pueblo Unido, the self-described alliance of leftist representatives of Marxism, Christianity, and social democracy, complained about lack of access to financing and threatened not to participate in future contests if the system is not reformed.

The new administration under Calderón represented little change. The PUSC leadership remained supportive of regional peace initiatives and refused, as did the PLN before it, to grant Cuba's request for landing rights. Regarding the establishment of diplomatic ties with Cuba, Calderón stated that he will only consider relations with Havana when "the country stops interfering in the internal affairs of other nations." (San José, Radio Relóz, 20 March; *FBIS-LAT*, 22 March.) Calderón, however, expressed admiration for reforms being implemented by Gorbachev and indicated that he expects Costa Rica to continue its cordial relations with the Soviet Union. (Hamburg, DPA, 8 May; *FBIS-LAT*, 22 May).

As for the left, Pueblo Unido (PU), which includes the Partido Popular Costarricense (PPC) and the Partido Vanguardia Popular (PVP), continued to suffer from the infighting that hampered efforts throughout 1989 to take advantage of an apparent popular desire for change. The platform emphasized socioeconomic programs responsive to the needs of the majority—particularly the marginalized population. It focused in particular on poverty and education and criticized the two leading parties for lack of concrete programs. Demanding respect for democracy and national sovereignty, the PU's presidential candidate, called "social democracy the flag for a rejuvenated left" and claimed that *peres-*

troika would actually help the leftist cause. (*Tico Times*, 26 January.)

Despite its weak showing at the polls, the PU coalition did not fall apart after the elections; rather, the PPC and the PVP determined to make the coalition more effective. The PU also hoped to achieve greater support from the popular masses it avers to champion. Rodrigo Gutiérrez, the lone PU representative in the National Assembly, spoke of creating a new PU, "a party for everyone, truly democratic." (*Adelante*, 9 February.) The PPC noted the necessity of creating "a new organization for political struggle . . . capable of bringing together the broad and diverse popular and patriotic movement existing" in Costa Rica (*Libertad*, 8 February).

Throughout the year, the leftist coalition supported various efforts to improve socioeconomic conditions. Both the PPC and the PVP focused on education and health care concerns. The PPC publication *Libertad* and *Adelante*, the PVP weekly, backed various strikes and protests for better pay and working conditions in sectors ranging from education to agriculture. The two parties' weeklies also criticized the rising cost of living and the government's economic reform measures. Internationally, the PPC and the PVP protested the U.S. "invasion" of Panama and claimed that "the U.S. plans other interventionist operations." (*Libertad*, 25 January.) Developments in Nicaragua and El Salvador were also closely followed, with the PVP and the PPC voicing support for their fellow leftists. The PPC and the PVP also sought to rationalize the major changes they saw sweeping the Soviet Union and Eastern Europe and to attempt to put them in a Latin American context. One article in *Adelante* (15 February) noted the "movement from authoritarian socialism to a democratic socialism."

With no congress planned for the near future, PPC general secretary Lenin Chacón called for a national assembly to address "urgent changes" that are necessary as the party seeks a "new national political image that will advance the movement and provide a progressive alternative to the existing government" (*Libertad*, 5 April). The PVP also noted the need for change. PVP general secretary Humberto Vargas Carbonell commented that the PVP lacked "a true feeling for the political reality of the country" and added that there was a "need for change, greater unity, revision." (*Adelante*, 15 February.)

Alicia Tompkins
Hoover Institution

Cuba

Population. 10,620,099 (July)
Party. Communist Party of Cuba (Partido Comunista de Cuba; PCC)
Founded. 1965
Membership. About 600,000 full and probationary members, one-third of whom are industrial workers, with managerial and office workers accounting for 20 percent of the total, professionals and technicians for 13 percent, and peasants for 2 percent. It is a middle-aged group: members aged 36 to 55 represent more than 60 percent of the total, with those over 55 accounting for 25 percent, and those under 37 for only 3 percent.
General Secretary. Fidel Castro Ruz, 64 (born 13 August 1926); title: first secretary
Politburo. 13 members: Fidel Castro Ruz, Raúl Castro Ruz (second secretary), Juan Almeida Bosque, Julio Camacho Aguilera, Osmany Cienfuegos Gorrián, Abelardo Colomé Ibarra, Vilma Espín Guillois, Armando Hart Dávalos, Esteban Lazo Hernández, José R. Ventura Machado, Pedro Miret Prieto, Jorge Risquet Valdés-Saldana, Carlos Rafael Rodríguez; 10 alternate members
Secretariat. 5 members: Fidel Castro Ruz, first secretary; Raúl Castro Ruz, second secretary; José R. Machado Ventura, Julián Rizo Alvarez, and Carlos Aldana Escalante
Central Committee. About 160 members and 70 alternates. That number is expected to be drastically cut in 1991; late in December Castro told the National Assembly that the Central Committee was a "monstrosity of peoples," with two-thirds more members and officials than it really needs (Miami, *El Nuevo Herald*, 29 December).
Status. Ruling party; no opposition party or dissident group allowed
Last Congress. Third, two sessions: 4–7 February, 30 November–2 December 1986; fourth scheduled for early 1991
Last Election. In 1986, all members of the National Assembly of People's Power approved and re-elected Fidel Castro Ruz and Raúl Castro Ruz as president and first vice-president of the Council of State for the 1987–1992 period. The council has a secretary and 23 members (ministers). The National Assembly's president is Juan Escalona Regueira.
Auxiliary Organizations. Union of Young Communists (Unión de Jovenes Comunistas; UJC), Union of Cuban Pioneers (Unión de Pioneros de Cuba; UPC), Federation of Cuban Women (Federación de Mujeres Cubanas; FMC), Committees for the Defense of the Revolution (Comités de Defensa de la Revolución; CDR), Confederation of Cuban Workers (Confederación de Trabajadores Cubanos; CTC), National Association of Small Farmers (Asociatión Nacional de Agricultores Pequeños; ANAP)
Publications. *Granma* (six days a week), official organ of the Central Committee, Jacinto García de Laserna, editor; *Juventud Rebelde* (daily), organ of the UJC

For the ruling Cuban communist party and President Fidel Castro Ruz, 1990 was the worst year since 1959, when the former guerrilla leader came to power after overthrowing the military dictatorship of Gen. Fulgencio Batista. The difficulties were principally economic. The Cuban economy, whose problems have been both endemic and serious practically since 1959, appeared to be in a free-fall, and the difficulties in 1991 are going to be even worse, according to Fidel Castro himself. The president, who used to rely economically and diplomatically on his East European "brothers," has discovered he has no friends in the former Socialist bloc. A clamor from East European capitals, as well as from Moscow, for changes in Cuba, Castro either rejected or ignored. Adding insult to injury, in December Czechoslovakia announced it would no longer provide an umbrella for the Cuban Interest Section in Washington. Although the population faced increased hardships in every area of daily life, there were few if any signs that popular discontent would affect Castro's firm control over the country: even though things were hard and even though people grumbled more than before, they were not demonstrating on the streets to vent their frustration, perhaps fearing the secret police and the ever-present vigilantes of the Committees for the Defense of the Revolution. Defying the tide of change in the communist world, the Cuban regime continued to adhere to the Marxist-Leninist principle of one-party rule, stressing the uniqueness of the Castrista revolution. Havana kept denouncing, often in bitter terms, political changes that were taking place in the Soviet Union and other former Socialist countries, as well as criticism of Cuba in those nations' media, now free from state censorship. Even though some Cuban leaders speaking to foreign newspapermen guardedly expressed support for changes in the Cuban political and economic system, none would do so in public as internal repression continued unabated.

> With the loss of allies in Nicaragua and Panama and the collapse of communism in the Soviet Union and Eastern Europe, Fidel Castro defiantly reinforced the Stalinist political system in Cuba and jailed all but a handful of some two hundred human rights activists. Castro strengthened his grip over the party, the military, and the government and reemployed the Committees for the Defense of the Revolution to squelch dissent. Castro suppressed religious processions and sabotaged a proposed visit to the island by His Holiness John Paul II,

according to Freedom House in its 1990 annual *Comparative Report of Freedom*, 22, no. 1. Other reports from Havana say that the pope's visit was rescheduled for late 1991.

Leadership and Party Organization. In the same speech in which he called the Central Committee a "monstrosity," Castro told the assembly that for him the communist party was "something that was close to being sacred because it is an indispensable instrument of the Revolution. God forbid that I should have an Anti-Party spirit, or that I should criticize the Party" (*Comparative Report of Freedom* 22, no. 1). Nevertheless, the party's role continued to erode as its cadres and bureaucracy at all levels were drastically cut. In June, Havana said that although the party's Politburo believed "in the one-party system and the socialist option," it was "not satisfied with how society functions, and that for that reason has called for a broad national debate to achieve even more democratic operations of political and state institutions." The main objective of the debate, the Politburo said, was to

> assure greater support by [party] members for their leaders. . . . Nor should we be surprised if tendencies dominant in the catastrophe in Eastern Europe emerge in one way or the other in the debates. . . . The limits of the discussions cannot be predetermined, [but] we must be ready for any level of discussions we may face. (*Granma*, 25 June.)

The interparty discussions apparently did not go

well for the leadership, and after a month or so they were discontinued or went unreported by the Havana media. In October, a committee charged with the preparation of the Fourth Congress, deciding not to wait for the event, issued a series of directives, which in effect cut communist leadership by 50 percent, affecting the municipal, provincial, and Central Committees and the secretariat. Also, during the next party leadership election—scheduled to take place in early 1991 and which Havana said would introduce direct, secret voting—the category of alternate, or associate, party members in the municipal, provincial, and Central Committees will be eliminated. The measure, Havana said, was intended to make party activities "more agile, economical and operational" by reducing bureaucracy and paperwork and eliminating many secondary party functionaries who would be sent to production. (*Granma*, 15 October.)

In a series of statements, Cuba made it clear that the Fourth Congress and a process of "rectification" of errors in the governance of the country would not lead to any substantive changes in the policies of the leadership of the country. If anything, Castro was more dominant than ever in every aspect of the country's life. Despite increased grumbling, he seemed to have the full support of the armed forces and the army-directed security apparatus, both of which were purged in 1989 of pro-Soviet officers who might have been inclined to follow the Gorbachev line. Castro was constantly adulated by the Cuban-controlled media. He was described as the only Cuban able to somehow lead the country out of its present predicament and the only one who was able to maintain a direct link with the general population. In view of the "exceptional historical circumstances now facing the Cuban Revolution," said a *Granma* editorial, the country was fortunate to have the "titanic guiding effort of Comrade Fidel Castro, in full maturity and at the peak of his mastery, to deal with the crisis of socialism and the aggressive euphoria of United States imperialism" (20 February). As not to leave any doubt about Castro's ideas of governing the country, the paper quoted the president declaring on 20 February, "we must progressively socialize more" and describing free agricultural markets as a "corrupt" institution. Maintaining its faith in Marxism-Leninism, Cuba was stressing the sui generis national genesis and character of its revolution, which it said was not imposed by the Red Army, as were the Socialist systems in Eastern Europe, but won by a group of

Cuban revolutionaries who were not Communists at the time, although they adopted a communist-style rule and Marxist ideas later. "We asked no one to make our Revolution," said Castro in October. "In these days when some people want to smash statues of Lenin into pieces, we feel the figure of Lenin growing in our hearts and our thoughts. . . . Well, they [East Europeans] call themselves socialists, social democrats, social whatsoever, in short, social nothings. . . . COMECON is a euphemism, it does not exist." (*Granma*, 14 October.) Throughout the year, Castro finished all his speeches with the slogan "socialism or death," which has been added to his former speech-ending phrase, "fatherland or death."

The Cuban Economy. The reorganization or the reduction in size of the communist bureaucracy, itself a cosmetic process, was a minor concern for the Cuban leaders. The economy, steadily if not precipitously declining, was their chief worry. Cuba had to face an entirely new situation in its economic involvement. "It is sad that this extraordinary effort for the development of the country and the consolidation of socialism in our homeland should coincide with the disaster in the socialist camp and the imperialist blockade which has already lasted more than 30 years," said Castro in his 26 July speech.

When our economy was chiefly based on the solid pillars of economic relations with the socialist camp and especially the Soviet Union, all these events take place, which lead to uncertainty about resources available to the country in the coming years. . . . We are working under very tense conditions, very tense, regarding the availability of essential resources, problems which we never had before. The situation is very difficult with regards to fuel . . . fertilizer, metal, wood, etc., for industry and agriculture. Trade with a few of the countries of the former socialist community has virtually disappeared while it continued with others. Why are we not complaining about the Soviets although deliveries of some products have been reduced by 50 percent? Because we know the Soviet government is doing all it can to fulfill its commitments. (*Granma*, 1 August.)

Earlier in the year, Castro criticized Czechoslovakia, Bulgaria, and Hungary for not signing new trade agreements with Cuba and for having sent Cuba shoddy goods in the past. He said that Hungarian and Bulgarian buses were gas-guzzlers (3.75 miles to a gallon), which were filling Cuban cities

with smoke. Cuban ire at its former allies manifested itself in other ways. In February, a Czech cameraman filming a street scene in Havana was beaten up by police agents, handcuffed, and arrested. He was later released and the government apologized for the incident.

The unreliability of Soviet supplies became evident in January when a delay in the shipment of Russian flour resulted in a month-long shortage of bread, which later was permanently rationed. Soviet-made, Sputnik brand razor blades disappeared from the stores and then were also rationed, two blades per month for each adult male. By mid-year, Havana began to prepare the population for wartime austerity. In September, Cuba added 28 food items to its ration list, which already contained 35 staples such as milk, beans, rice, and meat, and put severe restrictions on the sale of household goods, clothing, and electric appliances.

But the most economically damaging shortage was that of oil. For years, under barter agreements with the Soviet Union, Cuba received 90 percent of its annual petroleum consumption, in addition to some 700 industrial and agricultural products, from the USSR. In 1989, an average year, the Soviet Union supplied Cuba with 13 million tons of oil, 1.9 million tons of food, more than 1 million tons of fertilizer, over 1 million tons of heavy metals, and 80 percent of the island's transportation needs. In turn, Cuba basically exported sugar, nickel, manganese, and citrus fruit. In world market terms, this exchange of goods was beneficial to Cuba: its annual cost to Moscow was about $5 billion, not counting other development credits that over the years totaled some $10 billion. In 1990, with sugar production reaching 8.04 million tons, Cuba was apparently able to meet its scheduled sugar deliveries to the Soviet Union, as well as those of oranges and grapefruit, which had not always been the case in the past. In 1990, Cuba failed to fulfill its contract to deliver 300,000 tons of sugar to Bulgaria (Sofia, *DUMA*, 24 April; *FBIS*, 26 April).

As long as the Soviet media were strictly controlled, the cost of supporting Cuba was not publicly questioned in the Soviet Union. *Glasnost'* and Soviet economic difficulties changed all that, and Soviet citizens learned for the first time that Cuban-Soviet economic relations were one-sided. "If Soviet enterprises have alternative opportunities [to trade] they are not now interested in supplying Cuba," *Pravda* told its readers in April, complaining that "never-ending construction projects, obsolete design plans, laxness in fulfilling promises, disruptions in supplies, incompetent technical decisions and a mania for megaprojects are as familiar at our projects in Cuba as they are at home." Commenting on the cost of lengthy delays in unloading Soviet ships in Cuban ports, *Pravda* said, "The Soviet Union suffers losses in dollars. Cuba repays these losses in transfer rubles." (*FBIS*, 11 April.)

As the year wore on, Soviet questions became more pointed, as did Cuban complaints about the shortfalls in Russian deliveries of goods, especially petroleum. After the Havana press complained in August that Cuba had received 2 million fewer tons of Soviet oil than promised, *Komsomolskaya Pravda* sharply replied that the true total was 580,000 tons and that in the first eight months of 1990, Cuba actually received 100,000 tons more oil than during the same period of 1989. "So, what happened to the oil?" the Moscow paper asked rhetorically. "One can only guess: Either the oil supplied by us had been sold to third parties for foreign currencies, or Cuba's government has decided to create raw material reserves in anticipation of even harder times." (*FBIS*, 7 September.)

A week later, Castro attacked *Komsomolskaya Pravda* and *Izvestiia* for disputing Cuba's version of its energy crisis and the shortfall of Soviet oil deliveries and accused them of publishing "lies" about Cuba. Castro said he was obliged to respond "because we cannot accept them simply branding us as liars." The attack came at almost the same time as the Soviet Union announced that as of 1 January 1991 its trade with members of the Council for Mutual Economic Assistance, which includes Cuba, would be based on hard currency. Cuba was trying to obtain a special reprieve from Moscow, beginning with a 30 percent conversion to hard currency, so as to reach full convertibility in three years (*Miami Herald*, 13 September). Moscow has reportedly also notified Havana that beginning in 1995 Cuba would have to start repaying in dollars its accumulated trade imbalance debt, estimated by foreign sources at $30 billion.

The shortage of oil forced the Cuban government to adopt a series of stringent and economically damaging measures. As of October, the state sector began to receive 50 percent less oil than before, and the huge $1 billion Moa nickel plant, employing five thousand workers, was shut down. Work was also halted at a new, virtually completed oil refinery in Cienfuegos, which was to have had the capacity to produce 3 million tons of petroleum a year. A nuclear power plant at Cienfuegos, where 10,000 people worked, faced an uncertain future, according to Castro. Every family was told to reduce electricity consumption by 10 percent and warned that if they failed to do so their electricity would be cut off for one month. Similar electricity savings were established for all social and state agencies. In most production centers, work on Saturdays was halted. Offices in Havana eliminated lunch breaks, ending work by 3 P.M. to reduce electricity demand. In September, cuts were also made in the country's publications as a result of shortages of Soviet-supplied newsprint, leaving *Granma* the only daily newspaper circulating nationally. It was limited to eight pages on weekdays and six on Saturdays, when it was distributed only in Havana (*Granma* never published on Sundays). The government also announced that two Cuban paper factories were idle because of a lack of Soviet pulp and chlorine. Beginning 1 October, *Juventud Rebelde*, the communist youth newspaper, and the Cuban trade union daily *Trabajadores* became weeklies. *Bastión*, the armed forces publication and the fourth national daily, was closed down. Fifteen provincial dailies, including *Tribuna de la Habana*, the capital's local newspaper, and a trimmed-down version of the news weekly *Bohemia*, were to continue circulating, but all other newspapers, magazines, and publications were suspended. (*Granma*, 30 September.) Thousands of city workers, idle because industries had either to shut down or reduce production as a result of raw material shortages, began to be dispatched to the countryside in an effort to increase food production. Plans were announced to employ 100,000 in agriculture to save oil, and Cuba bought 200,000 bicycles in China and was negotiating to purchase 500,000 more to give to workers faced with the shortage of public transportation.

At the end of December, Cuba and the Soviet Union finally signed a trade agreement, but in the absence of any details from Havana or Moscow about the prices that each country was going to pay or charge for the two basic trading goods—sugar and petroleum—or about the overall value of the exchange, it was difficult to deduce the implications of the accord. The best guess of some experts was that Cuba received about six months' grace on the Soviet demand that all its former allies pay in convertible currency for Russian goods. It could be, the experts' argument goes, that the Soviet government has not yet decided what final shape its economic relations with Cuba was going to take. Castro suggested on more than one occasion that in Moscow there was a pro-Cuban faction within the leadership and an anti-Havana group centered mainly in academic and journalistic circles. Thus it appeared that, unable to resolve their dispute over policy toward the Castro regime, the Soviet leaders decided to continue slowly reducing deliveries of vital goods to Cuba but not to cut trade drastically. Experts assert, however, that under 1991 market conditions it would be more profitable for Moscow to sell oil for hard currency and then buy sugar on the world market rather than engage in barter with Cuba.

Whatever the details of the year-end deal, the Cuban leadership was apprehensive about the future of its trade and other relations with Moscow. "The word to define Cuba's relationship with the Soviet Union is uncertainty," wrote Cuban vice-president Carlos Rafael Rodríguez in a long article distributed by the *Los Angeles Times* syndicate.

The only certainty is that, in the immediate future, the situation will worsen. As a result of the U.S. trade embargo, Cuba conducts 70 percent of its total trade with the USSR and gets 90 percent of its oil from the Soviets. So we are prepared for the worst, for what I myself estimate will be five to six very difficult years. We must adjust to the changes in the world by mobilizing our society, hoping that the Soviet Union can sustain and reconsolidate itself while we put in place our own alternatives. Because we are not a rich country Cuba will always have a frugal socialism, even as we continue to develop. In the immediate future, as Fidel has correctly said, our women may have to wear the same clothes for five years. . . . One of the great uncertainties we face with the Soviets is that we must pay for their oil in hard currency beginning in 1991. . . . It would also mean selling sugar in hard currency. So trade in hard currency alone will not introduce a great difference—the difference will be in the price, which is what we are discussing with the Soviets now. . . . As a consequence of the uncertainty in their economy, the Soviets have told us that they are not going to negotiate a new five-year program in 1991 in regard to oil. Rather, we will come to an agreement for 1991, and in 1992 we will discuss the next four years. As a consequence, Cuba is prepared to consume the minimum amount of oil (*Miami Herald*, 7 December.)

Rodríguez also indicated that the major concern of the Cuban government was how the shortage of oil was going to affect the 1991 sugar production as thousands of tractors were replaced by oxen. He denied that sending thousands of city workers to the fields meant the "ruralization" of Cuba. "We are not Cambodians," he wrote. (Ibid.)

Cuba attempts to seek new markets. Unsure of economic aid from the Soviet Union and of trade with former East European Socialist countries, Cuba desperately began looking for markets elsewhere in the world, especially in Latin America and the Caribbean. Even though the Castro regime lost good friends in Nicaragua and Panama, Cuba had relations with seventeen Western Hemisphere nations, and Chile was also expected to resume ties with Havana. Although Castro was losing appeal among most Latin leftists because of his opposition to *perestroika* and *glasnost'* and his dismal human rights record, he was nevertheless received as a celebrity in Brazil during his March visit. There were about two dozen trade and diplomatic exchanges between Cuba and its neighbors, and Cuban cultural delegations traveled far and wide. Among the countries involved were Mexico, Argentina, Guyana, Venezuela, Bolivia, Ecuador, Peru, and the Bahamas. In 1989, Cuban trade with Latin America and the Caribbean countries totaled about $600 million. This total is believed to have declined in 1990 because Cuba was no longer reselling Soviet oil in the hemisphere, but Havana was looking for any avenue to expand commercial ties.

In November, Cubana Airlines announced new routes from Havana to Guayaquil, Ecuador, and Santiago de Chile. In the fall, President Castro met with Roderick Rainford, secretary general of the Caribbean community, to talk about tourism and scientific and medical cooperation. Cuba and Jamaica reestablished diplomatic relations in July, and in September Jamaica named a nonresident ambassador to Cuba. In 1983, after U.S. troops landed in Grenada, that country's U.S.-supported government expelled Cuban diplomats and severed relations with Havana. In 1990, Castro recognized the government of Prime Minister Nicholas Brathwaite and indicated a willingness to talk with Grenada about matters of mutual interest. Cuba hosted a delegation from the Bahamas and proposed a plan for the two countries to jointly market their tourist destinations to European tourists. In May, the 438-room Sol Palmeras Hotel opened in Varadero beach, the first Cuban-Spanish joint venture in tourism. A military mission from Bolivia visited Cuba and was shown the island's modern air force training facilities, possibly to offer Bolivians these services. (*Miami Herald*, 10 November.)

The country's economic structure is such that its agricultural products compete on the world market with those of many debt-ridden Western Hemisphere countries, meaning that Cuba has little to offer in trade or barter. Thus it promoted selling services, including some in the medical sector, that are inaccessible in a number of these nations, advertising them as cheaper than similar treatments in the United States. Havana said that people from 90 countries traveled to Cuba as part of a health tourism program, receiving treatment for vitiligo, kidney, and orthopedic problems and all types of surgery from more than 30 kinds of medical services available in a number of hospitals and clinics. Hundreds of Chernobyl radiation victims were also being treated in Cuba, which said it had the potential to take care of ten thousand such patients.

Trying to find oil on the island—something that U.S. companies in pre-Castro days and Soviet and Romanian experts after 1959 were unable to do—the Cuban government was seeking oil along the island's northern and southern coasts, according to José Yparriguirre, an official of the Cuban Center for Geological Investigations (*Latinamericana Press*, 22 November).

Foreign Affairs. Cuba, which in 1990 was a member of the United Nations Security Council, condemned the Iraqi invasion of Kuwait as an "unacceptable" action and voted in favor of the council's resolution demanding that Saddam Husayn withdraw his forces and reestablish the sovereignty of Kuwait. But the Cuban delegate abstained on the embargo resolution and voted against permitting the use of military force to remove Iraqi troops from Kuwait. Havana repeatedly said that the Iraqi action had resulted in great economic hardships for many Third World countries, especially those without oil, because of the rise in the price of petroleum.

Cuban troops continued to be withdrawn from Angola, where they have been stationed since 1975, and Havana announced that by 20 June 1991 the remaining soldiers would be brought back home, thus ending Cuban military interventions in foreign conflicts.

But the U.S.-Cuban "war" over the use of radio frequencies and television channels continued, with Havana getting, at least temporarily, an upper hand in that propaganda controversy. Cuba was able to effectively jam transmissions of TV Martí, a U.S. government–sponsored program that in March began to be beamed at Cuba from a balloon hoisted in the Florida Keys. The legality of the $30-million-plus project, produced under the umbrella of the U.S. Information Agency (USIA), became a matter of dispute under the terms of the 1982 International Telecommunications Convention. Havana reported in July that the International Telecommunications Union (ITU), at a June meeting in Geneva, supported the Cuban position on the issue—basically that no country could broadcast on channels in use by another country without first receiving permission for such transmissions. Although officials of TV Martí asserted that the program, broadcast between 3 A.M. and 6 A.M., was being received in some areas of Cuba, foreign journalists visiting the island did not confirm that assertion.

In April, retaliating against TV Martí, Cuba began jamming Radio Martí's AM signal, which had not previously been interfered with, and announced that the jamming was 90 percent effective. The U.S. officials said that although medium-wave Radio Martí broadcasts were being jammed, short-wave transmissions were not, and thus many Cubans could hear this program, which was also produced under the supervision of the USIA. According to Havana, its jamming of Radio Martí was due to the U.S. government's failure to fulfill its promise to give Cuba a radio frequency so it could broadcast its own medium-wave program to the United States (Radio Martí has been directing its broadcasts at Cuba since 1985). (*Granma*, 5 May.) In contrast, Cuba was showing a number of Hollywood-made movies and television programs on its two television channels that had been taken from satellite transmissions without paying usage rights. Among the movies taken from the air were *Crocodile Dundee*, *Wall Street*, *Police Academy*, *Beverly Hills Cop*, *E.T.*, *Platoon*, and *Star Wars* (TV Guide, 28 April).

Crime Wave in Cuba. Severe shortages of all types of goods in Cuba and what appeared to be a breakdown in the social structure in the country produced an alarming growth in crime, including the emergence of what Havana described as a large underworld that, at least in some cases, operated with the connivance of the authorities. This was a relatively recent occurrence in a nation whose regime had repeatedly claimed it had eliminated all "capitalist vices" by creating a new, exemplary Socialist society. In October, according to a *Granma* report, in a "combined" operation the Ministry of the Interior arrested a "group of notorious criminals belonging to networks in Havana involved in theft, speculation, embezzlement, trafficking in hard currency and objects of art and other criminal activity."

The report said that the arrest of three hundred Havana crime ringleaders would be followed by a roundup and arrest of many more underworld figures in other provinces and that the anticrime operations "will be continued and broadened."

Moreover, said *Granma*, investigations showed "complicity of some corrupt officials and administrators" in the activities of the persons arrested.

> Huge [black market] profits obtained by those hoodlums turned them into true crime lords whose ostentatious standard of living and constant squandering of money enabled them to pervert and corrupt people they came in contact with. . . . Many of them had succeeded in this way in buying homes, cars, electrical appliances, jewels and objects of art, as well as accumulating large amounts of both Cuban pesos and foreign currency. . . . One case involved a speculator who succeeded in setting up a ring through which he stole, transported and unlawfully sold thousands of bags of cement. Another example was a criminal called Leonardo "the Japanese," a drug trafficker who took teenagers to his home, drugged them and then got them involved in sexual aberrations. . . . A very small number of police officers and Ministry of Interior agents became accomplices of some of these criminals and this fact contributed somewhat to a climate of impunity in the Havana underworld. (*Granma*, 12 December.)

George Volsky
University of Miami

Dominican Republic

Population. 7,240,793 (July)
Party. Dominican Communist Party (Partido Comunista Dominicano; PCD)
Founded. 1944
Membership. 700 (estimated)
General Secretary. Narciso Isa Conde, 47
Central Committee. 21 members

Status. Legal
Last Congress. Fourth, 16–19 March 1989
Last Election. 16 May, no representation in Congress, boycotted the vote.
Publications. *Hablan los Comunistas* (weekly), Arsenio Hernández F., editor; *Impacto Socialista* (theoretical journal, appears every two months)

The Dominican Communist Party and other groups of the extreme left were generally inactive and in ideological disarray during 1990, the year in which the 16 May presidential and parliamentary elections were the focus of attention in the Dominican Republic. The country was also in the midst of a worsening economic crisis, which, however, did not add any strength to the splintered Marxist groups because, except for repeating the usual anti-American slogans, they had no solution to offer a population desperate for a light at the end of a dismal economic tunnel. In view of the well-known economic disasters in the Soviet Union and Cuba, Dominican leftists could not suggest, as they had in the past, that those countries' economic models be tried in the Dominican Republic. In addition, many supporters of Juan Bosch, a candidate for the presidency who early in 1990 was projected as a winner, were leftist militants or Marxist sympathizers. The 80-year-old Bosch had been a lifelong Marxist himself, although during the campaign he promoted capitalism as "the only way to achieve accelerated development of the Dominican economy."

In addition to the communist party there were scores of other leftist organizations, all, like the PCD, small if not miniscule. They were the Dominican Popular Movement (Movimiento Popular Dominicano; MPD); the Anti-Imperialist Patriotic Union (Unión Patriótica Anti-Imperialista; UPA); the Movement of the United Left (Movimiento de Izquierda Unida; MOU); the Party of the Dominican Workers–Ivan Faction (Partido de Trabajadores Dominicanos-Ivan; PTD-I); the Party of the Dominican Workers–Maria Faction (Partido de Trabajadores Dominicanos-María; PRD-M); the Socialist Bloc (Bloque Socialista; BS); the Militant Network for People's Power (Agrupación Militante pro Poder Popular); and the Resistance Front for the People's Liberation (Frente de la Resistencia pro Liberación del Pueblo). Several leftist parties were members of the Dominican Leftist Front (Frente Izquierdista Dominicano; FID), which was sponsored by the PCD, but they retained their individual party structures. In all, the Marxist groups had fewer than two thousand members. In 1986, the last time the left participated in an election, it received 0.28 percent of the total vote, or about five thousand votes.

Shortly before the 1990 election, eight Marxist-Leninist groups urged all Dominicans not to go to the polls on 16 May. They explained their decision to boycott the vote by arguing that neither of the two front-running presidential candidates, Juan Bosch and President Joaquín Balaguer, were capable of solving the problems affecting the Dominican people. The left was not the only one to complain, with the most criticism directed against President Balaguer. The frail, blind 83-year-old president, with more than half a century in the center of Dominican politics including the presidency, in 1986 defeated Bosch and other candidates by promising honest rule and quick economic reconstruction. But instead of reducing government spending and graft and in general tightening the economic belt of the country, Balaguer initiated a vast, wasteful public works program, constructing lavish monuments to celebrate, in 1992, the 500th anniversary of the arrival of Christopher Columbus in America, as well as other buildings without a redeeming economic value. As a result, inflation grew to over 60 percent annually, the once-vibrant middle class virtually disappeared, and the low standard of living of the lower classes declined even more.

It was not until four weeks after the election that the Central Election Board pronounced President Balaguer the winner over Juan Bosch by a margin of less than 25,000 votes out of a total of 1,800,000; thus Balaguer obtained 35.3 percent of the vote compared with his rival's 33.9 percent. Hundreds of foreign observers, headed by former President Jimmy Carter, were present in the country during the election and part of the vote-counting period to monitor the process. According to Carter, only minor irregularities were observed at the polling stations visited by his teams. But Bosch supporters, who had expected their candidate to win, alleged that the irregularities were massive and threatened to stage huge protests throughout the country. Disturbances were avoided by the intervention of José Francisco Peña Gómez, a third major candidate, who persuaded Bosch and Balaguer to agree to a supervised recount and to accept its results. Peña Gómez, the 54-year-old leader of the Dominican Revolutionary Party (Partido Revolucionario Dominicano; PRD) and a vice-president of the Socialist International, received 23.2 percent of the vote. He was seen by many Dominicans as a states-man who had averted a constitutional crisis and as a serious future presidential candidate.

Shortly after the election, it became clear that President Balaguer's rule was in deep trouble. His party, the Social Christian Reforming Party (Partido Reformista Social Cristiano; PRSC), received only 45 out of 120 seats in the Dominican Congress, leaving it short of a working majority. (The Socialist Bloc and the Dominican Workers' party, which did not boycott the election and whose candidates were helped by other parties, managed to obtain one seat each in Congress.)

As the economic crisis deepened, Balaguer's presidency was being increasingly contested not only by disgruntled political opponents and the extreme left but also by many business and labor leaders, his longtime supporters. In September, a few weeks after his inauguration, the country experienced one violent general strike in which fourteen people died and narrowly averted another. As inflation grew to close to 100 percent annually, the Dominicans witnessed the proliferation of grave shortages, from twenty-hour per day cuts of electric power and tap water to long lines for gasoline and to the disappearance from stores of basic foods, even sugar, the nation's principal crop.

In November, besieged by national labor strikes and by charges by the Catholic church that he had lost authority to deal with the nation's crisis, President Balaguer announced that he would seek a constitutional reform to move ahead the scheduled date of the next presidential election. In a speech to the nation, Balaguer proposed that the next election for president be held on 16 May 1992, two years earlier than the Constitution requires, "to guarantee democracy and put an end to accusations of illegitimacy against my government." (*Latinamerica Press*, 22 November.) Although the president was able to reduce the impact of a national strike that took place in November, not many observers took seriously Balaguer's proposal to change the Constitution; rather, many viewed the announcement as an astute political maneuver of the octogenarian president who is well known for his ability to outwit his opposition.

George Volsky
University of Miami

Ecuador

Population. 10,506,668 (July)

Party. Communist Party of Ecuador (Partido Co-munista Ecuatoriano; PCE), pro-Moscow, participates in elections as dominant member of the Frente Amplio De Izquierda (FADI) coalition; Popular Democratic Movement (Movimiento Popular Democrático; MPD), legal and electoral successor of former Marxist-Leninist Communist Party of Ecuador (Partido Comunista Marxista-Leninista de Ecuador; PCMLE); Ecuadorean Socialist Party (Partido Socialista Ecuatoriano; PSE); Popular Socialist Party (Partido Socialista Popular; PSP); National Liberation (Liberación Nacional; LN)

Founded. PCE: 1931; MPD: 1978 (from PCMLE: 1963); PSE: 1926; LN: 1987

Membership. PCE: 5,000; MPD: 3,000; PSE: 5,000—all estimates

General Secretary. PCE: René Maugé Mosquera; FADI: Xavier Garaicoa (president); MPD: Jorge Moreno Ordoñez (national director); PSE: Víctor Granda Aguilar

Status. Legal

Last Congress. PCE: Eleventh, 21–23 July 1988 in Quito; PSE: Forty-second, 26–28 May 1989 in Quito; FADI: 30 September 1989 in Guayaquil

Last Election. 17 June 1990 (for unicameral congress): FADI: 2 of 72 seats; PSE: 8 of 72 seats; MPD: 1 of 72 seats

Auxiliary Organizations. Workers' United Front (Frente Unitaria de Trabajadores; FUT), umbrella organization of three trade union confederations including the Confederation of Ecuadorean Workers (Confederación de Trabajadores del Ecuador; CTE), which is dominated by the PCE; Ecuadorean University Students' Federation (Federación de Estudiantes Universitarios del Ecuador; FEUE)

Publications. PCE: *El Pueblo*, weekly, editor, René Maugé Mosquera; *La Bandera Roja*, occasional; MPD: *Patria Nueva*

Economic problems, social unrest, and political conflict characterized the general state of affairs for Ecuador in 1990. The social democratic adminis-tration of Rodrigo Borja Cevallos encountered severe difficulty in alleviating the vicissitudes of daily life for most citizens. The political opposition was fragmented, as was the Marxist sector. The several Marxist parties devoted substantial effort to the struggle for partisan political advantage, with little real impact on national affairs. Meantime, the government and the non-Marxist parties also engaged in extended political battles that contributed little to the resolution of basic inequities in the society.

Domestic Party Affairs. The internal disunity and fragmentation of the Marxist left can be traced back to its origins in the decade of the 1920s. By 1990, there were three principal parties in addition to a handful of miniscule groupings. These consisted of the orthodox Communists and their electoral organization FADI; the Maoist PCMLE with the MPD; and the mainline Socialists of the PSP. The FADI and the PSP were willing, under certain circumstances, to cooperate with non-Marxist forces, whereas the Maoist organization was not.

The communist-dominated FADI first extended support to Rodrigo Borja for the second round of presidential elections in May 1988. Viewing the president and his ruling Democratic Left (Izquierda Democrática; ID) as providing a potential opening to progressive reforms, the FADI maintained its collaboration through the 17 June 1990 midterm congressional elections and after. Winning one seat while retaining its existing national seat (12 of the 72 seats are chosen on a national rather than provincial basis), the FADI thus contributed two votes to the progovernment bloc. As General Secretary René Maugé put it, "Without giving up Marxist ideology, our principles or our demands, we support the administration's efforts to alleviate the plight of the workers and of the people as a whole" (*WMR*, December 1989).

The rival PSE, while open to dialogue, has held itself more distant from government, which explained in part why it was among the few winners in the 1990 congressional contest. Doubling their popular vote, from 4.4 percent in 1988 to 8.9 percent, the Socialists increased their delegation from four to eight (including one national seat). The PSE, committed at least rhetorically to a unification of the left, remained in opposition to the government.

When the legislature convened for the first time following elections, the struggle to build a majority bloc and elect congressional officers was fierce. Antigovernment forces initially carried the day.

This soon broke down, however, in the face of a constitutional challenge to the authority of the president, which ultimately led, on 31 October, to a formal agreement including the ID, the PSP, and four other parties. The result was a six-party pro-government majority of 43 to 29. Crucial to the accord was the selection of the Socialists' Edelberto Bonilla as the president of the congress (*Latin American Weekly Report*, 15 November).

The only other Marxist party to gain congressional representation was the MPD, which had staunchly maintained an unbudging and dogmatic sectarianism since its founding in 1978. Although it joined with the FADI in an ill-fated electoral alliance in 1988, the MPD had soon gone off on its own again. In June 1990 its vote total was barely 3 percent, with its congressional representation falling from two to one. For Liberación Nacional, the noisy but miniscule faction that had rebelled and broken away from the FADI in October 1987, the elections proved fruitless.

Auxiliary Organizations. Notwithstanding well-established credentials as defenders of the worker, Izquierda Democrática and Rodrigo Borja were plagued throughout the year with labor unrest. Ecuador's three principal trade union confederations maintained their collaboration through the umbrella of the Workers' United Front (Frente Unitaria de Trabajadores; FUT). Public declarations, demands, and threatened work stoppages became routine. On 11 July the FUT called the third general strike against the government since its inauguration and set forth a lengthy laundry list of demands for policy reforms. Among those items were a substantial increase in the minimum wage, an end to weekly devaluations of the sucre, price controls for basic consumer goods, and a reversal of the policy to privatize state companies (*Latin American Weekly Review*, 19 July).

The basic thrust was directed at the economic program of austerity and gradualist adjustment that the administration had introduced shortly after taking office. Joined by organizations of teachers and Indians, the FUT insisted on direct conversations with Rodrigo Borja. The president declined. Viewing the policy alternatives as either shock or gradualism, he declared that those "disagreeing with gradualism . . . should admit that they are asking for the shock treatment of maxidevaluation" (*Vistazo*, 5 July). The 24-hour strike achieved only a partial work stoppage, after which the FUT returned to its campaign of public statements and denunciations of the government.

A growing force on the labor front during 1990 was the National Confederation of Ecuadorean Indians (Confederación Nacional de Indígenas del Ecuador; CONIAE). Drawing together numerous indigenous groups and challenging the state for the first time, CONIAE brought some one thousand Indians to Quito on 28 May to present a sixteen-point petition to President Borja, during which time the famous Santo Domingo cathedral was occupied by two hundred protesters. This was accompanied by the blocking of access roads in highland provinces and the seizure of a dozen soldiers as hostages. Only a mediating commission under Archbishop Antonio González of Quito resolved the immediate conflict.

The June National Uprising of Indigenous Peoples, as it was termed, effectively dramatized CONIAE's demands, among the more important of which were the return of community-held lands to the Indians, payment of official debts to Indian organizations, recognition of Quechua as an official language and compensation from oil multinationals for environmental damage to Indian-occupied territory. Although the government attempted to respond positively, it was reluctant to engage in direct negotiations. CONIAE insisted that, in addition to other demands, the first article of the constitution be reformed to declare Ecuador a multinational state recognizing the existence of nine major Indian nationalities (*Latinamerica Press*, 14 June).

This was highly controversial in the nation's political establishment, even when church leaders embraced the cause of reform. Ecuador was totally stunned by the mobilization of the Indians on behalf of these and other long-ignored rights or claims. The PCE was among those swift to seize on the conflict and was providing firm support well before the close of the year. Indian protests were unlikely to be muted in the future, thus providing a major issue on which the Marxists might focus attention.

Guerrilla Activity. Notwithstanding periodic bursts of publicity concerning Alfaro Vive, Carajo! (Alfaro Lives, Damnit!; AVC!), Ecuador was free from serious armed insurgency. The AVC!, which had initiated its activities in 1983, was subject to increasing factionalism and internal disunity. Confronted by the willingness of the Borja government to negotiate following its inauguration in August 1989 (*YICA*, 1990), AVC! members were divided over their future course of action. Whereas one group favored peace and sought an opening toward electoral participation, another was critical of the government and opposed any form of collaboration.

On 17 April the formation of the People's Armed Vanguard (Vanguardia Armada del Pueblo; VAP) was announced in Quito. This faction, headed by Elías Díaz Bustamante, called for policies similar to those of Peru's Shining Path (Sendero Luminoso) (*FBIS*, 23 April). Its opponents remained inside the AVC! and insisted on laying down arms and participating in electoral politics. In early June a news conference attended by AVC! leaders announced that they would inventory their arsenal and turn it over to the Andean parliament. The AVC! moving toward electoral status, also named its choices for the 17 June congressional elections. PSE and FADI candidates were tapped for Guayaquil and Esmeraldas, respectively (*FBIS*, 5 June).

AVC! spokesmen Pedro Moncada and Santiago Kingman followed up the news conference with a call for permanent dialogue among the government, workers, and "progressive businessmen" in the quest for a "truly participatory" democracy (*FBIS*, 11 June). This led in turn to a call on "all noncommitted citizens to form a party of independent people who are not registered with any political party" (*FBIS*, 27 June). In July the Executive Command of the AVC! announced plans to form a political party, as well as the preparation of specific proposals to be placed before the new congress (*FBIS*, 17 July).

For dissidents still clinging to the strategy of armed insurgency, there were efforts to publicize the so-called Batalión America (America Battalion), allegedly dominated by Colombian and Peruvian guerrillas. Characteristic was a September promise to "finish off" Chile's General Augusto Pinochet if requested by that country's leftist radicals (*FBIS*, 28 September). Timed to coincide with the state visit of Chilean president Patricio Aylwin, the threat was taken no more seriously than the self-proclaimed strength of the battalion. Even the AVC! never numbered more than a few hundred members. The future danger of antigovernment violence seemed to come more from the increasing activity of drug traffickers than from leftist radicals in Ecuador.

John D. Martz
Pennsylvania State University

El Salvador

Population. 5,309,685

Major Marxist-Leninist Groups

• Communist Party of El Salvador (Partido Comunista de El Salvador, PCES)
  Founded. March 1930; destroyed 2 years later; reorganized during the late 1940s
  Membership. Fewer than 1,000
  Leadership. Jorge Schafik Handal (general secretary since 1970)
  Governing Body. Central Committee
  Last Congress. Seventh, April 1979
  Status. Illegal
  Fronts and Auxiliary Organizations. The Armed Forces of Liberation (Fuerzas Armadas de Liberación, FAL) is the party's military branch. Together with elements of FARN and FPL the PCES controls the National Union of Salvadoran Workers (Unión Nacional de Trabajadores Salvadoreños, UNTS), established 8 February 1986 and led by Humberto Centeno and Marco Tulio Lima. The Nationalist Democratic Union (UDN) has been the PCES political front since 1965; after participating at cabinet level in the 1979 junta, it was declared illegal in 1980. During July–August 1988, its leaders, including General Secretary Mario Aguinada Carranza, Tirso Canales, and Aronette Díaz de Zamora, returned to El Salvador and became openly active once again.
  Publications. *Voz Popular* (irregular); *Fundamentos y Perspectivas* (theoretical, irregular)

• Farabundo Martí Popular Liberation Forces (Fuerzas Populares de Liberación Farabundo Martí, FPL)
  Founded. 1 April 1970 by dissidents from the PCES, led by the late General Secretary Salvador Cayetano Carpio and Central Committee member Mélida Anaya Montes ("Ana María")
  Membership. Ca. 1,200 cadres and fighters
  Leadership. Leonel González, first secretary of the Central Committee since August 1983, commander of the Popular Liberation Army (EPL; see below); Dimas Rodríguez, second in com-

mand of the EPL and the FPL; Ricardo Gutiérrez, chief of staff of the EPL; Salvador Guerra

Governing Body. Central Committee (membership unknown, except for above)

Status. Illegal

Last Congress. Seventh Revolutionary Council, August 1983

Front and Auxiliary Organizations. The People's Revolutionary Bloc (BPR) was established on 20 July 1975 as an FPL-controlled umbrella including unions and professional groups. The "subregional governments of people's power" in the department of Chalatenango were sporadically operative in certain areas until 1985, when the group lost permanent control over them; their leader was Evaristo López.

Publications. *El Rebelde* (irregular); *Farabundo Martí Weekly Informative* (external propaganda); since 1981 the BPR (see below) has irregularly published the *Popular Combat Weekly* (abroad) and the *Juan Ángel Chacón Bulletin*; the FPL also controls the second-most active radio station of the FMLN, Radio Farabundo Martí.

• People's Revolutionary Army (Ejército Revolucionario del Pueblo, ERP)

Founded. 1971 as an anonymous urban terrorist group known as The Group (El Grupo); following bloody internal purges in May 1975, it acquired its present name.

Membership. Ca. 2,000 cadres and fighters and as many as 20,000 civilian supporters and dependents

Leadership. Seven main leaders that double as the Political Commission of the PRS (see below): Joaquín Villalobos (alias of René Cruz), main leader; Ana Guadalupe Martínez; Ana Sonia Medina Arriola ("Mariana"); Mercedes del Carmén Letona ("Luisa"); Claudio Rabindranath Armijo ("Francisco"); Juan Ramón Medrano ("Balta"); Jorge Meléndez ("Jonas"); in addition, Francisco Mena Sandoval ("Manolo"), a former army captain who defected in 1981, is an increasingly prominent military leader on the northwestern front.

Governing Body. Political Commission of the ERP-PRS

Status. Illegal

Last Congress. Third Plenum, July 1981

Front and Auxiliary Organizations. The Party of the Salvadoran Revolution (PRS) and the front organization Popular Leagues—28 of February

(LP-28) were both established in 1977 as largely fictitious expansions of the militaristic ERP. Both are now largely defunct or inoperative.

Publications. The ERP controls (ensured by "Luisa") the FMLN Radio Venceremos.

• Armed Forces of National Resistance (Fuerzas Armadas de la Resistencia Nacional, FARN)

Founded. May 1975 by a group of dissident youth from the PCES, FPL, and Christian Democratic Party as a result of ERP purges. The Party of National Resistance (Partido de Resistencia Nacional, PRN), established in 1975 and supposed to control the military branch, remains ineffectual.

Membership. Fewer than 1,000 cadres and guerrillas; some 10,000 civilian supporters and dependents

Leadership. Fermán Cienfuegos (alias of Eduardo Sancho Castañeda) and "Luis Cabral," second in command

Governing Body. A seven-member National Leadership (equivalent of a Politburo) selects an "extended leadership" (Central Committee).

Status. Illegal

Fronts and Auxiliary Organizations. The United People's Action Front (FAPU) was established by Marxist Jesuit priests in the early 1970s and transferred to FARN; in 1981 it became largely nonexistent. FARN is by far the most successful FMLN group in infiltrating legal organizations, particularly student groups at both the National and Central American (Catholic) universities, as well as various human rights organizations, such as Committee of the Mothers of the Disappeared (COMADRES).

Publications. *Pueblo Internacional* (irregular); *Parte de Guerra* (war bulletin).

• Revolutionary Party of Central American Workers (Partido Revolucionario de los Trabajadores Centro Americanos, PRTC)

Founded. 26 January 1976 in San José, Costa Rica, as a regional, Trotskyist party, with branches planned in Costa Rica and Guatemala, which were never formed, and in El Salvador and Honduras, which were established and became officially independent on 29 October 1980

Membership. Fewer than 200 members, mostly urban, with some 1,000 sympathizers and dependents

Leadership. Francisco Jovel (alias Roberto Roca) is the supreme leader; Jaime Miranda is the representative to Mexico; important Central Committee members include Mario González ("Mario"), urban terrorist leader Ismaél Dimas Aguilar ("Ulysses"), and María Concepción de Valladares ("Nidia Díaz").

Governing Body. Central Committee (complete membership unknown)

Auxiliary Organization. The Popular Liberation Movement (Movimiento de Liberación Popular, MLP), established in 1979, had largely disappeared by 1981.

• Revolutionary Democratic Front (Frente Democrático Revolucionario, FDR)

Founded. 1980 as an umbrella alliance between the Marxist-Leninist guerrillas of the newly established FMLN, including all the above and their fronts, and a few minor civilian parties, including the allegedly social-democratic National Revolutionary Movement (MNR) led by Guillermo Ungo, a vice-president of the Socialist International, and the even smaller splinter from the Christian Democratic party, the Social Christian Popular Movement (MPSC), led by Rubén Zamora. As the Democratic Convergence, the FDR won less than 4 percent of the votes in the parliamentary and presidential elections of 1989.

Membership. A few hundred intellectuals and internationally connected professionals

Leadership. The Politico-Diplomatic Commission, led by Ungo and with Zamora as vice-president, includes representatives from the MNR, MPSC, UDN, FAPU, LP-29, BPR, and MLP, represented, respectively, by Ungo, Zamora, Mario Aguinada Carranza, José Rodríguez Ruiz, Ana Guadalupe Martínez, and Salvador Samayoa.

Status. Technically illegal under original name; however, in 1988 prominent members, including Guillermo Ungo, Rubén Zamora, Héctor Oqueli, and Mario Aguinada returned to El Salvador and formed a legal organization, the Democratic Convergence, while publicly retaining their links with and sympathies for the FMLN.

Fighting and the technological level of combat both increased during 1990 partly because the departing Sandinistas of Nicaragua overflew the FMLN arsenals and also because the FMLN retained a significant capability after its defeat in the November 1989 offensive. Furthermore, despite its increased aggressiveness, lethality, and combat capabilities, the FMLN obtained a high level of legitimacy, mostly due to U.S. congressional pressures on the Cristiani government and its military. To a decisive extent the Salvadoran internal conflict was decided by propaganda and public relations—a type of war in which the FMLN usually proves to be superior but that was lost at the last moment with the 2 January 1991 assassination of two wounded U.S. military advisers by the guerrillas.

Military Activities and Violence. The two major characteristics of the FMLN military operations during 1990 were the virtually unabated and massive attacks against military and civilian targets, despite the heavy losses incurred during the November 1989 offensive (see *YICA*, 1990) and the introduction of surface-to-air missiles, which not only resulted in significant losses to the Salvadoran Air Force but also escalated the level of warfare. At the same time, and despite their claims to the contrary, the FMLN continued to engage in terrorist actions, including the murder of civilians and assassination attempts against political personalities, including even President Alfredo Cristiani.

In January the military was forced to implicitly admit that massive guerrilla attacks had taken place against departmental capitals in the eastern part of the country but proudly proclaimed that Usulután and Santa Elena were not occupied by the FMLN. (*FBIS-LAT*, 10 January). On 24 January the chief of the armed forces, soon to become defense minister, Colonel (later general) René Emilio Ponce, admitted that the FMLN had a plan to attack the major cities, including the capital, thus implying that the November 1989 FMLN offensive had not destroyed the guerrillas' offensive capabilities (ibid., 25 January). As if to prove their omnipresence, the FMLN also attacked (unsuccessfully) the home of former Deputy Interior Minister Carlos Humberto Figueroa. The same month, while Vice-President Francisco Merino claimed that the FMLN had been virtually defanged, Ponce recognized that the guerrillas were once again ready for a widespread attack. (Ibid., 26 January.)

In February, the U.S. commander in Panama, General Maxwell Thurman, told the U.S. Congress that he doubted that the Salvadoran government could militarily defeat the FMLN (*NYT*, 9 February); a few days later the same source claimed that the air force had killed civilians in Chalatenango (ibid., 12 February). Also in February, Ponce claimed that 145 guerrillas and 53 soldiers had been killed in January—a spectacularly small kill ratio and one suggesting that the war was rapidly approaching a conventional level (ibid., 12 February).

On 6 March, following an attack against a civilian helicopter transporting Attorney General Mauricio Colorado, the FMLN claimed that "our anti-aircraft units fired on two military helicopters" (ibid., 7 March). It was a claim to be repeated later to excuse assassination attempts or simple murders of civilians or unarmed military personnel.

On 1 May, the FMLN once again tried to assassinate President Cristiani by staging an attack against his private residence, killing two policemen and producing eighteen casualties. At that moment the FMLN proclaimed its willingness to continue negotiations. (Ibid., 3 May.)

Although army accusations that the FMLN was engaged in forced recruitment were consistent, by May even the usually uncritical Americas' Watch admitted that the guerrillas were guilty of "several hundred executions" of civilians (*NYT*, 27 May). In June the army claimed that 38 insurgents had been killed in action in Chalatenango (*FBIS-LAT*, 18 June) and that the organization had tried to kill Assembly leader Ricardo Alvarenga on 27 June (ibid., 29 June). It also admitted responsibility for the murder of Colonel Carlos Figueroa Morales of the army's Legal Department on 9 July (ibid., 11 July). On 17 July, Captain Ramón of the Military Academy was murdered by an FMLN squad in Santa Tecla, an action claimed by the FMLN (ibid., 18 July). Up to the end of the year the FMLN continued its campaign of selective assassinations—attempts to murder politicians, their families, and officers—while also proclaiming its interest in negotiations.

On the military level, the guerrillas also used ground-to-air missiles to destroy helicopters and tactical aircraft, forcing the Salvadoran Air Force to limit or reduce the effectiveness of its sorties. In August another attempt to kill Cristiani took place, and in November the FMLN tried to take over the capital of the Chalatenango department. (Ibid., 21 November.)

Ideology. One of the important, albeit unconvincing, changes in the FMLN attitudes was the claim that the umbrella group is nationalistic and "democratic" rather than Marxist-Leninist. FMLN spokesmen in the United States consistently took that course in 1990, and even Fermán Cienfuegos claimed that "we do not consider ourselves either communists or Marxist-Leninists. We are the new democrats of the society." (*NYT*, 14 March.)

At the beginning of the year the FMLN came up with a new definition of its armed wing as the national army for democracy, trying to depict itself as nationalist, democratic, and thus non-Marxist—a line similar to Cienfuegos's.

As for the developments in the Soviet Union and Eastern Europe, Salvador Samayoa, former education minister and FPL ideologue, claimed that "with the change in the correlation of forces . . . we are in a better position to apply military pressure" (ibid., 6 February). A similar attitude was taken by PRTC's Nidia Díaz, who claimed that "we believe the Soviet Union and other countries of the socialist bloc are seeking their own formulas for change, and we will have to seek our own formulas" (ibid., 27 September). In all cases the new FMLN ideological claim was that the group is not communist, and never was; it cares not about the collapse of East European regimes because they have no local relevance and pursues "democratic" goals in any case rather than class warfare as defined in Havana, Moscow, or *Das Kapital*.

Leonel González claimed that because communism is no longer a threat the United States cannot claim that the FMLN is a threat (ibid., 19 March).

While PCES leader Handal seems to have been the main supporter of negotiations, followed by Cienfuegos (*FBIS-LAT*, 24 May), the military found it plausible to define intra-FMLN conflicts as leading to a Villalobos contract on Handal. It is also clear that the Handal-Cienfuegos opinion attracted some longtime supporters of other FMLN groups, like Belgian ex-priest Rogelio Ponceel of the ERP (*NYT*, 14 August).

Negotiations. According to the United Nations, U.N. negotiator Alvaro de Soto, brother of the famous Peruvian economist Hernando de Soto, was to be the mediator between the FMLN and the Cristiani government. The first and most direct negotiations between the FMLN and the Cristiani government took place in Caracas on 21 May, followed by a meeting in San José, Costa Rica, 20–26 July. The joint San José statement only claimed support for human rights, as defined by the Salvadoran legal code, and a pledge to eliminate torture, illegal arrests, and similar violations of human rights. In fact, however, the statement was intended to be (and was) a dead letter. (Text in *FBIS-LAT*, 27 July.) Neither the army—which consistently rejected the main FMLN demand to purge itself—nor the guerrillas ever took the San José statement seriously. That was the end of the much-talked-about "process" of negotiations.

In terms of propaganda, the FMLN continued to accuse the military as an institution and the Cristiani government as the government legally responsible for the killing of the Jesuit priests in 1989. In this, it seemed to have great success. The U.S. Congress limited U.S. aid to El Salvador, and U.S. public opinion seemed to be on the side of "peace," the goal of the guerrillas. However, on 2 January 1991, two wounded U.S. military advisers were killed by FMLN guerrillas after their helicopter was shot down. After denying the fact (*FBIS-LAT*, 4 January), rejecting U.S. accusations and local witnesses, the FMLN was forced to accept the idea of murder of noncombatants, and to promise a trial of those involved (ibid., 8 January). All the propaganda gains following the murder of the Jesuits were lost, and the Bush administration renewed full military aid to El Salvador—a serious setback for the FMLN.

Foreign Affairs. Clearly the hardest blow to the FMLN in terms of external and ideological affairs was the spectacular electoral defeat of the Sandinistas in Nicaragua. Like almost everyone, the FMLN expected a clear Sandinista victory, and on 21 February the FMLN sent a message to the FSLN hailing the coming victory as a triumph of "momentous, historic importance" for Latin America. (*FBIS-LAT*, 22 February.)

Michael S. Radu
Foreign Policy Research Institute

Grenada

Population. 84,135
Party. Maurice Bishop Patriotic Movement (MBPM)
Founded. 27 May 1984
Membership. 300 (mostly former members of the New Jewel Movement [NJM] and People's Revolutionary Government [PRG])
General Secretary. Dr. Terrence Marryshow (age 38, medical doctor)

Last Congress. May 1988
Last Election. 13 March 1990, 1.0 percent, no representatives
Publication. *Indies Times* (weekly)

The disintegration of the Soviet empire during 1990 had an impact on Grenada's small MBPM, as MBPM leader Dr. Marryshow moved the party away from its advocacy of the Cuban economic and political model and assumed a more social democratic political platform.

The MBPM's credibility was badly damaged by its poor showing in Grenada's 13 March general elections—deliberately chosen to coincide with the 11th anniversary of the island's Marxist coup d'état. Although the MBPM had announced that it would contest all fifteen of Grenada's parliamentary seats, it was able to field only six candidates—all of whom lost by substantial margins—and received less than 1 percent of the vote. A center-right coalition led by Prime Minister Nicholas Brathwaite formed the new Grenada government.

Marryshow had earlier expressed his deep disappointment at the Sandinista defeat in the Nicaraguan elections, which were held only two weeks before the Grenada polling. Deeming the results "a tremendous blow for the progressive forces of the region," Marryshow called for a meeting of leftist leaders in Latin America and the Caribbean to assess the major political changes taking place globally. (Bridgetown, CANA, 27 February.)

Influenced by the democratic changes in Eastern Europe, Marryshow had announced before Grenada's elections that the MBPM would advocate a mixed economic model of development. Although the state sector would play a dominant role, any future MBPM government would increase the island's tourism budget and would prefer that the private sector built and operated hotels. Marryshow stated that there would be no confiscation of private lands, as was the case during Grenada's rule by the PRG, and that the MBPM would offer incentives to owners of idle agricultural lands to bring them into production. (Bridgetown, CANA, 6 February.)

In a further indication of a more moderate trend for the left in the Caribbean, Marryshow and other MBPM officials were closely involved in persuading the Cuban government to grant diplomatic recognition to Grenadian prime minister Brathwaite and his government following the 13 March elections (Bridgetown, CANA, 24 April). Marryshow is reported to be among those who have formed close ties with reformist members of the Cuban government in anticipation of political change in Havana.

Timothy Ashby
Edinburgh, Scotland

Guadeloupe

Population. 342,175 (*World Fact Book*), 386,000 (French census)
Party. Communist Party of Guadeloupe (Parti Communiste Guadeloupéen; PCG)
Founded. 1944 as section of the French Communist Party (PCF), 1958 as independent party
Membership. 3,000 (estimated)
General Secretary. Christian Céleste
Politburo. 14 members: Henri Bangou; other members unknown
Central Committee. Christian Céleste (secretary)
Status. Legal
Last Congress. Ninth, 11–13 March 1988
Last Election. 24 April, 8 May 1988, president of France; 5 and 12 June 1988, French National Assembly, 1 of 2; 25 September, 2 October 1988, Guadeloupan General Council, 22 (members and allies; PCG's share, 10 of 22) of 42 seats
Auxiliary Organizations. Union of Guadeloupan Communist Youth (Union de la Jeunesse Communiste Guadeloupéenne; UJCG; Fred Sablon, general secretary), Union of Guadeloupan Women (Union des Femmes Guadeloupéennes; UFG), General Confederation of Guadeloupan Labor (CGTG)
Publications. *L'Etincelle* (PCG weekly), *Madras* (UFG monthly)

The PCG struggled to explain changes in Eastern Europe that led to the virtual disappearance of communist parties there. General Secretary Christian Céleste asserted that his party was healthy and strong—healthy because democratic and strong because of its membership and the fact that 7 out of 34 mayors, 21 out of 83 councillors, and 1 out of 2 members of the French Parliament were PCG.

In December a national conference of the party was held in the course of which members reaffirmed the program of the Ninth Congress, held in March 1988, proclaiming the goal of national independence with a Socialist orientation arrived at by democratic steps. PCG also participated in an all-Guadeloupe meeting, the Estates General of Guadeloupe, 19–22 July 1990. Its purpose was to discuss European Community (EC) integration in 1992. All groups and parties of the left were present; they concluded that Guadeloupe must be protected from complete integration with the EC. They said that efforts to integrate the various states of the Caribbean should be made and that Guadeloupe should negotiate a special relationship with the Europeans. Participants feared that the EC would make rules for Guadeloupe without Guadeloupan participation. It was noted, for example, that, beginning in 1993, rum from Guadeloupe and Martinique would not be protected from non-EC rum whereas Scotch whisky would be protected from U.S. bourbon.

A PCG delegation also traveled to Brussels for a Meeting of the Last European Colonies, which included the French Overseas Departments, the Portuguese Azores and the Spanish Canary Islands. Participants called for united action with respect to European integration. They wished for a special relationship with the EC that would take their particular problems into account.

The Popular Union for the Liberation of Guadeloupe held its Third Congress in March. The party, long denounced by Communists as petty nationalists, invited PCG attendance at the opening ceremony. Opposition to integration with the EC drew the former enemies together. Contributing to the sense of us versus them was the 1990 census report, which indicated an influx of Europeans. The increase was 40,000 from 1982 to a total of 386,000. A new phrase—genocide by substitution—was coined to dramatize the fears of 1992.

The PCG watched events in its former sister colony, Haiti. Max Bourjolly, one of the Haitian communist leaders, was expelled from Haiti at the beginning of the year and traveled to Guadeloupe. The PCG followed the elections of December in Haiti and denounced what appeared to have been efforts to thwart democratization there. The PCG issued its usual calls for solidarity with Cuba, and a delegation visited Havana.

The theme of the year, reiterated every week in the 46-year-old party newspaper, *L'Etincelle*, was that communism is not dead and that it must be reformed. Leaders were also concerned about Guadeloupan integration with Europe.

Brian Weinstein
Howard University

Guatemala

Population. 9,097,636

Major Marxist-Leninist Organizations

• Guatemalan Labor Party (Partido Guatemalteco de Trabajo, PGT)

Founded. 28 September 1949. The first Guatemalan communist party was created by the Comintern in 1922 and destroyed in 1932. On 29 September 1949 an illegal, new party was formed that became legal three years later under the present name, then became illegal again following the 1954 coup. The other PGT factions were established as follows: National Leadership Nucleus in 1978; PGT—6th of January in February 1988; OR in June 1987.

Membership. Unconfirmed estimates of 200–300 for all party factions

Factions and Leadership. PGT: Central Committee ("Camarilla") faction: Carlos Gonzáles (also general secretary of the Central Committee and head of the Political Commission); Elfidio Cano, Central Committee member; National Leadership Nucleus faction: Daniel Rios (supplanted in 1988 by José Manuel Díaz); new name PGT—6 de Enero (PGT—6th of January); main leader, José Manuel Díaz; Mario Sánchez, "in charge of general political questions"; membership unknown; no activities known in 1990; Revolutionary October (Octubre Revolucionario, OR) faction: main leader, a former EGP cadre, is known only as "Benedicto"; membership unknown; no known activities in 1990. Only the PGT—Central Committee faction is recognized by the Soviet Union and its allied communist parties.

Leading Body. PGT—Central Committee faction: Political Commission. The membership and size of the Political Commission are un-

known. The nature of the top structures of the other factions is also unknown.

Status. All illegal

Last Congress. PGT—Central Committee: Fourth, 1969; PGT—6 de Enero: First, 1988

Auxiliary Organizations. Autonomous Federation of the Guatemalan Trade Unions (FASGUA), Patriotic Youth of Labor (JPT)

Publications. PGT—Central Committee: *Verdad* (irregular, published abroad); OR: *Opinión Pública*

• Rebel Armed Forces (Fuerzas Armadas Rebeldes, FAR)

Founded. 1962; broke with PGT in 1968; largely inactive 1968–1978

Membership. Probably fewer than 800

Leadership. Jorge Ismael Soto García (alias Pablo Monsanto)

Status. Illegal

Auxiliary Organization. National Committee of Trade Union Unity (CNUS), founded in 1976, now practically defunct

Publication. *Guerrillero* (irregular, published abroad)

• Armed People's Revolutionary Organization (Organización Revolucionaria del Pueblo en Armas, ORPA)

Founded. 1971; militarily active after 18 September 1979

Membership. 600 (estimated)

Leadership. Rodrigo Asturias Amado (alias Gaspar Illóm), Héctor Nuila

Status. Illegal

Auxiliary Organizations. Infiltrated FAR's CNUS and EGP's CUC (see below)

Publication. *Erupción* (irregular)

• Guerrilla Army of the Poor (Ejército Guerrillero de los Pobres, EGP)

Founded. January 1972 in Mexico; militarily active since 1979

Membership. 700 (estimated)

Leader. Rolando Morán (alias Ricardo Ramírez de León)

Auxiliary and Front Organizations. Peasant Unity Committee (CUC), January 31st Popular Front (FP-31), Vicente Menchú Revolutionary Christians, Robin García Revolutionary Student Front (FERG). Most are now inactive or defunct.

Publications. *Compañero* (irregular, published abroad; sometimes translated into English); *Informador Guerrillero* (irregular)

• National Revolutionary Unity of Guatemala (Unidad Nacional Revolucionaria de Guatemala, URNG), an umbrella organization founded 7 February 1982 that includes FAR, ORPA, EGP, and the National Leadership Nucleus faction of the PGT. The URNG has never successfully unified the insurgent organizations, all of which continue to operate autonomously. The guerrillas' respective fronts, allied minor civilian groups of exiles, and other sympathetic groups, such as the Guatemalan Church in Exile, are more or less united under the political umbrella of the Representación Unitaria de la Oposición Guatemalteca (RUOG). RUOG's most prominent figures are Francisco Villagrán Kramer, a former vice-president; Rigoberta Menchú; and Rolando Castillo. It operates largely out of Mexico, Nicaragua, and Cuba.

Publications. URNG distributes its propaganda through *Noticias de Guatemala* (in Mexico); its press agency is Cerigua, and its clandestine radio station, La Voz Popular de Guatemala.

The year 1990 has been a very successful one for the Guatemalan revolutionaries. The level of activities by URNG groups has steadily increased throughout the year, with the number of actions, combatants, geographical scope of operations, and casualties inflicted on the armed forces higher and wider than at any time since 1983. At the same time, in the political realm the insurgent umbrella organization has obtained significant successes and greater legitimacy, if not popular support, than at any time since the beginning of guerrilla activities in 1962.

Military Activities. In January the then minister of defense, Héctor Gramajo, claimed that the guerrillas have been "decimated" and that the only ones left are "Cubans" (*FBIS-LAT*, 19 January). At the same time Rolando Morán claimed that, after the major army offensives of 1987 and 1988, the guerrillas had in fact come out strengthened, "expanded geographically, extending their influence, and... were now moving to the periphery of the major urban areas" (ibid.). Both claims are exaggerated, but the development in the field tended to suggest that Morán was closer to reality.

Although it is still unclear to what extent URNG groups have established actual tactical, let alone strategic, military cooperation, FAR, ORPA, and the EGP still retain their distinctive organization, and the PGT is a marginal element in military terms.

In terms of coordination, on 22 January, the eighteenth anniversary of the EGP, that group attacked army garrisons in its traditional area of operations the Quiche department and FAR engaged in combat in its stronghold in Peten, where it claimed to have destroyed a military plane. (Ibid., 23 January.) Conversely, in a campaign commemorating the 7 February 8th anniversary of URNG and 27th anniversary of FAR, again EGP and FAR coordinated their attacks in Quiche and Peten (ibid., 9 February); attacks against the Panamerican Highway and around the southwestern city of Escuintla may have been undertaken by ORPA (*Latin America Weekly Report*, 1 March). The latter attack apparently engaged large enough guerrilla units to warrant air attacks by the military.

In March, only days before the first meeting between URNG and government representatives in Norway, a number of bombs exploded in the capital and fighting took place in Peten, San Marcos, and Guatemala departments. In San Marcos an attack against the residence of the departmental governor resulted in casualties. (Ibid., 27 March.)

By the end of March the situation was dangerous enough for the conservative National Liberation Movement (Movimiento de Liberación Nacional, MLN) to accuse the government of "complacent passivity" and to claim that "the guerrillas are advancing at such a pace that they may halt the electoral process, either by seizing power, or by provoking a coup d'état" (*Latin America Weekly Report*, 30 March). On 29 March the army admitted that five men had been killed and two wounded by ORPA in San Marcos (*FBIS-LAT*, 30 March); at the same time three more soldiers were killed and two wounded in Solola, again by ORPA (ibid., 11 April). ORPA was also responsible for the killing of three policemen on 16 May, whereas the EGP killed nine soldiers in Huehuetenango on 24 May (ibid., 25 May). Toward the end of that month URNG was active in fourteen departments, including the capital and areas around it, and the army increased its estimates on guerrilla strength by almost a third compared to 1988, to 1,005; independent estimates range between 1,500 and 2,500 full-time combatants (*NYT*, 3 June). Illóm, however, claimed that there were between 3,500 and 4,000 combatants in URNG ranks (*FBIS-LAT*, 15 June).

On 2 August the military seized a large cache of weapons in Escuintla, including modern communication equipment (a cellular phone, for instance), explosives, and ammunition (*FBIS-LAT*, 6 August). At the end of that month the insurgents claimed that since January they had inflicted 1,633 casualties on the army, 110 in August alone (ibid., 31 August), an exaggerated claim. The military activities declined toward the end of the year, probably as a result of the rebels' promise not to interfere with the November elections.

Despite the increase in the pace of fighting, it is far from clear that the guerrillas were anywhere near a breakthrough. In fact, reports throughout the year tended to suggest that the URNG recruitment pool was steadily diminishing as more and more displaced Indians in Quiche (and some refugees in Mexico), who used to live under rebel control, were now surrendering to the army. (*Latinamerica Press*, 19 April; *CSM*, 4 September.) The relationship between the four groups that make up the URNG was not totally clear, but certain developments seemed obvious. The first is that the PGT, although now a full-fledged URNG member, was still not relevant militarily; indeed, URNG statements were always signed by Commanders Illóm, Morán, and Monsanto (an indication of their military activism) and by Comrade Carlos González. Furthermore, not a single incident of violence could reasonably be attributed to the PGT in all of 1990. Although the level of military coordination among the three major URNG groups increased in 1990, their geographical areas of operations were still jealously separated along the usual lines: ORPA in Solola, San Marcos, and the southwest; EGP in Quiche, Huehuetenango, and neighboring departments; and FAR in Peten, Alta, and Baja Verapaz.

Yet another important development of 1990 was the growing relationship between the URNG and the drug traffickers. Guatemala has not only become a major heroin and marijuana producer and exporter, but Colombian cocaine traffickers are using its territory. Significantly, most of the poppies are grown in remote mountain areas of Quiche and the Verapazes, guerrilla-controlled or -influenced areas. (*NYT*, 3 June.) Such a source of income, as well as suspected massive Sandinista supplies of weapons before the new Managua government took over, may well explain the obvious improvement in URNG equipment, supplies, and combat capabilities.

Political Developments and Negotiations. Steadily, without making any serious compromises, the URNG succeeded in becoming an accepted and legitimate political actor on the Guatemalan scene, despite the democratic process in the country, which culminated with the November congressional and first-round presidential elections. With each negotiation round the URNG became a more accepted, acceptable, and "normal" political interlocutor on the legal political scene of Guatemala. In accordance with the provisions of the Esquipulas accords, which the URNG implicitly rejected when it refused to obey the San Isidro declaration (see below), a first meeting between the guerrillas, their fronts, and representatives of the government and the legal opposition took place in Oslo, Norway, between 27 and 30 March. The delegation of the National Reconciliation Commission (CRN), the legal/government delegation, was led by Jorge Elias Serrano, who became the new president of Guatemala after the second round of elections in January 1991. The URNG delegation was led by URNG front leaders, including Luis Becker Guzmán and Francisco Villagrán. (*FBIS-LAT*, 2 April.) The meeting resulted in an agreement to meet again, this time with major representatives present.

In May the CRN delegation was broadened, at Serrano Elias's suggestion, to include representatives of all major political parties in the country and the leaders of the URNG. As a result, the Madrid meetings of 27 May–1 June between the two sides included major leaders such as Elias Serrano, Mario Sandoval Alarcon of the MLN, and Mario Solorzano of the Democratic Socialist party on the official side and Illóm, Monsanto, González, and Miguel Ángel Sandoval, Rolando Morán's representative. (*FBIS-LAT*, 11 June.) The agreement between the political parties and the URNG groups and their fronts provided for political and legislative reforms, reconciliation, respect for human rights, respect for the rule of law, an (undefined) peaceful solution to the civil strife in the country, and a promise by the URNG not to interfere with the electoral process. (Text in *FBIS-LAT*, 4 June.)

Neither the guerrillas nor the military seem to have taken the Madrid meetings seriously. Indeed, Illóm rejected the idea of the guerrillas' becoming ordinary political parties or at least not until there had been a radical purge of the military, the dismantling of the army's main counterinsurgency instrument (the civilian self-defense patrols), and revolutionary economic and political reforms (*FBIS-LAT*, 15 June). The military, however, claimed to see the Madrid discussions as the path toward a "Colombian" solution in which the insurgents would lay down their weapons and become political parties (interview with Defense Minister General Juan Leonel Bolaños Chávez, *FBIS-LAT*, 1 June). The army would also not entertain the notion of dismantling the civilian patrols, a key URNG demand, because, as military spokesman Colonel Isaacs Rodríguez stated, they were voluntary, legal, and justified (ibid., 2 July).

The collapse of the authority of the lame-duck Cerezo government as well as the URNG's increased legitimacy were demonstrated by meetings between influential legal groups in the country and the insurgents, all outside government policies. Thus 23–25 August a meeting took place in Ottawa between the URNG and representatives of the influential Coordinating Committee of Farming, Commercial, Industrial and Financial Associations (CACIF), Guatemala's main business group. (*FBIS-LAT*, 13 September.) On 29 September the URNG met representatives of the religious sector in Quito, Ecuador (ibid., 28 September). The latter meeting was important enough for the URNG to be represented by Illóm, González, Monsanto and Guzmán (ibid.). Finally, CNR members, again including Elias Serrano, met URNG representatives in Atlixco, Mexico, 27–29 October under the mediating of Bishop Arnulfo Quesada, once again with the goal of arranging direct talks between the incoming government and the URNG.

Despite the flurry of negotiations, meetings, and statements by guerrillas and official or legal representatives from Guatemala City, the outlook for a peaceful solution to the civil conflict remains unclear. Jorge Elias Serrano, the new president elected in the second round of presidential elections on 6 January, was heavily involved in talks with the insurgents, but he was also elected because of his anticommunism, law-and-order stance, and association with former President Efraín Rios Montt, the person that nearly obliterated the guerrillas in 1983–1984.

Foreign Relations. As far as the guerrillas' external connections are concerned, it is clear that their long-standing cooperation and identity of views with the Salvadoran Farabundo Martí National Liberation Front (FMLN) were strengthened during the year and their similarly close ties to the Sandinistas continued. Thus, at the end of December 1989 the URNG rejected the Central American presidents' San Isidro declaration, which condemned them and the FMLN for continuing their military activities; stated that they "fully support the struggle of the fraternal Salvadoran people, led by their vanguard, the FMLN"; and accused the Salvadoran and Guatemalan armies of "state terrorism." (Guatemala City, *El Grafico*, 29 December 1989.) Like the FMLN and various Honduran revolutionary groups, the URNG denied that the collapse of Eastern Europe had anything to do with their own legitimacy because, as Hector Nuila put it, the goal of the insurgents in Guatemala is to establish an original democracy and never to depend on foreign support, ideological influence, or control (*FBIS-LAT*, 3 June).

Michael S. Radu
Foreign Policy Research Institute

Guyana

Population. 764,649

Parties. People's Progressive Party (PPP); Working People's Alliance (WPA)

Founded. PPP: 1950; WPA: organized 1973, became formal party in 1979

Membership. PPP: 100 leaders and several hundred militants above non-Marxist rank and file (estimated); WPA: 17 leaders, with membership estimated in the hundreds

General Secretary. PPP: Cheddi Jagan, 73

Leadership. PPP, 9-member Secretariat elected August 1988: Cheddi Jagan, general secretary; Janet Jagan, executive secretary; Harry Persaud Nitka, organization secretary; Shree Chand, finance secretary; Clinton Collymore, information and publicity secretary; Feroze Mohamed, education secretary; Donald Ramotar, membership secretary; Clement Rohee, international secretary; Pariag Sukhai, mass organization secretary. WPA, 17-member collective leadership body announced May 1988: Eusi Kwayana, Rupert Roopnarine, Moses Bhagwan, Andaiye, Clive Thomas, Karen De Souza, Wazir Mohamed, Tacuma Ogunseye, Josh Ramsammy, Nigel Westmass, Ameer Mohamed, Stanley Humphrey, Bissoon Rajkumar, Danuta Radzik, Eric La Rose, Kassim Kamaludin, Vanda Radzik.

Status. Legal

Last Congress. PPP: Twenty-third, 30 July–1 August 1988

Last Election. 9 December 1985. PPP 45,926 votes, 16.84 percent, 8 of 53 seats in National Assembly. WPA: 4,176 votes, 1 seat in National Assembly

Auxiliary Organizations. PPP: Progressive Youth Organization (PYO), Women's Progressive Organization (WPO), Guyana Agricultural Workers' Union (GAWU)

Publications. PPP: *Mirror* (weekly), *Newsletter* (monthly), *Interior Special* (monthly), *Thunder* (quarterly); WPA: *Dayclean* and *Open Word* (weeklies)

Under increased international and domestic pressure, President Hugh Desmond Hoyte of the ruling People's National Congress (PNC) agreed to significant electoral reform in 1990, opening the possibility of the first relatively free election in Guyana since the PNC came to power in 1964. However, the unstable alliance between the PPP and the Social Democratic WPA (the two main opposition parties) and two smaller parties fell apart in the fall, leaving the PNC with a slight edge in the run-up to the election constitutionally due by 2 May 1991.

Despite initiating an economic liberalization program in 1988 as prescribed by the International Monetary Fund, the cash-starved Hoyte government continued to have trouble securing Western assistance, particularly from the United States. Although Canada and the United Kingdom had provided some support, Washington made it clear in 1990 that significant economic assistance would depend on political reform.

In February, the White House made public a message sent by President Bush to President Hoyte expressing the hope that the upcoming election would "reflect the democratic values shared by both our peoples" (*Caribbean Insight*, April). In March, Sally Cowal, deputy assistant secretary of state for inter-American affairs, reinforced the message after meeting with Hoyte in Guyana, stating at a press conference that she had received "every indication" the Hoyte administration was "very interested in having an open and free election" (ibid.).

At the same time, economic relations with Guyana's traditional allies in Eastern Europe and among Third World radical states continued to deteriorate. In September, Soviet ambassador to Guyana Mikhail Sobolev acknowledged that trade volume between the two countries was "practically nil because of the difficult financial and economic situation in both countries" and described 1990 as "a very unfortunate year" in Guyana-Soviet economic relations (CANA, 8 September; *FBIS-LAT*, 11 September).

In April, Guyanese foreign minister Rashleigh Jackson returned from Beijing with a disappointing US$6 million line of credit and two small loan agreements (*Caribbean Insight*, April). In June, the friendly rhetoric surrounding the four-day visit to Guyana by Cuban foreign minister Isidoro Malmierca could not disguise the fact that economic relations between the two strapped countries had become negligible (CANA, 13 June; *FBIS-LAT*, 14 June).

Before 1990, Hoyte had been able to fend off domestic pressure for a political opening, primarily because of divisions within the opposition. Following the fraudulent election of December 1985, the PPP, the WPA, and three small centrist parties—the Democratic Labor Movement (DLM), the National Democratic Front (NDF), and the People's Democratic Movement (PDM)—had allied in the Patriotic Coalition for Democracy (PCD) to press for electoral reform. But the PCD was weakened by constant internal squabbling (the PDM eventually dropped out), and Hoyte adroitly played the parties against each other. The PCD was unable even to agree on a coalition spokesperson until 1990.

In January 1990, however, an unprecedented civic movement for electoral reform was started independent of the PCD. The Guyanese Action for Reform and Democracy (GUARD), an initiative of the well-respected Guyanese Human Rights Association (GHRA), was backed by the Catholic and Anglican churches, independent labor unions and media, and business and professional groups. The GUARD pressed the government for an independent electoral commission, new voter registration rolls, vote counting at polling stations, and international monitoring. By midyear, the GUARD was attracting thousands of people to weekly rallies, the largest opposition gatherings ever under PNC rule.

At the end of the summer, Hoyte began making concessions. He invited electoral observer missions from the British Commonwealth and the Council of Freely Elected Heads of Government led by former U.S. President Jimmy Carter. Then, during a visit by Carter in October, Hoyte conceded on two more of the opposition's main demands—vote counting at polling places and a complete revision of the voter registration rolls. Hoyte also agreed to an independent electoral commission, although it was unclear how the PNC-dominated body would be reformed.

By the end of the year, however, Hoyte was angling to delay elections beyond May 1991. In December, he announced that because of the time necessary for conducting house-to-house voter registration, the life of the Parliament would be extended for at least two months beyond February 1991, with a new date for elections to be announced at some point early in 1991 (CANA, 19 December; *FBIS-LAT*, 21 December).

Hoyte had been encouraged when the PPP, the WPA, and the GUARD failed in the fall to unite around a single candidate. A divided opposition was to the PNC's advantage because the constitution, installed by the PNC in 1980, requires only that a candidate receive a plurality of the vote to be elected president. Nonetheless, Hoyte apparently wanted time to parlay his commitment to electoral reform into increased Western economic aid.

Despite Hoyte's recent liberalization measures, the economy had shown few signs of recovering from more than two decades of corrupt, inefficient socialism imposed by the PNC during the rule of the late Forbes Burnham (1964–85). Guyana remained one of the poorest countries in the Western Hemisphere, and Hoyte seemed reluctant to hold elections until his government secured the international aid necessary to convince the electorate that improvement under the PNC was possible.

PPP Ideology. The collapse of the Eastern bloc in 1989 and the internal changes in the USSR under Mikhail Gorbachev accentuated the traditional contradiction between the PPP's adherence to Marxism-Leninism and its advocacy of free elections at home. By the end of 1990, however, PPP leader Cheddi Jagan, gearing for the possibility of winning a free election in the coming year, was espousing private enterprise and the need for foreign investment to U.S. journalists and visiting delegations.

At the end of 1989, Jagan, founder and longtime PPP general secretary, stated at a press conference in Guyana: "We are not renouncing our beliefs. Marxism-Leninism is a working class ideology. . . . We are wedded to liberating the working people." (CANA, 21 December 1989; *FBIS-LAT*, 27 December 1989.) In response to questions from reporters, however, he said the PPP stood "firmly behind the forces of democracy and renewal in socialist Europe as it has always stood for democracy in Latin America, Guyana and other parts of the world" (ibid.).

During an interview a year later in December 1990, Jagan evaded questions about the PPP's communist ideology, calling it "irrelevant" in the post-cold war period (*Miami Herald*, 8 December). He said that, if he were elected president, he would continue the current government's efforts to attract foreign investment and divest state-owned enterprises. When asked by a visiting delegation to Guyana about his ideology and that of Soviet president Gorbachev, Jagan stated, "I was Gorbachev before Gorbachev in the sense of what we were doing and not adopting the traditional dogmas of Marxist parties" (ibid.). Nonetheless, contradictions were still evident as Jagan maintained in another interview just a month before that the PPP would follow "a democratic, anti-imperialist, and socialist course" if he became president (CANA, 3 November; *FBIS-LAT*, 6 November).

PPP Domestic Activities. After Hoyte in mid-1990 conceded to international election monitoring, opening the possibility of a fair electoral process, the four parties of the PCD tried to agree on a joint list of candidates. In early September, after eight weeks of negotiations, talks were abandoned because the PPP, backed only by the DLM, insisted that Jagan be the PCD presidential candidate. The WPA had proposed Alton Chase, a trade unionist and constitutional lawyer who was also being promoted by the GUARD.

In early November, the PPP announced that it would go alone to the 1991 election, with Jagan as the presidential candidate. Evidently, Jagan was confident the PPP could defeat the PNC without the support of other parties. The political base of Jagan, who is of East Indian heritage, and the PPP have always been in the Indo-Guyanese community, which accounts for about half the population. The black-led PNC is based in the Afro-Guyanese sector, which accounts for slightly less than a third of the population.

Although Jagan publicly stated that race had been overplayed as a political issue, it was known that he expected the full support of the Indo-Guyanese community, which would make him the winner if the PNC did not commit fraud. But he might have been mistaken. First, the WPA is Guyana's only truly multiracial party and has made significant inroads in recent years among those in the Indo-Guyanese community turned off by the PPP's Marxist ideology. Second, the GUARD also was receiving substantial support among Indo-Guyanese and appeared at the end of 1990 to be preparing its own list of candidates. Finally, Indo-Guyanese entrepreneurs, who make up a large part of the business community, were the primary beneficiaries of the Hoyte government's efforts to woo the private sector.

PPP International Activities. The PPP's main international activity consisted of lobbying the Caribbean Community (CARICOM), the United Kingdom, Canada, and particularly the United States to press the Hoyte government to hold free elections. Jagan's annual trips to Eastern Europe and Third World radical states became a thing of the past in 1990.

In the United States, the PPP's primary targets were the White House, Congress, and the U.S. business and human rights communities. On 27 February, two days after the Nicaraguan elections, Jagan issued a statement calling on the Bush administration to "lend its tremendous influence and prestige" to ensure that the Nicaraguan electoral model endorsed by the United Nations and the Organization of American States be "made applicable to Guyana" (CANA, 27 February; *FBIS-LAT*, 28 February). PPP lobbying efforts on Capitol Hill and among U.S.-based human rights groups helped generate public statements in support of free elections from Sen. Edward Kennedy (D-Mass.) and from the Western Hemisphere Subcommittee of the U.S. House of Representatives' Foreign Relations Committee (*Miami Herald*, 26 March; *Latin American Regional Reports-Caribbean*, 30 August).

In March, the PPP released an open letter to Canadian prime minister Brian Mulroney just before Mulroney's arrival in Barbados for a joint Canada-CARICOM meeting. The PPP urged Mulroney to support free elections to "ensure the restoration of democracy in Guyana" (CANA, 15 March; *FBIS-LAT*, 16 March). In May, Jagan sent similar letters to the heads of state of the CARICOM nations (CANA, 14 May; *FBIS-LAT*, 15 May).

In December, Jagan traveled to the United States to lobby Bush administration officials and Congress personally, as well as the business community in Miami, where he addressed numerous groups, including the Republican party's Elephant Forum (*Miami Herald*, 8 December). A month earlier, the PPP confirmed a report in the state-owned *Guyana Chronicle* newspaper that the PPP had hired the Washington firm of Reichler, Applebaum and Wippman but stated the firm would only represent the PPP's interests in Washington, not run its electoral campaign as the report alleged (*Latin American Regional Reports-Caribbean*, 13 December).

WPA Domestic and International Activities. Despite the WPA's commitment to collective leadership, Eusi Kwaya remained the party's most visible leader. During the negotiations to find a consensus PCD candidate for president, Kwaya argued for the nomination of a political independent to deprive the PNC of taking advantage of the nagging divisions within the coalition. As a compromise, he said the WPA was prepared to accept a PPP candidate for prime minister, the second-ranking position in Guyana's system of government.

After the PPP announced in November that it was going alone to the election with Jagan as its presidential candidate, the WPA decided that it would run separately as well. However, the WPA did not name a presidential candidate, leaving open the possibility that it might form an electoral alliance with the GUARD. During the summer, the WPA and the GUARD had agreed that the first task of a new government would be to overhaul the 1980 constitution, which states in its preamble that Guyana "is in the course of transition from capitalism to socialism" (*Carib News*, 31 July).

At the end of 1990, when it became evident that Hoyte was seeking to delay the election beyond May 1991, the WPA provided the most outspoken criticism. It charged the government with stalling for political reasons and protested the government's apparent refusal to create an independent electoral commission as Hoyte had promised Jimmy Carter in October (*Latin American Regional Reports-Caribbean*, 13 December). The WPA also issued a statement warning the United States that it would be "premature" to lift restrictions on economic aid to Guyana until the government had made good on its commitments to electoral reform (*Carib News*, 30 October).

In early October, the WPA sent Wazir Mohamed as its representative to a Socialist International Council meeting in New York City. The WPA became a "consultive member" of the Socialist International (SI) in 1986. As a result of Mohamed's efforts, the SI issued a statement calling on the Hoyte government "to respect the wishes of the great majority of the citizens of Guyana to have international observers present at the upcoming elections in numbers agreed upon in negotiations between the government and the opposition" (CANA, 10 October; *FBIS-LAT*, 11 October). The SI also stated that it would study the possibility of sending an SI observer delegation to the upcoming election.

Douglas W. Payne
Freedom House, New York

Haiti

Population. 6,142,141
Party. Unified Party of Haitian Communists (Parti Unifié des Communistes Haïtiens; PUCH)
Founded. 1968
Membership. 350 (estimated)
General Secretary. René Théodore
Politburo. René Théodore, Max Bourjolly (in exile), Gérard Joseph (?)
Status. Legal since 1985; in the open in Haiti with the return of Théodore in March 1986
Last Congress. 1979 (first)
Last Election. 16 December 1990
Publications. Publications in French and Creole: account of First Congress in 1978; explanations about PUCH

In January 1990, during the waning weeks of the presidency of General Prosper Avril, Max Bourjolly, the PUCH's number-two person, was arrested and expelled along with a dozen others from different parties and movements. The ostensible reason was the assassination of an army colonel and Avril's imposition of a state of siege on the country. Party secretary René Théodore condemned the actions and accused Avril, with whom he had had a courteous relationship, of dictatorial motives. With access to Radio Métropole and other privately owned media, PUCH expressed its views. It also participated fully in the political process, which included an action by twelve parties in March to rid the country of Avril and putting up candidates for the 16 December elections.

René Théodore early declared himself a candidate for the presidency, but instead of running under the banner of the PUCH, he ran as a candidate of the Movement for National Reconciliation. Other parties also formed coalitions in an effort to attract a broad spectrum of voters. In addition to the presidency, candidates ran for 555 seats on local councils and 110 seats in the legislature (27 in the Senate and 83 in the Chamber of Deputies).

Communist candidates were seriously weakened by the last minute entry of populist priest Jean-Bertrand Aristide into the presidential campaign. Aristide, removed from his parish by church authorities, spoke the language of liberation theology and called for extreme actions against the former Duvalierist regime. After Aristide declared his candidacy, the number of registered voters swelled by over a million, to a total of 3.27 million or all the country's eligible voters. Former members of PUCH such as the intellectual Dr. Gérard Pierre-Charles, an economist, joined advisers of Aristide. Reportedly, Pierre-Charles believed the communist party had lost its revolutionary spirit.

Correctly sensing that the immensely popular Aristide would take away his constituency of urban poor and workers, René Théodore vigorously attacked him during electoral rallies. On one occasion he accused Aristide of complicity with the Tonton Macoute, which led to threats of violence against the communist leader. Police had to disperse a crowd demonstrating against the communist candidate. The electoral losses of the PUCH underscored its weakness in Haiti.

Several candidates, including Aristide, traveled outside Haiti during the campaign to solicit financial assistance. Théodore seemed to receive little overt outside support, even from communist parties in Martinique and Guadeloupe. Cuba followed events leading up to the election and broadcast interviews with Théodore. Less stridently critical of the United States than Aristide, the PUCH leader proposed annulment of Haiti's foreign debt.

Brian Weinstein
Howard University

Honduras

Population. 5,259,699

Major Marxist-Leninist Organizations

• Communist Party of Honduras (Partido Comunista de Honduras, PCH)
  Founded. 1927, dismantled by 1932, reestablished 1954

Membership. Probably fewer than 100 permanent cadres in the country
General Secretary. Rigoberto Padilla Rush
Status. Illegal
Last Congress. Fourth, January 1986
Publications. *Vanguardia Revolucionaria, Voz Popular* (both irregular, published abroad)

• Revolutionary Party of Central American Workers (Partido Revolucionario de los Trabajadores de Centro America, PRTC)
Founded. 1976 in Costa Rica as Honduran branch of regional party, became independent in 1979.
Membership. Probably fewer than 100 cadres
Leader. Wilfredo Gallardo Museli
Status. Illegal

• Morazanist Front for the Liberation of Honduras (Frente Morazanista para la Liberación de Honduras, FMLH) The name of the group may be Morazanist Patriotic Front (Frente Patriótico Morazanista, FPM).
Founded. 1969 claimed, but inactive until 1980
Membership. Probably fewer than 100
Leadership. Gustavo Garcia España, Juan José Baca Núñez
Status. Illegal

• Lorenzo Zelaya Popular Revolutionary Forces (Fuerzas Populares Revolucionarias Lorenzo Zelaya, FPR-LZ)
Founded. 1980. According to reliable confidential sources, the organization was established by Nicaraguan intelligence cadres.
Membership. 100 (estimated)
Status. Illegal
Publication. *Lorenzo Zelaya* (irregular, published in Mexico)

• Cinchoneros Popular Liberation Movement (Movimiento Popular de Liberación Cinchoneros, MPL-Cinchoneros)
Founded. 1981 as successor to the People's Revolutionary Union; established in 1980 as Honduran front for the Salvadoran Popular Liberation Forces.
Membership. Some 300
Status. Illegal

Umbrella Organization

• Unified Directorate of the Honduran Revolutionary Movement (Dirección Nacional Unificada del Movimiento Revolucionario Hondureño, DNU-MRH)
Founded. 1982, largely ineffective
Membership. All the above parties and the Socialist Action Party (Partido de Acción Socialista de Honduras; PASOH) led by Virgilio Carias, previously headquartered in Nicaragua and closely linked to PRTC.

The level of political violence in Honduras increased during the year despite the fall from power of the Sandinistas in Nicaragua, the disarming of the contras and their departure from Honduras, and a peaceful change of government. Part of the reason for the escalation could have been the fact that, as in El Salvador, the departing Sandinista regime provided the last and largest shipments of weapons to the Honduran revolutionary groups, particularly the Morazanistas and the Cinchoneros. Another and probably more important explanation was the growing level of activities by the Salvadoran Farabundo Martí National Liberation Front (FMLN) in Honduran territory and, more generally, the continuous spillover of the Salvadoran conflict across the border. Finally, there seemed to be a growing level of ideological confusion, debate, and conflict within the already precarious umbrella group, the DNU-MRH.

This last point is made evident by the developments within two DNU-MRH groups—the PCH and the Morazanistas. In the *World Marxist Review*, PCH Central Committee member Randolfo Banegas admitted that "the mood of the popular masses in Honduras...is increasingly influenced by the situation in neighboring countries—Nicaragua, El Salvador, Guatemala—because sympathy for, or hostility towards certain forces in these countries is polarizing Honduran society." (*WMR*, February.) As for the situation inside the country itself, Banegas called for the broadest possible alliance of social forces, including church and army elements, behind a program including the elimination of U.S. military and contra presence, agrarian reform, state subsidies and price controls, a purge of the army and police, and "ideological and political pluralism" (ibid.). As for relations with other revolutionary groups—presumably those under the DNU-MRH umbrella—he rejected accusations that his party has "hegemonic pretensions," as well as the opposite claim—that by its very membership in the DNU-MRH, the party would lose its identity (ibid.). However, while calling for more "sensitivity" on the part of the PCH for the diversity of views within the coalition, he stressed the danger of the party being infected with "petty-bourgeois and other ideas" and clearly came down on the side of those demanding total independence for the party (ibid.).

The ambiguity—or confusion—in the ranks of the PCH was further demonstrated at the Havana meeting in late March, which included, in addition to the Cubans and the PCH, delegates from the communist parties of El Salvador, Costa Rica, and the Dominican Republic. In the "Open Letter to the Revolutionary and Progressive Forces of Latin America and the Caribbean" published at the end of the meeting, the participants claimed that the world faced the concomitant crisis of the "world capitalist system" and "the Socialist models, which turned bureaucratic, authoritarian and repressive." They said they supported *perestroika* and other similar processes" but also complained of a "worrying stagnation of anti-imperialism, of international-ism and of revolutionary positions." (*Latin America Weekly Report*, 10 May.) *Perestroika* had some negative aspects, they conceded, including the spawning of "Nazi-Fascist currents . . . and counter-revolutionary chauvinism," but the participants also stated that political progress involves "ideological, economic and religious pluralism" rather than sin-gle-party rule (ibid.).

The internal confusion and dissensions in the ranks of the PCH seem to have been replicated within the FMLH as well. On the one hand, on 8 May a faction led by Gustavo Garcia España announced from Managua that it was giving up armed struggle because "left-wing organizations espousing armed struggle have no place in Hondu-ras. Our people still believe in electoral processes." (*Latin America Weekly Report*, 24 May.) On the other hand, the same group, or at least its more radical faction, was one of the most active in terms of violence throughout the year, having been in-volved in the 31 March attack against a group of U.S. servicemen at Amarateca, wounding six, three of them critically (*Latin America Weekly Re-port*, 12 April; *FBIS-LAT*, 2 April). Furthermore, in December, the FMLH was involved in a cam-paign of bombings in Tegucigalpa and San Pedro Sula. Two FPM cadres—Baca Nuñez, training sec-retary of the Union of Workers in the Beverage and Related Industries, and Marco Tulio Funes Du-arte—were arrested as they were planting a bomb in a Tegucigalpa mall. (*FBIS-LAT*, 26 December.) Baca Nuñez was a founder of the FPM organization and also a PCH member (ibid., 27 December).

An FPM statement released a few days before the capture of the two militants justified the group's violence as a legitimate protest against imperialism and the government's economic policies. The state-ment went on to claim that "we . . . just like Jesus Christ and our supreme commander Jose Francisco Morazan are determined to struggle to improve the living conditions of the Honduran poor." (*FBIS-LAT*, 27 December.)

The other most active violent group was the Cinchoneros, longtime protégés of Nicaragua and, according to the Honduran military, based in Ma-nagua until its change of government. Indeed, docu-ments found on a captured member of the group, José Antonio Velasquez Vigil, clearly demonstrated Sandinista complicity. (*FBIS-LAT*, 18 January.) The Cinchoneros' most important action was the at-tempted bank robbery in El Zamorano on 15 Au-gust during which four soldiers, two civilians, and six terrorists were killed. According to the then chief of the armed forces, General Arnulfo Can-tarero López, two reasons for the increase in politi-cal violence in the country were the increase in drug trafficking, which allowed revolutionary groups to finance their operations, and the return of many leftists who had spent the last decade in Managua. (*Latin America Weekly Report*, 27 September.)

Yet another development mentioned by General Cantarero was the infiltration of the armed forces by leftist groups (ibid.). The seriousness of this prob-lem was demonstrated in June, when 36 noncom-missioned officers and privates of the elite Armored Cavalry Regiment in Las Tapias deserted, the largest such defection in years (*FBIS-LAT*, 15 Au-gust). Furthermore, army sources admitted that both the Cinchoneros and the Morazanistas had demonstrated good military skills "because they have been trained in Libya and Cuba" (ibid., 31 December).

Throughout the year the activities of the Salva-doran FMLN on Honduran territory continued una-bated, in cooperation with local radicals. Thus, on 10 April, a "logistical unit" of the FMLN was un-covered close to the Salvadoran border and a safe house discovered in Santa Rosa de Copan, leading to the capture of weapons, medical supplies, two Salvadorans, and a number of Hondurans. (Ibid., 11 April.) In May, another massive weapons cache was discovered in the village of Potrerillos, includ-ing many grenades, fuses, explosives, and rifles, and another FMLN member was arrested (ibid., 21 May). Finally, at the end of August, a French citizen was stopped on the Nicaraguan border on the way to

El Salvador after her car was found to contain mortars, ammunition, and FMLN military plans and documents (ibid., 31 August).

While the activities of both the local and the Salvadoran revolutionaries intensified during the year, the government of Honduras did not link them with the Soviet Union, as it has often done in the past. On the contrary, following the visit to Tegucigalpa of a Soviet commercial delegation in February, trade relations grew. (Ibid., 10 April.) In September, the mayor of San Pedro Sula visited Moscow and signed an agreement whereby the Soviets would install an electric trolley transportation system in his city (*Insight*, 17 September). Finally, following a New York meeting between President Rafael Leonardo Callejas and Eduard Shevardnadze, Honduras and the Soviet Union established diplomatic relations on 1 October (*FBIS-SOV*, 1 October).

Michael S. Radu
Foreign Policy Research Institute

Jamaica

Population. 2,441,396
Party. Workers' Party of Jamaica (WPJ)
Founded. 1978
Membership. 100 (estimated)
General Secretary. Dr. Trevor Munroe
Status. Legal
Last Congress. Fourth, 11–13 September 1988
Central Committee. 31 members (one-third women; one-third rural parishioners; one-third workers and small farmers)
Auxiliary Organization. University and Allied Workers' Union (UAWU)
Publication. *Struggle*

The People's National Party (PNP), headed by Michael Manley, reaffirmed its mandate by sweeping the 6 March local elections; the WPJ, continuing its focus on restructuring, did not participate.

Since his election in 1989, Michael Manley has not strayed from the mainstream agenda that allowed his PNP to defeat Edward Seaga's Jamaica Labor Party (JLP) and return to office after ten years. Manley, who was forced by illness to hand over the reins of power to Deputy Prime Minister P. J. Patterson for three months, focused on economic problems throughout 1990, reaching an agreement with the International Monetary Fund (IMF) early in the year. The once far-left leader did resume relations with Cuba—established by his government in 1972 but broken by Seaga on assuming office in 1980—but at a lower, nonresident ambassador level. At the end of the year, weekly charter flights between the two islands were also resumed after a ten-year hiatus. Manley showed no sign, however, of returning to the close relationship with Cuba that in the 1970s alarmed the United States and made his fellow citizens fear that Jamaica was becoming a Cuban surrogate. During a visit to Jamaica, a Soviet parliamentary delegation summed up the new Soviet philosophy toward the region, expressing a desire to cooperate in areas of mutual benefit but emphasizing it was not interested in imposing ideology or conduct on any nation. (Bridgetown, CANA, 27 April; *FBIS-LAT*, 30 April.)

Meanwhile, WPJ general secretary Trevor Munroe acknowledged that his party is reforming "to become more relevant," a move he claimed was in the works long before the sweeping changes occurred in Eastern Europe. In discussing the changing face of the left in the region, Munroe commented that he sees *perestroika* as "providing an opportunity to the region's left wing political parties to offer the electorate something new." (*Latin American Regional Reports: Caribbean*, 5 April.) He added that the Caribbean people "have had 300 years of experience with different types of capitalism [and] the present condition of the majority of our people is such that they would not consider the way of life we have as the way of life they desire" (ibid.). The WPJ leader further stated that "the challenge to the socialist and radical left is to revise, review, reform their program, their methods, in consultation with the people so a real alternative can emerge" (ibid.). To that end, the WPJ has abandoned its constitution and a number of centralized programs that are no longer appropriate in the current international economic and political reality, working toward becoming a "new patriotic, democratic and transformative organization" (Bridgetown, CANA, 24 February; *FBIS-LAT*, 27 February).

In March, in his role as president of the WPJ-associated University and Allied Workers' Union,

Munroe protested economic measures imposed by the PNP leadership and demanded that the "government reinstate free collective bargaining and get rid of IMF imposed wage guidelines which will further restrict the purchasing power of workers whose labor is key to the expansion of production." Failure of employers to heed these demands would have consequences, Munroe warned. (*Latin American Regional Reports: Caribbean*, 1 March.)

Continued government adherence to IMF-imposed measures could result in increased labor unrest but is unlikely to radically alter the political environment in the near term. The WPJ will therefore likely remain far behind the PNP and JLP on the political spectrum.

Alicia Tompkins
Hoover Institution

Martinique

Population. 359,800 (French census, *Justice*, 19 July), 340,381 (*World Fact Book*)
Party. Martinique Communist Party (Parti Communiste Martiniquais; PCM)
Founded. 1957
Membership. Less than 1,000
General Secretary. Armand Nicolas, 63, French citizen
Politburo. 3 members
Secretariat. 4 members
Central Committee. 33 members
Status. Legal
Last Congress. Ninth, 12–13 December 1988; Tenth planned for May 1991.
Last Elections. 24 April, 8 May 1988, president of France; 5 and 12 June 1988, French National Assembly, no seats; 25 September, 2 October 1988, Martinique General Council, 2 of 45
Auxiliary Organizations. General Confederation of Martiniquan Labor (CGTM); Martiniquan Union of Education Personnel (SMPE-CGTM); Union of Women of Martinique (Union des Femmes de la Martinique); Martiniquan Committee of Solidarity with the Peoples of the Caribbean and of Central America

Publications. *La Justice* (weekly newspaper)

Both the PCM and its labor union, CGTM, held congresses during the course of the year; the PCM held preliminary meetings to its Tenth Congress in December, and the CGTM, its Sixth Congress in June. In the course of the CGTM congress the labor movement split into two parts. Supporters of Combat Ouvrier, denounced as left wing or Trotskyite, disrupted the meetings and broke the organization into two.

More important for the Moscow-oriented PCM was explaining the changes in Eastern Europe, including the near disappearance of official communist parties. Armand Nicolas, general secretary of the party, told an audience that Marxism-Leninism was valid but that it had not been applied well in Eastern Europe. To draw the PCM closer to the people and to meet quickly any problems among the members, leaders instituted more democratic procedures at the local cell level. Open discussions and popular control over party elections would ensure support, in the leaders' views. The party program continued to emphasize one popularly elected assembly for the whole island instead of the present two. The PCM resolutely opposed Martinique's integration in the European Community (EC). An increase in the population from 315,000 in 1982 to 359,800 in 1990 led some to suspect that Europeans were already settling in the Caribbean and thus beginning to threaten the island's cultural distinctiveness.

In a 2 September meeting the PCM listed a five-point program, reaffirmed later at the Tenth Congress: (1) The association with Europe must be special and the result of negotiations, meaning that it must suit Martinique's needs. (2) Martinique land must be protected from speculation. (3) New jobs must be created. (4) Something must be done to prevent the influx of nonislanders; otherwise they might one day outnumber native Martinicans. (5) The present inequality of salaries, compared with metropolitan France, must be addressed.

On 14 December 1989 the European Parliament adopted the Program of Options Specific to the Distance and Insularity of the Overseas Departments (POSEIDOM), an ominous sign of future EC decision-making about Martinique, in the view of the communist party. This was one reason the PCM coordinated its stand on the Single European Act, which would integrate Europe and the overseas departments further with Guadeloupe during 1992.

A delegation traveled to Pointe-à-Pitre during the year.

PCM also cooperated with local Socialists and progressives in the election to the Regional Council in October. The Socialist party, the Progressive party of Martinique, and the PCM maintained their electoral Unity of the Democratic Left to ensure their strength in the election of the 41 members. As usual, the PPM was the strongest partner.

Municipal elections were also held in Macouba in June because the courts convicted PCM mayor Sévère Cerland of electoral fraud. Cerland lost the election, but litigation continued, as it usually does after local elections.

The PCM saluted efforts to bring democracy to Haiti. Members offered to help a visiting delegation from the newly formed National Confederation of Teachers of Haiti. The PCM newspaper, *La Justice*, which celebrated its 70th anniversary, denounced the military government until it gave up its power in March.

The party issued three new publications for the highly literate population. One, restricted to party members, was called *Le Militant*; its purpose is to encourage more democracy within the party by providing a forum for party members to express their opinions and suggestions. To inform the general public about party views about future relations with France and with the EC, the PCM published two booklets: *Rapport Ripert: Quelle Egalité Sociale? Quel Développement? Position du PCM et Nos Propositions* (Ripert Report [about relations with France]: What Social Equality? What Development? Positions of the PCM and our Programs) and *Refuser l'Intégration Européenne: Revendiquer l'Association et la Coopération* (Refusing European Integration: Demanding Association and Cooperation).

Brian Weinstein
Howard University

Mexico

Population. 87,870,154

Party. Partido Comunista Mexicano (PCM); during the 1980s, most Mexican Communists joined with other leftists to form a series of parties, most recently the Mexican Socialist Party (PMS), founded in 1987, which further broadened its base in 1989, when it became part of the broader leftist Democratic Revolution Party (PRD); some Mexican Communists continue to operate as the PCM.

Founded. PCM, 1919; PMS, November 1987; PRD, May 1989

Membership. PCM, unknown; PMS, 90,000; PRD, unknown

General Secretary. Juan Pablo Sainz Aguilar, of continuing PCM faction; Gilberto Rincón Gallardo and Pablo Gómez, of Communists, joined together in PMS and then PRD; noncommunist Cuauhtémoc Cárdenas, general coordinator of PRD

National Council. PRD, 100 members, 9 honorary members (*6 de Julio*, 30 November)

Status. All legal

Last Congress. PRD: First, 16–20 November 1990

Last Election. 11 November 1990, state representatives and municipalities in states of Mexico and Hidalgo.

Publications. *La Unidad* (PMS), ended May 1989; *6 de Julio, periódico de la revolución democrática* (PRD), a biweekly, commenced publication on 6 July 1989, editor, Gerardo Unzueta Lorenzana.

The majority of the left, including the PMS, threw in their lot with the PRD in 1989. Their rationale was simple. They believed that the political legitimacy of the PRI would continue to erode as the economic crises worsened. (*6 de Julio*, 20 December 1989.) At a certain point, the country would be ungovernable and the thoroughly discredited PRI would be swept into the dustbin of history. The symbolic rather than personal popularity of the son of Lázaro Cárdenas made the PRD the only choice of a desperate people.

Even before the year of the merger ended, there were a number of signs that the PRI might be able to rally under the unexpected political brilliance of President Carlos Salinas de Gortari or put together an alliance with the right-wing National Action Party (PAN) to share political power. Forced to act, the PRI leadership adopted an amazing degree of flexibility and demonstrated slight hesitation in dramatically changing its direction.

The strategy of the left formulated under the leadership of Cuauhtémoc Cárdenas relied on negative factors—a passive wait for economic collapse that would see power drop into its hands. PRD strategy thus allowed a frightened PRI to take aggressive steps to rescue the country and itself. Acting on the belief that the economic crises had precipitated the political problems, emphasis was placed on rapid recovery as well as a restructuring of the entire Mexican economic system.

By the end of 1990 it was clear that economic recovery was well under way and that an ambitious program to recast the entire economy had been outlined. The process has been called *Salinastroika*, defined aptly by the left as *perestroika* without *glasnost'*. In March a debt agreement with the United States reduced debt-servicing costs by $4 billion. Although modest, the agreement brought interest rates down to their lowest level since 1981. The unanticipated oil price increase helped also, and Mexico will probably close its books on 1990 with its trade in balance. Real wages increased in 1990, and although slight, was the first rise since 1982. In short the light at the end of a long and dark tunnel is now at least a strong glimmer.

The most important economic, social, and political event of the year was the rapid progress toward a free trade agreement with the United States. Movement toward its projected 1992 implementation required a dramatic break with the economic nationalism that has been a major feature of Mexican politics since the Revolution of 1910. In April, Mexico's trade secretary, Jaime Serra Puche, asserted that the country did not want to be part of a common market because it did not want to surrender an element of sovereignty, something a free trade agreement allegedly did not require. The extent of economic integration remains vague (*Latin American Regional Reports* [*LARR*], 10 May). In June, President Salinas de Gortari called on President George Bush to get talks moving on the agreement. It was his second visit to the United States in 1990 and his third since assuming office. On his return from Washington, President Salinas de Gortari dispatched his trade secretary to Canada and departed on a Pacific tour including Japan, Sin-

gapore, and Australia. Clearly the Mexican government had embarked on an aggressive trade offensive. (*Latin America Weekly Report*, 28 June.) Japan promised more investments and loans based on the possible elaboration of a future North American common market. The Mexican president visited Bolivia, Argentina, Uruguay, Brazil, Venezuela, and Honduras to stimulate bilateral economic ties as well as to indicate that Mexico had not turned its back on Latin America. (*LARR*, 1 November.) In the year 2000 the Mexican economy will be totally transformed and part of a wider international market.

The other part of the equation—reestablishing political stability and the dominance of the PRI—is entwined with economic restructuring and is every bit as Herculean a task. Holding onto political power while changing the system is a tricky business. The old political methods and the party machinery cannot be abandoned prematurely without a collapse of control. The PRD, meanwhile, hoping for that exact result, is attempting to put maximum pressure on the PRI by focusing publicity on PRI political practices both within Mexico and abroad, particularly in the United States and Europe. (*NYT*, 1 April.) Internally, the PRD has concentrated on municipal politics, an arena where the PRI is more likely to tolerate a degree of opposition activity, and within the chamber of deputies, where the publicity glare is sufficient to deter all but the most genteel anti-PRD tactics. On the municipal level, political violence is endemic. In Michoacán, members of the PRD kidnapped two PRI members during the installation ceremony of new mayors. The PRI mayor-elect of Irimbo and a state official were taken to the city hall, which had been seized earlier to prevent an alleged election fraud. (*FBIS-LAT*, 2 January.)

Meanwhile, the government has chosen to recognize a number of opposition victories. December municipal elections in Michoacán resulted in 59 PRD victories, and in Guerrero the PRD took 16 municipalities to the PRI's 22. In contrast, in the November election in Tlaxcala, the PRI conceded not one municipality to the opposition. (*LARR*, 18 January.) In Baja California Sur both the PRD and the right-wing PAN claimed fraud as the PRI claimed victory in municipal and legislative elections (*LARR*, 15 February).

Balancing off calculated concessions, the PRI has indulged in assassinations, disappearances, and intimidation. The PRD human rights commission listed 41 political murders, 13 of which occurred within the month of January 1990. Most of the murders occurred in Michoacán, Guerrero, Oaxaca, Morelos, and the capital itself. (*LARR*, 8 February.) The PRI denied involvement and called them coincidental deaths unrelated to politics. Police corruption, including that of the federal judicial police, is a major problem, although whether the police act in the interest of the government or not is a subject of debate. Demonstrations organized by the PRD in Acapulco and Ixtapa-Zihuatanejo, two important tourist centers, brought out the security forces, and, according to the PRD, one demonstrator died, eleven disappeared, and a number were injured. State authority insisted that airport security had been violated and that therefore they had to act against the demonstrators. Humberto Zazueta, head of the PRD human rights commission, claimed a rising number of violent incidents since Salinas de Gortari assumed office. Reprisals against the PRI resulted in the death of the PRI mayor of Turicato (Mich), and within days a clash with armed PRD members in Sixto Verde (Mich) caused another *priista* to lose his life. (*LARR*, 29 March.)

Mexico City's judicial police have been implicated in the intimidation and harassment of intellectuals seen as hostile to the government. Jorge Castañeda, a political supporter of Cuauhtémoc Cárdenas and son of a former foreign minister, had a death threat delivered through his secretary, who was apprehended by four armed men and told to deliver the message. Castañeda had criticized the government's economic and political policies in European and American publications and at numerous academic conferences in the United States. (*NYT*, 21 June.) President Salinas de Gortari subsequently telephoned Castañeda from Japan to assure him of protection. Political violence has enabled the PRD to claim the existence of an official policy to deny human rights. Such charges damaged the government internationally, and as a result the president established a National Commission on Human Rights in June just before he left on an official trip to Washington. (*Latinamerica Press*, 28 June.) Salinas de Gortari in fact has established a better human rights record than his predecessors: more than fourteen hundred political prisoners have been released in what has been called "a silent amnesty" (*Latinamerica Press*, 1 March).

PRI moves to change its corporate structure and reliance on sectors has been seized on by the PRD as an opportunity to develop a base within labor. Fidel Velázquez, secretary general of the Con-federación de Trabajadores de México (CTM)—the country's largest union and an important part of the PRI—has become an obstacle to economic restructuring. Don Fidel, now in his 90s, argues that sectors have constituted the backbone of the PRI and has threatened to withdraw from the party along with the CTM. (*LARR*, 23 August.) Earlier, a series of strikes embarrassed both the government and the CTM leadership. The Cerveceria Modelo brewery strike in Mexico City, involving a massive walkout of more than four thousand workers, and the strike at the Ford plant, according to the business newspaper *El Financiero*, indicated the breakdown of control over labor by Fidel Velázquez and the CTM. The CTM dissolved the striking unions and formed new ones. Strikers had nowhere to turn except to the PRD. (*NYT*, 8 April.)

A new electoral code opposed by the left passed both the Chamber of Deputies and the Senate, in part because of an agreement with the PAN and parties who had previously supported the PRD. Designed to make the structure more legitimate, it included two major features objected to by the PRD: control of the electoral machinery remains in government hands and, even more objectionable, a governability clause that automatically gives a party winning at least 35 percent of the vote a 51 percent margin in Congress. The PRD, however, did not present an alternative bill and only made a suggestion that Mexicans living abroad be allowed to vote. (*LARR*, 2 August.)

Salinas de Gortari criticized those that attacked the PRI efforts to reform. Without naming the leader of the PRD (Cuauhtémoc Cárdenas), he observed that the most critical were those who "when in positions of leadership contributed to its greatest vices," a comment that may indicate that the PRI is ready to make public details of Cárdenas's conduct as a former PRI governor of his home state of Michoacán. (*LARR*, 27 September.)

The extent that the left is forced to react to a political reality presented and formed by the ruling party is evident; moreover, their analytic formulation is oddly historical. For example, the umbrella group, the Patriotic Front (FP), which includes the PRD, PPS, PSD, and other minor groups, has resurrected Mexican nationalism as a major anti-establishment weapon. Modification of the state's petroleum monopoly (PEMEX) and the free trade agreement are portrayed as a sellout of national sovereignty. (*6 de Julio*, 13 January.) The PRI is denounced as a great obstacle to democracy because of its failure to live up to the Constitution of

1917 with its guarantee of effective suffrage. The left refers to the current government as a neo-Porfirian regime. (*6 de Julio*, 19 October.) (The opposition to the regime of Porfirio Díaz [1876–1911] made the same charge, although a different constitution, that of 1857, was being violated.) In the end the Porfiriato fell before the Revolution of 1910. All this indicates a tendency of the Mexican left to accept the romantic notion that history repeats itself and to cast Cuauhtémoc Cárdenas as a latter-day Francisco Madero, the "Apostle of Mexican Democracy."

In 1990 the PRD has been able to avoid splintering, although a minor number of defections have occurred. Holding Socialists, Communists, and populists together within the PRD has consumed a considerable amount of time and energy, including Cuauhtémoc Cárdenas's politically necessary trip to Cuba. Cárdenas carefully avoided any endorsement of Fidel while trying to appear somewhat sympathetic. (*Granma*, 16 September.)

The PRD newspaper *6 de Julio*, edited by Gerado Unzueta, formerly a top member of the communist party, mirrors the difficulty of spanning such a diverse constituency in its selection of articles. Circulation of the *6 de Julio* is said to be twenty thousand per issue. Financial problems continue to plague the newspaper, which has embarked on a program of selling shares to raise sufficient capital to continue publishing. Most of the advertising is placed by government agencies. (*6 de Julio*, 29 June.)

The First PRD Congress (16–20 November) drew 2,500 delegates reportedly representing 1,730,000 party members. Almost all top members of leading bodies of the communist party in its various transformations of the 1980s are among the one hundred members of the PRD National Council, whose president is Cuauhtémoc Cárdenas. Discussions at the congress reportedly centered on a document called the Political Proposal (Propuesta Política), which will provide a line of action leading to the 1994 presidential elections. The line of the proposal was developed by Cárdenas in his long speech to the inaugural assembly on 16 November. U.S. president George Bush's visit to Mexico during the conference drew repeated commentary from PRD members. According to *6 de Julio*, the PRD secretary of international relations, Gilberto Rincón Gallardo, a former top official of the communist party, and other PRD spokesmen charged that President Salinas was cooperating in Bush's "Initiative of the Americas," the objective of which is the "annexation of Mexico." (*6 de Julio*, 30 November.)

Among the 40 foreign organizations attending the conference as observers were the Palestine Liberation Organization and some social-democratic parties, but the vast majority were communist parties or Marxist guerrilla movements—including the Salvadoran Farabundo Martí National Liberation Front and the Guatemalan Unidad Nacional Revolucionara de Guatemala.

How to confront an extremely flexible PRI constitutes the major problem. Evidence of growing confidence within the PRI is indicated by the results of elections in the key state of Mexico. Elections on 11 November for state deputies and municipalities resulted in an announced 60 percent of the vote going to the PRI, a turnabout that is unbelievable. The PRD received only 15 percent. State elections in Hidalgo on the same date saw the PRI claim 81 of 84 municipalities. Earlier, on 28 October, in the state of Coahuila, the PRI won 36 of 38 municipalities. Manipulation of the vote seems undeniable, and the PRI itself admitted "some irregularities." PRI spokesman Maurico Valdes noted that the opposition only accepts elections when the PRI is defeated. Nevertheless, such "crushing success" raises questions about the fairness of the process. (*LARR*, 6 December.) These results indicate that the PRI believes that the worst is over, that Salinas de Gortari's program is working, and that therefore they can get away with claiming a larger share of electoral "victories" than in 1989. It also reflects the president's notion that a healthy economy and a better standard of living, brought about by dumping anti-Americanism, Mexican nationalism, and a state-directed economy, will enable the PRI to win fair elections. Pragmatic actions, or what Octavio Paz referred to as an end of fantasy, are hard to anticipate. The PRD reacts to a reality changed on a day-to-day basis by the government. As former Finance Minister Jesus Silva Herzog observed, Mexico is betting everything on the United States and private enterprise.

Colin M. MacLachlan
Tulane University

Nicaragua

Population. 3,722,683

Major Marxist-Leninist Organizations.

• Sandinista Front of National Liberation (Frente Sandinista de Liberación Nacional, FSLN)
Founded. 1961
Membership. 60,000 (statement by Luis Carrión, *Barricada*, 27 February)
National Directorate. 7 members: Daniel Ortega Saavedra, Víctor Tirado López, Tomás Borge Martínez, Bayardo Arce Castaño, Henry Ruíz Hernández, Jaime Wheelock Román, Luís Carrión Cruz
Executive Commission. 4 members: Daniel Ortega Saavedra (coordinator), Bayardo Arce Castaño (deputy coordinator), Tomás Borge Martínez, Jaime Wheelock Román
Main Party Organs. The Sandinista Assembly (105 members), is supposed to convene yearly. Routine party operations are under the control of 8 auxiliary departments: general affairs (René Núñez); organization (Lea Guido); agitation and propaganda (Dionisio Marenco); communication (Carlos Fernando Chamorro Barrios); political education (Vanessa Castro Cardenal); international affairs (Julio López Campos); finance (Plutarco Cornejo); studies of Sandinismo (Flor de Maria Monterrey).
Party-State Relationship. Until 25 April, the following top leaders of the FSLN were also in charge of the most important state institutions: Humberto Ortega Saavedra, minister of defense; Tomás Borge Martínez, minister of the interior; Víctor Tirado López, responsible for the labor movement and labor relations policies; Luís Carrión Cruz, minister of the economy; Henry Ruíz Hernández, minister of external cooperation; Jaime Wheelock Román, minister of agriculture and agrarian reform; Carlos Núñez Téllez, president of the National Assembly.
Status. Ruling party between 1980 and 1990; main opposition party since 25 April
Last Congress. FSLN Assembly, 18 February, 24 September 1989

Last Election. 25 February 1990. The FSLN won 38 seats out of 90 in the National Assembly; Daniel Ortega received 42 percent of the votes in the presidential election.
Auxiliary Organizations. FSLN activist membership estimated at between 12,000 and 16,000 (*La Prensa*, 27 October 1989); Sandinista Defense Committees (Comités de Defensa Sandinista, CDS), estimated membership, 11,000, led by Ajax Delgado; Luisa Amanda Espinosa Association of Nicaraguan Women (Asociación de Mujeres Nicaraguenses Luisa Amanda Espinosa, AMNLAE), led by Glenda Monterrey; Sandinista Workers Central (Central Sandinista de Trabajadores, CST), led by Lucio Méndez; Farmworkers Association (Asociación de Trabajadores del Campo, ATC), led by Edgardo García.
Front Organizations. Federation of Health Workers (Federación de Trabajadores de la Salud, FETSALUD), led by Gustavo Porras; National Union of Agricultural and Cattle Producers (Unión Nacional de Agricultores y Ganaderos, UNAG), led by Daniel Núñez; National Association of Teachers (Asociación Nacional de Educadores, ANDEN), led by Guillermo Martínez; National Union of Journalists (Unión Nacional de Periodistas, UPN), led by Lily Soto; National Council of Professional Associations "Heroes and Martyrs" (Consejo Nacional de Asociaciónes Profesionales "Heroes y Martires," CONAPRO); Union of Nicaraguan Writers (Unión Nicaraguense de Escritores, UNE), led by Michelle Najlis; National Union of Artists (Unión Nacional de Artistas Plásticos, UAP), led by Roger Pérez De La Rocha; Evangelical Commission for the Promotion of Social Responsibility (Comisión Evangélica de Promoción de la Responsabilidad Social, CEPRES), led by Miguel Ángel Casco (*Barricada*, 8 November 1989). Status Change: The auxiliary organization Sandinista Association of Cultural Workers (Asociación Sandinista de Trabajadores de la Cultura, ASTC) was renamed and became the front organization Institute for the Promotion of Culture (Instituto de Promoción Cultural, IPC), led by Rosario Murillo (*Barricada*, 2 February).
Publications. *Barricada* (party daily, circulation 120,000), *El Nuevo Diario* (government daily, 45,000), *Nicarahuac* (ideological journal), *Segovia* (army journal), *Bocay* (Interior Ministry monthly); all television stations and the two

major radio stations, Radio Sandino and La Voz de Nicaragua, are party-controlled and -owned.

- Socialist Party of Nicaragua (Partido Socialista de Nicaragua, PSN), oldest pro-Soviet communist party in the country

  Founded. 1937; first official congress, 3 July 1944

  Membership. 1,400 (estimated)

  General Secretary. Gustavo Tablada

  Political Commission. Luís Sánchez Sancho, Gustavo Tablada, Alejandro Solórzano, Roberto Guzmán, Adolfo Evertz, Juan Gaitán, José Luís Medina (elected by the plenums, which also elect the general secretary)

  Status. Part of the ruling coalition

  Last Congress. July 1989, 45th Anniversary Plenum

  Last Election. 25 February 1990; Sánchez and Tablada were elected deputies.

  Auxiliary Organizations. General Confederation of Workers—Independent (Confederación General de Trabajadores—Independiente, CGT-I), led by Alejandro Solórzano, 31,000 members (estimated), joined in November 1987 with the other three major independent labor union confederations (CUS, CTN-A, and CAUS) to form a coalition front, Permanent Congress of Workers (Congreso Permanente de los Trabajadores, CPT); Union of Construction Workers of Managua (Sindicato de Carpinteros, Albañiles, Armadores y Similares de Managua, SCAAS), led by Domingo Sánchez Salgado.

  Publication. *El Popular* (weekly, circulation ca. 7,000)

- Communist Party of Nicaragua (Partido Comunista de Nicaragua, PCN)

  Founded. 1970 as splinter of PSN

  Membership. 1,600 (estimated)

  General Secretary. Eli Altamirano Pérez

  Politburo. 7 members: Eli Altamirano Pérez, Ariel Bravo Lorio, Alan Zambrana Salmerón, Ángel Hernández Cerda, René Blandón Noguera, Manuel Pérez Estrada, Alejandro Gutiérrez Mayorga

  Status. Part of the ruling coalition

  Last Congress. June 1986, Second; December 1986, National Conference

  Last Election. 25 February 1990; Altamirano

  Auxiliary Organizations. Central for Trade Union Action and Unity (Central de Acción y Unidad Sindical, CAUS), led by Roberto Mor-

eno, 19,000 members (estimated); joined with the other three major independent labor confederations to form the coalition front, Permanent Congress of Workers (Congreso Permanente de los Trabajadores, CPT), in November 1987

  Publication. *Avance* (weekly, circulation ca. 20,000)

- Popular Action Movement—Marxist-Leninist (Movimiento de Acción Popular—Marxista-Leninista, MAP-ML); before 1989 called Nicaraguan Marxist-Leninist Party (Partido Marxista-Leninista de Nicaragua, PMLN)

  Founded. 1970 as a splinter of FSLN; expelled from FSLN in August 1972; after the 1979 revolution struggled for an independent political line until it adopted an ultraleft tactical support position toward the FSLN, with which it has a tacit alliance (*Barricada*, 8 September 1989).

  Membership. Unknown

  General Secretary. Isidoro Téllez

  Party Leaders. Fernando Malespín, Carlos Cuadra, Carlos Lucas

  Governing Body. Central Committee, last meeting, August 1985

  Status. Legal

  Last Election. 25 February 1990; received less than 1 percent of the vote.

  Auxiliary Organization. Workers' Front (Frente Obrero, FO), very small membership

  Publication. *Prensa Proletaria* (bimonthly)

Others

- The far-left Workers' Revolutionary Party (Partido Revolucionario de los Trabajadores, PRT) and the Central American Unionist Party (Partido Unionista CentroAmericano, PUCA) were founded in late 1984; neither was allowed to participate in the 1984 elections. Both had presidential and vice-presidential candidates running in the February 1990 elections: Bonifacio Miranda Bengoechea and Juan Carlos Leyton for the PRT, elected in their Fourth Congress (*Barricada*, 29 August 1989), Blanca Rojas Echaverry and Daniel Urcuyo Castrillo for PUCA. Other PRT leaders are René Tamariz and Leslie Pérez; other PUCA leaders include its founder, Alejandro Pérez Arevalo, and Giovanni D'Ciofalo. The PRT publishes a biweekly newspaper, *El Socialista*. The PRT had its origin in a small circle of radical students organized in the early 1970s as the Marxist Revolutionary League (Liga Marxista Revolucionaria, LMR), the Nicaraguan section of the Fourth International. The PRT had long criticized the FSLN for its alleged authoritarian-bureaucratic political line and for moving too slowly toward the consolidation of the dictatorship of the proletariat. In the electoral campaign, the PRT became a tactical ally of the FSLN, granting it legitimacy from the far left; the FSLN reciprocated by boosting this miniscule party of fewer than two dozen members to the proclaimed legitimacy and rank of the largest organization of the left with supposedly 2,585 members (*Barricada*, 29 August 1989). The PUCA, in contrast, according to its leader, Alejandro Baca Muñoz (*Barricada*, 10 February 1989), has publicly supported the FSLN, which has never challenged its obscure status as a miniscule organization. In the 25 February 1990 elections, none of these parties received more than 1 percent of the vote.

The 25 February elections were a turning point in the contemporary history of Nicaragua. The ruling FSLN, which was certain of victory and had used all the powers and resources of the state in their campaign against a disorganized and underfunded coalition of fourteen parties—the National Opposition Union (UNO)—lost decisively. Suddenly, after more than a decade of unchallenged rule, the Sandinistas found themselves out of power, although they retained a strong influence in the military, police, unions, and the media.

Party Affairs. Despite the election loss, Daniel Ortega had increased his control over the FSLN at the expense of other factions. To a large extent his reinforced position is due to the fact that his brother, Humberto, has retained the command of the military, although not his old job of defense minister, now assumed by President Violeta Chamorro. Although technically separated from the party and thus no longer a member of the National Directorate—a body now reduced to seven members following the death of Carlos Nuñez Tellez in Havana—Humberto Ortega still acts as a Sandinista. Thus, on 9 August he dismissed air force chief Javier Pichardo Ramirez (*Latin America Weekly Report*, 18 October), a close ally of Tomás Borge; that Borge's former instrument of power, the secret police, had now been incorporated in the army and was thus under Ortega's control further weakened the Borge faction of the party, to the advantage of Daniel Ortega.

The FSLN as a party was not mortally wounded by its electoral defeat. Not only did the army remain under FSLN control (although its numbers were drastically reduced by the Chamorro government), but numerous middle-level managers of state enterprises also retained their positions, as did most police and intelligence officers (*NYT*, 4 November). In addition, immediately after the elections and before the 25 April transfer of power, the Sandinista government did everything possible to reward its followers. Thus, on 10 March an amnesty law was passed by the lame-duck Sandinista majority in the assembly, with the pretext of reconciliation. Although the contras were included, as they would have been under the inevitable amnesty to be decreed by the new government, the main beneficiaries were Sandinista military men imprisoned for war crimes and officials jailed for common crimes, mainly theft. Even more significant, however, was what UNO described as "the sacking of the state." (*FBIS-LAT*, 12 March.) Indeed, the same lame-duck National Assembly transferred more than a thousand houses, formerly confiscated from opposition members, to Sandinista officials, including Miguel D'Escotto and Tomás Borge; cars, office equipment, printing presses, and more than three hundred former state enterprises were also transferred from the government to the FSLN (*Foreign Report*, 8 November). Similarly, radio transmission equipment was given to the 60 Sandinistas lucky enough to receive operating licenses for radio stations (ibid.). On assuming power, the new government found just $3 million in hard currency in the Central Bank—less than Somoza left to the Sandinistas in 1979 (ibid.).

The FSLN retained a strong, though diminishing influence among many of the unions, particularly those representing public sector workers, who were the most threatened by the new government's privatization policies. The newly established Front for Popular Struggle (FLP), a coalition of pro-Sandinista unions, had paralyzed the country through massive strikes in May and July, often using violence. (*Latin America Weekly Report*, 1 November.) When it called for a mass demonstration protesting the government's economic measures on 1 October, however, the FLP expected 60,000 participants; by its own admission, only 3,000 showed up (ibid.; *CSM*, 22 October).

On 12 June, the FSLN organized a meeting to assess the causes of the electoral defeat and reorganize the party. Tomás Borge admitted that the Sandinistas were arrogant, while Dora Maria Tellez stated that "verticalism created deafness in our leaders." (*Latinamerica Press*, 4 October).

The arrogance of the FSLN was demonstrated before the elections, when there was no hint that the party could lose and when it seemed that nothing less than an overwhelming victory would be satisfactory. *El Nuevo Diario* claimed that "the Sandinistas [had] conducted the most brilliant, pleasant and efficient political campaign in Central American history" (quoted in *FBIS-LAT*, 22 January). A few days before the elections, Bayardo Arce claimed that "we are still working toward the goal of 70 percent, and we believe that we can still hope to achieve that goal" (*FBIS-LAT*, 20 February). Not surprisingly, after the results were in, FSLN propaganda chief Dionisio Marenco stated, "I can't tell you what happened. . . . We didn't expect this at all." (*CSM*, 27 February.)

Mindful of their mistakes and miscalculations, the June meeting was devoted to changing the image of the FSLN. Among the changes approved were the direct vote for party leaders at all levels and the establishment of an ethics committee; there was almost no mention of Marxism, Leninism, or class struggle. Nevertheless, tensions continued to grow between the dogmatic revolutionaries, led by Tomás Borge, and the pragmatic followers of Daniel Ortega, with Ortega's the dominant faction. (*Latinamerica Press*, 4 October.)

The changes in the FSLN's ideological stance had started even before the elections. By the end of 1989 *Barricada* had rejected the association of FSLN with "Stalinist socialism, so easy to discredit"; defined the Sandinista version as one "aspiring to integrate free-market aspects with the possibility of planning" and claimed that the entire post-1979 period was one of Nicaraguan *perestroika* (*FBIS-LAT*, 9 February). Borge also claimed that "no one has yet realized that Nicaragua is the most important predecessor of Soviet perestroika. . . . A long time ago I told the Soviets that socialism should be modernized" (ibid., 16 February). Only a few days before, however, the same Tomás Borge, speaking in Havana about socialism's critics, stated that "those who laugh now will cry afterwards, when the final judgment of their arrogance is made" (ibid., 13 February). Similarly, Víctor Tirado defended Stalinism, claiming that "a strong state was needed. In those times it was understandable that the party should have to set itself up over civilian society" but concluded that "socialism

is not lost," although "each society thinks for itself and socialism is not exportable" (*FBIS-LAT*, 21 February).

Nor were all Sandinista leaders repentant after the elections, with Daniel Ortega promising to rule "from below" and Carrion referring to the UNO voters as "confused" (ibid., 1 March). The defeat of the Sandinistas was not limited to them alone; the entire Marxist left in Nicaragua was defeated. Of the eight parties that competed in elections (other than UNO and the FSLN), none obtained even 1 percent of the vote, including the Movement for Revolutionary Unity, the Revolutionary Workers' Party, the Marxist-Leninist People's Action Movement, and the Central American Unionist Party. The Socialist and communist parties, however, both renounced Marxism-Leninism and joined UNO, a shift that enabled them to be represented in the National Assembly for the first time.

Foreign Affairs. Not surprisingly, the most immediate and radical change in the wake of the Sandinistas' defeat was in the realm of foreign policy, with Nicaragua ceasing to be a supporter of revolutionary causes in Central America and elsewhere. Thus the year that started with the expulsion of twenty U.S. diplomats accused of espionage (*FBIS-LAT*, 4 January) ended with friendly relations with Washington, the lifting of the trade embargo, and renewed aid. The Sandinistas were vocal in their condemnation of U.S. intervention in Nicaragua and accused UNO of collusion for refusing to do the same.

Relations among the FSLN, communist countries, and leftist groups abroad continued as before, with the major exception of the Farabundo Martí National Liberation Front (FMLN). The FSLN campaign manager, Bayardo Arce, stated that the West German Greens provided 500,000 deutsche marks for the Sandinista electoral campaign and that "solidarity contributions" from foreign groups amounted to $3 million. (Ibid., 21 February.) The FMLN was the biggest loser abroad following the defeat of the Sandinistas. A few days before the vote it sent a message to the FSLN that read, "The Sandinista victory in the elections . . . will make it clear to the United States that it must respect the Nicaraguan people, lift the embargo and demobilize the contras." (Ibid., 22 February.) Before the elections, however, Daniel Ortega had promised to stop arming the FMLN (*NYT*, 2 February). One of the first measures taken by the Chamorro government was to close down the Salvadoran guerrillas' Managua headquarters.

Previous support for the Salvadoran revolutionaries came back to haunt the Sandinistas in January 1991. On 2 January the FMLN murdered two U.S. servicemen after their helicopter was shot down with a Soviet-made SAM-7 missile. Remnants of the missile, recovered by the Salvadoran military, led to the identification of its number; the U.S. State Department asked the Soviets for information, and Moscow confirmed that the weapon was part of a lot sent to Nicaragua in 1986. Humberto Ortega immediately came under attack of the UNO deputies, who asked for his resignation; however, he declared that he never ordered the transfer of the weapons, particularly since a Soviet condition for delivering them was precisely not to give them to a third party, and blamed a group of officers. (*FBIS-LAT*, 11 January.) Humberto Ortega also condemned the murder of the two Americans, blaming it on "extremists," and ordered the arrest of the officers involved, as well as eleven Salvadorans who had cooperated with them. Interestingly, one of those arrested, Odell Ortega, a former army major cashiered in August, claimed that "no one can condemn me, morally speaking, because I have been formed by revolutionary principles"; he assumed sole responsibility but did not explain why he accepted $11,500 for the sale. (Ibid., 4 January.)

Soviet involvement in the affair was strongly condemned by the Sandinistas and members of the extreme left. Daniel Ortega accused Moscow of caving in to U.S. pressures to take away the SAMs still in Salvadoran hands; Moisés Hassan described Soviet behavior as "unworthy," and Bonifacio Miranda, as "immoral, cynical and hypocritical." (Ibid., 14 January.) The FMLN denied that its leader, Joaquín Villalobos, was involved but implicitly admitted that it had received the weapons from Nicaragua, as an example of the Central American "feeling of solidarity and unity in the struggle for fair causes" (ibid., 4 January).

The furor over Soviet cooperation with San Salvador was only the latest example of the steady cooling of FSLN relations with Moscow. Thus the Soviets congratulated Violeta Chamorro, promised to continue trade and existing aid projects, and in June rebuffed a Sandinista request to establish a "parallel diplomatic office" in Moscow. (Ibid., 8 June.) It was also reported that Moscow had pressured Daniel Ortega to cooperate with UNO during the transition period (ibid.).

Michael S. Radu
Foreign Policy Research Institute

Panama

Population. 2,425,400
Party. People's Party of Panama (Partido del Pueblo de Panama, PPP) or People's Party (Partido del Pueblo, PdP or PDP)
Founded. PPP: 1930; PdP: 1943
Membership. 3,000 (*World Fact Book*, 1990); 500–1,000 militants estimated
General Secretary. Rubén Darío Souza Batista (commonly known as Sousa)
Politburo. Includes Cesar Agusto de León Espinosa, Miguel Antonio Porcella Pena, Anastacio E. Rodríguez, Cleto Manuel Souza Batista, Luther Thomas (international secretary), Felix Dixon, Dario González Pitti, Carlos Francisco Changmarín
Central Committee. 26 members
Status. Legal; regained status November 1989 after submission of approximately 25,600 signatures to the government electoral commission (Tribunal Electoral de Panama, TEP) (19,252 signatures required).
Last Congress. Eighth, 24–26 January 1986
Last Election. 1984, obtained less than 3 percent of the vote; no representatives in National Assembly 1984–1989; also participated as one of eight parties of progovernment Coalition of National Liberation (COLINA) ticket in elections of 7 May 1989, which were annulled on 10 May.
Auxiliary Organizations. Panama Peace Committee, Committee for the Defense of Sovereignty and Peace, People's Party Youth, National Center of Workers of Panama (Centro Nacional de Trabajadores de Panama, CNTP), Union of Journalists of Panama, Federation of Panamanian Students (Federación Estudiantil de Panama, FEP), National Democratic Women
Publication. *Unidad* (weekly), Carlos Francisco Changmarín, director

The People's Party of Panama (PPP) remained active as the democratically elected Endara struggled to recover from the effects of the economic embargo and the U.S. intervention that resulted in the ouster of military dictator Manuel Noriega in December 1989.

As the year passed, Panamanians grew increasingly frustrated with the slow pace of recovery. Promised U.S. aid was slow to arrive, and the euphoria following the U.S. intervention faded as the harsh reality of the country's severe socioeconomic problems settled in. Roman Catholic archbishop Marcos McGrath commented that "the principal problem in Panama is the lack of maturity of government officials who are not coming up with adequate programs to solve the country's problems." Throughout the year opponents and even supporters of the government criticized its lack of focus as it confronted economic problems. In December, the National Center of Panamanian Workers (CNTP) issued a communiqué criticizing what it called the government's intransigent attitude and denying reports linking labor leaders with the previous government. The CNTP voiced its support for a plan put forward by the National Council of Organized Workers to put pressure on the government. Among other actions, the plan called for a march on 4 December and a nationwide strike on 5 December.

The Endara government relations with Cuba were contentious. Havana had maintained a close relationship with the Noriega government and withheld recognition of the new government as well as promoted actions against it at the United Nations. At least once Havana referred to Panama as a U.S. puppet. Moreover, the Cuban embassy had granted asylum to Noriega's wife, two daughters, and close relatives. Several times during the year, Foreign Minister Linares characterized relations as being at an all-time low and intimated that diplomatic ties could be completely severed. In early July, the Endara government expelled several Cuban embassy employees, citing Havana's continued refusal to recognize the new government. The PPP, however, argued against any break in relations, saying that it would be against Panama's national interest. The PPP also pointed out that several other Latin countries, including Brazil and Mexico, had not yet recognized the Endara government. (*Unidad*, 13–19 June.) By November, tensions between the two countries appeared to be easing, with President Endara hinting at a rapprochement following a cordial exchange of greetings between the two leaders at the United Nations in mid-October. No further problems occurred between the two countries following the midyear expulsion of the Cuban diplomats.

President Endara also decided to honor a 1988 agreement establishing formal trade and consular relations with the Soviet Union, allowing Moscow to move ahead with plans to open a consulate and trade bureau in Panama before the end of the year. The Soviet Union apparently intends to expand its presence in the Colón Free Trade Zone and hopes to buy coffee, bananas, and seafood from Panama as well as sell tractors and heavy equipment. (Panama City, ACAN, 8 August; *FBIS-LAT*, 13 August.)

For its part the PPP issued several communiqués during the year calling for the departure of U.S. forces from Panama and questioning the legitimacy of the Endara government. In January the PPP Politburo demanded "the immediate withdrawal" of U.S. troops so that the country "can return to normal." The communiqué also said that it saw the U.S. military occupation as "the greatest obstacle" to the fulfillment of the canal treaties by the United States. (Panama City, ACAN, 13 January; *FBIS-LAT*, 22 January.) In September the PPP demanded that the United States "immediately end its occupation of Panama, the same way Bush and Gorbachev are demanding Iraq's withdrawal from Kuwait" (Panama City, *El Panama America*, 20 September; *FBIS-LAT*, 25 September). Finally, in December, yet another PPP communiqué questioned the legitimacy of the Endara government, stating that it was a government imposed on the country by "U.S. bayonets" and alleging that its origin was "an election in which no vote was counted . . . and which was annulled by the ruling authorities." The communiqué also appealed to Panamanian nationalism and called on the people to expel the "Yankee occupation forces." (Panama City, *El Periodico*, 19 December; *FBIS-LAT*, 26 December.)

With regard to its own future, the PPP addressed the changing international environment and its impact on leftist party struggles. PPP general secretary Rubén Darío Souza stated,

We Panamanian Communists see as our duty to articulate clearly the strategic objectives of the class struggle waged by working people and to show how the nation can really advance toward the socialist perspective. . . . We reject with a resounding "no" all advice to revise our ideology and strategic principles or to abandon our organizational structure.

Darío further espoused joint action by the left and "by all those opposed to the oligarchy and reactionaries," stating that "the record shows the need for organized cooperation among those sections of the working class movement that adhere to different ideologies and hold different views on important political issues." Darío denied that his call for joint action sprang from necessity owing to the small size of the PPP but said that cooperation was necessary if the "reactionaries are to be defeated or the main power structure changed." He also called for international assistance in Panama's struggle for freedom, independence, sovereignty, and progress. (*WMR*, January.)

Although desirous of cooperating with other like-minded movements, the PPP denied accusations that it supported activities of the M-20 guerrilla organization, including a plan to assassinate President Endara. PPP spokesman Carlos Changmarín stated the PPP "proposes a patriotic and political resolution" of the country's problems, adding "nobody can call us terrorists or an organization that enters into adventurous actions." (*Critica Libre*, 23 March; *FBIS-LAT*, 27 March.)

Alicia Tompkins
Hoover Institution

Paraguay

Population. 4,660,270
Party. Paraguayan Communist Party (Partido Comunista del Paraguay; PCP)
Founded. 1928
Membership. 4,000
General Secretary. Ananías Maidana
Status. Illegal, but tolerated
Last Congress. Third, 10 April 1971
Last Election. N/a
Publications. *Adelante* (a weekly newspaper); *Perspectivas* (an irregularly published magazine)

Life has improved for the PCP ever since Congress repealed two laws late last year that had allowed the old Stroessner dictatorship to ban any political activity it deemed to be "communist subversion." Although that was the first step toward legalizing the PCP, it will require changing the constitution to conclude the process; as it now stands, the constitution outlaws any party that owes an allegiance to a foreign power or that advocates the government's violent overthrow. But though it still lives in a legal twilight, the PCP has been acting as though it were fully protected.

The PCP's return to public activity in Paraguay for the first time since 1947 was hailed at a plenum of its Central Committee, held in Asunción in January. This meeting also saw a change in the PCP leadership, as Ananías Maidana took over as general secretary from the ailing, 78-year-old Júlio Rojas. Rojas, a longtime militant who had served more than twenty years in Stroessner's prisons, was moved to the largely ceremonial post of party chairman. He died in March.

During the year the PCP staged open rallies, published its newspaper, and issued communiqués about issues of the day. On 20 February it celebrated its 62d anniversary at an open ceremony attended by more than five hundred people (*Asuncion, Hoy*, 20 February; *FBIS-LAT*, 21 February). The PCP's dual strategy was to reach out to other opposition parties while keeping up a running criticism of the Rodríguez government's slow pace of reform. On 27 August representatives of the various opposition parties attended a night rally by about a hundred Communists, at which Maidana called for the formation of "a powerful front" to combat "the inhuman system of capitalism" and pressed for land reform (*FBIS*, 29 August). With the exception of the Febreristas, however, none of the opposition reciprocated the invitation.

The land reform issue offers the PCP its best opportunity. It is estimated that 2.2 million people (54 percent of the population) live in the rural areas; of these, 400,000 are landless. Several organizations are competing to represent them. It is not known to what extent Communists may have been involved, but there were many marches, demonstrations, and illegal occupations of the land during the year. The Rodríguez administration was busy ejecting squatters while agitation spread through the countryside. The president's patience was wearing thin, as evidenced by his dark warning, issued in late November, that future occupations would be punished with severe penalties.

Paul H. Lewis
Tulane University

Peru

Population. 21,905,605 (*World Fact Book*)

Party. Peruvian Communist Party (Partido Comunista Peruana, PCP)

Founded. 1928

Membership. 4,000 (estimated)

General Secretary. Jorge del Prado Chavez (b. 1910, member of the Senate, member of the National Executive Committee of the United Left coalition)

Coalition Partners. The PCP participates in the United Left (Izquierda Unida, IU) along with the Worker, Peasant, Student, and Popular Front (FOCEP), the Union of the Revolutionary Left (UNIR), and the Unified Mariateguista Party (PUM). Other small groups and individuals also identify with the coalition.

Opposition parties. The revolutionary guerrilla movements PCP—Sendero Luminoso and the Movimiento Revolucionario Túpac Amaru (MRTA)

Last Congress. Ninth, 27–30 May 1987

Last Election. April 1990; IU received 6 percent of the presidential vote and won 6 seats in the Senate and 16 seats in the Chamber of Deputies.

Publications. *Unidad* (newspaper of the PCP, Carlos Esteves, editor); *El Diario* (pro–Sendero Luminoso newspaper); *Cambio* (pro–Revolutionary Movement of Túpac Amaru magazine)

The installation of Alberto Fujimori as president on 28 July marked the second time in Peruvian history that three democratically elected presidents have succeeded one another. But 1990 was disappointing for the Peruvian Communist Party (PCP). Only a year before there had been speculation that Izquierda Unida (United Left, IU), a coalition created by the PCP and five other parties, could capture the presidency. The radical and moderate factions of the front, however, were unable to agree on a single slate of candidates, and in late 1989 they split. This cost IU the considerable credibility, influence, and political power it had attained in ten years. Confused and angered by IU's political infighting, many supporters abandoned IU and the dissident organization, Izquierda Socialista (Socialist Left, IS), and

on 8 April cast their votes for the unknown Fujimori and his eclectic movement, Cambio 90. Pollsters were stunned as the heavily favored and well-financed novelist, Mario Vargas Llosa of the Democratic Front (Fredemo), captured only 27.6 percent of the vote and was forced into a second round by the Nisei agronomist, who polled 24.6 percent. The left was thoroughly defeated, with IU and IS combined accounting for barely 10 percent of the vote. Although the divided left provided the vacuum from which Fujimori emerged to challenge the traditional elites of Fredemo, it also provided the margin of victory in the second round held 10 June. Fujimori swept 70 percent of the normally IU shantytown vote and did the same in the highland provinces, giving him a 57 percent to 36 percent victory over Vargas Llosa (*Latin American Press*, 14 June).

The new president's problems are monumental. Five years of Alan García's Aprista government ended in catastrophic failure. The nation was reeling from hyperinflation, which hit an historic high of 7,649.7 percent for the year (*Resumen Semanal*, 21 December–3 January 1991). All social indicators showed that Peruvians were worse off in 1990 than they had been before García took office. One-third of the population now lived in abject poverty; productivity was stalled with only the informal sector showing signs of growth; and the economy had become "dollarized" because of high inflation and an influx of drug money. These conditions continued to fuel the guerrilla revolution of Sendero Luminoso, which has been called the "strongest insurgency movement" and "democracy's most formidable enemy" in South America (*New Republic*, 18 June).

Fujimori called for a unified national effort to address these problems; his political situation was untenable without multiparty cooperation, given the magnitude of the problems and given that Cambio 90 had only one-quarter of the seats in Congress. Initially there were two ministers from IS and one from IU in the cabinet, but as Fujimori proceeded to implement economic readjustment programs that were as severe as anything attributed to Vargas Llosa in the campaign, two of the ministers resigned. By the end of the year, the rift between IU and IS had not been healed, but efforts were under way to reformulate a Socialist opposition bloc.

Leadership and Party Organization. In 1990, the Peruvian Communist Party faced readjustment on three fronts: (1) its relationship with

IU, (2) its position with regard to the new administration, and (3) its response to the "decline" of socialism in Eastern Europe and the USSR. For almost ten years the components of IU had cooperated in a loose parliamentary alliance (*YICA*, 1980–1989). The front had stimulated vigorous local organizations, experienced considerable success in regional elections, controlling four of the new regions, and accounted for one-quarter of each chamber in the national legislature. But when pressured to become a more coherent party in late 1989, its limitations became obvious. Moderate and radical factions disagreed on the answers to key questions about the use of political violence, electoral strategy, and organizational structure. The moderates argued that Peru's political and economic situation did not yet justify the use of political violence. The radicals placed more importance on ideological purity than on electoral strategy, and no one was certain whether members were *izquierdistas* or merely members of constituent groups who cooperated in opposition.

The moderates, which included the Revolutionary Communist Party (PCR), the regional Mariateguista committees, and the Socialist Convergence (non-Marxist Socialists and independents), withdrew from the coalition and created the IS as an electoral alliance to run Dr. Alfonso Barrantes Lingán, the former IU leader, for president. The radicals—members of the Union of Revolutionary Left (UNIR) and the Unified Mariateguista Party (PUM)—and members of parties committed to IU as an entity, such as the PCP, the Socialist Popular Action (APS), and the Revolutionary Mariateguista Party (PMR), maintained the IU coalition.

The split was fatal because the differences in platforms were too minor to attract new voters and because each group had a serious weakness. Despite Barrantes's personal following, IS had little depth nationwide. IU's national slate was a lackluster compromise, with independent Dr. Henry Pease García as president and Agustín Haya de la Torre (PMR) and Gustavo Mohme (APS) as vice-presidential candidates. Because the large parties (PCP, PUM, UNIR) had no one on the ticket, they concentrated on the legislative races. By the first week in January, IU had run only 18 television spots for president compared with IS's 141 and Fredemo's 967 (Caretas, 29 January; *FBIS-LAT*, 27 February). Attempts by PCP secretary general Jorge del Prado to reconcile the dissidents proved fruitless, and the left was soundly defeated. Even together Pease and Barrantes carried far less than IU's 26 percent in the 1985 election, and the congressional delegation declined from fifteen to nine senators (six IU and three IS) and from 47 deputies to 20 (16 IU and 4 IS).

When it came to the second round, the PCP decided that there was no choice but to support Fujimori. Even though Cambio 90's platform was sketchy and tentative, Fredemo's was definitely "antipopular." Only the Popular Democratic Union (UDP) called for a spoiled vote. The PCP and the rest of IU rejected that option because it played into Sendero's call for a boycott of the election, which they believed was not a true expression of the popular will. (*Resumen Semanal*, 18–24 May.)

The campaign cast Fujimori as the people's candidate, an underdog against the wealthy, white, coastal elite of Fredemo. He capitalized on his Japanese ancestry as the stereotype of honest, hardworking, and technologically competent people. He initiated his campaign in the *pueblos jovenes* of Lima and promised not to fight violence with violence but to use the "weapons of development" to counter misery and hunger (*Resumen Semanal*, 1–7 June). Yet Fujimori called himself a centrist, and his program was not much different from Fredemo's except in degree, timing, and emphasis. That is, he was a free market capitalist who wanted to reintegrate Peru into the international financial community but looked to the Pacific instead of Europe and North America. He wanted to attack hyperinflation but targeted 100–200 percent as a realistic first-year goal, not Fredemo's 10 percent. He also favored some privatization but said that strategic and public service industries would remain under state ownership. (*Latin American Weekly Report* [*LAWR*], 17 May.)

After Fujimori's victory there was considerable disagreement in IU as to the proper level of support and the propriety of participating in his government. IU member Gloria Helfner Palacios, a leader of SUTEP, the teacher's union, accepted the post of minister of education. Within one month, however, the National Executive Committee of IU forced her to renounce her membership as they wanted no direct affiliation with the regime. (*Resumen Semanal*, 17–24 August.) Her resignation in December reinforced the view that they were correct.

The various components of IS agreed to support a pluralist government. Carlos Amat y León took the agriculture portfolio, and Fernando Sánchez Albavera became minister of energy. In addition, Senator Enrique Bernales was elected first vice-president in Parliament. Sánchez Albavera claimed that he saw corresponding aims between IS and

Cambio 90, with their similar social base, priority to agricultural development, and modern socialism. He argued that socialism was compatible with a multiparty system, representative democracy, and the market economy. He criticized IU colleagues for their "lack of maturity and unwillingness to break with fixed ideologies" (*Expreso*, 19 August; *FBIS-LAT*, 25 September).

In their campaign, IS leaders argued that a strong state is obsolete and that the left must rationalize bureaucracy, decentralize, privatize, and democratize. Edmundo Murrugara said,

> Socialism's task in Peru is to help develop the domestic market. Our ills stem from too little capitalist development, not from too much. . . . Therein lies the difference between scientific socialism and utopian socialism, we need production and abundance before distribution. We must promote production before redistribution, so there is something to distribute. (*Equis x*, 22 January; *FBIS-LAT*, 9 March; *Expreso*, 29 April; *FBIS-LAT*, 21 June.)

By the end of the year, however, relations with Fujimori were strained. Amat y León had resigned as minister, and IS members found themselves at a greater ideological distance from Cambio 90 than from IU; cooperation, at least in Parliament, appeared possible.

The meaning of socialism within the Peruvian context and the question of IU's internal organization and its position vis-à-vis the Fujimori government will be discussed at the IU party congress in April 1991. Del Prado stated that the front had not discarded the notion that at some point they would realize a "pragmatic ideological unification of all the left that would culminate in one party." He also said that the PCP would make a detailed analysis of IU's defects. (*Resumen Semanal*, 23–29 November.) Who is invited and who attends will set the stage for leftist cooperation for the immediate future.

Domestic Affairs. Perhaps outgoing President Alan García's greatest achievement was keeping the nation together long enough to hold two elections and transfer power. Fujimori took over a virtually paralyzed nation, laced with what critics called "time bombs" laid by the Apristas. Debts with suppliers were to be paid with bonds after 28 July; the inflation rate for June was 42.6 percent, and international reserves, promised to be $800 million, were actually $144 million. At the time of the inauguration, economic uncertainty was so great that workers took to the streets; the violence increased as dollars and staples disappeared. (*Resumen Semanal*, 28 June–5 July, 20–25 July.)

Fujimori's initial actions surprised both those who supported him and those who opposed him. He enacted a harsh correction to gain international approval and initiated loan repayments to obtain much-needed credit and debt relief. IU opposed creating a program just to please the International Monetary Fund and the World Bank, and PCP leader Jorge del Prado criticized Fujimori's position that "the problem of debt is ours and ought to be resolved in Peru" (*Resumen Semanal*, 6–12 July). But Fujimori argued that the $500 million repayment would generate $750 million in investment and credits.

He launched the first "Fujishock" on 8 August, allowing prices to follow market forces, which meant fuel increased 3,000 percent, food was up 400–1,000 percent, and the cost of living in August was five times that of the previous month. Inflation in August was the highest ever recorded—397 percent. Prices and inflation did fall after August, but much of this decline was due to a recession. No one was buying anything, and stores closed half days to save on utilities. (*LAWR*, 20 September.) Government workers were told there would be no wage increases until 1991 because the state did not have sufficient revenue.

Those working were lucky; between 800,000 and 900,000 workers were unemployed, and another 1.6 million were underemployed (*Expreso*, 13 April; *FBIS-LAT*, 1 June). Fujimori's major problem was that those who had given him his wide margin of victory—the poor and middle classes—were the ones suffering under the measures that removed commodity subsidies and increased taxes (*Andean Newsletter*, 14 August). The Social Action Program (PES), which was created to provide a safety net for those in extreme poverty, was a failure. Fujimori had promised a program of $415 million to feed 7 million people through December 1990, with one-quarter of the funding to come from aid programs like Caritas, one-quarter from other nations, and one-half from the Peruvian government. But only $132 million materialized, and the number of needy persons skyrocketed to more than 13 million. (*Commonweal*, 11 January 1991.)

For most of the year labor unions were cautious, given the desperate economic situation, about disrupting the system; the General Confederation of Peruvian Workers (CGTP) actually tried to halt two miners' strikes that cost the nation a total of $70 million in lost revenues (EFE, 13 March; *FBIS-LAT*, 15 March). Labor's reaction to Fujishock, however, was violent. The whole approach of bringing down inflation with hunger was viewed as an attack on the workers. The communist CGTP and the Aprista Confederation of Peruvian Workers (CTP) led a demonstration in front of Congress that the police broke up with tear gas, water cannons, and batons, arresting two hundred participants. CGTP leader Pablo Checo labeled the measures "genocidal" and called a general strike for 21–22 August (Lima Television Peruana, *FBIS-LAT*, 17 August).

From that point on labor unrest spread, with the most severe impacts coming from the "indefinite" strikes of the public providers of social services. Health professionals were out for 70 days, and the welfare system was paralyzed for 35 days. In October alone, there were 93 strikes affecting more than 44,000 workers, 27 percent higher than October 1989. (*Resumen Semanal*, 9–15 November.) Fujimori attempted to regulate workers' right to strike in strategic and essential service sectors. The CGTP and IU quickly defended the constitutionality of this right and criticized the president's placing the population's right to services in conflict with workers' rights. Labor leaders threatened to challenge before the International Labor Organization any decree limiting strikes. (*Resumen Semanal*, 16–22 November.) Strikes were weakened, however, by workers who felt that the crisis was real and that there was no remedy other than to temporarily lower wages. There was also widespread support for dismissing inefficient workers (*Resumen Semanal*, 16–22 November).

IU's practical response to the August and October shock programs was to continue supporting community efforts, such as the "glass of milk" program, to provide food for the poor. It also pressed for the extension of these programs to rural areas and demanded that the government allocate three times the amount PES was planning to spend. (*Resumen Semanal*, 16–22 November, 23–29 November.) The importance of the popular organizations to the survival of thousands of persons was recognized by the government when it passed legislation that gave legal and juridical existence to organizations such as mothers' clubs, committees of "glass of milk," and popular kitchens (*Resumen Semanal*, 14–20 December). Proposed by IU and IS deputies, this status had long been sought, but Fujimori's interest was related to his counterinsurgency policy. Many beneficiaries of these self-help programs had fled the highlands to avoid the guerrillas; the organizations were, therefore, generally viewed as bulwarks against subversion in urban areas.

During the campaign, Fujimori supported the creation of a "unified pacification command" with civilian input into governance in the emergency zones. He recognized the need to curtail paramilitary organizations and to protect human rights. All these positions were encouraged by IU and IS legislators, and each tested president-military relations. (*La República*, 9 September; *FBIS-LAT*, 27 September.) Fujimori's first six months produced a mixed record. Immediately after taking office, he asserted his control over the military by passing over ranking officials to bring new individuals into positions of influence, and in September he initiated civilian oversight for governance in the emergency zones. In addition, he chastised the judiciary for its poor record in processing those accused of terrorism—in five years, of 2,237 persons arrested, only 608 had been tried and only 382 had been sentenced. In contrast, only one person has been charged with human rights violations.

Fujimori also supported having special tribunals for the military. General Clemente Noel y Moral was found guilty of abuse of authority and hindering justice in the 1983 Uchurraccay murders. But two other officers who had been under investigation—General Jorge Rabanal in connection with the 1986 prison massacres and General José Valdivia for the Cayara massacres—were actually promoted by the Senate despite the vigorous objections of IS and IU members. (*Andean News*, 10 December.) Fujimori demonstrated little ability, however, to rein in the military's continued "dirty war," symptoms of which are a record number of disappeared in Peru and the discovery of mass graves. A U.N. report released in October said that so far in 1990, 1,900 disappeared had been reported. For three years in a row Peru has led the world in disappearances (*LAWR*, 1 November); in 1990 attention was focused on some prominent disappeared individuals including a Caretas reporter, the founder of the national Committee of Families of the Disappeared, and a popular folk singer. Abuses were highlighted by discoveries of two common gravesites in Ancash and a police graveyard in Cuzco. (*Resumen Semanal*, 16–22 November.)

Fujimori's success will depend on his ability to make his multiparty cabinet continue to work toward their commitment to a national consensus to overcome the crisis. International economic reintegration must be accompanied by foreign assistance to alleviate the considerable suffering. To wield power over the military, he must demonstrate coherent civilian support. To keep social unrest from building into support for the guerrillas, Fujimori must keep channels for popular participation open and protected.

International Relations. Important changes in the international system and a new president forced Peru to readjust its global orientation. The Peruvian Communist Party prepared itself to vigorously oppose policies that undermined existing good relations with communist nations, that subordinated Peru to the dictates of international financial organizations, or that provided an opening for foreign troops to be used in a war on drugs.

The Soviet Union and the People's Republic of China continued important trade and aid relations. The Soviet fishing fleet met its contract, paying 17.5 percent of its catch to Peru (approximately 6,912 tons) and by July 1990 had donated an extra 600 tons to be distributed to the poor in the Andean highlands (*El Comercio*, 1 July; *FBIS-LAT*, 10 July). A visit by Chinese foreign minister Qian Qichen in September resulted in credit of $6.5 million for assistance to small and medium industries and a donation of $630,000 for aid to drought victims (Lima Television Peruana, 12 September; *FBIS-LAT*, 13 September).

Fujimori felt, however, that the needed level of assistance could only come from Peru's reintegration into the international financial community. Toward this end, he visited the United States before his inauguration and arranged for a bridge loan from an international consortium of the United States, Japan, and Spain to cover arrears of $1.5 billion. His advisers at that time argued that the plan was based on Peru's real capacity to pay and on the principle that no deal would interfere with reactivation plans (*LAWR*, 5 July).

Fujimori's Japanese ancestry may not automatically enhance Pacific basin relations, although he promised as such in his campaign. Peru had been the number one Latin American recipient of Japanese aid until 1984, when Peru stopped repayments. In 1988, Peru ranked number four, receiving $27 million, half of which was in grants and half in technical assistance. (*Japan Times*, 25 June– 1 July.) Only $400 million of Peru's $19 billion debt is owed to Japan (*Latin American Regional Report* [*LARR*], 24 May). This balance is not expected to change.

Regional relations became more prominent in 1990. At the Group of Eight meeting in April, discussion centered on the difficulties that Latin America would face as the developed world and international organizations turn their attention toward Eastern Europe and away from the developing nations. In May the Andean Pact met in Cuzco, where the presidents focused on the need for a strong Latin American bloc. It was the first time that an Ecuadorian president had visited Peru since 1941. The Machu Picchu accord included an agreement to coordinate economic and foreign debt negotiations commercial and industrial policies, energy policies, a directly elected Andean Parliament, and twice-yearly summits. (*LARR*, 28 June.)

Chile and Peru held their fifth meeting regarding arms reduction and limitation amid allegations that Chile had tilted the weapons balance by manufacturing and exporting powerful fuel-air explosive (FAE) bombs and cluster bombs from Cardoen Industries. IS senator Enrique Bernales called it "international folly" to spend money on weapons, stimulating an arms race. Allegations were made that Chilean cluster bombs had been sent to Iraq since 1982 and Ethiopia since 1989. (EFE, 17 October, *FBIS-LAT*, 19 October.)

The most complex and controversial international relationship was with the United States, and the most salient issue was drugs. In February the presidents of Bolivia, Peru, Colombia, and the United States met for a drug summit. García was pleased, saying that it was the first time a U.S. president had met with his South American counterparts to deal multilaterally on a problem. Differences in perspective, however, quickly surfaced. The Latins were skeptical of U.S. commitment and its supply-side analysis of the problem. U.S. emphasis was on the suppression of coca production, whereas the Peruvians wanted socioeconomic assistance with crop replacement and compensation. Of $216 million, 90 percent was targeted for military aid, of which Peru was to receive $35.9 million, marking the first U.S. military spending in Peru since 1968 (*Quehacer*, March/April).

The most modern base targeted against drug trafficking in Latin America, Santa Lucia in the Upper Huallaga Valley, was dedicated in January. The 100-acre base cost $1.5 million; part of the $35 million from the United States was to train five thousand soldiers, refurbish and relocate planes, and upgrade river patrols in this area. But neither García nor Fujimori signed the agreement, for they felt that their sovereignty was infringed on by the demand that all information be available to U.S. courts and that all suits be tried in U.S. jurisdiction. More important, both presidents agreed that eradication of coca plants by chemical or biological methods was too risky, the price too high both politically and environmentally. Finally, they wanted compensation for the social and economic disruption that eradication would inflict on the peasants. (*LAWR*, 5 July; *El Comercio*, 6 October; *FBIS-LAT*, 14 November.)

Fujimori, then, wanted a nonrepressive alternative that would emphasize the right to land ownership and investment in crop substitution and market development. He suggested that the United States help build a 350-mile railroad to connect the prime coca-growing area with the coast, so that it could become the "breadbasket" for Peru rather than the drug supplier for the United States (*LAWR*, 3 May; *LARR*, 15 November.)

Fujimori also rejected the aid package for fear of putting the peasants on the guerrillas' side. That Sendero is heavily involved in controlling drug-trafficking activities in the Upper Huallaga is well known; the U.S. State Department has said, "Since Sendero is a major part of the drug complex, we have to deal with them together" (*NYT*, 21 June). For Peruvians, the major problem in the Upper Huallaga Valley is Sendero Luminoso. Thus the military, in its efforts to undermine the guerrillas, has at times been charged by U.S. Drug Enforcement Agency (DEA) officers with warning the peasants of pending attacks. The PCP and IU have been vigilant in keeping the U.S. DEA role in drug control and counterinsurgency operations separated, believing that to confuse these two missions would fatally internationalize the conflict. (*Quehacer*, March/April.) There is evidence that Sendero Luminoso is counting on just such an eventuality. Luís Arce Borja, editor of Sendero's mouthpiece, *El Diario*, claimed that there was no way to avoid a confrontation between the Peruvian people and the U.S. interventionist forces: "You can count on the number of victims reaching 100,000 people in the next two years" ("Fatal Attraction: Peru's Shining Path," *NACLA Report on the Americas*, December/January 1990/1991).

Revolutionary guerrilla activities. The government and the media portrayed 1990 as a year of crisis for Sendero Luminoso. García argued that, after ten years of warfare, the guerrillas had achieved few of their goals and failed to affect the elections seriously. Although they wielded consid-

erable influence in three areas—Ayacucho and the Upper Huallaga and Mantaro valleys—they had made few lasting gains elsewhere. Moreover, support declined and recruitment lagged as Sendero suffered from desertions and counterinsurgency victories. Finally, there was evidence of a major theoretical split.

Nevertheless, political violence continued to devastate the national economy and to exact a horrifying human toll. In a country with a fragile infrastructure, entire regions can be isolated by strategic roadblocks or the destruction of key bridges and incapacitated by the downing of high-tension towers. The cost of replacing and repairing damage to electrical service in one five-month period amounted to $18 million (*Latin American Press*, 17 May). Attacks on research and experimental stations caused incalculable damage. In May, a sperm bank to improve cattle breeds was destroyed in La Molina (EFE, 3 May; *FBIS-LAT*, 4 May), and in June, the MRTA bombed the Japanese Center for Seismic and Disaster Research at the National Engineering University (Lima Television Peruana, 31 May; *FBIS-LAT*, 1 June).

According to the Senate Commission on Pacification, violence in Peru increased, with the number of deaths rising from 3,198 in 1989 to 3,452 in 1990. This brings the official total for the decade to 19,263. IS senator Enrique Bernales, commission chair, noted that this is a conservative figure because it only includes verified deaths. (*Resumen Semanal*, 4–10 January 1991.)

As conceived by Sendero Luminoso's founder and leader, Dr. Abimael Guzmán, who has not been seen since the armed struggle began, Sendero's goal is to create a "new democratic republic" by destroying the bourgeois state through a popular uprising. (For background, see *YICA*, 1980–1990.) Sendero's specific goal for 1990 was to sabotage the April congressional and presidential elections, thus undermining the legitimacy of the democratic system. Its tactics included assassinating government officials and candidates, disrupting the campaign and electoral process, and intimidating the population to boycott the elections.

During 1990, more prominent officials were assassinated than in any other year. In January, former Defense Minister Enrique López Albújar was killed; in September, former Labor Minister Orestes Rodríguez Campos; in November, a Cambio 90 party leader, Hector Montero; and on 16 December, Congressional Deputy Alejandro Victoria Mendoza. Others killed included 28 government officials, eleven mayors and vice-mayors, two district lieutenant governors, and one governor.

In election-related violence at least ten candidates for the legislature, one Aprista party leader, and two mayors were killed in March alone. The number of terrorist incidents that month—309—was surpassed only by the November 1989 electoral violence. Armed strikes paralyzed Ayacucho and Huanta. Although in Lima most people ignored the strike, transportation was impeded as private bus owners questioned whether the government could protect them. Of the ten thousand vehicles that normally circulated in the city, only seven hundred were operating (EFE, 28 March; *FBIS-LAT*, 29 March). Car bombs, fires, and dynamite attacks on political party offices and meeting halls, as well as candidates' homes, workplaces, or speaking sites, became almost everyday occurrences. But the guerrillas did not forsake the spectacular. Their psychological campaign included defacing more than a hundred stones at Sacsahuaman, the Inca fortress, with slogans against voting (EFE, 28 February; *FBIS-LAT*, 1 March).

In response, Garcia's government declared a state of emergency in Lima and Callao. It also offered police and military protection to the 3,487 candidates in the April congressional and presidential elections, along with providing life insurance for members of the national elections board (*Andean Newsletter*, 9 April).

The most direct influence of Sendero on the elections can be measured by blank and null votes. Abstentions in the emergency zone, where Senderista activity is most prominent, was the highest in the nation, with Huanuco at 50.1 percent, Junin at 49.5 percent, and Ayacucho at 47.5 percent in the first round. According to analysts, the percentage was high not only because of threats but also because of increasing migration from the area and lack of registration (*Resumen Semanal*, 18–24 May). Null and blank votes also indicate anti-systemic pressure on the democratic system. The Peruvian constitution states that an election is void if one-third of the ballots are blank or spoiled. Here again Sendero's influence is evident. In Ayacucho, in the first round 22.9 percent of the vote was spoiled. Nationwide, the invalid votes in the first round were 15.35 percent compared with 9.55 percent in the runoff (*Resumen Semanal*, 11–17 May).

At Sendero Luminoso's tenth anniversary celebrations in the Canto Grande prison, members announced that a new stage had begun—the war of movements. They said that until now it had been a war of guerrillas with dynamite, selective assassination, and cell work but that now companies and battalions would begin the people's war (*SI*, 18–21 May). In fact, in 1990 the most disturbing aspect of the decade-long guerrilla war was the extent to which larger units of civilians were drawn into battle on both sides. Sendero called it a new stage in their long-term strategy, and the military viewed it as more effective counterinsurgency measures; but it is more like war by proxy with, as human rights activists claim, peasants as cannon fodder.

Sendero forced campesinos into large columns of the "people's army," and the military sanctioned, trained, and armed *rondas campesinas* and self-defense committees. Both sides used intimidation to recruit support. In June it was reported that four hundred campesinos were put into columns led by 30 cadres, but that more than two hundred others were killed who would not participate (*LAWR*, 1 November). In Huanta, joining the military was supposedly voluntary, but those who did not volunteer were branded subversives; the Huanta military base was implicated in 127 disappearances in the first six months of 1990 (*San Francisco Chronicle*, 8 August; *Expreso*, 24 May; *FBIS-LAT*, 1 June).

The use of *rondas* has been criticized by the IU, the Andean Commission of Jurists, and human rights activists who claim not only that their role of "protection" makes them targets but that these organizations escalate the violence by giving vent to communal strife. The result has been more frequent confrontations with higher casualties because of poor equipment and training. In addition, peasant retaliation has proved just as brutal as Sendero's attacks, with *rondas'* sending the heads of their victims to the regional commanders to prove their effectiveness (*NYT*, 4 March).

Nevertheless, there is some indication that Sendero is losing this round. The use of conscripts has brought an increase in defections and intelligence leaks along with a decline in military performance. In Huanta and La Mar, 82 civil defense communities made up of more than three thousand peasants have pushed the guerrillas back; for the first time in many years vehicle traffic is going from Huanta to Ayacucho unharmed. This success is due in part to the deserters, who have good knowledge of Sendero's tactics and leaders and bring weapons with them. In Lima, people have used cadres from rural areas to organize armed strikes (*Latin American Press*, 17 May).

In June, the police scored their greatest success when they broke into Sendero's urban communication network, locating informants and Lima safe houses. One such house in Monterrico, which stored letters, records, plans, flyers, schedules, and gifts for Guzman, was described as the organization's archives (*Resumen Semanal*, 1–7 June). That information led to the breakdown of Sendero's urban organization, the Urban Revolutionary Movement of the People (MRDP), and provided intelligence on support groups in Lima. By October 35 people were arrested and identified as the central propaganda apparatus; one was a vice-rector of San Marcos University who was later released (*El Comercio*, 8 June: *FBIS-LAT*, 21 June; EFE, 5 October; *FBIS-LAT*, 5 October).

Sendero Luminoso's violence was also condemned by human rights organizations in 1990. Although thousands of poor, anonymous campesino communities have been caught in the crossfire between the military and the guerrillas, the plight of the Ashaninkas Indians gained international attention when that isolated tribe in Pasco mobilized to defend itself against the guerrillas of both Sendero Luminoso and the MRTA after its leader was murdered in late 1989. Fifty-three Indian communities united 12,300 people and declared war. The Indians proved no match for the Senderistas, however, who by mid-1990 had decimated the tribe. (EFE, 21 March; *FBIS-LAT*, 27 March; *NYT Magazine*, 2 December.)

On 17 May a pamphlet circulated in Ayacucho saying that the "time has come to end crime for crime's sake, the cult of personality and ideological fundamentalism." Announcing that the PCP-SL was temporarily retiring from the armed struggle but would continue the ideological fight, the flyer was immediately rejected as a government ploy by Sendero, and even the military doubted its authenticity. (*SI*, 21–28 May.)

But rumors of a split in Sendero were fed by a lull in activity around the group's tenth anniversary, disagreements in interviews of prison inmates, and *El Diario* acknowledging two lines of thought that they claimed were essential to the movement's progress. One group, "the blacks," are said to be older members who now question whether the tactics are worth the sacrifice and favor more traditional political activity; the other group, "the reds," are youthful radicals who want to pursue the military operations. Analysts feel that problems are arising because for so long the cadres only destroyed peasant communities, creating thousands of refugees, and did not rebuild anything. (*Latin American Press*, 17 May; Caretas, 21 May; EFE, 14 May;

FBIS-LAT, 16 May.) They have little support among the groups they supposedly champion because their violence is no longer directed against landlords or greedy merchants but toward delinquents and "dissidents." Peasants now cry, "punish don't kill," and the Unitary Peruvian Educators' Union (SUTEP) asks why they assassinate teachers, campesinos, and workers ("Fatal Attraction: Peru's Shining Path," *NACLA Report on the Americas*, December/January 1990/1991).

The same debate impinges on MRTA, which was created in 1982 by several radical left groups. Unlike Sendero, MRTA has close ties to the mainstream left in terms of goals and objectives, although it is committed to the use of arms. It has stressed cooperation with "patriotic" sectors of all national groups and has cultivated strong international ties with other revolutionary organizations, especially Colombia's M-19. (See *YICA*, 1987–1990.)

MRTA receives attention out of proportion to its size and influence because its activities are calculated to publicize its message. Throughout the year, the MRTA oscillated between terrorist activities and efforts at peace. In January, it took credit for the assassination of former Defense Minister Enrique López Albújar, claiming he had ordered the extrajudicial killing of 43 MRTA members in April 1989 (*LAWR*, 25 January). In November, the group killed Judge César Ruiz Trigoso, claiming that he stood for antilabor and repressive policies (*Andean Newsletter*, 10 December). Although MRTA has three guerrilla fronts in the field, they have had minimal success. In mid-1990, their second attempt to make gains in Cuzco failed (*Resumen Semanal*, 28 June–5 July). The military scored an important intelligence victory in Iquitos as well, capturing Sistero García Torres, alleged leader of the northeastern front. Because he was found with large amounts of U.S. dollars, he was charged with drug trafficking and terrorism. (*Andean Newsletter*, 10 December.)

But the government's successes were undermined by the spectacular escape of 48 MRTA inmates, including leader Victor Polay, from Canto Grande maximum security prison on 9 July. The nation was stunned by the high-tech escape, which required the acquiescence, if not support, of security guards and neighbors. A 250-meter tunnel, equipped with air compressors and lighting and excavated over two years, went up into a residential yard. Estimates were that 450 tons of earth had been removed. (*Resumen Semanal*, 6–12 July; *Latin American Press*, 12 July.)

At MRTA's Third Central Committee Plenary it was announced it would continue rural military action, but it also issued political demands that were similar to those of the legal left: reduce and freeze prices, index salaries and make the minimum wage equal to the "basic basket" of food for a family, dissolve the repressive military and paramilitary organizations, assign sanctions to war criminals, observe human rights, lift states of emergency, and create civilian-military commands (*Resumen Semanal*, 28 September–4 October; Lima Television Peruana, 15 October; *FBIS-LAT*, 16 October).

The group's response to Fujimori was mixed as well. When he sought international financial assistance, MRTA rejected a truce and made its goal one of "unmasking" Fujimori as an enemy of the people and "organizing the people against him, against imperialism, the criminal police and all injustice and abuses" (*Resumen Semanal*, 6–12 July). In October, however, Cambio 90 deputy Gerardo López Quiroz was kidnapped and held for eight days to discuss the possibility of a dialogue with a credible administration official (*Resumen Semanal* 28 September–4 October).

Efforts at dialogue were serious enough to bring together López Quiroz, CGTP leader Pacho, and former President Francisco Belaúnde Terry. But Fujimori wanted the guerrillas to first lay down their arms, even though his vice-president, Carlos García García, and IU representative César Barrera Bazan favored initiating dialogue as the first step (*Resumen Semanal*, 5–11 October).

Peruvian democracy was reinforced with the successful conduct of the 1990 general elections, and police intelligence coups and internal rifts have weakened both MRTA and Sendero Luminoso. Revolutionary guerrilla control is limited to areas where other organizations have been weak or where antigovernment sentiment is high and can be easily manipulated. The guerrilla influence, as many commentators have noted, is limited to exacerbating already serious problems, diverting scarce resources, unleashing repression, and creating an atmosphere in which confidence in the government is undermined. But the guerrilla's decline is relative to the strength of the abilities of the Peruvian system. Sendero's patient erosion of society may withstand many defeats, whereas Fujimori may not.

Sandra Woy-Hazleton
Miami University

Puerto Rico

Population. 3,291,207 (July)
Parties. Puerto Rican Socialist Party (Partido Socialista Puertorriqueño, PSP); Puerto Rican Communist Party (Partido Comunista Puertorriqueño, PCP)
Founded. PSP, 1971; PCP, 1934
Membership. PSP: 150; PCP: 100 (both estimated)
General Secretaries. PSP: Nestor Nazario, Carlos Gallisa, and Juan Mari Bras; PCP: Franklin Irrizarry
Status. Legal
Last Congress. PSP: Second, 1979; PCP: Fourth, 1954
Publications. PSP: *Claridad* (weekly); PCP: *El Pueblo* (monthly)

To hold or not to hold a referendum on the future political status of the island was the question that confounded Puerto Ricans in 1990. Whereas a year earlier the popular clamor appeared to favor the vote and leaders of the principal political parties were pressuring the U.S. Congress to pass a law authorizing it, near the end of 1990 many Puerto Ricans were expressing doubts about the wisdom of subjecting the island to such an emotional and divisive process.

Discovered by Columbus in 1593, Puerto Rico was a colony of Spain until 1898 when, as a result of the Spanish defeat in a war with the United States, it became U.S. territory. After a brief military occupation, Congress established a civilian government for Puerto Rico, which since 1952 has been a "commonwealth in free association with the United States." Puerto Ricans, who became U.S. citizens in 1917, elect the island's governor, whose term of office runs concurrently with that of the U.S. president. But they cannot vote in the presidential and congressional elections unless they live on the mainland. They generally do not pay federal income tax but can be drafted into the army and are eligible for a whole array of U.S. social services. Under congressional rules, the Senate Committee on Energy and Natural Resources has the primary responsibility for "territorial possessions of the United States," including Puerto Rico.

A bill to hold the referendum in September 1991 of the future status of Puerto Rico has been discussed in Congress since 1989. Under the 1990 House version of the bill, 3.6 million Puerto Ricans were to choose among four options: independence, statehood, a new commonwealth relationship, or the maintenance of the status quo. (There was disagreement about whether the more than 2.5 million Puerto Ricans who live in the United States would be allowed to vote in the plebiscite.) The third option would continue the island as a commonwealth, but its government would have more control than it currently has: it could ban, without federal approval, certain imports and would control landing rights at airports, enabling them to open up to European airlines and serve as a hub between Europe and Latin America. But after much debate in Congress, the bill died in the Senate and will have to be reintroduced in 1991.

In a similar referendum held in 1967, 60 percent of the islanders opted for commonwealth status. But at the beginning of 1990, polls indicated that 48 percent of the population favored statehood, and even President Bush expressed his support for that option. Support for the commonwealth status dropped to 44 percent, and that for independence, generally favored by leftist groups, declined to 7 percent. Governor Rafael Hernandez Colon, head of the Popular Democratic Party (PPD, politically similar to the U.S. Democratic party), has been opposed to the statehood option. The opposition New Progressive Party (PNP), led by Baltasar Corrado del Rio, akin to the Republican party, wants to see the island converted into the 51st state.

The fact that the referendum bill did not pass Congress in the 1990 session was probably owing to concerns expressed by several key legislators over the cost of statehood to the U.S. taxpayers. Because the welfare programs of the new state would have to be brought up to the level of other states, that cost alone was estimated at $2 billion. Also the eventual loss of tax exemptions for U.S. companies operating in Puerto Rico would lead to a loss of 100,000 jobs over ten years, creating approximately 30 percent unemployment on the island.

In Puerto Rico, a number of prominent businesspeople voiced opposition to the referendum, arguing that the vote, regardless of who emerged the winner, would divide the country and cause long-lasting social wounds. There was also a fear of the unknown. The businesspeople said that in the last few years the Puerto Rican economy has been making slow but steady progress and that any drastic change of status would unhinge the climate of stability that has existed in the island for several decades now.

Although President Bush supported statehood, some Republicans were not happy about his endorsement of that option, fearing that Puerto Rico would elect two Democratic senators and as many as five Democratic representatives, seats that would probably have to be carved out from those allotted to the other 50 states. As before, the idea of the plebiscite was opposed by the extreme left. Speaking in Havana, Nestor Nazario, described as "president" of the PSP, said that the referendum was a "new maneuver by the United States through which Washington wants to strengthen its political, economic and military grip on the island and give a new face to its colonial domination of the territory." He said that should the referendum take place, the PSP would urge Puerto Ricans to boycott the vote and reiterated the party's support of the island's independence. (*Granma*, 30 September.)

George Volsky
University of Miami

United States of America

Population. 250,410,000 (July)
Party. Communist Party U.S.A. (CPUSA)
Founded. 1919
Membership. 20,000 (claimed); 4,000–6,000 (probable)
National Chairman. Gus Hall
National Board. Gus Hall, Evelina Alarcon, Kendra Alexander, John Bachtell, Arnold Becchetti, Barry Cohen, Elsie Dickerson, Louis Diskin, Lee Dlugin, Joelle Fishman, Clyde Grubbs, James Jackson, Maurice Jackson, Judith leBlanc, Robert Lindsay, Carole Marks, Scott Marshall, George Meyers, Charlene Mitchell, Rick Nagin, Daniel Rubin, Betty Smith, James Steele, Sidney Taylor,

Jarvis Tyner, Sam Webb, Jim West, Michael Zagarell

Status. Legal

Last Congress. 24th National Convention, 1987

Electoral Activity. The party did not run a presidential candidate in the 1988 election. In the 1984 election, the last in which it had a national candidate, it polled under 0.1 percent of the vote. Candidates ran in local elections in 1990 (see below).

Publications. *People's Weekly World* (formerly, *People's Daily World*), New York, Barry Cohen, editor; *Political Affairs* (theoretical monthly)

The CPUSA remains the largest Marxist-Leninist organization in the United States. Founded in 1919 with the merger of two existing groups, the CPUSA attained a considerable if short-lived influence in the country during the 1930s and 1940s, with support in labor unions and liberal political circles. The party has also exercised an important influence in the black community, with a large share of today's elected black leadership consisting of individuals whose political careers began in the party's orbit (see Arch Puddington, "The Question of Black Leadership," *Commentary*, January 1991.)

The party reached its zenith at the close of the Second World War, when claimed membership hovered around 80,000 to 100,000. Party membership figures in the United States, at least since the mid-1930s, however, have had an ambiguous character because the bulk of the party supporters have been kept outside its formal structure, with a relatively small elite of tested prospects invited to full membership. Thus, the party milieu of active supporters may normally be estimated at around ten times the number of claimed or actual members.

Leadership and Party Organization. At the conclusion of 70 years of party history, it seems undeniable that although the organization has occasionally played a role in international communist affairs, it has, overall, failed to strike deep roots in the U.S. political environment, notwithstanding episodic influence. Although politicians in such left enclaves as the San Francisco Bay Area today include party members or supporters in coalition-building efforts, the party, its leaders, and its history remain unknown to the broad U.S. public. Thus, as in the British case, the CPUSA never overcame the burden of its origin as an artificial creation of the Soviet state.

The sole moment when the U.S. party on its own chose (unsuccessfully) to attempt to influence the world movement came in 1956, when the New York party leadership under John Gates, in control of the party's organ, the *Daily Worker*, came out in defense of the Hungarian insurrectionaries. Indeed, the U.S. party was perhaps the most avid in criticizing Moscow's intervention. In the wake of that crisis, the party was put under the control of loyalist Gus Hall, who remains at its helm today, but lost an overwhelming number of its basic cadre, including thousands of long-serving trade union activists. From that period to the present, the party has remained on the margin of U.S. life.

With the onset of *glasnost'*, the crisis of 1956 has been partially repeated as the party attempts to contend with the new reality in the East. That the relationship between the party and the center in Moscow has changed was demonstrated by the downgrading of the *People's Daily World* (*PW*) to a weekly, announced in the issue of 10 May and implemented with the issue of 9 June. (The paper had already been cut from five to four issues per week.)

Whereas the editors of *PW*'s British counterpart, the *Morning Star*, which announced a similar frequency reduction in January, admitted that their financial crisis was dictated by the cutoff of a Soviet subsidy in the form of subscriptions, *PW*'s editors ingenuously blamed their problems on the difficulties of running a daily in the United States with no advertising base (*PW*, 10 May). In an interview in the *New York Times*, *PW* editor Barry Cohen stated, "It just was a more sensible strategy for us to concentrate our resources on the once-a-week paper" (*NYT*, 19 October). In the same article, a regular press run of 62,000 was claimed for the paper, but the circulation of communist party papers has never been independently audited.

As grim news continued to come from the East, the CPUSA oscillated between condemnation of "CIA maneuvers" and a sheepish, often circuitous acceptance of the failures of the communist system. Michael Parenti, a polemicist who has emerged as the party's main younger ideologist, blasted "the anti-Marxist Soviets," noting, among other things, that one of his own books attacking U.S. democracy had been commissioned in 1987 for publication in Russian by Progress Publishers in Moscow but that by the end of 1988 Progress had become uninterested in the project, with no further notice to Parenti. In the same article Parenti slashed at the Soviet journal *Nauka i Zhizn* for publishing a pathbreaking historical analysis of Stalinism, Soviet universities for instituting courses based on Western sociological concepts, the Soviet press for praising Robert Conquest and others of the "most virulent anti-Communist academic critics in the West (who) have become something of heroes in the USSR," and the Soviet weekly *Argumenty i Fakty* for criticizing Lenin. Worst of all,

> The editor of the Minnesota-based Marxist Educational Press set up a book display at the Moscow International Book Fair...only to discover that none of the Soviet people who stopped...were interested in what American Marxists were writing. Instead, they repeatedly made disdainful and dismissive remarks....Some even asked, "What are you doing here?" When [Parenti] asked...what kinds of people voiced such sentiments [the answer was] "All sorts." (*PW*, 16 June.)

In the meantime, *PW* Moscow correspondent Carl Bloice, another major figure in the party's young cadre, wavered between reportages in praise of reform and articles supporting the tactical moves of the CPSU rightists. Occasional warnings about the bleak future purportedly facing the workers of the East under a free enterprise system also appeared, as in an article by Conn Hallinan, "Hungary at the Crossroads," in which it was argued that the dismantling of socialism was already producing an increase in poverty (*PW*, 1 December).

One of the most curious items in the saga of *glasnost'* and the U.S. left came in a report by a delegation from the leadership of the International Longshoremen's and Warehousemen's Union (ILWU), American Federation of Labor and Congress of Industrial Organizations (AFL-CIO), long a bastion of party activity, who had visited the 15–26 August reform congress of the Soviet Sea and River Workers' Union. ILWU had for decades maintained relations with this union in explicit defiance of AFL-CIO policy. But the report of the ILWU heads on *perestroika* in the Soviet maritime industry produced headlines in the union's newspaper, the *Dispatcher* (San Francisco), that would once have been inconceivable in those pages: "Soviet maritime workers try to form a real union," being but one example. Luckily, ILWU founder Harry Bridges, an unshakable admirer of Soviet communism, died 30 March, for such language in his union's paper might have killed him. (*Dispatcher*, 18 October.)

Domestic Party Affairs. Although the party did not outwardly betray the existence of major internal conflict, occasional signs indicated discon-

tent with Hall's continued leadership. Following a special joint meeting of the party's National Committee and National Council 4–5 August, Kendra Alexander, chair of the Northern California organization, traditionally a center of dissidence, criticized various aspects of party life, including electoral policy, "the level of struggle against racism within the Party..., the low level of sensitivity on this question," and the lack of follow-up on strategic decisions. (*PW*, 8 September.)

In the November elections, the party ran a number of local candidates, including CPUSA members running in California on the Peace and Freedom (P&F) ticket. California P&F gubernatorial candidate Evelina Alarcon, a member of the CPUSA's national leadership, won 2 percent of the state vote. Frank Lumpkin, a steelworker, ran for the Illinois State Legislature on the Independent Progressive ticket and won 12 percent of the vote with the endorsement of the radical South Chicago district of the United Steelworkers of America (AFL-CIO). Lorenzo Torrez ran for Arizona state representative and won 17 percent of the vote. These fairly large protest votes seemed to reflect a disenchantment among some voters with the rigidity of present-day U.S. electoral politics, dominated by incumbents. The party and the left in general expressed some pride that a 15 percent P&F vote in Northern California's First Congressional District resulted in the unseating of incumbent Democrat Douglas Bosco and his replacement by a moderate Republican, Frank Riggs (*PW*, 10 November, 15 December).

Louis Godena, who ran for Massachusetts state representative on the Peace, Jobs, and Justice ticket with a respectable degree of local support, declared on the basis of his experience that he was "convinced that the CP can be built into an electoral force to be reckoned with" (*PW*, 22 December).

Apart from such occasional sources of inspiration, however, the party seemed stricken for most of the year by a malaise issuing from the East. The only event that elicited true enthusiasm from the organization was the June visit of African National Congress leader Nelson Mandela, an occasion for much self-congratulation over Mandela's membership in the South African Communist Party, as well as Mandela's unquestioned political success in the United States (*PW*, 23–30 June).

Allied Organizations. As in the past, the party kept a fringe of front groups alive, including its youth section, the Young Communist League.

None, however, were very active on the national scene.

The party maintained its reduced network of foreign language organizations. See, for example, comments on the persistence of communist sympathies among some Finnish-Americans in "Sauna Culture: Michigan Has Finns, Not Just Tailfins," by Paul Ingrassia. (*Wall Street Journal*, 20 July.)

Also as in the past the one area in which the party had an apparently unfading attractiveness was among U.S. academic historians. Dissertations and related works on the party's history continue to appear. The flagship title among such books for 1990 was *Dorothy Healey Remembers: A Life in the Communist Party*, edited by the historian Maurice Isserman and published by Oxford University Press. This volume of memoirs by Southern California's proto-Eurocommunist was flatteringly reviewed around the country, although the individuals and conflicts described therein were unknown to anyone who had not been a party associate. (See, e.g., "At 76, Rebel with a Lifetime Cause—An American Communist: 'Part of the Conscience of the Country,'" by Nancy Scott, *San Francisco Examiner*, 5 August.)

International Views, Positions, and Activities. With the collapse of the socialist camp, the party found its international activities dramatically curtailed. One blow was the dissolution of *World Marxist Review*, the international monthly formerly published in Prague. The election of a democratic government in Nicaragua cut short the involvement of the party in that issue, while producing something approximating a shocked silence in the ranks. The party associated itself with ultraleftist initiatives in defense of Cuba (see, e.g., advertisement for U.S. Hands Off Cuba Coalition, in *East Bay Express* [Berkeley, Calif.], 9 November), joining with elements ranging from the Trotsko-Maoist Workers' World party to the Prairie Fire Organizing Committee, a remnant of the terrorist Weather Underground. The CPUSA maintained its lately improved relations with the North Korean government (*FBIS*, 18 October). Some agitation continued over El Salvador, and the party kept a presence in the small but loud movement against U.S. intervention in Kuwait.

Other Marxist-Leninist Organizations. None of the many sects in the U.S. ultraleft was unaffected by the demoralizing crash in the East,

the result being a concentration of energies on local issues.

Some Trotskyist groups, including the largest, Socialist Action, attempted to annex themselves to the process of Soviet reform but without much credibility or effect. The small, former Trotskyist Socialist Workers' party affirmed its loyalty to Castro's Cuba, while also sojourning in Pyongyang (*FBIS*, 4 October). Several North Korean junkets were undertaken by the Workers' World party, which seemed to gain some influence over a declining radical left owing to its fanaticism. The Spartacist League carved out a special niche by concentrating its energies on attacking the reform process in the East.

Of the Maoist tendencies, the cultlike League of Revolutionary Struggle continued its campaign of infiltrating student governments and grass roots protest movements in California, provoking a debate at Stanford University over its secret organizational methods (*Stanford Daily*, 18, 21, 22, 29 May and 7 June). This group has had some success in exploiting a Japanese-American constituency. The ultraextremist Revolutionary Communist Party (RCP), which in the past focused on associating itself with Peru's violent Sendero Luminoso movement, became involved in the national debate over flag burning, one of its members having been cited in a Texas case that reached the Supreme Court in 1989. Elsewhere, the RCP concerned itself with discussions of whether rap music produced by black teenagers expressed sexist views toward women.

A number of historic leftist groups continued to maintain an organizational life. The once significant Industrial Workers of the World (IWW), of anarchosyndicalist tendency and lately reduced to no more than two hundred members, became embroiled in a campaign by radical environmentalists to obstruct tree cutting in Northern California. The outcome of this for the IWW, however, mainly consisted in further chaos and internal decay.

The Socialist Labor party, a long-lived U.S. product, celebrated the 100th anniversary of its reorganization under Daniel De Leon, to whom Lenin looked for inspiration; but its audience had all but vanished (see its organ, *The People*, 22 September.)

Obituaries. The year 1990 saw the deaths of a number of prominent figures in the history of the CPUSA, its fellow-traveling milieu, and related activities. They included:

Jay Lovestone, founder of the CPUSA, leader of its "right faction" until 1929, later a leader in AFL-CIO international affairs, died 7 March at 91 (see *NYT*, 9 March).

Harry Bridges, founder of the ILWU, died 30 March at 89 (see the *Dispatcher*, 16 May).

Mark Zborowski, Soviet secret police agent infiltrated into the Trotskyist movement during the 1930s and believed responsible for the assassination of Soviet defector Ignace Porecki-Reiss, Trotsky's son Leon Sedov, and others, died 30 April at 82 (see *San Francisco Chronicle*, 12 May).

James F. Forest, second-level party leader—convicted in 1952 in the Smith Act trial of the Missouri state party leadership—and a member of the Secretariat of the World Peace Council, died in May at 79 (see *San Francisco Chronicle*, 7 June).

David Goldway, editor of the party-line Marxist quarterly *Science and Society*, died 25 July at 83 (see *NYT*, 28 July).

Martha Dodd Stern, accused Soviet spy who fled to Czechoslovakia, died 10 August at 81 (see *San Francisco Examiner*, 26 September).

Alden Whitman, party member from 1935 to 1940 and later obituary writer for the *New York Times*, died 4 September at 76 (see *PW*, 29 September).

Jack Kling, second-level leader, delegate to the 1935 congress of the Young Communist International in Moscow, and fugitive who spent four years underground in the United States during the 1950s, died 15 November at 79 (see *PW*, 1 December).

Archie Brown, national-level party leader, frequent electoral candidate in California, Spanish civil war veteran, and mainly known as organizer of riotous demonstrations against the House Committee on Un-American Activities, San Francisco, 1960—considered the beginning of the radical student movement at University of California at Berkeley. Brown, also protagonist in the 1965 Supreme Court decision affirming the right of communist party members to hold office in labor unions, died 23 November at 79. On 3 December, the San Francisco Board of Supervisors adjourned its meeting in

his memory (see *San Francisco Chronicle*, 24 November; *PW*, 8, 29 December).

Stephen Schwartz
Arguments & Facts International

Uruguay

Population. 3,036,660 (*World Fact Book*)
Party. Communist Party of Uruguay (PCU)
Founded. 1920
Membership. 50,000 (claimed; Bogotá, *Voz*, 25 October)
General Secretary. Jaime Pérez
Secretariat. 5: Jaime Pérez, Edgar Lanza, Daniel Baldassari (organization), Pedro Toledo (finances), Adolfo Drescher (propaganda) (Montevideo, *La Hora Popular*, 24 October.)
Executive Committee. 17: Jaime Pérez, Jorge Mazzárovich, León Lev, Ramón Cabrera, Marcos Carambula, Daniel Pazos, Thelman Borges, Eduardo Platero, Edgar Lanza, Gonzalo Carambula, Victor Rossi, Tabare Gonzáles, Andrés Toriani, Rafael Sanseviero, Frederico Martínez, Manuel Barrtios, Rubén Villaverde (ibid.)
Status. Legal
Last Congress. Twenty-second, 6–18 October 1990
Last Elections. November 1989. PCU ran with Frente Amplio coalition, with ca. 34 percent of votes and 22 of 99 seats (PCU's share, 10 percent and 11 seats)
Auxiliary Organization. Union of Communist Youth
Publications. *La Hora, El Popular*

The PCU entered 1990 flushed with the success of the Frente Amplio's (Broad Front) 21 percent showing in the November 1989 elections, 47 percent of which represented the PCU's list, Democracia Avanzada. In addition, the Frente had won the mayoralty (*intendencia*) of Montevideo, the second-most important elective office in the country. The new mayor, Dr. Tabaré Vásquez, is a Socialist. The communist party proudly reported that it had grown from some 5,000 members at the time of the restoration of democratic rule in 1985 to more than 27,000 by 1989.

Events in Eastern Europe and the Soviet Union, however, had a severe impact on the party's sense of self and its future direction. The PCU's internal debates grew heated during the year as did the dialogue between the party and the Democratic Socialist coalition, Nuevo Espacio. Nuevo Espacio, led by Senator Hugo Batalla of the Partido por el Gobierno del Pueblo (PGP), received 9 percent of the vote in 1989. A reconciliation between Nuevo Espacio and the Frente Amplio is deemed crucial if the left is to win the national elections in 1994.

At its Twenty-second Congress in October the PCU partially democratized its internal structure and spoke of the role of democracy on the path to socialism. But it did not alter its basic principles of Marxism-Leninism. Much of the internal debate over ideology (the nature of the class struggle, the vanguard role of the party, and so on) was in fact put off until the 1991 meeting. PCU general secretary Jaime Pérez, in his closing speech, recognized as much by saying that "so many problems have accumulated that it is impossible to solve them all in a single congress." (*Búsqueda*, 18 October; *FBIS-LAT*, 5 November.)

The biggest success of the congress might have been that the party did not split between its renovationist and its conservative wings, a possibility that had been hanging over the leadership for months. Notable, however, was that a leading revisionist, Estaban Valenti, the guiding light behind the brilliant election campaign commercials produced by the party, chose not to stand for reelection to the Central Committee. As reported by the respected newsweekly *Búsqueda*, the congress gave something to both factions:

For the revisionists, the congress was a victory for the "renewal" faction: Innovations were introduced, numerous young people were incorporated into the leadership, and a path was opened for a process of changes at the same time that a split was avoided.

For the conservationists, the results were not entirely unfavorable. "No current of thought has been disrespected, and the resolutions are not inconsistent [hibridas]," said [Hermés] Millan, who added that the new Central Committee "reflects the various internal positions." A veteran leader who asked not to be identified, said: "During the debate, all ideas were at stake. Nonetheless, Marxist-Leninist principles were preserved; at least we have that consolation." (*Búsqueda*, 18 October; *FBIS-LAT*, 5 November.)

Although there were some statements about less direct control of the unions by the party, PCU union leaders continued to be well represented on the Central Committee (CC).

In turn, trade union leaders such as Eduardo Platero from Montevideo's Association of Municipal Employees and Workers (ADEOM) and Jorge Silvano from the Federation of Transportation Workers (FOT) received a large number of votes that placed them in positions 4 and 11 on the new list of CC members.

The CC will include as full members 23 trade union leaders, seven of whom represent their trade unions on the PIT-CNT [Plenario Intersindical de Trabajadores—Convención Nacional de Trabajadores] Executive Secretariat. In addition to Platero and Silvano, they are Cristina Gonzalez (private health workers), Oscar Groba (UNTMRA), Ruben Villaverde (FFOSE) [expansion unknown], Manuel Barrios (construction workers), and Gerardo Rey (AUTE) [Officials Group of the Uruguayan Workers Union].

Only two communist trade union leaders, who are members of the PIT-CNT leadership are not included in the PCU CC: Bernardo Groisman (clothing industry workers) and Milton Castellanos (store workers). (*Búsqueda*, 18 October; *FBIS-LAT*, 5 November.)

Besides the eagerly awaited party congress, also newsworthy was a minor scandal that developed over charges by Pascual Latronico, a former leader of the Communist Youth Union (the youth wing of the PCU), that a paramilitary group and an information office kept watch over the armed forces and the traditional parties and that it had existed within the PCU even before the 1973 military coup. Latronico named León Lev and current Secretary General and Senator Jaime Pérez as involved in these organizations. This information may have been divulged as a result of the debate within the party between those who are sympathetic to the changes taking place in Eastern Europe and the Soviet Union and the hard-line conservatives.

The Socialist party held its congress the first weekend of December, with some 450 delegates attending. Despite expectations, and in the midst of the same debate as the PCU was having over the ideological legacy of Marxism-Leninism, the membership voted 275 to 162 to put off any modification of its declaration of principles until an extraordinary congress could deal with the matter some time next year. Nevertheless, the Central Committee was elected by secret ballot for the first time. Not unexpectedly, Tabaré Vázquez received the most votes for the party's highest body. Fourteen members of the Montevideo municipal government are members of the Socialist party's Central Committee.

Vázquez is the political man of the moment, but he has his hands full. With a $105 million annual budget (only $70 per capita) he cannot modernize Montevideo. Nevertheless, in his first few months in office he acted to lower the price of public transportation, distributed vacant lands to urban homesteaders, and acted to decentralize municipal government through the creation of so-called Centros Comunal Zonal. His decision to implement a progressive tax structure in Montevideo has been extremely popular with the working class. More important, the Socialist mayor of Montevideo has made it clear that he is his own man and will not take orders from the Executive Committee of the Frente Amplio, dominated by the PCU. Vázquez believes that the left must prove it can govern Montevideo and demonstrate responsible and effective executive leadership if it is to have a chance to win the presidency in the November 1994 elections.

The former Tupamaro guerrilla movement (Movimiento de Liberación Nacional—Tupamaros) held its annual congress in July. The meeting discussed past errors, organizational weakness, and the need to mobilize the masses. The new Executive Committee was reduced from thirteen to nine members. The Central Committee consists of 25 members, and not unexpectedly José Mujica, Julio Marenales, and Eleuterio Fernández Huidobro, old guard members of the organization, received the most votes. Nevertheless, 11 of the 25 members are new to the committee.

The armed forces remained quiet during 1990. The military leadership complained about low salaries and a reduced budget, but so did everyone in the public sector. The one ominous note was the creation of "symbolic units," which were defended as social or fraternal organizations or clubs. These clubs are composed of retired and active officers including generals, some of whom did not hesitate to describe the clubs as "defenders of the armed forces against anti-national groups." (*Búsqueda*, 9 August.)

President Luis Alberto Lacalle's first year in office was not an easy one for himself or his Blanco party. The economic adjustment plan he initiated in April was not an incremental scheme; exempting only the financial sector (an omission bitterly criticized by the left), the plan was meant to reduce the fiscal deficit from 6 percent of gross domestic product to only 2.5 percent. To accomplish this task, social security taxes were increased as were real estate transfer taxes and personal and business taxes. These revenue measures, coupled with a slash in government spending, resulted in a reduction of the central government deficit to only $8.9 million for the first nine months of 1990, compared with $178 million for the comparable period of 1989. Unfortunately, inflation, which according to Lacalle's economic team was to be reduced to 50 percent by year's end, rose steadily. The surge in oil prices after Iraq's invasion of Kuwait did not help. By November, inflation had reached 117 percent for 1990 and 127 percent for the previous twelve months. Triple-digit inflation historically ruptures the social contract in Uruguay. By year's end, Lacalle's parliamentary alliance with sectors of the Colorado party was being severely questioned, and serious reservations were expressed by the liberal wing of his own party, led by Senator Carlo Julio Pereyra. The gross national product was expected to be flat or slightly negative for the year. The left bitterly denounced the Lacalle program, but at year's end the government indicated that it would not alter its fiscal and monetary policies.

The soaring inflation in 1990 did not help Lacalle in his relations with the labor movement. Although not as unified or as tightly controlled by the PCU as before the dictatorship, the PIT-CNT is controlled by the left, with preponderantly communist leadership. In late September, Lacalle inaugurated a national dialogue to come to some agreement on wages between labor, entrepreneurs, and the government. With more than 20 percent of all workers employed in the public sector, the state has always played a significant role in salary negotiations. The aim of the talks, which continue to be inconclusive, is to avoid the social polarization and conflict of the late 1960s that helped produce the growing authoritarianism of the Pacheco Areco government and was a catalyst for the military takeover in 1973.

In 1991, the government's plan to privatize some state enterprises (telephones and the airline) and eliminate the monopoly enjoyed by some others (mortgage banking, insurance, and the production of alcohol and cement) will continue to be strongly resisted by the left in Parliament and in the union movement. But the Lacalle administration will find its most serious disagreement with labor will come when it attempts to pass legislation on union organization and activity, most especially the right to strike. Such legislation was postponed during 1990 but will be introduced when Parliament reconvenes in February. Uruguay has virtually no laws regulating union activity or strikes. As mild as the government's proposals may be, they will be denounced by labor; work stoppages, including general strikes, can be anticipated if and when the legislation is brought to a vote.

By the end of the year Uruguay and its creditor banks were near final agreement on restructuring its debt via the Brady Plan. Of the $1.6 billion in public debt held by private banks, it was expected that Uruguay would repurchase some $628 million at around 60 percent of its face value. The remainder of the debt will either be converted to bonds with a fixed interest rate of 6.75 percent or refinanced with a sixteen-year period of amortization and a grace period of seven years. Those banks that accept this last option will have to make a new commitment of fresh funds equivalent to 20 percent of the value of this portion of the loans.

President Lacalle's approval rating was at an alarmingly low figure after only eight months in office. Equipos Consultores, Uruguay's best polling organization, reported it at between 13 and 14 percent in November. The Parliament fared little better, with a positive rating of only 17 percent. Only Mayor Vásquez of Montevideo could claim a reasonable approval rating (46 percent) but this was down from 62 percent in March. (*Búsqueda*, 6 December.)

The early conflicts between Mayor Vázquez and President Lacalle over budget and decentralization issues concerning the municipal government turned into a sort of truce in the second half of the year. Nevertheless, the fact that Vázquez continues to be far more popular than the president implies that relations between the two men—expecially if there is no economic upturn in 1991—will be cool at best.

President George Bush's 22-hour visit to Montevideo 4–5 October proved to be a big nonevent for the left. After some debate about whether to demonstrate against the visit, the left agreed to some nonviolent protests, which turned out to be poorly organized and poorly attended. Mayor Vázquez took the opportunity to discuss social injustice and some North-South issues when he turned the keys of the city over to Bush. Bush responded with some extemporaneous comments indicating that everyone wants social justice and democracy. President Lacalle may have relished the spotlight that was turned on him for the day, but he received nothing concrete from the U.S. president.

As Uruguay enters 1991 it is safe to predict that if there is no improvement in the economic situation, tension between labor and the government will increase. Tabaré Vázquez will continue to be seen as a political threat to the two traditional parties, and talk of constitutional reform, especially of the electoral system, will become more prevalent. The left will look as if it were increasing in strength, but with more than three years to go until any elections, that strength will be difficult to operationalize. Uruguay will be drifting but, for the first time since the restoration of democracy in 1985, in a climate that is not beneficial to the economy or the polity.

Martin Weinstein
William Paterson College of New Jersey

Venezuela

Population. 19,698,104

Parties. Communist Party of Venezuela (Partido Comunista de Venezuela; PCV), formerly pro-Soviet; Movement to Socialism (Movimiento al Socialismo; MAS), democratic Socialist

Founded. PCV: 1931; MAS: 1971

Membership. PCV: 4,000, estimated; MAS: 267,000 (*El Nacional*, 7 August)

Party Leader. PCV: Trino Meleán, general secretary; Pedro Ortega Díaz, president; MAS: Freddy Muñoz, general secretary; Argelia Laya, president

Executive Committees. PCV: Politburo, 7 members; Central Committee, 41 principals, 3 alternates; MAS: Executive Committee, 23 members; National Directorate, 61 principals, 65 alternates

Auxiliary Organizations. PCV: Unitary Central of Venezuelan Workers (Central Unitária de Trabajadores Venezolanos; CUTV), Communist Youth (Juventud Comunista); MAS: MAS Youth (Juventud MAS), 60,000 members (*Diario de Caracas*, 25 July)

Last Congress. PCV: Eighth, 25–27 August; MAS: Seventh national convention, July, September, December

Last Election. 1988 (see *YICA*, 1990); PCV has 1 of 201 federal deputies; MAS has 1 state governor, 21 federal deputies, and 3 of 46 senators.

Publications. PCV: *Tribuna Popular*, weekly; *Canta Claro*, monthly ideological supplement of central committee

Windfall earnings from petroleum as a result of the Persian Gulf crisis did not stop Venezuela's slide into economic recession. Critics, in fact, point to continued deficit spending, as well as the government's slowness in implementing privatization plans and other administrative reforms, as fundamental causes of the malaise. At the same time, under the economic stabilization plan adopted in 1989, both prices and unemployment have increased dramatically (see *YICA*, 1990). Food riots began early in 1990 and were followed by protests against higher prices for gasoline and public transportation. The protests did not duplicate the violence of the 1989 conflicts, which left three hundred dead, but they were widespread and persistent. According to the Interior Ministry, the worst of the disturbances are orchestrated by "very small parties or insignificant movements . . . such as Union de Jóvenes Revolucionários and Venceremos" (*Diario de Caracas*, 2 August). A number of peaceful student demonstrations, including those protesting the visit of President Bush, degenerated into violence as a result of provocations by small groups of hooded persons (*El Universal*, 30 November).

PCV. A lot of *perestroika* was talked at the Eighth Party Congress. Unclear was how much of the talk represented genuine acceptance of the necessity for reform and how much simply a continuation of the ingrained tendency to follow Moscow's lead on all issues. Some changes were visible: the press was admitted to plenary sessions for the first time; a few long-estranged Communists were present by invitation; and elections were open and competitive. Trino Meleán, a psychiatrist and the PCV's only federal deputy, was elected general secretary by acclamation after Hector Mujica and CUTV president José Manuel Carrasquel withdrew their candidacies. Both Meleán and the new PCV president, Ortega Díaz, are described as party men; however, only somewhat less orthodox than their predecessors, Alonso Ojeda and Jesús Faría, respectively. Much of the old party machinery was also returned to the Central Committee.

If the political resolutions of this congress had been made twenty years ago, the MAS would have had no reason to leave the PCV. The 1968 Soviet invasion of Czechoslovakia was finally condemned, and the party aspires to the establishment of a Socialist regime that combines social welfare with democratic freedom: "not an authoritarian socialism like that which has failed but a democratic and humanistic socialism, supported by the immense majority of the people" (*Diario de Caracas*, 25, 27 August). In contrast, Hector Mujica, who is the most liberal PCV leader, had earlier refused to condemn outright the principle of democratic socialism. In a round table discussion of the subject, he said that it "is justified only when a socialist revolution is being consolidated, otherwise it eventually evolves into authoritarianism" (*WMR*, January).

The prospect of a fusion of the PCV with other small leftist parties, perhaps even dropping the name, remains likely. Although Alonso Ojeda would not comment on a name change when questioned earlier this year (*El Nacional*, 4 February), the presence of old defectors such as Eduardo Machado at the congress gave strength to the rumors.

In his closing speech to the congress, Meleán reaffirmed the decision of "the central committee and all the members of the party to resolutely support the Cuban revolution" (*Cubavision Network*, 29 August; *FBIS-LAT*, 29 August). Jesús Faría foreshadowed this result in June when he admitted that Gorbachev's opening in the Soviet Union was a brave and necessary move, which should not, however, be applied to Cuba. Aside from his opinion that "the fever of market economies will pass," he was convinced that Cuba "will not give perestroika the slightest chance, because the imperialists would use such an opportunity to get rid of Fidel Castro. Castro is very cautiously opening some channels for critics . . . without endangering his revolution." (*El Nacional*, 27 June.)

MAS. Honoring long-repeated calls for greater internal democracy, the Seventh National Convention of the MAS began in late July with elections for national leaders in which every party member's vote was counted. That ambitious project generated a not surprising amount of wrangling, recounts, and—in two states—new elections. MAS founder and former guerrilla Argelia Laya easily defeated Moisés Moleiro and Luis Bayardo Sardi for the presidency, and Freddy Muñoz won a second term as general secretary over Victor Hugo D'Paola. Plenary sessions, which followed two months later, approved a platform concerned primarily with opposition to the government's economic austerity measures and offering counterproposals for dealing with the widespread poverty and unemployment those measures had caused. In a third phase of the convention in December, remaining party offices were filled. Large numbers of seats on the Executive Committee and National Directorate went for the first time to regional delegates from all parts of the country. Much was made of the fact that, in addition to the new president, 20 percent of the new directors are women.

With its open elections, MAS anticipated norms of internal democracy demanded by the newly re-formed political parties law, part of a package of administrative reforms. In one of many discussions preceding its virtually unanimous passage in Congress, Freddy Muñoz lamented that internal power struggles had displaced ideological orientation in the mainstream parties (Democratic Action: Acción Democrática, AD, government party; COPEI: social Christian). Former MAS president Pompeyo Márquez said that the separate sessions of the MAS convention had been designed to avoid this, keeping the political aspects apart from the bureaucratic. In regard to MAS ideology, Márquez added that "socialism must be brought up to date, not rejected" and that "the failure of the authoritarian, centralized model" in Eastern Europe "in no way invalidates the quest for new forms of participation and property . . . to overcome the scourges of capitalism." (*Diario de Caracas*, 13 August.)

According to MAS deputy and former presidential candidate Teodoro Petkoff, Venezuela's windfall petroleum earnings should be used to pay off as much foreign debt as possible, not reinvested in wasteful state enterprises, many of which "must now be privatized" (*NYT*, 2 September). MAS nonetheless does not seem altogether easy with privatization. It has called for greater worker participation in some privatized companies, has proposed new antitrust legislation, and plans to introduce a privatization bill that defines more precisely the sectors that may be affected. Petkoff, for example, believes that the petroleum industry must remain in the hands of the state, with any eventual downstream participation of private capital subject to congressional approval (*El Nacional*, 6 September).

MAS has collaborated rather closely with COPEI in congressional opposition, and the association is expected to carry over into the next gubernatorial contests. There is also open discus-sion of MAS support for a ticket headed by former President Rafael Caldera (COPEI) in the 1993 presidential election. Within MAS, aspirants for that nomination include Petkoff, Muñoz, and Carlos Tablante, governor of the state of Aragua. Tablante was released from party dictates for the length of his term and has made no significant changes in the state government. He and other governors maintain that the decentralization of the national government, a reform passed in 1989 with much fanfare, is a farce as long as the administration refuses to release any part of regional investment funds to the states (*El Nacional*, 28 June).

Other Leftist Parties. Andrés Velásquez is Causa R's (Radical Cause) governor of the state of Bolívar. Although an opinion poll in June gave him good ratings for diligence, honesty, and capability, his administration has been the most embattled of all the opposition governors. A mixed commission—government, Guayana Development Corporation and labor unions—has been discussing privatization of the state-owned steel mill Sidor. Causa R would like a referendum, however, guaranteeing protection for the workers. Together with union leaders, the party has accused CVG president Leopoldo Sucre Figarella of provoking labor conflicts in order to paralyze the firm and thus hasten privatization (*El Nacional*, 6 September). Velásquez has also demanded complete decentralization of health services and said that inefficiency, "not sabotage," of the Health Ministry in meeting contract obligations has caused legitimate strikes that are shutting down services in Bolívar (ibid., 12 December). His administration has been criticized for the rough handling of *garimpeiros*, small-time gold prospectors who come by the thousands over the border from Brazil creating legal, social, and ecological problems.

It is not yet clear whether the split in the People's Electoral Movement (Movimiento Electoral del Pueblo; MEP) will be permanent. Adelso González Urdaneta claims he was reelected general secretary in the August elections. The faction led by Fernando Alvarez Paz, also a candidate for general secretary, said the elections never took place. González apparently boycotted makeup elections called in October. Luis Beltrán Prieto, MEP founder and president, supported Alvarez and considers González out of the party (*El Universal*, 5 December).

Carole Merten
San Francisco, Calif.

ASIA AND THE PACIFIC

Introduction

The communist-led states of Asia, with the exception of the Mongolian People's Republic (MPR), resisted the road to political pluralism and continued to limit the scope of economic reform. These Communist parties removed from their ranks those who dared mention political reform and they persecuted those who suggested a different form of political governance. Party leaders clung tenaciously to power, which sometimes led to vicious struggles over the future course of policies and the appointment of key party, government, and military personnel. Except in the Philippines, where the Communist Party remained active, the communist insurrectionary movement that had been so powerful in previous decades was over, although many left-wing parties espousing Marxism-Leninism continued to enjoy the liberties provided by their democratic societies. We can best review these developments by classifying communist activity into states with ruling communist parties, states with banned communist parties in opposition, and states with legal communist parties.

States with Ruling Communist Parties. In the People's Republic of China (PRC) the Communist party expelled 33,400 members from the party in 1989 and an unknown number in 1990. Its leaders also shifted a large number of officials at the provincial level and in the military, removing those who had demanded reform but not necessarily replacing them with hard-liners.

Meanwhile, the top leaders formed factions to advance their favorite personnel and pushed for policies they believed were in their personal interest and in the interest of preserving and consolidating party power. Although perhaps as many as three or four leadership factions bitterly competed, this power struggle was never resolved to the advantage of any particular faction, and compromise remained the order of the day.

For example, on 30 December 1990, after a six-day communist party plenum of 584 senior party members in Beijing, the guidelines for the 1991–1995 economic plan were announced: China will retain current economic reforms while looking for ways to keep most economic activity under government control. The PRC will welcome foreign investment on a selective basis aimed at importing technology to meet the needs of the government and factories making currently imported products. Officials declared that the party would adhere to building "socialism with Chinese characteristics," continuing change, promoting "socialist culture and ethics," and providing material benefits within the framework of a central planned economy in which the dominant sector would remain that of state enterprises and cooperatives.

The government also began holding trials in January 1991 for dissidents arrested in the 1989 anti-government protests. Top leaders like Zhao Ziyang who had been blamed for these disturbances were not put on trial, but a select number of lesser leaders were tried and given prison sentences ranging from lenient (three to five years) to severe (ten to thirteen years). To be sure, the remarks of hard-liners like Yang Shangkun attacking radical political and economic reforms for "impetuosity," a code word used by conservative officials to criticize the reforms pushed by former party chief Zhao, were played up in the press. Yet the presence of large numbers of reform-minded officials in both Beijing and the provinces attested to the provinces' continuing reluctance to remit more tax revenues to the central government.

The economy showed no significant signs of emerging from its doldrums. Mounting subsidies to bail out inefficient state enterprises and to keep grain and edible oil prices down forced the government to run an ever-larger deficit and print more money. According to Xiang Jingquan, a professor at the institute of Fiscal Sciences under the Finance Ministry, in 1989 about 60 billion renminbi (US$11.5 billion) were used to support poorly run enterprises and 37 renminbi (US$7.1 billion) for price supports. These amounts represent an incredible increase over the level of subsidies some ten years earlier.

Although beset by various crises, the Marxist-Leninist regime in North Korea, long ruled by the autocrat Kim Il-song, continued defiant even as other Marxist-Leninist regimes were overturned in Europe and the Soviet Union remained embroiled in difficulties. Kim Il-song announced on 24 May that the country would adhere to "our own style of socialism." Other leaders continued to celebrate the Kim cult, calling him "the first great leader in the Korean history of thousands of years."

The Nineteenth Plenum of the Sixth Congress, held in late May, brought a small but significant change to the top leadership of the Korean Workers' party: several technocrats returned to power, and Choe Kwang, the current chief of staff of the armed forces who had been purged after he was implicated in an anti–Kim Il-song incident in 1969, was returned to the fourteen-member Politburo.

Constrained by three years of poor harvests and dwindling trade, the economy remained weak, with the lowest growth rate since 1986. The Soviet Union stated that the barter system long used with North Korea would end in 1991 and that North Korea would have to pay for imports of Soviet goods and services with hard currency. The country's external debt is estimated at US$3–6 billion.

The regime's greatest setback of the year came when Moscow and Seoul normalized diplomatic relations in the fall. Pyongyang began negotiating with Japan over war reparations and normalizing relations, but these bogged down.

To prevent the spread of political pluralism, the republic of Vietnam continued to adhere to the policies of the recent past and to tolerate only minimal economic reforms to stimulate production and exchange. Tran Xuan Bach, a member of the Politburo, was expelled from that body when he publicly asked whether Vietnam should "think about" the idea of a multiparty system. Le Duc Tho, one of the most powerful figures in the party for the past decade, died on 13 October at the age of 79. Bui Tin, editor of the party newspaper *Nhan Dan*, was quoted in early spring 1990 as saying that the Communist party must learn to "persuade rather than rule" and that Vietnam already had pluralism in such matters as religious belief but would never allow political pluralism. Even though Bui Tin appeared to adopt an intermediate position, he was criticized, and in early December he announced that he would not return to Vietnam from Paris (although he denied that he was defecting).

In communist Laos, the party's general secretary, Kaysone Phomvihane, reportedly stated that the party "does not yet see any need for establishing other political parties." At the party's Ninth Plenum, 17–24 January, the party remained committed to its Leninist principles and organization and vowed to promote new economic enterprises to increase production and expand markets. In October the government arrested a small group for advocating a multiparty system to bring democracy, freedom, and prosperity to the people. Although the spring harvest appeared good, the trade deficit continued to rise. State enterprises still reported expanding output, but they made no mention of whether productivity had increased.

In Cambodia the Khmer Rouge continued their military attacks on the Vietnam-installed government in Phnom Penh. Despite Chinese assurances that Beijing had stopped sending military aid to the Khmer Rouge guerrillas in September, Chinese arms continued to flow to all factions fighting the Phnom Penh government, including the Khmer Rouge.

The most remarkable developments occurred in the MPR, a country much in the Soviet orbit of influence for 66 years. The Communist Party, under intense pressure from public demonstrations and concerned about economic difficulties, permitted the formation of opposition parties and introduced free elections to the chief legislative body, the Great People's Hural. In December 1989 the Mongolian Democratic Union emerged and called for the Communist Party to relinquish its monopoly on power, democratize, and allow a market economy to evolve. Massive resignations from the party in early 1990 paved the way for new leaders like Gombojabyn Ochirbat, a former trade union leader, who became the party's general secretary. The former general secretary, Tsedenbal, resigned in disgrace, and many party cadres who had been purged were rehabilitated.

On 10 April, 926 delegates were elected to the MPR's new party leadership. Party membership even increased modestly, from 90,000 to 100,000 by the year's end. Despite the shake-up among the party's top leaders, they could not agree on which reform policies to adopt. The debate remained mired in how to move to a market economy and how rapidly to make that adjustment. Then in April six opposition parties formed a coalition to take part in forthcoming elections. The economy continued to decline. A budget deficit helped to propel more inflation and produce more unemployment and social unrest. By year's end, bitter debate still raged over which reform package to adopt. In fact, the government even seemed to be backing away from previous measures calling for more privatization. The few bright spots, however, included the MPR's recognition of the Republic of Korea and increased Japanese investment in Mongolia's metallurgical industry. More foreign businessmen visited the country than ever before.

States with Banned Communist Party Opposition. Since the 1980s, Thailand has faced little danger from an indigenous communist insurgency, largely because of steady economic growth averaging around 7 percent per annum. The gradual liberalization of the political system has also discouraged organized leftist attempts to create instability and promote radical political change. Even right-wing military threats to interfere in government policy and personnel appointments have not reversed the liberalization trend.

In Burma the communist movement remains fragmented and in disarray. Some dozen members of the old party's Central Committee decided to return to China.

In Indonesia the government eliminated the communist movement and drove its leaders abroad. In 1990, Indonesia resumed normal diplomatic relations with the PRC. Leading officials announced that former communist leaders living abroad would be allowed to return to Indonesia but only under certain conditions. Probably only around ten former communist leaders live in China, and the PRC authorities forbid them from engaging in political activities.

In the Philippines, the Communist Party of the Philippines (CPP) took advantage of the government's economic difficulties and its periodic suppression of military coup attempts by encouraging its New People's Army (NPA) to continue its armed conflict. NPA rebels continued to attack foreign business companies and attempted to extort exorbitant "taxes" from at least 89 large firms in the metro Manila area. Similarly, the NPA burned farm equipment and farmland on Negros, destroyed buses in Davao del Sur, and killed a high-ranking police officer in Davao city. The party was also responsible for the murder of two U.S. servicemen and the kidnapping of U.S. and Japanese aid workers.

The CPP leadership postponed recommending Jose Maria Sison as party leader as long as he remained in exile in Europe. Although a leadership conference was allegedly held in Manila in the fall, it is still unclear who is the party's paramount leader.

The Philippine government announced in December that the number of NPA guerrillas had been reduced from more than 25,000 in 1985 to 17,900 and that in 1990 alone some 1,680 rebels had been killed and about 30 CPP leaders had been captured in the Manila area. The government also claimed to have reduced the number of CPP-controlled barangays from around 8,000 (out of some 40,000) to 5,752. Even so, the NPA remains a formidable force, and the precarious state of the economy as well as the uncertain loyalty of government military units combine to cripple government efforts to eradicate the NPA and eliminate the CPP as a serious threat.

States with Legal Communist Parties. There are no communist parties in the South Pacific, for few politicians in that vast region want such an affiliation. Socialist ideas, however, greatly influence the union movement, which has grown in strength in recent years.

The communist parties in New Zealand and Australia continued to assail their respective governments and their policies but failed to expand membership or influence the voting public to take their positions seriously.

In Sri Lanka, the pro-Moscow Communist Party and a Trotskyite party continued to exercise limited influence in the political system. Members of a radical Maoist group were hunted down and killed by progovernment death squads and security forces.

In India the communists tried to use the rise of militant Hinduism as a rallying cry to organize grass roots support for their cause. They also criticized the dominant Bharatiya Janata Party, the standard-bearer of militant Hindu nationalism, and worked within the National Front government to moderate the Bharatiya Janata Party's influence.

The Japanese Communist Party continued to advocate a parliamentary road to power, but it lost eleven seats in the 1990 election for Diet members. The party, which refused to align itself with other parties, supported a number of auxiliaries, which enjoyed little political influence. The party held its Nineteenth Congress in July. Kenji Miyamoto (82) remained chairman of the Central Committee. The only important change in leadership came with the election of 35-year-old Kazuo Shii as head of the Secretariat. Shii, who received an engineering degree from Tokyo University, joined the party in 1973. Miyamoto continued to defend his record and rebut critics who complained of his age and urged him to step down to allow a revitalization of party leadership.

Ramon H. Myers
Hoover Institution

Australia

Population. 16,923,478 (July; *World Fact Book*)
Parties. Communist Party of Australia (CPA); Socialist Party of Australia (SPA); Democratic Socialist Party (DSP); Communist Party of Australia—Marxist-Leninist (CPA-ML); Association for Communist Unity (ACU); New Left Party (NLP)
Founded. CPA: 1920; SPA: 1971; CPA-ML: 1964; DSP: 1972; ACU: 1985; NLP: 1989
Membership. CPA: 800–1,000 (1989); SPA: no current information; CPA-ML: 50 (1989); DSP: 250–500 (1989); ACU: no current information; NLP: 1,000 (*Tribune*, 13 June)
Leadership. CPA: Brian Aarons, Rob Durbridge (Australian Teachers' Union industrial officer), Michael Evans, Dennis Freney, Pat Ranald; SPA: P. Symon, Central Committee general secretary; NLP: Di Bolton (Canberra public servant), Brian Carey, Darryl Honor (Brisbane), Jack Mundey, Giselle Thomas (organizer of the Queensland regional branch)
Status. Legal
Last Congress. CPA: Thirtieth, 2–3 December 1989; SPA: Sixth, 3 October 1988; DSP: Eleventh, 2–6 January 1986; CPA-ML: Seventh, October 1988; NLP: Founding Conference, 9–11 June
Last Election. 24 March
Publications. CPA: *Tribune* (weekly; editorial collective includes Jim Endersby, Michael Evans, Dennis Freney, Gloria Garton, Phaedra Johnson, Carlotta McIntosh, Jan McKemmish, Peter Murphy, Sergio Scudery, Roderick Shaw, Jess Walker); *Australian Left Review* (monthly; David Burchell is part of editorship); SPA: no current information; CPA-ML: *Australian Communist* (bimonthly); *Vanguard* (weekly)

As Australian communism marked its centennial on 1 May, little remained to distinguish its agenda from that of the liberal mainstream. Australian government contacts with the Eastern bloc, meanwhile, continued throughout the year. On 3 January, Michael Costello, vice-minister of foreign affairs and trade, left for a second round of discussions on Foreign Minister Gareth Evans's proposal to resolve the Cambodia conflict and clear the way for elections there by replacing the Vietnam-backed Hun Sen regime with a U.N. administration and vacating the U.N. seat held by the Coalition Government of Democratic Kampuchea (CGDK). Costello's itinerary included meetings with Khmer Rouge representative Khieu Samphan, Vietnamese foreign minister Nguyen Co Thach, Cambodian prime minister Hun Sen, CGDK leader Son Sann, and Rafeedin Ahmed, U.N. special representative on Cambodia. (Hong Kong, AFP, *FBIS-EAS*, 2 January.) Heartened by changes in Eastern Europe and hoping to expand economic relations there, Australia opened an embassy in Prague on 30 January (Melbourne Overseas Service, *FBIS-EAS*, 2 February).

Prime Minister Nikolai Ryzhkov, the most senior Soviet official thus far to visit Australia, arrived on 13 February for three days of talks with Australian officials during which six agreements were formalized. Two of those compacts arranged access to Australian ports for the Soviet antarctic fishing fleet in return for guaranteed imports of Australian agricultural and mineral products. The other accords dealt with Soviet emigration to Australia, consular activities, the environment, and the peaceful use of nuclear energy. (*FBIS-EAS*, 13, 15, 22 February.) During his visit, Ryzhkov discussed economic issues and developments in Eastern Europe with Australian prime minister Bob Hawke (Hong Kong, AFP, 14 February; *FBIS-EAS*, 15 February) and inaugurated Melbourne University's new Centre for Soviet and East European Studies (Hong Kong, AFP, *FBIS-EAS*, 13 February). Soviet deputy foreign minister Igor Rogachev, who was among Ryzhkov's entourage of some one hundred persons, met with Gareth Evans for talks on Cambodia (Hong Kong, AFP, 14 February; *FBIS-EAS*, 15 February).

During an eight-day visit to Australia, Qi Yuanjing, the People's Republic of China (PRC) minister for metallurgical industries, officially opened a Western Australian iron ore mine in which the Chinese government holds a 40 percent share. The $A280 million project is expected to supply China with up to 10 million tons of ore per year over the next twenty years. (Melbourne Overseas Service, 5 May; *FBIS-EAS*, 8 May.) Qi, the first Chinese minister to visit Australia since the Tiananmen massacre of June 1989, held talks with various Australian government officials but was comparatively—indeed, pointedly—shunned by officials as a reminder that Canberra was not yet ready to overlook China's human rights abuses (Hong Kong, AFP, *FBIS-EAS*, 9 May).

In May, Australian wool exporters suspended shipments to the USSR, Australia's second-largest wool market, pending an overdue payment of $A100 million for earlier orders (Hong Kong, AFP, 7 May; *FBIS-EAS*, 9 May).

Foreign Minister Evans told Parliament on 10 May that he would press the Coordinating Council for Multilateral Control (COCOM) to ease restrictions on technology exports to Eastern Europe (Hong Kong, AFP, 10 May; *FBIS-EAS*, 15 May).

Prime Minister Hawke announced in June that the 19,400 Chinese students in Australia on 20 June 1989 who had subsequently been granted asylum would likely be required to return to China in 1994, though none would be forced to do so. The approximately twenty thousand students who had arrived in Australia after the Beijing crackdown would be expected to return home at the usual time. (Hong Kong, AFP, 12, 27 June; *FBIS-EAS*, 14, 27 June.) It is expected that Medicare entitlements will eventually be extended to all PRC students in Australia (*Tribune*, 4 July).

On 2 July the government announced that it would permit the reopening of the Yugoslav consulate general, which was closed following a November 1988 shooting incident (Hong Kong, AFP, 2 July; *FBIS-EAS*, 3 July). PRC vice–foreign minister Liu Huaqiu was allowed to open a new embassy building in Canberra on 10 August; a small group of protesters represented Chinese students and the Australia Tibet Council at the ceremony (Hong Kong, AFP, 10 August; *FBIS-EAS*, 13 August).

The Australian government's international telecommunications company, OTC, won a ten-year, $250 million contract to modernize Vietnam's local telecommunications network (Melbourne Overseas Service, 24 August; *FBIS-EAS*, 27 August). Trade Minister Neal Blewett, the first Australian minister to visit China since last year's crackdown, arrived in Beijing in early September for two days of talks on trade and economic issues (Melbourne Overseas Service, 2 September; *FBIS-EAS*, 5 September).

Also in September, Gareth Evans pressured the Phnom Penh government to accept Prince Norodom Sihanouk as chairman of an interim Cambodian ruling council, the Supreme National Council, with Cambodian premier Hun Sen to serve as vice-chairman (Hong Kong, AFP, 14 September; *FBIS-EAS*, 17 September). An Australian government economic delegation headed by New South Wales (NSW) prime minister Mike Glenard visited Guangzhou on 24 September to celebrate ten years of economic cooperation between NSW and Guangdong province (Guangzhou, Guangdong Provincial Service, *FBIS-CHI*, 25 September).

An Australian trade union delegation traveled to Vietnam for 21–31 October talks with the Confederation of Vietnamese Workers (Hanoi Domestic Service, 27 October; *FBIS-EAS*, 30 October). Vice-Minister Costello visited Pyongyang on 2–3 November to meet with Sihanouk for discussions aimed at resolving the Cambodia conflict. While there, he met with an unidentified Democratic People's Republic of Korea (DPRK) deputy foreign minister to continue the "existing dialogue" between Australia and North Korea and to express Australian concern over the DPRK's failure to meet its obligations under the nuclear nonproliferation treaty. Although their talks represented the highest-level government contact since diplomatic relations between the two nations were severed in 1975, Costello denied that the meeting indicated any Australian intention of restoring relations. (Hong Kong, AFP, 9 November; *FBIS-EAS*, 13 November.)

John Kerin, minister for primary industries and energy, arrived in Beijing on 29 November to urge officials there to increase Chinese imports of Australian wool (Melbourne Overseas Service, 1 December; *FBIS-EAS*, 5 December). Late in the year, Vo Van Kiet, first vice-chairman of the Vietnamese Council of Ministers, received representatives of the Australia and New Zealand Bank and a major Australian accounting firm, vowing to "positively consider" the firms' proposals to open offices in Vietnam and assist the country in its current economic restructuring (Hanoi, VNA, in English, 3 December; *FBIS-EAS*, 6 December).

Communist Party of Australia. Notwithstanding its 1989 decision to cease independent activity, the CPA appears still extant, at least in form. The *Tribune* is still described as its organ, and brief directories of CPA branches were published there as late as 30 October. The results of a late 1989 survey of *Tribune* readers indicated "much more support for the idea of a non-aligned, independent paper than . . . for one tied to the NLP" (*Tribune*, 31 January).

It is increasingly difficult to distinguish the CPA's aims from those of the liberal mainstream. The party focused throughout the year on environmental, aboriginal, women's, and gay and lesbian concerns. Labor matters also received considerable attention. The CPA supported Melbourne tram workers' protest over cost cutting in that government-run industry but suggested that they return to work and leave protests over staff trimming to the riding public (*Tribune*, 14 February). The party opposed the union consolidation proposals of the Labor party and the Australian Council of Trade Unions (ibid.).

In other domestic matters, the CPA was consistently opposed to privatization, particularly of the government-owned airlines and phone system. Like the CPA-ML, the CPA opposed, on grounds of both environmental protection and economic sovereignty, Japanese proposals for a high-speed train line and a Multi-Function Polis (MFP) technocity (*Tribune*, 2 May).

The CPA urged its members to vote for progressive, independent, and environmentalist candidates in the 24 March national elections; in the absence of such candidates, the membership was asked to vote for candidates of the ruling Australian Labor party (*Tribune*, 21 February).

Various *Tribune* articles during the year argued that current political developments signal a change in the mission of socialism rather than its demise. The CPA was pleased by the current de-Stalinization of Eastern Europe (*Tribune*, 13 December 1989), and a 14 February editorial welcomed the prospect of a multiparty Soviet system (*Tribune*, 14 February). The 6 June issue of the *Tribune* noted a 3 June march by ten thousand people, mostly Chinese students, to protest the 1989 massacre in Beijing. The CPA condemned Australian backing of the Aquino regime in the Philippines (*Tribune*, 13 December 1989), and U.S. economic pressure was taxed with the Sandinista defeat in Nicaragua's February elections (*Tribune*, 28 February).

Despite a price hike from 60 cents to one dollar per issue and a variety of fund-raising efforts, the *Tribune*'s financial troubles persist. Pleas continued throughout the year for contributions to the press fund, but the results were less successful than in previous years: As of 19 September the fund had accumulated a A$10,000 (33 percent) deficit; vegetable sales and other fund-raising activities, however, raised total press funds to A$29,186 by 31 October (*Tribune*, 31 October).

Socialist Party of Australia. P. Symon, general secretary of the SPA's Central Committee, held talks with DPRK president Kim Il-song on 6 January (Pyongyang, Korean Central News Agency, 6 January; *FBIS-EAS*, 10 January).

The SPA, which is in the process of amalgamation with the DSP, did not figure prominently during the year.

Communist Party of Australia—Marxist-Leninist. The CPA-ML's predictable denunciations of economic imperialism and capitalist exploitation continued. Domestically, the CPA-ML opposed privatization of government property and enterprises and government and private cutbacks intended to respond to a faltering economy marred by mortgage rates as high as 18 percent. The party condemned the privatization of child care (*Vanguard*, 28 March) and cuts in government welfare and infrastructure spending (*Vanguard*, 14 February). When the 24 March national elections came around, however, the CPA-ML reluctantly endorsed the ruling Australian Labor Party (ALP) as a lesser evil than the Liberal/National party (*Vanguard*, 7, 28 February).

The party, which expressed environmental, aboriginal, and industrial-safety concerns throughout the year, was particularly vociferous in its support of organized labor. Persistently decrying the "opportunism" (*Australian Communist*, January–February) of the Australian Council of Trade Unions (ACTU), the CPA-ML blamed the ACTU and its alleged ally, the ALP, for falling Australian living standards and the decline of union membership from 62 percent of the work force in 1986 (*World Fact Book*) to 42 percent in 1989 (*Australian Communist*, January–February). The CPA-ML also opposed the ongoing consolidation, backed by both Canberra and the ACTU, of unions into larger unions representing a minimum of twenty thousand workers (the ACTU's proposal calls for twenty union groupings).

During the course of the year, the CPA-ML backed the Melbourne tram workers' ultimately unsuccessful January–February opposition to government cost-cutting measures (*Vanguard*, 7 February), supported miners and striking pilots (*Vanguard*, 31 January), and endorsed teachers and truckers' demands for higher wages (*Vanguard*, 28 February). The "monopoly capitalism" of the Australian television networks was denounced repeatedly and at length (e.g., *Vanguard*, 24 January, 14 February).

Internationally, the CPA-ML reiterated its support for the Palestine Liberation Organization and condemned Foreign Minister Evans's proposal for resolving the Cambodia conflict (*Vanguard*, 24 January). Both "U.S. warmongering" in the Persian Gulf in response to Iraq's 2 August annexation of Kuwait and Canberra's support for U.S. actions were promptly denounced (*Vanguar '*, 15 August). Indeed, Australian surveys reflect .g widespread popular support for U.S. actions were denounced as rigged (*Vanguard*, 19 September).

Particular animus was reserved for U.S. and especially Japanese "interference" in the Australian economy and elsewhere. Japanese interest in building a high-speed rail line between Sydney and Melbourne and establishing a high-technology investment zone on the outskirts of Adelaide were condemned throughout the year (e.g., *Vanguard*, 18 July).

Foreign monopoly capitalists were excoriated as well for meddling in the affairs of China and Eastern Europe. Deriding the illusory defeat of East European communism, *Australian Communist* (May/June) warned against the predations of foreign monopoly capitalists there. The 24 January *Vanguard* noted with some satisfaction the difficulties in Poland's transition to a market economy; Albania's Socialist system, too, had been targeted by the imperialists (*Vanguard*, 31 January).

An article minimizing the death toll in the suppression of last year's Chinese democracy movement (*Vanguard*, 14 February) was followed by an assertion that reports of the crackdown had been exaggerated or fabricated: "The Australian government has played a particularly important role in the Western imperialists' ferocious anti-China campaign" (*Vanguard*, 2 May). The continuing mission of world communism is signaled, the 26 September *Vanguard* claimed, by that publication's substantially increased circulation over the past few years, among other things.

Democratic Socialist Party. The DSP, which is currently amalgamating with the SPA, last year denied any intention of joining the New Left party.

Association for Communist Unity. The ACU, which last year determined to merge its membership into the New Left party, appears to have ceased independent activity, though not to have disbanded as of June (*Tribune*, 13 June).

New Left Party. The NLP's National Organising Committee met 10–11 February to plan the party's Founding Conference. Agreeing "that the NLP lacks the resources and political base to be standing candidates," the committee urged NLP members to join "broad progressive alliances or stand as independents" in the 24 March national elections. The rank and file membership was urged to "support progressive independent and environmentalist candidates" or, absent those, the Australian Labor party. (*Tribune*, 14 February.)

In March the party issued a prounion industrial policy statement calling for greater union participation by women and "multi-lingual organisers" (*Tribune*, 21 March). The NLP, which intends to function internally along egalitarian lines, will work alongside unions and progressive organizations and take a gradualistic approach to building socialism (*Tribune*, 6 June).

Most NLP regional branches met 26–27 April to discuss a constitution, a platform outline, and the NLP's "Program for Political Action," all to be finalized at the Founding Conference. Attendance at the regional meetings totaled 75 in Sydney, 45 in Melbourne, 15 in Newcastle, and 20 each in Brisbane, Wollongong, and Perth. Regional representatives were also elected at various regional conferences; half of Sydney's delegates are women. (*Tribune*, 2 May.)

Attended by 150 delegates and "many other" members, the NLP's Founding Conference met 9–11 June in Sydney to debate the party's constitution, platform outline, and "Program for Political Action." The decentralized structure prescribed by the new constitution reflects the NLP's emphasis on action at the local and regional levels and allows lower-level groups greater decision-making power than in most Socialist parties (*Tribune*, 13 June). The platform outline expands on the "Time to Act for a New Left Party" statement that was distributed in April 1989, signed by some two thousand people, and endorsed as the fundamental policy statement at the NLP launching conference in July 1989. Almost a thousand people have taken out NLP membership. The platform outline covered a wide range of policy areas, including social justice, a radical expansion of democracy, an alternative economic development strategy, aboriginal and islander rights and sovereignty, a sustainable and livable environment, gender issues, and women's liberation. The platform outline also focused on multiculturalism and "a democratic, militant and interventionist union movement." (*Tribune*, 13 June.) Speakers at the conference included Canberra public servant Di Bolton, Wollongong teacher activist Mike Dwyer, NSW president of the National Union of Students Nadine Flood, ACTU Executive member Tom McDonald, and Adelaide environmentalist David Winderlich (*Tribune*, 13 June).

It was determined that women should be proportionally represented in all elected and representative party positions. The NLP was to concentrate over the next eighteen months on building and promoting its organization and increasing its financial resources and publication output. "A national recruitment drive through a media and leaflet campaign will be a top priority." The conference adopted various political strategies, including launching a proposed bill of rights, countering urban chemical hazards, and pursuing electoral work. The NLP vowed to learn from the "long overdue" collapse of Stalinist regimes in working for social equity and environmental prudence. (*Tribune*, 13 June.)

The NLP decided to "integrate diverse themes, particularly union, environmental and welfare movements" and to counterbalance the rightist tendencies of mainstream parties. The NLP's fundamental units are to be its regional constituencies, which may have as many as three hundred members each. Some NLP members have already been elected to local government councils; they and others will seek election to public office either as independents or in coalition with other progressive groups or individuals. Tom McDonald, federal secretary of the Building Workers' Industrial Union, said that members of both the CPA and the ACU are now active in the NLP; he urged the two organizations to disband and merge their membership into the NLP. Few NLP members, however, are said to belong to any other parties. (*Tribune*, 13 June.)

In July, citing environmental preservation and foreign control of Australian industries and resources, the NLP, represented by Rob Durbridge, joined with the Rainbow Alliance and the West Australia Greens in a campaign against the Multi-Function Polis proposed for the outskirts of Adelaide; the campaign wanted to solicit 1 million signatures to a statement of objection (*Tribune*, 25 July). In August the NLP's coalition with the Rainbow Alliance and the Greens was unable to agree to demand Iraqi withdrawal from Kuwait; the parties did, however, join in calling for self-determination and nonviolence (*Tribune*, 29 August).

The Adelaide regional group held meetings approximately monthly beginning 1 April, focusing on union and industrial issues. A meeting of local signatories of last year's charter, "Time to Act for a New Left Party," took place on 3 May. The Adelaide NLP branch took part in a May Day march on 5 May. Women members met on 2 September.

The Brisbane branch, which apparently was slow to organize, was active in gay and lesbian rights and environmental issues during the year (*Tribune*, 29 August). The first general meeting for 1990 was on 17 February, with several others held at irregular intervals thereafter. A Brisbane regional conference during 28–29 April discussed Founding Conference proposals and planned for the next eighteen months.

The Canberra branch began fortnightly meetings late last year to hear speakers and hold discussions. A regional conference was held on 18 March.

The Melbourne branch held its first general meeting on 25 February and others sporadically thereafter. A regional meeting on 29 April made plans for the Founding Conference. The Melbourne and Sydney branches took part jointly in a 6 May May Day march. A Melbourne NLP women's meeting was held 31 May.

Various local groups of NLP members in Sydney formed between late 1989 and early 1990 (*Tribune*, 14 February). On 25 February the Sydney branch convened a seminar on Australia's foreign debt that was attended by more than 80 people; its recommendations included reregulation of the finance sector, reintroduction of foreign exchange controls, changes in the tax system, and other forms of government intervention (*Tribune*, 28 February). A 12 August conference condemned both the Iraqi invasion of Kuwait and Canberra's dispatch of three Australian warships to the Persian Gulf as part of the international response (*Tribune*, 15 August). Various social functions were held beginning in September. The Wollongong branch met for discussions on 3 August.

Timothy J. McGuire
Hoover Institution

Bangladesh

Population. 118,433,062 (July)
Parties. Bangladesh Communist Party; National Socialist Party
Founded. Bangladesh Communist Party: 1948 as East Pakistan Communist Party; banned in 1954 to reemerge in 1971 after Bangladesh independence. National Socialist Party: unknown
Membership. 50,000 (1989 estimate)
General Secretary. Bangladesh Communist Party: Saifuddin Ahmed Manik; National Socialist Party: Mohammad A. Jalil
Status. Legal
Last Congress. Fourth Congress of the Bangladesh Communist Party was held in April 1987.
Auxiliary Organizations. Trade Union Centre, Cultural Front, Chatra Union, Jubo Union, Khetmozdur Samiti, Mahila Parishad
Publication. *Ekota* (in Bengali)

General Mohammad Ershad remained in control despite continued agitation by opposition parties and much violence throughout the country. Ershad's principal opponents continued to be Sheikh Hasina Wajed, daughter of Mujibur Rahman, Bangladesh's first president, and Begum Khalida Zia, widow of President Zia Rahman. Sheikh Hasina, as head of the Awami League party, and Begum Zia, at the helm of the Bangladesh National party, worked against Ershad at every turn.

During mid-March subdistrict elections— attended by violence that left eleven dead, more than two thousand injured, and some five hundred in custody—returns from four hundred contested positions revealed that Ershad's Jatiya party won 155 seats, the Awami League 101, and the Bangladesh National party 26, with the remaining seats captured by minor parties or independent candidates (*FEER*, 5 April).

Agitation and strikes against Ershad's rule and the corruption that characterized his regime continued through the year. In August, Ershad shuffled his cabinet, retaining for himself the portfolios of defense, national security, cabinet, and establishment. After the change the government included a vice-president, a prime minister, a deputy prime minister, and 25 cabinet ministers. (Hong Kong, AFP, 4 August; *FBIS-NES*, 7 August.)

Nevertheless, the changes proved too little too late, and anti-Ershad sentiment increased. By December, Ershad agreed to step down and call for fresh national elections. (*NYT*, 5 December.)

Party Affairs. The Bangladesh Communist Party maintained a relatively low profile throughout the year. Still reeling from 1989's internal struggles and resignations, the party was not able to present a unified position for the subdistrict elections. Although some splinter groups and party workers undoubtedly took part in the various agitations and strikes, their efforts were not of sufficient note to be remarked on by any observers.

Relations with the Communist World. The People's Republic of China continued to be an important source of political assistance and matériel. In early February, the chief of the Chinese air force, Wang Hai, visited Dhaka to call on Ershad and conduct technical talks with the Bangladesh air force. That service's need for equipment, spare parts, and training was undoubtedly high on the agenda. (Dhaka Domestic Service, 13 February; *FBIS-NES*, 15 February.)

Later the same month, Chinese Minister of Defense Qin Jiwei led a large delegation to Dhaka to meet with Ershad and the three Bangladesh service chiefs. These meetings undoubtedly focused on the equipment, spare parts, and training needs of the three arms of the Bangladesh defense forces. (Xinhua, 28 February; *FBIS-NES*, 1 March.)

Ershad reciprocated these efforts with a five-day state visit to Beijing in late June seeking to broaden existing and identify new areas for cooperation between the two countries (Dhaka Domestic Service, 20 June; *FBIS-NES*, 21 June).

Relations with the USSR continued to improve during the year. A Soviet goodwill delegation spent a week in Dhaka during January (Dhaka Overseas Service, 16 January; *FBIS-NES*, 18 January). In late March the two countries signed an agreement for barter trade worth approximately $40 million (Dhaka Overseas Service, 1 April; *FBIS-NES*, 3 April). Finally, the chambers of commerce of the two countries agreed to expand their relations and seek areas of cooperation (Dhaka Domestic Service, 7 April; *FBIS-NES*, 10 April).

Michael R. Potaski
Catholic University of America

Burma (Myanmar)[1]

Population. 41,277,389 (July)

Party. Burma Communist Party (BCP). At least three organizations have emerged from rebellions against the BCP leadership in March and April 1989: the United Wa State Army (UWSA), the Burma National Democratic Army (BNDA), and the Kokang Army (KA). UWSA rhetoric has shown some similarity to that of the BCP; however, none of the successor groups appears to retain any adherence to communist ideology.

Founded. 15 August 1939

Membership. 200 (estimated)

Chairman. Possibly [Bo][2] Kyin Maung, 67

Politburo. [Bo] Kyin Maung, [Yebaw] Kyaw Mya (Arakanese), [Ko] Pe Thaung (Rangoon Domestic Service, 10 July; *FBIS-EAS*, 17 July)

Central Committee. [Bo] Kyin Maung, [Yebaw] Kyaw Mya, [Ko] Pe Thaung, [Bo] Myo Myint, Kyaw Myint, ca. 68 (Sino-Burmese), [Saw] Ba Moe, 46 (Karen), [Saw] Ba Pho (Karenni), plus one or two unknowns. (Rangoon, *Working People's Daily*, 11 July)

Status. Illegal

Last Congress. Third, 9 September–2 October 1985

Auxiliary Organizations. Most of the BCP's former subordinate organizations have probably disintegrated. The following were reported in 1990: Shan State Nationalities Liberation Organization, Kayah New Land Liberation Council, and Democratic Patriotic Army.

Publications. None confirmed. Over the past year Rangoon authorities have claimed seizure of a number of publications put out by "BCP underground elements," including issue no. 6 of *People's Power*, in raids on opposition centers. The BCP formerly broadcast over the Voice of the People of Burma (VOPB), located near the Sino-Burmese border inside Burma. VOPB broadcasting facilities were seized by Wa rebels on 12 April 1989; the Burma Nationalities Broadcasting Service (BNBS) and the Voice of the People of Wa State (VPWS) subsequently broadcast at irregular intervals.

The remnants of party structure left after the 1989 near-total destruction of the BCP have further disintegrated during 1990 with the resignations or removal of much of the old leadership. Communist strength in Burma is now lower than at any time since the founding of the party. The three principal splinter organizations all claim an ethnic, rather than ideological, basis for existence. Despite initial indications that one or more of the three would join an opposition front, evidence is accumulating that all have reached agreement with the government to end hostilities and may be operating in tacit, if not explicit, alliance with Rangoon.

The BCP breakup preceded by some months a swelling of public protest against the Burmese government, the military-run State Law and Order Restoration Council (SLORC). The protests culminated in a stunning victory for an opposition coalition in the 27 May elections; however, the military leadership has refused to yield power and has even arrested many of the opposition leaders elected in May. The Rangoon regime continues to blame opposition activity on an alleged BCP underground organization and claims significant BCP infiltration of various sectors of Burmese society, especially education and religion. Although these assertions may well coincide with BCP desires, the capacities of the party even before its breakup were insufficient to permit the level of activity described by the SLORC.

Leadership and Organization. About a dozen members of the 1985 BCP Central Committee have decided to retire to China, according to Sai Aung Win, 53, another Central Committee member who defected to Rangoon 29 June. These include

---

1. The Rangoon government changed the country's name to Myanmar effective 18 June 1989, and this change has been adopted by the United Nations. The U.S. Board on Geographic Names has retained Burma as the English-language name, although it noted Myanma (using its standard Burmese language transliteration) as a native form. ("US Policy on Name of Burma," *Geographic Notes*. U.S. Department of State, Bureau of Intelligence and Research 11, [1 March].)

2. Honorifics are in brackets in this section. *Bo* connotes a military commander; *Saw* is a standard male honorific among the Karen and other ethnic minorities. The most common Burman honorifics (*U, Daw,* and *Maung*) are omitted. This article makes the standard distinction between *Burmese*, referring to the entire country, and *Burman*, referring to Burma's largest ethnic group.

two former chairmen, Thakin Ba Thein Tin and Bo Kyaw Zaw. In return for sanctuary, China reportedly requires the retirees to resign from the Central Committee and from the BCP. (Hong Kong, AFP, in English, 10 July; *FBIS-EAS*, 12 July.) Former Vice-Chairman Thakin Pe Tint, 74, died in September of throat cancer in a Beijing hospital. Ba Thein Tin was also reported hospitalized in Beijing late in the year. (*FEER*, 15 November.) Aung Win's defection after 27 years underground, possibly the first defection by a BCP Central Committee member, was announced in a SLORC news conference 29 June. According to the announcement, Aung Win resigned from the Central Committee on 3 March after deciding to surrender. (Rangoon Domestic Service, 29 June; *FBIS-EAS*, 6 July.)

According to Aung Win, only some two hundred party members remain, scattered around the country (Hong Kong, AFP, in English, 10 July; *FBIS-EAS*, 12 July). The three remaining Politburo members are Yebaw Kyaw Mya (Arakanese), Bo Kyin Maung, 67, and Ko Pe Thaung, a former paratrooper. The remaining Central Committee members include the above plus Bo Myo Myint, Kyaw Myint, about 67 (a Sino-Burmese from Moulmein), Saw Ba Pho (Karenni), and Saw Ba Moe, 46 (ethnic Karen and former Karen National Army member). Five Central Committee members are at central headquarters and four are in military regions, according to Aung Win. Other names mentioned as associated with the leadership are Than Gyaung (alias Aung Htet and brother of Sow Win, a victim of the BCP purges of the 1960s), Kyaw Zaw Oo (son of Bo Kyaw Zaw), and Khaing Aung. The effective, if not official, party leader is Bo Kyin Maung, who is also referred to in the BCP as "Yebaw Tun." (Rangoon, *Working People's Daily*, 11 July). Biographies of a number of past and current BCP leaders, including Kyin Maung and Myo Myint, were published in the *Working People's Daily* from 17 to 21 November 1989.

Information on the remnant BCP organization below the top leadership is fragmentary, reflecting the general disintegration since 1988. Most of the party leadership has been reported to be at Pang Wa in the 101st Military Region, an old BCP enclave on the Burma side of the Chinese border somewhat shielded from the Burma army by territory controlled by the ethnic insurgent Kachin Independence Army (KIA). There has been mention of a BCP attempt to establish a base area in the Shweli Valley but with no further details. The leadership allegedly retains substantial financial resources:

more than US$1 million and some 2.5 million yuan, according to SLORC (Rangoon, *Working People's Daily*, 12 September). Khin Maung has reportedly formed a new organization unit, Military Region 4828, under the command of Thet Khaing to direct BCP underground activities in the Burmese heartland. Thet Khaing and an associate, Kyaw Mya, have been given the authority of Central Committee members without the title, according to Aung Win. (Rangoon Domestic Service, 10 July; *FBIS-EAS*, 19 July). Among pre-1989 military regions, besides the 101st, Aung Win noted only the 202d Military Region, where the ten remaining cadre have become guerrillas (Rangoon, *Working People's Daily*, 11 July). Although the BCP leadership has lost contact with Tenasserim, some remnant of the Tenasserim Regional Command may exist; the SLORC claimed the surrender of two cadre from that organization in September (Rangoon Domestic Service, 21, 22 October; *FBIS-EAS*, 24 October).

On 20 June four organizations, at least three of which have been identified as BCP fronts, asked to join the opposition insurgent coalition, the Democratic Alliance of Burma (DAB). The four are the Shan State National Liberation Organization (SSNLO), the Kayah New Land Liberation Council (KNLC), the Karenni People's Liberation Organization (KPLO), and the Democratic Patriotic Army (DPA). (Bangkok, *Nation*, 16 August; *FBIS-EAS*, 16 August. For background on the SSNLO and the KNLC, see *YICA*, 1989; the BCP was reported forming the DPA after the 1989 mutinies [*YICA*, 1990].) No DAB decision on the offer has been noted. Thai Border Patrol Police (BPP) reported the 27 February surrender of a group of eight "ethnic Karen communist guerrillas," identified by the BPP as part of a larger group still operating in Burma opposite Thailand's Mae Hon Son province (*Bangkok Post*, 28 February; *FBIS-EAS*, 28 February).

Party Internal Affairs. The organization of Military Region 4828 and substantial BCP financial resources were two points cited by the SLORC during the year to describe a BCP underground organization that poses a true threat to the country. The BCP was portrayed as having planned the new underground before the mutinies, for instance, during a 10 September 1988 Politburo meeting, a full transcript of which was published in the *Working People's Daily* from 17 to 21 November 1989. Defector Aung Win described the BCP intention to use underground movements to organize in major ethnic Burman areas, particularly along the Irrawaddy River. If this succeeds, the armed struggle may emerge again, although "in the long-term and not in the immediate future," Aung Win said. (Rangoon Domestic Service, 10 July; *FBIS-EAS*, 17 July). He noted distribution by BCP underground groups of statements and pamphlets in the Mandalay area (Rangoon, *Working People's Daily*, 11 September). SLORC secretary Brig. Gen. Khin Nyunt, at an 11 September press conference, described Khin Maung's dispatching underground groups to the Mandalay, Madaya, Monywa, Meiktila, Myingyan, and Pyinmana areas to set up bases at the beginning of the year (Rangoon, *Working People's Daily*, 12 September); a SLORC spokesman cited a "Magwe District BCP administrator" named Thein Htike as working to undermine the May elections (Rangoon, *Working People's Daily*, 18 May). Aung Win noted, however, that there are few remaining hard-core cadre to carry out such plans. Only a "little over 10 people" remain under Bo Kyin Maung (Rangoon Domestic Service, 10 July; *FBIS-EAS*, 17 July). Elsewhere he was cited as declaring such BCP efforts doomed to failure "because of changing times and changing conditions" (Hong Kong, AFP, in English, 10 July; *FBIS-EAS*, 12 July). The current political situation certainly could have been fertile ground for a dynamic underground BCP organization, but the small numbers of cadre so far involved show minimal ability to take control of the existing massive discontent.

Showing more resilience are the groups that split off from the BCP in 1989, which show minimal, if any, signs of continued communist inclinations. All have been reported involved in talks with the SLORC during the year, disappointing DAB hopes that one or more might join the armed opposition. Following up earlier contacts with the KA and the BNDA (*YICA*, 1990), Brig. Gen. Maung Thint, head of the Burmese Northeast Command, met 10–11 March in the Kulong region with leaders of the KA and attended a ceremony to mark the KA revolt against the BCP (Rangoon Domestic Service, 14 March; *FBIS-EAS*, 21 March). The UWSA was left out of earlier negotiations with Rangoon, but, on 11 November 1989, UWSA leader Ta Cao Ngi Lai and some of his officers traveled by Burmese army helicopter to Lashio and met SLORC representatives to agree on an unofficial cease-fire. The arrangement reportedly included two thousand bags of rice per month and Burma army transportation for UWSA troops to fight opium warlord and drug-trafficking competitor Chang Chi-fu. (*FEER*, 28 June.) The

UWSA leadership, commemorating the 17 April anniversary of their own revolt, announced a general cease-fire with the Burma army in the Wa State and the formation of the Union of Myanma Democratic Front for Peace, which included the UWSA, KA, BNDA, and an unconfirmed Kachin organization (VPWS, 27 April; *FBIS-EAS*, 3 May). A Thai press report noted the Rangoon commission of the UWSA as a local militia force, following two meetings early in the year with SLORC commanders. This agreement was to include weapons and ammunition from Rangoon for the UWSA and SLORC's approval for the deployment of UWSA forces along the Thai-Burma border against Chang Chi-fu. (*Bangkok Post*, 5 May; *FBIS-EAS*, 9 May.) Fighting was reported between Chang's forces and the UWSA from late 1989 on, with particularly heavy clashes from January to March around the key narcotics-trafficking center of Doi Lang, on the Thai-Burma border. The Thai BPP reported a UWSA movement of sixteen hundred kilos of opium in mid-February to a border heroin refinery (*Bangkok Post*, 19 February; *FBIS-EAS*, 27 February), the security of which was probably a motivation for the fighting. Chang accused the UWSA of being the "ghost" of the BCP, called for Thai support, and threatened to attack Thai border areas if his situation worsened (Bangkok, *Nation*, 23 July; *FBIS-EAS*, 23 July).

SLORC propaganda remained focused on the alleged extensive BCP responsibility for 1989 demonstrations, as witness the 27 March speech by SLORC chairman Gen. Saw Maung (Rangoon Domestic Service, 27 March; *FBIS-EAS*, 28 March). As of late 1989, the SLORC reported distributing more than 250,000 copies of *The Burma Communist Party's Conspiracy to Take over State Power*, a book based on SLORC secretary Brig. Gen. Khin Nyunt's 5 August 1989 press conference (Rangoon, *Working People's Daily*, 27 October 1989). A series in the *Working People's Daily*, "Extracts from the History of Internal Insurgency," concentrating on the BCP, ran from November 1989 through April 1990. Repeated assertions of links between opposition leaders and the BCP boded ill for prospects for a power transfer. Maj. Gen. Khin Nyunt warned 26 August that BCP underground elements have infiltrated political parties (Rangoon, *Working People's Daily*, 27 August). Rangoon military commander Maj. Gen. Myo Nyunt gave the same warning to Rangoon garrison troops and described former military officers who were once ready to "work in any given role to oppose the BCP" but who now "have ignored the national cause and only look at how they can attain state power. Today they work under the instructions of their new masters—the old BCP people." (Rangoon Domestic Service, 16 May; *FBIS-EAS*, 18 May.) A *Working People's Daily* article of 9 October 1989, "They Are Totally the Same," noted that opposition leader Aung San Suu Kyi in 1989 had only repeated a 1962 BCP charge that soldiers were badly educated. Aung San Suu Kyi was formally banned on 17 February from running in the May general elections on the grounds that she had had contacts with "unlawful elements" (Tokyo, Kyodo, in English, 17 February; *FBIS-EAS*, 20 February). By late in the year, many of the opposition leaders elected in May were in jail, with six of the ten top leaders of the winning National League for Democracy in detention (*NYT*, 25 November).

The appearance of a campaign among Buddhist monks to refuse donations from soldiers was followed by a warning of BCP influence on religion and reports of BCP publications found during raids by soldiers on monasteries in Mandalay, the center of religious opposition. The *Working People's Daily* noted (29 October) that the raids again exposed "the perfidy and treachery of the BCP" and that opposition among students is no more than a "dance to the tune set" by the BCP (Rangoon, *Working People's Daily*, 25 August). The military themselves are not immune. Maj. Gen. Myo Nyunt described threats by "BCP underground elements" against families and relatives of military personnel and warned soldiers of "veteran BCP members . . . [who] returned to the legal fold, enjoyed all the privileges provided by the state, and now resort to all possible tricks to achieve the disintegration of the Defense Services" (Rangoon Domestic Service, 4 August; *FBIS-EAS*, 9 August).

Insurgency. The two above-noted reports of surrendered communist cadre evince the possible continued presence of a remnant of communist armed force in the field. Burmese summary reports on military actions, however, last referred to clashes with BCP forces in February 1989. The BCP front groups most recently noted as trying to join the main opposition insurgent alliance have never been of significant size and are probably close to disappearing. With this in mind, plus the understandings reached between the UWSA, KA, and BNDA and the military regime in Rangoon, the armed communist uprisings in Burma, which began in earnest

with the White Flag insurgency in 1948, may be considered at an end.

Evaluations by the Rangoon military leadership of BCP strength tend to confirm the lack of such strength, despite efforts to point to communist activity in regime propaganda. Gen. Saw Maung in January called internal disorder

> a long-term plan of the BCP Politburo. Some may say the Politburo has been smashed and there are no armed units left. No, it is not true. Whatever happened here was done by their hard-core elements. Who can say they no longer exist? Why should BCP cell members say they are BCP people? . . . This is not a minor problem. (Rangoon Domestic Service, 9 January; *FBIS-EAS*, 10 January.)

A month later, an SLORC spokesman told a press conference that the BCP is a head with no body and that therefore there was no need to launch a military strike against the remaining leadership and their families at the Pang Wa headquarters (Rangoon, *Working People's Daily*, 3 February). At a 19 October news conference, to a question on the strength of the BCP, a SLORC spokesman replied that, although BCP armed strength had disintegrated to an almost insignificant level, "they still have foreign currency, cash, and gems which they unjustly robbed from the people and are using in sending UGs [underground groups] to infiltrate mass and class organizations. . . . It is difficult to assess the strength of the infiltration of these UGs." (Rangoon Domestic Service, 19 October; *FBIS-EAS*, 22 October.) Maj. Gen. Khin Nyunt later reported the arrest during October of four BCP underground cadre (Rangoon Domestic Service, 7 December; *FBIS-EAS*, 10 December). Significant for the long-term position of the military regime was an SLORC representative's response to a foreign interviewer's question as to the military's biggest problem: "We cannot tell the rebels from the ordinary people" (Jakarta, Tempo, in Indonesian, 2 June; *FBIS-EAS*, 8 June).

International Views and Positions. According to the *Bangkok Post* (4 June), a Thai communist told his military captors in northeast Thailand that "the CPT has joined the BCP and minority groups on the northeastern border of China, and they are now operating near the western border of Thailand" (*FBIS-EAS*, 4 June). If it has any basis in fact, the statement might reflect a blurring of BCP remnants with splinter elements, particularly the UWSA.

Once a source of friction between the BCP and China is that the former key opium-trafficking elements of the BCP are now in tacit alliance with Rangoon, and thus opium may become an issue between the Chinese and the Rangoon military. The seriousness of the Chinese problem with opium may be indicated by the November creation of a State Anti-Narcotics Committee (Beijing, Xinhua, in English, 23 November; *FBIS-CHI*, 23 November) and multiple executions of drug traffickers reported in Yunnan and Guangzhou, whereas drug production in Burma has soared over the last two years (*NYT*, 11 February). The Sino-Burmese relationship, already of key importance to Rangoon, has grown still more important over the past year with the first direct Chinese supply of weapons and munitions to the Burmese military (*FEER*, 13 September). Thai press reports indicate China has agreed to supply $1.2 billion in arms to Burma (Bangkok, *Nation*, 27 November). Even before the arms deal, China was Burma's largest trading partner (Beijing, Xinhua, in English, 17 May; *FBIS-CHI*, 18 May). Rangoon sensitivity over reports of government involvement with opium traffickers and even over estimates of opium production in Burma reflect in large part military concern over the impact on their relations with Beijing. After Thai accounts of links between Rangoon and narcotics trading by the UWSA and KA, the *Working People's Daily* (11 March) replied: "The allegation that some Myanmar authorities are working in collusion with drug traffickers is a grave offense, tantamount to the basest defamation." During a Thai-Burmese border committee meeting, Burmese representatives rejected a U.S. estimate, presented by the Thai side, of Burmese 1990–1991 opium production (Bangkok, *Nation*, 25 March; *FBIS-EAS*, 27 March).

It is questionable whether Rangoon efforts, insofar as these are sincere, to reduce Wa and Kokang drug production will be any more effective than previous efforts by the BCP leadership. A Chinese drug control delegation was taken to witness the destruction of a heroin refinery in Kokang (Rangoon Domestic Service, 29 November; *FBIS-EAS*, 5 December), and both the KA (Rangoon Domestic Service, 23 November; *FBIS-EAS*, 26 November) and the UWSA (VPWS, 29 November; *FBIS-EAS*, 30 November) issued statements criticizing drug use and outlining long-term plans to eliminate opium production in their respective territories.

Charles B. Smith, Jr.
Department of State

Note: The views expressed in the preceding are the author's own and do not necessarily represent those of the Department of State or the U.S. government.

Cambodia

Population. 6,991,107 (July 1990), annual growth rate in 1990 was 2.2 percent.

Party. People's Revolutionary Party of Kampuchea (PRPK); also still called Kampuchean (Khmer) People's Revolutionary Party (KPRP). Since the official name of the country today is "State of Cambodia" to emphasize its inclusiveness of all factions, Phnom Penh party officials since early 1990, especially in conversation with foreigners, have begun speaking of the "Cambodian People's Revolutionary Party" (CPRP) as well.

Founded. The PRPK has its origins in the Khmer People's Revolutionary Party (KPRP), founded 28 June 1951, but since the mid-1980s PRPK leaders have assigned 30 September 1951, the date of the PRPK's first Central Committee meeting, as the party's formal birthday.

Membership. 11,000 regular members, 42,000 candidate members (June, estimated).

General Secretary. Heng Samrin (b. 1934), initially a senior cadre in the Pol Pot wing of the KPRP, served as commander of the Fourth Division, and, 1974–78, as chief political officer in the Central Command of Pol Pot's Revolutionary Army of Kampuchea. During his 1976–1978 tenure as a member of the party's Eastern Zone Executive Committee, he participated in an anti-Pol Pot conspiracy that ended in his flight to Hanoi for "retraining" during June–October 1978. On 23 January 1979 he was formally proclaimed in Phnom Penh as president of the Central Committee of the Kampuchean National United Front for National Salvation, the Hanoi-established umbrella organization of anti-Pol Pot PRPK elements.

On 4 December 1981 Heng Samrin abruptly took over from Pen Sovan the position of secretary general of the Hanoi-backed wing of the PRPK. Since the promulgation of the June 1987 constitution, Heng Samrin has been chairman of the Council of State.

Politburo. Currently 14 full and 4 alternate members (there is uncertainty about exact numbers because of the midyear political crisis): Heng Samrin (b. 1934), PRPK secretary general and Chairman of the Council of State; Hun Sen (b. 1951), chairman of the Council of Ministers and foreign minister until 6 November, when formally relieved of that post (he had been relieved de facto since July); Hor Nam Hong, alternate Politburo member and foreign minister; Chea Sim, chairman of the National Assembly; Mat Ly, vice-chairman of the National Assembly and since 30 July vice-chairman of the latter committee's Control Commission; Bou Thang, first vice-chairman of the Council of Ministers and chief of the Political Department of the Cambodian People's Armed Forces; Nguon Nhel, alternate Politburo member and since 15 August minister of agriculture; General Tie Banh, vice-chairman of the Council of Ministers and minister of national defense; Lieutenant General Pol Saroeun, alternate Politburo member, deputy minister of national defense, and Armed Forces General Staff chief; Ney Pena, alternate Politburo member and chairman of the PRPK Central Propaganda Commission; General Sin Song, minister of the interior; Chea Soth, vice-chairman of the Council of Ministers; Sim Ka, alternate Politburo member and secretary of the Phnom Penh municipal party committee; Say Chhum (b. 1945), since 15 August "standby vice-chairman" of the Council of Ministers; Sar Kheng (b. 1951), *chef de cabinet* of the PRPK Central Committee and chairman of its Organization Commission; Mem Sam-an (b. 1953), chairwoman of the Cambodian Federation of Trade Unions; Say Phuthan (b. 1925), chairman of the PRPK Central Control Commission; and Chea Soth (b. 1928), second vice-chairman of the Council of Ministers and minister of trade.

Secretariat. Heng Samrin, Hun Sen, Bou Thang, Mem Sam-an, Ney Pena, Sar Kheng, Mat Ly (replacing Say Phutang in July), Say Chhum.

Central Committee. 50 full and 17 alternate members (estimated; list incomplete). Full members, so far as known: Bou Thang, Politburo member; Chan Seng (b. 1935), member, PRPK Control Commission; Chay Sanguyn, deputy chief of staff, Cambodian People's Armed Forces, chief, Logistics Bureau; Lieutenant General Chea Sim, Politburo member and National Assembly chairman; Chea Soth, Politburo member; Chhay Than,

minister of finance; Chheng Phon, minister of culture; Chhim Chuon, PRPK Central Committee, member and vice-chairman of its Organization Commission; Dith Munti, deputy minister of foreign affairs and chief, PRPK's Foreign Affairs Commission; Do Sohan, secretary, PRPK Provincial Committee of Kompong Thom; Heng Sam Kai (b. 1930), brother of Heng Samrin, secretary, PRPK Provincial Committee of Svay Rieng; Heng Samrin, chairman, Council of State and PRPK secretary general; Brigadier General Hul Savoan, commander, Fourth Military Region, Cambodian People's Armed Forces; Hung Neng, secretary, PRPK Provincial Committee, Kompong Cham; Hun Sen, Politburo, chairman, Council of Ministers; Kham Len, member, Council of State and since February, minister of light industries; Kim Yin (b. 1928), director, Commission of Radio and Television (believed purged in early 1990); Kong Korm (b. 1941), former minister without portfolio, Council of State and, since mid-August, reported to be a deputy foreign minister; Major General Pen Vansarat, since mid-August, member, PRPK Central Control Commission; Koy Buntha (b. 1952), minister of social service and veterans' affairs, since mid-August, "standby member," Council of Ministers; Hong Longdi, since mid-August, deputy secretary of Phnom Penh municipal committee, and chairman of the capital's "People's Committee"; Lak On, secretary, PRPK Provisional Party Committee of Ratanakiri and chair, Cambodian Women's Revolutionary Auxiliary; Mem Sam-an, Politburo member, variously listed as "cochair" or "chair," National Federation of Trade Unions; Mean Sam-an (b. 1956), national chair, Cambodian Revolutionary Women's Auxiliary; Neou Sam, secretary, PRPK Provincial Committee in Siem Reap-Oddar Meanchey; Nguon Nhel, Central Committee member since mid-August, when appointed (interim?) minister of agriculture; Khoem Cheasoophan, since mid-August, deputy minister, State Affairs Inspectorate; Nhim Vanda, reported to hold unspecified flag rank in the Cambodian People's Armed Forces and chief, State Committee of Construction of Thai-Cambodian Border Defense since early March; Pol Saroeun, alternate Politburo member, deputy minister of national defense; Pen Navut, minister of education and sports; Phouk Gamoeun, since mid-August, deputy secretary, PRPK Provincial Committee in Svay Rieng; Ros Chhun, secretary general, National Executive, Cambodian National Defense and Development Front; Ros Sreng, secretary, PRPK Provincial Committee, Pursat; Say Chhum, vice-chairman, Council of Ministers; Sam Sundoeun (b. 1952), secretary general, Revolutionary Youth Front of United Cambodia, chairman, Cambodian-Vietnamese Friendship Society; Sim Ka, since mid-August, secretary, municipal committee of Phnom Penh; Som Kimsuor (b. 1949), editor of party weekly *Pracheason*, but reportedly purged and under house arrest since late June; General Sin Song, interior minister and alternate Politburo member; Tang Saroeum, minister for foreign economic and cultural cooperation and, since mid-August, reportedly a deputy foreign minister for international trade; Vong Kan, secretary, PRPK Province Committee of Bantay Meanchey; Thang Chhin, since mid-August, vice-chairman PRPK Central Committee Organization Commission; Ung Phan, reported purged since late July in government plot but reportedly reinstated in early November; Ung Sami, secretary, PRPK Provincial Committee, Battambang; Yos Son, chairman, PRPK Central Committee, chairman, foreign affairs commission, National Assembly. Alternate members (so far as published): Ung Phan; Chea Chanto, planning minister; Em Sam-an, vice-minister of education; Heng Khan, secretary, PRPK Provincial Committee in Kompong Speu; Khim Bo, secretary, PRPK Provincial Committee in Takeo; Lim Nai, secretary, PRPK Central Committee Organization Committee; Lim Thi, secretary, PRPK Provincial Committee in Kandal; Phang Saret, chairman, National Assembly Committee on Foreign Trade and Investment; Sam Sarit, director, Bureau of Estate Rubber Production; Say Siphon, general secretary, National Federation of Trade Unions; Som Sopha, secretary, PRPK Provincial Committee in Stung Treng; Thong Khon, general secretary, PRPK, Phnom Penh municipal committee and deputy interior minister; Um Chhunlim, vice-chairman, PRPK Central Committee Control Commission and reputed political section chief of the national secret police; Yim Chhaylim, health minister (sometimes described as regular Central Committee member); Yut Phuthang, secretary, PRPK Provincial Committee in Prey Veng, and member, National Assembly. *Note*: Virtually all regular and alternate members of the Central Committee also hold senior cadre positions in provincial or municipal "revolutionary committees" of Cambodian (Kampuchean) United Front for National Construction and Development.

Status. The PRPK remains the only officially recognized political party of the government headed by Heng Samrin. In anticipation of future power-sharing arrangements, the PRPK is seeking to place its key cadres in as many important State of Cambodia government bureaucracy positions as possible.

Last Congress. Fifth, 13–16 October 1985. The eleventh session of the PRPK Central Committee announced on 30 July that in view of the (unspecified) situation and because a conference of party cadres (presumed to have taken place in the second week of April), had "already summed up the situation" and had "set the goals for important tasks for the coming years," the normally quinquennial term of office of the Fifth Party Congress had been extended (Phnom Penh Domestic Service, 30 July; *FBIS-EAS*-90-147, 31 July; Russell R. Ross, ed., *Cambodia: A Country Study*, Federal Research Division, Library of Congress Area Handbook Series, 1990, pp. 215–218).

Last Election. The last general election for the National Assembly was held 15 May 1981; the 148 candidates of the PRPK and its main umbrella front, the KNUAUS, winning all 117 seats. More than 99 percent of the eligible electorate is said to have voted. Though the 27 June 1981 constitution prescribes a five-year term for the National Assembly, no elections have been held since 1981. On 5 February 1986, the sitting National Assembly voted to remain in function until May 1991, but that term will likely be extended if no Cambodian settlement is reached by then.

Front Groups and Auxiliary Organizations. The organized mass support base for the PRPK is the umbrella Cambodian United Front for National Construction and Defense (KUFNCD), with an estimated 1.6 million members in various subsidiary and interest groups representing virtually every aspect of community, economic, educational, and religious life. The KUFNCD Presidium is dominated by Council of State chairman Heng Samrin and his chief rivals, premier Hun Sen and National Assembly chairman Chea Sim.

Among the largest formal KUFNCD support affiliates are the officially 300,000-member Organization of Young Cambodian Pioneers (ages 5 to 9); the Revolutionary Women's Association of Cambodia (RWAK), with some 960,000 members and representation in the PRPK Politburo, Central Committee, and National Assembly; and Cambodian Revolutionary Youth Organization (KRYO), with about 750,000 members in the 9–17 years age group. KRYO members regularly participate in "officer cadet" training in the Cambodian People's Armed Forces (CPAF) in preparation for a (theoretically general) 5-year conscription of males aged 18 to 35; KRYO "cadet" service may in some areas be substituted for the required 3–6 months' service with local CPAF militia units.

The KRYO is also a training ground for a more selective front for older youths and young adults (17 to 26), the Cambodian People's Revolutionary Youth Union (KPRYU), a conduit for candidate membership in the PRPK. A more recently prominent ad hoc group is the Cambodian Branch (or Council) of the all-Asian Buddhist Peace Council, chaired by a longtime pro-PRPK Buddhist clergyman, Tep Vong, a vice-chairman of the National Assembly. Since April 1989, the Heng Samrin government, with the quiet support of Thai Buddhist circles, has been reaching out to leaders of the Cambodian Buddhist establishment. On 3 November a Cambodian Buddhist Council of Reconstruction was established with the approval of the PRPK leadership, but with as yet uncertain ties to the KUFNCD.

Little was heard during the year from the Kampuchean African-Asian People's Solidarity Committee, chaired until July 1990 by Khieu Kanharit or the Khmer-Soviet and Khmer-Thai Friendship Councils.

The Cambodian Journalists' Association (vice-chair, Khieu Kanharit) underwent purges and reorganization during the latter half of 1990 as the result of an attempt, first reported in early May, to democratize the Cambodian polity. Khieu Kanharit was dismissed from his various positions because of his allegedly liberal views and exposés of official corruption; he was replaced by Central Committee member Ros Chhun, and former director of the National Bank of Cambodia (*FBIS-EAS*, 3 July).

Media. With an estimated circulation of 5,000, the PRPK's Central Committee weekly, *Pracheachon* (The people), is the SOC's most authoritative official publication. Founded in 1983, its current editor is Central Committee member Som Kim Suor. Before Khieu Kanharit's purge, the weekly *Kampuchea* (founded 1981, KUFNCD official organ, estimated circulation of about 55,000) was probably the most widely read paper in the country; it had a reputation for careful criticism of government policies and carried exposés of inefficiency and corruption, including those submitted in readers' letters. The CPAF weekly *Kangthap Padevat*

(People's Revolutionary Army) and the now-irregular *Phnom Penh*, journal of the capital's municipal committee, with estimated circulations of 5,000 and 1,500 respectively, have little credence and are little read. Increasingly, the major source of news for urban Cambodians who have the radio equipment and the political-social connections to remain relatively unscathed are foreign, particularly Thai and Voice of America broadcasts. The daily radio reports of the "Voice of Cambodian People" (VOCP) and the radio bulletins of the government news agency Sapordamean Kampuchea (SPK), both in Phnom Penh, have limited audiences. Their respective directors, General Kim Yin and Em Sam-an, are both Central Committee members. The SPK's *Bulletin*, published for foreign embassies and journalists in English, French, Thai and Cambodian, primarily reiterated the text of earlier government news releases.

During the year, Cambodian media tended to evince a more pluralistic approach featuring, for example, announcements of religious activities. In addition, a more sympathetic tone was taken in reports about purported Cambodian refugees who had decided to return to their homeland under SOC rule.

A Cambodian-Japanese joint venture hopes to provide the State Commission on National Cambodian television with additional transmission capacity by late 1991, according to a commission announcement in late November.

Party Leadership and Organization. Party leadership during the year was characterized by a growing rivalry among the 39-year-old Hun Sen (premier since 1985 and concurrently chairman, Council of Ministers), the 61-year-old former Buddhist monk Chea Sim (chairman, the National Assembly), and Heng Samrin, the 57-year-old head of State and chairman, the Council of State; and by a rumored political "coup" or reform attempt during April and May involving up to 50 government, party, and military leaders (Tokyo, Kyodo, 13 June; *FBIS-EAS*, 14 June).

What these two factors signify, perhaps, is an effort to establish politically and economically modern reform policies that are West-oriented and more independent of Vietnam, policies that would presumably unshackle the economy from doctrinaire state control and give competitive opportunities to political parties outside the KNUFCD orbit. Chea Sim, probably the most Khmer-oriented and nationalistic member of the PRPK Politburo, appears to have been wary of any Cambodian-style *glasnost'*. Heng Samrin has tended to take a middle ground.

Rivalry among the KPRP triumvirate appears to have reached a new height at the end of May, when Hun Sen's ally, Transport and Communications Minister and Central Committee member Ung Phan, was arrested as the leader of an alleged antigovernment plot involving a number of subministerial senior officials and senior party cadres, among them Kan Man, deputy director, Foreign Ministry Bureau of European and American Affairs, and Nou Saing, the Communications Ministry's chief of planning; senior field grade officers were allegedly involved as well. Hun Sen was visiting Vietnam at the time of Ung Phan's arrest but was believed to have been aware of efforts to form a competitive Liberal Social Democratic party. (*NYT*, 11 August; Tokyo, Kyodo, 13 June; *FBIS-EAS*, 14 June.)

The arrest of Ung Phan, Kan Man, and other plotters reportedly was ordered jointly by Chea Sim and Heng Samrin. Party Politburo member and Interior Minister General Sin Song had gotten wind of Ung Phan's plans, which are said to have extended far beyond the five ringleaders arrested. According to Khmer Rouge sources, the plot even included KPRP Politburo member Defense Minister General Tie Banh, who was said to have been arrested during a mid-July visit to Hanoi (Voice of National Army of DK [clandestine], 15 July; *FBIS-EAS*, 16 July) but appears to have emerged unscathed despite his rumored sympathies for Hun Sen's reformist views judging from reports of his official activities on 24 July and 7 September.

The aftermath of the Ung Phan episode saw wholesale changes and transfers in ministerial, subministerial, and provincial party leadership positions (Phnom Penh Domestic Service, *FBIS-EAS*, 15 August), culminating in Hun Sen's official dismissal as foreign minister on 6 November and his replacement by Hor Mam Hong, a Heng Samrin protégé (Phnom Penh Domestic Service, 6 November; *FBIS-EAS*, 7 November). Other symptoms of the purge of Hun Sen's followers include the dismissal of Kieu Kanharit as editor of *Kampuchea* in late June and the "suspension from duty" and holding for "investigation" of He Kan, a KPRP vice-chairman in Phnom Penh on 6 September (*Bangkok Post*, *FBIS-EAS*, 3 July; Phnom Penh Domestic Service, *FBIS-EAS*, 6 September).

During the coup purges, attention focused on the views of the elusive Chea Sim, who, although re-

portedly "not opposed to the freewheeling economic laissez-faire" economy that has been transforming Phnom Penh and its environs into a modern, consumer-oriented society, is said to favor a much less open cultural life and far tighter political control than the Ung Phan (and thus, the Hun Sen) reform group (James Pringle, "Hard Liners Outflank Hun Sen," *Bangkok Post*, 25 October). Nevertheless, Chea Sim shares with Hun Sen, Heng Samrin, and other key KPRP provincial leaders a deep distrust of and desire to limit the Australian-proposed plan for a United Nations interim administration of Cambodia, which SOC and KPRP leaders agree would in effect legitimize, directly or by implication, a return of Pol Pot and the Democratic Kampuchea–Khmer Rouge regime and their guerrilla forces. On 3 December, Chea Sim emphatically rejected any U.N. peace plan that would usurp the authority of the SOC, stressing that any provisional regime should concern itself solely with directing and supervising fair national elections. (Tokyo, Kyodo, 3 December; *FBIS-EAS*, 3 December.)

Whatever their differences about a Cambodian variant of *perestroika*, party leaders throughout the year emphasized the need to guard against a return of Pol Pot, urging that the middle-echelon and local cadre levels of the KPRP leadership be strengthened. In his opening address to the National Assembly on 26 January, for example, Chea Sim stressed that even the noncommunist factions headed by Prince Norodom Sihanouk and former Premier Son Sann and now aligned with Pol Pot's Khmer Rouge in the Coalition Government of Democratic Kampuchea (CGDK) had become an "out and out tool of the genocidal Pol Pot clique" (Phnom Penh Domestic Service, 26 January; *FBIS-EAS*, 29 January). The mere possibility that it might entail the return of Pol Pot's Democratic Kampuchea (DK) made the U.N. proposal for an interim administration unacceptable. The same theme—the KPRP's centrality in warding off Pol Pot's return—was the subject of a special three-day party cadre school course directed by Politburo members in Phnom Penh in January (Phnom Penh Domestic Service, 1 February; *FBIS-EAS*, 2 February).

During much of 1990 the responsibility of maintaining the flagging morale of the military (Phnom Penh Domestic Service, 15 March; *FBIS-EAS*, 16 March) and of the public in the face of food and other consumer shortages, widespread hoarding, inflation, and widening Khmer Rouge guerrilla attacks fell to the part of cadres. This became all the more difficult because considerable public resentment was directed at the party triumvirate of Heng Samrin, Chea Sim, and Hun Sen over their infighting and refusal to share power and at the *nomenklatura* over its conspicuous consumption, corruption and favoritism (*Bangkok Post*, 14 March). Public disquiet over the persistent rivalries and alleged corruption within the party's leadership continued to weaken the KPRP's claim to a position of exclusivity and primacy and undoubtedly contributed to the Ung Phan plot to establish a rival and more openly competitive party system.

In late January Hun Sen found it necessary publicly to threaten to quit his prime minister's post if his relatives did not stop using his name in the furtherance of their various malversations (Bangkok, *Nation*, 5 February). The evident desperation that underlay Hun Sen's airing of his family problems was indirectly confirmed by his seeming absence from the Third National Congress of the KUFNCD, opened in Phnom Penh by Chea Sim and subsequently chaired by Heng Samrin. The premier, whose name was omitted from the customary listing of the Congress's presidium, was reported at various times to be "at the front" or "abroad," including in Hanoi and Beijing. His absence had been revealed as well a few days earlier, among the long, published list of top party leaders attending the official celebrations in Phnom Penh of the sixtieth anniversary of the Indochinese Communist Party, forerunner of the KPRP (Phnom Penh Domestic Service, 3 February; *FBIS-EAS*, 13 February). The only reference in the Cambodian media to Hun Sen's presence at the November National Assembly meeting came in a perfunctory mention of "a report read by Comrade Hun Sen" on an unspecified topic. At the ceremonial signing of the National Assembly's decrees by Chea Sim on 9 August, however, Hun Sen's name was listed after that of Heng Samrin on the long list of party leaders present—the first official reference to his name in several months (Phnom Penh Domestic Service, *FBIS-EAS*, 9 August).

At various party leadership conclaves during 1990, the premier's name only rarely made it into official print, unlike the names of lesser official figures. Meanwhile, beginning with the meeting of the tenth plenum of the KPRP's Central Committee in mid-January through the Central Committee's eleventh session in late June, various party pronouncements went out of their way to stress the unwavering solidarity of the SOC regime, the KPRP, and the CPAF with Vietnam, Laos, and the USSR (Phnom Penh Domestic Service, 9 January, 30 July; *FBIS-EAS*, 22 January, 31 July).

Heng Samrin emphasized during this period that KPRP cadres' patriotism and their solidarity with the CPAF had been the nation's strength, so that clearly "the genocidal Pol Pot regime" (and, by implication, substantive reform) were unwelcome (Phnom Penh Domestic Service, 16 May; *FBIS-EAS*, 17 May). Chea Sim voiced a similar theme throughout the year. Addressing the KUFNCD's Fourth National Council session in Phnom Penh in early August, for example, the National Assembly chairman counseled the opposition factions of Sihanouk, Son Sann, and the Khmer Rouge "to accept their bitter defeat in the country's interior" (Phnom Penh Domestic Service, 11 August; *FBIS-EAS*, 13 August). At the National Assembly's adjournment on 6 November, the very day that Hun Sen was formally relieved as foreign minister (actually, Hor Namhong's appointment to succeed him had already been announced on 3 October), Chea Sim argued the KPRP's centrality and warned against its opponents' attempts (Phnom Penh Domestic Service, 6 November; *FBIS-EAS*, 7 November).

In August and September there was extensive reshuffling of leading cadres in cabinet, subcabinet, and senior positions in the KPRP Central Committee and the party's provincial executive committees. At the close of September, for example, Tang Saroem, a former KPRP Control Commission member, was retired, and Li Soh, KPRP provincial secretary in Mondolkiri, and Chan Yoeun, chairman of that province's "People's Committee" were suspended from duty "for investigation." All were known Hun Sen allies. According to rumors circulating in Phnom Penh in August, Tang Saroem (demoted in mid-August from minister for economic and cultural cooperation to deputy foreign minister for international trade) had been implicated in the Ung Phan plot (Phnom Penh Domestic Service, 27 September; *FBIS-EAS*, 28 September). Most of the transfers tended to strengthen Heng Samrin, suggesting to some observers that the most important KPRP leadership struggle in the near future would likely involve protégés of Chea Sim and Heng Samrin.

Hun Sen, having lost his post as foreign minister to Nor Hamhong, a relatively obscure bureaucrat but a faithful Heng Samrin supporter, appeared by the end of the year to be becoming little more than a conduit for the routine, if uneasy, discussions between the Heng Samrin-Chea Sim duumvirate and the CGDK. Even in many critical issues affecting the international Cambodian discussions (e.g., the composition and chairmanship of the Supreme National Council), Nor Namhong, not Hun Sen, was beginning to emerge as the SOC regime's spokesman.

Faced with worsening security, economic, and political conditions, the party closed its organizational ranks as never before. In early July, foreign observers agreed that the SOC regime could remain in power only if it limited its concessions in the peace talks to settle the Cambodia problem (Voice of the Khmer [clandestine], 1 July; *FBIS-EAS*, 3 July). By late November, Cambodia's prospects had become still more grim. A November report attributed the "hardening" of government attitudes to an "impending disaster" that was the result of the civil war, the end of East bloc and other assistance to the Heng Samrin-Hun Sen regime, and of the regime's continuing international isolation (Voice of the National Army of DK [clandestine], 25 November; *FBIS-EAS*, 26 November). Party media called for an intensification of ideological indoctrination, purity of ideological commitment, and vigilance against the return of the "genocidal Pol Pot regime to power in Cambodia" (Phnom Penh Domestic Service, 18 August; *FBIS-EAS*, 21 August).

This year's Day of Hatred for Pol Pot on 20 May was accentuated by the inauguration of new KPRP "informational campaigns" in the lower ranks of the CPAF and in Western rural areas of the border provinces of Battambang and Siem Reap-Oddar Meanchey. In late October increased concern began to be expressed in *Pracheachon* editorials over the KPRP's ability to hold Cambodia's society together. The Pol Pot threat was trumpeted again and again as justification for KPRP primacy, and the KPRP line seemed to be moving rapidly toward the position that any suggestion of moderation or change in party policy could only benefit the Pol Pot enemy. To counter this threat, an expansion of membership in party and mass organizations, "both quantitatively and qualitatively," was recommended (Phnom Penh Domestic Service, 25 October; *FBIS-EAS*, 30 October).

Domestic, Political, and Economic Problems. The dominant reality of Cambodian life in 1990 was the intensified factional fighting among the 40,000-man National Army of Democratic Kampuchea (NADK), directed by the elusive and frequently ailing Pol Pot, with Presidium chairman of the Democratic Kampuchea and CGDK Vice-

President/Foreign Minister Khieu Samphan as its civilian frontman; the 8,000-man *Armée Nationale Sihanoukiste* (ANS), whose main current civilian front, Front Uni Nationale pour un Cambodge, Indépendent, Neutre, Pacifique et Cooperatif (FUNCINPEC), headed by Prince Norodom Sihanouk, the capriciously intermittent president of the CGDK; the 12,000-man Khmer People's National Liberation Armed Forces (KPNLF), commanded by General Dien Del under civilian head Son Sann; and the CPAF.

The first three factions are theoretically united against the fourth, but in early March and again in mid-August, both the ANS and the KPNLF in Battambang and Siem Reap-Oddar Meanchey provinces complained that units of their respective forces had been attacked or harassed by the NADK (i.e., the Khmer Rouge) (Bangkok, *Armed Forces Herald Weekly*, 10 March, 25 August). In early January, NADK accelerated its infiltration of disguised military units and party cadres throughout western Cambodia, apparently less with the intention of seizing and holding "liberated zones" rather than of creating an infrastructure of communications with the aim of "leapfrogging" further into the interior of Cambodia (see, e.g., Hong Kong, *Asia Yearbook, 1991*, p. 91).

Amid the welter of claims and counterclaims of victory by the different Cambodian military factions, perhaps the only constants were the fluidity of the battle lines, the relentless pressure of the NADK, and the CPAF's uncertain hold on much of the country (see, e.g., *FBIS-EAS*, 10, 18 January). The Khmer Rouge claimed that a number of explosions in Phnom Penh itself in early January had been facilitated by local inhabitants and even by "civil servants" of the SOC "puppet administration of Vietnam" (Voice of the National Army of DK [clandestine], 14 January; *FBIS-EAS*, 16 January). The Phnum Malay stronghold and other Khmer Rouge areas previously reported retaken by the CPAF were reported in late January and early April to have been seized again by the Khmer Rouge (Hong Kong, AFP, 3 April; *FBIS-EAS*, 3 April). This kind of indecisive conflict continued along most of the western Thai-Cambodian frontier throughout the year. During July–September, the NADK was said to be launching new offensives all over Battambang and Siem Reap-Oddar Meanchey, attacking provincial and district capitals and reportedly even getting ready to attack Phnom Penh. In response, the CPAF and its new Vietnamese "advisers" reportedly moved on the Khmer Rouge–

held town of Pailin and on NADK encampments along the main road to Battambang (*Indochina Chronology* 9, no. 3 [July–September]).

In the closing months of the year, with the coming of the dry season, the Khmer Rouge and the SOC further intensified their respective propaganda and military campaigns. During mid-October, the NADK's more aggressive use of Chinese-built tanks and armored vehicles was particularly evident in clashes around Tonle Sap lake in central Cambodia and as far away as the southeastern province of Kamput. As well, 24 T-59 Chinese tanks reportedly were deployed by the Khmer Rouge in fighting in Siem Reap-Oddar Meanchey province. The Phnom Penh authorities complained with some justification that the "stubbornness" of the Pol Pot forces was due to their getting a steady flow of Chinese and other foreign military assistance estimated to be worth about $100 million per year (Phnom Penh Domestic Service, 13 October; *FBIS-EAS*, 15, 18 October; Hong Kong, AFP, 18 October).

In late November, the Soviet embassy in Hanoi claimed that the USSR had stopped supplying arms to the Phnom Penh government; at about the same time, however, Thai sources reported recent shipments of "tons of ammunition" to Phnom Penh and the western frontier provinces, and massive shipments to remote areas of the country. Despite such efforts, at year's end the NADK not only still retained territory in the western provinces seized during a three-month offensive earlier in the year but had also laid down a logistical and communications infrastructure in the rural interior. The Khmer Rouge had bulldozed "hundreds of kilometres of road through thick jungle" in the direction of Siem Reap city and the nearby Angkor Wat temple complex. Meanwhile, CPAF forces continued their drive to secure the gem-mining town of Pailin and its environs, an area constantly subject to seesaw conflict and occupation by both sides (*Bangkok Post*, 19 October).

Reports from various sources, including the Khmer Rouge, persisted that, far from withdrawing its forces from Cambodia, as Hanoi claimed to have done two years earlier, Vietnam had been infiltrating specially trained and technical personnel (e.g., sappers and combat engineers) back into Cambodia in growing numbers since the January NADK offensive. In early October alone, for example, Thai military intelligence sources told the author that during the preceding month some 2,200 fresh Vietnamese troops had been sent to Cambodian combat areas, particularly in Battambang province (see

also Voice of the National Army of DK [clandestine], 4 October; *FBIS-EAS*, 5 October). The same sources subsequently claimed that the CPAF's much-publicized repulse of the NADK's mid-October attack on the vital Ban Nimit artillery and logistics support base complex in Banteay Meanchey province had been possible only because several battalion-strength Vietnamese units equipped with heavy automatic rifles and mortars had assisted the inexperienced CPAK forces. Road travel between Phnom Penh and the provincial or district capitals remained hazardous, another sign of the SOC regime's weakness. (*Indochina Chronology*, October–December.)

Another defining factor of Cambodian life, as fluctuating and uncertain as the nation's domestic security condition, was the state of its economy. The National State Bank devalued the riel three times during the course of the year: 218 riel=US$1 in May, 510 riel=US$1 on 15 September, and 600 riel=US$1 on 18 October. Between January and mid-October, civil service salaries were raised by more than 75 percent but public confidence in the regime's ability even to provide for its own cadres plummeted. Seemingly uncontrollable shortages of food and basic consumer goods, the collapse of basic utility services, and a flourishing black market made the daily struggle for existence a desperate one for many Cambodians. The erosion of the government administration itself was reflected in the habitual absence of many officials from their posts because of their need to take on second or third jobs in the private sector, including black market speculation and smuggling.

With the speedy devaluation of the riel, payment in various foreign currencies and even in commodities and precious objects in all but official transactions became steadily more commonplace. A State Council measure requiring prior approval by the National Bank of all such payments was largely ignored (*FBIS-EAS*, 15 October). SPK state radio commentaries scolded in late November that a trade system based on gems, barter, smuggling, and the black market was undermining the national economy. To stave off food shortages in the already restive ranks of the CPAF and the civil service, in early February the government announced a 250 percent increase in subsidies to rice farmers. By late June an additional 350,000 tons of rice (a 50 percent increase over 1989) had been purchased (Phnom Penh Domestic Service, 11 July; *FBIS-EAS*, 16 July).

Meanwhile, the Agriculture Ministry's optimistic reports on increased food production continued. (*Asian Survey*, January.) In Phnom Penh and southeastern provincial capitals, a superficial gloss of urban consumer prosperity was apparent, due to increased privatization of certain retail sectors (encouraged by official disregard of the underground economy), to a relaxation of import controls, and above all to the foreign speculation and joint ventures encouraged by the Kun Son reform policies.

In line with these reform policies, local party leaders were urged in late April to encourage the citizenry to apply for and to feel assured in "right to ownership of land," presumably in order to promote food production, but the absence of systematic and consistently applied agrarian reform legislation tended to give such general directives an uncertain effect. Meanwhile, increased guerrilla activity turned the Battambang Bambeay, Meanchey, and Siem Reap–Oddar Meanchey districts from food-producing areas into sparsely inhabited sources of new refugees, adding to the growing pressures of Cambodia's internal population displacement (some of it ordered by the Phnom Penh government).

At least 350,000 Cambodian refugees are already living in camps along the Thai-Cambodian border under the control of different CGDK factions. Refugee camp commands in DK-controlled areas continued to force thousands to resettle in "liberated villages" in the Cambodian border zone. Despite Khmer Rouge assurances to foreign relief agencies that they had moderated refugee treatment, both the U.S. Department of State in early February and various independent human rights organizations (Asia Watch, Amnesty International) reported harsh treatment of camp inmates by Khmer Rouge military units and camp authorities, including forcible impressment into the DK's armed forces.

The national economy—and popular confidence in the Hun Sen regime—was buffeted by a sharp decline in the usually substantial Soviet and Eastern Europe assistance and trade; total Soviet aid fell by about 45 percent. Equally seriously, the changing East European domestic political scene seemed to spell the end of tolerance for Cambodia's highly unfavorable annual trade balance with the USSR (1989 110 million rubles of imports versus 27 million of exports) and Eastern Europe. The Gorbachev regime appears to have written off the present Cambodian debt to Moscow of 800 million rubles, at least for the time being. The SOC regime has

suggested, however, that Cambodian economic development will be deferred, pending definitive settlement of the domestic factional conflict (Hong Kong, *Asia Yearbook, 1991*, p. 95).

International Developments. The year saw intensified peace efforts by the five permanent members of the U.N. Security Council, the Association of Southeast Asian Nations, Vietnam, China, the United States, and Australia, among others. Lower-profile contacts and relationships were also developed during the year, involving limited numbers of foreign executives, tourists, representatives of volunteer rehabilitation and humanitarian groups, and government agencies. In the latter category, for example, a six-member U.S. military team, the first to visit Cambodia since the fall of Saigon, examined the possible remains of American servicemen listed as missing in action (Phnom Penh, SPK, 24 July; *FBIS-EAS*, 24 July), one indication of U.S. interest in improving relations with the Indochina region generally and the SOC in particular (Singapore, *Indochina Digest*, 17 July).

A 16–17 July meeting of the U.N. Security Council achieved broad agreement on the need for some kind of U.N. transitional, supervisory administration pending general elections in Cambodia, for a complete pullout of foreign forces, and, above all, for a cease-fire, but the Paris gathering made little progress on determining the composition and powers of the U.N.-supervised interim Supreme National Council (SNC), on which all four Cambodian factions would hold seats; the geographic position and respective strengths of the Cambodian factional forces and the international peacekeeping army during a U.N. truce; the mechanics of the elections; the staffing of lower-echelon government posts; and guarantees of human and civil rights in all areas of the country, including those of returnees from the Thai border zone.

The SOC regime promptly objected to the idea of creating any interim SNC, on the grounds that it would deprive the Phnom Penh government "of all power to administer the country" (Hong Kong, AFP, 29 July; *FBIS-EAS*, 30 July). Shortly before, Prince Norodom Sihanouk also had attacked the SNC concept, saying that such a council could not be established so long as Vietnamese forces still occupied parts of Cambodia. He insisted further that Khmer Rouge participation in any future SNC was particularly essential, because the Hun Sen regime could not survive were it not for the backing of Vietnam and the presence of its "shock and special troops." Sihanouk went on to claim "they have been supported by the majority of the peasants who comprise most of the population of Cambodia" (Voice of the National Army of DK [clandestine], 24 July; *FBIS-EAS*, 25 July).

The prince's assertion came, however, just after the United States on 18 July had dropped a small policy bombshell by declaring that the United States would no longer recognize the CGDK, headed by Sihanouk, as the legitimate occupant of Cambodia's seat at the United Nations or, in fact, as Cambodia's legitimate government. U.S. secretary of state James Baker said that the U.S. policy shift was designed "to prevent the return to power of the Khmer Rouge," the most powerful CGDK military faction, but he added that the United States was ready to increase "humanitarian assistance" to Cambodia, including, presumably, all of its factions (Phnom Penh, SPK, 19 July; *FBIS-EAS*, 19 July.)

KPNLF leader Son Sann also was critical of the decision, a volte-face he thought indicative of U.S. readiness to help the Vietnamese through the Hanoi-installed Heng Samrin regime just when the Vietnamese seemed more willing to withdraw from Cambodia. Prince Norodom Rannaridh, Sihanouk's son and chief ANS field commander, warned that the decision to derecognize the CGDK would impel Sihanouk's organization "to move closer to China" (Paris, *Le Monde*, 20 July; *FBIS-EAS*, 20 July). A two-day meeting of ASEAN foreign ministers in Djakarta expressed concern that current peace efforts seemed to have bypassed Cambodia and disregarded the earlier consensus. Some ASEAN members clearly resented the continuing intervention in what had thus far been essentially a regional Southeast Asian dispute, and participants agreed that any attempt to exclude the Khmer Rouge would doom chances for a more enduring peace in Cambodia (Bangkok, *Nation*, 25 July; *FBIS-EAS*, 25 July).

Beijing, meanwhile, left no doubt that it would continue to support its Khmer Rouge client, at least for the time being. On 8 August, Premier Li Peng declared that his government intended to "assist" (including presumably with weapons) the DK and its NADK fighting force as long as Hanoi was aiding the SOC and its CPAF. He added, however, that the PRC had accepted the quadripartite Cambodian power-sharing arrangement as agreed to again at the mid-July Paris conference, avowing that China "will never support" Khmer Rouge dominance in a new Cambodia (*Indochina Chronology*, July–September). Nevertheless, Li indicated,

China advocated recognizing the CGDK as the legitimate occupant of the Cambodian seat in the United Nations, pending formal establishment of the Supreme National Council.

Despite such differences, all diplomatic quarters engaged in the search for a Cambodian peace formula grew increasingly impatient with the perceived intransigence of all four factions over the details of organizing the proposed SNC. After bilateral Vietnamese discussions with China and the United States resumed in mid-August, the three CGDK factions met in Beijing. That meeting resulted in a 21 August communiqué endorsing yet another intrafactional discussion to be held in Djakarta in September for the specific purpose of establishing an SNC, presumably to be headed by Sihanouk. (Phnom Penh, SPK, 22 August; *FBIS-EAS*, 22 August).

Meanwhile, the five permanent Security Council members went forward with their own agenda of peace compromise specifics, meeting in New York on 27 August to adopt their own five-point plan, which dealt with the establishment of an interim U.N. administration in Cambodia; pending general elections, coordination of a cease-fire and disarmament; U.N. supervision over future Cambodian elections; human, political, and civil rights under the interim administration; and the implementation of election results and the transition government's decision. The New York meeting also addressed the issues of domestic security and distribution of international humanitarian assistance. (Hong Kong, AFP, 30 August; *FBIS-EAS*, 30 August.)

Few details of this plan were actually worked out, however, in the face of the asserted need for a 10,000-man U.N. administrative-military contingent and a $3 billion annual expenditure to keep the U.N. commitment going (*Indochina Chronology*, July–September). Nonetheless, the CGDK reportedly agreed in essence to this latest set of proposals and hoped to pursue them at the Djakarta meeting the following month. The government in Phnom Penh was not so easily persuaded. After studying the 27 August proposal, Nor Namhong, the SOC's foreign minister-designate speaking on behalf of the Council of Ministers, demanded that the U.N. "show its impartiality beforehand" and guarantee "an effective disarmament of the Khmer Rouge" (Hong Kong, AFP, 30 August; *FBIS-EAS*, 30 August).

To a degree some SOC concerns already had been met because during the second half of July and most of August ASEAN members agreed to leave the Cambodian seat at the United Nations vacant. Compelling the Khmer Rouge to disarm, however, in view of China's pledge to continue to assist it, was another matter—not least considering the lucrative covert arms and related business along the border being conducted with the CGDK by Thai military and businessmen.

Meanwhile four days before the 10 September Djakarta conference, the United States exploded another minor diplomatic bombshell by announcing that the U.S. government had decided to open direct discussions with the Hun Sen government. U.S. secretary of state James Baker at the same time said, however, that "the jury is still out" as to whether the Cambodian factions themselves would fully accept the peace plan worked out in Paris and New York during their recent discussions (Phnom Penh, SPK, 6 September; FBIS-EAS, 6 September). Baker especially noted SOC reservations in this connection.

Secretary Baker proved prophetic. Though committing themselves to the "Permfive," a concept of a peace settlement, the Djakarta meeting's communiqué confined itself to future establishment of a twelve-member SNC and with the possibility of Sihanouk as a "13th" and presiding member. The CGDK and the SOC would each have six members on the SNC, which was described in the Djakarta communiqué as not only having authority to represent Cambodia "externally," including at the United Nations, but also as being "the unique legitimate body and source of authority" during the U.N. interim period (Phnom Penh, SPK, 11 September; FBIS-EAS, 11 September). Just what this all meant in terms of a "cease-fire in place" of the armed disputant factions in the country, let alone their voluntary disarmament, or what it signified in maintaining the lower levels of de facto SOC public administration, or in the organization of the elections, all remained unspecified.

On 12 October, the United Nations General Assembly adopted a resolution endorsing creation of an SNC by the disputing Cambodian parties, and, in effect, deferred the question as to who now occupied Cambodia's U.N. seat. (According to the ASEAN position, the SNC in fact was now doing so, whether it was "physically" present at the United Nations or not.) But the SNC members seemed to experience difficulty in settling the details of a peace formula. The twelve SNC members (among them Khmer Rouge leader Khieu Samphan, SOC foreign minister Nor Namhong, ANS commander Norodom Rannaridh, and KPNLF leader San Sonn)

met in Bangkok on 17 September but in four separate rooms, one room for each faction—hardly an auspicious beginning for those seeking unity and easy discourse (Hong Kong, AFP, 18 September; FBIS-EAS, 18 September). Progress in selecting a chairman and vice-chairman moved at a snail's pace in subsequent weeks. Sihanouk finally seemed to have accepted the Council's chairmanship at the close of October, with the SOC's Hun Sen as his vice-chairman, but just who would be the SNC's formal spokesman at the U.N. remained unclear at year's end.

A facilitating factor in settling the chair's position may have been the mid-September meeting in Bangkok of Sok An, the SOC's deputy foreign minister, with Zhang Qing, a senior official of the Asian Affairs Division of China's Foreign Ministry. The highly unusual SOC-PRC contact was viewed as being in accord with recent expressions of Chinese support for increased United Nations involvement in a Cambodian settlement, but these gestures should be placed in the context of authoritative reports in mid-November that the Khmer Rouge recently had received new shipments of heavy artillery from the Chinese (in fulfillment, the PRC claimed, of previous agreements) (Hong Kong, AFP, 20 November; FBIS-EAS, 20 November).

In early November lower-rank foreign affairs officials from the ASEAN and Security Council nations held discussions with Vietnamese and Laotian officials in Djakarta, but without Cambodians present. That attempt at a Cambodian peace plan was seen as possible preparation for another Paris International Conference on Cambodia (PICC). (J. M. van der Kroef, "Cambodia: Toward the Fourth Indochina War (II)," Asian Thought and Society 15, no. 44 [May].) But even this new approach appeared unpromising: The Laotian delegate, clearly speaking for the Indochina bloc, wanted "a significantly reduced role for the United Nations in a political settlement" of the Cambodian conflict (Hong Kong, AFP, 9 November; FBIS-EAS, 13 November). The USSR delegate to the Djakarta conference pressed for a United Nations draft peace proposal involving all nineteen PICC members, including the four Cambodian factions—an approach almost guaranteed to perpetuate the deadlock among the Cambodian factions. The United States and Indonesia, on the other hand, urged greater flexibility on all parties, stressing particularly the still unresolved issue of who would lead the SNC.

The continuous bickering clearly strained the patience of the Djakarta delegates: "Time is running out for everyone," acting French prime minister Michel Rocard declared. As the talks threatened to do little more than reveal the old fault lines of irreconcilable positions, threats were reportedly voiced that if the Cambodians could not even agree on who should head the SNC, the other proponents of a peace formula would desist from their efforts (Hong Kong, AFP, 11 November; *FBIS-EAS*, 13 November).

Meanwhile, as if to doom still further the chances of a settlement, relations between the Cambodian leaders themselves seemed to continue to deteriorate. On 5 December, Prince Norodom Sihanouk had to defend himself in a Paris courtroom against a $100,000 libel suit brought by the new SOC foreign minister, Nor Namhong, whom Sihanouk allegedly had accused in the *Journal du Dimanche* of having commanded a Khmer Rouge concentration camp. According to Nor Namhong, he had been an involuntary member of a camp inmate supervisory committee (*Indochina Chronology*, October–December).

Superpower impatience with the Cambodian leaders was evident in reports that the Security Council nations had agreed among themselves in late November to send some 10,000 U.N. administrators and security forces as an interim administration until free elections were held. The group reportedly agreed that the plan's success depended on the willingness of the four Cambodian factions to make it work. By mid-December the question of SNC leadership still was unresolved, however, even as the CGDK agreed to temporarily vacate its U.N. seat. (*NYT*, 26 November, 16 December.)

On 21–22 December, the four Cambodian factions met again in Paris and approved the Security Council plan. (The breakthrough of SOC endorsement came only after U.N. assurances that at least some SOC officials would be retained.) Further success eluded the conference when calls for actually disarming the four Cambodian military factions were sharply resisted by Hun Sen, who clearly distrusted the Khmer Rouge and their continuing military buildup in various sections of the country.

Another obstacle was the SOC's insistence on an explicit formal condemnation of the previous Pol Pot DK regime by reference to the term "genocide." France's foreign minister, Roland Dumas, declared at the end of the meeting (punctuated briefly by Hun Sen's collapse from fatigue, though he shortly resumed his participation) that Phnom Penh's demand

had threatened the signing of any final statement at all. In any event, the term "genocide" was omitted from the conference's concluding statement. The disputant factions agreed to meet again sometime in the future, but international concern with events in the Persian Gulf made new attention to the Cambodian peace effort seem less likely. (*FEER*, 3 January 1991).

The battlefield in Cambodia, not the conference table in Paris, Djakarta, or Beijing, had grown in significance as a determinant of a Cambodian peace settlement. Alarmed Western diplomats noted in late December that Chinese arms continued to flow to all four factions, including the Khmer Rouge. Indeed, one wire service report spoke of the Khmer Rouge loading "trucks and trucks of new Chinese ammunition" on the way to DK border camps and strongholds, though China, along with the other Security Council members, had repeatedly agreed to halt the flow of matériel to the Cambodian belligerents (*NYT*, 1 January 1991).

The Communist Opposition: The Khmer Rouge. As in the past, little reliable information was available about the PRPK's communist rival, the theoretically dissolved Party of Democratic Kampuchea (PDK), commonly called the Khmer Rouge. The same applies to Democratic Kampuchea (DK), the PDK's shadowy quasi-governmental structure, which became part of the CGDK in 1982. DK Council of State chairman Khieu Samphan remains CGDK vice-president and foreign minister, as well as the official chairman of the PDK.

Pol Pot (Saloth Sar), whose exact whereabouts rarely are reported, continues to be the PDK's and NADK's principal military strategist and chairman of the DK's obscure "Institute of Military History" (though he resigned all his PDK positions in August 1985). The memberships of the PDK's leadership organs are uncertain, if indeed they formally exist at all. The PDK, since its founding, has held no national congresses. Possibly because of its continued, if hidden, dominance by Pol Pot and his cadre, PDK literature disseminated today among NADK recruits says little about the current evolution of Khmer communism.

According to NADK instructional materials, 332 candidates stood for election to the People's Representative Assembly in the DK's only national elections, held on 20 March 1976. Of these candidates, 100 pre-approved "peasants, workers and soldiers" were declared elected.

There is considerable evidence that the PDK-NADK's overlapping top command structure remains in the hands of an inner circle called Angka (the term dates from the DK's reign of terror, 1976–78). This group consists of: Ieng Sary, a onetime senior Politburo member of the Khmer or Kampuchean Communist Party (KCP) and the DK's latest interior minister; Son Sen, another KCP veteran and former DK defense and foreign affairs minister; and Ieng Thirith, Ieng Sary's wife, commander of the PDK's women's youth front and rural women's auxiliary.

No overt tactical or political differences within this leadership group surfaced during the year, although there were reports of dissension about Angka's main rival, Chhit Choen (commonly known as Ta Mok), senior commander of the NADK's Battle Zone Command 1003, whose repressive recruiting methods in the Thai-Cambodian refugee border camps have led to protests by the Red Cross, the U.N. High Commission for Refugees, and the United Nations Border Relief Organization (UNBRO), as well as to reported displeasure in Beijing. In November, authoritative reports that about 150 of Ta Mok's NADK followers in Western Battambang had been "purged" a few weeks earlier by Pol Pot's NADK loyalists fueled speculation about strategy conflicts between the two PDK factions. The first one, comprising mostly Khieu Samphan and, for the moment, Pol Pot and their followers, seems ready to accept (under Chinese pressure) some sort of U.N. peace plan. Meanwhile, the Khmer Rouge power base, strengthened by dispersed but strategically placed PDK cadres, would lie low, ready to rise again once the U.N. had left and some nominally democratically elected Cambodian government had taken its place. The influential Ta Mok minority faction, however, seems determined to obstruct or at least postpone a U.N. interim settlement in order systematically to widen and strengthen the DK rural power structure, particularly in the arc of western provinces from Battambang to Preah Vihear. At the same time, this approach seeks to neutralize the KPNLF of Son Sann and the FUNCINPEC-ANS of Sihanouk as much as possible. Ta Mok also wants to intensify the guerrilla struggle (particularly through rural terrorism) to further discredit the SOC and develop a power base. The Ta Mok strategy does not rule out clashes even with U.N. peacekeeping forces.

For the moment, however, the Khieu Samphan "moderates" appear to have the upper hand in the PDK-NADK command. With its 40,000 well-armed and battle-tested forces, and with its brutal internal security and "discipline enforcement" squads, it seems unlikely that the NADK will agree to disarmament under U.N. supervision.

The PDK-Khmer Rouge administrative power is embodied in an interlocking network of sometimes overt, usually covert, controls reaching from isolated Khmer Rouge-dominated refugee camps inside Thailand that function as bases from which to project military power into Cambodia. The Khmer Rouge's "recruiters" periodically make their appearance at the KPNLF's huge Site 2 camp, opposite Banteay-Mean Chey. From these Khmer Rouge-controlled refugee camps a network of footpaths leads to clusters inside Cambodia of small "liberated zones" dominated by PDK committees or NADK squads. The zones, in turn, create a tightening circle of encampments around larger villages and district capitals, strategic areas around Tonle Sap lake and the Cardamom Mountains, enabling NADK forays further south or west and, with increasing frequency, across Kompong Chnnang toward Phnom Penh.

Defections of UNBRO-supervised refugee movements to sites outside NADK-Khmer Rouge control have continued, but reportedly at a much diminished rate. Apart from increased effectiveness of intimidation and terror in Khmer Rouge sites, the declining attrition rate also is attributed to the demonstrated strength of periodic Khmer Rouge military attacks and deep infiltration that underscore the SOC's weakness.

Khmer Rouge leaders have done their best to draw attention to the growing strength and size of Khmer Rouge units (up to 400 soldiers, with additional hundreds of "auxiliaries"). In their "liberated zones" local Khmer Rouge leaders and NADK forces attempt to refurbish their negative image through civic service campaigns of repairing buildings, clearing land, providing Chinese-style "barefoot" medical assistance, and so on. All this seems designed to create an impression of a gradually growing momentum of popular support and military strength. The PDK-NADK thus appears to be counting as much on developing a psychological momentum of inevitable victory as on displays of military power. (See *Asia Yearbook* 1991, pp. 91–92.) Meanwhile, it has been standard DK policy to blame Vietnam and the SOC for the continuing stalemate in negotiations (e.g., Phnom Penh Domestic Service, 17 November; *FBIS-EAS*, 19 November).

Media. The DK relies mainly on two self-identified radio stations operating from the same transmitter, believed to be located near the Chinese border. The first station, which broadcasts principally news of claimed NADK operations and successes, is the "Voice of the National Army of Democratic Kampuchea"; the second, which mainly reports general news, anti-SOC commentary, and official DK pronouncements, is the "Voice of Democratic Kampuchea."

Justus M. van der Kroef
University of Bridgeport (Connecticut)

China

Population. 1,133,682,501 (official 1990 census figure as of 1 July, excluding Taiwan and Hong Kong) (*NYT*, 31 October.)
Party. Chinese Communist Party (Zhongguo gongchan dang; CCP)
Founded. 1921
Membership. 48 million
General Secretary. Jiang Zemin
Central Committee. 175 full members and 110 alternate members
Standing Committee of the Politburo. 6 members, in rank order: Jiang Zemin (64), general secretary, chairman of party and state military affairs commissions; Li Peng (63), premier; Qiao Shi (66), first secretary, Central Commission for Inspection Discipline, member of Secretariat, vice-premier; Yao Yilin (73), oversees economic affairs, vice-premier; Song Ping (73), responsible for personnel matters; Li Ruihuan (56), in charge of propaganda, member of Secretariat.
Politburo. 14 full members: Wan Li, Tian Jiyun, Qiao Shi, Jiang Zemin, Li Peng, Li Tieying, Li Ruihuan, Li Ximing, Yang Rudai, Yang Shangkun, Wu Xueqian, Song Ping, Yao Yilin, and Qin Jiwei; alternate member: Ding Guangen
Secretariat. 4 full members: Qiao Shi, Li Ruihuan, Ding Guangen, and Yang Baibing; alternate member: Wen Jiaobao
Central Military Commission. Jiang Zemin, chairman; Yang Shangkun, first vice-chairman;

Liu Huaqing, vice-chairman; and Yang Baibing, secretary general
Central Advisory Commission. Chen Yun, chairman; Bo Yibo and Song Renqiong, vice-chairmen
Central Commission for Discipline Inspection. Qiao Shi, first secretary; Chen Zuolin, Li Zhengting, and Xiao Hongda, deputy secretaries
General Office. Wen Jiabao, director; Xu Ruixin, Yang Dezhong, and Zhou Jie, deputy directors
Department of International Liaison. Zhu Liang, director; Jiang Guanghua, Li Shuzheng, Li Chengren, and Zhu Shanqing, deputy directors
Department of Organization. Lu Feng, director; He Yong, Liu Zepeng, Meng Liankun, and Zhao Zongnai, deputy directors
Department of Propaganda. Wang Renzhi, director; Gong Yuzhi, Li Yan, and Wang Weicheng, deputy directors
Department of United Front Work. Yan Mingfu, director; Li Ding, Song Kun, Wan Shaofen, Wu Lianyuan, and Zhang Shengzuo, deputy directors
Work Committee for Government Organs. Chen Junsheng, secretary; Wang Chuguang, Zhang Jingyuan, deputy secretaries
Work Committee for Party Organs. Wen Jiabao, secretary; Gu Yunfei, Li Yan, deputy secretaries
Central Party School. Qiao Shi, president; Chen Weiren, Gao Di, Han Shuying, Su Xing, Xing Bensi, and Xue Ju, vice-presidents
Status. Ruling party
Last Congress. Thirteenth, 25 October–1 November 1987
Last Election. 1987
Auxiliary Organizations. The Communist Youth League of China (50 million members), led by Song Defu; the All-China Women's Federation, led by Chen Muhua; the All-China Federation of Trade Unions, led by Ni Zhifu; the Chinese People's Political Consultative Conference (CPPCC), the party's leading united front organization, led by Li Xiannian; and the eight democratic or satellite parties.
Publications. The official and most authoritative publication of the CCP is the newspaper *Renmin Ribao* (People's daily), published in Beijing. The Central Party School's biweekly theoretical journal *Qiushi* (Seeking truth) published its first issue in July 1988. Influential in recent years has been *Liaowang* (Outlook), the weekly publication of Xinhua (New China News Agency; NCNA), the official news agency of the party and government. The daily paper of the People's Liberation Army (PLA) is *Jiefangjun Bao* (Liberation army daily).

The weekly *Beijing Review* (*BR*), published in English and in several other languages, carries translations of important articles, editorials, and documents from various sources. *China Daily*, the first English-language national newspaper in the People's Republic of China (PRC), began official publication in Beijing and Hong Kong on 1 June 1981 and began a New York edition in June 1983.

Domestic Affairs. Chinese authorities were able to maintain the political and social stability that they earnestly desired throughout the year. The protracted period of martial law in Beijing was terminated in early January, and the unpopular government managed to survive the sensitive anniversaries of the April–June period and then successfully host the Asian Games in September, all without serious incident. Of course, extraordinary efforts were made to ensure these outcomes, with unprecedented numbers of security forces employed in Beijing and special restrictions imposed on the populace. Even so, the regime's success in maintaining order provided a psychological boost for the defensive political leadership. Meanwhile, people continued to play a waiting game with regard to politics as they waited out the continued longevity of the Eight Major Elders, all of whom lasted the year. There was a moderate recovery of the economy, with a strong rise in exports and foreign exchange acquisition. The government was compelled to raise some prices, however, and it was expected that inflation would again rise in the last quarter. Also the economy continues to have many structural problems that were not being addressed in a forthright and timely manner. Fundamental differences among top political leaders led to serious disagreements on a number of issues, including the appropriate use of propaganda and rectification efforts and the effect of such measures on reforms and the opening-up policy. Political reforms remained suspended or in some instances continued to be reversed, but some economic reforms were heralded again later in the year. In general, it appeared that the conservative elders under Chen Yun reasserted their dominance in the latter half of the year but were unable to achieve a consensus for their desired policy and personnel changes. Moreover, strong provincial leaders challenged the central government toward the end of the year, particularly over its efforts to retighten central controls and increase the transmittal of revenues to the center. As a consequence, disagreements over the Eighth Five-Year Plan and other matters repeatedly delayed the convening of the Central Committee's Seventh Plenum, originally scheduled for October or earlier, until late December.

On 10 January, Premier Li Peng announced the lifting of martial law, in effect in Beijing since 19 May 1989. That lifting, partly in response to international pressure, was seen as largely symbolic, inasmuch as other repressive measures continued in effect. (Seth Faison, Hong Kong, *South China Morning Post* [*SCMP*], 11 January.)

On 1 January the Organic Law of the Urban Neighborhood Committees of the People's Republic of China went into effect. Nearly 100,000 neighborhood committees have been established in urban areas in China, organized on the basis of regulations promulgated in 1954. Normally, one neighborhood committee is set up for each residential area of one hundred to seven hundred households. The leaders are chosen from among local residents, mostly retirees and housewives. (*BR*, 9–15 April.)

Vice–Foreign Minister Zhou Nan (62) succeeded Xu Jiatun as director of the important Hong Kong branch of the New China News Agency (Xinhua) in January (Chris Yeung, *SCMP*, 11 January). Zhou Nan, as vice–foreign minister, invited Hong Kong governor Sir David Wilson to visit Beijing from 10 to 12 January.

Asia Watch in New York announced in January that eighteen prominent intellectuals had been arrested in the past several months. Included in this list were Professor Wen Yuankai, a biophysicist at the China University of Science and Technology in Hefei, Anhui, and former adviser to Zhao Ziyang; Liu Xiaofeng, deputy director of the Research Institute for the Reform of the Economic Structure; Professor Tian Qing, a music scholar; and Zheng Di, a journalist with the banned *Economics Weekly*. Asia Watch also reported that workers and peasants have been detained in recent months and that at least 40 executions have been carried out. The number of arrests confirmed by official Chinese sources was put at over 6,000, while unofficial estimates range as high as 30,000. (Willy Wo-Lap Lam, *SCMP*, 11 January.)

Chen Muhua, vice-chair of the National People's Congress (NPC) Standing Committee and chair of the All-China Women's Federation, revealed in January that women leaders in China now total 8.7 million and represent 29 percent of the total leadership, an increase, it was said, of 24.3 times since the early years of the PRC (*Xinhua*, 23 January; *FBIS-CHI*, 25 January).

On 16 January the Chinese government made public the decision of the November 1989 Fifth Plenum of the Thirteenth Central Committee that China faced inflation, imbalances in supply and demand, an irrational economic structure, and an undesirable economic order despite the enormous achievements made during the ten years of reform (*BR*, 29 January–11 February).

Party authorities in Inner Mongolia sought to prevent news of prodemocracy developments in Mongolia, which might influence the large Mongol population in Inner Mongolia, and undertook other measures to prevent emergencies that might arise (Hong Kong, *Tang Tai*, 3 February; *FBIS-CHI*, 9 February).

Made public on 7 February was a document entitled "Opinions of the Central Committee of the Communist Party of China on Upholding and Improving the System of Multi-Party Cooperation and Political Consultation under the Leadership of the Communist Party of China" that had been issued on 30 December 1989. The document, hailed as a "major step towards socialist democracy," made clear that "political organizations that oppose the four cardinal principles and jeopardize the state power are absolutely not allowed to exist." (*BR*, 19–25 February.)

On 14 February, China announced the replacement of the entire leadership of the 600,000-member People's Armed Police. The police, regarded as ineffective during last year's student movement, occasioned the need to call in the PLA. Heeding the downfall of Romania's Ceauşescu and reflecting on the serious split in Romania between the Securitate police force and the army, China's hard-line leaders apparently decided to ensure that the People's Armed Police could be trusted. The new police commander is Zhou Yushu, a protégé of Defense Minister Qin Jiwei, who until this appointment was head of the 24th Army in the Beijing Military Region. The 24th Army had controlled the university area in Beijing without unduly resorting to violence. (Nicholas D. Kristof, 14, 15 February, *NYT*.)

A National Meeting of Advanced Representatives of Emulating Lei Feng was held in Beijing from 3 to 5 March (*Xinhua*, 5 March; *FBIS-CHI*, 6 March). The revival of a Lei Feng campaign at this time is hardly taken seriously by people, but it does underscore that hard-liners (in this case, Yang Baibing, the secretary general of the Military Affairs Commission) are in control of the institutions that can mobilize the resources for such a campaign.

Interestingly, however, many Chinese university students were currently embracing some of Mao's radical ideas as an indirect means of criticizing the political authorities, especially since it has become once again dangerous to quote just about anyone else. The new Mao vogue has seen the reappearance of Mao portraits in student dormitories along with copies of the former chairman's writings. (See, e.g., Ann Scott Tyson, Beijing, *CSM*, 22 February.)

The Sixth Plenary Session of the Thirteenth Central Committee was held in Beijing from 9 to 12 March. In wary anticipation of the impending anniversaries of events associated with last year's prodemocracy movement, the session adopted a seven-point decision on strengthening relations between the party and the people. (*BR*, 19–25 March.)

Of considerable embarrassment to hard-liners in the Chinese government was the escape to Paris on 24 March of Chai Ling, who had been "commander in chief" of the students who occupied Tiananmen Square in May and June of 1989, and of her husband, Feng Congde, both of whom had been sought in China by the police since the previous June (*SCMP*, *FBIS-CHI*, 4 April). Two other student leaders, Ms. Wang Chaohua and Li Gengyun, escaped to the United States at about this time. Ms. Wang was on the original 21 most-wanted list, and Li was leader and financial secretary of the Tiananmen College Students' Federation from Other Provinces. (Hong Kong, *Cheng Ming*, 1 April; *FBIS-CHI*, 3 April.)

The Third Session of the Seventh NPC was held in Beijing from 20 March to 4 April, with about three thousand deputies in attendance. Li Peng delivered the government work report on 20 March. He noted that despite the setbacks created by the "counterrevolutionary rebellion" in 1989 there had been some achievements. Inflation was held to 17.8 percent in 1989, gross national product grew 3.9 percent to 1,567.7 billion yuan, and national income rose 3.7 percent to 1,300 billion yuan. Foreign trade volume totaled US$111.6 billion, an increase of 8.6 percent, including US$52.5 billion of exports (up 10.5 percent). Total grain output reached an all-time high of 407.45 million tons, but per capita grain production fell short of the 1984 record. (Beijing Domestic Service, 20 March; *FBIS-CHI*, 21 March.)

The session adopted the Basic Law of the Hong Kong Special Administrative Region. It also passed an amendment to the Joint Venture Law, specifying among other changes that China will not nationalize any Sino-foreign equity joint venture. The session also accepted Deng Xiaoping's resignation from the state's Central Military Commission, his last remaining official position. (*BR*, 9–15 April.)

According to Chinese sources, an armed rebellion in early April in Xinjiang Province was put down, with 22 people killed and at least thirteen wounded. Western accounts said that about 50 people, mostly Kirghiz, were killed in clashes with security forces near Kashgar. (Beijing, Reuters, 22 April; *NYT*, 23 April.) Two months earlier, Ismail Amat, director of the State Nationalities Commission, blamed the "recent developments of ethnic conflicts in the Soviet Union, radical changes in the Eastern European countries and the awarding of the 1989 Nobel Peace Prize to the Dalai Lama" for Xinjiang's instability (Fan Cheuk-wan, *Hong Kong Standard*, 13 April; *FBIS-CHI*, 16 April).

The Shanghai-based *World Economic Herald* was formally closed in April. The publication was influential among students and intellectuals until its suspension one year ago. Its chief editor, Qin Benli, had been dismissed and confined to his home. (Beijing, *NYT*, 25, 26 April.)

On 30 April, martial law, imposed 8 March 1989 in Lhasa, ended in Tibet (Nicholas D. Kristof, Beijing, *NYT*, 30 April, 1 May).

A considerable stir was created when Xu Jiatun, the former head of Xinhua in Hong Kong, left for the United States about 1 May. Xu did not seek political asylum, but it seemed evident that he had in effect deserted the PRC, euphemistically making "an extensive inspection of capitalist society." (See, e.g., Hong Kong, *Pai Hsing*, 1 June; *FBIS-CHI*, 31 May.)

In May, China released another 211 people who had been detained for involvement in last year's protest movement, apparently to improve its image abroad, especially in the United States, where deliberations were under way regarding an extension of its most-favored-nation status. According to the Chinese government on 10 May, another 431 persons remained in custody, but the suggested total of 1,215 arrested by the government since June 1989 is much lower than the estimates of Western human rights organizations. (See Robert Delfs, *FEER*, 24 May.)

On 25 May, the organizers of the *Goddess of Democracy* radio ship broadcast project announced that because of the great political pressure that the Chinese government was exerting on several countries, they had decided to cancel plans to broadcast prodemocracy messages to the Chinese mainland (Taipei, NCNA, 25 May; *FBIS-CHI*, 29 May).

The months of April through June this year were particularly sensitive for China's political authorities. Hence, unprecedented security measures were imposed in Beijing and elsewhere, and various restrictions were applied to prevent any commemorative demonstrations or other manifestations sympathetic to the suppressed prodemocracy movement of the previous year.

Addressing three thousand youths in Beijing on 3 May, Jiang Zemin gave a speech that was somewhat conciliatory toward intellectuals. "In contemporary China," Jiang said, "patriotism is essentially the same as people's democracy or socialist democracy." He affirmed that young intellectuals as a whole were good and reliable, and he reiterated the "hundred flowers, hundred schools" theme. (Beijing, Xinhua, 3 May; *FBIS-CHI*, 4 May).

Three top Chinese leaders acknowledged that the party had made mistakes last year. Jiang Zemin implied as much during an interview with Barbara Walters of the American Broadcasting Company when he said, "There were different opinions among top CCP leaders on last year's turmoil, and this was a crucial issue." Deng Xiaoping told former German chancellor Schmidt on 21 May, "The students should not be blamed too much; the leadership and the party also made mistakes." Finally, Politburo Standing Committee member Li Ruihuan told leading Zhuhai cadres in May that he agreed with the remarks of Jiang and Deng: "We ourselves made mistakes and should not, as Li Peng has done, lay all the blame on the students, as this is wrong." (Hong Kong, *Ming Pao*, *FBIS-CHI*, 29 May.)

One means that hard-line authorities used to distract attention from the season's anniversary dates and from their own unpopularity was to invoke national pride and perhaps a measure of xenophobia by propagandizing the 150th anniversary of the First Opium War, drawing strained parallels between the narcotic and the "spiritual opium" of today's liberalism (see, e.g., James L. Tyson, Beijing, *CSM*, 31 May).

Three intellectuals—recently released activist Zhou Duo, Taiwan-born pop star Hou Dejian, and former university teacher Gao Xin—who had staged a hunger strike in Tiananmen Square last year planned to hold a well-publicized news conference at the end of May at which they were to release an open letter asking for the release of political prisoners, including Liu Xiaobo, the fourth member of their hunger strike. At the last minute, however, the three dissidents canceled the press conference. (Hong Kong, AFP, *FBIS-CHI*, 31 May.) The three were held for the next three weeks by police.

Despite the warnings and precautions of authorities, hundreds of students, determined that the anniversary of last year's brutal crackdown would be remembered, demonstrated at Beijing University on the nights of 3–4 June. Several foreign correspondents were roughed up in attempts to prevent them from reporting the demonstrations, which again included the smashing of small bottles (symbolizing dissatisfaction with Deng Xiaoping). Meanwhile, Tiananmen Square was closed, and security throughout Beijing was severely tightened. (See, e.g., Ann Scott Tyson and James L. Tyson, Beijing, *CSM*, 5 June.)

In Hong Kong more than 100,000 people took to the streets to mourn the victims of the previous year's Tiananmen massacre. The march, organized by the Hong Kong Alliance in Support of the Patriotic Democratic Movement, was much larger than had been expected. (*SCMP*, *FBIS-CHI*, 4 June.)

Despite such demonstrations, it was apparent that the Chinese government had managed to maintain control of the situation. In the somewhat relaxed atmosphere following the 4 June anniversary, the government announced on 6 June the release of another 97 participants in the prodemocracy movement. (Sheryl Wu Dunn, Beijing, *NYT*, 6, 7 June.)

On 25 June, one year after the party announced a purge of members who were involved in the democracy movement, it was apparent that the purge had fizzled. Although a significant number of the party's membership had to undergo a complex reregistration process and months of meetings, self-criticism, and essay writing, few offenders were actually removed from the party. The lack of success in this effort suggested that the party was stalemated over the issue and that hard-liners have not consolidated their gains by eliminating significant numbers of their antagonists. This lack of success may be because the high-level conservatives who want to remove more opponents from the party do not have control over the reregistration process at the grass roots. Among party liberals who have been prevented from reregistering (though not formally removed from the party) are Zhu Houze, formerly director of the propaganda department, and Du Runsheng, Li Rui, Li Chang, and Yu Guangyuan, all members of the Central Advisory Commission. (Nicholas D. Kristof, Beijing, *NYT*, 22, 23 June.)

It was also apparent, however, that in the year since June 1989 the central leadership had shifted a significant number of officials at the provincial level and in the military. New top officials had been appointed to more than a third of the provinces and to six of the seven military regions. Promotions seem to have been awarded to military officers who cooperated in the June 1989 crackdown. The most striking of these was the promotion of 55-year-old Zhang Gong, a spokesman for the martial law forces a year ago, to political commissar of the Beijing Military Region. But the civilian provincial changes presented a mixed picture. Although some officials who were removed had been identified with more rapid liberalization, not all the new appointees were hard-liners. (Nicholas D. Kristof, Beijing, *NYT*, 30 June, 1 July.)

Chen Yuan, deputy governor of the People's Bank of China, said at an investment seminar in Tokyo in June that China's total foreign debt was US$40 billion and that foreign exchange reserves exceeded $20 billion, while exports were an annual $50 billion. These figures suggest that China's debt burden was manageable and well below the safety ceiling set by the International Monetary Fund. Foreign banks were lending to Chinese banks and enterprises, but not to the government, according to Chen. China's loan repayments would be $4 billion to $5 billion in 1990, rising to $6 billion in 1991, with a peak of $7 billion in 1992, he said. (Tokyo, Reuters, 17 June; *NYT*, 18 June.)

China's number one dissident, astrophysicist Fang Lizhi, and his wife, Li Shuxian, were finally permitted, ostensibly to seek medical attention abroad, to leave the U.S. embassy in Beijing, where they had taken refuge on 25 June 1989 following the crackdown (Nicholas D. Kristof, Beijing, *NYT*, 25, 26 June).

In July it was announced that the number of Beijing University freshmen sent for military training would more than double, with the seven hundred and twenty-eight students graduating from the Shijiazhuang Military Academy in early July to be followed by sixteen hundred new ones in September (Seth Faison, *SCMP*, 9 July; *FBIS-CHI*, 11 July). Many observers in China expect that this effort by the hard-line authorities to instill discipline among young university students could backfire, inasmuch as the students will now have military savvy and connections.

In early July at the National Conference on Government Structural Reforms, Secretary General of the State Council Luo Gan said that the process of streamlining central-level units had been completed and that the exercise would thereafter be confined to local-level offices. The announcement was met with some skepticism, inasmuch as there remained indications of overstaffing in Beijing offices and especially since central planning has been re-emphasized in the last year and a half. Other goals of political structural reform stressed in the Thirteenth Party Congress resolution have also been shelved. (Willy Wo-Lap Lam, *SCMP, FBIS-CHI,* 6 July.)

China's fourth census since 1949 was completed on 10 July under a "relatively developed planned commodity economy," according to Shen Yimin, the deputy director of the State Council's Census Office. Shen noted that much of the rural population has moved toward nonagricultural industries and that the number of employees in the trades and occupations closely related to the commodity economy increased dramatically. The migrant population also has increased dramatically. As the household contract responsibility system is implemented, the number of people failing to register their residence has increased greatly. The problem of above-norm births in the countryside is even more serious than the impending baby boom brought about by the peak birth period of the 1960s, with a number of rural women having children at places other than home in order to avoid supervision. Work on the census is to be completed by September 1992. (*BR,* 24–30 September.)

On 30 October, Xinhua announced the precise figure of 1,133,682,501 as China's population as of 1 July (exclusive of Taiwan and Hong Kong), based on the results of the fourth national census. It was thought, however, that the population had increased by another 5.5 million or so since that date, based on the reported annual growth rate of 1.47 percent. (Nicholas D. Kristof, Beijing, *NYT,* 30, 31 October.)

Jiang Zemin made an inspection tour of Tibet from 20 to 30 July. He reiterated the line that "the central government will continue to implement special policies and flexible measures in the Tibet Autonomous Region" (*BR,* 13–19 August). The Dalai Lama declared, on 1 August in New Delhi, "I am not demanding complete independence from China," but he added that the current rule of Chinese authorities over Tibet was still unacceptable. He referred to his five-point peace plan that calls for Chinese control of foreign policy in return for Tibetan autonomy. (New Delhi, AFP, *FBIS-CHI,* 1 August.)

In early September, former party General Secretary Zhao Ziyang (71) was seen in public for the first time since his appearance among students in Tiananmen Square in May 1989 (Beijing, KYODO, 5 September; *FBIS-CHI,* 6 September).

On 7 September, Premier Li Peng was "relieved of his duties" as concurrent minister of the important State Economic Restructuring Commission, according to *Renmin Ribao.* His replacement was Chen Jinhua, president of the China National Petrochemical Corporation, who is known to have close ties with ousted General Secretary Zhao Ziyang. This personnel change was seen as an indication that moderate party forces are regaining control of the economic commission. (Ann Scott Tyson, Beijing, *CSM,* 10 September.) Subsequently, Chen Jinhua, "new reform chief," reaffirmed that "China would deepen its economic reform while maintaining the stability and continuity of the basic policies governing urban and rural reform, and strive for sustained, steady and coordinated development of the national economy." He specifically noted that there would be no deviation from central planning but added that what is "considered a comprehensive, all-inclusive plan is nothing but a bureaucratic fantasy." (*BR,* 5–11 November.)

During September conservatives made a number of public appearances, and their presence and perhaps increasing strength was again noted. For example, elders Bo Yibo (82) and Peng Zhen (87) spoke before the Japan-China Association on Economy and Trade in September. Bo urged a "special relationship" with Japan. Peng discussed the need to guard against U.S. attempts to turn China "into a vassal of the capitalistic world through peaceful evolution." Also, Chen Yun (86) was reportedly reemerging from a long illness and was being consulted by central planning advocates. In internal speeches recently, Chen had been blaming Deng Xiaoping's open door policy for corruption within the party. (*Insight,* 15 October.) In blaming Deng, Chen reportedly said that the corruption was the worst it had been in the 70-year history of the party (Chris Yeung, *SCMP,* 8 September; *FBIS-CHI,* 10 September). There were reports that Chen and Deng met together more than once beginning 8 September to discuss policy matters (Hong Kong, *Cheng Ming,* 1 November; *FBIS-CHI,* 2 November).

The best-selling 1989 novel *Snow White, Blood Red,* about the Liaoning-Shenyang Campaign during the Chinese civil war, sparked controversy during the year. Author Zhang Zhenglong is a PLA officer in a propaganda office in the Shenyang military region. Old cadres, whose views were reportedly compiled by General Wang Zhen, complained that the book presented a distorted picture of the war and reversed the verdict on Lin Biao. Beijing Municipal Committee secretary Li Ximing called it "anti-Party." In commenting on the book, Jiang Zemin asserted, "We cannot underestimate the influence of bourgeois liberalization in the army." The affair touched off an ideological investigation campaign within the PLA, so that all army writers are to have their works written since 1986 subjected to a "literary inspection." Colonel Zhang was arrested. (Hong Kong, *Wide Angle Monthly*, September; *Inside China Mainland*, November; and Ann Scott Tyson, Beijing, *CSM*, 27 September.)

The Asian Games that opened on 22 September were for the first time attended by all 38 members of the Olympic Council of Asia (*BR*, 24–30 September). When the games concluded on 7 October, China had won 341 of the 976 medals awarded, including 183 of 310 gold medals and 107 of 309 silver medals (*BR*, 15–21 October). The State Council afterward wrote to the games' organizing committee saying that much of the success of the Asiad was owed "to China's political and social stability" (ibid.). The *Beijing Evening News* later disclosed that as many as 650,000 people were involved in security work in Beijing alone during the games (Nicholas D. Kristof, Beijing, *NYT*, 11, 12 November).

The Administrative Procedure Law, China's first law enabling citizens to sue government organizations, went into effect on 1 October (see, e.g., *China Daily*, *FBIS-CHI*, 28 September).

In the fall, a new campaign against pornography was launched that had strong antiforeign overtones and threats that the death penalty would be imposed on those involved in the business. It was generally thought that hard-liners in the leadership were attempting to use pornography as the basis for a much broader campaign to propagate their own views. The new campaign also appeared to be unusual in that the previous campaign against pornography, begun last year, had already removed much flesh from magazines and videos in the marketplace and led to the closing of 12 percent of China's newspapers, 13 percent of social sciences periodicals, and 7.6 percent of the country's publishing houses. An editorial in *Renmin Ribao* on 27 October depicted the campaign against pornography as a matter of national survival as well as of socialism's

survival. (Nicholas D. Kristof, Beijing, *NYT*, 27, 28 October.)

On 31 October it was revealed that Wang Ruowang (72), a prominent writer and dissident, had been released after sixteen months of detention although still subjected to some restrictions (Nicholas D. Kristof, Beijing, *NYT*, 31 October, 1 November).

In late October–early November a week-long meeting was held on improving China's tarnished image abroad by improving overseas propaganda. The topic was considered sufficiently important that five of the six members of the Politburo's Standing Committee attended some of the sessions. It was agreed that more effort should be expended to better present China to the world, and plans to establish an office in charge of overseas propaganda were reported. (Nicholas D. Kristof, Beijing, *NYT*, 5, 6 November.)

On 17 November, China devalued its currency by 9.57 percent against the dollar in an effort to gain further profit from exports. The new exchange rate is 5.22 yuan to the dollar, down from the rate of 4.72 set after a 21.2 percent devaluation in December 1989. Foreign businesspeople applauded the move to bring the Chinese currency to more realistic levels but said the adjustment was too small to benefit exports substantially. (*WSJ*, 19 November.)

Deng Xiaoping appeared in public for the first time in about six months when he voted in the local NPC elections in Beijing on 26 December. The reappearance was especially significant because it coincided with the gathering of party leaders in the long-delayed and troubled Seventh Plenum. (Cable News Network, 26 December.) Indeed, it was later reported that Deng had given a private address on 24 December to Jiang Zemin, Li Peng, and Yang Shangkun and that his remarks were then relayed to the Central Committee, setting the tone for the plenum. Deng (characteristically) said that China's leaders should not quibble over whether the economy is running along Socialist or capitalist lines. (Beijing, Reuters, Honolulu, *Star-Bulletin*, 3 January 1991.)

The Seventh Plenum of the Thirteenth Central Committee then met in closed-door sessions from 25 to 30 December in Beijing. The plenum was attended by 171 full members, 107 alternate members of the Central Committee, and observers from the Central Advisory Commission, the Central Commission for Discipline Inspection, and "relevant departments." The communiqué of the plenum was a vague document that indicated the adoption of a cautious economic and social plan for the 1990s. The plan stresses stability and self-reliance rather than infatuation, it was reported, with the preceding reform decade. According to Xinhua, the plenum did not approve the drafts of the Eighth Five-Year Plan and the new Ten-Year Development Program that are to go into effect on 1 January 1991. Instead, the government is to "map out" the plans, presumably based on the communiqué. Priority is given in state spending to agriculture, basic industries, and infrastructure. Also, more attention is given to defense spending, which had received a shrinking share of the budget during the 1980s. Significantly, little attention was given in the communiqué to new economic reforms. Judging from the rhetoric it appears that the conservatives may have won the day, although such wording might have been necessary to secure passage while containing sufficient references to efficiency improvement to allow for needed changes. (Beijing, AP News, 30 December.)

Relations with Taiwan. On 20 May, President Lee Teng-hui announced in Taipei that his government's 40-year-old declaration of a "Communist rebellion" would soon be revoked, formally ending the state of civil war in China (David E. Sanger, Taipei, *NYT*, 20, 21 May). Lee also called for substantially expanding contacts once Beijing promotes democracy and a free economy, renounces the use of force against Taiwan, and tolerates Taiwan's efforts to broaden its relations with other countries. The announcement was the first time that a Taiwan leader had recognized the existence of the government in Beijing and suggested an end to the policy of the "three no's" (i.e., no official contact, no negotiations, and no compromise with the mainland). (James L. Tyson, Beijing, *CSM*, 21 May.) Yet, given the conditions, it is not surprising that Beijing did not respond favorably.

In September, the Kuomintang's Central Standing Committee on Taiwan resolved to establish a National Unification Council (NUC). Serving as the president's nonpartisan, ad hoc advisory team, it would correlate, originate, and stimulate ideas on mainland policy and unification strategy by means of consultations, consensus, and contact among the various sectors of society. (Taipei, *Free China Journal* [*FCJ*], 17 September.)

On 19 September, Chinese Red Cross societies on both sides of the Taiwan Straits announced a five-point agreement on procedures for the repatriation of illegal immigrants, the first such agreement between Taiwan and the mainland. Reportedly, top government officials on both sides approved of the agreement, although Taiwan authorities asserted that it did not constitute an official contact. (*FCJ*, 24 September.)

Auxiliary Organizations. The *Circular of the CCP Central Committee on Strengthening and Improving Party Leadership over the Work of Trade Unions, Communist Youth League (CYL) Organizations, and Women's Federations* received considerable attention early in the year, although there did not seem to be much actual follow-up in the months that followed (Xinhua, *FBIS-CHI*, 31 January).

The Third Session of the Seventh National Committee of the CPPCC, held from 18 to 29 March and chaired by Li Xiannian, entertained more than seventeen hundred proposals referring to 140 departments and institutions under the CCP's Central Committee and the State Council (*BR*, 9–15 April). In June it was reported that there were 2,931 CPPCC committees, with 410,000 members nationwide. There are also 1,666 local noncommunist party organizations with a total of 337,000 members, according to an official of the United Front Work Department of the CCP. (Xinhua, 8 June; *FBIS-CHI*, 11 June.)

The All-China Youth Federation, according to its chair, Liu Yandong, has some four million members and ties with more than one thousand youth organizations in some 140 countries worldwide. Liu said the federation was also developing ties with youth organizations in Taiwan, Hong Kong, and Macao, despite ideological differences. (Xinhua, 20 August; *FBIS-CHI*, 21 August.)

The National Congress of the Chinese Young Pioneers was held in Beijing beginning on 14 October, the 41st anniversary of its founding. The Young Pioneers have a membership of 130 million. (*Renmin Ribao*, 14 October; *FBIS-CHI*, 19 October.)

International Views and Positions. China made progress in regaining a measure of acceptance in the international community during the year despite the ascendancy of hard-line policymakers and their accusation that outside forces are employing a policy of "peaceful evolution" to lead China from the path of socialism. At the beginning of the year the Chinese government labored under the shadow of international sanctions (which Beijing claimed had little effect) that had been instituted following its bloody suppression of the prodemocracy movement in Beijing in June 1989. Much of the loss created by those sanctions was made up for by greatly expanded investments and large numbers of tourists from Taiwan. The termination of martial law in Beijing in January and the subsequent release of large numbers of persons arrested last year in connection with the prodemocracy movement improved the Chinese government's image abroad, as did the successful holding of the Asian Games in the early fall. These domestic measures were complemented by highly successful diplomatic maneuvering that garnered for China important formal ties with Saudi Arabia, Indonesia, and Singapore. By midyear, the United States indicated it would not oppose the resumption of Japan's large loan program to China. Moreover, the Chinese government made the most of the Persian Gulf crisis. Not only did that crisis help to distract attention away from China, but China was able to serve its own interests in voting with the U.N. Security Council majority in imposing sanctions on Iraq. Even its abstention on a U.N. sanction that would allow for the use of force was adroitly employed to gain advantage, inasmuch as it led to a meeting between the Chinese foreign minister and President Bush the next day and a World Bank loan the following week.

Relations with the Soviet Union. Relations with the Soviet Union continued to improve throughout the year, with important exchanges of party, government, economic, and military officials. Soviet deputy foreign minister Igor Rogachev visited Beijing 9–11 January in another effort to narrow the widening gap in Sino-Soviet relations engendered by the rapid liberalization of the Soviet Union and Eastern Europe. Rogachev also discussed the Cambodia issue. (Willy Wo-lap Lam, Hong Kong, *SCMP*, *FBIS-CHI*, 10 January; Hong Kong, AFP, *FBIS-CHI*, 11 January.)

On 8 February, China ended its official silence on news about recent developments in the Soviet Union when it reported on the 5–7 February plenum of the Central Committee of the Communist Party of the Soviet Union (CPSU). Xinhua noted that Gorbachev had said that the process of political pluralism in the Soviet Union "may lead at a certain stage to the establishment of parties." It also reported Gorbachev's call for a "rethink of democratic centralism" and the proposal to abolish Article 6 of the Soviet constitution, which defines the leading role of the CPSU. (*FBIS-CHI*, 9 February.) Meanwhile, there were many reports that older Chinese cadres

were anxiously watching developments in the Soviet Union, with many, including Deng Xiaoping, attacking Gorbachev in internal speeches and predicting his downfall (see, e.g., Ann Scott Tyson, Beijing, *CSM*, 13 February). In contrast, there was evidence of sympathy and support for Gorbachev among Chinese students (see, e.g., Hong Kong, *Cheng Ming*, 1 March; *FBIS-CHI*, 2 March).

Li Peng made an important official visit to the Soviet Union from 23 to 26 April, the first trip to the Soviet Union by a Chinese premier since Zhou Enlai's visit in 1964. The two countries signed six agreements during Li's visit: a long-term economic, science, and technology cooperation and development program; a peaceful use and study of space cooperation agreement; an agreement on mutual reduction of military forces in border areas and a guideline for enhancing trust in the military; a consultation accord between the two foreign ministries; a credit agreement on daily-use commodities provided by China to the Soviet Union; and a memorandum on the construction of two nuclear power plants in China with Soviet loans. (*BR*, 7–13 May.)

On 22 May, a delegation from the Central Committee of the CPSU led by B.K. Pugo, alternate member of the Political Bureau and chairman of the Control Commission, arrived in Beijing for a visit. It was the highest-ranking party delegation from the Soviet Union since party relations were restored one year earlier. (Xinhua, 22 May; *FBIS-CHI*, 23 May.)

General Liu Huaqing, vice-chairman of the Central Military Commission, made an official visit to the Soviet Union from 31 May to 14 June (Xinhua, 14 June; *FBIS-CHI*, 15 June). The Liu delegation was made up of senior aerospace experts, and the purchase of aviation equipment was discussed during the visit (see, e.g., Tai Ming Cheung, *FEER*, 19 July).

It was reported on 20 August that the Soviet Union has agreed to return Heixazi Island to China. The 300-square-kilometer island is situated at the convergence of the Heilongjiang and Ussuri rivers. It was also disclosed that the Soviet Union had agreed in 1989 to return to China the 1-square-kilometer Damansky (Zhenbao) Island, which is now occupied by Chinese farmers and military. (Tammy Tam, *Hong Kong Standard*, *FBIS-CHI*, 20 August.)

The two countries agreed in early September to establish general consulates in Khabarovsk and Shenyang (*Renmin Ribao*, 2 September; *FBIS-CHI*, 4 September).

It was reported in late October that China was in the preliminary stages of negotiating the purchase of state-of-the-art Sukhoi SU-27 jet fighters from the Soviet Union. The Soviet Union, which did not impose an arms embargo on China following the June 1989 crackdown, sent a delegation of about twenty aviation specialists to attend a biannual Chinese aeronautical trade show held for five days in late October. Chinese acquisition of such weaponry would represent a great leap in the firepower of China's antiquated air force and considerably affect the regional balance of military power in Asia. (Robert MacPherson, Beijing, AFP, *FBIS-CHI*, 29 October.)

The Chinese and Soviet foreign ministers, Qian Qichen and Eduard Shevardnadze, held a working meeting on 23 November in Urumqi, Xinjiang. They had an in-depth exchange of views on the situation in the Persian Gulf and briefed each other on related matters. They agreed to continue to consult with each other when the U.N. Security Council adopted additional measures. They also discussed bilateral relations, expressing satisfaction on the development of the relationship since normalization last year. (Urumqi, Xinhua, 23 November; *FBIS-CHI*, 26 November.)

Relations with the United States. In January the U.S. Congress voted to sustain President Bush's veto of a bill that would have given additional legal protection for Chinese students in the United States. For his part, Bush promised to issue an executive order that would afford the Chinese students extended protection, an order that was finally given on 11 April (deferring until 1 January 1994 any enforced departure of PRC nationals). On 30 January, the U.S. Senate readopted an amendment on sanctions against China to the State Department authorization bill. (*NYT*, 31 January). The number of Chinese students in the United States rose to 33,390, an increase of 15 percent over the year before (Robin Wilson, *Chronicle of Higher Education*, 28 November).

On 21 February, the U.S. State Department issued a human rights report that contained strong criticism of China's record. The report was in turn strongly criticized by Chinese sources (e.g., Meng Yi, "People of Various Circles in Beijing Denounce the U.S. 'Human Rights Report' for Interference in China's Internal Affairs," Hong Kong, *Liaowang Overseas Edition*, 26 March; *FBIS-CHI*, 3 April).

On 25 May, Bush announced the renewal of China's most-favored-nation trading status, again raising considerable congressional criticism, although efforts by the House to reverse this development or to make such renewal more difficult next year were unsuccessful.

American congressional criticism of China was sharply protested by the Chinese government as constituting interference in China's internal affairs, while the continued conciliatory gestures by the Bush administration were appreciatively noted. The Bush administration in turn regarded its policy to be justified by indications of Chinese responsiveness to foreign criticism.

Fang Lizhi and his wife, Li Shuxian, were allowed to leave China on 25 June, one month after Bush renewed China's most-favored-nation trading status. The departure of Fang and his wife removed what had been regarded as the single greatest obstacle to improved relations between China and the United States. (Nicholas D. Kristof, Beijing, *NYT*, 25, 26 June.)

Toward the end of the year it was apparent that a new point of friction was emerging in U.S.-China relations, as the U.S. trade deficit with China was expected to reach from $10 to $11 billion for 1990, compared with the deficit of $6.2 billion in 1989. This would make the shortfall second only to the U.S. trade deficit with Japan. (See, e.g., Takashi Oka, *CSM*, 25 October.)

On 30 November, Foreign Minister Qian Qichen met with President Bush for 45 minutes in the White House, the highest-level meeting of officials of the two countries in eighteen months. The meeting was held only one day after China cast its abstention vote (rather than a negative vote) in the U.N. Security Council on the use of force against Iraq. (*BR*, 10–16 December.) Three weeks later, Assistant Secretary of State Richard Schifter visited Beijing to discuss human rights with Chinese officials. Following Schifter's departure from China, Foreign Ministry spokesman Li Zhaoxing said, "To exchange views on human rights is one thing and to interfere in internal affairs under the pretext of human rights is another." He indicated that China would continue a dialogue on human rights but had no plans to free the imprisoned intellectuals. (Sheryl Wu Dunn, Honolulu, *Star-Bulletin*, 25 December.)

Relations with Japan. Japanese prime minister Kaifu received assurance from President Bush at the economic summit meeting of seven leading industrial nations in Houston in July that his administration would not oppose the resumption of Japan's aid program to China. The Japanese government, under pressure from the Japanese business community, was inclined to resume the $5.2 billion, five-year loan program in any case. (Maureen Dowd, *NYT*, 7, 8 July.)

The Japanese government decided to send its minister of education to attend the opening of the Asian Games in Beijing on 22 September.

On 17 September, during meetings in Beijing with a 60-member Japanese business delegation, Japan and China announced that they would extend the existing bilateral trade agreement for another five years. Under the agreement, Japan is to import some 60 million barrels of Chinese crude oil each year. (*Insight*, 15 October.)

On 21 October, naval and air units of the Japanese Maritime Self-Defense Forces blocked two Taiwan fishing boats from carrying a Taiwan Area Games torch onto the main island of the eight-island Tiaoyutai group, the object of a sovereignty dispute between China and Japan (*FCJ*, 25 October). By early November, however, it was reported that China and Japan had privately agreed to end the immediate dispute over the issue just before Japan's resumption of a 36.5-billion-yen development loan to China (Fan Cheuk-wan, *Hong Kong Standard*, 3 November; *FBIS-CHI*, 5 November).

Relations elsewhere. Jiang Zemin made a three-day visit to Pyongyang, North Korea, from 14 to 16 March, his first foreign travel since becoming party general secretary in June 1989 (*BR*, 26 March–1 April). In early September, Kim Il-song made a secret visit to Shenyang, meeting Li Peng and perhaps Jiang Zemin.

Relations with Vietnam appeared to improve later in the year, but the relationship was unclear by year's end. As late as 28 June, a leading official of the Asian Department of the Chinese Foreign Ministry said that recent exchanges of views between Chinese and Vietnamese officials in Beijing and in Hanoi had failed to narrow differences on the question of Cambodia. Vietnam's first vice-foreign minister, Diah Nho Liem, visited Beijing in early May, and Chinese assistant foreign minister Xu Dunxin visited Hanoi in June. (*BR*, 9–15 July.) By late August, however, China came to agree with the other major nations of the U.N. Security Council on a plan to enable the United Nations to play a major role in bringing the Cambodia conflict to an end.

Thus, on 3–4 September an important secret summit was held between top party and government leaders of both China and Vietnam, including Jiang

Zemin and Li Peng on the one side and Nguyen Van Linh and Do Muoi on the other. An understanding was reached at this meeting that led to subsequent meetings in Djakarta and Bangkok by representatives of the different Cambodia factions and to their acceptance of the U.N. Security Council plan for resolving the Cambodia conflict. China also opened the Friendship Gate on the Vietnam border for the Vietnamese athletes bound for the Asian Games in Beijing. Vice-Premier Vo Nguyen Giap went to Beijing for the games. (See, e.g., Nicholas D. Kristof, Beijing, *NYT*, 19, 20 September; Robert Delfs et al., *FEER*, 4 October.)

However, China-Vietnam relations began to sour again by November. In mid-December a large number of Vietnamese tourists were detained for a few days after crossing into China and were then returned to Vietnam even though they had visas for their visit. There were also reports by late December that China was supplying new military aid to Cambodia's Khmer Rouge, despite its claim to have halted shipments months earlier. (AP, 29 December.)

On 21 July, China and Saudi Arabia established formal diplomatic relations (*BR*, 30 July–5 August). However, China suspended diplomatic relations with Nicaragua on 6 November following Managua's announcement that day that it was establishing relations with Taiwan (Managua, Xinhua, 6 November; *FBIS-CHI*, 7 November). Yang Shangkun had met with a delegation from Nicaragua's National Assembly a few days earlier (Beijing, Xinhua, *FBIS-CHI*, 29 October). China and the Republic of the Marshall Islands established diplomatic relations at the ambassadorial level on 16 November (Beijing, Xinhua, 16 November; *FBIS-CHI*, 19 November).

China voted for all the U.N. Security Council resolutions calling for sanctions against Iraq but abstained on the 29 November resolutions permitting the use of force after 15 January 1991.

Premier Li Peng visited Indonesia 6–10 August, during which the 23-year break in diplomatic relations between China and Indonesia was formally ended on 8 August. Li was the first top Chinese official to visit Indonesia in 25 years. (*BR*, 20–26 August.) Li then visited Singapore 11–13 August, where he exchanged views with Prime Minister Lee Kuan Yew and First Deputy Prime Minister Goh Chok Tong, who would succeed Lee in November (ibid.). On 3 October, China announced the establishment of diplomatic relations with Singapore (*NYT*, 4 October).

On 23 October, Li Peng noted on behalf of the Chinese government the European Community's recent decision to restore its relationship with China (*BR*, 5–11 November).

On 4 December, the World Bank approved a $114.3 million loan to China, the first loan to go beyond the confines of meeting basic human needs since the June 1989 crackdown. This decision came less than a week after President Bush met with Chinese foreign minister Qian and only a day after China abstained from, rather than opposed, a U.N. Security Council vote authorizing the use of force to expel Iraq from Kuwait. Attila Karaosmaonoglu, the World Bank's vice-president for Asian Affairs, said that other loans by the bank to China were being prepared. (Stephen Labaton, *NYT*, 5 December.)

Stephen Uhalley, Jr.
University of Hawaii and the East-West Center

India

Population. 849,746,001
Parties. Communist Party of India (CPI); Communist Party of India—Marxist (CPM); minor Communist splinter parties
Founded. CPI: 1928; CPM: 1964
Membership. CPI: 467,539; CPM: 450,000; Communist extremist factions estimated at 15,000
General Secretaries. CPI: Indrajit Gupta; CPM: E. M. S. Namboodiripad
Politburo. CPI (Central Secretariat): 9 members: C. Rajeswara Rao, Indrajit Gupta, Avtar Singh Malhotra, Promode Gogoi, Chaturanan Mishra, N. E. Balaram, M. Farooqi, A. B. Bardhan, Homi Daji; CPM; 11 members: E. M. S. Namboodiripad, M. Basavapunaiah, Harkishan Singh Surjeet, Jyoti Basu, Samar Mukherjee, E. Balanandan, Nripen Chakravarty, Saroj Mukherjee, V. S. Achuthanandan, L. B. Gangadhara Rao, A. Nallasivian
Central Committee. CPI: National Council: 125 members; CPM: 70 members
Status. Legal

Last Congress. CPI: Fourteenth, 6–12 March 1989, in Calcutta; CPM: Thirteenth, 27–31 December 1988, in Trivandrum
Last Election. 1989. CPI: 12 seats; CPM: 32 seats; two CPM-allied communist parties (Revolutionary Socialist Party and Forward Bloc) won 8 seats (out of 524 contested seats in the 545-seat Parliament); CPM also dominates Left Front governments in two Indian states (West Bengal and Kerala), where CPI is a junior coalition partner.
Auxiliary Organizations. CPI: All-India Trade Union Congress, All-India Kisan Sabha, All-India Student Federation, All-India Youth Federation, National Federation of Indian Women, All-India Agricultural Workers' Union, National Federation of Progressive Writers; CPM: Centre for Indian Trade Unions, Kisan Sabha, Students' Federation of India, Democratic Youth Federation of India, All-India Democratic Women's Association
Publications. CPI: *New Age* (Pauly V. Parakal, editor); Indian-language dailies in Kerala, Andhra Pradesh, West Bengal, Punjab and Manipur; CPM: *People's Democracy* (M. Basavapunaiah, editor); Indian-language dailies in Andhra Pradesh, Kerala and West Bengal

Rise and Fall of the Singh Government. In November 1989, for the second time in India's independent history voters returned a non-Congress government to power. As with the Janata Dal government elected twenty-two years earlier, the fragile ministry of Prime Minister V. P. Singh proved short-lived. Singh's National Front government was an unstable coalition whose survival depended on support "from the outside"—from the Communists and the Bharatiya Janata Party (BJP), the standard-bearer of militant Hindu nationalism. Under this arrangement, the Communists and the BJP agreed to back Singh's centrist coalition without sharing the spoils of office.

Both the left and the right were uneasy with the arrangement from the outset. Nevertheless, both sides put their ideological differences aside and attempted to promote their own party interests in their political capacity as guarantors of the Singh government. Although the Communists performed respectably in the 1989 election, picking up 24 new seats for a combined strength of 52 seats in the 545-seat Parliament, the BJP's even more impressive performance was deeply disturbing to the Indian communist faithful (*YICA*, 1990). Throughout 1990, the Communists alternated between publicly vilifying the BJP as "reactionary" and "anti-national" and using their influence within the National Front to moderate BJP behavior. The Communists also shrewdly used the rise of militant Hinduism as a rallying cry to organize grass roots support in defense of secularism, a political staple of Indian communism.

Singh's downfall was the result of defections by the BJP and dissidents from within his own Janata Dal party. Singh's communist backers—CPI, CPM, and two allied communist factions—supported the embattled prime minister to the bitter end. In the final analysis, the left and right constituents of the National Front government proved more stable than the prime minister's own party. Unlike Indian centrist parties that are prone to infighting along caste lines and personality differences, the BJP and the Communists are disciplined, cadre-based organizations with rigorous ideologies.

The Communists and their BJP adversaries waged political battles on a number of explosive issues throughout the year. In the troubled states of Punjab, Jammu, and Kashmir, Indian security forces continued to battle Sikh and Muslim militants attempting to secede from the union. The Communists vigorously condemned secessionism but urged Singh to reaffirm constitutional safeguards and adopt conciliatory policies toward disaffected religious minorities. By contrast, the BJP urged stern police action to protect the Hindu population and ensure the nation's territorial integrity.

In August, Singh announced a plan to expand central government job reservations for "backward classes." The controversial policy was in part a bid to woo low-caste political support for his own party. The announcement sparked a violent upper-caste backlash throughout northern India. The Communists, longtime champions of job reservations and constitutional protection for the downtrodden, hailed the decision and mounted counterdemonstrations and rallies in support of Singh. The BJP was reluctant to throw its support behind the measure for fear of dividing its Hindu political base along caste lines.

The unraveling of the Singh government accelerated when the BJP marshaled its forces behind a divisive campaign to take possession of an Islamic mosque in the north Indian town of Ayodhya. The mosque was constructed in the sixteenth century on the site of a temple revered by Hindus as the birthplace of the deity Ram. The BJP hoped to divert attention from the job reservation stir by championing a cause that could unite Hindus on a common platform.

In September, BJP party leader L. K. Advani embarked on a month-long, ten-thousand-kilometer chariot procession across northern India to drum up support for the temple reconstruction drive. When the procession reached Ayodhya on 23 October, Singh ordered the arrest of Advani and thousands of his supporters. The action was almost certain to precipitate the collapse of the National Front government. Nevertheless, the Communists fully supported Singh's decision as a matter of principle. A week later, when Hindu militants attempted to storm the mosque, security forces fired on the crowd and killed scores of protesters. The confrontation triggered a wave of Hindu-Muslim riots across India.

Advani's arrest prompted the BJP to withdraw support from the Singh government. The fate of the government was sealed shortly thereafter when a rump of Singh's own Janata Dal party rallied behind dissident leader Chandra Shekhar and bolted the coalition. Singh lost a vote of confidence on 5 November and tendered his resignation, effective once a new government took office. The only votes he could muster were 82 of his own 141 party members and the 52 communist members of Parliament.

Once the ruling coalition collapsed, the Congress-I Party of former Prime Minister Rajiv Gandhi was the only party in a position to engineer the formation of a new coalition government. Although Congress-I had the largest bloc of seats in Parliament, it was still 80 seats shy of a majority. Because all major parties except the BJP were reluctant to call fresh elections to resolve the crisis, the contenders for power engaged in drawn-out negotiations to patch together a new coalition. The Communists, for their part, refused to join forces with their old Congress-I foe and announced their continued support for Singh's Janata Dal rump party. Indian president R. Venkataraman then invited the Congress-I, the BJP, and the Communists to form a coalition government. Each party either declined the invitation or failed to attract the necessary support. Chandra Shekhar, commanding a scant 10 percent of parliamentary seats, then agreed to form a government with the backing of Congress-I.

On 16 November, Chandra Shekhar was sworn in as India's eighth prime minister. Most political pundits believe this government will also be short-lived. New elections probably will be called later this year if Gandhi is confident that Indian voters will opt for stability and return to the Congress-I fold. Under the new political dispensation, the Communists find themselves in their accustomed parliamentary position as a loyal opposition. The Communists still retain a feeble alliance with V. P. Singh, but they no longer enjoy the sympathies of the central government. Once again, Indian Communists are in the political wilderness.

The CPI. As the weaker of the two Marxist parties, CPI was the junior partner in the so-called left group during the National Front's eleven-month rule. CPI commands a following in the critical Hindi-belt states of Bihar and Uttar Pradesh, including a member of Parliament from Ayodhya. Elsewhere, the party's base of support is thin, with a smattering of followers among urban workers and intellectuals in northern and western India. Although party chapters exist in almost all Indian states, CPI commands no appreciable support in the northeast and the south.

Unlike CPM, CPI has never ruled an Indian state, and its prospects for achieving such a breakthrough are poor. Consequently, the party has historically had to align itself with CPM and "progressive" non-Communist parties to make a political impact at both the state and the national level. Outside Parliament, CPI boasts an impressive network of political front organizations that carry the party's message to targeted constituencies such as workers, students, intellectuals, and women. CPI's rural support, except in Bihar, is extremely shallow.

Another source of support that CPI has traditionally tapped—the Soviet Union and its erstwhile East European allies—can no longer be counted on for political clout and financial sustenance. Indeed, as the Kremlin's role as the patron of international communism recedes, longtime pro-Soviet partners such as CPI are unsure of the ideological direction they should take in the future.

In April, CPI general secretary C. Rajeswara Rao resigned as party leader, though he still retains a seat on the National Council Central Secretariat. The 76-year-old Rao has been in failing health for some time, and his departure had been anticipated. The procommunist press noted, however, that Rao was an old-line, pro-Soviet Communist who was ill-equipped to guide the party in an era when international communism was undergoing dramatic decline. According to an editorial in the *Patriot*, the sea changes in international communism "left him helpless" (21 April).

Rao's successor as CPI general secretary was Indrajit Gupta, who had been groomed for the job for a number of years. The 71-year-old Gupta, scion of a wealthy family, followed the same political path

as many of his Indian comrades, imbibing Marxism while a student at Cambridge. On his return to India in 1941, Gupta dedicated himself to trade union organizing and the independence movement. He rose to become general secretary of the CPI trade union front and was arrested on several occasions for organizing strikes. When the Indian communist movement split in 1964, Gupta remained with the staunchly pro-Soviet CPI. He is the senior CPI parliamentarian, having won a seat in five of India's six national elections since independence. Like his predecessor, Gupta has impeccable "internationalist" credentials, having served as vice-president of the Soviet-sponsored World Federation of Trade Unions. He has maintained close personal ties with Soviet leaders and has generally endorsed Gorbachev's policies of *perestroika* and *glasnost'*. Owing to Gupta's advanced age and party background, however, he is an unlikely candidate to initiate the basic reforms that communist parties elsewhere in the world are undergoing.

No dramatic changes in party fronts occurred during the year. CPI supports at least seven such organizations. The most significant is the All-India Trade Union Council (AITUC), with a claimed membership of almost 3 million workers in public sector industries. Many of these industries rely on Soviet purchases of their output. Although CPI, CPM, and Congress-I have traditionally dominated India's powerful trade union movement, CPI activists are concerned over the inroads the Bharatiya Mazdoor Sangh, the BJP labor front, has made in recent years. *New Age*, the CPI organ, and a range of Indian-language dailies and theoretical journals advance the party line. Although CPI publications still decry "American imperialism" at every opportunity, the Soviets have apparently stopped using the Indian communist press to plant anti-American disinformation.

The CPM. With a solid bloc of seats in the national Parliament and as the driving force behind ruling Left Front coalitions in West Bengal and Kerala, CPM hoped that its backing for Singh's government would enable the party to protect its hard-won electoral gains at the state and national level. Throughout the year, CPM strategists such as West Bengal party boss Jyoti Basu pursued a pragmatic policy of quietly advancing CPM perspectives on minority rights, center-state relations, secularism, and foreign policy. Realizing that the BJP posed the most serious challenge to his government's survival, Singh courted CPM leaders and routinely sought their advice and support during his brief tenure in office.

Although some CPM cadres grumbled that political pragmatism had diluted the party's Marxist identity, Basu and other Politburo moderates managed to keep the party in line in the larger interest of expanding the CPM base at the expense of Congress-I and the BJP. By all accounts, CPM played a responsible, moderate role during the life of the National Front.

CPM patience ran out when BJP militants challenged Singh over the Ayodhya mosque/temple controversy. CPM met the challenge by backing Singh and rallying public opinion against the party's three political foes—the BJP, Congress-I, and what CPM termed the Congress-I "puppet government" of Chandra Shekhar. At a mammoth rally in Calcutta after Singh's downfall, Basu predicted the government would not last because of its "unprincipled alliance" based on "political opportunism." Basu then called on the party to agitate against the central government and the looming threat of Hindu fundamentalism. (*Telegraph*, 11 November.)

As it looks ahead to the next election, CPM probably will run on a domestic platform of communal harmony and government intervention on behalf of the disadvantaged. CPM's electoral prospects are limited, however, by the party's regional appeal. Despite decades of effort to broaden the party's mass base, CPM is confined almost exclusively to its "red fort" bastions in West Bengal, Kerala, and Tripura. Although seat adjustments with V. P. Singh's party could marginally improve CPM's position in the Hindi heartland, CPM is in no position to challenge the BJP and the Congress-I on the strength of its own following. CPM's other ally, CPI, also has little to offer.

Like CPI, CPM's focus throughout 1990 was on coalition making and breaking; few organizational changes occurred. Longtime Politburo heavyweight B. T. Ranadive died in April. Ranadive, the general secretary of the undivided CPI when India gained independence in 1947, was active in the Telengana armed struggle of the 1950s that was crushed by Indian security forces. He then went on to head the party's trade union front. Although a Maharashtrian, Ranadive joined his Bengali and Malayalee comrades in forming the breakaway CPM in 1964 (*Indian Express*, 7 April). Because Ranadive's seat on the Politburo remains vacant, the CPM inner circle remains a gerentocracy in the mold of the Chinese Communist Party. The average age of the CPM politburo is 74 years plus.

In regional party affairs, the powerful West Bengal branch of CPM remained solidly entrenched in power for its thirteenth straight year. CPM and its communist partners (CPI, Forward Bloc, and Revolutionary Socialist Party) control 36 of the state's 41 seats in the national Parliament. At the state level, the Left Front controls more than 80 percent of the West Bengal assembly seats. At the local level, CPM has used its many years in power to dole out government patronage and build a labyrinth of party-controlled administrative cells, particularly in rural areas. State assembly elections are due in 1992.

In the southern coastal state of Kerala, the CPM-dominated Left Democratic Front managed to ride out the year in power, though economic challenges threatened its survival in office. As in West Bengal, the CPM party apparatus runs deep in the state, particularly among urban intellectuals. The state's chronic unemployment problem has severely tarnished CPM's image, however. Moreover, the BJP has made political inroads among the state's Hindu population. To compound matters, the economic dislocations caused by Iraq's invasion of Kuwait in August seriously undermined Kerala's already hard-pressed economy. More than 100,000 Malayalee workers in Kuwait fled home with no jobs awaiting them; many more expatriate Keralans are expected to return home from the gulf if war breaks out.

To meet the crisis, CPM chief minister Narayan established a volunteer development brigade to put unemployed Keralans to work on economic development projects around the state. CPM coalition partners complained that the CPM youth front, the Democratic Youth Federation of India, formed the nucleus of the employment scheme. Many suspected the scheme was intended primarily to build CPM patronage. Congress-I, the CPM's chief political rival in the state, refused to participate altogether (*India Today*, 31 October).

In the tiny northeastern enclave of Tripura, the CPM remained in opposition, though the party retains strong support among the state's Bengali population. The Tripura state unit of CPM remains essentially a branch office of the Left Front government in Calcutta. The state's ruling ministry, a coalition of Congress-I and a local tribal party, greatly improved its political prospects with the arrival in power of a central government backed by the national Congress-I party.

Ideological and Foreign Policy Dilemmas.
The year's political dramas in the USSR, East Europe, and elsewhere in the communist world were deeply troubling to Indian Communists. Accustomed as they are to a bipolar world pitting the forces of "socialism" and "imperialism" against each other, both CPI and CPM were uncertain how to react to the global decay of Marxism.

CPI, the more pro-Soviet of the two, cautiously endorsed Gorbachev's radical program of domestic reform but resisted any hint that CPI was in need of repairs. In May, shortly after assuming his new post, General Secretary Indrajit Gupta journeyed to Moscow for consultations. In July, on the eve of V. P. Singh's routine state visit to the USSR, CPI issued a statement declaring that "we all have a stake in the success of *perestroika*, as it will unleash the full potential of socialism and give it a new face" (Hong Kong, AFP, 5 July; *FBIS-NES*, 12 July). Left unsaid, of course, was the fear that the end result of Gorbachev's reforms might be the scrapping of socialism, not its revitalization.

The ideological dilemma facing CPM was even more painful. Although the party had formerly sided with Beijing during the heyday of the Sino-Soviet split, CPM in recent years has pursued a more evenhanded approach in its dealings with fraternal parties. Events in 1990 revealed that CPM now belongs to a small fraternity of communist organizations that still cling to an inflexible, cold war party line. Indeed, portraits of Stalin still adorn CPM offices (*NYT*, 16 June).

In January, Jyoti Basu expressed the "consternation" of CPM cadres who bemoaned the demise of East European socialism. "The Indian leftist should draw a lesson" from the experience, he stated. "The socialist countries have failed to meet the basic needs of their people." To Basu, the need of the hour was not radical reform, but a rededication to Marxist dogma (*Hindustan Times*, 23 January).

In February, General Secretary E. M. S. Namboodiripad led a CPM delegation to Moscow for frank discussions with Soviet party officials. In June, the CPM Central Committee issued a statement calling the political upheavals in East Europe a "setback" that "negated the achievements of the socialist past." The following month, CPM went a step further when it branded Gorbachev a "deviationist" and called on the Soviet party to "reaffirm the basic principles of Marxism-Leninism" (*FBIS-NES*, 12 July; Hong Kong, AFP, 5 July).

On the foreign affairs front, the Communists issued ritual condemnations of Pakistani "interference" in communist Afghanistan, U.S. "intervention" in the Persian Gulf, and the depredations of multinational corporations. The latter themes were not in keeping with New Delhi's policies or prevailing public opinion in India. Indian leadership of the nonaligned movement, another pivotal element of communist foreign policy pronouncements, was seriously undermined by the winding down of the cold war.

The Chinese, for their part, attempted to keep relations with rival India on an even keel. Foreign Minister Qian Qichen led a Chinese negotiating team to New Delhi in March to probe for a settlement of the long-standing border dispute. A scheduled state visit to India by Premier Li Peng was canceled in December because of the change in government in New Delhi. CPM, Forward Bloc, Janata Dal, and Congress-I—each of which maintains formal links with the Chinese party—dispatched delegations to Beijing during the year.

Other Communist Parties. Small communist splinter groups exist on both the left and the right of CPI and CPM. On the right is the United Communist Party of India headed by former CPI general secretary S. A. Dange. The party promotes a policy of forging a united front with Congress-I and other noncommunist parties deemed sufficiently progressive. The party, confined almost exclusively to industrial pockets of Bombay and Tamil Nadu, enjoys little popular support.

On the left fringes of the Indian communist movement are an assortment of Maoists and underground revolutionary cells known collectively as Naxalites. Ideologically descended from those who waged a gruesome jacquerie in West Bengal in the late 1960s, the Naxalites in recent years have been relegated to a local security menace in a few Indian states. In 1990, however, the deeply divided Naxalite movement showed signs of renewed vigor.

Several trends were evident. First, a comparatively moderate group of Naxalites has forsaken revolutionary terror in favor of nonviolent direct action. Exemplified by the loosely structured Indian People's Front, these reformed Maoists seek to develop a mass base in backward tribal areas of Bihar, Orissa, Madhya Pradesh, Tamil Nadu, and West Bengal. Their tactics include strikes, demonstrations, nonpayment of taxes and rents, and standing candidates in local elections. CPI and CPM have each attempted to open a dialogue with these groups.

A second trend, championed by the legendary Naxalite leader Kanu Sanyal, stresses the importance of ideological unity and leaves the question of tactics to individual cells and leaders. Sanyal's umbrella organization, the Communist Organization of India—Marxist-Leninist, has staged unity conclaves in recent years in an attempt to forge a semblance of Naxalite unity. Some Naxalite constituents of the movement are still wedded to the 1960s doctrine of "annihilating class enemies" through the application of "revolutionary justice." Other factions are convinced that New Delhi's police powers are formidable enough to thwart another rural insurrection.

The third and most virulent brand of Naxalism is exemplified by the People's War Group (PWG) that is building strength in Andhra Pradesh. The PWG is based in the jungles of Telengana, a tribal region with a long history of revolt against police repression and landlord exploitation. The PWG closely resembles nihilistic bandit gangs such as Peru's Sendero Luminoso or Sri Lanka's Liberation Tigers of Tamil Eelam (for overviews of these groups, refer to country profiles elsewhere in the volume). PWG tactics include assassination, extortion, bank robbery, and sabotage. Police officials reported the PWG was responsible for more than two hundred kidnappings of public officials during the year (*NYT*, 21 October).

The PWG is reportedly headed by Kondepalli Seethharamiah, a 75-year-old firebrand cut in the mold of a latter-day Robin Hood. The group's most spectacular assault occurred in October when PWG saboteurs bombed a train carrying Indian army troops and equipment. The explosion killed 47 passengers and sent shock waves of revulsion across the nation.

The Congress-I state government in Andhra Pradesh attempted throughout the year to appease the PWG by granting amnesty to PWG members on trial, disbanding a police task force, and offering financial incentives to cadres willing to abandon the struggle and surrender their arms. The strategy failed. In December, New Delhi dismissed Andhra chief minister Chandra Reddy and ordered security forces to resume counterinsurgency operations against the PWG.

Tribal insurgents invoking communist rhetoric and organizational methods have for years tied down Indian security forces in the remote northeastern states of Nagaland, Manipur, and Assam. Although none of the guerrilla bands that operate in these states are believed to receive support from mainstream communist parties or China, their resort to secessionist violence remains a source of instability. In November, shortly after Chandra Shekhar took office, the Indian army mounted a large-scale counterinsurgency operation in Assam to root out extremists affiliated with the United Liberation Front of Assam, which seeks to carve out an independent Socialist state in Assam. Most of the guerrillas escaped the security dragnet, however, and fled to neighboring Myanmar.

Douglas C. Makeig
U.S. Department of Defense

Note: The opinions expressed in this article are the author's own and do not necessarily reflect those of the U.S. government or any U.S. government agency.

Indonesia

Population. 190,136,221 (*World Fact Book*)
Party. Indonesian Communist Party (Partai Komunis Indonesia, PKI)
Founded. 23 May 1920 (*Firsthand Information*, p. 71)
Membership. At its height (pre-October 1965), 1.5 million including intellectuals and workers. *World Fact Book*, 1990, states 1,000–3,000 members with less than 10 percent engaged in organized activity.
Party Leaders. Unknown. Tomas Sinuraya was at one time leader of the Moscow wing; Jusuf Adjitorop, of the Beijing wing.
Last Congress. Seventh Extraordinary, April 1962.
Publication. *Tekad Rakyat*, (People's Will) published abroad monthly (*Firsthand Information*, p. 76).

In 1990, although there was still official, principally military, concern about possible communist subversion, the PKI was less frequently accused of responsibility for domestic unrest or violence. Following the resumption of full diplomatic relations with the People's Republic of China (PRC), the government announced that, with certain conditions, former

PKI members living abroad would be allowed to return.

Leadership and Party Organization.
Chinese officials claim that only a handful, perhaps ten, former PKI members are still alive in China, and they are forbidden to be involved in politics. Furthermore, as the general secretary of the Chinese party assured President Suharto, the Chinese Communist Party (CCP) has no relations with the banned PKI. (*FEER*, 12 July; *Antara*, *FBIS-EAS*, 21 November.)

Satiadjaya Sudiman continued as the representative of the PKI on the *World Marxist Review* until the periodical's demise. In the February issue, Sudiman was one of eight Communists from different countries to comment on the December 1989 statement by five Warsaw Pact states apologizing for their role in sending troops into Czechoslovakia in August 1968. Unlike the other commentators, Sudiman did not deplore the 1968 actions but merely noted that the "new assessment is presumably accurate and correct." He reaffirmed that he and his fellow party members supported socialism "and all the steps taken to defend and strengthen it." He suggested that in the future more attention be given to "providing accurate, detailed, balanced and truthful information about various developments so as to enable an early objective analysis and proper conclusions." He added that the pact countries' emphasis on the need to observe the principles of sovereignty, independence, and noninterference in internal affairs in relations between states "are also important in relations between fraternal parties—big or small, ruling or in opposition, legal or working underground." (*WMR*, February.)

In Indonesia, despite some official concern that vestiges of the long-banned PKI remain active underground, there is no information about a clandestine party organization.

As of late 1989, 51 of those arrested after the 1965 abortive coup reportedly remained in prison, with 14 on death row. The movements and activities of seventeen thousand former detainees are still restricted. Four men who had been sentenced to death between 1969 and 1971 for their part in the 1965 events were executed in mid-February. The four, said to have been presidential guards believed to have taken part in the killing of six generals in the early hours of the coup, were identified as Noor Rohayen, 52; Satar Sujanto, 59; Yohannes Surono, 62; and Simon Petrus Sulaeman, 62. Reportedly, the four came from poor families and were only

subordinates; "there are still two or three on the 'waiting list' who were the real leaders." (Hong Kong, AFP, 16 February; *FBIS-EAS*, 16, 26 February.)

Reports that another six men on death row were likely to be executed during the year sparked diplomatic protests from the European Community countries, among others, and were believed to be the reason for heavy press coverage of this year's prison visits by family members at the end of Ramadan. The coverage included interviews with two prominent political prisoners—former Foreign Minister Subandrio and former Air Force chief Omar Dhani, both serving life sentences. Both men were described as looking fit and saying that they had found solace in Islam. Another prominent prisoner, Colonel A. Latief, the man many think knows most about the events of the night of 30 September 1965, is reported to have completed his memoirs and placed them in a bank for safekeeping. (*FEER*, 22 March, 10 May, 2 August.)

Domestic Party Affairs.
Allegations that remnants of the PKI were still trying to stage a comeback came principally from the military. The governor of the National Defense Institute, Major General Sukarto, warned that the new developments in Eastern Europe did not indicate any changes in communist ideology and might increase the threat of communism. Underground remnants of the PKI are still actively preparing for the time when they can reenter the state's political arena, he said. (*Antara*, 13 January; *FBIS-EAS*, 17 January.) On the 25th anniversary of the 1965 abortive coup, *Angkatan Bersenjata*, the armed forces daily, warned that although communism had lost ground in Europe, "Asian communist regimes hold their forts," an apparent reference to the PRC. (AFP, 1 October; *FBIS-EAS*, 2 October.) Some civilian political leaders also stressed that communism remained a threat to Third World countries. At a seminar sponsored by the International Forum of Indonesia, a leader of the United Development party proposed that Indonesia and the other countries in the Association of Southeast Asian Nations assist the Philippines in putting down the rebellion launched by the Philippine Communist Party (*Merdeka*, 23 May; *FBIS-EAS*, 6 June). Nevertheless, Indonesian leaders generally appeared to put less emphasis than in past years on the communist threat. In January, the coordinating minister for political and security affairs, Admiral Sudomo, predicted an increase in terrorism but did not single out

the Communists as the likely source. There seemed little inclination to attribute the unrest in Atjeh or in Timor to the PKI. The dissidents in Atjeh were rumored to be linked to a center in Libya (*FEER*, 28 June; *CSM*, 14 August.)

Efforts to root out remaining PKI sympathizers continued. A 29-year-old student from Central Java, Bonar Tigor Naipospos, was sentenced to eight years in prison for "spreading communism." He had been arrested in June 1989 for distributing "subversive" literature, including several banned books by Pramudya Ananta Toer (see *YICA*, 1989). Reportedly, the police had to use tear gas to disperse the crowd of approximately a thousand who gathered to protest the verdict. (*FEER*, 1 November.)

In preparation for the 1992 general elections, the government announced plans to review a 1985 policy allowing former communist party detainees to vote in national elections. Most former PKI members had been allowed to vote in 1987, but the planned review was seen as an opportunity to reassess the strength of the communist threat. All former communist detainees will have to prove they are no longer linked to communist ideology, and only those clearly found to have no further link with communism will be allowed to vote. They are to be screened by the state security agency and the armed forces Strategic Intelligence Agency. (AFP, Djakarta Domestic Service, 7 February; *FBIS-EAS*, *FEER*, 15 February.)

In April, a presidential decree provided for compulsory screening of officials for indications of communist sympathies. However, people will no longer be penalized for having relatives involved in the PKI. (*FEER*, 2 August.)

The government announced that former Indonesian Communists living in China and in Eastern Europe could return home but would have to account for their past actions before the court. President Suharto said that if they were not brought to court it would not be fair to other Indonesian Communists who had been punished. If they are proven innocent in court, he said, nothing would be done to them. (*Indonesia Times*, 20 July; *FBIS-EAS*, 2 August; *Antara*, *FBIS-EAS*, 21 November.)

Indonesian leaders, military and civilian, challenged a report in the *Washington Post* and several other U.S. papers that said that an American embassy official had supplied the Indonesian army with names of five thousand Indonesian Communists in October 1965. The leaders' main argument was that the Indonesian army did not need U.S. help to identify PKI members or to stamp out the communist uprising. (*Indonesia Times*, 25 May; *FBIS-EAS*, 1 June; *NYT*, 12 July; *FEER*, 2 August.)

International Views, Activities, and Ties. On 3 July, Indonesia and the PRC signed an agreement to restore diplomatic relations between the two countries the following month. Chinese support for the PKI coup attempt in 1965 led to the 23-year rift. At a news conference announcing the agreement, China's foreign minister, Qian Qichen, said that he had no idea whether Indonesia still had a communist party. At a later meeting, President Suharto assured the general secretary of the Chinese Communist Party that all PKI dissidents had been released. The Chinese press, hailing the formal resumption of relations as a "great event," did not explain the reason for the rupture of relations in the 1960s, attributing it only to "some complicated historical causes." (*NYT*, 4 July; *Antara*, *FBIS-EAS*, 21 November.)

Despite enthusiastic official statements about the resumption of formal ties with the PRC, there were signs that not everyone accepted Chinese assurances that the PRC no longer had an interest in the PKI. For example, just before Chinese premier Li Peng's much-heralded state visit to Djakarta, an official of Indonesia's Ministry of Youth and Sports Affairs announced the conditions under which Indonesians would be allowed to attend the Asian Games in Beijing: A total of five thousand Indonesians would be allowed to go to China to support the team. The government would screen the would-be supporters and give them security clearances before issuing them exit permits. Elderly supporters would not be allowed to go "because they may have known a lot about the PKI in their youth." (*Merdeka*, 26 July; *FBIS-EAS*, 6 August.)

Indonesia's continued ban on the circulation of printed material written in Chinese characters raised some awkward questions. More than a month after the resumption of formal ties, the Ministry of Information said that it had not yet received any request to place Chinese reporters in Indonesia. A ministry official said that the possibility that Chinese reporters or correspondents for China's news agency might be stationed in Djakarta was a consequence of normalization; however, permission for the assignment of foreign journalists was something that should be given selectively. He warned that circulating papers and magazines written in Chinese characters was still banned by the government. The official called on the press to report anyone keeping or trying to disseminate printed material written in Chinese. (*Antara*, 29 September; *FBIS-EAS*, 1 October.) During the year, Indonesia's ties with the USSR and Eastern Europe continued to increase, particularly cooperative trade arrangements, as did high-level exchanges with Vietnam.

Jeanne S. Mintz
Washington, D.C.

Japan

Population. 123,642,461 (*World Fact Book*)
Party. Japanese Communist Party (Nihon Kyosanto, JCP)
Founded. 1922
Membership. 500,000 (Tokyo, Kyodo, 5 July; *FBIS-EAS*, 5 July); industrial workers: 65.6 percent; women: 38.3 percent
Central Committee Chairman. Kenji Miyamoto
Presidium Chairman. Tetsuzo Fuwa
Central Committee. 150 full and 56 alternate members
Status. Legal
Last Congress. Nineteenth, 8–13 July
Last Election. February: 7.96 percent of popular vote in House of Representatives. The JCP holds 14 seats of 252 in the House of Councillors and 16 of 512 in the House of Representatives.
Auxiliary Organizations. All-Japan Student Federation, New Japan Women's Association, All-Japan Merchants' Federation, Democratic Foundation of Doctors, Japan Council of Students, Japan Peace Committee, Gensuikyo (Japan Council Against Hydrogen and Atomic Bombs)
Publications. *Akahata* (Red banner), daily circulation 550,000, Sunday circulation 2,500,000, total readership more than 3,000,000 in addition to frequent special issues and a poster, *Akahata Photo News*, 90,000 copies published twice a month; *Bulletin: Information from Abroad* (JCP Central Committee); *Gakusei shimbun* (Student newspaper), weekly; *Shōnen shōjo shimbun* (The boys' and girls' newspaper), weekly. *Zen'ei* (Vanguard), theoretical journal; *Gekkan gakushu* (Monthly studies); *Josei no hiroba* (Women's trib-

une); *Gurafu konnichiwa—Nihon kyōsanto desu* (Hello—we are the JCP); *Asu no noson* (The countryside tomorrow); *Bunka hyōron* (Cultural review); *Keizai* (Economics); and *Rōdō undō* (Workers' movement)—all monthlies. *Sekai seiji: Rompyō to shiryō* (International politics: Critical reviews and materials), fortnightly.

The JCP, which has suffered a serious image problem during the last two to three years because of being associated with terrorism, the Tiananmen massacre in China, and the fall of communist parties in Europe, changed its English name from Japan Communist Party. Its title in Japanese, however, remained the same, giving it the distinction of being Japan's oldest political party and the only party with the same name it had before World War II.

The JCP maintained its advocacy of the parliamentary, as opposed to the revolutionary, road to power. But in 1990 this strategy did not work: the JCP lost eleven seats in the election for the more important of the Japanese Diet's two houses, the House of Representatives, prompting the party to engage in serious introspection.

The JCP remained at odds with Japan's other political parties, making it all but impossible for it to gain political influence through an alignment of opposition parties. All indications during the year suggested that this will not change in the immediate future. The JCP continued to support a number of auxiliary and related organizations. It also maintained its internationalist stance, although, as in the past, its ties with foreign political parties were limited, as was its influence on Japan's foreign policy.

The JCP held its Nineteenth Party Congress in July. The mood of both the party leaders and the rank and file was not upbeat. Although the leadership was challenged, top party leaders remained in office and party policies and ideology remained generally unaffected.

Party Leadership and Meetings. Despite his age (82), Kenji Miyamoto remained chairman of the Central Committee. Miyamoto, who has been the party's top leader since the mid-1950s, was criticized during the year for staying in power too long, for the JCP's image problems, and for its loss in the July House of Representatives election, but this did not prevent his reelection at the July congress. Tetsuzo Fuwa, who is in his mid-50s, remained chairman of the Presidium. He was active during the year and still appears likely to be Miyamoto's successor.

The only important change in the party's leadership was the election of Kazuo Shii, 35, as the youngest person ever to serve as head of the Secretariat; he is also the youngest member of the JCP's 150-member Central Committee. Shii, an engineering graduate of Tokyo University, Japan's top university, joined the party in 1973 and was promoted to Central Committee membership in 1988. Miyamoto described him as an "excellent communist theoretician" (*FBIS*, 18 July).

At the Eighth Plenum of the JCP Central Committee, convened for three days beginning on 19 March at party headquarters in Tokyo, Miyamoto tried to play down the party's election defeat, noting that although the JCP had lost a considerable number of seats in the House of Representatives, it had suffered only a 1 percent decline in popular support. Given the coalitions of parties opposed to the JCP and the global decline in the prestige of communism, he argued that this was not a bad performance. (*Akahata*, 23 March.) Miyamoto also discussed ideological issues, changes in communism around the world, the JCP's relationship with other political parties in Japan, and foreign policy.

A rally on 5 May at Tokyo's Tatsuminomori-Hiroba Park commemorated the 30th anniversary of the party's paper, *Akahata*. Central Committee chairman Miyamoto gave the commemorative address, declaring that the JCP had performed quite well in the February election despite the "anticommunist rage" in Japan (*Akahata*, 8 May). He also discussed suggestions to change the party's name, "scientific socialism," and other issues (ibid.).

JCP leaders convened the Central Committee's Ninth Plenum on 22 May for two days in Tokyo. Kenji Miyamoto gave the opening address, discussing mainly issues to be considered at the Nineteenth Congress. A plenum draft resolution included the following main issues: the role of "scientific socialism" in the context of developments in Eastern Europe, the JCP's world role, the future of Japanese society, and party activities (*Akahata*, 25 May).

The JCP convened its Nineteenth Party Congress in Atami, Shizuoka prefecture, from 8 to 13 July. Approximately one thousand party representatives attended the meeting.

Miyamoto became leader of the JCP in 1958, when he was elected party general secretary at the Seventh Congress, and has been the party's boss ever since, though he subsequently moved to the positions of Presidium chairman and finally Central Committee chairman. Before and during the congress, Miyamoto's leadership was challenged. Before the meeting, *Akahata* carried editorials from rank and file members opposing Miyamoto's leadership. Some suggested he should step down because of his age (*FBIS*, 5 July) or because of his close association with deposed Romanian leader Nicolae Ceauşescu (*Economist*, 14 July).

Although it is difficult to ascertain the extent of party opposition to Miyamoto, the congress showed clear signs of dissatisfaction with top party leadership. The Presidium, however, is composed of Miyamoto supporters, and most showed no signs of dumping him. Indeed, some observers consider criticism of Miyamoto to have been a staged demonstration of party democracy (*FBIS*, 5 July).

At the congress, Miyamoto defended both the party line and his own record, pointing to his consistent reformism, his independence from both the Soviet Union and China, and his long-standing repudiation of a proletarian dictatorship in favor of "scientific socialism." He declared that "hegemonism, bureaucracy and great power policies of the two previous Soviet leaders—Joseph Stalin and Leonid Brezhnev—were responsible for the collapse of the Eastern European socialist states" (*FBIS*, 9 July). He argued that this does not mean that socialism itself is discredited. Miyamoto also took credit for having opposed Soviet and Eastern European communism in the past, saying that what was happening now showed the validity of his views. (Ibid.).

Nevertheless, Miyamoto admitted that the USSR's great power politics, hegemonism, and interventionism had caused problems the JCP had to overcome. He went on to note the challenge the party faced in promoting Socialist reform in a "highly advanced country such as Japan" (ibid.). He said that the JCP would uphold the system of democratic centralism and defended his friendship with Ceauşescu, saying that the JCP had "never praised the dictatorial domestic policies of Ceauşescu" (ibid.).

Fuwa's political report blasted Gorbachev's *perestroika*, calling it "an effort to seek harmony with imperialism and monopoly capitalism" (ibid.). He said that Gorbachev's "new thinking" had made the Soviet Union a "loyal ally of social democracy—a political theory not related to scientific socialism' (ibid.). He chided social democracy, pointing out that even in World War I it had supported the war by giving in to imperialists (ibid.).

Elections. In February, Japan had its most important election in four years for the National Diet's lower, more powerful chamber, the 512-member House of Representatives. The JCP suffered a major setback in this election, losing 11 of its 27 seats. The party's loss of popular votes, however, was much less significant, though it reflected a long-term decline in the JCP's popularity.

The JCP endorsed 131 candidates, many more than its size and support base justified. As in the past, the JCP stated that it hoped to "educate" the electorate during the election.

On 2 February, Presidium chairman Fuwa represented the JCP in nationally broadcast radio and television debates, speaking on the major campaign issues put forth by the JCP. This event was new for Japanese elections, but polls taken later suggested that few voters were influenced by the debate. Had this not been the case, the debate might have helped the JCP because of the attention and publicity and because putting the JCP leader with other party leaders gave the JCP a sense of legitimacy.

The JCP's campaign focused on the 3 percent consumption tax, the Recruit scandal, the U.S.-Japan defense treaty, and price supports for rice. The party also brought up its usual campaign issues: higher welfare payments, inequality, the status of women and minority groups, and the liabilities of capitalism—essentially social class issues. In addition, the party campaigned against the "emperor system." JCP candidates tried to explain or play down foreign policy issues, which seemed to hurt the JCP, but the party's platform continued to include opposition to U.S. bases in Japan, nuclear weapons, and the like.

In January, Fuwa called for a coalition of opposition parties to defeat the ruling Liberal Democratic Party (LDP) (*Japan Times*, 23 January), but no other opposition parties would consider this. In fact, they remained hostile to the JCP. Worse yet, the 8-million-member Japan Trade Union Confederation publicly called for an anti-LDP coalition that excluded the JCP (ibid.).

The JCP was the only party to unequivocally oppose the 3 percent consumption tax the LDP had pushed through the Diet in a less than democratic fashion. The tax, however, was not as strong an issue as it appeared because many businesses had already set up measures to collect the tax and because a number of business groups found the tax

advantageous (*FEER*, 11 October). Thus, while the JCP strongly supported repeal of the tax, as did a large segment of the population, its policy did not turn out to be as helpful as originally calculated.

The party also had the advantage on the Recruit scandal issue of being the only political party not implicated in the scandal, but apparently public outrage had diminished by February 1990.

The JCP was the only party to adamantly oppose the U.S.-Japan defense pact but on this issue was on the wrong side of the polls, with most Japanese supporting the treaty in its present form as well as defense spending at its present level, which the JCP also opposed. The JCP also sought to exploit farmers' discontent over U.S. pressure on Japan to open its rice market, but the JCP had difficulty appealing to the basically conservative farmers.

The party campaigned on various issues of class and fairness and on the nuclear issue. None of these, however, proved especially helpful in attracting votes. The JCP supported women's issues and ran more female candidates by a large margin—more than twice as many as the other four major parties combined (*Japan Times*, 4 February)—but the Japan Socialist party's leader was a woman who dominated nearly all debate on the subject and attracted a large female following.

The JCP won 5,226,986 votes of the 65,704,290 cast, for 7.96 percent of the total popular vote (*FBIS*, 22 February). This was a decline of almost 1 percent from the last House of Representatives election, when the party won 8.79 percent (ibid.). The JCP suffered a much bigger loss in seats because it fielded too many candidates and adopted a comparatively unsophisticated election strategy.

The party also suffered from the situation in the communist bloc, particularly in Eastern Europe, and the Tiananmen massacre in China, both of which sullied the JCP's reputation and image and made communism seem unworkable and inappropriate for Japan. The JCP failed to convince the electorate that it had long been at odds with these kinds of communist systems and that communism was still based on valid principles. Central Committee chairman Miyamoto noted that this was the most important reason for the party's setback, citing a poll showing 20 to 30 percent of the voters who supported the JCP in the previous election saying they would now vote for the Japan Socialist party because of events in Eastern Europe (*Akahata*, 23 March). Another poll he quoted showed that 42 percent of the voters said that developments in Eastern Europe would affect their vote (ibid.). The same was true of the June 1989 killing of students by the Chinese Communist Party, an event associated with the JCP in the minds of many voters, even though the JCP has been at odds with the Chinese leadership for nearly three decades.

Domestic Affairs and Issues. The JCP's major concerns in 1990 were the election to the House of Representatives and the party's defeat in that election, the JCP's relations with other parties, scientific socialism and other ideological issues, the decline of communism in Eastern Europe and elsewhere in the world, the consumption tax, the U.S.-Japan defense relationship, the antinuclear movement, the emperor, and labor's opposition to the JCP. Changing the party's name and its leadership were also central issues.

The defeat in the February election was a major setback for the JCP, but there was little that the party could do. For this reason party leaders endeavored to play down the defeat. Concerning the problem of the JCP's relationship with the other parties, its policy was not to budge unless and until the other parties—particularly the Japan Socialist party, which has in the past frequently aligned with the JCP—dropped their anticommunist stance (*Akahata*, 23 March).

Concerning theoretical matters, Chairman Miyamoto consistently described the doctrine of scientific socialism as stating that all worthwhile things produced by humanity should be inherited and further developed. That doctrine involves philosophy, economic ideas, and theories of social development, he said; it is not a dogma and is neither sectarian nor dogmatic. The Soviet Union, Miyamoto argued, had not in recent years advanced scientific socialism, and this was the cause of difficulties in the communist world (*Akahata*, 23 March, 24 May). He asserted that historical materialism and the theory of surplus value are essential to understanding the present world and that the argument that communism and socialism have collapsed "disregards the nature of world capitalism as it is" (*Akahata*, 24 May). Miyamoto went on to say that the millions of homeless in the United States, the withdrawal of capital from manufacturing industries there, and the "hollowing out" of the economy in the world's biggest capitalist country gives evidence of crisis in monopoly capitalism and that in this context it is an important task of the JCP to denounce the contradictions and limitations of capitalism (ibid.).

Miyamoto also devoted much time to explaining the apparent decline of communism in Eastern Europe and worldwide developments as stemming from the idea of infallibility and the absolutism of the Communist Party of the Soviet Union. Because of these "gross errors," he said, "the peoples came to strongly oppose these parties in power, leading to the fall of the Stalin-Brezhnev model regimes" (ibid.). He contended that these events demonstrated the past and present correctness of JCP policies. Pursuing this idea, Miyamoto noted that since the Eleventh Party Congress in 1970 the JCP has made it clear that the prospect for future socialism in Japan would be quite different from that in the Soviet Union (ibid.).

On the issue of the national consumption tax, Miyamoto declared at the Nineteenth Party Congress that petitions introduced by the JCP Diet Members' Group had been signed by more than 9 million people—more than those of any other party. He pointed out that the other parties had held "closed door sessions" with the ruling Liberal Democratic party and were not adamantly opposed to the tax, leaving the JCP as the only party in strict opposition (*Akahata*, 14 July). He challenged the ruling party's contention that it was needed because of the aging of Japanese society and vowed to continue to struggle against the tax (ibid.).

The JCP continued to assail the corruption that plagued the ruling party and implicated other parties, urging that scandals be investigated more thoroughly and openly and that the guilty be punished. The JCP advocated a limit on campaign contributions to help resolve this problem and noted the existence of such a restriction in the United States (ibid.). The party was unable, however, to parlay its detachment from major scandals and "money politics" into enough voter support to offset its other liabilities.

The JCP continued to oppose the U.S.-Japan security treaty, even though public opinion polls reflect majority support for it and all the other political parties endorse it. Party spokespersons during the year argued that the treaty is not justified by the so-called Soviet threat and pointed out that Japan has now become the third country in the world in military spending, compared to sixteenth twenty years ago. They also noted that the ruling party has doubled the area of U.S. military bases in Japan since the signing of the treaty, has given the U.S. military "privileges beyond world standards," and has, in violation of the law, allowed the United States to "freely bring into Japan" nuclear weapons

(*Akahata*, 14 July). Party leaders asserted that abrogating the treaty and taking the road of nonalignment and neutrality would make it possible for Japan to "make a great contribution to peace in Asia and the world" (ibid.).

On the issue of workers' welfare, the JCP condemned the long work hours in Japan and announced that income inequality has increased and that more and more wealth is held by the upper class (ibid.). The party also condemned the government and ruling party for the plight of women in Japan, pointing out that their average wage was 52 percent that of men, in contrast to 68 percent in England and 80 percent in France (ibid.). JCP leaders and candidates in various elections cited these figures and tried to relate them to sex scandals involving LDP leaders (ibid.).

JCP leaders also condemned the government's agricultural and environmental policies. They pointed out that Japan's self-sufficiency ratio for food was 79 percent in 1960 and is only 49 percent now—a decline that no other country with a population of more than 20 million has experienced. This, it was stated, has led to the decline of Japanese agriculture and left the nation with no rebuilding policies (ibid.). The party's apparent hope of attracting farmer support in the context of the ruling party's capitulation to U.S. pressure to import more agricultural products did not bring any noticeable successes in the February election, however. The JCP continued to criticize the nation's environmental record, noting that it threatened people's health and blaming big business, the Liberal Democratic party, and the government (ibid.).

Auxiliary Organizations. The JCP throughout the year maintained its usual contact with and support for its auxiliaries and fronts, many of which focus on nuclear weapons and nuclear war.

During 1990, however, more attention was focused on organizations not connected with the JCP. Several hard-left organizations gained considerable attention during the year, and some of their activities had a negative impact on the JCP's efforts to maintain a good image and win elections. In August, Chukakuha (Middle Core Faction), an extremist left group in Japan, claimed responsibility for firing three mortar shells at the Japan Broadcasting Corporation building to express its opposition to the Japanese imperial family (*FBIS*, 17 August). In October, the extremist Japanese Red Army warned Prime Minister Kaifu against involvement in the Middle East crisis, saying that such actions could

have serious consequences for the hostages held there (ibid., 12 October). In November, a secretive ultraleftist group, the Revolutionary Workers' Council (Kakurōkyō), claimed responsibility for a bomb attack on a police dormitory that killed one policeman and injured five (*FBIS*, 7 November). At nearly the same time, Chukakuha claimed it had attacked U.S. and Japanese military facilities in Tokyo and neighboring prefectures to protest the enthronement of Emperor Akihito. Japanese Red Army spokesmen in Lebanon denounced the ceremony and vowed to "fight to stop the revival of Japanese militarism," though they did not cite any actions the group had taken or might take (*FBIS*, 13 November). Although the JCP does not associate with these groups, it is often associated in the Japanese press and in the public mind with their activities because they are all viewed as leftist organizations with similar policies on the military, the emperor, and other issues, even though the JCP, unlike the other groups, does not advocate or practice violent means to attain its goals.

International Views and Activities. The JCP devoted a considerable amount of time, attention, and energy to international issues during 1990. Throughout the year, JCP spokespersons expressed the party's concern that the widespread perception of communism's collapse was hurting the JCP. Meanwhile, the party's relations with the Communist Party of the Soviet Union remained cool, relations with the Chinese Communist Party worsened, and relations with Communist parties elsewhere were unsettled and uncertain. JCP leaders tried to counter the notion that communism was in decline by quoting Marx: It "is important not to interpret but to change the world" (*Akahata*, 8 May). They argued that the Stalinist system in which groups of party and government bureaucrats give orders to the "completely neglected" people had nothing to do with Marx or Lenin. Miyamoto, Fuwa, and other top JCP leaders contended that the JCP had long ago espoused "scientific socialism" and that the Soviet Union under Stalin and subsequent leaders had not. In this context, Miyamoto asserted that the JCP at its Fourteenth Congress in 1977 had announced its view that socialism is in a "formative" stage and should not be judged by the present condition of Socialist countries (ibid.).

In March, the JCP reprinted *Akahata* articles delineating the party's relations with the countries of Eastern Europe. Miyamoto noted that the JCP had had good relations only with Romania and Yugoslavia, the two countries that did not take part in the 1968 invasion of Czechoslovakia. He noted more specifically that the JCP had severed relations with the Polish United Workers' party before martial law was declared, and he posed an agenda for Socialist countries: not to be satisfied with the simple abolition of the system of exploitation by the socialization of the means of production, to recognize the importance of Socialist democracy, to demonstrate democratic and flexible efficiency in the economy, to respect the right of national self-determination, to reject hegemonism, and to abolish nuclear weapons (*Bulletin*, March).

The JCP tried to distance itself from its former association with Romania by reprinting several previously published articles explaining its position. The JCP declared that the "massive, bloody" armed repression in Romania was a "gross misuse of government power" and that it had lodged a protest at the time with the Romanian Communist Party for "having trampled on socialist democracy" (*Bulletin*, January). The JCP subsequently rejected participation in an international conference called by Romania to defend socialism, calling it "contrary to the cause of scientific socialism as well as social progress" (ibid.). Throughout the year the JCP endeavored to publicize the fact that it no longer had close relations with Romania.

Relations between the JCP and the Soviet Union continued to be strained, as reflected in a long article by Presidium chairman Fuwa published in January in *Akahata* and reprinted for further dissemination in March (*Bulletin*, March). Fuwa pointed out, as JCP leaders have frequently done, that the Soviet Union's motivation in implementing *perestroika* and changing its relations with the capitalist countries was to improve economic conditions in the USSR. Fuwa's article, a response to Gorbachev's November 1989 "Socialist Ideas and Revolutionary Perestroika," observed that the Soviet Union no longer talks about imperialism and no longer condemns capitalist exploitation. Fuwa referred to the Soviet Union's "new thinking," reflected in Gorbachev's piece, as "new collaborationism" and noted that the Soviet Union has abandoned its long-standing commitment to eliminate nuclear weapons worldwide, allowing the capitalist countries to remain armed with such weapons. He used the term *Soviet firstism* to describe what he contends is Moscow's *perestroika* policy: anything to help the economy of the Soviet Union (ibid.).

The JCP continued this line of criticism at its Nineteenth Party Congress in July. Miyamoto averred that, in "a situation of the U.S. and the Soviet Union continuing to insist on military blocs," everything is left to negotiations between the great powers and the world cannot be set free of military power blocs and nuclear weapons (*Akahata*, 14 July). He said that the Soviet Union has "surrendered" to the U.S. policy of nuclear deterrence in arms talks with the United States (ibid.) and condemned the Kremlin for imposing that policy on peace movements (ibid.).

Relations between the JCP and the Soviet Union were further strained by Soviet problems in Estonia, Latvia, and Lithuania, countries whose bids for freedom the party said should be honored (ibid.). The JCP urged that the Soviet Union return not only the Northern Territories that were taken from Japan at the end of World War II but also territory beyond that, thereby taking the strongest and most anti-Soviet position of any of Japan's political parties. In midyear Shōji Nishihara, a member of the JCP Presidium, stated that the entire Kurile Island chain must be returned if Gorbachev wants to rid himself of Stalin's legacy, "restore socialism," and end the Soviet Union's "hegemonistic chauvinism" (*FEER*, 30 August). Subsequently, Presidium chairman Fuwa set forth a four-point proposal for Japan-Soviet talks on the issue: (1) territorial issues should be resolved in a peace treaty, (2) articles in the Yalta agreements and the San Francisco treaty should not be regarded as "preconditions," (3) settlement should be based on nineteenth-century negotiations between the two governments, and (4) "transitory measures" should be discussed leading toward a final treaty (*Akahata*, 4 September). The Soviet Union did not respond positively to these proposals.

Relations remained cool between the JCP and the People's Republic of China, with virtually no JCP–Chinese Communist Party contacts during 1990. Chairman Miyamoto, during the party congress, said that the Chinese leaders' June 1989 killing of students in Tiananmen Square and their suppression of the democracy movement were "inseparable from their great power chauvinism and hegemonism" (*Akahata*, 25 May).

On other international issues, the JCP continued to condemn the U.S. invasion of Panama in December 1989 (*Bulletin*, January). The party condemned Iraq for its invading Kuwait and taking hostages and supported U.N. sanctions against Iraq, saying that it is important for all nations to abide by the sanctions (*Akahata*, 7 September). But the party opposed the use of force, saying that military force would devastate the world economy, to the immediate detriment of Japan. The JCP adamantly opposed sending Japanese forces to the Middle East and expressed concern that the United States might use nuclear weapons if Iraq used poison gas (ibid.).

John F. Copper
Rhodes College

Korea
Democratic People's Republic of Korea

Population. 21,292,649
Party. Korean Workers' Party (KWP, Choson Nodong-dang)
Founded. 1946 (a united party since 1949)
Membership. KWP claims about 2 million, or about one-tenth of the population.
General Secretary. Kim Il-song
Presidium. 3 members: Kim Il-song, president, Democratic People's Republic of Korea; Kim Chong-il, Kim Il-song's son and heir designate; O Chin-u, minister of People's Armed Forces
Politburo. 14 full members: Kim Il-song; Kim Chong-il; O Chin-u; Yi Chong-ok, vice president; Pak Song-chol, vice-president; Yon Hyong-muk, premier; Kim Yong-nam; Choe Kwang; Kye Ungtae; Han Song-yong; Ho Tam; Chon Pyong-ho; Kang Song-san; So Yun-sok; 10 candidate members: Hyon Mu-kwang; Choe Tae-bok; Kim Cholman; Choe Yong-nim; Hong Song-nam; Kim Poksin; Kang Hui-won; Cho Se-ung; Hong Si-hak; Yi Son-sil
Secretariat. Kim Il-song, Kim Chong-il, Kye Ungtae, Han Song-ryong, Chon Pyong-ho, Choe Taepok, Pak Nam-ki, So Kwan-hui, Hwang Changyop, Kim Chong-nin, Ho Chong-suk, Yun Kipok, Kim Yong-son

Central Committee. 145 full and 103 alternate members
Status. Ruling party
Last Congress. Sixth, 10–15 October 1980, in Pyongyang
Last Election. 22 April 1990. All 687 candidates on the slate elected for Ninth Supreme People's Assembly, with government-reported voter turnout of 99.8 percent.
Auxiliary Organizations. General Federation of Trade Unions of Korea, Union of Agricultural Working People of Korea, Korean Democratic Women's Union, Socialist Working Youth of Korea, Friends' (Chongdogyo religion) Party, Korean Democratic Party, Committee for Peaceful Unification of the Fatherland
Publications. *Nodong Sinmum* (Workers' daily), KWP organ; *Minju Choson* (Democratic Korea); *Kulloja* (The worker), party theoretical journal; *Choson Inminkun Sinmum* (Korean People's Army news). English-language publications include the *Pyongyang Times* and *Korea Today*; in Japan the *People's Korea* generally follows the North Korean line. The official news agency is the Korean Central News Agency (KCNA).

Without doubt, 1990 presented the worst foreign policy crisis for the Democratic People's Republic of Korea (DPRK) in its 42-year history. Confronted by continuing *glasnost'* and *perestroika* in the Soviet Union and collapsing East European communism, North Korea was buffeted by powerful currents of openness and reform throughout the East bloc nations. The spectacular German unification of 3 October—the total absorption of an exhausted East Germany by a dynamic West Germany—was indeed a nerve-racking event for the leaders of communist North Korea, who had already been disturbed by a significant and widening gap between the two Koreas. In 1990, South Korea continued its successful Northern Diplomacy, opening formal diplomatic relations with the Soviet Union and all East European countries except Albania. In contrast, North Korea's relationship with the Soviet Union degenerated from mutual suspicion and mild criticism to outright denunciation and open hostility. Domestically, the DPRK was faced with economic difficulties of crisis proportions that could have serious repercussions for the current leadership structure and the credibility of Korean-style socialism. Both the Soviet Union and China, the DPRK's principal allies, sought to influence North Korea in favor of a more flexible foreign policy and greater domestic openness and pragmatism. There was evidence of incipient domestic political unrest. As the year progressed, the DPRK was caught between external and domestic demands for reform and openness, on the one hand, and the stubborn resistance of hard-liners evermore determined to strengthen North Korea's Stalinist regime, on the other.

Leadership and Organization. Power consolidation continued in the totalitarian leadership structure of the DPRK, which is based primarily on the absolute control of the three primary institutions of power: the party (KWP), the military (the People's Armed Forces), and the government machinery. Shell-shocked by the discomfiture of their East European communist allies and by the Soviet Union's program of *glasnost'* and *perestroika*, Kim Il-song and his supporters were more defiant than ever, making all-out efforts to maintain North Korea as a communist state built on the personality cult of Kim Il-song and the home-grown ideology of *juche* (self-reliance). External pressure for domestic political reform was considerable, but it made hardly a dent in the concentration of political power in the hands of the Kims and their hard-line supporters in the party, the military, and the government. Throughout the year, Kim Il-song proclaimed that North Korea would be the "last Eastern outpost of socialism" (KCNA, 1 January).

Recent rumors of Kim Il-song's deteriorating health proved untrue. The Great Leader celebrated his 78th birthday on 15 April with the usual month-long gaudy displays of the "world's first paradise on earth" (Pyongyang Domestic Service, 15 April). In apparent good health, Kim showed remarkable mental agility on 26 September when he met with former Japanese deputy prime minister Shin Kanemaru and Makoto Tanabe, vice-chairman of the Japan Socialist Party, at a mountain resort in Myohyangsan (Kyodo, 26, 27 September). The December *Vantage Point* carried a report on Pyongyang's Research Center for the Long Life of Comrade Kim Il-song, where some three thousand prominent doctors and medical personnel care for Kim Il-song and his son. A nearby special farm produces pollution-free rice, vegetables, and fruit exclusively for the Kims.

Nodong Sinmun on 14 and 15 April praised the Great Leader's achievements, saying that "without his great leadership our revolution would not be able to move a step forward" and calling Kim "our fatherland and our national destiny." In May the first plenum of the Ninth Supreme People's Assembly (SPA) elected Kim Il-song to his fourth five-year term as DPRK president and announced its "iron will and resolve to revere the Great Leader highly and follow him devotedly" (*Komsomol'skaia Pravda*, 27 May).

Kim Il-song's control of the government is largely through the Central People's Committee (CPC) and the National Defense Commission, both of which he chairs. The CPC, comprising senior party figures from Pyongyang and the provinces, is delicately balanced in Kim's favor. The Ninth SPA increased the CPC's membership from fourteen to seventeen and replaced twelve previous members. The real power of the DPRK government, however, rests in the eleven-member National Defense Commission (NDC), which Kim Chong-il now controls as its first vice-chairman (*FEER*, 29 November).

It was rumored for months that Kim Chong-il would be promoted to president or vice-president of the DPRK, thus finalizing his hereditary succession (*FEER*, 29 March, 29 November). Such speculation was given further credence when the Ninth SPA, which had been scheduled for November, was advanced by seven months (*FEER*, 7 June). When the SPA met 22–24 April, however, Kim Chong-il was elected to the newly created post of first vice-chairman of the NDC, on which he sits above Armed Forces Minister O Chin-u and Armed Forces Commander Choe Kwang. O and Choe were members of the partisan group that fought with the senior Kim during the anti-Japanese guerrilla war in Manchuria. In contrast, Kim Chong-il, who has no military experience, was given a pivotal position that empowers him to control the military—especially the fourteen-thousand-strong officer corps of the People's Armed Forces (which was rumored to oppose his succession). Kim Chong-il has been groomed for statecraft for seventeen years, and his succession was publicly announced ten years ago. Given this spring's developments in Pyongyang, DPRK specialists in Japan and South Korea now agree that the long-awaited formal transfer of power from Kim Il-song to Kim Chong-il is likely to take place in 1992, when the senior Kim celebrates his 80th birthday and his son turns 50 (*FEER*, 29 March; *Dong-a Ilbo*, 26 May; *Chungang Ilbo*, 18 June). Kim Chong-il remains "a mystical figure" even among the country's top elite. Despite the splendid contributions to ideological and economic matters that official propaganda attributes to him, Kim Chong-il's reputation rests on his enthusiasm for the cinema, his decadent lifestyle, and the many expensive and lifeless monuments he has erected in Pyongyang. The junior Kim, who is reportedly temperamental, has yet to show much aptitude for solving serious economic and political problems (*FEER*, 29 November).

The Eighteenth Plenum of the Sixth Congress, held on 23 May, brought about small but significant changes in the top echelons of the Korean Workers' Party, including the return to power of several senior cadres and technocrats (KCNA, 25, 26, 27 May; *Dong-a Ilbo*, 25, 26, 27, 31 May; *Chungang Ilbo*, 25 May). Two new members—Choe Kwang and Han Song-yong—were installed in the fourteen-member Politburo. Choe, who fought with Kim Il-song in Manchuria, is former (1963–69) and current (1988–) chief of staff of the armed forces. Purged in 1969 after being implicated in an anti–Kim Il-song incident, in 1977 he resurfaced as chairman of the People's Committee in Hwanghae province. Choe ranks second in the North Korean army after O Chin-u, armed forces minister and another member of the First-Generation Partisan Group. It is likely that Choe's new Politburo membership and his position as vice-chairman of the National Defense Commission (along with O Chin-u) are the result of his presumed support for the Kim Chong-il succession. Han Song-yong, a well-recognized specialist in the machinery industry, has steadily risen in the party hierarchy since he was elected a candidate member of the KWP Central Committee in 1980.

Three new candidate members were also named to the Politburo: Choe Tae-bok (party secretary), Kim Chol-man (National Defense Commission member), and Choe Yong-nim (vice-premier and chairman of the State Planning Committee). Another of the few remaining senior cadres and a professional soldier, Kim Chol-man has served as vice-commander of the armed forces. A technocrat, Choe Tae-bok has been party secretary in charge of educational and ideological affairs since 1986. Choe Yong-nim, another technocrat of recognized ability, was made a Politburo candidate member in 1980. He became a full Politburo member in 1981 and first vice-premier in 1984 but turned into a "forgotten person" in 1985, when he was dropped from both those positions. In 1990, Choe Yong-nim was appointed as second-ranking of the ten vice-premiers on the State Administrative Council, which is chaired by Premier Yon Hyong-muk (*Dong-a Ilbo*, 31 May).

In early January it was reported that Pak Song-chol, a Politburo member in charge of economic affairs, and another third-generation leader had been demoted or purged for advocating reform and openness (Seoul Domestic Service, 11 January). *Seoul Sinmum* reported on 24 January that in fall 1989 Pak had been demoted from the sixth rank in the Politburo to the eighteenth and that Chon Pyong-ho, a Politburo member since 1988, had been purged. The reshuffling of the KWP and government leadership in May 1990, however, proved the rumors false, as Pak was listed as the fifth-ranking Politburo member, as one of two DPRK vice-presidents, and as the second in rank to Kim Il-song on the powerful Central People's Committee. After May, Chon was listed as the thirteenth-ranking member of the Politburo, a party secretary, and the fourth-ranking member of the National Defense Commission. (Pyongyang Domestic Service, 24, 25 May.)

Also in May, Ho Tam was relieved of his position as party secretary in charge of inter-Korean affairs, but he retained his Politburo membership and was elected chairman of the Foreign Affairs Committee of the Supreme People's Assembly (SPA), reportedly in preparation for new parliamentary diplomacy toward South Korea and other countries. Ho is assisted in his new SPA position by Kim Yong-son, the new party secretary in charge of international affairs (*Chungang Ilbo*, 25 May).

The appointment of Han Song-yong, a specialist in the shipbuilding industry, to the Politburo and the promotion of Kim Tal-hyon, a specialist in external economic affairs, as a vice-premier, indicate the growing importance of state technocrats, who make up an estimated 64.5 percent of the current SPA (*Chungang Ilbo*, 25 May).

Domestic Developments. Kim Il-song opened 1990 with an emphasis on *juche*-based socialism. The "world's longest-surviving totalitarian leader" (*FEER*, 29 November) was nervous about the tide of change and reform sweeping the East bloc and about the effectiveness of South Korea's Northern Policy, but his New Year's message stressed that North Korea needed neither economic *perestroika* nor political *glasnost*' but the successful completion of Socialist construction. This dogmatic insistence on "our own style of socialism" continued throughout the year (e.g., *Hangyore Sinmum*, 29 May; *Nodong Sinmum*, 10 July, 7 August, 21 December). The Kim cult was further intensified when Kim Il-song was glorified as "the first great leader in [Korean history] of thousands of years" (*Minju Choson*, 31 May). A special 21 December *Nodong Sinmum* article suggested that, to complete Socialist construction in Korea, the people of North Korea have to carry out "a difficult and vast work of crushing the resistance of all sorts of enemies" and undertake the remaking of nature and society in conformity with the *juche* ideology (Pyongyang Domestic Service, 21 December). The ruling hierarchy was particularly concerned about demand for reform among the intellectuals. On 10 November, *Nodong Sinmum* warned:

> The legacies of the petit bourgeois individualism still linger in the mind of the old intellectuals. The remnants of this old society must be thoroughly removed from their minds so that they can remain faithful only to the leader and the Party. Young intellectuals have not experienced severe trials under imperialist and capitalist exploitation and therefore they do not know the harmful effect of capitalism.

There was evidence of acute concern, if not deepening paranoia, among the hard-line followers of Kim Il-song and Kim Chong-il about a spreading intraparty reform movement. The October issue of *Kulloja*, the KWP monthly magazine, quotes Kim Chong-il as having said that "pagan elements must not be allowed to exist in the party hierarchy. . . . Whatever changes may take place in the revolutionary environment, there can be no revision in the revolutionary principle of the Party." A few days after the Gorbachev-Roh summit in San Francisco on 4 June, the junior Kim warned against the "ideological and cultural infiltration of the imperialists" in the KWP leadership structure and demanded that the KWP consolidate the party organization and "strengthen the ideological education of the party members and working people" (KCNA, 9 June).

In 1990, North Korea stepped up its surveillance of some twenty thousand foreign residents, especially journalists. DPRK security agents secretly investigated the personal background, behavior, and traits of Soviet technicians and other foreigners in North Korea (*Choson Ilbo*, 19 April). Several foreign correspondents reported government harassment and interference with their activities in Pyongyang. On 12 May, Aleksandr Zevin, the chief Pyongyang correspondent of the Soviet press agency TASS, was expelled by the DPRK authorities for his critical articles about North Korea (*Yonhap, Chungang Ilbo*, 29 May). After the second Gorbachev-Roh summit in Moscow 13–16 December, North Korea closed the Pyongyang offices of *Komsomol'skaia Pravda* and the Novosti news agency and refused to grant a visa to a *Komsomol'skaia Pravda* correspondent (Seoul Television Service, 21 December; *Yonhap*, 24 December).

To halt the spread of ideological taint from abroad, North Korea by early 1990 had recalled about two thousand North Korean students and engineers from East European countries (*Yonhap*, 1 March). The eight hundred North Korean students and technical trainees flown back from Czechoslovakia around Christmastime (Prague, *Mlada Fronta*, 4 January) were reportedly held in a reeducation camp near Pyongyang before being sent to factories and educational facilities in remote areas (*Yonhap*, 1 March; *WSJ*, 2 March).

In April a well-informed South Korean source on North Korean affairs reported that in late March a "large-scale riot" had erupted in Hamhung, South Hamkyong province, after a student demonstration in Pyongyang. The incident was quelled by army troops. On 28 April *Dong-a Ilbo* reported several cases of Kim Il-song's portraits being torn down in Pyongyang. Such incidents seem to indicate that in 1990 the Kim Il-song regime was confronted with a previously unknown tide of popular disaffection and domestic unrest.

Rising demands for political reform and openness notwithstanding, the most serious domestic problem facing the DPRK in 1990 was its inefficient and frail economy. The Stalinist system of North Korea was left to manage its stagnant *juche* economy in virtual isolation from the Soviet Union and other East bloc countries. The DPRK could no longer continue its opportunistic, double-track diplomacy toward its two major allies and trading partners, the USSR and the People's Republic of China, which Kim Il-song had skillfully played off against each other. Its new, single-track diplomacy toward China, however, was severely limited by the rapid improvement of trade relations between China and South Korea. Economic détente with South Korea was deemed politically untenable, at least for the time being, and the DPRK's diplomatic overtures to the United States were constrained by a number of politically unacceptable U.S. preconditions. In light of these constraints, the DPRK turned in early fall to Japan, the sworn enemy of Korean nationalism, for the solution to its myriad economic difficulties.

The decline of the DPRK's command economy is indicated by a gross national product (GNP) growth rate during 1984–1989 averaging about 3 percent per year (*World Fact Book*, 1990, p. 171), compared with 10.2 percent for South Korea during the same period (*Chungang Ilbo*, 27 March). Estimates of real growth of the DPRK's GNP in 1988–1989 range from 2 percent (*FEER*, 29 November) to 2.4 percent (South Korea's National Unification Board, *Hankuk Ilbo*, 26 September). In 1990, North Korea registered its lowest growth rate since 1986, estimated by the *Far Eastern Economic Review* (29 November) at around 2 percent per year. In contrast, Marina Trigubenko, a prominent Soviet economist, stated that the DPRK economy actually suffered a negative GNP growth rate of 5.3 percent and a 10.6 percent decline in industrial output (Seoul, *Vantage Point*, December). In 1988–1989 the total value of North Korea's international trade sank 7.3 percent, from US$5.2 billion to $4.8 billion, with exports declining to US$1.95 billion (down 2.1 percent over 1988) and imports down to US$2.85 billion (a 10.9 percent drop over 1988) (*Vantage Point*, December).

The rapid deterioration of the DPRK economy is attributed to such reasons as three successive years of poor harvests, dwindling international trade caused by DPRK's low international credit rating, and military expenditures consuming up to 21 percent of the country's US$21 billion GNP (*Fortune*, 11 February 1991). Still more wealth has been squandered constructing giant monuments to the Kim cult and high-rise buildings and other nonproductive investments in Pyongyang (*FEER*, 29 November) designed primarily to enhance national prestige. The DPRK government reportedly spent US$4.7 billion, equivalent to 22 percent of GNP, on the Kim Il-song Stadium and other world-class facilities for the 1989 World Festival of Youth and Students (*Asian Wall Street Journal Weekly*, 14 January 1991).

According to the Japan External Trade Organization, as of 1989 North Korea was dependent on the Soviet Union and China for about three-fourths of its total external trade. An estimated 59 percent of North Korea's exports went to the Soviet Union and 15 percent to China. Some 57 percent of its imports came from the Soviet Union and 18 percent from China (*Dong-a Ilbo*, 12 October). As the Soviets tired of subsidizing exports and as the East European economies declined, however, North Korea's trade with the Socialist countries has dropped by some 10 percent; its trade with the Soviet Union has fallen from US$2.76 billion to $2.5 billion, or 10.4 percent (*FEER*, 29 November).

The Soviets were openly critical of the domestic and external economic policies of the DPRK government, faulting it for excessive spending on unproductive, showy projects, for mismanaging Soviet economic aid (*Insight*, 12 March), and for failing to live up to its trade agreements (Radio Moscow, 9 September).

Since 1949, North Korea has been paying between one-fourth and one-half of the world market prices for most of its imports from the Soviet Union, including crude oil. Until 1990 the Soviets conducted a barter trade system with North Korea and supplied about 40 percent of its crude oil at the "friendship price" of US$5 per barrel (*Yonhap*, 24, 29 December). Under the terms of a November trade agreement, however, the barter system will end beginning in 1991, and North Korea will have to pay hard currency at undiscounted prices for all its imports from the Soviet Union.

North Korea's total external debt at the end of 1989 was estimated at between US$3 and $6.7 billion (*Hankuk Ilbo*, 26 September), as much as 65 percent of it owed to Moscow (*Yonhap*, 24 December). North Korea's debt to Japan (in arrears since 1983) amounts to US$615 million, more than twice the value of its annual exports to Japan; the total volume of trade between North Korea and Japan declined by 12.8 percent in 1988–1989 (*Dong-a Ilbo*, 12 October).

In 1990 North Korea faced acute shortages of fuel, food, and most consumer goods. According to the *Korea Daily* (22 December), the oil shortage, caused principally by substantial cutbacks in Soviet petroleum to the DPRK (*Yonhap*, 24 April), was severe enough to close more than half of all industrial plants and radically limit military and civilian transport. It was reported that in 1989, despite facility expansion in the mining sector, factories had operated at only 45 percent of capacity because of shortages of fuel and materials (*Yonhap*, 25 September).

North Korea's agriculture, far from being privatized, moved to full state ownership, with farmers reduced to wage workers (*FEER*, 29 November). Since 1987 North Korea has suffered three consecutive years of poor crops due mainly to structural inefficiency and bad weather. In an effort to overcome the chronic shortages that in 1989 forced it to import more than 800,000 tons of food (*Yonhap*, 25 September), North Korea has adopted a "two meals a day" campaign (*Dong-a Ilbo*, 12 February 1991) and reportedly secretly accepted eight hundred tons of rice from a South Korean church group in July (*Yonhap*, 20 December).

Inter-Korean Affairs. Facing an imminent economic crisis and almost complete international isolation, North Korean leaders were concerned about the increasingly unfavorable position of North Korea in its economic, military, and diplomatic competition with South Korea. In particular, they were frightened by the prospect of a German-style reunification of the Korean Peninsula. For much of 1990, the DPRK's xenophobic leaders seemed more determined than ever to keep the country closed and "not to mix socialism with capitalism."

President Kim Il-song started the new year with demands that the South immediately remove "concrete walls" built south of the demilitarized zone (DMZ), which it alleged interfered with communication between the Koreas (KCNA, 1 January); South Korea maintained that the walls were defensive tank barriers. On 13 January, North Korea invited the president, the prime minister, and the heads of the three opposition parties in the South to take part in a joint North-South meeting of governments and political parties (KCNA, 9, 13 January). On 14 February, 23 March, and 23 May, the DPRK demanded the barriers' removal, a joint unification conference of politicians and party leaders from both Koreas, and the suspension of the 1990 Team Spirit joint U.S.-ROK military exercises. Brushing the proposed joint conference aside as a ploy to advance the North's united front strategy, South Korea countered with proposals for North-South summits and government-to-government meetings and invited the North to send observers to a smaller-scale exercise planned for spring 1990. On 3 March the ROK announced the discovery of a fourth North Korean invasion tunnel south of the DMZ in violation of the Military Armistice Agreement (*South-North Dialogue in Korea*, May).

The DPRK suspended North-South preliminary talks between 31 January and 3 July after lodging a complaint against the Team Spirit exercises. The Gorbachev-Roh summit on 4 June went unreported in the North, which rebuked the Soviets for embarrassing it by meeting its archenemy, President Roh, in the United States (*NYT*, 8 June). About three weeks after that summit, however, North Korea telephoned the South to accept its proposal for a 3 July session of the preliminary talks (Seoul Domestic Service, 26 June). The succeeding round, on 26 July, set the dates, venues, and agenda of the first two of three meetings of the North and South's prime ministers (KCNA, 26 July). President Roh Tae-woo's proposal for free travel across the DMZ

during 13–17 August (*NYT*, 20 July) was rejected by North Korea, which demanded a Pan-National Unification Conference at Panmunjom as a prerequisite. On 28 July, North Korea invited Chonminnyon (National Alliance of Democratic Movements), a federation of dissident organizations in the South, to send its representatives to the Pan-National Unification Rally to be held on 15 August. After initially agreeing, the South later declined to allow the Chonminnyon representatives to attend the DPRK-sponsored rally (*South-North Dialogue in Korea*, October).

The first North-South high-level talks were held in Seoul on 5 and 6 September. Each side's delegation included its prime minister and six members from the minister and vice-minister level. It was soon clear that the two sides were far apart (*NYT*, 6 September). Prime Minister Kang Yong-hun addressed his counterpart as "Premier Yon Hyong-muk," but Yon addressed him as "Chief Delegate of the South Side," a clear signal that the DPRK was still unwilling to talk with the Republic of Korea (ROK) on an equal footing. Reiterating old DPRK positions, Yon proposed a nine-point plan for military disarmament in Korea, including the withdrawal of 43,000 U.S. troops and nuclear weapons. He called on the South to stop joint military exercises with the United States, abandon South Korea's bid to enter the United Nations as a separate country, and release three South Korean dissidents jailed for their unauthorized trips to North Korea in 1989. Prime Minister Kang proposed that the two sides undertake a set of confidence-building measures—cultural and athletic contacts, family visits, and economic cooperation—to pave the way for military issues. Kang made no formal response to the North Korean proposals, but senior South Korean officials made it clear that the demands were unrealistic and unacceptable. (*NYT*, 5, 6, 7 September.)

As expected, neither side budged on any substantive issues at the first round of talks. The real significance of the 5–6 September encounter was that it took place at all and that the two delegations sat down face to face and expressed their disagreements with surprising cordiality (*Asia Wall Street Journal Weekly*, 10 September).

The second round of talks, held in Pyongyang 16–19 October, was preceded by two events of extraordinary significance: the 24–28 September agreement to diplomatic relations between North Korea and Japan and the 30 September announcement of formal diplomatic relations between the Soviet Union and South Korea. Although Pyongyang and Seoul both edged closer to improving diplomatic ties with each other's allies, the second meeting produced few results. Essentially reiterating his earlier proposals, Premier Yon demanded that the South halt the Team Spirit exercises and drop its National Security Law at once. The North's principal proposal was for a mutual nonaggression declaration, which Prime Minister Kang rejected as beyond his authority (*Yonhap*, 18 October). Kang proposed in a meeting with Kim Il-song that the two presidents hold a summit at an early date. Kim was noncommittal but said that he would seriously consider the proposal in light of the progress made in the prime ministers' talks (*Dong-a Ilbo*, 16–20 October; *Yonhap*, 16–19 October).

Unlike the Seoul round, the second meeting attracted no cheering crowds or public attention in Pyongyang. The official media reported at length on DPRK proposals but mentioned little about the South's. The delegation's unexpectedly cool reception by Pyongyang citizens—in sharp contrast to their enthusiastic welcome of the visiting soccer team and music delegation from the South—was explained by North Korean guides as caused by the continued imprisonment of student Yim Su-kyong and Pastors Mun Ik-hwan and Mun Kyu-hyon for their unauthorized trips to the North (*Korea Times*, 17 October).

At the conclusion of the formal session on 18 October, the two spokesmen neatly summarized the achievements of the second round of talks when they said in their joint statement: "All we have agreed is to hold the third talks" (*Yonhap*, 18 October). Although no progress was made on most substantive issues, the two Koreas agreed to another round 11–14 December as neither side was ready to be blamed for the failure of inter-Korean dialogue.

Despite earlier threats that the North would boycott the third round of talks (*Nodong Sinmum*, 4, 5 December), DPRK moderates, concerned about a possible disruption of talks on DPRK-Japan diplomatic relations, apparently prevailed over hardliners (Reuters, 5 December): the third round was held as planned. In the 11–14 December talks, the North again demanded a nonaggression pact, whereas the South insisted on cultural and economic ties as a precondition for arms discussions. Notwithstanding a complete lack of progress, however, neither side was prepared to discontinue the talks altogether; they agreed to hold another round 25–26 February 1991 (*NYT*, 14 December).

Relations with the Soviet Union and Eastern Europe. North Korea opened 1990 with a diplomatic affront to the Soviet Union by for the first time sending Kim Il-song's New Year's message only to Beijing, not to Moscow (*Dong-a Ilbo*, 8 January). DPRK relations with the Soviet Union deteriorated steadily throughout the year, apparently in direct and inverse correlation to improved economic and diplomatic relations between the Soviet Union and ROK. Two major blows to DPRK-USSR relations came in the form of the two highly publicized summits between Mikhail Gorbachev and Roh Tae-woo (4 June and 13–14 December) and the establishment of formal diplomatic relations between the USSR and the ROK on 30 September.

The cooling of DPRK relations was evident in the plummeting number of official visits: North Korea sent only 16 missions to the Soviet Union as compared with 41 in 1989, and Russian delegations decreased from 27 in 1989 to 15 in 1990. The exchange of delegations virtually ceased during the last three months of 1990 (*Vantage Point*, December 1989, December 1990).

Worsening North Korea–Soviet relations were also reflected in the volleys of increasingly vitriolic criticism from each side's government media and public commentators. On 22 January, Radio Moscow, quoting *Novoe Vremia*, attributed the DPRK's economic woes to "stubbornness and isolationism." On 16 February, the government-run *Moscow News* carried an article by Kang Sang-ho, former DPRK vice-minister of home affairs, who likened Kim Il-song to Stalin and pointed out the fate of Romania's Nicolae Ceauşescu. The 1 April issue of the weekly *Argumenti i Fakti* included a contribution by the editor of *Problemi Dalnovo Vostoka* (Problems of the Far East), who called North Korea a "museum to Kim Il-song" and asserted the wisdom of recognizing South Korea (*Korea Times*, 10 April). Indeed, during spring 1990, at least thirteen Soviet press reports found fault with North Korea and its mythic Great Leader.

Nodong Sinmum responded on 6 April by denouncing the new Soviet policy on Korea. On the same day KCNA labeled the Soviet Union "a friend of the enemy of our people" [South Korea] and asked why the USSR, which is committed to keeping nationality republics within its border from breaking away, hampers the union of North and South and helps "those who want to create two states."

On 12 April, Radio Moscow refuted the North Korean claim that Kim Il-song, as commander of all guerrilla units in Korea and Manchuria, had won Korea's independence from Japan. It downplayed his role in Korea's liberation by reporting that "the Soviet Armed Forces played a decisive role in liberating Korea in August 1945" and by noting that as a Soviet captain Kim had commanded only one of the partisan units fighting alongside the Soviet troops. On 20 April, Radio Moscow touched on still another sensitive subject: Which of the two Koreas started the Korean War? It quoted Soviet historian Mikhail Smirnov, who rejected North Korea's assertion that South Korea provoked the war in June 1950 and asked how the North could have seized Seoul within three days if it had not staged a surprise southward campaign.

North Korea showed its displeasure with Soviet criticisms in a variety of unfriendly acts. For the first time, not a single Soviet guest was invited to help celebrate Kim Il-song's birthday (his 78th) on 15 April (*Yonhap*, 29 May). Aleksandr Zevin, stationed in Pyongyang for seven years as *Pravda's* chief correspondent, was expelled from the DPRK (Radio Moscow, 24 April) for his critical reporting on North Korea and Kim Il-song and his 1988 trip to the Seoul Olympics (*Dong-a Ilbo*, 31 May). On 25 April, North Korea's ambassador to Moscow, Song Song-pil, was suddenly recalled to Pyongyang (*Dong-a Ilbo*, 6 June); he did not return to his post until late September (*Yonhap*, 27 September).

The 4 June summit between Mikhail Gorbachev and Roh Tae-woo in San Francisco was clearly a serious diplomatic slap at Kim Il-song. On 31 May a DPRK Foreign Ministry spokesman warned: "We consider the President of the Soviet Union, an ally of ours, is quite able to analyze and judge what a serious consequence will be entailed by his meeting with Roh Tae-woo who is seeking only the split of Korea" (KCNA, 31 May). Commenting on North Korea's reaction to the San Francisco meeting, Nikolai Shishlin, spokesman for the Communist Party of the Soviet Union's (CPSU) Central Committee, said: "The Soviet Union must maintain its own independent policy, not a 'great leaders' policy" (*Sankei Shimbun*, 1 June). There was obviously— and intentionally—no advance consultation on the San Francisco summit between Moscow and Pyongyang (*Yonhap*, 1 June; *NYT*, 7 June). A Soviet source reported that "the Soviet Union wants to prod North Korea into reforming itself by unilaterally promoting the normalization of diplomatic relations with the ROK" (*Asahi Shimbun*, 1 June). Likewise, President Roh stated that "we have no choice but to

open a road to Pyongyang via Moscow, as the direct road is blocked" (*Korean Times*, 1 June).

The Gorbachev-Roh summit, clearly aimed at establishing formal diplomatic relations between the Soviet Union and South Korea (*Sankei Shimbun*, 1 June; *Korean Herald*, 7 June), was roundly and repeatedly denounced as a "two Koreas plot" and an "anti-DPRK confrontation" on the parts of South Korea, the United States, and the USSR (e.g., KCNA, 6, 7 June; *Nodong Sinmum*, 6 June; Seoul Domestic Service, 7 June). On 13 June, the same day that North Korea said that two series of meetings with the South would be indefinitely postponed, it requested the resumption of counselor-level meetings with the United States in Beijing (*Chungang Ilbo*, 14 June).

After the San Francisco summit, Soviet media and commentators were increasingly critical of North Korea and demanded changes in Soviet policy toward the DPRK. Leonid Muletin, editor of *Novoe Vremia*, wrote on 23 June that there was a widespread infringement of human rights in DPRK and that the Soviet Union has "nothing in common" with North Korea. He proposed that the Soviet Union open diplomatic relations with South Korea as soon as possible (*Yonhap*, 23 June; Seoul Television Service, 28 June). On 28 June, *Moskovskii Komsomolents* described North Korea and Cuba as "Stalinist authoritarian states" and demanded that the Soviet Union sever its diplomatic ties with those two countries and stop supplying oil to them. There were indications that the usual 5 July celebration of the signing of the USSR-DPRK Treaty on Friendship, Cooperation and Mutual Aid did not take place in Pyongyang in 1990. On 6 August, the Moscow International Service, quoting a *Pravda* article by economist Natalia Vazanova, reported that "the [North] Korean colleagues are not always honest in fulfilling their duty" in DPRK-USSR trade relations and that "as a rule, payment[s] for the DPRK's debts are delayed, or sometimes have not been paid at all."

On 2 and 3 September, Soviet foreign minister Eduard Shevardnadze visited Pyongyang to inform the North Korean government of Moscow's intention to establish diplomatic ties with Seoul (*Yonhap*, 22 September). He also gave the DPRK official notice that no more large-scale Soviet investment and military aid to North Korea would be forthcoming and that, beginning January 1991, Soviet–North Korea trade would be settled in hard currency (Seoul Domestic Service, 28 September). Kim Yong-nam, vice-premier and foreign minister, strongly protested Moscow's establishing diplomatic relations with Seoul on the grounds that it would perpetuate the North-South division of Korea, a contention Shevardnadze reportedly challenged. Kim's reply was contained in a six-point memorandum dated 2 September and noting that the Soviet Union had been the first country to recognize the DPRK as the sole legitimate government of Korea, that the USSR's action would isolate the DPRK internationally and subvert its Socialist system, and that it would leave the DPRK no choice but to obtain military weapons independently (KCNA, 2, 3, 19 September). The Soviet government, more interested in a pragmatic association with the economically dynamic South Korea than with a bankrupt alliance with Kim Il-song's North Korea, retorted that the Soviet Union was free to pursue the foreign policy best suited to its needs and that "there is no need to ask for somebody's approval because it is [a] question to be decided by the Soviet Union itself" (*Vantage Point*, September). The USSR ignored North Korea's strong protest and established formal diplomatic relations with South Korea on 30 September, leading *Nodong Sinmum* (5 October) to refer to the Soviet–South Korea tie as "Foreign Relations Sold and Bought with the Dollar."

DPRK-USSR relations deteriorated further after ROK-USSR diplomatic relations were established on 30 September. During Roh Tae-woo's 13–16 December visit to Moscow—the first by a South Korean head of state—the Soviet Union and South Korea reportedly agreed to a major program of economic cooperation that included a US$3 billion South Korean aid package to the Soviet Union in 1991–1993 (*NYT*, 12, 14, 15 December; *Dong-a Ilbo*, 13–18 December); Gorbachev's first visit to Seoul for his third meeting with Roh Tae-woo was scheduled for April 1991 (*Dong-a Ilbo*, 18 December). The first Soviet ambassador to the ROK, Oleg Sokolov, was to arrive in Seoul on 7 December (*Seoul Sinmum*, 6 December).

The DPRK's relations with South Korea also worsened. Pyongyang accused Seoul of practicing "beggar's politics" in seeking better relations with Moscow (KCNA, 21 December). During 16–22 December, North Korea closed the Pyongyang offices of the Novosti news agency and *Komsomol'skaia Pravda* and refused to grant a visa to a TASS reporter. On 22 December, Pyongyang reported extensively on domestic Soviet criticism of *glasnost'*, broadly hinting that it was a failure (Seoul Television Service, 21 December; *Yonhap*, 24 December).

Despite the bitter denunciations of North Korea, all East European countries but Albania have opened diplomatic relations with South Korea; Mongolia joined that group in March (*FEER*, 5 April).

South Korea's rapidly expanding economic and diplomatic ties with East European countries were a sharp contrast to the virtual cessation of the DPRK's relations with its former allies. In 1990 only one East European delegation (an East German public health mission) visited North Korea, compared with a total of 28 in 1989. North Korea sent five delegations to East European countries and nineteen missions to Cuba alone. It has recalled all its diplomatic personnel, students, and trainees from most East European countries, including the united Germany, and after February no further delegations were dispatched to East European countries except Albania, to which one trade mission was sent in November. (*Vantage Point*, December 1989, December 1990.)

Relations with China. In 1990, North Korea tilted visibly toward China, the only neighboring Socialist country allied with it. North Korea's new relations with the People's Republic of China (PRC) were marked by a significant increase in the exchange of party and government delegations, including several secret visits of top leaders. North Korea sent a total of 37 delegations to the PRC, up 16 percent over 1989; China in turn sent 23 delegations, a 15 percent increase over 1989 (*Vantage Point*, December).

During 14–16 March, Jiang Zemin, general secretary of the Chinese Communist Party, made a goodwill visit to Pyongyang, his first overseas visit since the Tiananmen incident, arriving there just two days after South Korea's foreign minister, Choe Ho-chung, paid a brief visit to Beijing on his way to Pakistan (KCNA, 13 April). Choe reportedly continued his journey with Deng Pufang, the son of Deng Xiaoping. Chinese leaders are reportedly uneasy about the rumored transfer of power from Kim Il-song to Kim Chong-il that was to take place in April. (*The Economist*, 17 March; *FEER*, 22 March.) DPRK vice-premier and foreign minister Kim Yong-nam visited Beijing on 12 April to meet with PRC foreign minister Qian Qichen (KCNA, 13 April).

There were indications that, at the high-level policy consultations in March and April 1990, Chinese leaders made it clear that they did not share the views of North Korean leaders on improving economic and diplomatic relations between the Soviet

Union and South Korea or on closer economic ties between the PRC and South Korea. This difference of opinion surfaced again after the Gorbachev-Roh meeting of 4 June, where Beijing's official media commented that "China is not discouraging this process" (*Korea Times*, 9 June).

Shortly after Shevardnadze's disquieting visit to Pyongyang, 11–13 September, Kim Il-song made a secret visit to Shenyang for talks with Deng Xiaoping. A Beijing source reported that Deng had agreed in principle with the DPRK's "one Korea" line and that he had told Kim Il-song that China would take its cue in normalizing ROK-PRC relations from the progress of relations between North Korea and Japan and the United States (Seoul Domestic Service, 26 September). Kim also met with Jiang Zemin, who urged the improvement of DPRK-Japan relations (Seoul Domestic Service, 22 September). It was reported that Kim sought Jiang's assurances for a PRC veto on the ROK's separate entry into the United Nations (*Chungang Ilbo*, 12 October).

There is evidence that after the disastrous diplomatic setbacks in DPRK-USSR relations of the spring and summer, Kim Il-song became receptive to Chinese advice on economic reform and openness, but the PRC held to its policy of separating politics from economics in light of the growing importance of ROK-PRC trade relations for China's troubled economy. By 1989, ROK-PRC trade volume was almost five times the value of PRC trade with North Korea (US$665 million) (*Dong-a Ilbo*, 12 October; *Yonhap*, 29 December).

Disturbed by the prospect of a destabilized DPRK on its border, China has never publicly acknowledged two Koreas, but China's pragmatists want to be close to South Korea, a successful market economy. Hence, the Chinese advice to North Koreans has been "use capitalism to save socialism." The DPRK seemed to take China's advice to heart: two weeks after Kim Il-song's secret meetings in Shenyang, he received a Japanese party delegation to discuss the opening of formal diplomatic relations with Japan, a sworn enemy of North Korea (*Asian Wall Street Journal Weekly*, 17 December). North Korea has also shown greater flexibility in its dealings with the United States at the counselor-level meetings in Beijing.

During his 23–28 November visit to Beijing, Premier Yon Hyong-muk conceded that North Korea is facing "grave economic difficulties" (*Asian Wall Street Journal Weekly*, 17 December). A five-year agreement on economic cooperation was signed on 27 November under which China is to provide North Korea with US$150 million in economic aid in 1991 (*Dong-a Ilbo*, 2 February 1991). In the meantime, the PRC and South Korea agreed to open trade offices in each capital in January 1991 (*Dong-a Ilbo*, 6 December).

Relations with the United States. The sixth round of counselor-level contacts between the United States and the DPRK, held in Beijing on 5 January, brought little change or progress. The United States continued to demand more inter-Korean dialogue and reiterated its call for the DPRK to sign the safety clause of the International Atomic Energy Agency (IAEA). North Korea countered with its old demands for the withdrawal of U.S. troops and nuclear weapons from South Korea and the convening of a tripartite conference of North Korea, the United States, and South Korea. North Korea proposed that official contact between Pyongyang and Washington be upgraded (*Yonhap*, 6 January), a concession Washington was unwilling to make until ROK-DPRK relations improved (*Yonhap*, 15 January). On 13 January a ranking U.S. State Department official denied an *Asahi Shimbum* report that ambassador-level contacts with North Korea had been made (*Yonhap*, 15 January).

By April the DPRK showed cautious changes in its policy toward the United States as the breakthrough in Soviet–South Korean relations became evident. On 26 April, North Korea asked the United States to resume counselor-level contact in Beijing, which had been suspended since early January. For a change the DPRK agreed to consider returning the remains of U.S. soldiers who died during the Korean War. The next day, 27 April, four North Korean scholars requested entry visas to the United States to attend the Northeast Asian Security Symposium 17–19 May. North Korea also announced that it would send a delegation led by Choe U-chin, deputy director of the DPRK's Peace and Disarmament Research Institute, to an Atlantic Council–sponsored symposium 14–15 May (*Yonhap*, 28 April). Many Korean observers, however, saw North Korea's new diplomatic overtures toward Washington as "an attempt to drive a wedge between South Korea and the United States" (*NYT*, 29 May).

In early May, North Korea asked the United States to send a congressional delegation to Pyongyang to receive the remains of five U.S. soldiers killed in the Korean War, which Washington flatly rejected (*Chungang Ilbo*, 28 May). A compromise was struck when both sides agreed to the presence of five congressmen, including G. W. Montgomery, chairman of the House Veterans Committee, in the receiving ceremony at Panmunjom on 28 May. Although returning the remains of five servicemen out of an estimated 8,177 was at best symbolic, it nonetheless represented a concession to one of the U.S. preconditions for improved relations between Pyongyang and Washington (*Korean Times*, 15 May). The day the decision was made on the remains, the Bush administration allowed Ho Chong, the DPRK's deputy permanent observer to the United Nations, to travel to Washington to speak on North Korea's policy on inter-Korean relations at a symposium there (*Korea Times*, 22 May). It was reported on 30 May that Ho Chong told representatives of a U.S. veterans' organization that North Korea is willing to return the remains of another five U.S. soldiers and that it has located the remains of some one thousand others (*Yonhap*, 31 May).

On 30 May, after it became clear that the Gorbachev-Roh meeting would take place, U.S. and DPRK diplomats met in Beijing for a ninth round of counselor-level talks at which the United States is said to have reassured North Korea that neither Washington nor Seoul intended to isolate Pyongyang (*FEER*, 21 June). The same flexibility was conveyed on 4 June by Richard Solomon, assistant secretary of state for Asia and the Pacific, who said that the United States was ready to upgrade relations "if progress was made in U.S.-DPRK relations and inter-Korea dialogue" (*Yonhap*, 9 June). *Hanguk Ilbo* on 6 June reported Spence Richardson, chief of the Korea desk in the U.S. State Department, as saying that the United States was ready to open direct telephone lines with North Korea, to allow North Korean citizens to visit the United States on the basis of invitations, and to promote exchanges of scholars and students. In early July, a U.S.-ROK-DPRK arms reduction seminar was held at Stanford University. (*Choson Ilbo*, 8 July.)

On 28 September a high-ranking North Korean diplomat was quoted as saying that DPRK-USSR relations virtually came to an end in the wake of Shevardnadze's visit to Pyongyang in early September and that "it is inevitable to improve relations with the United States and Japan." The same diplomat also said that North Korea will disavow international terrorism in the interest of improved relations with the United States and that the issue of the IAEA agreement should be discussed in "closed dialogue"

with the United States. The United States insisted, however, that the ball was in North Korea's court (*Seoul Sinmum*, 29 September).

The U.S.-DPRK counselor-level meetings in Beijing continued in the fall but led to no evident breakthroughs.

Relations with Japan. The most significant diplomatic breakthrough for the DPRK in 1990 was the opening of bilateral talks on normalizing diplomatic ties with Japan. During 24–28 September, an 89-member Japanese interparty delegation led by Shin Kanemaru, former deputy prime minister and a powerful leader of the ruling Liberal Democratic Party (LDP), and Makoto Tanabe, vice-chairman of the opposition Japan Socialist Party (JSP), visited North Korea. Theirs was the first official LDP delegation ever to visit the DPRK. Kanemaru carried a letter from Prime Minister Toshiki Kaifu apologizing, in his capacity as LDP president, for Japan's colonial rule of Korea (1910–1945) (Kyodo, 24 September). On 28 September, Kim Il-song, Kanemaru, and Tanabe signed a joint KWP-LDP-JSP communiqué agreeing to establish formal diplomatic relations between North Korea and Japan. The communiqué said, "The Three Parties consider that in connection with the establishment of diplomatic relations, full compensation should be made by the Japanese Government for the past 35-year-long colonial rule and the losses inflicted upon the DPRK people in the ensuing 45 years." The three parties determined to initiate preliminary diplomatic talks in early November and urged that Japan and North Korea set up satellite communications links and inaugurate direct air flights between the two countries (Kyodo, 28 September). North Korea's new policy of normalized relations with Japan came two weeks after Kim Il-song's visit to Shenyang and less than a month after Shevardnadze's visit to Pyongyang.

North Korea's interest in improved relations with Japan was much in evidence by early spring. Between May and mid-September, North Korea received four JSP delegations, which the Kaifu government had asked to serve as an official channel for exploring improved relations with the DPRK.

North Korea removed an obstacle to improved relations with Japan by releasing two Japanese sailors of the *Fujisan Maru Number 18*. During November and December, North Korea and Japan held three rounds of preliminary talks in Beijing at which they agreed on a four-item agenda for the full intergovernmental talks set for 30–31 January

1991. DPRK vice-minister of foreign affairs Chon In-chol and Noboru Nakahira, former Japanese ambassador to Malaysia, were appointed to head the delegations. (KCNA, 22 December.) Two issues of major disagreement have surfaced since the 28 September meeting. The Japanese government has refused to compensate the DPRK for the period after World War II, saying it is not bound by the KWP-LDP-JSP agreement. The second stumbling block is the Japanese proposal that North Korea sign the IAEA accord as a precondition to normalized relations, a demand North Korea has rejected on the grounds that the United States has deployed nuclear weapons in South Korea. (*Dong-a Ilbo*, 18, 23 December, 29, 30, 31 January, 2 February 1991.)

Relations with the Third World. In 1990, North Korea made strenuous efforts to maintain its diplomatic initiative in the Third World, reportedly exchanging 190 official delegations with 59 Third World countries (27 in Africa, 10 in Latin America, 15 in Asia, and 7 in the Middle East). Still, the DPRK sent almost twice as many missions (118) to Third World countries as it received from them (63) (*Vantage Point*, December, January 1991.)

North Korea's immediate foreign policy objective in Third World diplomacy seems to have been to block South Korea's separate entry into the United Nations (*Korea Times*, 22 May). North Korea's diplomatic overtures focused on countries in which it has had more influence than South Korea. Its most active diplomatic contacts in Africa were with Ethiopia, Guinea, Tanzania, Zambia, Zimbabwe, and Angola. In the Western Hemisphere and, for that matter, in the whole south, Cuba was undoubtedly North Korea's closest ally. Vice-Premier and Foreign Minister Kim Young-nam visited the island nation in November. In Southeast Asia, North Korea sought to maintain close ties with Vietnam but was troubled by that country's growing economic cooperation with South Korea (*Korean Herald*, 6 January). North Korea accelerated its diplomatic overtures toward Thailand, with which it exchanged twelve delegations—a sixfold increase over 1989. North Korea received two parliamentary missions from Thailand in September and a military mission in October; the latter visit was returned in November by Armed Forces Minister O Chin-u. Two KWP delegations were sent there in December; and plans were made for Premier Yon Hyong-muk to travel to Thailand in early 1991 for talks on diplomatic and trade relations (*Seoul Sinmum*, 27 December).

Wonmo Dong
Southern Methodist University

Laos

Population. 4,023,726. Growth rate is 2.2 percent.
Party. Lao People's Revolutionary Party (Phak Pasason Pativat Lao, LPRP)
Founded. 22 March 1955
Membership. 40,000
General Secretary. Kaysone Phomvihane (70, Lao-Vietnamese, premier)
Politburo. 13 members: Kaysone Phomvihane, Nouhak Phoumsavan, Souphanouvong (president), Phoumi Vongvichit (acting president), Khamtai Siphandon, Phoun Sipaseut, Sisomphon Lovansai, Sisavat Keobounphan, Sali Vongkhamsao, Maichantan Sengmani, Saman Vi-gnaket, Oudom Khatthi-gna (alternate), Choummali Saignason (alternate)
Secretariat. 9 members: Kaysone Phomvihane, Khamtai Siphandon, Sisavat Keobounphan, Sali Vongkhamsao, Maichantan Sengmani, Saman Vi-gnaket, Oudom Khatthi-gna, Choummali Saignason, Somlat Chanthamat
Central Committee. 49 full members, 9 alternate members
Status. Ruling and sole legal party
Last Congress. Fourth, 13–15 November 1986, in Vientiane
Last Election. 26 March 1989 for 79 seats in the Supreme People's Assembly
Auxiliary Organizations. Lao Front for National Construction (LFNC), Lao People's Revolutionary Youth Union (LPRYU), Federation of Lao Trade Unions (FLTU), Federation of Lao Women's Unions (FLWU), Lao Buddhist Fellowship Organization (LBFO)
Publications. *Pasason* (The people), LPRP central organ, published in Vientiane (daily); *Alun mai* (New dawn), LPRP theoretical journal, published in Vientiane (quarterly), editor in chief, Mounkeo Olaboun; the official news agency is Khaosan Pathet Lao (KPL); Radio Vientiane, formerly Radio Pathet Lao (clandestine), celebrated 30 years of service to the party on 11 August.

In the face of confusion occasioned by the momentous events in Eastern Europe and the USSR, the LPRP gave renewed prominence during 1990 to the role of the party and to the justification of its unbroken monopoly of power. The year saw notable incidents of dissent both at home, where a number of officials were arrested for propounding a multiparty system, and abroad, where Laotian students in Eastern Europe held protest demonstrations demanding more democracy at home. Armed resistance also continued sporadically in various parts of the country. A number of important anniversaries were celebrated by the regime.

Party Leadership and Organization. The 35th founding anniversary of the LPRP was the occasion for a speech by General Secretary Kaysone on the theme of solidarity and harmony. In this lengthy speech delivered at a rally in Vientiane, Kaysone defined four "major conclusive points which are decisively significant to the victory of the revolutionary cause in the new stage":

1. Increasingly promote and expand the patriotic tradition of the multiethnic people, and adhere to the revolutionary objective, namely the consolidation, development, and perfecting of the popular democratic system in transition to socialism step by step. . . .
2. Strengthen the solidarity and harmony of the nation and rely on the people to extensively expand the implementation of democracy. . . .
3. Be determined to effect new changes in all respects with appropriate steps under the party's leadership. The new changes are the objectives and urgent requirements for defending and building the new system. Our party maintains that the new changes are the essence of a comprehensive, profound, and protracted revolution. . . .
4. Ceaselessly broaden and increase international solidarity and cooperation to gain extensive support for the cause of our national defense and construction. We have been victorious in our national liberation struggle because, in every victory of the revolution, our party has tightly combined genuine patriotism and internationalism; harmoniously linked national and epochal strengths; and resolutely fought every phenomenon of selfishness, idleness, and narrow-mindedness. (Radio Vientiane, 22 March; *FBIS-EAS*, 26 March.)

It is clear that the LPRP leadership under Kaysone intends to maintain equating the well-being of the LPDR and its people with the continued revolutionary successes of the LPRP and the experience of its Vietnamese mentors. An editorial in *Pasason* on

the LPRP founding anniversary repeated the formula that the party is "the organizer and leader of all victories of the Lao revolution and the continuator of the traditions of the Indochinese Communist Party, which was directly founded, educated, trained, and led by President Ho Chi Minh" (Radio Vientiane, 22 March; *FBIS-EAS*, 27 March). In Kaysone's first interview with a U.S. newspaper correspondent (another sign of the LPDR's increasingly open face to the outside world), Kaysone told Henry Kamm of the *New York Times* that "the Laotian people have faith in and agree with the LPRP's leadership, since the party belongs to the people, originates from the people and serves the people. Our Laotian party does not yet see any need for establishing other political parties." (*NYT*, 27 January.) Whenever questioned on the subject, party spokesmen have adopted the line of equating a multiparty system with anarchy in order to portray it as antidemocratic.

Kaysone's position as first among equals in the LPRP leadership was emphasized by the scale of the official celebration of his 70th birthday on 13 December. Representatives of various services of the LPDR brought bouquets of flowers to the Council of Ministers' meeting hall and delivered speeches of good wishes; a traditional *basi* ceremony was held, and a list of Kaysone's revolutionary achievements was on the front page of *Pasason*, along with his biography. (KPL, 13, 14, 15 December; *FBIS-EAS*, 13, 14, 18 December; Radio Vientiane, 13 December.) Previously, on 1 December, the Ho Chi Minh Medal, the highest distinction of the Socialist Republic of Vietnam (SRV), was conferred on Kaysone by visiting SRV state council chairman Vo Chi Cong, who declared that "over the past four decades, the name, life, and enthusiastic activities full of experiences of Comrade General Secretary Kaysone, under many different positions, have been closely related to each stage of the development of the Lao revolution, in particular since the founding of the LPRP" (Radio Vientiane, 3 December; *FBIS-EAS*, 6 December). The official announcement from Hanoi stated that the medal acknowledged Kaysone's "considerable contributions to consolidating and promoting the special friendship, militant solidarity and all-around cooperation between Laos and Vietnam" (Hanoi, VNA, 30 November; *FBIS-EAS*, 30 November).

In contrast, LPDR president Souphanouvong observed his 81st birthday on 13 July by receiving foreign ambassadors at his home in Vientiane (Radio Vientiane, 13 July; *FBIS-EAS*, 17 July). The message of good wishes from Vo Chi Cong was notably subdued, noting only his contributions to the people "under the leadership of the honorable and majestic LPRP" (Radio Vientiane, 13 July; *FBIS-EAS*, 17 July). In a rare report of his activities, Souphanouvong was said to have paid a three-day visit to Saravane province (KPL, 10 August; *FBIS-EAS*, 14 August).

Domestic Party Affairs. On New Year's Day, the LPRP organ *Pasason* editorialized that "1989 was a nightmare year for socialism" but expressed confidence that the Lao people would never lose faith in the Socialist countries (Radio Vientiane, 1 January; *FBIS-EAS*, 2 January). The LPRP Central Committee held its Ninth Plenum (Fourth Congress) 17–24 January and, speaking specifically of the rapid changes taking place in Eastern Europe, expressed assurances that "the genuine communists and people with ardent traditions and lofty ideals will manage to overcome all difficulties and to restore the people's faith in them, and will resolve the crisis and take their countries forward." In internal affairs, the plenum noted the success of a new economic structure and economic management mechanisms in promoting economic enterprises in the country to increase production and enlarge markets. People's living conditions had been improved, it said, and awareness of self-mastery had been consolidated. In the political field, people's democratic rights had been strengthened by the elections held in 1988 and 1989. The armed forces, although encountering numerous difficulties, were "able to smash all of the enemy's subversive schemes." The task at hand was to march firmly forward to make effective preparations for the convening of the Fifth Congress, probably in 1991. To translate the spirit of the Ninth Plenum into detailed plans, the Council of Ministers also convened an enlarged meeting for four and a half days beginning on 29 January. (Radio Vientiane, 3 February; *FBIS-EAS*, 5 February.)

As if to allay any lingering doubts about the party's leading role in the country's revolution, these were discussed in a radio talk on this particular theme on 29 January (Radio Vientiane, 29 January; *FBIS-EAS*, 30 January): "The party has not only provided clear guidance but also is capable of organizing every movement." On 7 February, the radio broadcast an editorial titled "The Leading Role of Party Members in the Cause of Restructuring in Our Country" (Radio Vientiane, 7 February; *FBIS-EAS*, 28 February). Another commentary empha-

sized the importance of party organization (Radio Vientiane, 27 February; *FBIS-EAS*, 6 March).

On the 60th anniversary of the founding of the Indochinese Communist Party on 3 February, the Executive Committee of the LPRP Central Committee sent a message of greeting to the Communist Party of Vietnam, calling it "a successor of the Indochinese Communist Party founded by President Ho Chi Minh, outstanding and well-known revolutionary of the international communist movement in the 20th century." The LPRP, it went on, was a successor of the ICP, and the Lao people "express satisfaction over the development of the special relations, great friendly solidarity and all-round cooperation between Laos and Vietnam based on Marxism-Leninism." (KPL, 3 February; *FBIS-EAS*, 7 February.)

In a three-part interview marking the LPRP's 35th anniversary, Phoumi Vongvichit, who like Kaysone was an ICP member before 1955, also dwelt on his meetings with Ho and the Vietnamese role in guiding the party's successful struggle for power (*Pasason*, 16, 17, 19 March; *FBIS-EAS*, 6 April). Phoumi returned to this theme in an interview with a Laos-based correspondent of the Vietnam News Agency and Vietnam television on 26 October, saying that "the fates of Vietnam and Laos are interrelated and inseparable." (Radio Vientiane, 29 October; *FBIS-EAS*, 31 October.)

Phoumi chaired a series of regional meetings of the LNFC during the year and gave a speech in Vientiane on 13 August commemorating the 40th anniversary of the founding of that organization (Radio Vientiane, 15 August; *FBIS-EAS*, 22 August).

Government Affairs. On 26 August, LPDR deputy minister of science and technology Thongsouk Saisangkhi resigned and in a letter to Premier Kaysone denounced the regime as a "communist monarchy" and a "dynasty of the Politburo." "Laos should change to a multi-party system in order to bring democracy, freedom and prosperity to the people," said Thongsouk's letter, copies of which were circulated to media outside Laos in October. (*Bangkok Post*, 20 October; Hong Kong, AFP, 22 October; *FBIS-EAS*, 22 October.) The newspaper reports said that Thongsouk was one of a group of midlevel LPDR officials who had been trying to form a movement, the Social Democrat Group, to campaign for multiparty democracy. One such report said that about half a dozen members of the group were arrested on 8 October.

Confirming the arrests, an article in *Pasason* said that "police arrested a number of bad elements," including Thongsouk, former Deputy Minister of Agriculture and Forestry Latsami Khamphoui, and Feng, a former official of the Justice Ministry.

> The three persons committed propaganda against the party and state policies and conducted activities aimed at overthrowing the regime and creating political disturbances in Vientiane capital. . . . They will be interrogated and tried according to the country's law. . . . Their acts also served the design of the reactionaries attempting to sabotage the LPDR, an achievement the Lao people scored through their great sacrifice, thus violating the law and affecting internal security, solidarity, and unity among the people in the country that the LPRP and the LPDR government have strived for during the past several years (Radio Vientiane, 5 November; *FBIS-EAS*, 6 November.)

It was not immediately clear from these sketchy reports whether the arrests in Vientiane were connected with a report from Thai military sources of the suppression by troops of antigovernment rallies in four provinces (Xieng Khouang, Sayaboury, Champassak, and Bolikhamsai) during March with the loss of 35 lives (*Bangkok Post*, *FBIS-EAS*, 27 April) or with reports, carried in the local press and on a clandestine radio station, of prodemocracy demonstrations by overseas Laotian students in front of the LPDR and Vietnamese embassies in Warsaw and Prague during July and August (Prague, *Mlada Fronta*, 17 August; *FBIS-EAS*, 30 August, 5, 13, 19, 20 September; Government for the Liberation of the Lao Nation [GLLN] Radio, 1, 8, 16 September). It seems, nevertheless, that the dramatic events in Eastern Europe are beginning to be felt in the LPDR despite the attempt of the party and government to isolate the country from such turbulence.

Of a different character than the dissent by mid-level government officials and that of the sons and daughters of the LPDR's ruling group studying abroad was the armed resistance to the regime mounted by guerrilla groups operating in the Laotian countryside. This resistance appears to be growing. Although difficult to evaluate on the basis of unilateral claims that may be inflated for their propaganda effect on the one hand and official denials on the other, resistance activities inside Laos were more in the news during 1990 than they have been since 1975.

The most solid report of resistance organization to date is a published eyewitness account of a ceremony held in Sayaboury province in December 1989 at which a "provisional revolutionary government" of Laos was created. The open-air, daytime ceremony was photographed by the author of the account, the Bangkok correspondent of a periodical devoted to military affairs. The "provisional government" named Chaofa Saisorivongsavang, a son of the late King Savang Vatthana, as head of state with the title of regent and Chao Pragna Luangmuangchanh Outhong Souvannavong as premier. The organization has adopted as its flag the three-headed white elephant on a red field of the former Kingdom of Laos. The military arm of the organization is a guerrilla force that calls itself the Lao Liberation Army (LLA).

According to this account, "Despite Vientiane's scoffing, there is little doubt that the LLA is active militarily in Laos, that it controls territory and that it administers civilian areas." The author noted, however, that barely a month after the ceremony he witnessed, LPDR helicopters landed troops and artillery in the region and began shelling and strafing attacks. At roughly the same time, air strikes were launched against areas deeper inside Laos, which, according to resistance sources, claimed 915 civilian casualties during 5–12 January. (Robert Karniol, "Laotian Resistance Emerges from Mist," Geneva, *International Defense Review* 23 [March].)

Appearing to confirm casualties in fighting in January, a pamphlet circulated at a conference sponsored by the Center for Strategic and International Studies in Washington, D.C., on 6 June contained photographs of what were described as victims of explosive and chemical weapons with specific locations and dates. A former Royal Laotian Army officer affiliated with the resistance also provided a list of Vietnamese army units stationed in Laos totaling more than nineteen thousand troops, plus another fourteen thousand Vietnamese integrated into LPDR units. Harvey Somers, a U.S. State Department officer at the conference, however, stated that he knew of fewer than five thousand Vietnamese military personnel in Laos, mostly in the south. He added that there was evidence of a low level of fighting, that he had no evidence of chemical weapons being used, and that the State Department had made its concerns in the matter known to the LPDR.

The flareup of fighting in January seems to have been concentrated in the southern Xieng Khouang–

northern Bolikhamsai area, which is the heartland of the Hmong people of Laos, the scene of heavy fighting during the war between 1960 and 1975, and the scene of severe reprisals by the new regime during 1977. According to one published report, 183 people were killed and 421 wounded during air raids in these two provinces (*Bangkok Post*, *FBIS-EAS*, 10 January). Among the indications of increased armed actions in various reports were stepped-up attacks on truck convoys along Route 13 between Vientiane and Luang Prabang and parts of Route 7 across the Plain of Jars, air strikes by MiG aircraft, large numbers of wounded soldiers in Vientiane's military hospital, and travel restrictions on foreign aid workers seeking to visit provinces north of Vientiane (*FEER*, 8 February). The LPDR, for its part, dismissed the reports as "ill-intended and groundless allegations" (KPL, *FBIS-EAS*, 23 February). Nevertheless, a brief item broadcast by Vientiane Radio in April praised security forces in Bolikhamsai province for carrying out three campaigns against "bad and vandalistic elements" in the region (Radio Vientiane, 10 April; *FBIS-EAS*, 11 April).

A clandestine radio station calling itself the radio station of the GLLN began broadcasting reports of guerrilla actions and government retaliation on 10200 kilohertz. This station broadcast a manifesto in August under the name of General Thonglit Chotbengboun (GLLN Radio, 15 August; *FBIS-EAS*, 21 August).

On 11 January, a group of 38 Vietnamese exiles, the survivors of the 68 armed men who crossed Laos from Thailand the previous August and were captured in Saravane province on their way into Vietnam, were found guilty and sentenced to varying prison terms. On 14 January, they were extradited to Vietnam (KPL, Radio Vientiane, 11 January; *FBIS-EAS*, 11, 12 January). LPDR commentaries gave detailed accounts of their safe bases in Thailand and the assistance they received from Thai military officers and blamed "reactionaries in the Thai ruling circles" for this infringement of neighborly relations (Radio Vientiane, 13, 23 January; *FBIS-EAS*, 16, 24 January). The Vietnamese ambassador in Vientiane later presented 88 medals to Laotians involved in foiling the infiltration attempt (Hanoi, VNA, 21 January; *FBIS-EAS*, 23 January).

The Supreme People's Assembly (SPA) held a three-day ordinary session in February to discuss and endorse the socioeconomic development plan and state budget for 1990 (KPL, *FBIS-EAS*, 12 February). Kaysone's 6,500-word speech highlighted Laos' favorable paddy production in 1989, which amounted to 1.4 million tons, and other economic achievements (*Pasason*, 10 February; *FBIS-EAS*, 2, 7 March). Later, the Standing Committee of the SPA issued a decree establishing a parliamentary committee of the LPDR to be a member of the International Parliamentary Union (Radio Vientiane, 26 March; *FBIS-EAS*, 29 March). An extraordinary three-day SPA session in June approved a number of laws (KPL, 28 June; *FBIS-EAS*, 2 July); another ordinary session was held from 24 to 29 November (Radio Vientiane, 29 November; *FBIS-EAS*, 30 November).

The major innovation expected from the SPA—ratification of the constitution of the LPDR—was apparently postponed until 1991. The text of the draft elaborated by the relevant committee of the SPA after many years' work was published and then circulated throughout the country for debate at meetings. The first of 73 articles in the draft as published stated that "the LPDR is a popular democratic state under the leadership of the LPRP." (*Pasason*, 4 June; *FBIS-EAS*, 12 June.) According to a party instruction, after its ratification by the SPA the constitution is to be submitted to the next party congress (Radio Vientiane, 10 May; *FBIS-EAS*, 15 May).

Chaleun Yiapaoheu, alternate LPRP Central Committee member, standing member of the SPA Constitution Drafting Committee, lectured on the draft article by article (Radio Vientiane, 2 June and following; *FBIS-EAS*, 18 June and following). Chaleun also explained that after the November SPA session the ratification of the constitution had been put off so as to allow "additional improvements" to be made to the draft, which had now been expanded to 82 articles (Radio Vientiane, 5 December: *FBIS-EAS*, 10 December).

Whether the SPA, under the chairmanship of Nouhak, the second-ranking figure in the party, can evolve into a deliberative body of members who are not only popularly elected but who dare to express a desire for change remains to be seen. So far, the contrast with the National Assembly of the former royal regime, with its lively debates on all aspects of government policies, could not be starker.

According to available indicators, the economy of the LPDR continued to perform relatively well in 1990, reflecting the incentive effects of financial and economic reforms carried out in recent years. An agricultural official was quoted as saying that the country plans to harvest 1.8 million tons of paddy in 1990 (KPL, 23 May; *FBIS-EAS*, 25 May). The trade deficit (an estimated $162 million in 1989) and external debt ($960 million, according to the Asian Development Bank), however, are still worrisome. Statistics released by the regime showed that there were 633 factories in the country in 1990 (compared with 100 in 1975), 19,000 factory workers (compared with 5,000), 831 million kilowatt-hours of electricity production (compared with 240 million), 363,000 square meters of textile production (compared with 40,000), 1,087,000 pieces of garment production (compared with 16,000), 11,000 tons of salt production (compared with 3,000), 600 tons of tobacco leaf production (compared with 75), 3,500 tons of coal production (compared with 225), and 1 million sheets of plywood (compared with 83,000). (Radio Vientiane, 23 November; *FBIS-EAS*, 30 November.) Domestic and external goods trade has expanded greatly (Radio Vientiane, 30 November; *FBIS-EAS*, 6 December). In August, the LPDR began preparatory meetings for drafting the third five-year plan (1991–1995) (KPL, 14 August; *FBIS-EAS*, 17 August). Decrees were issued by the Council of Ministers in the course of the year on conserving aquatic and wild animals (Radio Vientiane, 31 January; *FBIS-EAS*, 2 February) and forests and forestlands (Radio Vientiane, 29 January; *FBIS-EAS*, 8 February). The outlook for the economy of the LPDR is for reduced Soviet and East European aid in 1991 and a more difficult time ahead generally.

International Views and Activities. The LPRP has relations with more than 60 communist, workers', and progressive parties the world over, according to Thongloun Sisoulit, alternate member of the LPRP Central Committee, deputy head of the Foreign Relations Board of the LPRP Central Committee, and deputy foreign minister of the LPDR (Radio Vientiane, 27 November; *FBIS-EAS*, 29 November). In the same interview, Thongloun added:

In the last five years when numerous changes took place in many fraternal countries in Eastern Europe and Asia, our party came to understand the phenomena and readjusted our relations in line with the realities of these fraternal parties, on the basis of respect for their independence and self-determination. We sympathized with these fraternal parties, which faced confusion and difficulties. Even though some have not been able to continue normal relations, we have not severed our ties. On the contrary, we want to maintain ties, under present forms or any other for as long as they desire. As for relations with the communists, workers, and progressive parties in Western Europe, Asia, Africa, Latin America, and other countries, our party continues to support their struggles for peace, national independence, democracy, and social progress.

Thongloun also reported that the LPDR had established diplomatic relations with 74 other countries and contacts with numerous international organizations.

Ranking at the top of the LPDR's foreign relations priorities are Vietnam and Cambodia, countries in the unique category of "close solidarity and special relations." LPDR foreign policy during 1990 paid particular attention to the attempt to arrive at a negotiated solution to the Cambodian problem. Vientiane was the venue of the first direct meeting between an official of the U.S. government and the state of Cambodia. On 13 September, Cambodia's ambassador to the LPDR, Long Kem, met with U.S. chargé d'affaires in Vientiane Charles B. Salmon (Radio Vientiane, *FBIS-EAS*, 19 September).

LPDR organs supported the proposals of the state of Cambodia in the negotiations on that country, and Premier Hun Sen consulted in Vientiane with high party and government officials on his way to and on his return from Bangkok to meet Prince Norodom Sihanouk and other faction leaders. Laos and Cambodia exchanged reciprocal visits of delegations of parties and governments. SPA chairman Nouhak Phoumsavan, accompanied by Chaleun Yiapaoheu, visited Phnom Penh for discussions and an exchange of experiences with National Assembly chairman Chea Sim "with a view to improving and enhancing the time-honored relations of special friendship and all-around cooperation between the two peoples of Laos and Cambodia" (Radio Vientiane, 25 August; *FBIS-EAS*, 27 August). Cambodian National Assembly vice-chairman Mat Ly visited Vientiane in what was described as "a new step in the promotion and expansion of the special relations between our two countries"; it was stated that "the two sides unanimously agreed that only under the leadership of the party and state will the two peoples be able to march forward and succeed in defending, building, and further strengthening their respective countries" (Radio Vientiane, *FBIS-EAS*, 22 February).

Ties between the ruling parties were solidified. The LPRP's 35th anniversary was celebrated at a rally held in Phnom Penh at which the common roots of the LPRP and the Kampuchean People's Revolutionary Party (KPRP) were evoked by KPRP general secretary Heng Samrin (Radio Phnom Penh, 22 March; *FBIS-EAS*, 27 March); a delegation of the Organizational Board of the KPRP Central Committee paid a seven-day visit to Vientiane at the invitation of Oudom Khatthi-gna, the head of the organizational board of the LPRP Central Committee (KPL, *FBIS-EAS*, 20 February).

Kaysone was one of the speakers in Hanoi at the ceremonies observing Ho Chi Minh's 100th birthday on 18 May (Radio Vientiane, 17 May; *FBIS-EAS*, 18 May; text of speech in *Pasason*, 21 May; *FBIS-EAS*, 29 May). At a rally in Vientiane to mark the occasion, acting President Phoumi gave the main speech in which he recalled Ho's life in the service of international communism and his involvement in the revolution in Laos (Radio Vientiane, 19 May; *FBIS-EAS*, 21 May).

On 2 December the celebration of the fifteenth anniversary of the establishment of the LPDR provided the occasion for a summit meeting of Laotian, Cambodian, and Vietnamese leaders in Vientiane, during which the theme of "special relations" was noticeably downplayed. Acting President Phoumi and Foreign Minister Phoun Sipaseut were at Wattay Airport to greet the Vietnamese guests, led by Council of State chairman Vo Chi Cong and Foreign Minister Nguyen Co Thach, and the Cambodian guests, led by State Council chairman Heng Samrin and Council of Ministers vice-chairman General Bou Thang (Radio Vientiane, 30 November; *FBIS-EAS*, 4 December). After attending the mass rally and parade in the morning, the three Indochinese delegations held a meeting in the LPDR Council of Ministers' meeting hall on the afternoon of 2 December "in an atmosphere of profound friendship and close solidarity of fraternity and comradeship" (Radio Vientiane, 3 December; *FBIS-EAS*, 4 December). A news release was issued on 4 December in which the paragraph devoted to the Cambodian conflict was free of the polemics against the Khmer Rouge which similar high-level party-state delegation meetings have occasioned in the past (Radio Vientiane, 4 December; *FBIS-EAS*, 5 December). This moderation may reflect secret understandings reached by the Chinese and Vietnamese party general secretaries at their meeting in China in early September because it is only at that level that doctrinal arguments over the Cambodian party legitimacy can be resolved.

Laos and Vietnam exchanged numerous delegations during 1990. Among these were a delegation from the Foreign Relations Board of the Communist Party of Vietnam's Central Committee, a delegation from the newspaper *Nhan Dan*, a delegation from the magazine *Cong San*, and various economic, cultural, and scientific delegations. Both the chairman and the vice-chairman of the SPA visited Vietnam during 1990, and Nouhak's visit (Radio Vientiane, 23 July; *FBIS-EAS*, 25 July) was repaid by Vietnamese National Assembly chairman Le Quang Dao (Radio Vientiane, 20 September; *FBIS-EAS*, 21 September). In addition, there were various activities related to the border between Laos and Vietnam, including the signing of an agreement on border regulations by Phoun and Thach in Ho Chi Minh City on 1 March (Radio Vientiane, 2 March; *FBIS-EAS*, 5 March).

The LPDR's relations with Thailand continued to be up and down during 1990. Their common border disputes, which in prior years had led to fighting, were in the hands of various joint commissions for resolution. The sometimes monthly meetings of these were reported regularly in LPDR media to be occurring in an atmosphere of "mutual understanding." Despite a number of incidents, there was no renewal of open warfare across the border. In one area where the border is in dispute—along the Heuang and Heuang Nga rivers at the border between Sayaboury and Phitsanulok provinces, once the scene of vicious firing exchanges—joint inspections of the terrain were proceeding (Radio Vientiane, 7 December; *FBIS-EAS*, 10, 11 December; KPL, 11 December). The problem of "exiled Lao reactionaries" on the Thai side of the border continued to be raised sporadically by the LPDR. But at least in one instance the LPDR informed local Thai military commanders about a planned sweep operation in Laos near the border so as not to alarm the Thais (Bangkok, *Naeo Na*, 7 February; *FBIS-EAS*, 7 February).

Thai premier Chatchai Chunhawan visited Laos for the That Louang festival, an important Buddhist event (KPL, 2 November; *FBIS-EAS*, 6 November). Also, a visit to Laos by Thai princess Maha Chakkri Sirinthon, 15–22 March, during which she traveled extensively, helped dissipate tensions between the two countries (Radio Vientiane, 15 March; *FBIS-EAS*, 15 March and following). In recent years, due to changes in personnel in the Thai armed forces high command, the Lao have grown accustomed to hosting the large delegations from Bangkok that periodically arrive in Vientiane on get-acquainted visits. Comment in the LPDR media on bilateral relations accentuated the positive.

In one flashback to the past, a covert operation mounted from Laos succeeded in taking into custody on 17 November 1989 Colonel Khambou Phimmasen, a resistance leader recuperating from malaria in the Phu Phan Noi Mountains along the Nakhon Phanom-Mukdahan provincial border of Thailand, according to a Bangkok newspaper quoting Thai military intelligence sources. Khambou, now 57, was a lieutenant in the Second Paratroop Battalion on 9 August 1960 when that unit, under its commander, Capt. Kong Le, overthrew the Vientiane government in a neutralist coup d'état. Like Kong Le, Khambou is a southern tribesman. The Savannakhet radio station broadcast a statement by Khambou on 3 December 1989 in which he said that he had surrendered and appealed in the name of the Lao Neutralist Salvation Movement to "stop the counter-revolutionary national salvation struggle because it serves no purpose, either to the nation or to ourselves." Printed leaflets were also distributed to this effect on the Thai side of the Mekong. Khambou was reportedly the last neutralist active in the resistance. (Bangkok, *Khao Phiset*, 22–28 January, 5–11 February; *FBIS-EAS*, 5 March.)

The LPDR's relations with China were marked by numerous visit exchanges, with the highlight being Chinese premier Li Peng's visit to Vientiane 15–17 December during which official talks were held "in an atmosphere of intimate friendship, brotherhood, and mutual understanding." Both sides informed each other about their attitudes toward international and regional issues, but LPDR media made no mention of the issue of Cambodia. (Radio Vientiane, *FBIS-EAS*, 18 December.) The editorial in *Pasason* on Li Peng's visit was headlined "Lao-Chinese Friendship Flourishes Forever" (Radio Vientiane, 15 December; *FBIS-EAS*, 18 December). Li Peng invited Kaysone, whose usual summer vacation in the USSR was not reported in 1990, to "visit and rest" in China, an invitation that was accepted with pleasure.

Having decided to ignore their differences over the Cambodia issue, it was the common border between Phong Saly, Luang Namtha, and Oudomsai provinces of the LPDR and China's Yunnan province that emerged as the focus of concern in 1990. Not much has been said about a border problem, but during an official friendship visit to Vientiane, 19–25 August, by a Chinese delegation led by Deputy Foreign Minister Yuan Qihuai, the LPDR pressed the border matter and, indeed, in

reporting a courtesy call of the delegation on Foreign Minister Poun Sipaseut, called it "the main purpose of the visit by the Chinese Government delegation on this occasion." (Radio Vientiane, *FBIS-EAS*, 22 August.) A press release called the talks "an initial step leading to the permanent settlement of the border problem to be achieved in the spirit of friendship, justice, rationality, and compromise" and said that the two sides had decided to hold a second round in Beijing. Meanwhile, the two countries agreed to enforce an interim border accord signed in Beijing in late 1989. (Radio Vientiane, *FBIS-EAS*, 27 August.)

Border agreements were also featured in the LPDR's relations with Myanmar during 1990. A first round of talks about the common border of the two countries was held in Rangoon in August, and a second round concluded in Vientiane in December with a memorandum on a survey to be conducted in the near future. (KPL, 6 December; Radio Vientiane, 8 December; *FBIS-EAS*, 7, 10 December.)

Cuts in Soviet aid were the hallmark of LPDR-USSR relations in 1990. The five-year trade and aid program, which expired in 1990, will not be renewed, according to a Soviet embassy spokesman in Vientiane. Henceforth, there will only be annual plans. Only one aid project, repair of Route 8 in central Laos, will be maintained next year. The LPDR's imports from the USSR in 1990—oil, vehicles, fertilizer, and manufactured goods—totaled 59 million rubles ($98 million), whereas the LPDR's exports, mainly wood, coffee, and tin, totaled 22 million rubles ($36.5 million). (Hong Kong, AFP, 30 November; *FBIS-EAS*, 30 November.)

An Australian-aided satellite station in Vientiane began providing telephone, telegram, telex, and facsimile service, linking Laos through a Sydney-based company. Australia planned to give the LPDR $5.2 million in gratis aid for the 1989–90 fiscal year. (Radio Vientiane, 25 May; *FBIS-EAS*, 30 May.)

Japan and the LPDR began talks in 1990 on five economic aid projects: construction of a Ngum River bridge at Tha Ngon; a Se Katam hydroelectric dam project; a Vientiane sewer system; a rural development project in Savannakhet; and resuming the Japanese peace corps program. Japan is also repairing the Ngum River hydropower station, expanding the LPDR's telephone system, and constructing a $5 million river port facility in Vientiane. (KPL, 3, 7, 8, 15 February; *FBIS-EAS*, 5, 13, 14, 16 February.)

Relations between the LPDR and the United States continued on a positive note in 1990. An aide-mémoire for mutual understanding and cooperation in opposing the narcotics trade was signed in Vientiane on 9 January by Deputy Foreign Minister Souban Salitthilat and U.S. chargé d'affaires Salmon (Radio Vientiane, *FBIS-EAS*, 10 January). A State Department delegation visited Vientiane on 28 March and discussed the narcotics problem with LPDR officials (Radio Vientiane, *FBIS-EAS*, 29 March). Richard Solomon, assistant secretary of state for East Asia and Pacific affairs, led a delegation to Vientiane 14–15 May and signed a memorandum of understanding under which the United States agreed to provide $850,000 to produce artificial limbs in 1990–91, the second U.S.-funded project in the LPDR (Radio Vientiane, 15, 16 May; *FBIS-EAS*, 16 May). A U.S. delegation led by Carl W. Ford, Jr., principal deputy assistant secretary of defense for international security affairs, visited the LPDR 4–6 December and met with Deputy Minister of National Defense Lieutenant General Soulima Bounleut, the principal LPDR official concerned with narcotics matters (KPL, 7 December; *FBIS-EAS*, 10 December). Narcotics suppression remained a contentious issue in LPDR-U.S. relations, however, judging by a front-page article published in *Pasason* a few days later defending against U.S. charges that the mountainous region development company attached to the LPDR Ministry of National Defense is the main promoter of opium production in Laos (KPL, 10 December; *FBIS-EAS*, 11 December).

There was progress reported in 1990 on cooperation between the LPDR and the United States on the issue of information about and recovery of remains of U.S. servicemen missing in action in the war. A report from the National League of Families of American Prisoners and Missing in Southeast Asia pointed to increased cooperation from the LPDR in early 1990 (*Newsletter* [Washington, D.C.], 6 December). A spokesman said that as a result of three joint excavations in 1990, seven Americans were accounted for. Ann Mills Griffith, the league's executive director, paid another visit to the LPDR in August (*Newsletter*, 24 September). Meanwhile, the Texas-based Hunt Oil Company and the LPDR Ministry of Industry and Handicrafts signed an agreement for joint oil and gas exploration and survey in an area around Pakse (KPL, 24 February; *FBIS-EAS*, 2 March). Finally, during the U.N. General Assembly, Foreign Minister Phoun met with U.S. secretary of state James Baker on

3 October, the highest-level meeting to date between the two countries.

Arthur J. Dommen
Bethesda, Maryland

Malaysia/ Singapore

Population. Malaysia: 17,510,546; Singapore: 2,720,915

Parties. Communist Party of Malaya (CPM, renamed Malayan People's Party); North Kalimantan Communist Party (NKCP)

Founded. CPM: 30 April 1930

Membership. Malaysia: CPM: about 1,000 armed insurgents on Thai border and 100 in North Kalimantan and Sabah (*World Fact Book*); some 1,100 former CPM members turned in their weapons in February, and another 100 remain in China. NKCP: 53 former members surrendered to authorities in November. Singapore: 200–500; Barisan Sosialis infiltrated by Communists (*World Fact Book*)

Leadership. CPM: general secretary: Chin Peng (ethnic Chinese born Ong Boo Hwa, 68, also reported as 70); president: Rashid Maydin

Last Congress. Singapore, 1965 (last known)

Last Election. No data

Publications. No information

In 1990, CPM units laid down their arms in accordance with the agreements their general secretary had signed with the governments of Malaysia and Thailand in December 1989. Despite frequent reports that their leaders planned to form a legal party that would play a role in Malaysian politics, however, at year's end there was no sign of such activity.

Leadership and Party Organization. Chin Peng remained the acknowledged leader of the defunct CPM, heading the party's delegation at the February ceremonies on the Thai border at which the CPM's weapons were destroyed. Wu Ih Zu, a

Politburo member, and Rashid Maydin, president of the CPM, also attended the ceremonies.

Some one hundred CPM members—probably part of the 260 who, led by Chin Peng, advised the Malaysian government early in the year of their intention to return to Malaysia to wage a peaceful political struggle—reportedly still live in China. Chin Peng was expected to go to China after the February ceremonies to arrange for their return to Malaysia. He was variously reported to have re-named the CPM the Malayan People's Party and to be interested in heading a Labour-Socialist party of Malaysia. Despite these reports, Malaysia's Home Affairs Ministry claimed in late February that it had not received any applications from former CPM members wishing to return. (*Bangkok Post*, 20, 21, 25 February; *FBIS-EAS*, 20, 26, 28 February, 28 March; *Bernama*, 27 February; Bangkok, *The Nation*, 26 March.)

In late summer, the approximately 1,100 former guerrillas, most of them Thai-born, were still living in southern Thailand in four settlements near former CPM camps where the government provided them with land, shelter, and in many cases a small daily allowance. (For details about the group's ethnic composition, see *YICA*, 1990.) There was speculation that the former party leaders had maintained elements of the old logistic structure and that some of them had sizable bank accounts (*FEER*, 9 August).

The North Kalimantan Communist Party (NKCP) did not sign a peace accord with the Malaysian government until mid-October. Ang Chu Ting, secretary of the party's Second Bureau, and his deputy Wong Lian Kui represented the NKCP at the 17 October ceremony in Petra Jaya, Sarawak, at which 53 NKCP Second Bureau members—11 more than the Malaysian authorities estimated last year—surrendered. The government announced at the party's dissolution that the former guerrillas and their families would enjoy all the rights of legitimate citizens and be free to take part in political activities on the basis of the federal and state constitutions. Sarawak's chief minister added that the former NKCP members would undergo an orientation course for a few months and would not be accorded any special privileges. (Kuala Lumpur Television Network 1, 17 October; Kuala Lumpur International Service, *FBIS-EAS*, 18 October.)

It was November before Singapore members of the CPM announced that they intended to give up their armed struggle and return to society and stated their support for Singapore's sovereignty. Their spokesman was Fang Chuang Pi, 66, a longtime CPM leader who had been a fugitive since 1950. Fang declared his intention to return to Singapore, with the hope of contributing to Singapore's stability and progress. He said that 50 other CPM members hoped to return with him. The group included two former Barisan Sosialis members of the Singapore legislature, Chan Sun Wing and Wong Soon Fong.

Fang, now living in a hill town in southern Thailand, had fled Singapore in 1950 and lived in Indonesia, where he played a major role in directing communist activities in Malaysia and Singapore. After spending some time in Beijing, he had settled in Thailand. Fang told a journalist that over the years he had slipped in and out of Singapore, where he was called The Plen, and that after he moved to Thailand he changed his name to Li Bing. Prime Minister Lee Kuan Yew referred from time to time to Fang's influence and his efforts to get the People's Action party to work with the Communists in a united anticolonial front.

Fang confirmed that the CPM's former general secretary, Lai Teck, had been an agent for the French, the British, and the Japanese and had disappeared in 1947 with the party's funds (after which Chin Peng took over as general secretary). Fang said that the CPM had eventually tracked down Lai Teck and killed him but declined to say where the execution had taken place. He said that every 1 September, CPM members observed Martyrs' Day in memory of CPM comrades whom the Japanese had executed in Kuala Lumpur on 1 September 1942 after a tip from Lai Teck. (*Straits Times*, 8 November; *FBIS-EAS*, 13 November.)

Domestic Party Affairs. The deadline for the CPM rank and file to emerge from the jungle and lay down their arms was postponed twice to give the CPM more time to contact members still in hiding. It was finally set for 2 March. (*New Straits Times*, 14 January; *FBIS-EAS*, 22 January, 20 February; Hong Kong, AFP, 18 February.) Meanwhile, arrangements for the ceremonial destruction of CPM weapons at former party strongholds in southern Thailand stalled when Thai officials sought to record the occasion as one of historic interest. Chin Peng refused to permit photographs, videotaping, or the presence of journalists and turned down the Thai military's suggestion that CPM members themselves take pictures. When the ceremonies took place 22–24 February, the only incident to mar the occasion was an argument between CPM members and a Malaysian delegation member accused of secretly taking pictures during some of the events. CPM members wore their full party uniforms with red stars on the caps: this was the last time they would be permitted to wear their uniforms. (*Bangkok Post*, 20, 23, 25 February; *FBIS-EAS*, 20, 28 February.)

The issue of resettlement in Malaysia remained murky. Former CPM members, including those still in China, were to decide within a year of the signing of the 2 December 1989 accords whether they would return to Malaysia or remain in Thailand. Those still undecided at the end of the year would have to stay in Thai resettlement camps. The Malaysian government maintained that the Internal Security Act would not be invoked against CPM returnees, but the prime minister was quick to assert that they would be awarded no special privileges. He made clear that, unlike Thailand, Malaysia did not intend to provide former CPM followers with land on which to settle. Those who chose to return would have to prove that they were Malaysian citizens. Sensitive to domestic criticism of the accords from those who had suffered at communist hands, Malaysian authorities said they wanted six months to prepare for the resettlement of those who chose to return, and they asked returnees to refrain from political activities for a year after the accords "to avoid creating confusion" among Malaysians. Meanwhile, in Thailand ethnic Chinese Thais staged a demonstration protesting the alleged killing of their children by the CPM and demanding compensation. They claimed that CPM leaders had ordered the killing of new recruits in 1968 and 1969 on suspicion that some were Malaysian spies. (Kuala Lumpur International Service, 13 January; *FBIS-EAS*, 17 January, 26 February; *Bangkok Post*, 21 February.)

CPM members were to begin removing mines along the border in March, but in August Thai sources said that a Malaysian working party had been unable to reach agreement with the former guerrillas on dismantling booby traps on the Malaysian side of the border (*FEER*, 9 August). A high-ranking Malaysian police official warned in late August that communist ideology would continue to be a threat, especially from CPM members, even though they had agreed to lay down their arms. The police would continue to be on the lookout for communist underground activities that could influence individuals, political parties, youth organizations, and workers' unions, he said. (Kuala Lumpur International Service, 26 August; *FBIS-EAS*, 30 August.) There was little indication that CPM members would resettle in Malaysia, much less play a role in the general elections of 20–21 October. Indeed, in the spring, when it was widely expected that the government would call an early general election, the Partai Sosialis Rakyat Malaysia (Malaysian People's Socialist Party) chose to drop the word *Socialist* and renamed itself the Partai Rakyat Malaysia (*FEER*, 19 April).

The Singapore government maintained the position it had taken when the December accords were signed. In line with its constitution, it would accept all who were Singaporeans. However, the same constitution enabled the government to ensure that those who had engaged in violent attempts to seize power would have to satisfy the Internal Security Department that they had been rehabilitated. (*Straits Times*, 8 November; *FBIS-EAS*, 13 November.)

International Activities. The Malaysian government continued to expand its relations with the Soviet Union and East European countries. Offers of scholarships for Malaysian students were accepted from the Soviet Union and the People's Republic of China (PRC). In September the government lifted the last of its restrictions on travel to China. (Kuala Lumpur International Service, 13 April; *FBIS-EAS*, 13 April, 18 September; Kuala Lumpur RTM Television, 9 September.)

Singapore established diplomatic relations with the PRC in October, marked by an exchange of visits between Prime Minister Lee Kwan Yew and Chinese premier Li Peng. The PRC brushed aside Singapore's military ties with Taiwan as "a fact which we should not mind too much." The Singapore government had waited, as it said it would, for the restoration of ties between Indonesia and China, which took place on 8 August. (Tokyo, Kyodo, 12 August; *FBIS-EAS*, 13 August; *NYT*, 4 October.) Prime Minister Lee also exchanged official visits with the USSR prime minister (Singapore Domestic Service, 16 February; *FBIS-EAS*, 16 February; TASS, 23 September; *FBIS-SOV*, 24 September).

Jeanne S. Mintz
Washington, D.C.

Mongolia

Population. 2,187,275
Party. Mongolian People's Revolutionary Party (MPRP)
Founded. 1 March 1921
Membership. 100,049 (Montsame, 2 November); 1988 composition: 30.9 percent women; 32.9 percent workers; 17.3 percent Agricultural Association members; 49.8 percent intelligentsia. New recruits in 1990 included 50.9 percent intelligentsia, 42.4 percent workers, and 5.2 percent herdsmen.
Party Leader. Gombojabyn Ochirbat, 61
Politburo. Gombojabyn Ochirbat, former chairman of Trade Union Council and MPRP representative to the *World Marxist Review*; Myamyn Mishigdorj, 51, secretary, MPRP Central Committee; Tserenpiliyn Gombosuren, 47, foreign minister of the Mongolian People's Republic (MPR); Lodongiyn Tudeb, 55, Editor of *Unen*; Tsebeenjabyn Oold, 48, chairman, MPRP Auditing Commission
Central Committee. 91 members (no breakdown available on full or alternate status)
Opposition Parties. Mongolian Democratic Party (MDP), formed 18 February; Social Democratic Party (SDP), formed in March; Party of National Progress (PNP), formed in March; Free Labor Party (FLP), formed in March; Green Party, formed in May; Democratic Party of Mongolian Buddhists (DPMB), formed in June; Party of Mongolian Herdsmen and Farmers (MHFP), formed in December
Last Congress. 10 April 1990, extraordinary congress convened in Ulan Bator.
Last Election. 26 July 1990; of 430 seats in Great People's Hural, MPRP won 370; MDP, 23; PNP, 7; SDP, 7; FLP, 1; 22 uncertain and recontested.
Publications. *Unen* (Truth), MPRP daily organ. Montsame is the official news agency. The MPRP and opposition parties introduced several new publications during the year.

This year the Mongolian People's Republic (MPR) experienced the most dramatic changes in its 66 years as a Soviet satellite. The ruling communist MPRP overhauled its leadership, permitted opposition parties to form, introduced free elections for the MPR's chief legislative body (the Great People's Hural), and allowed nonparty figures to gain high government office for the first time. Unlike communist parties in Eastern Europe, however, the MPRP held on to power, only to preside over a deepening economic and political crisis.

Leadership and Party Organization. Influenced by events in Eastern Europe and the Soviet Union, opponents of the regime mounted demonstrations to press the government to make changes. The Mongolian Democratic Union (MDU), formed in December 1989, called for reforms that would force the MPRP to relinquish its monopoly on power, introduce democratization, and begin movement toward a market economy. The party responded with carrot-and-stick tactics, promising reform while threatening to suppress the MDU.

Unintimidated by government threats, the MDU organized successively larger demonstrations in January and February and announced the formation of a new political party, the Mongolian Democratic Party (MDP) on 18 February (Ulan Bator Radio, 18 February; *FBIS-EAS*, 20 February). The MPRP promised more reform, but its opponents remained unpacified. Confronting mass opposition, it convened an emergency plenum in early March. General Secretary Batmonh and his Politburo colleagues resigned on 12 March. On 16 March, the new Politburo was announced; Gombojabyn Ochirbat, a former trade union leader and Mongolia's representative to the *World Marxist Review* was named general secretary (Ulan Bator Radio, *FBIS*, 16 March). (The replaced Politburo members retired or assumed new positions: Batmonh, Dejid, and Lamdzab retired; Damdin is a media consultant; Sodnom heads the firm Mongoloil; Altangerel became a government official; Lantuu was elected chairman of the Gobi Altay province hural executive committee; and Namsray became editor in chief of a magazine.)

As part of its reform agenda, the MPRP continued its scathing review of former General Secretary Tsedenbal's tenure as party leader. The plenum stripped Tsedenbal and his wife of party membership and all awards and decorations, and party leaders and media attacked his legacy throughout the year. Furthermore, many of his purge victims, both living and dead, were formally rehabilitated.

On 10 April an extraordinary congress of the MPRP—consisting of 926 delegates, 88 percent of whom were elected for the first time—convened to review policy. Speeches at the congress strongly defended socialism and friendship with the Soviet Union and denounced opposition groups as uncooperative. The congress elected a 91-member Central Committee on 13 April (East Berlin, ADN, 13 April; *FBIS-EAS*, 16 April). General Secretary Ochirbat told a French newspaper that the MPRP had made mistakes but that it would not fail as had Eastern European communist parties (Paris, *Le Figaro*, 27 April; *FBIS-EAS*, 1 May).

In dealing with the opposition, the MPRP adopted a "bend but don't break" strategy that enabled the party to engineer free elections for the Great People's Hural (GPH) while maintaining its dominance (see below). Party membership increased from about 90,000 at the beginning of the year to more than 100,000 at the end.

Despite these gains, the political crisis in the MPRP deepened as the year progressed. Splits over economic policy were evident by the fall. General Secretary Ochirbat persisted in defending socialism and urged that collectively owned livestock in Mongolia's agricultural associations not be privatized (East Berlin, ADN, 22 November; *FBIS-EAS*, 23 November). Other leaders, however, called for more rapid transition to a market economy. Moreover, signs of political dissension became increasingly evident. The general secretary denied that the party was experiencing factionalism in an interview in November (Ulan Bator Radio, 8 November; *FBIS-EAS*, 17 November). Nevertheless, a few days later a group within the MPRP calling itself the For Democracy Club circulated an open letter to party members charging that opponents of democracy were running the party and calling on those who favored reform to unite to gain control (Montsame, 1 December; *FBIS-EAS*, 5 December).

Domestic Affairs. The most significant reform the Communists introduced was revising the MPR constitution to create a presidential system and to permit greater separation between party and state and free elections for the GPH. As early as January, party leaders considered allowing the development of a multiparty system. They initially rejected the idea but finally agreed to it in the wake of massive popular demonstrations. These reached a high point in late April and early May when nearly 50,000 protesters in Ulan Bator called for reform and democratization. The protests forced an abrupt conclusion of the MPR premier's state visit to China in early May.

The opposition MDU, estimated by its leaders to number more than 100,000, formed Mongolia's first opposition party, the Mongolian Democratic Party (MDP) in February. Although accused by the government of being unpatriotic and threatened with disbandment, the MDU persisted in sponsoring demonstrations, hunger strikes, and other mass actions to force change. It scored its first major victory when Batmonh stepped down and the new MPRP leadership took power.

Pressure on the government achieved progress toward separation of party and state when Batmonh resigned as chairman of the GPH Presidium and Sodnom resigned as premier on 22 March (Radio Ulan Bator, *FBIS-EAS*, 22 March). Punsalmaagiyn Ochirbat (not to be confused with General Secretary Ochirbat) became the new chairman, and Sharabyn Gungaadorj became premier. Chairman Ochirbat promptly announced that elections for the GPH would be held in July.

A flurry of political activity over the next two months resulted in the formation of several opposition parties and charges and countercharges between these parties and the Communists over election measures. In April, six opposition parties formed a coalition to contest the forthcoming elections. Several of them charged that the MPRP was manipulating the election laws to its advantage, a claim that subsequently proved accurate. They also demanded that the MPRP give up its constitutionally mandated "leading role" in Mongolia. In May, a special session of the GPH passed a law permitting the organization of political parties and establishing a small hural (baga) that would become the chief legislative and supervisory standing parliament for the MPR. According to the new rules, the GPH would be selected by popular vote; the GPH would then elect a president, vice-president, prime minister, and cabinet and would determine the membership of the baga. The baga would have 50 seats; each party would have one deputy for each 2 percent of the vote it received in the GPH election. (East Berlin, ADN, 10 May; *FBIS-EAS*, 11 May.)

The MPRP was the first to register under the new law, and other parties quickly followed. The MPRP's manifesto promised democratic elections, a state based on the rule of law, respect for human rights, and good relations with the Soviet Union and China (Montsame, 23 May; *FBIS-EAS*, 24 May). The Communists also promised to allocate 1.5 billion tugriks for increased wages and pensions and improving the supply of electricity. Other pledges included higher wages for technicians, nurses, and librarians, a 25 percent reduction in the charges for heating state-supplied housing, and more generous stipends for students, who would also receive discount tickets during vacations.

Angered by these pork barrel tactics, some opposition parties threatened to boycott the elections. The Communists persuaded them to participate by agreeing to suspend MPRP organizations within the army and security forces during the campaign.

The MPRP's tactics paid off. Communist dominance continued as 2,400 people vied in the primary elections to be among the 799 candidates selected to contest the 430 GPH seats: only 100 opposition candidates won. During the general election in late July, the MPRP received 60 percent of the vote and 86 percent of the seats. The opposition won 40 percent of the vote but only 14 percent of the seats. General Secretary Ochirbat won his seat by a scant 200 votes over his National Progressive party opponent. (Multiple sources; *FBIS-EAS*, 1 August.)

Following the elections, the GPH elected P. Ochirbat (MPRP) president by an overwhelming majority, 372 to 44. A Social Democrat, R. Gonchigdorj, was elected vice-president, and D. Byambasuren (MPRP), prime minister. President Ochirbat took the oath of office on 3 September during a colorful traditional ceremony reminiscent of the pledges of loyalty to the great khans. His inaugural speech emphasized political and economic reform and made no mention of Marxism-Leninism. Similarly, Byambasuren pledged to work for the creation of a market economy and promised to include representatives of all parties in his government. Despite these promises, a potential major difficulty for the new regime was the lack of participation in key leadership positions by the leading opposition party, the MDP.

The new government had no honeymoon from Mongolia's deepening economic crisis. Its heavy reliance on the Soviet Union for aid left it vulnerable to Moscow's economic travails. The Soviets have provided about $800 million annually in aid to Mongolia, or about $360 per capita in a country with an annual per capita income of about $900 (*Economist*, 17 March), and Mongolia now owes the USSR about $15 billion. In May, the Ochirbats visited Moscow to meet with President Gorbachev and appeal for a cancellation of the debt. Although terms of new arrangements were not specifically revealed, the Soviet Union apparently eased some of the requirements for repayment.

Mongolia's economic decline was accompanied by worsening inflation, a budget deficit of 20 percent, and growing unemployment and unrest. Serious shortages of food and energy were reported by fall (Ulan Bator Radio, 17 October; *FBIS-EAS*, 18 October). Yet debate over the introduction of market reforms kept the government from taking decisive action. By year's end, the government appeared to be retreating from previous reform measures when it called for a cessation of privatization in some sectors.

Probably the only bright spot in Mongolia's economy was its opening up to the outside world. Mongolia recognized South Korea in March and immediately sought South Korean participation in Mongolia's economy; some South Korean businesses showed interest. Japan agreed to provide $50 to $60 million in credits to develop the metallurgical industry. American, British, and other business interests explored the possibility of doing business in Mongolia. Although not immediately crucial in reviving the Mongolian economy, foreign investment may assist economic reform and development over time. The MPR also sought to join the International Monetary Fund, the World Bank, and the Asian Development Bank and could gain membership in some of these next year.

International Views and Affairs. Mongolia's crucial relationship with the Soviet Union became troubled, even as the Soviets moved into the second stage of troop reductions. (Withdrawal of all Soviet forces from Mongolia is to be completed by 1992.) The Soviet economic crisis led to stringent trading terms and difficult negotiations over repayment of Mongolia's debt. In February, the Soviet ambassador reminded Mongolians that about 60 percent of the MPR's gross industrial production and 20 percent of its agricultural production stemmed from enterprises built with Soviet assistance. He also noted that the Soviet Union supplied 80 percent of Mongolia's industrial and technical support. (Montsame, 27 February; *FBIS-EAS*, 1 March.)

Such assertions did not end accusations by the opposition that the USSR had exploited Mongolia. Many of the government's detractors urged an end to the special relationship between Moscow and Ulan Bator. One activist claimed that Soviet experts in Mongolia were worthless and had done more damage to the country than good (Budapest, *Népszabadság*, 18 September; *FBIS-EAS*, 26 September). In December employees of the joint Mongolian-Soviet Erdenet mining complex formed a "citizens' movement" urging that Mongolia nationalize the mine. The group claimed that outmoded Soviet technology and equipment would soon make the mines unprofitable. (Montsame, 1 December; *FBIS-EAS*, 5 December.)

The MPRP, increasingly concerned that such allegations could damage Soviet-Mongolian relations, persistently defended the advantages of close ties. General Secretary Ochirbat asserted that good relations with the Communist Party of the Soviet Union would be of paramount importance, and President Ochirbat declared that relations with the Soviet Union would be a key element of foreign policy. The November plenum of the MPRP adopted a resolution warning that "anti-Soviet tendencies" ran counter to the interests of the country and that Mongolia would "gain nothing" if relations further deteriorated. (Xinhua, 22 November; *FBIS-EAS*, 5 December.)

Additional measures were taken to improve relations with China. In addition to P. Ochirbat's state visit in May, numerous delegations were exchanged between the two sides, and more agreements were signed, including one on cooperation in science, technology, public health, and environmental protection (Xinhua, 3 May; *FBIS-CHI*, 4 May). In September, the first Chinese military delegation to visit Mongolia in 29 years arrived in Ulan Bator. Earlier, in July, the MPR reestablished a consulate in Huhehot, the capital of China's Inner Mongolia Autonomous Region. Mongolia also asked China to negotiate an agreement that would give Mongolia an outlet to the sea through a Chinese port. The Chinese agreed to consider the request.

Despite formal friendly relations and positive statements by both sides, press accounts suggested that China feared that Mongolia's democracy movement would spill over into Inner Mongolia (Hong Kong, *Ming Pao*, 7 May; *FBIS-CHI*, 7 May). A Mongolian oppositionist subsequently claimed that Mongols from Inner Mongolia participated in MDU meetings in Ulan Bator; the Chinese government protested.

An unprecedented outreach accompanied improving relations with the MPR's large immediate neighbors. The normalization of relations with South Korea—several months before the Soviet Union did so—was a marked departure from the MPR's past posture of following the Soviet lead in foreign policy. P'yŏngyang recalled its ambassador in a huff, but he returned quietly a few weeks later.

Mongolia sent delegations across Europe and to Southeast Asia in search of political and economic ties. In late July, Secretary of State James Baker became the first high-ranking U.S. official to visit Ulan Bator since Vice-President Henry Wallace in 1944. (Ulan Bator Radio, 31 July; *FBIS-EAS*, 2 August.) MPR foreign minister Gombosuren met with Secretary Baker in Washington in October to conclude a bilateral investment treaty.

Biographies. *Gombojabyn Ochirbat.* Ochirbat, general secretary of the MPRP, was born on 15 November 1929 in Dzabkhan Aimag. He graduated from Moscow State University in 1959 and returned to Mongolia to teach at a middle school in Gobi-Altay Aimag. During the 1960s he engaged in mass media and ideological work as secretary of the Union of Mongolian Journalists and chief of the Ideology Section of the MPRP Central Committee. In the early 1970s he became chairman of the Central Council of Mongolian Trade Unions and served until 1982, when he was removed after a dispute with MPRP leader Tsedenbal's wife. He then became an editor of educational publications until 1984, when he was appointed a deputy department head in the Central Committee. From 1988 until his current appointment he served as the MPRP representative to the *World Marxist Review* in Prague.

Punsalmaagiyn Ochirbat. Ochirbat, president of the MPR, was born into a herdsman's family in Dzabkhan Aimag in 1942. He graduated from the Institute of Mining in the Soviet Union and served in Mongolia's Ministry of Industry from 1966 to 1967. He became chief engineer of the Sharyn Gol mine, 1967–1972, and was promoted to deputy minister of Fuel, Power, and Geology. He became minister in 1976 and held that position until 1985. He headed the State Committee (which became a Ministry in 1987) for Foreign Economic Relations until his selection as chairman of the GPH Presidium in March and his election in July and inauguration as president in September.

Dashiyn Byambasuren. Byambasuren, prime minister of the MPR, was born in 1942 in Khentei Aimag, son of a herdsman. He graduated from the Institute for Economics and Statistics in Moscow in 1964. From 1965 to 1970 he served as director, Economic Department, Central Statistical Office. He served in the state price apparatus between 1970 and 1984, rising to become its chairman; he was also elected to the GPH. In 1984–1985 he was director of construction and renovation in the Ministry of Transportation; from 1985 to 1987 he was director of the Project and Research Center for Automated System Management; and from 1987 to 1989 he was the director, Institute for Administration and Management. He became deputy chairman of the Council of Ministers and a candidate member of the Politburo in 1989 and was elected prime minister on 10 September 1990.

William R. Heaton
Dumfries, Virginia

Nepal

Population. 19,145,800 (July)
Parties. Nepal Communist Party—Marxist; Nepal Communist Party—Marxist-Leninist; Nepal Communist Party—Maoist; Nepal Workers' and Peasants' Organization; Democratic Front; numerous factions of the above
Founded. Nepal Communist Party—Marxist: 1949; Nepal Communist Party—Marxist-Leninist: 1978; Democratic Front: 1980
Membership. 10,000 total (1988 estimate)
Leadership. Nepal Communist Party—Marxist: Man Mohan Adhikary; Nepal Communist Party—Marxist-Leninist: Radha Krishna Mainali; Democratic Front: Ram Raja Prasad Singh; many factions and offshoots are personality centered
Status. All legal
Last Congress. The Unified Nepal Communist Party held its third and last presplit congress in 1961. The various factions have held congresses, most notably in 1975 and 1986.
Auxiliary Organizations. Nepal Progressive Students' Union; Progressive Democratic Youth Association; All-Nepal National Free Students' Union; People's Front; Nepal National Student Federation; Nepal National Youth Federation
Publications. *Naya Janabad* (New democracy); *Nepal Patra, Barga Sangharsha* (Class struggle); *Mukti-Morcha* (Liberation front); *Mashal* (Torch); *Daily Diary Weekly*; *Samikshya Weekly*

The political dynamics of 1989 continued to make themselves felt, with India's protracted economic blockade of the landlocked kingdom causing considerable dislocation. New Delhi's initial goal of forcing Katmandu to renegotiate trade and transit treaties that would give India greater leverage, particularly over the kingdom's foreign policy, was supplemented by a desire to bring about a liberalization of Nepal's political structure.

Popular discontent with the monarchy and the government's defiance of Indian pressure grew alarmingly in 1990. Seven communist parties joined the Nepal Congress party—closely allied with the Indian National Congress—at a January political conference to plot a course of action; Indian politicians were in attendance, and Indian government officials and politicians lent their support to the proceedings. (*FEER*, 24 February; *NYT*, 17 April.)

Considerable changes were made in the executive and legislative structures of Nepal during the year. The political parties, particularly the Communists, were resurgent, and economic and other ties with India were restored. Although the full extent of India's covert political and intelligence intervention probably will not be known for some time, it is almost certain that Nepal's many extraregional ties, particularly its U.N. membership, were affected.

Party Affairs. This was a banner year for the various communist parties and the myriad of new factions and auxiliary groups that arrived on the scene. After years of operating underground, albeit with members serving in the National Panchyat (legislature), the parties and factions burst upon the scene to participate in the democratic fervor that gripped the country.

During the first half of January, an unprecedented effort to reunite the disparate factions occurred. The Manandhar, Verma, Fourth Congress—Nirmal Lama, and Amatya factions of the Nepal Communist Party; the Nepal Communist Party—Marxist; the Nepal Communist Party—Marxist-Leninist; and the Peasant-Worker party of Rohit Bhaktpur combined to form a United Left Front (*New Age*, 28 January).

The new front appointed Sahana Pradhan of the Nepal Communist Party—Marxist as its chairwoman, with Tulsi Lal Amatya of the Amatya faction of the Nepal Communist Party as honorary chairman. The Secretariat of the Action Committee was composed of Pradhan and T. L. Amatya plus a representative from each of the other parties and factions. The front announced its formation and platform at a 15 January press conference at which it laid out its commitment to overthrow the existing, partyless system and establish multiparty, participatory democracy. (New Delhi, *People's Democracy*, 28 January.)

Cooperation with the Nepal Congress party was highlighted in the front's agenda. The two groups quickly put together a plan of action that included mass action by mid-February. The congress and the front quickly began to mobilize their workers and student supporters for nationwide strikes beginning 18 February. The government reacted on 5 February with preemptive arrests of some two hundred political leaders and strike organizers. (Hong Kong, AFP, 7 February; *FBIS-NES*, 8 February.)

Despite those efforts, Katmandu was wracked by unrest on 18 February, with an estimated fifteen thousand people in the streets demanding a multiparty, democratic system. Riot police, it was reported, arrested five hundred students at Tribhuvan University, charged the marchers with batons, and used tear gas in an effort to disperse the crowd. Police opened fire on crowds in outlying towns, killing two and injuring several. As a result, the congress and the front were able to call successfully for a nationwide strike. (Hong Kong, AFP, 18 February; *FBIS-NES*, 21 February.)

The arrests at the university solidified student support of the congress-front efforts. By 27 February a Democratic People's Movement Students' Coordination Committee was operating. Claiming a membership of more than 70,000 students, the committee was composed of the prodemocracy Nepal Students' Union, the leftist All-Nepal National Free Students' Union (including both its pro-Moscow and its pro-Beijing factions), the Nepal National Student Federation, the Nepal Progressive Students' Union, and the Nepal Revolutionary Students' Union. (Hong Kong, AFP, 27 February; *FBIS-NES*, 1 March.)

The student committee organized sporadic demonstrations on their campuses and in the streets of Katmandu on 1 March. Those efforts were hit-and-run, being quickly staged and scattering before hard-pressed riot police could arrive on the scene. Even so, a number of students were arrested, and their relatives and student supporters gathered outside the jails to protest the detainees' treatment. (Hong Kong, AFP, 1 March; *FBIS-NES*, 2 March.)

On 9 March the front joined with the congress and student groups to launch widespread demonstrations. Commercial and other activities in the kingdom's cities and towns were brought to a virtual halt by the continued instability. Pradhan, Tulsi Lal Amatya, and other communist and front leaders were arrested along with the Congress party's leadership and various journalists. Party leaders announced that the prodemocracy agitation had left 30 dead, 150 injured, and eight thousand in jail. (Hong Kong, AFP, 9 March; *FBIS-NES*, 14 March.)

A call by the United Left Front and its congress allies to hold major demonstrations in late March was stymied when the government resorted to a heavy presence of security forces in the capital and to preemptive arrests of political leaders and activists (Hong Kong, AFP, 25 March; *FBIS-NES*, 26 March). Nevertheless, the winds of change were blowing across the kingdom, and by early April the king met with opposition leaders and agreed to make changes in the governing structure that would allow an interim government to form and a new constitution to be considered (*FEER*, 19 April).

Hoping to form the interim government, the United Left Front maintained its alliance, with the Congress party as a centrist block. This course led hard-line Communists to split with the front because they saw the mainstream Communists as too willing to compromise. The radicals formed a United National Democratic Movement and vowed to continue the agitation. (Hong Kong, AFP, 12 April; *FBIS-NES*, 13 April.)

On 16 April, King Birendra invited the United Front of communist parties and their Congress party allies to form a government. After a lengthy closed meeting the parties agreed to form a coalition government with the acting president of the Congress party as prime minister. (Hong Kong, AFP, 16 April; *FBIS-NES*, 16 April.) United Left Front chairwoman Sahana Prasad of the Nepal Communist Party—Marxist received the commerce and industry portfolios. Leaders of other communist factions received the justice, tourism, agriculture, forestry, and land reform portfolios. (Hong Kong, AFP, 18 April; *FBIS-NES*, 19 April.) The coalition began governing the country and preparing for popular elections, but it was beset by radicals from both the far right and the far left who opposed the interim government's centrist orientation. Violence resumed later that month. (Hong Kong, AFP, 27 April; *FBIS-NES*, 27 April.)

The king caused a brief stir in mid-May when he bypassed the newly installed interim government and ordered the formation of a panel to rewrite the kingdom's constitution. The move drew strong condemnation from the Nepal Communist Party, a participant in the interim government. In an effort to allay that criticism, the king appointed the party's chairman to the panel drafting the constitution. (*NYT*, 12 May.) Two weeks later, the king transferred legislative authority from himself to the interim government, thus empowering it to rule by decree until elections could be held to form a new legislature (Tokyo, Kyodo, 21 April; *FBIS-NES*, 22 May).

While attempting to set the domestic political scene in order, the interim government also attended to its most pressing issue. The interim prime minister arrived at an agreement with New Delhi for lifting the trade embargo as a precondition to negotiating fresh bilateral treaties. (*NYT*, 12 June.) Nonetheless, even that simple effort by the front-congress coalition drew barbs from the extreme left. The Nepal Communist Party's Flaming Torch faction demanded the abrogation of the agreement with India. (Hong Kong, AFP, 25 June; *FBIS-NES*, 27 June.) The following month, Flaming Torch was able to mobilize several thousand activists for anti-Indian demonstrations in Katmandu (Hong Kong, AFP, 13 July; *FBIS-NES*, 16 July).

Mainstream Communists cooperating with the congress had troubles of their own. The coalition of seven communist parties in the United Left Front was experiencing strain over the progress of the panel drafting the constitution and the election plans. The head of the Nepal Communist Party warned the interim government of possible unrest if an interim constitution were not quickly implemented. (Hong Kong, AFP, 29 June; *FBIS-NES*, 6 July.) The party specifically demanded guarantees of a multiparty democratic system, religious freedom, and an independent judiciary.

Concerned with the status of the monarchy, the Nepal Communist Party called repeatedly for constitutional provisions limiting the powers of the king (Hong Kong, AFP, 5 July; *FBIS-NES*, 6 July). It also warned, both independently and as a member of the United Left Front, that the royal family was plotting to undo the work of the democracy movement and return its retainers to positions of power (Hong Kong, AFP, 4 August; *FBIS-NES*, 7 August). In contrast, its blasts at the interim government continued to focus on the procedures and progress of the panel drafting the constitution (Hong Kong, AFP, 9 August; *FBIS-NES*, 10 August). It also periodically attacked the interim government, of which it was a part, on economic issues (Hong Kong, AFP, 15 August; *FBIS-NES*, 16 August).

By the end of August concerns about inflation and other economic difficulties, as well as differences between the United Left Front of Communists and their Congress party partners, led to renewed street protests. Radical communist leaders led crowds protesting the pace of domestic reform, the centrism of the interim government, and that body's attempts to reach a rapprochement with India. (*FEER*, 30 August; Hong Kong, AFP, 31 August; *FBIS-NES*, 5 September.) Labor strife paralyzed several key industries, and ethnic violence pitted Hindus against Muslims over proposed constitutional provisions declaring Nepal a Hindu state.

The constitutional drafting panel continued its work despite the protests and threats. The document was delivered to the king in November and promulgated by him. Mainstream Communists like the Nepal Communist Party and the Nepal Communist Party—Marxist-Leninist agreed to continue working with the United Left Front and the interim government to ensure that the gains made during the year were not lost. However, two radical left groups, the Flaming Torch faction and the National People's Liberation Front, rejected the draft constitution as reactionary and declared that they would not take part in elections scheduled for early 1991.

Relations with the People's Republic of China. Beijing sought throughout the year to balance its longtime friendship with Nepal against its desire for better relations with India. An eleven-member Chinese delegation visited Katmandu in January at the invitation of the Nepalese, who sought reassurances of Chinese support in their dispute with India. (Xinhua, 22, 24 January; *FBIS-CHI*, 23, 25 January.)

For its part, the interim government in Katmandu pressed its rapprochement with New Delhi in late May by canceling the last increment of an order of Chinese military equipment, as a small order in 1988 had factored heavily in India's decision to impose an economic blockade when the trade and transit treaties lapsed (Hong Kong, AFP, 25 May; *FBIS-NES*, 30 May, 6 June).

Michael R. Potaski
Catholic University of America

New Zealand

Population. 3,384,600 (*1990 New Zealand Year Book*)

Parties. Communist Party of New Zealand (CPNZ); Socialist Unity Party (SUP); Communist League (CL), known before June 1989 as the Socialist Action League (SAL); Left Currents (LC), known before January 1990 as the Workers' Communist League (WCL); Socialist Party of Aotearoa (SPA); Auckland Communist Left (ACL); Permanent Revolution Group (PRG); People's Party (PP); Organisation for Marxist Unity (OMU).

Founded. CPNZ: 1921, SUP: 1966, CL: 1989 (SAL, 1969), LC: 1990 (WCL, 1980), SPA: 1990, other groups: sometime during 1980s

Membership. CPNZ: 50, SUP: 60, CL: 25, LC: 25, SPA: 25, others: fewer than 10 each

Leadership. CPNZ: Ross Crook, chairman; Grant Morgan, general secretary; SUP: George Jackson, president; Ken Douglas, chairman; Marilyn Tucker, secretary; LC: David Steele and Robert Reid; CL: Mike Treen and Russell Johnson; SPA: George Harold ("Bill") Andersen, interim chairman; ACL: David Bedggood; PRG: Bill Logan; PP: Warrick Taylor, spokesman; OMU: Don Ross

Status. All legal

Last Congress. CPNZ: Twenty-fourth, 1–4 December; SUP: Eighth, 22–24 October 1988; CL: First, 3–5 June 1989 (Twelfth SAL); LC: First, January (Seventh WCL)

Last Election. 27 October (parliamentary), no representatives elected. The 10 CL and 4 PP candidates received a total of 404 votes for 13 seats (out of the 242,267 votes cast for a total of 97 seats). The SUP openly and actively supported the ruling Labour party, while many LC members concurrently belonged to the New Labour party or the Green party. In the last local government elections, held on 14 October 1989, no official representatives of communist or Socialist parties were elected, although a number of individuals from those parties did stand on various broad-based community tickets. In an Auckland city mayoral by-election on 8 December, the only Marxist candidate, Peter Bradley (CL), received a mere 189 out of the 123,456 votes cast.

Auxiliary Organizations. SUP: Youth in Unity, South Pacific United Youth Association, Workers' Institute for Scientific Education (WISE), Peace Council of New Zealand, New Zealand–USSR Society, considerable influence in Confederation of Trade Unions (CTU); CL: Latin American Solidarity Committee, Cuba Friendship Society, Nicaragua Must Survive committee; CPNZ: New Zealand–Albania Society, Trade Unionists Against the Compact (TUAC)

Publications. CPNZ: *People's Voice* (fortnightly; Grant Morgan and Peter Lusk, editors); SUP: *Tribune* (fortnightly; Jan Farr, editor), *Socialist Politics* (quarterly; Marilyn Tucker, editor); WCL: *Unity* (monthly until 16 March, when it ceased publication)

Throughout 1990 New Zealand, facing its worst economic recession since the 1930s, struggled to protect and expand its export markets in the Soviet Union, China, and Eastern Europe in the face of those countries' political and economic difficulties.

At home, the ruling Labour party, endorsed by the SUP-led CTU, went down to its worst defeat in the past 60 years. The various tiny communist and Socialist parties became even smaller and more divided than before.

CPNZ. The CPNZ benefited by being the most confident, trenchant, and consistent left-wing critic of the Labour government, which since 1984 had pursued arguably the most free market economic policies in the world. The other major communist party, the SUP, which held many top CTU posts, supported Labour as a lesser evil than the National party.

Particularly opposed by the CPNZ was a compact hammered out between the government and the CTU that prevented the unions from using industrial action including strikes to defend workers' jobs, wages, and conditions. CPNZ general secretary Grant Morgan was very prominent in the campaign of pickets and demonstrations organized by TUAC, described by the *People's Voice* as "an effective united front" of the CPNZ. (*People's Voice*, 1 October, devoted its whole 44 pages to the issue.)

Morgan and Peter Lusk turned the *People's Voice* from a small, boring paean of praise to Albania and Stalin into a well-researched, well-written, and topical critic of the government and a source of information on left-wing politics and industrial activity in New Zealand. The paper doubled in size, to some 36 to 44 pages an issue, and went from 50 cents to $1 a copy.

In foreign affairs the party and its paper remained resolutely pro-Albanian, as emphasized by a special statement from the CPNZ's national executive ("Albania Advances on Socialist Road," *People's Voice*, 23 July). The CPNZ also argues that it has consistently predicted, since the days of Khrushchev, that the Soviet Union's reform policies would lead to a restoration of capitalism and even fascism in the Soviet Union and Eastern Europe. It continues its dogmatic advocacy of a vanguard, revolutionary party creating a centralized Stalinist state and economy.

The CPNZ's chairman and former general secretary, Harold Crook, retired in October. He remained a member of the party's four-man national executive, which was reelected at the CPNZ's Twenty-fourth National Conference, held in Auckland 1–4 December. Crook, former president of the Huntly Miners' Union, has been a member of the CPNZ for 58 years. He was succeeded as chairman by his son, Ross Crook, with Grant Morgan (general secretary) and Barry Lee making up the executive. Delegates at the conference voted unanimously in favor of a new constitution for the party, though no substantial changes resulted. (For a full conference report and the text of the new constitution, see *People's Voice*, 10 December.)

SUP. The SUP's Central Committee met in early March to discuss developments in the USSR, Eastern Europe, Nicaragua, and New Zealand. The committee concluded that what was happening was a rejection not of socialism but of "the authoritarian bureaucratic methods adopted in the Stalin era and continued in various degrees." (*Tribune*, 12 March.)

A few weeks later the SUP's general secretary, Marilyn Tucker, told a seminar on The Future for Socialism, held in Sydney, Australia, from 16 to 18 March, that what the left needed was cooperation and unity among its factions. She stressed the importance of recognizing the growing diversity of society and the importance of producing, not simply redistributing, wealth. This theoretical line was subsequently developed in *Socialist Politics*, which Tucker edits. In one article, Paul Harris, writing on "The Relevance of Marxism," argued that "a future social democracy will have to go beyond old models by being: decentralised, multicultural, non-sexist, environmentalist, participatory and consensual." It

would include "a majority of Labour Party, NLP [New Labour Party] and SUP members, women, Maori and Pacific Island organisations, community groups, Greens, peace activists, and others." (*Socialist Politics*, no. 1.)

Despite all this stress on unity, by the middle of the year the SUP was itself seriously split by a major conflict over strategy. An SUP founder and former president, George Harold ("Bill") Andersen, 66,— chairman of the CTU's Auckland district council and of the Auckland SUP, president of the Northern Distribution Union, and from 1957 until 1990 secretary of the Northern Drivers' Union—opposed an SUP Central Committee decision to support only Labour party candidates in the October parliamentary elections. He described Labour as "one of the extreme right-wing governments of the world" (*Dominion Sunday Times*, 8 July) and argued that SUP members should be free to support other candidates from the NLP, Mana Motuhake, or Green party for seats such as Auckland Central, held by a particularly right-wing Labour cabinet minister.

Over the weekend of 2–4 June, some 40 members of the SUP's 16-strong Central Committee and others met at CTU headquarters in Wellington to discuss events in the USSR and the role and future program of the SUP in New Zealand. Andersen and fellow Central Committee member Doug McCallum, the 35-year-old SUP Auckland regional secretary and CTU Auckland regional coordinator, attacked the Labour government and said they could no longer support it.

The meeting, however, was dominated by supporters of CTU president and SUP national chairman Ken Douglas, who was afraid that the defeat of the Labour government would bring to power a National party government that would reintroduce voluntary union membership, deregulate the labor markets, destroy the welfare system, and realign New Zealand with the United States in foreign and defense affairs. The most prominent of those who agreed with Douglas appear to have been Marilyn Tucker (general secretary), Joe Tonner (assistant general secretary and Wellington regional secretary of the Public Service Association), Alan Ware (vice-chairman), Jan Farr (editor of *Tribune*), and Central Committee members Dave Arthur, Graeme Whimp, Frank McNulty, Simon Wallace, Joe Te Pania, and Richie Gillespie. Gillespie is chairman of the Wellington District Council of the CTU and secretary of the Wellington Drivers' Union. Most of the others are full-time CTU or trade union officials.

The decision to support all Labour candidates and to forbid SUP members' endorsing any other candidates was the last straw for Andersen. Although a further meeting between SUP central executive members and the Auckland branch of the SUP was held on 27 June, and although Douglas cut short a visit to the Soviet Union and returned for an emergency meeting of the central executive on 29–30 June, on 30 June Andersen submitted a letter of resignation from the party.

Within days McCallum had also resigned, as had Alec Morgan, the SUP's regional coordinator in Auckland, Peter Cross, vice-president of the Auckland Tramways Union and an SUP founder, and Pat Shepherd, a leader of the Auckland Unemployed Workers' Union. In all, thirteen Auckland SUP members sent letters of resignation, and others simply left the party. The SUP membership in Auckland dropped from 35 members in June to 9 in October. In effect this cut the SUP loose from New Zealand's industrial heartland, although the party still retains considerable influence in Wellington and in the central, paid bureaucracy of the CTU. In Auckland, where industrial militancy is now much more likely, Mike Jackson, general secretary of the Northern Distribution Union and one of the few Auckland unionists who remained loyal to the SUP, replaced Andersen, his onetime mentor, as SUP Auckland chairman. (See *Tribune*, 4 June, 4 July, and *People's Voice*, 11 June, for lengthy articles on the SUP's division.)

The conflict between Andersen's faction and most of the SUP's leadership appears to date back to 1986, when Andersen withdrew from the post of general secretary. He found it difficult to accept the SUP's support for a Labour government that was creating record unemployment, selling off state-owned assets and enterprises to local and foreign monopoly capitalists, and pursuing a strict monetarist policy. Until 1990 he tried unsuccessfully to convert his party colleagues not only by pointing out the incompatibility of their beliefs with Labour's actions but also by arguing that the SUP's reputation among the less well-to-do was being damaged and its membership decimated. A secret memorandum circulated among SUP leaders revealed that the party's membership had declined from 400 in 1984 to 75 in August 1990.

The party is also in financial difficulties. Although a fighting fund of $34,026 was subscribed during the financial year ending 31 March, during 1990 only the Wellington region paid its contribution to the fund, and the situation was worsened when the CPSU cut its order for the *Tribune* from several thousand copies to a hundred per issue.

Internationally, the SUP has remained loyal to the Soviet Union and the CPSU. Douglas, Ware, Arthur, and Angus McConnell all visited the Soviet Union during the year. Following Andersen's resignation and his formation of the new Socialist Party of Aotearoa (SPA), however, Boris Krotkov of the Soviet embassy in Wellington refused to endorse the SUP. He claimed that the Soviet Union was more concerned with the split in its own communist party and made the astonishing statement that the Soviet embassy "did not know" the local Communists and that "there was no contact with them." (*New Zealand Herald*, 5 July.)

Among a number of the SUP's aging membership who died during 1990 was John James ("Johnny") Mitchell. Mitchell, who died in May, was born in London in 1907. He joined the CPNZ in 1936, having supported the party for some years. An Auckland waterside worker, Mitchell helped found the Maritime Branch of the CPSU and was the publisher of an illegal news sheet during the 151-day waterfront strike of 1951. In later years Mitchell was president of the Stationary Engine Drivers' Union, chairman for 27 years of the Beresford Street Primary School Committee, chairman of the Auckland region of the SUP, and editor of the *Tribune*. During the 1980s Mitchell remained a prominent SUP member, was active in organizing community, unemployed, and beneficiaries' groups, and chaired the Auckland Trades Council's May Day committee.

SPA. The SPA was formed by former SUP members at an Auckland conference on 4 and 5 August. Bill Andersen, elected interim chairman of a five-person steering committee, claimed that the new party would be "socialist in structure and policy, with emphasis on building unity of the Left" (*New Zealand Herald*, 9 August).

The SPA joined with the CPNZ and the NLP in attacking the Labour party and criticizing the CTU's economic and industrial compact with that government and with the succeeding National government. The aim of the new party was "to help build an alliance of action of all the non-big business forces against the monopolies and their mates in both National and Labour."

During the October parliamentary elections the SPA refused to support any National party candidates and threw its support selectively to "a small number of Labour candidates," Mana Motuhake in the four Maori electorates, and some NLP and Green candidates.

In foreign affairs, Andersen claimed that Mikhail Gorbachev "has opened up a new world perspective" with his emphasis on peace and restricting nuclear weapons and by choosing "a democratic form of socialism." Andersen rejected claims that contemporary developments marked the end of communism, calling such assertions "nonsensical" and adding, "There are enough experienced communists [in the Soviet Union and Eastern Europe] to rebuild. The struggle to restructure socialism is desirable but the struggle to restructure capitalism is impossible." (*Dominion Sunday Times*, 29 April.)

CL (SAL). The remnant of the Trotskyite SAL, which in 1989 renamed itself the CL, nominated ten candidates in the New Zealand parliamentary elections held on 27 October.

The CL campaigned against the economic blockade and the military buildup against Iraq, advocated a shorter working week without loss of pay, and proposed radical measures to combat sexual and racial inequalities.

The ten candidates, who all stood in Labour party electoral strongholds in the main cities of Auckland, Wellington, and Christchurch, polled together 220 votes out of the 183,231 total votes cast for those seats.

Four other Marxist candidates who stood for Wellington constituencies under the banner of the People's party were similarly rejected by the voters, polling only 184 out of the 77,306 votes cast.

LC (WCL). The WCL, launched in 1980, decided in January at its Seventh National Conference to dissolve itself. During the 1980s the WCL, which had grown out of a group of Maoists who left the CPNZ when that party started to criticize China and align itself with Albania, had been very active in opposing athletic contact between New Zealand and South Africa, especially rugby. It was also prominent in the militant feminist and Maori movements, in antinuclear agitation, and in support of the Sandinistas in Nicaragua. One of its last major demonstrations was on 6 February, when various left-wing protesters tried to disrupt the Waitangi Day commemoration of the 150th anniversary of the signing of the treaty that ceded New Zealand to the British.

The WCL's newspaper, *Unity*, ceased publication after twelve years because the "financial burden . . .

is unjustifiable" (*Unity*, 16 March). The final issue (16 March) contained articles on the history of both the paper and the WCL.

The WCL was replaced by a new organization, Left Currents (LC), which promised to "build a revolutionary alliance of the forces struggling for Maori, women's and workers' liberation." The LC rejected the view that communist parties should have a monopoly of political power in a society. Although policy would be dictated nationally by a five-person national committee meeting every six weeks, each region would decide local strategy and tactics and cooperate with other progressive groups.

The word *communist* was rejected because of its "negative associations with monolithic, patriarchal, excessively hierarchical, racist and/or national chauvinistic, and environmentally exploitative actions of communist parties in power and . . . does not incorporate other key aspects of our policy, that is, the equal importance of liberation from the patriarchy, and the need for Maori self-determination" (*Unity*, 16 March).

The advocates of the new name and strategy, prominent among whom were David Steele and Robert Reid, stressed the need for an organization based on community activities and the goal of "social liberation." Many WCL activists had become involved either concurrently or totally in broader-based feminist, Maori rights, and workers' movements or in the NLP, whose vice-president for some time was a prominent WCL activist, Sue Bradford.

The NLP, however, tried to distance itself from its more left-wing minority. It expelled two tiny Trotskyite groups—the Communist Left, led by David Bedggood, and the Permanent Revolution Group, led by Bill Logan—from membership. Although the NLP officially deemed WCL and LC positions and membership as compatible with those of the NLP, a number of LC members including Bradford left the NLP during 1990 and became involved with the new Green party. In the elections the NLP gained only one seat, that of its leader, Jim Anderton (Sydenham). None of the NLP candidates previously identified with the smaller communist or Socialist parties polled particularly well.

New Zealand and the Soviet Union. The economic crisis in the Soviet Union was reflected in a drop in New Zealand exports to that country during 1989 and most of 1990 and in the difficulty the Soviet Union had in paying for what it did purchase. This was serious for New Zealand because the Soviets had become New Zealand's biggest market for wool and butter and one of its three major buyers of meat. By May concern was being expressed publicly about uncharacteristic Soviet slowness in paying for both current and past purchases. Despite a promise from Alexander Kovalev, the Soviet trade commissioner in Wellington, that the delayed payments would eventually be made and a threat that if New Zealand suspended deliveries the Soviets would look elsewhere for supplies, the New Zealand Wool Export Council decided to halt exports after the Soviets defaulted on large payments to twelve New Zealand wool exporters.

The Soviets started paying the overdue amounts in June but asked that New Zealand make available credit for all or part of the unpaid bills. By December, however, the amount owed New Zealand for butter and wool had risen to about NZ$150 million. Again the Soviets suggested further extensions of credit or gifts of food. Soviet ambassador Yuri Sokolov even proposed in November that New Zealand could accept surplus Soviet warships in lieu of the money owed. New Zealand's associate minister of trade, Philip Burdon, quickly pointed out that, in light of New Zealand's own NZ$40 billion external debt, critical economic condition, and 200,000 unemployed, it was impossible for New Zealand to waive the debt or give away its major export commodities. He went to Moscow in early December to discuss the matter with the Soviets, whose embassy in Wellington had responded to Burdon by commenting that in the future the USSR would remember who had been its friends and who had refused to help it in its hour of need.

New Zealand was also concerned at the suggestion that the European Community would donate meat and butter surpluses to the Soviets, a move seen as seriously damaging world demand and prices for those commodities.

In response to Burdon's visit to Moscow and intensive negotiations by officials of the New Zealand Dairy Board, the Soviets in mid-December agreed to pay the NZ$115 million owed for butter, though the payment of the NZ$35 million for wool remained unresolved.

A number of joint ventures continued to be discussed or implemented during 1990. The New Zealand Dairy Board, through its subsidiary SOVENZ, built three meat processing plants and a milk plant in the Altai region of the Soviet Far East. SOVENZ also built another milk plant in the Ukraine and peat-processing, peat moss, and fish meal plants on Sakhalin Island. An ambitious project to provide the USSR with New Zealand expertise in the use of compressed natural gas and liquid petroleum gas to fuel cars and trucks and to build a string of Soviet filling stations prefabricated in New Zealand also continued to be negotiated.

New Zealand visitors to the USSR during 1990 included in April Jim Bolger, leader of the National party and newly elected prime minister, and in September Sir Robert Muldoon, who had been New Zealand's vocal anti-Soviet and anti-SUP prime minister from 1975 to 1984. Muldoon, who is chairman of the privately funded Global Economic Action Institute (GEAI), cochaired, with the prominent Soviet economist Stanislav Shatalin, a conference in Moscow where academics, government officials, and financial and industrial experts from the Soviet Union, the United States, Europe, Japan, and elsewhere discussed the Soviet economy in the context of the world economy, especially world debt. Muldoon also had private talks in the Kremlin with the CPSU secretary, Aleksandr Iakovlev.

Two relatively minor matters clouded New Zealand–Soviet relations in 1990. The Soviet supertrawler *Baikovsk* was confiscated and its captain fined for illegally fishing in New Zealand waters, and Oleg Gordievsky's book, *KGB: The Inside Story of Its Foreign Operations*, published in October, asserted that the KGB had stepped up its activity in New Zealand and the nearby Pacific Islands after 1982. The comparative unimportance of New Zealand to the Soviet Union was indicated by the announcement that *Soviet News*, published fortnightly by the Soviet embassy in Wellington, would cease publication in August.

Relations with the Post-Socialist Countries of Central and Eastern Europe. The disintegration of the Soviet empire in Eastern Europe and the shift toward democracy and capitalism resulted in an upsurge of official and popular New Zealand interest in the region. In December 1989, the New Zealand government announced NZ$500,000 in technical assistance to improve agriculture and the environment in Poland and Hungary, NZ$250,000 for vocational education in the same countries, and NZ$100,000 to help expand New Zealand's agricultural technology exports to the region. In February 1990, New Zealand joined the European Bank for Reconstruction and Development, set up by the Organization for Economic Cooperation and Development to coordinate Western aid to, and investment in, the post-Socialist states. New Zealand agreed to contribute NZ$5 million over the next five years. Technical assistance to Poland and Hungary was subsequently extended to Bulgaria, Czechoslovakia, and Yugoslavia, New Zealand in September providing NZ$500,000 for projects in the latter three countries.

The New Zealand Trade Development Board (TDB) sponsored a business seminar on trade opportunities in Eastern Europe. Speakers at the seminar, held in Wellington on 15 February, included Mike Moore, the minister of external relations and trade; Peter Shirtcliffe, TDB chairman; Don Walker, New Zealand's former ambassador in Vienna; Don Gamble of the Ministry of External Relations and Trade; and Lajos Bokros, a director of the Hungarian national bank. Several New Zealand businessmen who had already developed successful business ventures in Eastern Europe, notably in agricultural expertise and technology, also addressed the 150-person audience.

The seminar was followed by a New Zealand economic mission to Hungary, Poland, Czechoslovakia, and East Germany from 26 March to 8 April. Moore, accompanied by business leaders, government officials, and representatives of various groups, traveled to Eastern Europe to promote New Zealand exports and to identify new commercial opportunities in those four countries, which in 1989 had taken NZ$33.5 million of New Zealand's exports. Almost two-thirds of New Zealand's 1989 exports to the region went to Czechoslovakia, mainly wool. During the visit Moore claimed he attended 100 meetings in eleven days, including a lengthy session with Poland's Lech Wałęsa. Contracts worth NZ$9.5 million were concluded and others worth NZ$6 million initiated.

In September, Stephen Diver took up a newly created position as New Zealand's trade commissioner for Central and Eastern Europe based in Vienna.

New Zealand's commercial and charitable contacts with Romania also continued. Some one hundred Romanian orphans were adopted into New Zealand families. In December a delegation of twenty Romanian officials visited New Zealand for talks. Hungary's foreign minister and Poland's deputy minister of agriculture visited New Zealand late in 1990.

Relations with the People's Republic of China. New Zealand's Labour government moved cautiously throughout 1990 toward the restoration of normal political, diplomatic, and economic relations with China. The cooled relations with Beijing in the wake of the June 1989 Tiananmen Square massacre were reflected in a drop in New Zealand exports to China, New Zealand's fifth largest trading partner.

In March, China's vice-minister for industry, Wang Zengjing, held talks in Wellington with New Zealand's trade minister, Mike Moore. In April, a delegation of New Zealand officials led by Graham Ansell, secretary of external relations and trade, visited China.

Dr. Don Brash, governor of New Zealand's Reserve Bank, was the guest of the People's Bank of China in June, when he met with Premier Li Peng. During the same month, ten New Zealanders from the New Zealand–China Friendship Society also visited China. Society president Professor Bill Willmott declined a request that his delegation on its return to New Zealand try to persuade Chinese students studying in New Zealand, including the 50 reportedly seeking political asylum, to return home.

Top-level political contacts were resumed when New Zealand prime minister Geoffrey Palmer met Vice-Foreign Minister Liu Huaqiu in Wellington in August and New Zealand minister of agriculture and forestry Jim Sutton visited China in September to meet Li Peng.

In December it was announced that Petrocorp, a subsidiary of New Zealand's largest corporation, would lead the first foreign consortium to win an oil exploration license in China, in which Petrocorp holds a 60 percent share.

Barry S. Gustafson
University of Auckland

Pakistan

Population. 114,649,406 (July)
Party. Communist Party of Pakistan
Founded. 1948 (banned in 1954; reemerged in 1989)
Membership. 200, with several thousand sympathizers (estimate)
General Secretary. Imam Ali Nazish

Status. Legal
Last Congress. Third, 25–27 May 1989

Pakistan's domestic and foreign affairs were in turmoil during the year. Domestically, continued ferment in the Sind, which many saw as the result of India's meddling, raised further doubts about Benazir Bhutto's ability to lead the country. Although Bhutto proved inept at dealing with her problems, she continually challenged the other members of the ruling triumvirate and tested the limits of her authority. In the end, she angered and alienated both President Ghulam Ishaq Khan and Chief of Army Staff Mirza Aslam Beg to the extent that the president prorogued Parliament, dissolved Bhutto's government, and called for fresh elections. In the November polls, Bhutto's Pakistan People's party was routed, Nawaz Sharif became prime minister, and Bhutto was relegated to the back benches as an opposition member.

Party Affairs. The Communist Party of Pakistan (CPP) cautiously began to rebuild after 35 years in the political wilderness, claiming a platform of agrarian reform, federalism, independent foreign policy, and economic stability (*WMR*, January).

The CPP claims that its support of Bhutto in the 1989 elections was instrumental in her decision to legalize it after she became prime minister. CPP Political Bureau member and Central Committee secretary Jam Saqi claims that the party operated openly in Bhutto's home province of Sind while it was technically illegal; that province is still being used to consolidate and expand the party into other provinces. The party is recruiting among peasants, workers, youth, students, and intellectuals and has particularly targeted the fragmented trade union movement. (*WMR*, January.)

Foreign Affairs. The past decade's preoccupation with Afghanistan was put on the back burner in the spring when relations with India seriously deteriorated. Pakistan's political and material support of the uprising by the Muslim majority in the Indian states of Jammu and Kashmir led to a rift between the two countries and again brought them to the brink of war. (Lahore, *Nation*, 9 May; *FBIS-NES*, 10 May.) International concern about the situation—especially the possibility that one or both of the two longtime adversaries might use nuclear weapons—prompted the U.S. government to dispatch Deputy National Security Adviser Robert

Gates on a last-ditch peace mission. (*FBIS-NES*, 2 July.)

By the end of the year, relations with India had improved somewhat after a series of political talks between New Delhi and Islamabad. Relations between Pakistan and the United States, however, cooled perceptibly as the Bush administration was required to cease aid under various congressional requirements regarding certification of the nature of Pakistan's nuclear program. (Delhi Domestic Service, 8 October; *FBIS-NES*, 9 October; *FEER*, 25 October.)

Relations with the USSR. Pakistan's relations with the USSR continued to improve during the year. With the Najibullah regime seemingly in control in Kabul and with the Afghan resistance making little headway, Moscow and Islamabad sought areas of possible cooperation. Foreign Secretary Tanvir Ahmed Khan traveled to Moscow in March and agreed to foster an intra-Afghan dialogue toward creating a broad-based government in Kabul. Although the accord drew considerable negative reaction from conservative elements in Pakistan and among the Afghan resistance, it did set the stage for further dialogue. (*FEER*, 29 March.)

In late February and early March a delegation of Pakistani parliamentarians paid the first such visit to Moscow in thirteen years. The visit was touted as representative of the normalization of Pakistani-Soviet relations following Moscow's withdrawal from Afghanistan. The Pakistanis expressed their gratitude for a recent Soviet loan to finance the expansion of a steel mill and agreed to establish a joint ministerial commission to promote cooperation in economic, scientific, and technological matters. (Lahore, *Nation*, 7 March; *FBIS-NES*, 9 March.)

Soviet-Pakistani ties received a further boost in the spring when the USSR agreed to provide development assistance to Baluchistan. Soviet aid and technical assistance will be used to build a major dam on one of the desert province's few rivers, a source of water that will bring an estimated 40,000 acres under cultivation and provide hydroelectric power to the impoverished region (Islamabad Domestic Service, 5 May; *FBIS-NES*, 9 May).

By summer, members of the Soviet Muslim Religious Board for Central Asia were in Islamabad for a conference sponsored by the Pakistan government's Ministry for Religious Affairs. The two bodies reached an agreement under which Pakistan will set aside 10 million rupees for the propagation of Islamic teachings in Central Asia, the construction and repair of mosques, and the distribution of religious literature (Islamabad Domestic Service, 29 July; *FBIS-NES*, 1 August).

Relations with the People's Republic of China. China remained the linchpin of Pakistani foreign policy. In early May, at the height of Indo-Pakistani tensions, the chairman of the standing committee of the Chinese National People's Congress, Wan Li, paid a five-day visit to Islamabad for discussions of bilateral and regional issues. Speaking about the situation with India, Wan Li expressed China's support of the "just aspirations of the people of Kashmir" and encouraged India and Pakistan to resolve their dispute peacefully. (Islamabad Domestic Service, 5 May; *FBIS-NES*, 8 May.)

In September, shortly after the gulf crisis began and amid the turmoil that followed Bhutto's ouster, President Ghulam Ishaq Khan made an unexpected visit to Beijing. There he sought, and evidently gained, reassurance that the traditionally close ties between Pakistan and China would not be endangered by the changing security situation in Southwest Asia or by Beijing's growing rapprochement with New Delhi. (Islamabad, *Muslim*, 20, 25 September; *FBIS-NES*, 21, 28 September.)

Sino-Pakistani defense cooperation continued through the year both bilaterally and in conjunction with Iran and Saudi Arabia. With the reduction of the superpowers' support for their respective proxies in the Afghan civil war and the end of U.S. military assistance to Pakistan because of the latter's nuclear program, the search for alternative sources of aid and matériel became more critical for Islamabad. Beijing will be looked on as Pakistan's stalwart friend, and Islamabad will seek to build further linkages between itself, Beijing, and various third parties.

Michael R. Potaski
Catholic University of America

The Philippines

Population. 66,117,284 (*World Fact Book*)
Parties. Communist Party of the Philippines (CPP); Philippine Communist Party (Partido Kommunista ng Pilipinas; PKP)
Founded. CPP: 1968; PKP: 1930
Membership. CPP: 25,000 (CPP claims 35,000); PKP: 5,000 (estimated)
Leadership. CPP: Jose Maria Sison, chairman in absentia; Benito Tiamzon, acting chairman; Ricardo Reyes, general secretary; PKP: Felicisimo C. Macapagal, chairman; Merlin Magallona, general secretary
Central Committee. CPP: members: Jose Maria Sison, Benito Tiamzon, Romolo Kintanar, Wilma Austria-Tiamzon, Ricardo Reyes, Leo Velasco, Arturo Tabara, Antonio Cabanatan, Prudencio Calubid, Sotero Llamas, Armando Teng, Allan Jasminez, Ruben Balistoy, Salvador Bas ("Choy"), Geronimo Pasetes, Julius Giron, Noel Etabag, Miel Laurenaria, Antonio Zumel, Fidel Agcaoili, Juliet De Lima-Sison, Sixto Carlos, Luis Jalandoni; alternate members: Rafael Paredes, Maria Eugenia Magpantay-Topacio, Adelberto Silva ("Tonyo"), Nilo de la Cruz, Elizabeth Principe, Enrico Esguerra, Eduardo Quitoriano, Alexander de Vera, Jose de Vera; captured in 1990: Antonio Cabardo, Caridad Magpantay-Pascual, Edsel Sajor, Antonio Tujan, Randal Echanis, Vicente Ladlad, Vicente Martinez, Manuel Homena. PKP: Felicisimo C. Macapagal, Merlin Magallona, Alejandro Briones, Jesus Lava, Jose Lava, Aurora Evangelista
Status. CPP: illegal; PKP: legal
Last Congress. CPP: has never held a full congress; PKP: Ninth, December 1986
Auxiliary Organizations. CPP: New People's Army (NPA), National Democratic Front (NDF). Under its National United Front Commission, the CPP controls or influences many other organizations, listed here by sector. Religious: Christians for National Liberation (CNL); Ecumenical Movement for Justice and Peace; National Ecumenical Forum for Justice and Peace; Ecumenical Partnership for International Concerns (EPIC); Mindanao Interfaith Pastoral Center; Ec-

umenical Forum for Church Response. Environment: Philippine Environmental Action Network (PEAN); CODEV. Education, youth: Youth for Democracy and Nationalism (KADENA); League of Filipino Students (LFS); National Union of Students of the Philippines; Association of Nationalist Teachers (KAGUMA); Association of Youth for a Free Philippines (KAKAMPI); Association of Concerned Teachers (ACT); Progressive Organization of Teachers for Enlightenment and Nationalist Transformation (POTENT). Labor: May First Movement (Kilusang Mayo Uno, KMU); Peasant Movement of the Philippines (Kilusang Magbubukid ng Pilipinas, KMP); National Federation of Sugar Workers (NFSW); Small Farmers' Association (SFAN); Federation of Small Fishermen. Women: Patriotic Movement of Women (Makabayang Kilusan ng Bagong Kababiahan, MAKIBAKA); General Association Binding Women for Reforms, Integrity, Leadership and Action (GABRIELA). Human rights: Task Force Detainees (TFD); Philippine Alliance for Human Rights Advocates (PAHRA); Mothers and Relatives Against Tyranny (MARTYR); Families of Victims of Involuntary Disappearances (FIND). Professional: Medical Action Group (MAG); Concerned Artists of the Philippines (CAP); Confederation for Unity, Recognition and Advancement of Government Employees (COURAGE); Citizens' Alliance for Consumer Protection (CACP). General political: New Nationalist Alliance (Bagong Alyansang Makabayan, BAYAN); People's Party (Partido ng Bayan, PnB); Alliance for New Politics (ANP); Volunteers for Popular Democracy (VPD); Nuclear-Free Philippines Coalition; National Alliance for Justice, Freedom, and Democracy. CPP foreign auxiliaries and support groups: United States: Alliance for Philippine Concerns (APC) and its affiliates; Washington Forum, APC—Chicago; Philippine Workers' Support Committee; Church Coalition for Human Rights in the Philippines; Friends of the Filipino People in Honolulu; Friends of GABRIELA; Canada: Canada-Asia Working Group; Austria: Philippines-Austrian Committee; Belgium: Philippine Group—Ghent; Philippine International Center for Human Rights (PICHR); Britain: Philippine Resource Centre; Philippine Support Group; Denmark: Philippine-Danish Support Group; Italy: Friends of the Filipino People in Italy (Solidarietà con il Popolo Filipino); Ireland: Filipino-Irish Support Group; Netherlands: Filipino People's Committee (Komite ng Sambayanang Pilipino, KSP); Commission for Filipino Migrant Workers; Dutch Philippines Support Group; Simbayan; Sweden: Swedish-Filipino Association; Switzerland: Samahang Pilipino; Gruppe Schweiz-Philippinen; West Germany: Aktionsgruppe Philippinen (AGPHI); Japan: Resource Center for Philippine Concerns; Australia: Philippine Action Support Group; New Zealand: Philippine Solidarity Network. PKP: Association of Agricultural Laborers; National Association of Workers (Katipunan); Philippine Committee for Development, Peace and Solidarity; Democratic Youth Council of the Philippines. CPP and PKP joint membership: Forward Looking Organization of Women (FLOW); Freedom from Debt Coalition; National Movement for Civil Liberties; Congress for People's Agrarian Reform (CPAR).

Publications. CPP: *Ang Bayan* (The nation), monthly (restricted availability). NDF: *Liberation*, monthly (sporadic); *NDF Update*, bimonthly, published in the Netherlands; *Balita ng Malayang Philipinas*, (Free Philippines news service), bimonthly. NPA: *Pulang Bandila*, (Red flag), bimonthly. Alex Bocayao Brigade: *Ang Partisano* (The partisan); *Taliba ng Bayan*, biweekly; *Larab*, monthly, published in Samar. Solidarity group publications: United States: *W Forum*, irregular, published by the Washington Forum; *Philippine Witness*, published by the Church Coalition for Human Rights in the Philippines; Netherlands: *Filippijnenbulletin*, monthly, published by the Dutch Philippine Group; West Germany: *Pintig*, irregular, published by the Aktionsgruppe Philippinen; Australia: *Philippine Brief*, irregular, published by the Philippine Action Support Group; New Zealand: *Philippines Update*, monthly, published by the Philippine Solidarity Network; Japan: *Solidardad II*, quarterly, published by the Resource Center for Philippine Concerns. Books: Benjamin Pimentel, Jr., *Edjop: The Unusual Journey of Edgar Jopson* (Quezon City: KEN, Inc., 1989); Alfredo B. Saulo, *Communism in the Philippines: An Introduction* (enlarged edition) (Manila: Ateneo de Manila University Press, 1990).

CPP. Asia's largest communist insurgency, the CPP in 1990 showed signs of continued deterioration and reduced political support. CPP fortunes, however, could be reversed by the crumbling government of President Corazon Aquino, beset by military coup attempts, natural disasters, and a sharp economic decline. The CPP took advantage of the government's distraction by military rebels to continue NPA military attacks and experiment with an insurrectionary strategy designed to grab power in the capital city. Military rebels and the CPP entered into an ominous but inconclusive dialogue. The U.S. military bases remained the focus of CPP political propaganda. Internationally, the CPP sought to justify its revolution in the face of communism's continued decline. Despite embarrassing setbacks, the CPP appeared to increase overseas solidarity work, especially in Western Europe.

Leadership and organization. While still in Europe, Jose Maria Sison, reputed chairman in absentia, kept a high profile, maintaining an active lecture schedule, making numerous statements, and defending himself from charges made by the Philippine government and the Armed Forces of the Philippines (AFP) (*FEER*, 25 January). In a June interview, Sison stated that Aquino "could not have become president without soliciting the support of the national democratic movement," but Sison later said that "Marcos and Aquino are the same. They are both the highest bureaucrats representing the big bourgeoisie and the landlord class, and subordinate to the United States." He also claimed to be living on a budget of about $373 a month. (*Katipunan*, July–August.)

Sison's option to reside in the Netherlands may end soon, as his application for political asylum there had not been approved by midyear. A report of Sison's imminent expulsion, however, was immediately denied by the Dutch government and by Sison himself (*Philippine Newsday*, 19 June; *FBIS-EAS*, 21 June). Denying reports that he was planning to move to North Korea (ibid.), he later told a radio interviewer that "many sectors" in the Netherlands are working to obtain political asylum for CPP leaders (*Diario Filipino*, 20 June; *FBIS-EAS*, 27 June).

Then on 13 July, the Dutch government made a surprise decision to refuse Sison's request for political asylum. Dutch law provides for an appeal process during which Sison may continue to reside in the Netherlands for at least a year (*News Weekly*, 8 December). The outgoing Dutch ambassador to Manila said that Sison most likely will be expelled from the Netherlands once he exhausts the appeal process (*Manila Standard*, 3 August). Apparently, Dutch authorities changed their attitude toward Sison after CPP activists in Europe were discovered

to be counterfeiting U.S. money (*News Weekly*, 21 July).

Toward the end of 1990, there was speculation that Sison might move to Belgium. Sison has long been close to the leadership of the Maoist-oriented Belgian Labor party. Sison participated in the Belgian Labor party's May First activities and was scheduled to give them a lecture on 10 March (*Pacific Newsletter*, no. 590).

The CPP appears willing to continue deferring the question of Sison's position while he is abroad. In early November, military officials stated that a large number of top CPP leaders had converged on Manila for a leadership conference (*Manila Bulletin*, 9 November; *FBIS-EAS*, 14 November). Amid reports that Central Committee (CC) member and National Democratic Front (NDF) leader Antonio Zumel had fled to the Netherlands for medical treatment, the NDF announced after its first national congress that it had named Zumel its chairman (*Philippine Daily*, 12 July; *FBIS-EAS*, 16 July; *Newsday*, 1 August). It was speculated that Zumel is not able to perform party tasks and that the NDF is now being led by its new general secretary, Frank Fernandez, secretary of the Negros Regional Party Commission.

Acting CPP chairman Benito Tiamzon kept a low profile in 1990. Press reports alleged that the CPP had spent 1 million pesos to bribe the soldiers who allowed his wife, Wilma Austria-Tiamzon (age 37), to escape from Manila's Camp Crame during a 1989 Christmas party (*Manila Chronicle*, 13 May; *FBIS-EAS*, 16 May). Austria-Tiamzon, who apparently has resumed her position in the CPP Political Bureau, may now be acting head of the Central Luzon Commission (*FEER*, 23 August).

In contrast to Tiamzon, NPA chief Romolo Kintanar made several statements to the press, issuing threats to foreigners, proposing cooperation with military rebels, and making statements during a flurry of peace negotiation proposals later in the year.

Ricardo Reyes, CPP general secretary, is also secretary of the Manila-Rizal Regional Commission, which, with about 4,000 members, is the CPP's largest territorial commission. The 500-member-strong Alex Boncayao Brigade (ABB) urban partisan unit is controlled by the commission. (*FEER*, 23 August.)

A CPP order of battle compiled in midyear by Philippine authorities identifies the following active Political Bureau members: Jose Maria Sison, Benito Tiamzon, Wilma Austria-Tiamzon, Arturo

Tabara, Leo Velasco, Romolo Kintanar, Ricardo Reyes, Salvador Bas, Luis Jalandoni, and Sixto Carlos. The Political Bureau's Executive Committee, which is responsible for day-to-day decision making, comprises the Tiamzon couple, Sison, Reyes, and Kintanar. Political Bureau members captured in 1990 include Antonio Carbardo, Caridad Magpantay-Pascual, and Antonio Tujan.

The National Military Commission, which is responsible for overall military policy, is chaired by Benito Tiamzon, with Romolo Kintanar as vice-chairman. Other members include Leo Velasco, Jose de Vera, Antonio Cabardo, Prudencio Calubid, Randal Echaniz, and Eduardo Quitoriano. The NPA General Command includes Romolo Kintanar, chief of staff; Antonio Cabardo, vice-chief of staff; Randal Echaniz, political director; Alfredo Simbulan; Ramon Ramirez; Virgilio Maceda; Nilo de la Cruz; and Franklin Realiza.

Leaders of major territorial commissions identified by the order of battle include Leo Velasco, chairman, Northern Luzon Commission (NLC); Arturo Tabara, chairman, Visayas Commission (VISCOM); Antonio Cabanantan, chairman, Mindanao Commission; Armando Teng, secretary, Southern Tagalog Regional Committee (STRC); and Manuel Homena, secretary, Panay Regional Committee. Alfredo Mapano is secretary of the Northern Mindanao Commission. (*Manila Bulletin*, 7 April; *FBIS EAS*, 11 April.)

Several high-ranking CPP members were captured in 1990. On 9 April, Political Bureau member and NPA deputy chief Antonio Cabardo was captured (*Daily Inquirer*, 10 April). Cabardo, who had just returned from Europe, had briefly assumed command of the NPA while Romolo Kintanar was in jail in 1987. Press reports later alleged that several party members were investigated in relation to Cabardo's capture, including CC members Ricardo Reyes and Jose Luneta (*Manila Chronicle*, 4 August; *FBIS-EAS*, 6 August).

On 21 April authorities captured Caridad Magpantay-Pascual, CC member and head of the strategically important Central Luzon Commission (*Philippine Daily*, *FBIS-EAS*, 23 April). She is also the second-highest ranking woman in the CPP (*NYT*, 5 May). Edsel Sajor, CC member, chairman of the Manila-Rizal Commission, and chairman of the National Propaganda Commission, was captured on 16 May (*FBIS-EAS*, 21 May). On 5 June, AFP intelligence operatives captured Political Bureau member Antonio Tujan (Manila Broadcasting Company, 2 June; *FBIS-EAS*, 6 June). On 3 August

the AFP captured Randal Echanis, CC member, member of the National Military Commission, and head of the NPA's Political Commission (*Manila Chronicle*, 4 August; *FBIS-EAS*, 6 August). On 14 August, Philippine constabulary officers captured Vicente Ladlad, CC member and secretary of the CPP's National Education Commission (Quezon City Radio, 14 August; *FBIS-EAS*, 16 August). In Manila on 7 November military operatives captured Vicente Martinez, CC member and head of the NPA command for the Eastern Visayas Regional Party Committee (*Manila Bulletin*, 9 November; *FBIS-EAS*, 14 November). On 27 December in Iloilo, constabulary troops captured Manuel Homena, alternate CC member and head of the Panay Regional Party Committee (*Manila Chronicle*, 28 December; *FBIS-EAS*, 31 December).

The CPP lost many more important midlevel leaders, including Alfredo Atienza, Executive Committee member of the Negros Regional Party Committee, who was captured on 15 June (*Philippine Daily*, 16 June; *FBIS-EAS*, 19 June) but released on 20 December for lack of evidence (AFP, *Negros News and Features*, 26 December). Alfredo Simbulan, member of the Executive Committee of the NPA General Command, was captured along with Echanis (*Manila Chronicle*, 4 August; *FBIS-EAS*, 6 August). On 3 November, the military captured Reynaldo Bernardo, number two man in the ABB (*Manila Bulletin*, 9 November; *FBIS-EAS*, 14 November).

The military released a profile of Nilo de la Cruz, head of the ABB, an NPA partisan unit responsible for many high-profile assassinations. In 1968 he was a member of the CPP front Kabataang Makabayan. During the 1970s, he was active in trade union activities and was deployed to the Visayas region and then to southern Luzon. In 1985 he was made an alternate member of the Central Committee, supervised "anti-infiltration" campaigns, or purges, in the Manila area in 1988, and in 1989 became head of the Regional Operations Command of the Manila-Rizal Regional Commission. (*Newsday*, 31 July.)

The order of battle also revealed the membership of the CPP's International Department (ID). The secretary is Sixto Carlos, who is based in Europe. However, Carlos is believed to have resigned from this post following the exposure of the CPP's counterfeiting of U.S. dollars to fund its activities (*News Weekly*, 21 July). The ID's deputy secretary is Nathan Quimpo, also known as "Marty Villalobos," under which name Quimpo is believed in 1986 to have written internal CPP reports criticizing the party's revolutionary strategy and calling for Sandinista-style tactics. Other ID members listed include Luis Jalandoni, Rolando Simbulan, Alexander Aquino, Byron Bocar, Jovy Celestial, Eliseo Tellis, Arturo Balagat, Lydia Orbea Schmidt, George Baviera, Christine Ebreu Carlos (wife of Sixto Carlos), and Ed de la Torre.

To coordinate its affairs, the ID maintains a Home Front Bureau in Manila with at least 52 members. Also identified are the following ID Solidarity Support Groups and numbers of known members: U.S.-Canada (24), Asia-Pacific (11), Japan (5), Hong Kong (6), Australia (6), Saudi Arabia (19), Middle East (1), Western Europe (12).

Domestic affairs. In December 1989, the CPP said that the outcome of the failed coup attempt, due largely to overflights by U.S. jets, "demonstrated that the United States held the ultimate extraterritorial power in a neocolony" (*Manila Times*, 5 January; *FBIS-EAS*, 12 January). An NDF assessment issued two months after the coup attempt said that the crisis offered the NDF "the possibility of a return to center stage politically. This can only be done by sharpening the political alternative it offers.... National democratic organizations have to overcome ideological and organizational obstacles that have limited united front work in the past." (*Balita ng Malayang Pilipinas*, January–February.)

Although the CPP had in the past viewed the military rebels as Fascists, in 1990 it entered into a sporadic dialogue with some rebel factions. The degree of future cooperation, however, is unclear. Most reports of potential cooperation revolved around the Young Officers Union (YOU), a group of AFP officers who graduated from the Philippine Military Academy in the late 1970s and early 1980s and who figured prominently in the December coup attempt. The YOU was reported to have an extremely nationalist foreign policy, a Socialist economic agenda, and a communist-style organization (*LAT*, 11 September). The rebels, at times more feared than the CPP, conducted a campaign of bombings in Manila throughout the year and were widely suspected of being ready to lead another coup attempt in late summer or the fall (*FEER*, 6 September).

On 11 March, NPA chief Romolo Kintanar appealed to the military rebels, saying, "We consider patriotic officers and men and women of the armed forces as potential allies and comrades in our revolutionary struggle ... [and together we should]

coordinate moves against the real enemies of our people, the despotic big landlords, comprador bourgeoisie and bureaucrat capitalists" (Hong Kong, AFP, 11 March; *FBIS-EAS*, 12 March). On 19 June, Sison said that it was possible for the CPP to cooperate with rebels led by "Gringo" Honasan if they adhered to the CPP's objective of total independence for the country (*Diario Filipino*, 20 June; *FBIS-EAS*, 27 June), but CPP cadre and military rebel statements indicated that a full alliance was not imminent. After her capture, CC member Caridad Magpantay-Pascual ruled out a CPP-rebel alliance, accusing the rebels of merely wanting to "grab power" (Quezon City Radio and Television, 20 April; *FBIS-EAS*, 24 April). In May, a YOU spokesman called on the CPP to drop the "foreign ideology of Marxism-Leninism" as prerequisite to joining forces (*National Midweek*, 2 May; *FBIS-EAS*, 11 May). Perhaps reacting to adverse publicity over the alleged alliance, reports in December alleged that the YOU had demoted one of its leaders over the decision to cooperate with the CPP (Manila, DWIZ Radio, 26 December; *FBIS-EAS*, 27 December).

CPP interest in cooperating with military rebel forces in the future may complement the party's apparent decision to intensify urban warfare. In a 1 April interview, Romolo Kintanar said, "It is to be expected that the mass movement and partisan operations will be heightened in urban areas" (*Philippine Daily Inquirer*, 2 April). Kintanar and key members of the Manila-Rizal Regional Commission are said to favor an increased emphasis on urban warfare (*FEER*, 23 August). Documents captured from Manila cadres are said to promote a new political-military strategy that advocates the "concrete integration of political and military struggle," particularly in the Manila area. In May, an issue of the ABB's *Ang Partisano* urged cadres to organize workers and students into "the backbone of insurrection which will be launched in the near future ... [the] ultimate direction of our struggle in the capital region for the actual grabbing of political power" (*Philippine Daily Inquirer*, *FBIS-EAS*, 25 May). It is also speculated that this new emphasis is designed to increase tensions within the AFP, possibly prompting further coup attempts that would further weaken the government (*Manila Bulletin*, 1 June; *FBIS-EAS*, 7 June).

Manifesting this new strategy were frequent assassinations in Manila by the ABB and other NPA units. For example, on 11 June, Col. Saturnino Dumlao, an AFP intelligence officer responsible for the capture of several high-ranking CPP leaders, was killed. Perhaps reflecting their frustration at not being able to stem CPP attacks, on 28 June masked police in Manila mounted a highly publicized terrorist attack on the funeral march of an NPA "sparrow" assassin. Two marchers were killed. (*Manila Bulletin*, *FBIS-EAS*, 29 June.)

More ominous manifestations included open ABB participation in strikes led by the CPP-controlled May First Movement (KMU) labor union federation on 24 October. ABB units were said to be responsible for burning 24 buses during the strikes, but the ABB claimed responsibility for only 5 (Quezon City Radio, 29 October; *FBIS-EAS*, 30 October, 7 November; *Manila Bulletin*, 7 November).

It is feared that the CPP's Political Bureau, apparently still committed to the more balanced "protracted people's war," is now so far underground (to escape detection) that it cannot enforce its directives, a situation that hard-liners are exploiting (*FEER*, 23 August). In a January interview, captured CC member Satur Ocampo listed the errors and weaknesses of the CPP, among them inadequate political training of CPP cadres, "bureaucratism," the laxity of security that has led to the arrest of leading cadres, and "recurrent hysteria in anti-infiltration campaigns." He added that "legal and paralegal training is being undertaken" to correct these errors. (*Manila Times*, *FBIS-EAS*, 12 January.)

In 1990 the CPP expanded its violence against foreigners. On 6 March a 76-year-old American rancher on Masbate Island was killed for not paying "revolutionary taxes" (*WP*, 9 March). On 1 April, Romolo Kintanar threatened U.S. and Japanese citizens in the Philippines, claiming that Japanese aid was being used to mask counterinsurgency (*Philippine Daily Inquirer*, 2 April).

On 13 May, the eve of preliminary talks between Manila and Washington on the future of U.S. military bases, the NPA killed two U.S. airmen in Angeles City, near Clark Air Base (*WP*, 14 May). The next day the NPA issued a statement threatening more violence against Americans, saying, "All our officers and men will carry out, to the last man if necessary, our mission to drive away U.S. aggressors from Philippine soil" (*WP*, 15 May). There were many other threats against Americans, one forcing the head of the U.S. Chamber of Commerce to leave Manila (*FEER*, 23 August). The U.S. government responded by condemning the NPA attacks, issuing hazard pay to U.S. personnel, confin-

ing its military personnel to the bases, and reducing the size of its military exercises in the Philippines (*FEER*, 31 May; *Washington Times*, 4 June).

The CPP on Negros kidnapped Japanese aid worker Fumio Mizuno on 29 May and U.S. Peace Corps worker Timothy Swanson on 13 June. The United States did not learn until 1 July of Swanson's capture (Tokyo, Kyodo, 1 July; *FBIS-EAS*, 2 July), which the AFP said had been planned by the NRPC's leader, former priest Frank Fernandez (*FBIS-EAS*, 10 July). There were reports that the CPP was asking for about $250,000 to release Mizuno, but they did not receive any ransom (*Visayan Daily Star*, 8 June). A CPP court tried and acquitted Mizuno of crimes (*Visayan Daily Star*, 7 July). NRPC conditions for releasing Mizuno and Swanson on 2 August included a 72-hour cease-fire in the release area, CPP statements to be read on local radio, and discussion of their political demands with authorities. The Negros NPA called the Peace Corps a Central Intelligence Agency front (*Philippine Daily Inquirer*, 4 August).

The CPP kidnapping did succeed in reducing foreign confidence in the Aquino government, including a 27 June U.S. announcement that its 261 Peace Corps workers would be withdrawn from the Philippines (*NYT*, 28 June), a move Defense Secretary Fidel Ramos criticized as premature (Manila, Radio Veritas, 28 June; *FBIS-EAS*, 28 June). After Mizuno's release, his sponsor, the Organization for Industrial, Spiritual, and Cultural Advancement, hinted that it might withdraw from the Philippines (*Manila Times*, 4 August). West Germany withdrew a $14.7 million road construction project on the Bondoc Peninsula, a CPP stronghold, following NPA opposition to the project (*NYT*, 15 July). The project was also opposed by the German Green party (*Philippine News and Features*, 1 July). Negros businessmen claimed that the CPP kidnapping deterred much potential foreign investment (*Visayan Daily Star*, 6 July).

Despite a year of considerable CPP activity, the Philippine government claimed significant progress against the party. In January the military claimed to have cut the number of NPA guerrillas from more than 25,000 in 1985 to 19,000 and guerrilla fronts from 75 to 60 (Quezon City, *Malaya*, 21 January; *FBIS-EAS*, 24 January). By December, Aquino said that these had declined to about 17,900 NPA guerrillas and 54 guerrilla fronts (Quezon City Radio, *FBIS-EAS*, 21 December). For 1990, the AFP claimed that it had killed about 1,680 CPP rebels and captured about 30 CPP leaders in the Manila area (Manila, DWIZ Radio, 2 January 1991; *FBIS-EAS*, 2 January 1991). AFP statistics for January through June indicated an average of 8.9 insurgency-related fatalities per day, down from 10.2 in 1989.

The government claimed that since 1987 it had reduced the number of CPP-controlled *barangay*s from about 8,000 (out of some 40,000) to 5,752 (*FBIS-EAS*, 21 December). In April the military claimed that the CPP controlled 227 *barangay*s in the mountainous Cordillera region. Acknowledging that the CPP had three "shadow governments" in Bataan, a military officer claimed that his anti-insurgency efforts were hampered by the "luke-warm attitude of the municipal and barangay officials." (*Manila Bulletin*, *FBIS-EAS*, 17 April). In August the government claimed to have dispersed CPP "shadow governments" in three towns near the provincial boundary of Cagayan and Kalinga-Apayao (*Manila Bulletin*, 29 August; *FBIS-EAS*, 31 August).

Government success in quelling the insurgency was largely a function of the CPP's inability to advance a successful revolutionary strategy, obtain increasing public support, and raise sufficient funds. One indicator of the lack of funds was the sparse availability of CPP publications like *Ang Bayan* and *Liberation*. One government report said that in 1990 the CPP raised about $63 million from all sources, but documents alleged to have been captured with Wilma Austria-Tiamzon showed that in 1987 the CPP generated about $1 million, with nearly 70 percent coming from foreign nongovernment organizations (*Manila Chronicle*, 21 June; *FBIS-EAS*, 22 June).

The government claimed progress against the CPP despite the effects of the December 1989 coup attempt, the threat of additional coup attempts, a major earthquake on 16 July, and a decline of gross national product growth from 5.7 percent in 1989 to about 3.0 percent in 1990. Taking advantage of the government's preoccupation with the December coup attempt, the CPP increased its attacks, including the 5 January NPA assassination of the mayor of Mexico City, Pampanga province (*Manila Bulletin*, 8 January; *FBIS-EAS*, 9 January). AFP statistics show that insurgency-related incidents rose from a daily average of 7.4 in January to 10.3 in February and 10.5 in March.

The CPP's economic warfare continued as well. On 27 March members of a southern Luzon counterpart to the ABB, the Maria Lorena Barros Brigade, shot Froilan Pablo, a senior vice-president of the Nestlé Corporation (*Philippine Daily*, 28 April;

FBIS-EAS, 1 May). On 28 June, NPA rebels raided a Philippine National Oil Company drilling site in Sorsogon province, stealing equipment and medicine (Manila Broadcasting Company, *FBIS-EAS*, 29 June). The military claimed in July that the ABB had targeted at least 89 large firms in the metropolitan Manila area for "revolutionary taxation" (*Manila Chronicle*, 31 July; *FBIS-EAS*, 2 August). In the first quarter of 1990, NPA guerrillas on Negros burned $200,000 worth of farmland and equipment (AFP, *Negros News and Features*, 17 April).

On Negros, although CPP strength continued to decline, the party continued economic sabotage, urban assassinations, political organizing, and attacks on the AFP. On 10 July, NPA guerrillas ambushed and burned sugar plantation owner Ike Ballesteros, a prominent leader of sugar planters organized to oppose the CPP (*Visayan Daily Star*, 11 July). The most notable indicator of decline was the party's decision in early 1990 to collapse its central guerrilla front, one of three on Negros (AFP, *Negros News and Features*, 20 November). The NRPC appeared to be concentrating its forces in northern Negros (ibid., 18 September). The new bishop of Bocolod continued to isolate priests allied with the CPP in his diocese, formerly a major base of support for the CPP in Negros. The secretary of a southern CPP district on Negros, captured in June, said that CPP strength on Negros had declined 30 percent since 1986 as a result of economic development and the popularity of the local government (interview, Bocolod City, 6 August).

On 6 August, NPA guerrillas killed Davao, Mindanao, Police Brig. Gen. Antonio Teves (*Manila Chronicle*, *FBIS-EAS*, 13 August). On 25 October, NPA guerrillas burned two buses in Davao del Sur as a show of support for the Welgang ng Bayan (National Strike) called by the KMU (*Manila Bulletin*, *FBIS-EAS*, 7 November).

The most active period for CPP-government peace efforts came after the 16 July earthquake. On 21 July the CPP authorized territorial commands to issue temporary unilateral cease-fires in earthquake-affected areas (Hong Kong, AFP, 21 July; *FBIS-EAS*, 23 July). Aquino welcomed the unilateral cease-fire but initially rejected CPP appeals that the government follow suit (*Manila Bulletin*, *FBIS-EAS*, 24 July). Under pressure from leftist senators like Wigberto Tanada, however, she announced in late August that she was willing to negotiate cease-fires with the CPP and military rebels (*NYT*, 30 August). Peace activists, led by

Tanada, then engaged the government in a dialogue aimed at promoting discussions between the government and the CPP. Tanada is chairman of BAYAN. (*National Midweek*, 27 June.)

At times there was confusion in the attitudes of both the government and the CPP toward this process. Disregarding the military's reluctance, on 12 September Aquino ordered a halt to military offensives in the three provinces hardest hit by the earthquake (*NYT*, 13 September). On 16 September an ABB spokesman rejected the "piecemeal" cease-fire (Hong Kong, AFP, 16 September; *FBIS-EAS*, 17 September), while CPP chairman Rudolfo Salas affirmed the NDF's intention to participate in the "new peace effort." However, three of the four members of the NDF panel (Satur Ocampo, Carolina Malay Ocampo, and Rudolfo Salas) were in jail (Manila, Radio Veritas, 14 September; *FBIS-EAS*, 21 September).

Jose Sison began by rejecting military suggestions that the NPA lay down its arms and suggesting that the government must first implement "just" agrarian reform, remove foreign powers, and "reorient" the armed forces (Manila Broadcasting Company, *FBIS-EAS*, 18 September), but he soon offered to lead peace negotiations if the government would return his passport and ensure his safe passage to the Philippines (Quezon City, ABSKBN Broadcasting, 20 September; *FBIS-EAS*, 21 September). On 24 September, Romolo Kintanar declared an end to the NPA's unilateral cease-fire in the earthquake-affected areas, saying, "In the face of the government's insincerity and high-handedness, the NPA has no other recourse but to intensify military operations" (Hong Kong, AFP, 24 September; *FBIS-EAS*, 24 September).

In mid-October the NDF issued a nine-point "peace agenda," which included removal of the U.S. military bases and troops by 1991; abandoning the economic program drawn up by the government and the International Monetary Fund; implementation of "genuine agrarian reform"; protection of human rights and the reorientation of the military; weeding out corruption in the government; upholding self-determination and the grant of genuine autonomy to cultural communities; ending destruction of the environment; suspending debt service payments for the next five years and selectively repudiating foreign loans; and adjusting the wages of private sector workers, government employees, and teachers. Secretary Ramos rejected this agenda. (*Manila Bulletin*, 16 October; *FBIS-EAS*, 17 October.)

In early February, Aquino hinted that the CPP could be legalized if it renounced the use of violence (Quezon City Radio, *FBIS-EAS*, 13 February). Former President Diosdado Macapagal, who in October called for the legalization of the CPP (*Manila Chronicle*, 19 October), led discussions of that possibility with the Aquino government. However, on 16 December that dialogue was broken off by the government due to the CPP's continued attacks and its refusal to accept democracy (*FBIS-EAS*, 18 December).

The CPP marked its 22d anniversary by proposing the following tasks to advance its struggle: "completely expose and isolate the U.S.-backed Aquino regime; expose the U.S. role in the severe economic crisis; advance mass protest actions such as strikes; organize and mobilize the broadest united front; intensify urban guerrilla warfare in urban centers and tactical offensives in the countryside." The CPP was reported to say that it would "play a secondary role in the next military attempt to unseat President Corazon Aquino." (Tokyo, Kyodo, 26 December; *FBIS-EAS*, 26 December.)

Auxiliary and front organizations. From 13 to 21 July, the NDF held the first national congress since its founding in 1973, electing CC member Antonio Zumel as chairman, Frank Fernandez as general secretary, and Luis Jalandoni, head of the NDF office in Europe, as vice-chairman for international affairs.

Several NDF statements highlighted the main CPP political theme of 1990: removal of the U.S. military bases. In an early May interview, Luis Jalandoni said that, if the Aquino government closes the bases in 1991, "it can immediately count on the support of several forces, including the NDF. We will declare a unilateral cease-fire" (*Manila Chronicle*, 6 May; *FBIS-EAS*, 8 May). On the eve of the May talks on the future of the bases, the NDF called the talks "one of the biggest charades ever" and urged Filipinos to "vigorously resist the extension of the bases treaty" and use the talks to serve notice of termination of the bases agreement (Hong Kong, AFP, 13 May; *FBIS-EAS*, 14 May). In an early June interview, Jalandoni called the May killing of U.S. servicemen by the NPA the "regrettable consequence of an unjust and aggressive policy on the part of the U.S." (*Manila Chronicle*, *FBIS-EAS*, 6 June). A press report alleged that CC member Jose de Vera visited Libya for advice on attacking U.S. facilities (*Manila Bulletin*, *FBIS-EAS*, 3 May).

In March several CPP fronts led a 92-km protest walk against the bases. CPP fronts involved included the Alliance of Concerned Teachers—Central Luzon (ACT-CL), BAYAN, the League of Filipino Students—Central Luzon (LFS-CL), the Peasant Movement of the Philippines (KMP), and the KMU. (*FBIS-EAS*, 12 March.) CPP fronts like the KMU and the LFS led several antibases demonstrations throughout the year (Manila Broadcasting Company, 26 January, 14 May, 30 November; *Philippine Daily*, 2 May; *Manila Chronicle*, 3 May; *FBIS-EAS*, 26 January, 2, 3, 14 May, 30 November).

Despite the government's attempts to marginalize the May First Movement (KMU) trade union federation, in 1990 it appeared to flourish. The KMU now claims to have about three hundred member unions with a total membership of about 100,000. The KMU's staying power in the Manila area is attributed to its willingness to employ the NPA to fight antiunion "goons" hired by companies. The CPP's emphasis on union work is said to come at the expense of cultivating support among students and professionals, which accounts for the CPP's loss of popularity in those groups. (*FEER*, 23 August.)

On 30 October the military reacted to the KMU's leading role in the 24 October strike by arresting KMU chairman Crispin Beltran (Manila Broadcasting Company, *FBIS-EAS*, 1 November). At a Senate hearing in late November, Vice-Chief of Staff Rudolfo Biazon asked unsuccessfully for a law declaring the KMU illegal (Manila Broadcasting Company, 29 November; *FBIS-EAS*, 30 November).

In late October military officials said that they were preparing to file charges against the National Federation of Sugar Workers (NFSW), one of the largest KMU affiliates, for associating with the CPP (AFP, *Negros News and Features*, 30 October). In early November, about seven hundred former CPP rebels staged a protest against the NFSW, calling the union a CPP front and demanding the return of union dues (ibid., 6 November). The NFSW, which claims about 86,000 members on Negros, Leyte, Cebu, and Panay, has gained some political ground on the issue of sugar plantations' refusal to pay the minimum wage (*FEER*, 25 January).

In May, KMP chairman Jaime Tadeo was jailed after being convicted of embezzling government funds. The KMU and the Ecumenical Forum for Church Response protested Tadeo's plight. (Manila Broadcasting Company, 10 May; *FBIS-EAS*, 11 May; *National Midweek*, 18 July.) In June the KMP refused to join Kabisig, an Aquino-led coalition of nongovernment development organizations designed to accelerate rural development (*Manila Chronicle*, 14 June; *FBIS-EAS*, 18 June).

Several CPP fronts and civil libertarians protested a 25 July Supreme Court ruling that allowed "warrantless arrest" of suspected subversives. Speakers at an 8 August rally at the Supreme Court denounced the ruling as a "return to Marcos style repression." The rally included GABRIELA, SELDA, the National Movement for Civil Liberties, the Medical Action Group, the Philippine Alliance of Human Rights Advocates (PAHRA), and Task Force Detainees (TFD). (*Philippine Human Rights Update*, 15 July.)

In late October, TFD charged that between January 1989 and September 1990 there were 4,408 political detentions, of which 4,149 were illegal (*Manila Chronicle*, 29 October; *FBIS-EAS*, 30 October). The U.S. State Department's annual report on human rights in the Philippines said for the first time that TFD has a "close association" with the CPP.

A captured CPP document titled "Political Orientation of the Philippine Human Rights Movement under the U.S.-Aquino Regime" offered insights into the CPP's attitude toward the human rights issue: "The principal task of the Philippine human rights movement is to help expose, oppose and isolate the U.S.-Aquino regime. . . . Whenever and wherever possible, it should help in aggravating and exploiting splits among the reactionaries to advance the revolution."

International affairs. As communist regimes fell in Eastern Europe and Nicaragua in late 1989 and early 1990, the CPP sought to justify its continued revolution by differentiating itself from the "failed" revolutions. According to Sison, "revolutionary forces in the Philippines . . . look down with contempt on those forces of capitalism in Eastern Europe" (*Katipunan*, July–August). In early January, captured CC member Satur Ocampo told an interviewer that the ruling parties in Eastern Europe had failed to sustain their "leading role in revolutionizing their societies." Ocampo praised Gorbachev, saying his "socialism with a human face" will preserve socialism from Western hegemony. (*Manila Times*, 7 January; *FBIS-EAS*, 12 January.) In its December 1989 anniversary political assessment, however, the CPP Central Committee criticized Gorbachev's détente policy, which "proposes that super rivals can become super partners," and blamed him for "weakening . . . the anti-imperialist and proletarian bond of the Warsaw Pact countries." Attributing the fall of communist regimes to capitalist excess, the CPP was determined to learn from their mistakes (ibid.). One captured CPP official on Negros said that the decline of international communism depressed party intellectual circles but had little impact on the party's reputation in the countryside (interview, Bacolod City, 6 August). The CPP praised the Soviet withdrawal from Afghanistan and the Vietnamese withdrawal from Cambodia (*Manila Times*, 5 January; *FBIS-EAS*, 12 January).

During a February visit to Manila, Soviet Foreign Ministry spokesman Gennadii Gerasimov urged the United States to withdraw from Philippine military bases (*Manila Chronicle*, 22 February; *FBIS-EAS*, 23 February). After an April visit to Moscow, Vice-President Salvador Laurel said he had been assured that the Soviets no longer extend assistance to the CPP and the NPA (*Manila Bulletin*, *FBIS-EAS*, 23 April).

In midyear, Foreign Minister Manglapus disclosed that he had contacted North Korean officials seeking Pyongyang's pledge of nonsupport to the NPA (*Manila Bulletin*, *FBIS-EAS*, 13 June). A congressional delegation to Pyongyang reported that North Korea was willing to consider formal diplomatic ties and cut its contacts with the insurgents (Hong Kong, AFP, 16 June; *FBIS-EAS*, 18 June).

On 11 February, the CPP Central Committee congratulated Nelson Mandela and the African National Congress, saying that they are "justified to conduct all forms of revolutionary struggle to achieve their freedom" (*Balita ng Malayang Pilipinas*, January–February).

The CPP's 15-year campaign for support in Europe received embarrassing setbacks in 1990. In a February speech before the U.N. Commission on Human Rights, Foreign Secretary Manglapus said that "a network" in Western Europe and North America "has succeeded in raising millions of dollars for remittance to the Philippine Maoist rebels. . . . The money comes from those . . . unwitting institutions which often go to the extent of resorting to theology in order to justify their naivete." (Hong Kong, AFP, 6 February; *FBIS-EAS*, 6 February.)

His charges were confirmed by two scandals that rocked the CPP's European network. On 22 February, Swiss authorities arrested Dutch citizen Dolf Haustvast when he tried to deposit about US$1.5

million in $100 bills, 10 percent of which were counterfeit (*News Weekly*, 21 July). Haustvast, who said he obtained the money in Belgrade, is the husband of Hanneke Haustvast-Haaksma, founder of the Philippine Group–Netherlands, a secretive, pro-CPP solidarity group. Swiss authorities said they were convinced the money, once laundered, was meant for the CPP (*Bangkok Post*, 22 July). Documents relating to the counterfeiting scheme are said to have been captured along with CC member Cabardo (*Philippine Daily Globe*, *FBIS-EAS*, 27 June). Sison denied any NDF involvement in Haustvast's activities (*Manila Bulletin*, *FBIS-EAS*, 2 May).

The second scandal to emerge caused a public furor in the Netherlands, where the government had suppressed an internal report stating that between 1982 and 1990 some $1.9 million in Dutch government funding for the Interchurch Coordination Commission for Development Projects (ICCO), which administers development projects in the Philippines, had been given to the KMU. The report also said that the CPP would receive up to 20 percent of the money given to the KMU. The network that helped funnel Dutch government aid to the CPP included two pro-CPP employees in the Dutch foreign aid office, who assured their director that money was not going to the CPP. (*Manila Chronicle*, 21 June; *FBIS-EAS*, 2 May, 25 June.) One reported outcome of the scandals was the resignation of Sixto Carlos as ID leader due to his failure to handle CPP illegal activities in Europe. He was also reported to have divorced his wife Christine Ebro and married a Dutch citizen to protect his status abroad. (Manila Broadcasting Company, 15 June; *FBIS-EAS*, 18 June.)

The Dutch Ministry of Foreign Affairs also reported that a secretive radical Dutch group, X min Y, gives between $25,000 and $50,000 annually to the NDF (*FBIS-EAS*, 25 June). On 5 September, X min Y held a Philippines issues coordination meeting in the offices of the Dutch Philippine Group (FGN) in Utrecht. The meeting included the president of the FGN; members of the Transnational Institute, an affiliate of the Washington, D.C.–based Institute for Policy Studies; and Ed de la Torre. He is the founder of the CPP front Christians for National Liberation and now works for the Catholic Institute for International Relations in England. Current Dutch development minister Jan Pronk helped found X min Y.

Pro-CPP activities appeared to increase in Belgium, where the Philippine International Center for Human Rights (PICHR) was founded in June. It is housed in the building of the National Center for Development Aid (NCOS), Belgium's largest church-based development aid organization. Among PICHR's sponsors are Task Force Detainees and the Protestant Lawyers' League of the Philippines. In 1990, NCOS and the Belgian Labor party cosponsored several Philippine projects, including a grant of about $90,000 to the KMP. KCOS also provided about $10,000 to the NFSW and about $20,000 to TFD. Possible reasons for increased NDF activity in Belgium include its growing importance as a center for commerce and finance after 1992 and the greater importance of the European Parliament.

A document captured in an April raid on a Manila safe house proposed an ASPAC NLM Dialogue, a conference of national liberation movements to be sponsored by the ID Asia-Pacific Committee in July 1990. Intended guests included members of the NDF, New Caledonia's Front de Libération Nationale Kanake et Socialiste, the Fiji Labor party, Indonesia's Partai Komunis Indonesia, the OPM of Papua New Guinea, and South Korea's National Democratic Alliance. Proposed areas of cooperation listed by the document include "cooperation in solidarity work in the various countries; Regular consultation/caucus; Joint lobby at the Non Aligned Movement and other international bodies."

Also captured in the safe house raid was a document titled "Tactical Program for the Party in North America for 1990," which set forth the goals of raising the theoretical level of the entire North American party organization and consolidating the party in North America. Among the specific tasks enumerated in the document are building and strengthening alliances with progressive groups or individuals and systematically and aggressively disseminating NDF materials and publications. The document also called for strict collection of monthly party dues of 3.5 percent of take-home pay.

Another document, "Some Questions on the Overseas Mass Movement in the U.S.," assessed the CPP network in the United States, noting that "our open organizations are quite small. . . . Our influence has been quite limited. . . . The NDF has no open projection in the U.S. until now." The leading pro-CPP solidarity group in the United States, the Alliance for Philippine Concerns (APC), was involved in several events in September to highlight the last remaining year of the U.S.-Philippine Military Bases Agreement. On 16 Sep-

tember, the APC affiliate Washington Forum organized a Run/Walk for a Bases-Free Philippines. In San Francisco on 17 September, a meeting of the Coalition for Peace and Sovereignty in Asia-Pacific was held to discuss why the Philippine bases should be closed. This coalition includes the APC, the Philippine Resource Center, and the Young Koreans' United Church Network on the Philippines. (*W Forum*, October–November.)

The Washington, D.C.–based Church Coalition for Human Rights in the Philippines (CCHRP) asked supporters to write letters requesting the release of Alfredo Simbulan, a member of the NPA General Command captured on 3 August (*Urgent Action Alert*, 6 August). In July the CCHRP named Rev. Kathryn Johnson as its new director (*Philippine Witness*, no. 32). However, in May the International Affairs Committee of the Service Employees' International Union criticized the KMU's "support of violence by the New People's Army" (*W Forum*, October–November).

PKP. *Leadership.* No major changes were reported. Jesus Lava, 78, returned to the Philippines after nineteen years of self-exile in Czechoslovakia as consultant to the *World Marxist Review*. He is reported to be in good health.

Domestic affairs. Regarding the issue of a possible CPP-PKP merger, Lava stated during a Manila roundtable, "It is no secret that the NDF International Department head Luis Jalandoni and myself have been having talks." The CPP and the PKP have no disagreement over a political program, but they failed to unite on the "forms of struggle." Lava further stated, "We sincerely believe that legal struggle is the correct form of struggle," but added that he plans to work for national unity and reconciliation among all "patriotic forces who may wish to fight against U.S. imperialism." (*Philippine Daily*, 19 June; *FBIS-EAS*, 21 June.)

In mid-July, Philippine constabulary units in Pampanga province killed two leaders of the People's Liberation Army (HMB), which in recent years has turned to criminal activities. The two dead leaders were said to have also been targeted by the NPA because crimes committed by the HMB had been blamed on the NPA. (*Diario Filipino, FBIS-EAS*, 18 July.)

International affairs. At the aforementioned forum, Lava criticized Soviet and Eastern European leaders who made Joseph Stalin their "whipping boy," saying, "Stalin had his good points and evaluation of his record should be even handed." During Gennadii Gerasimov's visit to Manila, responding to the question of whether Philippine Communists were worried about Soviet reforms, he said, "The General Secretary of the Communist Party of the Philippines-PKP whom I met at a reception, didn't raise the subject" (*Manila Chronicle*, 22 February; *FBIS-EAS*, 23 February).

Richard D. Fisher, Jr.
Asian Studies Center, Heritage Foundation

South Pacific Islands

Populations. Commonwealth of the Northern Mariana Islands: 22,719; Cook Islands: 18,187; Federated States of Micronesia: 104,937; Fiji: 759,567; French Polynesia: 190,181; Kiribati: 70,012; Nauru: 9,202; New Caledonia: 153,215; Papua New Guinea: 3,822,875; Republic of the Marshall Islands: 43,417; Solomon Islands: 335,082; Tonga: 101,313; Trust Territory of the Pacific Islands (Republic of Palau): 14,310; Tuvalu: 9,136; Vanuatu: 165,006; Wallis and Futuna: 14,910; Western Samoa: 186,031 (*World Fact Book*)

Regional Overview. The year 1990 saw the continued undermining of the South Pacific governments' capacity to maintain political stability. This has led in many cases to formal reviews of, or demands for change to, existing political structures. The independent states of the region for the most part have Westminster-style political systems, with varying levels of participation. Although some systems are becoming less open (Fiji, Vanuatu), others are becoming more pluralist in outlook (Western Samoa, Tonga). Everywhere in the region there is disquiet about the ability of governments to meet popular demands for improvements in living standards.

The failure of governments to meet these demands creates the potential for instability in the region, most notably in Papua New Guinea, where one can chart the decay of Port Moresby's capacity to guide political and economic development. A view is growing in the region that the 1990s will be the crucial test of the islands' capacity to peacefully manage change.

One should not overestimate the opportunity for the development of revolutionary or communist ideologies. The islands' leadership remains pro-Western, religious, and conservative. The region's tradition of managing peaceful transitions of government has seldom been broken and is unmatched in the rest of the developing world. Island political parties tend to lack ideological conviction, revolving instead around the ability of prominent people to attact supporters.

There is no communist party in the South Pacific. Few politicians would find it beneficial to claim such an affiliation. But socialism influences the union movement, which has grown in significance this year in Papua New Guinea and Fiji and finds a natural home with supporters of the Nuclear Free and Independent Pacific (NFIP) movement, the champion of the anticolonial and antinuclear cause. (Michael Easson, "Labor and the Left in the Pacific," in Dennis L. Bark and Owen Harries, *The Red Orchestra: The Case of the Southwest Pacific* [Stanford: Hoover Institution Press, 1989]; *Islands Business*, August.)

The NFIP movement is a loose coalition of trade unions, church groups, journalists, academics, and other activists. In November their sixth conference was held in New Zealand, with 154 delegates from some 26 Asian and Pacific nations attending. The conference produced the usual raft of motions condemning the U.S. presence in Palau and supporting independence movements in New Caledonia, East Timor, and West Papua (Irian Jaya). The meeting split over supporting indigenous movements, with some delegates signing a declaration saying that justice, not "indigenousness of ethnicity," should be the NFIP priority. Fiji's coup leaders are clearly not progressive enough for some in the movement. Some NFIP members are also concerned that a Maori nationalist group has hijacked the movement's agenda and would like to see their headquarters moved. The agenda was not the only hijack victim; money has unaccountably been disappearing from the NFIP's Auckland bank account. (*Pacific Islands Monthly*, December.)

Organizations associated with the NFIP movement, such as the World Council of Churches, frequently make comments to the media on South Pacific political issues and undertake training programs and small aid projects in the islands. Australian and New Zealand unions are particularly active in island unions, and several organizations compete for membership and regional influence. For example, the New Caledonian Union des Syndicats des Travailleurs Kanaks et Exploités (USTKE, United Union of Kanak and Exploited Workers) is affiliated with the World Federation of Trade Unions (WFTU), a communist front organization.

With the exception of opening their embassy in Papua New Guinea, there was little Soviet activity in the region in 1990. In December 1989, Australian foreign minister Evans stated that "we should expect continued manifestations . . . of Soviet attempts to gain influence and supporters and to erode the strong pro-western bias of the region" (Gareth Evans, *Australia's Regional Security: Ministerial Statement* [Canberra: Government Printer, 1989]). But the USSR's domestic problems suggest that the South Pacific may receive even less attention in the future.

One surprising feature of Soviet interest in the region is the number of Soviet academics with South Pacific research interests—around 40 to 50, one commentator estimates—compared with fewer than a dozen South Pacific specialists in the United States (John Dorrance, *The Soviet Union and Oceania* [report produced for the State Department, 9 July]).

One manifestation of Soviet regional activity concerned Moscow's shortwave Radio Peace and Progress, which began broadcasting to Latin America on the same frequency that Radio New Zealand used for the South Pacific. New Zealand's weaker transmitter was drowned out, and the islands were left listening to Spanish spoken with a Russian accent. The problem had apparently been rectified by November, by which time the New Zealand service looked to be in severe financial difficulty. (*New Zealand Herald*, 10 May; *Pacific Islands Monthly*, November.)

If Soviet interest in the region is declining, the People's Republic of China has become much more active, principally in competing with Taiwan for diplomatic recognition. The island leaders soon found that money and development projects could be squeezed out of one, and sometimes both, of the Chinas. But there are limits to such manipulation. Beijing has indicated its displeasure with the South Pacific Forum's decision to investigate ways of involving Taiwan in forum activities (Radio Australia,

1 August). As the larger of the two aid donors, Beijing has some regional weight with which to press its claims.

Papua New Guinea. Papua New Guinea (PNG) faced its worst-ever political crisis in 1990 with a debilitating counterinsurgency war on Bougainville Island. More than 150 lives have been lost in combat operations, and other deaths have resulted from human rights violations committed by government and rebel forces. Since March, the Bougainville Revolutionary Army (BRA, referred to as the Bougainville Liberation Army in *YICA*, 1990), has been in control of the island.

On 11 January, Prime Minister Rabbie Namaliu announced that the Papua New Guinea Defence Force (PNGDF) was launching "Operation Footloose" to wipe out the BRA. Despite claiming to have captured the BRA headquarters, the PNGDF clearly underestimated the BRA's strength and level of popular support. The BRA continued to attack workers at the giant Panguna copper mine, destroying the police headquarters there on 15 January. BRA attacks in the north and south of the island demonstrated that security forces had control only of the main towns of Arawa and Kieta. (*Australian Financial Review*, 12 January; *Islands Business*, February.) Bougainville Copper Limited (BCL), the owners of Panguna, announced in early February the withdrawal of all personnel from the mine and the evacuation of non-Bougainvillians to the PNG mainland. Information later revealed showed that the Australian Operational Deployment Force was within hours of being sent to evacuate expatriate nationals (*Canberra Times*, 12 February; *Pacific Islands Monthly*, March).

A crucial factor in strengthening local support for the BRA was the extent of human rights violations committed by the security forces against Bougainville islanders. A November Amnesty International report gave accounts of nineteen extrajudicial executions and more than 50 cases of torture or ill-treatment by the security forces in late 1989 and early 1990. More worrying still was the random destruction of villages and property. In the Kieta district around the mine alone, more than 1,600 houses were burnt down by security forces. (Interviews with BCL sources, Amnesty International, *Papua New Guinea: Human Rights Violations on Bougainville, 1989–1990* [London, November].)

A cease-fire was negotiated in early March; on Port Moresby's instruction security forces were withdrawn from the island pending negotiations, against the advice of the controller of the Bougainville emergency, Police Commissioner Paul Tohian. Back in the capital on 15 March, a drunk Tohian went on radio calling on the police to stage a coup d'état. Some two hundred police surrounded Parliament, but the coup attempt fizzled out, with the PNGDF remaining loyal to the government. (*Washington-Pacific Report*, 15 March; *Pacific Islands Monthly*, April.)

From April to July the government engaged in sporadic talks with the rebels to arrange a venue for negotiations. A blockade of the island was mounted, and the BRA made a declaration of independence on 17 May. Conditions on the island worsened with the absence of medical supplies and the lawless and often brutal behaviour of BRA members toward those suspected of being sympathetic to Port Moresby. (Hong Kong, AFP, 4 May; *FBIS-EAS*, 4 May; *Pacific Islands Monthly*, June.)

Eventually talks were held on the New Zealand Navy vessel *Endeavour*. In early August it was agreed that services essential to the island would be resumed in return for a deferral of claims to independence. In early September, PNGDF forces attempted to land supplies at Kieta but were not allowed to disembark. The BRA maintained that the PNGDF presence violated the *Endeavour* agreements. (*Islands Business*, September; *Time Magazine*, 17 September; Radio Australia, 4, 20 September.)

By late September, Port Moresby was again contemplating a military solution. PNGDF troops landed on Buka Island, off the northern Bougainville coast. Some 23 lives were lost in fighting that lasted until early October. Around four hundred troops are now stationed on Buka. (Radio Australia, 3, 4, 19, 21 October.)

On 28 December, BRA supreme commander Francis Ona rejected further talks with Port Moresby, stressing that Bougainville had been independent since May. A request from the nongovernmental Australian Council for Overseas Aid that medical supplies and doctors be sent to Bougainville was rejected by Port Moresby on 2 January 1991. (Australian Associated Press Wire Service, 2 January 1991.)

There is no solution in sight to the Bougainville situation, which undermines Port Moresby's capacity to govern. In January, Namaliu announced severe spending cuts following the loss of income from Panguna. At the same time he was compelled to spend more on the military, announcing plans to

boost the size of the army by 60 percent, to around 5,200, over five years. Australia offered to help begin the process by providing funds to train an additional 450 troops and by giving extra aid for police training. In September it was announced that PNG and Australia would jointly conduct a review of the role and capabilities of the PNGDF. (*Sydney Morning Herald*, 11 January; Department of Foreign Affairs and Trade [Canberra], *Monthly Record*, January; *Australian Financial Review*, 26 January; *Australian*, 7 September.) Skeptics might say that the measure came too late to be of any use, but lack of discipline within the PNGDF is a problem that needs to be addressed before it threatens national stability.

On the other side of PNG, the border with Indonesia's Irian Jaya province saw a growth in activity of the Organisasi Papua Merdeka (OPM, Free Papua Movement), which is demanding independence from Indonesia. Several times during the year members of the Indonesian armed forces crossed illegally into PNG in hot pursuit of OPM guerrillas. Such border crossings have caused problems in the bilateral relationship in the past but may be alleviated by the signing of an agreement in early November to establish a Joint Irian Jayan Border Security Committee. Prospects of mounting joint patrols, maintaining joint border posts, and allowing Indonesian hot pursuit into PNG now seem more likely. (Radio Australia, 5 November; Melbourne Overseas Service, 26 July; Hong Kong, AFP, 10 August; *FBIS-EAS*, 26 July, 10 August.)

In domestic politics, the political opposition mounted two no-confidence motions against the Namaliu government, one in July that was withdrawn because of lack of support and one in early November that was not voted on because Namaliu adjourned Parliament for eight months. The adjournment may have saved the government, but it killed the prospects of passing drafted legislation designed to protect the executive from influence brokering on the floor of Parliament. (*Islands Business*, August, December; *Pacific Islands Monthly*, August, December.) PNG politics continues to be dominated less by ideology than by personality. In September, John Ramoi resigned from Parliament citing his failure to attract support for his Socialist party. A contributing factor may have been an investigation into Ramoi's alleged misuse of public money (Radio Australia, 24 September).

In sum, PNG continues to suffer from a "crisis of ungovernability." The level of crime in urban centers, the degree of violence in society, the lack of discipline in the armed forces, and Parliament's incapacity to deal with these problems all raise doubts about the country's future political stability.

Foreign relations. PNG continued to diversify its overseas contacts, emphasizing ties with Southeast Asia. In March the Soviet Union opened its first resident embassy in the insular Pacific. It is understood that the USSR requested diplomatic positions for 28 people but was given accreditation for only 15. In May the foreign minister, Sir Michael Somare, said that an embassy would open in Moscow by the end of the year, but this has not yet happened. (*PACNEWS*, 20 March; Radio Australia, 29 May.)

In June the two countries signed a fishing agreement granting port access for Soviet fishing and research vessels and providing training for PNG nationals at Soviet fishery research centers. The agreement led to the sacking of Allan Ebu, fisheries and resources minister, who claimed that his department was not keen on the deal, that no studies had been conducted into its dollar value, and that a deal with South Korea would be much more beneficial. (Radio Australia, 6 June; *Pacific Islands Monthly*, October.) In September a PNG Parliamentary delegation visited Moscow and conducted talks with the chairman of the Supreme Soviet, A. I. Luk'ianov (*Izvestiia*, 2, 9, 13 September; *FBIS-SOV*, 5, 12, 14 September).

In April, the People's Republic of China (PRC) granted A$4.5 million toward building a sports stadium (Radio Australia, 1 May). Some A$11 million had already been handed over, and more than a hundred Chinese construction workers are at the project site. In September, PRC/PNG relations soured with the visit to Port Moresby of Frederick Chien, the Taiwanese foreign minister, to attend independence anniversary celebrations. His presence at one function prompted the walkout of PRC ambassador Zhao Wei. The PRC protested that countries recognizing Beijing should not have formal or informal links with Taiwan. Foreign Minister Somare demanded an apology from Zhao Wei, saying that "as the Founding Father of the nation, I have every right to invite who I want" to the independence celebrations. Chien's visit was the first of a Taiwanese foreign minister to a country that recognizes the PRC. Taiwan opened a representative office in Port Moresby in February. (Radio Australia, 13, 17–18 September; *Melbourne Age*, 19 September.)

Relations with the PRC appeared to have been smoothed over by December, when a memorandum of understanding on economic and trade cooperation was signed in Beijing (Radio Australia, 4 December).

Fiji. The adoption on 25 July of Fiji's new constitution culminates a process that began with the coup d'état of May 1987. As was expected, Fiji now has a constitution that enshrines the political dominance of ethnic Fijians at the expense of the Indo-Fijian population.

The constitution provides for a 70-seat House of Representatives, with ethnic Fijians holding 37 seats, Indo-Fijians, 27 seats, Rotumans, 1 seat, and General Electors (people of "mixed race"), 5 seats. The Great Council of Chiefs (GCC) will select a 34-member senate that will include 24 ethnic Fijians and 1 Rotuman. The GCC will also appoint a president, who in turn will appoint a Fijian prime minister from the House of Representatives. The constitution also reserves half the positions in the judiciary, the Legal Services Commission, public service, and the Political Services Commission for ethnic Fijians. (*Constitution of the Sovereign Democratic Republic of Fiji, 25 July 1990* [Suva: Government Printer].) A related recasting of electoral boundaries gives emphasis to rural areas, reducing the number of urban seats, which in 1987 had a greater propensity to vote for the Labor party.

Although biased against the Indian community, the constitution could have been much worse. Unlike earlier drafts, the final document keeps the government and the Fiji Military Forces (FMF) separate by not giving the FMF commander a cabinet seat. Separation of powers is guaranteed, as is a listing of personal rights and freedoms. More important, there is no proscription of political parties. Although there will always be a majority of ethnic Fijians in Parliament, the constitution does not specify the party to which they must belong. The Labor party can still run in elections but will have to make policy changes to woo the rural ethnic Fijian vote.

On balance, the constitution offers a positive, though flawed, return to constitutionalism and lays the foundation for elections in 1991. Opponents of the constitution should remember that the alternative is military rule, not a return to precoup days.

India has mounted strident opposition to the constitution, whereas Australia and New Zealand have expressed more muted concern. Most important for Fiji, the South Pacific Forum states have expressed satisfaction with the document (Melbourne Overseas Service, *FBIS-EAS*, 3 August). The strongest overseas opposition to the interim government, led by Ratu Sir Kamisese Mara, comes from the Australian and New Zealand union movement, their NFIP colleagues, and the various communities of "émigré" Fijians associated with the deposed Labor party/National Federation Party (NFP) coalition. (*Islands Business*, August.) The Australian Labor Party (ALP)—as distinct from the Labor government—has developed links with the Labor/NFP coalition. In November a grant of some A$5,000 and a promise of A$10,000 more was given by the ALP national secretariat to establish a Labor/NFP office. This embarrassed an Australian government trying to follow a less partisan policy (Parliamentary Debates, *Senate*, 27 November). Curiously, a September meeting of the World Council of Churches in Geneva urged acceptance of the constitution (Radio Australia, 21 September), but the Pacific Council of Churches, a founder of the NFIP movement, criticized the constitution, saying that it contained basic violations of human rights (John Whitehall, "The Nuclear Free and Independent Pacific Movement," in Bark and Harries, *Red Orchestra*; Radio Australia, 27 July).

Domestically, the Labor/NFP coalition rejected the constitution and said that they would boycott elections held under it (*Islands Business*, August). But since July the coalition has begun to fragment. Its November annual meeting delayed a boycott decision until July 1991. Already, a splinter group from the Indian-dominated NFP has said that it will contest all 27 Indian seats. Fijian Muslims may try a power grab for the Indian seats if the predominantly Hindu NFP abstains. (*Pacific Report*, 6 December.)

FMF major general Sitiven Rabuka and two colonels relinquished cabinet positions in the interim government on 5 January. This was seen as a victory for Ratu Mara's attempts to return Fiji to a civilian administration. But Rabuka has not hesitated to remind Fiji that the FMF continues to watch the political situation. In May Rabuka warned against the power of the trade union movement and suggested that the FMF could be used to break a threatening strike of sugarcane harvesters (Radio Australia, 15 June). As the constitution was being released, Rabuka made public his intention to resign from the military and contest the next election. This worried some in Australia and New Zealand who would prefer to deal with a Fijian leader not tainted by association with the coups.

There were other worrying developments in the behavior of the FMF. Rabuka was reluctant to accept cuts in defense spending and made the comment that he would only accept cuts ordered by an elected government. But a compromise had been reached by year's end. (Hong Kong, AFP, 18 November; *FBIS-EAS*, 19 November; *Pacific Report*, 22 November; Radio Australia, 31 October.) Throughout the year there were reports of lawless and violent behavior on the part of FMF soldiers, culminating with the admission that five soldiers had beaten an Indian academic opposed to the constitution. Charged with abducting and torturing the academic, the soldiers were given suspended sentences (Radio Australia, 22 November; *Melbourne Age*, 8 November).

With the news that an internal intelligence organization was being established and that a South Pacific news service was being expelled from Fiji in May, there are legitimate concerns that Fiji is slipping into an authoritarianism not associated with the earlier, largely peaceful coups. The return to constitutionalism may have come too late to stop this process. (Hong Kong, AFP, 7 May, 26 September; *FBIS-EAS*, 8 May; 28 September.)

Foreign relations. Fiji politicians spent 1990 cultivating ties with countries able to replace some of the aid, trade, and military contacts enjoyed in precoup times with Australia and New Zealand. France and Malaysia have supported the interim government and have developed military links that compensate in part for the loss of training with Canberra and Wellington.

The year saw a warming of relations with the PRC, although Fiji tried also to maintain a diplomatic balancing act with Taiwan. In January, Taiwan agreed to loan Fiji US$2 million to buy equipment for the FMF (*Washington-Pacific Report*, 1 February).

Prominent figures in the interim government visited both China and Taiwan. In April, Ratu Mara led a delegation to a number of Asian states including the PRC and Taiwan. In May, President Ganilau went to Taiwan for the inauguration of President Lee Teng-hui. In October, Apisai Tora, the minister for infrastructure and public utilities, visited China. (Radio Australia, 7 April; *New Zealand Herald*, 17 May; Hong Kong, AFP, 3 October; *FBIS-EAS*, 3 October.) On his visit Mara met, among others, President Yang Shangkun, Premier Li Peng, and General Secretary Jiang Zemin. Fiji was granted a F$10-million interest-free loan for constructing a convention center in Suva. (Chengchu Sichuan Provincial Service, 18 April; *FBIS-CHI*, 23 April; Radio Australia, 19, 20 April.)

The most significant visit to China was made by Major General Rabuka in April and May, his first overseas trip since the May 1987 coup. The nine-day visit, financed by the Chinese government, reportedly involved discussions on purchasing equipment and receiving military training. Rabuka met Yang Shangkun as well as the chief of staff of the armed forces, General Chi Haotian, and the defense minister, General Qin Jiwei. (Radio Australia, 22, 30 April; 1, 3 May.) Yang assured Rabuka of PRC support and expressed his hope that military ties between the two countries would be strengthened.

While the general was in China, three Taiwanese warships arrived at Suva for a goodwill visit. It is a measure of the seriousness with which the PRC treats Fiji that no official protest was issued. (Radio Australia, 4 May; *FEER*, 31 May.)

On 1 June, the Chinese president made a one-day official visit to Fiji, stopping over after a five-nation tour of Latin America. Yang Shangkun expressed his hope for boosting relations with Fiji through further high-level contacts. He pledged support for the South Pacific Nuclear-Free Zone, preservation of marine resources, and maintenance of regional stability. (Hong Kong, AFP, 1 June; *FBIS-EAS*, 5 June; Radio Australia, 1, 2 June.)

A few days after Yang Shangkun's departure, the FMF took delivery of fourteen Japanese trucks bought with the money secured from Taiwan in January (Radio Australia, 7 June). The NFP/Labor coalition criticized the government for cultivating China, "meeting with people who practice straight raw communism" (Hong Kong, AFP, 9 May; *FBIS-EAS*, 9 May).

Vanuatu. In 1990 Vanuatu celebrated its tenth anniversary of independence. In power for all that time, Prime Minister Father Walter Lini and his Vanua'aku Pati (VP, Our Land Party) further consolidated their dominance of the political system. Lini has already nominated his successor, former foreign minister and now VP general secretary Donald Kalpokas, but has yet to decide whether he will stand down before the election set for late 1991 (*Pacific Report*, 22 November).

The principal opposition parties—the Union of Moderate Parties (UMP), led by Maxime Carlot, and the Melanesian Progressive Party (MPP), led by VP rebel Barak Sope—have had no representa-tion in Parliament since their July 1988 walkout. After by-elections, the VP has 40 of Parliament's 46 seats, the remainder being held by a UMP splinter group, the Tan Union.

Proposals for a merger of the UMP and the MPP have been abandoned. Sope is reported to be cultivating a constituency among the MPP's pre-dominantly francophone supporters and in this way has earned the MPP's animosity. (Ken Ross, *Prospects for Crisis Prediction: A South Pacific Case Study* [Canberra: Australian National University, 1990].) Also fragmented is UMP/MPP resolve to boycott participation in VP-dominated political activity. In December, the general secretary of the MPP, George Carlo, resigned his position and, abjuring his earlier criticisms of the VP, applied to join the ruling party (*Pacific Report*, 6 December). Carlo's move appeared to further weaken Barak Sope's capacity to challenge the VP's political supremacy, highlighting the point that significant political debate in Vanuatu takes place not between parties but rather within the VP.

One cannot write off the possibility of an electoral upset in 1991; swings in popular support can be drastic in island politics. But unlike other South Pacific parties, the VP's long tenure in office has allowed it to consolidate its hold on power. The top level of the public service, for example, comprises around 50 to 60 VP figures. As one researcher notes, this group is "a cadre of the most well educated ni-Vanuatu [people of Vanuatu] and by default, the only group with any executive experience in bureaucracy." (Ross, *Prospects for Crisis Prediction*.)

In mid-October the first meeting was held of the Constitution Review Committee (CRC), a body created to recognize customary Melanesian political practice in conjunction with Westminster-style constitutionalism. Twenty of the 31 CRC members are from the VP. Notwithstanding their decision to boycott the CRC, in December the president of the UMP, Jean-Marie Leye, decided to take up a seat on the CRC.

Concern has been expressed that the CRC will be used to undermine political freedoms. Father Lini has denied the charge but stressed also the inapplicability of some Western political norms. Among the mooted constitutional reforms are proposals to weaken the judiciary and give more power to customary village chiefs in resolving land and other disputes. It is less easy to see how principles enshrined in the existing constitution, such as freedom of speech, will be reconciled with some aspects of

Melanesian custom. (*Pacific Report*, 12 April; *Islands Business*, September.)

In foreign relations, Vanuatu is the only South Pacific state to be a member of the nonaligned movement. Father Lini was not present at the October summit meeting between President Bush and eleven island leaders in Honolulu. At the time of the summit, President Fred Timakata was paying a ten-day visit to the PRC, where he met the Chinese president and premier. (Xinhua, 19 October; Guangzhou Guangdong Provincial Service, 27 October; *FBIS-CHI*, 22, 30 October.)

One month earlier, the then foreign minister, Donald Kalpokas, visited Beijing and stressed his country's maintenance of a "one-China policy" (Xinhua, *FBIS-CHI*, 18 September). Vanuatu is reported to have borrowed US$7.5 million toward the construction of a new Parliament House. The building is being designed by a Chinese engineering team and is planned for completion in November 1991. (Radio Australia, 13 June.)

Notwithstanding China's close ties with Vanuatu, Vietnam accredited its first ambassador to Port Villa in March. The nonresidential post will be filled by the Vietnamese ambassador to Australia. (Radio Australia, 21 March.)

Solomon Islands. The conduct of politics in the Solomon Islands remained hectic and confusing in 1990. The focal point of the year's events was Solomon Mamaloni, the prime minister and leader of the People's Alliance Party (PAP).

In May, the government defeated a parliamentary no-confidence motion by Andrew Nori, leader of the opposition group. The opposition—in fact a loose coalition of five separate parties—expressed concern about the government's capacity for sound financial management. (*Pacific Islands Monthly*, March.)

Mamaloni was criticized for negotiating, independent of cabinet approval, a loan for US$250 million from an Italian organization known as ESCA. A US$1-billion loan from Hong Kong and Middle Eastern sources has also been reported.

By October, opposition to Mamaloni's leadership had spread within the PAP. A week before a PAP party convention was reportedly going to sack the prime minister, Mamaloni resigned from the party, announcing that he would rule as an "independent Prime Minister" leading a government of "national unity and political reconciliation." Five cabinet ministers were sacked, their positions being filled by four opposition members and a PAP back-

bencher. Nori maintained that the opposition had a paper calling for Mamaloni's resignation with the signatures of a majority of parliamentarians. At least two of the signatories, however, subsequently took up cabinet posts. (*Islands Business*, November; *Pacific Islands Monthly*, November; *Pacific Report*, 25 October; Radio Australia, 13–17 October.) The November sitting of Parliament saw the remnants of the opposition, led by Nori, and the disaffected elements of the PAP, led by the sacked deputy prime minister, Danny Philip, attempt to pass a no-confidence motion, which was disallowed by the speaker on legal grounds (Hong Kong, AFP, 16 November; *FBIS-EAS*, 16 November).

One commentator noted that these developments left the Solomon Islanders "puzzled but probably not over-anxious" (*Islands Business*, November). On balance, Mamaloni has consolidated his position. Four of his new ministers come from the populous and influential Malaita province; one, Sir Peter Kenilorea, is a former prime minister. For the moment at least the new cabinet has the talent, and accommodates sufficient interests, to keep Mamaloni in power.

The Labor party maintained a low profile. In January the party reportedly withdrew from the opposition group following a lack of consultation on political tactics (*Pacific Islands Monthly*, January).

In 1990 the Solomon Islands' most difficult foreign policy problem was to maintain good relations with PNG over the secessionist movement on Bougainville Island, only a few miles northwest of the Solomons. Amid problems caused by Bougainville rebels crossing into Solomon Islands territory, the two countries have been able to reach an agreement on joint surveillance of the narrow straits separating the two countries.

Taiwan is the Solomons' third-largest source of aid after the European Community and Japan and maintains an embassy in Honiara. A treaty to provide Taiwanese fishing access to the Solomons' exclusive economic zone was reportedly under negotiation in May (*Islands Business*, May).

In October, the Solomons' representative at the U.N. General Assembly reiterated the call to reinscribe French Polynesia on the U.N.'s list of non-self-governing nations. This move is designed to provide support for the vocal group calling for self-government in the French territory (Radio Australia, 9 October).

New Caledonia. A calm political year in the French territory of New Caledonia raised hopes that the Matignon accords did indeed provide a formula for reconciling the interests of the pro- and anti-independence factions. The accords provide for a program of economic development and political education leading to a referendum on self-determination in 1998.

In March, a special congress of the proindependence umbrella organization Front de Liberation Nationale Kanak et Socialiste (FLNKS, Kanak Socialist National Liberation Front) elected as president 38-year-old Paul Neaoutyine, a leading figure in one of the more radical groups in FLNKS, the Parti de Liberation Kanake (Palika, Kanak Liberation Party). The FLNKS leadership has usually gone to a senior figure from the largest of its constituent groups, the Union Caledonienne (UC). On this occasion the UC had to settle for the newly created position of vice-president, filled by Rock Wamytan.

Since his election Neaoutyine has presented a moderate image, stressing the need to consult with all parties. However, Neaoutyine acknowledges that many in Palika "ideologically have adopted Marxism" (*Islands Business*, May). In a recent interview, Neaoutyine ascribed the South Pacific's political problems to colonialism and neocolonialism and said of his own views: "I know some see me as a revolutionary. I'm not renouncing my convictions, nor my militant past. But today I am obliged to represent all of the FLNKS. And the struggle takes different forms at different stages. We tailor our strategy to the circumstances of the struggle." (*Pacific Islands Monthly*, October.) At present, the struggle has involved attempts to improve the economic lot of the indigenous Kanaks. The most imaginative step has been for a Kanak regional council to purchase, with French aid, New Caledonia's largest privately owned nickel mine from Jacques Lafleur, leader of the anti-independence party, the Rassemblement pour la Caledonie dans la Republique (RPCR, Assembly for New Caledonia in the Republic). (*FEER*, 2 August; Radio Australia, 21 September.)

Among the proindependence groups rejecting the Matignon accords are the USTKE, which in September chose not to nominate a candidate for a seat on the Kanak-controlled South province council (Radio Australia, 7 September), and the Front Uni de Liberation Kanak (FULK, United Kanak Liberation Front), led by Yann Celene Uregei. The latter was briefly detained for questioning by Noumea police in July when he returned to New Caledonia after more than a year overseas. Uregei has long been suspected by the FLNKS of com-

plicity in the assassination of Jean-Marie Tjibaou, their former president (Hong Kong, AFP, 15 July; *FBIS-EAS*, 17 July). Never short of resources for travel, Uregei was in New York in October to petition the U.N. Fourth Committee on Decolonization about the dangers of the Matignon accords (*Pacific Islands Monthly*, November).

In March, the leader of the Kanak Socialist Liberation Party (LKS), Nidoish Naisseline, announced the formation of a new umbrella organization to coordinate the radical opposition to the FLNKS. Calling themselves the Anti-Neocolonialist Front, the LKS and FULK picked up 23 percent of the vote to the FLNKS's 45 percent in local elections on Ouvea Island in February (Hong Kong, AFP, 19 March; *FBIS-EAS*, 19 March).

The FLNKS failed in its bid to be accepted as an observer at the annual meeting of the South Pacific Forum, which gathers the leaders of the independent island states, Australia, and New Zealand. However, FLNKS leaders met the forum group informally and got the support of the meeting to call on France to permit regular visits from the United Nations to monitor progress toward self-determination. This accords with the FLNKS's apparent desire to place less emphasis on the role of the Matignon agreements and more on the U.N. Fourth Committee on Decolonization. (*Pacific Islands Monthly*, September; *Pacific Report*, 5, 16 August.)

French Polynesia. Amid problems caused by the French desire to reduce the amount of direct financial support given to Papeete and increasing pressure on the local Legislative Assembly to provide for the needs of a rapidly growing urban population, French Polynesia is looking to elections in March 1991. The current indications are that the Polynesian Liberation Front (PLF), led by Oscar Tumaru, will increase the number of seats it holds in the assembly without winning enough to form a government. The PLF remains staunchly proindependence and opposes French nuclear testing. Its somewhat more radical advocacy of these issues has reportedly led to declining support for the other proindependence party, Ia Mana Te Nuaa, led by Jacqui Drollet (*Islands Business*, January).

The prospective winner of the March election is Gaston Flosse, leader of the pro-French Tahoeraa Huiraatira party. Flosse favors a progression for French Polynesia to greater administrative autonomy while still remaining a French territory (*Is-*

lands Business, October). This position is likely to receive a sympathetic hearing from Paris, which has worked hard (and spent much) to improve its image in the region this year. President Mitterrand, Prime Minister Michel Rocard, and eight other ministers visited Papeete in May to commemorate that city's centennial. Mitterrand stressed that French Polynesia would be given greater administrative autonomy but would also be expected to take more responsibility for financial management. (Radio Australia, 19 May; *Pacific Islands Monthly*, June.) Mitterrand's visit was protested by the PLF, which declared three days of national mourning to protest nuclear testing and the "loss of the local people's homeland to France" (Radio Australia, 16 May).

Nauru. In September, Taiwan joined Australia in being one of only two countries to maintain diplomatic missions on Nauru, approximately 8 percent of whose population is ethnic Chinese (*Pacific Islands Monthly*, October). Nauru's president, Bernard Dowiyogo, visited Taiwan in May for President Lee Teng-hui's inauguration (*Bulletin*, 12 June).

Relations between Nauru and Australia, its former colonial administrator, continue to be poor. On 20 April, Nauru filed a ten-volume legal brief against Australia in the International Court, seeking US$54 million in compensation for damage to the Nauru environment caused by phosphate mining before independence. Australia maintains that all its obligations were settled at the time of Nauru's independence in 1968. If successful, Nauru plans to bring similar suits against New Zealand and the United Kingdom, which shared in the U.N. postwar territorial mandate.

A decline in phosphate prices this year cut export earnings by one-third, from A$35 million to about A$25 million, forcing a major reduction in government spending and a closure of overseas missions in Tokyo, Honolulu, Hong Kong, and a number of island states. With remaining phosphate stocks due to be exhausted within the decade, Nauru faces a worrying period of economic decline. (*Islands Business*, July; *Pacific Islands Monthly*, July; Radio Australia, 2 May; Hong Kong, AFP, 1 July; *FBIS-EAS*, 3 July.)

Cook Islands. The Cook Islands' relationship of "free association with New Zealand" began to chafe against the political ambitions of the ruling Cook Islands party, led by Geoffrey Henry. Under

the agreement, New Zealand has responsibility, after consultation, for the Cooks' defense and foreign affairs. The Cook Islanders also enjoy New Zealand citizenship and access to New Zealand social services. But the Henry government has found that quasi-independent status limits its access to international aid programs, such as that administered under the Lome convention. The Cooks have also made preparations to host U.S. Coast Guard port calls, something contrary to New Zealand's antinuclear policy. In August, after months of discussion, the Cooks government announced an agreement with the French to carry out maritime surveillance patrols of Cook Islands' exclusive economic zone using aircraft flying out of French Polynesia. New Zealand welcomed the move, but it is clear that Wellington, irritated by developments in the relationship, has reduced the level of financial aid to the islands. (*Pacific Islands Monthly*, July; *Pacific Report*, August; *Australian Society*, December.)

In August it was reported that the Soviet Union offered the Cooks a number of scholarships for individuals to undertake study in the USSR. There have been no reports as to whether the offer was taken up (*Pacific Islands Monthly*, August). There were also reports that Taiwan had made unofficial inquiries about the possibility of establishing diplomatic ties (Radio Australia, 24 November).

Tonga. A politically eventful year in Tonga saw the growing influence of a reform movement seeking a more democratic political system. The February elections saw proreform commoners win six of the nine available seats in a Parliament dominated by the royal family and Tongan nobles. The leader of the reform group, 'Akilisi Pohiva, was elected by a substantial majority after campaigning on the need for greater accountability. Pohiva's election was challenged in the Tongan Supreme Court by a group of conservative members of Parliament alleging bribery and corruption during the campaign. The court dismissed the charges in May. (*Islands Business*, March; Radio Australia, 20 May.)

Among the reformers' supporters has been the Catholic bishop of Tonga, Patelisio Finau, who in March was quoted as saying, "I think there will be a coup d'état if there is no change" (*Islands Business*, March). For his trouble, the king called Finau a Marxist and an agent of the Vatican who advocated a political coup (Hong Kong, AFP, 29 October; *FBIS-EAS*, 30 October; *Islands Business*, November). Pohiva has been the subject of similar attacks.

In fact the political agenda of the reformers is modest. Pohiva wants to increase the number of commoner seats in Parliament and reduce those allocated to the nobles to create a parity between commoners on the one hand and nobles and the nonelected cabinet on the other. No one advocates overturning the monarchy, but Pohiva is pessimistic about prospects for change under 72-year-old King Tupou IV. Crown Prince Tupoutu'a is said to be more sympathetic to reform.

Reformers have most discomfited the government with their allegations of corruption and financial mismanagement. Pohiva, who has advocated pay cuts for politicians and more exacting standards of accountability, is pursuing an injunction in the Supreme Court to stop the sale of passports to non-Tongan nationals. It is rumored that such sales have totaled US$25 million, but the king refuses to specify the amount or to make the money available to the government because, he says, "they would only spend it." It is believed that large numbers of Hong Kong and Taiwanese Chinese have bought passports, now selling for US$30,000, but few countries have recognized their validity. (*Pacific Report*, 15 February, 6 December; *Islands Business*, December.)

On 1 April—appropriately, as it turned out—Police Minister George Akau'ola went on Tongan radio to defend the sale of passports and to deny rumors of a coup. Members of a Christian fundamentalist organization, the Tokaikolo Fellowship, claimed to have evidence of a U.S.-backed coup planned for 6 April. A fellowship member said she had been kidnapped by the plotters, drugged, and interrogated by men in dark glasses and by a witch with computers strapped to her chest, only to be rescued by an angel dressed in shining white. Amid reports of devils loose in the kingdom, the Tongan Defense Force was armed and put on alert. Nothing happened. Later, four New Zealanders, accused of spreading rumors against the king, were deported—none of them wearing dark glasses. (*Pacific Islands Monthly*, May; Radio Australia, 14 April; *Washington-Pacific Report*, 1 April; Hong Kong, AFP, 2 April; *FBIS-EAS*, 2 April.)

Tonga remains Taiwan's staunchest ally in the South Pacific. King Tupou visited Taiwan for Lee Teng-hui's inauguration in May. (*Pacific Islands Monthly*, July; *Bulletin*, 12 June.)

Western Samoa. Following a year of heightened political debate, Western Samoa held a referendum on 29 October in which a narrow majority voted in favor of a universal franchise. Previously the vote was restricted to those recognized to be *matai*, or heads of extended family groups. In February the influential Roman Catholic cardinal Pio Taofinuu commented that the *matai* system had been so eroded by political influence buying that the government should adopt a universal franchise. Both government and opposition had earlier gone on public record as favoring an extension of the franchise (*Islands Business*, February; *Pacific Report*, 1 February.)

Amid confusion about the procedures for enrolling, the October vote produced an inconclusive result. Of an estimated 75,000 potential voters, 53,000 registered and 39,328 voted. Some 19,392 voted in favor of the wider franchise, 17,464 against. A collateral proposal for an upper house reserved for traditionally elected *matai* titleholders was rejected, 21,428 against to 13,930 for. (Hong Kong, AFP, 29 October; *FBIS-EAS*, 1 November; *Islands Business*, November.)

The opposition National Democratic Party (NDP) leader, Tupua Tamasese Efi, argued that this was not a sufficiently clear mandate for the government to act. The NDP opposed the passage of the Electoral Amendment Bill through the Legislative Assembly (Fono), claiming that Prime Minister Tofilau Eti Alesana's Human Rights Protection party was using the bill to bolster its own support for the election in early 1991. Amid peaceful street protests the bill was enacted into law on 10 December. (Radio Australia, 8, 11, 16 December.)

Following the 1989 visit of Tofilau Eti Alesana to Beijing, China announced an interest-free loan to Samoa of US$5.5 million. This followed an earlier loan of US$2.75 million for a new complex of government buildings (*Pacific Islands Monthly*, January).

Tuvalu. Tuvalu has continued the process of diversifying its sources of foreign aid. In April it put forward a request for an A$76-million development package. Japan and, to a much lesser degree, South Korea have recently become aid donors. (*Pacific Islands Monthly*, April; *Canberra Times*, 30 April.) In 1990 there was no record of aid discussions or other forms of contact with communist countries.

Kiribati. In May the PRC extended a $3.2-million (currency not specified) interest-free loan to upgrade Bonriki airport and build a new Parliament House. It was reported that repayment was to be through the trade of Kiribati goods to China. This will take some time because the total value of Kiribati exports in 1988 was US$5.1 million. Kiribati also has a fishing agreement with Taiwan that provides access to Kiribati's two-hundred-mile exclusive economic zone. (*Islands Business*, September; *Pacific Report*, 16 August; Radio Australia, 23 May.)

Trust Territories of the Pacific Islands (TTPI). On 22 December the U.N. Security Council voted to terminate U.N. trusteeship over the Marshall Islands and the Federated States of Micronesia. This act ends the U.S.-administered TTPI. It also indicates a change of policy on the part of the Soviet Union, which in past years might have exercised its veto over the termination of the trusteeship as a way of embarrassing Washington. However, both the Soviets and the PRC overcame their objections, leaving it to Cuba to criticize the United States for abusing the island populations and ruining their culture at the same time as they used the region for nuclear testing. Palau remains under U.S. trusteeship pending resolution of the status of the Compact of Free Association. (*Canberra Times*, 24 December.)

Commonwealth of the Northern Marianas Islands (CNMI). Political debate continued in the CNMI about the degree of autonomy the islands could enjoy from the United States. A similar issue arose this year in American Samoa, a non-TTPI U.S. territory in the South Pacific. Debates about the status of semi-independent territories are a normal part of the conduct of politics in these islands and should not be interpreted as potentially undermining their links with the United States. (*Washington Pacific Report*, 15 May.)

Federated States of Micronesia (FSM). The FSM have continued to diversify their range of diplomatic contacts. Following the establishment of diplomatic relations in 1989, the PRC announced in April the opening of an embassy in the FSM, with a resident chargé d'affaires reporting to the PRC embassy in Canberra. In November, the president of the FSM, John Haglelgam, visited China, had discussions with President Yang Shangkun, and signed two agreements on economic and technological cooperation. Haglelgam reportedly asked for China's support in the U.N. Security Council in voting to end U.S. trusteeship formally. This China did in late December. (Radio Australia, 3, 5 November;

Melbourne Age, 5 November; *Washington-Pacific Report*, April.)

In domestic politics, the FSM engaged in an inconclusive review of their constitution, which, if adopted, will devolve power to its states but not fundamentally change the U.S.-modeled political system (*Islands Business*, December).

Republic of the Marshall Islands. A constitutional convention held during the first half of the year rejected proposals aimed at strengthening the power of traditional chiefs. The government, led by President Amata Kabua (who is a Marshallese paramount chief), sponsored the proposals to take account of customary political values. Among those proposals rejected by the convention was one to weaken commoners' claims to equal distribution of rental from land, significant because of the US$6 million paid annually for the Kwajalein missile range facility.

One proposal accepted by the convention is to increase the status of the Traditional Rights Court and to ensure that it, rather than the High Court, deals with all land disputes according to Marshallese custom. These reforms will be put to a plebiscite in 1991. (*Pacific Report*, 12 April; *Islands Business*, June.) Radio Australia reported in November that China has given diplomatic recognition to the Marshalls, thus strengthening the Marshalls' claim to be treated as a fully sovereign state (Radio Australia, 25 November).

Republic of Palau. Palau's seventh referendum in nine years on the status of the Compact of Free Association with the United States was held in February, failing once again to attract the necessary 75 percent of the votes needed for ratification. The turnout was low, some 7,747, or around two-thirds of Palau's 11,200 voters (Charles Scheiner, "Palau: Recent Developments," *Bulletin of Concerned Asian Scholars*, January–March).

At 60.8 percent, the procompact vote was the lowest of the seven referenda. Nevertheless, seven affirmations of support by large majorities for the compact have not deterred commentators from describing the situation as a case of overbearing U.S. pressure on a defenseless island state. At issue is Palau's "anti-nuclear" constitution, which limits U.S. use of Palauan land for military bases. The possibility of establishing a naval base seems increasingly remote, given the U.S. strategic drawdown in the Pacific, but Washington maintains that the price for receiving a substantial aid package under the compact is that the constitution must change. A decade of political bumbling in Palau demonstrates that the 75 percent vote needed either to change the constitution or to adopt the compact cannot be mustered.

Following the referendum's failure to resolve the issue of Palau's relationship with the United States, Washington has reestablished a measure of administrative control over the islands. In October, the Palauan government accepted a U.S. Department of the Interior order that will make it possible for the department to veto laws and block expenditure. Some 90 percent of Palau's budget comes from U.S. aid. (*Pacific Islands Monthly*, March; Radio Australia, 23 October; *Canberra Times*, 4 January 1991.) Predictably, the order was greeted with outrage by members of the NFIP lobby, which characterized the U.S. action as a "shocking display of arbitrary power" (*Pacific Islands Monthly*, December).

Peter Jennings
Parliament House, Canberra

Sri Lanka

Population. 17,196,436 (July)
Parties. Communist Party of Sri Lanka (CPSL, pro-Moscow); Janatha Vimukthi Peramuna (JVP, Maoist)
Founded. CPSL: 1943; JVP: 1968
Membership. 5,000 (estimated)
General Secretary. CPSL: Kattorge P. Silva
Politburo. CPSL: 11 members, including Silva and Pieter Keuneman (president)
Status. Both legal
Last Congress. CPSL: Thirteenth, 22–26 March 1987; Extraordinary Congress, 9–11 December 1989
Last Election. CPSL: parliamentary, 1989; ran with 3 other parties as United Socialist Alliance (USA) (2.9 percent; 3 MPs elected); presidential, 1982: did not run a candidate; presidential, 1988: did not run a candidate, but supported USA candidate Ossie Abeygoonasekera, who received 4.6 percent of the vote. JVP: presidential, 1982: 4.2

percent; presidential, 1988: did not contest; parliamentary, 1989: did not contest.
Auxiliary Organizations. CPSL: Federation of Trade Unions (24 affiliated unions), Public Service Workers' Trade Union Federation (100 affiliated unions), Communist Youth Federation, Kantha (women's) Peramuna
Publication. *Aththa* (major daily newspaper; editor, A.U.M. Abeyratne; 28,000 circ.)

The Sri Lankan political left experienced another bad year in 1990. The three major leftist groups in the country experienced setbacks during the year or were unable to reestablish lost influence. The nonviolent left, made up of the pro-Moscow Communist Party of Sri Lanka (CPSL), the Trotskyite Lanka Sama Samaja Party (LSSP), and several smaller parties, continued to exercise limited influence in the political system. The members of the Maoist JVP continued to be hunted down and killed by progovernment death squads and security forces. The most radical of the Tamil leftist guerrilla groups, the Eelam People's Revolutionary Front (EPRLF), was militarily decimated by its Tamil rivals, the Liberation Tigers of Tamil Eelam (LTTE), and ultimately several of its leaders were massacred by the LTTE in India.

By the end of the year, the left was seeking to reorganize, to mobilize the significant support it still held in the country, to once again seriously challenge the governing United National party.

Several leftist parties attempted to broaden their coalition. A tentative union was made between the Sri Lanka Freedom party (the dominant opposition party in the country), the CPSL, the LSSP, and two smaller leftist movements, the Desha Vimukthi Janatha Pakshaya and the Bahujana Nidahas Peramuna. The parties planned to form a united party list in the next elections. If successful, the "old left" might once again be able to exert a strong influence on Sri Lankan politics.

Despite the death or capture at the end of 1989 of all its Politburo and district commanders, the "new left," the JVP, continued to be a presence in Sri Lankan politics. Throughout 1990, members of the JVP began to reorganize the underground movement. Their military actions against the government were reduced to sporadic attacks on government supporters. The progovernment death squads that were so instrumental in the JVP's defeat, however, were still active. Burning bodies of youths were still found throughout the country as the death squads continued their indiscriminate attacks on anyone suspected of being a JVP supporter.

In the northern and eastern sections of the country, the truce with the last tiger group fighting the government, the LTTE, came to an end in June when the LTTE launched a series of attacks on Sri Lankan police posts in the Eastern province. Open warfare ensued as the government found itself unable to militarily defeat the Tigers. In the Eastern province, the LTTE withdrew to the jungles after giving up the major towns and cities. In the North, it was much more successful and by the end of the year still controlled most of the Jaffna peninsula.

The LTTE, the least ideological of the tiger groups, began a campaign to destroy its chief Tamil opponent, the EPRLF, which dominated the elected government of the Northern and Eastern Provincial Council. The LTTE had defeated most of the EPRLF's Tamil National Army by the time the Indian peacekeeping force had completed its withdrawal in March. During this time, the Sri Lankan government provided the LTTE with logistical support in its attacks. After defeating the Tamil National Army, the LTTE sought to assassinate the EPRLF leadership. Sam Thambimuttu, a popular EPRLF member of Parliament from the Eastern province, was assassinated on 7 May in Colombo by the LTTE. Fifteen other EPRLF leaders were killed by the LTTE on 19 June in Madras, India. The dead included EPRLF leader Kandaswamy Pathmanabha and Member of Parliament V. K. Yogasangary. The chief minister of the Northern and Eastern Provincial Council, Varatharajaperumal, had fled the country in March to avoid assassination.

Government support for the LTTE backfired when the LTTE attacked the government and resumed the ethnic conflict in June. The major difference now was that the LTTE was the only strong force left in Tamil politics. The EPRLF and its allies, the Popular Front for the Liberation of Tamil Eelam, the Tamil Eelam Liberation Organization, and the Eelam National Democratic Liberation Front, had all been seriously weakened by the LTTE attacks. In addition, the leaders of the EPRLF and most of its allies had all been killed in the previous three years by the LTTE or other groups.

By the end of the year, the violence in the country had changed. The southern conflict of the JVP was largely over, while the war in the North was at its bloodiest. The parties of the left were faced with the prospect of rebuilding their movements and regaining the influence and strength that they had once held in the country.

Robert C. Oberst
Nebraska Wesleyan University

Thailand

Population. 56,000,000 (July)
Party. Communist Party of Thailand (CPT)
Founded. 1942
Membership. 250–500 members (estimated); armed communist insurgents, 300–500 (estimated)
General Secretary. Thong Jaensri (unconfirmed, pseudonym?)
Status. Illegal
Last Congress. Fourth, March–April 1984 (clandestine; met in four regions of the country)
Last Election. No communist party candidates allowed to participate in the 1988 nationwide election
Publications. *Thong Thai* (Thai flag) and *Prakai Fai* (Flame) (intermittent underground publications)

Since the 1980s Thailand has faced little danger from either indigenous communist insurgency or Vietnamese invasion, largely because of steady economic growth, averaging 7 percent during the 1980s and a remarkable 10 percent during 1987–1990. The progress of Thai-style semidemocracy has also helped dispel those threats but has been complicated by the military's repeated attempts to reassert its traditional control. Indeed, military pressures forced Prime Minister Chatichai Choonhavan to dissolve his cabinet in December.

Reflecting U.S. disengagement from Southeast Asia and the reduced threats to Thai security, Thailand's foreign policy has moved toward "omnidirectionality," cultivating close ties with nations of different ideologies. For example, Thailand has improved its relations with Vietnam and the Phnom Penh government as well as strengthened ties with its neighbors Laos and Burma. Nevertheless, relations with the United States provide the basis for Thai security policy.

Relations with Communist States. The increasing trade between Thailand and the Soviet Union resulted in a $200 million surplus in Thailand's favor for 1989, the latest year for which figures are available. Soviet prime minister Nikolai Ryzhkov visited Thailand in February to discuss trade relations and to encourage Thai investment in Soviet joint ventures for textile, garment, and consumer goods production. Trade delegations from Czechoslovakia, Poland, and Hungary also visited in 1990 to pursue improved trade ties. Premier Li Peng and air force head Wang Hai of the People's Republic of China arrived to strengthen economic and trade cooperation, discuss Cambodia, and negotiate weapons purchases. The Royal Thai Air Force had canceled its plan to purchase Chinese-made F-7M jet fighters because the fighters are guaranteed for only five hundred operational hours before requiring a complete checkup. The navy agreed to pay China $40 million for antiship missiles to equip its Chinese-made frigates. In general, however, Thailand backed off from its policy of buying Chinese weaponry because of disillusionment with its quality, preferring to look to the United States and Europe for fighters, ground-attack aircraft, battle tanks, antisubmarine helicopters, torpedoes, and a helicopter carrier. (*FEER*, 4 October 1990.)

During 1990, Bangkok hosted monthly conferences with Cambodian and Vietnamese delegations in a largely futile search for a peaceful settlement to the Cambodian imbroglio. Vietnamese delegations also came to Thailand to capitalize on Chatichai's policy of turning Indochina from a battlefield into a marketplace. Much of the initial euphoria of that policy passed, however, as Thai business executives found that Vietnam lacked the infrastructure to sustain foreign investment.

Communist Party Activity. There was little communist activity in Thailand in 1990, although nine key members of the CPT have not yet surrendered to Thai authorities (Wirat Angkhathawon, Thong Jaensri, Prasit Taphianthong, Pluang Wannasi, Luan Iamsakun, Huang Chaichumchon, Sun Ungthong, Hu Saelim, and Phairat Suphakanchana-khanti). It is not known how many of these nine are still living in Thailand or whether they coordinate their activities. Meanwhile, CPT members continued to take advantage of the amnesty law that applies to communists not charged with or convicted of criminal offenses. Sun Ungthong (alias Comrade Chom or Comrade Amphon), an ostensible CPT Central Committee member, and four other party members surrendered in Yala province. Sun is believed to have been general secretary of the CPT Central Regional Headquarters. (*FBIS-EAS*, 28 March.) Taengon Chandawong, a longtime CPT member and the widow of Khrong Chandawong, also defected in 1990.

In January, Chin Peng, leader of the Communist Party of Malaya (CPM), returned to China after spending three months in southern Thailand supervising truce talks with Thai and Malaysian authorities to end a 40-year armed struggle against the Malayan (and subsequent Malaysian) government. The December 1989 truce agreement included a five-year assistance program under which Thailand will provide support for the resettlement of CPM members and their families from their former strongholds, in exchange for the destruction of their weapons. Many former insurgents were thought to be in Thailand because the Malaysian government refused to allow them to settle in Malaysia; it subsequently agreed, however, to allow CPM members claiming Malaysian origin to return to Malaysia. Chin Peng himself returned to China, while his 1,100 comrades remained in southern Thailand.

For all practical purposes, the CPT exists in name alone because mass defections have reduced it to a few hundred activists operating mostly in southern Thailand. The party receives no support from abroad and has not held a congress for six years.

Clark D. Neher
Northern Illinois University

Vietnam

Population. 66,170,889 (*World Fact Book*, July)
Party. Vietnam Communist Party (Viet Nam Cong San, VCP)
Founded. 1930 (as Indochina Communist party)
Membership. 2,195,824 (*Nhan Dan*, 3 February 1989); 80 percent male, 20 percent female (estimated); about 99 percent ethnic Vietnamese; aver-

age age, early 50s (estimated); 40 percent *ban co* (poor peasant); 25 percent peasant/farm laborer; 15 percent proletariat; 20 percent other

General Secretary. Nguyen Van Linh (b. 1915)

Politburo. Nguyen Van Linh, Vo Chi Cong (b. 1912), Do Muoi (b. 1917), Vo Van Kiet (b. 1922), Le Duc Anh (b. 1910?), Nguyen Duc Tam (b. 1920), Nguyen Co Thach (b. 1920), Dong Sy Nguyen (b. 1920?), Nguyen Thanh Binh, Doan Khue, Mai Chi Tho (b. 1922), Dao Duy Tung.

Secretariat. Nguyen Van Linh, Nguyen Duc Tam, Dao Duy Tung, Tran Kien, Le Phuoc Tho, Nguyen Quyet, Dam Quang Trung, Vo Oanh, Nguyen Khanh, Tran Quyet, Tran Quoc Hoang, Pham The Duyet

Central Committee. 124 full and 49 alternate members

Status. Legal, ruling party

Last Congress. Sixth, 15–18 December 1986

Last Election. 19 April 1987, Eighth National Assembly, 98.8 percent, 496 seats, all VCP-endorsed (*Indochina Chronology*)

Auxiliary Organizations. Vietnam Fatherland Front (Nguyen Huu Tho, chairman), Ho Chi Minh Communist Youth Union (Ha Quang Du, general secretary)

Publications. *Nhan Dan* (The people), VCP daily, (cir. 500,000); *Tap Chi Cong San* (Communist review), VCP theoretical monthly; *Quan Doi Nhan Dan* (People's army), army newspaper

The year 1990 was a difficult one for the Vietnamese Communist Party and its highest-level Politburo leadership, primarily because of the influences filtering into the country from USSR and Eastern European political upheavals. This force for change represented to Vietnam's leaders a clear and present danger to the sociopolitical edifice they had erected during years of wartime sacrifice and a high price in lives and treasure. The ruling Politburo felt beleaguered by external and internal forces largely beyond its control and made it determined to avoid all policy change. Internal political controls were tightened on all groups and institutions that might even inadvertently threaten the inviolable rule of Vietnamese politics: the party monopolizes all political power. A party line was set down—no political pluralism for Vietnam—that no one could cross, not even Politburo members. Although the political scene was grim, there was some economic improvement during the year, chiefly the result of a more laissez-faire policy in the agrarian sector (which is 85 percent of the entire economy).

This in turn reflected a changed attitude by top leadership toward economic incentives as well as loss of faith in the notion that the best way to increase rice production is through moral exhortation. Improved living conditions made political inequities more acceptable.

Intimations of reform and renovation of the economic sector continued unabated, the rhetoric differing little from that heard in Hanoi since 1975. The intent to *doi moi* (reform) remained but was largely a matter of promises. Vietnam's foreign policies were marked by few initiatives and little change. The People's Army of Vietnam (PAVN) returned to Cambodia but in small numbers and apparently with the understanding that its stay would be temporary. The maneuvering with China to define a new, more equitable relationship continued, as did diplomatic maneuvering with the United States. Efforts were mounted to discourage Moscow from significantly distancing itself from Vietnam, which was important to Hanoi in economic terms.

Looking back on Vietnam during 1990, there were no significant policy changes in any state or party sector, be it economic, internal, political, or foreign relations, and this had been accomplished at no particular political price. In those few instances where change did occur, it was for defensive purposes (a crackdown on intellectuals), because of irresistible outside pressure (Cambodia policy), or a case of apparent change rather than changed reality (China, U.S. foreign policies).

Leadership. The highest (Politburo level) leadership during 1990, viewing itself as increasingly beset by both external and internal forces largely beyond its control, responded by avoiding where possible all major policy decisions and particularly those that could bring in unintended influences.

The doctrinal line that no Vietnamese could cross was political pluralism. The loyalty test was total opposition to the idea of a multiparty ruling system for Vietnam. No one was above this restriction. A top figure on the Hanoi scene, Tran Xuan Bach, learned this in February when he was unceremoniously expelled from the Politburo for publicly inquiring whether Vietnam should "think" about the idea of a multiparty system.

Although the party encouraged suggestions for improvement from all Vietnamese and would entertain criticism on occasion, it would not share political power with any nonparty element. The rationale was that the genius of the Leninist system of government in Vietnam was the concept of a vanguard party monopolizing political power; if the monopoly was broken, both the system and the party automatically collapsed. There appeared to be no doubt in the minds of the top leaders, judged by their public statements and their private conversations with foreign visitors, as to the wisdom and the propriety of this position.

The major development in the leadership during the year was the death of Le Duc Tho on 13 October at the age of 79. He was the paramount political figure on the Hanoi scene, to the extent that any single individual could be the leading figure in a system of collective leadership. Inevitably his passing led to a realignment of the Politburo factions, a sorting-out process that was continuing at the year's end.

Another major development in the leadership during the year was Tran Xuan Bach's expulsion in March. It was the first time that a member had been removed in such an abrupt manner and under a deliberately engendered cloud of disgrace. The handling of the matter violated the long-standing principles of collective leadership. What appears to have triggered his expulsion was his article "Reflections on the Road to Renovation" in the January issue of *Tap Chi Cong San*. It harshly criticized the party's current performance, permissible at his level and frequently done by all members in the same vein, but also challenged the concept of the party monopolizing political power—"passing itself off as a government" was the way Bach put it. Hence he crossed the boundary line into the forbidden territory of political pluralism by implying that Vietnam might do better with a multiparty system.

A second major development at the higher reaches of leadership was the revolt and apparent defection of Bui Tin, editor of the party newspaper *Nhan Dan* and longtime senior spokesman for the party among foreign visitors to Hanoi. Early in the year (in a Reuters 5 March *Bangkok Post* interview), Bui Tin said that the VCP should change its ways drastically and learn to "persuade rather than rule" if it hoped to stave off the upheaval visited on Eastern Europe. He insisted that Vietnam already had pluralism in some forms, giving religion as an example, but said it would never adopt political pluralism. He also said that the party must remain faithful to Marxist economic principles because the only option was capitalism, which he equated with exploitation. Bui Tin appeared to be taking an acceptable middle position, but his interview immediately drew high-level criticism and put him into a

dangerous political posture. In early December, while in Paris on official business, Bui Tin announced that although he was not defecting, he had decided not to return to Vietnam despite official orders. It appeared that he was repositioning himself in anticipation of major political change in Vietnam, and his action was seen by some observers as a weathervane of coming Vietnamese political developments.

VCP chief Nguyen Van Linh in January was reported planning to retire the following month. In March he was again reported ready to retire, this time in early 1991. It was the third year in a row that Linh had indicated his early retirement.

Surfacing publicly for the first time in an interview was Major General Duong Thong, deputy general director of the Interior Ministry's counterintelligence general department (*tong cuc phan gian*), the first public acknowledgment that Vietnam has a counterintelligence service. In October Do Phuong was named director general of the Vietnam News Agency (VNA), a veteran (b. 1930) party figure in party journalism.

Deaths during 1990, in addition to Le Duc Tho, included Admiral Giap Van Cuong, commander in chief of the SRV navy (27 March, age 68); Nguyen Lam, former Socialist Republic of Vietnam (SRV) deputy prime minister (1 April, age 68); and Dang Viet Chau, former Democratic Republic of Vietnam (DRV) finance minister (21 May, age 70).

Domestic Affairs. Vietnam's internal malaise, described by some observers as a condition of neither faith nor fear, had these general characteristics. There was decay in its institutions, especially in the once-vaunted party, now suffering from loss of elan and a tarnished reputation. The party was no longer seen as the unquestioned leading institution; questions concerning its legitimacy were being asked for the first time. Social controls were reasserted but much of the effort was so delicately conducted (iron fist in velvet glove) that it appeared to many, especially those in the North, that the coercive organs were losing their effectiveness. The struggle continued between the forces of ideology and those of pragmatism/rationality, the language of both sides being widely regarded as "pseudo-reform" talk. The party monopoly on communication of ideas continued to lose ground. The cumulative effect of all these was a decline in authority.

Three plenary meetings of the VCP Sixth Congress Central Committee were held during 1990: the Eighth, 12–27 March; the Ninth, 16–28 August; and the Tenth, 17–26 November. Specific actions by the Eighth Plenum included Tran Xuan Bach's removal from the Politburo, as Central Committee secretary, and from the Central Committee (but not from the party); the announcement that the Seventh Party Congress would be held in the second quarter of 1991; and promulgation of a vaguely stated plenum communiqué designed as a comprehensive plan to prevent a repetition of the East European political upheaval in Vietnam.

The plenum plan was in three parts: Part One instructed party leaders and cadres to improve their mass mobilization efforts using various standard mechanisms such as mass meetings, agitprop sessions, and criticism and self-criticism sessions to energize the masses, tap the latent force they represented, and above all motivate the general population by addressing their needs and aspirations. Cadres are now told to break from past appeals, be "diverse and innovative" in their motivational work. Part Two ordered the reorganization of mass organizations so as to make them better instruments for mobilization. The two organizational matrices here are (1) the mass organs, the Fatherland Front and the many *van hoi* (interest groups) (youth, women, workers, farmers, students, intellectuals, and so forth) and (2) the state organizations, the bureaucracy (especially in the economic sector), and above all the military. Part Three set forth the specific tasks required to mobilize Vietnam, motivating all Vietnamese to continue to accept the party's monopolization of political power and, most important, accept and obey the high leadership. In brief the Politburo told cadres to jack up the people with mobilizational devices using every persuasive argument to buy time.

The Ninth Plenum, reportedly marked by much heated discussion, was devoted to long-range party policy programs and plans using the eighth draft of a plan begun in late 1989 that, after vetting by the Ninth Plenum, was submitted in near final form to the Tenth Plenum. Presumably it would be submitted to the Seventh Congress and, on approval, become the major guideline for the party into the year 2000. The Ninth Plenum also considered a short-run plan and program that addressed such pressing problems as increased efforts to prevent smuggling and intensify the anticorruption drive. The Ninth Plenum, informally labeled by some in Hanoi as the "purification" plenum, was largely devoted to party morality matters. If there was any weakening of party commitment to total centralized planning, as opposed to opening the economy to free market forces, it was not evident in the communiqué. The tone of the Ninth Plenum document was grim and did not exude the confidence common in earlier plenum resolutions.

The Tenth Plenum had before it the long-awaited, often rewritten, vastly ambitious master plan for the future of the Communist Party of Vietnam that would accomplish the following by the year 2000: increase Vietnam's per capita income from $210 to $420 per year, increase rice production to 30 million tons (a 50 percent increase), treble electricity production, increase export values five times (to $5.3 billion per year), and cut inflation back to a single digit (in 1990 it ran at about 50 percent per year). This would be done by offering individual Vietnamese greater economic incentives, developing the five-sector economic system (a mix of state, private, and state-private enterprises), and decentralizing some economic controls to the provincial level, thus lessening day-to-day central management of the economy. Also published in draft form were two other documents: a VCP Party Building Plan and a draft of the new VCP bylaws.

The year also witnessed a steady tightening of internal security controls in party affairs, education, publishing, veterans' activities, religion, art, literature, and the courts. The Hanoi press in April announced the start of a major campaign to crack down on dissenters in which Vietnamese were warned that the army would be used to suppress any attempt to destabilize the regime. The control measures were all in the name of national security, indeed, in the name of Vietnam's survival. Operative throughout the year was Politburo Directive 135, Mass Movement Activity to Safeguard National Security, that bluntly ordered the suppression of organized political dissent and warned that military force would be used to quash public activities that destabilize the regime.

Supervising this defense of the status quo was party general secretary Nguyen Van Linh, a major figure in the reform faction of the Politburo. During the year he became increasingly hard-line in his public utterances, arguing that *coi mo* (openness, the Vietnamese equivalent of *glasnost'*) was to be postponed until greater internal security could be assured.

Throughout the year the question that continued to nag the party was, can it successfully contain the forces for change and preserve the status quo without fundamental or even significant alteration? The prospects for doing so appeared promising at least for the short run. But if it was impossible to maintain the status quo, the prospect appeared to be either genuine reform or substantial instability or possibly both.

The leadership's determination was reflected in a party purge. Throughout the year there were numerous statistical reports, usually by province, of the numbers disciplined, either by reprimand or expulsion. Typical were Song Be province "removed" 204; An Giang "disciplined" 167; Thai Binh province expelled "hundreds"; Tien Giang, 16 percent of members rated unsatisfactory; Hai Hung, 6,000 of 55,600 members disciplined; Ben Tre expelled 230; Hau Giang expelled 467 but found no members in 136 villages of the province; and Haiphong deemed 20 percent of membership inadequate. Reasons given were abusing power, diverting funds, or general sloth or incompetence. The February issue of *Tap Chi Cong San* said that 60 percent of the party's 2 million members "care only for their personal interests, show little interest in Party matters"; that 30 percent are performing satisfactorily; and that 10 percent are "degenerate, deviants who abuse power, engage in corruption and follow decadent life styles." Eighteen percent were described as "elderly pensioners"; proletariats totaled only 8 percent. (*Nhan Dan*, 28 March.)

What was informally termed the *democracy debate* raged inconclusively among upper-level party cadres and intellectuals during the year. This was not a debate over the merits of democracy; the parameters of such discussion had been firmly established by General Secretary Nguyen Van Linh's 60th VCP anniversary address (3 February), which specifically rejected the notion that opposition parties were a required necessity of democracy. Linh reiterated this in October when he told a group of senior military officials that "the Party must resolutely expel all who seek to abolish democratic centralism in favor of political pluralism and a multi-party system." The democracy debate, then, centered on possible new definitions of democratic centralism, broadening the orthodox "freedom in debate, unity in action" concept. Party theoretician Tuan Minh, in *Tap Chi Cong San* (March) in an article entitled "Right to Stick with One's Opinion," argued that "even after debate if you still don't agree, why can you not go on holding to your opinion?" He urged the party not to "crudely dismiss minority opinions and don't crush them." That his line of reasoning was published in a major party journal was in itself significant.

The most sensitive intellectual issue faced by party theoreticians during the year was explaining to the rank and file the reasons for and the meaning of the "political earthquake" in East Europe and the USSR—"this caduceus of power slipping from the Party grasp," as it was put. Various doctrinal explanations were offered by party thinkers in Hanoi including the following:

1. Leninist systems and ruling communist parties "disintegrated" because new leaders broke with past orthodoxy, even to the point of severing ties with the theoretical basis of Marxism-Leninism. The sense of this explanation seemed to be that the offending regimes had proceeded from a faulty model of Socialist construction to compound the original error by incorrectly implementing reform and renovation programs.

2. Proletarian internationalism as a concept had been dissipated by a spirit of resurgent nationalism. Often this was put down to an incorrect interpretation by the masses as to what was actually happening and who later discovered they had been duped into believing that political pluralism was in their interests.

3. Plots and destructive acts by imperialist powers and reactionaries who had become increasingly skilled in exploiting Socialist world contradictions and in fielding their new anti-Socialist strategy that "seeks to divide, sabotage, exacerbate, buy off."

4. A "ruinous psychology" that led to loss of confidence in the Leninist political system in general and the party in particular. This resulted in individual misbehavior, dogmatism among cadres, demands for special privileges by upper-level cadres, disregard for the law, theft, and "oppression of the masses." As a result the people lost confidence in the party: true party members became indignant, the masses complained, social discipline was poor, and society was in turmoil.

5. Flaws in the system itself: a dense bureaucracy that was the product of excessive bureaucratic centralism, a cumbersome state economic subsidy system, and "legalisms" that impede weeding out the corrupt and incompetent from party ranks or prosecuting them in the courts.

This dissatisfaction extended into the ranks of the party young. Ho Chi Minh Youth League membership dropped during the first eight months of 1990 from 4.0 million to about 3.5 million; only 70 percent of the remaining membership were rated as "active" by party leaders (*Tien Phong*, 28 September). Editorials in party youth journals worried that young Vietnamese regarded Marxism-Leninism as "obsolete" (VNA, 2 November).

In summary, party affairs in Vietnam during 1990 suggested that significant changes were in the offing. As the year ended reports from Hanoi indicated that the Seventh Party Congress—officially scheduled for some time in the second quarter of 1991—would launch a bold new program that would, in effect, attempt to co-opt the reform sentiment by seizing the initiative and becoming the banner of the reform movement. Strenuous efforts were made to prepare the rank and file for the forthcoming Seventh Congress; district-level party secretaries came to Ho Chi Minh City and Hanoi for week-long conferences at which plans were outlined for "filling the membership with militancy." Minister of Defense Le Duc Anh reportedly headed a high-level party committee that drew up a list of people who would stand for election to the Politburo. Many observers predicted major leadership changes would come at the Seventh Congress, a few predicting "a showdown" over the future of the party.

International Activities. Major foreign policy developments of the year included

- Efforts to improve Vietnam's all-important association with the USSR, which since 1979 has been a military alliance in all but name.
- Laying the ground for improvement of regional relations with the Association of Southeast Asian Nations, particularly Thailand and Indonesia; determining exactly what is the reality, the status, and the future of the Sino-Vietnamese relationship; and exploring prospects for improved or "normalized" relations with the United States.
- Moving to divest Vietnam of the Cambodian millstone, distancing itself to some degree from the State of Cambodia (SOC), and disassociating itself from the continuing struggle between the SOC and the Government of Cambodia (GOC).
- Mounting a campaign to solicit promises from foreign governments, international funding agencies, and capitalist world investors to supply Vietnam with technology transfer and massive sums of capital investment.

Both qualitative and quantitative changes occurred in the Soviet-Vietnamese-USSR relations during the year. As the year began, Hanoi owed the USSR 9 billion rubles, one-third of which it had agreed to write off; the USSR was trying to collect some if not all of the remaining two-thirds (Vietnam is the USSR's third-largest debtor). Moscow had largely halted funding aid projects in Vietnam, instead seeking to invest in those projects deemed mutually beneficial, such as food and industrial crop (rubber, kenaf, lacquer) production. The USSR during the year announced a drawdown of its military presence in Vietnam. Foreign Ministry spokesman Vadim Perfiliev told a press conference in Moscow 19 January that all MiG-23 and TU-16 planes departed Vietnam in late December 1989, leaving one squadron (six to ten planes) of "varied types." He added that the Soviet naval presence at Cam Ranh was "being reduced."

Throughout the year Vietnamese officials were openly critical of internal developments in the USSR having to do with *glasnost'* and *perestroika*. An unnamed Foreign Ministry official interviewed by Japanese journalists obliquely criticized the USSR for abandoning the "dictatorship of the proletariat" and opening the way for a pluralistic political party system (Tokyo, Kyodo, 7 February; *FBIS-EAS*, 7 February).

There was considerable official traffic between Hanoi and Beijing during the year, the significance of which was not at all clear at year's end. Both sides seemed interested in ending the cold war that has existed between them since the late 1970s, but neither appearing willing to sacrifice much in the name of better relations. There were two formal high-level meetings during 1990 (and two in 1989). SRV deputy foreign minister Dinh Ngo Liem went to Beijing in early May, officially "to inspect the work of the Vietnamese embassy," and met with People's Republic of China foreign minister Qian Qichen and others for discussion of bilateral problems. Party chief Nguyen Van Linh, Prime Minister Do Muoi, and former Prime Minister Pham Van Dong made a "secret" trip to Beijing in early September, according to SRV Foreign Ministry sources in Hanoi. The report was "confirmed by diplomats in Beijing," according to Chinese journalists. SRV Foreign Ministry officials "declined to confirm" the report, implying that the visit did in fact take place but could not be acknowledged because of a Vietnamese request.

The chief U.S.-Vietnam bilateral development during the year was the announcement by U.S. secretary of state James Baker in Paris (18 July) that the United States would open a "dialogue" with Hanoi on the Cambodian peace process. Baker also announced that the United States would free up restrictions on dispatching U.S. private humanitarian aid to Cambodia and would not vote for the Coalition Government of Democratic Kampuchea to take the Cambodia seat at the U.N. General Assembly in the fall. The first meeting (6 August) was in New York (Deputy Assistant Secretary of State Kenneth Quinn for the United States, SRV ambassador to the U.N. Trinh Xuan Lang for Vietnam). A second meeting between the two was held in New York on 31 August.

Earlier the United States had said that it would like diplomatic relations with Vietnam but not before a political settlement in Cambodia. State Department spokeswoman Margaret Tutwiler said on 30 April that the precondition was an acceptable Cambodian political settlement, which included verified withdrawal of PAVN troops from Cambodia.

The White House issued Presidential Determination No. 90-38, known as the trading with the enemy act (on 5 September), which extended for one year the economic embargo on Vietnam (and Cambodia and North Korea). Had the president not done this, the embargo would have lapsed automatically (it need not last a year; he could remove the restriction at any time). The move was a blow to U.S. traders in Asia who wanted to begin serious economic activity in Vietnam. During the year U.S. business and veterans' lobbies renewed their campaign for U.S. diplomatic recognition of the SRV and abandonment of the economic embargo and other restraints on intercourse. The Asia-Pacific Council of the American Chambers of Commerce in Djakarta announced plans to lobby in Washington to persuade Congress and the administration to lift U.S. trade sanctions against Vietnam.

The third formal U.S.-SRV "dialogue" was held in New York (20 September) between U.S. assistant secretary of state Richard Solomon and SRV deputy foreign minister Le Mai, one notch higher on the diplomatic ladder. Also present were General John Vessey, presidential emissary on missing in action/prisoner of war (MIA/POW) affairs; U.S. secretary of state James Baker; and SRV foreign minister Nguyen Co Thach, who also met for 30 minutes in New York (29 September, Waldorf-Astoria Hotel). A U.S. spokesman said that Baker sought to acknowledge the progress made by the U.N. "permanent five" in the Cambodian peace process, including forming the Cambodia Supreme National Council to take the Cambodian seat in the U.N. General Assembly and to accelerate activity on the MIA/POW issue. A communiqué said afterward that the two countries agreed "to take concrete steps that are conducive to the normalization of relations." The State Department later waived travel restrictions to permit Thach to come to Washington to discuss the resolution of casualties issue. At the meeting Thach suggested that General Vessey be stationed in Vietnam to deal with the resolution of casualties issue; the State Department official replied the United States would take the suggestion under advisement.

Douglas Pike
University of California at Berkeley

EASTERN EUROPE AND THE SOVIET UNION

Introduction

The first full year of peaceful revolution in East-Central Europe marked further progress toward completely eliminating the communist *nomenklatura* from key governmental agencies, displacing two state presidents through national elections, and strengthening a broad movement toward free market economies. This phase has been aptly described as "the end of the beginning."[1]

The USSR began withdrawing its armed forces from Hungary and Czechoslovakia, signed an agreement with the Federal Republic of Germany to follow suit, and commenced negotiations with Poland toward the same end. It appeared a foregone conclusion that the Warsaw Treaty Organization (WTO) would be disbanded in 1991; the same fate awaited the Council for Mutual Economic Assistance (CMEA), which had become moribund.

The Soviet Union. Transfer of power from the ruling communist party's Politburo started with the introduction of a new presidential council, to which eighteen individuals were appointed during March 1990 by Mikhail S. Gorbachev. Nine of them belonged to the old Politburo of the Communist Party of the Soviet Union (CPSU).[2] This organization did not even last to the end of the year but was abolished under a new reorganization plan that placed the Council of Ministers under the USSR president. The Congress of People's Deputies approved the following: a veteran apparatus worker as vice-president and a former KGB general as interior minister. These and other changes precipitated the 20 December 1990 resignation of Eduard A. Shevardnadze, who warned of a forthcoming dictatorship.

These dramatic developments had been preceded on 13 March by the repeal of Article 6 in the Soviet constitution, which had guaranteed the "leading role" of the CPSU, thus legalizing the establishment of other political parties. An "executive" presidency was established the same day, which laid the foundations for Gorbachev's rule by decree. He also survived the Twenty-eighth CPSU Congress held at midyear.

Gorbachev's choice for deputy general secretary, Ukrainian party leader V. A. Ivashko, defeated "conservative" E. K. Ligachev, who had criticized many of the foregoing moves as emasculating the CPSU. The party congress elected an enlarged Politburo of 24 members, eleven secretaries, and five members of the secretariat.[3] No direct challenge to Gorbachev materialized because some 40 percent of the congress delegates were party officials.

However, Gorbachev's chief rival, Boris N. El'tsin, head of the Russian Soviet Federated Socialist Republic, warned that a party based on the apparatus alone would collapse and that only a "renewed party" capable of uniting democratic forces could survive. Gorbachev made the first choice, and El'tsin resigned from the CPSU on 12 July 1990. He was followed by the director of the Moscow party school, the mayors of Moscow and Leningrad, and others.

Three days later about 50,000 residents of Moscow denounced the CPSU at a mass rally in Red Square and called for more party resignations. During the preceding six months, some 186,000 members had left its ranks. The number of Soviet citizens who "fully trust the CPSU" dropped from 27 percent in December 1989 to only 14 percent in July 1990,[4] according to a government public opinion poll.

That may have been one reason for the ensuing divisions within republic communist parties. Parliaments in all three Baltic states proclaimed their intention to leave the Soviet Union, and this precipitated splits into pro-USSR communist and nationalist communist factions. The violence in the Caucasus led to Moscow's use of armed forces, special State Security Committee (KGB) units, and regular Interior Ministry troops, actions that also took place in the Baltic republics.

The CPSU continued to control international communist front organizations, although their monthly magazine, *World Marxist Review*,[5] closed down in mid-1990. Other setbacks included the ouster of Soviet-line fronts for trade unions, journalists, and students from Prague by the new Czechoslovak government; of the Women's International Democratic Federation from East Berlin by the unified German government; and of the World Federation of Democratic Youth from Budapest by the Hungarians. The new East-Central European governments have ended their former annual subsidies to the World Peace Council.

East-Central Europe. The transition away from command economies and monopolies over political power by local communist parties has not affected all countries in this region. Neither the regime in Albania nor the one in Romania permitted political pluralism to gain a foothold in their countries. Widespread unemployment, inflation, and rising foreign indebtedness were some of the by-products in all parts of the former Soviet bloc.[6]

Albania. The collapse of other bloc regimes did not affect communist rulers in Tiranë until early 1990, when reports of antigovernment demonstrations reached the West. Despite superficial reforms, during the first few days of July, some five thousand Albanians sought asylum in eight foreign embassies or escape abroad. Party leader Ramiz Alia shook up his Politburo, blaming former colleagues for the disturbances. During the fall, a new electoral law still restricted candidates for parliamentary seats to the ruling Albanian Party of Labor and its mass organizations.

When the army had to put down mass demonstrations during early December in three major cities, Alia removed five members and two candidates for membership in the Politburo. Some of them had been demoted earlier. A day later, it was announced that independent political organizations would be permitted. The first one, called the Democratic Party, came into being on 12 December at a mass rally in Tiranë. This did not prevent demonstrators at Shkodër from dynamiting a statue of Enver Hoxha only three days later. On 21 December the council of ministers gave its permission for state-owned enterprises to remove the name and symbols of Joseph Stalin.[7] National elections were announced for 31 March 1991, the first multiparty ones since the communists seized power.

Bulgaria. The ruling movement replaced the word *communist* with the word *socialist* in its name on 3 April 1990. Elections held during June gave the ruling party a plurality of 47 percent and 211 of the 400 seats in Parliament. Nevertheless, round-table discussions resulted in an agreement to recognize other political parties that had little time or funds to compete with the renamed communists.

The Union of Democratic Forces (UDF), however, provided a leader in the person of Zhelyu Zhelev. The UDF had emerged as the second strongest party, with 36.2 percent of the vote and 144 seats in Parliament. That body, with communist support, elected Zhelev president of Bulgaria. Separation between the Bulgarian Socialist Party (BSP) and the state continues to progress.

At its Thirty-ninth Congress toward the end of September, the BSP adopted a platform admitting responsibility for "past distortions in every sphere of life," although it refused to apologize to the Bulgarian people. The congress abandoned Lenin's "democratic centralism" and any claim to a monopoly of power in the state. The Fortieth Congress will probably be held in March 1991, just before the next parliamentary elections in May. During the last six months of 1990, the BSP lost three-fourths of its membership.[8]

Czechoslovakia. In early November 1990 the local communists changed their designation to Federation of the Communist Party of Bohemia and Moravia and the Communist Party of Slovakia (KSCS). The active membership has dropped to somewhere between 300,000 and 500,000 from 1.7 million a year earlier. In the June elections, it won 40 seats out of 300 in Parliament.

Since ceding power in December 1989 the "de-communization" of Czechoslovakia has not been contested by the KSCS. The most visible former high-ranking communists in the new government were the federal prime minister, Marian Čalfa, and the defense minister, Miroslav Vácek. The latter was dismissed in October after his compliance with armed forces mobilization plans during the November 1989 "velvet revolution" was revealed. Reform communists (those purged following the August 1968 invasion by Soviet troops) occupying high-level positions include parliamentary chairman Alexander Dubček and the foreign minister, Jiří Dienstbier.

Property of the communist party has been expropriated so that by midyear 1990 the organization controlled no more than 10 to 15 percent of its previous assets. A law adopted on 16 November nationalized 85 to 90 percent of these holdings without compensation. Early in the new year, Czechoslovakia became the first country in East-Central Europe to return property confiscated after the February 1948 communist coup d'état.[9]

East Germany. Up to 100,000 Soviet troops are scheduled to leave the five eastern provinces in the Federal Republic of Germany during 1991, together with military equipment and dependents. This process will continue well into 1994, according to agreement. With unemployment soaring throughout the former German Democratic Republic and with some ten thousand people moving west every month, it has been estimated that Bonn will spend more than $1 trillion over the next decade to rebuild its newly absorbed provinces.[10]

The two communist parties, one in the east and the other in the west of Germany, decided not to merge because of differences in structure, theory, and practice. The Second Congress of the eastern Party of Democratic Socialism (PDS) convened during 26–27 January 1991 in Berlin, where Gregor Gysi was reelected chairman. He claimed to base the new PDS program on "democratic socialism" in contrast to the previous "real socialism," which was condemned. Gysi admitted that about 70,000 had left the party and that only 3,000 had joined since May 1990, leaving the claimed total around 214,000 members.[11] The total loss from the time its predecessor, the Socialist Unity Party of Germany, held power numbered more than 2 million.

Hungary. The former ruling communist movement, renamed the Hungarian Socialist Party (HSP), won just 10.9 percent of the vote during the March 1990 parliamentary elections.[12] It had previously split, with only 50,000 (formerly 700,000 members) remaining in the HSP. Even the communist newspaper, *Népszabadság*, was sold to foreign investors. However, in local elections during the fall, more than 70 percent of the five hundred former communist council chairmen were reelected as independents. This has resulted in a divided government.

Budapest is moving away from Moscow in the direction of Western Europe and its neighbors, with the USSR becoming only one of five "legs" in Hungarian foreign policy. Although the Soviets have acknowledged the immorality of the Hitler-Stalin pact and apologized to Czechoslovakia for the 1968 invasion, they have refused to do the same regarding the suppression of the 1956 Hungarian uprising as of this writing. In response to a claim for damages to the environment by USSR occupation forces, Admiral Iurii Grishin told his counterpart that Budapest should apply for money in Washington, D.C.[13]

Poland. Here also the former communists changed their name to the Social Democracy of the Republic of Poland (SDRP) at the end of January 1990. A smaller rival group calls itself the Social Democratic Union of the Polish Republic. Neither plays any significant role in government, and both should be completely swept out of Parliament after the fall 1991 national elections. The SDRP claimed about 60,000 members,[14] a drop from 2 million in July 1989.

Owing to public demand, Parliament adopted a law in November 1990 that nationalized 95 percent of the former communist party's wealth and left the remainder for SDRP use. The state expropriated 1,869 buildings. Former communist leader and president of Poland, General Wojciech Jaruzelski, agreed to step down, which paved the way for Lech Wałęsa to be elected on 9 December 1990 to the presidency. He was sworn in before Christmas, and a new government followed.[15]

Romania. The former communist party of 3.8 million members disappeared after the execution of its leaders, Nicolae Ceauşescu and Elena Ceauşescu, on Christmas Day 1989. The successor organization, now in power, is called the National Salvation Front (NSF) and is made up of 1 million former communists. Although other political movements are now legal, no power sharing has materialized. National elections for president were won on 20 May 1990 by Ion Iliescu, former NSF head and before that secretary for ideology in the communist bureaucracy, who had fallen into disfavor. The same lopsided majority resulted in 263 NSF deputies out of 396 in the legislature.[16]

Protest demonstrations in Bucharest were put down by riot police and some ten thousand miners (brought in by railroad), who used wooden clubs and wire bludgeons on 14 June 1990. None of them was detained for brutalizing unarmed civilians and destroying offices of the opposition. The United States has refused to extend most favored nation treatment to Romania because of such human rights violations.

Yugoslavia. The League of Communists of Yugoslavia (LCY) held its Fourteenth Congress in January 1990. With almost 2 million members, this organization is more of a façade than the powerful instrument it was in the hands of Tito, who led it until his death in 1980. The congress ended abruptly after the Slovene delegation demanded a confederation of independent, republic organizations "freely united" in the LCY. When voted down, the Slovenes walked out, and the other delegates returned home.

With or without the LCY, the government of Yugoslavia continued to function. Other political movements prepared to compete in the first postwar, multiparty regional elections. In both Slovenia and Croatia, center-right coalitions defeated reform communists. Although one of the latter won the Slovene presidency, a nationalist became the first noncommunist president (of a Yugoslav republic) in Croatia. The born-again Serbian communists, now the Socialist Party of Serbia, won control of Parliament, and their leader became president with 65 percent of the vote. The victory in Montenegro was similar. However, communists lost in Macedonia.[17] Although the federal government at Belgrade continues to issue orders, nobody seems to be paying attention. To date, the army has threatened to intervene but has not yet done so.

The future looks grim for what is left of communist parties throughout East-Central Europe. Their days appear to be numbered even in such former Stalinist strongholds as Albania and Romania. Changing names or faces of leaders will not fool the electorate, which blames, rightly so, the communists for decades of mismanagement not to mention criminal activity. To paraphrase Karl Marx, that system is destined for the garbage can of history.

Richard F. Staar
Hoover Institution

NOTES

1. Ronald Linden, "The End of the Beginning," *Report on Eastern Europe* 2, no. 1 (4 January 1991): 1–4.

2. For identification of the members, see table 2.2 in Richard F. Staar, *Foreign Policies of the Soviet Union* (Stanford: Hoover Institution Press, 1991), pp. 29–30.

3. For biographic sketches, see "Politbiuro i sekretariat tsentral'nogo komiteta KPSS," *Izvestiia TsK KPSS*, no. 8 (August): 7–61.

4. "Komu narod doveriaet," *Izvestiia*, 29 November 1990, p. 2.

5. The *World Marxist Review* at its height claimed a circulation of 500,000 copies. At the very end, only the Soviets and Mongolians continued to subsidize the journal. *Pravda*, 23 May 1990, p. 7.

6. Richard F. Staar, ed., "Introduction," *East-Central Europe and the USSR* (New York: St. Martin's Press, 1991).

7. See the two articles by Louis Zanga, "New Economic Ideas," *Report on Eastern Europe* 2, no. 2 (11 January 1991): 8–10, and "A Watershed Year," *Report on Eastern Europe* 2, no. 6 (8 February 1991): 1–6.

8. Compare figures in Richard F. Staar, ed., *YICA*, for 1989 and 1990, pp. 329 and 345, respectively.

9. "Czechoslovaks to Return Property Confiscated in the Communist Era," *NYT*, 27 February 1991, p. A-12.

10. Ferdinand Protzman, "Germans Lower Expectations on East's Economic Recovery," *NYT*, 12 February 1991, pp. A-1 and C-2.

11. "PDS and DKP Presidiums Meet," *Neues Deutschland*, 7 January 1991, p. 3; M. Podkliuchnikov, "PDS: Strategiia na zavtra," *Pravda*, 28 January 1991, p. 4.

12. Vladimir V. Kusin, "The Elections Compared and Assessed," *Report on Eastern Europe* 1, no. 28 (13 July): 38–47.

13. "Hungary Wants Soviets to Pay for Damages," *Insight*, 4 March 1991, p. 30.

14. Radio Warsaw, 23 August; *FBIS-EEU*, 24 August.

15. Louisa Vinton, "Walesa Forms a New Government," *Report on Eastern Europe* 2, no. 3 (18 January 1991): 17–20.

16. Vladimir Socor, "NSF Produces Electoral Landslide," *Report on Eastern Europe* 1, no. 27 (6 July): 24–32.

17. V. V. Kusin, "Elections Compared and Assessed."

Albania

Population. 3,237,131 (*World Fact Book*)
Party. Albanian Party of Labor (APL, Partia ë Punës e Shqipërisë)
Founded. 8 November 1941
Membership. 135,000. The social breakdown of party membership is as follows: 38.9 percent, blue-collar workers; 25.5 percent, cooperativists; 33.2 percent, women.
First Secretary. Ramiz Alia
Politburo. Ramiz Alia, chairman of the People's Assembly, chief of state, commander in chief of the armed forces, and chairman of the defense council; Adil Çarçani, chairman, Council of Ministers; Besnik Bekteshi, minister of industry, mines, and energy; Hekuran Isai, deputy premier and minister of the interior; Pali Mishka, deputy premier and minister of agriculture; Kiço Mustagi, minister of defense, chief, General Staff; Vangjel Çerava; Xhelil Gonji; Abdyl Backa, Tiranë party chief. Candidate members: Llambi Gjegprifti, chairman, People's Council, Tiranë district; Xhemal Dymyla; Niko Gjizari, chairman, State Bank. There are two vacancies in the alternate list of Politburo members. The Politburo normally consists of 13 full members and 5 candidates, almost all of whom occupy top government posts. Purges conducted in July and December have left several vacancies, which will probably be filled in the next party congress scheduled for June 1991.
Secretariat. Ramiz Alia, first secretary; members: Xhelin Gjoni; Spiro Dede; Abdyl Backa.
Party Control Commission. Pilo Peristeri, chairman
Status. Ruling party
Last Congress. Ninth, 3–8 November 1988
Last Parliamentary Elections. 1 February 1987
Other Parties. Democratic Party (Partia Demokratik)
Founded. 12 December 1990
Chairman. Gramoz Pashko
Vice-Chairman. Sali Berisha
Auxiliary Organizations. Albanian Democratic Front (ADF), Adil Çarçani, chairman; Central Council of Trade Unions of Albania (CCTUA), Sotir Koçallari, chairman; Union of Labor Youth of Albania (ULYA), Lisen Bashkurti, chairman; Albanian War Veterans, Shefqet Peçi, chairman
Main State Organ. Council of Ministers, 22-member cabinet, which includes a post of minister secretary general to the Council of Ministers and the chairman of the State Planning Commission. Several individuals hold more than one position.
Composition of the Cabinet. Adil Çarçani, prime minister; Hekuran Isai, deputy prime minister and minister of interior; Pali Mishka, deputy prime minister and minister of agriculture; Ismail Ahmeti, public works; Skender Gjinushi, education; Besnik Bekteshi, industry, mining and energy (holds two portfolios); Qemal Dysha, finance; Ylli Bufi, food industry; Reiz Malile, foreign affairs; Shane Korbeçi, foreign trade; Pajtim Ajazi, internal trade; Enver Halili, justice; Bashkim Sykaj, light industry; Kiço Mustaqi, people's defense; Ahmet Kamberi, public health; Salvador Franja, transportation; Farudin Hoxha, minister to the presidium of the Council of Ministers; Fatos Nano, minister, secretary general to the Council of Ministers; Buhar Kolaneci, chairman, State Planning Commission
Publications. *Zeri i Popullit*, daily organ of the Central Committee of the APL; *Bashkimi*, daily organ of the Democratic Front; *Rilindja Demokratik* (Democratic Renaissance), organ of the newly founded Democratic party (publishes twice a week); *Zeri i Rinisë*, daily organ of ULYA; *Puna*, weekly organ of CCTUA; *Lluftetari* and *10 Korrik*, weekly organs of the Ministry of Defense; *Nentori*, monthly organ of the Albanian Writers and Artists League; *Drita*, monthly literary magazine; *Laiko Vema*, organ of the Democratic Front for the Greek Minority. The Albanian Telegraphic Agency (ATA) is the official state news service.

Internal Party and Government Affairs. The collapse of communist regimes in 1989 in most of Eastern Europe initially appeared to pose minimal threats to the steadfastly pro-Stalin leadership in Albania. Confident that their grip on power would not be broken and that the winds of change that uprooted feared dictators elsewhere had no direct implication for them, Ramiz Alia and his cohorts dismissed these events as proof of the collapse of revisionism, not of true socialism. In the spirit of Enver Hoxha, Alia greeted the Albanian people with a vociferous 1990 New Year message in defense of Stalinism: "The general line of our party, which is elaborated in Albania and by Albanian communists alone, with Comrade Enver Hoxha at the head is the correct line of freedom, independence and absolute people's and national sovereignty" (GMT Domestic Service, 1 January; *FBIS*, 3 January). News stories about "upheavals" in Albania reported in the Western media were dismissed by Alia as the work of sinister forces, aimed at undermining the "people's power." He stated that "the events that have occurred recently in Eastern Europe have inspired certain known anti-Albanian forces to resume the campaign of slanders against our country. . . . They cannot succeed in doing us harm; we have never allowed and will never allow anybody to dictate our laws and norms." (*WP*, 2 January.) "The crisis that has swept over the East European countries is a crisis of what is called the socialist community but not of socialism in theory and practice" (*Zeri i Popullit*, 1 January). Nevertheless, Alia's assertions that he and Enver Hoxha had devised the "perfect" socialist system and that there was therefore no need to alter its course rapidly lost credibility as 1990 continued. A search for acceptable cosmetic changes then began, with some of the innovations suggested at the Eighth Plenum (September 1989) revived to offer the appearance of reform without jeopardizing the party's control.

The Ninth Central Committee Plenum (22–23 January) was called into session to "carry further some recommendations made months earlier" by Lenka Çuko, a member of the Secretariat (*YICA*, 1990). Alia found in these proposed changes the "wisdom of Enver Hoxha" and reiterated that they had "nothing to do with events in Eastern Europe" (ATA, 3 February; *FBIS*, 7 February). Among the steps taken in January were the following: (a) opening meetings of all base party organizations to the masses "to bring them closer to the party," (b) limitations of "four or five years" for all terms of office, including newly elected cadres, secretaries, and party bureau chiefs, and (c) rotating cadres of state and party organs. At the same plenum, it was decided that at least one-third of the members of both the legislature and the Central Committee would be replaced after they had served "one or two terms" (ibid.). A total of ten "innovations" were introduced at this time, which taken together seemed to preempt all the demands that reformist movements in Eastern Europe had presented to their regimes. The critical difference, however, was that Alia wanted to have his cake and eat it, too; Article 3 of the Albanian constitution, which legitimizes the party's monopoly of power, was not affected.

At the beginning of the year, the situation in the country was tense and rumors of upheavals pervasive. Although the regime seemed shaken by the overthrow of Ceauşescu in Romania, one of Albania's closest East European allies, it nevertheless tried to weather the storm. Alia denounced accounts of mass demonstrations in the northern city of Shkodër (*WP*, 2 April) as "fabrications designed to overthrow the people's power in Albania and to destroy its independence" (*NYT*, 9 February). To assure the world that the situation at home was under control, he revived a tested method of public relations: he invited prominent Western fellow travelers to visit Tiranë and chaperoned them around the country. As planned, they made the expected "authoritative, eyewitness" assessments to the effect that everything seemed peaceful in Albania. Senator Giulio Orlando (Italy) in particular proved a convenient guest at a critical time. While visiting Albania, the Italian politician stated (and was widely quoted in the Tiranë radio and press) that he "saw nothing unusual; there was the normal presence of soldiers. Nothing to astonish me. No signs of state of emergency." (*NYT*, 20 January.)

On the diplomatic front Alia also took action. He dispatched two of his senior diplomats, Sokrat Pliaka to Athens and Mohammed Kaplani to Ankara, to brief their Balkan neighbors on Albania's commitment to Balkan cooperation and to continued reform as initiated by the communist party (*WP*, 17 February). While on the road, Pliaka announced Albania's willingness to restore relations with the superpowers and to consider joining the Conference on Security and Cooperation in Europe (CSCE) process.

At the Ninth Plenum, Alia had acknowledged "shortcomings in the Albanian economy" but still persisted in his belief that central planning would remain the pillar of communist economics for the foreseeable future. Despite all efforts to deflect external pressures and fine-tune the process of "soft landing," however, the government and the communist party faced dire difficulties during 1990. These were made worse by the complete dislocation of foreign trade, the loss of European ideological partners, and the intense scrutiny the country received as the last "Stalinist domino still standing" (*The World & I*, June). By April the regime concluded that it had to undertake measures that would give the impression of more serious change and thus increase the likelihood of Western assistance.

The Tenth Central Committee Plenum (17 April) was called into session to examine a variety of critical issues. It also served to carry forth some of the suggestions made at the January gathering of the CC, which dealt with the "democratization of the socioeconomic life and to strengthen the thinking and action of the people" (*Zeri i Popullit*, 19 April). By then Alia had succeeded in dubbing himself the besieged "reformer," fighting against the hardliners who insisted on the perpetuation of "outdated approaches." While Alia was peddling his reformer's image, the State Security Committee (Sigurimi) commenced, with Alia's approval, intimidating operations to prevent mass demonstrations in Tiranë. On 30 April, Sigurimi agents forced their way into the Greek embassy and dragged away a young student who had sought asylum there (UPI Wire Service, 30 April; Athens News Agency, 3 April). In another instance, men of the dreaded Sambisti, a section of the Sigurimi trained to infiltrate opposition groups and cause havoc among their members, manhandled the French ambassador and his wife (*Hamburg Bild*, *FBIS*, 12 June). France lodged a strong protest, as did the Italian, French, Greek and West German embassies for persistent violations of diplomatic norms. The Albanian Foreign Ministry in turn denied the incidents ever happened. (*CRS: Reports for Congress*, 90–456, 7 September.) Frustrated, Greece recalled its ambassador to Tiranë, Spyros Dokianos, for consultations.

The key proposals put forth at the April plenum dealt with the restoration of long-denied elementary freedoms, as well as the revision of the penal code to make this restoration possible. The plenum also formally endorsed the desirability of restoring relations with the superpowers and the European Community (EC) and of joining the CSCE process (*Zeri i Popullit*, 19 April; *FBIS*, 24 April). As usual, Alia took the high road on relations with Moscow and Washington: "If, as they say, the United States changed their attitude toward Albania, we have no reason not to welcome this" (ibid.).

To solidify his image as a reformer, Alia instructed the government to take the necessary administrative steps to revive the Ministry of Justice, whose abolition he had vociferously supported in 1967 because it was an "impediment to intensification of class struggle." Manush Myftiu, a former member of the Albanian Fascist party (he converted to communism in 1941), was charged with the task of redrafting the penal code to accommodate this change. The seventh legislative session of the people's assembly then formalized the party's resolution. Myftiu's recommendations on the "improve-

ment of the democratization of the penal legislation as well as some organizational measures" passed in the usual unanimous fashion (ATA, 9 May; *FBIS*, 10 May). The legislative session also "validated" other recommendations from the Central Committee such as freedom of conscience, decentralization of power, limited private property, productivity incentives, limitations of terms of office at the state, enterprises, and party levels, multiple candidacies, and contested elections. Also, for the first time in postwar history, Albanians were given the right to have passports. Other significant changes were made in the area of civil rights. The number of crimes punishable by death was reduced from 33 to 11 (*Zeri i Popullit*, 9 May), and religious expression was decriminalized. However, although the state retained the right to "conduct atheist propaganda," the church was not granted the right to proselytize (RFE/RL, *Report on Eastern Europe*, 25 May). Once these reforms were in place, Tiranë received Javier Perez de Cuellar, the first visit to Albania by the secretary general of the United Nations (*NYT*, 12 May).

The "reforms" introduced in May to impress the world with the regime's intention to end its isolation had one serious drawback: the APL was both the sole initiator and the director of their execution. In some areas, the changes seemed ludicrous by Western standards, even though they were heralded as great strides toward democratization. For example, agitation that aims at the overthrow of the regime is punishable if voiced publicly but not considered a crime if voiced privately (AFP, 11 May). Given the ambiguity of the definition of *private* and *public* in the law, expressing unorthodox views remains risky, even among family members. Another change heralded by Myftiu as evidence of "the humanistic character of socialist justice" was the abolition of the death sentence for all women, not just pregnant ones, as was previously the case (ibid.).

In a transparent attempt to add credibility to his policies and to forestall further demands for changes, Alia then undertook another partial reshuffle of his cabinet. Aranit Cela, the procurator general and chief judge (nicknamed "the Butcher" in dissent circles) who for twenty-three years had played the role of the "Albanian Andrei Vyshinski," was relieved of his duties and retired. His position was given to a woman, Kleanthi Koço. Enver Halili was shifted from the position of minister/secretary general to the Council of Ministers and made minister of justice; Niko Gjizari, chairman of the State Planning Commission, was elevated to the post of secretary to the cabinet and party chief of Elbasan (the industrial center of the country). Finally, Bujar Kolaneci was assigned the post of chairman of the State Planning Commission (ATA, 9 May; *FBIS*, 10 May).

However, the changes initiated by the Tenth CC Plenum and adopted by the people's assembly were not wholly believable, nor did they go far enough. The key people of the Hoxha era were still in full control, and Alia had difficulty persuading anyone that he was sincere in his reformist intentions.

Summer of Upheavals. The "reforms" introduced in an incremental manner since January, even though essentially superficial, had a profound impact among intellectuals, workers, and ordinary citizens. Students in particular intensified their demands and persisted in testing the parameters of the promised freedoms. By midsummer, they had begun street demonstrations, and some attempted to cross the borders into Greece. Several were shot at the borders in the Mourgana Mountains, eliciting a women's march to the site of the shooting (accounts of refugees, interview by the author, 9 January 1991). Word of the shooting quickly reached Tiranë, and students and workers devised new methods to achieve a mass exodus from Albania: they entered foreign embassies in large numbers while their associates made maximum use of the telephone links Albania had established with AT&T (*NYT*, 12 April) by calling foreign journalists to draw attention to their plight. The virtual invasion of embassies started in earnest on 2 July and, by a calculated selection of the date, reached its peak on 4 July. Initially, a few students entered the compound of the Greek embassy after a worker smashed his truck through the wall. In the next few days, approximately five thousand Albanians of all ages sought asylum in the embassies of Germany, Italy, Czechoslovakia, Poland, France, Greece, Turkey, and Egypt (*NYT*, 4 July). Two students who sought asylum in the Cuban embassy were turned over to the police. One of them allegedly committed suicide by banging his head against the wall while in custody in a Sigurimi prison. After days of stalemate and brutality, the government relented and provided passports to those who wanted to leave the country (*NYT*, 6 July). Word of the availability of passports was disseminated quickly, and tens of thousands of young people, workers, and even children of high party officials made their way toward the center of the city attempting to enter embassy compounds (ibid., 6 July). Refugees who reached

Greece at the end of December intimated that the son of Muho Asllani, a Politburo member, was among those seeking refuge in the German embassy. (This rumor, which was circulating among Albanian circles in Priština Kosovo as well, was never confirmed.)

The summer events in Tiranë left a number of people dead. According to news accounts, routinely denied by the regime, a mass grave at the foothills of Dajti Mountain was dug to bury the dead. The French news agency reported 23–30 fatalities (*FBIS*, 6 July); Italian television quoted sources within Albania and placed the number of dead in the hundreds (*FBIS*, 10 July). In the chaotic situation prevailing in Tiranë, no one knew who was in charge of the security forces. Certainly it was not Simon Stefani, who was subsequently relieved of his position.

The Aftermath of the Embassy Siege: Purges and Reforms. In the chaos of mass exodus Alia called into session the Eleventh CC Plenum to deal with the "new situation." In secret proceedings, the first secretary ingeniously fired those who failed to predict and prevent the events and parlayed changes at the top as a victory against the hard-liners. Alia dismissed those who sought asylum in foreign embassies as "hooligans" and the pawns of a broader conspiracy. In his report to the plenum he said:

> It is clear that their aim was to create distrust in the laws which have been and will be enacted in the road to democratization; which our party has chosen and will follow to the end. Of course the people seeking shelter in the Embassies are neither patriots, nor honest citizens of this country. (ATA, 7 July; *FBIS*, 17 July.)

Nevertheless, an analysis of the July purges does not support the official interpretation of the changes as "victory" over the hard-liners.

Three members of the Politburo, Prokop Mura (minister of defense), Rita Marko (deputy chairman, people's assembly), and Manush Myftiu were relieved of their posts and retired; Simon Stefani, minister of interior and deputy premier, was relieved of both posts and assigned to the position of chairman of the State Control Commission; a fifth member, Lenka Çuko, the sole woman in the Politburo and Secretariat, was made the party chief of Fier; and, although not mentioned in the official communiqué, Muho Asllani, party chief of Durrës, was demoted to manager of a cooperative farm. Before we deal with their replacements (some of them temporary, as we shall see below), we must note that a significant body of evidence suggests that the losers had failed, in their respective areas of authority, to sell the public on the new policies being "democratic," thus undermining the party's image among the masses. A case-by-case review shows the following:

Lenka Çuko. She was the first person to talk about the need for multicandidacies in elections and limitations in the term of office of party and state officials at the Eighth CC Plenum (*Zeri i Popullit*, 27 September 1989; *YICA*, 1990). She was supported by Alia who at that time found "merit" in her report.

Simon Stefani. He was assigned the position of minister of interior in February 1989 for the sole purpose of bringing the Sigurimi under the party's control. During his watch the first and only public criticism of the secret police was published; the novel *Thikak* (Knives) mocked the Sigurimi's practices of viewing every ordinary crime as a political plot and an opportunity for its agents to get promoted. The novel received rave reviews by none other than Ismail Kadare, Albania's most prominent writer, who in October defected to France because he doubted Alia's sincerity about reforms (*AP*, 25 October; *NYT*, 6 December). In his review of the novel Kadare said that "it will disturb people's conscience and will prove its emancipating effect" (*Drita*, 15 October 1989; *YICA*, 1990). The author of *Thikak*, Neshat Tozaj, himself a Sigurimi man, concluded his novel with the promise that the "demythologizing" of the dreaded security apparatus was under way: "The Party would need to work hard and for a long time to strip this Ministry [Interior] of its mythology and destroy the cult of security. . . . What the enemy has done in forty years must be undone in a very short time." (Neshat Tozaj, *Thikat* [Tiranë: Shtepia Botuesë "Naim Frasheri," 1989], pp. 259–60.)

Manush Myftiu. Deputy Premier Myftiu was placed in charge by the Tenth CC Plenum and by the seventh legislative session to draft a new penal code and to institutionalize legality in Albania. His proposals, which included the issuance of passports for the first time in postwar Albania, were enacted enthusiastically by the people's assembly and give evidence of the reappearance of legality in a land

that, for 40 years, was ruled by the totalitarian Enver Hoxha. As it turned out, issuance of passports was the spark that caused the exodus to the embassies. Although the law was in place, few were actually given passports, which led people to find other ways of getting out of the country.

Prokop Mura. The first civilian to serve as minister of defense, Mura assumed the position in the aftermath of Prime Minister Mehmet Shehu's assassination (see *YICA*, 1983), replacing the latter's brother-in-law, General Kadri Hazbiu. Mura could hardly qualify as the typical Stalin loyalist, and his tenure as defense minister confirmed his mediocrity.

None of the individuals listed above fits the category of *hard-liner*, even though they all qualify as opportunists. Their appointments, taken in conjunction with the changes introduced at the Twelfth Plenum, suggest that the genuine reformers lost out, that the hard-liners succeeded in parading as reformers, and that, for the time being, Alia achieved what other East European regimes failed to accomplish: a "soft landing" bolstered by intense nationalism and renewed patriotism. This interpretation is also supported by an analysis of the careers of the replacements in the Ministries of Defense and Interior.

Stefani's successor at the Ministry of Interior and deputy premier is Hekuran Isai. He held the same position for seven years under Enver Hoxha and was replaced in February 1989 by Stefani, ostensibly to bring the dreaded Sigurimi under party control. Isai was in charge of the bloody and massive purges of Shehu followers and is responsible for physically eliminating an unspecified number of senior army officers accused of being foreign spies. He was and remains a Hoxha clone.

Mura was replaced as defense minister by his deputy, Gen. Kiço Mustaqi, a vocal Hoxha supporter who also played a critical role in purging the army of Hazbiu and Shehu supporters and who rose in party and government ranks with Hoxha's support. A total of twelve cabinet changes were initiated by the Eleventh CC Plenum. The critical ones in the Politburo and key ministries involved individuals with the capacity and stature to challenge Alia but who were not necessarily opposed to reform. The pattern of changes introduced in the aftermath of the embassies siege suggests that Alia sought to punish those who failed to maintain public order and those who could easily be blamed for failures in the economy and shortages in consumer goods (for a list of these changes, see *ATA*, 7, 9 July; *FBIS*, 9 July).

Albanian Reforms under Alia. Following the purges of July, approved by the Eleventh CC Plenum and the Council of Ministers, Alia supported the enactment of a series of legislative acts and decrees that suggested a more serious commitment to the democratization process, albeit under party control. With the embassy refugee crisis essentially resolved (all protesters having been exiled), he spent the rest of the summer consolidating his position and reinforcing his image as a true nationalist and democrat. In August, he enacted two decrees regulating and protecting foreign investments (*Gazeta Zyrtarë*, no. 6, August; *FBIS*, 17 October). In October, he visited New York to address the General Assembly and used the opportunity to visit the grave of Bishop Fan Noli, a nationalist famous in Albanian history books for facilitating the education of young Albanians in Comintern schools in the twenties (*Bashkimi*, 3 October).

To carry out the recommendations of the Ninth, Tenth, and Eleventh plenums of the Central Committee, Alia, who behaved increasingly as a one-man reform movement, called on the Democratic Front to debate the means of implementing Albanian-style pluralism. On 9 October, the presidency of the Democratic Front, still under the chairmanship of Nexhmije Hoxha, the widow of Enver Hoxha, met to discuss the draft electoral law. With Alia present, the mass organization discussed and adopted an electoral law that de facto perpetuated the old-style Albanian democracy. Nevertheless, it too was seen as evidence of expanding pluralism.

According to the proposed law, the right to field candidates was reserved for the APL and the known mass organizations. Specifically, it stated that "according to the draft law, this right [to field candidates] belongs to the Party of Labor of Albania, the Democratic Front of Albania, the Trade Unions, the Women's Union, the Youth Union, the Veterans Association, the Writers and Artists League, as well as other organizations recognized by the law" (*ATA*, 9 October; *FBIS*, 17 October).

These were the same mass organizations used as fronts by the APL and could hardly be accepted by genuine reformers as serious vehicles of pluralism. However, even half measures needed appropriate constitutional changes. Article 3 of the 1976 constitution finally had to be modified to implement changes in the parliamentary elections. This

was recommended by Mrs. Hoxha, with Alia's approval.

On 6–7 November, the Twelfth Plenum of the CC was called to discuss constitutional revisions and to fine-tune the mechanisms for the control of new organizations. Alia's report, "The Consolidation of the People's Power and the Perfection of the Entire Political System Stimulates the Democratic Development," recommended three basic changes be taken up by the people's assembly: (*a*) the leading role of the party was to be redefined but not abandoned because "it responds to our concrete reality," (*b*) foreign investment, prohibited by Article 28 of the constitution, was now welcomed, and the Parliament was to be instructed to provide enabling legislation, and (*c*) Articles 37 and 55 of the 1976 Constitution, which declared atheism the state norm, were to be revised since they "violated freedom of conscience" (*ATA, FBIS*, 8 November).

The eighth legislative session of the people's assembly was called into session soon after the Twelfth CC Plenum and given a heavy agenda. It had to deal with a total of eleven proposals, including setting up a commission to revise the constitution (*ATA*, 9 November; *FBIS*, 13 November). Although the agenda seemed heavy, the Parliament still functioned as essentially a CC rubber stamp and approved with only minor modifications all submitted recommendations. The process of democratization seemed to be moving quickly, but the intelligentsia, the students (who returned to the University of Tiranë and found living conditions deplorable), and the workers were not ready to accept the notion that Alia and his associates, all of whom made their careers as Hoxha men, should be taken seriously. Distrust of Alia's intentions was confirmed when his protégé, prominent Albanian writer Ismail Kadare, defected to France and accused his former friend of reneging on his promises to introduce legality in the land. The prominent author eloquently expressed what many of his compatriots felt. In a press release Kadare revealed not only had he had many meetings with the president but he had exchanged letters with Alia in which he had expressed "very clearly the necessity for a rapid, profound and complete democratization of the country." He continued that, "because there is no possibility of legal opposition in Albania I have chosen this course [defection] which I never wished to take and which I will not recommend to others" (*NYT*, 26 October).

Then, in the first week of December, mass demonstrations occurred in three major cities, including the capital, and army units were called to impose law and order. In the midst of the confusion caused by student demonstrators, Alia called the Thirteenth CC Plenum ostensibly to reorganize the party at the top and proceed with democratization. Five full Politburo members and two candidate members were removed. Some of them, as we have seen, had already been demoted in the July purges. Simon Stefani, who had lost his government job in July but still retained membership in the Politburo, was fired from all positions; Lenka Çuko had the same fate, along with Muho Asllani (party chief of Durrës) and Hajredin Çeliku (minister of transportation). The big surprise was the elimination of Foto Çami, a member of the Secretariat and often mentioned in Western analyses as "Albania's most prominent liberal." Two candidate members, Piro Kondi and Qirjako Mihalli, were also cashiered. (ATA, 12 December; *FBIS*, 12 December.) On 12 December, a day after the latest purges, the Democratic party was formed.

Birth of the Albanian Democratic Party. After three days of mass political unrest and demonstrations in several cities, the new leadership agreed to open up the political system to independent parties. The CC announced that "the Thirteenth Plenum was of the opinion that the creation of independent political organizations according to the law in force is to the good of the further democratization of the life of the country and pluralism" (AP, 11 December).

The change in tone during the week of unrest among the Albanian communist leadership was stunning. Almost until the last moment, the leadership maintained that the unrest was caused by "hooligans" and "criminals." When security forces proved unable to suppress unrest, government authorities then sent troops to crush the revolt.

On 12 December, at a huge rally in Tiranë, the first independent party came into existence after 44 years of uncontested communist control. The new Democratic party applied for official acceptance at the newly created Ministry of Justice amid uncertainty and unfolding political drama in this Muslim-dominated Balkan nation. The provisional leader of the new Democratic party is Gramoz Pashko, a university professor of economics. Pashko, 35, is the son of a former CC and cabinet member and has been a communist party member (AFP, in English, 19 December; *FBIS*, 20 December). The vice-chairman of the party, Dr. Sali Berisha, comes from a prominent Albanian clan in Kosovo and escaped

from a Yugoslav prison two years earlier. One of his relatives, Tome Berisha, is president of the Democratic Alliance of Albanians in Croatia, with headquarters in Zagreb, Yugoslavia (*Slobodna Dalmacia*, 9 September; *FBIS*, 17 September). The birth of the new party was greeted with massive protests in five major cities and the ensuing police brutality. Yet Pashko praised Alia for "having avoided imposing martial law" (AFP, in English, 19 December; *FBIS*, 20 December).

In Shkodër, a city of 72,000, demonstrators allegedly attacked government buildings and dynamited the statue of the once feared tyrant, Enver Hoxha, three days after students in Tiranë began their protests. On 14–15 December, when several hundred protesters took to the streets in Elbasan, communist authorities sent tanks to this major industrial city (Vienna International Service; *FBIS*, 15 December). Unable to control the fast-spreading unrest in other Albanian cities, including Durrës and Kavajë, the government appealed to Albanian nationalism and patriotism to stop those who threatened the democratic process in Albania (Belgrade, Tanjug, in English, *FBIS*, 15 December). The new party joined in that appeal, which then raised questions about its independence. More than three hundred protesters were arrested, and trials were staged in several major cities. (Tanjug, in English, 18 December; *FBIS*, 19 December). Thus far, 177 students have been tried in Elbasan, Durrës, and Shkodër and given sentences of up to ten years in prison.

On 18 December more than a thousand people demonstrated in Tiranë demanding the release of all political prisoners, the removal of the statue of Stalin (to be replaced with one of Fan Noli), and the postponement of the date of legislative elections (initially scheduled for 10 February 1991) to give the new party time to organize (AFP, *FBIS*, 18 December). The latter was necessary because the Democratic party had failed to define either its ideology or its program in a coherent manner. Since its founding on 12 December it had avoided a confrontational approach with the communist leaders and in so doing has limited its credibility as an alternative. There were also questions about the credentials of some of the leaders of the Democratic party and whether some of the mass demonstrations were not carefully planned "spontaneous events." There is at least one area, however, in which the APL and the Democratic party seem to agree: the value of nationalism as a substitute for orthodox Marxism-Leninism. In an article published in

Bashkimi, a leader of the new party saw the emergence of "democratic structures" as a "valuable contribution to the struggle of our brothers in Kosovo" (*Bashkimi*, 17 September; *FBIS*, 27 September). For the Greek minority and for thousands of Albanians, however, the new party did not provide assurances of democratization. In fact, many of them were frightened by the revival of Muslim nationalism and sought asylum in Greece and Yugoslavia. More than seven thousand refugees crossed the borders in a matter of three days during the last week of 1990. Many of those who entered Greece (this author interviewed a large number of them) said that "they did not trust the new party, because most of its leaders are known communists." The response of the authorities to legitimate protest seems to reinforce the view that democracy still has a long way to go in Albania. Although significant steps have been taken toward democratization and although elections were indeed postponed until 31 March, communist authorities continued to arrest demonstrators and to impose sentences for participating in the December uprising (Tiranë Domestic Service, *FBIS*, 19 December).

Nevertheless, after two weeks of ambivalence the government and Alia opted to grant legal status to the Democratic party. On 19 December the people's assembly adopted several measures regarding the recognition of independent parties and announced that once a political organization has applied at the Ministry of Justice, authorities will render their decision on its acceptability within 30 days. An application for acceptance could be rejected on several grounds, such as the party's ideology espousing a "fascist, racist, warmongering, and anti-national character." Moreover, foreign citizens or Albanians who are not permanent residents are not permitted to take part in the formation of the party or to become members. Further, no financial assistance is to be accepted from foreign countries, associations, individuals, or Albanians residing in foreign countries. At the same time, the government made available to the new party the equivalent of $100,000 and allowed it to publish its own newspaper, appropriately titled *Rilindja Demokratik* (Democratic renewal).

De-Stalinization Reaches Albania. On 21 December, the Council of Ministers declared, on the recommendation of the ruling Politburo and taking into consideration that circumstances have changed, that the people were free to remove all vestiges of Stalinism and that state-owned enterprises can now remove the name and symbols of Joseph Stalin and the agricultural cooperatives, if they so decide (ATA, 21 December: *FBIS*, 22 December). Since the East European uprisings, former communist governments made it a ritual to remove the statues of Stalin, their once beloved leader, around midnight when the people are at home. The same was done in late December in Tiranë, a city that once worshiped Stalin and looked on him as a national hero.

Economic and Social Reforms. The year 1990 witnessed cautious yet important developments in Albania's social and economic spheres. It also witnessed unprecedented social upheavals beginning in the summer of 1990. During the Tenth CC Plenum, President Alia informed his comrades that noncommunists were increasingly occupying key positions in the economic sectors as decided during the Ninth Plenum. Alia announced that "nearly 17.5 percent of the total number of cadres and engineering technical staff who run the economy and culture in companies, plants, factories, agricultural enterprises, and cooperatives in the district of Tirana are communists, whereas 82.5 percent are non party members." (ATA, in English, 19 April; *FBIS*, 20 April.) In addition, for most of the year, the communist leadership emphasized that central planning was there to stay. By the end of 1990, however, official thinking had changed significantly, and the Tiranë government now opted for a market economy. In a speech to the workers' party *aktiv*, Alia stated that "the new economic mechanism, replacing the system of central command and administration, will lead toward a market economy on which the large sector will compete with the cooperatives and the private sector." (Albania GMT Domestic Service, *FBIS*, 26 December.) But how this mechanism would be established remained unclear.

Albania has been cautiously trading with some European countries for some time. In December, President Alia announced that joint ventures with Western governments were being undertaken. He disclosed that both a joint Albanian-French firm for various goods and a joint Albanian-Swiss bank have been created. He also said that talks were under way with German, Italian, Canadian, and American firms for joint efforts on offshore oil drilling. Other Western companies are also exploring ways to invest in the Albanian economy.

Mass Organizations. For almost the entire year, mass organizations continued applauding the party's policies. One of the most consequential changes at the top echelons of the communist leadership was the resignation of Nexhmije Hoxha, the 71-year-old widow of the later Enver Hoxha, from the chair of the Democratic Front. Her replacement, Prime Minister Adil Çarçani, apparently intends to use the same structure to contest the next parliamentary elections. Far from being out of favor, as some Western news organizations have indicated, Mrs. Hoxha remains a member of the CC; on 26 December she was selected to join 23 top party members to draft the APL's program. This committee will work closely with another group of party stalwarts to redraft the new APL statutes (GMT Domestic Service, *FBIS*, 26 December).

The CCTUA has been subject to intense criticism by workers for not defending their rights and by the party apparatus for not "educating" the masses in socialist ways. On 22 December, the union's 201-member CC adopted a text resolution declaring that it will no longer act as "a transmission belt of the party." The announcement was made by Genc Pusuli, head of the 800,000-member strong organization, who has joined the Democratic party (*NYT*, 23 December). A few days later, the youth organization also declared its independence. What is remarkable about these defections from the ranks of the APL is that the same people remain in power as before and that the youth organization seems to have adopted a highly nationalistic attitude.

Foreign Relations. With the collapse of the Eastern bloc at the end of 1989, the Albanian leadership took steps to force the country out of its self-imposed isolation. Early in the year, a spokesman at the Foreign Ministry paved the way for the restoration of relations with Moscow and Washington and for Albania's participation in the CSCE process (*WP*, 17 February). Relations with Moscow were finally restored in late July (*Izvestiia, WP*, 31 July), and direct contacts with Washington were established in early May to work out the restoration of ties (*WP*, 15 May). By late 1990 Albania had been granted observer status in the CSCE and accepted the Helsinki accords, which it had rejected for many years. In late summer two U.S. congressional delegations visiting Tiranë found the country's human rights situation appalling. In a formal statement the delegation, headed by Senator Dennis DeConcini, rejected full membership of Albania in the CSCE process: "We are of the opinion that as a full member, Albania would be glaringly out of step with the rapidly developing process toward democratization, political pluralism, the rule of law and free market economies that is taking place throughout Europe" (AP, 23 August). In October the Albanian government hosted the inter-Balkan conference in Tiranë, despite initial reservations on the part of Greece following the execution-style shootings of two would-be escapees at the Greek-Albanian border (BBC, Current Affairs Unit, 26 October). Greek foreign minister Andonis C. Samaras took that opportunity to launch an attack against Albania's persistent atheism and its poor record on human rights.

Relations with Neighbors. Although Albania improved relations with the superpowers and ignored the former socialist states, relations with its Balkan neighbors took a turn for the worse at the end of 1990. During Christmas week, agents of the Sigurimi roamed through Greek villages in the south of Albania spreading rumors of the impending closing of the Greek borders and issuing veiled threats to the Greek minority to abandon their homes or "face unspecified consequences." In a two-week period, eight thousand refugees (in some cases entire villages) fled to Greece, terrified and confused. The Greek government accused Tiranë of spreading fears to force the Greek minority to emigrate, and an urgent visit by the Greek prime minister to Tiranë was scheduled (Athens News Agency, 29 December). Refugees in Filiátes, Igoumenítsa, and Ióannina recounted that the Sigurimi was spreading rumors among the Greek community and other minorities in Albania. In some villages, Greeks were reminded of the Muslim pogroms of the 1920s and the pillage of villages by Albanian Nazi collaborators in World War II.

Archbishop Seraphim of Greece denounced Tiranë in a radio broadcast (9 January 1991) for reviving the idea of a "mono-ethnic Muslim state" in the Balkans. The regime denied such intentions, however, and "looked forward" to Prime Minister Mitsotakis's visit to Tiranë. However, the exodus of refugees from Albania continued as planned by the regime, causing serious social turmoil at the Greek-Albanian borders. Greek officials interviewed by this author are certain that the exodus represents a calculated effort by the Alia regime to "soften" the Greek-Albanian borders; an influx of refugees into Greece would relieve internal pressures from overpopulation and unemployment in Albania.

Although relations with Greece and Yugoslavia took a decided downturn (owing to the revival of intense Albanian nationalism), relations with Turkey improved dramatically, reminding the Balkan neighbors of the interwar era, when Turkey acted as Albania's protector. In late June, Prime Minister Çarçani paid an official visit to Ankara (ATA, *FBIS*, 29 June); by the end of the year Turkey had become Albania's most visible ally and economic investor.

Nikolaos A. Stavrou
Howard University

Bulgaria

Population. 8,933,544 (*World Fact Book 1990*, p. 43.)

Party. Bulgarian Socialist Party (Bŭlgarska sotsialisticheska partiya; BSP); name changed from Bulgarian Communist Party on 3 April.

Founded. Bulgarian Social Democratic party founded in 1891; split into Broad and Narrow factions in 1903; the Narrow Socialists became the BCP and joined the Comintern in 1919.

Membership. 501,790 claimed as of 1 May 1991. According to a report of the BSP Supreme Council, 122,096 left the party between 1 January and 30 June, while 44,180 new members joined. Figures on the social and ethnic composition of the party were not given, but the report described an "alarming decline" of membership in urban areas. (*Duma*, 7 August.) After the BSP congress in September, the party leadership announced that an exchange of party cards would be carried out to determine how many wished to continue their membership. Although originally scheduled to be completed by 30 November, the exchange was continued indefinitely owing to the tumultuous conditions in the country (BTA, 4 December; *FBIS*, 5 December).

Chairman of Supreme Party Council. Alexander Vasilev Lilov (b. 31 August 1933)

Leadership Groups. Supreme Party Council: 150 members. All-party Control Commission: 71 members. Chairman: Deyan Ignatov Rizov (b. 1937). Presidium of Supreme Party Council: 22

members. Chairman: Alexander Lilov; deputy chairmen: Chavdar Kiuranov, Liubomir Kiuchkov, Alexander Tomov, Dimitŭr Yonchev; Secretariat: Blagoi Dechev, Nencho Temelkov; members: Georgi Bliznashki, Filip Bokov, Georgi Bozhinov, Apostol Dimitrov, Ivan Dinkov, Anton Grigorov, Doncho Konakchiev, Alexander Marinov, Svetoslav Minchev, Svetlin Rusev, Petia Shopova, Ivan Stanev, Anzhel Vagenshtain, Zhan Videnov, Krasimir Zheliazkov

Last Congress. The Thirty-ninth Congress was held 22–25 September. At that time a new system of enumerating party congresses was adopted. Earlier in the year (30 January–2 February) the party held its Fourteenth Congress, using the old numbering system. The next congress is scheduled for March 1991.

Last Election. 10, 17 June 1990. The BSP won a plurality (47 percent) of the popular vote and a majority of seats (211 of 400) in the Grand National Assembly.

Publications. During the year the party's daily newspaper changed its name from *Rabotnichesko delo* (Workers' cause; *RD*) to *Duma* (Word). *Dŭrzhaven vestnik* (State gazette) contains texts of laws and decrees. Bŭlgarska Telegrafna Agentsiya (BTA) is the official news agency.

Bulgaria continued the movement toward democracy that began with the fall of Todor Zhivkov on 10 November last year. Although the Bulgarian Communist Party changed its name to Socialist and managed to win a plurality in the country's first free elections since 1931, its hold on the country declined steadily, and its leaders were unable or unwilling to take responsibility for harsh reforms to meet the country's economic crisis. Its best known statesmen, President Mladenov and Prime Minister Lukanov, were both forced from government office. Mladenov was succeeded by the leader of the opposition and Lukanov by a nonparty jurist. Polls showed a steady decline in the party's popular support, and there were numerous signs of internal conflict and disarray.

Domestic Developments. *The "Congress of Renewal."* The processes of change within the Bulgarian Communist Party that began with the fall of Todor Zhivkov on 10 November 1989 (see *YICA*, 1990) continued to develop at the BCP's Fourteenth Congress, dubbed the "Congress of Renewal," held 30 January–2 February. The prevailing tendency was for delegates to attack the "totalitarian regime" of Zhivkov and to accept a generalized collective guilt for the sins of the past. Some longtime members of the old leadership who had turned on Zhivkov the previous November were no longer able to avoid responsibility for their own past roles. Georgi Atanasov, a BCP Central Committee secretary since 1977 and prime minister since Zhivkov's fall, was sharply criticized and offered his resignation on the third day of the congress. Petur Dyulgerov, Dimitŭr Stanishev, Petko Danev, Mincho Yovchev, and Panteley Pachov were also unable to survive the transition to the post-Zhivkov era and saw their careers in the party leadership come to an end.

The congress adopted a "Manifesto on Democratic Socialism" to serve as a statement of the party's program. Describing Bulgaria as being in "an acute economic and political crisis," it called for the BCP to transform itself into a "modern Marxist party of democratic socialism." To this end it specifically recognized the legitimacy of organized "ideological currents and associations" within the party and guaranteed them the right to express their views openly. The manifesto recognized the desirability of political pluralism in society and called for movement toward a market economy and the legalization of new forms of property. The manifesto also proposed changing the party's name as an important symbol of its break with the Zhivkov era. This was later accomplished through a referendum completed on 3 April. Eighty percent of the party membership was said to have voted, with the change of name to Bulgarian Socialist Party being approved 629,522 to 72,609 (*PR*, 5 April). At the same time, the party's newspaper, *Rabotnichesko delo* (*RD*), changed its name to *Duma* (*RD*, 3 April).

The Fourteenth Congress made a number of structural changes in the party. The Central Committee was replaced by a Supreme Party Council. This body in turn elected a Presidium headed by a chairman. Initially, the Supreme Party Council was to number 131. When the congress elected its members, however, most of the leaders of reform factions were defeated. The leadership then persuaded the congress to expand the council to 153 members to include most of those who had been defeated on the first ballot. Several of the reformers added in this way later resigned, stating that they did not want to be the beneficiaries of "manipulation" (*RD*, 6, 8 February). Only about twenty members of the new governing body had been members of the old BCP Central Committee.

Petŭr Mladenov, who had to this point combined party and state leadership, supported the separation of these functions and announced his resignation as party leader. On 3 April the National Assembly elected him to the post of president of the republic in a series of political reforms. Mladenov was succeeded in the party leadership by Alexander Lilov, who was made chairman of the Presidium. Two deputy chairmen were named: Georgi Pirinski (b. 1948) and Alexander Strezov (b. 1935), both of whom had been involved with Bulgarian diplomacy and were closely associated with Mladenov during his years as prime minister. This was also true of Rumen Serbezov (b. 1939), who became the Presidium's secretary. The Presidium also included Petŭr-Emil Mitev, leader of the Road to Europe faction, and Chavdar Kiuranov, a prominent dissident during the Zhivkov era. The congress also elected Stefan Prodev as editor of *Rabotnichesko delo*, the party newspaper. Prodev had been purged from the party under Zhivkov but was rehabilitated by the new leadership.

Andrei Lukanov, generally regarded as the party's most able and experienced statesman, was nominated to replace Atanasov as prime minister and was confirmed in this position by the National Assembly on 3 February. Lukanov, Mladenov, Lilov, and Defense Minister Dobri Dzhurov were clearly the dominant figures at the congress, which nearly always endorsed their views. (*RD*, 30 January–4 February; RFE, *Report on Eastern Europe*, 20 April.)

While the party was struggling with its process of renewal, several of its former auxiliary organizations collapsed or underwent drastic change. Trade unions declared their separation from party control, forming a Confederation of Independent Bulgarian Trade Unions on 18 February. Krŭstiu Petkov, a professor of economics elected chairman of the confederation, called for a complete internal democratization of Bulgarian unions and the rejection of the *nomenklatura* principle (Sofia Domestic Service, 17 February; BTA, 18 February; *FBIS*, 28 February). The Dimitrov Communist Youth League (Komsomol) disintegrated at its congress 24–26 February. A successor organization, Bulgarian Democratic Youth, was created under Rosen Karadimov, who had led the reform movement in the Komsomol; nearly half the delegates refused to join, and several new youth organizations, some affiliated with the political opposition, gathered strength. (*Narodna mladezh*, 27 February; RFE, *Report on Eastern Europe*, 16 March.) The Bulgarian Agrarian National Union (BANU), which had earlier thrown off communist party control, completed a purge of its old leadership at a congress 27–28 February. Its new chairman, Viktor Vŭlkov, declared his commitment to making BANU a "center party" independent of both the communists and opposition forces. (*Zemedelsko zname*, 1 March; Sofia Domestic Service, 6 April; *FBIS*, 10 April.) The mass Fatherland Front organization, which traditionally nominated the candidates for the National Assembly, also separated itself from the BCP, and under its new chairman, Ginio Ganev, declared itself a nonparty organization dedicated to promoting "patriotism and mutual toleration" (*RD*, 21, 22 February).

Roundtable negotiations. While the communist party and its former auxiliaries were attempting to deal with the legacy of the Zhivkov era, opposition groups were also making rapid progress. More than 50 political parties were organized in the period between Zhivkov's fall and the elections in June, but the most influential of these formed an alliance, the Union of Democratic Forces (UDF), headed by Zheliu Zhelev, the country's most prominent dissident. The UDF was officially formed on 7 December 1989 by ten parties and organizations. These included the Discussion Clubs for the Support of *Glasnost'* and *Perestroika*, now renamed Clubs for the Support of Democracy and Eco-*glasnost'*, whose constituency came primarily from the intelligentsia; two revived traditional parties, the Social Democrats and the Bulgarian Agrarian National Union-Nikola Petkov (BANU-NP) (the BANU-NP is separate from the official BANU described above); four human rights organizations; the Independent Students' Society; and the trade union *Podkrepa*. Soon thereafter, three more organizations were admitted. Two, the Democratic and Radical Democratic parties, were revivals of precommunist political forces. The third, the Green party, was a new formation made up of those who found Eco-*glasnost'* insufficiently radical. Several other groups and parties also subsequently announced their solidarity with the UDF. (Valentin Danevski, *Politicheski partii, dvizheniia i organizatsii v Bŭlgariia i tekhnite lideri* [Sofia: Sofia Press, 1990], pp. 26–27.)

With some of Bulgaria's leading intellectuals as spokesmen, and showing an impressive ability to organize mass demonstrations, particularly in the capital, the UDF gained the BCP's agreement to enter into roundtable discussions on the future of the country. The roundtable, whose sessions were televised, came to function almost as a substitute parliament. Composed of representatives of the BCP/BSP, UDF, and BANU, with several other groups accorded observer status, the roundtable saw intense negotiations lasting from the end of January through March that produced agreements on a number of basic issues. The first of these institutionalized the role of the roundtable itself, providing that significant legislation be agreed on there before being sent to the National Assembly for approval. The second provided for specific constitutional changes, eliminating references to socialism and communism and creating the post of president of the republic. The National Assembly promptly enacted the changes and elected Mladenov to the presidency.

The roundtable also reached decisions intended to make Bulgaria a multiparty democracy, establishing formal procedures allowing parties to be formed and gain official recognition. Its terms were liberal, granting recognition to a party on the basis of little more than an individual declaration that it possessed more than 50 supporters. The law did, however, ban the formation of parties on an ethnic or religious basis, a measure aimed at preventing the organization of a separate, and perhaps separatist, party to represent the country's ethnic Turks and Muslims. Despite this provision, the Party of Rights and Freedoms (PRF), led by Akhmed Dugan, became the de facto Turkish party, although its charter proclaimed general goals.

The roundtable also agreed that elections would be held for a Grand National Assembly (GNA) of four hundred members, half to be elected in two hundred single-member districts and half to be selected by proportional representation. The GNA would sit for a term of eighteen months during which it would function both as a parliament and as a constitutional assembly to design a new political structure for the country. Elections were scheduled for 10 June with runoffs on 17 June in single-member districts where no candidate received more than 50 percent of the votes cast. A neutral body, the Central Electoral Commission, chaired by law professor Zhivko Stalev, a nonparty member, was formed to prepare the machinery for the election. Finally, the roundtable reached an agreement on the conduct of the election campaign that required the government to provide basic resources to the opposition and to allow it equal access to the media. Although some local authorities resisted implementing this agreement, it was adhered to on the national level. Newsprint was made available to the opposition press, which in the absence of censorship launched vigorous attacks on the governing socialists, and time on television was assigned to the individual parties and made available for debates between representatives of the major political forces.

The June elections. The UDF entered the campaign with a high degree of confidence, assuming that in free elections the overwhelming majority of the population would reject the BSP. Consequently, it sought to make the election a referendum on the past 45 years of communist rule. This tendency was reinforced by the discovery of mass graves, containing the remains of hundreds of victims, located near the sites of concentration camps and prisons, thus focusing public attention on the Stalinist era.

With regard to current and future policies, however, the UDF had difficulty speaking with a single voice. This was particularly evident concerning the question of the future of the BSP. Some UDF leaders expressed sympathy for the BSP's efforts to reform itself, advocated eventual reconciliation, and opposed the idea of reprisals against BSP officials. In this vein, Zheliu Zhelev and others in the UDF advocated a "Spanish policy," that is, following the example of Spain's transition from fascism under Juan Carlos. Others, however, adopted a far more strident tone, frequently characterizing the BSP as "murderers" and a "Mafia," giving the impression that the UDF would conduct a wholesale purge of the government if it won. The economic program of the UDF advocated "shock therapy"— an immediate and complete transition to a market economy—without making it clear how this would be effected or how the most vulnerable elements in the population would be protected. In their overconfidence, UDF leaders rejected offers to join a coalition government and repeatedly pledged that they would never compromise themselves by cooperating with the BSP. In the last days of the campaign, they even turned down a BSP proposal to sign a pledge of mutual nonviolence, a decision that the socialists used as proof of their opponents' extremism.

The BSP sought to distance itself from its past record, running a campaign that was totally devoid of Marxist ideology. Indeed, BSP spokesmen rivaled the UDF in their denunciation of totalitarianism and stressed their role in bringing down the Zhivkov regime. The party's new symbols—a

red rose and a cartoon boy who resembled Pinocchio—thumbs-up gesture, and Good Luck for Bulgaria slogan replaced the heavy-handed mottoes and portraits of party leaders characteristic of past campaigns.

The BSP presented itself as the party of "responsible, conservative change," stressing the experience of its leaders and minimizing its policy differences with the UDF. It denied seeking a monopoly of power and called for the formation of a coalition with the opposition either before or after the elections. The BSP also pledged a gradual transition to a market economy during which no one would suffer. The party's claim that old-age pensions would be endangered by a UDF victory apparently carried great weight among the elderly.

While cultivating a new image designed to appeal particularly to middle class, urban voters, the BSP conducted a more traditional campaign in the countryside. There, local party and government officials put heavy pressure on the village population, whose habits of subordination, developed over the past 45 years, were not easily broken. This pressure was admitted by BSP leaders, who attributed it to overzealousness on the part of local activists while denying that it was a tactic promoted by the national party leadership.

Results of Elections Held 10, 17 June 1990			
Party	*Votes*	*Percent*	*Seats*
BSP	2,886,363	47.15	211
UDF	2,216,127	36.20	144
BANU	491,500	8.03	16
PRF	368,929	6.03	23
Others	158,279	2.59	6

The election results, shown in the accompanying table, were a shocking disappointment to the opposition but hardly represented the "overwhelming socialist victory" that was reported in much of the Western press. The BSP failed to get a majority of the popular vote, and some of its leading figures, like Prime Minister Lukanov, were forced into embarrassing runoffs or, like Defense Minister Dzhurov, were actually defeated. The opposition dominated Bulgaria's cities, winning 24 of 26 seats in Sofia, scoring a clean sweep in Plovdiv and Varna, and enjoying a commanding level of support from professionals and the young. Both the BANU and the PRF distanced themselves from the BSP and refused to entertain any proposals for parliamentary cooperation. Because decisions of the GNA required a two-thirds majority, the opposition could exercise a veto on any socialist proposals. (John D. Bell, "'Post-Communist' Bulgaria," *Current History*, December; John D. Bell, Ronald A. Gould, and Richard Smolka, *The 1990 Bulgarian Elections: A Pre-election Technical Assessment* [Washington, D.C.: International Foundation for Electoral Systems, 1990]; John D. Bell et al., *An Orderly Rebellion: Bulgaria's Transition from Dictatorship to Democracy* [Washington, D.C.: International Foundation for Electoral Systems, 1990].)

Mladenov's resignation. Victory in the June elections was the high point in the BSP's fortunes during the year, for the party showed itself unable to govern the country, and its leading position quickly deteriorated. Political tension actually increased after the elections, and in the streets of major towns protesters established "communist-free zones" in tent cities and demanded full investigations of past communist crimes. A student strike at the University of Sofia spread to the provinces. Increasingly, protests focused on a statement made by President Mladenov the preceding December when, unable to gain a hearing from a hostile demonstration, he had told the defense minister that "the best thing is to let the tanks come." Although this statement was not acted on, it was captured on a videotape that was made available to the opposition and broadcast during the election campaign.

Mladenov's immediate response was to charge that the tape had been fabricated by the opposition. When its authenticity was upheld by a panel of experts, he maintained that his remark was "being taken out of context." Finally, he admitted having made the statement but pleaded that it was due to the passion of the moment and that he had never authorized the use of force against his opponents. Although this last argument was valid, the opposition focused on Mladenov's long effort to cover up the truth and called for his resignation. Even the BSP newspaper suggested that presidential dignity required Mladenov to leave office. With support eroding even in his own party, Mladenov resigned on the evening of 6 July, stating that he had no wish to be "a cause of tension." (RFE, *Report on Eastern Europe*, 3 August.)

Several votes in the GNA resulted in a political deadlock, as no party could gain the necessary two-thirds majority to elect a successor to Mladenov. After behind-the-scenes negotiations, the various

nominees withdrew in favor of UDF leader Zheliu Zhelev, who was elected president with the support of a majority of the BSP's deputies. Zhelev promptly nominated General Atanas Semerdzhiev of the BSP for the vice-presidency, and he was elected with opposition support. Semerdzhiev, who had been minister of the interior, was credited with depoliticizing the police and ending censorship.

If the BSP leadership believed that the election of Zhelev would promote the organization of a coalition government, it was quickly disappointed. Dr. Petŭr Beron, Zhelev's successor as president of the UDF, maintained the commitment to noncooperation with the socialists. Moreover, Zhelev acted vigorously to take the political initiative from the socialists, particularly in the sphere of foreign affairs, where the constitution gave him extensive authority. His role as national spokesman soon led to his overshadowing the BSP leaders in the surveys of public opinion.

Separating the party from the state. The BSP pledged, and the opposition demanded, that the party carry out a "secularization," separating the instruments of government and other aspects of national life from party control. To a degree this was carried out without controversy. Compulsory courses in Marxism-Leninism were removed from school curricula; the mummy of Georgi Dimitrov, the first communist prime minister and the leader of the BCP until 1949, was removed from its mausoleum and cremated; the national anthem was shorn of its references to communism and the USSR; and the national holiday was changed from 9 September, the anniversary of the communist seizure of power, to 3 March, the anniversary of Bulgaria's liberation from the Turks. The sections of state security that dealt with censorship and internal subversion were disbanded, and a number of figures closely associated with that institution were dropped from the government and even expelled from the BSP. Party cells in the army and the workplace were disbanded. In August the GNA passed legislation replacing the incumbent people's councils, dominated by BSP members, with interim councils more broadly representative, to sit until new local elections could be held in 1991 (BTA, 29 August; *FBIS*, 30 August). A commission of the GNA was established to change place-names of alien, that is, Soviet or Marxist, inspiration.

Some changes proved more difficult. The BSP's reluctance to remove the illuminated red star over party headquarters led to a threat by two members of the opposition to immolate themselves (BTA, 20 August; *FBIS*, 21 August). On 26 August an anti-BSP demonstration turned into a riot in which the crowd broke into the party building, ransacked many of its offices, and burned its first floor. All political parties condemned this act, which was the main exception during the year to the absence of violence that prevailed despite the tense political situation. On 4 October, following the BSP's second congress of the year, a helicopter lifted the star from its pylon and carried it away. The BSP leadership proposed to place it in a museum of socialist memorabilia, but many in the opposition called for its public destruction (BTA, 4 October; *FBIS*, 5 October).

The BSP's Thirty-ninth Congress. During the election campaign, the BSP leadership announced its intention to hold a postelection party congress to continue the renewal process. It took place 22–25 September, in the Sofia party house, where the smells of fire damage were still in the air. To emphasize the continuity of the present BSP with its predecessors (organized Marxism in Bulgaria will be one hundred years old in 1991), the delegates voted to number this congress as the party's 39th. There were 1,328 delegates, 70 percent of them attending a party congress for the first time, and 77 percent were under age 50. The preponderance of new faces, however, did not translate into an unequivocal backing of reform. There was a clear sentiment that control of the party should be given to the younger, "post-Zhivkov" generation of leaders, but at the same time overwhelming majorities rejected proposals for radical change and consistently voted against most of the figures associated with reform factions in the party. One fact that emerged clearly was that such groups as the Road to Europe and the Alternative Socialist Association, which received a great deal of media attention, were composed almost exclusively of Sofia intellectuals with little following in the provincial party apparatus.

The congress adopted a platform that acknowledged responsibility for past "distortions in every sphere of social life" but massively rejected a proposal that it apologize to the Bulgarian people for past crimes and mistakes. The platform endorsed the BSP's transformation into a "modern, left-wing party of democratic socialism," a favorite phrase of Lilov's, and explicitly abandoned the Leninist principle of "democratic centralism" and any claim to a monopoly of power in the state.

Drama at the congress was provided by a falling-out between the party's two strongest figures, Lukanov and Lilov. Lukanov joined with reformist groups in recommending that Lilov be replaced as party leader to symbolize the BSP's complete break with the Zhivkov era. Lilov surprisingly seconded Lukanov's proposal to give power to the younger generation. He asked the congress to choose a new leader, promising to "rejoice from the bottom of my heart at your selection." Lilov, who has a fondness for sarcasm, went on to argue that Lukanov, however, was too valuable to be lost to the party leadership and recommended that he be retained despite the fact "that he, too, is of the generation in question." During the debates, most of Lilov's erstwhile rivals dropped out of the running for the chairmanship, and eventually Lukanov ended the contest by throwing his own support to the chairman. Lilov was reelected with 833 votes in contrast to 286 for Alexander Tomov and 180 for Dimitŭr Yonchev.

In the election of the party's Supreme Council, there appeared to be considerable resentment toward the men who had ended the Zhivkov dictatorship. Petŭr Mladenov, Dobri Dzhurov, and Stanko Todorov were all voted down. The defeat of Dzhurov, who also resigned as defense minister, was particularly surprising, for he had been called "the most beloved man in the country" at the time of the party's February congress. Election to the Supreme Council was also denied to the leaders of the reform factions, with the single exception of Alexander Tomov. (*Duma*, 25, 27 September; RFE, *Report on Eastern Europe*, 26 October.)

At the first session of the BSP Supreme Council, Lilov and Lukanov, warning of the dangers of a split in the party, were able to persuade a majority to invite the leaders of the defeated reform factions to take part in council activities and to participate in working groups of experts devoted to the main issues of party affairs. For the time being, this appeared to satisfy the reformers, who in postcongress meetings decided to continue to work for change within the party rather than to leave it. (*Duma*, 26 September; BTA, 29 September; *FBIS*, 1 October.)

Lilov and Lukanov temporarily minimized the importance of their disputes during the congress, both men admitting the existence of "differences" but denying that they were either fundamental or personal (*Pogled*, 8 October; *FBIS*, 10 October). Lukanov, however, took part in a renewed effort to remove Lilov in a session of the BSP's Supreme Council that was extended over the period 8–13

November. In a letter, the full text of which was not published, sixteen members of the council, including Lukanov, Alexander Tomov, Stefan Prodev, and two-thirds of the party presidium, accused Lilov of holding back the renewal process in the party and of establishing an "authoritarian style" of leadership. Lilov refused to resign, and after intensive debates, in which the critics were accused of plotting an illegal seizure of power, he prevailed in the Supreme Council by a vote of 58 to 50. Lilov consolidated this victory through the addition of ten new members to the Presidium at a meeting of the Supreme Council on 22 November. It is also likely that some of Lilov's critics withdrew from the leadership, but only Stefan Prodev's resignation as editor of *Duma* was reported. At this meeting it was also announced that the Fortieth BSP Congress will be held immediately after the elections for local authorities, probably in March 1991. The internal BSP leadership crisis was rapidly overshadowed by the crisis in the government and the fall of Lukanov's cabinet. (*Duma*, 14, 22 November; *FBIS*, 16, 23 November; *Otechestven vestnik*, 15 November; *FBIS*, 19 November.)

Economic decline and Lukanov's resignation. It was Lukanov's goal after the BSP's victory in the June elections to bring the opposition, or at least a significant part of it, into a BSP-led coalition that would share responsibility for the measures that needed to be taken to rebuild the Bulgarian economy on a free market foundation. The opposition, however, refused to cooperate, taking the position that the socialists should have full responsibility for the situation they had created during their years in power. Lukanov vacillated while the economic situation rapidly deteriorated.

In its election campaign the BSP had promised a painless transition to a market economy. Under the Lukanov government the pain materialized but the transition did not. The mechanisms of the old command economy dissolved, but no new system was adopted in their place. Lukanov suspended payments on the principal of Bulgaria's $10 billion foreign debt at the end of March and stopped making interest payments in June. This made it almost impossible to finance imports, and soon after the elections basic commodities such as sugar, cooking oil, and detergent began to disappear from the shelves, forcing the government to introduce rationing. An energy crisis loomed as the USSR decreased its deliveries of oil and announced that after 1 January 1991 Bulgaria would have to pay for Soviet oil at world market prices and in hard currency. The hope that energy needs would be met by Iraq, which had accumulated a $1.3 billion debt to Bulgaria during the Iran-Iraq war, was dashed by the crisis in the Persian Gulf. Shortages of fuel and power, combined with the inability to finance the importation of raw materials, led to sharp declines in industrial and agricultural production. According to the government's office of statistics, during the first three-quarters of 1990 there was a decline of 11 percent in total domestic production, which included a 13 percent decline in commodity production. This was accompanied by a rapid rise in prices, averaging 36 percent in the months from May through November. (BTA, 10 December; *FBIS*, 11 December.) Problems in the operation of the Kozlodui atomic power complex also caused sharp reductions in the generation of electricity.

In October, Lukanov proposed a comprehensive economic reform based on six hundred pages of recommendations prepared by a team of U.S. experts headed by Richard Rahn, vice-president of the U.S. Chamber of Commerce. It called for the rapid denationalization of major state-owned holdings, the privatization of agriculture, and reliance on the market to set prices and wages. Lukanov warned that there was no alternative to this program and that it inevitably would be accompanied by sharp dislocations, increased unemployment, and a decline in living standards for the majority of the population. Because of the hardships involved, Lukanov refused to ask the National Assembly to approve the plan unless the political opposition would agree in advance to support it. The opposition, however, was aware that the popularity of the BSP had fallen drastically; public opinion surveys found that only 25 percent of the population would vote for the BSP and that 78 percent expressed approval of President Zhelev (BTA, 13 October; *FBIS*, 15 October). Despite the fact that Lukanov's reform program largely coincided with their own proposals, opposition leaders withheld their support and moved to topple the government. The *Podkrepa* trade union took the lead, issuing a call for a general strike, which was followed by two weeks of expanding strike activity and large antisocialist demonstrations in Sofia and other cities. On 29 November, after the Confederation of Independent Trade Unions announced that its members, too, would take part in the general strike, Lukanov and his government resigned (*NYT*, 30 November).

After negotiations between the parties, the GNA assigned the task of forming a new government to

Dimitŭr Popov, a nonparty jurist who had won general approbation for his performance as secretary of the Central Electoral Commission that had administered the June elections. On 20 December, Popov gained the approval of the GNA for his cabinet. It contained three deputy prime ministers: Dimitŭr Ludzhev, an adviser to President Zhelev, from the UDF; Viktor Vŭlkov, who also became foreign minister, of the BANU; and Alexander Tomov, of the BSP. Tomov, whose star rose rapidly in the last months of 1990, was now the highest-ranking socialist in the Bulgarian government. Of the remaining ministers, seven were from the BSP, two from the UDF, one from the BANU, and five were not members of any party. The Ministry of the Interior was placed in the hands of Khristo Danev, who like Popov was a jurist without party affiliation. (*NYT*, 21 December; RFE, *Daily Report*, 20 December.) Popov's government was expected to remain in office to preside over elections for local authorities, scheduled for late February or March 1991, and new parliamentary elections in September.

The opposition press headlined Lukanov's resignation as the fall of Bulgaria's "last socialist government." It was clearly the hope and expectation of the opposition that the next elections for the National Assembly would bring the popular repudiation of the BSP that failed to materialize this year. The BSP was obviously in internal disarray and declining in both membership and popular support. The "Bulgarian exception" to the collapse of communism in Eastern Europe that was observed by some Western journalists after the June elections now seemed to have been no more than an illusion. If this year's trend continues, the BSP will soon share the fate of its counterparts in Czechoslovakia, Hungary, and Poland. It is, at least, hardly likely to gain a significant measure of public trust without spending time out of the government.

The UDF, however, was not without setbacks of its own. Dr. Petŭr Beron, Zheliu Zhelev's successor as head of the UDF's governing council, resigned suddenly on 3 December, following allegations that he had once worked for the state security service. He was replaced by Filip Dimitrov, a 35-year-old attorney and vice-president of the Green party. His election, by a vote of eight to seven, with the representatives of the largest components of the UDF opposed, was evidence that the political opposition was little more united than the BSP. (*NYT*, 4, 12 December.) The individual parties in the UDF, however, enjoy their own popularity and would survive the breakup of the umbrella organization, particularly since President Zhelev serves as a unifying symbol.

International Situation. The drastic changes occurring throughout Eastern Europe and in the Soviet Union created a new international environment for Bulgaria. The breakup of the Warsaw Pact and the Council for Mutual Economic Assistance and the expanding economic crisis in the USSR made it clear that Bulgaria could not look to its traditional partners to provide military security, reliable sources of raw materials, or secure markets. The Soviet decision to ask for payment for its exports at world prices and in hard currency presented Bulgaria with serious problems for the future.

There was a general consensus among all political groups that Bulgaria had to strengthen its relations with the West and reduce its reliance on the USSR, a position that even the Soviet leadership endorsed during Lukanov's visit to Moscow in March (RFE, *Report on Eastern Europe*, 13 April). President Zhelev expressed the new situation much more bluntly later in the year, stating that although Bulgaria's territorial integrity was in theory secured by its membership in the Warsaw Pact and through a bilateral treaty with the USSR, the pact was already a "political corpse" while the Soviet Union was in the process of disintegration and could hardly be considered a dependable ally (BTA, 8 October; *FBIS*, 9 October).

Bulgaria applied for membership in the International Monetary Fund and the World Bank in February (*RD*, 20 February), but its chances were hurt by its inability to make payments on its foreign debt and by continuing political instability (*Financial Times*, 5 April).

The election of Zheliu Zhelev to the presidency had a marked impact on the conduct of Bulgarian diplomacy because substantial influence over foreign policy was clearly provided within the vaguely drawn prerogatives of that office. Zhelev quickly made visits to Western Europe, the United States, and Japan to demonstrate that Bulgaria had firmly entered the "postcommunist era" despite the result of the June elections and to plead for economic aid. In the United States, Zhelev met with President Bush and reached agreements that provided for Bulgaria to receive most-favored-nation status and a contribution of 1 million tons of seed corn.

Western economic support became especially critical following the Iraqi occupation of Kuwait. Bulgaria endorsed the economic sanctions against Iraq and agreed to send a token military force to the region, but the loss of Iraqi oil deliveries struck Bulgaria more severely than any other European country. By the end of the year, the European Community announced its intention to include Bulgaria in a program of assistance to the East European states (*WP*, 3 January 1991). Prospects for the future were also considerably improved with the announcement that the USSR would accept Bulgarian manufactured goods in exchange for 6.5 million tons of gasoline during 1991. This would supply about one-third of Bulgaria's projected needs (*WP*, 3 January 1991).

In regional affairs, Bulgaria appeared to have successfully reestablished good relations with Turkey. The principal issue between the countries was the treatment of Bulgaria's Turkish minority, for in some areas of heavy Turkish population ethnic Bulgarians feared that coming elections would give the Turks control of the local government; consequently they demonstratively opposed the extension of full civil rights to the Turks. Presidential adviser Dimitŭr Ludzhev made a goodwill visit to Ankara to assure the Turkish government that on the national level Bulgaria was committed to full equality for its Turkish and Moslem minorities. (BTA, 24 October; *FBIS*, 24 October.)

Biographies. *Alexander Lilov.* For nearly ten years, between 1974 and 1983, Alexander Lilov was one of the most powerful figures in Bulgaria, becoming the BCP's chief ideologist and the expected successor to Todor Zhivkov. But as often happened to "heirs apparent" under Zhivkov, Lilov was suddenly purged. He spent the next six years as director of the Institute for Modern Social Theories, which had a reputation for harboring party dissidents. (Danevski, *Politicheski partii*, pp. 10–11; RFE, *Report on Eastern Europe*, 20 April.)

Born 31 August 1933, Lilov earned a doctorate in philosophy and literature and is the author of several books dealing with aesthetics as well as political themes. In 1986 he published a book on imagination and creativity that, though couched in Marxist vocabulary and structure, defended the importance of intellectual liberty. The book also discussed the ideas of Bulgarian and foreign Marxist philosophers without once mentioning the name of Todor Zhivkov, suggesting that Lilov did not intend to seek peace with Bulgaria's leader.

After Zhivkov's fall, Lilov was quickly added to the BCP Politburo and then became chairman of the party at its Fourteenth Congress in February. He regularly spoke of the importance of "renewal,"

internal party democratization, and joining the "modern European left." The pace of change under his leadership, however, was too slow for some advocates of reform, who also found him aloof and arrogant. Party conservatives, on the other hand, were uncomfortable with his character as an intellectual and saw him as too defensive.

Despite the fact that he only narrowly beat back challenges to his leadership from Lukanov and others, he was the only one of the BSP's "big four"—Mladenov, Lukanov, Dzhurov, Lilov—to remain in office at the end of the year.

Andrei Lukanov. Born in 1938, Lukanov comes from a communist "dynasty," both his father and grandfather occupying important places in the history of the Bulgarian party. He is well educated, and his fluency in Western languages particularly impresses Western diplomats and journalists. He held many positions during the Zhivkov era, particularly in the field of economic relations with foreign countries, and was a candidate member of the BCP Politburo for ten years before Zhivkov's fall. He was supposedly a proponent of reform during that period, and when he was elevated to the post of prime minister after the party's February congress he was hailed as a reformer "in the Gorbachev mold." There is perhaps more truth in this judgment than was intended by those who expressed it, for while Lukanov was frank in describing the problems that Bulgaria faced, he was unwilling to accept the responsibility for adopting the harsh measures—price reforms, privatization of the land, legalization of free markets, and so forth—needed to put the country on the road to recovery.

When Lukanov resigned his office at the end of November, President Zhelev praised him for his efforts and called him a resource too important for Bulgaria to waste. It is not unlikely that he will find a place as a technocrat in some future government organized by the UDF. It would be a role more suited to his character than national leadership proved to be. (RFE, *Report on Eastern Europe*, 6 July.)

Stefan Prodev. In the mid-1980s, Stefan Prodev (b. 1927) was the editor of the journal *Narodna kultura*, which became known for its liberalism in cultural issues and exposure of political corruption. In late 1988 he was a founder of Sofia's Discussion Club for the Support of *Perestroika* and *Glasnost'*, one of the first examples of open, organized dissent in the country. As a result, Zhivkov's regime removed him from his post, but after Zhivkov's fall, Prodev was almost immediately reinstated as editor of *Narodna kultura*. On 29 January he was elected chairman of the Bulgarian Journalists' Union. Unlike many of his intellectual colleagues who were leaving the party to join the opposition, Prodev expressed commitment to the cause of reformed socialism, and at the congress in February he was elected editor of the party newspaper *Rabotnichesko delo*, soon to be renamed *Duma*. Under his direction, *Duma* completely changed its character, becoming no less lively or informative than the emerging opposition press. Prodev did not hesitate to engage in polemics with the UDF or other parties or avoid disagreeing with BSP positions. He dissented, for example, from the BSP's decision to back Zheliu Zhelev for the presidency.

During the year Prodev apparently became disappointed with the slow pace of internal party reform and joined the effort in November to force Alexander Lilov from the BSP chairmanship. When this failed, Prodev announced that he could no longer serve as editor of *Duma*. By the end of the year, it had not yet become clear what his future role would be, but he remained an influential spokesman for reform within the party. (RFE, *Report on Eastern Europe*, 9 March.)

Alexander Tomov. During 1990 Alexander Tomov (b. 1954) emerged as one of the leading figures of the younger generation. A graduate of Leningrad State University, Tomov is a specialist in "political economy," a subject he taught at Sofia University while also serving as a consultant to the council of ministers. Shortly after Zhivkov's fall, Tomov founded the Movement for Democratic Socialism, often called Demos, dedicated to opposition to Stalinism and neo-Stalinism in Bulgarian life.

Tomov rose to prominence at the Thirty-ninth BSP Congress in September, where he ran against Alexander Lilov for the party chairmanship. Although defeated badly, he was elected a deputy chairman of the Presidium. In November, he played a leading part in the unsuccessful effort to persuade the party Supreme Council to oust Lilov. After the fall of the Lukanov government, Tomov became the top BSP representative in the new cabinet of Dimitŭr Popov. His new prominence makes him a likely successor to Lilov as party leader, if support for the BSP's chairman continues to deteriorate. (Danevski, *Politicheski partii*, pp. 12–13.)

Todor Zhivkov. Bulgaria's former dictator spent the year under house arrest at the mountain villa of his granddaughter. There was some expectation that he would testify before the Grand National Assembly, but his appearance never materialized after jurists objected that it might prevent his receiving a fair trial in the future. He gave several press interviews denying any wrongdoing and pointing out that the shops had been full while he was in power. In November, not long after the anniversary of his removal from power, he gave an interview to Western reporters in which he stated that socialism had from the beginning been based on incorrect premises. "If Lenin were alive today," he added, "he would say the same thing." Zhivkov went on to say that Bulgaria's survival depended on developing close ties to the West and that the country's sufferings were due fundamentally to the decisions made by Roosevelt, Churchill, and Stalin after the Second World War. (*NYT*, 28 November.)

At the end of the year, the state prosecutor's office filed charges against Zhivkov that accused him of embezzling $23,000 in government property.

John D. Bell
University of Maryland in Baltimore County

Czechoslovakia

Population. 15,683,234 (July)
Parties. Federation of Communist Party of Bohemia and Moravia and Communist Party of Slovakia. Name changed in November 1990; day-to-day usage will continue to be Communist Party of Czechoslovakia (Komunistická strana Československa; KSČS). Czech Party: Communist Party of Bohemia and Moravia (Komunistická strana Čecha Moravy; KSČM); Slovak Party: Communist Party of Slovakia/Party of the Democratic Left (Komunistická strana Slovenska; KSS).
Founded. KSČ: 1921; KSČS; April 1990
Membership. 700,000 (November; note, however, Chairman Mohorita's statement in September that active membership may be 300,000 to 500,000); Age structure: 6 percent under 30; 58 percent, 31–60; 36 percent over 60 (ČTK, 15 June). Oc-

cupational structure: 31 percent manual laborers; 25 percent intelligentsia (ČTK, 5 September). KSS: 192,000, with 25 percent estimated inactive.

Chairmen. KSČS: Pavol Kanis, Slovak, 42 (KSS Institute of Marxism-Leninism). Rotating chairman Miroslav Grebeníček (Czech, age 43). KSČM: Jiří Svoboda, 45 (film director). KSS: Peter Weiss (researcher, KSS Institute of Marxism-Leninism).

Presidium. Abolished, along with the Central Committee, at the Eighteenth Party Congress, November 1990. A Federal Council is composed of twelve KSČM and twelve KSS members.

Status. Legal

Last Congress. KSČS: Eighteenth, 3–4 November 1990, in Prague; KSČM: 13–14 October, in Olomouc; KSS: 20–21 October

Last Election. 8–9 June. 300 seats in the Federal Assembly as follows: Civic Forum-Public Against Violence, 168 seats; KSČS, 48 seats; Christian and Democratic Union, 40 seats; Association for Moravia and Silesia, 16 seats; Slovak National party, 15 seats; Coexistence, 12 seats; Liberal Democrats, 2 seats

Auxiliary Organizations. Most dissolved or radically reorganized. Revolutionary Trade Union Movement dissolved in March. Communist Youth Union founded in March.

Publications. *Rudé právo*, KSČS daily. Bratislava *Pravda*, now an independent left-wing paper, is no longer the KSS daily. The following major party organs ceased publication: the KSČS ideological weekly *Tribuna*; the theoretical weekly *Nová mysl*; and the fortnightly *Život strany*, devoted to organizational and administrative matters. Československá Tisková Kancelář (ČTK) is the official news agency.

The KSČS, emerging from the schism of the Czechoslovak Social Democratic party, was formally constituted at a merger congress of left-wing groups in 1921 and admitted to the Communist International the same year. Continuing tensions with the international movement were resolved with the bolshevization of the party in 1929. Enjoying a legal status throughout the democratic first Czechoslovak republic (1918–39), unprecedented in the other countries of East–Central Europe, the party emerged from illegal underground activity after World War II with a popular following strong enough to garner 38 percent of the vote in free elections and the prime ministership under party leader Klement Gottwald.

Eroding party support and the cold war division of Europe culminated in the party seizure of power in February 1948 and the entrenchment of a Stalinist political and economic structure. The general record of party subservience to Moscow was punctuated by a single major liberalization, the Prague Spring of 1968, only to see normalization restored after the Soviet-led Warsaw Treaty Organization (WTO) invasion in August of that year. Two decades of subterranean discontent were strictly repressed by an aging party leadership whose claims to governance would be abrogated by a revaluation of 1968. Gorbachev's reform initiatives, therefore, met with mere lip service, and no clear departure from party control predated the spectacular toppling of the regime during the Velvet Revolution of November and December 1989 (*YICA*, 1990).

The collapse of communist power was officially validated by the formal recision of Article 4 of the Czechoslovak constitution, which had defined the party's leading role. The political vacuum was filled by a transitional Government of National Understanding, with limited communist participation under the presidential leadership of dissident playwright Václav Havel, who set a conciliatory tone permissive of subsequent communist participation in the political life of a pluralizing polity. The mobilizing vehicles for the transition were two umbrella organizations that had served as coordinating centers for the Velvet Revolution in late 1989: the Czech Civic Forum (*Obcanské forum* [OF]) and the Slovak Public against Violence (*Verejnost' proti nasiliu* [VPN]).

Party Affairs. The party's power-sharing agreements and the ceding of its leading role in December 1989 were only the start of an ongoing and still incomplete process of retrenchment in the communist position. The penetration of KSČS organizational control of all aspects of life could not be instantly annulled by fiat. Instead, the "decommunization" of Czechoslovakia continued through 1990 in a series of interrelated areas, the most important of which were the question of the responsibility of individual communist leaders for past conduct of power and policy, the validity of communist and former communist participation in governance, and the proprietorship of the party's extensive assets.

The KSČS took the lead in fixing blame and jettisoning the most clearly discredited leaders: in early 1990, the Central Committee launched a wave of expulsions that included almost two dozen former presidium members and party secretaries. The formal expulsions, most of them finalized at the 17 February Central Committee plenum, targeted former KSČS first secretary Gustáv Husák, Miroslav Štěpán, Vasil Bil'ák, Miloš Jakeš, Antonín Čapek, Jozef Lenárt, Karel Hoffmann, Petr Colotka, and Josef Kempný, among others. The aim of this high-level housecleaning was to deflect public opprobrium and to clear the decks for less tainted figures to begin the emergency overhaul of the party's mission and goals. The Central Committee mandated continuing efforts to purge the party of compromised lesser officials (*Rudé právo*, 26 March).

Prominent members of the old regime also faced investigation and prosecution for corrupt or repressive abuse of power and, in several cases, for treason in connection with possible collaboration with the Soviet invasion of 1968. Key party figures were taken into custody throughout the spring for interrogation; the most dramatic instance was probably the temporary detention on the eve of the June parliamentary elections of Bil'ák, Jakeš, Lenárt, and others for a new round of interrogation in connection with the 1968 invasion (ČTK, 7 June). The only notable major prosecution, however, was that of former Prague party chief Štěpán, who was first taken into custody in late December 1989 and sentenced to two and a half years in prison in October for abuse of power in conjunction with his role in suppressing the demonstrations of 17 November 1989 (ČTK, 23 October). His case remained the only high-visibility accounting.

A wide cleavage between the masses and the elite was apparent on this issue of retribution for past damage to the nation. Actions such as the Štěpán prosecution caused significant unease in a government leadership troubled by the equity of calibrating guilt and singling out individual malefactors, however culpable (*Lidové noviny*, 11 July). First articulated in January, the Havel approach — rejecting collective guilt while asserting universal public responsibility for past wrongs — discouraged a renewed round of uncomfortably communist-tinged show trials. The president's message appeared to meet with considerable sympathy among deputies of the Federal Assembly, most of whom were concerned that they not penalize everyone "who was a communist party member even for a day" (ČTK, 23 October).

Mass opinion, however, reflected a pronounced tendency to settle past scores, thereby leaving open the continuing possibility of further retribution. An opinion survey conducted in October indicated that some three quarters of the population felt that the relevant party functionaries deserved punishment for past criminal acts or, more generally, for political mistakes and malfeasance tantamount to criminality (*Rudé právo*, 23 October). Respect for the institutional rights of the party, however, was substantially higher, with 72 percent of those polled affirming that the KSČS should enjoy equal standing with other parties (ČTK, 16 May).

The second area of ongoing concern was that of communist participation in the construction of the new order. In the interests of continuity and inclusiveness, the Havel leadership had sought to retain reform-minded communist officials in key positions in the transitional Government of National Understanding. The twelve-member Czech government installed in late 1989 also contained three KSČS members (*Rudé právo*, 6 December). The most visible of these figures were federal Prime Minister Marian Čalfa and Defense Minister Miroslav Vaček. Čalfa, a 43-year-old Slovak lawyer, came into the legal department of Prime Minister Strougal's office in 1972, where he served in various capacities until a 1988 cabinet reshuffling won him the post of minister without portfolio for coordination questions. During the post-November transition, he became prime minister of the new noncommunist majority but left the KSČS without comment in mid-January amid vociferous party criticism that his high office represented a partisan rather than a personal mandate (Bratislava, *Pravda*, 22 January).

Mounting pressure during 1990 for more thorough decommunization, however, posed a challenge to the continuing exercise of responsibility by communist bureaucrats and economic managers at all levels. On 17 October, apparently in response to such sentiments as well as to specific evidence of Vaček's compliance with military mobilization plans during November 1989, Havel announced the general's dismissal, with appreciation for his service in the transition (*Mladá fronta dnes*, 19 October). Čalfa, now the only surviving official of the pre-November regime, was in a highly exposed political position despite his relative popularity and Havel's continued support; criticism of his communist past, however, put the prime ministerial position in continued jeopardy at year's end.

Even the former communists of Prague Spring were surprised to discover that twenty years in the political wilderness had not insulated them from being lumped with postinvasion "normalizers" as participants in the destructive machinery of communist power. This was a sizable group; according to a KSČS accounting in 1990, the party purges of the postinvasion period created a substantial "shadow party" of some 465,000 evicted members, about four thousand of whom were readmitted between 1976 and 1989 (*Rudé právo*, 26 January). The visibility of these reformers—among them Federal Assembly chairman Alexander Dubček and Foreign Minister Jiří Dienstbier—in the transition government brought complaints that their rehabilitation had taken precedence over that of noncommunist victims of the high Stalinist period. Many viewed the Prague Spring as a communist holding operation that failed to challenge the essential premise of party dominance and control (*Lidové noviny*, 30 June; *Literární noviny*, 20 September).

Broad public and official concern about the survival of the party's *nomenklatura* Mafia and the tentative nature of personnel changes was reflected in a stream of media stories about opportunist local party members landing on their feet (*Literární noviny*, 17 March; *Občanský deník*, 1 September) and federal legislation facilitating the replacement of entrenched managers and civil servants from the former regime. KSČS warnings of the dangers of discarding desperately needed expertise, a selfserving but not invalid point, were not likely to carry the day, but similar concerns within the government have thus far moderated any wholesale purges. Efforts to be evenhanded and discriminating in the treatment of communist managers has been politically sensitive, however. Czech prime minister Petr Pithart described a no-win situation in this regard: "When I speak about Communist mafias, I receive hundreds of letters about decent communists, specialists in the right places. When I do not mention a word about these people, then I receive hundreds of letters about Communist mafias." (Prague Domestic Service, 17 July.)

A special issue in the debate over communist participation was the attempt to utilize a nonjudicial screening process to assure some minimal standards of political probity among elected officials by eliminating those who had previously succumbed to pressures to inform for the communist regime. Such screening was widespread in the parliamentary electoral campaign; over a hundred candidates withdrew as a result of such findings, the most shocking of which implicated VPN chairman Jan Budaj and Czechoslovak People's party chairman Josef Bartončik. Electoral postmortems, however, raised second thoughts about the process; Slovak prime minister Vladimír Mečiar reflected a broader concern when he bemoaned the difficulty of assessing the motives and extent of collaboration, the danger of accepting fabricated evidence, and the converse possibility that some culprits evaded scrutiny because some fifteen thousand files had disappeared (Bratislava, *Pravda*, 26 June). Then Interior Minister Sacher charged that the missing files had been destroyed by the remnant of ancien régime sympathizers within the security apparatus (Prague Domestic Service, May 20). The full complexity of the screening issue, however, receded in prominence during the November local elections.

As the issue of party assets had fomented heated debate in Poland and Hungary well before the autumn of 1989, it was not surprising to find KSČS stewardship of its holdings under fire. The party was quick to try to seize the initiative and to pledge voluntary restitution of state subsidies, hoping to deflect censure and moderate the extent of loss with a show of cooperation. For example, the Central Committee acquiesced in the return of its headquarters to the Ministry of Transportation and Communications in mid-January (*Rudé právo*, 17 January). Public suspicion of this approach, however, sparked a series of anticommunist rallies and a ten-minute general strike in April and May, as the Federal Assembly first debated the assets question and reviewed progress in the divestiture of an estimated nine and a half billion korunas of party property. Chairwoman of the Federal Control Commission Koriňková projected that by midyear the party would retain only 10 to 15 percent of its former holdings (*Lidová demokracie*, 10 May).

Controversies over the issue and over discrepancies in accounting continued to dog the resolution of the problem, however, and on 16 November, after months of discussion, the Federal Assembly finally passed a constitutional bill to nationalize KSČS assets without right to compensation—despite repeated communist protests that this action violated constitutional due process guarantees (*Rudé právo*, 18 October).

Amid the external battles the KSČS waged to fend off further inroads into its weakened position, the party's primary concerns were to adapt effectively to the radically altered political environment, to retain a party membership base, and to redefine the party's goals and procedures so as to remain viable in the new pluralist context. The cataclysmic events of 1989 brought to the fore a new leadership headed by Vasil Mohorita. Mohorita, at 38 representative of a post-1968 generation of party functionaries, made his career in the party youth movement, joining the KSČS Secretariat in 1988 and the Presidium only in November 1989. He continued at the helm of the party until the Eighteenth Party Congress in November. His voice would be most prominent in defining the tone and direction of party policy and tactics throughout the year.

The KSČS membership base inevitably shrank as disillusioned and opportunist members jumped ship. Sixty-six thousand had already left the party in 1989, most of them in the fall (ČTK, 8 January), and the hemorrhage continued at an accelerated pace in 1990. By autumn, party leaders announced a shrinkage from 1.7 million to 700,000, and Mohorita candidly acknowledged that the actual figures might fall into the range of 300,000 to 500,000 (*NYT*, 14 October).

During 1990, the party would also be denuded of much of its organizational empire as well as its membership, as one social organization after another—women's groups, trade unions, professional organizations—gained autonomy or simply dissolved. The KSČS Central Committee's Advanced School of Politics, which had educated thousands of the party *aktiv*, closed its doors at the end of June; other training facilities ceased operations as well.

The erosion of the party's extensive base in journalism proceeded apace throughout 1990, with many party publications ceasing publication (*Zemědělské noviny*, 18 January) and others handed over to local governments. Even the surviving organs faced severe cuts in the supply of newsprint, as independent journalism blossomed (*Lidová demokracie*, 9 March). The most portentous developments occurred in November, however, when the Bratislava edition of *Pravda* announced the severance of its connection with the KSS-DLS to become an independent left-wing daily published by an editorially directed joint stock company (Bratislava, *Pravda*, 27 November). Earlier in November, the KSČS daily *Rudé právo* made a contested change of masthead, designating itself a "left wing" rather than a "Communist" paper (ČTK, 7 November).

Amid the deteriorating organizational resources and external challenges, finding an appropriate response to the unavoidable burden of responsibility for the debasement of Czechoslovak political and economic life was a particularly sensitive task for an organization not trained to sensitivity. The new party leaders sought a formula that would acknowledge serious mistakes while preserving credibility for the future.

Forced to reappraise the party's past record, Mohorita recognized the impossibility of averting a crisis in a leadership formed and tainted by the 1968 invasion, a leadership for whom "any advancing reform would have revealed the harmfulness and political wrongness of the then normalization processes, as well as the unlawfulness" of the initial Warsaw Pact invasion (ČTK, 23 February). The party's "deep crisis," then, was not merely a function of individual aberration but of systemic failure to respond to public needs and interests. Rejecting any renewed attempt to gain a monopoly of power, the KSČS avowed the need to "shed neo-Stalinist ballast" (Bratislava, *Pravda*, 25 January) and the previous mindset, in which "the party mainly knew how to give orders" (Prague Television, 17 January). The proper tone was elusive, as veteran communists chafed under the unaccustomed mandate for humility, evoking Mohorita's reminder after the elections that "we cannot escape our past" (*Rudé právo*, 15 June).

Although confessing past errors, the KSČS refused to repudiate the legacy of the February 1948 coup, seeing it as a popular movement with majority support and idealistic goals (*Rudé právo*, 2 February). The party was also quick to manipulate the rhetoric of pluralism in its own defense, lashing out at "self-appointed judges" who engage in "personal scoresettling and discrimination" behind the shield of the Civic Forum (*Večerník*, 23 January). With surprising self-righteousness, party organs compared communist dismissals to the postnormalization purges and recited tales of psychological pressure and intimidation alien to the pluralist credo (Bratislava, *Pravda*, 15 January).

The party's major test of survival was, of course, the June parliamentary election, mobilization for which began as soon as the date was set. Keeping a carefully low profile, the KSČS adopted the defensive slogan No Democracy without Pluralism; No Pluralism without the Communist Party. Its very existence was nevertheless challenged twice during the campaign. The first challenge was the Prague prosecutor's investigation, eventually terminated, of the party as a fascist movement within the meaning of the criminal code (*Svobodné slovo*, 18 April). Late in the campaign, the four reconstituted "historical parties" of the first republic launched a joint appeal for the outlawing of the KSČS for its continuing intimidation of voters, eliciting sharp party protests at this affront to pluralism (*Rudé právo*, 19 May). The ban attempt was doomed to failure by the refusal of Civic Forum and President Havel to cooperate. Shunned as a coalition partner, the KSČS nevertheless maintained a statewide electoral and parliamentary foothold with nearly 14 percent of the vote and 48 seats in the Federal Assembly, finishing as the second-strongest party. The approximately two and a half million party voters represented a much broader base than the party membership; Mohorita acknowledged, however, the dearth of laborers and youth in the electoral constituency (*Rudé právo*, 15 June). Nevertheless, the showing was strong enough to allow the party leadership to read the results as confirming the KSČS's "justified place in our society" (*Rudé právo*, 11 June), despite rival partisan attempts to "unleash anti-communist hysteria."

The postelection Fifth Central Committee Plenum expressed satisfaction with the parliamentary results and continued the organizational pruning of the apparatus. Responsive to the state's name change from the Czechoslovak Socialist Republic (ČSSR) to the Czech and Slovak Federative Republic (ČSFR), the party also altered its abbreviated form from KSČ to KSČS in acknowledgment of the enhanced recognition thereby accorded Slovak identity (*Rudé právo*, 25 June).

The KSČS postelection position was hardly enviable, however, despite ongoing contacts with government officials, including Havel. Continued isolation in influence, even from the electorally unsuccessful left wing parties, met party professions of constructive opposition and willingness to cooperate in common goals. The party was thus marooned, left to pick its way through a hostile political landscape seeking opportunities to champion social justice in ethnic relations and in the allocation of the burdens of economic transformation without true allies.

The autumn brought a leadership change—the resignation of Ladislav Adamec from the party chairmanship (to be replaced by First Secretary Mohorita until the November party congress) and an intensification of pressure on the party. At the October Central Committee session, Mohorita stirred up a firestorm of controversy by asserting that the government blueprint for economic reform spelled "the end to national understanding and the beginning of a hard and uncompromising struggle." Although party spokesmen and Mohorita argued that these pugnacious words were taken out of context, KSČS officials were by no means unanimous in rising to his defense. Undoubtedly appalled by the apparent revelation of the wolf under the party's sheep's clothing, Jíří Svoboda, newly elected leader

of the KSČM and his Central Committee pointedly reaffirmed the need for national understanding and rejected "hard and uncompromising" politics as alien to the vocabulary of party pluralism (*Rudé právo*, 12 October). The KSS Executive Committee regretted that the remarks provided a ready pretext for a renewed "round of anti-communist hysteria" (Bratislava, *Pravda*, 12 October).

Outside the party, criticism was universal: the Civic Forum's press release on the incident chided that "the Communist Party has had ten months to recognize its guilt and to join in democratic life. It has not used this chance." (ČTK, 8 October.) Tens of thousands of demonstrators rallied against communist resurgence in the week following Mohorita's combative remarks (*NYT*, 12 October); deputies in the Federal Assembly retaliated by dismissing him from the parliamentary presidium on 22 October over communist protests that this was an affront to the principles of proportional representation (ČTK, 22 October). The response to this effort at assertiveness is worth careful note, as the incident tapped wellsprings of deep-seated public fear and antagonism.

The capstone of the yearlong party struggle to redefine itself was the Eighteenth Party Congress held in Prague 3 and 4 November. The chief organizational consequence of the congress was the federation of the party. Henceforth, a KSČS Federal Council comprised of twelve KSČM members and twelve KSS members would replace the Central Committee; the post of first secretary was also abolished, with a council chairmanship rotating between the KSČM and the KSS. By secret ballot, delegates narrowly elected Miroslav Grebeníček as the KSČM candidate for chairman. Grebeníček, a 43-year-old historian at Masaryk University in Brno, edged out Mohorita for the post. The KSS candidate was Prague-born Slovak Pavol Kanis, of the KSS Central Committee's Institute for Marxism-Leninism. Kanis, who startled a Western journalist with the proposition that "we no longer have any communist ideas" (he himself was denied admission to the party until 1981 for his heterodoxy), looked to Austrian-style social democracy as a model for the KSČS (Vienna, *Der Standard*, 24 November). Grebeníček yielded the first rotation to Kanis on grounds of national sensitivity and superior party organizational experience. Substantive discussion at the congress, although described as "stormy" at times and enlivened by a bomb scare, provoked no significant policy departures. Party reports acknowledged past mistakes, hewed to the value of the

February 1948 Revolution, reviewed its critique of government policy, and refused the petitions of the old guard for readmission to the party.

A final achievement of the year was the KSČS's surprising gains in the late November local elections, as the second-strongest party in the Czech lands and third in Slovakia. Analysts attributed this unexpectedly strong showing to heavier turnout in the countryside, where political affiliation was less significant than individual rapport and where the community standing of local communists was considerably higher than that of the party bosses in the center (ČTK, 27 November).

Political Affairs. Although the KSČS no longer plays a decisive role in determining public policy in Czechoslovakia, its impact continues in three important respects: the continuing concern with extirpating surviving remnants of the framework of communist power; the influence of the contemporary KSČS, as it responds from a still-strong bureaucratic and electoral base to political issues; and, perhaps most important, the shaping of the policy agenda by the problems generated by communist rule in both domestic and international affairs. Even the most radical reorientation must proceed from a base constructed by previous party hegemony.

The Government of National Understanding functioned with the formal public legitimation of electoral choice, but President Havel strove to make it as broadly representative as possible, with dissident intellectuals in key positions but including seven reform communists and three former communists among its ministers (*Report on East Europe*, no. 2, 12 January). The government had of course to work in tandem with the Federal Assembly, still functioning with a communist majority at the beginning of 1990. Through the mechanism of resignation and recall, 120 spaces in the assembly fell open, to be filled by interim elections in late January; the revised 350-member parliament then contained 152 unaffiliated deputies, 138 communists, and a residuum of largely National Front parties. Only eight of the newly elected deputies were communist (ČTK, 30 January). This partially refurbished assembly would function until its replacement by a freely elected body in June.

Idealized aspirations for democracy proved easier to evoke than to actualize. Generalized guarantees of free speech, for example, yielded in practice to arguments about the boundaries of fair criticism, quarrels over journalistic practice, and the poisoning of the political atmosphere with charges and countercharges of communist-style polemics (*Rudé právo*, 24 February). Nevertheless, a range of civil rights were revitalized during the spring of 1990. On 27 March, a package of laws granted freedom of association, petition, and publishing. Legislation passed 28 March restored continuous citizenship rights to those deprived during the communist era (ČTK, 28 March). An amendment to the existing press law abolished censorship; radio, television, and the film industry remained under the state's regulation, although by summer the government had taken the first steps toward licensing independent broadcast stations.

Suspicions were understandably hard to eradicate, however. There was continuing public distrust regarding the extent and sincerity of restructuring in the security agencies throughout the year (*Zemědělské noviny*, 2 November); Richard Sacher, interior minister until the June elections, was under continuous fire for "insufficient and slow purification" of his organization (ČTK, 8 May; *Report on East Europe*, no. 20, 18 May). Indeed, all organizations associated with communist rule were sullied by that connection. The National Front umbrella of social organizations, long a transmission belt of communist policy rather than a forum for dialogue, was suspended on 7 February and reorganized at each government level under the designation Association of Political Parties and Social Organizations (*Národná obroda*, 7 and 12 July; *Report on East Europe*, no. 31, 3 August). The discredited National Committee structure of local government succumbed to local assemblies and elected mayors with considerably greater independent authority.

The central task of the interim government was to establish and carry out a procedure to guarantee free elections. Legislation passed in late February provided for proportional representation with a 5 percent threshold (3 percent in Slovakia) of the popular vote necessary to win parliamentary seats (ČTK, 27 February). An organization that could obtain ten thousand signatures could mount a candidate slate and receive a government campaign subsidy, depending on electoral performance. The KSČS was barred from this subsidy.

A lively and confusing campaign, marked by some two dozen parties all generally committed to a return to Europe and to economic transformation, culminated in a resounding victory for the Civic Forum/Public against Violence (OF/VPN) coalition: 46 percent of the popular vote and absolute majorities in both houses of the Federal Assembly.

The KSČS was the only left-wing party to cross the 5 percent threshold. Considerable negotiation brought the Christian Democrats into the federal coalition, but the OF/VPN's continued postelection dominance assured that there was considerable continuity in ministerial responsibilities after June: remaining in their key positions were Prime Minister Čalfa, Finance Minister Václav Klaus, Minister of Economics Vladimír Dlouhý, Foreign Minister Jiří Dienstbier, Labor Minister Petr Miller, and Defense Minister Miroslav Vaček.

The existing party structure was by no means equivalent to the highly institutionalized party system of interwar Czechoslovakia or western analogues. Neither programmatic coherence nor established party identification could be expected overnight, but the aftershock of communist rule has left its mark here as well. Public aversion to the mere concept of partisan organization, in the wake of decades of KSČS control, had a profound effect on the electoral organization of power, with fledgling organizations displaying a penchant for less hierarchical authority and the looser designation of "movement" or "forum" as opposed to party. The stresses this attitude produced were particularly pronounced in the electorally successful but ideologically and organizationally unwieldy OF/VPN, mandated to lead the governing coalition without partisan discipline and cohesion. The floundering movement, its goals and direction "fuzzy" and "barely legible" even according to its own adherents (Bratislava Domestic Service, 29 September; *Rudé právo*, 26 September), came to a point of resolution at the October OF conference, where Finance Minister Klaus was the surprise winner of the movement's chairmanship. Klaus defined his victory as "clear approval for radical economic reform" and a mandate for greater organizational coherence and responsiveness to local branches (*Lidové noviny*, 2 November).

Facing a decline in popularity from the honeymoon period of early 1990 (ČTK, 14 November), the OF/VPN axis nonetheless remained the central political force in Czechoslovakia. Its eventual character remained unclear at year's end, however, with the Civic Forum congress rescheduled from December 1990 to January 1991 to permit further consideration of structural changes (ČTK, 9 November).

Despite the strong communist showing, the November local elections were notable primarily for their contribution to maintaining the existing balance of power. Government coalition parties retained their strong footholds, while their ethnic challengers, particularly the Slovak nationalist SNS and the Moravian Self-Government-Democracy Movement, fared poorly. In Slovakia as well, the governing Public against Violence/Christian Democrat/Democratic party coalition won just over 50 percent of local seats (ČTK, 27 November).

National and Ethnic Issues. Although many of Czechoslovakia's transitional problems are shared in some form by neighboring postsocialist regimes, the national question is dictated by the often tortured seven-decade relationship between Czechs and Slovaks. The original union of two kindred Slavic nations separated by a millenium of separate political history was troubled by the centralist constitution of the interwar period and stringent Stalinism. The federal framework accepted as a legacy of the Prague Spring eroded under normalization. The Velvet Revolution brought new Slovak demands for an "authentic federalism" and greater accommodation to Slovak interests.

Slovak sensitivities to their status within the state first struck Czech awareness in the heated controversy over the renaming of the state; after an intensive struggle that resulted in the designation Czech and Slovak Federative Republic (ČSFR), the shocked Czech public came to regard the national question as the single most important issue facing the country, outpolling even economic concerns. The Czech-Slovak controversy has not taken the form of violent outbursts seen in Romania or Yugoslavia; some three-quarters of both Czechs and Slovaks are clearly committed to the continuation of a joint state. The difficulty in harmonizing national interests, however, took center stage in the last half of 1990, featuring Slovak conflict with its Hungarian minority over language rights and, in particular, a hair-raising dispute over the problem of federal competence vis-à-vis the republics.

A general consensus on the necessity of striking a new federal bargain had crystallized rather early in the year but was not accompanied by equal consensus on the specific form of the relationship or even by a common theoretical conception of the legal basis on which power should rest. In June, the federal government transferred authority for a number of ministries to the republic level. By the summer, it had become apparent, however, that the initial expectation of a two-year period of constitutional negotiation over federal competence before extensive revisions of the federal bargain would seriously hamper the progress of economic transformation.

A meeting in Trenčianské Teplice on 8 August was the first of a series of high-level conferences at which federal and republic officials tried to hammer out practical guidelines for the division of power between the center and the two republics. These ongoing sessions, vexed by "too many surprises," personality conflicts, and recurrent issue crises, were impelled by the recognition that ethnic strife impaired international investor confidence and that continued failure to allocate economic power authoritatively was taxing public patience. During the fall, Havel issued repeated pleas and warnings that Czech-Slovak misunderstanding imperiled the country's international standing and the very existence of the state (*Rudé právo*, 26 October). The context for these complicated negotiations was multifaceted, but an enduring theme was the extent to which the distortions of past years could be attributed to the pathologies of communist bureaucratic centralism rather than to "Czech haughtiness and incorrigible Pragocentrism" (*Národná obroda*, 26 June).

The negotiation process resolved several questions, including the division of the modest budgetary pie (*Zemědělské noviny*, 1 December). General agreement to reserve core functions in finance, defense, and foreign policy to the federal government nonetheless left questions of specific definition. On 13 November, the three governments finally approved a jointly sponsored constitutional amendment allocating fiscal and policy authority. Although the Czech and Slovak National Councils both approved the so-called competency statute in late November, the Czech version drew banking, the post office administration, and the protection of minority rights back into the center. In early December, the affronted Slovak government declared that unless the Federal Assembly approved the November understanding without centralizing amendments, it would assert the sovereignty of its own republic's laws over those of the federation. Havel, who had taken a determinedly balanced stance on the national question, now responded sharply, warning of the ČSFR's "disintegration as a state" and calling for emergency powers to avert constitutional crisis (*NYT*, 11 December). To everyone's apparent relief, the Federal Assembly approved a satisfactory version of the competency statute on 12 December (ČTK, 12 December).

Economic Affairs. Communist rule left an immediate crisis of lowered productivity and growth. In the case of lowered productivity, this stasis severely constrained government financial resources. Budgetary stringency was the hallmark of fiscal policy at all levels. Only the category of social expenditures was slated for growth, as the government planned to rectify past wrongs and to ease the shock of economic transition with a range of transfer payments. Specially targeted were compensation to rehabilitated victims of the communist regime, unemployment benefits, consumer subsidies to compensate for energy and heating cost increases, and cost-of-living increases for pensioners.

Although the economic dislocations of 1990 were not as severe in Czechoslovakia as elsewhere in the former bloc, uncertainty and reconstruction did take its toll. Official inflation figures of 7.2 percent announced in November, driven by food and fuel price increases, met with skepticism from some analysts as too low (*Hospodářské noviny*, 22 November). Third-quarter statistics registered unemployment levels of 0.5 percent in the Czech lands and 1.1 percent in Slovakia through the end of October (*Hospodářské noviny*, 9 October; *Verejnost'*, 13 November). A moderate decline of 3.7 percent in industrial output compared with 1989 over the first three quarters did not provoke undue alarm about the secular trends in this area (*Hospodářské noviny*, 12 October).

The immediate economic situation inherited from communist rule, however, was less important than the task of dismantling the cumbersome and stagnant centrally planned economy that had driven Czechoslovakia out of the ranks of the world's top industrial economies after 1948. The Government of National Understanding that took power in December 1989 had a clear, though highly general, mandate to engage in massive economic reconstruction. Perhaps unduly regardful of its provisional standing, however, the government was slow to undertake major systemic reform, deferring to the democratically elected bodies due to emerge from the June elections. This posture later came to be seen by many as an unfortunate squandering of the opportunity to act while a massive popular consensus still reigned in the place of politics as usual (*Lidové noviny*, 17 September). However, considerable preparatory groundwork was laid in the spring. For example, parliamentary action ended the state monopoly on foreign trade in April; by June the government had issued more than six hundred permits for foreign trade activity (Bratislava, *Pravda*, 26 June). Provisional liberalization of enterprise laws also allowed for the proliferation of small businesses.

Immediately after the parliamentary elections, the new federal government mapped out a fairly detailed timetable for economic reform that was refined and often enacted over succeeding months (*Hospodářské noviny*, 9 July). Currency and pricing reforms were central goals of the market transition. An internal convertible currency law, passed in November and slated to take effect on 1 January 1991, allowed enterprises to exchange korunas for foreign exchange to buy imports and make payments abroad (Prague Domestic Service, 28 November). Price liberalization, scheduled to become operational the same day, included a package of safeguards to mitigate the inflationary pressures inherent in the monopoly structure of Czechoslovak industry and to cushion the impact of the simultaneous Council for Mutual Economic Assistance (CMEA) transition to world market prices (ČTK, 20 November; *Hospodářské noviny*, 23 November).

Privatization, a pressing concern throughout the region, posed problems of equity and efficacy in dismantling the state-controlled economy. The approach eventually adopted in Czechoslovakia in the fall of 1990 was to divide the formidable task into two components: the so-called small privatization process of auctioning off small businesses and the big privatization process of transferring ownership of larger state enterprises by converting them into joint stock companies. Citizen stockholders, who were issued coupons for the purpose, could then buy shares of the enterprises (*Svobodné slovo*, 4 October). An additional law, passed on 25 October, established a framework for the reprivatization of immovable assets confiscated by the state in the nationalization of 1955 to 1961.

The working class, with much at stake in the progress of economic transformation, faced rising unemployment and price levels and an uncertain return for the social insecurity they were asked to tolerate in the interest of eventual prosperity. After the Communist Revolutionary Trade Union Movement (ROH) dissolved itself on 2 March, organized labor interests were represented by the Czechoslovak Confederation of Trade Unions (ČSKOS), which evolved from the strike committee in November 1989. The new trade unions voiced periodic dissatisfaction with government responsiveness throughout the year. In April, ČSKOS demanded fuller partnership with the government "in questions that concern the substantive interests of working people" (ČTK, 5 April). In November and December, the unions launched their strongest challenge to government industrial policy during the parliamentary consideration of laws on unemployment and collective bargaining and amendments to the Labor Code. Unions went on temporary strike alert to protest insufficient guarantees of worker participation in labor-related management decisions. The utilization of the symbolic strike continued to be an instrument of labor communication in politics throughout the year.

The communist response to these massive projected changes was guardedly critical. Without ever challenging the essential need for economic reconstruction, the KSČS continually questioned the march to capitalism and the equity of specific arrangements. Party spokesmen argued that the "government's blueprint gives disproportionate influence to private ownership relations" (*Rudé právo*, 24 October). In November, the party submitted its own "large privatization" bill that gave a greater role to cooperative forms of ownership (ČTK, 8 November). Party organizations, disbanded in state bodies in December 1989, continued to operate, largely on an informal basis, in the workplace. The Eighteenth Party Congress championed worker interests in the transition, warning of the dangers of inflation, unemployment, and "the selling out of national wealth and property" (ČTK, 3 November); there was no indication that party economic policy had made an impact on either the public or the government.

Environmental and Energy Policy. The catastrophic dimensions of Czechoslovakia's environmental problems finally attained full recognition in 1990. Decades of industrial pollution driven by a Stalinist production fetish, heedless of environmental damage, had wreaked havoc, particularly in desolated North Bohemian regions often described as moonscapes. More than 35 percent of the population live in a severely polluted environment, surrounded by forests dying of sulfur dioxide exposure, toxic wastes, largely untreated water pollution that severely affects 70 percent of the country's rivers, and contaminated arable land (*Report on East Europe*, no. 12, 23 March). Environment Minister Josef Vavrousek reckoned the costs of rectifying the ecological disaster at some 650 billion korunas over the next two decades (*Hospodářské noviny*, 9 July). Preliminary efforts are under way to seek pollution control and cleanup technology from the West and to scale back production of the brown coal that most seriously affects air quality (*Hospodářské noviny*, 16 November; ČTK, 22 November).

Czechoslovakia faces a Hobson's choice in energy policy, each major alternative posing its own dilemma. Hydroelectric power is available only in limited quantity, curtailed still further by the Hungarian and Czechoslovak suspension of the controversial Gabčikovo-Nagymaros dam project. Utilization of domestic reserves of brown coal, which currently fuels 68 percent of the country's thermal power plants, has been a disastrous source of pollution. The nuclear industry, equipped with Soviet-type reactors, provides one-fifth of the country's electricity; although the ČSFR is too dependent on this energy source to permit its abandonment, the nuclear alternative has faced mounting scrutiny in the post-Chernobyl period and is slated for expensive safety overhauls. Equivocal nuclear safety power standards have been a source of considerable diplomatic stress with neighboring Austria (*Národná obroda*, 20 July). Finally, the vital delivery of petroleum products from the Soviet Union is increasingly expensive, uncertain, and erratic. The successful search for alternative energy sources is curtailed by a distribution system oriented to Soviet suppliers and by the lack of storage facilities. Nevertheless, the government has been canvassing prospects for oil and natural gas purchases from the Middle East, Algeria, and Tunisia and from Britain's North Sea reserves, among others. The gulf crisis and the continued turmoil in the Soviet Union that has heavily disrupted fuel deliveries have administered twin jolts to an energy situation already in dire straits; the government estimated in November that energy costs had risen between 44 and 74 percent in 1990 (ČTK, 30 November), with more increases to come.

Religion. After decades of religious repression, the government acted quickly to abolish the 1949 law constraining religious activities on 23 January. With President Havel championing the moral utility of religion for the life of the state, mutual independence, rather than full separation of church and state, was the base from which to develop a revitalized religious role. For example, the government authorized religious instruction to begin in the schools as early as September 1990.

Freedom of religious expression has been guaranteed for all faiths. With two-thirds of the population at least nominally Roman Catholic, however,

the Catholic church has been at the center of Czechoslovakia's religious revival. By April, all thirteen bishoprics, most of them vacant for years, had been filled, and the incarceration of monks (1949) and the seizure of monastic property (1950) were reversed with a statute on relegalization and property restitution (ČTK, 19 July).

The religious highlight of the year was the 34-hour visit of Pope John Paul II to Czechoslovakia on 21 April, his first to a former bloc country outside of Poland. He was met by the church's prime survivor, 91-year-old František Cardinal Tomášek, archbishop of Prague, a living historical embodiment of the travails of a church that had survived communist rule. Ordained in 1922, secretly elected bishop in 1949, and relegated to the labor camps of the 1950s, Cardinal Tomášek reemerged as apostolic administrator of the Prague archdiocese in 1965 at the age of 66. Never as visible as his Polish or Hungarian counterparts, he became increasingly assertive in his eighties and survived to preside over the reemergence of a beleaguered church.

International Affairs. The reordering of Czechoslovakia's international relations, only partially completed in 1990, was designed to replace a bloc-oriented socialist reference group with a pan-European, broad global frame of reference. The reestablishment of diplomatic ties with previously ideologically unacceptable states, notably Israel, heralded the broadening of the country's foreign policy ambitions from the more restricted base of the communist years. An enhanced Czechoslovak contribution to the international community was symbolized by its cooperation in the United Nations–sponsored economic sanctions against Iraq and the preparation of token peacekeeping forces in the event of regional conflict.

The central thrust of Czechoslovak international efforts, however, was continental rather than global. The "return to Europe" was reflected both in a general aspiration to regain the pluralist economic and political heritage lost in 1948 and in a specific agenda for establishing linkages with West European integrationist institutions and promoting broader cooperation across an undivided continent from the Atlantic to the Urals. In March, Foreign Minister Dienstbier went to the two-day session of the Council of Europe in Lisbon to request full Czechoslovak membership in that body, returning with a favorable response and an interim guest status (Prague Television Service, 24 March). In May, in anticipation of fuller future involvement, the ČSFR concluded a trade and economic cooperation agreement with the European Community designed to lift all trade restrictions by 1995 (ČTK, 7 May). An active program to develop ties with each of the major West European countries within both the European Community and the European Free Trade Association framed a relentless travel schedule for diplomatic and economics officials (*Hospodářské noviny*, 26 November).

In the context of defining the position of the ČSFR within the European Community, the unification of Germany was potentially the most significant diplomatic concern for the ČSFR, affecting the country's relationship with its largest Western trading partner (West Germany), its second largest bloc trading partner (East Germany), and, not least, the historically dominant nation that shaped the Central European landscape throughout the nineteenth and twentieth centuries. Although ČSFR officials accepted unification and hastened to encourage new ties, historical issues loomed in the background of the dialogue, particularly with regard to the rights of Sudeten Germans evicted from Czechoslovakia after World War II (Prague Television Service, 30 November).

The KSČS's loss of power orphaned a partisan organization accustomed to act with state prerogatives in foreign affairs. The most important task left to the party, therefore, was fence-mending, that is, reestablishing stable ties with the Western left and finding new grounds for cooperation with former partners in governance. Thus, the KSČS sought in the new year to reestablish its international standing on the left with a series of explanatory talks with West European left-wing parties and with intensive bilateral contacts with successor communist parties in Hungary, Poland, Yugoslavia, and East Germany (*Rudé právo*, 14 February). On 14–15 November, leaders of the successor communist parties of Hungary, Poland, Germany, Bulgaria, and Czechoslovakia gathered in Moscow for the first joint meeting since the cataclysmic events of 1989 to compare notes on their common plight and to reaffirm their faith in the continuing relevance of socialism to the interests of working people (TASS, 15 November).

The KSČS warned against a "one-sided" tilt to the West (ČTK, 4 November) and looked to Moscow as the "chief guarantor" of Czechoslovakia's security. The dismissal of the KSČS old guard eliminated some serious tensions that had strained Communist Party of the Soviet Union/KSČS rela-

tions in the Gorbachev era. The party-to-party relationship, however, has lost most of its centrality and all of its capacity to produce authoritative results. Neither party is a sure pathway to influence in the country of the other. In October, Gorbachev responded to KSČS overtures for a strengthening and renewal of ties with cordiality but with the proviso that "mutual solidarity and the broad possibility of common operations" proceed in the context of respect for noninterference in the internal affairs of sovereign states (*Rudé právo*, 2 October). In short, the Czechoslovak communists are at best functioning informally in the interstices of the formal state diplomacy that produces results, even with the Soviet Union.

Economic Relations. The year 1990 was a transitional year for fuller Czechoslovak participation in the international economic community, a process of breaking through the shackles of the cold war and those of the cumbersome, centrally planned economy. Assistance and cooperation from the West were still constrained by CMEA regulations, with the expectation that cooperation between such corporations as IBM and Czechoslovak educational and industrial organizations would increase as international restrictions eased. In addition to the economic ties forged with Western Europe, further significant aid and trade were anticipated with the reactivation of the General Agreement on Tariffs and Trade membership and admission to the International Monetary Fund (IMF) and the World Bank in September.

Relations with the United States warmed considerably after the communist demise and the accession of the popular President Havel, who visited in February. That same month, U.S. secretary of state Baker offered an economic assistance package comparable to those provided Hungary and Poland. In April, the signing of a bilateral trade agreement to lower tariffs was accompanied by promises of most-favored-nation status for Czechoslovakia, subsequently approved in November. President Bush proffered a final assistance proposal in a speech to the ČSFR Federal Assembly during his brief visit to Czechoslovakia on 17 and 18 November: some $60 million for a U.S.-Czechoslovak enterprise fund to promote privatization, as well as support for the ČSFR in the IMF and the World Bank.

The pivotal relationship, however, remained that with the Soviet Union, Czechoslovakia's largest trading partner, largest debtor, and supplier of 90 percent of the ČSFR's oil and natural gas imports.

The importance of this relationship of historically conditioned economic dependence was slated for radical redefinition on both sides; Soviet spokesmen talked of the "deideologization of foreign trade," meaning that its vital raw materials would go to the highest bidder in hard currency now that the political reasons for supplying East Europe had evaporated. Czechoslovak trade officials showed equal interest in diversifying their trade base. Trade was, in fact, crucial to the state's economic health, as the Ministry of Foreign Trade estimated that one-third of national income was generated in that sector (Prague Television Service, 13 July).

The beginnings of disengagement were far from smoothly executed, however. Ongoing official negotiations designed to set broad guidelines for future economic interaction between the USSR and the ČSFR often bogged down in disagreement and constantly shifting estimates of Soviet capacity to meet its delivery contracts, particularly of oil. The conduct of business in freely convertible currencies as of January 1991 raised innumerable practical problems in calculating the value of Czechoslovak assets in the Soviet Union and in handling Soviet indebtedness of roughly four billion rubles. At year's end, agreement eluded the two countries on a range of issues including the future of joint projects and the mode of payment for Soviet forces still based in the ČSFR. The larger question—that of the future stability and even survival of the Soviet Union—loomed constantly in the background for government officials troubled by the country's continuing dependence on the disintegrating superpower, particularly in the sphere of fuel supplies.

Relations with neighboring countries in the former Soviet bloc have undergone a process of differentiation corresponding to the problems and, more rarely, opportunities raised by the painful parallel processes of democratization and economic transition. A key area of ongoing discussion and negotiation is the economic dislocation produced by the massive unilateral cancellation of contracts by firms in former East Germany, with estimated losses of about $1 billion (ČTK, 4 October; *FBIS-EEU*, 10 October, 30 November; Prague Television Service, 29 November); Czechoslovakia is appealing to the Federal Republic of Germany in this regard, in the interests of a long-term economic relationship. Further problems include tensions over travel and purchase restrictions, particularly with Poland, and, of course, the fate of the CMEA. Czechoslovakia, which maintains trade surpluses with all the CMEA countries except Hungary and Vietnam, chafed un-der multilateral agreements that permitted manipulation of exchange rates and delay in payment to the disadvantage of the more solvent and less inflationary Czechoslovak economy (Bratislava, *Pravda*, 22 March). The ČSFR has therefore been at the forefront in proposing a radical restructuring of the CMEA and in seeking bilateral agreements to modulate the economic shocks generated by internal economic dislocations (*Mladá fronta*, 12 January).

The reordering of Czechoslovakia's international allegiances had a striking impact on unpaid aid to developing socialist countries. In June, the government decided to phase out such assistance, meeting ninety million korunas of existing commitments to Vietnam and others through 1992 and postponing the award of any additional assistance pending the installation of a freely elected government (*Hospodářské noviny*, 8 June). Experts expressed general disillusionment with the record of aid to developing countries, likening the cooperative experience to "playing the lottery" and noting the Czechoslovak help had made little impact on Third World developmental progress (*Práce*, 17 March). Relations with Cuba were particularly troubled, with Castro's complaints about the quality of Czechoslovak manufactured goods (no doubt sharpened by the ČSFR's desertion of socialism) (*Rudé právo*, 16 March), escalating to an informal severance of commercial relations in May (Belgrade, Tanjug, 23 June).

In an echo of Gorbachev's "new thinking" on Third World alliances, Czechoslovakia too has sought to deepen relationships with those developing nations whose resource base or economic success makes them a beneficial partner. Thus, for example, Dienstbier visited India, Japan, South Korea, and Thailand in his October Asian tour in search of closer cooperation, while Čalfa toured the Maghreb countries of North Africa in early December, mindful of both their interest in Czechoslovak technology and their oil and natural gas reserves.

Military/Security Issues. The decommunization of the military and security policy has developed along three dimensions over the course of 1990: the internal restructuring of the armed forces, the withdrawal of Soviet troops from Czechoslovakia, and the pending resolution of the future role of the Warsaw Treaty Organization (WTO).

The restructuring of the armed forces has been an especially delicate issue. Budgetary constraints and a transformed international environment in which, in the words of the deputy defense minister, "Czechoslovakia has no potential enemies" (ČTK, 31 October) mandated a budgetary cut of about 12 percent for 1990 (*Hospodářské noviny*, 3 July) and severe manpower cuts—a reduction of the army by 60,000 to 140,000 soldiers. But this widely approved retrenchment has been insufficient to counter public doubts or avert plummeting status for the military, whose role in social control under communism was resented and whose stance during November 1989 continued to be investigated. Professional soldiers, including an officer corps that was 82 percent communist at the time of the regime's downfall, underwent continued competency screening in 1990; some ten thousand soldiers had left or been discharged by mid-October (ČTK, 16 October). A ban on political activity in the military was undertaken in late 1989.

The second critical issue, in both symbolic and practical terms, was the withdrawal of the 73,500 Soviet troops stationed on Czechoslovak territory since the 1968 invasion. The abuse of Czechoslovakia's sovereignty by invading WTO troops quickly became, after the Velvet Revolution, a starting point from which to redefine the country's independent international position. The official repudiation of the invasion in December 1989 by the governments involved was heralded in Czechoslovakia; thereafter, the legal basis for Soviet garrisons lost its original rationale, which could be publicly disavowed as "null and void." After intensive negotiations, Soviet forces began to leave on 26 February in a series of phased withdrawals slated for completion in June 1991; the withdrawal was proceeding on schedule at year's end. A constellation of important ancillary issues surrounded the withdrawal, the most important being the problem of compensation for environmental damage left in their wake. Cleanup costs are estimated to run to some $2 million per site (Soviet troops occupied about 150 military installations in the ČSFR). A general protocol covering these financial claims, not scheduled to be concluded until 1993, augurs a protracted period of bargaining and disagreement (*Mladá fronta*, 4 October).

The fate of the WTO was by no means as definitive. In March, Prime Minister Čalfa made it clear that Czechoslovakia saw no reason for undignified and possibly destabilizing haste in exiting the pact "until such time as the bipolar European alliance structure gave way to a broader security framework." Instead, Czechoslovak officials sought to reconstruct the alliance as a consultative body and a political instrumentality for disarmament talks, anticipating the speedy abrogation of the pact's integrated military command. This goal was not fulfilled at consultative meetings in March and July. The USSR postponed a WTO summit scheduled for November to confront the alliance's military role because of "domestic and international problems" that no alliance partner had cause to doubt. As two-thirds of the population favor neutrality and only 16 percent approved continuance in the pact (*Lidové noviny*, 14 May), ČSFR membership seemed destined for eventual termination.

Although years of communist rule were instrumental in creating the issues just discussed, the current KSČS has raised no serious challenge to government approaches to resolving them. Nor does it fundamentally challenge the need to transform the European security system in coming years into a common enterprise inclusive of all countries; Havel and Dienstbier have been adamant about the need to avoid a Soviet "Versailles," a posture the party surely approves.

Carol Skalnik Leff
University of Illinois at Champaign-Urbana

Germany
German Democratic Republic

Population. 16,307,170 (July)
Party. Party of Democratic Socialism (Partei des Demokratischen Sozialismus, PDS). Note: The Sozialistische Einheitspartei Deutschland—Partei des Demokratischen Sozialismus (SED-PDS) changed its name in February to Partei des Demokratischen Sozialismus (PDS). The SED-PDS (then the PDS) was the principal governing party in coalition governments until the general elections of 18 March. After 12 April it was in opposition in the German Democratic Republic (GDR). After 3 October, when the GDR ceased to

exist, it entered the Bundestag as an opposition party.

Founded. 1918 (SED, 1946; SED-PDS, 1989; PDS, 1990)

Membership. 345,000 (interview with Gregor Gysi, *Rudé právo*, 19 September; *FBIS-WEU*, 10 October); only 214,000 claimed in *Pravda* by 8 January 1991

Chairman. Dr. Gregor Gysi, 42

Honorary Chairman. Hans Modrow, 62, resigned November 1990

Deputy Leaders. Hans Modrow, prime minister until 12 March; Wolfgang Berghofer, resigned January; Wolfgang Pohl, resigned October; André Brie from February 1990.

Presidium of the Executive Council. (Parteivorstand) (March 1990) Monika Werner, head of party delegation in Volkskammer (until March); Marlies Deneke, head of commission for youth and women's policy; Lothar Bisky, head of commission on press and media; Klaus Höpke, head of commission for culture and science; Hans-Joachim Willerding, head of commission for international affairs; Helmar Hegewald, head of commission for Third World policy.

Arbitration Committee. 20 members (July)

Executive Council. 101 members (July)

Parliamentary Organization in Volkskammer. (March 1990) 66 members: Executive Board; chairman, Gregor Gysi, deputy leader, Dr. Dietmar Keller; parliamentary business organizer, Bernd Meyer; Executive Committee of the Delegation: Executive Board plus Eva Maria Förtsch, Dr. Uwe-Jens Heuer, Dr. Käte Niederkirchner, Dr. Martina Schönebeck, Dr. Fritz Schulmann, Dr. Klaus Steinitz, Dr. Hans-Joachim Willerding; Volkskammer Presidium representative: Dr. Käte Niederkirchner (also a deputy president); Chamber Presidium members: Dr. Dagmar Enkelmann, Bernd Meyer.

Last Election. Bundestag, 2 December 1990; 17 members of 662

Last Congress. 24 February, First Congress of PDS; reconvened as the "Congress of Renewal" 16 September.

Publications. Previously, *Neues Deutschland* (now independent), *Einheit*

At the beginning of the year the prospects for the survival of the German Democratic Republic (GDR) were not good. The unification of Germany seemed to many observers the most likely way out of the near total collapse of the country's social, political, and economic order. The flight of hundreds of thousands to the Federal Republic of Germany (FRG) ruled out a return to stability. Huge street demonstrations also continued to be a central feature of political life, just as they had in the last months of 1989. Long before the monetary union of 1 July, the GDR's economic dependence on the FRG was an established fact. Any formula for the future would have to take that dependence into account. There was no chance for the GDR to reestablish a viable economy without massive support from the West. This was well understood by ordinary people as well as by the country's leaders. Judging from the mood and slogans of the street, the demand for unification was irresistible and the elections that were called for the spring would, in effect, be a referendum on unification.

In view of the turmoil, it was apparent that the country could not bear the tension of a prolonged transition to the promised democratic system. The general elections, which had been scheduled for 6 May by the communist-led government of Hans Modrow, were moved forward to 18 March. No one believed that the communists could hope for an outcome that would keep them in power. Yet many, both in the party and outside it, continued to believe that democratic elections would somehow accomplish the salvation of the GDR. They looked forward to a transformation that would leave the country as a humanized and democratic socialist alternative to the FRG. For the first two months of the year these ideas were central in the policy pronouncements of the Modrow government and of the party. Yet any hope for such a result had passed long before.

The idea that the GDR could be rescued discounted the unique character of the old regime and failed to take into account the GDR's dependence on the Soviet Union and its unequal competition with the economic power and values of West Germany. In the GDR the state and "developed socialism" were intimately bound together. Without its hard-line socialist system, backed by Soviet power, little remained to define and defend the distinct character of the GDR. Both Hans Modrow and the party's chairman, Gregor Gysi, recognized as much when, at the end of January, they announced the party's acceptance of some form of German unification. Yet the countertendency persisted. Almost to the moment of unification, the party fought for a slower-paced transition period and an outcome that would not result in a straightforward extension of the FRG's institutions into the territories of the GDR.

In promoting a cautious approach the party was in broad agreement with its former enemies. New Forum, Democratic Awakening, and other parties of the opposition shared the communist suspicion of unification and preferred an approach to inter-German relations that would concede as much as possible to what they believed were the unique values of East Germany. There were many in the Evangelical church who also held these sentiments. (For a review of the attitude of the church, see an interview with the consistorial president of the Evangelical church, Manfred Stolpe, in *Maerkische Volksstimme*, 13 January; *JPRS-EER*, 6 April.) The noncommunist opposition was united on most central issues but hopelessly fragmented and poorly organized. By the end of February no fewer than 38 parties and political groupings were in existence in the GDR, and 24 parties and alliances were registered for the elections (East Berlin, ADN, 9 March; *FBIS-EEU*, 9 March).

The leadership of the small parties, although often idealistic and energetic, lacked electoral and parliamentary experience. Except for the communists, none of the GDR's parties had an adequate organization or a strong political tradition. Besides the communists, only the church had possessed a quasi-independent and nationwide structure under the old regime, which was why the church was able to exercise a strong influence on the formation of an opposition in the GDR during 1989 and why church leaders continued to be an influential element in opposition and government parties throughout the year (*YICA*, 1990; RFE/RL, *Report on Eastern Europe* 1, no. 28 [15 July]).

During the campaign for the general elections of 18 March, the political parties of the FRG played a commanding role. With the exception of the unexpectedly strong showing of the communists, now the Party of Democratic Socialism, the election had been an overwhelming success for the parties with strong organizational ties with the FRG. The election campaign was in fact largely fought by West German party machines and with the direct involvement of West German leaders. All the GDR's own leaders except Gregor Gysi were overshadowed.

The CDU-dominated Alliance for Germany won the elections with 40.6 percent of the vote and formed a CDU-led coalition with Lothar de Maizière as prime minister. In view of the strong links between the CDU and the Federal Republic, it seemed likely that the GDR would follow Bonn's lead. The government of Helmut Kohl expected no less; yet the new government took a strong and frequently independent line. In negotiating the state treaties that prepared the way for the economic and monetary union of 1 July and the political unification of 3 October, the GDR representatives frequently adopted stances that were much different from those of the FRG. The differences were not always resolved in Bonn's favor. In the realm of foreign affairs, the GDR also showed that it was capable of acting independently.

In the round of international negotiations that cleared the way for unification, the attitudes of the Soviet Union toward its interests in Germany were especially important. During the first half of the year the Soviet leaders came to accept the inevitability of German reunification. Mikhail Gorbachev and Eduard Shevardnadze looked to Bonn to represent the German side in all dealings with third parties. Yet on several pivotal issues, such as the role of a united Germany within the North Atlantic Treaty Organization (NATO), the East Germans took significantly different positions from those of FRG and succeeded in exerting more influence than most observers expected.

Whatever the differences in policy preferences between the two German governments, the overpowering impact of the FRG's political parties, institutions, and economic power assured that the end result of negotiations would conform closely to the FRG's concept of a united Germany. By the time of the all-German elections on 2 December, it was possible to see the irony of the last days of the GDR. New Forum and the other indigenous East German political movements, which had done more to pull down the old regime than anyone, left the political scene regretting the GDR's demise, for the direct-line successors of their old antagonists had managed to find a place in the new Germany. As an additional irony, many of the ideas and values of the opposition were now claimed by the communists.

As for the last GDR government, it is difficult to imagine a more complicated political environment than the one that de Maizière and his cabinet had faced. Working within a turbulent multiparty system in the absence of a strong democratic culture, they faced a disintegrating society and economy. They thus had to take on a vital round of international negotiations that would eliminate their country and accept that their own status was transitional and limited. Having to cooperate with the state that had so thoroughly penetrated and deeply influenced policy considerations in their own country, it is not surprising that the painstakingly built coalition was not fated to survive for the remaining lifetime of the GDR. Under the strain of economic collapse and disagreements over the timetable for unification, it fell apart at the end of the summer. The CDU minority government lasted only a little longer, and the last government of the GDR was finally dissolved on 3 October.

Leadership and Party Organization. The Extraordinary Congress of 8–9 December and 16–17 December 1989 was the last for the Socialist Unity Party (SED), which reorganized and re-named itself first the Socialist Unity Party of Germany—Party of Democratic Socialism (SED-PDS) and later the Party of Democratic Socialism (PDS). For a short time it remained the most influential force in the GDR government. Despite its parliamentary role, however, the party's status as the ruling party was at an end. In December it renounced its "leading role" (*YICA*, 1990), and the erosion of communism's political fortunes could not be halted in the emerging democratic environment.

The dramatic decline that had begun in the last months of 1989 continued unabated; by the beginning of the year the party's morale had been shattered at all levels. The communists, uncertain about their goals and their future, were in a state of organizational chaos. Between December and the general elections of 18 March, the party proved incapable, even under the able leadership of Gregor Gysi and Hans Modrow, of accomplishing the goals it had set at the Extraordinary Congress. Despite impressive progress in its campaign of internal reform, it could not complete the transition to a democratic socialist party with an effective electoral strategy and program. Fated to have an ever-diminishing influence on the political life of the country and to see its policy preferences overtaken by events, the March elections left the PDS in opposition. Its attempts to slow the pace of German reunification and to preserve something from the GDR's former social and economic priorities largely failed. Throughout the year, the future of the country was more and more in the hands of those, both in the GDR and in the FRG, who wanted the unequivocal and rapid unification of Germany on terms that conceded little to the PDS point of view.

The crucial steps for restructuring and reorienting the party were taken at the Extraordinary Congress. The congress delegates' four main objectives were to

1. Elect the members for new leading organizations to replace the Central Committee, Politburo, Secretariat, Central Auditing Commission, and Party Control Commission

2. Choose a new name for the party

3. Decide on a new party statute that would formalize the organizational changes and redefine the rules governing party membership

4. Work out a new program that would reflect the democratic and parliamentary aspirations of the party

Only the first two objectives were completely met in the short time provided by the two sessions of the congress; the party statute and the program were announced some weeks later. The new name SED-PDS was agreed on through a compromise between those who insisted on retaining the existing title, Socialist Unity Party, and those who demanded a name that symbolized a complete break with the past (*ND*, 18 December 1989). Another important symbolic issue was the new party statute, with heated debates over whether Leninist should be retained as part of the basic definition of the party's principles in the statute's preamble (*ND*, 19 December 1989). Such details reflected the still powerful presence of conservative forces that would continue to impede the party's transformation.

On 4 February the party underscored its attempts to break with the past by dropping SED from its name (*ND*, 5 February; Hamburg, DPA, 30 January; *FBIS-EEU*, 31 January). Further organizational changes were announced in mid-February when the new draft statute was published (*ND*, 17–18 February). The name, statute, and PDS program were formally adopted at the First Congress of the PDS 24–25 February. The statute approved the changes in the organs of central leadership that had been adopted at the Extraordinary Congress (*YICA*, 1990) and in other ways expressed a democratic organizational model for the party. In the preamble the PDS was defined as a "German socialist party" dedicated to "humanistic democratic socialism." No mention was made of Leninism or Leninist organizational ideas. Accordingly, the statute defined a relationship between the central leadership and the local party committees that differed significantly from the old "democratic-centralist" model of the SED. The essential change was a reduced role in the work of local organizations. Below the central organs three levels of local leadership were identified: the basic organizations (Basisorganisationen), district organizations (Kreisorganisationen), and regional/state organizations (Bezirks/Landesorganisationen). All levels were to be established on the basis of elections and operate democratically. A crucial change at the grass roots level was that the Leninist "cell" of the primary organizations was abandoned; these organizations were no longer firmly anchored in the workplace but in residential areas and communities. In consultation with the district committees, members were free to form their own organizations in these localities or in their factories and other places of work, "when conditions are appropriate" (*Statut Partei des Demokratischen Sozialismus* [*SPDS*], *ND*, 17–18 February). The practical effect of this change at the grass roots level can be seen in the Berlin organizations. Statistics released in June showed that only 6.2 percent of the Berlin membership remained organized in the workplace, whereas 75 percent participated in the residential groups (*ND*, 11 June).

The move toward democratic procedures at the local level was convincing because the restructured organs at the center did not easily lend themselves to the meticulous supervision of party life. Even if the party had been in a less chaotic state, the return to centrally directed discipline would have been difficult. A new style of leadership had almost certainly to follow, given the now genuine role of elections in choosing the leadership and the Central Committee being replaced by an Executive Board (Parteivorstand) with a limited number of policy-oriented commissions in place of the former Central Committee departments and the large bureaucracy of the Secretariat (*YICA*, 1990). The full-time staff of the central apparatus declined in numbers during January alone by 25 percent, from 855 to 622 (*ND*, 20–21 January). The Politburo, Central Control Commission, and Central Auditing Commission were also replaced with organs that were less likely to work for rigid centralization. Instead of the Control and Auditing commissions there was now one twenty-man board, the Arbitration Committee, that was to exercise fewer supervisory and executive functions than its predecessors and that was more open to the influence of lower party organizations (SPDS; *ND*, 17–18 February). In the Presidium, which took over the functions of the Politburo, the power of the chairman was balanced by the presence of three deputy chairmen and the heads of the Executive Commissions (*YICA*, 1990). The congress also appointed a potentially influential 24-member Council of Elders to assist the chairman. The council included the former intelligence chief, Markus Wolf, the distinguished economist, Jürgen Kuczynski, and the GDR's preeminent historian,

Ernst Engelberg (*ND*, 18 December 1989, 13–14 January).

The potential for personal power in Gregor Gysi's chairmanship was further restricted by the fact that one of his deputies, Hans Modrow, was also the prime minister; another, Wolfgang Berghofer, had chaired the sessions of the Extraordinary Congress and, until his resignation at the end of January, enjoyed almost as much influence among the rank and file as Gysi and Modrow. In short, the chairman's ability to lead the party seemed anchored more in his ability to maintain the confidence of his colleagues than on his control of the bureaucratic apparatus. Democracy was also encouraged by the break in continuity in the leadership. Among the 101 members of the Executive Board, only 4— Hans Modrow, Hans-Joachim Willerding, Gerd Koenig, and Herbert Richte—had been members of the defunct Central Committee. Besides the few district chairmen who were included, the rest of the Executive Board were elected from the rank and file, not from the apparatus. (Eberhard Schneider, "Der letzte Parteitag der SED," *Berichte des Bundesinstituts für ostwissenschaftliche und internationale Studien*, 1990.)

Although there was much discussion of the party's new ideology and policy orientation at the Extraordinary Congress, the program was left in preliminary draft and not published until 14 February ("Programm der Partei des Demokratischen Sozialismus," *ND*, 10–11, 14 February). The new program pledged itself to the principles of social democracy and abandoned the party's previous self-image as a "class party." Reiterating the commitments undertaken at the congress toward democracy, human rights, social justice, and the rule of law, it also endorsed the principle of a "market economy dedicated to the social and ecological interests of the people" and a mixed system of public and private ownership. The sections concerned with the economy also called for worker democracy at the trade union level and, through elected management committees, in the enterprises. On this last point there was friction between the previously communist-dominated Federation of Trade Unions (FDGB) and the party. The trade unions were suspicious of any movement toward worker democracy in the factories which might undermine their own ability to represent the workers or compromise their possible future relationship with the German Trade Union Federation (DGB) in the FRG. (*Frankfurter Allgemeine*, 12 February; *JPRS-EEU*, 3 April.)

In international affairs the program underscored that strong ties with the Soviet Union were vital for the continued existence of the GDR and the stability of Europe, stressed that the GDR's eastern neighbors would remain important partners, and reaffirmed the party's "ties of active solidarity with the people of the Third World." On the question of the party's attitude toward German unification, the program called for a relationship between the two Germanies in the context of a demilitarized and united Europe. Because there was to be no unity through a simple incorporation into the Federal Republic's political and parliamentary system, there was some shift of emphasis on the unification issue as between the program and the documents of the congress. At the congress the German question had not received much attention; the final document of the first session simply concluded that "a union of the GDR and the FRG is not on our agenda" and went on to note that the GDR anticipated a treaty-based relationship with the FRG and was "open to the idea of confederative structures." (*ND*, 11 December 1989; Eberhard Schneider, "Der Letzte Parteitag der SED," *Berichte des Bundesinstituts für ostwissenschaftliche und internationale Studien*, 1990.) The unification issue was definitely on the party's agenda by 14 February, and the program largely confined itself to stressing the dangers and obstacles but without rejecting the idea. By the end of the month, although still stressing the difficulties and the need to proceed slowly, both Gysi and Modrow had accepted the inevitability of reunification. On 29 January, Gysi referred to the unification process as "unstoppable" (DPA, 29 January; *FBIS-EEU*, 30 January). On 1 February, Hans Modrow made it clear at a news conference that the party accepted the idea of an eventual federation of the two Germanies providing there were sufficient safeguards for both Germanies, for European security, and for Germany's neighbors. He borrowed the slogans of the street demonstrations when he proclaimed that the party was "for Germany for a united fatherland." (*ND*, 2 February.)

In January the SED-PDS was still a mass party, with perhaps a million members, although in view of the turmoil in the communist ranks, which continued unabated after the party's Extraordinary Congress in December, nobody could be sure of the numbers. Estimates varied from 1.0 to 1.4 million, approximately half the 2.3 million that were members as of January 1989 (*YICA*, 1990). Gysi admitted the party's impaired ability to interpret or even gather information on its remaining strength (*Der Spiegel*, 18 December 1989). The party's precipitous and continuing decline was obvious. In the first six weeks of the year there were further losses, somewhere between 250,000 to 750,000 (East Berlin, ADN, 15 February; *FBIS-EEU*, 16 February). As a consequence, the party mustered only 600 delegates for its February congress, as against the 2,600 who had been present in December (East Berlin, ADN, 24 February; *FBIS-EEU*, 26 February). By the beginning of July the membership had been further reduced to approximately 345,000. Those numbers remained relatively stable to the end of the year. (RFL/RL, *Report on Eastern Europe*, 7 September; *CSM*, 28 November.)

In its public utterances the party tried to put the best face on these losses, arguing that the decline could indicate a qualitative improvement. According to this view, many who were leaving were unwanted by the party; there was no room for people who could not accept the commitment to democracy and openness or who had compromised themselves under the previous Stalinist leadership. In contrast, the people who remained were likely to be the best; personal courage and idealism were needed to remain active in the face of so many difficulties. It was also true, according to Gysi, that the party was successfully expanding its efforts to recruit new members. (*ND*, 24–25 February.) Opposed to the leadership's claims, however, were indications that too many of those who remained in the ranks were those least likely to conform to the desired image of a reinvigorated and democratic party. Thus as it declined, the SED-PDS was increasingly made up of a disproportionate number of older cadres and others who, because of their career dependency on the party, saw a doubtful place for themselves in the emerging new order. Estimates for the Berlin organization indicated that, by June, 35 percent of the membership was older than 60 and only 10 percent was under 30 (*ND*, 11 June). Such a conclusion is also supported by election results. The PDS did best in Berlin and other large urban centers, probably because SED functionaries and state bureaucrats were most highly concentrated there (RFE/RL, *Report on Eastern Europe*, 23 March).

The loss of membership was not the only symptom of the crisis that had overtaken the party, whose problems reflected the general crisis of the GDR. The open political atmosphere that began in the last months of 1989 destroyed the institutional and ideological barriers that had formerly protected the party from the scrutiny of the public and the party's own rank and file. The party was confronted with one scandal after another until the full extent of the SED's mismanagement, dishonesty, and repressive character were fully exposed. The party tried to clean house and thus free itself from its Stalinist legacy, but it was a gargantuan task. In the first six weeks of the year no fewer than a thousand comrades who had been the victims of past injustices were officially rehabilitated, and 1,587 past resolutions of the party were rescinded (East Berlin, ADN, 12 February; *FBIS-EEU*, 27 February; *ND*, 12 February). The rehabilitation process continued until the end of the year. In December the party rehabilitated KPD and SED members who had been victims of Walter Ulbricht's regime in 1950 and 1951 during the biggest purge in the GDR's history (RL, *DR*, 11 December). The party also aggressively investigated the past records of its own functionaries, and many were expelled. The emergency meeting of the Executive Board on 22 January purged Egon Krenz and thirteen other members of the old Politburo. Expulsions also affected the Central Committee and executives at the regional levels. In total, approximately one thousand leading functionaries had been removed by mid-February. (*ND*, *NYT*, 22 January.)

Party expulsions were frequently followed by criminal proceedings launched from the GDR's public prosecution office. The charges included crimes against the human rights provisions of the GDR's constitution, high treason, and the misappropriation of state property. During the first six months of the year, arrest warrants were issued and court actions launched against Erich Mielke, Werner Krolikowski, Hermann Axen, Harry Tisch, Günter Mittag, Willi Stoph, and Gerald Götting, all former members of the Politburo. Many other lesser functionaries, state officials, and state security personnel were also charged. (*ND*, 19 January; East Berlin, ADN, 30 July; *FBIS-EEU*, 31 July.) These were people who months or weeks before had been beyond the reach of public criticism, so it is not surprising that so many in the country and the party never accepted that the PDS could ever dissociate itself from its past record.

Another difficulty lay in the party's inability to find a place on the political spectrum that clearly distinguished it from other socialist forces; neither the program nor subsequent policy and ideological pronouncements provided sufficient clarification. Yet such clarification was necessary as a rationalization for the party's continued participation in GDR and German politics for the party to hold and recruit

members and attract an electoral following. The leadership was to discover that there were no halfway measures between communism and social democracy and that communism could not be reformed. Any move toward democracy destroyed everything that had defined the unique character of the SED.

Gregor Gysi and other PDS spokesmen tried to define a third way for the party that was neither communist nor capitalist (*Der Spiegel*, 18 December 1989). From the outset the formulation lacked a sharp focus and suggested everything at once. The party stood for an alliance with all democratic forces, for environmental protection, for cooperation and eventual unity with the FRG, for saving some measure of GDR sovereignty, for a socialism different from that of the social democrats, and for preserving the major features of the GDR's past achievements. The only effect of such a confusing formulation was to isolate the party both from the social democrats and other moderate left-of-center forces and from the hard-line left.

According to Gysi, the third way placed the PDS to the left of the social democrats (SPD) (East Berlin, ADN, 21 January; *FBIS-EEU*, 22 January). Nevertheless, in the eyes of the diehard Leninist and radical elements in the PDS, the new course was not far enough to the left and represented a betrayal of principle. Following the Extraordinary Congress, a group of SED functionaries formed a communist platform and worked to preserve communist ideology and Leninist organizational principles within the SED-PDS (*ND*, 3 January; East Berlin, ADN, 8 January; *FBIS-EEU*, 25 January). The communist platform survived to the end of the year, but as the reform process gained ground, some hard-liners found new political homes in the many small radical left and sectarian parties that appeared in the first three months of the year. For example, a spokesman for *Die Nelken* (Carnations), a left communist splinter group that formed in mid-February, noted the presence among his comrades of many disillusioned former members of the SED (East Berlin, *Wochenpost* 37, no. 2 [12 January]; *JPRS-EEU*, 16 February).

On the left the political landscape came to resemble that of the Weimar Republic. Parties with familiar pre–World War II names reappeared. The Spartacists, the Communist Party of Germany (KPD), and the Independent Social Democratic Party (USDP) were established in January and February and began to organize for the elections (*ND*, 7 February; East Berlin, ADN, 31 January; *FBIS-*

EEU, 31 January). Of the 24 parties and alliances that were officially registered for the March elections, 7 were to the left of the PDS (East Berlin, ADN, 9 March; *FBIS-EEU*, 9 March): the Action Alliance United Left (Carnations, United Left); the Alternative Youth List (German Youth Party, Green Youth, Marxist Youth Association, Free German Youth); the League of Socialist Workers (Fourth International); the Green Party, Independent Women's Association; the Communist Party of Germany (KPD); the Spartacist Workers' Party; the Independent Social Democratic Party of Germany.

Before the March elections none of these splinter groups showed much enthusiasm for cooperation with the PDS, and most rejected the idea out of hand (East Berlin, ADN, 18 February; *FBIS-EEU*, 27 February). The alienation of left fundamentalist opinion was not important for the PDS electorally but did serve to point out that the party was in trouble with its young and idealistic cadres. More significant for the party's electoral prospects and for its future place in the new parliament was its relationship with the SPD; the PDS might reasonably assume that its reform efforts had made it an acceptable ally for the socialists, as revealed on 27 February by André Brie, the PDS election campaign manager. Brie looked forward to "at least 10 percent" of the PDS share of the vote and hoped that after the election left-wing forces would "coalesce." According to Brie, the party had stretched out its hand to the SPD and was prepared for a "partnership." (Hamburg, DPA, 27 February; *FBIS-EEU*, 28 February.) The SPD responded immediately by rejecting any suggestion of an alliance (Hamburg, DPA, 28 February; *FBIS-EEU*, 1 March).

The tactical setbacks that faced the PDS in the first three months of the year only served to point out how restricted its choices were. Given the enormous burden of its Stalinist past, nothing short of a fresh start offered hope for survival. Two strategies were available: The SED-PDS could continue on the path of renewal through reform, or the SED-PDS could admit that it was totally compromised, dissolve itself, and then build an entirely new "social democratic" party. Then the way might be open for a direct organizational amalgamation with the SPD and other opposition forces. Such an outcome, however, was by no means certain, whatever the fate of the SED-PDS. Former communists who joined or tried to join the SPD confronted an ambivalent attitude: Early in the year the SPD seemed willing to accept them and expressed regret that many capable and reform-minded people were tied to the fate of a dying communist party (ADN, 21 January). Not until some months later, however, did the eastern SPD drop its formal prohibition against accepting former communists into its ranks (RFE/RL, *Report on Eastern Europe*, 20 June). Other disaffected party members rejected all versions of socialism and moved to the right. The SPD campaign promised that their party would not join any coalition that included the German Social Union (DSU); in the interparty negotiations that followed the March elections, the SPD chairman, Ibrahim Boehme, complained that the right-wing DSU was full of former communists (ibid., 23 March).

The PDS's decisive moment for choosing an overall strategy came in the second half of January with a general crisis of confidence within the party. On 18 January a resolution was adopted in Berlin by the executives of several influential party committees including the district executive of the GDR Academy of Sciences. Their statement demanded the unconditional disbandment of the party and the reconvening of the Extraordinary Congress to oversee the dissolution process. The statement pointed to the SED-PDS's failure to halt the worsening crisis in the country or to implement fully the decisions of the Extraordinary Congress. (ADN, 19 January; *FBIS-EEU*, 19 January.) On 20 January the party executive (Parteivorstand) met in an emergency session to consider the dissolution issue. After a lengthy and often stormy debate, the executive decided to preserve the party in the best interests of the country and because, as Gysi explained, "the treaty-based community between the two German states and the development towards a united Europe require strong left-wing forces in the political spectrum" (ADN, 21 January; *FBIS-EEU*, 22 January).

The crisis reached its climax on 21 January when Gysi received word that the demand for immediate dissolution had been taken up by Wolfgang Berghofer, the SED-PDS deputy chairman and widely respected mayor of Dresden. Berghofer resigned along with 39 other leading Dresden functionaries. The Berghofer group declared that the party had "ruined the GDR politically, economically and morally." Their statement went on to assert that the party lacked the strength "to change itself fundamentally and to help overcome the deep crisis in our country at the side of the democratic forces." It also endorsed a phased unification with the FRG within the framework of European unity, and it looked forward to "an ecologically oriented social market economy." (ADN, 21 January; *FBIS-*

EEU, 21 January; *ND*, 22 January.) The PDS's decision to keep the party intact seemed vindicated by its relatively strong showing in the general elections. With 16.3 percent of the vote and 66 candidates elected, the PDS finished a strong third and could thus form a convincing opposition in the Volkskammer.

The transition of the PDS from a Leninist cadre party to an electoral parliamentary party was virtually complete when it took up its opposition role after the new administration was installed in April. Gysi was elected as the party's parliamentary chairman by the PDS caucus (East Berlin, ADN, 26 March; *FBIS-EEU*, 26 March). Modrow, who reluctantly agreed to lead the PDS list into the elections, might have been thought of as the natural choice to lead the caucus (Hamburg, DPA, 22 February; *FBIS-EEU*, 23 February). He had the prestige of the premiership, which he continued to enjoy as interim prime minister while negotiations were under way for the formation of the de Maizière coalition. Modrow's position was, however, not as strong as it appeared to be. As a result of the party's minority opposition role, the PDS delegation in the Volkskammer had become the main focus of the party's efforts to influence the policy direction of the GDR. The fact that it was Gysi, the party chairman, who was selected also as parliamentary leader was consistent with the relative increase in status that the caucus had gained within the overall organization of the PDS.

Modrow's role both in parliament and in the party was diminished after the March elections. Although he was named honorary chairman of the PDS (East Berlin, ADN, 26 March; *FBIS-EEU*, 26 March) and was also nominated for the post of president of the Volkskammer (*ND*, 27 March), this bid failed and Modrow finished third to the Alliance and SPD candidates. Sabine Bergmann-Pohl (CDU) was elected. But Modrow's candidacy had not been frivolous. As prime minister and leader of the "government of national responsibility," he had been widely regarded, both at home and abroad, as honest and capable. On his government's last day in office, all members rose to give him a standing ovation (East Berlin, ADN, 7 March; *FBIS-EEU*, 7 March). During the election campaign he gained widespread respect for his determination to keep the interests of the country first, which was why he initially refused to lead the party into the election. His low-key campaign adopted a moderate, nonpartisan approach. His reputation had, however, been tarnished by allegations in the West German press

concerning his record as first secretary of the Dresden party organization under Honecker wherein he was accused of playing a leading role in launching police attacks in October 1989 on thousands of peaceful demonstrators and of authorizing the arrests and brutal detentions that followed (*Der Spiegel*, 12 February; *ND*, 5 March). Gregor Gysi rushed to Modrow's defense, saying that the PDS would not tolerate such an attack (*ND*, 5 March). Modrow seemed secure in the confidence of the party, but even without the suggestion of scandal in his background, a PDS candidate, especially one with Modrow's prestige, would be unacceptable in an important parliamentary role. The CDU and the SPD, with the backing of their western partners, would allow no risks in the crucial timetable for unification. It is therefore not surprising that parliament not only denied him the presidency of the chamber but also rejected him for the lesser position of one of the deputies to the president (each party except the CDU was to receive a deputy post and each party submitted two candidates). Käte Niederkirchner (PDS) won decisively against Modrow (Hamburg, DPA, 5 April; *FBIS-EEU*, 6 April), and thus Modrow was left with no special function either in the PDS nine-member parliamentary executive or in the party's committee structure. Gysi named Dr. Dietmar Keller as his parliamentary deputy and Bernd Meyer as caucus manager. (*ND*, 10 May.) Modrow, who was left with his party offices, assumed a special role in the party's attempts to extend its organization into the Federal Republic. He also announced that he was ready to carry the PDS Bundestag election campaign into the Federal Republic in the fall (*ND*, 19 March).

The parliamentary influence of the PDS was sharply curtailed after 3 October when, under the second treaty of union between the two Germanies, the PDS entered the Bundestag with its allocated 24 deputies (*ND*, 26 September). Gysi presided over a PDS Bundestag delegation that lacked the strength to qualify as a parliamentary group according to the Bundestag rules. Only through an interim arrangement, which was to lapse following the all-German elections of 2 December, did the party receive any group privileges (Hamburg, DPA, 16 October; *FBIS-WEU*, 19 October; *ND*, 18 October); these included the right to bring motions before plenary sessions of the Bundestag and the right to a portion of debating time and one-half the monetary stipend available to fully fledged groups. It was not, however, able to vote in committees or in the Bundestag's Council of Elders. As a result of the all-

German elections, the PDS representation was reduced to fourteen seats, and it lost, despite Gysi's vigorous appeals, even those privileges that it had possessed after 3 October (*NYT*, 3 December).

Beginning in March the initiative to extend the party beyond the borders of the GDR became an important priority, indicating the presence of important new problems and organizational challenges for the party (Hamburg, DPA, 14 March; *FBIS-EEU*, 16 March). After the formation of the de Maizière government, the political climate had somewhat improved for the party's alliance-building strategy, although this was not obvious when it came to the largest possible allies of the PDS. Overtures toward the SPD, such as Gysi's open letter in May, did not lead to any breakthrough in the relations between the two parties (*ND*, 29 May). Similar initiatives toward the Greens met with little more success, although the Greens showed less suspicion of the PDS than did the SPD; nevertheless, they showed little inclination for open collaboration (*CSM*, 28 November).

Yet as a partner the PDS possessed a relatively large membership, financial resources, organizational skills, and considerable popular support. Even after unification on 3 October, and even though its share of the vote had declined from 16.3 percent in March to 11.6 percent in the Länder elections of 14 October, it still had the third-largest following in the east (*ND*, 16 October). Even the SPD took account of these strengths, and during the year a noticeable difference in attitude toward the PDS was detectable between the western and the eastern branches of the SPD. In the west, any form of cooperation with the PDS remained anathema. In the east, a much more positive position emerged, especially when it came to recruiting from the PDS membership. At the East German SPD Congress on 10 June, the party reversed its policy of not admitting former PDS members. (RFE/RL, *Report on Eastern Europe*, 20 June.) This move was understandable because, with a membership of approximately 30,000, it was scarcely one-tenth the size of the PDS.

The prospects for collaboration on PDS terms were only marginally better when it came to the smaller left-wing groups. With the accelerated timetable for unification, there was more reason for parties and individuals who had no hope for political survival in an united Germany to consider ways of cooperating with the PDS. If West German electoral laws were to apply in the upcoming all-German elections, then any party that did not obtain at least 5 percent of the vote would be excluded under FRG law from representation in the Bundestag. Under these conditions the PDS might be seen as an attractive political partner for many small left-wing splinter groups in both parts of Germany. The decision to look for partners was given fresh impetus by an agreement reached in Bonn in early August between the SPD and the CDU that would allow smaller parties to run on the same ticket with larger parties (except the major West German parties—the CDU, SPD, and FDP) (*NYT*, 2 August). This arrangement was designed to protect the small East German parties. To the extent that they were in fact protected, the PDS lost potential votes because nearly all the splinter groups were on the left. If the PDS could succeed in creating a joint ticket, it could conceivably turn this potential problem into an advantage.

When it came to cooperating with the splinter groups, however, the PDS also had to overcome some considerable handicaps. For the splinter groups in the east, the strong, ideologically based objections to cooperation with the PDS, which had been obvious from the beginning, were unlikely to be overcome by the threat of the 5 percent rule. In the FRG there was a bewildering variety of attitudes toward the PDS on the part of more than a dozen left-wing splinter groups. Some, such as the United Socialist Party (VSP) and the Marxist-Leninist Party of Germany (MLPD), had been more sympathetic to the "revolutionary people's movements" in the GDR than to the reformed communist party and, while rejecting reunification, welcomed the fall of the old order. Others, for example, the Workers' Federation for the Reestablishment of the KPD (AB), the League of West German Communists (BWK), the Autonomous Communists (Autonome), and the Communist League (KB), saw developments in the GDR and the move toward reunification as a catastrophe for socialism and a victory for imperialism. They were suspicious, too, of the direction of change in the PDS, especially the party's acceptance of German unity. (*Innere Sicherheit*, no. 1 [23 March].) At best the PDS could hope to build fragile and limited alliances with these groups. The German Communist Party (DKP) offered more promise. The DKP, although extremely weak electorally, had gradually built up a considerable network of influence on the left of West German politics (Wolfgang Rudzio, *Die Erosion der Abgrenzung; Zum Verhältnis Zwischen der Demokratischen Linken und Kommunisten in der Bundesrepublik Deutschland* [Westdeutscher Verlag, 1988]). The collapse of communism in Eastern Europe and especially in the GDR had thrown the DKP into confusion both organizationally and ideologically. The party, which had been dependent on the SED, took time to work out its attitude to the PDS (*Innere Sicherheit*, no. 1 [23 March]). By the time of the elections in December the DKP was instructing its members to support the PDS, and eight of its members had joined the open PDS lists (*ND*, 13 November).

Despite the difficulties the PDS had little choice but to pursue an aggressive alliance-building strategy, for it was by no means certain that it could survive the 5 percent rule. Expansion was essential if the PDS were not to face marginalization and "regionalization." The campaign of westward expansion continued throughout the year with limited results. PDS organizations were established in several major cities including Hamburg in March and West Berlin in July (*ND*, 19 March, 3 July). There was more success with alliance building, which partly offset the difficulties encountered in establishing the PDS's own organizations.

In July the PDS announced plans to open a second session of the congress that it had held in February; this second session, or "renewal conference," was to be held in September. At the same time the party announced the theses that would be adopted at the congress, which would define its place in a united Germany. The theses identified the PDS "as a socialist party and part of the left in a united capitalist Germany" and called for the party to work for an alliance with other left-wing forces throughout Germany (*ND*, 17 July). The alliance took shape when the PDS entered into a new political formation in the Federal Republic, the Left List/PDS. On 16 September four hundred PDS delegates—fifty from left groups in the FRG and three hundred and fifty individual delegates—decided on a joint election program. The program was then adopted at the reconvened party congress, which also met on 16 September (East Berlin, ADN, 16 September; *FBIS-WEU*, 18 September). According to Gysi, what had been achieved was not the program of a new political party but rather a combined election ticket to ensure a strong voice for the left in the Bundestag (*ND*, 27 September; *Süddeutsche Zeitung*, 17 September). The joint ticket, however, had only been achieved by deliberately avoiding contentious issues and, during the short time that it held together, was full of tension and disagreement. As it happened, the Federal Constitutional Court ruled that only the parties from the GDR could run

in the December elections on two separate lists—one for the FRG and one for the territories that made up the former GDR. The 5 percent rule would, therefore, not affect the outcome for the PDS, and the rationale for the Left List/PDS collapsed (*ND*, 13–14 October). Consequently, the PDS leadership decided to run on the party's own ticket throughout Germany. Nonparty members and organizations of the Left List were free to run under PDS banners. (*ND*, 13–14, 15 October.) In any case the PDS was bound to do badly in the Federal Republican Länder; the result ranged from 0.2 percent in Saarland to 1.1 percent in Bremen and Hamburg. In the east the party did well only in Mecklenburg-Pomerania (14.2 percent) and Brandenburg (11 percent). In Saxony, Saxony-Anhalt, and Thuringia its share ranged from 8 percent to 9.5 percent; in Berlin its share was 9.7 percent. (*NYT*, 4 December.)

The disappointing result—fourteen seats in the Bundestag—was less affected by the absence of effective electoral allies than it was by the party's own internal problems. On the eve of the election the PDS experienced its single most damaging crisis: in October it was revealed that Deputy Chairman Wolfgang Pohl, in his capacity as party treasurer, had arranged the transfer of 107 million deutsch marks from party funds. The money had been placed in the trust of Putnik, a Soviet company that operated in the GDR and Western Europe. Pohl and PDS financial director Wolfgang Langnitschke were arrested on 26 October amid a crisis involving a police raid on PDS headquarters in Berlin on 19 October. (*This Week in Germany* [*TWiG*], 2 November, 26 October.) In his testimony, Pohl admitted that he had arranged the transfer and that he and Langnitschke acted on their own without the knowledge of Gysi. Pohl claimed that he had diverted funds to protect them from the growing pressure for the confiscation of the party's assets. This story was compromised when it was revealed that another official, Karl-Heinz Kaufmann, tried to make a cash withdrawal on the account. The party at first denied the allegations of fraud and vigorously protested the arrests and police raids. As the weight of evidence became apparent, the party was forced to admit the truth of the allegations. (Berlin, ADN, 26, 27 October; *FBIS-WEU*, 29 October; *NYT*, 27 October.)

The scandal rocked the central leadership. Two members of the Presidium, Bernd Meyer, former parliamentary manager, and Bärbel Adam did not survive a vote of confidence in the Executive Committee. Gysi submitted his resignation, but when it seemed that the PDS would dissolve if he left, he was persuaded to remain. (Berlin, ADN, 27 October; *FBIS-WEU*, 29 October). Modrow announced that he was stepping down from his post of honorary chairman (Hamburg, DPA, 6 November; *FBIS-WEU*, 7 November). On 11 November, as part of its effort to contain the damage, the party announced that it would surrender 80 percent of its assets. Gysi was to prepare a comprehensive settlement of financial questions with the independent public commission that had been established to take inventory of the assets of parties and organizations of the former GDR (Berlin, ADN, 11 November; *FBIS-WEU*, 14 November).

At the end of the year the party's future was in doubt. It could be seen from the election results that it had not escaped being merely a regional party, nor had it buried its past. There is no end to the revelations concerning the activities of the Stasi and former communist officials, and every such incident reminds the public of the party's unhealthy roots. The PDS has few political assets. It can draw some strength from the continuing economic hardship and dislocation in the east, but this is a precarious and probably temporary political advantage. The party can hope to work more closely with the Greens in the Bundestag, but a more important place for it in German politics seems out of the question. The party still lacks a clear identity and has been accused more than once of plagiarizing the SPD's program and policies. If it continues on a moderate left-of-center course, it faces the prospect that its following and membership will eventually be absorbed by its powerful social democratic rival.

Domestic Affairs. *Social and political affairs.* For East German society the new year began as the old had ended, in complete chaos. Emigration continued at a rate of approximately 2,000–3,000 a day; by the end of January, 74,000 people had left (*WP*, 29 January). The emigrants, by and large, were young skilled workers and professionals, and the impact on the economy was disastrous. Massive public protests were still the principal feature of political life, and many people had become completely disoriented. Some qualified observers thought they detected symptoms of a generalized moral panic and a mass neurosis in a situation of insecurity and uncertainty parallel to that of 1944–1945. (*Der Spiegel*, 12 February; West Berlin, *Die Tageszeitung*, 9 March; *JPRS-EEU*, 9 May.)

Any arrangement for governing such a society was bound to be fragile. From its inception in December the first Modrow coalition which was based on an alliance between the PDS-SED and the "satellite" parties that had formerly been completely subservient to the SED, was unstable. The PDS-SED held sixteen cabinet posts; the Liberal Democrats (LDP), four; the Christian Democrats (CDU), three; and the National Democrats (NDPD) and Farmers' Party (DBD), two each (*WP*, 26 January). Although the SED-PDS was still the dominant force in the coalition, a number of factors compromised the ability of the communists to set the political agenda.

Modrow steadily lost ground in his effort to manage his partners in the government. Within the coalition, the smaller parties, especially the CDU, were gaining self-confidence. The Christian Democrats in the FRG were a powerful magnet for the East German CDU. As the bonds between the two parties gradually strengthened, the CDU in the east was under increasing pressure to complete the break with the communists (RFE/RL, *Report on Eastern Europe*, 9 March; *NYT*, 22 January). Early in January the indications were that some of the GDR's parties would, thanks to their allies in the west, emerge as powerful new political forces in the GDR. The newly resurrected Socialist Democratic Party of Germany (SDP) was already forging an alliance with the SPD (*YICA*, 1990). In the first two months of the year it profited enormously from the assistance it received from the west. By the beginning of March, the party had approximately 100,000 members and had gained, according to several opinion polls conducted at the end of February, the support of 35–50 percent of the electorate (*CSM*, 27 February). The close connection with the SPD seemed to account for its popularity. In January it changed its name from SDP to Socialist Party of Germany (SPD) to match that of its sister party; on 24 February, Willy Brandt accepted the position of honorary chairman, a post he also held for the SPD in the FRG. (RFE/RL, *Report on Eastern Europe*, 9 March.)

The CDU was handicapped by its former status as an official and subordinate ally of the communists, but its future, too, lay with its western counterpart. In January, the German Social Union (DSU) was formed from eleven small conservative groups with the help of the West German Christian Social Union (CSU), the CDU's Bavarian ally (*LAT*, 21 January). With the encouragement of the West German CDU, a new alliance of political parties was formed in early February from the CDU, the

DSU, and one of the early opposition groups, Democratic Awakening. The new party was to run in the elections as the Alliance for Germany and enjoyed the full support of the CDU political machine. (*NYT*, 6 February.) The West German Free Democratic Party (FDP) also found an ally in the LDP. In March, the liberals formed a wider alliance, the League of Free Democrats—The Liberals (BFD), which continued to be backed by the West German FDP (East Berlin, *Der Morgen*, 30 March; *FBIS-EEU*, 6 April). According to opinion polls, the Alliance for Germany commanded 24 percent of the vote and the Liberals 3 percent. Together the major western-backed parties commanded about 75 percent of the decided voters at the end of February. (RFE/RL, *Report on Eastern Europe*, 9 March.) The indigenous opposition parties also began to consolidate, and a number of alliances were formed. The most important of these were Alliance 90, which was made up of New Forum, Democracy Now, and the Human Rights Initiative, and the Greens, Green Party, and the Independent Women's Union. In the weeks leading up to the elections, the communists were ever more conscious of their weak minority position.

An additional constraint on the Modrow government stemmed from the complicated decision-making process that had emerged at the end of 1989. Government policy had to be set within the context of ongoing roundtable talks that began on 7 December 1989 between the government and the opposition parties (*YICA*, 1990). Modrow had pledged government cooperation with all democratic forces to push through the economic and political reforms that were necessary to save the country. This promise made the party prisoner to endless negotiations with the opposition. The roundtable was for many purposes the effective seat of government; the power of the opposition rested on the fact that it, not the SED-PDS, held whatever influence could be said to exist over the streets. In January, the then largest opposition group, New Forum, claimed to have 200,000 members and was able at any time to call for massive public protests (*NYT*, 4 January).

During the second week of January the turbulence in the GDR's governing arrangements almost destroyed the coalition and the roundtable. The crisis centered on the attempt by the communists to reestablish an effective security service. The old State Security Service (Stasi) was the most hated symbol of the old regime and the first target of the opposition in the drive for reform. In December 1989 the Modrow government, with the support of the other roundtable members, agreed to dissolve the Stasi and create two new security agencies, one for intelligence gathering and the other for the "protection of the constitution." At the beginning of the month the opposition, led by New Forum, withdrew their support for a new political police force and expressed unhappiness with the progress of the dissolution of the old one. A government report, which was released at the roundtable on 9 January, revealed that approximately 85,000 of the Stasi were still employed (*LAT*, 13 January), and it appeared that the government intended to reemploy former Stasi members in its new organizations. The New Forum and other opposition groups threatened to leave the roundtable if Modrow did not drop his plans and agree to consider them again only after the general elections. The minority parties in the coalition also supported the demand and threatened to resign from the government. (RFL/RL, *Report on Eastern Europe*, 2 February.)

Although the Stasi issue was at the center, the opposition also thought it saw a general effort on the part of the government to stall reform and to shore up the SED-PDS's position. The opposition complained that the existing coalition arrangement lacked proper legitimacy because it had not been put in place through elections (*NYT*, 4 January). It worried about communist control of the public media and about the absence of adequate resources on the opposition side for conducting an election campaign (*CSM*, 11 January). The government responded by promising to make resources available to the opposition parties, by pointing to the democratization of the party press, and by trying to persuade its critics of its good democratic intentions. The democratic rhetoric may have been more convincing had the communists taken a different line on the security issue; instead, the stance of the SED-PDS leadership was that the security services were essential in view of the growth of right-wing sentiment and activity in the GDR. Fascism and ultranationalism, according to the communists, posed a clear and present danger. In the name of the democratic reform, which the government claimed it was leading, that danger had to be contained.

There is no doubt that the open border did encourage elements of the West German and West Berlin right-wing Republican party to make as much out of the confusion in the GDR as possible. In the first three months of the year, the Republicans established several groups in the GDR (Hamburg, DPA, 24 March; *FBIS-EEU*, 26 March). The collapse of communist hegemony had awakened some ultranationalist and racist sentiment in the GDR—witness the emergence of the skinhead cult and the sporadic outbursts of racist, antiforeign, and anti-Semitic sloganeering—but the SED-PDS press made as much as it could out of the issue, to the point of calculated exaggeration. *Neues Deutschland*, the party's daily, strove to broaden the issue so that an equation could be made linking the growing public demand for reunification with radical right-wing sentiment. The images and language of the past were evoked to lend emotional weight, with the party warning against a Fourth Reich, *Anschluss*, and a new round of German domination of Europe. At the same time it presented itself as the natural barrier against such evils.

The intentions of the government became clear when on 11 January the LDP paper, *Der Morgen*, reported that the new security service, the Bureau for the Protection of the Constitution, had already been established (*NYT*, 11 January). The response was immediate. During 11–12 January, thousands demonstrated throughout the country against the government, the SED-PDS, the Stasi, and the communist-controlled media. The Volkskammer was blockaded by thousands of demonstrators, and there were warning strikes. The flag of the Federal Republic and the slogan Germany United Fatherland were much in evidence. (East Berlin, ADN, 11–12 January; *FBIS-EEU*, 12 January.) Previously, when faced with attacks from their coalition partners and the opposition, Modrow and Gysi had threatened to seek a vote of confidence by holding a referendum seeking approval for the government and its policies (*NYT*, 11 January). This time, however, the government abandoned this tactic, probably because of the double threat posed by the furious demonstrations and the prospect of a disintegrating coalition. On 12 January it announced that plans for replacing the Stasi would be dropped and that no further consideration would be given to new security arrangements until after the elections (*LAT*, 13 January).

Despite this retreat, mass demonstrations continued, and it was doubtful that sufficient order would remain to allow an election campaign (East Berlin, ADN, 14, 16 January; *FBIS-EEU*, 16 January). In a desperate attempt to restore stability, Modrow invited the opposition to join the coalition; it is a tribute to his diplomatic skill that, following lengthy negotiations, the opposition reluctantly agreed (*NYT*, 27 January). A "government of national responsibility," as it was called by Modrow,

was formed on 5 February. One minister without portfolio was allocated to each of the eight main opposition groups: Democratic Awakening, the SPD, New Forum, Democracy Now, the Green League, the Green Party, the Independent Women's Association, and the Peace and Human Rights Initiative. (RFE/RL, *Daily Report*, 6 February.) The formation of Modrow's second government marked a turning point in the GDR's political development; the "government of national responsibility" was in every sense an interim arrangement.

On 20 February an electoral law was passed that reduced the number of seats in the Volkskammer to four hundred from five hundred and the term in office to four years from five years (RFL/RL, *Report on Eastern Europe*, 9 March). The date for the elections was advanced from 6 May to 18 March. Local council elections were scheduled to follow on 6 May. Although the PDS was ready to accept its role as the opposition, it had some slender hopes that a new postelection coalition could be formed between the PDS, the SPD, and other left-of-center parties. The chance that such a partnership could be realized was a powerful motivating factor in the party's attempt to democratize itself. These hopes, however, soon dissipated during the election campaign when it became clear just how thoroughly the West German parties had penetrated the GDR's political life and how thoroughly the other parties rejected the idea of forming an alliance with the PDS. Gysi reluctantly admitted that "no one wishes to cooperate with us" (*ND*, 7 March). That statement, with minor exceptions, was to remain true for the rest of the year.

Although no opposition group was willing to enter an alliance with the communists, the PDS found limited common causes with some of them. At the end of January, during the roundtable negotiations that led to Modrow's second government, there had been efforts to reach an agreement that would have blocked the participation and interference of the West German parties in the campaign. Although a majority of the smaller parties stood together with the PDS in opposing West German involvement, the CDU, the SPD, and the LDP refused to bind themselves to any agreement (RFE/RL, *Daily Report*, 6 February). There was a great deal of bitterness among the smaller parties concerning the degree to which the campaign was dominated by the western parties and western political leaders (*NYT*, 28 February).

The western parties' most prominent leaders campaigned intensively. Although the PDS launched a slick modern campaign under the able direction of André Brie, the party's campaign manager, only Gregor Gysi drew anything like the crowds that flocked to hear Helmut Kohl, Willy Brandt, Oscar Lafontaine, and Hans-Dietrich Genscher. The smaller parties could not compete; their electioneering was overly intellectual and lacked mass appeal, nor did they have the resources to match the efforts of the large parties. New Forum and Democracy Now, which had played the leading roles in the struggle against Honecker, now found themselves caught in the middle. The PDS, with its powerful organization and its democratized image, managed to capture most of the votes of those who were suspicious of unification. In fact the campaign became a referendum for unification, and the unequivocal promotion of a rapid pace toward that goal was likely the major reason for the success of the CDU campaign. (East Berlin, *Neue Zeit*, 20 March; *FBIS-EEU*, 23 March.) The CDU overtook the SPD, advancing from an estimated 24 percent in popular support in February to the election result of 40.6 percent (*ND*, 19 March).

The SPD was less straightforward on the reunification issue. At the SPD Party Congress, which was held at the end of February, Ibrahim Boehme, the party's chairman, endorsed the idea of a fast-track schedule for unification. The western SPD, in contrast, was ambivalent on the timetable question. The western leaders placed more emphasis on the difficult bargaining that lay ahead and the consequent necessity for not "plunging headlong into it," as Kohl and the alliance wanted. The stance that the SPD leaders took was in large part conditioned by their strategy for the Bundestag elections, scheduled for December, for there was a good chance that the SPD might be able to defeat Chancellor Kohl on unification. Public opinion polls in the FRG showed that a majority of the West German electorate were worried about the probable financial and social costs of a rush to unity (RFL/RL, *Report on Eastern Europe*, 18 May). Oscar Lafontaine, the SPD's most likely candidate to be the next West German chancellor, hoped to mobilize those fears both in the FRG and in the GDR. The resulting SPD position was blurred. Throughout the negotiations between the two German governments, the western SPD continually advocated a gradual approach that they claimed would avoid the worst economic and political dangers of Kohl's policy. Strategies aimed at the December Bundestag elections did not mean much to the eastern SPD at this early stage, and there was a noticeable difference

between the two parties on the problem of the timetable. The differences surfaced in April after the SPD entered the de Maizière coalition; the SPD members of the government endorsed de Maiziere's policy declaration of 19 April, which called for a rapid pace in the all-German negotiations, and made it clear that the government had a mandate to end the separate political existence of the GDR at the earliest possible date. (*ND*, 19 April.)

In the minds of the GDR electorate the Alliance for Germany best represented the break with the past that so many fervently wanted. The SPD had misjudged the mood of the electorate and underestimated the PDS's ability to win the support of those who were less happy with the promise of a single German state. The PDS successfully mobilized this sentiment and did better than had been anticipated even by its own organizers. André Brie, the party's campaign manager, had predicted 10 percent of the vote, and some earlier polls had given the PDS less. As it turned out, the party received just over 16 percent, which left them with 66 seats in the 400-member parliament, the third-largest number of deputies in the Volkskammer. The alliance parties polled just over 48 percent; the CDU, 41 percent and 163 seats; the DSU, 6 percent and 25 seats; and Democratic Awakening, 1 percent and 4 seats; the SPD polled 21.8 percent and 88 seats; the BFD obtained 21 seats; Alliance 90, 12; DBP, 9; the Greens, 8; and the smaller left-wing parties together, 2. (East Berlin, ADN, 23 March; *FBIS-EEU*, 23 March; *NYT*, 19 March.) The elections left the CDU and its allies with a clear majority.

In the negotiations leading up to 12 April, de Maizière worked for a "grand coalition" solution to the problem of forming an effective cabinet. A widely based government that included the SPD and the Liberals would allow the widest possible consensus for the difficult issues on the legislative agenda and ensure the necessary two-thirds majority for dealing with the constitutional problems of unification. One obstacle to building the expanded coalition arose out of the SPD's election promises: The socialists had promised that they would not enter into a coalition agreement with either the PDS or the right-wing DSU (*NYT*, 20 March). The solution was for the three alliance parties to enter the cabinet separately. The SPD was thus spared an agreement with the DSU. There was, however, a much more difficult question that needed to be answered before the coalition could be formed.

During the weeks leading up to the election, a number of allegations appeared in the press concerning the past careers of many leading GDR politicians. The West German weekly *Der Spiegel* printed a story that criticized Hans Modrow for his part in the brutal suppression of protesters when he had been mayor of Dresden under Honecker (*Der Spiegel*, 26 March). Ibrahim Boehme, chairman of the SPD, was accused of having been an informer for the Stasi and betraying the well-known novelist Rainer Kunze and other leading dissidents to the Stasi. The Boehme story was given to *Der Spiegel* by a man who claimed to have been Boehme's Stasi controller for more than ten years (*Der Spiegel*, 26 March). Although Boehme steadfastly proclaimed his innocence, the scandal destroyed him both politically and personally and stalled the coalition talks. He resigned on 27 March, having nominated Markus Meckel, his deputy chairman, to replace him (*WP*, 27 March). Ten days earlier, on the eve of the election, much to the embarrassment of the Alliance for Germany, Wolfgang Schnur, the chairman of Democratic Awakening, had been expelled from the party after he admitted that he had worked for the Stasi (*WSJ*, *Berliner Zeitung*, 16 March; *FBIS-EEU*, 23 March). He was replaced by Rainer Eppelmann, deputy chairman of Democratic Awakening. Lothar de Maizière, also accused of being a police informer, hesitated before accepting office. According to Werner Fischer, the government representative on the Committee for the Dissolution of the GDR State Security Service, evidence showed that de Maizière may have worked as an informer. The Munich newspaper *Süddeutsche Zeitung* also raised embarrassing questions about his past career. (Hamburg, DPA, 22 March; *FBIS-EEU*, 23 March.) The scandal widened when the citizens' committee examining the Erfurt Stasi files reported that 40 of 56 deputies from Erfurt had had some kind of contact with the Stasi. Werner Fischer claimed that at least 10 percent of the members of the new parliament had formerly worked for the Stasi. (RFE/RL, *Daily Report*, no. 58 [22 March]; *WP*, 27 March.)

It took nearly a month in an atmosphere of charges, countercharges, and denials for the coalition to take shape. A major impetus to find a new basis of trust came at the end of March when the West German press announced that the Bundesbank had recommended a one for two exchange rate for the eastern mark as a basis for monetary union and that the recommendation had the backing of Kohl's government (RFE/RL, *Report on Eastern Europe*, 11 May; ADN, DPA, 31 March, 1 April; *FBIS-EEU*, 2 April). This news was greeted with outrage in the GDR; all parties united to condemn the suggestion as an unacceptable betrayal. (East Germans believed that Helmut Kohl had explicitly made the promise of a one for one exchange rate during the election campaign.) This powerful incentive for a more orderly transition to the new government temporarily deemphasized the Stasi issue. All parties then agreed to submit the background of their parliamentary deputies to an inquiry (ADN, 4 April; *FBIS-EEU*, 5 April).

Although the scandal haunted the last months of the GDR, it did not prevent the formation of the coalition. As the Stasi disintegrated and the days of the GDR drew to a close, a vicious subculture arose. Unemployed security operatives resorted to blackmail to earn a living, frequently offering incriminating information about former comrades who had managed to find employment outside the service. As the new prime minister put it, the government not only had to take responsibility for a daunting domestic and international policy agenda but was also asked to bear the burdens of the past, to make amends for wrongs that had been committed years and even decades before. The investigations into the Stasi files and interviews with former SED functionaries revealed the worst abuses of the old regime. Alexander Schalck-Golodkowski, former deputy minister of foreign trade, testified that he had kept huge private accounts, stocks of precious metals, and other valuables in Switzerland for senior members of the regime, including Erich Honecker and Willi Stoph, Honecker's prime minister. (*FBIS-EEU*, 5 April.) The world learned of the SED's support for the Red Army Faction and other terrorist organizations that had operated in the West and of arms and drug deals conducted by senior officials; it also learned of Soviet death camps, set up at the end of World War II, where thousands of detainees had been killed. (*NYT*, 28 March; *CSM*, 5 April.) Those who wanted to argue that something of value was being lost with the demise of the GDR had an uneasy time. At the end of the year, two months after the GDR had passed into history, the story of intrigue, fraud, and betrayal seemed only half told.

On 6 May, less than three weeks after the new government took office, the country went to the polls again, this time to contest the seats of 7,787 local councils. The results indicated that after 18 March no dramatic changes in voter alignment had taken place. The CDU remained the strongest party in the country, with 34.4 percent of the vote, down from 40.6 percent in March. The CDU's major partner, the DSU, also suffered losses and managed only 3.4 percent, down from 6.3 percent. The SPD and the PDS suffered similar setbacks. The PDS showing varied. In Frankfurt an der Oder it finished first with more than 74 percent of the vote and did relatively well in most major cities. The PDS took considerable satisfaction from indications that its role as the principal opposition force in the country had been confirmed by the electorate. The SPD share of the vote dropped only 0.5 percent, to 21.3 percent, whereas the PDS fell almost 2 percent, to 14.6 percent. The outcome showed that the smaller parties had been the winners at the expense of the three major parties. The DBD and the newly formed Farmer's Association did especially well; together they obtained nearly 6 percent of the vote, up from 2.2 percent in March. (ADN, 7 May; *FBIS-EEU*, 7 May.)

The advance of the smaller parties could be an indication that local and special interests were now more important than they had been at the beginning of the year. The gains of the farmers' parties illustrated this point. In some parts of the country the DBD polled more than 10 percent of the vote, reflecting the concern that most farmers felt as they faced competition from the FRG's agricultural products. Unregulated competition would be ruinous without large public subsidies to protect the inefficient East German industry. There had already been a number of large-scale public protests organized by farm groups, and more were threatened. (RFL/RL, *Report on Eastern Europe*, 25 May.) Other concerns of the electorate also gained in electoral significance, mainly to the benefit of the smaller political groups. Women's groups, for example, led public protests to prevent the GDR's permissive abortion laws from being replaced by the more restrictive ones of the Federal Republic. By the terms of the State Treaty on Monetary, Economic and Social Union, the GDR's abortion regulations were to remain in force in the jurisdiction of the East German Länder. The environment provided another area of public concern as the degree of mismanagement of the old regime and the horrific extent of environmental degradation were increasingly exposed to public scrutiny.

The final draft of the State Treaty on Monetary, Economic and Social Union was finalized on 14 May. Although the treaty offered some protections for the East German economy, it basically involved the complete acceptance of the FRG's "social market economy." The treaty came into effect at midnight on 30 June. For many GDR citizens the immediate consequences were negative; with the removal of most subsidies, and the exposure of East German enterprises and farms to free market competition with the West, the country faced large-scale dislocations in both the industrial and the agricultural sectors. As unemployment and insecurity increased, so did the incidence of strikes and public protest. In this political environment there were new opportunities for the opposition and increased pressure on the government to clear the way for the unification process.

In the government's program statement of 19 April, de Maizière formally accepted that the route to unification would be based on Article 23 of the FRG's Basic Law, which allowed the GDR's parliament or the East German Länder to incorporate into the Federal Republic by passing legislation to that effect with a two-thirds majority. The terms and modalities for incorporation were to be defined in a state treaty, agreed on between the two governments, before being submitted for approval in both parliaments. The actual date for the accession required the approval of the GDR's parliament or the approval of the East German Länder governments that would be in place after 14 October. As it turned out, the date for incorporation proved to be a contentious issue, for the unification timetable had to take into account the ongoing discussions at the "2+4" talks between the two German governments, the Soviet Union, the United States, Great Britain, and France. Those talks, which were to define the place of a united Germany within the alliance and economic structures of Europe, had opened on 5 May, and the likely date for the conclusion of the treaty arrangements was mid-September. So there could be no accession until after that date.

Another consideration was the timing of the elections in the Federal Republic, which were scheduled for 2 December; any change in that date would have required an amendment of the FRG Basic Law. If the date for unification was before 2 December, then the resulting all-German elections would likely mean that the small East German parties would fail to gain seats under the FRG's 5 percent rule. The most important consideration from the point of view of the coalition government was the fate of the PDS; if the date were set after 2 December, then the PDS would probably survive in the united Germany and continue as a serious rival of the SPD. If, however, the SPD and the PDS were to face elections on 2 December, the SPD was likely to do better than the PDS in the east because voters would perceive that only the SPD, with its nationwide resources, could defend their interests in the Bundestag. A similar problem confronted the CDU's other major coalition partner, the BFD, which also could benefit from the resources of its FDP sister party at the expense of the small East German parties. One final factor related to the accession date was that each of the three coalition partners was scheduled formally to merge with their western counterparts before 2 December. Any decision on the date for unification and the timing of the elections, therefore, could not avoid being affected by the election strategies of the western parties.

At the end of July the questions surrounding the unification timetable provoked a crisis. De Maizière announced his preference for a unification date after 2 December (*NYT*, 25 July) for obvious partisan political and tactical reasons. Following heated discussions with his coalition partners, the attempt to reach a compromise or to get the CDU to back down failed, and the BDG left the coalition on 24 July (*CSM*, 26 July). The SPD remained, and an agreement was reached for the 2 December election date. It seemed for a time that the coalition minus the BDG could continue to be sure of the two-thirds majority that was required to take advantage of Article 23. This was not to be; the pressure to advance the date of the election faced a severe test from a different quarter. By August the costs of unification for the West German electorate were being revised upward. From the point of view of the Kohl government, it would be better to have the elections before too high a price were put on them and before the West German public became even more worried. Also, by the end of July, the economic situation in the GDR had completely collapsed. The uncertainty had to end in the interests of the GDR's economy and to forestall any serious erosion in East German support for a united Germany and the CDU.

When faced with the economic collapse of the country, de Maizière fired the finance minister, Walter Romberg, and the agricultural minister, Peter Pollack, on 15 August, and the SPD and four more cabinet ministers resigned (*CSM*, 17, 21 August). Although this turn of events left the government in an even more difficult situation with respect to the date for unification, it also cleared the way for negotiations. Everyone was now committed to a compromise. A bewildering array of proposals and counterproposals suggested a number of dates: 15 September, 14 October (the same date as the scheduled Länder elections), and, finally, 3 October. The 3 October date seemed plausible given the expectation that the "2 + 4" talks would deliver the draft treaties on unification for ratification before that date. The amalgamation of the GDR's political parties with their western counterparts was completed before 3 October.

The results of the Länder elections confirmed the preelection party alignment. The CDU gained over its March and May results with 43.6 percent; the SPD also gained with just over 25 percent; the PDS continued its decline, dropping more than 2 percentage points from its May results to 11.63 percent; the FDP and the Greens increased their share by approximately 2 percent; and the DSU lost 2 percent. The greatest change was in the category of others: in March, the small parties that made up this category took 25 percent of the vote; in May that figure had declined to 8.25 percent; in October it was under 6 percent. (ADN, 15 October; *FBIS-WEU*, 18 October.) The loss of electoral support for the lesser parties reflected the tendency to amalgamation that was stimulated by the realization that only through amalgamation was political survival possible. In August and September a number of such mergers took place. Of the larger parties, only the PDS lacked a viable counterpart in the West. The CDU, the SPD, and the Liberals all went into the elections as united national parties. The Greens, too, had merged with the Green forces in the west. The small DBD, which had done well in the local elections of May, split, with a majority entering the ranks of the CDU while a minority went to the SPD (for a review of party mergers see Meredith Heiser, "The Unification of East and West German Parties," RFE/RL, *Report on Eastern Europe*, 20 July). In the territories that made up the former GDR, the December elections once again conformed to the same alignment. The CDU emerged the winner, with the largest share on both eastern and western lists. The SPD was a powerful second with 240 seats. The FDP returned 79 deputies, the Greens 7, and the PDS 14. (*NYT*, 3, 4 December.) Once more the PDS declined in the public's esteem and managed only fourteen seats in the expanded Bundestag. Had the 5 percent rule been applied without the safeguard of the separate lists for the eastern Länder, the PDS would most likely have been wiped out along with every other East German party that was not by now part of a powerful nationwide machine.

Economic affairs. At the beginning of 1989 it was possible to survey the GDR economy within the old terms of reference, when it was still the Soviet Union's most important East European trading partner. Producing the best-quality industrial goods anywhere in Eastern Europe, the GDR had the most developed social security system and the highest standard of living of any communist-style society. Even western economists sometimes allowed that the East Germans had achieved a level of productivity and consumption comparable to that of some western economies. (*YICA*, 1990.) One year later the most favorable comment concerning the past achievements of the GDR had been badly compromised, and the GDR's economy was in deep crisis. The strains of the revolutionary changes at the end of 1989 not only exacerbated existing economic difficulties but gave a clearer picture of past levels of economic achievement. By virtually every measure the economy had been mismanaged, and its problems were structural and systemic, not simply induced by the extraordinary strains of mass migration and political turmoil. Under Honecker and "real existing socialism," the systems of economic management and production had almost totally failed. The extent of the failure had long been obscured by a system of performance measurement different from that used in the west and by an artificial exchange rate that made it difficult to assess production values. Analysis was further complicated by the deliberate falsification of economic data by the most senior levels of the GDR's party and state administration. (*Berichte des Bundesinstituts fuer ostwissenschaftliche und internationale Studien*, 1990.) During 1990 a more accurate estimate of past economic performance gradually emerged. At the end of the year, however, the picture was still incomplete, and the full costs facing the German economy for rescuing and integrating the territories of the defunct GDR were still not entirely clear. In the last months of 1990 estimates for the capital investment bill, for the costs of servicing the GDR's debt load, and for improving services and social support were being steadily inflated.

Some indication of the GDR's poor industrial performance can be gained by comparing it with that of the FRG. When East German industrial productivity is measured over several key sectors against that of the FRG, a ratio of approximately 1:2–2.5 is indicated (*Saechsische Zeitung*, 9 March; *JPRS-EEU*, 4 May). In March, the FRG Steel Trade Association announced that it was ready to help the steel industry in the GDR by means of management retraining and new investment. At that time the

association estimated that the productivity of West German plants was 2.5 times the average for the GDR and that low productivity resulted from poor quality control and obsolete equipment. (*Die Welt*, 13 March; *FBIS-WEU*, 23 April.)

In the housing and construction industry, productivity was even lower; by one estimate 70 percent of the equipment deployed in this sector was hopelessly antiquated (*Die Welt*, 16 March; *FBIS-WEU*, 23 April). The extreme disparity between the levels of performance of the two Germanies was attributable in large part to the inflexibilities in the GDR's central planning machine, its rigidity in establishing industrial investment priorities, and its notorious inability to provide incentives for technological innovation and increased labor productivity. The GDR automotive industry, for example, was using plant and production techniques that had not changed since the 1930s.

The entire communication and transportation infrastructure was frozen at FRG 1950 levels. The telephone system had only a few electronic data centers; lengthy delay was the rule on the degraded and obsolete rail and road networks. The weakness of the GDR's infrastructure was a significant disincentive to outside investment. (*Süddeutsche Zeitung*, 30 January; *JPRS-EEU*, 7 March.) The banking system, too, was unsuited to a modern industrial economy. Credit institutions were nonexistent, and the range of services offered by the Central Bank through its undeveloped network of branches offered few modern banking services. The expansion of western credit banks into the GDR was essential to expedite a private market, economic union, and western investment. (ADN, 17 April; *FBIS-EEU*, 18 April.)

The acute labor shortage, which had been frequently cited as a major obstacle to increased productivity, was revealed to be related to obsolete and labor-intensive technology rather than to a high rate of expansion. As the economy opened itself to market forces after 1 July, few East German industrial enterprises were able to survive competition without subsidies. Plant closures, bankruptcies, and rising unemployment were the result. In April, the GDR's finance minister, Walter Romberg, reported that 70 percent of the GDR's firms could not compete with the FRG without some level of subsidy. According to Romberg, 20 percent required massive aid, 50 percent substantial aid, and only 30 percent might remain competitive. (East Berlin, ADN, 23 April; *FBIS-EEU*, 24 April.)

One of the weakest sectors in the economy was agriculture. After economic union, when most food and agricultural subsidies were removed, western food products entered in direct competition with East German production. Almost immediately the GDR's agriculture began to collapse, competing with goods of higher quality, more reliably distributed, and often cheaper. Given their access to superior West German products, retail chains in the GDR refused to buy East German foodstuffs. Farmers were forced to offer their produce from the back of trucks and makeshift stalls. (RFE/RL, *Report on Eastern Europe*, 3 August.)

The energy industry was in a far worse state than most observers had thought. The GDR depended on the Soviet Union for most of its energy needs in the form of gas and oil; the rest came from East Germany's abundant resources of lignite and from nuclear power plants. These indigenous resources had been hopelessly mismanaged: Burning lignite without modern defenses against air pollution had led to one of the worst air-quality records in Europe, with a sulfur dioxide emission rate of four to five times the average for the European Community (EC) countries. One of three lakes in the GDR was biologically dead; 80 percent of its rivers could not be fished; 20 percent of its forests were destroyed and another 40 percent were dying. The health costs of heavy air pollution were also without parallel in Western Europe and only matched in Czechoslovakia, Poland, and parts of the USSR. One estimate suggested that as much as 40 percent of East Germany's population suffered ill-effects from air pollution. In Leipzig, where air pollutants are heavily concentrated, one out of two children are treated annually for illnesses associated with poor air quality. (*CSM*, 16 March.)

Nuclear energy plants were also well below EC standards. The establishment at Greifswald on the Baltic had hundreds of significant nuclear-related accidents, and the machinery was poorly maintained and of dangerous design. Following a safety inspection by western experts, one plant was closed. (*WSJ*, 20 February.) In September, when the EC standards for nuclear power generation were applied to the GDR, two plants could not be brought on-line. In addition all but two lignite-burning plants in the country were shut down. (*Süddeutsche Zeitung*, 17 September; *FBIS-WEU*, 18 September.) There could easily have been an accident of Chernobyl proportions. (*WSJ*, 30 January.)

An interview with Professor Helmar Hegewald, director of the Commission on Environmental Policy of the PDS Executive Committee, revealed that the environment had received almost no attention from the Honecker regime. According to Hegewald, both industrial and agricultural enterprises had been allowed to operate with few restrictive regulations, even though such regulations were in place. (*Junge Welt*, 9 March; *JPRS-EEU*, 25 April.) In its destructive impact on water quality the indiscriminate and massive use of chemicals by collective farms rivaled the bad pollution record of industry. (East Berlin, *Wirtschaftwissenschaft*, March; *JPRS-EEU*, 11 May.) The SED, in an extreme example of the "smoke-stack socialism" mentality, saw investment in environmental protection as an unnecessary diversion of capital from heavy industry. Honecker and Günter Mittag reportedly became irritated at the mention of the word *environment*. Reports from Hans Reichelt, the environment minister under Honecker, that catalogued the extent of the damage were labeled "top secret" by Security Minister Erich Mielke's office and never influenced industrial policy in any significant way. The well-publicized attention that the Honecker regime had given in recent years to environmental protection legislation and international accords for limiting pollution contained, according to these sources, deliberate falsifications, evidence of a cynical disregard for the consequences of GDR-generated wastes on neighboring countries. (*Junge Welt*, 9 March; *JPRS-EEU*, 25 April.)

The positive side of the management of East German economic resources lay in its extensive social security and social services system, which had taken shape in the 1970s and 1980s. Although extensively damaged by the emigration of doctors, dentists, and other skilled professionals, the GDR's medical system still offered comprehensive, free, and reasonably high-quality health care. The standards were the best in Eastern Europe and in some respects rivaled those of the FRG. Infant mortality, for example, was substantially lower in the GDR than in the FRG. Social services in some sectors offered more to the GDR citizen than did the highly developed welfare legislation in the Scandinavian countries. Abortion was free and unrestricted. Day-care services were extensive and well run. Maternity leave provisions were the most generous in Europe. With provisions aimed at the welfare of women, the GDR had a much higher proportion of its female population employed than did the FRG. In addition, rent and food subsidies and guaranteed employment offered cradle-to-grave security to the

GDR's work force, albeit at low levels of consumer consumption.

During 1990 the threats to the GDR's social security system posed by the prospect of unification with the FRG became important politically. Both the Modrow and the de Maizière governments tried to respond to the concern that the people of the GDR were about to lose their security network by having aspects of the GDR's social policies guaranteed in the contractual arrangements of the State Treaty on Monetary, Economic and Social Union. These efforts met with limited success. Subsidies for rents, transportation, and some foodstuffs were to be phased out gradually. GDR regulations on abortion were to remain in place in the East German Länder. The opposition exploited the threats posed by unification to the social security arrangements in the GDR as major parts of their electoral and parliamentary strategies. As the time for unification drew near there was a concerted attempt, sponsored by opposition forces in the Volkskammer, to guarantee some of the main features of the GDR's social security system. A draft for a new constitution was worked out in the Volkskammer on the initiative of the opposition that contained guarantees for security of employment and other provisions of GDR social welfare legislation.

The strategy of seeking constitutional guarantees depended on Article 146 of the FRG's Basic Law. By following Article 146, unification would have been achieved after both Germanies had drafted an all-German constitution to replace the Basic Law and the GDR constitution of 1949. When it became clear after 19 April that Article 23 was to be followed by the de Maizière government, the new draft constitution presented to the Volkskammer in April became redundant (*ND*, 18 April). The government majority voted down the New Forum motion to debate the document, and it became a dead letter (Hamburg, DPA, 26 April; *FBIS-EEU*, 26 April). According to a public opinion poll conducted in the GDR in April by the Infas Institute, 42 percent of those polled favored a new independent constitution; 38 percent, an all-German constitution; and only 9 percent said they would prefer the FRG's Basic Law (*Der Morgen*, 11 April; *FBIS-EEU*, 18 April). (This is the same population that made Helmut Kohl the most popular political leader in East Germany and returned a government that was intent on a fast pace toward unification.) The poll probably indicates that there was some strong support for the opposition stance on the unification issue. At the time of the poll there were approxi-

mately 38,000 unemployed in the GDR, and the numbers were increasing rapidly (DPA, 24 April; *FBIS-EEU*, 25 April). The opposition charges that the social policy of the GDR was being sacrificed and that the East German population stood to lose something of value to them contributed substantially to the relatively strong electoral strength of the PDS. The opposition was confident enough of their support to demand a referendum to determine the route to unification. An opposition motion in the Volkskammer calling for such a referendum was defeated by a narrow margin. (Hamburg, DPA, 26 April; *FBIS-EEU*, 26 April; *ND*, 17–18 March.)

At the beginning of the year the first Modrow coalition government announced wide-ranging plans to reform the economy. The minister for the economy, Christa Luft, and other officials outlined plans to transform the centralized economic structure into a mixed economy that would involve, according to the government, cutting subsidies, establishing a more realistic price structure for the state sector, and allowing private enterprise and joint ventures. Luft also stated that the Bundesbank and the GDR's State Bank were working on convertible currency and discussing other ways to stabilize the east mark. (*ND*, *WP*, 14 January.) The GDR side placed its faith in the joint venture idea as a quick way to expand and improve East German production; in mid-January, Luft announced that the GDR's constitution would be amended to permit joint ventures (*CSM*, 11 January). Yet the government, fearing an overly extensive penetration of the GDR's economy, limited joint ventures to majority foreign control for companies with five hundred or fewer employees. A 49 percent limitation was placed on larger companies. FRG companies were not permitted to buy land or buildings. (*WSJ*, 26 January.) Besides the restrictions on joint ventures, there were other indications that the government was ambivalent about capitalist-style reforms. When the administration announced legislative measures that would clear the way for a larger role for free enterprise, the PDS press launched attacks on the FRG's capitalist system (*ND*, 17–18 March).

The response to the GDR initiatives on the part of West German and other foreign businesses was at first encouraging. High-profile deals were struck early in the year in the automotive industry, as Volkswagen, Opel, and BMW explored the possibilities for dealership networks and joint ventures with East German manufacturers. Volkswagen outstripped the other West German car companies when Carl H. Hahn, chairman of the managing board of Volkswagen AG, announced on 3 March that his company planned a 3 billion deutsche mark investment in a Trabant plant that would manufacture Volkswagen Polo cars. According to Hahn, production would reach 250,000 cars a year by 1994. (*NYT*, 13 March; *Süddeutsche Zeitung*, 29–30 January; *JPRS-EEU*, 7 March.) Another large-scale project was revealed in March when Opel AG announced a joint venture with the East German automobile plant Automobil-Werk Eisenach to build 150,000 cars. By late March, 383 joint ventures had been approved by the GDR's Office for Joint Venture Consulting and Authorization for companies with turnovers under 20 million east marks and less than two hundred employees (*ND*, 28 March). Implementation of agreements, however, lagged behind formal approvals and expressions of interest. According to a poll conducted in March by the Federation of German Employer Associations (BDA), 25 percent of the companies in the FRG had expressed an interest in expanding their operations into East Germany, but only 1 percent had actually done so (East Berlin, *Aussenwirtschaft*, 28 March; *JPRS-EEU*, 22 May). The same poll, however, found that there were 1,100 cooperative agreements that had been negotiated between FRG and GDR companies across a range of service, consultative, and manufacturing-under-license activities. These figures indicate the trend that would continue for the rest of the year. The unification of the economies was under way long before the State Treaty on Monetary, Economic and Social Union came into effect on 1 July. The growing number of private arrangements inexorably drew the two economies together, so that even at the beginning of the year their final integration appeared certain.

Both before and after the state treaty came into effect, one barrier after another fell to economic integration. The banking system was modernized; the State Bank dissolved its network of branches and adopted the model of the Bundesbank, confining its attentions to managing the money supply. West German credit banks expanded their operations into the GDR. A host of legislative adjustments, many of them minor, were continuously introduced to smooth the path. The regulations that restricted private and foreign ownership were removed after the de Maizière government entered office. (Mainz ZDF television, 19 April; *FBIS-EEU*, 23 April.) In the first six months of the year, 100,482 applications for privatizing state property were received; of these, 1,102 led to reprivatization (ADN, 23 July;

FBIS-EEU, 24 July). This unacceptably low ratio gave rise to continual complaints concerning the slow pace of privatization. The real barrier to investment did not have as much to do with legislation as it did with the uncertain debt load and inefficiency of most GDR companies. (*International Herald Tribune*, 2 May.) Both before and after 1 July, work was done on the harmonization of welfare, social security, environmental protection, and pension regulations in an effort to make the two economic systems more compatible.

By far the most important issue faced by the two governments was that of currency convertibility. Discussions started in January between Economics Minister Christa Wolf, the FRG economics minister, Helmut Hausmann, and the heads of the two central banks, Horst Kaminsky of the State Bank and Karl Otto Pöhl of the Bundesbank. The objective of the talks was to stabilize the east mark and to find a formula for convertibility and monetary integration. (*ND*, 14 January; *NYT*, 6 February.) A formula for convertibility was a major sticking-point in the unification process. On several occasions the talks were nearly shipwrecked, and both governments were placed under great strain by coalition partners and by electoral considerations. The obstacles were removed on 23 April when Helmut Kohl presented terms that were acceptable to East Berlin.

In January and early February the convertibility issue centered on finding a currency formula that would provide an incentive for GDR citizens to remain where they were. Mass migration was placing stress on both economies. In the Federal Republic public opinion was swinging against the government as the strain on employment, housing, and social services increased. In this context the idea of introducing a one to one exchange rate was first broached by Kohl. The focus broadened when it became clear during the East German election campaign that the drive toward early political union had gained overwhelming momentum. The currency question was, therefore, somewhat altered at the end of February. A formula was needed that would make it possible for the Bundesbank to exercise full control over monetary policy for the whole of Germany, which would require removing the virtually worthless East German marks from the economy.

Again there were strong political reasons for suggesting a one to one rate. It offered the best way of protecting East German savings, wages, and pension funds. During the East German elections, Kohl was perceived as promising that the one to one rate would be the monetary foundation for unification. The population expected that rate, as did the State Bank, the government, and the opposition. It was a shock, therefore, when, at the end of March, the press learned that the president of the Bundesbank, Karl Otto Pöhl, had suggested a two to one rate to the government and that that proposal had been accepted by the minister of finance, Theo Waigel, and backed by Kohl. Because the average wage rate in east marks in the GDR was approximately half that paid in the West in deutsche marks, and because the purchasing power of the east mark in the GDR was approximately equal to that of the deutsche mark in the FRG, the average East German worker's wages would be reduced to 25 percent of the average in the FRG. (RFE/RL, *Report on Eastern Europe*, 11 May.) The effect on the estimated 180 billion east marks of GDR private savings would be less drastic; savings can be considered as targeted for consumer durables, not the average basket of goods on which wage equivalents are calculated. The purchasing power of the east mark in a marketplace of consumer durables was estimated as 1.6–1.8 to 1. The two to one conversion rate thus represented a net loss of savings of 20–40 percent. (Ibid.)

The formula that was presented on 23 April adopted the one to one rate for wages and pension funds (after these had been adjusted upward to meet FRG levels) and for savings up to 4,000 marks for working people, 6,000 for pensioners, and 2,000 for persons under 15 years of age. All savings above these amounts were to be converted at the two to one rate. The debts owed by state enterprises were to be converted at two to one as was the state debt. Both exchange rates amounted to the FRG treasury paying a considerable subsidy to the East German economy.

In the three months that remained to the GDR, the impact of increased competition took a heavier toll than anticipated on East German industry and agriculture. Unemployment rose by 100,000 in the month following economic union. At the end of July, 224,000 were out of work and another 500,000 had applied for government-sponsored relief work (*WSJ*, 20 July). The labor minister, Regine Hildebrandt, forecast a rise in unemployment to 1,000,000 in industry and an additional 250,000 in agriculture (*CSM*, 31 July). Forecasts for the agricultural sector predicted that up to half of all cooperative farms would fail owing to inefficiency, high costs, and low product quality (*CSM*, 1 August). In an effort to control the flow of West German agricultural goods into the GDR, licensing agricultural imports was introduced on 2 May. This measure, however, had little effect given the massive quantity of goods and the difficulty of enforcing the regulation. (*Berliner Zeitung*, 5–6 May; *FBIS-EEU*, 11 May.) As the GDR's economy collapsed, Bonn channeled almost $2.5 billion to the GDR, which was paid out by the GDR authorities in emergency loans to the agricultural and construction sectors. There were plant closures, bankruptcies, and strikes. By midsummer the GDR's agriculture faced total ruin. All hope was now centered on an early date for unification; the disastrous economic situation was the background factor in the collapse of the de Maizière coalition and the hurried round of negotiations that finally brought the date for accession forward to 3 October.

At the end of the year the final costs of the difficult transition were still not clear. There was no model that the Germans could look to; nowhere had there been such a complete and sudden transition from a planned to a market economy. The strategy adopted by Kohl sees massive direct investment as the solution. The government recovery plan calls for $70 billion in direct government aid over the next four years, and this figure is subject to significant upward adjustment (*CSM*, 18 October). So far the Bundesbank has managed to keep the inflationary effect of such large-scale expenditure under control, and the forecast is for 3–4 percent inflation in 1991. Private investment, despite the flurry of initial interest, has so far been disappointingly slow, probably because of the huge debt load that burdens many East German firms. The opportunity for direct investment was still restricted until midsummer, when the last legal restrictions on foreign ownership were removed (*NYT*, 17 August). East Germany's major economic advantage is that its wage rates are much lower than in the West. This competitive advantage is, however, likely to be rapidly eroded as demands for wage parity fuel industrial unrest. Major strikes in the transportation industry suggest that the two to one wage differential will not be sustained for long. The crippling rail strikes at the end of November may be a harbinger of worse unrest to come (*NYT*, 27 November, 2 December). Outdated technology is the other major problem; there is simply no demand for many products of East German industry, no matter how cheaply they can be produced. Yet despite the catalogue of economic woes, the results of the elections on 2 December suggest that there is still considerable optimism in East Germany. A majority of East

Germans continue to believe that their hopes for security and eventual prosperity lie with Chancellor Helmut Kohl and the CDU.

Foreign Affairs. The beginning of the year found the GDR with a range of foreign policy interests that had narrowed dramatically from what they had been during 1989, although at the rhetorical level not much changed at first. The government's foreign policy statements continued to emphasize the GDR's established priorities. There was, for example, to be no change in policy toward the Third World, where the GDR's communist foreign policy tradition had led it to a special relationship. Successive SED administrations had assiduously cultivated good relations with the revolutionary movements of national liberation on every continent; the GDR had good relations with the radical Arab states, with the Palestine Liberation Organization, with the Sandinista regime, and with Cuba. It had been GDR policy to expend considerable resources on nurturing and providing material support to these and other governments and political movements that shared the "anti-imperialist" point of view. (*YICA*, 1990.) Suspicions that the GDR had harbored terrorist organizations were well founded. The Honecker regime had provided training, funds, and refuge for the Red Army Faction and a variety of Arab terrorist organizations and coordinated some of their operations. Interviews with former intelligence chief Markus Wolf and other former members of the GDR's secret services revealed an extensive involvement of the Honecker regime with terrorism. (See, for example, Vienna, *Neue Kronen Zeitung*, 22 June; *FBIS-WEU*, 25 June; DPA, 21 June; *FBIS-EEU*, 22 June; *Der Morgen*, 18 July; *FBIS-EEU*, 24 July.)

In January the Modrow government took an initiative that could have, everything else being equal, dramatically changed its relations with its former associates in the "anti-imperialist" camp. While in Vienna at the end of January, Modrow announced that he anticipated establishing diplomatic relations with Israel (*NYT*, 27 January). In a move designed to pave the way for improving relations, Modrow reversed the long-standing GDR position on responsibility for the persecution of the Jews under Hitler. In February, in a letter to Edgar Bronfman, the president of the World Jewish Congress, Modrow admitted the responsibility of all Germans for the Holocaust and stated that the GDR was ready to assume its share of the burden of guilt. He went on to pledge material support to the survivors; the

government would enter into negotiations with Israel and the Conference on Jewish Material Claims Against Germany. (*WSJ*, *NYT*, 9 February.) The de Maizière government developed these initiatives and, as it came into office, issued an emotional apology to Israel, the Soviet Union, and the Jews of the world for Germany's past crimes (*WP*, 13 April). At the same time the de Maizière government tried to maintain good relations with the Arab nations and to limit any damage to Arab-GDR relations that might result from the overtures to Israel. In Cairo on 21 May, Foreign Minister Meckel assured the Egyptians that good GDR relations with Israel did not signal a change in the GDR's stance on the Palestinian question. (ADN, 21 May; *FBIS-EEU*, 23 May.) In other areas the de Maizière government also moved away from the old priorities. For example, in July, despite the strenuous efforts of the Cubans to prevent a change in relations, the GDR suspended its Cuban aid program. The former SED daily *Neues Deutschland* took an unusually strong antigovernment stand on this matter, using language more appropriate to the Honecker years than to mid-1990. (*ND*, 31 July.)

The PDS government's insistence on the importance of the GDR's place in the Warsaw Pact and the Council for Mutual Economic Assistance (CMEA) was another point that did not match the existing situation of the GDR. The importance of the CMEA and the Warsaw Pact was highlighted in the PDS program that was adopted at the party's founding congress at the end of February. (*ND*, 14 February). The Modrow government worked hard to reassure its East European partners that its relations with the FRG would not compromise its long-standing trade relations within the CMEA. For example, at the January session of the CMEA in Sofia, Modrow emphasized that the GDR was confident about its trade relations with the other East European countries (ADN, 13 January; *FBIS-EEU*, 16 January). Modrow offered similar assurances to the Warsaw Pact commander in chief, General Lushev, when the two met in Berlin on 12 January. (TASS, 11 January; *FBIS-SOV*, 12 January). The special relationship with the Soviet Union, however, was soon to be altered beyond recognition, and the alliances themselves were fated soon to disintegrate. On 20 September the GDR representatives on the Warsaw Pact Joint Chiefs of Staff left Moscow. The last meeting of the alliance with GDR representation was 2 October. (*Krasnaia zvezda*, 20 September; *FBIS-SOV*, 5 October.) After the PDS left the government in April, it continued to pursue a foreign policy that relied on the network established under the SED regime. In June, when the party faced the forced trusteeship of its assets, Gysi traveled to Moscow, Athens, Rome, and Vienna seeking the support of communist and socialist parties to resist the government's measures (*ND*, 15, 17 June).

In January it was apparent that the foreign policy resources of the GDR were almost entirely devoted to one problem: the GDR's relationship with the FRG. In the first three months of the year the political systems of the two Germanies had merged into one political landscape, and it became impossible to separate foreign from domestic policy considerations. For the first time the GDR's relations with the Soviet Union and its East European allies were fully subordinated to its German policy.

On 1 February, Modrow announced a four-stage plan for gradually constructing all-German institutions. This was the first full-scale response to Helmut Kohl's "Ten Points" speech establishing confederative structures between the two Germanies (*YICA*, 1990). The first stage in Modrow's plan was negotiating a series of bilateral treaties of cooperation in the areas of economic policy, currency convertibility, transportation, and the harmonization of the two judicial systems. At the second stage a confederation would be created with some common institutions including a joint parliamentary committee and joint executive organs in specified areas of jurisdiction. At the third stage some sovereign rights would be transferred to the confederal institutions. Finally a unified German federal state would be established through elections in both Germanies to produce a unified parliament that would decide on a constitution and a unified government with its seat in Berlin. Modrow attached the conditions that all obligations to third parties would have to be honored and that there was to be no interference in the internal affairs of the state. Each German state would be neutral as the new united Germany took shape. (*NYT*, 2 February.) The Soviet position on German unification now accepted something like Modrow's scheme, although the initial Soviet response to Kohl's "Ten Point" speech had been cool and on balance negative (*NYT*, 6 December 1989.) By February, that no longer appeared true. Gorbachev found merit in Modrow's plan, which was similar to Kohl's ten points except that Modrow introduced the neutrality condition and underscored the interests of third parties. Two days after Modrow's announcement, Gorbachev talked about the "inevitability" of German reunification but drew

attention to the need for caution and a step-by-step approach (*WSJ*, 2 February).

The suggestion of neutrality that Modrow introduced was a sticking point in finalizing the treaty that reconciled a united Germany with the security and economic structure of Europe. Gorbachev appeared wedded to German neutrality as a precondition for a united Germany. Modrow, in contrast, showed more flexibility. A few days after his plan had been announced, he stated in an interview that neutrality was a matter for "discussion" and was not to be regarded as "something hard and fast" (RFE/ RL, *Daily Report*, 5 February). Modrow sought to link his plan for a united Germany with a general plan for European security and disarmament that was adopted by the SED-PDS and the government at the beginning of January. This "Security Model 2000" envisioned a united, federal, and neutral Germany within a confederated Europe that stretched "from the Urals to the Atlantic." In its Europewide vision the plan was a more specific version of Gorbachev's "common European home." The "Security Model 2000" and Modrow's four-stage plan made little impression in the West, if only because the Modrow government would not be long in office. The overall concept of Europe that was embedded in Modrow's position had a following that extended beyond the ranks of the PDS and continued to be influential for the remainder of the lifetime of the GDR. Rainer Eppelmann, de Maiziere's minister of defense and disarmament, was a strong advocate of German neutrality as was, for a time, Markus Meckel, de Maiziere's foreign minister. (ADN, 2 July; *FBIS-EEU*, 3 July.)

In April, in preparation for the upcoming "2+4" talks on the future of Germany, the GDR and the FRG worked to coordinate their policy positions (ADN, 24 April; *FBIS-EEU*, 25 April). Despite the expectation that the East German CDU-dominated government would be subservient to Kohl, the GDR delegation and in particular Meckel showed a surprising independence (RFE/RL, *Report on Eastern Europe*, 13 July). The most pressing problem was a united Germany's relationship to NATO. The Soviet position in April was adamantly opposed to extending NATO to the Oder-Neisse frontier. The Western powers, especially the United States and Britain, were equally determined that Germany remain in NATO, and this position never changed (*NYT*, 18 May). The argument on the Western side held that a neutral Germany would raise new security problems for Europe rather than solve existing ones. European security could only be guaranteed by firmly anchoring Germany within the existing alliance structure. Poland, Czechoslovakia, and Hungary also accepted that logic (RFE/RL, *Report on Eastern Europe*, 2 March). Only the Soviet Union's objections stood in the way.

At the Ottawa Open Skies Conference in February, Shevardnadze's commitment to the neutrality condition seemed less rigid. When interviewed by journalists, he said that "the ideal solution is a neutral Germany," but he wondered "how realistic that [proposal] is" (ibid.). An ambivalence in the Soviet position as early as February indicated that under some circumstances the Soviets might be willing to accept NATO membership for Germany. In the inter-German talks in April and at the "2+4" meetings, the East German delegation helped remove Soviet concerns with Meckel's concept of the GDR's place in the negotiations for a united Germany as a "bridge to the East" with a special mission to interpret Soviet and East European interests for its West German partner. He sometimes spoke of a "Berlin-Warsaw-Moscow axis" that would continue to be influential in the design of policy after unification. (ADN, 24 April; *FBIS-EEU*, 25 April.) Meckel resented that the idea of the GDR as a bridge did not provide the GDR with a more central place in the talks. As the talks progressed and final agreement seemed nearer, the Soviet delegation found little need for a bridge and negotiated with Bonn as if Helmut Kohl, alone, represented the German side. From time to time Meckel complained bitterly that the bilateral understandings, reached between the Soviets and Bonn, completely ignored the GDR. Meckel expressed disappointment that the GDR had "been able to bring less than we imagined at the start" into the German unification process. (ADN, 19 July; *FBIS-EEU*, 19 July.)

In April, Meckel presented a position paper that said that the GDR would support German membership in NATO, provided that the NATO strategic design dropped the forward defense doctrine. NATO forces were not to be stationed in eastern Germany. The GDR position also saw NATO as a transitional structure that would endure until a Europeanwide security system evolved. This position which contained part of what was eventually going to emerge from the "2+4" talks, was adopted by the West Germans. (RFE/RL, *Report on Eastern Europe*, 13 July.)

In May, in an attempt to put pressure on the Western delegations to the "2+4" talks, the Soviet Union called a halt to the troop withdrawals that Gorbachev had announced in December 1988. According to Rainer Eppelmann, the Soviet motive was the deterioration in the Soviet military posture that had developed as a result of the unexpectedly large number of troops that the Hungarians and Czechs were insisting be withdrawn from their territories. Eppelmann warned that, given heightened Soviet security sensitivities, no agreement on the future level of Soviet forces in Germany could be reached until a broader agreement was concluded on European security issues at the Vienna conventional arms reduction talks. (RFE/RL, 1 June.) If Soviet concerns were to be met, a seemingly impossible compromise had to be found that would provide both for German membership in NATO and for a Soviet military presence in Germany. The major initiatives came from the Soviet side. There was a breakthrough in June because of a proposal by Gorbachev that Germany remain in NATO providing two conditions were met: First, that NATO would transform itself into a political rather than a military alliance. Second, that the Länder of the GDR be given a special status within NATO whereby NATO troops would not be stationed in the East while Soviet troops remained deployed there. The special status of the GDR territories was to be transitional, pending the construction of a new security system. Gorbachev hoped to see the beginnings of NATO's transformation into a political alliance at the July NATO summit. (*Süddeutsche Zeitung*, 11 June; *FBIS-EEU*, 12 June.)

On 4 September, in the final round of talks, the delegations were in the final stages of drafting an agreement that incorporated most of Gorbachev's suggestions. The final draft treaty was signed on 12 September. Under its terms Germany remains a member of NATO with the condition that the Soviet garrison will remain for now, withdrawing on a timetable that will see all forces removed by 1994. NATO forces are not to be stationed in the former territories of the GDR at least until 1994. Germany will contribute 12 billion deutsche marks toward the costs of rehousing, retraining, and transporting the Soviet garrison as it leaves Germany. The 12 billion deutsche marks are part of the overall package of Western aid for the Soviet Union. Germany is to remain fixed within its present borders. (*ND*, 12 September.) The prerogatives of the Four Powers in Berlin and in Germany are rescinded with the ratification of the treaty by Germany and the Four Powers. Ratification is expected in 1991 (DPA, 4 September; *FBIS-WEU*, 6 September). In November a border treaty was signed between the German and Polish governments that was the final recognition of the existing frontiers, replacing existing treaties between the GDR and Poland (*NYT*, 1 November). In a separate treaty the German government assumed part of the cost of maintaining the Soviet garrison.

The GDR's participation in the "2+4" talks was its last serious involvement in foreign policy. Long before 3 October, a single German foreign policy was rapidly emerging. In connection with the "2+4" talks, Meckel and Genscher had worked to coordinate policy. There was ample evidence that the coordination was not complete and that independent GDR initiatives were present. Even so, most of the time the GDR followed Bonn's lead from April until its demise. In April agreements were struck to combine diplomatic resources. Embassies and consulates were closed where they duplicated FRG facilities. Retiring foreign service personnel were not replaced. The only diplomatic representations that were begun by the GDR in 1990 were establishing diplomatic relations with Israel and South Korea. In both cases the decisions were important only in that they marked a symbolic break with the policies of the old regime. The dissolution of the GDR's diplomatic apparatus was quickly accepted by the diplomatic representatives of other countries. Dr. István Horváth, Hungary's ambassador to Bonn, also acted as ambassador to Berlin (ADN, 19 July; *FBIS-EEU*, 20 July). In July rumors circulated that the GDR's Foreign Ministry was to be closed before 3 October. Although Mickel denied such suggestions, the GDR's diplomatic corps, most of whom had been appointed under Honecker, was melting away (*Neue Zeit*, 2 August; *FBIS-EEU*, 7 August). After the SPD left the de Maizière coalition, there was no replacement for Markus Mickel (RFE/RL, *Research*, 7 September). At the end, the Federal Republic's foreign service was inundated with applications for reemployment from former members of the GDR service. Most of them were turned down when it was discovered that they had used their positions to gain access to their files to remove incriminating materials (*Die Welt*, 19 October).

Davis W. Daycock
University of Manitoba

Hungary

Population. 10,568,686 (July)

Party. Hungarian Socialist Workers' Party (HSWP, membership unknown, hard-line faction not represented in Parliament); Hungarian Socialist Party (HSP, 50,000 members, reform communists represented in Parliament)

Membership. HSWP: no data, hard-liners, former policemen, former party activists, officers of the Workers' Guard and Interior Ministry; HSP: 37,500 dedicated reform communists and technocrats

Founded. HSWP: 1918; HSP: October 1989

Party Leader. Gyula Thurmer, president, HSWP; Gyula Horn, HSP; HSP: Miklós Németh, Gyula Horn, Imre Pozsgay, Mátyás Szürös (all members of Parliament)

Governing Coalition. Hungarian Democratic Forum (HDF, 25,000 members); Independent Smallholders' Party (ISHP, 50,000 members); Christian Democratic People's Party (2,000 members)

Opposition Parties. Association of Free Democrats (AFD, 34,000 members); Federation of Young Democrats (FIDESZ, 5,100 members); HSP; Agrarian Coalition; and Independents. (Note that the HSWP is not represented in Parliament.)

Last Congress. HSWP, Fourteenth, second session, 27 January 1990. HSP, meeting of the Coordinating Committee, January 1990.

Last Election. HSP ended up with 10.9 percent of the vote in March 1990 and 8.55 percent in the second round in April 1990. The HSP thus holds 33 seats in Parliament out of 386 seats. The HSWP received 3.68 percent of the vote in March and thus has no seats in Parliament.

Publications. The party daily *Népszabadság* has been sold to foreign investors and is now operated as an "independent socialist daily." The party theoretical journal, *Társadalmi Szemle*, has been transformed into a social democratic monthly with a mildly Euro-socialist tilt. The Socialist Workers' Party has published *Szabadság* since 1989.

Summary. The HSWP which had ruled Hungary in various incarnations since the late 1940s, ceased to exist as a relevant political force in October 1989 when the party split. The reformist HSP took about 80,000 members of the HSWP, which had more than 700,000 and transformed itself into a democratic, socialist, and European leftist party. The government of Miklós Németh presided over Hungary's democratic transition in early 1990, dissolving Parliament and supervising Hungary's first free elections since 1946.

The hard-liners in the HSWP faded into irrelevance as 1990 progressed. The most significant political events of 1990 included several rounds of elections, the formation of a coalition government, the continuation of economic reforms started under the Németh government, and Hungary's orientation toward joining Western Europe. Not insignificant were the collapse of the Council for Mutual Economic Assistance (CMEA), the impending end of the Warsaw Pact, and ongoing Soviet withdrawal.

The communist-socialist era in Hungary came to an end in May 1990 when the centrist government of Prime Minister József Antall was formed. This essay will reflect mainly on significant political changes in Hungary as they affected the two successors to the communist party, alluding to the overwhelming task of economic transformation only where it is relevant to this issue.

Democratic Elections. Two rounds of parliamentary elections in March and April of 1990 put the Socialist Party into opposition and transformed the HSWP into an extraparliamentary interest group that occasionally makes critical comments about "bourgeois restorations" and "reaction" but is largely ignored as a political force by the population and polity alike.

Hungary's unique electoral law stipulated a unicameral Parliament of 386 seats, with 176 elected on individual lists and 152 mandates on county lists. The remaining seats were allocated from surplus votes of the winners and all the votes of the losers for a total of 58 seats on this modified "national list."

More than 45 parties took part in the elections, but only 12 were allocated votes on the national list. The campaign involved frequent personal attacks by members of the Democratic Forum and the Free Democrats on one another. Who engaged in the worst mudslinging or unfair campaigning was controversial but irrelevant to the results of the first round held on 25 March 1990, where the results were as follows (*Magyar Nemzet*, 30 March):

Hungarian Democratic Forum	24.7 percent
Free Democrats	21.93 percent
Independent Smallholders	11.73 percent
Hungarian Socialist Party	10.89 percent
Young Democrats	8.95 percent

Several parties, including the social democrats and the hard-line Socialist Workers' Party, did not achieve the 4 percent required to make it into the second round and eventually into Parliament. Even with a voter turnout of nearly 65 percent, few seats in the individual districts went to a clear winner.

The second round of elections on 8 April 1990 produced a voter turnout of nearly 46 percent and gave the Democratic Forum an overwhelming mandate:

Democratic Forum	164 seats
Independent Smallholders	44 seats
Christian Democratic People's Party	21 seats
Free Democrats	93 seats
Young Democrats	21 seats
Hungarian Socialist Party	33 seats
Others	11 seats

The governing coalition controls 229 seats out of 386, and interim President Árpád Göncz called on József Antall to form a government on 2 May. The Free Democrats, who became the most vocal and vociferous critics of the Antall government, struck a deal with the Democratic Forum and named Árpád Göncz, a Free Democrat, as interim president and György Szabad from the Democratic Forum as the acting speaker. Göncz and Szabad were confirmed in August. A socialist, Mátyás Szürös, became a deputy speaker. Szürös played a key role in Hungary's peaceful transition to democracy while he was acting president of the Hungarian republic from October 1989 to May 1990.

Since May the Antall government has replaced its interior, finance, and agricultural ministers, but given the overwhelming difficulties of economic transition, foreign debt, fluctuating oil prices, and an opposition eager to exploit difficulties to its own advantage, the low turnover is commendable for Hungary's first democratic government since the end of World War II.

The Antall government is as follows: József Antall, prime minister; Péter Boross replaced Balázs Horváth as interior minister in December; Elemér Gergátz replaced F. J. Nagy as agriculture minister in January 1991; Lajos Für, minister of defense; István Balsai, minister of justice; Péter Ákos Bód, minister of industry and trade; Sándor Keresztes, minister of environment; Csaba Siklós, minister of transport; Géza Jeszenszky, foreign minister; Gyula Kiss replaced Sándor Györiványi as labor minister in January 1991; Béla Kádár, minister of international economic relations; László Surján, minister of welfare; Mihály Kupa replaced Ferenc Rabár as finance minister in December.

Three ministers without portfolio were replaced also in December 1990. None of the cabinet posts are held by members of the opposition. Significantly, most former communist functionaries have been cleared out of the professional staffs of ministries, causing many critics of the Antall government to assert that "experts" were replaced by mere political appointees. That key positions such as trade, finance, foreign affairs, and international economic relations are held by individuals with extensive experience and academic credentials in their fields is often ignored by the loudest critics, in most cases the Free Democrats, who claim to be a "party of experts."

Despite the absence of socialists from cabinet posts, Gyula Horn, the former foreign minister responsible for opening Hungary's borders months before the Berlin Wall fell, holds the key post of chairman of the parliamentary Committee on Foreign Affairs. He and his successor, Géza Jeszenszky, collaborate in public and private to shape and defend Hungarian foreign policy. The head of the State Property Agency (Állami Vagyonügynökség), Lajos Csepi, a former member of the HSWP, is responsible for privatizing and selling off Hungary's extensive state sector. In October 1989 some 600,000 to 700,000 members of the former HSWP, including Csepi, quit without joining either successor party. Now more than 0.5 million professionals out of a population of 10.5 million continue to hold key jobs based on qualifications, not party membership. Csepi himself asserted that he only joined the HSWP to gain access to important jobs, not out of ideological conviction (Heti Világgazdaság, 16 February 1991). His example is repeated throughout Hungary.

Although the Socialist Party gave up most of its assets, including its prized office building on the Danube, the White House, and sold its daily paper, Népszabadság, to foreign investors, its reformist members continue to enjoy the respect of the Antall government, and there have been few cries for retribution against the communists.

The Socialist Party, like all major Hungarian political parties, has established many private foundations and profitable firms. For example, the socialists made 43 million forints on a newspaper publishing operation (Heti Világgazdaság, 27 October). The socialists own hotels, travel agencies, consulting companies, publishers, and regional newspapers. In fact, most of the regional and small-town newspapers that were sold to Axel Springer, Rupert Murdoch, and others were previously owned by the socialists. The party newspaper Népszabadság was sold to private investors, netting the party a tidy sum of 108 million forints in common stock. The hard-line HSWP also publishes a newspaper, Szabadság, through Press Foundation X, a private company it owns.

Led by Gyula Thurmer the hard-liners have resorted to launching broadsides in interviews, visiting Mikhail Gorbachev, and citing "reactionary forces" that are "making an attempt to forge political capital out of the anti-communist and anti-Soviet hysteria" (MTI, in English, 28 August). When the unfortunate Antall government tried to double gasoline prices in late October as a result of the war in the gulf, the hard-liners agitated during a five-day taxi strike that crippled transportation throughout Hungary and led to the resignation of the interior minister. The taxi and transport strike almost brought down the Antall government as the Free Democrats and others called for Antall's resignation after a mere five months in power.

Through "covert" mayors the Socialist Party controls a large number of local governments throughout Hungary. In the local elections in September and October, more than 70 percent of the five hundred former local council presidents were reelected as "independents." Local politicians, who deliver the goods to constituents much like politicians throughout the world, recast themselves as independents and gained reelection on personal popularity and ineffective campaigns on the part of the Democratic Forum. On the county level, however, the Free Democrats gained control of fourteen of Hungary's eighteen county seats. (Heti Világgazdaság, 22 December.) Thus Hungary has a truly divided government: a centrist, essentially Christian-Democratic coalition in Parliament; overwhelmingly "bourgeois radical and liberal" control of the provincial seats; and covert socialist mayors in the small towns and villages.

The socialists made one last grab for power in July by advocating a referendum stating that the president of the republic should be picked by popular vote. Because only about 35 percent of the population took the socialists' part, the referendum was an unmitigated disaster.

Intense debates raged from May to December in the Hungarian Parliament about which coat of arms to adopt, arms sales to Croatia, alleged anti-Semitic remarks, Jeszenszky's statements on the sale of newspapers to foreigners, foreign investment, the 1991 budget, land privatization versus reprivatization, and so forth. Given the overwhelming problems that faced any government taking over the reins of power in Hungary, it is not surprising that the debates were passionate and often totally counterproductive. But after more than 40 years of restricted speech and economic frustration, such parliamentarianism is not surprising.

The Antall Era. The Antall government's philosophy is based on four principles: freedom, popular sovereignty, economic transformation, and Europeanization (*FBIS-EEU*, 24 May). In the economic sphere, Antall's critics at home and abroad denounce his slow approach to privatization and monetary reform. Antall, however, does not wish to follow the Polish shock therapy of inflation in the four digits and drastic currency devaluation and fears the social backlash of rising homelessness, inflation, unemployment, and general misery. The transport strike, a reaction to moving Hungarian gasoline prices to world market levels in October, crippled the country, thus confirming Antall's worst fears. The Free Democrats freely propose "drastic" and "rapid" privatization, draconian budgets, and steep devaluation because consequent misery could propel them to power in an extraordinary election.

The Socialist Party's reformers laid the groundwork for Hungary's current economic misery by borrowing in excess of $20 billion to support the standard of living in the 1970s and 1980s. Yet the major pieces of legislation that guide privatization, enterprise creation, foreign trade, and investment were proposed and passed by the lame-duck Németh government during its last years in power.

A public opinion poll held at the end of 1990 placed the ruling Democratic Forum behind two of its opposition rivals, the Young Democrats and the Free Democrats (*Heti Világgazdaság*, 2 February 1991). The poll indicated that, despite political frustration and disappointment, nearly two-thirds of the public would take part in an election, even after having voted six times in less than a year since November 1989. Of those polled, 23 percent supported the Young Democrats, 22 percent, the Free

Democrats, and only 14 percent, the Democratic Forum. The socialists and the two coalition parties also lost support. But in terms of personal popularity, this poll revealed that the chairman of the Socialist Party, Gyula Horn, the former foreign minister, remained the third most popular figure in the country, with a sympathy index of 74 versus 47 for the prime minister.

In domestic and international economic policy, the Antall government, which came to power in May 1990, had to contend with the following serious difficulties, any one of which would challenge any possible alternative ruling coalition in Hungary:

1. Privatizing the state-owned sector by selling off assets to domestic and foreign investors
2. Creating incentives for stimulating the private sector
3. Modernizing the country's totally inadequate communications infrastructure
4. Meeting foreign debt service obligations
5. Borrowing foreign funds to finance technical modernization
6. Dealing with impending poverty, inflation, and unemployment
7. Settling accounts with the Soviet Union and other trading partners when CMEA switched to hard currency accounting in 1991
8. Dealing with wildly fluctuating oil prices and the other consequences of the Persian Gulf war
9. Finding alternative supplies of oil to the Soviet Union, which can deliver only a fraction of its previous shipments to Hungary
10. Negotiating the financial terms of Soviet withdrawal
11. Creating adequate incentives for foreign investment in Hungary without distorting the domestic economy
12. Adjusting to the loss of East German markets
13. Dealing with land reprivatization, a key condition for Smallholder Party participation in the coalition in that the Supreme Court has declared a certain form of reprivatization unconstitutional because it discriminates on the basis of when land was seized by the state
14. A serious drought during the summer of 1990 that reduced the harvest of most of Hungary's crops

Foreign Policy. In addition to the difficulties of transforming an economy distorted by more than 40 years of central planning, Hungary in 1990 had to deal with the crumbling of order in the Soviet Union, the crackdown in the Baltic states, the dissolution of the Warsaw Pact by April 1991, ethnic tensions in Romania, Czechoslovakia, and Yugoslavia, and the reunification of Germany. But foreign policy has produced concrete results. Hungary joined the Council of Europe in November, is seeking associate membership in the European Community (EC), and has engaged in cooperative discussions within various Central European forums such as the Pentagonal and the Alps-Adriatic groups. The Antall government, with Foreign Minister Jeszenszky's leadership, has met repeatedly with leaders from Czechoslovakia and Poland to coordinate a response to the crackdown in the Soviet Union and to discuss applying for EC membership.

Hungary's primary foreign policy intention is to join the EC, first as an associate member and then as a full member. The overall de-Sovietization of Hungarian foreign policy lies in its explicit East-Central European orientation, which by most definitions excludes the current Soviet Union. On a diplomatic front, Hungary actively promotes at least four forms of such cooperation: the Alpine-Adriatic group (parts of Bavaria, Austria, Italy, Yugoslavia, Hungary); the Pentagonal group (Austria, Italy, Yugoslavia, Hungary, Czechoslovakia); the newest, the Tisza-Carpathian group (Hungary, eastern Slovakia, Transylvania, Ukraine); and finally a Czechoslovakia-Hungary-Poland group advocated by Václav Havel. This last tripartite group may add the Baltic states in the future. Prime Minister Antall has also called for an "East-Central European Union," to come into being after the dismantling of the Warsaw Pact, as a balancer between the West European Union and the USSR. (RFE, *Daily Report*, 31 August.) Poland is expected to act as a bridge to the Balkans, Yugoslavia, and to the Baltic states.

A critical principle of Hungarian participation in these multilateral consultations is protecting the linguistic, educational, cultural, and collective rights of ethnic minorities. Yet enthusiasm for these potential forms of East-Central European cooperation does not replace Hungary's number one foreign policy goal, namely, rejoining Europe. Prime Minister Antall has declared unequivocally that no form of regional cooperation is an alternative to all-European unity. Instead, regional cooperation simply invigorates historical and economic ties on a geographic basis. In other words, Hungary, an enthusiastic supporter of East-Central European cooperation, will not place regional efforts above the goal of joining the EC and other Western bodies. (*Magyar Hirlap*, 2 August.)

The Europeanization and simultaneous Central Europeanization of Hungary's foreign policy orientation explicitly de-Sovietizes Hungary's foreign relations by excluding the USSR from regional associations and by abandoning organizations that the USSR established to dominate its sphere after 1945. Some versions of East-Central European cooperation, however, include the possibility of expansion in two directions: (1) incorporating various regions or republics of the USSR (2) inviting newly independent Soviet republics to join, such as the three Baltic states. Thus, in the long run confederal proposals include what is left of the Soviet Union after a range of independence and sovereignty movements has been implemented.

Just as the EC legitimized and made acceptable German reunification, some form of non-EC and non–North Atlantic Treaty Organization confederation in East-Central Europe may legitimize total independence for various Soviet republics seeking it and allow Moscow to shed the union of restive republics while saving face (the new association is friendly and nonthreatening to the USSR). Hungary hosted a meeting on 25 February 1991 that decided to disband the Warsaw Pact military alliance on 1 April 1991, achieving a goal proclaimed by the revolutionary government of Imre Nagy in 1956.

As defined by Foreign Minister Géza Jeszenszky, the Soviet Union becomes one leg of a five-legged Hungarian foreign policy (its other limbs are Germany, France, the United States, and Hungary's neighbors) (*FBIS-EEU*, 11 September). The Soviet Union has apologized to Czechoslovakia for the 1968 invasion and conceded that the Molotov-Ribbentrop agreement was immoral. No official state or party organ has apologized for suppressing the 1956 revolution, however, which killed thousands of Hungarians, including Prime Minister Nagy, during the fighting and several years of retribution thereafter. In August 1990 the Hungarian Parliament requested that the USSR Supreme Soviet declare the 1956 intervention illegal. Lack of a formal reconciliation could prevent a full redefinition of Hungarian-Soviet relations. Popular and official frustration is growing in Hungary at the weak Soviet responses to Hungarian concerns. An investigation of 1956 remains a critical issue blocking full normalization of Hungarian-Soviet relations.

Recognition of Sovereign Soviet Republics.
Hungary greets the declaration of independence
and sovereignty by most Soviet republics with enthusiasm, meaning that Budapest is willing to conduct relations with those republics as long as they
approach Hungary first. Political sympathy and solidarity is most evident with the Baltic states: direct
contacts exist, and recognition is likely. The centrally planned trading system cannot deliver enough
energy to Hungary and to the rest of Eastern Europe; therefore, Hungary, Poland, and the Czech
and Slovak governments are ready to negotiate directly with the local governments of the other oil-
producing regions in the USSR.

There are indications that Hungary will support
moves toward independence and sovereignty among
various republics of the Soviet Union. After announcing bilateral relations with the Ukraine,
Prime Minister József Antall pointed out the following in a speech to the Council on Foreign Relations:

> We support the attempts of other republics in the
> Soviet Union to regain their sovereignty, in particular
> the Baltic countries. . . . We trust that Mr. Gorbachev,
> who in his own thinking has moved away from reform
> of an incurable political system and now endorses
> democratic pluralism, will definitely adopt the think-
> ing of those Russians who propose sovereignty and
> fair relationships of [for] republics within a new kind
> of Soviet Union. (József Antall, "Hungary's Place
> among the Western Democracies," speech to the
> Council on Foreign Relations, New York, 16 October
> 1990, p. 8.)

The prime minister hinted that Hungary and other
Central European states would have a role in reshaping the Soviet Union into a voluntary democratic confederation of independent states.

If democracy and market economics emerge in
the republics and overall in the Soviet Union, then
Hungary is ready to expand friendly ties (*Magyar
Hirlap*, 2 August). In late September, Hungary and
the Ukraine expanded consular ties in preparation
for possible full democratic relations. The Ukrainian government also promised "cultural autonomy" for the Hungarian minority in Transcarpathia.
Also in late September, Estonia and Hungary
agreed to establish consular ties. The possibility of a
new web of direct political and economic ties among
the former states of the outer empire could be interpreted as threatening by Moscow or could form the
basis of a peaceful transition to a confederation in
place of the Soviet Union.

Foreign Policy Goals. Hungarian relations
with the USSR have become a sideshow to three
major concerns of Hungarian foreign policy:

1. Rejoining Europe through association and
   eventual membership in the EC
2. Ensuring the rights of nearly 4 million Hungarians living in areas that became parts of
   Yugoslavia, Czechoslovakia, and Romania
   after World War I
3. Supporting new forms of cooperation
   through several East-Central European regional groupings.

Hungary and the Soviet Union have to settle the
untidy business of the cold war: Soviet troop withdrawal and compensation. The burden of socialism,
inadequate infrastructure, and outdated industries
will remain long after the CMEA formally comes to
an end. Once the shock of these nonrecurring issues
is over, there is much hope for friendly relations.
These relations may be with the USSR or its de-
volved republics, which have a range of legal and
effective degrees of sovereignty and independence.

Rejoining Europe. Rejoining Europe in an
economic sense is both a desired result and a
method of supporting transformation. As a goal,
becoming a capitalist, prosperous, democratic
country like Austria or the Federal Republic of
Germany is paramount. Thus EC membership is
seen as a magical formula for achieving prosperity
as well as economic transformation. Associate and
eventual full EC membership is supposed to propel
Hungarian exports and pull in capital investment,
training, and technology. Painful and comprehensive reforms, however, are required for entry into
the EC. Hungary has obtained the support of several West European states for its membership effort,
including Germany and Britain.

The goal of EC membership motivates industrial
restructuring and privatization. But EC membership (or associate status) alone does not alleviate
the impending inflation and unemployment, and
privatization and the creation of an entrepreneur
sector should take place regardless of potential
membership. Creating favorable conditions for domestic and foreign investors and building an infrastructure to attract investors can take place without EC membership.

Hungary and Its Neighbors. Hungary's other
foreign policy priority affects the Soviet Union and

Transcarpathia, a part of the Ukraine since the end of World War II. Roughly one-third of ethnic Hungarians live in the countries surrounding Hungary. Some are concentrated in compact, homogeneous communities; others live near the Hungarian border in cities and villages that have experienced a large influx of non-Hungarians since 1920. Prime Minister Antall declared shortly after his victory that he is the spiritual head of government for 15 million Hungarians; some 14 million in the Carpathian Basin and the rest in diaspora. Hungary is intent on enforcing the promises of the former dissidents who share power in Czechoslovakia and Romania regarding the institutionalization of protection for all ethnic and linguistic minorities. Hungary provided moral and substantive support to Václav Havel and Alexander Dubček, and refuge for tens of thousands of Romanian citizens, regardless of ethnicity, for several years before the transformations in Czechoslovakia and Romania. Foreign Minister Jeszenszky does not hesitate to point out the generous humanitarian, medical, and logistic assistance that all levels of Hungarian society provided to the Romanian revolution in December 1989, in the hope of ending the inflamed animosity exploited by the Ceauşescu dictatorship.

Certain unofficial elements and government officials among Hungary's neighbors react to attempts to even discuss the situation of ethnic minorities with a chorus of accusations—revisionism, fascism, revanchism—reminiscent of the communist days. It has become difficult to conduct a rational discussion without these responses, which serve propaganda purposes and distract attention. Speaking of Hungarians outside Hungary was taboo until the 1980s, and Hungary's neighbors introduced freedom of speech only in late 1989. Therefore nationalist emotions, which were suppressed for nearly 50 years, are coming to the surface. Any mention of minority rights is regarded by some as revanchism and others as an attack on national legitimacy or sovereignty. (*Financial Times*, 23 October; *Süddeutsche Zeitung*, 8, 27 October.) Declining standards of living inspire extremists to blame the usual suspects, in this case the Gypsies. In Romania and Slovakia, the scapegoats and targets of nationalist newspaper articles are Gypsies, foreigners, fascists, and Hungarians.

Soviet-Hungarian relations are directly affected by the status of Hungarians living in Transcarpathia. Although in World War II the USSR used Transylvania to entice Romania to abandon Germany in 1944, the Soviet Union will most likely remain neutral in Hungary's discussion of minority rights with Romania, Czechoslovakia, and Yugoslavia.

Prospects. In foreign policy the Antall government is expanding Gyula Horn's and the reform communists' attempts to open Hungary to the West. In domestic matters, the Hungarian Socialist Party has transformed itself into a Central European incarnation of a leftist, social-democratic movement. The discredited communists are concentrated in the Hungarian Socialist Workers' Party, a group not represented in Parliament and totally discredited in the eyes of the public. Although the old communist party had to give up sizable assets as well as clear out its primary organizations from all enterprises and offices, several of its leaders, such as Gyula Horn, Mátyás Szürös, and Imre Pozsgay, enjoy the respect of the public and hold important positions in Parliament.

Economic data released for 1990 give some cause for optimism (MTI, *Econews*, 18 January 1991). For example, Hungary had a record convertible currency trade surplus of $945 million, with an 18 percent growth in exports, and the EC now accounts for more than a third of Hungary's foreign trade. Reflecting plummeting exchanges with the Soviet Union, only a third of Hungary's trade in 1990 was done in rubles. Germany has surpassed the Soviet Union as Hungary's largest trading partner. Regarding direct foreign investment, Hungary leads both Czechoslovakia and Poland, states with one and a half to four times Hungary's population.

If the opposition's Free Democrats were to form a government, they would face the same overwhelming economic and political hurdles that the Hungarian Democratic Forum government does at the start of 1991. A strong opposition is needed in democratic society, but given the extraordinary nature of economic and political transformation, a coalition between the Forum and the Free Democrats may be needed in the interests of stability and the continued legitimacy of democratic government.

Biographies. *Béla Kádár.* Minister of international economic relations, Béla Kádár was born at Pécs in 1934. He graduated in 1956 from the University of Economics in Budapest with a degree in financial affairs and worked for the National Bank of Hungary and then briefly for the Elektroimpex Foreign Trading Company.

His career as an economist began at the Institute of Economics and Market Research, where he studied developing countries. Later he headed the research department of the Research Institute of World Economy, studying advanced capitalist countries. In March 1988 he was appointed director of the Institute of Economic Planning in the National Planning Office.

In 1980 his thesis on structural changes in the world economy won him a doctorate in economics. The special features of the economic development processes, the economic policies of small countries, and ideas for Hungarian strategies in external economy were his main interests.

Dr. Kádár was guest professor at a number of universities abroad. He is the author of many books and professional articles, several of which have been published in foreign languages. He has passed state examinations in English, Spanish, German, Russian, and Portuguese. Dr. Kádár is not affiliated with any party.

Géza Jeszenszky. Minister of foreign affairs, Géza Jeszenszky was born in November 1941. After graduating from secondary school, he was denied admission to the university because of his family background and political beliefs. He worked for two years as a manual worker and eventually was admitted to the University of Budapest, where he did both graduate and postgraduate work. He taught school and then joined the staff of the Széchényi National Library and the faculty of Eötvös Lóránd University. In 1973, he was accepted for a postgraduate fellowship sponsored by the Hungarian Academy of Sciences and was appointed in 1976 to teach in the Department of International Relations of the Budapest University of Economics.

He has published a number of papers on Hungarian and American history and on Hungary's international relations from the mid-nineteenth century until World War II. He is especially interested in the international image of Hungary abroad as conveyed by the refugees and emigrés of the 1848 and 1956 revolutions, a subject on which he published a book and several studies. In the early 1980s, he spent two and a half years as a Fulbright visiting professor at the University of California at Santa Barbara.

Dr. Géza Jeszenszky is a founding member of the Hungarian Democratic Forum. In his capacity as the head of the party's Foreign Affairs Committee, Dr. Jeszenszky was appointed minister of foreign affairs by Prime Minister Antall in the first demo-cratically elected Hungarian government in 40 years.

József Antall. Prime minister of the Republic of Hungary, József Antall is a third-generation politician who was born in 1932. His grandfather was secretary of state. His father was a government commissioner who, between 1939 and 1944, was responsible for refugee affairs and thus in charge of the undercover operations that protected Polish and French prisoners of war, as well as Jews who fled to Hungary from other parts of Europe. After the war, József Antall, Sr., was a prominent member of the Smallholders' Party, a member of Parliament, and later minister of reconstruction and minister of finance.

Dr. Antall received his degree in history from the Eötvös Lóránd University in Budapest. He worked as a librarian, archivist, and secondary school teacher and then was appointed director of the Semmelweis Museum, Library, and Archives of Medical History in 1984. He has published more than three hundred papers on history and political science and is a member of a number of Hungarian and international learned societies.

József Antall has been active in public life since his youth. In October 1956, during the Hungarian revolution, he helped reorganize the Independent Smallholders' Party and was a founder of the Christian Youth Federation. Because he had been chairman of the staff's revolutionary committee at Budapest's Eötvös Gymnasium, he was arrested and dismissed from his teaching post after 1956.

Dr. Antall has written extensively on the history of the nineteenth century, the evolution of liberal thinking, the American Civil War and Abraham Lincoln, and American-Hungarian political relations. He is widely read in twentieth-century history and an admirer of Winston Churchill. His political philosophy also reflects the influence of leaders such as Konrad Adenauer and Ludwig Erhard, who felt that cooperation could supersede conflict in relationships among nations. His favorite Hungarian writer is Baron József Eötvös, novelist and essayist, minister of education, and founder of the modern Hungarian educational system. Among earlier prime ministers of Hungary, he especially admires Batthyány and Kossuth.

József Antall is a founding member and president of the Hungarian Democratic Forum, the largest opposition party to emerge from the revolutionary changes of 1988–1989 in Hungary. He played a key role in drafting the party's platform, which closely reflects his political philosophy. In 1989 he assumed a leading role in the Opposition Round Table, which redrafted Hungary's constitution and paved the way for Hungary's first democratic election in 40 years.

He has been president of the Hungarian Democratic Forum since October 1989, and in the general elections of 1990, he received his mandate to Parliament. Hungary's new coalition government was sworn in on 23 May, with József Antall as prime minister. Dr. Antall is married with two sons.

Charles Jokay
Hudson Institute, Indianapolis, Indiana

Poland

Population. 37,776,725
Head of State. President Lech Wałęsa (elected on 9 December 1990)
Main Political Parties. Center-right agrarian parties: Polish Peasant Party; Polish Peasant Party—Rebirth; other center-right parties: National Party, Christian National Union, Christian Democratic Labor Party, Democratic Party; center-left parties: Polish Socialist Party; left-wing parties: Polish Socialist Party—Democratic Revolution; other parties: Social Democracy of the Republic of Poland (SDRP, formerly the communist party or Polish United Workers' Party, PZPR), Union of the Social Democracy of the Republic of Poland (USDRP, breakaway faction of the former PZPR).
Founded. SDRP, 1990; USDRP, 1990
Membership. SDRP, 60,000 claimed; USDRP, 5,000 claimed (Radio Warsaw, 23 August)
Party Leadership. SDRP: chairman, Aleksander Kwaśniewski; general secretary, Leszek Miller. USDRP: Tadeusz Fiszbach
Political Pressure Groups. Roman Catholic Church, Confederation for Independent Poland (KPN, nationalist group), Solidarity (trade union), All Poland Trade Union Alliance (OPZZ, populist program), Clubs of Catholic Intellectuals (KIKs), Freedom and Peace (WiP, a pacifist group), Independent Student Union (NZS) (Central Intelligence Agency *World Fact Book* [Washington, D.C., 1990], pp. 253–54)
Last Parliamentary Election. June 1989; Solidarity won a majority in parliament. New elections scheduled for fall 1991.
Last Congress. First/founding, 29 January (also Eleventh and last of PZPR)

In the summer of 1989 Poland became the first independent nation in Eastern Europe. The Solidarity-led coalition government embarked on a transition from communism to democracy and from a command to a market economy. Several tangible results have already been achieved. The inflation rate has been reduced, and the rate of exchange between złoty and dollar was stabilized (US$1 = 9,500 złotys) when the government introduced unrestricted internal convertibility and pegged all transactions to the prevailing rate on the free market. Stores are now brimming with food and clothing, and the queues that once dominated every storefront of communist Poland have disappeared.

This conversion to a market economy, however, generated recession and a painful decline in the standard of living. Whereas salaries have been frozen and governmental price supports and other subsidies eliminated, prices have been allowed to comply with supply and demand routine. Within a short period of time prices stabilized at a West European level, but the average wage in Poland still parallels that of Third World countries. Restructuring the economy imparted immense social discomfort to the major segment of the population.

Sweeping changes dominated the political scene. The nation participated in two thoroughly democratic elections—one on the local level and another for a new president. This pace of return to Western civilization is without a historical parallel and can be seen as one of the great events of the twentieth century.

The New Party of the Polish Left. The rise and fall of the PZPR was coupled with the advance and retreat of Soviet influence in Poland. Despite its illegitimate origin and its criminal past, however, the rout of the communist party in Poland was a self-made disaster. In part, the death of the PZPR had its roots in the Leninist principles of artificial unity, "democratic centralism," "dictatorship of the proletariat," and "socialist internationalism," that is, in the orthodox and petrified foundation of communism. The PZPR had had several opportunities to modernize and align its program and methods with the socioeconomic aspirations of the Polish nation, but it had declined them all.

Many times the party betrayed its own ideals and aspirations, becoming an obedient instrument of Soviet rule in Poland. Beginning with the Polish October of 1956, the party systematically pledged to reform itself and its political agenda but rapidly retreated into ideological conservatism and monopolistic customs once the domestic situation stabilized and the threat to its hegemony abated. Its shameful activities culminated in the imposition of martial law and the effort to crush Solidarity in the 1980s. The communists have never admitted responsibility for the painful state of affairs in Poland.

The communists were also not known for honest self-criticism, a weakness fully evident during the final official meeting of the party. To cover up its historical record, they shifted the focus to founding a "new party of the Polish left." The Eleventh PZPR Congress was not seen as a burial but as a birth, a constituent meeting of the country's left-wing forces. Mieczysław Rakowski, PZPR's last first secretary, began his speech by stating that

> We want to start building a new party. Its creators will be faced with an enormous effort. Tough and selfless people will be required, people who can take a lot. Those who attack us today are already saying that the new party will be a repainted Polish United Workers' Party (PZPR). We have to prove, to ourselves and to them, that we are among the people who have understood the rhythm of time and its needs.
>
> We regard the presence of PZPR in the nation's and the country's life as past, but it would be a bad thing if the 11th congress were to become the author of an act of indictment against it. (Warsaw Domestic Service, 27 January: *FBIS-EEU*, 29 January.)

The end of the PZPR was concurrent with the introduction of its successor, the Social Democracy of the Republic of Poland (SDRP). Out of 1,633 delegates who attended the Eleventh Congress, 1,157, including 20 Sejm deputies, enlisted in the SDRP. About 150 deputies, including 25 Sejm deputies, joined the rival organization, the Social Democratic Union of the Polish Republic, headed by well-known communist liberal Tadeusz Fiszbach. (*NYT*, 1 February.)

It was not the first such mutation in the history of Polish communism, as J. B. de Weydenthal explains:

After all, the party has changed its name several times in the past but remained faithful to its ideological principles: in 1925 it changed its name from the Communist Workers' Party of Poland to the Communist Party of Poland; in 1942 it changed to the Polish Workers' Party; and in 1948 it called itself the Polish United Workers' Party. Might the change to the Social Democracy of the Polish Republic be no more than a new name for basically the same group? (RFE, *Report on Eastern Europe* 1, no. 87 [16 February].)

A decisive majority of the party's former members fully realized that a communist or a neo-communist organization in Poland had no chance of political survival; they had to regroup and modify their profile, assuming the appearance of a European social democracy. This alteration, however, did not prevent division into orthodox-hierarchical and liberal-democratic organizations. Supported by a majority of delegates, the Social Democracy of the Polish Republic adopted a new political platform stressing nationalism and warning against capitalism. The splintering Social Democratic Union of the Polish Republic, however, proceeded to distance itself from its communist heritage. "A neo-Communist Party has no chance and no credibility," argued Tadeusz Fiszbach. "You cannot become Social Democratic today when that was what you were fighting against yesterday." (*NYT*, 29 January.) A handful of hard-liners decided to remain "pure" and refused to associate themselves with either group, but they failed to establish an alternative organization.

Key elements of the political manifesto adopted by the Social Democracy of the Republic of Poland include the following:

• The good of Poland represents our highest aspirations. We serve Poland. We consider the will of the people, expressed in democratic elections based on proportional representation, to be the only source of authority.

• We want Poland to be a fatherland of the free and equal who possess solidarity and a state in which there is social justice. We see its future being linked to democratic socialism.

• We deem tolerance to be an inalienable value in public life. We find the following to be inviolable: freedom of expression, conscience, and religion. We support the separation of church and state and the neutrality of the state with respect to the religious conviction of citizens. We believe that the rights of minorities in every field—political, cultural, religious, and ethnic—should be respected.

• We link our ideas to the Polish socialist tradition, the present-day work of the Polish left, and the achievements of the Socialist International.

• There can be no freedom without social justice, which cannot be accomplished without the honest distribution of what has been rationally and efficiently produced.

• We are in favor of a market economy with elements of interventionism and state social responsibility; of an economy in which there are a variety of sectors; and of the gradual replacement of state property by public property, which will assume various forms and will ensure that the most efficient use possible is made of production assets.

• Although we recognize the need to expand the private sector, we reject the dogma that only private ownership is compatible with the logic of the market economy and that only it can ensure the highest degree of efficiency.

• The change from state ownership cannot be turned into the speculative selling off of national wealth.

• We are in favor of the just distribution of the cost of socioeconomic changes among various social groups and property sectors.

• We are against depriving people of social achievements and withdrawing their guarantees of a stable life.

• We are an integrated part of the European and world left. We support the development of cooperation with all leftist formations that are striving for democracy and the just resolution of global, national, and social problems. We particularly value association with the Socialist International. (*Trybuna kongresowa*, 30 January: *FBIS-EEU*, 9 February.)

This declaration, the party's attempt to "paint itself in a new political color," is a blend of nationalism, populism and watered-down Marxism intended to create the impression of a complete turnabout in the party's orientation. The legacy of the PZPR, however, continues to permeate the way political and social goals are defined, and the stigma of Stalinism, chauvinism, anti-Semitism, anti-intellectualism, economic mismanagement, duplicity, and servility toward Moscow is likely to be an unsurmountable barrier against any political comeback in the future. In August, the party claimed to have no more than 60,000 members. (Warsaw, PAP, 23 August; *FBIS-EEU*, 24 August.)

In contrast, Fiszbach's group was less tainted by the communist bequest. The Social Democratic Union of the Republic of Poland declared that it would be guided by the following intentions:

• We are standing on the grounds of parliamentary and self-governing democracy, and we want to participate in the creation of a new political, economic, social, and ecological order in Poland.

• We dissociate ourselves from a monopolistic political system. We are for pluralism. We declare readiness for dialogue with other social democratic and socialist groupings, along with those that until recently were repressed.

• We are for national agreement, the binding element of which should be the guarantee of sovereignty and safe existence within the current borders and dialogue and constructive cooperation among the main social and political forces. Poland's relations with close and distant neighbors should be based on agreement, cooperation, and mutual respect for national interests. There is no other alternative for Poland but to actively join the European integration process. (Warsaw, PAP, 29 January: *FBIS-EEU*, 30 January.)

Besides ideological matters, the communist legacy also consists of enormous material assets formerly commanded by the PZPR. Among these assets are information centers, publishing houses, buildings and premises, means of transportation, and numerous other resources. Control of these resources could give the communists a head start in any political contest in Poland. Nevertheless there are ethical considerations in assessing rights to the communists' wealth. More than 40 years of political monopoly and exemption from outside supervision allowed the communists, unhampered by legal restraints, to engage in highly profitable economic activities.

The public demanded immediate nationalization of communist wealth. Such a step, however, would appear as an act of revenge on the defeated foe and was rejected at first by the Polish Parliament. Instead, the communist party Central Committee agreed to submit an inventory of party property, and in November the Sejm passed a law turning 95 percent of the former PZPR's assets over to the state treasury, leaving the remaining 5 percent for the use of the Social Democracy of the Republic of Poland. The state had taken control of 1,869 PZPR buildings with a total area of more than 490,000 square meters.

The same method was applied to the assets of two former allies of the communists; the United Peasant Party and the Democratic Party. The law passed, with 167 deputies voting for, 120 against, and 32 abstentions, because several political groups felt strongly that all assets were acquired illegally, which meant that these groups had no legitimate right to anything. As expected, the Social Democracy of the Republic of Poland labeled this action a "confiscation" and "an act of political revenge and burdening of people of the left with a collective responsibility for the past." (Warsaw, PAP, 9 November; *FBIS-EEU*, 13 November.)

With this step the PZPR became a thing of the past, but its former members continue to claim that they saved Poland from becoming a Soviet republic and from losing the western territories. They also credit themselves for economic successes during the first three decades of communism. That arrogance and the condescending attitude means that the PZPR would never admit to being a trespasser on the Polish political scene, having usurped power with the assistance of Soviet tanks.

Solidarity. A propensity for political fragmentation was never a distinctive feature of communism. Differences between the intellectually inclined segment of Solidarity and the trade union–oriented wing were already evident during the inception of this movement in 1979. The requirements of the united front strategy against the communists compelled these two groups to cooperate. After the defeat of communism, however, this temporary "halo effect" evaporated, and the groups drifted apart. Solidarity was evolving from a vast umbrella of anticommunism to an organization of competing political factions.

After simmering for a while the split was formalized at the end of June when 63 top Solidarity figures resigned from the Lech Wałęsa–dominated Citizens' Committee, the main political body of the union, and promptly introduced their own organization, the Citizens' Movement for Democratic Action (Polish acronym, ROAD). Wałęsa and his supporters organized under the political label of the Center Alliance. (*Chicago Tribune, NYT*, 29 July.)

Political discrepancies between the two organizations did not entail any vital elements of postcommunist evolution but focused instead on the procedures for its implementation. The main theme of the Center Alliance's political program was "acceleration" of reforms. Solidarity's leader criticized the Mazowiecki government for its lofty style, its slow implementation of economic reforms, and its reluctance to hold presidential elections before the end of the year. "Acceleration" also meant removing from the political and economic establishment members of the former *nomenklatura*, as well as more rapid privatization of state enterprises and greater commitment to extending an effective safety net for workers. The Mazowiecki forces appeared to harbor former communists and offer them an unfair advantage in difficult times.

In addition, the new leadership remained entangled with the former *nomenklatura* and its lifestyle, which included the accumulation of expensive real estate and automobiles and disdain toward the masses. Lech Wałęsa appeared prepared to challenge Prime Minister Mazowiecki in April after Wałęsa's reelection as chairman of Solidarity, during which he won 77.5 percent of the votes cast, making him eligible to compete in the presidential contest. (*CSM*, 23 April.)

The other side embraced a more gradual dismantling of communist structures, including a slower approach to presidential elections. This faction favored Prime Minister Tadeusz Mazowiecki for president and did not hesitate to accuse Wałęsa of a conversion "from the leader of Solidarity, a mass movement of Polish democracy... into a Caesar," as well as attempting to destabilize the political situation in the country. (*NYT*, 8 June.) They feared Wałęsa's populism and disrespect for an orderly, methodological transition to democracy. According to ROAD, Wałęsa's stress on "acceleration" jeopardized the democratic character of changes and amounted to a declaration of a civil war. Wałęsa's critics feared, in fact, that he was the best candidate for the first postcommunist dictator in Central Europe.

Wałęsa's alleged short temper and rough treatment of his associates were cited as ominous character traits for a national leader. His public accentuation of pluralism contrasted sharply with his propensity to individualism and determination to carry out his own ideas. In essence, Wałęsa's disapproval of the government was presented as his dislike of democracy.

Lech Wałęsa responded to these accusations in the following manner:

Well, they are no longer taking the right path, they have spoiled it. They have been unable to take advantage of the enthusiasm which society displayed last year and the confidence which society had vested in them. I am the only man to visit factories. Every week

I meet various work forces and communities and listen to what people have to say. None of the others do so. And people tell me the reforms are not fair, the costs thereof are unfairly distributed, that mafias and cliques continue to rule the provinces, and that schemers belonging to the old nomenklatura, who stuffed themselves at society's expense while the Communists were in power, have fared even better under "Solidarity" because they have formed companies, taken over state property, and are living like kings. What is more, they burned all incriminating documents. (Quoted in *Tygodnik Gdański*, 19 August.)

As a social organization, Solidarity was also facing some structural problems. Despite its evident aspirations to become a political party, it claimed to be a trade union interested only in defending its members' bread-and-butter needs. As a union it opposed the government it helped to establish after the collapse of communism in the summer of 1989. The emerging political cleavage reflected polarization of the general public into the center-left (pro-Mazowiecki) and the center-right (pro-Wałęsa), but both sides refused to institutionalize political parties, as Anna Sabbat-Świdlicka explained:

> The conflict within Solidarity cannot be dismissed as an exchange of insults between rival factions jostling for position: it involves a fundamental difference of view over the strategy to be used in building a democratic Poland. . . . The partisan politics normal to a democracy are being blocked on the grounds that the "historic experiment" in a peaceful transition from communism to democracy must not be disputed. In Wałęsa's view, however, political differences are not being articulated and aired publicly but suppressed by an elite political group. Wałęsa, in this somewhat awkward way, is trying to help Poland break out of this vicious circle. ("Wałęsa Moves to 'Tidy Up' Solidarity," RFE, *Report on Eastern Europe* 1, no. 25 [22 June].)

Initially, the public expected that the "war at the top" could be averted by diplomatic negotiations, a "summit meeting" between Mazowiecki and Wałęsa. The impression was created that the meeting would be in the best interests of the union leader because all "big names" sided with Mazowiecki and because Wałęsa's "excessively rigid stance toward a popular premier might be condemned as a manifestation of [his] . . . political brutality." (*Gazeta wyborcza*, 6 July.) Unity within the leadership

could advance the cause of reforms and guarantee the consensus necessary for stability. Finally, it was not in the best interest of Prime Minister Mazowiecki to attack Wałęsa, a powerful symbol of victory over communism from the Elbe to the Urals. Sixty-eight percent of the participants in a public opinion Research Center survey said that the divisions and differences of opinion within Solidarity had a negative impact on the situation in Poland, and 84 percent concluded that the disagreement had a negative effect on the nation's morale. (*Gazeta wyborcza*, 11 July.)

Preparing for the summit, Prime Minister Mazowiecki decided to preempt Wałęsa's arguments by firing three communist ministers, including General Czesław Kiszczak, the interior minister who jailed and hunted Solidarity activists, and General Florian Siwicki, the defense minister. Mazowiecki also announced that presidential elections should not be postponed for too long, failing to realize that he was playing into his opponents' hands by implicitly admitting that Wałęsa's accusations were valid. (*WP*, 7 July.) The Lech Team, in contrast, gained evidence that their antiestablishment campaign would pay tangible political dividends by exposing the prime minister's tendency to make tactical mistakes. Lech Wałęsa then could popularize his "acceleration" and induce President Jaruzelski to consider resignation. Marian Turski, a well-known Polish commentator, wrote in *Polityka*:

> Lech Wałęsa possesses a very special political instinct like no one else's. . . . Wałęsa is capable of changing his position from one day to the next, depending on the public mood, which—it must be admitted—he can read like no one else can. In his own way he resembles Chairman Mao-Zedong in his maneuvering. After all, the "cultural revolution" was nothing other than an attempt to steer a new political course against one's own establishment. (30 June.)

The Wałęsa-Mazowiecki meeting took place on 7 July under the mediation of a Roman Catholic archbishop and resulted in a declaration stating that both leaders would work together (*WP*, 8 July). The political reality, however, was that the entire Polish society was already polarized into those in favor of continuity and stability and those in favor of acceleration and instability. The question of how well Wałęsa and Mazowiecki could get along was of no consequence. The true outcomes of the meeting were that the prime minister failed to integrate the

Solidarity chairman into his camp and that a presidential campaign was inaugurated in Poland.

An equally important development was Mazowiecki's failure to take control of the local political organizations that assisted the union during elections to local governments. The prime minister's idea of a new federation designed to support his government floundered, as the regions reaffirmed their allegiance to Wałęsa. (*NYT*, 2 July.) This development went hand in hand with changes in the public perception of both leaders. Although Mazowiecki was perceived as more trustworthy than his opponent (47 vs. 21 percent), Wałęsa received more credit for being courageous and determined (70 vs. 13 percent) and better able to express the interests of Poles (40 vs. 27 percent). The prime minister scored only a few points above Wałęsa on such questions as Who could better represent Poland abroad? and Who was more responsible for what he said and did? The most important consideration, however, was loss of public confidence in the Mazowiecki government.

Presidential Elections. Legal provisions for elections were set in late September when President Wojciech Jaruzelski signed a decree that defined electoral procedures. The democratic nature of the elections was secured by strict adherence to such principles as universal suffrage, equality, and direct and secret balloting. The right to nominate candidates was granted to political and social organizations and to eligible voters, providing that at least 100,000 supporters signed the nominating petition. To win the elections, a presidential candidate had to receive more than half the valid votes; if no candidate could muster an absolute majority, the runoff elections between the two candidates who received the largest number of votes were to be held after fourteen days. (*Dziennik ustaw*, no. 67 [2 October].)

The presidential race began in the middle of July when General Wojciech Jaruzelski expressed a willingness to resign before his seven-year tenure expired in favor of a freely elected president. Familiar with the political realities in Poland, General Jaruzelski had no intention of obstructing rapid changes but expressed his surprise "not by the changes. . . . as such, but by their pace and depth." (Quoted in *NYT*, 20 July.) Formal notification was delivered one month later, clearing the way for new elections. Among the reasons behind his decision, the general stated his "concern to prevent undesirable public sentiment" and to "promote democracy,"

that is, to expedite the transition to a fully democratic system. (*NYT*, 18 September.)

Assessing his achievements as president at his first anniversary in office General Jaruzelski pointed out that

> In Poland during this period, a great historical turn took place. I attempted, within the framework of my constitutional powers and capabilities, to advance this process in such a way so as to make it take place in an evolutionary way, in social calm, in a spirit of national agreement, and with a feeling of civic responsibility. (Warsaw Domestic Service, 19 July; *FBIS-EEU*, 20 July.)

At the beginning of the presidential campaign it was assumed that the contest would be confined to only two candidates, Mazowiecki and Wałęsa. The prime minister was expected to attract supporters who had academic educations, who lived in medium and large cities, who were nonworking (students and housewives), and who were generally satisfied with their material situation. Also, his followers were thought to include individuals who opposed both compulsory religious teaching in schools and prohibiting abortion. The chairman of Solidarity, in contrast, attracted individuals who had lower academic credentials, who lived in villages and small towns, and who were farmers and workers, backers of compulsory religious instruction, and antiabortion activists. Also, voters under 25 years of age liked him, as well as those who feared high unemployment. (*Gazeta wyborcza*, 10 July.) A key to Wałęsa's political strength was the trust he enjoyed among the disaffected working class, whereas Mazowiecki was counting on such achievements as the control of hyperinflation, the newly plentiful supply of goods, and the rapid development of the private sector. These successes, however, did not satisfy those who faced unemployment and an approximately 30 percent decline in the standard of living.

Eventually six candidates entered the presidential contest: Roman Bartoszcze, a 44-year-old farmer by profession, associated with the Polish Peasant Party; Włodzimierz Cimoszewicz, a 40-year-old professor of international law at the University of Warsaw; Tadeusz Mazowiecki, a 63-year-old lawyer representing the Citizens' Movement for Democratic Action (ROAD); Leszek Moczulski, a 60-year-old lawyer, leader of the Confederation for Independent Poland; Stanisław Tymiński, a 43-year-old technician, politically independent; and of course Lech Wałęsa, a 47-year-old electrician backed by Solidarity and the Center Alliance. Initially, it was expected that the elections would be confined to a duel between Mazowiecki and Wałęsa, but it did not take long to discover that a dark horse had surfaced as a threat to the front-runners.

Prime Minister Mazowiecki entered the race rather reluctantly, feeling uncomfortable running against a man with whom he had been closely associated for more than a decade. His electoral platform was based on his record as a prime minister, having supervised the peaceful transition from communism to democracy, and his foreign policy achievements, especially his having gotten Poland included in the "2+4" talks on the German-Polish border. He presented an image of a responsible, determined, and capable politician who valued stability and enjoyed recognition abroad.

With his supporters, Mazowiecki orchestrated malicious indictments of Wałęsa. The Union leader was accused of equivocation, lack of loyalty, unpredictability, irresponsibility, incompetence, demagogy, and inability to reform: Wałęsa was presented as a man who needed democracy to initiate personal dictatorship and whose commitment to democracy was contrasted with his courting workers with unrealistic expectations. Contradictory campaign promises and an occasional call for a constitutional amendment to authorize acceleration by decree prompted further doubts concerning Wałęsa's integrity and the extent of his personal ambition. Adam Michnik, a well-known Solidarity activist who sided with Mazowiecki, did not hesitate to compare Wałęsa to anti-intellectual and charismatic revolutionary leaders, including Lenin and Khomeini, and warned that a Wałęsa presidency could lead to a Latin American populist-style dictatorship in Poland. He summarized his anti-Wałęsa stance by saying that

> Lech Wałęsa will not be president of democratic Poland. Rather, he will become a destabilizing factor, creating chaos and isolating Poland from the rest of the world. . . . Wałęsa is a politician with a great talent for setting people at odds. That is why he is so dangerous. His merits will change into their opposites. They will become a curse for Poland. As president, he'll torpedo democracy. (*NYT*, 23 November.)

A similar attitude was expressed by Jerzy Turowicz, representing *Tygodnik powszechny*, who stated that

> The "acceleration" campaign has already generated a certain amount of political instability, it has dimin-

ished our country's international credibility. Poland, which was the first to free itself from communist domination and was considered the most stable country in the postcommunist part of Europe, now appears to be occupying third place after Czechoslovakia and Hungary, and that has already had a number of negative economic consequences.

> . . . Poland's future lies with Europe. However, we can only return to Europe as a modern democracy, as a state based on the rule of law, and not as an authoritarian state. We believe that the Polish path to a modern democracy rests with Tadeusz Mazowiecki's candidacy for the office of president of the Republic of Poland. (28 October.)

In contrast, Prime Minister Mazowiecki's supporters called him a man with respect for legal and parliamentary procedures and the principles of a free market. He was said to be a peacemaker and a true statesman without autocratic tendencies who could reconcile various conflicting interests and promote stability in Poland as well as on the entire European continent. (*Gazeta wyborcza*, 29 October.) ROAD's Coordinating Commission issued a letter to its sympathizers to secure as many votes as possible for Mazowiecki:

> We are convinced that our candidate will be a good president. We know what experience he has; we value his character, his authority, and his ethics, and we share most of his views on public issues. We want to go forward resolutely; without disputes and illusion.
>
> The support that the Citizens' Movement for Democratic Action [ROAD] accords Tadeusz Mazowiecki as a future president does not mean that we approve of all the present government's moves and policies. After the president is elected, it will be possible to form a new government that will continue those aspects of the work of the present cabinet that have been successful and to do so in a bolder and more consistent manner. (*Gazeta wyborcza*, 29 October.)

The final argument on behalf of Prime Minister Mazowiecki focused on the limits of presidential power within the constitutional framework derived from the ideas of separation of power. These tactics worked for a while because, as of the middle of November, the prime minister continued to enjoy a 49.3 to 33.9 percent advantage over Wałęsa and was thus optimistic about his presidential prospects. (*Insight*, 19 November.)

Wałęsa, in contrast, showed no predisposition to academic disputes and legal matters. For him a future president would have to be a "regulator," never confined to "shake hands like the German president" (Warsaw, PAP, 29 October; *FBIS-EEU*, 30 October). The question of presidential powers has not yet been settled in Poland, however, because the 1952 Constitution currently in force does not specify presidential prerogatives; a new constitution is not expected before the end of 1991.

Lech Wałęsa focused his attention on the daily needs of an average family in Poland. Entitling his electoral program the "New Beginning," he denounced the Mazowiecki government for its lack of fairness in social apportioning economic hardship and for its departure from the Balcerowicz plan of economic reforms in favor of former communists and other privileged groups. Wałęsa acted as an independent candidate—free of loyalty to special interests or pressure groups and as a grass roots democrat and empiricist free of "legislative scholasticism." Mazowiecki's "government by journalists," Poland's new ruling class that had come to power by compromising with the communists, was criticized for its authoritarian propensities in that "all totalitarian systems are the work of intellectuals, because it satisfies their demand of 'ordering' the world from above in accordance with a particular philosophy" (Polish journalist Stefan Kisielewski, *Gazeta wyborcza*, 7 November).

Wałęsa's strength had its source in his political instincts and his recognition that voters were much less interested in what the issues were than in what they should be. He ran as an achiever and an accomplished steward of the nation, able to turn around the economic situation. Wałęsa's lack of logic and his exaggerated expectations, his simple language and political manipulations, could not hurt him within his constituency. His independence, personification of Catholic ethics, working-class roots, and common sense could inspire the average voter struggling with harsh economic realities.

Before the 25 November elections a third candidate surged into the contest, and the presidential race became more than a duel "between a barbarian and a bore." A political survey released about ten days before the elections showed Stanisław Tymiński to be the third-most popular candidate, with 17 percent of the popular support, 1 percent less than Mazowiecki. The Solidarity chairman had already moved to first position, with 35 percent approval. (*NYT*, 18 November.)

Tymiński was a total stranger to the Polish political scene. His background is elusive as he holds Polish, Canadian, and Peruvian citizenships, and he introduced himself as a millionaire who made a fortune in a computer company in Canada and a cable television company in Peru. Together with a former correspondent in Mexico for the communist *Trybuna ludu*, he wrote a book entitled *Sacred Dogs*, and in 1990 he had been elected president of the 3,500-strong Libertarian Party of Canada.

In his political campaign, Tymiński glorified hard work and entrepreneurship, as evidenced by his own financial successes. "He's very appealing to people who would like to live in a rational world," concluded Polish sociologist Jadwiga Staniszkis (*NYT*, 18 November), and he advanced a triumphant image of a Pole who could prosper under adverse conditions. His electoral platform exploited popular hostility toward the government: he criticized Mazowiecki for selling national assets below the market price to foreigners and for heavy taxation, while offering to reduce the size of government. Among other things, in his book he recommended that Poland develop its own medium-range nuclear force. (*NYT*, 30 November.)

The first round of elections ended with a bitter defeat for Prime Minister Mazowiecki. With a turnout of only 60.6 percent, Wałęsa finished first with 39.9 percent, Tymiński second with 23.1 percent, and Mazowiecki third with 18.1 percent. The popular rejection of Mazowiecki was stunning, and the popularity of Tymiński startled the majority and prompted the Roman Catholic church to abandon its tradition of political neutrality and throw its prestige behind Wałęsa. Polish bishops issued a statement in support of Solidarity and charged Tymiński with "impudence." (*NYT*, 4 December.) Prime Minister Mazowiecki, who handed in his resignation after the defeat, also urged people to support Wałęsa and warned that Tymiński's victory would be disastrous for the country. Because none of the candidates achieved an absolute majority in the first round of elections, the runoff elections on 9 December concluded the contest.

The second round ended with an overwhelming victory for Wałęsa. The official results submitted by the State Electoral Commission determined that 53.40 percent of the electorate participated, casting 74.25 percent of its votes for Wałęsa and 25.75 percent for Tymiński. (Warsaw, PAP, 10 December; *FBIS-EEU*, 11 December.)

In his first interview following the elections, President-elect Wałęsa stated what this great lesson in democracy had taught him:

We must implement the Polish reforms together with the people. I do not mean we have to teach people complicated economic theory and win them over by means of figures. I mean we have to talk to them and provide them with information so that they can see what it is we want, what we are doing, where we have succeeded, and where we have failed. Poles, therefore, are underinformed; this has to be changed by means of straightforward information, or else everyone will become suspicious. (*Słowo powszechne*, 7–9 December: *FBIS-EEU*, 11 December.)

The Third Republic of Poland was born on 22 December 1990. In his first presidential address Lech Wałęsa noted that the "bad times when our country's authorities were appointed under foreign pressure or as a result of forced compromises are coming to an end." He assured Poland's neighbors that the country "wishes to be an element of the peaceful order in Europe [and] . . . an equal partner for others." For his people, Wałęsa promised to implement "the modified program of Deputy Prime Minister Balcerowicz" and to pursue nationwide privatization to make Poland "a nation of owners, everyone can and should become the owner of a fragment of the national assets, a fragment of our fatherland." (Warsaw Domestic Service, 22 December; *FBIS-EEU*, 24 December.)

The inauguration ceremony saw the insignia of state authority, which had been removed from the Royal Castle in Warsaw on 2 September 1939, returned from exile. It was a profound moment in national history, a closing page in the 50-year-long chapter of German and Russian brutality against the Polish nation that symbolized the beginning of Poland's return to democracy and European civilization.

The harsh political reality of Poland reemerged as soon as the ceremonies were over. Forming a new government became a complicated issue not only because of political divisions within the country but because of President Wałęsa's insistence that Leszek Balcerowicz continue to hold the positions of both deputy prime minister and finance minister and maintain autonomy from the prime minister. For this reason President Wałęsa found it difficult to replace Mazowiecki until, at the end of December, Jan Krzysztof Bielecki agreed to become Poland's next prime minister. (*NYT*, 30 December.)

The choice of this relatively unknown individual indicated Wałęsa's strong interest in appointing young, politically weak professionals with strong backgrounds in a free market economy and no political roots in Warsaw. Bielecki has a degree in economics from Gdańsk University and experience in private business, but his government, if confirmed by Parliament, is not likely to last longer than the next parliamentary elections, scheduled to take place before the end of October 1991.

Local Elections. The presidential contest in Poland was preceded by elections to local governments. But the importance of the 27 May voting was not in the fact that the nation expressed itself freely for the first time in decades, for the 1989 roundtable agreement had introduced political changes at the top, leaving the rest of the country still in the hands of the communist *nomenklatura*. Thus elections on the local level were aimed at dislodging communist strongholds throughout the entire country. This "second half of the revolution" was expected to institute a grass roots democracy, a guarantee that the country would not be governed as it had been under communism.

An additional purpose of the elections was to stop widespread corruption on the local level. Territorial elites—local party bosses, administrators, police, business managers, and their spouses—monopolized politically critical and lucrative positions and used the newly adopted law on the transfer of public property into private hands for unprecedented private acquisition. As Jerzy Regulski, the plenipotentiary for local governments, explained: "Terrible things are going on right now. They are buying flats and houses according to the established prices and getting ready to sell them for more. Speculation, you understand. There is terrible corruption. It is robbery what is going on now." (*NYT*, 30 March.)

Public participation in the voting for more than 50,000 new local officials was light as preoccupation with economic matters and a wildcat strike of railway workers attracted political attention. According to the General Election Commission, the nationwide participation was only 42 percent. The distribution of votes broke down to about 36 percent for Solidarity, 17 percent for the Peasant Party, and the remainder for numerous smaller political groups, with less than 2 percent of the votes cast for former communists. The democratic character of the elections was acknowledged by the standing Conference of Local and Regional Authorities (CLRAE) at the Council of Europe, which states that "the Polish elections to local self-government were democratic, free, just and very well organized." This positive evaluation is expected to expedite Poland's admission to the Council of Europe. (Warsaw, PAP, 31 July; *FBIS-EEU*, 1 August; *NYT*, 27 May.)

Restructuring the local authority in Poland, that is, the transition from a centralized *voivodship*-level state administration where the power flow was from the top down to a *gmina* (borough) self-government was a remarkable political achievement. Now, power on the local level is vested in the council authorized to pass ordinances, the *gmina* board, an executive body made up of four to seven members elected from *gmina* council members and headed by the chief executive officer; the *wójt* for villages, the *burmistrz* for towns, and the president for cities with populations over 100,000 perform day-to-day administrative functions. (*Rzeczpospolita*, 29 May.)

The Balcerowicz Plan. The most critical phase in implementing the Balcerowicz plan started on 1 January 1990. Its immediate objectives were to arrest the hyperinflation of the previous year as well as to

• Stabilize the economy by suppressing inflation and restoring the economic equilibrium.
• Shift to an open market economy along with activating the process of transformation in the ownership structure of national wealth.
• Balance the state budget.
• Alleviate the social hardships accompanying the suppression of inflation.
• Achieve a 50 percent reduction of governmental subsidies for large, publicly owned enterprises. Approximately 90 percent of the trade turnover should occur at free market prices, although certain areas were designated to be subsidized such as coal, fees for central heating and hot water, rents, and railroad transportation.
• Secure internal convertibility of the Polish złoty with a stable hard currency exchange rate to "harden" the złoty and equalize domestic prices with those of the international market.
• Increase the interest rate by the Polish National Bank above the rate of inflation to create strong incentives for savings in domestic currency.
• Abandon preferential loan interest rates and curtail the printing of money ("hollow currency policy").
• Avoid reduction in competitiveness in the domestic and foreign markets through an increase in costs dictated by excessive pay increases and, tied to this, price increases.

This "shock therapy" was tailored to steer the country through the bumpy road from a centralized to a free market economy and to justify unpopular decisions during the formation of the free market. Ending the open black market, illegal currency exchange, and food rationing were among the first positive results of fighting hyperinflation, but the side effects of the cure were at least a 30 percent drop in production and a more than 30 percent reduction in real income. The economy was not expected to show any signs of improvement until the end of the year.

The effectiveness of Poland's fight against inflation and its governmental administration of economic reform hinged on the proper structure for the program and consistency in its implementation. Social conditions were not conducive to a prolonged transition period. Lingering egalitarian and populist attitudes were intensified by mistrust of privatization. The public in Poland feared that the transfer of wealth would result in the so-called proprietization of the *nomenklatura*, that is, an unfair advantage enjoyed by the former elite in acquiring state property. Two additional roadblocks to a free market included a deeper than expected recession, which had a dampening effect on the public's enthusiasm for capitalism, and the reluctance of individual citizens to become involved in the economy through private investments. The economic culture in Poland still shows strong traits of socialism such as expecting full economic security and hesitating to seek out economic opportunities.

The first phase of the conversion to capitalism was completed in the summer of 1990. The monthly inflation rate was reduced from 78 percent in January to about 4 percent in May. The country achieved the growth of hard currency reserves of $3.2 billion, whereas the growth of credits by some 26 trillion złotys and the notorious budget deficit were replaced with a surplus of more than 7 trillion złotys. (*NYT*, 7 June; *Rzeczpospolita*, 25 June.)

At the end of the year, Poland reported 172 percent inflation, a 33 percent reduction in personal consumption, a 36.4 percent drop in real wages, and a 13 percent reduction in gross investments. Nonetheless, hard currency exports increased 24.6 percent and imports declined by 24.3 percent, resulting in a hard currency surplus of more than $3.4 billion. At the same time, a 40 percent cut in imports within the Council for Mutual Economic Assistance (CMEA), a consequence of the sharp drop in Soviet oil deliveries, resulted in a 3.2 billion surplus in transfer rubles. An expected 15 percent decline in the gross national product (GNP) may reduce this year's GNP to $176 billion, or $4,648 per capita, from $207 billion and $5,468 in 1989. (*Financial Times*, 20 November.)

All things considered, the first strides toward capitalism were nevertheless encouraging. Professor Jeffrey Sachs concluded that

> In just 75 days, some stunning successes have been achieved. After a final burst of price increases when price controls and subsidies were eliminated at the beginning of the year, hyperinflation has stopped dead. Under the pressure of tight credit and a balanced budget, and with prices now free to balance supply and demand, products returned to the shops—no more lines, bribes or running between empty shelves. (*WSJ*, 21 March.)

But this triumph did not come peacefully. Several strikes fractured the social harmony that is imperative for crossing over from one economic system to another. The most serious disruption appeared in May when the rail workers requested a 20 percent pay increase and threatened a wildcat hunger strike. Lech Wałęsa's personal mediation between the striking workers and the government helped restore tranquility, but several potential foreign investors, including a Japanese car company, abandoned a possible joint venture because of "economic chaos" in the country. (*NYT*, 25 May.) Two additional waves of strikes involving farmers in July and municipal transportation workers in November, rocked the Polish economy before the end of the year, and both were harmful to Poland's reputation on international markets.

The scale of unemployment, however, never exceeded 6 percent of the labor force. Only in selected regions did the level of unemployment approach West European proportions of 8 to 10 percent. In September there were more than 700,000 jobless in Poland, including close to 200,000 people who had never worked before. (*NYT*, 3 September; RFE/RL, *Daily Report*, no. 105 [1 June].) The government set up a network of unemployment bureaus, retraining centers, and several other forms of assistance to assist the unemployed without discouraging them from looking for work.

The top priority in the postinflationary period in the development of the Polish economy (after the collapse of domestic demand) was stimulating the supply side of the economy. Instead of printing money, a policy that would quickly result in another spiral of inflation, the Balcerowicz plan envisioned accelerating privatization under the conditions of the hard money, that is, noninflationary economic growth. Unwarranted wage expansion, a premature retreat from economic austerity promoted by the Balcerowicz plan, would renew the threat of inflation and reverse progress toward a free market economic system. During a televised interview Deputy Prime Minister Leszek Balcerowicz stated that it would be erroneous to believe that

> the higher the level of wages at present, the better the point of departure. That is not how it will be, and this type of action could worsen rather than improve the point of departure, worsen it because . . . this leads to the consumption of essential financial reserves. The main issue is whether [the enterprises] will exploit, maintain, the often quite considerable reserves which exist within these enterprises . . . in order not to reduce their competitiveness in the domestic and foreign markets through an increase in costs directed by excessive pay increases, and tied to this, price increases. (Warsaw Television Service, 16 November; *FBIS-EEU*, 19 November.)

To achieve this end, continuing economic reform in Poland will focus on establishing an independent central bank, a network of commercial banks, a stock exchange (located in the building previously occupied by the Central Committee of the communist party), and an internationally compatible accounting system. These institutions should function as agents of structural change in the economy and the key instruments in promoting the largest possible public confidence in the process of privatization. The nation's economic rebirth depends on the efforts of individual entrepreneurs and the public at large, as well as on the development of a business atmosphere sympathetic to investments. As Anne Applebaum, *The Economist*'s correspondent in Warsaw, concluded, "The desire to produce—the instinct to compete—has not yet received the oxygen it needs. No amount of pro-capitalism rhetoric will revive it: only capitalist practice will do it." (*WSJ*, 6 June.)

Another important task of economic conversion is replacing the existing tax system. Revision of the tax law aims at equalizing the tax load for the public and private sectors of the economy, eliminating all tax exemptions, and lowering the tax ceiling for enterprises. Typical for socialism turnover, the tax will be replaced by the value-added tax and the five existing personal income taxes will be replaced by one uniform tax law.

Privatization of the Polish economy begun in the summer when the Polish Parliament introduced legislation authorizing a wholesale disposal of its economic enterprises. The new law created a Ministry of Property Transformation empowered to break down large state enterprises, to transform them into joint stock companies with their shares to be sold within 24 months, to auction companies or to mediate sales to individual buyers, and to sell shares to the population, with the workers of a privatized company entitled to buy up to 20 percent of the shares at half price (10 percent of the shares can be bought by foreigners without special authorization). (*Financial Times*, 2 August.) The seven companies offered for sale were selected from more than seven hundred enterprises after their financial health was confirmed by Western accountants. The best buy was considered to be Exbud, a construction company that in the first seven months of this year registered sales of $57.9 million and $8.4 million in profits. (*NYT*, 7 September.)

Two strategic goals of privatization are, first, a complete restructing of the economic base and, second, creating small and medium Polish capital. The government made a decisive move to promote the private sector and to give it preferential conditions for development. Again, Leszek Balcerowicz argued that "the adopted laws create conditions under which enterprises will stop being no one's property and the economy will find its owners. The privatized enterprises will be managed by people who will be genuinely concerned with thriftiness and thereby good labor management, low costs, and high quality of products." (Warsaw, PAP, 15 July; *FBIS-EEU*, 16 July.)

It is important to realize that the economic reforms in Poland have been taking place under unfavorable international conditions. Poland's trade with the Soviet Union and several other members of CMEA had disintegrated, resulting in a lower than expected supply of oil. Besides the general economic collapse of the Soviet bloc, the road to economic recovery was further complicated by the Persian Gulf crisis, including higher prices of oil and the loss of some $500 million from Iraq for the purchase of Polish weapons and other goods. In September fuel prices in Poland went up by 30 percent, and the cost of gasoline is expected to climb during the next year. (Interview with Leszek Balcerowicz in *Głos poranny*, 5 November; *FBIS-EEU, WSJ*, 12 September.)

Poland's foreign debt (more than $40 billion) continues to weigh heavily on the economy despite Western willingness to defer scheduled payments (Roman Stefanowski, "Government Determined to Continue on Economic Course," RFE, *Report on Eastern Europe* 1, no. 26 [29 June]). Poland's overall debt in hard currency consists of about $27 billion in credits guaranteed by the governments of seventeen Western countries (the Paris Club), more than $9 billion owed to Western commercial banks (the London Club), and a $4 billion debt to other states, including the USSR and countries of Eastern Europe. About 40 percent of that sum, approximately $16 billion, is unpaid interest. Poland's chief creditors are Germany (20 percent), France (11 percent), Austria (8 percent), and Great Britain (8 percent). The service on the debt cost Poland $46 billion between 1971 and 1989. (Warsaw, PAP, 4 July; *FBIS-EEU*, 5 July.) In January, Poland missed a $70 million payment to the Paris Club, but the country managed to reschedule almost $10 billion over fourteen years with an eight-year grace period. During this time Poland would pay only the interest on this amount, with the principal to be paid off within the remaining six years.

Despite the foreign debt of about $1,050 per capita, Poland's creditworthiness abroad is not expected to be impaired as long as Warsaw is inclined to follow guidelines issued by the International Monetary Fund. As long as Poland moves ahead with its privatization program, the World Bank will extend it some $1.1 billion in new loans with which to modernize the food, transport, and gas industries. Meanwhile, Deputy Prime Minister and Finance Minister Leszek Balcerowicz strives for a permanent 80 percent reduction in Polish debt repayment, to around $800 million per year, which would bring payments down from around 7 percent of the national budget to about 2 percent. Minister Balcerowicz expressed optimism that "some interlocutors will seriously consider our proposal" but added that "in any case, this is no Marshall Plan. All that is left for us to do is to count on our own efforts and on a greater degree of understanding from the world during the final, difficult decade of the 20th century." (*Trybuna*, 11 May; *FBIS-EEU*, 16 May.) Professor Sachs concurred:

In this year of German unification, the U.S. should tell West Germany—by far Poland's leading creditor— that respecting Poland's borders is not enough. Germany, together with the U.S. and other creditors, must sharply reduce its debt. The World War II allies did just that for Germany itself in 1953. (*WSJ*, 21 March.)

The overall balance sheet of the Polish economy at the end of the year appears to be positive despite there being many small companies and a few large private enterprises still struggling with legal obstacles and the public sector still playing a central role until privatization is finalized. Many observers argue that more concessions for the free market are needed to stimulate private business and discourage the illegal labor market. It is up to the new president and his government to see that the promised "acceleration" of economic reforms promptly creates stable legal and fiscal conditions for a free market economy.

National Security Affairs. An opportunity for a fresh look at national security matters came along with changes in the international environment in Europe and in East-West relations. Poland ceased to behave as a member of an unequal alliance and is structuring its defense consistent with a lack of threat from the West. The country feels uneasy about the potential disintegration of the Soviet Union and the unclear direction of the political changes taking place in the USSR. This situation has prompted Poland to act cautiously, to avoid unnecessary entanglement in Soviet affairs, and to prepare for such contingencies as a total breakdown of the Soviet empire as well as for a comeback of the conservative forces determined to maintain the USSR by force.

Poland's approach to Moscow shows its anxiety over the future of the Soviet state and its hesitation to take the end of the cold war for granted. In Poland's view, the division of Europe cannot be erased within a year or two: the Helsinki process is welcomed, but it is weak and may become another League of Nations. As a consequence, Poland became the only East European state seriously interested in retaining the Warsaw Pact's political structure until an all-European security system is well established. (RFE/RL, *Daily Report*, no. 129 [10 July]; *WP*, 22 March.)

This unexpected Polish-Soviet thaw at the beginning of the year may explain Polish sluggishness in dealing decisively with the issue of the Soviet troops deployed on Polish territory. Both the Polish and the Soviet governments expressed the opinion that these troops should leave Poland and that due to their size (58,000 troops stationed in 35 garrisons located in seventeen *voivodships* [*Żołnierz rzeczypospolitej*, 9 May]), the Soviet armed forces cannot play a meaningful role in domestic politics. The timing of the Soviet withdrawal was not on the agenda until the

end of the year. The Polish position was summarized in a statement of the National Defense Committee, which "considered these matters in light of the as-yet-unclear new system of European security. The withdrawal of Soviet forces from our country should be coordinated with the developing international situation." (Warsaw Television Service, 13 March; *FBIS-EEU*, 14 March.) At the end of the year Poland proposed that the Russians should leave within twelve months' time but discovered that Moscow had already created its own five-year timetable.

Events taking place in the USSR brought in focus Poland's dilemma vis-à-vis the Soviet empire. Poland's long-term aspiration is full membership in the European Community (EC), with the expectation of becoming an associate member in a few years and a member in ten years. But this ambition presents the Poles with a choice of either building a Berlin Wall along its eastern border or of playing a role in Soviet politics. This second option, however, presupposes that Poland has decided either to ally itself with the Russians against the western republics of the USSR or to promote the political aspirations of Lithuanians, Ukrainians, and the White Russians against Moscow.

Unresolved domestic disputes in the USSR pushed Poland to search for good relations with the central government in Moscow and the simultaneous improvement of bilateral ties with the Soviet republics. In this way, Poland was trying to promote the idea of converting the USSR into a loose confederation of sovereign republics linked together by common defense and foreign policies. As a confederation, the future Soviet Union would retain enough vitality to counterbalance the newly reunited Germany, but as a highly decentralized state the USSR would lose its capacity to mobilize for imperial pursuits outside its own borders.

Complete disintegration of the Soviet Union into independent states would promote instability in the region and have an adverse impact on Poland's security. Unrestrained by Moscow, these newly created states might exhibit quarrelsome international tendencies, plus the entire region east of Poland might fall under German influence.

Poland's economic impoverishment is not seen in Warsaw as a serious handicap to an active foreign policy. Its central geographic location on the European continent guarantees relevance in regional equilibrium; in the "new Europe," Poland finds itself between two economic and military giants. The Poles would like to model their foreign policy on de Gaulle's intensely nationalistic postwar France, a country that became a great power and achieved reconciliation with Germany despite its relative economic weakness.

Among its top foreign policy objectives, Poland counts on improving and expanding Polish-American security cooperation in Europe. Because France is likely to continue its somewhat anti-U.S. stance and because a united Germany will be tempted to search for balance between Washington and Moscow, Warsaw hopes to be recognized as a valuable European partner of the United States.

Poland is firmly in favor of the North Atlantic Treaty Organization (NATO), the only guarantee of a U.S. presence in Europe and the principal constraint on German and Russian nationalism. According to Foreign Minister Krzysztof Skubiszewski, Poland's foreign policy has moved away from that of a "satellite country" into a stance worthy of an "independent country" and thus has the right to voice its own foreign policy preferences. (RFE/RL, *Daily Report*, no. 66 [3 April].) Return of sovereignty means that

> the conditions for entangling Poland in some global conflict no longer exist. Earlier, while this country pursued a bloc policy and had extremely strong ties to Soviet Union, such a threat did exist, if only in the form of a retaliatory strike—following a Soviet attack—against Poland by NATO. (*Żołnierz rzeczypospolitej*, 6 September; *JPRS-EEU*, 16 October.)

Normalization of relations with a united Germany dominated Poland's diplomatic activities in 1990. Warsaw advanced the idea of Polish participation in talks on the unification of Germany and received support from the governments of East Germany, the USSR, and France. The Poles had feared an ambiguous settlement of the Polish-German border issue that would leave Poland to face Germany without the assistance of the great powers. Renewed attention to the border issue was prompted by Chancellor Kohl's initial evasion in pledging respect for the Oder-Neisse line before Germany's unification. The Poles felt that only war could bring about territorial changes in Europe and emphasized that there is a direct linkage between the Oder-Neisse border and peace on the entire continent. This policy mobilized public opinion in Europe against Kohl's stance and put pressure on the most conservative constituencies in Germany to recognize postwar borders as a condition of international support for reunification. (*NYT*, 21 February.)

In addition, Poland was determined to avoid having its borders again defined by superpowers as had happened during the Second World War. Although Poland failed to secure a permanent place at the "2+4" talks, it was invited to discuss the Polish-German territorial issues. Both German governments pledged to conclude without delay a treaty between a united Germany and Poland and to recognize the Oder-Neisse line as a permanent legal border between two sovereign states. (*CSM*, 19 July.)

This commitment was not contingent on solving any other aspect of mutual relations, however, such as the issue of the approximately 300,000 ethnic Germans living in Poland (*NYT*, 9 March). Nor did it influence the Polish demand that Germany pay up to $284.6 billion in compensation to the victims or their heirs of the Nazis' crimes and slave labor policies in Poland during World War II (*WSJ*, 7 March).

The Polish-German border treaty was signed in Warsaw on 14 November 1990. Key provisions of the treaty are included in Articles 2 and 3:

> The parties to the treaty declare that the border existing between them is inviolable now and in the future and undertake to respect each other's sovereignty and territorial integrity without restriction.
>
> The parties to the treaty declare that they have no territorial claims whatsoever against each other and will not assert such claims in the future. (Warsaw Domestic Service, 14 November; *FBIS-EEU*, 15 November.)

Poland's principal concession to the Germans was admitting that territorial changes after the Second World War resulted in "the great suffering . . . , particularly the loss of . . . homes suffered by numerous Germans and Poles." But speaking to the German audience Poland's foreign minister, Krzysztof Skubiszewski, noted that

> I am sorry that it came to this as the result of the war. Poland did not want this war. Our borders were determined at Yalta by the three great powers. Poland was not present at Yalta, but we also accepted large losses of territory in the East, Polish losses. (Hamburg, DPA, 14 November; *FBIS-EEU*, 15 November.)

Thus ended the most recent round in more than a thousand years of Polish-German relations. Since September 1939, the country had suffered millions of casualties under combined Nazi and Soviet occupations but in the end succeeded in preserving its national identity, its cultural values, its pro-Western orientation, and its place in Europe. Put simply, Poland was a victor in the cold war and joined the community of independent European nations. During his 1990 visit to Poland, West German president Richard von Weizsäcker assured the Poles that

> Today's western border of Poland remains untouched. We respect it and do not have now or in the future any territorial claims against Poland or any other neighbor.
>
> Between Poles and Germans, however, as in all of Europe, the aim is not to recognize borders so that they can better divide us from one another. Quite the contrary: they should lose their dividing character. Borders should become bridges. We do not want to tear down the Berlin Wall in order to build it anew on the Oder and Neisse. (Hamburg, DPA, 2 May; *FBIS-EEU*, 3 May.)

Poland's relations with its eastern neighbors were complicated by the two-tier approach of the Soviet empire and by the unresolved status of such issues as the fate of Poles in the USSR, the Polish debt to the USSR, and the still not fully resolved problem of the Katyń Forest massacre of World War II. In April, the Sejm of the Polish Republic adopted a resolution on Katyń stating that

> the Polish nation and state are interested in friendly relations with the Soviet Union. They can develop only on a foundation of truth. That is precisely why the Sejm of the Republic is convinced that the Government of the Soviet Union, after the statement on the Katyń crime, will also clarify other, previously unexplained issues and will address the problem of compensation. The whole truth about the past will be a reason for hope, understanding, and reconciliation for Poles. (Warsaw Domestic Service, 28 April; *FBIS-EEU*, 30 April.)

Polish authorities expect Soviet assistance in determining the location of other places where Polish officers were murdered. To date, only the Katyń Forest near Smolensk has been identified as the place where Soviet internal security forces executed more than four thousand Polish nationals. Now, after 50 years of denials, the Soviet Union has assumed responsibility for this crime but so far has shown little inclination to identify places where another eleven thousand Polish officers were murdered.

A similar lack of cooperation on the part of the Soviets has characterized Poland's attempt to reach Poles living in the USSR. Those living in the western republics of the USSR are usually well informed about political developments taking place in Poland, including the opportunity to return, but the Poles living in some remote districts of the Soviet empire have limited access to such information. More than one and a half million Polish citizens were deported into work camps in Siberia and Kazakhstan, and few were allowed to return. The Polish government is now seeking to open a consulate in Kazakhstan to assist Polish nationals in maintaining their Polish identity and supporting those trying to return. (*Życie Warszawy*, 22 January.)

Negative attitudes toward Russians are prevalent in Poland, with various public opinion polls showing that only 21 percent of Poles claim to like Russians (*Rzeczpospolita*, 11–12 August). Anti-Russian feelings were amplified by Soviet troops stationed in Poland and their disregard for Polish law. Most frequent violations include soil contamination, hardships involved with operating the Soviet military airports, violations of Polish airspace, disregarding the rules on forests and game laws, robberies, frequent car collisions, and Soviet attacks on the Polish population. The greatest resentment centers on the large subsidies provided by Poland for the Soviet troops. The legal status of the Soviet troops stationed in Poland was first defined by the 1956 agreement between both governments on the "temporary" deployment of Soviet troops on Polish territory. The newly concluded follow-up agreement addressed these issues and established an office of a government plenipotentiary attached to the Soviet troops in Poland. (*Żołnierz rzeczypospolitej*, 9 May.)

Little progress, however, has been achieved in negotiating a Soviet withdrawal from Poland. The Polish side would like the Russians to leave no later than 31 December 1991, but Moscow demands more time to provide logistic support for its forces stationed in former East Germany. A related but more complicated issue is the transit through Poland of the Soviet forces returning from Germany to the USSR. Close to 400,000 heavily armed troops and their families, about 1 million people, are expected to cross Polish territory, creating the danger of confrontation with the Polish population, roadblocks, and serious damages to the transportation systems in Poland. (*Życie Warszawy*, 30 November.)

The stationing of Soviet troops has had an emotional and symbolic meaning for the Poles, who view the Russians as an invading force. At the end of the year the Polish government adopted a firm attitude on a speedy Soviet withdrawal, but for practical reasons it focused attention on the political status of the Soviet army in Poland and on the question of damages caused by the Soviet military presence. Meanwhile, Polish sources emphasize that membership in the EC is by no means contingent on the removal of the Soviet armed forces from the Polish territory; the Poles may have to wait until the German troop evacuation is completed and coordinate the Soviet departure with cutbacks in the Bundeswehr.

Development of relations between Poland and its immediate neighbors to the east assumed a form of "understandings" between "sovereign states" without the establishment of diplomatic relations. Both Polish-Ukrainian and Polish-Lithuanian agreements specified that the countries involved have no territorial claims on each other. In addition, both demonstrate a willingness of the Soviet republics to pursue independent foreign policies. Only Belorussia has refused to conclude such a treaty with Poland, claiming rights to some provinces in northeastern Poland. (BBC-CARIS Talk no. 252/90.)

In other matters, diplomatic relations between Poland and Israel were resumed for the first time since the 1967 war in the Middle East (NYT, 28 February). This diplomatic breakthrough was followed by a stance adopted by the Senate of the Republic on the 1968 anti-Semitic campaign that stated that the Polish citizens of Jewish descent were the main target of this anti-intellectual and anti-academic campaign, "a tool in the struggle that was being waged within the ruling communist camp, but the odium prompted by those shameful deeds and injustices affected all of Polish society, and caused great political and moral harm to the Polish nation and state." The Senate "expressed profound regret over the disgraceful excesses" and invited individuals expelled to "return to the republic, which is now the fatherland of all who have links with Poland." (Gazeta wyborcza, 5 March.)

The improvement of mutual relations received further encouragement after Poland opened its borders to the Soviet Jews escaping from the USSR for Israel. Poland offered to fly Soviet Jews from Warsaw to Israel after Malev, the Hungarian airline, terminated such flights for fear of terrorism. Speaking at an American Jewish Congress dinner, Prime Minister Mazowiecki explained that "just as in the Middle Ages, Poland gave refuge to Jews fleeing persecution, so today Poland will not evade humanitarian assistance to Jews emigrating from the Soviet Union." (NYT, 27 March.) The Poles, however, have a long way to go before the perception of anti-Semitism no longer taints Poland's international image and obscures domestic issues.

Throughout the year there was a steady improvement in Polish-U.S. relations. In February, Lech Wałęsa addressed a joint session of the U.S. Congress, and later Prime Minister Mazowiecki arrived for a visit to Washington. Poland has satisfied four basic preconditions set up by the United States to qualify for U.S. economic assistance. Under the policy of a "new democratic differentiation" each East European state is expected to demonstrate:

• Progress toward political pluralism, based on free and fair elections and an end to the monopoly of the communist party.
• Progress toward economic reform, based on the emergence of a market-oriented economy with a substantial private sector.
• Enhanced respect for internationally recognized human rights, including the right to emigrate and to speak and travel freely.
• A willingness on the part of each of these countries to build a friendly relationship with the United States. (Focus on Central and Eastern Europe, no. 26 [19 October].)

Respect for human rights qualified Poland for $227.5 million in cash assistance and a $1 billion stabilization fund to support the convertibility of the złoty (NYT, 1 February). These grants were independent from support advanced by the International Monetary Fund and the World Bank.

Also, the federal, state, local government, and private institutions in the United States formulated a vast array of programs to address particular needs in Poland. The most significant, perhaps, is the U.S.-Polish initiative in military matters. On 4 December, U.S. defense secretary Richard Cheney visited Warsaw to discuss closer military ties, Polish interest in purchasing F-16 fighters, and sending Polish officers to study in the United States. (Warsaw, PAP, 4 December; FBIS-EEU, 5 December.) A definitive U.S. decision with respect to these requests is not likely to be made before the end of the gulf crisis, but the door to military cooperation is clearly open.

The balance sheet of the first full year of democracy in Poland includes several reasons for optimism. Progress toward democracy was marked by two unfettered elections and remarkable political stability despite economic hardship. Democracy may not as yet have become a way of life in Poland, but encouraging experience with democratic institutions has strengthened public confidence in self-government and decreased frustration with democratic procedures.

Economically, for the time being the country succeeded in curbing inflation and eliminating the dollar's black market exchange rate. The second stage of the economic recovery program is already under way, designed to create conditions to invigorate the economy without setting off new hyperinflation. Commercialization of the large state enterprises has reached a takeoff stage and is expected to proceed without delays during the next year. These structural changes should be expedited by new credits, and Poland is cautiously optimistic that reduction of its foreign debt is only a matter of time. Preconditions for turning these assets into economic prosperity are already in place.

In the area of foreign affairs, Poland took an active part in the "2+4" talks over the future of Germany and settled the issue of the Polish-German border in a treaty with a united Germany. This places Poland among the key international players in Europe. Reorientation of Poland's foreign policy from East to West is being achieved without a serious strain on Polish-Soviet relations and has resulted in the improvement of Polish-German ties. Poland's leading role in dismantling decades of communism is an inspiring accomplishment.

Arthur R. Rachwald
U.S. Naval Academy

Romania

Population. 23,273,285
Party. National Salvation Front (Frontul Salvarii Nationale, NSF)
Founded. 22 December 1989. The NSF came into existence at the time of the overthrow of Nicolae Ceauşescu, the former president of Romania and general secretary of the Romanian Communist Party (Partidul Comunist Român, RCP).
Membership. No official figures have been published on NSF membership or its ethnic and socioeconomic composition. Visitors returning from Romania in April were told it had a membership of "about 1,000,000." (Vladimir V. Kusin, "How Many Communists Now?" RFE, *Report on Eastern Europe* 1, no. 30 [7 September].) Although the NSF denies that it is the successor to the RCP, it has inherited a significant portion of the former party's membership, many of its leaders, and most of its assets. Just before the overthrow of Ceauşescu in November 1989, the RCP had a membership of 3,813,000, as reported at the Fourteenth RCP Congress (*Scînteia*, 21 November 1989).
Party Leadership. On 29 December 1989, Ion Iliescu was formally named chairman of the NSF just one week after the group came into existence. Iliescu remained chairman of the party until shortly after his election as president of Romania on 20 May. On 5 July he resigned as party chairman in keeping with the requirement that the country's president be politically neutral. During the year, no new NSF chairman was chosen. Two first deputy chairmen of the NSF continue to serve in these positions: Nicolae S. Dumitru, a former professor of Marxism at the Bucharest Higher School of Construction, and Claudiu Iordache, who was never a member of the RCP. Other prominent leaders of the NSF who continue to hold positions in the Romanian government are Prime Minister Petre Roman and Dan Marţian, who was named secretary of the NSF on 29 December 1989 and elected chairman of the Assembly of Deputies (the lower house of the Romanian Parliament) on 18 June.
Opposition Parties. Some 80 political parties participated in the elections of 20 May 1990, but most are small organizations of little importance. The two major opposition parties are the Liberal Party and the National Peasant Party/Christian Democracy. The Hungarian Democratic Federation of Romania, an organization of Romanian citizens of ethnic Hungarian nationality, does not consider itself a political party, although it received the second-highest number of votes in the parliamentary elections. In August, after the overwhelming victory of the NSF in the May elections, segments of the National Peasant Party, the National Liberal Party, the Social Democratic Party, the Hungarian Democratic Federation, and several other groups

established the Democratic Antitotalitarian Forum (DAF) in an effort to unite the opposition against the NSF. The DAF is linked with the institutionalized or parliamentary opposition. The Civil Alliance, an umbrella organization of the noninstitutionalized or extraparliamentary opposition, was established in November. Although the DAF and the Civic Alliance have much in common, significant differences in their philosophical outlook have prevented the two from forming a united opposition.

Status. From 1948 until 31 December 1989, the RCP was the only legal political party in Romania. Following the overthrow and execution of Nicolae Ceauşescu, the provisional government (the Council of the National Salvation Front) issued a decree on 31 December 1989 permitting the operation of political parties. Although the NSF continues to be the dominant political force in the country, other political parties continue to function.

Last Congress. The NSF has not yet held a party congress. The first conference was held in Bucharest 7–10 April 1990, although the organization came into existence on 22 December 1989.

Last Elections. On 20 May 1990 elections were held for the president of Romania and for members of the restructured bicameral parliament. The election campaign and the results of the voting are discussed at greater length below.

Publications. *Adevărul* (formerly the RCP daily *Scînteia*), *Dimineaţa*, and *Azi*, NSF-controlled dailies; *România Liberă*, independent daily (formerly the RCP political front organization's daily of the same name); *Dreptatea*, daily of the National Peasant Party/Christian Democracy; *Liberalul*, daily of the Liberal Party. *Adevărul*, *Dimineaţa*, *Azi*, and *România Liberă* are national mass-circulation newspapers. *Democraţia* is a political weekly (formerly *Munca de Partid*, the RCP Central Committee weekly); *Viaţa Capiţalei* is a Bucharest-oriented cultural weekly (formerly *Săptămâna*); and *Lumea Azi* is a foreign affairs weekly (formerly *Lumea*, the RCP foreign affairs weekly). Rompres is the Romanian telegraphic agency.

Political Evolution of the NSF. *NSF becomes the provisional government after the collapse of the Ceauşescu regime.*

The NSF announced that it was assuming power as the provisional government of Romania on 22 December 1989, the day Nicolae Ceauşescu fled Bucharest. There was no indication that the NSF existed before the uprising against Ceauşescu, although claims were later made that clandestine groups involving some of its leaders had been active well before the December revolution. On the evening of 22 December, Ion Iliescu, who was later given the title president of the NSF, read a communiqué from the NSF announcing that "all power structures of the Ceauşescu clan have been dissolved. The government is dismissed. The State Council and its institutions are ceasing activity. All state power has been assumed by the Council of the National Salvation Front."

The program presented by the NSF called for abandoning "the leading role of a single party"; free elections in April; separate legislative, executive, and judicial powers; limited terms for government officials; changing the country's name from the Socialist Republic of Romania to Romania; drafting a new constitution; restructuring the national economy "in accordance with the criteria of profitability and efficiency"; a return to small-scale peasant production; redirection of education along democratic and humanistic lines, eliminating "ideological dogmas"; "observing the rights and freedoms of national minorities and ensuring their full equality with Romanians"; reorganizing trade to satisfy the daily needs of the population, including an end to the export of domestically scarce foodstuffs and oil products; observance of Romania's international commitments, "primarily those to the Warsaw Pact"; and promoting domestic and foreign policies that are subordinate to the interests of the people, including the "complete observance of human rights and freedoms, including the right to free movement" (Radio Bucharest, 22 December 1989; see also Dan Ionescu, "The National Salvation Front Starts to Implement Its Program," RFE, *Report on Eastern Europe* 1, no. 5 [2 February]).

The leaders of the NSF and the government they appointed were a self-designated group. Although NSF councils were subsequently established throughout Romania at the local level, the national council in Bucharest was established first; the local organizations developed later to replace the local RCP organizations and the RCP-led Socialist Democratic and Unity Front. The initial leadership of the NSF was a combination of prominent former communists who had fallen out of favor with Ceauşescu, dissident intellectuals and human rights activists, and military officers who supported the anti-Ceauşescu forces during the revolution.

The NSF, which took over much of the structure of the disintegrating RCP, quickly emerged as the leading political force in the country. The NSF was initially welcomed, but its autocratic method of operation and the large number of former communists in its ranks quickly raised popular doubts about its commmitment to democracy and reform. The NSF soon was perceived as the successor to the RCP (*NYT*, 8 January; *CSM*, 10 January).

The NSF becomes a political party. On 31 December 1989, just a few days after the NSF assumed control of the government, it issued a decree on the registration and operation of political parties in preparation for democratic, multiparty elections initially scheduled for April 1990 (Radio Bucharest, 31 December 1989). Within days of the collapse of the Ceauşescu regime, a series of new political parties were established, many claiming descent from historical Romanian parties that had been forcibly abolished in 1948.

When it came into existence, the NSF announced that it would serve only as an interim government until free elections could be held. On 23 January, however, just a month after the NSF came to power, NSF spokesman Silviu Brucan announced a reversal of policy: the front would run candidates in the election and would not disband after elections as it originally promised. At the time the announcement was made, the NSF made an effort to placate the emerging political parties by meeting a number of their demands. First, the NSF agreed to their request to postpone elections by one month to give them additional time to organize. The election date was set for 20 May. Second, the NSF invited the United Nations to send an observer team to monitor the campaign and the voting. Third, the NSF Council voted to convene a roundtable with representatives of the new political parties to agree on ground rules for the election (Radio Bucharest, Rompres, 23 January; *NYT*, 24 January; *WP*, 26 January; AFP, 31 January).

A fire storm of protest followed the announcement that the NSF would field candidates in the election. The National Peasant, National Liberal, and Social Democratic parties, the most important of the emerging political parties, called the NSF decision to participate in the elections an "abuse of power." Doina Cornea and Dumitru Mazilu, leading dissidents during the Ceauşescu era and members of the NSF Council, and the poet Ana Blandiana resigned in protest. Two thousand Romanians staged a mass demonstration at the front's offices in Bucharest, accusing the NSF of using communist tactics and charging that it had simply replaced the old one-party state with a new one. A few days later another rally of an estimated twenty thousand people continued the protest. The NSF responded by issuing a decree severely restricting all public demonstrations. The new regulations were protested by the opposition parties and by the U.S. government. A few days later the NSF, ignoring its new regulations, staged a mass rally in Bucharest that it swelled with tens of thousands of workers who were bussed in from factories and paid to participate in the rally. (*România Liberă*, 26 January, 1 February; Rompres, 24 January; [Paris] *Libération*, 29 January; *WP*, 25, 27 January; *NYT*, 27, 29, 30, 31 January, 1, 8 February.)

On 6 February, the NSF officially registered as a political party and unveiled its political program for the upcoming elections. The program endorsed political pluralism, a free market approach to economic reform, freedom of speech and religion, and protection of rights for ethnic minorities. The front also announced that its candidate for president would be Ion Iliescu (Rompres, 6 February).

NSF assumes leadership of the provisional Council of National Unity. The wave of popular unrest that accompanied the NSF decision to become a political party required some structural changes in Romania's provisional government. The Council of the National Salvation Front, which had been the provisional government since shortly after the collapse of the Ceauşescu regime, was formally replaced by the provisional Council of National Unity. The council, established under terms of an agreement reached on 1 February between the NSF and the emerging political parties, was to be composed of "active participants in the [December] revolution," scientific and cultural figures, workers, peasants, intellectuals, young people and students, representatives of the national minorities, and representatives of the counties. The body was to have 180 members, with half to belong to the political parties and the other half to the NSF (Rompres, 1 February).

After its first session on 9 February, it became clear that the NSF still dominated the new provisional government. Each of the 37 political parties received three representatives on the new council, whereas the NSF received 112 seats. Furthermore, most of the county representatives selected were NSF supporters. When the composition of the council finally emerged, as many as two-thirds of the 250-member body were front supporters. The newly emerging political parties were quick to criticize the continued leading role of the NSF in the provisional council. (Rompres, 9 February; Radio Bucharest, 10 February; *NYT*, 4, 5, 11 February; see also Michael Shafir, "The Provisional Council of National Unity: Is History Repeating Itself?" RFE, *Report on Eastern Europe* 1, no. 9 [2 March].)

Signs of dissatisfaction with the NSF multiplied. A number of prominent leaders of the NSF resigned. Intellectuals and dissidents who had associated themselves with the NSF in the aftermath of the December revolution quit as the NSF consolidated its position using tactics and personnel associated with the discredited RCP. (*NYT*, 4, 8 February; *LAT*, 5 February.) Mass popular demonstrations against the NSF demanded the resignations of the ministers of defense and internal affairs; ultimately they were forced to resign because of their previous association with the Ceauşescu regime (*NYT*, 15, 16, 17, 18, 19 February). Mass protests continued, with demonstrators occupying government buildings and NSF headquarters and demanding the ouster of Iliescu. Although the emerging political parties contributed to the unrest, they were more the beneficiaries of the wave of anti-NSF sentiment than the cause of it. There was genuine national concern that the NSF was simply replacing the RCP as the single ruling party.

The NSF sought to bring the situation under control with a number of steps. First, there was an effort to demonstrate that individuals associated with the Ceauşescu regime would be removed from office. The dismissal of the defense and interior ministers, who had contributed to the success of the December revolution but were linked with the Ceauşescu regime, was an important element in this effort. Second, the hated Securitate (secret police) was disbanded and its functions given to the Defense Ministry. (Previously it had been part of the Interior Ministry.) The new defense minister announced that an agency to assure national security would be organized along the lines of the U.S. Federal Bureau of Investigation. Some three thousand Securitate officers were put on reserve duty, a number of officers were placed under arrest, and investigations were said to be under way involving some 70,000 former Securitate personnel (*NYT*, 22 February). Third, the government proceeded quickly with a few show trials of some of the leading villains to show that efforts were being made to eliminate Ceauşescu holdovers. At the same time that the change was made in defense and interior ministers, it was announced in Cluj that two former

Securitate officers had been sentenced to nineteen years in prison for serious crimes; a few days later a major trial of 21 Securitate officers began in Timişoara (Rompres, 22 February, 2 March; *NYT*, 3 March). Fourth, the provisional council adopted regulations to protect government buildings from public demonstrations and to allow police officials to control protesters.

The new policies, however, were not successful in controlling the demonstrations. Anti-NSF demonstrators continued to protest regularly in Bucharest. In April, opposition leaders, principally intellectuals and students, began a long-term protest demonstration at University Square in Bucharest to challenge and publicize the government's "neocommunist" policies and personnel. During this time, the NSF organized its own rallies to show its support, although the pro-NSF demonstrations were government-organized affairs reminiscent of those of the Ceauşescu era. In February, the NSF brought some three thousand miners from the Jiu Valley to Bucharest by train for such a support rally. This was the second time the government had called the miners to Bucharest to help it put down opposition protests. Because the government had doubled the miners' wages, improved their working conditions, and provided transportation to Bucharest for the rallies, the miners were willing to support the government (*NYT*, 20 February).

The opposition parties. Among the first actions of the provisional government after Ceauşescu's overthrow in December 1989 was to call for an election with the participation of multiple political parties. Within a week of Ceauşescu's death, a decree law on the registration and operation of political parties was issued by the NSF. The provisions of the law, however, were ambiguously worded to permit government limitations on the right of opposition parties to function, permitting the formation of political parties with the exception of "fascist parties or parties propounding ideas that run counter to state order." The law also specified that political activity must be "predicated on respect for national independence, sovereignty, and territorial integrity" and must "affirm the nation's dignity." These phrases have no precise legal meaning and could easily be used to hamper legitimate political activity if the government should wish to do so. (Rompres, 31 December 1989; *România Liberă*, 4 January.)

The process of establishing political parties was under way even before the decree law was promulgated on the operation of parties. On 26 December 1989 a number of pre-1947 party leaders and prominent human rights activists reestablished the National Peasant Party, which had been Romania's largest interwar political party. It had won an estimated 70 percent of the vote in the last free election in Romania in 1946 but was outlawed by the communist government in 1947. The party merged with the Christian Democratic Youth Movement, which had sprung up among a segment of university students within a few days of Ceaușescu's overthrow. The youth movement had intended to establish a Romanian Christian Democratic Party, but the National Peasant leadership convinced the youth group that the two shared the same goals. Thus the Christian Democratic Youth Movement became the youth wing of the National Peasant Party. Another group to merge with the party was the Christian National Peasant Party, which was founded on 22 December 1989. The party was renamed the National Peasant Party/Christian Democracy after the two mergers and began publishing a daily newspaper, *Dreptatea* (Justice), on 7 February. The party's program focused principally on rural concerns—establishing a market economy, distributing land to individual peasants, greater investment and government support for agriculture, separating church and state (but reinstituting religion as a subject of study in schools and universities), reestablishing Christian values in society, recognizing workers' rights including the right to strike, and equal rights for ethnic minorities and all religious groups. (For the party program, see *Adevărul*, 27 January, and *Dreptatea*, 14 April.)

On 31 December 1989, the Liberal Party, Romania's oldest political party, was reestablished at a conference of former party members and younger sympathizers. The Liberal Party had previously governed longer than any other party and had given Romania some of its most prominent political leaders. Although the party had been disbanded by force in 1948, some of its previous leaders continued to live in Romania, and toward the end of the Ceaușescu era some had made occasional protest statements. The Liberal program called for decollectivization of agriculture, private ownership of land and industry, trade union rights including the right to strike, respect for human rights and equal rights for all national minorities, separation of church and state, and resumption of traditional ties with Western Europe. (For this party program, see *Adevărul*, 12 January.) The party also resumed publication of *Liberalul* (The liberal), its daily newspaper, which had been forcibly closed in 1947.

The Social Democratic Party was a small but respected party in pre-1948 Romania. In 1948 the party merged with the RCP, and most of its leaders were promptly pushed aside. A group of anticommunist social democrats, trade union members, and youth reestablished this party shortly after the December revolution. The focus of the party's program was on the establishment of parliamentary democracy and a market economy, use of experts in economic management, free trade unions with the right to strike, and improvement of social and economic benefits for society. (For this party program, see *Adevărul*, 6 February.)

There were 82 political parties established in the five months between Ceaușescu's death and the elections, but most of them were small groups that focused on a particular ideological issue or a particular individual leader. After the elections, another twenty political parties were officially registered. (Rompres, 24 April, 17 August; *NYT*, 3 February; *WP*, 4 February; Vladimir Socor, "Political Parties Emerging," RFE, *Report on Eastern Europe* 1, no. 7 [16 February].)

The election campaign. The elections, which were set for 20 May, were to select the president and members of Parliament. Only three parties nominated candidates for the presidency. The NSF nominated Ion Iliescu, a former RCP official who had fallen out of favor with Ceaușescu and held a minor position in the regime for the previous decade and a half. The Liberal Party nominated Radu Câmpeanu, who was imprisoned under the communists and been in exile in Paris for the previous seventeen years. The National Peasant Party nominated Ion Ratiu, who had spent the last four decades in exile in London, where he became a wealthy businessman. (For a summary of the positions of the three candidates, see the debate of the presidential candidates, Radio Bucharest, 17 May, 19:10 Greenwich Mean Time.) The new Parliament was a bicameral body, unlike the unicameral Grand National Assembly of the Ceaușescu era. The elections were to select 396 members of the Assembly of Deputies, or lower house, and 119 members of the newly created Senate. The principal task for the Parliament is preparing a new Romanian constitution. The three major parties fielded candidates for most seats in the Parliament, but in addition some 80 political parties ran candidates for parliamentary seats.

As the parties organized to contest the elections, they requested and were granted a one-month extension to better prepare. Once the NSF decided to participate in the elections, however, the political parties and the NSF became involved immediately in controversy and countercharges. The democratic parties were handicapped by a serious lack of resources with which to conduct the campaign, whereas the NSF took over most of the organizations, much of the personnel, and the resources of the RCP. The democratic parties were given only limited and strictly controlled access to the news media, whereas the NSF controlled the media. (*CSM*, 10, 18 May; interview with Vladimir Fulger, vice-president of the Christian Democratic Union, *România Liberă*, 30 March; Crisula Ştefănescu, "Romania Radio and Television Coverage of the Election Campaign," RFE, *Report on Eastern Europe* 1, no. 23 [8 June].)

Furthermore, as the election day drew closer, the campaign became increasingly violent. Although the NSF was quick to accuse its political opponents of abuses and violence, it was clear that the NSF allowed, encouraged, and possibly even organized a campaign of intimidation against the democratic parties. There were reports that gangs of NSF thugs prevented opposition parties from establishing local offices. The presidential candidates running against Ion Iliescu seemed personally targeted for much of the violence. Raţiu and Câmpeanu were subject to mobbing, harassment of family members, at least one alleged murder attempt, and other types of intimidation. The opposition parties issued a joint statement criticizing the "climate of violence" and threatening to boycott the elections unless the harassment and intimidation ceased (Bucharest, AFP, 9 May). Acting President and NSF presidential candidate Ion Iliescu described the joint statement as "an insolent ultimatum," and Prime Minister Petre Roman claimed to have been the subject of death threats, which he blamed on the opposition parties. The NSF-controlled mass media also systematically slandered the democratic parties and their presidential candidates. The U.S. State Department publicly condemned the violence and slander in the election campaign, eventually recalled the U.S. ambassador to Washington for consultations to protest the violence, and warned Romania of the consequences for future relations and assistance. (*NYT*, 28 April, 1, 7, 8, 14, 20 May; *WP*, 20 May; Dan Ionescu, "Violence and Calumny in the Election Campaign," RFE, *Report on Eastern Europe* 1, no. 21 [25 May].)

Table 1: Results of the 20 May 1990 Parliamentary Elections

Party	Number of Seats Assembly of Deputies	Senate
National Salvation Front	263	92
Hungarian Democratic Federation	29	12
Liberal Party	29	9
National Peasant Party	12	1
Romanian Ecological Movement	12	1
Alliance for Unity of Romanians	9	2
Democratic Agrarian Party	9	–
Romanian Ecological Party	8	1
Independent	–	1
Romanian Social Democratic Party	5	–
Social Democratic Party of Romania	2	–
Labor Democratic Party	1	–
Free Exchange Party	1	–
National Reconstruction Party	1	–
Free Democratic Youth Party	1	–
"Bratianu" Liberal Union	1	–
German Democratic Forum	1	–
Romanies' (Gypsy) Democratic Forum	1	–
Ethnic representation for nine nationalities	9	–
Total	**396**	**119**

Election results. Under these conditions, the results of the election were predictable. In the presidential race, NSF candidate Iliescu received an overwhelming majority—85.1 percent of the votes cast. Liberal candidate Câmpeanu received 10.6 percent, and National Peasant candidate Raţiu received 4.3 percent.

In the parliamentary elections voting was on the basis of party lists as well as voting for individual candidates. Seats were allocated according to proportional representation within electoral districts. The NSF also won overwhelmingly in both the Senate and the Assembly of Deputies. The Hungarian Democratic Federation of Romania, an alliance of Romanians of ethnic Hungarian nationality, came in a distant second in the vote, while the Liberal Party came in third and the National Peasant Party came in fourth. Nine seats in the Assembly of Deputies were allocated to specified national minorities that failed to win representation in the open voting (see table 1). Those minorities allocated a representative were the Armenians, Bulgarians, Serbs, Lippovan, Czechs and Slovaks, Greeks, Poles, Ukrainians, Turks, and Tatars. (Rompres, 25 May; *Adevărul*, 26 May; *Dimineaţa*, 27 May; Mihai Berindei and Ariadna Combes, "An Analysis of the Romanian Elections," *Uncaptive Minds*, August-September-October; Vladimir V. Kusin, "The Elections Compared and Assessed," RFE, *Report on Eastern Europe* 1, no. 28 [13 July]; Vladimir Socor, "National Salvation Front Produces Electoral Landslide," RFE, *Report on Eastern Europe* 1, no. 27 [6 July].)

Political observers both inside and outside Romania acknowledged that the results of the elections were not an accurate reflection of the balance of political forces in Romania. Although the NSF received three-quarters of the seats in Parliament and won the presidential contest with 85 percent of the vote, there was still strong opposition to the NSF. A number of questions were raised about fraud in the election, and Western correspondents suggested irregularities in the voting process. Western observers in Romania for the voting called the election generally valid, but they were critical of the unfair advantages the NSF held throughout the campaign through its control and manipulation of the media. Ultimately, however, even the U.S. State Department declared the vote valid despite these "flaws." (*LAT*, 22 May; AP, Reuters, 21, 22, 23 May; *WP*, 20, 23 May; *NYT*, 21, 22, 25, 26 May.)

Government-inspired violence against protesters. Just three weeks after the elections, even before the swearing in of the new president and the formation of a new government, Iliescu and the NSF encouraged violent clashes with antigovernment demonstrators that shocked Romanians and the rest of the world. The violence was the worst since the events of December 1989 when Ceauşescu was overthrown. Since 22 April a peaceful demonstration had been under way in Bucharest's University Square. Shortly after the demonstration began, a number of the protesters began a hunger strike to call attention to their cause. Protesters demanded that all former communist officials be banned for ten years from political office and civic participation. The anticommunist demonstration was clearly intended to criticize the NSF, acting President Ion Iliescu, Prime Minister Petre Roman, and the provisional government because most of them had held responsible positions at one time or another during the Ceauşescu era (*NYT*, 1 May).

In mid-June, the government decided to bring the protest to an end for several reasons. First, the government had shown some restraint during the election campaign and not put down the demonstrations despite its obvious disapproval of the protesters, but when the NSF won a resounding victory in the elections, it was in a strong position to act. Second, Iliescu and most of those in the government had no great commitment to pluralism, freedom, or democracy. Because all those leaders were products of the communist system and because few if any had been part of the democratic or human rights opposition, they were inherently suspicious of pluralism and expressions of opposition against the government. Third, there were indications of dissent within the NSF itself. Silviu Brucan, initially one of the leading figures in the NSF, and other NSF leaders had distanced themselves from Iliescu, and there were signs of other internal problems. Taking action against the demonstrators proved helpful in promoting unity within the NSF.

Government attempts to end the protest. The government engaged in discussions with the protesters' representatives, who demanded the establishment of a television station not under government control, the dismissal of Interior Minister Mihai Chitac for obeying Ceauşescu's orders to open fire on demonstrators in Timişoara in December 1989, and a full disclosure of events before and during the December revolution. The government's initial response was unacceptable to the demonstrators, and on 11 June there were protests outside the government building and the following day outside the main television building. Although the government then offered a positive response, the protesters did not trust its promises and announced that they would continue the demonstrations until the government actually authorized the independent television station.

On 12 June government authorities issued directives for government forces to restore public order in University Square. At 4:00 A.M. on 13 June, truncheon-swinging riot police sealed off University Square with trucks and buses, arrested the demonstrators, and forcibly cleared protesters from the area with electric cattle prods. Later that afternoon, a small group of protesters gathered around the square. A student leader, Marian Munteanu, spoke from the balcony of a university building and called on those present to free demonstrators who had been arrested that morning and were being held at the Bucharest city police headquarters and the Interior Ministry. Eyewitnesses reported that he urged nonviolent protests. Police forces, who could have easily controlled the situation at that time because of the small number of protesters involved, did not act, and the violence began. (The interior minister was dismissed the following day for the police forces' poor performance in controlling the demonstrators.) Seeking to tear down the police cordon, demonstrators then moved from University Square to police headquarters, where they gathered in increasing numbers, seizing the garage and first floor of police headquarters, then moving on to the Interior Ministry where they again attempted to storm the building. Military forces were called in to protect the Interior Ministry building and the surrounding area. The insurgents then marched on the television headquarters, causing considerable damage; reportedly, the head of Romanian television had to be rescued by paratroopers. Substantial evidence shows that the way in which the protests were handled and the approval of certain provocative actions by government forces were calculated to increase the violence and sharpen the conflict. During this time, several hundred people were seriously injured and official statistics reported at least four deaths.

The miners intervene. On the evening of 13 June, Acting President Ion Iliescu made a nationally broadcast speech in which he charged that the legally elected government was in danger of being overthrown by force. He said that country was facing a "legionary rebellion" and called on loyal citizens to come to the aid of the government (Rompres, in English, 13 June; Radio Bucharest, 13 June). His use of the term *legionary rebellion* referred to Romania's Iron Guard (also called the Legion of the Archangel Michael), which was a Fascist influence in Romania before and during World War II. This reflex branding of his opponents as Fascists was the kind of response that would have come from Ceauşescu.

At dawn on the morning of 14 June, some ten thousand miners from the Jiu Valley arrived in Bucharest armed with wooden clubs and wire bludgeons. Their appearance was hardly spontaneous; they had been brought to Bucharest on trains, and substantial evidence exists that they were led by former Securitate officers. The government, however, claimed that the miners had "come of their own will" and that the authorities had not provided transportation or other assistance. The miners' rampage was vicious and brutal. They attacked the demonstrators in the area around University Square, began randomly destroying university facilities, and then began assaulting and beating anyone suspected of opposing the government. Miners went on to ransack and burn the offices of the National Liberal and National Peasant parties (the leading opposition parties) and the homes of party leaders as well. The miners then demanded the closing of the country's only independent mass circulation newspaper, *România Liberă*. Helmeted miners patrolled the center of Bucharest, searched for suspected protesters in tandem with soldiers, and punched, kicked, and bashed with clubs those they found before marching them into waiting police vans. Foreign reporters and camera operators were also attacked and beaten by the miners to stop them from reporting on events. Reports said that more than a thousand Romanian protesters were arrested in the aftermath of the violence, including student leader Marian Munteanu. No miners were arrested. (*NYT*, 14, 15, 16, 18, 19, 20, 22 June; *WP*, 14, 15, 16, 17 June; *CSM*, 18 June; Crisula Ştefănescu, "Marathon Demonstration in Bucharest's University Square," RFE, *Report on Eastern Europe* 1, no. 24 [15 June]; Michael Shafir, "Government Encourages Vigilante Violence in Bucharest," RFE, *Report on Eastern Europe* 1, no. 27 [6 July].)

International outrage. The miners' violence in Bucharest provoked a major outcry from the international community. The White House spokesman said that "the United States condemns in the strongest possible terms . . . the Government-inspired vigilante violence that departs from the commonly accepted norms of democracy and the rule of law." The United States also withheld nonhumanitarian economic aid from Romania, announced that it would not act on Romania's request for most-favored-nation trade status, and sent the U.S. ambassador to Romania to Bucharest with instructions to deliver a high-level protest (*NYT*, *WP*, 15, 16 June). The countries of the European Community (EC) likewise condemned the violence, announced that the EC would postpone signing a trade and economic cooperation agreement that was within days of completion, and decided to exclude Romania from a Western aid package for Eastern Europe (AP, 17 June). Official protests were also made by Great Britain, France, Spain, Sweden, Italy, Switzerland, Canada, Denmark, and Austria, as well as by representatives of other Central and East European countries. Although the Soviet Union reacted less sharply than other countries to the events, Soviet officials and news media were critical of

Romania and characterized the violence as being in the spirit of Ceaușescu (TASS, 15 June; *Pravda*, 18 June; see Mihai Sturdza, "Worldwide Indignation in the Miners' Rampage in Bucharest," RFE, *Report on Eastern Europe* 1, no. 27 [6 July].)

Inauguration of the president. Ion Iliescu was sworn in as president of Romania at a joint session of the newly elected bicameral Parliament on 20 June. This brought an end to nearly six months of the provisional government that had replaced that of Nicolae Ceaușescu. The ceremony was delayed for almost a week because of violence and was marred by its aftermath. The U.S. ambassador to Romania and other diplomats boycotted the ceremony to protest the actions of the miners. On the day of the inauguration, students and professors at Bucharest University started a three-day strike to protest the continued detention of students who were arrested during the police actions against demonstrators.

In his inaugural speech, Iliescu promised free market economic reforms, the rule of law, full recognition of individual and minority rights, and improvements in social protections for the population. He defended the government's use of violence to end protests the previous week but also attempted to distance the government from the miners' violence. This was significant because he had previously warmly praised and thanked the miners for their action. Iliescu noted that the events of the previous week exposed serious weaknesses in the military and law enforcement agencies and called for strengthening the security apparatus and for greater discipline in the armed forces (Radio Bucharest, 20 June; *Adevărul, NYT,* 21 June).

Ion Iliescu is something of an anomaly among the new group of Central and Eastern European leaders who came to power during 1989–1990. He was a prominent communist official under the Ceaușescu regime: from 1967 to 1971, he was minister of youth in the government and concurrently head of the RCP youth organization, and in 1971 he became RCP Central Committee Secretary for ideology but lost that post later that same year, reportedly for disagreeing with a major Ceaușescu ideological initiative. Demoted to Timiş County RCP secretary for propaganda, he was partially rehabilitated by his appointment as Iaşi County RCP first secretary. From 1974 to 1979 he was a candidate member of the RCP Political Executive Committee, and from 1979 to 1984 he was a member of the State Council, the standing presidium of the Romanian Parliament. He once again fell from

favor as a result of one of Ceaușescu's notorious whims and was demoted to the directorship of a technical publishing house in Bucharest. During his political heyday, he acquired a degree of popularity, particularly among members of the intelligentsia. After Ceaușescu's overthrow, it emerged that Iliescu was a member of a small group of conspirators who had been plotting at least since the early 1980s to overthrow the Ceaușescu regime (*WP*, 24 August). Until the popular uprising in December 1989, however, the group was ineffective in winning support among the Securitate and the military. When Ceaușescu fled Bucharest, some of Iliescu's group emerged as an organized political alternative with enough of an action program to fill the political vacuum created by Ceaușescu's overthrow. Iliescu, unlike some of the better-known leaders in Eastern Europe, was never a dissident, public opponent, or even a critic of the existing communist regime. In fact, until the December revolution, he was a quiet, low-level cog in the party machine. He benefited from his known association with Soviet leader Mikhail Gorbachev during their student days in Moscow in the early 1950s, but there was no indication of his supporting any of Gorbachev's reforms before the death of Ceaușescu. (On Iliescu's background, see Rompres, 20 June; Vladimir Socor, "The New President," RFE, *Report on Eastern Europe* 1, no. 23 [8 June].)

Iliescu, as president of the NSF Council (the interim government) and provisional head of government, has shown no great enthusiasm for democracy, pluralism, a free press, or an open society. In many regards he has simply continued to rule Romania through a somewhat more benign form of the previous communist system. Although a number of political dissidents and human rights activists were given prominent positions in the NSF soon after it became Romania's provisional government, power in the NSF and the provisional government was exercised by former communist officials. The NSF took over the local institutions of the RCP, and often the new local leader was the second-ranking, and in some cases even the first-ranking, former RCP official. NSF tactics were reminiscent of the modus operandi of the RCP, and genuine political dissidents and human rights activists resigned from the NSF to protest its neocommunist policies and practices.

Even the rhetoric Iliescu uses on critical occasions suggests that his ideological outlook is generally that of an unreformed communist. As stated earlier, in his urgent call on 13 June for help from the miners to put down demonstrations in Bucharest, he branded the protesters as "Fascists" who were taking part in a "legionary rebellion"—a typical communist description of the opposition (Radio Bucharest, 13 June). Following the rampage, Iliescu thanked the miners for displaying "workers' solidarity" in the face of a plot by forces inside and outside the country who believe that "right-wing forces should come to power in all East European countries." He said the workers must show "vigilance" in defending a democracy that "serves the masses," not one that serves "the rich of those who want to become rich" (Radio Bucharest, 15 June). Iliescu and the NSF leadership have also used appeals to national interests in much the same fashion as Ceauşescu, but they have compounded this manipulation by drawing on religious sentiments. (Vladimir Socor, "The New President," RFE, *Report on Eastern Europe* 1, no. 23 [8 June]; Michael Shafir, "The Leadership Yet to Prove its Credibility," RFE, *Report on Eastern Europe* 1, no. 28 [13 July].)

Formation of the new government: The prime minister and the cabinet. One of Iliescu's first actions after his formal inauguration as president was to name Petre Roman as prime minister. Roman has served as interim head of government since December 1989 and was closely identified with Iliescu during the six-month period of the provisional government. His appointment was therefore hardly a surprise. On 28 June Roman introduced his new cabinet to the Parliament and presented the new government's program (Radio Bucharest, 28 May; *Adevărul*, 29 May; *LAT*, 28 May). The 23 ministers in the new cabinet reflected some significant changes from the provisional government (only 5 had been ministers and 5, deputy ministers in the provisional government), but in some aspects it represented less of a change from the past than had been the case with the other former Soviet allies in Eastern Europe.

The new cabinet has an average age of 48, whereas many members of the former government were in their 60s or older. In the new government, three ministers are in their 60s, seven are in their 50s, ten are in their 40s, and two are in their 30s. Most new officials have technical backgrounds and in many regards are strikingly similar to Petre Roman. Of the 23 ministers, 10 are engineers, 5 are lawyers, 4 are economists, 1 is a physician, 1 is an architect, and 1 is an aesthetician. Fourteen of the ministers hold doctorates. Because the main task of

the new government, as spelled out in the prime minister's initial speech to Parliament, is to transform Romania's centralized command economy to a market-oriented one, the educational and generational composition seems appropriate. A young, technically trained group not identified with past policies is likely to guide the transition smoothly.

At the same time, however, it would be wrong to see the new government as representing a fundamental break with the past. The fact that most of the new officials have not held such rank previously probably has more to do with age than with ideology. Under the Ceauşescu regime, most of them held important second-level managerial positions in factories and research institutes and a number of them were considered sufficiently reliable to permit them to study abroad. Some of the new government members have family connections with prominent members of Ceauşescu's inner circle. Prime Minister Roman is the son of Valter Roman, a longtime communist who enlisted in the International Brigade in the Spanish civil war in the 1930s and returned to Romania after World War II to become a senior RCP official with Ceauşescu. Minister of Health Bogdan Marinescu is the son of Voinea Marinescu, the minister of health under Ceauşescu in the 1960s. Foreign Minister Adrian Năstase is the son-in-law of Angelo Miculescu, former deputy prime minister, minister of agriculture, and Romanian ambassador to China.

Before the election, Iliescu said that, whatever the results of the election, the new government should be composed of a broad coalition. He quickly forgot that statement, however, after the election successes of the NSF. All members of the government are linked with the NSF, with the sole exception of the minister of culture, Andrei Pleşu, an independent who had been a member of the provisional government.

The members of the cabinet presented to Parliament on 28 June were: prime minister, Petre Roman, 44; minister of state for industry and trade, Anton Vătăşescu; minister of state for quality of life and social security, Ion Aurel Stoica; minister of state for economic guidance, Eugen Dijmărescu; minister, assistant to the prime minister for reforms and relations with Parliament, Adrian Severin; agriculture and the food industry, Ion Tipu, 53; communications, Andrei Chirică, 51; culture, Andrei Pleşu; education and science, Gheorghe Ştefan, 42; secretary of state in the Ministry of Education and Science (with rank of minister), Andrei Ţugulea, 62; environment, Eugen Valeriu Pop, 51; finance,

Teodor Dumitru Stolojan, 47; foreign affairs, Adrian Năstase, 40; secretary of state in the Foreign Ministry (second-ranking official at the ministry with rank of minister), Romulus Neagu, 60; health, Bogdan Marinescu; interior, Dorel Viorel Ursu, 37; justice, Victor Babiuc, labor, Cătălin Zamfir, 49; national defense, Victor Stănculescu, 62; public works, transportation, and regional development, Doru Pană, 53; resources and industry, Mihai Zisu, 53; trade and tourism, Constantin Fota, 55; youth and sports, Bogdan Nicolae Niculescu Duvăz, 42. (On the government leadership, see *Adevărul*, 29 June; Vladimir Socor, "The New President," RFE, *Report on Eastern Europe* 1, no. 23 [8 June]; Michael Shafir, "The Leadership Yet to Prove Its Credibility," RFE, *Report on Eastern Europe* 1, no. 28 [13 July].)

The new Romanian Parliament. The Parliament elected in the 20 May elections has had to cope with a series of serious institutional questions that have limited its ability to play the traditional role of checking executive power in a democratic society. The Romanian Grand National Assembly under the Ceauşescu regime was a unicameral body, but the new Romanian Parliament is bicameral, with a 396-member Assembly of Deputies and a 119-member Senate. This is similar to the parliamentary system established in the 1923 Romanian constitution, but there is an important difference in how the members of the Senate are selected. In the interwar Senate, some members were directly elected and others were appointed on the basis of their previous government service, elected indirectly by local officials, or designated ex officio. In the new Romanian Senate, all members are elected in much the same way that representatives are chosen for the Chamber of Deputies. There is no effort to assure proportional representation for the national minorities, although minority groups are assured a single representative in the Chamber of Deputies. Although there are certain procedural differences between the two houses, these differences are not sufficient to distinguish the two bodies.

The Parliament has the responsibility to oversee actions of the government and the president, but procedural and practical difficulties limit this ability. The initiative clearly lies with the president and the government. The procedures of the Romanian Parliament are very similar to those of the French National Assembly under the constitution of the Fifth Republic and are not undemocratic, but whether they will encourage responsive democratic government depends on how they are implemented. Several issues suggest that it will be difficult for the Parliament to function as a democratic deliberative institution. First, few Romanians now alive can remember Romania's last freely elected parliament, which means there is little democratic tradition on which the new deputies can rely. Second, the NSF has a 75 percent majority in both houses, which makes it even more difficult to overcome the rubber-stamp tradition of the Parliament under the Ceauşescu regime. Third, the principal task of the Parliament is to adopt a new Romanian constitution. New elections will be held twelve months after the Parliament adopts a new constitution, and if no constitution is adopted, an election will be held no later than eighteen months after the original Parliament was elected. The present Parliament is therefore a transitional body. At the same time, however, the country is going through radical changes that will have a profound impact on the nature of the political and economic system well into the future. (For the text of the legislation establishing the conditions under which the Parliament functions, see *Monitorul Oficial al României*, no. 35 [18 March]. See also Radio Bucharest, 15 March; Michael Shafir, "The Electoral Law," RFE, *Report on Eastern Europe* 1, no. 18 [4 May]; and Michael Shafir, "Romania's New Institutions: The Parliament," RFE, *Report on Eastern Europe* 1, no. 42 [19 October].)

Continuing protests and the opposition. Despite the fact that Iliescu and the NSF government had questionable democratic credentials and showed an incredible lack of judgment in handling the June riots in Bucharest, they represented major progress in comparison with the bleak repression of the Ceauşescu era. The overwhelming success of the NSF in the May elections, however, was less a show of support for Iliescu and his policies than it was a vote for the familiar and least risky choice. The manipulation of the mass media and the use of intimidation that produced the NSF landslide did not give the NSF a true popular mandate. The result was that a strong, politically mobilized, and vocal segment of society—primarily urban and intellectual—remained dissatisfied with the electoral outcome and willing to voice their objections through the international media and the domestic press. The domestic press is still a vehicle for opposition views despite the fact that large segments of it are subject to government control. The most obvious and dramatic way this extraparliamentary opposition made its views known was through protest demonstrations, and these continued during the year.

In the period following the June demonstrations, students and intellectuals in Bucharest continued a campaign for freeing those arrested in the June miners' rampage, including student leader Marian Munteanu and engineer Nica Leon. International protests against the continued detentions increased the pressure on the NSF government. On 21 July several thousand peaceful demonstrators in Bucharest also called for their release, and a week later more than a thousand demonstrators in Iaşi issued a similar call. On 1 August both *România Liberă* in Bucharest and *Le Monde* in Paris published an appeal on behalf of Munteanu and Leon signed by two hundred prominent Romanian and French intellectuals. Finally on 3 August—some six weeks after the demonstrations—Munteanu was released; the following week, on 9 August, Leon was also released, but another 175 people were reportedly still in prison.

At the end of August, for the first time since June, hundreds of protesters marched through Bucharest, barricaded themselves on a central street, and demanded Iliescu's resignation. Police and Interior Ministry forces in riot gear attempted to break up the demonstration with cattle prods and batons. The week-long protests focused on food shortages and other deprivations. Before things returned to normal, some 80 people were arrested (*NYT*, 27, 28 August). In mid-September thousands of demonstrators marched through Timişoara shouting anticommunist slogans and protesting that the revolution had been seized by former communists. The demonstrators also protested articles in the nationalist newspaper *România Mare* (Great Romania) that referred to the Timişoara revolution that had sparked the December overthrow of Ceauşescu as the "work of hooligans and foreign agents."

On the first anniversary of Ceauşescu's overthrow, some ten thousand people demonstrated in Timişoara demanding the resignation of the NSF government. Dissatisfied with the government's economic policies, which had led to price increases not offset by wage increases, and the presence of former Ceauşescu supporters in the NSF regime, they also strongly remonstrated against the fact that leaders of the Ceauşescu regime have not been brought to trial. Police and Securitate forces had killed 170 people in the December 1989 demonstrations in Timişoara, and those involved in the shootings were still on trial; but the legal proceedings

were moving at such a slow pace that many people feared that their old cronies were protecting them from the criminal penalties they deserved. The Right Reverend László Tökés, bishop of the Hungarian Reformed church and the leader who had triggered the Timişoara revolt in December 1989, said on this occasion that the "government did not fulfill its promises. . . . The Hungarian minority is not satisfied, and neither is much of Romania" (*NYT*, 17 and 19 December).

Domestic Issues. *Coping with the Ceauşescu legacy: The demise and revival of the RCP.* Following the death of Ceauşescu and the collapse of his regime, the NSF assumed most of the organizational resources of the RCP, including many of its leaders, but the NSF made a major effort to disassociate itself from the RCP. Within a week of Ceauşescu's death, an "initiative group" of the RCP issued a statement welcoming the December uprising. They dissociated themselves from the previous regime and condemned Ceauşescu and his associates, calling for the convening of an extraordinary party congress to dissolve the party and place "all of its property in the hands of the people, through the Council of the National Salvation Front." (Agerpres, 30 December 1989; AFP, 30 December 1989; *NYT*, 1 January; *WP*, 1 January.) Following mass demonstrations on 12 January, Iliescu announced to the protesters that the RCP would be outlawed because under Ceauşescu it had acted contrary to Romania's national traditions and spirit. The following day—in an abrupt about-face—the NSF council withdrew the decree banning the RCP and announced that the question of outlawing the RCP would be decided at a referendum on 28 January (*NYT*, 13 January; UPI in the *San Francisco Chronicle*, 13 January; *San Francisco Examiner*, 14 January). On 18 January, the NSF reversed itself again and canceled the referendum. That same day, however, the NSF council adopted, and provisional President Ion Iliescu signed, a decree confiscating all material assets and funds of the RCP on behalf of the Romanian state. The assets included 21 palaces and villas, 41 residential villas (party guest houses) in the various counties, 22 hunting lodges, 55,000 hectares of farmland, and the party's economic trust Carpaţi, which consisted of 60 enterprises with 48,000 employees (Radio Bucharest, 18 January; *NYT*, 18, 19 January; LAT, 19 January). Throughout the year, public protests and demonstrations denounced the continued presence of high-level Ceauşescu-era figures in responsible government positions. Occasionally, officials who had been in good standing at the time of Ceauşescu's death were dropped from government posts or forced to resign "for reasons of health," but prominent second-tier officials continued to dominate the government.

In November, a group of former prominent leaders of the RCP announced the creation of the Socialist Labor Party to revive liberal left-wing socialism with the aim of bringing stability and prosperity to Romania. The individuals—Ilie Verdeţ, Constantin Pârvulescu, Gheorghe Apostol, Cornel Burtică, and others—were all prominent RCP leaders during the Ceauşescu era and were not out of favor when the former party leader was overthrown in the December revolution (*Dimineaţa*, 2 November; Radio Bucharest, 17 November; *Adevărul*, 18 November). Popular demonstrations were held throughout Romania to protest the new party, and some opponents charged that the new party was created by the NSF to divert criticism from the NSF leaders' own communist credentials (Radio Bucharest, 18 November; Rompres, 19, 20, and 21 November; *România Liberă*, 20 November; *Dreptatea*, 22 November; *NYT*, 20 November). Ilie Verdeţ gave a status report on the party at the end of November (Rompres, 24 November):

> Since the RCP has not been dissolved, neither legally nor statutorily, it just ceased its activity after the events of and after 22 December 1989, some members of the former RCP Central Committee and of the Auditing Commissions from 32 counties have jointly agreed upon the reorganization of the RCP into a socialist party on different bases and structures. And the socialist party merged with the Democratic Labor Party at the latter's convention attended by 575 delegates and representatives, of which 356 [were] of the DLP. At present the new party numbers 123,000 enrolled members.

Coping with the Ceauşescu legacy: Trials of Ceauşescu-era officials. Another key domestic policy effort of the NSF was to demonstrate its distance and separation from the RCP and the Ceauşescu legacy by bringing prominent officials of the previous regime to trial. This was part of a concerted effort to raise NSF standing with the population, which wanted revenge against the leaders of the hated regime. In a trial that began on 27 January and lasted one week, four associates of Ceauşescu who held top government positions— Emil Bobu (former RCP Central Committee secre-

tary), Ion Dincă (first deputy prime minister), Manea Mănescu (vice-president of the State Council), and Tudor Postelnicu (former interior minister)—were found guilty. All four were sentenced to life imprisonment, had their property confiscated, and were stripped of their civil rights (Rompres, 27 January). On 13 February a court in Sibiu sentenced seven former senior Securitate officers to prison terms ranging from fifteen to twenty years for "conspiracy to commit genocide" during the December events. On 22 February in Cluj, two former Securitate officers were each sentenced to nineteen years in prison for serious crimes. On 2 March, a Securitate department chief from Bucharest and 21 former high-ranking officers of the Timiş County militia and Securitate units were put on trial for complicity in genocide and for brutally suppressing the uprisings in Timişoara in December 1989 (Rompres, 10 February; *NYT*, 3 March). Nicu Ceauşescu, son of the former dictator and head of the RCP organization in Sibiu County, was put on trial in May, though the trial was delayed because the younger Ceauşescu had a "progressive liver disease." (*Dimineaţa*, 26 May; *NYT*, 27, 29 May.) Nicolae Andruţă Ceauşescu, brother of the dictator and former head of the Securitate school, also went on trial in May, although his trial was delayed several times in order to get additional witnesses. Ultimately he was convicted and sentenced to fifteen years imprisonment (Rompres, 22 February, 22 June). In late summer legal proceedings were begun against former Prime Minister Constantin Dăscălescu and 23 former members of the RCP Political Executive Committee who had been arrested on grounds of complicity in genocide. In August indictments were filed against the former head of Securitate, General Iulian Vlad, and against former Interior Minister Postelnicu (Rompres, 23 July, 11, 12 September).

In countries of Eastern Europe where the replacement of the old regime was done more gradually or through generally nonviolent means, there was not the same kind of vindictive demand for retribution that was evident in Romania. The onerous repression of the Ceauşescu regime left a population demanding the punishment of those responsible. With almost half a century of experience with a judiciary that had served the politically powerful, fair and impartial trials were not the norm. The summary execution of Nicolae Ceauşescu and Elena Ceauşescu on 25 December 1989 established the pattern for the trials of other former prominent leaders of the regime. (See Dan Ionescu,

"Old Practices Persist in Romanian Justice," RFE, *Report on Eastern Europe* 1, no. 10 [9 March].)As the trials progressed during the year, proceedings took more time, trials adjourned for lack of evidence, and procedural motions from the defendants began to delay the speed of verdicts. The question was raised as to whether these were legal procedures designed to assure fair trials for the defendants or simply further manipulation of the courts by a neocommunist regime to avoid punishing those involved in the vicious activities of the previous government. Public protests frequently were staged when various legal proceedings were delayed.

Coping with the Ceauşescu legacy: Reorganizing the Securitate forces and gaining control of the military. The secret police (Securitate) was a key element in Ceauşescu's control of Romania; thus disbanding the old institution and securing the loyalty of the Securitate was a key problem for the NSF. Furthermore, there was the problem of winning and keeping the loyalty of the Romanian military authorities. The problem assumed great urgency because it was the stubborn resistance of the Securitate forces that prolonged Ceauşescu's overthrow and turned the revolution into a bloodbath. The regular military forces were initially loyal, but they ultimately joined the side of the rebellion, sealing the fate of the Ceauşescus and their regime. For the NSF, gaining control of the Securitate and military forces was critical to retaining control of Romania. (*România Liberă*, 16 February; Radio Bucharest, 20 February; Rompres, 28 February; Paris, *Le Monde*, 23 February; London, *The Times*, 29 May; *Dreptatea*, 20 September; Mihai Sturdza, "How Dead Is Ceauşescu's Secret Police Force?" RFE, *Report on Eastern Europe* 1, no. 15 [13 April].)

In February, the provisional government announced that the Securitate would be disbanded and its functions taken from the Interior Ministry and given to the Defense Ministry. The defense minister announced that an agency modeled after the U.S. Federal Bureau of Investigation would be organized to assure national security. At the same time, three thousand Securitate officers were put on reserve duty, a number of officers were arrested, and investigations were undertaken on 70,000 former Securitate personnel (*NYT*, 22 February). The trials of a large number of Securitate officers were a further step to break up the old institutional relationships and make clear the identity of the new leaders.

Despite these efforts, however, there was a persistent and probably justified public paranoia that the Securitate as an institution still existed and that many of its key personnel were still in positions of power. One persistent demand that was reiterated at most of the public demonstrations throughout the year in Romania was that the Securitate be disbanded.

In October in an interview in New York, President Iliescu conceded that "a few thousand" members of the Securitate were still being used to help maintain public authority, but he insisted that these individuals had been screened, were not guilty of crimes of repression during the Ceauşescu era, and were performing "technical" functions. He said that the secret police forces, as well as "20,000 special troops subordinated to the *Securitate*" had been dismissed and their commanders put on trial (*NYT*, 4 October).

Assuring control over the military was a persistent problem for the NSF government. The defection of the military forces to the anti-Ceauşescu cause was a critical element in the success of the December 1989 revolution (Michael Shafir, "New Revelations of the Military's Role in Ceauşescu's Ouster," RFE, *Report on Eastern Europe* 1, no. 19 [11 May]); in recognition of that fact several key military officers were named to the leadership of the NSF when it assumed the role of provisional government in December 1989. Among those who assisted the revolution were Major General Ştefan Guşă, chief of the general staff and first deputy minister of defense since 1986; Lieutenant General Victor Stănculescu, first deputy minister of defense since 1985; Major General Gheorghe Voina; and two other lower-ranking officers. At the same time, the NSF needed the military to remain loyal to the new government. There was also strong popular dissatisfaction with and distrust of the old military leadership who had been promoted under the Ceauşescu regime. Among the lower levels of the military—enlisted personnel and junior officers—there was close identification with the aims of the anti-Ceauşescu regime and opposition to the old officers. In addition, ambitious officers used dissatisfaction in the ranks and popular protests as opportunities to advance their own careers and deal with their opponents.

On 16 February, Nicolae Militaru was replaced as minister of defense by Victor Stănculescu, whom Ceauşescu had appointed a first deputy defense minister but who had joined the revolution and then served as economics minister in the NSF provisional government. The change was the result of a week-long demonstration by some three thousand junior and midlevel officers. (Rompres, 15 February; Radio Bucharest, 16, 17, 18 February, 1 March; *România Liberă*, 17 February; AFP, 16 February.) At the same time, President Iliescu established a commission to investigate the military's role in the December revolution and review all of Militaru's appointments. Stănculescu played a double game in the whole process. He apparently participated in the military action against the civilian population in Timişoara in December 1989, faked a broken leg to avoid involvement in Ceauşescu's order to open fire on the civil population of Bucharest on 21 December, supervised Ceauşescu's departure by helicopter from the Central Committee building in Bucharest on 22 December, and then two days later was present for the trial and execution of the Ceauşescus. He seems to have played the same game as minister of defense. He initially supported the drive for democratization of the army but used it to purge his personal enemies in the military. He then switched sides again and joined Iliescu's attempts to tighten control and depoliticize the military.

Within the military a Committee for Action to Democratize the Army was established soon after the December revolution to deal with military problems of the Ceauşescu era. The fact that the committee had some initial support within the leadership of the Defense Ministry suggests that it may have been set up to channel military discontent in ways that could be controlled by the leading officers. (Paul Gafton, "Armed Forces Seek to Democratize," RFE, *Report on Eastern Europe* 1, no. 14 [6 April].) On 4 June, however, when the committee called for the dismissal of Internal Affairs Minister Mihai Chitac, both the Defense Ministry and the Interior Ministry disassociated themselves from the demand (Rompres, 4, 5 June). On 14 June, in the wake of the army's inability to restore order when the government demanded action to stop the protest at University Square in Bucharest, Iliescu criticized the committee, and the Defense Ministry abolished it. On 25 July, however, a communiqué from the committee announced that it would continue its effort to democratize the Romanian military forces. On 9 October another reform group, the Action Group for the Modernization of the Army, was established that called for the purge of military officers compromised by association with the Ceauşescu regime and demanded the removal of Defense Minister Stănculescu (*România Liberă*, 8

November). In a newspaper interview in October, Stănculescu said that as far as he knew the Committee for Action to Democratize the Army no longer existed and at the same time described leadership efforts to restore discipline in the military and end these efforts at "democratization" (*Adevărul*, 13 October). Although it is apparent that the NSF and the government have succeeded in achieving a degree of control over the military, there are still serious questions about its full reliability.

Economic reform and the status of the economy. Reforming the Romanian economy was one of the first priorities identified following the overthrow of Nicolae Ceauşescu in December 1989. The NSF provisional government on 22 December called for restructuring the national economy "in accordance with the criteria of profitability and efficiency" by returning to small-scale peasant production in the countryside and reorganizing trade to satisfy the daily needs of the population, including an end to exporting foodstuffs and oil products (Radio Bucharest, 22 December 1989). The first concrete steps in this direction were taken with the creation of a National Commission for Small-Scale Industry and Services, which was to develop the program of economic changes necessary to bring Romania toward a market economy (Decree Law 56/1990, *Monitorul Oficial al României*, no. 10 [15 January]). On 5 February, the council of the NSF issued a decree allowing private individuals to set up profit-making enterprises that could employ up to twenty people (*România Liberă*, *NYT*, 6 February; Decree Law 54/1990, *Monitorul Oficial al României*, no. 20 [6 February]). The next day, the Romanian national bank announced the devaluation of the Romanian currency by 58.38 percent, and the tourist (noncommercial) rate and the commercial rate were both set at the same level—21 lei to the dollar. These changes were made following consultations in Romania with experts from the International Monetary Fund and the World Bank (*NYT*, 6 February). In April, provisional Prime Minister Petre Roman announced the establishment of a State Secretariat for Privatization to focus on procedures for privatizing large state enterprises. (Radio Bucharest, 27 April; see also Rompres, 8 March.)

All these steps were taken by the provisional government before the elections, but they were consistent with popular wishes. In June, following the elections and the inauguration of the new government, Prime Minister Roman presented the government's program to the newly elected Parliament.

He said that its "foremost mission" would be to ensure "an historic transition of unprecedented scope, namely, the transition from a supercentralized economy to a market economy." He indicated that the next two years would be decisive in this process and that it would be difficult, but necessary, to break with "structures, mentalities, and practices accumulated in so many years of dictatorship." During his report, Roman acknowledged that in the six months since Ceauşescu's overthrow, little had been done toward making the necessary changes. Managers feared taking risks because they were used to central authorities telling them what to do, and Roman noted that fear of labor unrest led the management of certain economic enterprises to reduce production levels and increase wages. The only solution, Roman told Parliament, was to encourage free market principles and let the market bring about productivity and efficiency. Romania could not hope to have the status of a European country unless it unleashed the "forces of change," which he identified as "entrepreneurship, competition, free initiative, privatization." At the same time the government acknowledged that these changes would bring hardship and social unrest. Roman proposed a six-month moratorium during which labor unions would refrain from demanding higher wages and better working conditions and during which the government would institute enterprise funds to compensate those whose incomes were likely to be reduced. Roman also suggested several possibilities for the privatization of the economy, giving workers priority in purchasing shares of their enterprises. He also warned that, with the exception of basic food items and energy, prices would be determined by the free market. Other currency reforms were also necessary, including establishing the full convertibility of the leu, creating a stock market, and introducing a greater role for banks in financing economic activity. In this presentation to Parliament, Roman promised that the government would present an initial package of reform legislation for approval within six months. (Radio Bucharest, 28 June; *Adevărul*, 29 June; London, *Financial Times*, 29 June.)

The economic situation, however, deteriorated. In July the government attempted to link workers' pay with their output and ordered banks to release money from special enterprise funds according to the fulfillment of production programs established by the enterprises. At the same time the government announced that the Romanian economy would not be able to provide jobs for all high school and university graduates; during the first half of the year some enterprises were unable to provide work for all employees and paid only half their wages. Officials said that legislation on unemployment benefits should be drafted. Less than a month after Prime Minister Roman's presentation to Parliament, the president of the Senate criticized the government for failing to present a package of legislation to the parliament for quick action (*CSM*, 31 July, *NYT*, 1, 6, 22 August).

On 18 October, Roman submitted a report on the economy to a joint session of the two chambers of Parliament on the serious condition of the economy and requesting extraordinary powers to implement the necessary reforms. The performance of the economy during the first nine months of the year was dismal: industrial production was down almost 28 percent, and exports dropped by 46 percent in comparison with the same period the previous year. Roman said that acceleration of the transition to a market economy was essential and that some controls on wages and prices would be lifted, the leu devalued, and the transition to a convertible currency introduced on 1 January 1991. The government adopted provisions reducing taxes on foreign-owned enterprises in an effort to encourage foreign investment. The government program for privatization initially only involved converting state enterprises into joint stock companies, not selling shares to individuals. Faster and more extensive privatization was permitted in the agricultural, food-processing, and service sectors of the economy. Private ownership of land in rural areas would be permitted by those who would be farming it and by others in the countryside, but the amount of land a single owner could purchase would be limited. As a consequence of these reforms, the prime minister expected an increase in unemployment. He reported that 700,000 were underemployed and that 120,000 (of whom 80 percent were women) were fully unemployed. The number of underemployed and unemployed could rise to 1,220,000 in 1991, when an additional 300,000 young people enter the labor market after completing high school and college. (Rompres, 18 October; *Dimineaţa*, 23 October.)

On 1 November the government deregulated some prices; the immediate result was doubling the price of clothing, public transportation, and furniture and tripling the price of footwear. The leu was devalued by 70 percent, from 21 to 35 per U.S. dollar, but even so drastic a change may not have been enough because on the black market lei were being exchanged at the rate of about 100 to the dollar. Popular response to these economic policies, however, reflected concern for the personal impact, for these policies to bring about free market pricing did not include a counterbalancing increase in wages. Romanians again took to the streets in Bucharest's University Square to protest the price increases. (*WP*, 6 November; *CSM*, 8 November.) The protests unsettled the government to the point that Prime Minister Roman threatened to resign if protests against his government's economic policies did not cease (Radio Bucharest, 5 November).

The proposals for reform were not welcomed across the board. Managers of economic enterprises, many of whom were appointed by the Ceauşescu government, were reluctant to implement the changes. Two weeks before Roman's report to Parliament on 18 October, Minister for Economic Guidance Dijmărescu said that the government planned a wholesale purge of managements elected by factory workers after Ceauşescu's December 1989 overthrow. The workers had unfortunately "elected nice guys, not good managers," who refused to take responsibility for market reforms and allowed theft of factory property. The government said that it would appoint their successors. ("Romania to Sack Managers Chosen by Factory Floor," *Independent*, 5 October.) The day before Roman's 18 October report to Parliament, sixteen secretaries of state in economic ministries were dismissed and several new officials were appointed (Rompres, 17 October). Foreign correspondents said that members of Parliament were not particularly in favor of implementing the tough, unpopular decisions that were necessary for economic reform and that representatives were concerned with the social consequences of privatization, price increases, and unemployment for their constituents (Reuters, 18 October; London, *Financial Times*, 18 October; Paris, *Le Monde*, 19 October; *NYT*, 19, 30 October).

The effort to encourage investment of foreign capital to bolster the economy was a high priority of the government. On 14 March, even before national elections, the provisional government issued a decree law taking "certain steps to attract foreign capital investment." The new legislation relaxed restrictions on foreign capital, permitting joint ventures with the proportions of foreign and domestic ownership decided on by the foreign and Romanian owners as well as permitting completely foreign-owned ventures. Although certain bureaucratic and tax requirements were imposed, it appears that these were not intended to be obstacles to investment, and other requirements were eased in an effort to encourage the influx of foreign capital (Decree Law No. 96/1990, *Monitorul Oficial al României*, no. 37 [20 March]). Within a few months the minister of trade reported the signature of agreements with 24 companies and ongoing discussions with a large number of other potential investors (interview with Alexandru Mărgăritescu, *Tribuna Economică*, 20 April; Paul Gafton, "New Provisions for Foreign Investment in Romania," RFE, *Report on Eastern Europe* 1, no. 24 [15 June]).

There was progress toward privatization of economic assets during the year, but Romania was the East European country with the most stringent restrictions on private economic activity before the 1989 revolution. Shortly after Ceauşescu was overthrown, the government liberalized the sale of agricultural products and granted peasants the use of half a hectare of collective land to expand private farming. During 1990 some 320 cooperative farms were closed and the land taken over by individual farmers. By the end of the year the land privately farmed by members of cooperatives had increased by two and a half times.

In the private trade sector, growth was even more spectacular. The law permitting small private enterprises with up to twenty employees by July had generated 50,000 requests for licenses; 32,000 had been permitted, and 20,000 firms were established. The principal area in which such firms operated was the service sector; 75 percent of the private firms were in this area. By November, the number of applications had reached 140,000; 50,000 were approved, and only 20 percent of those were in nontrade sectors of the economy. By November the total number of requests reached 140,000; some 50,000 had been approved, 80 percent of which were in the trade sector. (Rompres, 22 May, 12 September, 28 November; *România Liberă*, 21 July.)

On 20 September, a new law on commercial companies was adopted by Parliament. The legislation, based on pre–World War II commercial codes, permits the establishment of five types of companies, ranging from simple partnerships to joint stock companies. All Romanian enterprises must convert to one of these new commercial categories within six months (Rompres, 20 September). Enterprises that convert to joint stock companies will be required to turn over 30 percent of their shares to a state privatization agency, which will then issue vouchers with a nominal value of five thousand lei to each adult Romanian citizen resident in Romania. These vouchers can be sold or transferred after a year but only to resident Romanian citizens. The goal of the legislation is to privatize half the country's capital within the next three years. (Rompres, 20 September; *Monitorul Oficial al României*, 7 August.) Although the Romanian government has begun implementing a number of programs to move the economy toward private ownership with increasing emphasis on market forces, those programs are in the incipient stages, and there is a great deal that must be done to bring about a truly market-oriented economy.

Freedom of the press and freedom of expression. A key element in bringing about political reform and democratization in Romania is developing a free press. Although there is far greater freedom of expression and freedom of the press permitted in Romania now than under the Ceaușescu regime, there are still serious problems. During the initial months after the December revolution, the Romanian press was the principal forum through which the political opposition criticized the NSF. Romanian television was a particular focal point of the struggle. In early February there were mass demonstrations at television headquarters protesting that news coverage was biased against the new political parties and for the NSF, and the union of radio and television workers protested the appointment of writer Aurel Dragoș Munteanu, who had been spokesman for the NSF, as head of Romanian radio and television. A demonstration by some three thousand journalists and others against NSF control of the media led Munteanu to resign on 9 February. These earlier skirmishes, however, ultimately gave way to concerted NSF efforts to dominate television and radio. The media struggle sharpened with the approach of the 20 May elections, and the opposition political parties charged that the NSF was manipulating the state-run television service and controlling other mass media for its own benefit in the campaign. Foreign observers generally agreed with the charges of media manipulation. The two-month-long demonstration in University Square in Bucharest, which began 22 April, started over demands that Romanian television be freed from NSF control through the establishment of an independent television station, but Iliescu adamantly refused to permit a truly independent television station to compete with NSF-controlled television.

There was greater success with the daily newspaper *România Liberă*. It had been controlled by the RCP under Ceaușescu, but under the leadership of two crusading journalists, Octavian Paler and Mihai Petre Băcanu, *România Liberă* became the leading independent newspaper, unaffiliated with any political party. As an independent voice, it gained great popularity in Bucharest, reaching 1.5 million people daily. NSF authorities systematically attempted to prevent its distribution elsewhere and, in an effort to reduce its effectiveness, tripled the price of newsprint overnight and cut newsprint supplies in half. The journalists on *România Liberă's* staff took advantage of the government's laws on privatization to become the first private enterprise in Romania. They divided themselves into six separate companies of twenty or fewer individuals in order to meet the requirements of the initial privatization law.

The miners' rampage in Bucharest in June seriously threatened the freedom of the press. The miners, mobilized by the NSF government to end demonstrations in University Square, were also used to intimidate the media. During the violence, the miners ransacked the offices of *România Liberă* and other independent newspapers, as well as the offices and homes of opposition politicians. The progovernment printers' union denounced the "irresponsibility" of independent journalists and threatened to refuse to print offending publications. *România Liberă* demanded that the NSF reaffirm its commitment to press freedom as an essential element of democracy. Reluctantly, on 17 June, the government declared its commitment to "total freedom of operation for the democratic institutions of the press, radio, and television," and newspapers that had ceased publication during the miners' rampage began to reappear. (On the media in Romania, see Kevin Devlin, "Postrevolutionary Ferment in the East European Media," RFE, *Report on Eastern Europe* 1, no. 28 [13 July].)

Attacks by government agencies were part of the effort to control the free press. At the end of August, the Romanian intelligence service issued an intimidating warning to the Romanian press: "The circulation of false information, rumors, or misinformation or the disclosure of legally protected data, as well as the insults and calumnies circulated by certain publications, is not only incompatible with the freedom of the press but are also offenses punishable by the penal code" (*România Liberă*, 1 September).

About that same time, the Justice Ministry proposed new legislation on the press that contained democratic-sounding provisions but that also had serious loopholes that could allow government action against the media. Although granting journalists the right to receive public information and banning precensorship, the legislation also provided for sanctions under circumstances that could be manipulated by the government to harass or silence journalists. The legislation also gave rights to "professional" journalists that would appear to favor those "trained" in the RCP's Ştefan Gheorghiu Party Academy, whereas the new independent journalists, many of whom supported the opposition political groups, would not have similar rights. The legislation clearly favored the state-controlled television and Rompres, the official news agency. Peter Galliner, director of the International Press Institute of Zurich and London, sent a letter to President Iliescu formally protesting the draft law and charging that it seriously threatened press freedom in Romania. A newly established association of independent journalists responded to the government's proposed legislation by drafting a charter on freedom of the press to air their views on the necessity of freedom of the press and specifying the principles to assure such freedom (*România Liberă*, 21 September). The international condemnation as well as outspoken domestic criticism led the government to withdraw the draft law in early October. (The text of the draft law and criticism of its provisions appeared in *Curierul Ziariştilor* [Journalists' mail], no. 1, a new periodical for journalists that began publication in September. See also Crisula Ştefănescu, "The New Press Law," RFE, *Report on Eastern Europe* 1, no. 38 [21 September], and Crisula Ştefănescu, "Government Withdraws Controversial Draft Law on the Press," RFE, *Report on Eastern Europe* 1, no. 43 [26 October].)

The government's decision to withdraw the draft law on the press, however, was only a tactical setback in the NSF's efforts to control the media. In mid-October, the government reversed an earlier decision to make 30 publications independent and combined them as part of a state-owned national publishing house. The independent journalists union criticized this government effort to subordinate the independent press to its totalitarian interests. In the other former communist-ruled countries of Eastern Europe, freedom of the press was more firmly institutionalized during 1990 than it was in Romania. The tenacity of the country's independent journalists, however, has thus far thwarted the government's effort to control the press.

Freedom of movement and migration from Romania. The Ceauşescu government was one of the most restrictive in Eastern Europe in limiting travel. After the collapse of the Ceauşescu regime, travel restrictions were quickly lifted in response to popular pressure. The decision to grant all citizens passports on request, however, created such a backlog that government officials were unable to process all the requests. Within one month, 450,000 passports were issued, four times the number issued during the entire previous year. By April more than 1 million Romanians had been issued passports; by the end of May the number had climbed to more than 1.5 million (AFP, 8 February; Rompres, 14 April; 8 June). Although large numbers of people wanted to travel outside Romania, they were able to get only limited amounts of foreign currency because of the country's economic situation. Many Romanians went abroad to find jobs and economic opportunities, but Western countries soon established tighter visa requirements for Romanian travelers. In just 24 hours on 14 March, some five to seven thousand Romanians entered Austria before the tighter visa requirements on Romanians came into force (*NYT*, 15 March). Austria was the last Western European country to impose visa restrictions on Romanians. Thereafter, journalists reported lines of Romanian vehicles several kilometers long on the Bulgarian side of the border with Turkey as Romanians sought to go to the last country they could visit without a visa. By the end of the summer, the Bulgarians closed their border with Romania, using as an excuse a minor cholera outbreak in the Danube delta (Tanjug, 21 August).

The migration of ethnic Germans from Romania to Germany that has been under way since the end of World War II greatly increased after the lifting of travel restrictions. West German foreign minister Hans Dietrich Genscher, during a visit to Romania three weeks after the overthrow of Ceauşescu, said he expected 60 to 80 percent of Romania's ethnic Germans to migrate to Germany (Rompres, 15 January). By May the German government had established consulates in Timişoara, Braşov, and Sibiu to handle the flood of visa applications from Romanian citizens, and five hundred to a thousand ethnic Germans arrived each day at the Nürnberg center for processing emigrants from Romania (*România Liberă*, 31 May). In addition to ethnic Germans migrating to Germany from Romania, large numbers of Romanian Gypsies also sought to migrate there. In May some seven hundred Romanian refugees, mostly Gypsies, were crowded into an army barracks outside East Berlin, while another two thousand sought refuge in and around the railroad station in Dresden. German authorities reported that between 1 January and 12 August some 86,623 emigrants from Romania had come to West Germany, although they did not specify the number of ethnic Germans (DPA, 18 August).

Romanian citizens who were ethnic Hungarians continued to flee to Hungary. From 1987 until the overthrow of Ceauşescu, some 25,000 Romanian citizens, of whom three-quarters were ethnic Magyars, fled to Hungary (see *YICA*, 1990). With the lifting of travel restrictions, it became easier to migrate, and the number leaving Romania for Hungary continued. Hungarian officials estimated that through February about one thousand ethnic Hungarians per month were arriving in Hungary from Romania (Radio Budapest, 22 February). In March, with the flare-up of dangerous ethnic violence in the region of Tîrgu-Mureş (see below), the migration increased dramatically. Some reports suggested that shortly after the violence, as many as five hundred ethnic Hungarians per day were pouring into Hungary (*LAT*, 30, 31 March).

The size of the migration was obviously a concern to the Romanian government. Radio Bucharest (2 September) reported that as many as 800,000 Romanians had left the country since the December revolution. The Interior Ministry, however, denied that such a large-scale migration was taking place. It said instead that only 60,000 Romanians had emigrated legally between January and October 1990 and that another 25,000 individuals failed to return to Romania from visits abroad (Rompres, 11 October). The migration, however, was unquestionably much greater than the government was willing to admit and remains a sensitive matter. (Dan Ionescu, "the Exodus," RFE, *Report on Eastern Europe* 1, no. 43 [26 October].)

Religion and church-state relations. Government interference in religious affairs was substantially reduced after Ceauşescu's overthrow. On 19 January the Department of Religious Affairs, the regime's instrument for controlling the country's religious life and organizations, was replaced by the Ministry for Religious Affairs headed by Nicolae Stoicescu, a distinguished historian and a former political prisoner (Radio Bucharest, 19 January). When the government was reformed in June after the elections, the Ministry for Religious Affairs had disappeared from the new, streamlined government.

Political upheaval produced an upheaval in the Romanian Orthodox church, the largest religious denomination in Romania. The Orthodox church cooperated closely with Ceauşescu and the Romanian Communist Party (RCP) after the consolidation of communist power in Romania in 1948. Patriarch Teoctist, the head of the church in recent years, was regarded by Romanians as a supporter of Ceauşescu and his government because he, as well as other Romanians who collaborated with the regime, had lavishly praised Ceauşescu. The most blatant and outrageous example occurred as the Romanian revolution was already under way. On 19 December 1989, at the conclusion of the annual meeting of the National Church Assembly that occurred two days *after* the bloody Securitate massacre of innocent protesting civilians in front of the Orthodox Cathedral in Timişoara, Teoctist sent a telegram to Ceauşescu praising his "brilliant activity, wise guidance," and "daring thinking." The telegram proclaimed that Romanians were living "in a golden age appropriately and righteously bearing your [Ceauşescu's] name." (Agerpres, 20 December 1989.)

Three days later, Ceauşescu fled Bucharest and Patriarch Teoctist hastily attempted to atone for his previous excesses. During the first few hours after the NSF announced its assumption of power, the patriarch addressed Romanians on national television and urged support for the NSF. After the revolution, the church was given increased opportunity to broadcast religious services on radio and television, opportunities that it had never had under Ceauşescu. Teoctist and others in the Orthodox hierarchy issued belated denunciations of the Ceauşescu regime from the pulpit and, with the lifting of state restrictions, took a number of actions to revitalize the church. At an extraordinary synod of the church on 3 and 4 January, the decision was made to energize the church's charitable work, recognize the Lord's Army (a popular religious movement established in 1923), resume religious instruction for children, revitalize theological training for the clergy, lift bans against priests who had opposed the Ceauşescu regime, establish parishes and churches in new communities, and seek reconciliation with Romanian Orthodox communities in Europe and the United States (Rompres, 6 January). Teoctist also announced that the church would legally seek to reclaim property and assets seized during communist rule.

Patriarch Teoctist's repentance was too little and too late. The Orthodox public was critical of his role under Ceauşescu, and reform forces within the church demanded a change. Distinguished intellectuals, religious scholars, and others established the Group for Reflection on Renewal within the Church on 9 January. The group's aim was to renew the church through purging members of the hierarchy who were identified with the Ceauşescu regime. The day after it formed, the group called for the resignation of the members of the Permanent Synod, the church's leading executive body. On 18 January, Patriarch Teoctist resigned for "reasons of health and age." A few days later, the bishop of Alba Iulia (Transylvania) also resigned, reportedly at the demand of some one hundred priests of his diocese (Radio Bucharest, *Le Monde*, 18 January).

Another blow to the Orthodox church was the reestablishment of ties between the Vatican and Romania and the restoration of the Uniate dioceses in Transylvania that involved almost 3 million ethnic Romanians. The Uniates, or Greek Catholics, accept the authority of the Roman Catholic pope, but their liturgy is Byzantine, or Greek rite. Most ethnic Romanians in Transylvania before 1948 were Uniate, but as the Romanian communists consolidated their hold on the country, the Uniate parishes and dioceses were forcibly merged into the Romanian Orthodox church and papal authority over Eastern rite believers was terminated. In Romania there are 870 Latin rite priests and 540 Byzantine rite priests, many of whom had been ordained clandestinely during the Ceauşescu era. Almost as soon as the Ceauşescu regime ended, negotiations began with the Vatican to resume ties. Special papal envoy to Eastern Europe, Archbishop Francesco Colasuonno, arrived in Romania on 3 January and remained in the country for more than a week, meeting with officials of the Romanian Orthodox church, the government, and Roman Catholic leaders in Transylvania. During that visit the Orthodox church accepted in principle the restoration of rights to the Uniate church. Vatican envoys were in Romania again in February for a two-week visit, and a third delegation visited in March.

The full restoration of Roman Catholic rights in Romania and the establishment of diplomatic relations with the Vatican were probably set back by the Vatican's decision on 14 March to name a number of high church leaders without consulting with the Romanian government. New bishops were named for all six Latin rite and all five Byzantine rite (Uniate) dioceses. Minister of Religious Affairs Nicolae Stoicescu characterized the naming of the new bishops as "a serious transgression of the principles of international law" (Rompres, 16 March). Two months later, however, the Romanian government and the Vatican formally reestablished diplomatic relations after a lapse of 42 years, and the rights of the Uniate church were formally restored (Rompres, 14 May; *NYT*, 16 May).

The Rise of Romanian Nationalism and the Resurgence of the Ethnic Minorities. Romanian nationalism was carefully manipulated by Ceauşescu and the RCP to legitimize communism in Romania and give Ceauşescu and the party a measure of popular support and authority among the Romanian people. Paranoia about the Hungarian minority was manipulated to mobilize Romanian support against the regime's opponents. One of Ceauşescu's initial frantic efforts to suppress the unrest in Timişoara that triggered the Romanian revolution in December 1989 was to brand it as an effort of Hungarian irredentists and separatists to dismember Romania. Although Ceauşescu and the RCP stimulated Romanian nationalism for their own benefit, they always kept it under control. Following the overthrow of Ceauşescu, the NSF tried to utilize Romanian nationalism to its own advantage, but the forces of democracy and free expression made that nationalism difficult to manipulate. Romanian nationalism also contributed to spontaneous outbursts of violence against the ethnic Hungarians, which made it difficult for the NSF to keep its promises of providing ethnic minorities full and equal rights as Romanian citizens. At the same time, intense popular Romanian sentiment for the return of Bessarabia (Soviet Moldavia) to Romania hampered relations with the Soviet Union, which was having difficulties containing the nationalistic feelings of its many peoples. During the elections, the NSF and its allies used false claims that the opposition parties were willing to permit the dismemberment of Romania and the return of Transylvania to Hungary in an effort to present the NSF as the best defender of Romanian national interests (*România Liberă*, 11 April).

The NSF's appeal to Romanian nationalism made it difficult to contain popular enthusiasm. The designation of a new Romanian national holiday is a good example. The communist National Day was 23 August, the anniversary of the 1944 coup d'état that marked the beginning of communist participation in Romanian governments. All parties agreed that the old national day should be dropped but disagreed over which day should replace it. Ethnic Hungarians and others favored 22 December—the anniversary of the overthrow of Ceauşescu. The NSF government finally decided on 1 December—the anniversary of the 1918 merger of Transylvania and Bessarabia with the traditional Romanian provinces to form greater Romania. That date brought to the surface Romanian nationalism of the interwar period, as well as strong anti-Hungarian and anti-Russian sentiment. At a mass rally attended by more than 100,000 in Alba Iulia on 1 December—the first celebration of the new national holiday—President Ion Iliescu praised the selection of "this symbolic day" when Transylvania joined the old kingdom. The nationalistic crowd applauded militant nationalist speakers and jeered opposition leaders, who subsequently protested the incidents in Parliament. The Democratic Federation of Hungarians in Romania issued a statement questioning the nature of the festivities (Rompres, 29 November, 1 December).

Resurgence of the Gypsies. Under Ceauşescu, Gypsies (or Roma, as they prefer to be called) were denied the status of a separate ethnic group and forced to live a marginal existence with poor housing, inadequate health care, little education, and high unemployment. With the collapse of the Ceauşescu regime, the Gypsies began to assert themselves aggressively. Initially, they challenged the accuracy of the most recent national census, which numbered Gypsies in Romania at fewer than 230,000. Gypsy leaders estimated their numbers to be at least ten times that high. As Gypsies have taken a more forceful posture, racial prejudice has emerged against them in the press and other public forums. In keeping with the new, more democratic awareness in post-Ceauşescu Romania, in February an umbrella organization of Gypsies was founded—the Democratic Union of Romanies in Romania. There has been a proliferation of Gypsy organizations, with six political parties legally registered, in addition to various other cultural and social organizations. (*CSM*, 14 June; Dan Ionescu, "The Gypsies Organize," RFE, *Report on Eastern Europe* 1, no. 26 [29 June].)

Rising tensions between Romanians and the Hungarian minority. Ethnic Hungarians in Romania welcomed Ceauşescu's overthrow as an opportunity to achieve full rights as Romanian citizens, as well as the right to use their language. The NSF provisional government initially supported these

claims, and several prominent Hungarians were members of the NSF Council, including the Reverend László Tökeś, the ethnic Hungarian pastor of the Hungarian Reformed Church in Timişoara whose attempted arrest by the Securitate triggered the initial protests that culminated in the overthrow of Ceauşescu. Shortly after the collapse of the regime, ethnic Hungarians founded the Democratic Federation of Hungarians in Romania. At its first national conference on 14 January, the group called for recognition of the rights of ethnic Hungarians in Romania but opposed revisions in the Romanian-Hungarian border. At that same conference, the federation announced that it would run candidates in the forthcoming parliamentary elections but would not become a political party (Rompres, 14 January; *WSJ*, 3 January).

The Hungarians sought to reestablish the extensive system of Hungarian cultural institutions that were sytematically suppressed and abolished under Ceauşescu, particularly Hungarian-language educational institutions. In the early postwar period, a large number of Hungarian-language schools at all levels flourished in Transylvania, where Hungarians were a substantial portion of the population. After 1958, those schools were merged with Romanian-language schools, and fewer and fewer subjects were taught in Hungarian. In 1958, the Hungarian Bolyai University in Cluj, the cultural center of Transylvania, merged with the Romanian Babes University, and Hungarian language instruction declined significantly. After the December revolution, Hungarians sought to reestablish their cultural identity, and in the more open conditions of post-Ceauşescu Romania, they publicly advocated and worked for change. The Ministry of Education announced that it would reinstate instruction in minority languages, and there was even a promise that Bolyai University would be reestablished. (Rompres, 20 January; Judith Pataki, "Free Hungarians in a Free Romania: Dream or Reality?" RFE, *Report on Eastern Europe* 1, no. 8 [23 February].)

Although the NSF provisional government initially appeared to be sympathetic to these Hungarian demands, it gradually assumed a more critical line as Romanian nationalist opposition to these Hungarian efforts began to emerge. An ethnic Hungarian official in the Education Ministry was fired for announcing increased education in minority languages (Radio Bucharest, 27 January; Rompres, 27 January). In January, Western reporters visiting Romania in the aftermath of Ceauşescu's overthrow reported ethnic conflicts between Romanians and Hungarians in the Transylvanian cities of Cluj and Tîrgu-Mureş (DPA, 26 January). In a January speech, Iliescu referred to "separatist trends" in Transylvania and called for overcoming national conflicts (Rompres, 25 January). On 8 February, tens of thousands of ethnic Romanians protested against Hungarian-language schools; the same day similar numbers of ethnic Hungarians demonstrated in favor of such schools. The demonstrations followed inflammatory press reports about the expulsion of ethnic Romanians from schools with a majority of Hungarian students. Károly Király, a former vice-president of the NSF council and an ethnic Hungarian, criticized the NSF for failing to establish the Ministry for Ethnic Minorities as promised. The following day Reverend Tökeś suggested that the animosity between the two groups had been incited by Ceauşescu supporters. On 13 February representatives of eleven ethnic minority groups issued a joint declaration urging the newly established provisional Council of National Unity to take quick steps to support individual and group rights of members of minority groups. Pressure from nationalist Romanians led the NSF provisional government to postpone implementing such measures.

During this period of ethnic unrest, an extreme Romanian nationalist organization, Vatra Românească [Romanian hearth], was established in Transylvania. It found particular support among some local leaders of the Ceauşescu regime who were being absorbed by the local councils of the NSF. The first indications of the goals of Vatra Românească appeared in a Romanian press agency report where it was identified not as a political party but as "an organization of the Romanian spirituality of Transylvania" that "will militate against any manifestation of separatism, chauvinism and nationalism, expresses its protest against the attempts at harming state unity and the culture of the Romanian people, to combat any tendency of distorting and destroying the assets of the Transylvania Romanian." It also called for "the use of the Romanian language as the only official language throughout the country's territory" (Rompres, 21 February). Another version of Vatra Românească's program was more sinister. A manifesto—apparently not publicly disseminated, stamped "Vatra Românească, Tîrgu-Mureş National Headquarters," and dated 20 February—claimed that "unhappily, the holy land of Romania has been soiled by the Asian feet of Huns, by Gypsies and other underlings. . . .

Do not be afraid to rise up and spill their impure blood." It called Transylvania "the most unclean" part of Romania "because of the Hungarians, but unfortunately because of others, too." It called for concentrating first on cleansing Transylvania but said that later other parts of Romania would be purified of Gypsies, Jews, and Tatars (AFP, 11 April). In an interview later in the year published by a leading Budapest newspaper, Ion Coja, deputy chairman of Vatra Românească, said that the organization "was created as an expression of the spontaneous popular reaction of Romanians in Transylvania to the separatist manifestations of Hungarians." He accused the Democratic Association of Hungarians in Romania of being "anti-Romanian" and "separatist" and said that Hungarians in Romania "demand privileges which do not exist anywhere—not even in Western democracies." He concluded that "ultimately, the minority has to be loyal to the majority, because in no country is it tolerated that minorities live their own lives." Coja claimed that 4 million Romanians were members of Vatra Românească (Budapest, *Népszabadság*, 5 September). The organization had access to local media and the logistical help of the local government organizations, which it used to publish articles with the threatening message that Hungarians were seeking to tear Transylvania away from Romania and in general to incite ethnic hatred. This radical nationalist organization sought to continue the Ceauşescu regime's policies of forced assimilation of ethnic minorities and the homogenization of Romanian society.

The escalating conflict between Vatra Românească and the rising expectations of the Hungarian minority produced an outburst of ethnic violence in the Transylvanian city of Tîrgu-Mureş. The city is the center of the Székely region, an area of eastern Transylvania inhabited predominantly by Hungarians. Tîrgu-Mureş was the capital of the Hungarian Autonomous Region until it was abolished in 1968 by Ceauşescu, who then began systematically settling ethnic Romanians in the area to dilute the Hungarian proportion of the population. Over the past two decades, Tîrgu-Mureş has been transformed from a predominantly Hungarian city to one divided between Hungarians and Romanians. Furthermore, the Romanians who migrated to the area were principally from distant parts of eastern Romania, many of whom were struggling with intense nationalistic feelings of their own. These circumstances made them particularly susceptible to the nationalistic appeals of Vatra Românească.

On 19–20 March, attacks by ethnic Romanians against ethnic Hungarians in Tîrgu-Mureş left eight dead and 365 injured. Among those seriously injured was András Sütö, the foremost Hungarian-language writer in Romania. The attacks on Hungarians appear to have been carried out primarily by peasants from outlying mountain villages, who were given alcohol and bused into Tîrgu-Mureş for the occasion. The implements used in the attacks—pitchforks, scythes, and axes—reflected the background of the perpetrators. For two consecutive days, despite constant appeals from besieged Hungarians, the army and the police made no serious attempt to stop the attacks or protect those targeted for violence. There were reports that the army was equipped only with batons and thus unable to stop the attacks. Not until the evening of the second day did army reinforcements finally arrive and restore order. What role the NSF in Bucharest or local NSF officials played in the affair is not clear; however, the headquarters of the Romanian Liberal Party and the Romanian Social-Democratic Party were also attacked and ransacked by the Vatra Românească mob. Let us emphasize that the attacks against Hungarians were not supported by all Romanians: many ethnic Romanians in Tîrgu-Mureş attended a rally of ethnic Hungarians called to protest the provoking of interethnic hatred; representatives of several ethnic Romanian groups spoke at another rally to show solidarity with Hungarians; and several independent Romanian organizations reaffirmed their support for Hungarian minority rights. (Radio Bucharest, 21 March; Rompres, 21, 22, 23 March; *NYT*, 18, 26 March; *WP*, 23 March; AFP, 21 March; Vladimir Socor, "Forces of Old Resurface in Romania: The Ethnic Clashes in Tîrgu-Mureş," RFE, *Report on Eastern Europe* 1, no. 15 [13 April].)

The official Romanian government response to the events in Tîrgu-Mureş was reminiscent of the worst offenses of the Ceauşescu regime. A government statement issued on 21 March blamed the clashes on provocations by Hungarian citizens who it said crossed the border on 15 March to celebrate the anniversary of the Hungarian revolution of 1848. (Several key events of the 1848 revolution took place in what is now Romania.) Prime Minister Roman made a number of inflammatory charges against citizens of Hungary, most of which could not be substantiated and others of which were contradicted by Romanian sources (Rompres, 21 March). On 23 March, the government began to change its line. A communiqué published in Bucharest "disassociated" the government from accusations made in the mass media "regarding separatist and nationalist tendencies" among the Hungarian minority. The communiqué also said that accusations that the Hungarian minority intended to "harm Romania's territorial integrity" were "groundless." The government threatened action against those who published or disseminated assessments or reports that "incite hatred and violence between ethnic communities." That same day, however, a message from Prime Minister Roman to the U.N. secretary general, European prime ministers, and other international organizations reiterated the allegations concerning the participation of citizens of Hungary in the violent incidents in Tîrgu-Mureş and spoke of the seriousness of the "nationalist-chauvinist and revisionist instigations carried out by certain circles from Hungary against Romania" (Rompres, 23 March; *Adevărul*, 24 March). In a response to foreign journalists' questions on 24 March and in an address to the nation on 25 March, Iliescu used language reminiscent of the Ceauşescu era to describe the response to events in Tîrgu-Mureş when he said that "problems of the relations between the Hungarian minority and the majority Romanian population" was "a problem the Romanian state alone has to settle" and emphasized the "unitary character" of the Romanian state (Rompres, 24, 25 March, 7 April).

The excessive violence in Tîrgu-Mureş brought an uneasy calm to the ethnic Hungarian and ethnic Romanian tensions. At a conference of the Democratic Federation of Hungarians in Romania, held in the city of Oradea in April (less than a month before the Romanian elections), Hungarians conducted a spirited debate on how best to gain the minority rights they sought under existing conditions in Romania and what role they should play in the forthcoming election (*Romániai Magyar Szó*, 24, 25, 26, 27, 28 April). With the approach of the elections, the NSF had decided to appeal to Romanian nationalism. In the voting the Democratic Federation of Hungarians in Romania received the second largest number of votes, which had certain negative aspects because the leading opposition group was an ethnic Hungarian federation.

A week before the elections, the interim government modified the basic Ceauşescu-era education law but did little to liberalize or improve restrictive provisions on education in the student's mother tongue and did not move toward expansion of Hungarian-language schools. The Hungarian and other minorities strongly protested the decision. The week after Iliescu's landslide election, János

Fazekas, a former deputy prime minister under Ceauşescu and a leading ethnic Hungarian, addressed an open letter to the new president condemning the government for having done little on minority issues (see Carmen Pompey, "Decision on Education Protested by Minorities," RFE, *Report on Eastern Europe* 1, no. 27 [6 July]). In July, Vatra Românească organized demonstrations in Bucharest and four Transylvanian cities protesting the alleged favoritism of Hungarians in Transylvania, while the Democratic Federation of Hungarians in Romania called for an open and rational dialogue (Rompres, July 8). The Ministry of Education rejected the federation's demand for a Hungarian-language university in Cluj on the basis that there were already numerous courses in Hungarian at Babes-Bolyai University and that university-trained professionals should study in Romanian because they would eventually be working among Romanians (Rompres, July 25). The Hungarian federation joined a number of other organizations representing ethnic groups and established the League of Ethnic Minorities of Romania, which met with President Iliescu to urge minority rights (Radio Bucharest, Rompres, July 29).

While the Hungarians voiced their demands for full rights for the minority, the NSF government fostered nationalist sentiments that incited anti-Hungarian feelings. Major commemorations were held in northern Transylvania on 30 August, the 50th anniversary of the Vienna Diktat, under which the northern half of Transylvania was given to Hungary by Hitler and Mussolini. In the town of Ip, where 157 Romanians were killed by Hungarian soldiers in 1940, Prime Minister Roman as well as the foreign and interior ministers participated in a special commemoration. This was the first time in the half-century since those events occurred that any official commemoration had been held (*NYT*, 2 September). The calls for a separate Hungarian-language university continued, and a major meeting on the issue took place in Cluj in late November, with Congressman Tom Lantos, cochairman of the U.S. Congressional Human Rights Caucus, supporting the creation of a separate Hungarian-language institution.

Soviet Moldavia and relations with the Soviet Union. The disputed territory of Bessarabia (Soviet Moldavia), to which both Romania and the Soviet Union have laid claim, is another complex issue that is entwined with Romanian nationalism, Romania's relations with the Soviet Union, Soviet domestic nationality policies, and the problem of the Hungarian minority in Transylvania. Bessarabia, which makes up the bulk of the Soviet Socialist Republic of Moldavia, lies between the Prut and Dniester rivers; Turkish until 1812, when the area was added to the Russian Empire, it became part of Romania in 1918 when Russia was convulsed with revolution. The Soviet Union never accepted that change of ownership, and in 1940, under the infamous Molotov-Ribbentrop pact, Soviet troops took it back. Romania joined Hitler's armies in the attack on the Soviet Union in 1941 to retake the disputed territory, but the Soviets again occupied it in 1944 when they drove out Nazi and Romanian troops. The Soviets have been in possession of the territory since World War II. Shortly after retaking the area for the last time, the USSR established the Moldavian Soviet Socialist Republic as a republic of the Soviet Union. The population of Moldavia, which numbers 4.3 million, is ethnically mixed: about 64 percent are "Moldavian," 14 percent are Ukrainian, 13 percent, Russian, the Gagauzi, almost 4 percent, and Jews and Bulgarians, 2 percent each (*1990–1991 Statesman's Yearbook* [New York: St. Martin's Press], p. 1275). Although the Romanians consider the Moldavians to be Romanians, in the past the Soviets emphasized that they are a separate and distinct nationality. The Moldavians speak Romanian, although the Soviets call it Moldavian. Until 1989 the official alphabet was Cyrillic, whereas the Romanians use the Latin alphabet.

Under Ceauşescu, veiled Romanian claims to Bessarabia were periodically raised as a means of rallying Romanian nationalism or irritating the Soviet Union, but Ceauşescu's repressive, austere regime held little attraction for the Moldavians. The Soviet Union opposed any boundary changes, and in the past there was little serious consideration of altering frontiers. The recent national assertiveness of Lithuania, Latvia, Estonia, Armenia, Georgia, and Azerbaijan, however, has raised new questions about Soviet Moldavia, particularly when coupled with the fall of Ceauşescu and the election of the new government in Bucharest. In 1988, Moldavians held mass demonstrations to demand that Moldavian/Romanian be made the official language of the republic and that it be written in the Latin script. In August 1989, Soviet authorities finally agreed to these demands. A reflection of the complex ethnic problems in the Moldavian republic came in October–November 1990, when the Gagauzi minority opposed the increasing assertiveness of the Moldavian/Romanian majority and ethnic Russians came to the aid of the Gagauzi. Moldavian militants mobilized to prevent Gagauzi separatism and to reinforce their demands for greater ethnic recognition (*NYT*, 26 October, 1, 3, November; *WP*, 27 October, 3 November).

After the fall of Ceaușescu, contacts between Romania and Soviet Moldavia increased substantially with the blessing of both the Soviet and the Romanian governments. In a demonstrative gesture just days after Ceaușescu's execution, Iliescu and Foreign Minister Sergiu Celac met with a group of Romanian-speaking writers from Soviet Moldavia in the presence of the Soviet ambassador to Romania. Under Ceaușescu, even cultural contacts were discouraged by the Soviet Union. Soviet authorities began removing barbed wire fences along the frontier with Romania and relaxed restrictions to permit people in frontier regions to move back and forth across the border. Romanian authorities have likewise allowed greater contacts. In May, eight border crossings were opened by Soviet authorities, the first time in half a century that Romanians were able to enter Soviet Moldavia at these locations. In June, tens of thousands of Romanians entered Moldavia and met with Moldavians who came from as far away as Kishinev. Soviet border troops restored order after a few hours and forced the Romanians to return (AFP, 24 June). The leader of the Moldavian Popular Front, a mass movement pressing for greater Moldavian autonomy, reported crowds chanting for reunification at a nationalist rally in Soviet Moldavia. The same reaction had been observed by journalists in Romanian territories adjacent to the Soviet border. (Paris, *Le Monde*, 3 January, *LAT*, 12 January; *WP*, 16 January; AFP, 24 June; Mihai Carp, "Cultural Ties between Romania and Soviet Moldavia," RFE, *Report on Eastern Europe* 1, no. 30 [27 July].)

At the same time, however, the Romanian government was particularly cautious not to alarm the Soviet Union by making claims to Soviet territory. (It also served Romania's interest to avoid raising border questions because of its fear that Hungary might raise border adjustments in the context of the Hungarian minority in Transylvania.) At the end of January, the new Romanian ambassador to the Soviet Union, Vasile Șandru, said that the new Romanian government withdrew reservations made by the Ceaușescu regime when it signed the Helsinki Final Act. Romania's reservations at that time related to the status of Soviet Moldavia, and Șandru wanted the Soviet government to know that Romania was committed to Europe's current boundaries.

Much the same position was taken by President Iliescu in an election rally speech in Turnu-Severin. Although he called the Soviet seizure of Bessarabia "a historical injustice," he said that redrawing Romania's present borders was not in the country's best interest (Rompres, 4 May).

Despite the government's best intentions, however, the growth of nationalist sentiment among the ethnic Romanian population in addition to the greater freedom of expression in post-Ceaușescu Romania resulted in popular demands for the return of Bessarabia. In April, some three hundred prominent writers, journalists, and orthodox priests from Romania and Soviet Moldavia gathered in Bucharest to demand that Bessarabia be permitted to rejoin Romania. The Soviet ambassador to Romania rejected their demand. Nevertheless, both sides continued to encourage contacts. In July discussions were held between the Soviet Moldavian foreign minister, the Soviet ambassador in Bucharest, and Romanian Foreign Ministry officials at which the possibility of "diplomatic and consular" ties between Romania and Soviet Moldavia were discussed (Radio Bucharest, 3 July). In September, Romanian and Moldavian officials signed an agreement to automate and expand telephone and telegraphic communications and extend other contacts between Romania and Moldavia (Rompres, 7 September). The reunification of Germany with Soviet approval raised hopes and led some Romanians to call publicly for the reunification of Bessarabia with Romania (*Viitorul*, 6 October).

During the disruption and upheaval in Moldavia in October, some fifteen thousand Romanians marched through the streets of Bucharest to show support for the territorial integrity of Soviet Moldavia and to protest the attempt to establish a Gagauz republic. The marchers handed a petition to a Soviet embassy representative. Most of the protesters were from the Free Democratic Party, the National Christian Democratic Party, the Bucharest-Kishinev Association (an organization favoring closer ties between Romania and Moldavia), and other groups. Vatra Românească expressed support for the protest, and other Romanian organizations adopted formal resolutions of support for the Moldavian cause against the Gagauzi (Rompres, 9, 11 September, 24 October; *Dreptatea*, 26 October).

Because of popular Romanian nationalist sentiment for the reunion of Bessarabia with Romania, the government has been caught on the horns of a dilemma: seeking to rally and manipulate Romanian nationalism to strengthen its position among the Romanian masses but at the same time balancing that with the urgent need to avoid antagonizing the Soviet Union. The result has been public statements strangely reminiscent of Ceauşescu's carefully measured manipulation of the issue. For example, in his speech on the first celebration of Romanian National Day on 1 December in Alba Iulia, President Iliescu could not avoid mentioning Bessarabia because the 1 December anniversary marks the date in 1918 when Transylvania and Bessarabia were united with the old kingdom. He said that "history will find a way of correcting the injustice of Romania's loss of its former territories," but he did not call for changing borders (Rompres, 1 December).

Foreign Relations. For the past three decades, Romania's principal claim to international attention was its foreign policy, which was distinctly separate from that of the Soviet Union. Although Romania remained within the Soviet orbit as a member of the Warsaw Pact and the Council for Mutual Economic Assistance (CMEA), Romanian leaders frequently emphasized their differences with the Soviet Union. Romania pressed against the limits of Soviet tolerance and occasionally provoked an angry Soviet reaction but managed to avoid Soviet military intervention. During the last decade of Ceauşescu's rule, however, Romania's international distinction was overshadowed by its atrocious human rights policies, its treatment of its ethnic minorities, and its abusive domestic policies. During 1990, with the government struggling to maintain domestic order, reorganize the political system, conduct elections, transform the national economy, and deal with severe domestic problems, international relations assumed a clearly subordinate role.

The aftermath of the bloody and violent overthrow of Ceauşescu was the first occasion for the new government to deal with international politics. Soon after the end of the revolution, a series of foreign ministers from the Soviet Union, the European communities, and the United States visited Romania to show support for the new government and assess the country's need for assistance in the aftermath of the revolution and 25 years of Ceauşescu's repressive domestic policies. Soviet foreign minister Eduard Shevardnadze was in Bucharest within two weeks of Ceauşescu's overthrow with promises of increased deliveries of oil, gas, electricity, and other assistance. That help was reiterated to Prime Minister Roman by Soviet prime minister Nikolai Ryzhkov on 10 January when the two met in Sofia in connection with a CMEA meeting (Rompres, 7 January). Western foreign ministers who visited Bucharest in January included Hans Dietrich Genscher of West Germany, Roland Dumas of France, Sten Andersson of Sweden, Antonia Samaras of Greece, and William Waldegrave, minister of state in the British Foreign Ministry. In mid-February, U.S. secretary of state James Baker was also in Bucharest. Hungary made a particular effort to assist the Romanian people and the new government in the aftermath of the overthrow of Ceauşescu, providing food and medical assistance as well as logistic support for other countries sending aid.

The Hungarian government made an effort to place relations with Romania on a better level. During the last few years of the Ceauşescu era, relations with Hungary had been openly hostile, mainly because of the Romanian treatment of its ethnic Hungarian minority. Ceauşescu had been absolutely unyielding on that issue despite public condemnation of Romanian policies in a number of international conferences and by many Western governments. With the new Romanian government, both sides appeared to be interested in improvement. One of the early visitors to Romania on 16 January was Hungary's minister of culture and education, who met to work out a program to provide educational materials and satisfy other educational needs of the Hungarian minority. At the end of February the Hungarian defense minister met with his Romanian counterpart in Bucharest, a marked contrast to the cancellation of a similar visit by Hungary before Ceauşescu's demise. The rise of ethnic tension between Romanians and Hungarians in Transylvania, which culminated in the March violence in Tîrgu-Mureş, led to a cooling of relations. The Romanian government's knee-jerk reaction—blaming citizens of Hungary and indirectly the government of Hungary for the problems—was both wrong and destructive to mutual trust. Furthermore, Hungary led the international outcry against the ethnic violence in Tîrgu-Mureş, and this did not help bilateral relations.

Exchanges over Transylvania continued to flare up during the rest of the year. In the fall, Hungarian president Árpád Göncz was attacked by the Romanian foreign minister for his translation of a volume on Transylvania (Rompres, 4 October). The Romanian ambassador to Hungary made a plea for reconciliation with Hungary but began his appeal with an attack on the Hungarian president's translation of the "Horthyist book" on Transylvania. He also questioned Hungarian prime minister József Antall's controversial statement claiming that he had a responsibility for ethnic Hungarians in Romania, Czechoslovakia, and Yugoslavia as well as Hungary. The Romanian diplomat also suggested that the minority's drive for its rights could not deny the majority its legitimate rights (*Tineretul Liber*, 28 November; Rompres, 28 November). Although Romania's government-controlled media seemed to fan the flames of Romanian chauvinism, the independent press took a more balanced and moderate position vis-à-vis the minority issue and relations with Hungary. There was criticism of instances of extreme nationalism in Hungary (in the nationalist Hungarian paper *Szent Korona* [Holy crown]), but there was also recognition of Hungarian aid during the December revolution and a more balanced assessment of the possibility for better bilateral relations (*România Liberă*, 14 November).

The approach of the Romanian election in May and NSF campaign tactics provided another occasion for Western expressions of concern with the electoral process. The United States and the countries of Western Europe all lodged complaints with Romanian officials about government interference in the democratic process and government manipulation of the press, which limited the ability of the opposition parties to participate effectively in the electoral process. United States' concern reached the point that the U.S. ambassador to Bucharest was called back to Washington for consultations to show displeasure with the electoral campaign.

The next outpouring of international criticism of Romania came in June in connection with the above-mentioned brutal miners' rampage in Bucharest, which broke up a public protest against the NSF government and was used to intimidate opposition political parties, opposition politicians, and the independent media. The unanimous condemnation of the Romanian government left the country isolated internationally for its antidemocratic actions.

Following the criticism of its domestic activities, Romania attempted to bring itself back into the international mainstream after the Iraqi invasion of Kuwait by supporting the international condemnation of Iraq and agreeing to observe the U.N. economic sanctions against Baghdad. Romania also offered to produce jet fuel for the United States in connection with the stationing of U.S., Arab, and Western European troops in the Persian Gulf.

After the installation of the new government, an effort was made to move back to a more normal pattern of international relations. In early September, for example, President Iliescu and Foreign Minister Adrian Năstase paid an official visit to Yugoslavia (Rompres, Radio Bucharest, 5 September). The United States and Western Europe, however, continued to criticize the Romanian government's activities that restricted freedom of the press, freedom of expression, and minority rights in violation of internationally recognized human rights. President Bush pointedly did not meet with President Ion Iliescu when the Romanian president was in New York for the U.N. General Assembly meeting in October, although he met with all other leaders from Eastern Europe (*NYT*, 4 October), and the United States refused to extend most-favored-nation trade status to Romania despite clear indications that the Romanian government eagerly sought this economic benefit (Rompres, 28 September).

Robert R. King
Washington, D.C.

Union of Soviet Socialist Republics

Population. 290,938,469 (*World Fact Book 1990*)
Party. Communist Party of the Soviet Union (*Kommunisticheskaia Partiia Sovetskogo Soiuza*; CPSU)
Founded. 1898 (CPSU, 1952)
Membership. 16,900,000 claimed, January–October; 800,000 left the party, and 200,000 joined (*Literaturnaya Gazeta*, 30 January 1991). Women, 30.2 percent of membership; workers, 27.6 percent; collective farmers, 7.6 percent (*Izvestiia TsK KPSS*, 7 May).
General Secretary. Mikhail S. Gorbachev
Politburo. 24 members: Mikhail S. Gorbachev, Russian, b. 1931, president, USSR, and general secretary, CPSU Central Committee (CC);

Vladimir A. Ivashko, Ukrainian, deputy secretary general, CPSU CC; Mikolas M. Burakiavicius, Lithuanian, b. 1927, first secretary, Lithuanian CC; Stanislav I. Gurenko, Ukrainian, b. 1936, first secretary, Ukrainian CC; Aleksandr S. Dzasokhov, Russian, b. 1934, secretary, CPSU CC; Islam A. Karimov, Uzbek, b. 1936, first secretary, Uzbek CC; Petr K. Luchinskii, Moldavian, b. 1940, first secretary, Moldavian CC; Kakhar Makhkamov, b. 1932, Tadzhik, first secretary, Tadzhik CC; Anatolii A. Malofeev, Belorussian, b. 1933, first secretary, Belorussian CC; Avtandil Margiani, Georgian, b. 1944, first secretary, Georgian CC; Absamat M. Masaliev, Kirgiz, b. 1933, first secretary, Kirgiz CC; Stepan Pogosian, Armenian, b. 1932, first secretary, Armenian CC; Ayaz Mutalibov, Azeri, b. 1938, first secretary, Azerbaijani CC; Nursultan A. Nazarbaev, Kazakh, b. 1940, first secretary, Kazakh CC; Saparmurd A. Niiazov, Turkmen, b. 1940, first secretary, Turkmen CC; Ivan K. Polozkov, Russian, b. 1935, first secretary, Russian CC; Iuri A. Prokof'iev, Russian, b. 1939, first secretary, Moscow city party committee; Alfreds P. Rubiks, Latvian, b. 1935, first secretary, Latvian CC; Galina V. Semenova, Russian, b. 1937, secretary, CPSU CC; Enn-Arno Sillari, Estonian, b. 1944, first secretary, Estonian CC; Egor S. Stroev, Russian, b. 1937, secretary, CPSU CC; Ivan T. Frolov, Russian, b. 1929, editor in chief, *Pravda*; Oleg S. Shenin, Russian, b. 1937, secretary, CPSU CC; Gennadii I. Ianaiev, Russian, b. 1937, vice-president, USSR

Secretariat. 13 secretaries and five members (*indicates member of Politburo): *Mikhail S. Gorbachev, general secretary; *Vladimir A. Ivashko, deputy secretary general; Oleg D. Baklanov, Ukrainian, b. 1932, defense industry; *Aleksandr S. Dzasokhov, ideology; Valentin M. Falin, Russian, b. 1926, foreign affairs; *Ivan T. Frolov, editor in chief, *Pravda*; Boris V. Gidaspov, Russian, b. 1932, first secretary, Leningrad oblast party committee; Andrei N. Girenko, Ukrainian, b. 1936, nationalities policy; Valentin A. Kuptsov, Russian, mass organizations; Iuri A. Manaenkov, Russian, b. 1936, Russian Soviet Federated Socialist Republic (RSFSR) affairs; *Galina V. Semenova, women's issues; *Oleg S. Shenin, party organizational work; *Egor S. Stroev, agriculture. Members: Viktor Aniskin, chairman of the Gorkii kolkhoz near Moscow; Valentin Gaivoronskii, worker; Ivan Melnikov, secretary of the Moscow State University party committee; Aleksandr Teplenichev, secretary of an industrial party committee in Lipetsk; Gulchakhra Turganova, collective farmer.

Central Committee. 412 members. The CC has been organized into 6 commissions and 9 departments. At the October CC plenum, it was announced that the CC would be reorganized with 11 commissions and 12 departments.

Status. Ruling party (other parties legal)

Last Congress. Twenty-eighth, 2–13 July, in Moscow

Last Election. Congress of People's Deputies, March–April 1989, 2,250 members; 87.6 percent of elected candidates were CPSU members against 71.4 percent in the Supreme Soviet elected in 1984. The working legislature, the Supreme Soviet (chosen from the congress membership), was elected in May 1989 and contains 542 members.

Presidential Council. 16 advisers to president of USSR, March–December; Vadim V. Bakatin, Russian, b. 1937, public order; Valerii I. Boldin, Russian, b. 1935, staff work; Aleksandr N. Iakovlev, Russian, b. 1923, law enforcement and ideology; Veniamin A. Iarin, Russian, b. 1940, trade unions; Dimitri T. Iazov, Russian, b. 1923, military affairs; Albert E. Kauls, Latvian, b. 1938, agriculture; Vladimir A. Kriuchkov, Russian, b. 1924, state security; Iurii D. Masliukov, Russian, b. 1937, economic planning; Vadim A. Medvedev, Russian, b. 1930, media; Iurii A. Osip'ian, Armenian, b. 1931, science and technology; Evgenii M. Primakov, Russian, b. 1929, foreign policy; Valentin G. Rasputin, Russian, b. 1937, ecology and culture; Grigorii I. Revenko, Ukrainian, b. 1936, nationalities; Nikolai I. Ryzhkov, Russian, b. 1929 (chairman, USSR Council of Ministers), economy; Stanislav S. Shatalin, Russian, b. 1934, economy; Eduard A. Shevardnadze, Georgian, b. 1928 (USSR minister of foreign affairs; resigned 20 December), foreign policy. **Note:** On 26 December, the USSR Congress of People's Deputies approved a reorganization that places the Council of Ministers directly under the USSR president and abolishes the Presidential Council.

Auxiliary Organizations. All-Union Leninist Communist Youth League, 30 million members, led by Vladimir Ziukin, b. 1954; Voluntary Society for the Promotion of the Army, Air Force, and Navy (DOSAAF), more than 65 million members; Union of Soviet Societies for Friendship and Cultural Relations with Foreign Countries. The All-

Union Central Council of Trade Unions, 140 million members, was formerly affiliated with the party. On 26 October, the trade union organization was reorganized as the General Confederation of Soviet Trade Unions, independent of party and state.

Publications. Main CPSU organs are the daily newspaper *Pravda* (circulation 7.7 million), the theoretical and ideological journal *Kommunist* (appearing 18 times a year, with a circulation of about 1 million), and the semimonthly *Partiinaia zhizn'*, a journal of internal party affairs and organizational matters (circulation about 1 million). *Kommunist vooruzhennykh sil* is the party theoretical journal for the armed forces. The *Komsomol* has a newspaper, *Komsomol'skaia pravda* (6 days a week), and a monthly theoretical journal, *Molodaia gvardiia*. Each USSR republic prints similar party newspapers in local languages and usually also in Russian. Specialized publications include *Rabochaia tribuna*, *Dialog*, and the weekly *Ekonomika i zhizn'*. The party also publishes the weekly *Glasnost'*.

The year 1990 was one of critical challenges for both the CPSU and the Soviet state. In February, the party agreed to renounce its constitutional guarantee as the sole legal party in the USSR, only two months after party leader Mikhail Gorbachev had adamantly rejected the idea of multipartyism. Thereafter, the formation of various political movements proceeded apace amid indications that the CPSU's hold on the country was slipping, owing to an acceleration of defections from party membership.

Most union republic party organizations moved toward some sort of autonomy vis-à-vis Moscow, and in the RSFSR a separate organization was set up with Ivan Polozkov, a conservative cool to Gorbachev's reforms, elected as the Russian party's first leader. There were other signs of a conservative backlash within the party against Gorbachev, and the Twenty-eighth CPSU Congress, which assembled in Moscow in July, contained many delegations dominated by hard-line regional leaders. Nevertheless, Gorbachev was able to get most of what he wanted from the conclave, including the establishment of a new, much less powerful Politburo to be devoted strictly to party affairs as well as the defeat of conservative leader Egor Ligachev.

For most Soviet citizens, the party congress was largely irrelevant to their concerns. The most excitement was generated by the resignation of Boris

Eltsin from the party on the penultimate day of the meeting. Eltsin's election as president of the RSFSR in May capped the remarkable comeback of the former Moscow party chief and made him the most important political figure in the country other than Gorbachev.

Although one union republic after another issued declarations of sovereignty or autonomy, moves toward secession were at least temporarily contained, and the increasingly fragile union somehow held together. Gorbachev sought to stem the tide by proposing a new treaty of the union that might provide a measure of real federalism. But when the Russian republic, under Eltsin, asserted its supremacy over Kremlin-made laws, the union and Gorbachev faced the most serious challenge to date. Gorbachev was forced to negotiate with Eltsin as a virtual equal on such issues as the planned reform of the economy. Eltsin held out for the plan, identified with economist Stanislav Shatalin, for a "500-day" transition to a market economy. Gorbachev at one point seemed to endorse the Shatalin plan but then reneged and temporized, opting for a compromise between radical reform and a more moderate course advocated by Prime Minister Nikolai Ryzhkov. Eltsin and Gorbachev were again on a collision course at year's end as the RSFSR parliament announced that it would contribute only 24 billion rubles to the union budget in 1991, rather than the 119 billion demanded.

Any plan or combination of plans seemed unlikely to revive quickly the moribund Soviet economy. *Perestroika* was widely viewed as an abject failure, and shortages of consumer goods, including the Soviet staple, bread, were the worst in decades. The distribution system had largely broken down, and the economic situation became critical in the latter months of the year.

Ethnic and national conflicts continued to simmer, sometimes bursting into bitter open conflict. Adding to Soviet woes, there was a massive escalation of ordinary crime. In short, the Soviet Union appeared to be falling apart, and observers both within and outside the USSR speculated that Gorbachev's delicate balancing act might not be able to hold the union together much longer.

Gorbachev did, however, enhance his already considerable formal authority within the political system during the year. In March, he was elected to a strengthened "executive" presidency and was consistently able to dominate the Supreme Soviet on important matters until the usually complaisant deputies staged a brief, surprising revolt in November. Also in March, a Presidential Council, composed of advisers to Gorbachev, was established, and after the Twenty-eighth CPSU Congress, it had clearly supplanted the Politburo as the real "cabinet" of the country. The Presidential Council was destined, however, to be a short-lived institution. In December, another governmental reorganization plan approved by the Congress of People's Deputies called for abolition of the Presidential Council and the placement of the Council of Ministers directly under the USSR president.

In external affairs, the USSR's world power continued to shrivel, although Moscow was able to function as a kind of secondary superpower. The year saw the definitive collapse of the Soviet bloc in Eastern Europe, a development clearly prefigured by events of 1989. At the Twenty-eighth CPSU Congress and elsewhere, there were rumblings about the "loss" of Eastern Europe. With the congress behind him and after months of shifting positions on the issue, Gorbachev agreed, in July, to the inclusion of a united Germany within the North Atlantic Treaty Organization (NATO). The deal with Bonn promised substantial economic benefits to the USSR, but Gorbachev came away empty-handed when he sought additional economic aid from German chancellor Helmut Kohl in Bonn in November. The two leaders did, however, sign a nonaggression treaty, pledging to honor the postwar borders of all European states.

Relations with the United States were generally harmonious, and Gorbachev and U.S. president George Bush met for a major summit in the United States in late May and again for a minisummit in Helsinki in September. The Iraqi invasion of Kuwait on 2 August posed perhaps the most crucial test to date of the "new political thinking" and of the developing relationship with the United States. The Soviets sought a peaceful resolution to the crisis and dispatched presidential adviser Evgenii Primakov to Baghdad twice for discussions with Saddam Husayn. At the United Nations, the United States and the USSR voted together on sanctions against Iraq, and in general the Persian Gulf crisis was marked by cooperation between Washington and Moscow.

Gorbachev was awarded the Nobel Peace Prize in October, further embellishing his international image. But within the USSR, the award only emphasized the disparity between Gorbachev's achievements in the world arena and his failures at home. He had, of course, produced a striking transformation of the Soviet polity, but this in turn unleashed a flood of problems. The nationalities issue

and the difficulties involved in reforming the political system and the economy had all been underestimated by the Soviet leader, and he was now paying dearly for earlier misjudgments. Highly unpopular with the Soviet masses, Gorbachev saw his authority slipping away. Finally, confronted with rising anarchy in the country, Gorbachev followed the traditional pattern of Russian reformers whose reforms turn sour: he veered sharply to the right.

As *poriadok* (order) replaced *perestroika* (restructuring) in Gorbachev's priorities, reformers became alarmed. Foreign Minister Eduard Shevardnadze resigned on 20 December with a dramatic speech warning of approaching dictatorship. The Congress of People's Deputies gave Gorbachev additional powers in December and reluctantly approved his choice as vice-president, Gennadi Ianaiev, a veteran *apparatchik*. With Boris Pugo, a former State Security Committee official, installed as the new interior minister and with leading reformers in limbo, Gorbachev seemed to be hunkering down for a tough approach to the USSR's problems, backed by the army, the police, and the party apparatus.

Leadership. Party leader Gorbachev had faced some heavy opposition within the party during 1989 but had weathered all storms, particularly challenges at the June and December CC plenums. While advancing his program for the transfer of functional power from party to government, he continued to rely on his position as party leader. In December he vehemently rejected suggestions for ending the communist party's monopoly on power. He was compelled, however, to abandon this position and accelerate the movement from party to government control as a result of three developments: party cohesion was eroding rapidly, with the central apparatus losing control of regional and union republic parties; the party's position in Soviet society was weakening rapidly under the impact of *glasnost'* and the multiplication of political groups within and outside the CPSU; and the economy and law and order were breaking down while the central authorities seemingly lacked the will or means to reverse processes of disintegration.

The first hint of a shift by Gorbachev came during a January visit to Lithuania when he indicated that he would not necessarily oppose multipartyism. Thereafter, events moved rapidly. On 6 February, the CC agreed to repeal of Article 6 of the USSR Constitution, which guaranteed the "leading role" of the party. Gorbachev also called for a "rethinking" of the principle of "democratic centralism" (*Pravda*, 7 February). One day later, the party leadership called for the establishment of something resembling a Western-style presidential government with a strong executive and separation of powers.

The political reforms of 1988–1989 left Gorbachev with inadequate power when confronting critical situations. On 13 March, the Congress of People's Deputies voted for the repeal of Article 6 by a vote of 1,771 to 164 and on the same day voted the creation of the "executive" presidency by a vote of 1,817 to 111 (ibid., 14 March). The latter legislation gave the president several important new powers, including the rights to make war in certain circumstances, to veto legislation, and to declare states of emergency and also authorized a Presidential Council to assist the chief executive (TASS, *Izvestiia*, 14 March). Gorbachev had to withdraw a proposal allowing him to appeal a veto override, however, and also promise that any imposition of a state of emergency would be preceded by an official warning and prior approval of local authorities (AP, 13 March). Two days later, Gorbachev was elected to the restyled presidency by a vote of 1,329 to 495, with the remainder of the deputies abstaining (TASS, *Pravda*, 16 March).

Gorbachev's vote was less than 60 percent of the total membership and not much more than the 1,123 needed to win. This was duly noted by Western analysts, who saw signs of increasing opposition to the party leader. Clearly, there was discontent with Gorbachev from both left- and right-wing elements in the party, but decades of democratic centralism and monolithism in the CPSU had led both Soviet and Western observers to regard anything less than total unanimity as a Pyrrhic victory for the party leader. With the advent of "democratization," however, opposition to the leader could be expected, and Gorbachev's vote total would have been regarded as a landslide in Western democratic systems. The major political significance of the events of February and March from Gorbachev's standpoint was that the overwhelming majority of CC members and legislators, including many critics of his policies, were convinced that they could not manage without him. Neither "radicals" nor "conservatives" were capable of holding party and country together under conditions of *glasnost'* and *perestroika*. The impotence of the party professionals was clearly demonstrated when, despite their grumbling, they bowed to obey the party leader's call for a renunciation of their monopoly of power.

The CC vote on 6 February was preceded by a massive demonstration in Red Square demanding the end of one-party rule. Significantly, the authorities aided the demonstrators, providing them with equipment such as public address systems. This fueled speculation that Gorbachev and his closest associates were attempting to exert irresistible pressure on reluctant party officials, as well as using both "revolution from above" and "revolution from below" to sustain the momentum of political reform and to protect Gorbachev's power. Certainly the events of February and March demonstrated that Gorbachev now saw the necessity of accelerating the changeover from party to government rule because the party was becoming an increasingly shaky foundation for a leader's authority. Contrary to speculation that was rife in Moscow during the late winter, however, Gorbachev did not give up his party leadership during the year. This course, however, remained a distinct possibility for the future.

A major step in the switch to presidential government came with the introduction of the Presidential Council (*NYT*, 25 March), which held its first meeting on 27 March (Moscow Central Television, 27 March; *Report on the USSR*, 6 April). Major figures in the leadership—Aleksandr Iakovlev, Premier Nikolai Ryzhkov, Foreign Minister Eduard Shevardnadze, KGB chief Vladimir Kriuchkov, Defense Minister Dimitrii Iazov—were named, as were Interior Minister Vadim Bakatin and First Deputy Premier Iuri Masliukov. Otherwise, Gorbachev cast a rather wide net, obviously intending to make the council inclusive of various attitudes and interests. Other appointees included Latvian agrarian reformer Albert Kauls, Kirgiz novelist Chingiz Aitmatov, novelist and environmentalist Valentin Rasputin, conservative trade unionist Veniamin Iarin, Armenian Iuri Osipian, vice-president of the USSR Academy of Sciences, and economist Stanislav Shatalin. More conventional appointees included Evgenii Primakov, a Gorbachev adviser on foreign policy and president of the Council of the Union prior to his selection for the council; Grigorii Revenko, first secretary of Kiev oblast party committee from 1985 until his selection for the council; and Valerii Boldin, head of the CPSU CC General Department.

Notably, three of the sixteen original council members represented the army and the police, reflecting both the urgency of the problem of domestic disorder and the degree of Gorbachev's dependence on the coercive instrumentalities. A fourth member, Masliukov, was a product of the military-industrial complex.

The precise role of the Presidential Council was not initially clearly defined, but it quickly emerged as a powerful arm of the presidency, performing functions previously carried out by the Defense Council, the Politburo, and the Secretariat of the CC. After the reorganization of the Politburo at the Twenty-eighth CPSU Congress, the council clearly displaced the Politburo as the main center of decision making. But the Politburo had been in decline well before the congress. In 1989, the Politburo met only 34 times, rather than once a week as in former years (*Izvestiia TsK KPSS*, no. 1, January). In March, less than two weeks after the Presidential Council began functioning, First Deputy Premier Leonid Abalkin said that the Politburo had "stopped making any decisions" (AFP, 9 April; *Report on the USSR*, 1 June).

Egor Ligachev, who had maintained his role as chief spokesman for party conservatives despite his September 1988 demotion to commissioner for agriculture, continued his rearguard action against Gorbachev. At the February CC plenum, he criticized "serious errors and mistakes" committed under Gorbachev's leadership and said that "destructive forces are threatening our society with chaos and destruction, moral and physical terror" (TASS, 6 February; *WP*, 7 February). On Gorbachev's left, Boris Eltsin, cochairman of the Interregional Group of Deputies, was an outspoken dissenter at the February plenum and also opposed an early change in the presidency because "it is unknown what he is to preside over." Eltsin said that "it is not only premature but also dangerous to introduce the presidency until there is a union treaty, a treaty of the union republics" (*Argumenty i fakty*, no. 9, 3–9 March). Ligachev, however, endorsed Gorbachev's election to the executive presidency, hailing it as a "truly positive development" (TASS, *FBIS-SOV*, 15 March).

The Congress of People's Deputies amended the Soviet constitution in March to legalize the existence of parties other than the CPSU (*Izvestiia*, 17 March). Thereafter, alternative political movements accelerated their organizational processes. The various Popular Front movements in the outlying republics continued to gain in strength, and *Rukh*, in the Ukraine, became an increasingly powerful competitor of the Ukrainian Communist Party. Local elections in March produced majorities in the city soviets of Moscow, Leningrad, and other major cities for Democratic Russia, an offshoot of the Interregional Group of Deputies (*Report on the USSR*, 6 April). The rise of alternative political formations exacerbated the left-right division in the political system, making it more difficult for Gorbachev to play a centrist role.

Gorbachev, however, faced more serious problems. Even as he was engaged in a high wire act, attempting by a combination of pressure and persuasion to keep the increasingly fractious union from falling apart, Gorbachev's personal popularity plummeted, primarily because of the dismal condition of the economy. On May Day, an unprecedented incident occurred in Red Square, when demonstrators at the end of the parade carried banners denouncing Gorbachev and the leadership, causing Gorbachev and other officials to retreat from the Lenin mausoleum (*NYT*, 2 May).

"Radical" forces were growing restive under Gorbachev's leadership, fearing that the initial reform impulse of his administration had been dissipated or rendered outmoded. Iuri Afanasiev, a cofounder of the Interregional Group of Deputies who had left the CPSU in April, bitterly denounced Western "Gorbymania" at a May conference in Copenhagen. Afanasiev criticized Gorbachev on four grounds: his failure to cooperate with the "democratic opposition"; his behavior as an "out-and-out colonialist" on the issue of Lithuania; the introduction of direct presidential rule in Moscow; and the "half-hearted" nature of economic reform (Copenhagen, *Berlingske Tidende*, 15 May; *FBIS*, 16 May).

The "democratic opposition" won a signal victory in May when Boris Eltsin was elected president of the RSFSR. Gorbachev took a personal hand in the proceedings of the RSFSR Supreme Soviet and attempted to have his longtime ally, RSFSR premier and candidate Politburo member Aleksandr Vlasov, elected to the presidency. Vlasov withdrew, however, after a poor showing in the early balloting, and Eltsin won decisively on the final round against Krasnodar *kraikom* first secretary Ivan Polozkov (*Izvestiia*, 30 May). Eltsin's election followed the installation of radical reformer Gavril Popov as mayor of Moscow and the election of Anatolii Sobchak as mayor of Leningrad (ibid., 24 May). These electoral results meant that the government of the two largest Soviet cities and of the huge Russian republic had slipped out of Gorbachev's control. His dominance of the two cities was already questionable, but the presence of his loyal comrade Vlasov in the RSFSR premiership had been a guarantee of his position in the Russian republic. Over the following two months, as Eltsin organized his government, Gorbachev's exclusion from the administration became even more obvious. Vlasov was replaced as RSFSR premier by Eltsin's nominee, Ivan Silaev, and the RSFSR government squared off against the central government, with USSR prime minister Ryzhkov a particular target.

There were, however, some indications that Eltsin was willing to cooperate with Gorbachev and that Eltsin's supporters viewed his election primarily as a means for pushing Gorbachev further to the left. In any case, for the short run, the major thrust against the party leader came from the right. At the June congress of sovkhoz and kolkhoz directors, old foes Eltsin and Ligachev dueled once again. Ligachev said that he would not permit the disintegration of the Soviet Union and charged that his warnings to Gorbachev had been ignored and that the leadership was "far too permissive." Soviet television reported neither Ligachev's speech nor the appearance of Eltsin at the congress (Vienna Domestic Service, *FBIS*, 15 June).

Ligachev followed this blast with an interview sharply critical of Gorbachev. The conservative stalwart said that he was firmly against the establishment of private property and was concerned that the country might be headed for a restoration of capitalism. In addition, Ligachev called for a referendum on whether the country should follow a socialist or a capitalist path (*Pravda*, 18 June).

Matters came to a head at the organizational conference of the new Russian Communist Party. (Since 1925 there had been no separate party organization for the Russian republic; the RSFSR party committees had been directly supervised by the CPSU CC apparatus in Moscow.) Speaking on the opening day of the conference, Gorbachev strongly defended his leadership, while acknowledging shortcomings in its program and practice. He attacked Ligachev without naming him, saying that "nothing could be more absurd" than the idea that movement toward a market means a return to capitalism. Keenly aware of his slipping popular support, Gorbachev also assailed the public's "narrow-minded attitudes" after decades of totalitarian rule (*NYT*, *WP*, 19 June).

Gorbachev's critics, led by Ligachev, responded with a furious assault on the party leader. Ligachev made an implicit demand for Gorbachev's resignation as general secretary, saying that "one cannot head the party, this leading force, without dedicating all one's time to it" and charged that "many crucial problems are now discussed neither in the

Politburo nor at plenary meetings of the party Central Committee." Turning to foreign policy, Ligachev thundered that "the socialist community has disintegrated while the positions of imperialism have been dramatically consolidated." A Leningrad party official, Viktor Tiulkin, said that *perestroika* had "given nothing to the people over the past five years." Delegate Ivan Osadchi called on the congress to fight the "suicide" of the Soviet Union and the CPSU. Ligachev's longtime protégé Aleksandr Melnikov accused Gorbachev of having created a "cult of personality" for himself. The most ominous challenge came from army general Albert Makashov, who reflected widespread disgruntlement in military ranks. Makashov denounced the decisions that led to Soviet troop withdrawals from Eastern Europe, "countries that our fathers liberated from fascism," and said that "we are not ready for ideological surrender." Nettled, Gorbachev retorted that "some comrades are treating the General Secretary and President very casually" and hinted that he might resign from the party leadership (TASS, *NYT*, *WP*, 19, 20 June). Boris Eltsin, however, appeared quite friendly toward Gorbachev at the conference and in a newspaper interview defended the leadership against what he called the "one-sided" discussion at the meeting (*Pravda*, 21 June).

The most important immediate result of the conference was the election of Ivan Polozkov as first secretary of the Russian Communist Party. Polozkov, party first secretary of Krasnodar *krai*, an important region that had once been controlled by Gorbachev supporters, had emerged as one of the leading conservative voices in the party. Polozkov narrowly defeated Oleg Lobov, a former Eltsin associate from Sverdlovsk, for the new leadership post (*Izvestiia*, 24 June).

The Russian Communist Party conference sent shock waves through the party, leading to a wave of resignations by liberals. With conservative forces in full offensive, a major struggle was foreseen for the upcoming Twenty-eighth CPSU Congress. Politburo member Vadim Medvedev was said to be taking soundings about the possibility of postponing the congress, and Boris Eltsin said that he leaned toward a postponement "so it will not be held in the same great haste" as the Russian gathering (*NYT*, 27 June). However, the congress proceeded as scheduled, opening on 2 July.

As expected, the congress was stormy, with some of Gorbachev's closest associates becoming special targets (see below). The conservative forces concentrated on trying to win the new post of deputy general secretary and thus restrain Gorbachev within the party apparatus. Ligachev was defeated for the post by Gorbachev nominee Vladimir Ivashko and departed for Siberia, ostensibly to retire and write his memoirs; however, the old conservative warhorse remained active in the USSR Supreme Soviet and in agricultural organizations.

Some important party restructuring came out of the congress. The Politburo was reorganized, with the fifteen union-republic party leaders included ex officio on the 24-member committee. The new Politburo was to concentrate on internal party affairs and would have little of the wide-ranging power held by the old body. The CC was increased to 412 members, with the category of candidate member abolished (*Pravda*, 13, 14 July). Boris Eltsin resigned from the party, but most Democratic Platform members elected to remain for the time being.

The defeat of Ligachev and the reorganization of the party leadership gave Gorbachev some breathing space but did nothing to enhance public confidence. A poll released by the All-Union Center for the Study of Public Opinion, with more than 1,400 respondents, contained devastating news for the leadership. Forty-six percent expressed no confidence "at all" in the country's leadership, and 46 percent supported the demand that the government resign. Eighty-four percent approved the election of Boris Eltsin as president of the RSFSR. Respondents were asked, "If we had a multiparty system, which party would you vote for?" Only 18.8 percent said the CPSU, while 10.9 opted for the Democratic Platform; 29 percent were undecided, and the remainder chose other groups (*Moscow News*, 15–22 July).

The principal beneficiary of the public mood was Boris Eltsin, who used his position as president of the Russian republic to challenge central control over the economy of the RSFSR. He also opposed USSR premier Nikolai Ryzhkov, pushing on several occasions for the resignation of the Council of Ministers chairman. Eltsin and Ryzhkov had both been products of the old Kirilenko machine in Sverdlovsk, and it is believed that Ryzhkov was mainly responsible for bringing Eltsin to Moscow in the spring of 1985, first as a department head, then as secretary of the CC. Their relationship apparently soured after the bitter conflict at the October 1987 plenum that led to Eltsin's departure from the leadership of the Moscow city party.

Some observers concluded that Gorbachev was using Eltsin as a lever to get rid of Ryzhkov. The prime minister was widely blamed for the economic crisis and was by late summer clearly the most unpopular politician in the country. Rumors circulated in Moscow that Ryzhkov would be replaced by Foreign Minister Eduard Shevardnadze or Deputy Premier Leonid Abalkin. However, Gorbachev made no overt move to discharge Ryzhkov and, in fact, seemed reluctant to part with him. Nevertheless, Gorbachev's moves in a high-stakes game on the future of the Soviet economy sometimes left the prime minister in a position of considerable embarrassment.

Gorbachev's big political problem was Eltsin. The Russian president was too powerful and too popular to be ignored, yet a complete yielding to Eltsin's demands would leave Gorbachev as a ceremonial president with little control over the USSR. In these conditions, Gorbachev carried out several rounds of negotiations with Eltsin, featuring flip-flops between apparent complete agreement and angry confrontation over the issues.

In early August, Gorbachev and Eltsin agreed to formulate a joint program for transition to a market economy. This program was to be based on the "500-day" plan prepared by Stanislav Shatalin and RSFSR deputy premier Grigorii Iavlinskii. The economic plan was to become, in turn, part of the basis for a new "union treaty" that would give greater freedom to the republics (*CSM*, 14 August). By the end of the month, the entente between the two leaders had broken down over Gorbachev's abrogation of a 9 August RSFSR resolution that claimed control over Russian resources (ibid., 28 August). Gorbachev and Eltsin met 29–30 August for wide-ranging discussions on internal problems and "some international issues" (TASS, *FBIS-SOV*, 29, 30 August), but the two leaders remained at odds over important issues.

In September, the economic downturn intensified and the USSR appeared increasingly ungovernable. In this atmosphere, rumors spread of an impending military takeover, and publications such as *Moscow News* and *Literaturnaia gazeta* examined the possibility of an army coup. *Komsomolskaia pravda* (26 September) spoke of military plans to take over strategic points such as power stations, television offices, and military terminals and reported that troops from Ryazan and Tula had been put in a state of combat readiness. Defense Minister Dimitri Iazov responded with a speech to the Supreme Soviet emphatically denying these rumors. Iazov confirmed that there had been troop movements in Moscow in recent weeks but said they were related to the soldiers' participation in the 7 November Revolution Day parade or gathering the harvest (TASS, 26 September; *NYT*, 27 September).

Gorbachev attempted to meet the crisis by requesting additional powers. On 24 September, the USSR Supreme Soviet, by a vote of 305 to 36, agreed to grant emergency powers to the president for 500 days. Gorbachev was empowered to issue decrees on property rights, the budget and financial systems, price increases, and measures to maintain law and order. The Supreme Soviet also authorized Gorbachev to work out a compromise plan for the economy by 15 October (TASS, 24 September; *NYT*, 25 September). The first use of his new powers was a decree on 28 September ordering all state enterprises to fulfill their contractual obligations until the end of 1991 or face heavy fines (*Pravda*, 29 September).

The Russian republic went ahead with the 500-day program for economic reform, but Gorbachev won an overwhelming mandate on 19 October for a compromise plan. The USSR Supreme Soviet approved, by 333 to 12, a plan emphasizing strict budget control but to a much less radical degree than the so-called Shatalin plan. Gorbachev made an urgent call for national discipline and delivered a scorching attack on Eltsin, whom he portrayed as a destructive opportunist. Within hours of the plan's approval, Eltsin denounced it as a catastrophe and insisted that economic reform should be in the hands of the leaders of the individual republics (ibid., *NYT*, 20 October).

Eltsin appeared with Gorbachev at the 7 November Revolution Day celebration, and the two leaders appeared to be quite convivial. The occasion was marred by a shooting incident. According to early KGB reports, a man armed with a sawed-off shotgun fired from about 100 yards away from the Lenin mausoleum but posed no real threat to the Soviet leader. Subsequently, Sgt. Andrei Milnikov, the policeman who overpowered the gunman, said that the man had been armed with a hunting rifle and pointed it toward the mausoleum where Gorbachev, Eltsin, Moscow mayor Gavril Popov, and other officials were reviewing the parade (*LAT*, 15 November).

In mid-November, Gorbachev and Eltsin met for another summit and appeared ready to cooperate to meet the deepening crisis. Eltsin called for a coalition government to confront the emergency, and it seemed likely that Gorbachev would accede to the demand. Gorbachev at this point, however, faced a threat from an unlikely quarter—the new Russian government. An order freeing prices on luxury goods was rejected by the RSFSR Supreme Soviet, which announced that the measure would not take effect in the Russian republic. On the same day, the usually passive USSR Supreme Soviet demanded, by a vote of 362 to 0, that Gorbachev deliver a state of the union address to parliament.

Izvestiia (15 November) deplored the governmental disarray, scorning "political spectaculars," while another Moscow newspaper carried the headline "Revolt in the Kremlin" (*Vecherniaia Moskva*, 14 November). The seriousness of the situation was underscored in an article by Marshal Sergei Akhromeiev, which warned that while the army would remain subservient to legitimate political rule, it was ready to "protect our federal socialist state" from violent and illegal efforts to dismember it (*Sovetskaia Rossiia*, 14 November).

Confronted by a rebellious parliament, Gorbachev hastily cobbled together an emergency restructuring plan. Under the proposal, the office of USSR prime minister would be abolished and the Federation Council, composed of the leaders of the fifteen republics, would be transformed into the chief executive agency. The president's powers would be enhanced by a new security council overseeing the army, the police, and the KGB and by a network of presidential representatives around the country to enforce orders from the center. The Supreme Soviet promptly and overwhelmingly gave preliminary approval to the plan (*NYT*, 18 November). In December, the Congress of People's Deputies approved the main outlines of the reorganization plan, with the Council of Ministers to be directly under the USSR president. In addition, the Presidential Council was to be abolished. But the congress refused to set up a Presidential Supreme State Inspectorate to monitor compliance with orders from Moscow (ibid., 29 December).

In late December, Gorbachev warned that he would impose direct presidential rule on rebellious areas, confirming the sharp turn to the right that may have begun after a difficult meeting on 15 November with irate army officers. On 2 December, Gorbachev replaced the reformist Interior Minister Vadim Bakatin with Boris Pugo, head of the Party Control Commission and former head of the KGB in Latvia; the outspoken conservative Col. Gen. Boris Gromov was installed as his deputy (*Izvestiia*, 3 December). In effect, the KGB and the army had taken over the civilian police. The message was unmistakable: Bakatin had been under severe attack from the right for the breakdown of order and for his proposal that party cells be eliminated in the militia.

Reacting to the rightward trend, Foreign Minister Shevardnadze stunned the congress and the world on 20 December when he resigned, delivering an emotional speech in which he charged that "reformers have gone and hidden in the bushes. Dictatorship is coming." (*NYT*, 21 December.) Gorbachev denounced Shevardnadze for quitting at such a difficult time and appeared ruffled but unshaken in his positions. If Shevardnadze aimed to influence Gorbachev to maintain the movement toward democratization, the tactic evidently did not succeed. The Soviet president continued his thrust toward centralization and restoration of *poriadok*.

Moderates were dismayed when Gorbachev nominated the veteran apparatchik Gennadi Ianaiev for the new post of vice-president. During the year, Ianaiev had risen to the leadership of the trade unions and had then been elected to the CPSU Secretariat and Politburo. His public statements during the year had indicated that, from the standpoint of party traditionalists, he was a safe officeholder.

Gorbachev was rebuffed when Ianaiev failed to win election on the first ballot. Following a lecture from the leader and some Gorbachevian lobbying, the colorless bureaucrat was elected by the Supreme Soviet on the second ballot (*NYT*, 27, 28 December). Indicative of the way things were going, Gorbachev relied heavily on the conservative Soiuz group of deputies to accomplish this goal.

Premier Ryzhkov was hospitalized following a heart attack during the congress (TASS, 26 December). Under the governmental reorganization plan, he was unlikely to play much of a role, if any, in the USSR government during 1991.

With the abolition of the Presidential Council, the influence of prominent reformers was doubtful. Bakatin was already out, and Shevardnadze apparently continued in his post until a successor could be appointed. Stanislav Shatalin was almost certain to be a casualty of the rightward turn, and the political future of Aleksandr Iakovlev was most uncertain.

Twenty-eighth Congress of the CPSU. The 4,683 delegates to the Twenty-eighth CPSU Congress assembled in Moscow on 2 July in a tense atmosphere produced by the double threat of a conservative counteroffensive against Gorbachev and his reformist policies and the prospect of a breakaway from the party by "radical" and liberal elements. The former threat was the more immediate one. Some 2,800 delegates represented the Russian Communist Party, which had established its own organization two weeks earlier. Only 2.1 percent of the delegates had entered the party since 1985 (*Pravda*, 5 July), and more than 40 percent were party officials. The general mood at the outset seemed mostly conservative, even rebellious, but the expected direct challenge to Gorbachev did not materialize.

One of the more outspoken conservatives, Boris Gidaspov, Leningrad party leader, strongly defended Gorbachev at the congress, perhaps thereby assuring his election to the Secretariat at the conclave's conclusion. Even the hard-line leader of the Russian Communist Party, Ivan Polozkov, sought to present himself as a moderate. There was plenty of criticism directed toward Gorbachev's policies and those of some of his closest associates. But party conservatives were constrained by a growing awareness that a full-scale victory over Gorbachev would lead to an immediate rupture in the party's ranks and leave them without popular support. At the same time, a hard core of conservative delegates was determined to restrain "liberal" tendencies as much as possible.

The moderate stance of the congress was indicated on its first day when Gorbachev easily turned aside two proposals from the floor, one on devoting a special session of the congress to discussion of the CPSU's "guilt before the people" and another demanding resignation of the entire CPSU CC and Politburo (TASS, *NYT*, 3 July).

In his opening speech to the congress, Gorbachev strongly defended *perestroika*, appealed for calm while the process of drawing up a new union treaty proceeded, and upheld the principles of the "new political thinking" in foreign policy. He also warned that unless the CPSU put forward realistic and attractive policies, the populace would move toward other competing parties (*Pravda*, 3 July).

On the second day of the congress, Politburo members Nikolai Sliunkov and Vitalii Vorotnikov, candidate member Aleksandra Biriukova, and CC secretary Gumer Usmanov submitted their resignations (ibid., 4 July). Subsequently, Aleksandr Iakovev and Eduard Shevardnadze announced that they would not be candidates for reelection to the Politburo, thereby somewhat defusing conservative opposition.

Much of the work of the congress was devoted to reports by commissions, selection of committees, and other routine activities. Probably the most important business was conducted off the floor in a meeting between Gorbachev and city and district first secretaries on 4 July. The party leader was asked to renounce *perestroika* and to "put things in order at last." This demand was flatly rejected by Gorbachev, who insisted that the "political line" would not change while he was in charge (*Izvestiia*, 7 July). This was the first turning point of the congress, evidently convincing many moderate delegates that the unreconstructed right must be spurned.

Several key speeches marked the first week of the congress. On 3 July, Iakovlev and Shevardnadze strongly defended their roles in shaping Soviet foreign policy. Egor Ligachev attacked the leadership's "thoughtless radicalism, improvisation, and swinging from side to side" and also blasted the Soviet media. Somewhat contrasting views were offered by Defense Minister Iazov and KGB head Kriuchkov. Iazov endorsed the new defensive doctrine and the lowering of international tensions. Kriuchkov, in contrast, said that the security organs should act more resolutely to maintain law and order and contended that "the danger of war continues to be a real one" (TASS, Reuters, 3 July; *International Herald Tribune*, 4 July).

A second major event was the speech by Boris Gidaspov on 4 July. Gidaspov favored the granting of additional powers to Gorbachev and proposed the empowering of presidential representatives to maintain order in various parts of the country. He also strongly endorsed the move from party to soviet rule (TASS, 4 July; *Pravda*, 5 July).

A third key moment at the congress was the address by Boris Eltsin on 6 July. The RSFSR president warned that there were only two alternatives: either a party of the apparatus that would shortly collapse or a "renewed party" capable of uniting democratic forces. Eltsin proposed changing the party's name to the Party of Democratic Socialism to compete on an equal basis with other parties. He also favored working toward a "federation of national units," postponing the adoption of a new platform and party rules, and eliminating all party cells in the armed forces, police, and KGB (ibid., 7 July). Eltsin, in effect, warned the party that, in the event of a rightward turn, its fate might well be decided by nonparty forces.

The three significant events noted above gave the right few options and virtually assured an outcome favorable to Gorbachev. The party leader's stern rejection of low-level secretaries' demands demonstrated that the right could expect no yielding by the

leader on general policy. Gidaspov's speech demonstrated further that the apparent conservative majority was not united. Finally, Eltsin's address threw into the balance the rising pressures from outside the party. The hard-line conservatives then sought to salvage something on certain key votes.

A proposal—that in the event of a party conference between congresses delegates would be chosen from those attending the Twenty-eighth Congress—was defeated by a vote of 2,582 to 1,357 (*NYT*, 10 July). A major change in the composition of the Politburo was approved, with 15 of the 24 members to be party leaders of the union republics (*Pravda*, 10 July). Both votes were defeats for the conservatives. The proposal on party conferences would have virtually guaranteed a conservative majority at any such meeting; the size and composition of the new Politburo assured that it would fit neatly into the ongoing transition from party to government domination and would pose no real check on the party leader.

Gorbachev was reelected as general secretary on 10 July by a vote of 3,411 to 1,116; his only opponent, Teimuraz Avaliani, Kiselevsk *gorkom* first secretary, received 501 votes (ibid., 11 July).

On 11 July, the right made its last attempt to influence the outcome of the congress when Egor Ligachev ran for the new post of deputy general secretary. Because this official was expected to supervise the work of the party apparatus, the election of Ligachev would effectively undercut Gorbachev's leadership of the CPSU. This last challenge by Ligachev was turned back decisively. Vladimir A. Ivashko, former Ukrainian party leader, defeated Ligachev by a vote of 3,109 to 776 (TASS, 11 July; *NYT*, 12 July).

A resolution adopted on 10 July based on Gorbachev's report to the congress called for continuing support for *perestroika*, backed the presidential system and multipartyism, and rejected proposals for removal of party organizations from the workplace (*Pravda*, 11 July).

Boris Pugo, chairman of the Party Control Committee since September 1988, was elected chairman of the new CPSU Central Control Commission on 11 July (ibid., 12 July).

On 12 July, Gorbachev outlined the draft of the new party rules. The draft gave greater power to republican party organizations and to lower-ranking bodies generally but nonetheless rejected the principle of federalism (Central Television, 12 July; *Report on the USSR*, 20 July). On the following day, TASS reported that the congress had established a commission, headed by Gorbachev, to draft the new party program. This program is scheduled to be adopted at a party conference or congress to be held not later than mid-1992 (Central Television, 13 July; *Report on the USSR*, 20 July).

Boris Eltsin provided the greatest excitement of the congress on 12 July when he announced that he was resigning from the communist party. On the same day, Viacheslav Shostakovskii, rector of the Moscow party school and a leader of the Democratic Platform, announced his resignation and was promptly fired from his position as rector. Mayors Gavril Popov of Moscow and Anatolii Sobchak of Leningrad also left the party and, like Eltsin, said that they would not join any particular new political party (*NYT*, *WP*, 13 July).

The Twenty-eighth Congress concluded by electing a new Central Committee of 412 members; the category of candidate member was abolished. Only 59 of the members had served on the previous Central Committee, yielding a turnover of about 85 percent (*Pravda*, 14 July).

Given the turmoil preceding it, the congress was something of a disappointment. But with the congress behind him, Gorbachev was able to proceed with his negotiations on German unity and Germany's membership in NATO (see below). Commentary on the congress by both media and public was sometimes scathing. On 6 July, the evening news program *"Vremiia"* complained that it was difficult for journalists to cover the event because the speeches delivered at the congress contained so few new ideas (*"Vremiia,"* 6 July; *Report on the USSR*, 20 July). The public apparently largely ignored the proceedings, and Muscovites interviewed by the Western media tended to dismiss the congress as simply a matter of intraparty struggling for power that had no relevance to their daily lives or to the pressing problems of the country (NBC News, 10 July).

Party Policies, Organization, and Personnel. In 1990 the CPSU's dominant role in the political system was challenged as never before in the history of the communist regime. The party's cohesion and clout were reduced by several threatening phenomena: defections from the party and its youth affiliate, the Komsomol; decline of regional party organizations and the weakening of central party control over those organizations; growing separatist tendencies in the predominantly non-Russian union republics in response to local de-

mands for independence or autonomy; and the rise of new, competing political parties.

These indications of party decline were related to *glasnost'*, political reform, the economic crisis, and Gorbachev's style of governance. Although the party continued to be the most important political force in the country, its strength was now mainly concentrated in the ranks of apparatchiks in party and government, most of whom had a vested interest in opposing or slowing reform. But with the rise of political alternatives, Gorbachev could not dispense with this solid core of party members. This political imperative reduced Gorbachev's freedom of action on policy and rendered him more vulnerable to criticisms by progressives who had earlier seemed to be his natural allies.

The new commission system introduced in September 1988 had still not jelled, and the reduction in size of the Central Committee apparatus had coincided with its general loss of directing power over the economy. The Russian Buro, established in 1989 and accepted by Gorbachev as an alternative to a separate RSFSR party organization, had blurred lines of authority; moreover, the Buro met as a body only once a month and showed little potential for acting as an integrative mechanism for the party in the Russian republic. Gorbachev had been named as head of the Russian Buro, but this mostly served to give him another title. Like Khrushchev during the years of his roles as premier and first secretary, Gorbachev's holding of state positions necessarily made for a downgrading of his supervision of the party.

Defections from the party were already apparent at the beginning of the year, and the number escalated over the following months. However, not all loyal party members regarded this as a problem. Key figures on the party's right saw the growing exodus as a positive development, enhancing their own weight in the organization. In the Soviet press in January, Lt. Col. V. Tokarev, a party official in the army, admitted that some of those departing were "mature and sensible people" but claimed that there was a more exacting standard for new members and contended that "restructuring" was speeding up the "natural processes of purification and affirmation" (*Krasnaiia zvezda*, 6 January; *FBIS-SOV*, 10 January). In contrast, Aleksandr Ilin, in a *Pravda* front-page editorial (25 January), attributed much of the loss of membership to the fact that "an atmosphere of party comradeship has not yet replaced the stilted official climate of relations between the 'top' and the 'bottom.'"

Gorbachev's most immediate problem in the party at year's outset was the split of the party in Lithuania into two separate organizations, one loyal to Moscow, the other strongly proindependence. Speaking in Vilnius on 13 January, the general secretary stepped back from his previous vigorous rejection of multipartyism, saying that he saw "no tragedy" in a multiparty system (Central Television, 13 January; *NYT*, 14 January; *Report on the USSR*, 2 February).

This concession was followed a week later by the founding conference of the Democratic Platform of the CPSU in Moscow. Participants in the conference included prominent progressives Boris Eltsin, Sergei Stankevich, Gavril Popov, Iuri Afanasiev, Igor Chubais, and Vladimir Lysenko. The group issued a declaration calling for a multiparty system, the abolition of Article 6 of the USSR Constitution, the end of "democratic centralism," and the reconstitution of the CPSU as a parliamentary party (*NYT*, 21, 22 January). More than 40 percent of the deputies in the Congress of People's Deputies in December had favored a vote on Article 6. Pressure for abandoning the party's constitutional monopoly on power mounted, climaxing with a demonstration by some 100,000 people in Red Square immediately before the CPSU CC plenum in early February. At this plenum Boris Eltsin served as the main speaker. The CC, at Gorbachev's urging, voted in favor of invalidating Article 6 (*Pravda*, 7 February).

Meanwhile, popular protest was playing havoc with the power of regional secretaries, traditionally the bulwark of power in the CPSU. In a seven-week period beginning 1 January, thirteen regional first secretaries resigned or were dismissed from office. Those ousted included Gennadii Bogomiakov, first secretary of Tiumen *obkom* since 1973. Most revealing was the dismissal of Vladimir Kalashnikov in Volgograd (ibid., 28 January, 5 February), ostensibly due to a housing scandal involving Kalashnikov's family but more generally attributable to the regional leader's arrogance and tendency to treat the huge oblast as a feudal barony. Kalashnikov had been Gorbachev's protégé in Stavropol, and Kalashnikov's appointment as Volgograd first secretary in 1984 added an important region to Gorbachev's growing "organizational tail" in his drive for party leadership. Evidently supremely confident because of his ties to the party leader, Kalashnikov changed from a zealous reformer in his first two years in office into an old-style party boss. Thus, in the summer of 1989, Kalashnikov was denied a seat

in the Supreme Soviet and was rejected as a nominee for first deputy chairman of the USSR Council of Ministers in charge of agriculture. The criticisms of Kalashnikov in the Congress of People's Deputies at that time left no doubt about the state of affairs in Volgograd, clearly one of the worst-run provinces in the USSR. Still Gorbachev took no action, perhaps because he could not afford to lose a loyal local leader when confronted with growing conservative opposition among regional secretaries.

Izvestiia (3 February), commenting on the dismissals of first secretaries in Tiumen, Volgograd, and Chernigov in the Ukraine, said that "democratization and *glasnost'* are doing their work" and that "even ruling circles nowadays are by no means fully aware of the immeasurable increase in the potential of the 'real power.'"

Besides the internal challenges, the party confronted outside threats as well. Formation of new parties accelerated following the CC decision of 6 February to approve repeal of Article 6. Social democratic parties had been established in Georgia, Belorussia, Estonia, Latvia, and Lithuania (*CSM*, 9 March), and these were soon followed by social democratic parties in Russia and the Ukraine. In Russia, the Social-Patriotic Movement linked various nationalist groups, and many splinter parties also emerged. Democratic Russia brought together social democrats, reform communists, and other proreform elements. In parliamentary and local elections held in early March, Democratic Russia emerged as the big winner in the RSFSR.

As multipartyism gathered steam, *Izvestiia* commentator Stanislav Kondrashov (10 March) said that "the historical need for a multiparty system is long overdue" and called the CC platform for the Twenty-eighth Congress "characteristically half-hearted" on the issue.

As the meeting of the parliament approached that would deal with the proposals on the presidency and Article 6, a CC plenum was held to prepare both for the legislative session and for the upcoming party congress. The CC endorsed several Gorbachev proposals on reorganization and "democratization." However, on the important matter of delegate election to the party congress, which progressives regarded as a crucial test of intraparty democracy, Gorbachev opted for a compromise proposal that allowed local party organizations to choose the precise details of electing delegates (*NYT*, 12 March). This provided an opening to local party officials cool to reform and led to the election of an apparent conservative majority at the Twenty-eighth Congress.

The party newspaper *Pravda* did not escape the party turmoil. The CC adopted a lengthy resolution in April calling for a restructuring of the newspaper and giving detailed instructions on its future operation (*Pravda*, 7 April). Ivan Frolov had been hand-picked by Gorbachev in 1989 to refurbish the sagging party organ; however, *Pravda*'s circulation continued to decline, dropping to 7.7 million. A fall to 3 million was predicted for 1991. In October, *Pravda* employees demanded Frolov's resignation. Seeking to head off a revolt by his subordinates, Frolov announced a plan for a new and more autonomous newspaper to be independently managed and financed by a *Pravda* Association. Because the plan depended on advertising, particularly by foreign companies, prospects for its success seemed dubious (*Time*, 5 November).

In the spring, the fragmentation of the party continued. An independent Latvian party held its constituent congress in mid-April, following a walkout by dissidents at the regular Latvian party congress the previous month. The independents rejected subordination to any other organization, endorsed private property, and supported Latvia's independence from the USSR (ibid., 15 April). Rumblings were heard in other union republic communist parties, and a public opinion poll showed that respondents having "full confidence" in the party had dropped from 22 percent in September to 4 percent (*WP*, 3 April).

Within the party the main concern of conservatives was the Democratic Platform. In an interview published on 8 April, Egor Ligachev condemned the platform's positions as "utter revisionism" and said that "there are forces operating in society which oppose socialism. Such forces are also present within the CPSU" (*Selskaiia zhizn'*, 8 April; *FBIS-SOV*, 9 April). Two days after Ligachev's blast, the CC issued an "open letter," read on Soviet television, denouncing the Democratic Platform and implying that its adherents should be read out of the party: "The time has come to decide what to do about those who put themselves outside the party. How can they stay in the Communist Party of the Soviet Union?" (Reuters, 10 April; *NYT*, 11 April.) The open letter presumably was approved by Gorbachev, whose motives in this case were unclear. The declaration appeared just as the process of electing congress delegates was getting under way, and it seemed that local party bosses had

been given their marching orders to get rid of the radicals (*CSM*, 16 April).

Igor Chubais, a leading member of Democratic Platform, contended that the letter showed that there had been a "conservative coup" led by Ligachev. Several expulsions from the party immediately preceded or followed publication of the letter, including the dismissal of Chubais himself on 10 April. Purges against Democratic Platform members appeared to be under way in Belorussia and in Cheliabinsk. Iuri Afanasiev and two other prominent Democratic Platform members, Nikolai Travkin and Georgii Khatsenkov, resigned from the party within days of the letter's publication (Reuters, 19 April).

While party leaders concentrated on the Democratic Platform, another group emerged in the party. The Marxist Platform was an alternative program developed by the Federation of Marxist Party Clubs; the program was published just six days after the announcement of the CC open letter (*Pravda*, 16 April). The Marxist Platform rejected both the CPSU draft program and the social democratic orientation of the Democratic Platform. The Marxist Platform envisioned a return to "classical Marxism" and the ownership of property by collectives and regions rather than the state (*Report on the USSR*, 15 June).

Responding to the splintering of the party, *Pravda* (18 April) published an article by Vladimir Markov that contended that the "very existence" of factions "drastically reduces the opportunities for intraparty democracy." Markov argued that membership in a faction carries an obligation to adhere to group assessments and promotes distrust of others not in the faction.

A possibly greater threat than the factions appeared with the first move toward organization of a Russian Communist Party. Six hundred and fifteen delegates representing 1.5 million party members from more than 50 regions met in Leningrad 21–22 April and declared their determination to revive the republic's communist party. Plans were set for a constituent congress to meet on 19 June (*Krasnaiia zvezda*, 24 April; *FBIS-SOV*, 25 April).

The conservative Leningrad organization would presumably play a crucial role in any separate organization, and the *obkom*'s first secretary, Boris Gidaspov, had been one of Gorbachev's more outspoken critics. The open letter of 10 April had taken aim at the Leningrad organization as well as the Democratic Platform, and the province's communists, meeting on 25 April, denounced the open letter (TASS, 25 April; *FBIS-SOV*, 27 April).

The Russian Federation's social democratic party held its inaugural congress in Moscow in early May (TASS, 4 May; *FBIS-SOV*, 7 May), and the Democratic Platform voted to split from the CPSU if its reform proposals were not accepted by the party congress (BBC-CARIS, 18 June). The Democratic Platform also presented its reform proposals at the organizational congress of the RSFSR Communist Party in June only to have the conservative-dominated conclave reject or ignore them. The Democratic Platform's candidate for leader of the new Russian party, Vladimir Lysenko, received only 90 votes in the first round of balloting (*NYT*, 23 June). The congress dealt a rebuff to Gorbachev in the runoff election when hard-liner Ivan Polozkov, first secretary of Krasnodar *kraikom*, was elected first secretary of the RSFSR Communist Party. Polozkov won 1,396 votes and lost 1,251; his opponent, Oleg Lobov, second secretary of the Armenian Communist Party, won 1,066 votes and lost 1,581 (TASS, 23 June; *FBIS-SOV*, 25 June). Before the vote, Polozkov made clear his attitude toward Gorbachev by saying that "the crisis is not in the party but in its leadership"; Polozkov extolled Leninism, centralized government, and collective farming and denounced the "fetish" of a market economy (*NYT*, 23 June).

Polozkov's successor as Krasnodar first secretary was Aleksandr V. Maslov, 41, former first secretary of Timashevsk *raikom*. Maslov had worked in the CPSU CC apparatus since 1987 (*Trud*, 10 August; *FBIS-SOV*, 17 August).

The Democratic Platform confirmed its decision to leave the CPSU on 12 July but urged members to go slow on resignations until the group's founding congress met in the autumn (BBC-CARIS, 13 July). A major reason the Democratic Platform opted for independence despite the setbacks for conservatives at the Twenty-eighth CPSU Congress was Gorbachev's continuing opposition to factions within the party. On 15 July, some 50,000 Muscovites rallied on Red Square, denouncing the CPSU and calling for more resignations from the party. Meanwhile, party officials admitted that 186,000 of its members had quit from January to mid-June (*LAT*, 16 July).

As the CPSU continued to decline in numbers and prestige, multipartyism took on more substance. A meeting of a "centrist" bloc including the Union of Democratic Forces, the Russian Democratic Forum, the radical faction of the Moscow Popular Front, and the Liberal Democratic Party

was held in Moscow in early August. Attending as observers were the chairmen of the Peace Party, the Democratic Party, the Party of Urban and Rural Proprietors, and the Blue Movement (Moscow Domestic Service, 4 August; *FBIS-SOV*, 6 August). Leningrad activists broke away from the Democratic Party of Russia to organize the Free Democratic Party of Russia (TASS, 5 August; *FBIS-SOV*, 6 August).

The tendencies toward radical splintering of noncommunist forces figured to leave the CPSU with an overwhelming advantage in a multiparty system. However, the party continued to have problems of cohesion within its ranks, and, despite the departure of Ligachev, the left-right struggle was still evident. When the RSFSR held its first regular congress in September, conservatives had a field day criticizing Gorbachev. Delegate Ivan Vtorushin called for "returning the nation to 1985," and First Secretary Polozkov told cheering delegates that Gorbachev's reform program was "on the brink of collapse" (AP, 4 September).

Gorbachev's troubles mounted, both within and outside the party. A government poll published in November showed that respondents who "fully trust" the CPSU fell from 27 percent in December 1989 to 14 percent in July (*Izvestiia*, 29 November).

In the first truly multiparty elections held in the USSR, the Round Table/Free Georgian coalition of seven parties won 54.03 percent of the vote and 114 of the 250 seats in the Georgian Parliament. The Georgian Communist Party, with 29.42 percent of the vote, elected only 60 deputies (TASS, 1 November; *Report on the USSR*, 16 November).

Viktor Vichkanov resigned as first secretary of the party in the city of Magadan, saying that he no longer believed that a transition to a market economy would improve the life of the people (Radio Moscow, 28 October; *Report on the USSR*, 9 November).

Gorbachev told delegates to the Twenty-eighth Moscow City Party Conference in November that he had no intention of quitting as party leader and was firmly committed to maintaining the party's dominance in society. However, in a dramatic mea culpa address to the Moscow communists, Gorbachev acknowledged that problems of food supplies, ethnic conflicts, crime, and the "paralysis of power" were due to errors of central organs, particularly the CPSU, the CC, and "the actions of the General Secretary and President" (AP, TASS, 29 November; *Pravda*, 30 November).

In December, the Georgian Communist Party split from the CPSU and declared its intention to work toward the republic's independence. Givi Gumbaridze resigned as first secretary of the Georgian party and was replaced by Avtanti Margiani, a 46-year-old engineer. Meanwhile, the Lithuanian Communist Party held a congress and prepared to change its name to Democratic Labor Party (AP, 8 December).

Efrem Sokolov did not stand for reelection as first secretary at the Thirty-first Congress of the Belorussian Communist Party. Anatolii A. Malofeev, 57, former first secretary of the Minsk *obkom*, was elected to the post, narrowly defeating Vladimir Brovikov, former USSR ambassador to Poland and a leading critic of Gorbachev's policies (TASS, 1 December; *Report on the USSR*, 14 December).

Government and Law. The USSR Council of Ministers received much of the blame for the worsening economic situation, and Prime Minister Nikolai Ryzhkov was a particular target. After Ryzhkov opposed the Shatalin 500-day plan for reform of the economy, demands for his resignation mounted, with Boris Eltsin leading the charge. On 11 September, Gorbachev endorsed the Shatalin plan but defended the prime minister, albeit in a rather halfhearted fashion. Ryzhkov responded by threatening to resign if the Shatalin plan were approved (*CSM*, 13 September). On 16 September, a crowd of about 30,000 people marched from Gorki Park to the Kremlin to demand Ryzhkov's resignation (*NYT*, 17 September).

When Gorbachev moved for a compromise plan on the economy in October (see above), he appeared to be yielding to Ryzhkov, and the much-maligned premier's survival prospects brightened. However, when Gorbachev was confronted by the sudden rebellion of the USSR Supreme Soviet in November, he indicated a willingness to sacrifice Ryzhkov, proposing that the office of prime minister be abolished and that the Federation Council become the chief executive board for the country. Eltsin quickly announced opposition to the plan.

Eltsin was also the key figure in an earlier challenge to the central government. The Congress of People's Deputies of the RSFSR approved a draft declaration on the priority of the RSFSR constitution and laws on 8 June by a vote of 544 to 271 (TASS, *FBIS-SOV*, 8 June). Five days later, the RSFSR congress formally approved the final draft of the declaration of sovereignty (*Sovetskaiia Rossiia*, 14 June). The RSFSR Supreme Soviet followed on 9 August with a declaration on the "RSFSR's sovereignty over the protection of its economic foundations" (ibid., 10 August). On 23 August, Gorbachev issued a decree invalidating the 9 August declaration, and the RSFSR Supreme Soviet Presidium responded by asserting that Gorbachev's decree was illegal and did not have "the force of law" (TASS, 25 August; *FBIS-SOV*, 27 August). The impasse continued and blended into the broader question of a new union treaty.

In September, Gorbachev issued a decree ordering the political organs of the Soviet armed forces and the KGB to reform. Instead of indoctrinating them in Marxist-Leninist ideology, the political organs were ordered to ensure that the state policy of the USSR was explained to the troops (BBC-CARIS, 5 September). But Gorbachev consistently refused to consider disbanding party organizations in the military and security forces. Indeed, he could scarcely afford to do so. Under conditions of growing fragmentation of the political system, Gorbachev was increasingly dependent on the army and the KGB; any reduction of party influence in the coercive instrumentalities would serve to strengthen their independence.

As democratization proceeded, it was not surprising that the KGB's role in Soviet society became a major issue. But the source of the year's major controversy over the security agency was when former KGB major general Oleg Kalugin told a conference of Democratic Platform members in June that the KGB's image had changed but its activities had not. According to Kalugin, the KGB continues to infiltrate every workplace, church, artistic union, and political organization in the USSR (*NYT*, 17 June). KGB head Vladimir Kriuchkov denounced Kalugin, claiming that the former major general was bitter because he had been pensioned off owing to incompetence. Kalugin's charges evidently struck a responsive chord in the populace: in August, he led in the first round of a by-election for a Supreme Soviet seat in conservative-dominated Krasnodar *krai* (*Pravda*, 21 August).

Democratization also struck *Glavlit*, the censorship agency that had survived the early stirrings of *glasnost'*. In June, the USSR Parliament approved a law on freedom of the press that ended decades of government censorship and allowed individual citizens to start newspapers. But the immediate effects of the law were limited because the government's monopoly on printing paper remained unaffected (*NYT*, 13 June).

Two more major acts of democratization came in October. The USSR Law on Freedom of Conscience and Religious Organizations was adopted by the Supreme Soviet on 1 October by a vote of 341 to 1, with 1 abstention. This law grants legal status to parishes, monasteries, and schools but not to churches as a whole. Theological students are given the same status as other students, and there are guarantees against discrimination on the basis of religion (TASS, 1 October; *Pravda*, 9 October; *Report on the USSR*, 23 November).

Following months of discussion, the USSR Supreme Soviet finally passed, on 9 October, the Law on Public Associations, which gives all political parties legal status. Passage of this law marked the legal end of the CPSU's monopoly of power (BBC-CARIS, 10 October).

Demonstrations by thousands of students in Kiev led to the resignation of Ukrainian prime minister Vitalii Masol on 17 October. Masol, who had been under fire for weeks, had been sharply criticized on grounds that his economic planning did not take into account the basic principles of a market economy (ibid., 17 October).

Chingiz Aitmatov, one of the original members of the Presidential Council, resigned from that body in October to accept an appointment as USSR ambassador to Luxembourg (*Report on the USSR*, 2 November).

Economy. The economy, weak at the outset of the year, moved inexorably toward disaster, raising the specter of widespread hunger during the winter of 1990–1991, threatening Gorbachev's political power and even the survival of the USSR. Villains were identified on all sides: black marketers, sabotaging bureaucrats, panic buyers, obstreperous republican governments. But the most important cause of the sudden economic crisis was probably Gorbachev's inept leadership. Partial reform and contradictory policies had left the populace confused and economic mechanisms in disarray.

Although urged by some advisers and by Boris Eltsin to move rapidly toward a market economy, Gorbachev apparently could not make up his mind. The risks in moving toward a market economy worried the Soviet leader, and, indeed, many Western analysts were highly skeptical about such a transition, given the absence of a supporting social infrastructure. But Gorbachev's stop-and-go performance, now heralding the market, next recoiling from it, made economic reform largely a rhetorical issue. At the same time, political reorganization had

taken place, which effectively removed the strong hand at the center that had directed the command economy. Politics no longer dictated economics, and, without a rational economic mechanism to operate more or less autonomously, the result was anarchy. The prevailing view at home and abroad was that *perestroika* had failed, and by December the USSR was soliciting emergency aid from abroad. Ironically, the greatest urgency concerned food supplies, although the grain harvest had come in at around 240 million tons, the largest in years.

Two preliminary steps toward the market economy had been taken in the early months of the year. In late February, the USSR Supreme Soviet approved the lifetime leasing of land with a right of inheritance but not of buying or selling (*Izvestiia*, 28 February). One week later, the Parliament passed a bill on property that opened the way for stock markets and ownership of small businesses as long as there was "no exploitation of man by man" (*WP*, 7 March; *Pravda*, 10 March).

High-level planning was reportedly proceeding in late winter on major proposals to move toward a market economy. But Gorbachev's earlier hesitations on marketization colored this endeavor. Reacting to criticisms of the cooperative movement, Gorbachev in 1989 yielded regulation of it to local authorities. In some areas, this had meant open season on free enterprise; in Krasnodar *krai* local officials led by *obkom* First Secretary Ivan Polozkov had dismantled one thousand cooperatives (*NYT*, 2 March).

The only area where capitalism succeeded was in the black market, which was growing by leaps and bounds. The official economy, in contrast, was yielding danger signals. In the first two months of the year, Soviet industrial production reportedly fell by 5 to 6 percent, due in part to the fact that the number of work days lost due to strikes or other reasons in January and February 1990 was more than for all of 1989. Production of consumer goods likewise fell 5 percent. Economist Andrei Orlov, an aide to Deputy Premier Leonid Abalkin, warned that resistance to reform could force a return to the old system of rigid central planning (BBC-CARIS, 5 April).

In April five Soviet economists, including Oleg Bogomolov, director of the Institute of Economics of the World Socialist System, participated in a conference hosted by the American Enterprise Institute. They painted a picture of "very deep crisis," saying that their estimates indicated a worse situation in the USSR than that reported by the Central

Intelligence Agency (CIA). The economists made these major points about the economic situation: (1) farm production was much lower than official figures showed; (2) the system of distributing food and other products to consumers had almost completely broken down; (3) economic links between regions were being destroyed and replaced by attempts at self-sufficiency; and (4) as much as 50 percent of the industrial output and 40 percent of agricultural production was consequently "lost" (*WP*, 24 April).

Gorbachev did encourage one basis for a market economy with a decree promoting private home ownership. The decree, issued on 20 May, directed the government to let individuals build, buy, and sell their own houses and own the lots on which they stood (*NYT*, 21 May). But when the government presented a proposal for a "regulated market" that would triple the price of bread on 1 July, double other food prices as of 1 January 1991, and raise prices of other goods by 43 percent at the beginning of the new year, Gorbachev hesitated and said that this proposal should be submitted to a national referendum (*Pravda*, *NYT*, *WSJ*, 25 May).

On 13 June, the USSR Supreme Soviet postponed a decision on raising the price of bread (*NYT*, 14 June). With no possibility of the broader proposal winning voter approval, its main effect was to stimulate panic buying and worsen shortages.

The city of Moscow was already particularly affected by hoarding and by the arrival of a stream of non-Muscovite shoppers from areas even more strapped than the capital. Moscow deputy mayor Iuri Luzhkov said that anxious consumers, set in motion by Premier Ryzhkov's announcement of the price rise plan, had increased purchases of flour and vegetable oil seven- or eightfold (ibid., 27 May). The Moscow City Council responded by placing limits on purchases of dozens of basic food and household items and requiring shoppers to show their passports to prove Moscow residence (ibid., 29 May).

Negative public attitudes continued to hamper all efforts toward reform. A. Kiva, in an article in *Izvestiia* (2 June), said that marketization was inhibited by the "lumpen" mentality, "leveling the desire to have things shared out." Kiva maintained that private property is more public than state property because state property is arbitrarily managed by a bureaucracy pursuing its own interests.

European Community leaders meeting in Dublin agreed to consider providing some $15 billion in aid to the Soviet economy, but Britain's reluctance led to a decision to study the matter carefully before making definite commitments (BBC-CARIS, 26 June). As the economic downturn became more alarming, Premier Ryzhkov warned that social tensions would probably increase because of worsening food problems and the limited supply of hard currency available to purchase grain overseas (*Izvestiia*, 23 July).

The midyear economic report contained more bad news. In the first half of the year, gross national product dropped 1 percent and labor productivity fell 1.5 percent. At the same time, consumer prices for goods and services rose 14.2 percent (TASS, 29 July; *Pravda*, 30 July; *Ekonomika i zhizn'*, no. 32, August).

Soviet consumers, used to hardships, soon confronted a shortage of basic goods surpassing anything experienced in the postwar period. Widespread shortage of vegetables was reported (*Pravda*, 15 August), and a summer-long cigarette shortage finally led to a demonstration in Revolution Square near the Kremlin (AP, 22 August). Cigarette rationing was introduced in the capital on 1 September (BBC-CARIS, 29 August). Gorbachev issued a decree dismissing First Deputy Premier Vladlen V. Nikitin and blaming him for the cigarette shortage (TASS, 30 August; *FBIS-SOV*, 31 August); the problem was temporarily relieved by massive purchases abroad. Ration cards for bread were introduced in Tarusa (*Pravda*, 16 August), and in early September bread largely disappeared from stores in Moscow (*NYT*, 4 September). *Izvestiia* (3 September) saw the bread shortage as a sign of the continuing breakdown of the state-run economy and pointed out that a similar problem had led to the March Revolution in 1917. Leningrad was also reported to be near a "food crisis" (*Pravda*, 30 August).

In late August, the USSR was reported to have sold as much as $1 billion in gold over several days, compared with $2 to $3 billion in an average year; foreign observers saw this as a desperate sign (*CSM*, 23 August).

The economic crisis was exacerbated by the political problem of separatist tendencies among the union republics. The republics began concluding economic agreements with each other, and some republics raised prices, drawing consumer products away from areas that had not done so. The Baltic republics all considered plans to print their own money, and the Ukraine included plans for a separate currency in its declaration of sovereignty (AP, 30 July). But the biggest problem was the RSFSR, which threatened to go it alone on economic planning under President Boris Eltsin.

Gorbachev was compelled to deal with Eltsin, and, over four months, they engaged in numerous negotiations on economic and other matters. At the beginning of September, they reportedly agreed on a plan to move to free markets in 500 days (*NYT*, 2 September); on 11 September, Gorbachev formally endorsed what came to be known as the Shatalin plan (ibid., 12 September). However, in October, Gorbachev opted instead for a compromise plan that proposed less privatization and the retention of more central economic levers than provided for in the Shatalin plan (TASS, 16 October; *Izvestiia*, 17 October; *Report on the USSR*, 26 October). The RSFSR threatened to go ahead with its own economic plan, but on 11 November Gorbachev and Eltsin met in the Kremlin and reportedly agreed on questions concerning property, natural resources, and banking (TASS, 11, 12 November). These talks were to serve as the basis for agreements in advance of the signing of an all-union treaty. But this one of many apparent agreements between Gorbachev and Eltsin was soon put in jeopardy by Eltsin's rejection of Gorbachev's plans on the union treaty.

Trade talks between Moscow and the Baltic republics broke down, reportedly because of the Kremlin's "uncompromising attitude" toward the republics' independence or economic autonomy (Reuters, 14 November). Lithuanian prime minister Kazimiera Prunskiene expressed fears of a new economic blockade by the USSR (*Report on the USSR*, 23 November).

First Deputy Premier Iuri Masliukov, introducing the government budget proposal for 1991, recommended a cut of 75 percent in foreign aid and a 10 percent reduction in defense expenditures. For the first time, a distinction was made between national and republic revenues, and the proposed national expenditures were to be about half the union budget. A national deficit of $23 billion was envisioned for 1991. Finance Minister Valentin Pavlov reported that gross national product had dropped by 1.5 percent during the first nine months of the year (TASS, 27 November; *Izvestiia*, 28 November).

The Russian Parliament took an important independent step in the first week of December when it legalized the private ownership of land. The legislation contained some restrictions on the right of peasants to dispose of their land, including a minimum of ten years' ownership before it can be resold and a requirement that it be resold only to local governments. The bill was passed despite lobbying against it by Gorbachev, who had declared a week earlier that he could not accept the private ownership of land, although he favored leasing arrangements (*WP*, 4 December).

Two emergency actions were taken in early December to meet the deepening crisis in food supplies. Gorbachev issued a decree on 1 December ordering the creation of worker vigilante committees with unusual powers to monitor the food industry and punish those involved in theft and speculation (*NYT*, 2 December). The USSR Supreme Soviet three days later granted Gorbachev emergency powers to begin reorganizing the government to meet the critical situation.

In October, the Italian government approved $2 billion in economic aid for the USSR (AP, 16 October). But as the dimensions of the USSR's food crisis became more apparent, aid poured in, especially from private sources. Vienna promised 100,000 food parcels for Moscow's children, and organizations in the United States, Italy, and Scandinavia prepared shipments of milk, flour, canned goods, and other staples. German chancellor Helmut Kohl issued a strong appeal for "good neighborly" help for the USSR, and German food aid from private donors was expected to reach $400 million. The first shipment of food from Germany arrived in Leningrad on 30 November, just one day before the beginning of food rationing in Leningrad, Cheliabinsk, and Nizhnii Novgorod (formerly Gorki) (ibid., 1 December). Aid in some form was also soon forthcoming from Australia, Israel, Japan, Switzerland, Spain, France, Canada (*NYT*, 13 December), and even India (NBC News, 12 December).

Gorbachev's procurement of emergency food supplies from abroad produced a predictable backlash at home. "Having to ask for food is shameful," said Leningrad party leader Boris Gidaspov. "If I were President, I would reject the advice of foreign experts" (*U.S. News and World Report*, 10 December). A group of hard-liners in the USSR Supreme Soviet accused Gorbachev of "presenting the Soviet Union as a beggar country" and demanded an immediate end to the aid from abroad (AP, 8 December).

As the December meeting of the Congress of People's Deputies neared its end, a new economic problem confronted Gorbachev. The RSFSR Parliament announced that the Russian republic would contribute only 24 billion of the 119 billion rubles demanded by the central government for the 1991 budget (*NYT*, 28, 29 December). After the action by the RSFSR Parliament, Boris Eltsin departed on a trip to Siberia (NBC News, 29 December), leaving Gorbachev trying to figure out how to pry the needed rubles from the Russian republic.

Nationalities and Problems of the Union. *Glasnost'* uncorked the bottle of nationalism in the USSR, resulting in the expression of long-smoldering resentments. Political reform compounded the problem; the transfer of power from party to soviets provided a multiplicity of platforms for airing ethnic grievances. Ethnic demands blended with the debate on Soviet federalism to produce an explosive mixture, culminating during the year in proclamations of sovereignty and demands for autonomy that even reached city and district level. Gorbachev sought to hold the country together with a new draft treaty of the union, presented for consideration in November, but five of the fifteen union republics rejected the treaty outright.

At the beginning of the year Gorbachev journeyed to Lithuania to try to curb that republic's move toward independence. The Soviet president reiterated his opposition to independence but said that he had ordered the writing of a law providing a mechanism for secession. On the first day of Gorbachev's visit, some 300,000 Lithuanians jammed central Vilnius in a candlelight demonstration for independence (AP, 11 January). Following Gorbachev's visit, events moved rapidly. On 11 March, Lithuania's Parliament issued a declaration of sovereignty, voting 124 to 0 with 9 abstentions for independence. On the same day, the Parliament elected Vytautas Landsbergis president and Landsbergis in turn named economist Kazimiera Prunskiene as prime minister. The two leaders of the new noncommunist government were commissioned to negotiate terms of future relations with Moscow (*NYT*, 11 March). Lithuania's action was followed by an Estonian declaration on 30 March, setting a slow move to independence (ibid., 31 March), and by a Latvian declaration, on 4 May, charting a gradual restoration of independence (*NYT*, 5 May). Gorbachev declared the declarations by Estonia and Latvia to be illegal (ibid., 15 May), but Lithuania was a more immediate concern.

Gorbachev responded to Lithuania's declaration with a tough stance designed to pressure the republic into backing down. The pressure tactics finally worked after more than three months of high tension that complicated Soviet relations with the United States. Warned by Washington against using force in Lithuania (*NYT*, 24 March), Gorbachev chose his methods carefully. The Lithuanians found, however, that they could not count on assistance from the West; the United States and its allies were unwilling to jeopardize the new order in Central Europe for a quixotic drive in support of Lithuania's independence.

Gorbachev gave the Lithuanians a deadline of 19 March for renouncing their independence declaration. Lithuania rejected the demand and appealed to democratic nations to recognize the newly declared state (*WP*, 19 March). The Soviet president followed with an order for Lithuanian citizens to turn in their guns and told the KGB to strengthen controls on the republic's border (AP, 21 March). On 23 March, an armored column of almost a hundred military vehicles rolled through Vilnius as the war of nerves escalated, and U.S. diplomats were ordered out of Lithuania (*WP*, 24 March). On 27 March, Lithuania's leaders accused Moscow of "inexcusable aggression" and kidnapping its citizens after Soviet troops stormed two hospitals in a roundup of army deserters (AP, 27 March).

On 31 March, Gorbachev turned up the heat, saying that Moscow would not negotiate unless the declaration of independence were annulled. He warned of "grave consequences" if Lithuania refused (*NYT*, 1 April). Two weeks later, Gorbachev set another deadline, threatening to cut off vital supplies if Lithuania did not back down within two days. U.S. president Bush and British prime minister Margaret Thatcher, meeting in Bermuda, urged Gorbachev to call off the threatened economic sanctions (ibid., 14 April). On 18 April, Soviet authorities fulfilled the threat and stopped the flow of oil to Lithuania's only refinery (*WP*, 19 April). The Soviets also cut back on deliveries of coal, natural gas, and other supplies. The Lithuanian government announced that it would try to circumvent the economic blockade by seeking direct trading links with Soviet cities, particularly Moscow, Leningrad, and Lvov, all controlled by radical political groups.

Fruitless calls by Prime Minister Prunskiene to Western capitals convinced the Lithuanians to trim their sails. A suggestion by FRG chancellor Helmut Kohl and French president François Mitterrand that Lithuania suspend some of the laws passed after the independence declaration (AP, 28 April) became the basis for new negotiations with Moscow. On 16 May, the Lithuanian government formally agreed to suspend all laws passed after the independence declaration and to discuss a transition period to full separation from the USSR (*NYT*, 17 May). Following more negotiations and continuing economic pressure from Moscow, Lithuania went a step further in June, finally offering to suspend the independence declaration (ibid., 17 June). The Lithuanian Parliament agreed to a 100-day moratorium on independence, and the USSR reopened the oil pipeline to Lithuania (*NYT*, 1 July). On 2 July, Premier Ryzhkov announced that the economic blockade of Lithuania had been completely lifted (Reuters, 2 July).

While Gorbachev sought to calm the Baltic republics, the situation in the south threatened to get completely out of hand, repeating the pattern of the previous year. The year 1990 began with fighting on the Iranian border as elements of Azerbaijan's majority Shiite population demanded free movement between Azerbaijan and Iran. In the enclave of Nakhichevan, thousands of protesters camped along the border demanding incorporation of that region into Iran (*Izvestiia*, 3 January). Meanwhile, armed conflict continued between Azerbaijanis and Armenians along the border of those two republics, and militant nationalists demonstrated in Baku.

Gorbachev declared a state of emergency on 15 January, and the Soviet government dispatched 11,000 army and police troops to the affected areas (*NYT*, 16 January). The troops moved in on 20 January as the ruling council of Nakhichevan declared independence (*LAT*, 21 January). Clashes ensued with militants of the Azerbaijani Popular Front. The situation was reported as returning to normal one week later after more than 100 people had been killed and 80 Popular Front leaders arrested.

USSR defense minister Dmitrii Iazov claimed that the Popular Front had detailed plans for the seizure of power and had scheduled a mass rally to announce the takeover. Only the Soviet army's move into Baku on 20 January had prevented the takeover, Iazov said (ibid., 27 January).

Military intervention did not end violence in the south. On 25 July, Gorbachev issued a decree requiring that armed Armenian nationalist groups turn in their arms and disband within fifteen days (TASS, 25 July). The Armenian Supreme Soviet rejected Gorbachev's decree on 30 July, declaring that it "contradicts the Armenian people's right to self-defense." USSR interior minister Vadim Bakatin estimated that ten thousand to twenty thousand Armenians were involved in illegally armed groups and said that private armies also existed in Moldavia, Georgia, Azerbaijan, Latvia, Lithuania, Estonia, and the central Asian region, where clashes between Uzbeks and Kirghiz had resulted in

more than two hundred deaths in recent months (AP, *LAT*, 31 July).

Militants found easy access to weapons via raids on arsenals, black market activity, and collaboration with fellow ethnic members of the armed forces (*CSM*, 26 July). As the violence spread, Soviet authorities were forced to put down one flash fire after another. In February, rioting broke out in Uzbekistan between Moslems and Armenians in the city of Samarkand; Interior Ministry troops were sent in to quell the violence (*WP*, 17 February). By June, the situation in Central Asia was so tense that Interior Minister Bakatin said that Kirghizia and Uzbekistan could be on the brink of war. In four days of violence in Kirghizia in early June, 48 people were killed and more than three hundred injured; three thousand extra troops were dispatched to the area to restore order (BBC-CARIS, 7 June).

In Georgia, rocked by violence the previous year, sentiment for independence gained momentum, but nationalist forces in the republic were fragmented into many competing groups. In July, militant nationalists blockaded rail transport into the Caucasus to protest slowness of the government in arranging multiparty elections (ibid., 31 July). When elections were finally held, major opposition groups managed to put aside their differences to form a fairly cohesive bloc in opposition to the Georgian Communist Party. The Round Table/Free Georgia coalition of seven parties won 54.03 percent of the vote and 114 of 250 seats in the Parliament (TASS, 1 November; *Report on the USSR*, 16 November). Spurred by memories of the April 1989 Tbilisi massacre, Georgians strongly resisted Gorbachev's plans for a new union treaty.

By the end of the year, all fifteen union republics had issued some form of sovereignty declaration. But these republican actions could not conceal the often bitter divisions within the republics. Moldavia particularly illustrated the complexity of the nationality problem. The Moldavian Parliament had changed the republic's name to Moldova and passed a language law requiring Russian speakers in top government and industry positions to learn the Moldavian language by 1994 or face losing their jobs (*WSJ*, 24 July). In response to what it regarded as discrimination, the mainly Russian city of Tiraspol voted in a referendum in favor of becoming a separate autonomous republic within Moldavia (BBC-CARIS, 30 January). Tiraspol's example was followed by a number of other regions and cities in the USSR during the year, the most bizarre being a declaration of autonomy by the Kronstadt district in Leningrad province. Here, the people of Kronstadt claimed jurisdiction over the USSR naval base in their district.

Moldavian Communist Party first secretary Piotr Luchinskii was defeated for the republic's presidency in April by Mircea Snegur, a communist closely identified with the Moldavian Popular Front. Thereafter, the Popular Front used a small parliamentary majority to begin to erect its own political structures, apparently without interference from the Kremlin (*CSM*, 29 May). The border with Romania was thrown open, apparently in the hope that this would relieve some of the pressure on both sides of the border for reunification with Romania. In October, President Snegur denied any ideas of reunification with Romania (TASS, 13 October; *Report on the USSR*, 26 October), but tensions between Moldavians and ethnic Russians and Ukrainians remained high.

By November, the Moldavian leadership and Moscow faced an attempt to form two autonomous republics, the Turkic-dominated Gagauz and the mostly Russian Dniester, on the left bank of the Dniester; the two would-be republics planned to secede from Moldavia (TASS, 2, 6, 7 November). This time, troops were sent in to Moldavia to end disturbances. At the end of November, Gorbachev canceled a trip to Moldavia after Gagauz and Russian Dniester deputies threatened to boycott his scheduled speech to the republic's Parliament (*WP*, 1 December). At year's end, the fractious forces in Moldavia were under a one-week deadline from Gorbachev to cease and desist or face direct presidential rule (NBC News, 26 December).

More distressing for the Soviet leadership than the events in the outlying republics were the separatist tendencies displayed in predominantly Slavic parts of the country. In the Ukraine, the nationalist movement *Rukh* had, within months of its formation, posed a serious challenge to the Ukrainian Communist Party. *Rukh* and other democratic forces exerted great influence in the Parliament elected in early 1990 and moved toward an early confrontation with Moscow. On 16 July, the Parliament voted 355 to 4 for a declaration asserting the precedence of Ukrainian laws over those of the USSR. The Parliament claimed total control over all of the republic's economic and natural resources and demanded reparations for the 1986 Chernobyl disaster. Further, the Parliament also declared that the republic has the right to declare itself a neutral state, to withdraw from military alliances, and to ban the presence of nuclear weapons on its soil (*Chicago Tribune*, 17 July).

After the declaration, the Ukraine remained relatively quiet for two months, but in September *Rukh* and its allies organized a demonstration of tens of thousands of nationalists in Kiev and a one-day warning strike. The demonstration and strike were designed to support demands that Ukrainian men drafted into the Soviet army serve only in the Ukraine, that the Ukraine refuse to sign a new union treaty, and that the communist party be declared a "criminal organization" and stripped of influence in the republic's government (AP, 30 September).

Eleven days after the Ukrainian declaration in July, the Belorussian Parliament approved, by a vote of 230 to 0, with 120 members absent, a similar document asserting the supremacy of Belorussian laws and the right to establish the republic's own armed forces and security police (*NYT*, 28 July).

The most important of the republics, the RSFSR, had already weighed in with its blast at the central government. On 8 June, the RSFSR Congress of People's Deputies approved a draft declaration on the primacy of republic laws by a vote of 544 to 271 (*WP*, 9 June). Five days later, the Parliament gave final approval to the draft and on 9 August issued its declaration asserting control of the republic's resources. Perhaps more important was Eltsin's mode of operation as he negotiated directly with other republics and even moved toward direct relations with foreign countries. When Belorussia issued its sovereignty declaration in July, Eltsin was meeting with the presidents of Latvia, Estonia, and Lithuania in Latvia and promised to sign treaties with the Baltic republics recognizing their sovereignty (*NYT*, 28 July). Later, Eltsin negotiated directly with the Ukrainian government and was hailed as a hero when he visited Kiev in the fall. However, Eltsin faced his own sovereignty problems, as a number of smaller political units within the RSFSR put forward claims similar to those advanced by the republics. Particularly troublesome were the independence movements in the Tuva and Buriat autonomous soviet socialist republics (*FEER*, 13 September). Eltsin also lacked control over the economy and the coercive agencies. As he frequently complained, real control, such as it was, still resided in the Kremlin.

Gorbachev's promise of a new union treaty may well have had a calming effect on some of the republics; but well before the official presentation of the treaty in November the outlines of the projected federation were fairly clear, and even at this stage

Georgia and the Baltic states were opposed to it, with Moldavia and Armenia expressing reservations. The proposed draft treaty appeared to contain a design somewhat similar to that of the German Empire (1871–1918). Under this plan, defense, foreign affairs, and some economic and police matters would continue to be controlled by the central government. The Congress of People's Deputies approved the draft treaty in December and authorized referendums to vote on the treaty in the union republics (*NYT*, 26 December).

Nonetheless, in December, Kirghizia became the last of the fifteen republics to seek greater autonomy when it declared itself an "independent and sovereign state." The republic's Parliament declared that future national laws will be enacted in Kirghizia only after it has ratified them (TASS, 12 December).

In the year's final weeks, the tug of war between Moscow and the Baltic states came to the fore again. Gorbachev's decrees were consistently ignored by the three republics, and Latvia authorized a cutoff of supplies to Soviet forces in the republic. Defense Minister Iazov ordered troops to seize key installations if supplies were threatened. KGB chief Kriuchkov then appeared on Moscow television and vowed to wage an all-out struggle against growing separatist and criminal elements ("*Vremiia*," 11 December).

An early crackdown in the Baltic states and elsewhere was widely expected, and a change in the Interior Ministry fueled such speculation. Boris Pugo was shifted from the Party Control Commission to minister of the interior, and Col. Gen. Boris Gromov, the former commander in Afghanistan, was named as his deputy (*U.S. News and World Report*, 17 December). The appointment of the hard-line Gromov, the most outspoken Soviet general since Nikolai Ogarkov, also signaled a further rise in military influence and a strong commitment by the brass to maintaining the national union.

In the climate of national animosity, anti-Semitism surfaced, fueled by right-wing extremist groups. On 18 January, a meeting at Moscow's House of Writers was disrupted and several people were beaten by attackers shouting anti-Jewish epithets. In Leningrad, leaflets appeared promising a hunt against Jews on 5 May, St. Georgii's Day. In Kharkov, apartments of several Jews were burglarized and anti-Semitic leaflets were distributed. *Literaturnaia gazeta* reported rumors of pogroms in the offing (*Newsday*, 25 February). Konstantin Smirnov-Ostashvili, leader of one branch of *Pamiat*, the ultranationalist movement, went on trial in July for allegedly leading the disruption in January (*LAT*, 17 July). Smirnov-Ostashvili, the first person in the USSR to be charged with inciting ethnic strife, was convicted after a lengthy trial.

More than 50,000 Jews left the USSR in the first half of the year, and the number was expected to triple by January. The historian S. Rogov, writing in *Pravda* (24 July), warned that anti-Semitism had reached alarming levels and threatened the process of political reform.

Auxiliary and Front Organizations. Organizations affiliated with the CPSU experienced difficulties similar to those of their parent body. The Komsomol had lost about 10 million members from its high watermark in the early 1980s and was down to about 30 million members. A name change and some reorganization had not helped the youth affiliate, which had fared poorly in recent years in competition with the new unofficial groups.

Anatolii Bliudin, writing in the organization's newspaper in January, said that the policy and practical actions of the Komsomol since its Twentieth Congress had been a "passive reflection" of reality (*Komsomolskaia pravda*, 16 January). Vladimir Ziukin, a secretary of the Komsomol Central Committee, urged that the organization learn from the experiences of youth affiliates in Eastern Europe and push for full-scale internal democratization (ibid., 10 February).

When the Komsomol held its Twenty-first Congress in April, a major question concerned the place of the new Russian Komsomol in the all-union organization. Because the Russian Komsomol had not completed its organizational setup, a makeshift arrangement was worked out for its temporary representation (*Komsomolskaia pravda*, 20 April). The congress adopted a resolution providing procedures for the recall of the Komsomol CC members and condemning the practice of "substituting apparatii for elective Komsomol bodies" (ibid., 24 April). Vladimir Ziukin was elected as new first secretary of the Komsomol CC replacing Viktor Mironenko (Moscow Television, 20 April; *FBIS-SOV*, 24 April).

The regime's troubles with labor were reflected in the actions of the All-Union Central Council of Trade Unions (AUCCTU). An April meeting set plans for a new confederation of Soviet trade unions (TASS, *FBIS-SOV*, 18 April), and on 14 May the Central Council approved the platform calling for the organizational change at the Nineteenth

AUCCTU Congress in October. At the congress, leaders admitted that the organization was out of touch with the workers, and President Gorbachev attended the session at which the AUCCTU voted itself out of existence (AP, 24 October). The delegates set up a new body, the General Confederation of Soviet Trade Unions, which will be independent from state, political, and public structures (TASS, *FBIS-SOV*, 26 October).

International Views, Positions, and Activities. The USSR confronted a profoundly different international reality during the year. The "new world order" had been partly shaped by Soviet foreign policy, and Gorbachev was still frequently described as its architect. But the new political environment was also the result of underlying trends that dictated a more flexible arrangement of world forces. Gorbachev had sensed the movement toward diffusion of power in the world and sought to direct the processes of change that were producing a loose, multipolar international system in place of the tight bipolarity that had dominated the international scene for 40 years after World War II. For a time, he had appeared to be spectacularly successful, but in 1990 the USSR was clearly no longer an energizing center of international politics; rather, Moscow's role was now largely reactive.

The USSR's diminished clout was largely a function of domestic and bloc politics. The Soviet political and economic crisis sharply reduced the USSR's leverage on a variety of international issues, and the definitive collapse of the East European bloc left Gorbachev with few cards to play. At home, critics duly noted the sudden decline in Soviet world power, but Gorbachev and his closest associates chose to put the best face on matters and claimed that the new relationship with the United States and the other Western democracies was a triumph for the "new political thinking."

There was certainly some justification for the leadership's claims. Earlier leaderships' security policies had in fact bred insecurity, whereas now the USSR had no cause to fear any outside force. Gorbachev's summit meetings with U.S. president George Bush in May and September, his epochal agreement with German chancellor Helmut Kohl in July, and the Conference on Security and Cooperation in Europe (CSCE) gatherings in June and November signaled the end of the cold war. This denouement was generally welcomed in both East and West, and Gorbachev was awarded the Nobel Peace Prize for his contribution to its achievement. But the end of the cold war had been partially produced by the decline of the USSR as a superpower; it now proved incapable of continuing to play its former role.

In the emerging new world order, there appeared to be three major points of concern for the USSR: the political and military position of Germany, international economic relationships, and the new locus of conflict. When Gorbachev accepted the membership of a reunified Germany in NATO in July, the move sanctioned Germany's rise toward a position of dominant power on the European continent. The reunification of Germany gave added impetus to the growing entente between Moscow and Washington: the United States needed the USSR as a weight against Germany, and the USSR needed the United States for the same purpose. The major powers were reverting to balance-of-power politics, and the political geography of Europe bore some similarity to that of the late nineteenth century. But the new order was still in process of formation, and Gorbachev's policies figured as a key component of the process. This provided a reason for Western governments, particularly that of the United States, to throw their support behind the political survival of the Soviet leader. Gorbachev, in turn, encouraged the Western perception of dependence on him.

There were, of course, other reasons for U.S.-Soviet cooperation than the changing political order in Europe. Arms control negotiations continued to be emphasized and culminated in the Conventional Forces in Europe (CFE) treaty, signed by 22 nations at Paris in November. Progress was also reported toward a treaty on strategic arms, but the previous urgency on arms control was lacking as perceptions of threat diminished on all sides. Without the political conditions that had fueled earlier drives, Soviet policy focused on two other major concerns of the new world order: economic considerations and the locus of conflict. As predicted by Soviet international relations specialists, world frictions turned more toward a North-South orientation than the old East-West axis, with the Third World providing a major point of tension.

In the 1970s, Soviet analysts had viewed successes in the Third World as tangible indicators of USSR gains in the world correlation of forces. By the late 1980s dreams of reflected glory from Third World "liberation" struggles had long since vanished, and Soviet spokesmen now maintained that even if the USSR had been successful in such conflicts it would not have been sufficient to tilt the world correlation in Moscow's favor. Accordingly, the Third World came to play a secondary role in Soviet policy, subordinate to other concerns such as the U.S.-Soviet relationship, the prevention of international economic disruptions, and avoidance of nuclear proliferation. The new approach was most evident in Moscow's cooperation with Washington on the transition to a democratic government in Nicaragua and in its pronounced coolness toward Cuba's Fidel Castro.

Iraq's Saddam Husayn presented a crucial challenge to the "new political thinking" and the emerging irenic relationship with the Western powers just three weeks after the epochal agreement on a reunified Germany. When Iraq invaded Kuwait on 2 August, it was suddenly apparent that projections of the "end of history" were premature and that accord among the great powers had not been sufficient to forge a new world order. Symbolic of the dramatic changes was that U.S. secretary of state James Baker and USSR foreign minister Eduard Shevardnadze were conferring in Siberia when news arrived of the Iraqi onslaught against Kuwait. The United States and the USSR cooperated in placing economic sanctions against Iraq. The unprecedented near unanimity on the use of force vote in the United Nations was made possible by the earlier transformation of the political environment among the great powers.

For Moscow, support for the Washington-inspired U.N. reaction to Iraq's aggression involved junking an old ally; its willingness to do so spotlighted its new priorities. But the USSR still pursued its own policy, seeking a negotiated settlement of the Persian Gulf crisis, with Gorbachev's foreign policy adviser Evgenii Primakov as the point man in diplomatic efforts to avoid war.

When Gorbachev and Bush met in Helsinki in September, the Soviet leader reportedly exerted pressure on the U.S. president to slow the movement toward war. But as the crisis continued with no sign of resolution, the Soviets voted with the United States on a resolution authorizing the use of force as of 15 January 1991 if Saddam had not withdrawn from Kuwait by that time. When Moscow agreed on the use of force, there was widespread speculation of an at least implied promise of economic payoff. But at this point a bribe was probably unnecessary.

Moscow's posture on the gulf crisis was the result of several considerations. The crisis was a test of the new U.S.-USSR relationship, but, in any case, given the USSR's domestic troubles, Moscow had little to gain by opposing Washington. The imbroglio gave the Soviets a chance to demonstrate their vaunted new peacemaking role in the world, and they dispatched members of their refurbished diplomatic corps to play a new role in the Middle East. Washington's invitation to the Soviets to send military forces to the Persian Gulf demonstrated how international politics had been turned upside down in ways that might be to the USSR's advantage. At the same time, a stoppage of Middle East oil supplies to Western Europe threatened to plunge that area into economic recession or depression, and, given the Soviets' growing dependence on the Western democracies for a bailout of their faltering economy, such an outcome could prove disastrous. Thus, the Soviets had strong reasons for supporting the United States but also had an imperative interest in avoiding an all-out war.

Although the European scene and relations with the United States took center stage, the Soviets were also active in the Far East with inconclusive results. Normalization of relations with China proceeded slowly as Beijing's hard-line leadership remained suspicious of Gorbachev's domestic reforms. Diplomatic contacts with Japan were stepped up, but the issue of the Kurile Islands remained a stumbling block; Tokyo was reluctant to give economic or technological aid to the Soviets without a settlement in its favor of the Northern Territories dispute. The USSR also courted South Korea, thereby alienating Stalinist North Korea but at the same time gaining leverage against both China and Japan.

At year's end, foreign policy no longer supplied the political plus for Gorbachev that had helped sustain his leadership in earlier years. Soviet domestic disarray pointed once again to the truism that success in foreign affairs is ultimately grounded in domestic politics. A country that must beg for foreign handouts to keep its people from starvation is in no position to exert great influence abroad.

Evidence of Soviet internal disintegration and fears of reversion to dictatorship raised alarms in the West. The USSR's potential absence from the ranks of the great powers and its possible rejection of "new political thinking" would have a severe destabilizing effect on world politics.

For this reason Western aid poured into the USSR in December, one component of which was food supplies stockpiled in Berlin as a precaution against a new Soviet blockade of the city. The significance of the gesture was apparent in every world capital and painfully evident in Moscow. Gorbachev hailed the Western charity as a victory for *perestroika*; his critics viewed it as the most appalling proof of Soviet decline.

It seemed possible that, with a new tough approach to domestic problems, Gorbachev might still succeed in holding the USSR together. If so, the methods necessary to that end might irreparably damage Gorbachev's carefully cultivated image in the West. To some observers, however, the governance of the USSR during crisis was necessarily incompatible with the "new political thinking."

U.S.-Soviet Relations. Washington moved toward close collaboration with Moscow on various matters in several arenas during the year. The relationship had gone beyond détente to entente, mutual understanding about vital interests. The relationship was not without its frictions, however, and there was some backlash in Moscow as critics of the new political thinking saw Moscow being reduced to Washington's junior partner. There was some truth in such charges because most major diplomatic initiatives now came from capitals other than Moscow.

Soviet and U.S. leaderships did much to maintain and broaden the relationship between the two countries. One area providing an early test of the new links was Central America. At the end of the previous year Moscow had loudly denounced Washington for "gunboat diplomacy" following the U.S. invasion of Panama. But Soviet opposition turned out to be rhetorical and did not inhibit cooperation on Nicaragua; behind-the-scenes activities in tandem by Washington and Moscow in the early months of the year paved the way for the transition to democratic government in Managua. The rapport that had developed between U.S. secretary of state James Baker and USSR foreign minister Shevardnadze during their Wyoming meeting in September 1989 also played an important role. The new U.S.-Soviet tie was also responsible for the unexpected revival of the United Nations as a political force in the world, and one Soviet initiative accounted for the revival of the U.N.'s Military Staff Committee.

Soviet spokesmen noted with approval the hearings before the U.S. Senate Armed Services Committee that indicated a decline in the "Soviet threat," particularly Sen. Sam Nunn's summary statement that the hearings showed a "substantial decrease in the danger of military confrontation between the superpowers" (*Izvestiia*, 26 January). U.S. president George Bush's proposal for cuts in U.S. and Soviet troop levels to 195,000 each in Central Europe and an additional 30,000 U.S. troops elsewhere in Europe was hailed by Foreign Ministry

spokesman Gennadii Gerasimov as a "step in the right direction" (Paris, AFP, 1 February; *FBIS-SOV*, 2 February), but Moscow reacted angrily to U.S. newspaper reports of continuing Soviet arms shipments to Nicaragua. *Izvestiia* (4 February) termed the reports "patent fabrications" and "drops of poison" on the eve of Secretary Baker's visit to Moscow.

Cuba's alleged transshipment of weapons to Nicaragua was a prickly issue during Baker's visit to Moscow during the second week of February. Nevertheless, both sides affirmed commitment to a peaceful settlement in Central America. Baker made an unprecedented appearance before the USSR Congress of People's Deputies committee on international affairs, and plans were made for a June summit in the United States between Bush and Gorbachev. The two sides agreed on a phased reduction of chemical weapons and reported progress on strategic weapons and air-launched cruise missiles. They also expressed the hope that the Vienna negotiations on conventional forces would lead to an agreement by the end of the year (TASS, 10 February; *NYT*, *Pravda*, 11 February).

Bush rejected Gorbachev's proposal but predicted a "major success" on arms control at the June summit (AP, 12 February). In March, the United States proposed a ban on land-based missiles; in April, Shevardnadze delivered a reply from Gorbachev rejecting the proposal. Gorbachev complained that the proposal excluded sea-based ballistic missiles, which the USSR had long wanted the United States to cut. The reply came at the conclusion of three days of talks in Washington between U.S. and Soviet specialists that failed to narrow the differences on technical disputes. These disputes held up completion of a broad treaty on reduction of long-range nuclear weapons.

U.S. officials ascribed the tougher Soviet stance to a reassertion of military power in Moscow (*NYT*, 8 April). Despite the slowing of negotiations, Gorbachev and Shevardnadze told seven visiting U.S. Democratic senators that the arms treaty was on course and that they expected that all issues would be resolved before the summit. But the situation in Lithuania had now become an irritant to U.S.-Soviet relations, and the senators were told that the secession crisis would be resolved peacefully without "lectures" or "interference" from Washington (*WP*, 13 April).

The Kremlin's reaction to U.S. statements warning against the use of force in Lithuania was predictable, but the United States had no intention of letting the Baltic situation interfere with resolving broader issues. When Lithuanian premier Kazimiera Prunskiene visited the White House for a talk with Bush in early May, she was required to get out of her car, show her Soviet passport, go through a metal detector, and walk up the driveway on her own. White House officials asserted that the incident occurred because the driveway gate was broken (*NYT*, 4 May).

U.S.-Soviet arms negotiations continued, with time running out for a summit agreement. Senior Soviet arms negotiator Viktor Karpov was dispatched to Washington for talks with Baker and Undersecretary of State Reginald Bartholemew. The talks were described as "productive," but substantial differences remained, with sea-launched missiles still a major stumbling block. Baker agreed to meet Shevardnadze in the Soviet Union 16–19 May, and the summit was advanced, at Soviet request, from the second half of June to 30 May–3 June (AP, 20 April).

Ronald Lehman, director of the U.S. Arms Control and Disarmament Agency, told a Senate panel in May that "now is not the time" for linking naval weapons with other arms in negotiations. Admiral Carlisle A. H. Trost, chief of naval operations, said that elimination of all tactical naval nuclear arms might be in the interest of the United States if bombers assigned to naval fleets were also banned but expressed pessimism on "the likelihood of ever concluding such an agreement." Sen. Edward Kennedy (D-Mass.) took issue with the Bush administration's position, saying that he could not understand why there was willingness to deal in all areas except naval arms (ibid., 12 May).

When Baker journeyed to the USSR in May, cooperation on the transition to democratic government in Nicaragua had dispelled much remaining frost in relations. But the evident bonhomie did not resolve the remaining issues of arms control. Baker reportedly discussed with the Soviet leaders arms control, regional and international issues, human rights, and bilateral contacts, but no major breakthroughs were claimed (Moscow Domestic Service, 18 May; *FBIS-SOV*, 21 May; *Pravda*, 19 May).

As negotiations proceeded on various fronts, USSR ambassador to the United States Iuri Dubinin pointed out that economic ties were unsatisfactory, witness the trade imbalance and the small share of U.S.-USSR exchanges in both countries' foreign trade. Most rankling was the continuing U.S. refusal to grant most-favored-nation status to the

USSR. Dubinin declared "that economic interaction is an organic part of the whole set of relations between the USSR and the United States and that a lag there behind other fields impedes the progress of our relations as a whole" (*Pravitelstvennyi vestnik*, no. 19, May; *FBIS-SOV*, 25 May).

Dubinin's criticism appeared in the midst of a controversy over a new U.S.-USSR trade agreement concluded in Paris in late April. Under the agreement, the United States would grant most-favored-nation status to the USSR. Various regulations for trade were also agreed on, some of which were contained in "side letters" to the main body of the agreement. Some members of Congress complained that the side letters represented a lower degree of commitment on concessions wanted by the United States (*NYT*, 1 May). Three weeks later, Bush announced that he was withholding most-favored-nation st .us from the Soviets as long as the Lithuanian question remained unresolved. At the same time, he confirmed that he was renewing most-favored-nation status for China, setting off a fire storm in the U.S. Congress (ibid., 25 May).

Gorbachev's arrival in late May was another public relations triumph for the Soviet president, but the summit was not spectacular in terms of substantive results. Four days of meetings yielded arms, trade, commercial, environmental, and cultural accords. Bush indicated, however, that the trade agreement they initialed would not go to Congress until the Soviets enacted liberalized immigration laws. The leaders expressed hope that an agreement on conventional forces in Europe could be reached by the end of the year. They agreed to halt production of chemical weapons and to slash their stockpile of long-range nuclear weapons, although the latter agreement was only in principle. It was hoped that a Strategic Arms Reduction Treaty (START) could be signed at a summit meeting in Moscow later in the year, possibly in December. Bush and Gorbachev remained at loggerheads over Lithuania and Germany. The U.S. president continued to insist that a united Germany have membership in NATO, a position that Gorbachev adamantly rejected (*NYT*, 1–4 June).

Following the summit, Gorbachev and his wife, Raisa, made a whirlwind visit to Minnesota and then flew to California. In San Francisco Gorbachev renewed acquaintance with former U.S. president Ronald Reagan, and then, in a major address at Stanford University, the Soviet leader said that "the Cold War is now behind us. Let us not wrangle over who won it." He also called for a "new approach to the structures of security . . . and alliance building" that would result in a "unity . . . worthy of the life of a human being" (AP, 4 June).

The Soviet media hailed this summit as a major success: *Literaturnaia gazeta* (6 June) said that "many people believe that this has been the most productive meeting in the history of Soviet-American relations since the war," while *Izvestiia* (17 June) said that "Soviet-American dialogue is in many respects the determining factor in world life today."

Gorbachev's agreement with German chancellor Helmut Kohl on German reunification in July removed one source of U.S.-Soviet discord just as the splintering of the CPSU added another area of friction. After U.S. secretary of state Baker said on 16 July that he thought it would be appropriate to "touch base" with opposition leaders, Gorbachev spokesman Arkadii Maslennikov warned U.S. officials not to offer CPSU opponents "encouragement or assistance" (AP, 18 July).

At the economic summit of major industrialized democracies in Houston 9–11 July, West Germany and France pushed for economic aid to the USSR. Reluctance of the United States to commit resources in prevailing conditions of economic inefficiency in the USSR led to an "agreement to disagree": each state was free to offer aid to the Soviets if it wished to do so (*NYT*, 10, 12 July). President Bush had also pointed to certain "legal and political problems" inhibiting aid, among them Soviet aid to Cuba, which, he said, "could be used to help the Soviet people" (*Sovetskaia Rossiia*, 1 July; *FBIS-SOV*, 5 July).

Other irritants were evident in Soviet press comments. Bush's speech at the launching of a new aircraft carrier was criticized as filled with the "phraseology of force" and "superpatriotism" (*Pravda*, 24 July). Bush's 25 July speech on Captive Nations Day was also described as peppered with "cold war terminology" (TASS, *FBIS-SOV*, 26 July).

Although some frictions continued to surface, the main course of relations between Moscow and Washington remained on track. Secretary Baker was welcomed to Irkutsk by Shevardnadze for wide-ranging discussions on major issues (*Pravda*, 1 August). While their talks were under way, they were suddenly confronted with a major international crisis as Iraq invaded Kuwait on 2 August. The two foreign ministers then extended their conclave and moved to Moscow, concluding the talks on 3 August. It was announced that progress had been

made on 50 percent cuts in the two countries' strategic offensive weapons and that START was expected to be signed at the next summit. The foreign ministers pledged to seek agreement on conventional forces in time for the CSCE meeting in Paris in November and said that they had narrowed their differences on the issues of Afghanistan and Cambodia. Shevardnadze said that on 1 January 1992 the USSR would stop production of mobile strategic missiles based on railway platforms (Moscow World Service, 2 August; *FBIS-SOV*, 3 August).

The big payoff on the Irkutsk and Moscow talks was felt almost immediately in cooperation on the Persian Gulf crisis, already promised on 3 August in statements made at Vnukovo-2 airport by the foreign ministers. The USSR voted with the United States on resolutions condemning the Iraqi invasion of Kuwait and on economic sanctions against Iraq. At the suggestion of the Soviets, the Military Staff Committee of the United Nations was revived to assist coordination.

In the first week of the crisis, responding to a U.S. request, the USSR froze arms shipments to Iraq (*Izvestiia*, 7 August). The Soviets did not, however, remove their military advisers from Iraq, maintaining that the USSR had contractual obligations to meet. This maintenance of a foothold in Iraq aroused some suspicion in Washington, which proved groundless as the Soviets, while sometimes differing with the United States over methods, demonstrated a firm commitment to the U.N. coalition and against Iraq, their former client.

Moscow emphasized a peaceful settlement of the crisis, and Presidential Council member Evgenii Primakov served as Gorbachev's personal envoy in shuttle diplomacy that continued for several weeks, with stops in Baghdad, Washington, Cairo, Damascus, and West European capitals. Primakov's travels apparently produced no movement toward a settlement, although he did obtain Saddam Husayn's agreement to a schedule for Soviet citizens to leave Iraq (TASS, 1 November; *Report on the USSR*, 9 November).

With U.N. forces, mostly American, rapidly deploying in Saudi Arabia, a hurry-up summit was scheduled between Presidents Bush and Gorbachev, who met in Helsinki on 9 September. In their joint communiqué, they agreed that nothing short of the complete implementation of U.N. resolutions was acceptable, and they called on Iraq to withdraw unconditionally from Kuwait, to allow the restoration of Kuwait's legitimate government, and to free all hostages (*Pravda*, 10 September). In a press conference following the meeting, however, Gorbachev stressed the search for a peaceful solution and said that military action "would draw us into unpredictable consequences." Further, he maintained that the United States, the USSR, and United Nations had "an enormous arsenal of approaches to reach a political solution to the problem" (Moscow Television Service, 9 September; *FBIS-SOV*, 10 September).

Moscow appeared to tilt toward a more forceful stance on the gulf crisis in late September. Foreign Minister Shevardnadze, in New York for a meeting of the U.N. General Assembly, said that "we will comply with any decision, with any resolution of the Security Council. . . . And that would include anything regarding the involvement of the Soviet troops under the flag, under the auspices, of the United Nations." (AP, 29 September.) Baker and Shevardnadze held another round of talks in New York, reportedly concerned mostly with the reduction of conventional arms in Europe (Moscow Domestic Service, *FBIS-SOV*, 4 October). They issued a joint statement supporting the peacekeeping activities of the United Nations and declaring their intention to encourage "the trend away from theoretical excess towards efforts to deal pragmatically with the major issues of the 1990s" (TASS, 3 October; *FBIS-SOV*, 4 October).

Primakov continued to stress a peaceful solution at a 19 October meeting with Bush at the White House. The Soviet envoy claimed that the USSR had no military advisers in Iraq, only 80 specialists there in connection with the supply of equipment. On the prospects for a settlement, Primakov said that "I cannot say that after the meeting with the President I became less modestly optimistic than before." While Primakov was meeting with Bush, Baker was voicing a positive opinion of U.S.-Soviet cooperation on the gulf crisis in a speech to the U.S. Committee on USSR-U.S. Relations. Baker said that Soviet-U.S. relations are now characterized by "hitherto unprecedented opportunities for cooperation" (TASS, 19 October; *FBIS-SOV*, 22 October).

In the following weeks, the USSR voted for the U.S.-sponsored resolution authorizing the use of force as of 15 January 1991 if Iraq did not withdraw by that date. But the Soviets continued to prefer a peaceful solution and, given their domestic troubles, were in no position to become directly involved militarily in the gulf region. Meanwhile, the lengthy negotiations on conventional forces in Europe paid off with the signing at the CSCE meeting in Paris of a treaty dramatically reducing weapons on the continent (see below).

When Shevardnadze and Baker met again on 9 December in the latter's hometown of Houston, emergency economic aid for the USSR was at the top of the agenda. On the Persian Gulf crisis, Shevardnadze said that the USSR would not send military forces to the area. "This option is nonexistent," the foreign minister declared, but he supported U.S. insistence that U.S.-Iraqi talks be held well before the 15 January deadline. The two diplomats reportedly moved closer on issues involving Angola and Afghanistan but were unable to resolve all problems on START (*NYT*, 12 December).

Baker and Shevardnadze moved on to Washington for an important session with President Bush. The president waived the Jackson-Vanik amendment on export credits for six months and approved up to $1 billion in federally guaranteed loans to allow the USSR to buy agricultural goods in the United States. Bush also said that he would propose that the World Bank and the International Monetary Fund give the USSR "special association" status in order to provide economic assistance and advice. The Bush-Gorbachev summit was scheduled for 11–13 February 1991 (*WP*, 13 December).

Shevardnadze's resignation as USSR foreign minister less than two weeks after the meetings with Bush and Baker cast a pall over U.S.-Soviet relations. But both sides insisted that there would be no change in policy (*NYT*, *Pravda*, 21 December).

Western Europe and Germany. The problem of German unification occupied center stage during the first half of the year. As late as November 1989, the Soviets had categorically rejected German reunification, and in March Gorbachev had called membership in NATO by a unified Germany "out of the question." But Moscow's weakening clout in world affairs produced an erosion of the Soviet position amid various proposals and counterproposals. In June, Gorbachev proposed associate membership for Germany in both NATO and the Warsaw Pact; this idea was dismissed by the NATO allies. Finally, in July, Gorbachev and German chancellor Helmut Kohl came to an understanding on reunification and NATO membership.

Under terms of the agreement worked out in meetings in Stavropol and Moscow, a united Germany would be allowed to have NATO membership but no foreign NATO troops could be stationed on the territory of the former German Democratic Republic. Kohl agreed that the future all-German army would be limited to 370,000, in contrast to the 480,000 troops under arms in the current Bundeswehr. The length of mandatory service would be reduced from fifteen to twelve months. Soviet troops would be withdrawn from East Germany over a period of three to four years.

The bonus for Moscow came in the form of economic concessions from Bonn, including $3 billion in credits and $750 million to pay for the stationing of Soviet troops in East Germany for the remainder of the year. The Federal Republic of Germany also agreed to build housing for returning Soviet troops in the USSR and to fulfill all the German Democratic Republic's economic commitments to Moscow (*Pravda*, 17, 18 July; *NYT*, 16, 17, 18 July; *Insight*, 6 August).

The last major obstacle to German reunification was removed immediately after the Kohl-Gorbachev meeting when the "2+4" (the two Germanies plus the four World War II allies) negotiators in Paris announced a treaty guaranteeing the Oder-Neisse line as the border between Germany and Poland (*NYT*, 18 July).

Although Gorbachev's yielding on German unification brought something of a conservative backlash at home, Germany continued to be the centerpiece of his European policy. In November, the Soviet leader traveled to Bonn, where he signed a treaty on nonaggression and on general German-Soviet relations with Kohl, now the chancellor of a united Germany. Two other treaties on social and economic cooperation were also signed, but Gorbachev failed to get a commitment on a big new package of economic aid that he wanted (Reuters, DPA, *NYT*, 10, 11 November). While in Bonn, Gorbachev expressed concern about the tensions associated with the continuing presence of Soviet troops in the territory of the former German Democratic Republic. In the previous week, Oleg Bogomolov, director of the Institute for International and Political Research, said that Soviet troops may leave Germany before their 1994 deadline (*Bild am Sonntag*, 4 November; *Report on the USSR*, 16 November).

The Bonn government was somewhat strapped financially because of the massive costs involved in the reconstruction of East Germany, but Gorbachev was more successful elsewhere in his solicitations. In October, the Italian government approved an aid package worth $2 billion for the USSR (AP, 16 October). Less than two weeks later, when Gorbachev visited Madrid, he signed sixteen agreements, including one providing a $1.5 billion credit from

Spain over three years (TASS, 27 October; *NYT*, 28 October).

After his stop in Madrid, Gorbachev went on to Paris, where he signed a treaty of friendship and cooperation with French president Mitterrand. The treaty provided that, in the event of a threat to peace, the two countries would consult each other without delay and would hold regular political consultations. French assistance was promised as the USSR begins to shift to a market economy, as well as help in arranging accords between Moscow and the European Community. The Soviets also promised to reimburse French holders of bonds issued by the czarist government between 1822 and 1917 (AP, 30 October).

When Gorbachev visited Italy in November, he signed a treaty of friendship and cooperation with Premier Giulio Andreotti. On 18 November, Andreotti announced a credit line worth $900 million for the USSR, and the October deal was augmented. It was then announced that the total credit package over five years would amount to more than $6 billion, including $1.9 billion in direct loans and $4.3 billion in export credit guarantees (TASS, 18 November; *Report on the USSR*, 30 November).

The Soviets had envisioned the Conference on Security and Cooperation in Europe (CSCE) as a framework for a new order in Europe and, to some extent, as a replacement for the crumbling Warsaw Treaty Organization (WTO) and possibly as a substitute for NATO. Toward that end, the USSR in June signed a declaration committing it for the first time to multiparty democracy. The CSCE document, signed by 35 nations, commits member states to pluralism, free elections, an independent judiciary, and the separation of the state from political parties (*NYT*, 30 June).

Following up on the June agreement, the Soviets committed themselves further at the big CSCE summit in Paris in November. Thirty-four nations signed a new European charter supporting democracy, human rights, the rule of law, and free market economics as norms for the continent (AP, 23 November). Deputations from the three Baltic republics showed up at the conference but were denied admission at Soviet insistence. Presidents Bush and Gorbachev conferred on the Persian Gulf crisis, with the Soviet leader reportedly still pressuring the U.S. president for restraint.

The most spectacular result of the CSCE summit was the signing of the long-awaited agreement on conventional forces in Europe. NATO and WTO negotiators reached accord on terms on 15 November in Vienna (*NYT*, 16 November), and the agreement was signed by the 22 nations making up the NATO and WTO alliances on 19 November. The treaty limits each side to 20,000 main battle tanks, 30,000 armored combat vehicles, 20,000 pieces of artillery, 6,900 combat aircraft, and 2,000 attack helicopters. Nevertheless, the negotiators were unable to agree on personnel limits. Further talks were scheduled in Vienna to deal with the matter; however, some negotiators said that troop cuts had become a relatively unimportant issue (AP, 15 November; *NYT*, 20 November).

Although Britain was less disposed than the continental countries to offer aid to the USSR, relations between the Soviets and British were quite cordial. United Kingdom foreign secretary Douglas Hurd journeyed to Moscow in April for two days of talks with Foreign Minister Shevardnadze that dealt mostly with the matter of German reunification; Hurd also met with Gorbachev. An accord was signed on emergency notification about nuclear disasters, on the exchange of information about operating and controlling nuclear installations, and on cooperation in cultural, educational, and scientific matters. Hurd noted a "serious improvement in Soviet-British relations and between the East and West generally" (TASS, 10 April; *FBIS-SOV*, 11 April).

British defense minister Tom King followed with a trip to Moscow in May. King conferred with USSR defense minister Dmitrii Iazov on problems connected with German unification, the reduction of conventional forces in Europe, and the future of NATO and WTO (TASS, 14 May; *FBIS-SOV*, 15 May). Three weeks later, Prime Minister Margaret Thatcher was warmly welcomed to Moscow by Gorbachev and discussed with him results of the Washington summit (Moscow Television Service, 8 June; *FBIS-SOV*, 11 June). Thatcher said that she was "very satisfied" with Soviet-British relations. "I even think that they are better now than they have ever been in the past, and this is largely due to President Gorbachev" (*Pravda*, 8 June).

Iuri I. Karlov was named USSR representative to the Vatican with the rank of ambassador (*Izvestiia*, 31 March), a follow-up to President Gorbachev's visit with Pope John Paul II the previous year. One week after the announcement of Karlov's appointment, TASS and Radio Vatican signed an agreement on the supply of English-language information to the Vatican radio station (TASS, 6 April; *FBIS-SOV*, 11 April). When Gorbachev visited Italy in November, he met again with Pope John Paul II and

was quoted as saying that his next meeting with the pope would probably be in the USSR (TASS, 18 November; *Report on the USSR*, 30 November).

Gorbachev's European policy showed dividends in December when the heads of government of the twelve European Community countries, meeting in Rome, agreed to send $1 billion in new emergency aid to the USSR. German chancellor Kohl and French president Mitterrand were the most vocal proponents of the proposal. New British prime minister John Major was more cautious, worrying about the risk of squandering supplies and overburdening the dilapidated Soviet transport network (*WP*, 15 December).

The provision of aid, both public and private, was not inspired entirely by altruistic motives. There was considerable alarm in Europe about the possibility of an influx of millions of refugees from the USSR in the event of widespread hunger in that country (*European Journal*, 8 December).

Eastern Europe. Soviet relations with the Eastern European countries during the year were conditioned by the reunification of Germany, the decline in East-West tensions, the rise of democratic governments in the area, and the dismantlement in all but name of the Warsaw Treaty Organization (WTO). With the collapse of the Soviet bloc, it was necessary to forge new relationships with the former satellites, and the Soviets insisted that their approach was based on the "new political thinking." But some very practical problems emerged in this transitional period. The downturn of the Soviet economy had a serious negative effect on regional trade; Hungary was particularly affected. Withdrawal of Soviet troops was also a complex matter. In eastern Germany, the continued presence of Soviet forces led to heightened tensions with the local populace. Generally, East Europeans wanted to speed the exit of the Soviet military. But in Poland the prospect of a reunified Germany brought a turnaround, with Warsaw welcoming Soviet troops as a surety against its now more powerful neighbor. Nevertheless, "gradual" withdrawal of Soviet troops from Poland began in June (Moscow Television Service, 1 June; *FBIS-SOV*, 4 June).

Lech Wałęsa, in January, demanded the total withdrawal of Soviet troops from Polish territory by the end of 1990, a demand that was spurned by the Polish government (*Krasnaia zvezda*, 21 January). Wałęsa's election as Poland's president in December raised the possibility of more prickly relations with Moscow. But one long-standing issue had apparently been defused with the Soviet admission that the Katyń Forest massacre had indeed been carried out by Soviet secret police forces during World War II (Warsaw Domestic Service, *FBIS-EEU*, 13 April).

The Soviet economic crisis and the relaxation of border controls led to a thriving black market in barter exchanges, with Soviet "tourists" trading Russian vodka for consumer goods available in Warsaw (*European Journal*, 8 December). This cross-border traffic was no great concern for Poland, but as the frontline state bordering the USSR, Poland figured to be the first country affected by any massive Soviet emigration. Thus the critical situation in Soviet cities produced some nervousness on the Polish side of the border.

Czechoslovakia and the USSR reached an agreement on Soviet troop pullout, which began on 26 February. All 73,500 Soviet troops were scheduled to be out by 30 June 1991. Arrangements were agreed on during Czechoslovak president Václav Havel's visit to Moscow for talks with Gorbachev (Moscow Television Service, *FBIS-SOV*, 26 February). Two weeks after the beginning of the troop withdrawal from Czechoslovakia, Moscow and Budapest agreed on the withdrawal from Hungary of all 49,700 soldiers and equipment by the same date of 30 June 1991 (AP, 10 March).

Leaders of the Warsaw Pact countries, meeting in Moscow in June, decided to convert WTO from a military to a political organization (*Izvestiia*, 27 June). On 3 November, representatives of WTO states met in Budapest and decided on a division of pact tanks and other weapons. The USSR was to keep 13,150 of the 20,000 tanks, and the other states would have between 1,000 and 2,000. The move by WTO cleared the last major hurdle to the Conventional Forces in Europe (CFE) agreement signed in Paris on 19 November. Hungarian foreign minister Géza Jeszenszky assessed WTO prospects: "As a military organization, I would not bet that it would last as long as the end of next year" (AP, 3 November).

The Soviet economic decline and the Persian Gulf crisis combined to put extra pressure on the rebuilding of economies in East-Central Europe: oil supply became a major concern. On 30 October, the USSR informed Hungary that it would no longer accept rubles as payment for oil deliveries as of 1 December. Two days later, in a letter to the USSR Supreme Soviet, the chairman of the Hungarian Parliament's Foreign Affairs Committee, Gyula Horn, complained that the USSR's failure to keep commitments was straining bilateral relations (Radio Budapest, 30 October, 2 November; *Report on the USSR*, 9 November).

Also concerned about oil, Czechoslovakia sent its prime minister to Moscow in October to confer with USSR premier Ryzhkov. After the meeting, it was announced that the USSR would supply 13 million tons of oil to Czechoslovakia in 1991, down 20 percent from 1990 (BBC-CARIS, 31 October). Two weeks later, Czechoslovakia's finance minister, Václav Klaus, was in Moscow for talks with USSR finance minister Valentin Pavlov. The two finance ministers signed an agreement to take effect on 1 January 1991 providing that trade payments will be made in convertible currencies (TASS, 16 November; *Report on the USSR*, 23 November).

China. Sino-Soviet relations showed a modest improvement during the year as border tensions continued to decline and several meetings of consequence were held. But the great hopes aroused by Gorbachev's 1989 visit to Beijing had not been realized. The brutal crackdown on dissidents in China and the collapse of the Soviet bloc in Eastern Europe gave each side an additional reason for distrusting the other. The Chinese leadership also gave strong indications of its opposition to Gorbachev's domestic policies, although these reservations were mostly expressed in private.

The USSR Ministry of Foreign Economic Relations reported in January that the volume of trade between the USSR and China topped 2 billion rubles in 1989, a more than ninefold increase since the early 1980s (Moscow International Service, 6 January; *FBIS-SOV*, 25 January). In March, Konstantin Katushev, chairman of the USSR State Committee for Foreign Economic Relations, reached agreement in Beijing with Chinese officials on the current year's exchanges and projected a 36 percent increase in trade volume over 1989 (Moscow International Service, 15 March; *FBIS-SOV*, 16 March).

Another round of border talks concluded in Beijing in February. The Soviet delegates professed to be pleased with the results, but Soviet media reported that the talks were not easy and that many problems remained (Moscow International Service, 24 February; *FBIS-SOV*, 26 February).

The first official military visit from the People's Republic of China (PRC) in 30 years was a positive sign. Major General Song Wen-zhong, head of the Foreign Affairs Bureau of the PRC Ministry of National Defense, led a delegation on a ten-day visit in April (TASS, *FBIS-SOV*, 12 April). Less than two weeks after the military delegation departed, Chinese premier Li Peng, accompanied by Foreign Minister Qian Qichen, arrived in Moscow to return Gorbachev's May 1989 visit (*Pravda*, 24 April). Li Peng signed an agreement for cooperation on various projects with Premier Ryzhkov, including construction of a nuclear power plant in China. Qian Qichen signed a separate agreement with USSR foreign minister Shevardnadze on further reductions of troops along the two countries' common border. The Soviet side maintained its policy of not criticizing China's crushing of prodemocracy demonstrations in June 1989 (*Pravda*, 23–25 April; *NYT*, 25 April). About two hundred protesters in Moscow denounced Li as a "bloody butcher" for his role in the antidemocracy crackdown (Reuters, 26 April).

The visit, the first by a Chinese premier to the USSR since 1964, represented only a small step forward in Sino-Soviet relations. No formal communiqués were issued. One Soviet official said that the visit's main achievement was the avoidance of an open ideological split (*FEER*, 10 May). Prospects were not bright for an early upsurge in USSR-PRC contacts. In internal documents, Chinese leaders attacked Gorbachev for supporting radical change in Eastern Europe, for eliminating Article 6 of the Soviet Constitution, and for allowing a multiparty system. Beijing's ongoing campaign against liberalism was likely to inhibit contacts, and it was clear that Soviet leaders had scaled down their expectations for Sino-Soviet cooperation (*CSM*, 27 April).

Although inhibitions remained on both sides, Foreign Minister Shevardnadze said that "the turnaround in relations between our countries is a major achievement of the policy of peace and dialogue" and that "qualitatively new Soviet-Chinese relations" will "increasingly act as a stabilizing factor not only in Asia and the Pacific region but also in the international arena as a whole" (*Izvestiia*, 16 May).

In June, Premier Ryzhkov received Col. Gen. Lu Huaqing, deputy chairman of China's Central Military Council, in the Kremlin while Qian Qichen talked with the USSR's deputy minister of foreign affairs, Igor Rogachev, in Beijing (TASS, 13, 14 June; *FBIS-SOV*, 14 June). Further simultaneous meetings were held in July. USSR Supreme Soviet chairman Anatolii Lukianov welcomed a delegation led by National People's Congress of China vice-chairman Peng Chong while USSR first deputy premier Iuri Masliukov attended the meeting of the joint Soviet-Chinese Commission on Economic, Trade, and Scientific-Technological Cooperation in Beijing. At the Beijing conference, agreements were signed on protecting investments and avoiding double taxation (TASS, 21 July; Moscow Television, Moscow Radio, 22 July; *FBIS-SOV*, 23 July).

Foreign Minister Shevardnadze met with Qian Qichen in Harbin on 1 September during his Far East tour that also included North Korea and Japan. The meeting was scheduled before the Iraqi invasion of Kuwait, but the Persian Gulf crisis apparently dominated the talks. The foreign ministers expressed agreement on the issue of foreign hostages in Iraq and Kuwait and on peaceful means for settling the crisis. Other matters discussed included Afghanistan, Cambodia, and Korea. The ministers set 10 September as the date for the start of the next round of talks on reduction of forces along the border (*Izvestiia*, 3 September). They also scheduled a new round of talks on delineating the USSR-PRC border for the end of October. Shevardnadze said that the USSR and China had agreed on 90 percent of the total frontier in two years of border talks (TASS, 1 September; *CSM*, 11 September).

In early November, a Chinese Foreign Ministry spokesman was quoted as saying that the border talks had been under way for two weeks "in an earnest and realistic atmosphere, and progress was made" (AFP, 3 November; *Report on the USSR*, 16 November).

Foreign Minister Shevardnadze visited China in November to discuss with Chinese leaders Sino-Soviet relations and the gulf crisis (Radio Moscow, 22 November; *Report on the USSR*, 30 November). In the following week, a Soviet delegation headed by Genrikh Kireev, head of the USSR Foreign Ministry's department on relations with socialist countries in Asia, resumed talks in Beijing on mutual reductions in armed forces along the border (TASS, 30 November; *FBIS-SOV*, 7 December).

Japan. Although diplomatic activities gave an impression of movement, the essentials of the Soviet-Japanese relationship remained as they had been for some years. The USSR needed Japanese economic aid and investment, and Tokyo wanted the return of the Northern Territories. Japan aimed to withhold its economic carrot until some movement was evident on the issues of the Kuriles; on the Soviet side, domestic political considerations precluded a rapid hand over of the islands. The strategic balance in the northern Pacific was also a complicating factor, and there were internal divisions in both governments over the approach to the islands issue. The two sides could only agree on innocuous "confidence-building" measures while awaiting some possible breakthrough during President Gorbachev's scheduled April 1991 visit to Japan.

Despite the USSR's internal troubles, the cards were definitely not all in Tokyo's hands. The USSR still held the islands, and their value as a bargaining chip was unlikely to diminish, while a hand over would produce great resentment among conservatives in the USSR. Moreover, Moscow's relations with other major powers had warmed just as Tokyo was facing the bill for its long-term inflexibility on foreign economic relations and other matters. Japan's guarded position on the Persian Gulf crisis, its continuing economic friction with Washington, and its approaching problems with Europe related to European Community unification all added up to the danger of long-term Japanese isolation. Keeping Moscow at arm's length compounded the potential problem, and the Soviets were unlikely to forget quickly the Japanese foreign minister's delivery of a gratuitous insult to the USSR at the July economic summit in Houston. Soviet overtures to South Korea (see below) seemed designed in part to undercut Japan's bargaining position and its influence on the Asian continent; these overtures offered better immediate prospects for Moscow than did negotiations with Japan. Thus, Gorbachev and Shevardnadze had good reasons for going slow in their dealings with Tokyo.

On the Soviet side, Boris Eltsin threatened to become a wild card. While still a mere member of the USSR Supreme Soviet, he spent ten days in Japan in January and carried out his own personal diplomacy independent of the USSR government. He met with Japanese premier Toshiki Kaifu and advocated a five-stage movement requiring twenty years for settlement of the issue (Moscow Radio, 20 January; *FBIS-SOV*, 22 January; *New Times*, no. 6, 6–12 February; *FBIS-SOV*, 1 March). Subsequently, after becoming RSFSR president, Eltsin indicated that he favored joint Soviet-Japanese administration of the Kuriles. When Moscow mayor Gavril Popov visited Tokyo in October, he said that the RSFSR was ready to negotiate over the islands and rejected the idea that resolution of the island dispute should be linked to Japanese economic aid for the USSR (AFP, 29 October; *Report on the USSR*, 9 November).

Within the Soviet government, there were also reported differences on the issue. The Institute of World Economics and International Affairs (IMEMO) had developed a special interest in Japanese affairs and was said to be pushing a U.N. trusteeship for the islands; Gorbachev was believed to be favorably disposed to such a scheme as a long-range solution (*FEER*, 21 June). The USSR Foreign Ministry reportedly resented IMEMO's intrusion, and the Soviet military was also disgruntled. *Krasnaia zvezda* (5 June) warned that some Japanese publications were calling for special forces to retake the islands.

Vsevolod Ovchinnikov, a prominent political commentator, went public with the proposal for a U.N. trusteeship at the beginning of July (*Pravda*, 1 July). But another commentator, Leonid Mlechin, pointed to the Soviets' tactical advantage. As a result of Gorbachev's meeting with the president of South Korea, Mlechin said, "Soviet diplomacy has secured a firmer foothold in the Far East, and Shevardnadze will have vast room for maneuver." Further, he noted that "what the Soviet economy would like to get from Japan is readily available—on easier terms—from Korea." (*New Times*, no. 27, 3–9 July; *FBIS-SOV*, 11 July.) On the Japanese side, the Foreign Ministry insisted on unconditional return of all four islands, whereas some leading politicians of the ruling Liberal Democratic party showed readiness to accept a compromise deal, perhaps one involving initial return of only two of the islands (*FEER*, 21 June).

The USSR's domestic crisis did have a negative impact on economic relations with Japan. Export insurance rates on trade with the USSR doubled due to lateness in paying bills by Soviet trading organizations (*WSJ*, 15 May). Because of Soviet payment problems, two-way trade fell 6 percent in the first half of the year, to $2.77 billion (*FEER*, 30 August).

Four major events marked the summer months. In the first week of July, Japanese premier Kaifu said that it would not be possible for his government to take part in economic assistance to the USSR until the Kurile Islands dispute was settled (*NYT*, 7 July). At the economic summit in Houston, Japan again refused to promise immediate economic aid to the USSR. Japan's foreign minister, Taro Nakayama, added insult to injury by commenting in what he apparently thought was a private session that giving aid to the USSR would be like "treating a diabetic with sugar"; Soviet press comment was predictably scathing (*Izvestiia*, 23 July).

After the strained Houston meeting, Gorbachev gave a frosty reception to Yoshio Sakurauchi, speaker of the lower house of the Diet, in Moscow on 25 July. When Sakurauchi urged that the USSR return the islands, Gorbachev appeared to deny any possibility of compromise and even hinted that he might cancel his scheduled 1991 visit to Japan (*FEER*, 9 August).

The events of July did nothing to smooth the way for Shevardnadze's September visit to Tokyo, and the meeting was most notable for its lack of results. Shevardnadze and Nakayama signed a memorandum of cooperation in overcoming the consequences of the Chernobyl disaster and firmed up plans for Gorbachev's 1991 visit (TASS, *FBIS-SOV*, 6 September). On the question of a peace treaty and the "well-known territorial linkage," however, Shevardnadze stated that "I cannot say that some meaningful progress was achieved on this question" (TASS, 6 September; *FBIS-SOV*, 7 September).

When the USSR's domestic crisis hit with full force in December, Tokyo offered aid, but Japan was parsimonious compared with the other major democracies. Assistance on transportation and distribution was promised, and the city of Kawasaki sent $92,300 worth of medical supplies (*NYT*, 13 December). Gorbachev announced on 3 December that he still planned to visit Japan in April 1991 (*Report on the USSR*, 14 December).

North and South Korea. Moscow skillfully exploited an opening to South Korea during the year, looking to Seoul for economic benefits. The warming trend in USSR-South Korea relations was also a means of gaining leverage vis-à-vis Japan, China, and the Stalinist regime in North Korea while extending Soviet influence generally in East Asia.

Events during the winter pointed toward a rapid development of Moscow-Seoul ties. South Korea's Hyundai group agreed to a joint venture to produce 1 million cubic meters of lumber each year in the Soviet Far East (*Insight*, 5 February). Aeroflot also signed an agreement with Korea Air on air routes and Aeroflot flights to Seoul from Moscow and Khabarovsk were scheduled to start on 29 March (TASS, 22 February; *FBIS-SOV*, 27 February). Kim Yong-sam, cochairman of South Korea's governing Democratic Liberal Party (DLP), visited Moscow in late March for conferences with Aleksandr Iakovlev and other officials. Kim said that "astonishing progress, both qualitatively and quantitatively, has been made in Korean-Soviet relations in various areas" (Moscow Radio, 27 March; *FBIS-SOV*, 30 March).

While Kim was in Moscow, reports circulated that the USSR and South Korea would soon establish diplomatic relations, and Moscow noted ap-

provingly the establishment of such ties between Mongolia and South Korea (TASS, 26 March; *FBIS-SOV*, 29 March).

A week after the Kim visit, Seoul announced that it would exchange ambassadors with the USSR during the year. At the same time, Soviet relations with North Korea took a nosedive. Two North Korean defectors arrived in Seoul after fleeing from Leningrad, and the North Korean embassy in Moscow began confiscating students' passports to prevent more defections. Meanwhile, the Soviet press blasted Kim Il-sung's regime. The Soviet periodical *Argumenty i fakty* dwelt on the feeble state of North Korea's economy, its external debt, and the people's "miserable existence" (*Washington Times*, 4 April). *Moscow News* carried an article comparing Kim Il-sung to Stalin and Ceauşescu (*Insight*, 26 March). Moscow Radio on 20 April quoted historian Mikhail Smirnov as casting doubt on Kim Il-sung's assertion that the South provoked the 1950–1953 war; this was the first time that this claim had been officially disputed in the USSR (*FEER*, 3 May).

As with Japan, the USSR's domestic economic crisis complicated matters. South Korean sources reported that slow payments by the USSR were becoming a serious problem; payments were said to be two to five months late, with the USSR owing seven Korean conglomerates about $30 million (Seoul, Yonhap, 12 May; *FBIS-EAS*, 15 May). A positive note was provided when the Korea Chamber of Commerce and Industry requested a lowering of South Korean tariffs on East bloc raw materials in order to expedite exports to the socialist nations (*Korea Herald*, 12 May; *FBIS-EAS*, 15 May).

Pyongyang inveighed against the Moscow-Seoul rapprochement, but the Soviets lightly dismissed North Korean protests (*NYT*, 31 May). During his visit to San Francisco, Gorbachev met with South Korean president Roh Tae-woo (*Izvestiia*, 6 June), raising alarms in Pyongyang. Seeking to discourage the idea of a rush to "normalization," Gorbachev said that diplomatic relations "may arise as bilateral ties develop and in the context of the general improvement of the political situation in the region and on the Korean Peninsula" (TASS, 5 June; *NYT*, 6 June).

Despite Gorbachev's public caution, USSR-South Korean links continued to grow. One week after the Gorbachev-Roh meeting, a visiting delegation from the South Korean Foreign Trade Association signed an agreement on cooperation with the Soviet Chamber of Commerce and Industry (TASS,

12 June; *FBIS-SOV*, 13 June). The first official exchange of students and faculty between the two countries was announced in August (*FEER*, 30 August). Soviet and South Korean officials, meeting in Moscow in early August, agreed to announce a timetable for normalizing relations at their next meeting in Seoul in September. Diplomatic "normalization" was almost explicitly tied to economics, as Soviet officials submitted a list of major investment projects and the two sides discussed possible agreements on protection of foreign investments and avoidance of double taxation (TASS, 3 August; *FBIS-SOV*, 7 August; *FEER*, 23 August).

Attempts were made in August and September to defuse the growing hostility between Moscow and Pyongyang; there was also need for Soviet input with North Korea to encourage processes of normalization and lowering of barriers between North and South Korea. Gorbachev and Ryzhkov sent greetings to North Korean leaders on the 45th anniversary of the liberation of Korea from Japan (Moscow Domestic Service, 14 August; *FBIS-SOV*, 15 August), and a detachment of the Soviet Pacific fleet visited North Korea for the celebration (Moscow International Service, 13 August; *FBIS-SOV*, 15 August). On his Far Eastern trip, Shevardnadze met in Pyongyang with North Korean foreign minister Kim Yong-nam, and they signed an agreement on border issues (TASS, 3 September; *FBIS-SOV*, 4 September). The Soviet foreign minister said afterward that there was "mutual understanding" on two issues, the situation in the Persian Gulf and the state of affairs on the Korean peninsula (*Komsomolskaia pravda*, *FBIS-SOV*, 4 September).

In November, the USSR and North Korea signed an agreement in Moscow basing trade on payment in hard currency, effective 1 January 1991 (*Report on the USSR*, 16 November). The agreement followed establishment of full diplomatic relations between the USSR and South Korea in September. In late October, South Korea officially opened its embassy in Moscow (ibid., 9 November).

Presidential Council member Vadim Medvedev headed a delegation to Seoul in November. Several agreements on trade and cooperation were announced; the pacts were to be formally signed during South Korean president Roh Tae-woo's visit to Moscow in December (AP, 23 November).

Further cementing the new ties with Seoul, the USSR in December apologized to South Korea for its role in the Korean War and for the downing of a South Korean airliner in 1983 (ibid., 18 December).

East Asia and the Pacific. The USSR and the Mongolian People's Republic (MPR) agreed in March on the complete withdrawal of Soviet forces from Mongolia in 1991–1992. The main combat strength of the Soviet forces is to be withdrawn in 1991 and the remaining troops in 1992 (TASS, *FBIS-SOV*, 2 March). Earlier, in February, the last monument to Stalin was dismantled in Ulan Bator (Moscow Television, 22 February; *FBIS-SOV*, 2 March). Hoping to give reform in Ulan Bator a forward push, Gorbachev welcomed Mongolia's new leader, Punsalmaagiyn Ochirbat, to Moscow in May (TASS, 16 May; *FBIS-SOV*, 17 May).

In accord with the new Soviet policy on trade in convertible currency, the USSR signed an agreement with the MPR in August to convert trade to that basis in 1991 and to bring prices and reciprocal settlements into line with international practice (TASS, *FBIS-SOV*, 20 August).

The phased removal of forces from Mongolia plus the earlier withdrawal from Afghanistan put increased pressure upon Vietnam in regard to Cambodia. Foreign Minister Shevardnadze was active in pushing for a Cambodian settlement. In January, he said that favorable opportunities were being opened up for progress toward a "lasting and balanced solution" of the protracted regional conflict and touted a Soviet initiative on a moratorium on military aid to all sides in Cambodia (*Izvestiia*, 6 January). In June, Shevardnadze met with Cambodian premier and foreign minister Hun Sen in Moscow and expressed approval of agreements in Tokyo between Hun Sun and Prince Norodom Sihanouk on the creation of a Supreme National Council and on measures to achieve a cease-fire (TASS, 8 June; *FBIS-SOV*, 11 June).

A settlement in Cambodia was important to Moscow because that country had long been a source of friction with Beijing. The Soviet approach was also in line with Gorbachev's general objective of extending Soviet influence in Asia while lowering military tensions. The cutback in Soviet forces in Asia and the USSR's decision to wind down its base at Cam Ranh Bay, Vietnam, had convinced many in the Association of Southeast Asian Nations that the Soviets no longer presented a security threat and opened up new possibilities for various kinds of cooperation (*FEER*, 17 May). The importance of the region to Moscow was further demonstrated by Premier Ryzhkov's February trip to Thailand, Singapore, and Australia (*Izvestiia*, 12 February; *Pravda*, 16 February; TASS, 17 February; *FBIS-SOV*, 20 February).

The diplomatic thrust into Southeast Asia was given added impetus by the souring of relations with Hanoi. The Democratic Republic of Vietnam (DRV) had rejected reform, and its leadership had openly criticized the domestic policies of Gorbachev. Moreover, one phase of Soviet-DRV economic cooperation was rapidly playing out. The agreement on Vietnamese "guest workers," due to expire in 1995, was already being repealed in practice. The head of the foreign workers' department of *Gostrumtrud*, G. Peschanaia, said that "this year 2000-3000 of them will leave and we are not going to object if it turns out to be more than that" (*Komsomolskaia pravda*, 2 August; *FBIS-SOV*, 13 August).

India. Soviet relations with India remained close, featuring increased contacts during the year. Ties were reaffirmed in January during the visit of TASS general director Leonid Kravchenko to New Delhi and the talks between Shevardnadze and Shailendra Kumar Singh, foreign secretary of the Indian Ministry of External Affairs, in Moscow (TASS, 23, 27 January; *FBIS-SOV*, 23, 29 January). USSR Supreme Soviet president Anatolii Lukianov met top Indian officials in New Delhi in April bearing the message that *perestroika* contained an "immense potential" for joint actions and broadening of contacts between the two countries (TASS, 8 April; *FBIS-SOV*, 11 April).

Several Soviet financial officials followed Lukianov on the Moscow–New Delhi shuttle. Indo-Soviet trade was expected to reach $5.21 billion in 1990, and a proposal for a joint project to produce the IL 96/300 airliner was under consideration (*FEER*, 17 May). On the diplomatic front, Soviet deputy foreign minister Igor Rogachev held consultations with Indian foreign minister Inder Kumar Gujral in New Delhi on Afghanistan, Cambodia, the situation in Kashmir, and relations of the two countries with China (TASS, 17 April; *FBIS-SOV*, 18 April).

A bit of controversy sparked the relationship in July when *Moscow News* (no. 26, 8–15 July) reported that the USSR was about to sell a nuclear submarine to India, supplementing the one leased in 1988. *Moscow News* said that deliveries of nuclear technologies should be strictly banned and called on the USSR Supreme Soviet to raise serious objections to the deal. Questions were also raised about India's $9 billion debt to the USSR, but trade representative G. A. Shcherbakov maintained that New Delhi had always paid its credits and interest on time and that there was no problem for Soviet-Indian economic relations (*Izvestiia*, 20 July).

Vishwanath Pratap Singh, India's prime minister, was welcomed to Moscow in July for talks with Gorbachev. At the conclusion of their talks, they issued a vague communiqué endorsing nuclear disarmament and the peaceful settlement of regional disputes (TASS, *FBIS-SOV*, 24 July). Shevardnadze and Indian foreign minister Gujral also held talks and reported agreement in principle on several issues, including Afghanistan, Cambodia, and Kashmir (TASS, 25 July; Delhi Domestic Service, 26 July; *FBIS-SOV*, 26 July). Following the meetings in Moscow, Premier Singh visited Tashkent, where he expressed satisfaction with the state of business contacts between Uzbekistan and India (TASS, 25 July; *FBIS-SOV*, 26 July).

Afghanistan. The USSR had gained substantial diplomatic advantages as a result of its withdrawal of forces from Afghanistan. During the year, Moscow sought to salvage what it could in Afghanistan and shore up the Kabul regime without sacrificing those advantages. The continuing turmoil in Afghanistan produced some frictions in U.S.-Soviet relations, but these were not sufficient to hamper the trends toward cooperation between Moscow and Washington.

The USSR continued to send food and fuel to Afghanistan and military aid "in line with bilateral commitments and treaties"; it also supported Afghan leader Najibullah's policy of "national reconciliation" (*Sovetskaia Rossiia*, 16 January).

Najibullah in February called for a cease-fire under U.N. supervision and claimed that around 40,000 armed troops of the opposition had accepted "national reconciliation" and come over to the government side in the year since the Soviets' withdrawal (Moscow Domestic Service, 5 February; *FBIS-SOV*, 6 February). Shevardnadze met Afghan ambassador Sayed Mohammad Ghulabzoli and endorsed active cooperation toward "a comprehensive political settlement in Afghanistan" (TASS, 2 February; *FBIS-SOV*, 6 February). Meanwhile, a Soviet military correspondent reported that there were still 82 members of the Soviet armed forces alive in Afghanistan, mostly held as prisoners by the armed opposition (*Krasnaia zvezda*, 2 February).

During the winter, Saudi Arabia was criticized by *Pravda* for continuing to finance arms and ammunition for the Afghan mujahideen (*Insight*, 5 March).

In May, Kabul upped its claims of opposition defections to 150,000. *Izvestiia* (14 May) blamed Washington for the continued fighting and political impasse in Afghanistan. Following the failed coup by former Defense Minister Shahnawaz Tanai in March, *Izvestiia* said the United States had followed a "two-track" policy, slowly pursuing the search for a political settlement while rapidly pushing military support for the opposition: "The upshot is a standstill and continuing bloodshed."

The ninth meeting of the permanent intergovernmental Soviet-Afghan commission on economic cooperation was held in early August, spotlighting the Soviet decision to resume participation in the construction and operation of joint projects in Afghanistan (TASS, 2 August; *FBIS-SOV*, 3 August). Also in August, the USSR Ministry of Foreign Economic Relations confirmed that the Soviets had agreed to provide $300 million in financial aid to Afghanistan. It was reported that the USSR had supplied 230,000 tons of grain and 100,000 tons of aviation fuel to Afghanistan during the year (TASS, 15 August; *FBIS-SOV*, 16 August).

Afghanistan was a topic of discussion during U.S. secretary of state Baker's meeting with Foreign Minister Shevardnadze in Irkutsk in early August. According to their communiqué, they narrowed their differences on Afghanistan but still had some "discord" on the ways to reach a truce and prepare general elections under U.N. supervision, especially in regard to the powers to be exercised during a transitional period by Najibullah and by a coordinating committee of Afghan political forces (Moscow World Service, 2 August; *FBIS-SOV*, 3 August).

Najibullah was welcomed to Moscow in late August by Gorbachev and Premier Ryzhkov. The Afghan leader described their talks as characterized by "sincerity and comradely openness." He said that Afghan armed forces had recently cleared three vital routes and was upbeat about Western attitudes toward his regime. Najibullah reported that France and Italy had reopened their embassies in Kabul and said that the tone of the U.S. press had changed, with some papers questioning "the military road to solution of the Afghan problem" (TASS, 24 August; *FBIS-SOV*, 27 August).

Middle East. The Persian Gulf crisis overshadowed other Soviet activities in the region, long a highly complex area for USSR policymakers.

Moscow's position on the crisis helped somewhat in sorting out the tangled threads of Soviet policy in the Middle East and had the additional benefit of making it more consistent with the USSR's general approach to world politics. Earlier Soviet support for the expansionist Saddam regime had been incompatible with the line of "new political thinking." The new political thinking, however, had been largely grounded in perceptions of relative Soviet weakness and the inefficacy of projecting Soviet military power abroad. These considerations had not applied to relations with Iraq. Moreover, the USSR's new approach to world affairs after 1985 had not precluded selective support for clients in the Third World.

In the case of Iraq, Soviet concerns had involved maintenance of a foothold in the Middle East and the establishment of a profitable outlet for the USSR arms industry. The association with Iraq, however, posed difficulties for the growing rapprochement with Iran, for the often ticklish relationship with Syria, and for the recent slight openings to Saudi Arabia and the gulf states. The minimal benefits from the association with Iraq counted for little against the USSR's new relationship with the United States and other Western powers. Additionally, Moscow's tilt in the crisis meshed neatly with the slowly evolving realignment between the USSR and other actors in the region. The Soviets' emphasis on diplomatic settlement left open the possibility that Moscow would still have more influence in Baghdad after the crisis than any other major power. Thus, the Soviet stance on the crisis was not surprising. Nevertheless, in the early weeks the USSR's position was somewhat ambiguous, leading to speculation that there was serious infighting within the Soviet leadership on basic decisions.

Immediately after the invasion, the USSR announced the suspension of arms delivery and military hardware to Iraq (*NYT*, 3 August). Over the next four weeks, Moscow endorsed U.N. resolutions on the invasion of Kuwait, while quietly tolerating the buildup of U.S. military forces in the gulf region. But on 30 August two prominent Soviet officials questioned the mounting U.S. military presence in the region. Deputy Foreign Minister Aleksandr Belonogov told a parliamentary committee that "there are no guarantees that the United States will leave Saudi Arabia after the crisis is over." General Vladimir N. Lobov, chief of staff of the Warsaw Pact alliance, said that the U.S. presence had drastically changed the strategic balance in the region and could scuttle disarmament talks in Europe (TASS, 30 August; *NYT*, 31 August).

Despite public support for the U.S.-led campaign against Iraq, the USSR maintained its 1972 treaty with, and military trainers in, Iraq. Some Western observers thought that Moscow's mixed signals indicated conflict within the leadership; others suggested that the USSR was pursuing a "two-track" policy, courting the West while not burning its bridges to Baghdad (*Insight*, 17 September). More persuasive was the view that Moscow had its priorities ordered but could not control events. Despite often conflicting statements by Gorbachev, Shevardnadze, and Primakov, it seemed clear that the Soviets preferred a peaceful resolution of the conflict.

Primakov's second mission to Baghdad in late October appeared at first to be a vindication of the Soviets' diplomatic efforts. By mid-November, it had become clear that the expected results had not been achieved and that Primakov's mission had actually been a failure. Thereafter, the Soviets turned reluctantly toward acceptance of the force option. Gorbachev and Bush discussed the crisis at the Paris CSCE summit, and on 29 November, the USSR voted in favor of the U.N. resolution authorizing the use of force against Iraq (*NYT*, 30 November).

By mid-December, with most Soviet "guests" out of Iraq, the USSR had apparently decided to limit its role to rhetorical support. It was now made clear that Soviet forces would not go to the gulf under any circumstances, reversing Shevardnadze's 29 September position on the matter. Whatever Moscow's position might have been in other circumstances, the USSR could not afford to dispatch military forces abroad at a time when troops might be needed at home to curb domestic violence.

Despite official denials, it seemed likely that the resignation of Shevardnadze as foreign minister on 20 December would have some effect on Soviet policy on the gulf region. This was partly a matter of the hard-line forces that had gained influence within the Soviet leadership. Also important was the role of foreign policy technicians. Regardless of the identity of the new foreign minister, Evgenii Primakov and Valentin Falin were likely to have more clout in the formation and execution of policy. Primakov, an Arabist, was much more favorably disposed toward Iraq than was Shevardnadze. Falin, head of the CPSU International Department, has been sharply critical of the United States on a number of occasions.

The Soviet position on the gulf crisis under Shevardnadze's direction alienated Libya and the Palestine Liberation Organization (PLO), but relations with both had been troubled for some time. Earlier, the USSR had accorded embassy status to the PLO mission in Moscow, a move welcomed by Yassir Arafat as demonstrating the USSR's solidarity with the Palestinian people (TASS, 16 January; *FBIS-SOV*, 17 January). If the USSR lost ground with these former clients, this loss was more than balanced by gains in relations with Iran, Egypt, Syria, and Turkey.

The Soviets had earlier sought to smooth relations with two of these countries during the visit of Syrian president Hafiz al-Assad to Moscow in April (*Pravda*, 29 April) and Egyptian president Hosni Mubarak in May (ibid., 16 May). The gradual détente between Moscow and Teheran, featuring commercial ties, had apparently reached a higher level with joint cooperation on quelling the unrest on the Azerbaijan border in January (*CSM*, 9 January). A Soviet break with Baghdad could only be welcomed in Teheran, despite Iran's own "two-track" policy in the crisis. Soviet-Turkish collaboration also seemed likely to be promoted by common positions on Persian Gulf matters. Vladimir Georgiev, a senior Soviet diplomat in Ankara, lavishly praised Turkey's position on the crisis, saying that "the Soviet Union and Turkey are following similar policies" (Ankara, Anatolia, 11 August; *FBIS-SOV*, 13 August).

In recent years, some small steps have been taken toward normalization of relations with Israel. The slow process of normalization was threatened during the year by the issue of the settlement of Soviet emigrés in Israeli-occupied Arab territories. The USSR strongly protested (*Izvestiia*, 19 February, 31 July, 1 August) and threatened to halt emigration to Israel unless assurances were given that no Soviet Jews would be settled outside Israel proper.

The issue did not slow the outflow of Jews from the USSR, however. Emigration actually accelerated substantially in the final months of the year in response to economic conditions and the growth of anti-Semitism in the USSR. By the end of the year, 172,000 Soviet Jews had arrived in Israel since 1 January. On Christmas Day, consuls of the two countries presented their credentials in Moscow and Jerusalem, marking the first time that such relations had existed since 1967 (AP, 26 December).

One Third World country that remained a Soviet outpost was Yemen. The merger in May of North and South Yemen brought no reduction in aid from the USSR. Fifteen hundred Soviet specialists were reportedly still in North Yemen, including physicians, nurses, construction supervisors, and electrical engineers (*Insight*, 6 August).

Africa South of the Sahara. Foreign Minister Shevardnadze attended ceremonies in March marking Namibia's independence and also toured Angola, Mozambique, Nigeria, Tanzania, Zambia, and Zimbabwe. In Lusaka, Shevardnadze was received by Zambian president Kenneth Kaunda, who shared the Soviet foreign minister's views on recent successes in "overcoming the atmosphere of confrontation in the international arena." In Zimbabwe, Shevardnadze hailed recent tendencies toward a dialogue in South Africa and said that a clash in that country would be "an inordinately high price to pay" for the abolition of apartheid. Zimbabwean president Robert Mugabe expressed support for *perestroika*, saying that "socialism is not giving ground but . . . a certain reassessment of values is taking place" (Moscow World Service, 17 March; TASS, 20, 22 March; *Izvestiia*, 25 March).

In the year's second half, Soviet interest in the African continent concentrated on a settlement in Angola. The USSR, along with the United States and Portugal, worked behind the scenes to promote a peace plan that would end the fifteen-year civil war between the Soviet-backed government and the U.S.-supported Union for the Total Independence of Angola (UNITA).

During his December visit to the United States, Foreign Minister Shevardnadze met with UNITA leader Jonas Savimbi in Washington. Shortly afterward, Savimbi announced approval of a five-point peace plan to end the civil war. The plan provides for multiparty democracy, an internationally supervised cease-fire, internationally monitored elections, setting a date for elections before signing the cease-fire, and the end of all outside military assistance following the signing of the cease-fire (*LAT*, 15 December).

Latin America. At the outset of the year, the U.S. invasion of Panama appeared to be an irritant with considerable negative potential for the broadening U.S.-USSR relationship. Washington was denounced for "gunboat diplomacy," "shameless" treatment of Latin America, and "imperial" thinking. Most significant was the linkage between Panama and Nicaragua in Moscow's assessment of the region. The Soviet press played up a statement by U.S. secretary of defense Richard Cheney, which, it

was said, did not rule out "strong-arm" tactics in Nicaragua (*Pravda*, 8 January).

A blowup over Central America did not materialize, however, as Foreign Ministers Baker and Shevardnadze worked closely behind the scenes to facilitate the transition to democratic government in Nicaragua. Following the election of Violetta Chamorro as Nicaragua's president, the Soviets expressed concern about lack of progress on demobilization of the contras (*Izvestiia*, 7 April) but promised "good, friendly relations" with the Chamorro government (Moscow Radio, 21 March; *FBIS-SOV*, 30 March). V. G. Komplektov, USSR deputy foreign minister, pointed out one practical benefit to the Soviets from the change of leadership in Managua: lifting the U.S. blockade and the inflow of U.S. aid would mean that Nicaragua would not need Soviet aid. "We ourselves," said Komplektov, "could use some of the Soviet goods exported to Nicaragua" (*Pravda*, 22 April).

Pravda (10 January) reported that diplomatic ties with Chile would probably be restored soon; the new Chilean president had indicated that he would pursue this goal.

A CPSU delegation headed by Iuri Litvintsev, first secretary of Tula *obkom*, visited Costa Rica in February for meetings with prominent politicians and public figures (TASS, 13 February; *FBIS-SOV*, 15 February).

Cuba continued to be the primary Soviet focus in Latin America and also the most troublesome country for Moscow. Castro's opposition to *perestroika* and firm resistance to reform at home nettled the political leadership in the Kremlin. Moreover, Castro complicated the increasingly close Moscow-Washington relationship; this was particularly evident early in the year in regard to the Nicaraguan issue. Nevertheless, Moscow seemed reluctant to discard Cuba entirely, and there were some indications that the Soviet military leadership was particularly interested in maintaining a foothold in the Caribbean.

The chiefs of the general staffs of Angola, Cuba, and the USSR met in Moscow in January to discuss implementation of the 1988 New York agreements on the withdrawal of Cuban forces from Angola (TASS, 10 January; *FBIS-SOV*, 11 January). Meanwhile, negotiations were under way on a new aid agreement, with Moscow looking for ways to cut its $6 billion plus annual subsidy to Cuba (*Report on the USSR*, 12 January).

The Cuban Council of Ministers reported in late January that for the previous two months Cuba had not received its deliveries of grain from the USSR, causing rises in the prices of bread and eggs and affecting distribution. Moscow responded that two days before the report was issued, two Soviet ships had arrived in Cuban ports carrying 43,000 tons of wheat (*Komsomolskaia pravda*, 30 January; *FBIS-SOV*, 12 Febi ary). Although Moscow rejected the implication that the USSR was responsible for Cuba's food problems, a Soviet official subsequently admitted that economic reform was adversely affecting economic relations with Cuba. V. Zaykin, head of the Cuban department at the USSR International Cooperation Bank, said that "if Soviet enterprises have alternative opportunities, they are not now interested in supplying Cuba" (*Pravda*, 9 April).

Deputy Premier Leonid Abalkin set out for Havana on a negotiating mission in April, days after *Pravda* had called for a "radical overhaul" of Soviet aid. Abalkin signed a trade agreement for 1990 worth $14 billion but did not reveal the terms of trade. The question of future subsidies was apparently left up in the air (TASS, 19 April; *CSM*, 20 April).

Two weeks after Abalkin's visit, CPSU CC secretary Oleg Baklanov led a Supreme Soviet delegation to Havana. Baklanov conferred with Fidel Castro, briefing him on *perestroika* and the upcoming Twenty-eighth CPSU Congress (TASS, 4, 5 May; *FBIS-SOV*, 7 May). Upon his return to the USSR, Baklanov denied that there had been a decline in Soviet-Cuban economic ties (*Pravda*, 17 May). Others were not so sanguine. An article in *Moscow News* (no. 19, 20–27 May) pointed out that Cuba produced only 55.5 tons of sugar per hectare, as opposed to 100–120 tons in other leading exporter countries. As a result, sugar deliveries to the USSR had been lower than envisaged for several years running.

Cuba was the leading debtor to the USSR, owing approximately $24.78 billion. When Konstantin Katushev, USSR minister of foreign economic relations, met Cuban officials in Havana in June for another economic negotiating session, he attributed the massive credit outflow to the fact that "the potential of the Cuban economy is, unfortunately, insufficient to balance our export and import relations." The purpose of Katushev's visit was to work out the transition to a new system of exchanges. He admitted that the two sides had not agreed on figures and that problems remained to be solved (TASS, 9 June; *FBIS-SOV*, 13 June). The two sides had still not agreed on the hoped-for five-year plan for aid and trade. Cuba would remain, at year's end, an exception to the new policy of conducting trade in convertible currencies; Cuba simply did not have access to enough hard currency to make such a program work.

While Havana and Moscow haggled over economic matters, other considerations affected the relationship. Castro's opposition to reform and the changing Soviet-U.S. relationship figured in a growing conflict between "liberals" and "traditionalists" in the USSR over Moscow's ties with Cuba. Conflicting signals emanated from the Soviet government indicative of the tensions aroused by Castro. USSR ambassador to Cuba Iuri Petrov said that commercial ties between the two countries would increase and denounced the United States for trying to oust Castro through military and economic pressure. But Foreign Ministry spokesman Gennadii Gerasimov, in an interview, contradicted Petrov and indicated that the USSR planned to phase out aid to Cuba (*Fort Lauderdale News and Sun-Sentinel*, 22 July).

Reflecting "liberal" opinion, Andrei Kortunov, a foreign affairs adviser to the USSR Supreme Soviet, said that the Soviet leadership was aware of the declining strategic value of Cuba. Kortunov also noted that "liberal" economists believed that the terms of trade between Cuba and the USSR were excessively favorable to Havana (*Latin American Regional Reports—Caribbean Report*, 21 June). Supporting the "liberal" position, *Izvestiia* (25 August) published a letter urging Castro to take "a step toward the people of the United States."

In late July, Castro said that Soviet petroleum shipments were down to "a very tense" level (*Newsweek*, 6 August). The economic situation looked even bleaker a month later when the Cuban government announced emergency measures due to a shortfall of 2 million tons in Soviet oil deliveries (*Komsomolskaia pravda*, 1 September; *FBIS-SOV*, 7 September).

Given the Soviet domestic crisis, further economic strains between Cuba and the USSR seemed unavoidable. But there were some indications that "traditionalists" were gaining the upper hand in Moscow on future relations with Havana. Chief of the General Staff Mikhail Moiseev traveled to Cuba in October and announced that the USSR would honor all contractual agreements on economic, political, and military cooperation established during Gorbachev's visit to Cuba in April 1989 (Reuters, 9 October; *Report on the USSR*, 19 October). Politburo member and CPSU secretary for organizational matters Oleg Shenin visited Cuba later in the month. While in Cuba, Shenin denounced criticism of the Soviet-Cuban relationship in the Moscow press, saying that "wholesale vilification is an insult to the Cuban people." Acknowledging past mistakes in economic matters, Shenin said that "I believe it is our side that deserves the most criticism" (*Pravda*, 2 November).

A development in December indicated a further meshing of policy toward Cuba with the general rightward trend in Moscow. Valerii Nikolaenko, head of the USSR Foreign Ministry's Latin American Department, and Georgii Mamedov, new head of the Foreign Ministry's USA and Canada Department, told a news conference in Moscow that the USSR wanted the United States to drop its demand for democratic change in Cuba as a precondition for normalizing relations. Nikolaenko also said that a possible future reduction in Soviet military aid to Cuba would depend on progress in normalization of ties between Washington and Havana (Reuters, 3 December; *Report on the USSR*, 14 December).

Party International Contacts. Relations with other parties were affected by the collapse of the Soviet bloc and the general downturn of international communism. The CPSU sought to salvage something from the overturning of communism in Eastern Europe, to maintain ties where possible with ruling communist parties, and to make points for Soviet foreign policy initiatives. Not surprisingly, the overall level of contacts was down not only in Eastern Europe, where the ending of communist rule in most countries had disrupted relations between parties, but elsewhere as well, particularly in the Third World. Nevertheless, the CPSU was still able to concentrate on key areas, and a steady stream of contacts was maintained with the communist parties of China, Bulgaria, and Mongolia. The mechanisms for relations with other communist parties were, however, in a transitional stage, and prospects for the future were as cloudy as those for the party as a whole.

The CPSU CC Secretariat announced in November that it would transfer planning and organization of cooperation with foreign parties to republican and local party organizations (TASS, 11 November; *Report on the USSR*, 23 November). This was evidently in part a response to the increasing demands for autonomy by these organizations. Whether intended or not, it might also serve Soviet foreign policy goals by dissociating the political leadership from the international communist movement, in much the way that Stalin's dissolution of the Comintern in 1943 had buttressed the wartime alliance. In contrast, Stalin's action on the Comintern left untouched Moscow's primacy in international communism; the November action by the Secretariat might mark finis to any international communist movement. But it remained to be seen how the new arrangements would work out and whether they would last. In the final analysis, external relations of the CPSU would depend on the party's fate in the USSR and its role in Soviet society. A conservative resurgence would surely end tendencies toward decentralization; a victory for noncommunist democratic forces would render the CPSU's foreign contacts largely irrelevant.

Three days after the Secretariat announcement, the leaders of five former ruling communist parties—those of Poland, Czechoslovakia, Hungary, Bulgaria, and the former East Germany—met with CPSU officials in Moscow to discuss the situation in Eastern Europe and the future role of the renamed and somewhat restyled communist parties in the region (TASS, 14 November; *Report on the USSR*, 23 November). What guidance the CPSU might offer these parties so recently thrust into opposition was unclear because the Soviet party was itself operating under siegelike conditions.

Most parties accepted reluctantly the realities of a post–cold war and postcommunist era, often conducting postmortems on the vanished communist power. Some ruling communist parties manned the barricades, resisting reform as the sure route to dissolution of communist party-states. These differences were reflected in a May symposium in Moscow, sponsored by *Pravda*, that brought together representatives of eighteen communist party newspapers and journals from Bulgaria, Hungary, China, Vietnam, East Germany, Cambodia, Cuba, Laos, Mongolia, Poland, Romania, Czechoslovakia, and Yugoslavia. Representatives of East European parties soberly assessed the crisis of socialism and sought to analyze the mistakes of development that had produced it. Zheng Mengxiang, deputy chief editor of *Renmin Ribao*, asserted that "socialism has tremendous potential and great prospects" and that "we are for preservation in the courses of reform of the leading role of the Communist Party," while acknowledging that "in order to see a socialist future, each country has to undergo reforms and *perestroika*." Lodongiyn Tudev, chief editor of the Mongolian Communist Party newspaper *Unen*, said that "in such a country as Mongolia, where political culture is as yet relatively slight, democracy and a multiparty system could have undesirable consequences." Representatives from Vietnam and Cuba attributed much of the crisis to the machinations of "imperialism" (*Pravda*, 29 May).

Andrei Lukanov, Bulgaria's premier and member of the Bulgarian Communist Party Supreme Council, visited Moscow in March for conversations with Gorbachev concerning "major transformations of state and public life in the Soviet Union and Bulgaria, prospects for Soviet-Bulgarian relations, and the situation in Europe" (*Pravda*, 20 March). In April, R. P. Fedorov, first deputy head of the CPSU CC International Department, met in Sofia with Aleksandr Lilov, chairman of the Bulgarian Supreme Council (TASS, 2 April; *FBIS-SOV*, 3 April). Lilov was welcomed to Moscow by Gorbachev in May, and Bulgarian communist officials met *Pravda* editor in chief and Politburo member Ivan Frolov at the beginning of June (*Pravda*, 1 June).

Numerous contacts were made between the CPSU and the refurbished Socialist Unity Party (SED) of Germany, now retitled Party of Democratic Socialism (PDS). Moscow city party leader Iuri Prokofiev met a delegation from the Berlin branch of PDS in Moscow in January for discussions on restructuring in the USSR and the German Democratic Republic (TASS, 10 May; *FBIS-SOV*, 12 January). PDS party leader Gregor Gysi visited Moscow in February and conferred with Gorbachev. Gysi said that the previous leadership's rejection of *perestroika* was responsible for the deep crisis in the country (East Berlin, ADN International Service, *FBIS-SOV*, 2 February). He also said that unification of Germany should proceed along confederation lines "within the European process" (TASS, 14 June; *FBIS-SOV*, 15 June). Gysi was still talking of German Democratic Republic sovereignty in June when he returned to Moscow for talks with Aleksandr Iakovlev (TASS, 14 June; *FBIS-SOV*, 15 June). A letter was handed to Gysi from the CPSU general secretary assuring the PDS of the CPSU's continued support just a month before Gorbachev's meeting with German chancellor Kohl; the letter was published at the beginning of August (East Berlin, ADN International Service, 1 August; *FBIS-SOV*, 2 August).

The PDS was involved in scandal during the autumn when police raided its party headquarters following allegations that the party had transferred about 100 million marks abroad using a Soviet firm as a conduit. A chastened Gysi visited Moscow again in October, supposedly to clear up Soviet questions about the affair (*Report on the USSR*, 2 November).

In March, CPSU CC secretary Georgii Razumovskii welcomed Jenö Kovács, member of the Hungarian Socialist Party Presidium, to Moscow for talks on cooperation between the two parties. Kovacs also met with officials of the CPSU CC International and Ideology departments (*Pravda*, 7 March).

Aleksandr Iakovlev received Leszek Miller, general secretary of the Social Democracy of the Polish Republic (SdRP) Central Executive Committee, on Miller's working visit to the USSR in May. The two party officials stressed expansion of dialogue with "all political tendencies in both countries working in the interest of Soviet-Polish good-neighborliness" (ibid., 22 May). Miller also met Gennadi Ianaiev, CPSU secretary for foreign affairs, while on vacation in the USSR in September (Moscow Television Service, 4 September; *FBIS-SOV*, 6 September).

Vladimir Kuptsov, CPSU CC secretary for mass organizations, visited Prague 15–19 October for conversations with top officials of the Czechoslovak Communist party (*Pravda*, 20 October).

Contacts with nonruling European parties outside the bloc area were considerably more limited than in previous years. Most contacts were perfunctory or involved exchanges of party journalists. Roland Leroy, member of the French Communist Party Politburo and political director of *l'Humanité*, was welcomed to Moscow by *Pravda* editor in chief Ivan Frolov in January (ibid., 23 January). A delegation from the West German Communist Party, headed by party cochairman Rolf Primer, also visited *Pravda* headquarters in May at Frolov's invitation (*Pravda*, 18 May). The CPSU wired congratulations to the Spanish Communist Party on its 70th anniversary (ibid., 15 April). Gorbachev sent congratulations to Alvaro Cunhal on his reelection as general secretary of the Portuguese Communist Party (TASS, 30 May; *FBIS-SOV*, 1 June) and warm greetings to the Italian Communist Party newspaper *L'Unità* on the occasion of its "festival" (TASS, 3 September; *FBIS-SOV*, 5 September).

One contact that might be a harbinger of future exchanges under the decentralization plan announced in November was the visit of V. I. Vyalyas, first secretary of the Estonian Communist Party to Helsinki. Vyalyas met Yrjo Håkanen, general secretary of the Communist Party of Finland (Unity) in January; the Finnish communists proposed cooperation with the Estonian party on preserving the

Baltic Sea (TASS, 17 January; *FBIS-SOV*, 18 January). Later, Soviet press comment was favorable when delegates from Hakanen's party attended the Finnish Communist Party congress, the first significant contact between the two parties since they split in 1987 (*Pravda*, 3 March).

CPSU CC secretary Kuptsov attended the Seventeenth Congress of the Cyprus Communist Party, the Progressive Party of the Working People (AKEL), in October. Kuptsov addressed the congress, touching upon the domestic problems of the USSR and admitting that "we really are living through a difficult time now" (ibid., 6 October).

There were a number of exchanges with the Chinese Communist Party (CCP), with no appreciable effect on interparty relations. Valentin Falin, head of the CPSU CC International Department, was in Beijing during the last week of 1989 to brief Chinese officials on the Malta summit and other matters (*FEER*, 4 January). A CCP delegation, led by Wang Renzhi, head of the CCP CC Propaganda Department, was welcomed to Moscow in March by Aleksandr Kapto, head of the CPSU CC Ideological Department (*Pravda*, 21 March). International Department deputy head R. P. Fedorov led a delegation to Beijing in April (Moscow International Service, 17 April; *FBIS-SOV*, 19 April). Another delegation led by Boris Pugo, chairman of the CPSU Party Control Committee, visited China in June and toured the Shenshen Special Economic Zone (Moscow International Service, 2 June; *FBIS-SOV*, 4 June). The CCP sent greetings to the CPSU at the opening of the Twenty-eighth CPSU Congress (TASS, *FBIS-SOV*, 2 July). Two weeks after the close of the party congress, Li Shuzheng, deputy head of the CCP CC International Liaison Department, arrived in Moscow for talks with CPSU CC secretary Ianaiev (*Pravda*, 26 July).

The Mongolian Communist Party's new leader, Gombojabyn Ochirbat, visited Moscow in May and conferred with Gorbachev on questions of reform and the political situation in East Asia (TASS, 16 May; *FBIS-SOV*, 17 May).

A delegation of the Workers' Party of Korea, CC International Department, arrived in Moscow in late April just as Soviet–North Korean relations were becoming strained. The delegation had meetings with CPSU CC International and Ideological Department officials and with the Ulyanovsk *obkom* (*Pravda*, 4 May).

Relations with the Japanese Communist Party were, for all practical purposes, nonexistent. The Japanese party's resistance to "new political thinking" and its hard line on the Kuriles issue had alienated the CPSU. Soviet reportage of the Japanese Communist Party's Nineteenth Congress at Atami in July was exceptionally harsh (ibid., 10 July).

Although there were some problems in Soviet-Vietnamese relations at the state level, there were several contacts between the CPSU and the Communist Party of Vietnam (CPV) without obvious friction. In February, a public meeting in Moscow celebrated the 60th anniversary of the founding of the CPV (*Pravda*, 2 February). In March, a CPSU delegation headed by A. A. Nizovtseva, deputy chairman of the Central Auditing Commission, visited Vietnam and Cambodia (ibid., 2 March), and in May another delegation led by A. S. Pavlov, chief of the CPSU CC State Law Department, made the trip to Hanoi (*Pravda*, 8 May).

Visits were exchanged in May in connection with the celebration of the 100th anniversary of Ho Chi Minh's birth. Dao Duy Tung, CC secretary and member of the CPV Politburo, led a delegation to Moscow and signed an agreement with CPSU CC secretary Vadim Medvedev on ideological, scientific, cultural, and educational cooperation between the two parties (Hanoi, VNA, 24 May; *FBIS-SOV*, 6 June). CPSU CC secretary and Politburo member Lev Zaikov visited Hanoi and talked with CPV leaders about improving the efficiency of economic cooperation between the USSR and Vietnam (TASS, 18 May; *FBIS-SOV*, 22 May).

A CPSU delegation led by A. S. Kamay, second secretary of the Belorussian Communist Party, visited Bangladesh in April at the invitation of that country's party (*Pravda*, 18 April).

Regular contacts were maintained with the Communist Party of Afghanistan. In January, Afghan party leader and president Najibullah received a delegation led by Aleksandr Mokanu, member of the CPSU Central Auditing Commission and deputy chairman of the USSR Supreme Soviet Chamber of the Union, for a briefing on "national reconciliation" policy (TASS, 27 January; *FBIS-SOV*, 1 February). In August, Najibullah, while on vacation in the USSR, met with Gorbachev and Shevardnadze for talks on the situation in Afghanistan, the progress of *perestroika*, and international issues (TASS, *FBIS-SOV*, 23 August).

The CPSU CC sent greetings in May to the 21st Israeli party congress (*Pravda*, 22 May).

South African Communist Party general secretary Joe Slovo was welcomed to Moscow by CPSU CC secretary Gennadi Ianaiev in August. Ianaiev reaffirmed the CPSU's solidarity with South African communists and the African National Congress in their struggle against apartheid (TASS, 16 August; *FBIS-SOV*, 21 August).

Two CPSU CC secretaries visited Cuba during the year. Oleg Baklanov, secretary for the defense industry, conferred with Fidel Castro in May and discussed *perestroika* and the upcoming Twenty-eighth CPSU Congress (TASS, 4, 5 May; *FBIS-SOV*, 7 May). Secretary for Party Organizational Matters Oleg Shenin visited Cuba in October and denounced criticism of the Soviet-Cuban relationship in the Moscow press (*Pravda*, 2 November).

Biographies. *Evgenii Maksimovich Primakov.* A Russian, born 12 October 1929, Primakov joined the CPSU in 1959. An unknown scholar and midlevel apparatchik during the Brezhnev years, Primakov's career took off following the elevation of Mikhail Gorbachev to the general secretaryship of the CPSU. In 1985, Primakov was named director of the Institute of World Economics and International Relations (IMEMO) and quickly became one of the principal spokesmen for the "new political thinking."

Primakov was elected a candidate member of the CPSU CC at the Twenty-seventh CPSU Congress in 1986 and was promoted to full membership at the CC plenum of April 1989. In June 1989, Primakov was elected chairman of the USSR Supreme Soviet Council of the Union and in May 1989 was elected a candidate member of the CPSU CC Politburo. In March 1990, Primakov was named to the Presidential Council, with general responsibilities in the area of foreign policy, and left the post of chairman of the Council of the Union.

A close adviser to President Gorbachev on foreign policy, with special expertise on the Middle East, Primakov has frequently accompanied the Soviet leader on trips abroad. Following the Iraqi invasion of Kuwait in August 1990, Primakov became the principal Soviet negotiator pursuing a peaceful solution to the gulf crisis in Baghdad and Western capitals. (*Report on the USSR*, 1 June; *NYT*, 6 October; *RL Research*, 1 April 1986; *Pravda*, 26 April, 21 September, 1989.)

Boris Nikolaevich Eltsin. A Russian, born 1 February 1931, Eltsin graduated from the Ural Polytechnic Institute in 1955 and joined the CPSU in 1961. He worked as a construction engineer in Sverdlovsk until his co-option into party work in 1968. From 1968 to 1976, Eltsin served as a secretary of the Sverdlovsk oblast party committee and in November 1976 was elected as first secretary of the Sverdlovsk *obkom*. Elected to the CPSU CC in 1981 at the Twenty-sixth CPSU Congress, Eltsin was reelected in 1986 at the Twenty-seventh CPSU Congress.

Eltsin was called to Moscow in March 1985 to head the CC Construction Department and was promoted to the CC Secretariat at the July 1985 plenum. In December 1985, he was named head of the Moscow city party committee, replacing the deposed Viktor Grishin. Eltsin proceeded to shake up the corrupt and inefficient Moscow party organization but encountered stiff resistance from entrenched officials.

Promoted to candidate member of the Politburo in February 1986, Eltsin emerged as a principal spokesman for radical reform and the most vocal opponent of conservative party secretary Egor Ligachev. Dissatisfied with the pace of reform, Eltsin made a controversial speech at the October 1987 CC plenum in which he asked to be relieved of his duties in Moscow and attacked Ligachev. Three weeks later, Eltsin was fired as Moscow party leader, denounced by party leader Gorbachev, and demoted to a deputy minister's post in the government. Eltsin lost his candidate membership on the Politburo at the CC plenum of February 1988 and made a vain plea for rehabilitation at the Nineteenth CPSU Conference in July.

Despite a small, loyal following in the party, Eltsin appeared to be finished in all-union politics. Democratization made possible the revival of his career. Running in Moscow district for the Congress of People's Deputies in March 1989, Eltsin won more than 90 percent of the vote against a party-backed candidate and was elected to the Supreme Soviet in May 1989. Chosen as cochairman of the Interregional Deputies group, he emerged as a leader of the "loyal opposition" and was called on by Gorbachev to appeal to striking miners in the summer of 1989.

In May 1990, Eltsin scored his most notable success, winning election as president of the RSFSR. Subsequently, he pushed for Russian republic autonomy. He also championed Stanislav Shatalin's 500-day plan for transition to a market economy against Gorbachev's temporizing. A major speaker at the Twenty-seventh CPSU Congress, he announced his resignation from the party near the end of the conclave. Although no longer a party member, as the most prominent politician other than Gorbachev, he was invited to review the November Revolution Day parade with party and government leaders. (*Pravda*, 30 May; *CSM*, 6 June, 28 August; TASS, 29 August; Alexander Rahr, *A Biographic Directory of 100 Leading Soviet Officials* [Munich, 1984], p. 57; Boris Lewytzkyj, *Who's Who in the Soviet Union* [Munich, 1984], p. 88; *Pravda, Izvestiia*, 25 December 1985; *Pravda*, 19 February 1988; *WP*, 27 March 1989.)

R. Judson Mitchell
University of New Orleans

Yugoslavia

Population. 23,841,608 (July)

Party. League of Communists of Yugoslavia (Savez Komunista Jugoslavije, LCY)

Founded. April 1919 as the Socialist Workers' Party of Yugoslavia; disbanded and replaced by the Communist Party of Yugoslavia (CPY) in June 1920. After being expelled from the Cominform in 1948, the CPY changed its name to the League of Communists of Yugoslavia at the Sixth Party Congress in 1952. The LCY dissolved May 1990; its self-proclaimed successor party, League of Communists—Movement for Yugoslavia (LC-MY), held a founding conference 24 December. An estimated 400 delegates took part (Belgrade, Tanjug, 24 December; *FBIS-EEU*, 27 December).

Membership. LCY: 1,167,203 estimated (*Report on Eastern Europe*, 7 September). LC-MY, unknown, although according to a member of the Executive Committee, Stevan Mirković, 140,000 "applications" have been received (*Delo*, 14 December; *FBIS-EEU*, 27 December).

President of the LCY Presidium. Milan Pančevski, Macedonian from Macedonia; replaced in May 1990 by Miomir Grbović (Montenegro) as "coordinator."

Secretary of the LCY Presidium. Stefan Korošec, Slovene from Slovenia; two-year term began June 1988

LCY Presidium. 23 members representing the republics, autonomous provinces, and the LCY organization in the armed forces. When the Four-

teenth Congress "suspended" operations in January, the presidium continued in office until the federal party went out of business at the May session of the congress.

Committee for the Preparation of the Congress of Democratic and Program Renewal of the LCY. Chairman, Miroslav Ivanović (Montenegro). Members: Bosnia and Hercegovina, Ivan Brigić, Nijaz Duraković, and Dževad Tasić; Montenegro, Momir Bulatović and Momir Vukotić; Serbia, Petar Skundrić, Radoš Smiljković, and Bogdan Trifunović; Kosovo, Jagos Zelenović and Rahman Morina (died 12 October); Vojvodina, Predrag Jereminov and Nedeljko Šipovac; the Yugoslav People's Army (JNA), Simeon Bunčić and Božidar Grubišić

LCY Central Committee. 165 members: 20 from each republic, 15 each from the two Serbian autonomous provinces, and 15 from the army's party organization. Also dissolved in May 1990.

Status. Began the year as ruling party. Accepted the need for a multiparty system at the Fourteenth Congress in January. Federal party dissolved when Fourteenth LCY Congress reconvened at the end of May.

Last Congress. LCY Fourteenth Extraordinary Congress; January 1990. Congress deadlocked and was suspended until end of May.

LC-MY Leadership. Composed of a 52-member Main Yugoslav Committee; president, Dragan Atanasovski, engineer from Kumanovo; other members unknown; an eight-member Executive Council: military members, army officer Vukota Popović, former JNA-LCY party secretary Admiral Božidar Grubišić, retired Col. Gen. Stevan Mirković, retired Adm. Branko Mamula. Civilian members, Nikolay Kaloper, author from Osijek, Dr. Mirjana Marković (Slobodan Milošević's wife), a professor at Belgrade University, Dr. Nikola Matovski, professor at Skopje; and Borislav Mikelić, an engineer from Petrinja. Plan is to have 14 members, with 5 seats reserved for 2 delegates each from Montenegro and Bosnia and Hercegovina and 1 from Slovenia.

Last Elections. May 1986. The Yugoslav Parliament has two chambers: the 220-member Federal Chamber and the 88-member Chamber of Republics and Provinces. President of the Assembly, Slobodan Gligorijević (Serbia); vice-president, Ms. Suada Muminagić (Bosnia and Hercegovina). The term of office is currently one year.

Auxiliary Organizations. As the LCY withered away, the Socialist Alliance of Working People of

Yugoslavia (Socijalistički savez radnog naroda Jugoslavije, SAWPY) also fragmented into contending regional parties and groups; in Serbia it merged with the LC Serbia to form the Socialist Party of Serbia (SPS). The League of Socialist Youth of Yugoslavia (Savez socijalističke omladine Jugoslavije, LSYY) splintered as well. The trade unions sought an independent identity and battled for salary increases as soon as the government's June deadline passed.

Government Bodies. An 8-member collective state presidency was elected in May 1989 for a five-year term. The president and vice-president serve for one year, and these positions rotate among the membership. On 15 May, Dr. Janez Drnovšek (39), Slovenia, was replaced as president of the Socialist Federal Republic of Yugoslavia (SFRY) by Dr. Borisav Jović (62), Serbia. The current vice-president, Stjepan Mešić (Croatia), nominated by the Croatian Democratic Union (CDU) to replace Dr. Stipe Šuvar, will become the first noncommunist president of Yugoslavia in May 1991. The other members are as follows: Bosnia and Hercegovina, Bogić Bogićević; Montenegro, Nenad Bućin, 55; Macedonia, Dr. Vasil Tupurkovski; Kosovo, Riza Sapundzija; Vojvodina, Dr. Dragutin Zelenović, 61. The general secretary of the presidency is Anton Stari (Vojvodina). Because this is an administrative position, Stari is not a member of the state presidency.

Day-to-day government is in the hands of the Federal Executive Council (FEC), headed by its president, Prime Minister Ante Marković, 65, Croatia. Vice-presidents of the FEC are Aleksandar Mitrović and Živko Pregl. Among the most important federal secretaries are Budimir Lončar, foreign affairs; Col. Gen. Veljko Kadijević, defense; and Petar Gračanin, internal affairs.

Publications. The main LCY publications, *Komunist* (weekly) and *Socijalizam* (monthly), went out of business along with the federal party. Other major publications include daily newspapers, *Borba* (formerly a SAWPY organ, subsequently financed by the federal government); *Politika* (Serbian strongman Slobodan Milošević's party line), *Vjesnik* (Zagreb); *Delo* (Ljubljana); *Oslobodjenje* (Sarajevo); *Nova Makedonija* (Skopje); *Rilindja* (Priština), banned by Serbian authorities 9 August; and an Albanian-language weekly in Macedonia, *Flaka e Vellazermit* (Skopje). The first privately published daily, *RI Telefax* (Rijeka), appeared in October. Prominent weeklies are *Nedeljne informativne novine* (*NIN*)

(Belgrade), *Vreme* (Belgrade), *Danas* (Zagreb), and *Novi forum* (Zagreb). Controversial religious material continued to appear in the biweekly Catholic journal *Glas Koncila*. Philosophical and social controversy is covered by the Belgrade biweekly *Književne novine*. Military views are often expressed in the JNA weekly *Narodna armija*.

Leadership and Party Organization. In 1989 popular revolutions transformed the leading role of East Central European communist parties into one of minority partners in coalition governments. Those communist politicians who had managed to transfer their loyalties to "revolution from below" developed major credibility problems and faced rising popular pressure to resign. The tornado of change did not stop at the borders of Yugoslavia, however. As neighboring communist regimes in East Germany, Bulgaria, and Czechoslovakia fell and the violent collapse of Nicolae Ceaușescu's "socialism in one family" became the main attraction on late-night Yugoslav television, those who fought to limit systemic change to pluralism within the party could not hold the line.

At the January 1990 Extraordinary Fourteenth Congress of the LCY, the ruling party gave up its 45-year monopoly of power. The proposed congress declaration admitted that "the first condition of our social reform is to rid the political system of anyone's monopoly, even that of the LCY . . . in a democratic society nobody can be the exponent of exclusive political truth" (*Politika*, 24 January; *FBIS-EEU*, 31 January).

This step was not enough. Outvoted in their demands that the League of Communists reconstitute itself into a confederation of independent republic organizations "freely united" in the LCY, the Slovene delegation walked out. Congress delegates turned a deaf ear to Serbian president Slobodan Milošević's demands that they continue with or without Slovenia and went home. The congress was officially suspended. Morning-after assessments in the Yugoslav media were divided as to whether the LCY was "definitely dead" (Split, *Slobodna Dalmacija*; Belgrade, Tanjug, 24 January), "the departing political party" (*Borba*, 24 January), or "the only true Yugoslav-oriented party in Yugoslavia" (*Politika*, 24 January).

Whatever the result of the aborted congress for the federal party, Prime Minister Ante Marković stated flatly that Yugoslavia would continue to function with or without the League of Communists (*NYT*, 24 January).

The Fourteenth Party Congress resumed in May under less than auspicious conditions. The session was presided over by Miomir Grbović (Montenegro). Grbović had replaced LCY president Milan Pančevski when Pančevski—having resisted demands of his republic party organization to resign for failing to respect the "stands of the League of Communists of Macedonia" (*Borba*, 23 May; *FBIS-EEU*, 29 May)—rotated out of office 17 May. Grbović took over as a coordinator, destined to go down in party history as the leader who directed the dissolution of the LCY during his ten-day term in office.

On the eve of the May congress, the 31st consultative session of the LCY Central Committee (CC) essentially rubber-stamped the proposed document of the congress and the composition of the committee charged with preparing a congress of LCY democratic and program renewal (Belgrade, Tanjug, 25 May; *FBIS-EEU*, 29 May). Notwithstanding the plans for reorganizing the LCY, in reality these moves paved the way for the federal party to go out of business.

Technically there was a quorum when the Fourteenth Congress reconvened (Belgrade, Tanjug, 26 May; *FBIS-EEU*, 29 May). However, the fact that Slovenia, Croatia, and Macedonia boycotted the session both undermined its credibility and boded ill for its effort to rebuild as a modern, democratic political party able to compete in the emerging multiparty political arena.

With the federal party organs dissolved, the Committee for the Preparation of the Congress of the LCY Democratic and Program Renewal attempted, largely unsuccessfully, to bridge the institutional gap. This committee was made up of two members from each republic party and one member from each provincial party and from the party organization in the armed forces. Presidents of the republic, provincial, and JNA parties were to participate in an ex officio capacity. This permitted boycotting parties to delegate members to the committee and set 29 September 1990 as the target date for the "congress of renewal."

Members of the boycotting party organizations subsequently did attend meetings of the preparatory committee as observers, but efforts to reorganize the LCY came too late. The communist electoral defeats in Slovenia and Croatia further diminished interest on the part of these regional parties in reconstituting the federal League of Communists (Belgrade, Tanjug, 5 June; *FBIS-EEU*, 7 June).

By July the preparatory committee's draft documents for the renewal congress could not be adopted because of the absence of Slovenia, Croatia, Serbia, and Montenegro. Moreover, the regional communist parties were proceeding with their own versions of democratic renewal without waiting for the federal party to get itself organized (Belgrade, Tanjug, 26 July; *FBIS-EEU*, 27 July). Most important, the staunchest advocate for pluralism within the LCY as an alternative to multiparty competition, Slobodan Milošević, had given up on the LCY. Consequently, the Serbian League of Communists disappeared in a merger with its own mass organization, the Socialist Alliance of Serbia, and Milošević became the president of the Socialist Party of Serbia.

By August those charged with solving the remaining financial problems were in fact leasing eight floors of the former CC building in New Belgrade to anyone who could pay the bills (*Pravda*, Moscow, 4 August; *FBIS-SOV*, 6 August). League of Communist organizations began disappearing from republic government organizations, restricting party organizing to local communities. Those among the more than twenty thousand party members working in justice administration, the public prosecutor's office, public security, and other state bodies who held their jobs on the basis of political rather than professional qualifications had reason to fear for those jobs (Belgrade, Tanjug, 12 August; *FBIS-EEU*, 14 August).

According to some reports, the LCY preparatory committee recommended that the party take the name Yugoslav Socialist Party (JSP) and considered creating a Yugoslav leftist alliance (*Borba*, 10 September; *FBIS-EEU*, 13 September; *NIN*, 28 September; *JPRS-EEU*, 23 October). Just which factions of the former League of Communists favored such a solution was unclear, however.

Then, in November, an initiative committee, reportedly composed of concerned individuals and groups (including the party organization in the armed forces), pursued another direction. Tired of waiting for official renewal, this group launched the League of Communists—Movement for Yugoslavia (LC-MY) (*Politika*, 14 November; *FBIS-EEU*, 19 November). Dedicated to federalism, socialism, and the mission of the Yugoslav armed forces as the foundation of "social self-protection," the LC-MY appeared to express dissatisfaction on the part of communists in the armed forces with the other available political options (*NIN*, 9 November; *FBIS-EEU*, 19 November).

The proclamation issued by the founding meeting of the new party made no mention of its relationship to the preparation committee, which had been charged with leading the transformed LCY back into political life (*Borba*, 21 November; *FBIS-EEU*, 30 November). According to unconfirmed reports from Belgrade, an attempt of its somewhat shadowy founders to recruit the chairman of the officially constituted LCY renewal committee had been turned down.

Domestic Affairs. Yugoslav politics in 1990 left many Western and Yugoslav observers deeply confused. In Yugoslavia, as throughout postcommunist Europe, the road to multiparty democracy was full of economic hardships, territorial conflicts, and ethnic strife. Communist and noncommunist politicians alike campaigned against command economies on platforms of economic reform and national identity.

In Yugoslavia this political dynamic revolved around the struggle of parties, alliances, movements, and groups in search of constituencies and other political support from which to compete in the first postwar, multiparty, regional elections. On this new political stage, the "nation" increasingly became the source of legitimacy, reinforcing ethnic identities and worsening ethnic, interrepublic, and provincial tensions.

In the turmoil that followed it was easy to lose sight of the economic success of the Marković government. Paradoxically, as the federal League of Communists "withered away," the still official communist government made good on the prime minister's promise that Yugoslavia would continue to function, with or without the party.

Economic performance. During 1989 the Marković government had pushed through the federal assembly the laws necessary to establish a legal infrastructure for market-oriented reform. Insisting that anti-inflation measures required a legal foundation in a market economy, the prime minister created amendments to existing laws on enterprises, banks and other financial institutions, and accounting. New laws on labor relations, foreign trade, commodity reserves, securities, money, and capital markets were fought through the assembly. As the year ended inflation skyrocketed to 2,666 percent (Tanjug, 12 September; *FBIS-EEU*, 13 September), and Marković abandoned his long-term strategy in favor of "shock treatment."

The January 1990 anti-inflation program, worked out in collaboration with the International Monetary Fund (IMF) along the lines of Harvard professor Jeffery Sachs' "cold turkey capitalism," went into place. Among other things this program called for convertible currency, pegging the dinar to the deutsche mark at a ratio of seven to one (the U.S. dollar would be twelve to one). This rate was not to change until June 1990 (*Borba*, 19 December). Meanwhile, Yugoslavs could exchange dinars for foreign currency at the official rate.

Other pieces of the anti-inflation package included a tight monetary policy, a program to obtain a balanced budget, a floating interest rate, and, for the most part, market-determined prices, although prices for infrastructural services such as energy and utilities remained frozen until June 1990. Wages were also frozen until June at the November 1989 rate.

The Serbian leadership condemned the Marković program as soon as it became public. Slovenes would not agree to the taxation measures. Other groups had their own complaints. However, none of the detractors could offer an alternative strategy. In contrast, Sachs, an architect of Poland's "shock therapy," enjoyed a solid reputation in international financial circles. Thus, the Marković program had international credibility and support. It would facilitate debt rescheduling and tap whatever financial resources were available. With the population and Parliament alike at the end of their patience, the federal assembly signed off. When agreement could not be reached, they settled for temporary emergency measures.

Within three months inflation had been slowed to a virtual crawl. Compared to a 65 percent monthly inflation rate in December 1989, prices went up only 2.6 percent in March and then actually fell by 0.2 percent in April. Annual estimates then ranged from 15–20 percent (Belgrade, *Politika: International Weekly*, 12–18 May). In July monthly inflation was zero.

Despite increases due to summer wage hikes, republic feuding within the Yugoslav domestic market, and the damaging repercussions of the U.N. blockade against Iraq, year-end inflation held at 118 percent (Belgrade, Tanjug, 7 December; *FBIS-EEU*, 10 December). In contrast to the 1989 figures, this represented a substantial accomplishment. However, on the road to a market economy, 771 bankruptcy proceedings (688 in industry) were filed against enterprises and legal entities with 7.5--

billion-dinar debts and 455,091 employees (*Borba*, 24 October; *FBIS-EEU*, 21 November).

In short, Prime Minister Marković made substantial headway on his promise to deliver economic reform with or without the League of Communists. Indeed, during the spring he ranked number one among politicians "pulling Yugoslavia forward" in every republic. Percentages in the polls indicated support for him that ranged from 61 percent in Serbia (compared with Milošević's 50 percent) to 79 percent in Slovenia (Kučan, 53 percent) to 92 percent in Bosnia and Hercegovina (*Borba*, 21 May; *FBIS-EEU*, 29 May). Marković appeared on the way to becoming Yugoslavia's most popular politician.

But for the reform package to succeed, the prime minister needed cooperation from the country's squabbling republics, which did not seem forthcoming. In his November report to the federal assembly, the prime minister strongly condemned, as violations of the General Agreement on Tariffs and Trade (GATT), the internal import barriers and duties passed by the Serbian Parliament in October and Slovenia's retaliatory taxes on meat and dairy produce as endangering the Yugoslav united market (*Borba*, 16 November; *FBIS-EEU*, 16, 21 November). Moreover, according to Marković, Serbia was 2.14 billion dinars in arrears on paying its federal taxes from sales tax and customs duties; Vojvodina, 293 million dinars; and Slovenia, 164 million. Combined with the refusal of some republics to continue contributing to the fund for underdeveloped republics and Kosovo, the prime minister calculated that by October the federation was owed 5.12 billion dinars by republic and provincial governments. Conversely, those defending Serbia's protectionist measures argued that the federal government had not met an estimated 2.6 billion dinar obligation to Serbia (Belgrade, Tanjug, 1 November; *FBIS-EEU*, 2 November). Clearly, federal and republic policymakers were deeply divided as to who owed what to whom.

Nonetheless, as the year ended, Western debt had been held to an estimated $16.5 billion. Despite the $1.3 billion cost to Yugoslavia of the crisis in the Persian Gulf and a drought that brought some $1.7 billion in agricultural losses (Belgrade, Tanjug, 15 November; *FBIS-EEU*, 16 November), hard currency reserves were up to roughly $9 billion (Belgrade, Tanjug, 9 December; *FBIS-EEU*, 10 December).

Although they still lagged behind imports, exports to convertible currency markets had increased roughly 55 percent (Belgrade, Tanjug, 11 December; *FBIS-EEU*, 12 December). When tourist services were added in, this gave Yugoslavia a favorable balance of payments. According to the federal secretary for development, Boža Marendić, from December 1989 to August 1990, Yugoslav firms brought in some 1.7 billion deutsche marks in the form of 2,250 joint investments with foreign partners (Belgrade, Tanjug, 12 September; *FBIS-EEU*, 12 December).

Unfortunately, these accomplishments were seriously jeopardized by financial scandal in the wake of the 28 December secret decision of the Serbian Parliament to issue $1.8 billion in new money without informing the federal government. This money—estimated at about half the planned federal government credit expansion—was then loaned to the Serbian government, which spent it on safety nets for unprofitable enterprises, pensions, and farm supports.

There was outrage at home and abroad. The World Bank warned Yugoslavia that it faced a credit cutoff if the prime minister's market-based reform program was abandoned. As one Western diplomat assessed the situation, "The tragedy is that Yugoslavia had the most consistent economic reform of all the East European countries, and it has been ripped to shreds" (*NYT*, 10 January 1991).

The multiparty elections. As the federal League of Communists crumbled, the political action of 1990 was in the regional (republic) electoral arena, where a confusing array of parties, movements, groups, and associations fielded candidates. The results effectively eliminated the "leading role" of any party and have undoubtedly made more difficult the government's effort to achieve agreement on political direction and economic reform.

In the April and May multiparty assembly elections in Slovenia and Croatia, center-right coalitions defeated reform communists by substantial margins. The Slovene opposition coalition Demos received 55 percent of the vote compared with 17 percent for the Slovene Communist Party of Democratic Renewal. The Croatian Democratic Union (CDU, also known as the Croatian Democratic Community) took 205 of the 356 seats in the three-chamber Croatian parliament. However, this election was a complicated three-round process in which the CDU received slightly less than one-third of the total vote, while the left bloc trailed by roughly 10 percent. This led to ongoing challenges to the mandate of the CDU for constitutional change (*Danas*, 17 July; *JPRS-EEU*, 30 August).

Meanwhile, the presidency of Slovenia went to the leader of the former Slovene League of Communists, Milan Kučan, now heading the reformed Slovene party. In Croatia the nationalist leader of the Croatian Democratic Union, 68-year-old wartime partisan Dr. Franjo Tudjman, became the first noncommunist president of a Yugoslav republic.

Prime Minister Marković attempted to translate his growing popularity into political capital, announcing his plans for a coalition of parties in support of the government reform program (*Borba*, 29 May; *NYT*, 30 May). By July it was clear that the government-sponsored Alliance of Reform Forces would run in the coming republic elections. Although the prime minister's decision was greeted with enthusiasm abroad, internal reactions ranged from approval to ambivalence and hostility (*Borba*, 25 July; *CSM*, 31 July).

As most observers expected, President Slobodan Milošević held on to his job with roughly 65 percent of the vote in the much-disputed Serbian elections. His party of born-again Serbian communists—the Socialist Party of Serbia (SPS)—took 194 of the possible total 250 seats in the republic Parliament. Of the 56 victories that went to his opposition, the largest number, 19 seats, went to the Serbian Movement of Renewal.

The left-oriented parties also dominated in Montenegro and made a respectable showing in Macedonia. The Communist Party of Montenegro won 83 of the possible 125 assembly seats, and its leader, Momir Bulatović, took the presidency with some 64 percent of the vote.

Of the 120 seats in the Macedonian assembly, 31 went to reform communists (League of Communists of Macedonia—Party for Democratic Transformation, LCM-PDT), 18 to the Alliance for Reform Forces for Macedonia (ARFM), with the Socialist Party taking four seats. Thirty-seven seats went to the Internal Macedonian Revolutionary Organization—Democratic Party for Macedonian National Unity (IMRO-DPMNU), and 25 seats went to the Albanian-based Party for Democratic Prosperity (PDP). In short, a left-wing coalition had a simple majority but lacked the two-thirds necessary to form a government or to elect a president of the republic (Belgrade, Tanjug, 12 December; *FBIS-EEU*, 13 December).

Contrary to early predictions, ethnically based parties swept the elections for the 240 members of the two-house assembly in Bosnia and Her-

cegovina. A year-end tally reported that the Muslim Party for Democratic Action (PDA) took 86 seats, the Serbian Democratic Party (SDP), 72, and the Croatian Democratic Union (CDU), 44. The League of Communists—Social Democratic Party (LCBH-SDP) came in with fourteen seats plus five in coalition with the Democratic Socialist Alliance of Bosnia and Hercegovina; Alliance for Reform Forces Bosnia-Hercegovina (ARFBH) won another twelve; and one was won in a coalition with the Democratic Party of Mostar (Belgrade, Tanjug Domestic Service, 12 December; *FBIS-EEU*, 13 December). However, the left parties were squeezed out of the republic's collective presidency by a narrow margin in which the ethnic-based parties took all seven seats on the presidency. These parties are therefore in a position to decide who will represent Bosnia and Hercegovina in the Yugoslav state presidency.

In the meantime, Alija Izetbegović, leader of the Muslim PDA, became head of the republic presidency. A representative of the Serbian Democratic Party took the position of president of the assembly, while the Croatian Democratic Union filled the post of head of government. (Belgrade, Tanjug Domestic Service, *FBIS-EEU*, 20 December.)

The overall showing of Prime Minister Marković's Alliance for Reform Forces at the republic level did not bode well for the government party in a national, multiparty election. Yet the party was not put to the test because the federal election scheduled for the end of the year was postponed owing to lack of agreement on the rules of the electoral game.

Moreover, should a federal election be held, it is unclear how many of the proliferating parties, alliances, movements, and coalitions would be better off competing on the national level. Under the existing circumstances, parties might well be considerably less important than personalities. If so, Marković has both name recognition and a respectable record. Although he could suffer the fate of his Polish counterpart, Tadeusz Mazowiecki, the Yugoslav prime minister's main rival, Serbian president Slobodan Milošević, is no Lech Wałęsa.

Meanwhile, on 31 December the Yugoslav Parliament formally extended Marković's term of office until mid-May 1991 and that of the federal chamber of the national assembly until a new, multiparty federal parliament can be established. Conversely, the chamber of republics and provinces will expire when its term ends on 15 May 1991 (Tanjug, 1 January 1991).

Constitutional disarray. In November, Marković reported to the national assembly that the constitutional amendments that his government has presented in December 1989 to establish a legal basis for the reforms were still unpassed. Even worse, rewriting amendments and republic constitutions was going on without regard for the consequences to the federation (Belgrade, Tanjug, 15 November; *FBIS-EEU*, 16 November).

According to the prime minister, the provisions of the Serbian constitution concerning the republic's status, the powers of the president of the republic, the status of autonomous provinces, and property rights—notwithstanding the provision of the Serbian constitution that pledges to perform its duties in accordance with the SFRY constitution—conflicted with the federal constitution. In his view, the amendments to the Croatian constitution were also in conflict with the SFRY constitution and federal constitutional amendments. The prime minister rejected the so-called constitution of Kosovo—passed by a secret meeting of the Albanian members of the disbanded provincial assembly (*NYT*, 14 September)—as a "threat to the territorial integrity of both Serbia and Yugoslavia" (ibid.).

Somewhat ironically, Bosnia and Hercegovina, Macedonia, and Montenegro were also constitutionally out of order because they had included the as-yet unpassed amendments to the SFRY constitution in their own republic constitutions. Until these federal amendments are passed, the new republic constitutions conflict with the federal constitution.

The prime minister's warnings did little to stem the tide of constitutional change at the republic level. And as the year ended, the new Croatian constitution was approved by the Croatian assembly (*NYT*, 24 December).

The constitutional confusion, the failure to implement federal laws, the demands of Serbs in Croatia for autonomy, and the Slovene referendum in which 88.5 percent of the voters expressed their preference for independence (*NYT*, 26 December) are part of the political struggle over the nature of postcommunist Yugoslavia.

The Slovene solution. With the midsummer declaration of Slovene sovereignty, policymakers in Ljubljana served notice that a federation (in the Slovene mind associated with Serbian hegemony) was unacceptable. According to Slovene politicians, any Yugoslavia that includes Slovenia must be a confederation in which Slovenes remain masters of their own republic's fate.

Yet there was room for political maneuvering. Slovenia officials also insisted that the December vote for independence was not a vote to break with Yugoslavia per se. Rather, the plebiscite was to be seen as the start of a six-month process intended to produce agreement on a confederation for republics of Yugoslavia similar to that for the member nations of the European Community. In the words of Slovene secretary of foreign affairs Dimitzij Rupel, this was a search for "a new form of coexistence" (*NYT*, 24 December).

It remains to be seen whether or not Serbia's reelected president, Slobodan Milošević, can be won over to the Slovene view. Throughout the year, Milošević continued to demand a strong federation as the basis for any multiparty political system. Yet, given Serbia's duties on imports from other republics and its refusal to pay federal taxes, it appeared that in practice the Serbian leadership was as confederal as the Slovene politicians it attacked. Moreover, buried in dire accounts of interrepublic relations was a statement by Slovene representative Janez Drnovšek that he had met with the Serbian president to discuss the possibilities for cooperation between their republics and would do so again because Milošević had "shown readiness for future cooperation" (*Delo*, 19 December; *FBIS-EEU*, 20 December).

Soldiers in politics. The Yugoslav military had a constitutionally defined role in the complex power-sharing arrangement that Tito had left behind. The JNA party organization was represented in the LCY presidency and Central Committee, legitimizing politicians in uniform as partners in the search for solutions to political and economic crisis. In this way, contrary to Western thinking or for that matter the Leninist model on military-civil relations, the Yugoslavian army had been deliberately included in national politics.

Its channel of access, however, was the League of Communists. Thus, the collapse of the federal LCY intensified what was an already agonizing reappraisal of the army's political mission. Fearing that communists within the military establishment would move in to save the LCY or otherwise obstruct the transformation to a multiparty system, the opposition parties demanded the depoliticization of the military's mission.

Even before the January LCY congress, Yugoslav soldiers in politics equated such demands with an attack on the integrity of Yugoslavia. Fearing that the true agenda was "to silence the armed forces, to shut them into garrisons and thereby remove them from sociopolitical life. . .[so as to] break up Yugoslavia as a federal state and head it in the direction of a confederalist concept," they were "against the armed forces being depoliticized in every respect." (Interview with Dimitrije Baucal, *Narodna armija*, 18 January; *JPRS-EEU*, 9 May.)

The army delegation at the Fourteenth Congress totaled 68 members: 32 Serbs, 8 Montenegrins, 8 Croats, 10 Yugoslavs, 3 Muslims, and 2 Slovenes. Of this group, sixteen admirals spoke to the congress. Their message was one of unambiguous support for a federal state in which the JNA would continue to participate in a Yugoslavia capable of making policy and paying for defense. They held that neither succession nor confederation was acceptable and that democratic reform of the state was the only possible solution. In addition, the army would continue to play a part in social and political development.

Clearly, their preference was for the LCY to continue as a unified Yugoslav communist organization. However, this was not put forward as a condition for military support of the government, and some army speakers stressed that the JNA could adjust to democratic progress in the form of a multiparty system. Indeed, when the Slovene delegation walked out, the former president of LC-JNA, Petar Simić—unlike Milošević—supported postponing the congress, noting that "all the blame does not belong to Slovenia alone. . . . Ultimatums, blockades, pressure, and faits accomplis have never resulted in resolution of problems between peoples." (*Danas*, 6 February; *FBIS-EEU*, 30 April.)

Nonetheless, the army adopted a gradual approach to the departure of the LCY from the political scene. On the matter of party cells in the army, JNA spokesman Col. Vuk Obradović stressed that the LCY in the army would be dealt with in relation to the new constitutional and legal provisions for a multiparty system and the law on political association. Until that time LCY organizations would remain active in army units and headquarters. (Tanjug, 28 March; *FBIS-EEU*, 29 March.)

Thus the issue became not whether the LCY should end such activity but when. Army spokesmen insisted that the army had not been against a multiparty system but only warned against it being introduced too fast. In May the former head of the general staff of JNA and a member of the LCY CC, Stevan Mirković, said somewhat plaintively that "if a stand is taken in society that LCY should leave the army, it will do so. But the army

cannot be put back into the barracks so suddenly." (Interview, *Borba*, 19–20 May; *FBIS-EEU*, 20 May.)

Although there was no time frame for disbanding the LC-JNA organizations, the federal secretariat of defense's new plan for moral education of recruits, which emphasized "defence of our common land, Yugoslav patriotism, and the combat traditions of our nations and nationalities" (Belgrade, Tanjug, 18 May; *FBIS-EEU*, 21 May), signaled that the army was preparing for that day.

Still, an explicit exception was made for the JNA when the presidium of the LCY representing party organizations in federal agencies announced that the LCY would end party cells in all federal agencies by 5 November (RFE/RL *Daily Report*, 24 September). In fact, this issue was resolved by the LC-JNA's decision to dissolve its organizational work in the armed forces and merge with the recently founded League of Communists—Movement for Yugoslavia (Belgrade, Tanjug Domestic Service; *FBIS-EEU*, 17 December). The LC-JNA supported the position of the federal secretariat for national defense that all parties and political organizing should be banned from the armed forces (Belgrade, Tanjug Domestic Service, 13 December; *FBIS-EEU*, 14 December) in principle.

Notwithstanding this formal renunciation of former political advantage, the session announcing the dissolution of such LCY-JNA organizations concluded by sending a letter to LC members in the army inviting them to join the new party. Presumably they would not have the right to continue organizing within the armed forces should the SFRY presidency accept the proposal of the secretariat of national defense banning such activity.

In sum, the issue appeared to be not so much the survival of the LC-JNA as an army sanctuary for the party as a shortage of viable national parties with whom to reestablish a party-army partnership that would allow the JNA to retain, in some form, the political mission that has kept Yugoslav soldiers in politics since 1945. With political parties proliferating at dizzying speeds, the army has had to relate to an increasingly complex array of socialist, radical, liberal, democratic, regional, nationalist, religious, and environmental movements and parties.

Throughout these developments the military leadership positioned itself on the side of cohesion, emphasizing that until civilian politicians could agree on the legal basis of the emerging multiparty political system, the army's job was to defend the existing constitution. This then brought the military leadership into the political struggle surrounding the conflicting confederal/federal constitutional agendas.

Not surprisingly, the secretariat for national defense formally condemned Slovene constitutional amendments (Belgrade, Tanjug Domestic Service, 29 September; *FBIS-EEU*, 1 October). The secretariat's statement bluntly reminded policymakers in Ljubljana that the JNA intended "to carry out its constitutional obligations on the entire territory" of Yugoslavia and said flatly that separate republic armies would "not be tolerated."

Repeated warnings from the secretary for national defense, General Veljko Kadijević, and other high-ranking officers that the army would not "allow the break up of the nation" (Belgrade, Tanjug, 28 September; *FBIS-EEU*, 1 October) fueled rumors that the JNA was plotting a military coup to prevent the disintegration of Yugoslavia (*Danas*, 17 October; Milan Andrejevich, "The Military's Role in the Current Constitutional Crisis," RFE *Report on East Europe*, 9 November).

Indeed, the military establishment had trouble explaining where it would draw the line. Defense Secretary Kadijević insisted that the army "would not impose political solutions" (Belgrade, Tanjug Domestic Service, 16 November; *FBIS-EEU*, 19 November). The former chief of the general staff of the JNA, Gen. Stevan Mirković (retired) went further, assuring the anxious that "the army will not prevent republics in their attempts to decide on succession through constitutional and legal means" (Belgrade, Tanjug, 21 November).

Both Kadijević and Mirković also qualified such assurances with a restatement of the army mission to prevent violent attempts to change the state system or to push the country into civil war. Then, on the eve of the Serbian elections, Kadijević responded to the rising national/ethnic and territorial/bureaucratic tensions with an explicit threat to disarm "national armies" by force if need be (Belgrade, Tanjug Domestic Service, 2 December; *FBIS-EEU*, 3 December).

At the same time the Slovene secretary for national defense, Janez Janša, suggested that there was continued room for dialogue when he revealed that military circles had "recently issued several assurances" that the outcome of the Slovene plebiscite for independence will be "respected by everyone [although]. . . Slovenia cannot on its own decide on the manner in which it will secede from Yugoslavia, if it decides to do so" (Belgrade, Tanjug

Domestic Service, 13 December; *FBIS-EEU*, 14 December).

Thus, as the year ended, it was impossible to tell whether the Slovene defense minister was engaging in wishful thinking or whether the Western media were quoting Kadijević out of context on the willingness of the army to keep the federation together by force if necessary (*NYT*, 26 December).

In either case, such warnings from Yugoslav politicians in uniform are as likely to be psychological deterrents as they are a clear statement of immediate intent. The Slovene referendum—in which 88.5 percent of those voting opted for an autonomous, independent Slovenia—is best understood as an indication of discontent. Whether the system acts on this referendum depends on whether republic politicians disputing the federal or confederal nature of the country's future political system can agree on the rules of the game for multiparty federal elections in time.

The Slovene minister of foreign affairs has stated that "[Slovenia] has neither the intention to secede nor any interest in such a move. I think it is possible to reach an agreement on a confederation in Yugoslavia, that is a union of independent Yugoslav states" (*Borba*, 10–11 November; *FBIS-EEU*, 19 November). Indeed, notwithstanding the subsequent formal Slovene declaration of independence on 26 December, this view was reiterated, albeit somewhat more conservatively, by the president of the Slovene assembly, Dr. France Bučar: "Our decision concerning an independent Slovenia is neither a negation of Yugoslavia nor an a priori option for it" (Belgrade, Tanjug, 26 December; *FBIS-EEU*, 27 December).

Slovene politicians were well aware of the costs of secession. If independence meant going it alone, Ljubljana faced the loss of the Yugoslav market, a potential blockade by international financial circles that recognize the integrity of Yugoslavia, and prolonged negotiations on property issues—all of which would substantially worsen conditions that Deputy Prime Minister Jože Mencinger had already described as on the verge of collapse (Belgrade, Tanjug, 21 November; *FBIS-EEU*, 23 November).

Ultimately, the role of the military in the transformation of Yugoslavia depended less on the preferences of the military leadership than on the willingness and ability of new and old civilian politicians alike to weather the uncharted difficulties of multiparty politics. Sectarian political rhetoric aside, there were some positive signs. Take, for example, the announcement of the Croatian Defense Ministry that it was disbanding its civil defense youth volunteer units. These had been created during the height of the tensions between Tudjman's government and the republic's 600,000-strong Serbian minority (Zagreb, Tanjug, 28 November) due to "misunderstandings and negative political connotations" in ethnically mixed regions. In these circumstances the best that could be expected of the Marković government was an effort to facilitate conflict containment, not conflict resolution.

Foreign Policy. Throughout 1990 Yugoslav foreign policy mirrored the domestic tensions created by the imperatives of economic reform and the search for national self-determination. Yugoslav federal policymakers struggled to control an export-driven economy, to restrain proliferating republic foreign policy initiatives, and to contain the economic and political damage caused by widely publicized human rights violations in Kosovo.

Europe. In this regard, the embarrassing expulsion from Kosovo of members of the International Helsinki Federation for Human Rights—which Serbia officially insisted that the group had brought on itself by bringing medicine and propaganda into Kosovo—did not help matters. Despite its defensive reaction, the Serbian government stressed that it would "do everything in its power to prevent such incidents from happening again" (Belgrade, Tanjug Domestic Service, 8 September; *FBIS-EEU*, 10 September). In his zeal to take the high ground, Croatian president Franjo Tudjman renewed his August invitation (Belgrade, Tanjug, 21 August; *FBIS-EEU*, 22 August) to the European Parliament and other public and private institutions for human rights to come to Croatia and see for themselves the conditions of the republic's Serbian minority (ibid.).

The furor over Serbian treatment of the Helsinki group broke during the visit of a Council of Europe delegation to Belgrade to meet with members of the Yugoslav national assembly. Members of the visiting delegation took the occasion to remind their hosts that the council considered progress on the road to democracy and security of human rights to be preconditions for Yugoslav membership in that body (Belgrade Domestic Service, 6 September; *FBIS-EEU*, 7 September). SFRY president Jović responded that he expected all conditions for full Yugoslav membership in the council to have been met by the end of the year (ibid.).

The subsequent statement of the head of the European Community (EC) delegation, Ambassador Marc Janssens, in Zagreb for a roundtable meeting on cooperation between Yugoslavia and the EC, indicated that continued commitment to Prime Minister Marković's economic reforms and steady progress in the transformation of Yugoslavia into a multiparty, parliamentary democracy were also prerequisites of "qualitatively higher forms" of cooperation between Yugoslavia and the community (Belgrade, Tanjug, 20 September; *FBIS-EEU*, 21 September).

To what degree that linkage extends to protecting human rights in Kosovo will become manifest during talks on Yugoslavia's becoming an associate member of the EC, set to begin in 1991. In the meantime, the Spanish representative from the Council of Europe pinpointed a key factor for cohesion when he said that "the Council of Europe is needed by Yugoslavia as an outside factor of its unity" (Belgrade Domestic Service, 6 September; *FBIS-EEU*, 21 September).

By early November, Slovenia had opened missions in Washington, Brussels, and Vienna, with a statement of intent to do so in Moscow before the end of the year. Although these offices do not have diplomatic status, they underlined the seriousness with which policymakers in Ljubljana viewed Slovene foreign policy agendas.

The growing dilemma such initiatives posed for Yugoslavia's foreign policy establishment was evident during the 19–22 November Paris Conference on Security and Cooperation in Europe (CSCE). The official Yugoslav delegation, headed by SFRY president Borisav Jović, included Foreign Secretary Budimir Lončar and one representative from each of the six Yugoslav republics. Notwithstanding the CSCE rejection of separate Slovene representation at the Paris summit (BBC, Gabriel Partos, "Central Talks and Features," no. 274/90, 7 November), Slovene foreign minister Dimitrije Rupel issued a statement dissociating Slovenia from President Jović's official speech. A spokesman for the federal delegation characterized Rupel's statement as overstepping "the bounds of international practice and [exceeding] the limits of civilized behavior" (Belgrade, Tanjug, 20 November; *FBIS-EEU*, 23 November).

Competition from the unrecognized Slovene delegation complicated Yugoslav bilateral activities as well. The Slovene minister of foreign affairs held meetings with Czechoslovak president Václav Havel, Austrian foreign minister Alois Mock, members of the U.S. delegation, and representatives of the French Commission for Cooperation with Eastern Europe. In this regard, Rupel complained bitterly about efforts on the part of the official Yugoslav delegation to deny the Slovenes media access and prevent them from making contacts.

However, the rejection of the Slovene delegation as a CSCE participant was in line with Rupel's assessment of the reaction of international forums toward Slovene independence. The Slovene foreign minister realistically acknowledged that it would "be difficult and take a long time to gain international recognition because Europe fears a possible chaotic situation and wants, above all, peace in this part of the continent" (Belgrade, Tanjug, 22 November; *FBIS-EEU*, 23 November).

In its morning-after assessment, the collective state presidency supported the model of development that came out of the CSCE summit—that is, a pluralist democracy, the rule of law, a market economy, and respect for human and national rights—welcomed the progress in creating institutional prerequisites for constant political consultation and cooperation, and approved SFRY president Jović's dialogue with foreign policy partners in search of increased economic cooperation and understanding for Yugoslavia's difficulties in implementing economic and political reform (*Politika*, 28, 29, 30 November; *FBIS-EEU*, 12 December).

As the year ended, the Yugoslav republics joined the march to Europe 1992. Croatia, Macedonia, Serbia, and Slovenia were admitted to the Community of European Regions (Bosnia and Hercegovina and Montenegro have observer status) (Belgrade, Tanjug, 7 December; *FBIS-EEU*, 10 December). More important, Foreign Secretary Lončar reported that the Brussels meeting of the Council for Yugoslavia-EC Cooperation was a turning point for Yugoslav relations with the EC: Yugoslavia both entered the category of those countries to receive EC aid and "kept its Mediterranean position within Europe" (Belgrade, Tanjug, 20 December; *FBIS-EEU*, 21 December).

The United States. Officially the United States applauded the progress brought about by the Marković government's anti-inflation program and supported the prime minister's market-oriented reforms. The long-standing U.S. commitment to the integrity of Yugoslavia remained. However, President George Bush's decision to receive Croatian president Franjo Tudjman created some nervousness on the Yugoslav side (Belgrade, Tanjug Domestic Service, 27 September) and signaled that

the White House might be making contingency plans in the event that Yugoslavia failed to make the transition to a multiparty democracy without falling apart.

Moreover, following the midsummer drama in which the Albanian members of the Kosovo assembly voted to declare the province a republic with or without the agreement of Serbia or the federal government only to have Serbia suspend the Kosovo provincial government all together (*NYT*, 6 July; Milan Andrejevich, "Serbia Cracks down on Kosovo," RFE *Report on Eastern Europe*, 27 July), human rights concerns for the 90 percent Albanian majority led to demands that Congress move against what was increasingly seen as Serbian repression.

U.S. congressional apprehension became anger when riot police beat back Albanian demonstrators during a visit to the province by a senate delegation headed by Republican leader Robert J. Dole (*NYT*, 30 August). That anger has expressed itself by a congressional amendment to cut off all aid to Yugoslavia except in republics where democratic, multiparty elections had been held. In fact Yugoslavia was not receiving U.S. aid, but there could have been serious repercussions if the U.S. Export Import Bank were to suspend credits for exports to Serbia or if U.S. representatives to the World Bank were to oppose credits for Serbian projects. The Yugoslav government could take small comfort in the State Department's "sharp disagreement with the amendment" (Belgrade, Tanjug, 25 October; *FBIS-EEU*, 26 October), for the souring of Serbian relations with Congress had placed key participants in the U.S. foreign policy establishment at loggerheads concerning future relations with Yugoslavia.

In this context of bureaucratic contradictions, the role of the Central Intelligence Agency report predicting the breakup of Yugoslavia and civil war within eighteen months was unclear. Indeed, leaked on the eve of the Serbian elections (*NYT*, 28 November), the report potentially contributed to what some U.S. scholars feared could be the "Lebanonization" of Yugoslavia (*NYT*, 3 December).

The Soviet Union. In contrast, throughout 1990 Soviet and Yugoslav political and security interests largely coincided. Moscow's withdrawal from Afghanistan removed a major source of tension between them. The Soviets' upgrading of the nonaligned movement (NAM) was gratifying, and their interest in expanding the CSCE as the infrastructure of a collective European security in the wake of the October German reunification was compatible with the long-standing neutral and nonaligned positions developed by Yugoslavia.

Nonetheless, a number of economic issues centered on the remaining roughly $2 billion trade surplus with the USSR. In January reports circulated that the trade surplus would be balanced over the next two years in the context of a projected $30 billion, five-year trade turnover program between the two countries (Tanjug, 18 January; *FBIS-EEU*, 19 January).

By July the timetable for phasing out what both sides described as "the debt" had been extended to four years and was scheduled to begin in January 1991. The Soviet side agreed to pay back in goods over a three-year period. If, after a one-year grace period, that deadline is not met, hard currency payment will be required (Tanjug, 1 July; *FBIS-EEU*, 2 July).

To facilitate Soviet repayment, the Yugoslavs agreed to early repayment of $230 million in commercial and $650 million in interstate state credit and to take over an unspecified amount of debt securities that Soviet banks had bought in London and Paris. The second-largest Yugoslav trading partner next to West Germany (Belgrade, Tanjug, 11 December; *FBIS-EEU*, 12 December), the Soviet Union was to increase deliveries of goods and to construct a natural gas pipeline system in Yugoslavia. A separate protocol agreed to shift to hard currency payments for services as of August 1990; a general shift to hard currency payments in Soviet-Yugoslav economic relations was set for January 1991. (*Pravda*, 20 July; *FBIS-SOV*, 26 July.)

Meanwhile, Soviet-Yugoslav relations increasingly reflected initiatives from republic political actors. In July, Serbia established relations with the Russian federation (Tanjug, 27 July; *FBIS-EEU*, 31 July), followed by an agreement on economic cooperation in September (Belgrade, Tanjug, 29 September). Shortly thereafter, the Slovene "representation" was set up in Moscow as well (Belgrade, Tanjug, 6 September; *FBIS-EEU*, 7 September). However, in the Slovene case, it was not clear that such representation was targeted at the Russian federation as opposed to the USSR as a whole.

Nonaligned priorities. At the ninth NAM summit in Belgrade, 1989, Yugoslavia made substantial headway in steering the movement on the path to modernizing and adapting to the rapidly changing international political system. Whereas the Yugoslav conception of the need for such modernization was accepted in principle, in practice what

was to be done remained an open question, creating serious difficulties for Yugoslav policymakers in Yugoslavia's role as "coordinator" of the nonaligned movement between NAM summits.

Bojana Tadić, a leading Yugoslav scholar of nonalignment, concluded that the program of the ninth summit was not "sufficiently operationalized" and summed up the dilemma facing the movement: "This question boils down to . . . where is the place and what are the possible functions of nonalignment today in the completely changed structure of the international community and almost completely superseded models of international relations?" (Bojana Tadić, "The Non-aligned Movement and the Priorities of Yugoslav Foreign Policy," *Review of International Affairs* 961 (Belgrade), 20 September).

As Tadić acknowledged, Yugoslavia's nonaligned foreign policy reflected the tensions of the country's domestic political environment in which there was concern not to miss opportunities in the 1992 European integration–dominated priorities in Slovenia and Croatia. Yugoslavia worked to mobilize "timely condemnation of Iraq" for its aggression against Kuwait and nonaligned requests for immediate withdrawal. There was a foreign ministers' meeting of Yugoslavia, India, and Algeria in Belgrade as well as Yugoslav networking among the nonaligned at the United Nations. (Belgrade, Tanjug, 13 September; *FBIS-EEU*, 14 September.)

As country chairman of the nonaligned movement, Yugoslavia launched a peace mission in the gulf that took Foreign Secretary Lončar to Iran, the United Arab Emirates, Syria, and Jordan. At that time Lončar was not invited to Baghdad—most likely as a sign of Iraqi displeasure at Yugoslav support for unconditional withdrawal and the U.N. blockade.

Yet as tension mounted, Baghdad signaled that the Yugoslav foreign secretary was welcome "at any time." Iraqi foreign minister Tariq Aziz stressed the Iraqi expectation that as chairman of NAM Yugoslavia could contribute to peace and stability in the gulf as he bid farewell to outgoing Yugoslav ambassador Stojan Andov (Belgrade, Tanjug, 18 December; *FBIS-EEU*, 19 December) who was returning to Yugoslavia "to commit himself to political activities at home." (Tehran, Islamic Republic News Agency, *FBIS-EEU*, 14 November.)

Yugoslav diplomacy responded to the Iraqi change of heart over Lončar's visit by mobilizing a serious initiative for a diplomatic settlement of the gulf crisis. In turn, the foreign secretary's reports of his 30 December talks with Iraqi foreign minister Aziz and Saddam Husayn subsequently played a role in European Community efforts (*Politika, International Weekly*, 12–18 January 1991). Thus, during the last days of December what Tadić referred to as the "marginalization" of the nonaligned movement (Tadić, "Non-aligned Movement," as cited above) had at least been slowed, and Yugoslavia's peace initiatives in the Persian Gulf as chairman of the movement were a plus in Yugoslav efforts to be included in the "common European home."

Biographies. *Ante Marković, prime minister.* Born in 1924, Marković, a Croat from Bosnia and Hercegovina, joined the partisans in 1941 and reportedly, the CPY in 1943. He graduated from the Technical Faculty University of Zagreb in 1953 with a degree in electrical engineering; from 1953 to 1961 he was a construction and planning engineer at the Rade Končar enterprise. From 1961 to 1982, he was the executive director of the enterprise that became one of Yugoslavia's largest manufacturers of electrical equipment. His political career began in the 1960s in local government and party organizations in Zagreb, and he was a member of LCY CC. He was prime minister of Croatia from 1982 to 1986 and president of the Croatian state presidency from May 1986 to May 1988. (RFE *Report*, 23 March 1989; *NYT*, 20 January 1989.)

Dr. Janez Drnovšek. Born in 1951, he was president of the SFRY Presidency until May 1990 and then continued as Slovene representative on that body. He has a doctorate in economics and was manager of a branch bank in Ljubljana. His diplomatic experience includes assistant to economic counselor in Egypt, a term as president of the Slovene Trade Union Committee for International Affairs, and a member of Slovene Assembly. Since 1984 he has served as one of Slovenia's representatives to the federal chamber of republics and provinces. Considered one of Yugoslavia's experts on the foreign debt crisis, he is fluent in Serbo-Croatian, English, French, and Spanish and has some knowledge of German. (*Delo*, 8 April; RFE *Report*, 15 April 1989.)

Dr. Borisav Jović. Born in 1928, he was the Serbian representative on the SFRY presidency and replaced Janez Drnovšek as president of that body 15 May. Between 1963 and 1971 he held a range of economic posts including secretary of Serbia's Economic Chamber and Serbian secretary of trade and industry. During the 1970s Jović also served as president of the federal government's commission for relations with the Council for Mutual Economic Assistance and then as federal director of planning. In 1975, he was Yugoslav ambassador to Italy; in 1984 he became vice-president of the Serbian national assembly; in 1986 he was a member of the Serbian LC CC and presidium; and in 1988 he was president of the Serbian national assembly. He was Ante Marković's main competitor for the job of prime minister in 1989. (Milan Andrejevich, "Yugoslavia's New President," RFE *Report*, 25 May.)

Slobodan Milošević. Born in Pozarevac, Serbia, on 29 August 1941, Milošević graduated with a law degree in 1964 from the University of Belgrade, where he became active in politics. His first executive position in 1968 was at the state-owned Tehnogas company, where his interest in politics increased and where he met Ivan Stambolić, who became first his mentor, later his political rival in Serbian politics. Milošević was promoted to director general of Tehnogas in 1973; in 1978 he received the prestigious post of president of Beobanka (the Belgrade bank).

His political activity began in 1969 when he joined the League of Communists of Yugoslavia (LCY); by 1984 he was head of the Belgrade city party committee. That same year his mentor, Stambolić, became president of the League of Communists of Serbia (LCS). Given Milošević's personal charisma and the emotional appeal of his Serbian nationalism, he easily succeeded Stambolić to the LCS chairmanship in 1986 and established populist rapport more on the strength of his personality than on ideology and institutions.

As he rose in politics and gathered power, Milošević undermined his erstwhile colleague Stambolić, having him removed from the Serbian presidency, which in May 1989 Milošević assumed. To further his political advantage, Milošević exploited the Serbian popular concerns of nationalism, economics, and religion by manipulating the press, Serbia's public loan program, and even the Serbian Orthodox church.

His legal, banking, and technocratic background did not temper his basic philosophy of emotional nationalism. His political talents and maneuvers made it possible for Serbia to assert control over its autonomous provinces. The goal seems to be Serbian supremacy in whatever federation or confederational form the other republics eventually choose. However, his steamrolling politics and style, despite his concession (under pressure) to permit opposition parties, began to worry responsible politicians, students, and intellectuals. Milošević's attempt to crush the early March 1991 demonstrations in Belgrade with army units is symptomatic both of his approach and of Serbian concerns.

He is married to Dr. Mirja Marković, the Belgrade communist party committee's chief ideologist and a Marxist sociology professor who was his high school sweetheart and who is currently a member of the self-proclaimed successor to the LCY, the League of Communists—Movement for Yugoslavia (LC-MY) party's leadership.

(Sources: Sabrina P. Ramet, "Serbia's Slobodan Milošević: A Profile," *SAIS Review* 11, no. 1 [Winter/Spring 1991]: 93–105; Milan Andrejevich, "The Yugoslav Crisis: No Solution in Sight," *Report on Eastern Europe*, 22 February 1991; Andrejevich, "Unrest in Belgrade: A Symptom of Serbia's Crisis," *Report on Eastern Europe*, 29 March 1991.)

Robin Alison Remington
University of Missouri at Columbia

Council for Mutual Economic Assistance
The Last Year before Its Final Demise?

Introduction. Because of a simultaneous collapse of the communist political order in Eastern Europe, the disappearance of the German Democratic Republic from Europe's political map, and the economic crisis throughout the former Soviet bloc, the institutional framework of the Council for Mutual

Economic Assistance (CMEA) has been disintegrating. As of January 1991, there were nine full members of CMEA: Bulgaria, Czechoslovakia, Cuba, Hungary, Mongolia, Poland, Romania, Vietnam, and the USSR. Albania joined the CMEA in 1949 but since 1961 has not participated in CMEA activity nor has it paid dues (Richard F. Staar, *Communist Regimes in Eastern Europe*, 5th rev. ed. [Stanford: Hoover Institution, 1988], p. 292). Its raison d'être as a tool of Soviet economic domination has disappeared as a consequence of political developments in Eastern Europe in turn triggered by a dramatic change in the Soviet approach to relations with Eastern Europe. As a result, 1990 may be the last year before its final disappearance.

The developments in economic cooperation, trade, and investment point to the demise of the organization. In the area of trade, the decisions already taken by CMEA members to shift to world market prices and payment in hard currencies beginning in 1991 will effectively dismantle most previous "isolationist" arrangements. In addition, the CMEA special agreements on trade of specific products (e.g., steel) have unraveled. Cooperation in the areas of investment, research, and development has been almost nonexistent since its peak in the mid-1970s. Joint investment projects, popular in the 1970s, were starved of resources in the 1980s, and an ambitious program of technological cooperation, fashioned after the European Community's Eureka program, has never taken off. Thus, the organization has effectively collapsed, although its headquarters still exist in Moscow and a vast bureaucratic personnel is still on the payroll.

The unraveling of CMEA has been accompanied by plummeting trade and its reorientation toward Western Europe. Intra-CMEA exports and imports fell substantially in 1990; the fall was not restricted to trade with the Soviet Union but also encompassed trade between smaller Central European economies. Several CMEA countries have already embarked on the path of shifting their trade away from their traditional CMEA markets. They have also increasingly relied on payments in hard currencies in their mutual trade dealings.

The changes to be implemented in 1991 will effectively redesign the institutional framework of economic interaction among CMEA members. A traditional primacy of politics over economics will be replaced by a subordination of these relations to the imperative of economic efficiency. Although the links that have emerged as a result of the integrationist efforts of the last 40 years will remain bind-

Table 1: Economic Performance of European CMEA countries
(Annual percentage change)

	Industrial Output					Agricultural Output			
	1986	*1987*	*1988*	*1989*	*1990*	*1986*	*1987*	*1988*	*1989*
Bulgaria	4.0	4.2	5.2	2.1	−1.2	11.7	−5.1	−0.1	0.4
Czechoslovakia	3.2	2.5	2.0	2.0	−5.0	0.6	0.9	2.2	1.1
Hungary	1.9	3.5	0.0	−2.0	−10.0	2.4	−2.0	4.3	−2.0
Poland	4.7	3.4	5.3	−2.0	−15.0	5.0	−2.3	0.6	2.0
Romania	7.7	4.5	3.6	−2.0	−22.0	12.8	2.3	2.9	—
USSR	4.4	3.8	3.9	1.7	−24.0	5.3	−0.5	1.7	0.8

SOURCES: "RWPG '88," Warsaw, *Życie gospodarcze*, 16 April 1989; Moscow, *Pravda*, 12, 19 June 1989; *Economic Survey of Europe in 1989–1990* (New York: United Nations, 1990); and PlanEcon, Washington, D.C.

ing, they will become weaker at a considerable short-term cost to Eastern Europe. Whatever framework emerges, it is not likely to foster integration within the CMEA area, as they all will gravitate toward the European Community, the source of capital and modern technology. Although there is a need to expand mutually profitable intraregional trade, a shift to the Western international trading regime will do more than a reformed integrationist group encompassing CMEA members.

The Economic Crisis and CMEA. Because of constraints to foreign trade generated by administrative systems of CMEA economies, the intraregional trade has never been buoyant. The crisis— the disintegration of central controls in the Soviet Union and trade liberalization in some reform-minded CMEA countries—has added new constraints on regular commercial transactions. Faced with growing domestic and external imbalances, several CMEA governments introduced measures suppressing import demand. The Soviet inability to compensate for the losses in its CMEA terms of trade by increasing export volumes resulted in cuts of exports by other CMEA countries unwilling to finance Soviet excessive consumption through the accumulation of transferable rubles. Last but not least, the liberalization of import controls in Hungary and Poland triggered substituting Western imports for East European manufactured goods.

Symptoms of the crisis of CMEA economies include the unraveling of the CMEA trade network and the acceleration of the movement away from the organization of member countries as well as from its traditional leader, the Soviet Union. Although the Soviet Union has retained its dominant position within CMEA and continues to be a major trading partner of all CMEA members, CMEA trade for other partners has lost much of its relevance. Czechoslovakia, Hungary, and Poland significantly reoriented their trade to Western Europe. So of course did the Soviet Union, which cut its CMEA energy exports to maintain its share on Western markets. Thus, the economic crisis accelerated long-observed trends that have been pushing CMEA toward disintegration. (See "CMEA," *YICA*, 1990.)

Economic performance in 1990 continued to be disappointing in all CMEA countries. The fall of domestic output growth rates was shared by all countries, and they all recorded absolute contractions in their gross domestic product (GDP). Poland, Hungary, and East Germany, the "negative growth generators" of 1989, were joined by their other CMEA partners, the Soviet Union, Bulgaria, Romania, and Czechoslovakia. The decline occurred no matter whether a government had adopted drastic measures to replace an administrative economic system with one based on a market mechanism or had carefully refined its administrative mechanism. Countries that did nothing to dismantle the administrative economic system (e.g., Romania and the Soviet Union) fared almost as poorly in industrial output as those countries that have already started the transition to a market economy (Hungary and Poland). See table 1.

The contraction in economic activity in 1990 reflected a number of factors, some common to all CMEA economies and others specific for different countries. The common denominator was a systemic limbo that most CMEA countries found themselves in; the problem was that the collapse of the administrative economic system has not been accompanied by the emergence of a new market-based mechanism of stimulating and coordinating economic activity. In addition, they all faced balance-of-payments constraints. Specific factors reflected diverse economic policies as well as diverse approaches to reform the economic system, shaped to a large degree by domestic political situations. The inability of governments to discipline economic actors led to inflation in all CMEA countries, to a breakdown of distribution systems in some of them (the Soviet Union, Bulgaria, and Romania), and to economic decline in all of them.

Although economic decline and inflation spared not a single CMEA country, there were different underlying circumstances and policy approaches. In many of them (e.g., Romania, Bulgaria, and the Soviet Union) deteriorating economic performance was simply the result of the absence of a coherent economic system and policy framework, but in others (especially Poland and Hungary), economic contraction is the outcome of an effective program of economic reform and restructuring. The economic decline in the latter group of countries reflects an inevitable result of cleansing the economy from accumulated distortions and inefficiencies of a centrally planned economic system. In the former, the steep decline results from chaos in the economy. So far only the Polish government has introduced measures that will genuinely open the economy, and that move, as we shall see, has contributed to a significant improvement in foreign trade performance, both in the West and East.

Although the fall in Soviet exports was not the biggest among CMEA countries, its negative impact on other CMEA countries was by far the largest. The rapidly eroding ability of the Soviet government to control its domestic political and economic actors, as well as a legacy of ill-conceived investment programs, contributed to supply and transportation bottlenecks that resulted in the fall of domestic aggregate output and reduced Soviet export deliveries to European CMEA countries in 1989 and 1990. For instance, Soviet deliveries of timber to East Europe fell short of that contracted by 267,000 cubic meters, of coal by 100,000 tons, and of fuel by 46,000 tons in 1989 (*Izvestiia*, 8 May). In the first half of 1990 Soviet exports to Eastern Europe declined by about 11 percent. The fall in Soviet exports was exacerbated by the improved terms of trade of European CMEA members vis-à-vis the Soviet Union. For instance, its exports in value terms to Poland fell by 4 percent in 1988 (see *Gospodarka światowa i gospodarka Polska w*

1988 roku, Central School of Planning and Statistics [Warsaw, 1989], p. 42).

Because of the dependence of smaller CMEA countries on Moscow, growing shortages of raw materials and energy traditionally supplied by the Soviet Union spilled throughout CMEA. The fall in Soviet exports of energy was particularly steep, contributing to an energy crisis in Eastern Europe. Moscow unilaterally cut supplies of fuel to Czechoslovakia by 20 percent in January and by 30 percent to Poland in January–March. (*Financial Times*, 14 February.) Overall, according to Ievgienij Chartukov of the Moscow Institute of World Energy and Prognoses, the Soviet oil export is estimated to fall by more than 20 percent in 1990, to about 100 million tons. (*Życie gospodarcze*, no. 39, p. 12).

The Soviet cuts in exports, accompanied by the decline in Soviet terms of trade, depressed trade with CMEA economies. The only exception was Romania, whose exports and imports from the Soviet Union increased during the first quarter of 1990 (see table 2). Soviet exports and imports from other European CMEA countries plummeted. Faced with rapidly expanding surpluses in their trade with the Soviet Union, European CMEA members sought to cut their Soviet exports. Bulgaria reduced its exports by 20 percent, and Poland introduced three separate exchange rates and a system of licensing designed to keep its exports within the amounts stipulated in trade protocols and to encourage imports from the Soviet Union. These changes made exports above trade protocol quotas unprofitable for Polish enterprises. As a result, ruble exports stood in August at 64 percent of their levels in August 1989. (See Keith Crane, "Polish Foreign Trade in 1989 and the First Seven Months of 1990," Plan-Econ *Report*, nos. 42–43.)

Faced with the soaring surplus, which reached 1.1 billion rubles in 1989 and fearing that a fall in domestic demand would be combined with rapidly expanding Soviet demand for imports, the Hungarian government also resorted to restrictive compulsory export licensing. Hungarian ruble exports to the Soviet Union fell by 20 percent in the first half of 1990 and imports by 14 percent. (*Statisztikai Havi Közlemények* [Statistical monthly bulletin] 1.) The contraction in exports aggravated Hungarian economic problems and pushed some enterprises (e.g., Ikarus, a bus producer) to the brink of bankruptcy.

The contraction in the trade with the Soviet Union was accompanied by suppressed trade among smaller CMEA-5 countries. No reliable data for

Table 2: Developments in Intra-CMEA Trade in the First Half of 1990
(percent change as compared with the first half of 1989)

| | Reported from: | | | | | | | |
| | Soviet Union* | | Czechoslovakia | | Hungary | | Poland‡ | |
To	Export	Import	Export	Import	Export	Import	Export	Import
Soviet Union			−11.4	−16.7	−19.9	−14.0	25.3	−11.5
CMEA-5	−9.2†	−3.9†	−26.4	1.1	−18.5	−20.9	21.7	−42.3
East Germany	−15.1	4.3	−17.2	10.8	−14.9	−13.1	9.4	−32.6
Bulgaria	7.2	−7.3	−17.9	−29.7	−57.2	11.2	4.5	−44.9
Czechoslovakia	−13.6	−7.4			−23.0	−27.0	39.6	−40.2
Hungary	−10.6	−19.7	−5.5	−20.8			10.7	−57.2
Poland	−20.2	14.9	−48.3	21.6	−62.0	−22.0		
Romania	7.8	−26.8	−10.3	−42.7	107.0	49.1	20.5	−67.8

* For the first three months of 1990 as compared with the same period in 1989.
† For Soviet exports and imports, CMEA-6 including all East European CMEA members and the former German Democratic Republic.
‡ For the first seven months of 1990 as compared with the same period in 1989.
SOURCE: PlanEcon *Reports*, nos. 24, 29–30, 34–35, 42–43, 44–45

1990 are available for Bulgaria, Romania, and former East Germany. However, because their trade with the four reporting countries fell (see table 2), there is no reason to suspect that they increased their mutual trade in 1990. On the import side, only Czechoslovakia increased its purchases from smaller European CMEA members. The surge of imports from Poland and East Germany outweighed sharp cuts from other countries. At the other extreme, Poland's import demand for merchandise produced in other European CMEA countries recorded the largest contraction—42.3 percent during the first seven months of 1990.

With the exception of Poland all other CMEA members recorded a steep decline in their CMEA exports in 1990. The reasons for Poland's export success lie in the coincidence of Poland's transition to a demand-constrained open economy and expanding *shortageflation* (inflation combined with shortages) in other CMEA countries. The stabilization program implemented by Poland's Solidarity government in January 1990 has almost completely dismantled administrative controls over foreign trade; quantitative restrictions have been replaced by tariffs and the exchange rate. The sharp contraction of domestic demand combined with a total dismantling of the state monopoly of foreign trade and the financial autonomy of enterprises turned out to be powerful forces in stimulating the search for foreign markets. This situation created conditions enabling domestic economic factors (state- and private-owned firms) to exploit unique opportunities offered by the economic crisis and CMEA's disintegration. Inflation, combined with growing

Table 3: Share of the Soviet Union in CMEA Trade of CMEA-5 in 1988–1990
(percent of CMEA exports/imports)

| | Exports | | | Imports | | |
	1988	1989	1990	1988	1989	1990
Bulgaria	77.6	—	—	72.9	—	—
Czechoslovakia	59.9	58.3	62.8	59.5	56.6	51.8
GDR	57.1	51.4	—	59.2	51.4	—
Hungary	61.9	63.1	57.6	57.2	57.6	88.9
Poland	60.2	61.7	62.6	57.6	43.6	66.5
Romania	58.8	58.9	—	49.3	58.8	—

SOURCES: For 1988: author's calculations from data in Martin Schrenk "Future of the CMEA," *Socialist Economies in Transition* (World Bank) 1, no. 1, April 1990; for 1989 and 1990: from data in PlanEcon *Reports*, nos. 24, 29–30, 34–35, 42–43, 44–45

**Table 4: Changes in the Directions of Trade of Selected CMEA Members
(shares in 1989 and 1990)***

	Socialist Countries		Developed West		Developing Countries	
	1989	*1990*	*1989*	*1990*	*1989*	*1990*
Czechoslovakia						
—Exports	52.2	46.2	38.0	44.4	9.8	9.4
—Imports	55.4	48.3	36.0	43.2	8.6	8.5
Hungary						
—Exports	50.8	39.3	39.1	49.0	10.1	11.7
—Imports	47.3	38.1	43.6	52.2	9.0	9.6
Poland						
—Exports	43.6	29.8	45.7	60.5	10.8	9.7
—Imports	43.9	32.2	48.8	62.8	7.4	4.9
Soviet Union						
—Exports	62.3	61.8	24.0	25.1	13.7	13.0
—Imports	63.1	59.1	28.5	30.4	8.4	10.5

* For comments and sources, see table 2.

shortages in the Soviet Union and to a lesser extent in Czechoslovakia as a result of the collapse of central controls, boosted domestic demand because consumers and producers sought to spend money before it lost more of its value. Thanks to the liberalization of foreign trade, Polish firms were able to take advantage of a lack of competition on CMEA markets and increase their exports.

Poland's exports to European CMEA members expanded rapidly during the first seven months of 1990, dramatically outweighing the fall in its imports. Because imports contracted much more, Poland, with a surplus of 1.6 billion rubles accumulated during this period (as compared with a 68-million-ruble deficit in the same period in 1989) and 2.1-billion-ruble surplus with the Soviet Union, became the main creditor of its CMEA partners.

Poland's CMEA export performance brings to the fore two points. First, the liberalization of trade and currency convertibility in other countries is likely to provide a boost to intraregional trade, although there may be large shifts in its composition and direction. Therefore, the transformation of economic systems in other countries and recovery may reverse the trend of declining intraregional trade. Second, Poland's trade performance has clearly demonstrated the payoffs of the liberalization strategy in foreign trade. The piled-up ruble assets are not worthless; for instance, the East German deficit of 230 million rubles is to be settled in deutsche marks (DM) at a favorable rate of DM 2.34 per ruble, and the surplus with the Soviet Union will be used to cushion the transition to hard currency oil prices.

The decline in trade between European CMEA members and the Soviet Union did not alter a traditional radial pattern of economic interaction within CMEA. On the contrary, because the fall of trade among European CMEA members was larger than their trade with the Soviet Union, this pattern has been magnified. Thus, despite the decline in volume and value (because of the Soviet worsening terms of trade in the late 1980s), the Soviet Union remained their major trading partner.

The share of the Soviet Union in the trade of smaller CMEA members increased in 1990 (see table 3). For instance, the share of Czechoslovak CMEA exports to the Soviet Union increased from 58.3 percent in 1989 to 62.8 percent in 1990. The removal of controls on all machinery imports in 1990, effected under the pressure of the International Monetary Fund (IMF), resulted in a dramatic decline of imports from CMEA countries as Hungarian firms substituted Western imports for them. (Keith Crane, "Hungarian Foreign Trade during the First Half of 1990: Ruble Trade Collapses; Hard Currency Exports up Sharply," PlanEcon *Report*, nos. 44–45.) The share of Hungarian imports from European CMEA members fell from 42.4 percent in 1989 to 11.1 percent in 1990. The weight of the Soviet Union in intraregional trade will clearly increase once their oil price is set at the world level in 1991.

As the growth of intra-CMEA trade lagged significantly behind the growth of trade of CMEA countries with other partners in 1990, there was a reorientation of trade toward the West. This shift was especially visible in the case of three post-communist countries: Hungary, Poland, and Czechoslovakia (see table 4). Their exports increased during the first six months of 1990 by 17.1, 21.5, and 10.2 percent, while imports increased for Czechoslovakia (27.9 percent) and Hungary (5.6 percent), and fell in the case of Poland by 28.1 percent. Exacerbated by the contraction in intra-CMEA trade, the share of the developed west increased by 17 percent for Czechoslovakia's exports (20 percent for imports), by 25 percent for Hungary (19 percent for imports), and by 32 percent for Poland (28 percent for imports).

In all, the crumbling of intra-CMEA trade is the result of two processes. One is related to the negative growth rates and the collapse of central controls indispensable for the traditional administrative economic system to coordinate economic activity. This system has not been replaced by an effective new one. The other derived from the growing mismatch between Soviet export capabilities and the CMEA trade regime. Because of the Soviet inability to balance its trade through increased volume of exports, the Soviet trade partners were unwilling to "honour agreed export volumes where this involved incurring substantial current account surpluses in transferable roubles, which are difficult to mobilize, even over time, and so constitute involuntary, quasi interest-free loans to the partners in deficit" (*Economic Survey of Europe in 1989–1990*, Economic Commission for Europe [New York: United Nations, 1990], p. 144).

In Search of Solutions: Is CMEA beyond repair? The crisis of CMEA institutions is not the result of the massive collapse of communist regimes in 1989. Except for orchestrating the economic dependence of Central–East European countries on the Soviet Union and partially decoupling them from the world economy, the organization—as a Western analyst succinctly observed—"has never succeeded in developing an economically coherent or politically feasible plan for promoting increased interaction on a multilateral basis" (Karen Dawisha, "Eastern Europe and Perestroika under Gorbachev: Options for the West," in *Pressures for Reform in the East European Economies*, vol. 2., Joint Economic Committee, Congress of the United States [Washington, D.C.: U.S. Government Printing Office, 1989], p. 529). As I argued in the last edition of this volume (see "CMEA," *YICA*, 1990), the limited

progress in integration was derived mainly from the inherent features of the administrative economic system, which displayed a strong aversion to foreign trade in the absence of supranational authority. Because of political stability considerations, the latter has been declined by smaller CMEA members fearful of total Soviet domination.

Conflicting interests and official disenchantment with CMEA surfaced dramatically in the late 1980s. Following earlier CMEA summits devoted to fundamental changes in CMEA, the third economic summit of the 1980s to approve new measures and to celebrate the 40th anniversary of the organization, initially slated for March 1989, has been postponed indefinitely. The Forty-fifth Council session initially to be held in June was first deferred until October; it finally convened in Sofia in January 1990. Contrary to speculations preceding the session, the council has not dissolved the organization. Instead, it has set up a commission to present a "concept of new system of economic cooperation among member countries of the Council" by the end of the first quarter of 1990.

The commission has faced a daunting task as it had to reconcile divergent interests of its members and solve fundamental obstacles to integration. The former relate to different approaches to economic reform and the reorientation of their foreign economic policy toward the West and the Western economic multilateral organizations (the World Bank and IMF). The latter are insurmountable without a full transition to a market economy. In a nutshell, they relate to the absence of common currency or currency convertibility, to the lack of equivalence between domestic prices and foreign prices, to the absence of effective financial institutions, to the existing domestic price distortions, to the irrelevance of the official exchange rate that has never been based on purchasing power parities as stipulated by the 1973 Karl-Marx-Stadt Agreement (Zdenek Drabek, "CMEA: The Primitive Socialist Integration and Its Prospects," in *Economic Aspects of Regional Trading Agreements*, ed. David Greenway, Thomas Hyclak, and Robert J. Thornton [New York: New York University Press, 1989], p. 244), and to the foreign trade monopoly.

Thus, not surprisingly, the draft of the document—which so far has not been published—is very general and offers few clues on how to revive CMEA. (Based on the Polish translation of CMEA internal working document *Koncepcja nowego systemu współpracy gospodarczej krajów członkowskich Rady*, April.) Interestingly, the integration of

CMEA members is not stated as the goal of the organization. Instead, the document argues that one of the main objectives of cooperation is "to generate new impulses to integrate the economies of member states with the world economy, including European and other regional economic structures, as well as to overcome the economic division of Europe" (ibid., p. 1). Emphasizing the sovereignty of national decision making, it retains the "old" CMEA principle of "interested parties" according to which governments participate only in selected integrationist schemes. States may enter into bilateral as well as multilateral arrangements. The statements pointing to a necessity of developing cooperation in various spheres are not accompanied by any suggestions as to how to accomplish it.

The document is clearly a compromise between various approaches to economic policies and institutional change. On the one hand, it asserts that cooperation and integration with the world economy are to be accomplished through the development of market economies and the withdrawal of the state from direct controls. On the other hand, in phraseology strongly reminiscent of central planning, it calls for the identification of priorities, an extensive exchange of economic information, forecasts as well as the development of programs related to environmental protection, research and development, production, and so forth. It thus assumes that the state, not firms and individuals, should continue to take direct responsibility for cooperation. This situation is clearly incompatible with the removal of direct central controls and a market-based economic system.

Similar incompatibilities and generalities are found in a section on foreign trade. CMEA trade is to be conducted according to the rules of the General Agreement on Trade and Tariffs (GATT) regime, and "member countries will gradually remove trade controls based on export-import licenses and other nontariff trade barriers" (ibid., p. 5). Member countries pledge to dismantle the state monopoly of foreign trade and to phase out the administrative nontariff barriers to trade. Yet, it is noted that Bulgaria, Vietnam, Mongolia, and the Soviet Union deem it necessary to create privileged access to their markets and administrative establishment of sectoral markets.

Actual developments outpaced the recommendations of the Reform Commission. Although the Soviet delegation at the Sofia meeting indicated that the transition to a new accounting system in world prices and convertible currencies would be spread over several years, the support for this position quickly evaporated in Moscow. On 31 July 1990, Moscow withdrew from the system of agreements on nontrade payments with other CMEA countries and announced the transition to hard currency and world prices in mutual settlements beginning 1 January 1991.

The conditions, timing, and scope of the transition to settlements in hard currencies have been left to bilateral negotiations. The basic forms include bilateral clearing in convertible currencies, bilateral clearing in transferable rubles, payments in national currencies, and payments in convertible currencies. Other instruments and barter arrangements between interested parties are also allowed.

With the exception of fusing the International Bank for Economic Cooperation and the International Investment Bank and floating it as a joint stock company, there is a conspicuous absence of any reference to any forms of cooperation outside of trade or to the organizational underpinnings of integration. Sections on capital and labor mobility and taxation and the transformation of legal rules of economic cooperation could be inserted into any general agreement between any two countries. They set no framework calling for a gradual transfer of sovereignty to a supranational organization, indicating that there is neither interest nor political will to discuss integration seriously.

There is little popular support for CMEA in Eastern Europe. According to popular perception, CMEA is a symbol of Soviet domination and exploitation of their economies. The Soviets remain ambivalent about the organization; for some it remains an imperial symbol (and potentially useful channel for controlling political outcomes in East–Central European countries), while for others, it is a vehicle for transferring resources from the Soviet Union. The noncommunist officials from Eastern Europe see little economic value in the organization, even if reformed. Their eyes are turned to the source of technology, capital, and viable politico-economic institutional design, that is, to the West. The remark of Poland's minister of privatization, Waldemar Kuczyński, is noteworthy. He observed that a new "CMEA must in no way restrict the economic freedom of its member states nor hinder their contacts with the European Community." (In the same interview, he also added that "the unrealistic plan of forming a CMEA free market should be given up." See *FBIS-SOV*, 31 July.) In other words, CMEA may exist as long as it is irrelevant for member countries.

For most European CMEA members, the most important issue was not how to reform CMEA but how to design the pace and conditions of the transition in their bilateral economic relations with Moscow. Because of accumulated ruble assets and liabilities, several questions arose: what exchange rate should be adopted for converting transferable rubles into US dollars? what portion of trade should be cleared in convertible currencies? how should previous contributions to joint CMEA projects be estimated? and over what time period could the accumulated assets be used to finance purchases? All these questions suddenly became politically and financially important.

The choice of a ruble exchange rate, which was overvalued in CMEA commercial transactions, is relevant because hundreds of millions of rubles to be converted to convertible currency are at stake and because all of their holders are faced with a prospect of a sudden worsening of their terms of trade with the Soviet Union. For instance, the Soviet debt to Hungary, amounting to 780 million rubles, would generate $1,443 million at the official rate ($1.62) instead of $708 million at the actually negotiated rate of $0.92. Another more pressing issue for Central–East Europeans is the time framework over which ruble assets converted into dollars could be used to cushion their soaring Soviet import bills in turn triggered by the switch to the world oil price. Under these circumstances, it is not surprising that neither they nor the Soviets were particularly preoccupied with the reform of CMEA.

The fact that most pressing issues discussed in earnest by CMEA members address various ways to withdraw from constraints imposed by CMEA indicates that CMEA is beyond repair. CMEA was based on concepts that had become obsolete as a result of economic and political change in the Soviet Union and its former European empire. The Soviet Union no longer has the capacity (or is willing) to impose the traditional CMEA rules of the game. With the exception of Cuba, they all now declare the establishment of a market economy as their goal. Because they all seek to integrate with the Western international economy, there is no political support for developing the organization based on the principle of insulation from the world economy; as a Soviet economist put it, the task now is to draw "the East European countries and the Soviet Union into the system of European division of labor" (see I. Frantseva, "Trudnoe vozvrashchenie v Evropu," *Izvestiia*, 23 July).

Under these circumstances, it is tempting to characterize the developments that took place in CMEA in 1990 as a search to find the least costly way to dismantle the organization. Yet CMEA, with its enormous and increasingly obsolete bureaucracy, still exists, and some Soviet officials even hope the change in pricing and accounting systems will help restore the organization. O. Mozhayskov, chief of the USSR Gosbank's Foreign Currency Economics Administration, is quoted as saying that "CMEA indeed no longer feels important, but hard currency settlements are capable of reviving it" (B. Mikhaylov, "Proshchai uslovnyi rubl'," *Izvestiia*, 1 July). Hungarian minister of external economic relations Béla Kádár declared that it is premature to bury CMEA because "the preservation of economic relations with the Soviet Union remains of vital importance for the countries of East Europe" (interview with Moscow Radio International Service; *FBIS-SOV*, 29 June). In this context, an interesting question addressed in the next section is whether there is in fact a demand for a reformed CMEA.

Conclusion: Is There a Need for CMEA?

Although all delegates (except Cuba) expressed their dissatisfaction with the organization at the Sofia council meeting, they backed away from the idea of CMEA's dissolution as suggested, for example, by the outspoken new finance minister of Czechoslovakia, Václav Klaus. The meeting brought to the fore the realization that the overhaul of CMEA—although an indispensable step toward integration with the Western world economy—would entail significant cost at least in the near future. Therefore, the compromise calling for the creation of an ad hoc committee charged with drawing a blueprint for putting CMEA relations on a new footing was reached.

The agreement has been prompted by Central European short-term economic considerations, as the use of world prices and convertible currencies in CMEA trade would impose severe costs on non-Soviet members. Therefore, all Central–East European CMEA members favored an incremental approach that would assure a transition cushioning the inevitable terms of trade shock. (For instance, Polish Solidarity prime minister Tadeusz Mazowiecki called for government guarantees of agreements "till 1995 to ensure stable supplies of raw materials and fuels" [Warsaw, PAP, 9 January].) With the switch to world prices and convertible currency, Moscow effectively rejected an incremental approach to dismantling the CMEA trade accounting system. Under these circumstances, it remains a puzzle what advantages CMEA members can derive from the organization.

Stability of trade agreements, a point raised by Mazowiecki in Sofia in January 1990 mainly in reference to Soviet supplies of energy and fuels, can be assured by bilateral intergovernmental arrangements outside the CMEA framework. Similarly, to integrate the economies of, say, Czechoslovakia, Poland, and Hungary, respective governments do not have to resort to CMEA channels. On the contrary, a much more effective method would be direct negotiations without interference of other CMEA members.

Another argument in favor of continued existence of CMEA relates to the intensity of trade links. When asked by a Hungarian radio reporter why a useless organization should be reformed instead of letting it fall apart, then Prime Minister Németh said:

> Because there are certain objective facts; it is enough if I refer to the area of raw material and energy deliveries, which vary from country to country, but by and large the closeness of economic links may be measured at around 50–70 percent. To switch this or shunt it over onto another rail belongs, I think, to the sphere of fantasy." (*FBIS-EEU*; 11 January.)

Indeed, CMEA has achieved a significant level of sufficiency—about 68 percent of their imported capital equipment, 96 percent of their petroleum and ferrous raw materials, and 65–80 percent of their nonferrous metals come from mutual deliveries (Warsaw, *Trybuna ludu*, 6 January). But these exchanges, organized around bilateral patterns, can be carried on without the bureaucratic structure of CMEA.

Moreover, a system of bilateral arrangements with CMEA is an impediment to developing links with international markets by forcing CMEA domestic producers to adjust to world standards. For instance, East Germany had a CMEA-sanctioned agreement to buy buses exclusively from Hungary (see *The Economist*, 31 March). Similar monopoly-type arrangements still exist for some products. Because they provide suppliers with no incentive to improve quality or to technologically update their products, their unraveling is an important step in creating an environment conducive to integration with the world economy.

CMEA economies have been unable to keep up with technological progress without Western im-

ports. Economic crisis and declining competitiveness compel CMEA members to seek ways of reintegrating with the world economy. This in turn calls for a rapid expansion of links with the West and a steep decrease in the level of CMEA's self-sufficiency.

Because of geographical proximity and the infrastructure in place, Central–East Europe will remain an important market for Soviet oil and other raw materials. The Soviets had a stake in keeping CMEA as a conduit for supplies of raw materials but only when they are supplied at subsidized prices. Moscow's motives, which were mostly political, will become economic once the transactions are conducted on a commercial base. Because the bulk of their CMEA exports is immediately salable in capitalist international markets, the Soviet Union will be an immediate beneficiary from normalizing CMEA trade relations, that is, putting them on the rules governing interaction in the world economy. Thus a linkage between the continued existence of CMEA and "the preservation of economic relations," as suggested by Béla Kádár, is tenuous at best.

Yet the Soviet delegation to the Sofia meeting of CMEA argued vehemently against CMEA's dissolution. (For an analysis of Soviet policies toward CMEA, see Bartlomiej Kaminski, "The Disintegration of Comecon: Can It Survive the Collapse of Command Economic Systems?" *Journal of Social and Behavioral Sciences*, forthcoming.) Soviet prime minister Nikolai Ryzhkov suggested that "we are integrated and interlinked to such an extent, that to destroy these [intra-CMEA] links today one would have to destroy one's whole economy" (Moscow, TASS International Service; *FBIS-SOV*, 11 January). This is a veiled threat; according to this interpretation, the disappearance of CMEA would amount to the termination of trade ties. This would be so only if the Soviet Union decided to cut its CMEA trade because there is nothing in the organization per se that would prevent individual countries from trading as usual even if CMEA offices in Moscow were closed (which would cut transaction costs). With the switch to world prices and convertible currency in their trade with CMEA members, the collapse of exports would also impose severe costs on its originator, the Soviet Union.

A final factor that keeps CMEA from dissolution is bureaucratic inertia. The organization was established not out of pressing economic need but out of political reasons. Over its 42-year existence, it has done little to integrate the economies of its members. With the transition away from artificial prices and the transferable ruble, Central–East European countries have no economic and political stakes in prolonging the existence of the organization. Although non-European members would like to see continued subsidies and assistance flowing from Central–East Europe, the Soviet Union will have little leverage to compel them to provide assistance. Therefore, whether Moscow likes it or not, the survival of the organization is no longer in its hands but depends on the actions taken in the capitals of East-Central European countries.

Bartlomiej Kaminski
University of Maryland at College Park

The Warsaw Treaty Organization, 1955–1990

The epochal events of 1990 are examined in other sections of the *Yearbook*: the unification of Germany; the rebellions of the union republics of the USSR; the reorientation of Poland, Czechoslovakia, and Hungary toward the European Community (EC) and the North Atlantic Treaty Organization (NATO) states; and the re-Balkanization of the Balkans. In November 1990 the Conference on Security and Cooperation in Europe (CSCE) represented the venue for adoption of a treaty on Conventional Forces in Europe (CFE) that established a post–cold war military balance in Europe and the Charter of Paris, a ten-point program reminiscent of Woodrow Wilson's Fourteen Points. To describe these changes as Warsaw Treaty Organization (WTO) developments makes no more sense than calling them Ottoman, Hapsburg, Hohenzollern, or Romanov developments.

If the Warsaw Pact had not actually collapsed in late 1989 it had certainly disappeared by the June 1990 session of the Political Consultative Committee. Four democratically elected noncommunist governments—Poland, Hungary, Czechoslovakia, and East Germany—constituted a voting majority of the seven-member communist military alliance. This majority lasted until October, by which time the Defense and Foreign ministries of the German Democratic Republic (GDR) had been merged into the bureaucracies of the Federal Republic. Before the disappearance of the National People's Army, the GDR defense minister was Rainer Epplemann, a clergyman who had previously led the pacifist movement in East Germany.

Georgi Arbatov, a Gorbachev adviser on East-West relations, summed up the essence of the summer of 1990 for the WTO by telling Western correspondents in June that "the Warsaw Pact is ceasing to exist like the Cheshire cat from Alice in Wonderland, but there are still some traces of the smile" (Colin McIntyre, "Warsaw Pact Dying or Already Dead, Diplomat Says," Reuters, 4 June, from Nexis). The smile that Arbatov was referring to was the temporary agreement of the East Germans, Czechs, Poles, and Hungarians to continue the life of the Warsaw Pact so that the WTO disarmament commission could maximize the influence of the Central Europeans on the CFE talks among 23 or 22 nations (depending on the number of Germanies). CFE had the mandate to negotiate in-theater parity between the bloc of NATO states and the bloc of WTO states. To conclude the CFE agreement, the WTO states met at a contentious arms control caucus in which the East European states tried to reduce the proportion of WTO forces made up of Soviet forces.

Once the CFE negotiations were concluded, the Central Europeans stopped smiling. By early November, the WTO members saw no point in continuing the debate over the survival of the Warsaw Pact. Representatives of the Warsaw Pact met for their last working session in mid-November of 1990 in Budapest. (*FBIS-EEU*, 16 November.) The meeting agreed to complete legal dissolution of the pact by 1 July 1991. The Council for Mutual Economic Assistance (CMEA) outlived the WTO by six weeks, surviving into early January of 1991 before its representatives agreed to disband their organization (*FBIS-SOV*, 8 January 1991).

Before the final working session, the Soviet commander of the WTO, P. G. Lushev; his chief of staff, V. N. Lobov; and Soviet defense minister D. T. Yazov made a series of arguments that by November had exhausted the patience of the new governments in Warsaw, Prague, and Budapest and even embarrassed the renamed communist regimes still in power in Bucharest and Sofia. The Soviet arguments included the following: (1) the Warsaw Pact remains a vital part of the European security system; (2) the WTO should not dissolve unless NATO is dissolved; (3) the two Germanies should not unite; (4) if they do unite, Germany should not be allowed to remain in NATO; (5) the Warsaw Pact should survive as a political counterweight to NATO in the aftermath of German unification and German membership in NATO. It should also continue to conduct joint military exercises. (See *FBIS-SOV*, 14, 16, 21 May, 4 June, 1, 8 August.)

During the intra-WTO debate in the summer of 1990 Czechoslovakia argued that a temporary preservation of the WTO could maximize the influence of the East Europeans on the creation of a post-CFE European security system. The Hungarians replied that the quickest way to create a new European system was to disband the Warsaw Pact as soon as the CFE treaty was concluded. But none of the East European members of the WTO, not even Bulgaria, supported the Soviet position that the Warsaw Pact should be preserved as long as NATO existed.

As the debate developed, the WTO gradually ceased its principal activity, conducting joint military exercises. There were several limited joint military exercises during the spring of 1990. (*FBIS-SOV*, 2 February; *FBIS-EEU*, 6, 9, 28 March.) The last scheduled WTO joint exercise—Soviet–East German maneuvers—were conducted in August as purely USSR maneuvers ("NVA Cancels Participation in Pact Exercises," *FBIS-EEU*, 19 July). In early October, Czechoslovakia, Poland, and Hungary rejected General Lobov's call for the resumption of joint WTO exercises (*FBIS-EEU*, 9 October).

The history of the Warsaw Pact in 1990 consists of a series of brief and slightly comic footnotes to the East European revolutions of 1989. The serious business of European security in 1990 was carried out through "2+4" talks on German unification, the 23 or 22 state negotiations over CFE, and the 35 or 34 government discussions over the CSCE Charter of Paris.

The CSCE documents constituted a legal end to the NATO–Warsaw Pact confrontation. The CFE treaty set equal limits to the overall number of specified types of military equipment that could be maintained in the Atlantic to Urals area by sixteen members of NATO and six members of the WTO. The key issue in the negotiation was the number of

weapons to be allocated to the USSR, which obtained approximately two-thirds of the total allotted to the six WTO states. This total was broken down into sublimits covering different military districts in the vast space between the Urals and Soviet borders with Eastern Europe. The gross totals are as follows:

Category	NATO	WTO	USSR
Battle tanks	20,000	20,000	13,150
Armored vehicles	30,000	30,000	20,000
Artillery pieces	20,000	20,000	13,700
Combat aircraft	6,800	6,800	5,150
Attack helicopters	2,000	2,000	1,500

SOURCE: ACDA, *Treaty on Conventional Armed Forces in Europe* (Washington, D.C., 1990), pp. 1–10.

The Charter of Paris attempted to lay the basis for a post–cold war order by establishing three new agencies based in Central Europe: a CSCE Secretariat in Prague to serve a newly created permanent council of the CSCE, an Office for Free Elections based in Warsaw, and a Conflict Resolution Center based in Vienna to deal with issues of military security. (After considerable debate over the selection of the proper host city, London became the location of the Western-backed European Bank for Reconstruction and Development, whose mission was financing postcommunist development in Eastern Europe.)

The CSCE session had seated a united Germany, the greatest economic power on the entire Eurasian continent. It did not seat the representatives of Lithuania, Latvia, or Estonia, who demanded recognition from Moscow of their status as independent sovereign states dating back to the same Versailles conference that had created modern Poland, Czechoslovakia, Hungary, and Austria. Warsaw, Prague, and Budapest extended de facto but not de jure recognition to the Baltic states. Both Prague and Budapest wanted to assure the completion of Soviet troop withdrawals; Warsaw was still negotiating over the timing of a Soviet troop pullout. As the USSR disintegrated, its former allies showed no more commitment to the preservation of the USSR than they had to the preservation of the Warsaw Pact.

CSCE had in effect charged Warsaw, Prague, Budapest, and Vienna with the task of constructing bridges linking Brussels with Moscow. Almost immediately, construction work on the new European order came to a halt because of the crisis in the Baltic states.

The Formal Dismantling of the Warsaw Pact. The January issue of *Voennaia mysl'* published an article (signed to the press 26 December 1989) by WTO commander in chief General of the Army P. G. Lushev. In this article the Warsaw Pact commander claimed that the guiding principle of the WTO remained "socialist internationalism, manifested most vividly and visibly in [the member states'] joint struggle against imperialism's aggressive policy and in the resolution of questions of joint protection of the gains of socialism and the prevention of war." (*JPRS*, 22 February.) Similar statements came from high-ranking Soviet officers until the conclusion of the CFE agreement. On the 45th anniversary of the WTO, Soviet defense minister Yazov and WTO commander Lushev argued that both NATO and the WTO should jointly build a new European security structure in a "common European home." They also argued that a united Germany should not be permitted to remain in NATO. (*FBIS-SOV*, 14 May.)

16 January–5 February. In Vienna, the highest-ranking NATO and WTO officers gathered for a three-week seminar on military doctrine scheduled before the revolutions of 1989. The original purpose of the seminar was to clarify Eastern understanding of NATO doctrines of forward defense and flexible response and Western understanding of Gorbachev's concept of "reasonable sufficiency." Instead, NATO states listened to East European delegations announce their intentions to adopt national military doctrines, restructure their armed forces to assert national control, and confine WTO cooperation to purely political matters, that is, the negotiation of a CFE agreement. According to one U.S. participant, between the formal sessions, East German participants at the seminar asked West German officers if they could try on West German uniforms. Soviet participants gave lectures on "reasonable sufficiency" and a defensive doctrine, one of whose critical requirements was substantial cuts in U.S. naval forces. (Interviews with staff members of the U.S. delegation to the Vienna doctrine talks. For coverage of the seminar see the January issue of *Defense and Disarmament Alternatives* 3, no. 1. See coverage of the seminar in Alan Riding, "Hungary Seeks Withdrawal of Soviet Forces in Two Years," *NYT*, 19 January. See also "Draft of New Military Doctrine Published," *Volks-*

armee, no. 50 [December 1989]; *JPRS-EEU*, 12 February. See also "Organization of Czechoslovak Army Revamped," *FBIS-SOV*, 8 February. See also "Vacek, Mohorita Discuss Democratization of Army," *FBIS-EEU*, 13 February; "[Bulgarian] Army Chief Announces Military Cuts," *FBIS-EEU*, 15 February; "[Polish] Defense Committee Adopts Defense Doctrine," *FBIS-EEU*, 26 February.)

February. A Polish debate began on whether Poland should delay seeking a Soviet military withdrawal until it receives legal assurances from a united Germany to respect the Oder-Neisse boundary (Roman Stefanowski, "Soviet Troops in Poland," RFE, *Report on East Europe* 1, no. 9 [3 March]. See also "Solidarity Daily on Benefits of Troop Presence," *FBIS-EEU*, 23 February; "Siwicki Speaks on Withdrawing Troops from Poland," *FBIS-EEU*, 16 February; "Daily Questions USSR Military Presence," *FBIS-EEU*, 10 April).

23 February. Foreign Minister Gyula Horn, a communist, suggested that Hungary might join NATO's political organization (*NYT*, 24 February).

26 February. A Soviet-Czechoslovak agreement on the withdrawal of the Central Group of Forces from Czechoslovakia by 1 July 1991 is signed (*FBIS-EEU*, 26 February. See also "Text of USSR-CSSR Troop Withdrawal Accord," *FBIS-SOV*, 5 March).

10 March. Soviet-Hungarian agreement on the total withdrawal of the Southern Group of Forces by 30 June 1991 is signed. Soviet troops began the withdrawal on 12 March. (*FBIS-EEU*, 13 March. See also *FBIS-EEU*, 12 March.)

17 March. At the meeting of the WTO Committee of Foreign Ministers (CFM), Eduard Shevardnadze was the only person opposing the membership of a unified Germany in NATO. All the East European members of the WTO supported both German unification and German membership in NATO. (*FBIS-EEU*, 19 March.) At the CFM session, Jiři Dienstbier of Czechoslovakia and Skubiszewski of Poland both affirmed support for Lithuania's declaration of independence (ibid., 11 March).

9 May. The Alliance of Free Democrats submitted a bill to the Hungarian National Assembly calling for Hungary's withdrawal from the Warsaw Pact (*FBIS-EEU*, 9 May. See also "Hungary's Warsaw Pact Membership Analyzed," *FBIS-EEU*, 16 May).

7 June. At a meeting of the Political Consultative Committee (PCC) in Moscow, the East Europeans rejected a Soviet draft communiqué. The Hungarians and Czechs later argued over which East European delegation deserved credit for the communiqué issued. (*FBIS-EEU*, 8, 21 June.) In any case, the PCC declared an end to the NATO–Warsaw Pact confrontation ("Pact Declaration Published," *FBIS-SOV*, 8 June). In subsequent statements President Václav Havel and Foreign Minister Dienstbier of Czechoslovakia emphasized the temporary preservation of the WTO as a device to maximize the influence of the Central Europeans on fashioning a new CSCE security system and for drawing the USSR into the new system (*NYT*, 13 June). Prime Minister József Antall of Hungary argued that the pact should be phased out as soon as the CFE talks were concluded so that his country and its neighbors could cooperate more fully with the European Community.

At the PCC session Gorbachev made an appeal to pact members to revitalize WTO by reorganizing its military structure and by emphasizing it as a political organization. The East Europeans, though polite, ignored him. (*FBIS-SOV*, 11 June.) Gorbachev's argument was that the WTO should continue to exist as long as NATO existed. Soviet journalists later attempted to present the "capture" of the WTO by the Central European democracies—all noncommunist—as a reason for resurrecting the alliance. ("Further Reportage on Warsaw Pact Meeting," *FBIS-SOV*, 11 June. See also "Advantages, Disadvantages of Warsaw Pact Viewed," *FBIS-SOV*, 28 June.)

The new missions for the Warsaw Pact, as defined by the dominant East European majority of Warsaw, Prague, East Berlin, and Budapest, were to (1) negotiate radical cuts at the Vienna talks on Conventional Forces in Europe (CFE) and (2) dissolve the WTO. (There was continued Czechoslovak-Hungarian disagreement on the proper timing of the Warsaw Pact demise). For the CFE negotiations, the PCC authorized an existing disarmament committee to work out the WTO position. This committee had been established in 1987 at the time of the adoption of the new "defensive doctrine." It also established a provisional committee to prepare plans for abolishing the WTO, to be approved by a PCC meeting in November. (The

PCC never bothered to meet in November; lower-level officials met on 14 November and announced the end of the WTO.)

Symbolic of the change in pact affairs were the actions of Soviet deputy foreign minister Yulii Kvitsinskii, who symbolically surrendered to the Czechs the rubber stamp used by the chairman of each PCC session (*FBIS-SOV*, 8, 11 June; *FBIS-EEU*, 8 June).

14 June. The Hungarian defense minister announced that Hungary will no longer participate in joint WTO exercises (*FBIS-EEU*, 12 July).

15 June. The last meeting of the WTO Committee of Defense Ministers took place (*FBIS-EEU*, 18 June).

18 June. Prime Minister Antall of Hungary announced that his country will not remain in the WTO (*JPRS-EEU*, 13 July).

27 June. The Hungarian Parliament voted to withdraw from the Warsaw Pact by the end of 1991 (*FBIS-SOV*, 3 July).

16 July. The provisional committee of the WTO met outside Prague for three days of talks on the future of the WTO (*FBIS-SOV*, 27 July. See also *FBIS-EEU*, 17, 18 July).

18 July. The National People's Army canceled all further joint military exercises with Soviet forces in Germany (*FBIS-EEU*, 18 July).

6 September. The Polish Senate (a largely ceremonial body) passed a resolution demanding that Soviet troops leave Poland as soon as possible. Foreign Minister Skubiszewski requested the initiation of Polish-Soviet negotiations on a complete USSR troop withdrawal. (Ibid.)

10–11 September. The WTO Disarmament Commission met in Bratislava. The USSR had demanded 80 percent of the total number of tanks, artillery, and aircraft to be allotted to the WTO under a CFE agreement. Warsaw, Prague, Budapest, Bucharest, and Sofia wanted to limit Moscow to a lower percentage (precise figure not available). NATO insisted that the Soviets receive no more than 66 percent. (RFE/RL, *Daily Report*, no. 172 [10 September]. See also *FBIS-EEU*, 27 September.)

14 September. CFE talks resumed in Vienna.

18 September. The provisional committee of the WTO met in Sofia and failed to agree on the future of the WTO. (*FBIS-SOV*, 19 September.)

18 September. The National People's Army (NVA) of the GDR formally ceased its membership in the WTO. The NVA officers terminated their service at the Moscow headquarters of the joint staff of the WTO. (*FBIS-SOV*, 19 September.)

22–23 September. The WTO Disarmament Commission met in Prague and failed to agree on a formula for allocating force levels under a prospective CFE agreement (*FBIS-SOV*, 21, 24 September).

27–30 September. Officials from the Defense and Foreign ministries of Warsaw, Prague, and Budapest met to coordinate security and military policy. The Soviets were deliberately excluded from the meeting. (*FBIS-SOV*, 24 September.)

2–4 October. In Bucharest, the last meeting of the WTO Military Council took place. The WTO commander, supported by the USSR and Romania, proposed continuing joint military exercises. Poland, Czechoslovakia, and Hungary rejected the proposal. (*FBIS-EEU*, 9 October.)

9 October. East Germany ceased its participation in the WTO Disarmament Commission (*FBIS-EEU*, 12 October).

4 November. The WTO Disarmament Commission endorsed the USSR-NATO formula for allocating the USSR some 13,150 of the WTO's 20,000 tanks; another 13,700 of the WTO's 20,000 artillery systems; 20,000 of the WTO's 30,000 armored personnel carriers; 5,150 of the WTO's 6,800 combat aircraft; and 1,500 of the WTO's 2,000 attack helicopters. At a press conference the Hungarian foreign minister, Géza Jeszenszky, refused to use the term Warsaw Pact and instead referred to "a group of states participating in the Vienna [CFE] talks." The Polish foreign minister, Krzysztof Skubiszewski, declared that Warsaw would no longer remain in the Warsaw Pact: "To have good relations, we don't need the Warsaw Pact. It will disappear because it no longer corresponds to the international situation existing in that part of Europe." (*NYT*, 4 November.)

14 November. Representatives of the six remaining WTO states met in Budapest and agreed to the complete legal dissolution of the military structure of the Warsaw Pact by 1 July 1991 (*FBIS-EEU*, 16 November).

An Obituary for the Warsaw Pact. The CSCE session of November 1990 had declared an end to the cold war. But although the cold war was over, its anomalies remained. At that time nearly as many people still lived under communist regimes as did at the beginning of 1989—in China, North Korea, Vietnam, Laos, Cambodia, Romania, Bulgaria, Albania, much of Yugoslavia, and even most parts of the USSR.

As historians fashion explanations for the end of the cold war in 1989–1990, they will undoubtedly renew unresolved debates about the origins of the cold war. In retrospect, the phrase *cold war* may be understood as an imprecise term for a global Soviet-U.S. military confrontation. From the perspective of 1990, events previously located at the center of the cold war—the Chinese civil war of 1945–1949, the Korean War, the Vietnam conflict, the wars in Laos and Cambodia—appear to have been East Asian wars irrelevant to the outcome of the global Soviet-U.S. military standoff. The armed conflicts in Angola, Mozambique, Ethiopia, Somalia, Nicaragua, and Central America appear in retrospect to have been even less important to the outcome of the cold war.

Why the Soviet-U.S. military confrontation began and ended is usually addressed as a global question because the cold war conferred vital strategic significance on places that happened to be located near disputed areas: Korea, Laos, Mozambique, Grenada, the Greenland-Iceland–United Kingdom gap, El Salvador, Somalia. Asking the more modest questions of when and where the cold war began and ended, however, yields a surprisingly clear answer: Eastern Europe.

During the 1989–1990 period indigenous communist parties fell from power in Poland, Hungary, East Germany, and Czechoslovakia but not Romania, Bulgaria, Yugoslavia, or Albania; the two Germanies united; the USSR agreed to withdraw its troops from Eastern Europe; the Warsaw Pact disintegrated; a CFE agreement codified a tremendous reduction in the East-West military equipment in Europe, concluding negotiations begun in 1973; and the United States and the USSR almost concluded a strategic arms reduction treaty (START) under negotiation since the early 1980s.

What precipitated the events of 1989–1990 was Mikhail Gorbachev's decision to reverse a 73-year policy of using armed force—whether the Workers' and Peasants' Red Army, the Soviet Army, or the Warsaw Pact—to crush the political opponents of the "ethnic" communist parties of the non-Russian union republics and people's democracies that made up what Brezhnev had called "the socialist commonwealth" (*sotsialisticheskoe sodruzhestvo*) (*YICA*, 1989). According to this argument, the Warsaw Pact since its inception had been primarily concerned with keeping East European communist parties in power.

This explanation of course overlooks the issues at the center of East-West strategic analysis: capacity for massive retaliation; flexible response; no "first use"; the air-land battle; Strategic Arms Limitation Talks (SALT) I and II and START; Soviet military strategy as a doctrine for fighting and winning a nuclear war; the USSR "conventional option" for a European war, featuring operational maneuver groups; Marshal Ogarkov's high-technology non-nuclear theater warfare; the balance of intermediate-range nuclear forces (INF) and the impact of the INF treaty; and emerging technologies including the Strategic Defense Initiative.

The above formulation also overlooks the great strategic issues of 1988: the impact of the INF treaty on nuclear deterrence and the enhanced importance of British and French nuclear forces; CFE negotiations that made nuclear arms control look like simplicity itself; the use of exotic technologies for "discriminate deterrence"; and the impending demographic imbalance between NATO and the Warsaw Pact.

But the thesis of "keeping communist parties in power" does focus on the fact that all the strategic issues disappeared in 1989–1990 with the collapse of communism in East-Central Europe and the unification of Germany. There were no compelling economic or strategic-military reasons for the Soviets not to agree to the rapid withdrawal of their garrisons from the region. The USSR military presence appears to have disappeared because its political mission, maintaining the leading role of ethnic communist parties in East-Central Europe, had disappeared.

This argument does not deny that the costs, dangers, deployments, and actual conflicts of the cold war were global in scope. It proposes instead that this conflict was the unintended consequence of the peculiar political, conventional, and nuclear dynamics of the Soviet-U.S. confrontation in East-Central Europe.

That analysis also argued that the revocation of the Soviet security guarantee to ruling ethnic parties was the unforeseen result of Gorbachev's effort to construct a "common European home" (*YICA*, 1989). In this region between the Atlantic and the Urals, Gorbachev hoped to resolve the socio-economic problems of the CMEA states by shifting both Eastern and Western economic resources from the East-West arms race to the revitalization of the economies and societies of the socialist commonwealth. The critical requirement for construction of the common European home became the renunciation of the use of Soviet armed force in East-Central European affairs, which Gorbachev pledged on several occasions: in Prague 10 April 1987, in Belgrade 18 March 1988, in Strasbourg to the Council of Europe 6 July 1989, and, finally, his most unconditional pledge in Helsinki 26 October 1989.

According to this analysis, the military dimension of Gorbachev's common European home was the revised WTO doctrine of "reasonable sufficiency" promulgated by the PCC session of 1987. The events of 1989 revealed the military-political contradictions of "reasonable sufficiency": for the Warsaw Pact, the price of peace with the nations of Western Europe proved to be the virtual surrender of the nations of East-Central Europe.

The practical application of the Gorbachev doctrine of reasonable sufficiency appears to have broken the previous linkage among the maintenance of communist regimes in East-Central Europe, the division of Germany, the NATO–Warsaw Pact military standoff in Europe, and the Soviet-U.S. global nuclear confrontation. If so, the question arises as to how the previous WTO strategy—which can perhaps be described as the Grechko doctrine of "unreasonable sufficiency"—had for decades linked these four issues together. The section below offers an explanation.

The origins and outcomes of unreasonable sufficiency. After the Federal Republic of Germany (FRG) joined NATO in early May 1955, the Soviets retaliated by forming the Warsaw Pact on 14 May and then promoting the East German barracks police to the status of National People's Army (January 1956). Possessing a national military force gave the GDR the symbol of sovereignty enjoyed by the other people's democracies.

Sandwiched between the entry of the FRG into NATO and the creation of the WTO was the hastily concluded Austrian state treaty, a USSR effort to prevent a fusion of pan-German issues with the Soviet-NATO confrontation. The Austrian state treaty secured the withdrawal of Moscow's troops from Austria in return for Vienna's pledge not to join NATO or to merge politically with the FRG.

But in finalizing the status of the GDR as a separate German and socialist state, the Soviets also fused the chronic threat posed by the instability of East-Central European regimes to the recurring question of German reunification. From 1956 to 1961 the response of the GDR to its new status as a permanent part of the East-Central European system was a mass flight of its population to West Germany through Berlin, legally an open city under four-power occupation.

The size and composition of this frantic emigration was so great that it threatened the survival of the GDR. Khrushchev's repeated failures to find a diplomatic solution to the Berlin crisis finally ended with the construction of the Berlin Wall, a barrier that East and West eventually came to regard as a distasteful but useful device to stabilize inner-German relations and interalliance tensions.

During the same period (1955 to 1961) East-Central Europe as a whole also experienced tremendous turmoil. In October 1956 the communist party and the army in Poland almost went to war against the USSR over the installation of Wladyslaw Gomulka as the new leader of the Polish party. In November 1956, the Hungarians rose up in an anticommunist revolt that the Soviet army had to suppress.

In 1957, Tito launched a second Yugoslav campaign against Soviet hegemony over the world communist movement. During 1959–1961 the Albanians broke with the USSR, carried out a de facto withdrawal from the Warsaw Pact, and won Chinese support for their stand against the USSR.

In the early 1960s the Romanians vocally rejected Khrushchev's plans for the economic integration of the USSR and East-Central Europe; Bucharest even had the temerity to pose as a mediator between the Soviet Union and China.

From the late 1950s to the early 1960s, the independent communist states of Yugoslavia and Albania (a WTO member de jure until 1968) began modernizing their "territorial defense doctrines." The Romanians undertook similar measures, and the Polish military sought to establish an independent front within the Warsaw Pact. These efforts to adopt independent national military doctrines posed a threat to the internal cohesion of the Warsaw Pact.

During the East-Central European and inner-German crises of 1955–1961, the NATO allies armed the Bundeswehr and encouraged it to assume the role of NATO's premier conventional force. At the same time, the United States carried out extensive deployments of strategic and tactical nuclear weapons systems throughout Europe. These systems were supported by even more powerful nuclear weapons based in North America and at sea.

In sum, by 1961 the "German question" had fused with the problem of political instability in East-Central Europe, the risk of conventional war with NATO, and the threat of nuclear war with the United States.

In the period after the formation of the Warsaw Pact, the USSR lacked a declaratory military doctrine that addressed the interlocking security problems the USSR faced in Europe. In 1960, Khrushchev announced a new Soviet military doctrine based on the primacy of nuclear weapons in both theater and global conflicts. The elaboration of the new doctrine was codified in the 1962 volume *Military Strategy*, edited by Marshal V. D. Sokolovsky, former chief of the Soviet General Staff.

The doctrine of unreasonable sufficiency. The doctrine promulgated during the 1960–1962 period sought simultaneous solutions to the military-political problems of political instability in East-Central Europe, the movement toward independent military doctrines by WTO members, the possible revival of the German question, and the military-technical demands of conventional conflict with NATO and nuclear war with the Americans. By the time Gorbachev came to power, this doctrine had proven to be one of "unreasonable sufficiency."

If any one Soviet figure deserves to be associated with this doctrine, which remained in effect until 1987, it is Marshal A. A. Grechko, commander of the Warsaw Pact from 1960 to 1967 and Soviet minister of defense from 1967 to 1976. This doctrine squarely faced up to two military-political requirements: (1) The necessity for Soviet conventional forces sufficient to intimidate and repress political upheaval in East-Central Europe and to prevent de facto withdrawals from the WTO such as that carried out by Albania and (2) the necessity for sufficient Soviet military forces to intimidate both Germanies and enforce the continued separation of the FRG and the GDR.

But Soviet conventional military power sufficient to meet these military-political requirements generated two additional military-technical problems. First the credibility of the Soviet threat to both Germanies required negating the NATO doctrine of forward defense of the West German border. This in turn required a Soviet capability for conventional victory over the whole of NATO Europe. The Soviets had to win this victory quickly or not at all, for in a long war of conventional attrition NATO's superior economic resources would probably prevail. (See Harriet Fast Scott and William F. Scott, *Soviet Military Doctrine: Continuity, Formulation and Dissemination* [Boulder, Colo.: Westview, 1989], pp. 28–43. Michael MccGwire, in *Military Objectives in Soviet Foreign Policy* [Washington, D.C.: Brookings, 1987]; William T. Lee and Richard F. Staar, *Soviet Military Policy since World War II* [Stanford: Hoover Institution Press, 1986].)

From the Soviet point of view, a credible conventional threat to the FRG was not a bid for overturning the status quo but a necessary condition for preserving it. The Soviets objected to the U.S./NATO commitment to the FRG because it undercut the credibility of the Soviet capacity to enforce the division of Germany.

The second problem was that the credibility of the Soviet conventional threat to NATO in Europe in turn required the negation of the U.S. nuclear guarantee to NATO's conventional forces as expressed in the doctrines of "massive retaliation" and "flexible response." The Soviets sought to negate the U.S. nuclear guarantee by successive combinations of nuclear war–fighting doctrines in Europe, by putting the U.S. homeland at risk of nuclear devastation, and by arms control agreements that called into question the credibility of the U.S. doctrine of flexible response. From the USSR point of view, deterrence of nuclear war required unilateral Soviet deterrence of the limited use of U.S. nuclear weapons, above all in the European theater. During the era of U.S. nuclear superiority at the theater and global levels, the only way the Soviets could make a reasonably plausible claim of neutralizing U.S. nuclear superiority was to adopt declaratory strategies of preemptive attack or launch under attack.

As the USSR approached global nuclear parity, such claims became highly provocative in the European theater, particularly because of Soviet conventional superiority. Once the USSR had achieved undisputed nuclear parity, as recognized by the SALT II treaty of 1979, Soviet leaders let the fact of parity speak for the neutralization of U.S. nuclear

forces. In public, they took the position of abjuring the first use of nuclear weapons. (Scott and Scott, *Soviet Military Doctrine*, pp. 124–25.)

The Americans, not the Soviets, were responsible for the globalization of European security policy. Under the doctrines of "massive retaliation" and "flexible response," the United States attempted to offset the regional Soviet advantage in European theater conventional forces with a global threat of nuclear retaliation. The U.S. policy was based in part on what one author has called "hegemony on the cheap" (David Calleo, *Beyond American Hegemony* [New York: Basic Books, 1987], pp. 41–43), that is, a primarily fiscal decision to substitute "cheap" nuclear weapons for the expensive conventional forces needed for conventional deterrence of a Soviet attack on Europe.

But the underlying logic for U.S. reliance on global nuclear deterrence as the solution for NATO's security problem probably grew out of the U.S. understanding of the political reasons for U.S. participation in two world wars. Americans had come to believe that a battle for domination of Europe was in fact the central front of a battle for world domination.

Thus it made sense to Washington, from both strategic and fiscal standpoints, to regard nuclear deterrence in Europe as tantamount to deterring a world war. Not to commit U.S. nuclear weapons to deterring a Soviet attack on Europe was seen as the equivalent of a U.S. invitation to Moscow to conquer NATO by conventional means.

For the USSR, the dynamic of the Soviet-U.S. global deterrence since 1960 maintained a gross and irrational disproportion between the limited, conservative political objectives of the USSR in the European theater and the apocalyptic military means employed to pursue these objectives. The globalization of Soviet security policy in Europe also brought with it two additional problems. Globalization replicated in regions of slight political importance to the USSR the same gross disproportion between military means and political ends. It also risked importing Third World Soviet-U.S. military conflicts into Europe because the logic of global nuclear war had transformed Europe from the primary political arena of East-West conflict into the globe's decisive military theater by virtue of the concentration of enormous conventional and nuclear firepower in East-Central Europe.

Every high-level Soviet critique of NATO policy over the last 35 years has presented this analysis of the Soviet security dilemma, albeit in a polemical and vitriolic fashion that has obscured the underlying contradictions of Soviet policy. The official line has been that the peace-loving Warsaw Pact states sought only to preserve the post–World War II status quo. According to the Soviets, "revanchist forces" in the FRG sought to change "the territorial and political realities" of postwar Europe. Germany's imperialist ally, the United States, immensely aggravated the security threat to the WTO by organizing a global anti-Soviet coalition that planned to use U.S. nuclear weapons, especially in Europe. (See I. I. Iakubovskii [WTO commander, 1967–1975], *Boevoe sodruzhestvo bratskikh armii i narodov* [Moscow: Voenizdat, 1975], chaps. 1–3; V. G. Kulikov [WTO commander, 1975–1988], *Varshavskii dogovor—soiuz vo imiia mira i sotsializma* [Moscow: Voenizdat, 1982], chap. 2; V. G. Kulikov, *Nadezhnyi shchit mira i sotsializma* [Moscow: Voenizdat, 1985], chap. 3.)

Until the Gorbachev era, a gingerly understated component of this analysis was that political upheavals in East-Central Europe played directly into the hands of German revanchists and U.S. imperialists intent on reversing the results of World War II. (These arguments were restated in a 1985 article by WTO commander V. G. Kulikov, "Varshavskii dogovor na strazhe mira i sotsialisticheskikh zavoevanii," *Novaia i noveishaia istoriia*, no. 2 [1985].) Since Gorbachev came to power, authoritative Soviet military spokesmen have bluntly pointed out the connection between political instability in East-Central Europe and NATO's alleged strategic objectives (M. E. Monin in G. V. Sredin, ed., *Internatsional'nyi kharakter zashchity sotsialisticheskogo otechestva* [Moscow: Voenizdat, 1988], pp. 168–69).

During the 1960s and 1970s, when Grechko was in office, Soviet military doctrine provided a unilateral military solution to the security problems faced by the USSR in both halves of Europe. The solution provided by Grechko's declaratory doctrine was that of assuming a conventional nuclear offensive posture against East-Central Europe, both Germanies, NATO, and the United States.

This offensive posture, enshrined in a common WTO doctrine, also preempted independent East-Central European capabilities for the defense of national territory. The East-Central European states that had adopted such doctrines of "territorial defense" (Yugoslavia, Albania, and Romania) denied the USSR use of their national military forces and territories to enhance the WTO threat to NATO.

There was, however, a basic military-political contradiction within the doctrine of unreasonable sufficiency. As the 1962 doctrinal compilation edited by Marshal Sokolovsky pointed out, the center of gravity of the political conflict (Eastern and Central Europe) did not coincide with the center of gravity of the military conflict (the global nuclear forces of the United States and the USSR). (See V. D. Sokolovsky, ed., *Military Strategy: Soviet Doctrine and Concepts* (New York: Praeger, 1963), pp. 203–4.) In short, the decisive arenas for the pursuit of the USSR's European security objectives were the global nuclear confrontation with the United States and the continental confrontation with NATO.

Similarly, maintaining the Soviet military forces necessary to keep communist parties in power in East-Central Europe and to keep the two Germanies divided did not make unreasonable demands on USSR economic resources. The primary requirement for Soviet military intervention in East-Central Europe was preempting organized resistance, a requirement that could be met through imposing a common doctrine on the WTO states.

But the requirements of inflicting a rapid conventional defeat on NATO in the event of the outbreak of war on German soil and of neutralizing the U.S. nuclear guarantee to NATO committed the USSR to a perpetual global arms race with NATO and the United States. In this arms race, the U.S. strategy was to shift the terms of the competition into exotic technologies that the Soviets found ruinously expensive. (Matthew Evangelista, *Innovation and the Arms Race* [Ithaca, N.Y.: Cornell University Press, 1988].) In this global confrontation, areas of little intrinsic importance acquired significance because of their relationship to the overall global balance.

It should be noted that after 1960 most of the time, energy, and money of the USSR Ministry of Defense was dedicated to matching or surpassing the military power of the United States and its allies and to confronting the United States and its allies at points across the globe. At the same time, what drove Soviet military policy in Europe was not a USSR political objective of defeating the West on its own soil or the soil of Third World battlegrounds.

Instead, Soviet military policy in Europe was fueled by the military-technical requirement of undercutting the NATO doctrines of forward defense and flexible response. This military requirement developed out of the political requirement of guaranteeing the division of Germany as well as the security of the ruling East-Central European communist parties, including the Socialist Unity Party of the GDR.

The contradiction between the limited, conservative political objectives of the USSR in Europe and the global nuclear challenge the Soviets posed to the United States (in response to the U.S. policy of globalizing the NATO–Warsaw Pact confrontation) accounts for the contradictions between Soviet military and political policies in Europe from 1955 to 1985.

Soviet diplomacy sought the codification of the European status quo (see Robin Remington, *The Warsaw Pact* [Cambridge, Mass.: MIT Press, 1969] and Raymond L. Garthoff, *Detente and Confrontation: American-Soviet Relations from Nixon to Reagan* [Washington, D.C.: Brookings Institution, 1985], chaps. 4, 9, 10, 14), whereas Soviet military programs attempted to neutralize the Western military forces that NATO deployed in defense of the same status quo. The best examples of this contradiction are seen during the early 1970s, when Grechko was Soviet defense minister. During this period the USSR simultaneously pursued the following policies:

- A massive buildup of Soviet conventional forces in Europe, mainly through the establishment of the Central Group of Forces in Czechoslovakia but also through extensive modernization. This buildup considerably enhanced the Soviet threat to both Eastern and Western Europe.
- The pursuit of *Ostpolitik* with the Federal Republic and détente with Western Europe.
- The negotiation of the Helsinki Final Act of 1975 in an effort to codify the European status quo.
- The buildup of Soviet theater nuclear forces as an effort, in conjunction with the SALT I and II treaties, to undermine the credibility of flexible response.

The inherent tension between the military and political dimensions of Soviet doctrine during the 1960s and early to mid-1970s was partly hidden by the fact that during this period Soviet nuclear and conventional capabilities did not match the requirements of doctrine.

The self-destruction of unreasonable sufficiency. In the late 1970s, following Grechko's death, Soviet military capabilities finally began to match doctrinal requirements, and the doctrine of unreasonable sufficiency proved self-defeating in regard to its military and political objectives. Grechko's unilateral military solution to the USSR's political problems in Eastern and Central Europe produced three counterproductive military results.

The first is what Soviet analysts writing during the Gorbachev era have called "self-encirclement." That is, the USSR provoked the formation of a global anti-Soviet coalition consisting of all the states threatened by USSR global capabilities, including China and Japan. By Soviet accounts, this coalition possessed four or five times the economic and technological resources of the Soviet bloc. The costs of conducting an arms race against this anti-Soviet coalition wreaked enormous damage to the Soviet economy. (Viacheslav Dashichev, "The Search for New East-West Relations," *Literaturnaia gazeta*, 18 May 1988 in *CDSP* 40, no. 24 [13 July 1988].)

Second, Grechko's doctrine accepted the U.S. strategy of globalizing the NATO-WTO confrontation and shifting the terms of the European standoff to a competition in high technology. The Americans thus were able to "set the rules of the game," a frequent complaint lodged against U.S. policymakers by Soviet analysts. (Ye. Primakov, "A New Philosophy of Foreign Policy," *Pravda*, 10 July 1987 in *CDSP* 39, no. 28 [12 August 1987].)

The Americans constantly forced the Soviets to validate their European strategy by countering the U.S. global strategies and new technologies aimed at vulnerable Soviet flanks inside and outside Europe. This meant that the pursuit of limited objectives in Europe required a global military posture based on high technology. To be sure, the acquisition of a global military capability supported Soviet security objectives in regions outside Europe. But this benefit came at the cost of importing risks in these regions into the European security equation. (Ibid.)

Third, Grechko's doctrine set in motion a recurring and futile cycle of conventional and nuclear strategies. USSR conventional capabilities in Europe provoked a U.S. nuclear war–fighting strategy aimed at Soviet forces both in Europe and throughout the USSR. The Soviets responded with nuclear war–fighting capabilities aimed at Western Europe and North America. Fear of nuclear war drove both sides toward arms control policies based on mutual nuclear deterrence.

The Soviets found that mutual deterrence at the nuclear level implied mutual paralysis at the conventional level in Europe. This paralysis undercut the validity of the Soviet security guarantee to the ruling East-Central European parties. This realization forced the Soviets to reaffirm a conventional option for the European theater. The Americans then responded with new concepts of nuclear war fighting and even more exotic conventional technologies. The cycle then repeated itself.

Politically, the Grechko security program for Europe had the unintended effect of generating a permanent political requirement for large Soviet conventional forces in Eastern and Central Europe. This was because the USSR security guarantee to the communist regimes of East-Central Europe freed these regimes from the responsibility of efficiently managing their economies and societies.

The inherent deficiencies of Leninist central planning compounded the irresponsibility of the East-Central European leaders. As Valerie Bunce argued in an article aptly titled "The Empire Strikes Back" (*International Organization*, Winter 1984/85), the more inept the East-Central European leaders, the greater the claims they were able to make on Soviet resources. Their open dependence on the Soviet Union further compounded the crisis of legitimacy suffered by these parties.

The mismanagement of East-Central European affairs by leaders protected through the Soviet security guarantee perpetuated the crises of instability in the region. Political instability perpetuated the need for large Soviet conventional forces. The credibility of these forces in turn required perpetual challenges to the NATO doctrines of forward defense and flexible response.

By 1985 the Grechko legacy had revealed that there were no permanent military solutions to the linked problems of political instability in East-Central Europe, the "German question," and the confrontation with the military allies of the FRG. Grechko's military solution had only compounded the underlying socioeconomic causes of instability in East-Central Europe and had fused these volatile processes to a global arms race that promised economic ruin in peacetime and catastrophe in war.

Gorbachev and his advisers began a search for political solutions to the linked problems of instability in East-Central Europe, the division of Germany, and the NATO-WTO confrontation. The transition between the Grechko and Gorbachev solutions to the USSR's European security dilemma required a new USSR-WTO military doctrine. This emerged in 1987 as the doctrine of "reasonable sufficiency." In 1989–1990 the practical application of the new doctrine brought about the collapse of communism in East-Central Europe, the unification of the Germanies, the end of the Warsaw Pact, and the conclusion of the cold war.

Christopher Jones
University of Washington

International Communist Organizations

WORLD MARXIST REVIEW

The *World Marxist Review* (*WMR*), since its 1958 inception the only permanent institutional symbol of unity for the world's pro-Moscow and independent communist parties, shut down on 15 May after having produced issue no. 5–6 (May–June) of 1990 (*YICA*, 1990; *Pravda*, 23 May). During the first four and a half months of the year, this theoretical monthly, controlled by the International Department of the Communist Party of the Soviet Union, had developed into a true forum of debate for Marxist issues, a trend that had been noted since 1988 (*YICA*, 1989, 1990). Extremes ranged from the March issue's reprint of Fidel Castro's dogmatic speech of December 1989 entitled "Socialism or Death" to the April issue's carrying a Zbigniew Brzezinski article that criticized the Marxist underpinnings of the Soviet regime. Still, there was enough specific "new thinking" on its pages to cause a Japanese Communist Party spokesman to reiterate in the spring his organization's traditional complaint that the *WMR* was nothing more than a Soviet mouthpiece (*Report on Eastern Europe*, 1 June; *YICA*, 1984). Nevertheless it is ironic that just as this magazine of 68 communist parties reached its high point of pluralistic debate, it went out of business, with its officials claiming that circulation had dropped to "zero" (from an estimated high of more than 500,000) (*Report on Eastern Europe*, 1 June).

The magazine's closure was more likely the result of the Soviets' inability or unwillingness to control its Czech hosts, especially because the Czech government announced its intention of ousting such Soviet-line fronts as the World Federation of Trade Unions, the International Organization of Journalists, and the International Union of Students. These, like the *WMR*, were all headquartered in Prague (see below). It has been alleged that the Soviets, who furnished more than half of the 400 persons once on the *WMR* staff, were, along with the Mongolians, the only financial supporters of the magazine at the end (*NYT*, 3 July). In any case, the Czechs appear to have presided over its demise: Lubomír Molnar took over from Aleksandr Subbotin as the first non-Soviet chief editor early in the year; at the time of its closing Jaroslav Preček was identified as the magazine's "liquidator" (ibid.; *Report on Eastern Europe*, 1 June).

FRONT ORGANIZATIONS

Introduction. Despite the continued decline of direct Soviet confrontation with the West or, more accurately, with the developed capitalist countries, not a single major Soviet-line international front formed during the 25-year period following World War II and calling itself a "closely cooperating nongovernmental organization" (see chart 1) is known to have gone out of business, although the major ones have reduced the size of their operations (*YICA*, 1990). Five of them held their highest level meetings during the twelve-month period from February 1990 to January 1991:

- World Peace Council (WPC), Triennial, Athens, February
- International Association of Democratic Lawyers (IADL), Thirteenth Congress, Barcelona, March
- World Federation of Trade Unions (WFTU), Twelfth World Trade Union Congress, Moscow, November
- World Federation of Democratic Youth (WFDY), Thirteenth General Assembly, Athens, December
- International Organization of Journalists (IOJ), Eleventh Congress, Harare, January (1991)

This is about average for the period because such meetings are usually held every three or four years and we have identified eighteen such organizations.

In addition, at least six new types of front or semifronts formed since 1980 and characterized by official communist sources as "new social movements" and by British commentator Clive Rose as "Soviet-influenced organizations" were noted as having held major meetings during the year (*WMR*, December 1986; Clive Rose, *The Soviet Propaganda Network* [London: Pinter, 1988]): International Foundation for the Survival and Development of Mankind (cosponsored meeting in Moscow, January), International Trade Union Committee for Peace and Disarmament (Copenhagen, May), International Teachers for Peace (Budapest, June), Peace Wave Action Committee (worldwide, August), International Physicians for the Prevention of Nuclear War (Coventry, September; Bonn, October), and International Association of Lawyers Against Nuclear Arms (Berlin, November). These, plus the aforenoted major meetings and additional minor ones of the traditional fronts held during the year, suggest that the Soviets have not given up on "citizens' diplomacy" as a means of promoting their policies.

That at least the traditional fronts still reflect Soviet policies or the Soviet environment became increasingly clear during 1990 in at least three ways: (1) as the East European nations slipped away from Soviet control, they loosened or broke their ties with these fronts; (2) as the Soviets stressed securing of financial assistance and technical aid from the developed nations at the expense of supporting "liberation struggles" and economic development in the Third World, these fronts have tended to decentralize so that the Soviets could more easily concentrate on their new interests; and (3) as the Soviets continue to criticize themselves for past political rigidities, the traditional fronts have also (especially for their past support for now discredited Soviet policies). The new type of front tended to be weak on Eastern Europe (as distinct from the Soviet Union) and directed against developed capitalist countries from the beginning. Not having a pre-1980 history, however, there was less need for self-criticism.

Two issues arise here with respect to the traditional fronts. First, to what extent are their self-criticisms sincere and to what extent are they merely meant to garner aid from the developed countries? Second, to what extent are the anti-Western positions (especially those promoted by

Chart 1: Major International Communist Front Organizations (Traditional)*

Organization (president, general secretary, or equivalent)	Year founded	Headquarters	Claimed membership[†]	Affiliates	Countries
Afro-Asian Peoples' Solidarity Organization (AAPSO) (Murad Ghalib, Nuri Abd-al-Razzaq Husayn)	1957	Cairo	no data	87	no data
Asian Buddhist Conference for Peace (ABCP) (Kharkhuu Gaadan, G. Lubsan Tseren)	1970	Ulan Bator	no data	15	12
Berlin Conference of European Catholics (BCEC) (Franco Leonori, Hubertus Guske)	1965	Berlin	no data	no data	45
Christian Peace Conference (CPC) (Richard Andriamanjato, Kenyon Wright)[1]	1958	Prague	no data	no data	ca. 80
Continental Organization of Latin American Students (OCLAE) (Jorge Arias Diaz, Angel Arzuaga Reyes)	1966	Havana	no data	34	26
International Association of Democratic Lawyers (IADL) (Stefano Rodota,[2] Amar Bentoumi)	1946	Brussels	25,000	no data	ca. 101[3]
International Federation of Resistance Movements (FIR) (Arnaldo Banfi, Alex Lhote)	1951	Vienna	5,000,000	78	27
International Institute for Peace (IIP) (Erwin Lanc, Max Schmidt)	1957	Vienna	no data	no data	no data
International Organization of Journalists (IOJ) (Armando Rollemberg, Gerard Gatinot)[4]	1946	Prague	ca. 260,000[5]	101[5]	90[5]
International Radio and Television Organization (OIRT)	1946	Prague	no data	29	23
International Union of Students (IUS) (Josef Scala, Georgios Michaelides)	1946	Prague	40,000,000	117	110
Organization of Solidarity of the Peoples of Africa, Asia, and Latin America (OSPAALA) (Susumu Ozaki? Rene Anillo Capote)	1966	Havana	no data	no data	no data
Women's International Democratic Federation (WIDF) (Freda Brown)	1945	Berlin	200,000,000	142	124
World Federation of Democratic Youth (WFDY) (a South African, a Hungarian)[6]	1945	Budapest	150,000,000	ca. 270	123
World Federation of Scientific Workers (WFSW) (Jean-Marie Legay, Stan Davison)	1946	London	1,000,000+	ca. 46	70+
World Federation of Teachers' Unions (FISE) (Lesturuge Ariyawansa, Gérard Montant)	1946	Berlin	26,000,000+	ca. 150	79
World Federation of Trade Unions (WFTU) (Ibrahim Zakariya, Aleksandr Zharikov)[7]	1945	Prague	214,000,000	92	81
World Peace Council (WPC) (Evangelos Maheras, Ray Stewart)[8]	1950	Helsinki	no data	no data	145

* All those ever noted as having attended meetings of the "closely coordinating nongovernmental organizations" (*YICA*, 1990)

[†] As of 1989. These and the figures on affiliates and countries do not take into consideration East European (and other) defections or 1990 additions because the full extent of either is presently unknown.

[1] Prague, *CPC Information*, 28 June
[2] Paris, *Est et Ouest*, December
[3] U.N. Economic and Social Council, Congo, E/C 2, 1991, Add. 1, 9 August.
[4] Harare, SAPA, 30 January 1991; *FBIS*, 1 February 1991
[5] U.N. Economic and Social Council, Congo, E/C 2, 1991, Add. 2, 2 September.
[6] Athens, *Rizospastis*, 12 December. The names of the officeholders were not given.
[7] Moscow, *Trud*, 21 November
[8] Helsinki, *Peace Courier*, no. 3 (March)

Third World elements) considered by the Soviets to be useful pressure on the developed nations and to what extent are they viewed as likely to endanger the receipt of foreign aid? The foreign aid question is perhaps most germane in the case of Cuba, which is certainly less "reformed" than the USSR, anxious to play on the residual anti-U.S. feelings of many Latin Americans, and a major beneficiary of the front decentralization process. But, as we will see below, it is also applicable to the Libyans as well as Indian and French leftists.

Eastern Europe: Undesired Disconnection.
Late in the year it was announced that the Czech government had asked the WFTU, the International Union of Students (IUS), and the IOJ to vacate their Prague headquarters by May or June 1991 (Prague, ČTK, 5 October; *FBIS*, 10 October; Prague, *Svobodné slovo*, 6 December; Helsinki, *Sanomalehtimes*, c. 12 December). An initially unconfirmed report in April indicated that the Women's International Democratic Federation (WIDF) was also to be forced out of its East Berlin headquarters; this was confirmed by the WIDF statement that a decision on a new headquarters location would be made at its March 1991 congress in Sheffield (New York, *People's Daily World*, 18 April; Berlin, *Women of the Whole World*, no. 6). It appears that the two East European–based religious fronts, the Christian Peace Conference (CPC, Prague) and the Berlin Conference of European Catholics (BCEC, Berlin), are being allowed to stay put for the present and that the WFDY will remain in Budapest.

Withdrawal, wholly or in part, of East European national affiliates from their respective international fronts has reached a serious level. Two extremes here with respect to the WPC are Romania, which was unique in sending only an observer to the February Athens WPC meeting, and Bulgaria, which emerged from that meeting as the only East European nation with representation at either the policy or the working level (in fact, it had positions on both) (Session of the WPC, Athens, 6–11 February 1991, *Documents* [Helsinki: WPC Information Center, 1991]; Helsinki, *Peace Courier*, no. 2). The German Democratic Republic (GDR), Hungary, Czechoslovakia, and Poland were said to have ended their annual subsidies to the WPC by May (Moscow, *Komsomolskaia pravda*, 29 May). The Hungarian Peace Committee announced its complete withdrawal from the WPC just after the Athens meeting on the grounds that it had not suffi-

ciently reformed (Budapest, MTI, 17 February; note that all those listed in the WPC's new headquarters liaison office were holdovers from the old Secretariat and that only 6 of the 40 members on the new WPC Executive Committee had not been on the old Presidential Committee [Session of the WPC, *Documents*; Helsinki, *New Perspectives*, no. 1]).

According to London's *Morning Star* of 26 November, the affiliates from Bulgaria, Czechoslovakia, Hungary, the former GDR, Poland, and Romania had left the WFTU. Although correct in general, this picture was misleading in the case of Poland, whose National Trade Union Alliance (NTUA) was the only East European national trade union federation to attend the Moscow world trade union congress and thus was represented in that meeting's 30-member Presidium (Twelfth World Trade Union Congress, *List of Participants*). Of course, Solidarity is now a legal Polish trade union federation as well. Just the same, a residual popularity of communism in the Polish trade union movement allows the NTUA to play the same sort of role in the WFTU that the Bulgarian Peace Committee does in the WPC (which can be better explained in view of the traditional relative popularity of the USSR among Bulgarians).

The Hungarian Lutherans and two small Czech sects withdrew from the CPC (Prague, *CPC Information*, 25 July). The Czechs and East Germans had left the IOJ by the middle of the year (Prague, *The Democratic Journalist*, no. 7–8). In view of the aforenoted certainty that the IUS had been asked to leave Czechoslovakia and the probability that the WIDF was being forced out of Berlin, we assume that the former host affiliates of these two internationals have also withdrawn. In an apparently unique case, one of the new fronts, the International Mineworkers' Organization, lost its Hungarians, East Germans, and a small breakaway group of Bulgarians (London, *Independent*, 6 September).

Finally, several top East European front leaders left their posts in 1990 to be replaced by persons from other regions. Most noticeably, the CPC underwent a reorganization in June during which Madagascan Richard Andriamanjato was made moderator, replacing Hungarian president Károly Tóth, and Britisher Kenyon Wright was made coordinating secretary, replacing Czech secretary general Lubomir Mirejovský (Prague, *CPC Information*, 28 June). Earlier, in May, France's Gérard Gatinot replaced Czech Dušan Ulčák as secretary general of the International Organization of Journalists (IOJ), though he won by only one vote over East German Brend Rayer (Prague, *Democratic Journalist*, no. 7–8). Former Hungarian WFTU president Sándor Gáspár, who had resigned in March 1989, was finally replaced in November 1990 by Sudanese Ibrahim Zakariya (Moscow, *Trud*, 21 November). The exception here appeared to be the WFDY, whose December General Assembly retained its secretary general's slot for a Hungarian, even though no other East European nation aside from the USSR was given space on the new fourteen-member WFDY Coordinating Council (Athens, *Rizospastis*, 12 December).

The Third World: Desired Disconnection. During 1989, there were suggestions that the Soviets were trying to oust Romesh Chandra (India) from the WPC presidency at the same time that Third World affiliates were trying to keep him in that position. In February 1990 Chandra was, as predicted, "kicked upstairs" to the position of honorary president; in November he was involved in an abortive and Soviet-derided attempt to put President Bush and U.S. policy "on trial" for their involvement in the Persian Gulf area (*YICA*, 1990; Helsinki, *New Perspectives*, no. 3; Moscow, *Izvestiia*, 30 November). Similarly, in early 1989 we noted the Soviet annoyance with the strident anti-imperialist rhetoric involved in the preparations for the Pyongyang world youth festival. In addition, following an extremely "Third Worldish" WFTU General Council meeting in November 1989, WFTU published an inflammatory anti-U.S. and anti–South Korean bulletin supporting North Korea in early 1990. Moammar Khadafy was rumored to be willing to help make up the WFTU deficit as of the middle of the year, when his fellow Arab "anti-imperialist" Ibrahim Zakariya (Sudan) was "promoted" from secretary general to president of the WFTU. Zakariya was replaced by the Gorbachevian Aleksandr Zharikov (USSR) (*YICA*, 1990; London, *ITF News*, May–June; Moscow, *Trud*, 12 November; Paris, *Est et Ouest*, December). The secretary general is the working head of such organizations and, given the nationalities involved, this action apparently allows the Soviets to get a strong handle on day-to-day operations of the organization. It is unusual, however, in that the Soviets have never before directly taken over either the presidency or the secretary generalship of a traditional front because doing so destroys the traditional front characteristic of concealed control. The presence of a Soviet secretary general makes the WFTU more

like one of the new fronts, where open Soviet leadership is apparently used to impress on the West the strength of the organization and its clout in the Soviet power structure. That presence might also serve to reassure the Third World majority in the WFTU that the Soviets have not lost interest in the organization, however unenthusiastic they may be about some Third World issues it has pursued. Zharikov had formerly been vice-president and presumed de facto Soviet controller of the IUS, and the new director of the WFTU-related International Center for Trade Union Rights, Fathi al-Fadl (another Sudanese), is a former IUS secretary general (*YICA*, 1984; Twelfth World Trade Union Congress, *List of Participants*).

Whatever conflicts between the Soviets and the Third World are implied by these reorganizations, 1990 saw an increased awareness of North-South tensions within the classical fronts. Such tensions seem a fitting context in which to consider their concurrent regionalization. For example, the CPC Working Committee statement—that the principal confrontation in the world had changed from East-West to North-South—was accompanied by the selection of Madagascan Richard Andriamanjato as temporary head of the organization (Prague, *CPC Information*, 28 June). In the September *Peace Courier*, Indian professor Satish Chandra criticized Soviet WPC secretary Vladimir Orel's proposal that reconciliation be a major slogan for the organization; Chandra said that the reconciliation objective would disarm the "people's movement" against foreign domination and control of the Third World and complained that the Soviets and other former supporters had given up on the New International Economic Order (NIEO) to redress the balance between rich and poor nations. In the November *Peace Courier* another Indian, former WPC secretary O. P. Paliwal, reiterated the primacy of the North-South issue and, although not as inflexible as Chandra on the Orel position, urged that the WPC explain why the "onus of reconciliation" must rest on the North.

In April 1989 and the following November, Soviet Peace Committee leaders proposed that the WPC regionalize and do most of its decision making at that level; the WPC decided to do just that at its February meeting (*YICA*, 1990; Session of the WPC, Athens, 6–11 February 1990, *Documents*, p. 36; *Peace Courier*, no. 3). The stipulation that these new regional structures be self-financing is undoubtedly intended to provide the Soviets with financial relief because they are directly involved only in the European region. It would also seem to ensure that the Third World centers be small-scale operations (Session of the WPC, *Documents*, p. 38).

The following is a summary of the Third World region administration:

1. Arab Regional Center (Cairo, set up in May)
a. WPC Executive Committee members (policymakers): Khalid Muhyi-al-Din (Egypt), regional coordinator; Abd-al-Fattah Yasin (Iraq); Abd-al Atti Obaydi (Libya); Mohamed el-Eafa (Morocco, originally in African group?); Abdallah Hurani (Palestine); and Hasan Maki (Yemen)
b. Permanent staff (full-time): Bahig Nassar (Egypt), secretary; an assistant to the secretary (unidentified); and a typist (unidentified). The preexisting Cairo WPC Information Center is to be incorporated into this office. Perhaps they are identical in personnel. (Session of the WPC, *Documents*, pp. 41–42; Helsinki, *Peace Courier*, nos. 6 and 7.)

2. Asian Regional Center (New Delhi, set up in July)
a. WPC Executive Committee members: Chadrajit Yadev (India), regional coordinator; Abdul Basir Ranjbar (Afghanistan); Mitsuhiro Kaneko (Japan); Li Mong Ho (North Korea); Nageshwar P. Singh (Nepal); and Tahira Mazhar Ali (Pakistan); there are open slots for Mongolia and Vietnam.
b. Permanent staff: unknown. The center operates out of the offices of the All-India Peace and Solidarity Organization, and the Asian center appears to have incorporated the Pacific one (Sonja Davies [New Zealand], coordinator) for the time being. (Session of the WPC, *Documents*, p. 42; Helsinki, *Peace Courier*, nos. 8 and 11.)

3. Latin America and Caribbean Regional Center (Havana or Mexico City, set up in August–September)
a. WPC Executive Committee members: Luis Echeverria (Mexico), regional coordinator; Jorge Alberto Kreyness (Argentina), vice-coordinator; Antonio Pinheiro Machado Neto (Brazil), vice-coordinator; Orlando Fundora Lopez (Cuba), executive secretary; Hugo Mejias Briceno (Nicaragua); Jose Solis Castro (Ecuador); Marcelino Jaen (Panama); and Eneida Vasquez (Puerto Rico)
b. Permanent staff: unknown. The preexisting WPC Information Center will remain in Havana no matter where the regional center is finally placed. (Session of the WPC, *Documents*, p. 43; Helsinki,

Peace Courier, no. 9; Porto Alegre, *Zero Hora*, 3 September.)

4. African Regional Center (Dakar, set up in October)
a. WPC Executive Committee members: Vital Balla (Congo), regional coordinator; Boubacar Seck (Senegal), vice-coordinator; Pascual Luvualu (Angola); Felike Gelde Giorgis (Ethiopia); Agadzi (Ghana); Francesca Pereira (Guinea-Bissau); and Joseph Musoli (Zambia)
b. Permanent staff: Mamadou Sako (Mali), secretary; Donatien Okombi (Congo), secretary; and a secretarial slot for an Anglophone country. The preexisting WPC Information Center in Brazzaville will remain there. (Session of the WPC, *Documents*, pp. 41, 72, 74; Helsinki, *Peace Courier*, no. 11.) Because the identified regional secretaries—Nassar, Sako, and Okombi—had previously been WPC secretaries at the Helsinki headquarters, it is possible that former WPC secretary Jesus Reyes Arencibia (Cuba) has the same job at the Latin America center (Washington, *Problems of Communism*, March–April 1987; Session of the WPC, *Documents*, p. 100). It is also likely that Bhagat Vats (India), former editor of the WPC's Helsinki-based *New Perspectives* (closed down early in 1990), is the secretary at the Asian center (ibid., p. 105). Three of the aforenoted regional coordinators—Muhyi-al-Din, Yadav, and Balla—are on the highest WPC body, the nine-member Standing Committee (Session of the WPC, *Documents*, p. 44), as is Regional Executive Secretary Orlando Fundora, who had been regional coordinator until displaced by Echeverria in August or September (ibid.; Helsinki, *Peace Courier*, no. 9).

The July–September issue of *Teachers of the World* (East Berlin) indicated that the FISE planned to set up regional centers in the Third World (in Dakar, New Delhi, Santiago, and Tunis); at the WFTU's November congress similar centers were announced for Brazzaville, New Delhi, Havana, and an undetermined place in the Middle East (London, *Morning Star*, 26 November). We assume that in these cases the overall headquarters will concentrate more heavily on the developed world, especially because the new WFTU secretary general, Aleksandr Zharikov, is a Russian and the new WFTU deputy secretary general (a new position), Alain Stern, is a Frenchman, as is the secretary general of the FISE, Gérard Montant.

The IOJ, in contrast, apparently planned to expand regional centers for all areas: in December its president suggested that the organization might become an umbrella for continental journalist organizations, and the July–August *Democratic Journalist* (Prague) stated that more of the organization's activity should be undertaken at the regional level (Helsinki, *Sanomalehtimes*, 12 December). We assume that the IOJ will build on the regional centers it already has (e.g., in Paris, Mexico City, and Addis Ababa) (*Yearbook of International Organizations, 1990/91* [Munich: Saur, 1990], entry no. BB2325). The CPC, which completed its regional coverage of the world by setting up a European center in January, announced in June that from henceforth the bulk of its work would be undertaken by these decentralized units (Prague, *CPC Information*, 28 June). In a report submitted to the U.N. Economic and Social Council's (ECOSOC's) Committee on Non-Governmental Organizations and published in July, the IUS said it was planning to decentralize, with no further explanation given (U.N., ECOSOC, E/C 2/1991/2, 23 July).

In return for the apparent financial savings that will result from the dispersal of the classical fronts (along with an almost universal reduction in the size of their respective central headquarters), the Soviets will have to tolerate more radical and more anti-Western policies than they might prefer. The cases of the outspoken Indians and the North Koreans have already been mentioned; Cuba and Libya might also cause problems. Cuba, like India a major beneficiary of the front decentralization policy, has been highly critical of the Soviet "new thinking" in general and its lack of "anti-imperialist" drive in particular. At the November WFTU congress, Cuba pushed for a more "ideological" and "class-based" variety of trade unionism than the Soviets desired (*YICA*, 1990; BBC-CARIS, no. 277/90). Libya is well-funded, aggressive, and next door to both the WPC center in Cairo and the projected FISE center in Tunis; its alleged offer to fund the WFTU has already been noted. Libya also offered to hold a joint seminar with the WPC's Arab center as soon as it was set up, and Libya's international front complex threatens to overwhelm the WPC (e.g., Libya participates in the WPC through the Tripoli-based Arab People's Congress (APC) and International Secretariat for Solidarity with the Arab People and Their Central Cause—Palestine, as well as through its peace committee) (Helsinki, *Peace Courier*, no. 7; Session of the WPC, *Documents*). Note also that the Arab center secretary, Bahig Nassar, represented both the WPC and the APC at the APPS

Congress of 1984 (6th Congress of AAPSO [Cairo: AAPSO Secretariat, undated]).

Libya was not responsible, however, for the apparent failure of the WPC Arab center in the gulf crisis. The peace committees of Iraq, Libya, Yemen, and Palestine, all representing their respective governments and constituting a majority of the Arab members of the WPC executive, would not condemn the Iraqi invasion, so the center would not either (Helsinki, WPC Information Center, *Present Crisis in the Middle East—Reactions of the Peace Movements, I and II*; Helsinki, *Peace Courier*, no. 8). WPC president Maheras issued calls for a peaceful settlement within the Arab "framework" with Arab regional coordinator Muhyi-al-Din (not the whole center) in Cairo on 20 August and for military restraint on the part of North Atlantic Treaty Organization nations with WPC executive secretary Stewart in Helsinki on 27 August (ibid.). It took an early October meeting in Athens of Arab WPC member organizations in addition to undesignated members of the Cairo-based Afro-Asian People's Solidarity Organization (AAPSO) and a high-level WPC contingent (President Maheras, Honorary President Chandra, Executive Secretary Stewart, Secretary Orel, and *Peace Courier* editor Sadhan Mukherjee) to come out with an acceptable statement (ibid., no. 10). Even though the *Peace Courier* stated that there was virtual unanimity (except for the Iraqi representative) that Iraq and the United States should withdraw simultaneously and that a Middle East conference be called to find a settlement for all outstanding issues, including the Palestinian one, the periodical published no verbatim conference statement to that effect (ibid.). Instead it published the WPC Standing Committee's statement making these same points and attributing them to conference decisions (ibid.).

The "both out" line was identical to that taken by "eleven Arab Communist organizations" in mid-August and was essentially the same as that stated by CPC coordinating secretary Kenyon Wright in late August and by the WFTU's *Flashes from the Trade Unions* in early September (London, *Morning Star*, 17 August; Prague, *CPC Information*, 20 August; Prague, *Flashes from the Trade Unions*, 7 September). It could thus be considered as the line approved by the Soviets for others but not for themselves because of likely complications in their relations with the West. By contrast, the Libyan (Khadafy) line has been "with Kuwait against Iraq and with Iraq against America" and to chide the USSR for not having played a more prominent role in the current gulf crisis to offset U.S. influence in the area (Moscow, *Izvestiia*, 19 January 1991).

The Developed Capitalist Countries: Focus of Soviet Attention.

The WPC's Europe/North America Regional Center was set up in April in Paris and was the first such body to be established by the peace organization (Helsinki, *Peace Courier*, no. 6). The Executive Committee members supervising it were Evangelos Maheras (Greece), WPC president; Jacques Denis (France), European regional coordinator; Libby Frank (United States), regional coordinator for North America when that unit is set up; Genrikh Borovik (USSR); Georgi Dimitrov-Goshkin (Bulgaria); Konrad Lubbert (West Germany), Rosemary Belcher (United Kingdom); and as yet undetermined representatives from Finland, Sweden, and Portugal (*World Peace Council* pamphlet). Maheras, Denis, Borovik, and possibly Frank are also members of the WPC's eleven-member Standing Committee, its top body (Session of the WPC, *Documents*).

In May, an embryonic European group was formed by the IOJ, again presumably located in Paris. It included representatives from France, the USSR, Bulgaria, Finland, and Portugal—all countries represented in the aforenoted WPC group—plus Hungary, Poland, Romania, Spain, and East Germany (since withdrawn) (Prague, *Democratic Journalist*, no. 7/8). It would appear that this group has not fully developed; it was specifically stated by the WPC's Arab regional coordinator in August that the biggest obstacle to his center's cooperation with outside regional bodies was "the absence of effective WPC European and North American regional and sub-regional centers" (Helsinki, *Peace Courier*, no. 7). This, together with the failure of the WFTU and FISE to set up European regional centers and the continued predominance of Europeans at the central headquarters of the fronts, raises the distinct possibility that the Soviets intended regionalization to be a mere facade to rid themselves of any responsibility for the Third World.

The French Communist Party (PCF) reelected its "Stalinist" leadership at its December party congress; to the extent that it provides input to the fronts, the result would appear to be potential conflict with the Soviets (Paris, AFP, 22 December, *FBIS*, 24 December). Although we have no specific indication that PCF Central Committeeman Denis is at odds with Borovik in the WPC, there is tension between the liberal Soviet WFTU secretary general, Aleksandr Zharikov, and his dogmatic French

assistant, Alain Stern (*Est et Ouest*, December). Another source noted that reelected WFTU vice-president Henri Krasucki, PCF Politburo member and General Confederation of Labor (CGT) chairman, had clashed with the Soviets at the November WFTU congress in pushing for a more "class-based" and "ideological" brand of trade unionism (BBC-CARIS, no. 277/90). We might expect even more tension between French secretaries general Gérard Montant (FISE) and Gérard Gatinot (IOJ) and their respective Soviet secretaries, Mikhail Kolesnikov and Vladimir Artemov, because the Soviet secretaries, though technically subordinate, are generally thought to have had the final say in running these organizations (*YICA*, 1988, 1990). In any case, the Soviets seem to be stuck with the French in their European front activities because they apparently provide the largest pool of leftists in the area willing to participate in such activities and, at least in the case of the WFTU, appear to render financial aid to the effort (London, *Morning Star*, 20 November; London, *ITF News*, May–June). The Soviets' interaction with the French at these front headquarters also gives the Soviets the West European exposure that they seem to want.

Another and earlier indication of Soviet concern with the developed capitalist countries is seen in the composition of the leadership in the new kind of front organizations noted from 1980 onward (see chart 2). Note that the replacement of French communists as the main Soviet partners here by Americans, Swedes, Germans, and Britishers who are for the most part noncommunists is significant in the light of the potential their countries have as donors of economic aid and technical expertise. The attraction of Sweden is obvious—a prosperous and essentially capitalist country using a socialist "fig leaf."

It is not yet certain whether the European House organization, set up in Budapest in March 1990, belongs to one of these new type of fronts, which have generally supported the Soviet propaganda line, or is one of the neutralist or pro-Western organizations that are described below as targets for Soviet entry (Helsinki, *Peace Courier*, nos. 4–5; Rose, *Soviet Propaganda Network*). It is in Europe that the Soviets and their allies have most notably concentrated on infiltrating such organizations. East Asia and the Pacific, the other area for developed capitalist countries, is secondary for such activity. European Nuclear Disarmament (END), still officially the "equal responsibility" organization (United States and USSR both to blame), was finally joined by the Soviet Peace Committee (SPC) in

Chart 2: New Social Movements (Selected)

	Founded	Leadership
International Physicians for the Prevention of Nuclear War (IPPNW)	1980	United States, USSR
International Lawyers Against Nuclear Arms (ILANA)	1988	United States, USSR, Sweden
International Foundation for the Survival and Development of Mankind (IFSDM)	1988	United States, USSR, Sweden
Performing Artists for Nuclear Disarmament (PAND)	1983?	United States, USSR, Sweden, Finland
International Scientists for Peace	1986?	West Germany
Teachers for Peace	1985	West Germany, Denmark
International Trade Union Committee for Peace and Development (Dublin Committee)	1982	United Kingdom
International Mineworkers Organization (IMO)	1985	United Kingdom, USSR, Australia, France
Peace Wave	1987	Japan-based (United States, USSR instigated)
Ecoforum for Peace	1986	No Third Worlders on board
Generals for Peace	1981	All North Atlantic Treaty Organization countries

SOURCE: U.S. Department of State, *Soviet-Controlled Front Organizations in Crisis* (1991)

1990, and Tallinn cohosted the site for the organization's conference that year along with Helsinki (Copenhagen, *Information*, 6 July). The SPC followed WPC affiliates from Finland, Greece, and Hungary into END during 1986–1987. It must also coexist with the now legalized (Soviet) Civic Peace Coalition of WPC critic and former official Tair Tairov, who was apparently instrumental in getting Moscow as the site for the 1991 CND conference (Helsinki, *Peace Courier*, nos. 4–5, 7). (The Civic Peace Coalition allegedly has the support of the "liberal" Moscow city council, the cooperative movement, and the new, independent trade unions; the SPC is apparently backed by more "conservative" groups [Copenhagen, *Information*, 6 July]. A meeting of old-line END leaders with former East European dissidents in a new "grass roots" Helsinki Assembly in Prague in October may have been an attempt to exclude the more conservative WPC elements that had recently entered the neutralist international [Helsinki, *Peace News*, November].)

The year also saw renewed attempts by the French communist CGT, a WFTU affiliate, to enter the European Trade Union Confederation (ETUC), which is close to the WFTU's two rivals, the socialist-oriented International Confederation of Free Trade Unions (ICFTU) and the religiously oriented World Confederation of Labor (WCL) (London, *Morning Star*, 3 April). The ETUC has generally opposed membership by communist unions but did allow the Eurocommunist Italian General Confederation of Labor (CGIL) in after it had disaffiliated from WFTU and secured the support of its ICFTU and WCL national counterparts for the move (Golrick and Jones, *The International Directory of the Trade Union Movement* [London: Macmillan, 1979]). As of now, the CGT has neither of these advantages, but the British Transport and General Workers' Union is said to be supporting its entry nonetheless (London, *Morning Star*, 3 April).

A third case of attempted "entryism" is in the journalism field. The IOJ proposed in January that the neutralist, pro-Western International Federation of Journalists (IFJ) join it in setting up a new European journalist organization independent of each sponsor and that in May the two internationals cooperate in setting up a "common European home of journalists"; neither offer was accepted (Prague, *IOJ Newsletter*, no. 3, February; Prague, *Democratic Journalist*, nos. 7–8). In early December, then IOJ president Nordenstreng suggested that the IFJ serve as the European regional organization under an IOJ that would merely be an umbrella for such continental groups (Helsinki, *Sanomaleh-times*, 12 December. Note that, as of late 1989, 21 out of the 38 IFJ affiliates were European whereas only 14 out of the 90 were IOJ [*Yearbook of International Organizations, 1990/91*, entries BB2325, CC1937].).

In the Far East and the Pacific, END's counterpart appears to be the Nuclear Free and Independent Pacific (NFIP) network coordinating committee. It has a correspondent with *International Disarmament Campaigns*, put out by END affiliates, and it has indirect WPC participation through its Australian host affiliate, the Australian Coalition for Disarmament and Peace (also linked to the International Peace Bureau, an old-line Geneva-based organization affiliated to END) (Alan J. Day, ed., *Peace Movements of the World* [Harlow, Essex: Longman, 1986]). In the trade union field, leftwing affiliates of the ICFTU and WCL are combined directly with those of the WFTU in a new-type front, the Asian-Pacific Trade Union Coordination Committee. This organization met in Kuala Lumpur in March (as did the NFIP in Auckland in November).

Self-criticism. The year appears to have been a banner one for front self-criticism, although this represented a continuation, not the start, of a new policy (see *YICA*, 1990). Apparently designed to keep dissatisfied affiliates and their individual members within the fold and to enhance future credibility, this self-criticism was characterized by understatement. The adjective *some* was a favorite in official publications: WPC president Maheras noted early in the year that the support of the "socialist countries," the hostility of the United States, and the indifference of the West in general "resulted in *some* [italics added] one-sided positions which damaged its [the WPC's] credibility" (Helsinki, *Peace Courier*, nos. 4–5). The CPC stated: "It is true that during the difficult period of the Cold War and in an atmosphere of strong ideological pressure, the CPC accepted *some* [italics added] compromises, made mistakes, and in *some* [italics added] cases gave way to pressure. We need to do penance for this." (Prague, *CPC Information*, 3 January.) Then WFTU secretary general Zakariya noted that "WFTU is invariably associated in the minds of *some* [italics added] people only with the trade unions of Eastern Europe" (Prague, *Flashes from the Trade Unions*, 2 March).

This last example illustrates the "public opinion" approach, which elucidates little. It has been used elsewhere by the front apologists: AAPSO secretary general Abd-al-Razzaq stated: "We were *looking as if* [italics added] there is a patronage to AAPSO and that [*sic*] the movement is working under that patron" (Cairo, *Afro-Asian Solidarity*, no. 1).

Soviet spokesmen, however, appear to have been a bit more candid: then All-Union Central Council of Trade Unions International Department chief Aleksandr Zharikov noted: "A lot of people consider the WFTU as an organization representing only the interests of the world communist movement and the socialist system . . . *and to a certain extent this was true*" (italics added) (Prague, *Flashes from the Trade Unions*, 27 April). Soviet WPC secretary Orel was even more forthright when he stated that "the great role played by peace committees of socialist countries in the life of the WPC from its very birth *is undeniable* [italics added]. The ideology, politics, and organizational and financial resources of the 'socialist camp' *have become one of the pillars on which the basic concept of the WPC has stood* [italics added]. This pillar no longer exists." (Helsinki, *Peace Courier*, no. 1.)

Still, the USSR is never specifically identified in the above statements concerning the past. It was left to the AAPSO secretary general, Nuri Abd-al-Razzaq Husayn, to link up the statements with Soviet direction, or at least example setting, for, following his "patronage" statement (above), he attested: "We cannot take credit for what we are saying now. The changes came from the Soviet Union and were started by Gorbachev." (*Afro-Asian Solidarity*, no. 1.)

As a footnote to the above we might note that the fronts appear to have begun to criticize some aspects of Soviet government policy, although whether sincerely or as a credibility-building ploy is not known. In April, the IOJ protested to Gorbachev the decision to bar journalists from Lithuania (BBC-CARIS, no. 131/90). In October, the SPC (the more conservative of the two major Soviet peace coalitions—see above) expressed "profound concern" over the underground nuclear test in the Novaya Zemlya archipelago (Radio Moscow, 25 October). Earlier, in February, the SPC was involved in forming the Nevada-Semipalatinsk Movement, which called for closing the nuclear testing ground at the archipelago (Helsinki, *Peace Courier*, no. 6).

Wallace H. Spaulding
McLean, Virginia

Soviet Foreign Propaganda

Moscow continued to use the mass media of radio, television, press, films, and videos; personnel (government officials, Communist Party of the Soviet Union [CPSU] cadres, journalists, academics, and cultural figures); exchanges in government, culture, education, science, technology; and, to a lesser extent in 1990, foreign aid in support of its foreign objectives. Because Lenin had designated the press as the most effective instrument—"a collective propagandist and a collective agitator"—that medium has lost none of its stature in Soviet dissemination of propaganda abroad. Gorbachev's policies of *glasnost'*, *perestroika*, and new political thinking made a positive impression on foreign governments, the mass media, and the general public. In the latter part of the year, however, Gorbachev's image became tarnished as a result of mounting domestic problems and his threats of employing repressive measures. As in previous years, the Soviet president was the Kremlin's most effective official propagandist. Accompanying him on his foreign visits, his wife, Raisa, enhanced Gorbachev's image as no previous leader's spouse had done.

Despite some reported reductions, the Kremlin's investment for foreign propaganda remained high. Although no updated figures have been furnished since the $4 billion cited in past years (see *YICA*, 1990), U.S. officials continued to see no reduction of effort, and any quantitative reductions were offset by the qualitative gains of receptive foreign environments.

USSR foreign minister Eduard Shevardnadze, reporting to the Twenty-eighth CPSU Congress as a Politburo member, indicated the magnitude of Soviet expenditures devoted to foreign activities by revealing that, after assuming the Foreign Ministry portfolio and "gaining access to the relevant information," he discovered that over the previous twenty-year period "ideological confrontation" with the West had added 700 billion rubles to the cost of military confrontation. In addition to human casualties and suffering, the Afghanistan war cost 60 billion rubles and the confrontation with China another 200 billion rubles. He cited a "peace dividend" of 240–250 billion rubles during the current five-year plan from implementing the policy of new thinking. The clear lesson, Shevardnadze declared, is that, together with dialogue, cooperation, and interaction, "defense sufficiency" will suffice for Soviet security (*Pravda*, 5 July).

Despite *glasnost'* and Moscow's adherence to the Helsinki process, Soviet authorities still considered information to be a "delicate sphere" and delayed the two-way flow of information. According to the editor of *International Affairs* (March), information is "much more pervaded and fettered with ideology than other spheres." The editorial pointed out that at the 1989 Information Forum in London, where the Soviet delegation presented a package of proposals, the USSR government had only recently approved those proposals. Difficulties remained, however, such as requiring payment in foreign currency for foreign publications.

According to Leonid P. Kravchenko, then director general of TASS, broadening East-West cooperation with "free, unimpeded information exchanges" is due to "dynamic changes" in Soviet mass media, the result of *glasnost'* and *perestroika*. He said that *glasnost'* is a "very efficient and effective tool of *perestroika*." Previously ignored social problems were now said to be reported "honestly and openly." International information also has been affected by new political thinking, with the mass media "destroying stereotypes in the coverage of Western countries and shedding simplistic judgments on life there."

Addressing a foreign audience, Kravchenko admitted that the mass media is "deeply ideologized." Although not wishing to count "stubborn ideological weeds" planted during the cold war, he emphasized the importance of understanding realities and journalists' not falling behind their political leaders. Nevertheless, he said, common ground is possible (e.g., the Intermediate-range Nuclear Forces [INF] Treaty), and journalists should help "build bridges of trust between nations, break down die-hard prejudices and clear the logjams . . . of mistrust, abandon slanted, narrow, negativist approaches to covering life in our countries."

According to Kravchenko, the mass media are duty-bound to increase the flow of objective information. The mass media can be either constructive or destructive, depending on their objectives, and "can serve as a means of strengthening or subverting trust between nations." Kravchenko concluded that the mass media possess "vast power over people" in portraying countries as friends or enemies and that the Soviet media are prepared to use that power for a good cause. (Address delivered on his behalf by Vladimir N. Matyash, TASS bureau chief, before the Satellite Communications Users' Conference in Washington, D.C., 22 November 1989.)

While Kravchenko was perceived in the West as attempting to modernize TASS, domestically his objectivity and political persuasion were suspect. For example, his own deputy, A. Krasikov, criticized Kravchenko for TASS's conservative posture, charging that numerous staffers disagreed with the position of the director general. At the October plenum of the Central Committee, Kravchenko criticized *glasnost'* (*Moscow News*, no. 42), but the previous month he had been castigated by *Izvestiia* writer Anatolii Druzenko for his remarks on the mass media. Addressing the plenum, Kravchenko attacked "opposition forces" interfering in the country's affairs, and although he recognized prohibitions in the new press law (see below), Druzenko chided him for, in effect, substituting prohibition for the "cadre lever" (i.e., CPSU leaders in the media using "dialogue" to convey guidance). To Druzenko, this was reminiscent of the historical language, such as "collective propagandist," "transmission belt," and "assistant." The attack on Kravchenko was especially disturbing because it was conducted by a member of the Central Committee (*Izvestiia*, 14 October).

Organization. Dramatic changes occurred in the CPSU, the government structure, and the leadership during the year. Although the locus of power was shifting from party to state—both of which were headed by Gorbachev, who had accumulated unprecedented formal power—the CPSU Secretariat still appeared to be the most important body guiding the internal and worldwide Soviet propaganda campaigns.

Of the six commissions established in 1988, the one for ideology is the primary instrument of policy guidance. Vadim A. Medvedev headed this unit until the Twenty-eighth Party Congress elected Aleksandr Dzasokhov to replace him. The other important body is the International Policy Commission headed by Aleksandr N. Iakovlev until the Twenty-eighth Congress, when he was succeeded by Gennadii Ianaiev. Like their predecessors, Dzasokhov and Ianaiev were elected Politburo members as well as secretaries. (For the makeup of the two commissions and the background of the former chairmen, see *YICA*, 1990.)

An Ossetian, Dzasokhov (b. 1934) has been a CPSU member since 1957, a people's deputy, a chairman of the USSR Supreme Soviet International Affairs Committee, but on the Central Committee only since 1990. A Russian, Ianaiev (b. 1937) joined the CPSU in 1962 and advanced to Central Committee member and a people's deputy in 1990. Both Iakovlev and Medvedev were appointed by Gorbachev to the new Presidential Council, with Iakovlev responsible for ideology.

The commissions, which meet several times yearly, are responsible for submitting proposals and analyses directly to the Politburo. The Ideology and International departments are under jurisdiction of the commissions and conduct daily operations in areas assigned to them. Staffed by specialists, the departments prepare analyses and proposals. The Ideology Department, headed by Aleksandr S. Kapto, prepares guidance for the mass media; one of its sections arranges for propaganda carried worldwide by TASS, Novosti, Radio Moscow, and other organizations. At the conference of CPSU ideological workers, Kapto said that one aim of his department was to develop recommendations on how CPSU committees and mass information media should work most effectively. He admitted that in some cases ideological work lagged behind *perestroika*. (Radio Moscow, 23 April; *FBIS*, 24 April.)

Valentin M. Falin (b. 1926) continued as head of the International Department. An experienced propagandist, Falin served as ambassador to West Germany during 1971–1978, first deputy chief of the International Department (1978–1983), editor of *Izvestiia* (1983–1986), and chairman of Novosti (1986–1988). He became a CPSU member in 1953, a candidate for membership on the Central Committee in 1986, a full member in April 1989, and was elected a secretary at the Twenty-eighth CPSU Congress. He is a people's deputy and a member of the Council of the Union and of the Supreme Soviet's International Affairs Committee. Not insignificant is his membership on the CPSU International Policy Commission.

The International Department is responsible for foreign communist parties, fronts, friendship societies, foreign affairs branches of the USSR Academy of Sciences, and mass organizations. Not clear is the extent of the International Department's role in cadres abroad, foreign affairs, and arms control and disarmament negotiations. Thus the Ideology and International departments direct the Soviet propaganda mechanism that includes, in addition to the CPSU apparatus, the State Committee for Television and Radio (Gostelradio) and the Committee for Publishing, Printing Plants, and Book Trade (Goskompechat).

The foregoing, as can be expected, are committed to supporting Gorbachev in *glasnost', perestroika*, and new political thinking. The division of responsibilities between Ianaiev's commission and Falin's department had, according to Ianaiev, yet to be worked out. Also not clear was the power relationship between Dzasokhov and Presidential Council appointee Iakovlev, whose responsibilities included ideology. Gorbachev's proposal to abolish the Presidential Council and establish a National Security Council was approved on 5 December, but certain officials (e.g., Middle East envoy Primakov) continued to be identified as members of the Presidential Council. Nor was it obvious what input Shevardnadze's successor as foreign minister would have; Shevardnadze had been a member of the Presidential Council and an influential figure in foreign affairs.

In its first session the Ideology Commission, chaired by Dzasokhov, made eight recommendations to overcome the Stalinist legacy: the first was to organize ideological ties and defend "humane democratic socialism," the sixth, to make recommendations for the CPSU mass media and establish contact with others, and the eighth, to promote cooperation with domestic organizations and foreign "progressive parties" (*Pravda*, 21 November).

During Gorbachev's leadership, official spokesmen for the president and the Foreign Ministry gained in importance. The longtime (since 1986), well-known, and effective Foreign Ministry spokesman Gennadii Gerasimov, who became an ambassador, was succeeded by Vitalii Churkin, a former adviser at the ministry and Shevardnadze's close aide. The spokesman is head of the Information Directorate. News conferences are held at the ministry's press center.

President Gorbachev again was applauded by the West as an effective politician, when, on 2 April, he chose Arkadii A. Maslennikov (b. 1931) to fill the new office of presidential press secretary. Maslennikov had been head of the Supreme Soviet press center since August 1989 and on the editorial staff of *Izvestiia* and *Pravda* (capitalist countries desk). Earlier he was a *Pravda* correspondent in India, Pakistan, and Great Britain; before that (from 1965) he worked at the Institute of World Economics and International Relations (IMEMO). Maslennikov explained that the press office's responsibility is maintaining contact with the mass media and communicating through them accurate information from the president, Presidential Council, and Federation Council. He rejected "suppressing" information broadly considered secret, saying that Gorbachev is interested in disseminating information (*Izvestiia*, 14 April).

In the aftermath of the Bush-Gorbachev summit, on 28 August Maslennikov was replaced by Vitalii Ignatenko, editor in chief for the last four years of *Novoie vremia* (New Times). Earlier, the 49-year-old press chief had been a deputy general director with TASS and first deputy editor in chief of *Komsomol'skaia pravda*. He said that Gorbachev recognizes that in the past journalists had inadequate sources of information; thus, a main function of the press office would be to inform the public. Ignatenko, with a staff of ten to fifteen, planned to hold news briefings every Tuesday, or as events warrant, at the Foreign Ministry press center. He also stated that Gorbachev would maintain direct contact with the media as well (TASS, 28 August; *Izvestiia*, 3 September).

According to TASS, another unprecedented development was the 28 July admission of journalists to the meeting of the CPSU Secretariat, chaired by General Secretary Gorbachev, that discussed implementing the resolutions of the Twenty-eighth Congress.

On 14 November, President Gorbachev appointed Mikhail F. Nenashev, former chairman of the USSR Committee on Television and Radio Broadcasting, as chairman of the USSR State Committee for the Press. In accordance with the new press law, Gorbachev's decree directed a radical reorganization of the press and information structure. Nenashev was given two weeks to submit proposals. Because of economic conditions, the decree provided for state support as well as legal protection (TASS, 14 November; *Pravda*, 15 November).

Telegraphic Agency of the Soviet Union (TASS). Seizing on new opportunities, several news agencies opened during the year (see below). TASS, however, occupies the premier position. The official government news agency maintains correspondents in 127 countries as well as at home. TASS receives and transmits more than ten thousand pages daily and distributes more than five million photographs yearly. Thousands of clients use its photo library, which lends negatives and slides. (*YICA*, 1990.) These figures are the same as earlier figures, but Director General Kravchenko, cited above, said that photographs numbered 6.5 million; dispatches, more than 4 million words daily to more than four thousand newspapers and radio and TV stations within the Soviet Union; and foreign subscribers, in Russian or any of eight other languages, more than 1,100. According to Kravchenko, TASS has agreements with 125 wire services in 93 countries (110 by December, see below) and has recently modernized its system with computers, video terminals, and communications facilities. TASS is also developing an automated satellite communications system and extending its database to more than three hundred users (*Izvestiia*, 14 April; the TASS bureau chief in Washington, Matyash, said on 3 January 1991 that all information in Kravchenko's report was essentially valid at the end of 1990).

The director general expressed gratification that improvements in the international situation and U.S.-Soviet bilateral relations had enabled TASS to form fruitful business contacts in satellite communications with firms from capitalist countries. The modernization of the mass media, he said "should help update information policy in the spirit of new political thinking." (Ibid.) TASS finally issued its first publication, *Ekho planety*, a weekly targeted for family reading. According to its editor in chief, N. K. Setunskiy, TASS had accredited correspondents in 110 countries (confirmed by Matyash) and was planning to receive stories on South Korea, Israel, and South Africa—countries not previously covered.

As noted above, Kravchenko was severely criticized for his conservative and orthodox viewpoint. On 14 November, Gorbachev announced several personnel changes in the mass media, including Kravchenko's transfer to his previous organization, Gostelradio (USSR State Committee for Television and Radio Broadcasting) as chairman, where he had been first deputy chairman from 1985 to 1988 (*Pravda*, 15 November). The new director general of TASS, announced on 28 November, is Lev Spiridonov (TASS, 28 November), former deputy editor of *Pravda*. Spiridonov is considered to be conservative.

Beginning in January, a TASS economic weekly, *Ecotass*, began to carry business advertisements for foreign and Soviet firms in addition to their proposals on cooperation. A year's advertising in *Ecotass* costs 450 foreign currency rubles a column, with discounts for repeats. This weekly, founded 25 years ago, is published in English, French, German, and Italian as well as Russian. Subscribers are promised the information businesspeople need to operate in the Soviet market. (TASS, 2 January.)

Novosti. In 1961 during the period of "ideological confrontation," the Novosti Press Agency (Novosti or APN), was created solely for propaganda purposes and as a "product of the Cold War," as one of its officials acknowledged (*Izvestiia*, 2 August). Until 1990 the organization was formally called a public organization, but in reality it was controlled totally by the CPSU and subsidized by the state. APN, the major disseminator of foreign-language propaganda materials all over the world, targeted selected geographic areas and audiences. By means of a 1990 presidential decree, Novosti came under the jurisdiction of the Presidential Council and was renamed Novosti News Agency (Informatsionnoie Agenstvo Novosti, IAN).

In addition to the change in name, Chairman Albert Vlasov acknowledged that APN had been established for "commentary and propaganda," leaving it to TASS and newspapers to report current developments. Under *perestroika*, however, IAN "does not impose our ideas about life," being conscious of the world's judgment of Soviet deeds rather than declarations. Accordingly, Novosti's main responsibility is timely reporting of *perestroika*. Vlasov, who before becoming chairman in 1988 had been first deputy chief of the CPSU Propaganda Department, explained IAN's multifaceted activities beyond publishing (i.e., using video, television, and a worldwide computer network and providing services on request). For example, its TV section films events especially for American, German, Japanese, and Italian networks. The photographic unit has the satellite computer capability to transmit color photographs to newspapers worldwide from anywhere in the USSR within seventeen minutes. As for its 100-million-ruble annual budget, which is approved by the Supreme Soviet, Vlasov admitted it was high but only if compared to past "ineffective ideological campaigns." He cited yearly assistance to some four thousand foreign journalists accredited to or visiting the USSR. (*Argumenty i fakty*, 2 August.)

IAN has been an enormous foreign propaganda machine, with its 100-million-ruble budget, offices in more than 100 countries (145 cited in other Novosti sources), and 39 illustrated magazines and ten newspapers in 46 languages, totaling approximately 3 million copies. The agency produces news bulletins, articles, essays, commentaries, interviews, and photographs; hosts roundtable discussions; holds briefings and news conferences; conducts radio broadcasts, telecasts, and telebridges; and sells its own film documentaries and videos (*YICA*, 1990). Its assistance to foreign reporters includes tours. For example, in August, 58 correspondents from Western countries, including the United States, visited units in Leningrad, Kiev, and the Belorussian military districts. TASS (7 August) attributed favorable comments to the visitors.

Novosti publishes books in numerous foreign languages, by itself or in conjunction with foreign publishers; the titles, covering a variety of subjects, including Soviet foreign policy and international affairs. The most widely distributed (140 countries) is the weekly *Moskovskie novosti* (Moscow news), published in cooperation with the Union of Soviet Societies of Friendship and Cultural Relations with Foreign Countries (*YICA*, 1990). For 1991, *Moskovskie novosti* appears to have gone from nine to five languages: English, French, Spanish, Arabic, and Russian.

Developing countries and youth continued to be primary targets for Soviet materials. Illustrated magazines cover domestic and foreign policies, life, problems, and achievements in various spheres of activity and ideology, as well as Soviet ties and cooperation with countries around the globe. The following English-language publications are promoted by Novosti: *Soviet Life* (see below), published in the United States; *Soviet Weekly* (Great Britain), an illustrated newspaper; *Soviet Land* (India), a biweekly published in twelve languages; *Sputnik Junior*, a monthly magazine for children, and *Youth Review*, a weekly newspaper, both published in India in English and in Hindi; *New Dawn*, a monthly appearing in eight African countries; and *Polar Star* (Uganda), a monthly magazine.

Other foreign-language periodicals distributed by *Mezhdunarodnaia kniga* in 1991, are the following (number of languages in parentheses): *Soviet Union* (22), *Sputnik* (8), *Travel* (5), *Soviet Woman* (14), *Misha* (7, the first Soviet children's magazine to appear in other languages), *Ukraine* (1), *Perestroika* (3), *Socialism: Theory and Practice* (4), *Social Sciences* (5), *Culture and Life* (5), *Soviet Literature* (5), *Soviet Film* (5), *Science in the USSR* (4), *Books and Art in the USSR* (5), *Soviet Theater* (5), *Sport: USSR and World Arena* (5), *Olympic Panorama* (5), *New Times* (7), *International Affairs* (3), *XX Century and Peace* (5), *Asia and Africa Today* (5), *Far Eastern Affairs* (4), *Foreign Trade* (5),

America Latina (2), *Soviet Soldier* (5), *Muslims of the Soviet East* (5), *Soviet Uzbekistan* (11), *Reborn Armenia* (6), *Business Contact* (4), and *News from Ukraine* (1). All, except *America Latina* (Russian and Spanish), publish in English and are either weekly, quarterly, semiannual, or annual. Subscriptions range from US$10 (*XX Century and Peace*) to US$53 (*Foreign Trade*); most are in the US$20 range.

USSR Yearbook '90, published in English, French, German, Spanish, and Swedish (the latter replaced Italian), solicited advertisements for its periodicals and other publications as well as large-scale ads for domestic publications and radio programs. One such ad, a full page, appeared in *Soviet Life*, published in the United States by the *Christian Science Monitor*'s monthly *World Monitor*. During the year Novosti also published a series of booklets: "*Perestroika: What's New in Legislation*," on property in the USSR, joint ventures, cooperatives, the judiciary and the law; *Documents and Materials*, including speeches by Gorbachev and other leaders and CPSU documents such as those from the Twenty-eighth Party Congress and the USSR-U.S. summit (May–June); other writing on *perestroika* topics included *Religion and Society*. Several other titles follow: *The People and the Party Are United*; twelve volumes of *Vladimir Ilyich Lenin: A Biographical Chronicle, 1870–1924*, prepared by the Marxism-Leninism Institute of the CPSU; *Human Rights in the USSR*; *Lessons of Andrei Sakharov*; *Violence: Sources and Limits*; and *The Turning Point*, about Stalin.

Other News Agencies. After a year's preparation, the independent news agency Interfax began operations in September 1989. A Soviet-French-Italian joint venture—Interquadro—had invested rubles and hard currency in the enterprise and supplied the equipment. The agency's office was in the Radio Moscow building. According to its new director, Mikhail V. Kommissar, Gostelradio assisted with recruiting professional journalists. Kommissar said that Interfax was created because foreign diplomats and specialists complained about the inadequacy of reliable information in the USSR and that they disliked TASS because of "its tendentious reporting, political bias, and inefficiency," thus prompting the creation of an agency for efficient and objective reporting of Soviet events.

The goal of Interfax, according to Kommissar, is "objectivity, accuracy, and non-ideological information. We report facts." (*Argumenty i fakty*, no.

30.) During its relatively short period of operations, Interfax has gained a reputation among foreign subscribers as timely, accurate, objective, and professional and is popular in the Soviet Union as well. This agency has more than one hundred correspondents throughout the USSR who communicate by fax machine. According to Kommissar, Interfax is the only news agency capable of reaching the majority of the Soviet people through newspapers, radio, and television. The rapidity of reporting, he said, is due to Interfax's freedom from the "disinformation" system of the past. (Ibid.)

The newest statewide news agency, founded in 1990, is Postfactum, an independent commercial undertaking connected with *Kommersant* (The Merchant), a new business journal. Postfactum, which is sponsored by the Komsomol (the Communist Youth League), the Union of Cooperatives, and several business organizations, has as its objective enhancing the transformation to a free market economy. NINFA, an independent news agency, was established by an association of various industrial and "creative" organizations to provide information to subscribers about the Soviet Union, claiming lucrative contracts for several defense enterprises (TASS, 2 July). There were news agencies in a number of Soviet republics, including SIA in the Siberian city of Novosibirsk; IMA in the Baltics; DANA in Kazakhstan, the first officially recognized independent news agency in the Central Asiatic republics; Tatar in Kazan; and Infonovosti.

***World Marxist Review* Is Discontinued.** The editorial board at *Problems of Peace and Socialism* (*PPS*) announced in its June issue that, after 32 years, it was ceasing publication. The English-language edition of *PPS*—the *World Marxist Review*—was published in Toronto by Progress Books. Edited and printed in Prague since 1958, *PPS* was the theoretical and information journal of communist and workers' parties worldwide. In 1989, *PPS* appeared in 41 languages and was distributed in 145 countries, with a circulation at one time estimated at half a million (the figure was never made public). Circulation was dwindling, however, and by the end of its existence *PPS*'s influence was thought to be minimal.

The journal was funded mainly by the CPSU and controlled by the Kremlin through its dominant position on the editorial board; the staff of up to four hundred members was reduced to about forty near closing. (*YICA*, 1985; Kevin Devlin, "International Communist Journal Closing Down," *Report on Eastern Europe*, 1 June; *Facts-on-File*, 18 August.) The June issue of *PPS* listed communist parties from 68 countries as making up the *PPS* editorial council.

Like its predecessors (*The Communist International* and *For a Lasting Peace, For a People's Democracy*), *PPS* served as a global communications channel for the CPSU, communist, and left-wing organizations. However, the sharply rising costs of publishing; the dissatisfaction of foreign communist parties with the journal's orthodoxy; changes in Eastern Europe, and Gorbachev's policies of *glasnost'*, *perestroika*, and new political thinking all contributed to *PPS*'s end. Foreign disapproval, led since the early 1980s by the Japanese comrades, was supported by others who objected to Soviet control and called for PPS dissolution. Limited changes for modernization, announced by the International Department's first deputy head, Vadim V. Zagladin, in April 1988, led to a wider spectrum of subjects and views—including interviews with Henry Kissinger and John Kenneth Galbraith, as well as answers to questions by the Vatican; that restructuring, however, was insufficient to offset the dynamic changes in the world and the aforementioned problems. (Devlin, "International Communist Journal Closing Down.") *Pravda* (25 May) said: "Changes in the international communist and workers' movements, new world conditions, the stormy and multifaceted processes taking place in Eastern Europe, and the developing difficulties there, both material and technical, have made further publication of this journal practically impossible."

Pravda. The proliferation of new, interesting newspapers and journals—in addition to a sharp rise in the cost of newsprint, distribution, and the newspapers themselves—affected new ventures as well as the traditional press. Moreover, the Ministry of Communications announced that the post office would cease delivering newspapers, including *Pravda* and *Izvestiia*, on Sundays and holidays (*Pravda*, 21 December).

As the organ of the CPSU, with a multilanguage digest distributed in European countries and the United States, *Pravda* continued to be the flagship of party publications; its new task is to represent the authoritative platform for new thinking. *Pravda* experienced serious problems, however, when it ran an editorial admitting current interpretations of Lenin's legacy. Taking into consideration the organ's low standards, loss of popularity, and increasing competition, the CPSU directed *Pravda* and the party press generally to undertake a renewal program, to abandon "dogmatic thinking, stereotypes, and conventionalism." (*Pravda*, 24 April.)

Pravda's editor in chief, Ivan T. Frolov, said that the press has done little to improve its prestige and that "substantial *perestroika* is required" (*Pravda*, 1 July). Frolov (b. 1929) occupied high positions in the CPSU and the government and was hand-picked by Gorbachev, whom he had served as an assistant on ideology. A member of the party since 1960, Frolov had extensive experience within the party and in publishing, including *Voprosy filosofii*, *Problems of Peace and Socialism*, and *Kommunist*. He became a Central Committee member in 1986, is a member of its Ideology Commission, and was elected to the Politburo by the Twenty-eighth Congress. He is also a people's deputy and was a member of the Presidential Council.

Despite the criticism leveled against Frolov, including calls for his resignation, Gorbachev continued to support him. Significantly, criticism came not only from various commentators but from within *Pravda* itself; Interfax cited Vladislav Iegorov, deputy secretary of the organ's editorial party committee, as reporting that "in the opinion of the majority of the newspaper's collective, it is impossible to work with Frolov." Interfax concluded that *Pravda* and *Sovietskaia Rossiia* have become "symbols of the anti-*perestroika* forces." (Moscow Television, 12 October; *FBIS*, 17 October.) The dissatisfaction with conservatism became so great that editors reportedly mutinied, demanding independence (*Moskovskie novosti*, no. 41).

The CPSU admonished *Pravda* to be truthful and to make people its focus. Frolov and his editorial page requested that activists propagandize *Pravda*, conduct readers' meetings, organize clubs, mount exhibits, and stage festivals on its behalf. Also, the Central Committee called for closer press-committees relations and for moving away from rule by edict. (*Pravda*, 24 April, 1 July.)

All unionwide publications experienced a drastic reduction in subscriptions for 1991: newspapers by 69.4 percent and journals by 45.4 percent. *Pravda*'s subscriptions fell by some 4 million in 1989, 6.7 million in 1990, and 2.8 million in 1991. This "alarming" development pointed to the need for an "interesting and substantial" paper. (*Pravda*, 12 October; *Izvestiia*, 24 November.)

Despite the "distressing" reduction of subscriptions, Frolov stressed that the organ's circulation would remain high and that it would continue to be a "world-class" newspaper. He revealed that the Central Committee had approved a plan for *Pravda* to become a "combine or association," freeing it from CPSU economic management. Frolov said the paper was earning millions of dollars from advertising, which helped modernize, obtain new printing equipment, and improve staff housing. (TASS, 24 October.) Soliciting foreign advertising, *Pravda* contacted some 150 U.S. companies offering a full page for $50,000. In a letter, the organ's representative, I. N. Filipov, said that "*Pravda* is certainly the most influential newspaper in the USSR.... Gorbachev himself starts his day with reading *Pravda*." *Izvestiia* began carrying Western advertising in January (*WSJ*, 17 May).

Joint and Other Ventures. Joint ventures, especially in collaboration with hard currency partners, were encouraged by the Soviet leadership. After a long delay (see *YICA*, 1990), *The Literary Gazette International* (*LGI*) began publication in February. The first English-language publication of the well-known Soviet journal, *LGI* is a joint undertaking of Moscow's *Literaturnaia gazeta* and the Sun World Moscow of El Paso, Texas, a printing and distribution agency. Each issue costs US$2.00; a one-year subscription (26 issues) sells for $29.99. At the end of the year, subscriptions totaled "a little over 3,500" (telephone interview in December with Cynthia Neu, president of Sun World Moscow). Fyodor Burlatsky, editor in chief of the Moscow journal, is board chairman. The 24-page *LGI* is a literary and socio-political journal generously sprinkled with black-and-white and color photographs. Its ad claims that *LGI* is "Russia's only uncensored newspaper" now available in the United States. Printed on top of the first page is "Uncensored News."

An English-language translation of *Izvestiia TSK KPSS* made its appearance in the spring. Printed by Nova Science Publishers (New York), it comes out quarterly, whereas the Russian version is a monthly. Nova publishes two other quarterlies—*Current Politics of the Soviet Union* and *Political Archives of the Soviet Union*—that are each sold by subscription at $95.00 a year. The number of subscribers is unavailable, but Nova is satisfied enough to be planning a third quarterly. (*Pravda*, 20 April; telephone interview with Nova spokesperson.)

The French version of the U.S. monthly *Rolling Stone* was preparing, with a cooperative, a Russian edition, *Perusta Oy*, to be distributed in the Soviet Union beginning in January 1991. Reportedly 2 million copies will be sold at three rubles each. The French editor said that the magazine will create a network of communication and exchange among musicians and youth and that he hopes to "open the minds of young people" carrying such stories as "Crime in the United States, in Europe." In its March issue the French edition had a story about a teenage rape in New Jersey; its regular column, "America, America," was headed "Vision of Horror." The editor said he had the required financing ($1.5 to $2 million) and advertising commitments from various companies, including McDonald's. The venture, which the Soviet cultural attaché in Paris called a "great event," was negotiated with the USSR minister of culture. (*WP*, 14 March.)

The Hearst Corporation and *Izvestiia* were planning a weekly, "uncensored" American-Soviet newspaper, *We-My*, to be distributed in both countries. A prototype was published on 4 July. According to Hearst president Frank A. Bennack, such a newspaper could "contribute significantly to mutual understanding and help foster democratic ideals." The paper covers political, economic, and social issues and developments in both countries. (*Washington Times*, 23 May; *USA*, 24 May.) As negotiations progressed another test issue was readied for early 1991 (telephone interview with Hearst in Washington).

A joint publication, *Russkii kurier* (Russian Courier), "of progressive Soviet journalists" and Russian emigrant representatives was intended for both domestic and foreign (Paris, Ottawa, and California) distribution. The weekly was to have 24 pages with a 16-page art supplement. The editor in chief, Aleksandr Gleyser, said that the editorial council would include Viktor Korotich and that despite Ernst Neizvestny's participation the newspaper "will not be extremely left-wing" (Radio Moscow, 18 April; *FBIS*, 18 April).

In the fall U.S. *Business Week* test printed 50,000 copies, with a normal schedule of publications in the USSR to begin in January 1991. This undertaking was negotiated between McGraw-Hill, Inc., and Kniga Publishing House, a Soviet enterprise. *Business Week* is printed monthly in Minsk. The articles are translations from *Business Week* and *Business Week International* (*Izvestiia*, 8 July).

The Soviet weekly *Kommersant* (Merchant) published a special summit issue intended for the U.S. market. Within the Soviet Union, *Kommersant* aimed at foreign as well as domestic business. Said to be a continuation of an earlier (1908–17) publication, it was suspended until January when the cur-

rent one made its appearance in Russian and English. Its domestic circulation was reported to be 350,000, and the hope was for 60,000 U.S. subscribers beginning in September. The subscription price was $165 a year (*USA*, 30 May).

Other ventures included the Soviet-German *Vsia Moskva* (All Moscow), an informational advertising annual; *Megapolis*, an international weekly, published by Moscow's International Research Institute of Management with help from TASS and Novosti and the German Pro Public International Sales and Advertising; *Menedzher* (Manager), a bimonthly published by the Soviet-American Information Computer Enterprise; and *Vestnik* (Herald) a Soviet Foreign Ministry and Austrian effort that includes an English-language version. Some were already in existence or planned including a Russian-language publication of the *Reader's Digest* to commence in 1991. *Pravda* was preparing an international edition in cooperation with major U.S., British, French, and Japanese publishers (TASS, 24 October).

Several Soviet journals are aimed at foreigners operating in the Soviet Union, including *Face to Face, Business in the USSR, Link, Business Contact*, and *Moscow Business*; the latest is *Russian Business Review Quarterly*, whose first issue appeared 1 November. Published in English the quarterly was to be distributed in 50 countries, with the Menatep Inter-Bank Association giving financial support. Sergei Fedyukhin, the commercial director, said that his journal, which will include advertising, differs from others in that it is targeted only to professionals; he claims that it has access to the most valuable sources of business information in the USSR. The quarterly was seeking a foreign partner for the anticipated profitable venture. (TASS, 1 November.)

Official Moscow was indeed searching for foreign partners. According to D. F. Mamleyev, deputy chairman of the State Committee on the Press, who attended the annual convention of the Association of American Publishers in New York, new contracts were being concluded. He cited the association's president as saying that contacts must be developed since both sides favor them and opportunities exist. (*Pravda*, 22 October.)

Radio and Television Broadcasting. Important developments altered radio and television as instruments of information and propaganda. In addition to the press law on the media, President Gorbachev made leadership changes and signed a decree on "Democratization and Development of Television and Radio Broadcasting in the USSR." Although that decree officially depoliticized these media, abandoned state and CPSU control, and provided for independent enterprises, the realities of the political and economic situation caution against optimism for true democratization.

Gorbachev's decree, signed 14 August, singled out television and radio as having the largest viewing public and thus the largest capability to influence public opinion. Radio and TV, the decree stated, should assist in the country's transformation, promote its consolidation, strengthen its stability, and "secure the protection of state interest, the humanization of interpersonal relations, law and order, and concord among nationalities." Internal development—including republican sovereignty and political pluralism—made a radical change necessary.

The decree recommended that the USSR Supreme Soviet legislate regulations and establish the jurisdiction of Gostelradio as well as its relations with such organizations at republic and lower levels. Rights and powers of committees at the lower levels should be expanded. Monopolizing airtime by any party, trend, or group is impermissible as is the propagation of employees' political views on state stations.

The decree provided for limitations on independent enterprises as well. Licensing authority was given to Gostelradio and the Ministry of Communications. Soviets, organizations, and parties can establish centers or stations only with "their own financial and technical resources." Also, the decree stated that any acts by republic, kray, and oblast organs to change the legal and property status of Gostelradio's subdivisions were invalid. (Text in *Izvestiia*, 16 July.) Mikhail F. Nenashev, chairman of Gostelradio, pointed to the "independents" clause as the most important, admitting to past "party monopoly." He also favored protection from demands by groups and parties to prevent the situations that exist in "bourgeois democracies." (TASS, 16–17 July; Moscow Television, 16 July; *FBIS*, 18 July.) Earlier, Nenashev stressed his opposition to an unrestricted "fourth power" such as exists in "bourgeois democratic states" (Moscow Television, 12 April; *FBIS*, 23 April). As a result of the decree, he said a new structure of Gostelradio would replace the decades-old "rigid centralization" (Radio Moscow, 13 November; *FBIS*, 14 November).

With reorganization came changes in leadership. In November, President Gorbachev ap-pointed Nenashev to be chairman of the Soviet Committee on the Press and Leonid Kravchenko (52) to be chairman of Gostelradio, where he had earlier served as first deputy chairman. Both were directed to submit reorganization proposals within two weeks. (Decrees in *Pravda*, 15 November.) In an interview with *Pravda*, Kravchenko declared that Gostelradio must be abolished and quickly replaced by two independent state companies, possibly named All-Union State Television Company and Radio Broadcasting Company. The interviewer said that there were 90,000 television staffers throughout the country and a budget of 2.7 billion rubles, of which 2 billion is allocated to the technical sector. Kravchenko said that this paradox must be corrected. (*Pravda*, 27 November.)

As seen above, Kravchenko had been criticized as general director of TASS and was not free from criticism in his new position. *Moskovskie novosti* challenged him about pretensions of pluralism in view of his past opposition to repeal of Article 6 of the constitution, his objections to the capricious press, and his concern with party scrutiny by the media. Despite his defense of the CPSU, the paper pointed out, TASS communists failed to elect him as delegate to the party congress; he was elected in Azerbaijan. (*Moskovskie novosti*, 25 November; *FBIS*, 3 December.)

The Kremlin's capability to exercise its substantial control despite *glasnost'* was illustrated before and after passage of the press law. Most recently the popular television show "*Vzglyad*" (View) was banned when it announced a show devoted to Shevardnadze's resignation. According to *Komsomol'skaia pravda*, close aides of the foreign minister were to appear on the 27 December program; instead, Kravchenko canceled the show. (Moscow Radio Rossiia, 29 December; *FBIS*, 31 December.) When questioned on television, Kravchenko said simply that "this program does not exist" and explained at length that Shevardnadze's assistants said the minister would not appear; at the People's Congress the president asked people not to become involved in the debate. In editorial discussions with Kravchenko, no formula could be found for "*Vzglyad*" and thus the program was not shown. (Moscow Television, 30 December; *FBIS*, 31 December.)

In recent years Radio Moscow has decreased its external broadcasts from 2,252:15 hours per week at the end of 1988 to 2,178:45 hours (in 84 languages) at the end of 1989. These figures included transmissions by Novosti's Radio Peace and Progress (RPP) and external broadcasts by republic radio stations. (U.S. Information Agency [USIA], *Communist International Radio Broadcasting Decreases in 1989*, 25 May 1989.) By May external broadcasts—excluding those of RPP, the Russian service, and the republics—totaled 1,573 hours weekly. RPP broadcast 80:30 hours in ten foreign languages and 171 hours in Russian. The republics are not included because, in gaining greater independence, their programming may reflect an outlook different from Moscow's.

Radio Moscow's foreign language output for 1991 decreased 21 percent from the 1,573 hours in May. The Malay service (seven hours) was discontinued, and seven other languages were reduced, with Pashto and Dari to Afghanistan cut from six to three hours. Moscow also ended a separate service to North America, Africa, and Great Britain, with the remainder absorbed by the existing Moscow English service. Altogether English transmissions were reduced from 232 to 168 hours weekly. Moscow, however, increased its French output from 91 to 105 hours weekly, inaugurating a French service to Canada. (Personal and telephone interviews with USIA specialist.)

In line with Gorbachev's policy of improving foreign relations, clandestine radio broadcasts had been reduced (see *YICA*, 1990) and ceased entirely when the Turkish-language "Our Radio" went off the air 11 June 1989. "Our Radio" was the last clandestine transmission out of the USSR and Eastern Europe. (*FBIS Trends*, 6 July 1989.) Jamming foreign broadcasts into the Soviet Union, which ended in November 1988 (see *YICA*, 1990), has not resumed nor have there been reports of any intention to do so.

Gorbachev and other Soviet spokesmen appeared on foreign television programs, including many times on U.S. networks. Accessible, English-speaking, and generally personable, they have been effective in propagating the Kremlin's policies. For example, on Sunday, 3 June, following the Bush-Gorbachev summit in Washington, the familiar Georgii Arbatov (director of the USA and Canada Institute) appeared on CBS with Dan Rather. Arbatov declared that there was no alternative to Gorbachev and that the only criticism was that the Soviet leader was not moving fast enough on *perestroika*. Foreign Ministry spokesman Gennadii Gerasimov appeared on ABC's "David Brinkley Show" and likened the Kremlin's position on the Soviet republics to the United States going to war to maintain the union. He said that the USSR is now more democratic because the republics have the right of secession. This came at the end of the program, with no time for rebuttal.

The Kremlin has pursued bilateral and multilateral activities in the media as elsewhere. One such relationship is with CNN, whose broadcasts continued to be received in the Soviet Union. Moscow utilized the U.S. network for its own advantage. For example, when the United States invaded Panama in December 1989, the Kremlin's protest was first given to CNN in Moscow for immediate broadcast worldwide, not to the U.S. embassy as protocol dictates. (*Time*, 12 February.) Ted Turner, called a "leading visionary of our time" by *Soviet Life*, was the recipient of the first *glasnost'* award, presented in Los Angeles by the magazine and the Volunteers of America of Los Angeles. The award was "in recognition of his pioneering achievements on behalf of Soviet-American relations," including staging the Goodwill Games. (*Soviet Life*, May.)

Propaganda Themes. Over the years slogans for May Day and the Great October Revolution were indicators of current Soviet domestic and foreign policies. Prepared by the Central Committee propaganda section, the slogans which appear in speeches and commentaries, reflect Gorbachev leadership's policies of *perestroika* and new political thinking and serve as guides for foreign propaganda. During Gorbachev's era the slogans have been reduced in number and in militancy. Gone from the year's slogans were confrontational epithets such as "imperialism," "fascism," and "class struggle." Not repeated was the previous year's "People of the planet! Fight for a nuclear-free and nonviolent world."

Between 1989 and 1990 the number of slogans increased by 2 (16 to 18) for May Day but decreased for the October Revolution from 22 to 17. Those for May Day were published in *Pravda* and *Izvestiia* on 18 April. The party appealed to people and workers, among others, to create "humane, democratic socialism," to help form "a socialist state based on the rule of law," to "hasten economic reforms," and to support *perestroika*. With demands in the republics for self-determination, the citizens were exhorted to say *nyet* to "nationalist and separatist forces" so as to strengthen the Soviet federation.

Party members were called on to affirm the CPSU's "vanguard role through concrete deeds" and to "consolidate the Party's ranks." In accordance with celebrating May Day as a "day of international solidarity," the first slogan called on the proletariat of all countries to unite and pledged "solidarity with foreign fighters for social progress, democracy, and rights of the working people."

The slogans for the 73d anniversary of the Great October Revolution were issued by the Politburo and published in *Pravda* 24 October. The Politburo called on members to be loyal to October's ideals, to defend Lenin, and to fight for the CPSU's renewal and, as in May, for "humane, democratic socialism." The major goals of the party's policies were rule of law, economic progress, and "spiritual rebirth." Citizens were told that the future of the USSR is "unity of sovereign republics" and that they should say yes to a new union treaty; as in May the population was exhorted to say no to "nationalism and separatism." Workers, peasants, intelligentsia, women, and youth were asked to implement *perestroika*. The military was called on to strengthen organization and discipline, as well as to protect labor. Fraternal greetings were directed to communists, supporters of socialism, and all progressive forces in the world.

Many propaganda themes were a carryover from the previous year (see *YICA*, 1990). The major themes for the reporting year are to

- Achieve global peace
- Arrive at new political thinking
- End the cold war
- Pursue disarmament
- Set up nuclear-free zones
- Cooperate, not confront
- Withdraw from East Europe
- Expand East-West ties
- Build on U.S.-Soviet relations
- Set up a common European home
- Agree to German unification
- Solve regional problems
- Deideologize
- Practice humane, democratic socialism
- Implement *perestroika*
- Continue *glasnost'*
- Defend with "reasonable sufficiency"
- Appeal for Western aid
- Unify and make sovereign the republics

These themes seek to reflect Soviet domestic transformation and the Kremlin's new attempts to achieve peace and disarmament through coopera- tion. Stalin's command methods were denounced; *perestroika* and a market economy were to be achieved by democratic means as exemplified by constitutional amendments and new laws. Although legislating political pluralism and allowing formal "sovereignty" and "secession" rights to the re- publics, the leadership attempted to persuade audi- ences, not always successfully, that the CPSU had given up its leading role and that a new union treaty was beneficial to all nationalities.

People's Diplomacy. *Perestroika* and new po- litical thinking have mobilized millions of Soviet people to actively participate in a variety of external activities with "persistent efforts to have plans and interests translated into actual government policy." People's diplomacy supplements traditional diplo- macy in some matters and occasionally precedes it. (*USSR Yearbook '90*, pp. 341–43.) Organizations meeting with the Union of Soviet Societies of Friendship and Cultural Relations with Foreign Countries (SSOD) at the Diplomatic Academy stressed the "interdependence" of people's and offi- cial diplomacy (*Komsomol'skaia pravda*, 17 May). A candid objective of people's diplomacy was given by Vadim Zagladin, former first deputy chief of the International Department, an adviser to President Gorbachev, and chairman of the Supreme Soviet, when he said that the aim is to appeal to public opinion, which would respond by pressuring gov- ernments on issues where traditional diplomacy is not succeeding (see *YICA*, 1990).

As Zagladin pointed out, people's diplomacy is not new, having been practiced by nineteenth- century socialists and in 1917 by the Bolsheviks, who invoked the human desire for peace. Under Gorbachev, people's diplomacy has been revived, with dialogue replacing confrontation. No sector is spared in the attempts to enhance the new Soviet image in the promotion of peace, cooperation, and security. Numerous foreign contacts and links have been established by such organizations as the Soviet Peace Committee, the SSOD, the Soviet Women's Committee, and the Soviet Committee for Security and Cooperation in Europe (CSCE).

Contacts between cities, universities, and nu- merous other institutions are common, as are re- ciprocal visits, conferences, and roundtable discus- sions involving specialists. Joint peace marches are favorite events. Youth is a primary target, not only in colleges and universities but in lower schools. Even an exchange of military cadets materialized; in February Soviet cadets visited West Point, and the following month U.S. cadets visited the Moscow High Combined Arms Command Acad- emy (*Soviet Life*, June).

Organizations such as the SSOD and its branches, however, have been criticized about their modus operandi; according to A. Ignatov, a corresponding member of the Council of the USSR-France Society, *perestroika* has broken the SSOD's monopoly on relations with foreigners. Ignatov stressed the need for SSOD and other groups to change from being "propaganda services" to recruiting members genuinely interested in foreign countries. (*Literaturnaia gazeta*, no. 14.)

Third World countries have traditionally received a great deal of attention, but Europe has been the object of Gorbachev's attention. Not forgotten, however, is Latin America, where new political thinking has energized people's diplomacy. The guiding organization is the Soviet Committee of Solidarity with the Peoples of Latin America (SCSPLA); its recently elected chairman, Karen Khachaturov, said that the "stereotype of the enemy is crumbling" due to Soviet policies, changes within Latin America and new Soviet–Latin American relations based on "trust." SCSPLA's priority is to establish and develop contacts with a broad spectrum of political parties and with "peace-making" cultural, scientific, ecological, human rights, and religious movements and to have a dialogue with the Organization of American States and its branches. Familiarity with the Soviet people, especially the youth, is considered especially a "rewarding field of activity." (Karen Khachaturov, "People's Diplomacy and Latin America," *Socialism: Theory and Practice*, March.)

Common European Home. The Kremlin continued to develop its major foreign policy objective of a common European home (see *YICA*, 1990, for previous activities), marked by favorable Western response. The fall of the Berlin Wall became a symbol of overcoming the split on the continent and creating a united Europe. Europe's construction, according to Soviet publicists, is based on universal values of freedom; national, ethnic, religious, and other forms of tolerance; and pluralism. The participation of the Soviet Union and East European countries in the Council of Europe is an example of concrete deeds of the Helsinki process.

In addition to Gorbachev's past proposals (e.g., in Strasbourg 6 July 1989), the Kremlin proposed a Committee of Foreign Ministers of CSCE countries, a European human rights institute, a European nuclear risk reduction center, and other programs.

Moscow points to the unification of Germany as linked with overcoming the split of Europe. In Warsaw (13 April), Gorbachev characterized the military-political status of Germany as of "exceptional importance." Germany's commitments regarding the Soviet Union and Eastern Europe, linked with the all-European process, are believed to preclude war emanating from Germany. Citing concrete moves it has taken toward European security in creating a common European home and in line with its new doctrine of sufficient defense, Moscow began reducing its military by 500,000 personnel and 10,000 tanks and other military equipment. Moreover, it favors turning the North Atlantic Treaty Organization (NATO) and the Warsaw Treaty Organization (WTO) from military-political blocs into predominantly political alliances. The Kremlin also stressed the importance of reducing U.S. and Soviet troops in Central Europe to 195,000, a figure agreed on in Ottawa in February, and proposed withdrawing troops to each country's borders by 1995–1996 as well as eliminating all foreign military bases by the year 2000. Moscow signed agreements with Hungary and the Czech and Slovak Federal Republic for withdrawal of its troops in 1991. After Gorbachev's suggestion in Italy (November 1989) that an all-European (Helsinki II) meeting be held, Soviet publicists have urged support for such a gathering. Gorbachev cited the need for a new structure, new organizations, and new mechanisms, all in line with new political thinking and a major step toward the creation of a new European home. (Kremlin's position detailed in "Soviet Concept of a Common European Home," background information distributed by the Soviet delegation at the Bush-Gorbachev summit in Washington, May–June.)

Gorbachev continued to conduct his personal diplomacy. During 29–30 May he made a state visit to Canada, where he said that Soviet-Canadian relations have been upgraded since the removal of "ideological blinkers and Cold War fears" and ranked their bilateral interaction as "an integral and crucial part of a future European home." Prime Minister Brian Mulroney viewed Gorbachev's visit as "very important and very helpful for our relations." Gorbachev, of course, spoke very favorably of the Canadian people. (*Visit of Mikhail Gorbachev to Canada* [Novosti, 1990].)

At the invitation of King Juan Carlos I, Gorbachev made an official visit to Spain 26–28 October, the first ever by a Soviet head of state. He addressed the Cortes Generales (parliament) and signed a political declaration with Prime Minister Felipe Gonzalez; other documents were also signed. President Gorbachev, who was awarded honorary doctorates by Madrid and Complutens universities, cited the misfortunes of the past in keeping the two countries apart and expressed his high regard for the hospitable, "proud and talented" Spanish people and the indispensable role of Spain and the Soviet Union in building a new Europe. The prime minister said that Gorbachev's visit was of "enormous importance" for bilateral relations, for a new international order, and for a new order in Europe. In the political declarations the leaders pledged to develop political dialogue at summit and other levels, increase economic relations, broaden personal contacts, and update cooperation in various spheres including the mass media. Moreover, the sides would begin preparing a bilateral treaty. (*Visit of Mikhail Gorbachev to Spain* [Novosti, 1990].)

In Paris, Gorbachev and President François Mitterrand signed a Treaty of Understanding and Cooperation and five other documents on exchanges. The two countries pledged to consult one another in case of security threats, and France pledged $1 billion of loans and credits. (Text in *Pravda*, 30 October.) Shevardnadze said that, ever since Gorbachev's first visit to France in 1985, the Kremlin had never doubted French assistance or that its leadership supported Soviet reforms (*Izvestiia*, 30 October).

At the invitation of Chancellor Helmut Kohl, President Gorbachev visited the Federal Republic of Germany (FRG) 9–10 November, the first anniversary of the collapse of the Berlin Wall, for which Gorbachev was praised. He was the first head of state to visit Bonn since unification. The major signed document was the Treaty of Good-neighborliness, Partnership and Cooperation between the USSR and the FRG. The two leaders had agreed on German unification in July, for which Gorbachev was applauded. In the treaty (22 articles) the countries declared no territorial claims on anyone (Article 2); should a threat to peace arise, they will coordinate their positions (Article 7). Gorbachev said that the "era of confrontation" had finally ended; Kohl remarked that "German-Soviet relations have a new, forward-looking quality extending far into the next century." The other two treaties promoted economic cooperation and provided for cooperation between labor and social services. (*Visit of Mikhail Gorbachev to the FRG* [Novosti, 1990]; New York, German Information Center, *This Week in Germany*, 16 November.)

The Kremlin's relations with Italy continued to be active as well. Prime Minister Giulio Andreotti's visit to Moscow in July was "an affirmation of our meaningful and continuing dialogue" (*Pravda*, 29 July). On his way to Paris for the CSCE conference, Gorbachev visited Rome, where he was presented with the Fiuggi International Prize by President Francesco Cossiga, who said that "relations between the Soviet Union and Italy increasingly resemble those of allies" (TASS, 18 November). Gorbachev and Andreotti signed a Treaty of Friendship and Cooperation, while the foreign ministers of the countries signed agreements on credit and the environment (text of treaty in *Pravda*, 19 November). On 18 November, Gorbachev met with Pope John Paul II, their second such meeting (the first was in December 1989). The president was "very much satisfied with their conversation" and commented that their next meeting "probably" will be in Moscow. (TASS, 18 November.)

On 19 November leaders of the 22 NATO and WTO countries met in a historic session in Paris to sign the Conventional Armed Forces in Europe (CFE) Treaty, seen by some as the most significant since Versailles. The treaty, which seeks to establish parity in major conventional forces between the alliances in the area from the Atlantic to the Urals, limits each side to 20,000 tanks, 20,000 artillery pieces, 30,000 armed combat vehicles, 6,800 combat aircraft, and 2,000 attack helicopters. It also places country ceilings and includes "unprecedented" verification measures. The Soviet Union, with its huge array of armaments, agreed to the largest cuts. In his remarks, President Bush said that "this is a glorious day for Europe." Gorbachev declared that the "breakthrough in Soviet-U.S. relations was decisive here" and that the notion of European area transcends geographic boundaries. In an answer to a question, he said that a door has been opened into the twenty-first century and that new words have appeared in the vocabulary— "partnership, cooperation, concord and friendship." Defense Minister Dmitriy Yazov denied that the treaty was detrimental to the Soviet Union. Earlier, a *Pravda* (14 October) correspondent concluded that concessions were common sense, pointing out that conventional arms consume some 84 percent of the military budget. The 34 CSCE leaders in Paris adopted the comprehensive "Charter of Paris for a New Europe," which included articles concerning human rights, democracy, the rule of law, economic liberty, security, culture, and the environment. They also endorsed German unification. The U.S. congressional Helsinki Commission said that the charter "heralds a new era of democracy, peace, and unity in Europe." (Text of President Bush's remarks and fact sheet on the CFE Treaty in U.S. Department of State, *Dispatch*, pp. 202–3; Mikhail Gorbachev: *Address at the Meeting of the Leaders of States Participating in the CSCE* [Novosti, 1990]; U.S. Helsinki Commission, *Digest*, December; *The Economist*, 24 November; *U.S. News & World Report*, 26 November; TASS, 17, 19 November.)

For the Kremlin, meetings between Prime Minister Margaret Thatcher and Gorbachev had become a "constant and substantial element in today's international politics." The Soviet leader informed Mrs. Thatcher about his visits to Canada, the United States, and the WTO meeting, and she expected a positive response from NATO to WTO's transformation. (*Pravda*, 9 June.) As a strong supporter of the Soviet leader, Mrs. Thatcher's resignation came as a surprise to Moscow. Spokesman Gerasimov said she would be remembered for making "a great contribution to the development of good relations between the Soviet Union and the European continent. She was a historic figure who helped bring the USSR closer to Europe." (*Izvestiia*, 23 November.)

United States: Pro and Con. The Gorbachev leadership has been careful not to exclude the United States from the European process. President Gorbachev's 1987 book *Perestroika: New Thinking for Our Country and the World*, was cited for confirmation, and Gorbachev's comments since then have reaffirmed this official position. Background material prepared for the Bush-Gorbachev summit (*Soviet-American Relations*, April) cited the "highest priority" for Soviet foreign policy as being "to ensure the best possible external conditions for the advance of *perestroika* inside the USSR." To accomplish this, a dialogue with all countries is needed and "confrontation has to be abandoned." The Soviet Union was prepared to cooperate with the United States on new ideas, broadening interaction on the basis of new thinking, realism, equality, and mutual benefit.

In his 1990 New Year's message to the American people, Gorbachev said that the USSR and the United States had chosen cooperation, agreeing at Malta (December 1989) to abandon the "instruments of the Cold War." Moreover, he said, "we shall start building a world excluding undermining activities, pressure, interference and armed inva-

sions." (*Pravda*, 2 January.) Gorbachev announced that the immediate Soviet foreign policy objective is progress in negotiations on all major weapons to achieve concrete results (ibid., 16 March). The summit has been a gauge, Gorbachev said, for the possibilities of narrowing the gap between words and deeds (ibid., 8 April).

After Gorbachev's ascension in 1985 and before the 30 May–3 June summit, six other summits had been held, with Malta a testament to the "viability of the new thinking." Since 1985, Gorbachev has also had 37 meetings with U.S. officials, Foreign Minister Shevardnadze has held 40 with secretaries of state, and five meetings took place between Defense Minister Iazov and U.S. defense secretaries. These were all proof of "noticeably improved" bilateral relations. Dialogue and cooperation led to several important steps, including the February agreement at Ottawa on troop limitations in Central Europe and German unification. Gorbachev viewed the agreement on armed force reductions as "important and positive," proposing an extension of the 195,000 limit to all Europe outside the USSR, as well as the withdrawal of troops to their own borders by 1995–1996 and elimination of all foreign military bases by the year 2000. (Ibid., 21 February.)

At the Washington summit, the two leaders signed documents on trade, chemical weapons, nuclear testing, peaceful uses of atomic energy, and university student exchanges. There were statements on a 50 percent reduction in strategic offensive weapons and on the Vienna conventional arms talks. Ministerial documents addressed the oceans, civil aviation, maritime transportation, and grain sales. Before the summit, on 22 May, Gorbachev met with several *Time* reporters and gave them written answers to their previously submitted questions. His activities in Washington included meetings with congressional leaders and intellectuals and interviews with Soviet television and Novosti. Both presidents were interviewed at Camp David and met jointly with reporters following the summit. After Washington, Gorbachev traveled to the Midwest for a meeting with business representatives and to California for a speech at Stanford University and a meeting with business and political leaders. (All activities are detailed in *USSR-US Summit, Washington* [Novosti, 1990].)

More than seven thousand foreign and U.S. media representatives covered the summit. Soviet reporting was overwhelmingly favorable. Gorbachev was quoted as saying that the agreements were the most important accomplishment, the result of the transition to "constructive interaction" and "interdependence" (*Izvestiia*, 2 June). A *Pravda* (4 June) correspondent hailed the meeting as a "major milestone" and quoted Primakov: "the most fruitful in the entire history" of U.S.-Soviet relations. In *International Affairs* (September), a deputy foreign minister ranked it as a "history-making event." In the Novosti interview, Gorbachev acknowledged some rivalry but said that "signs of partnership are emerging" (*Pravda*, 4 June). A number of Soviet reporters portrayed Gorbachev as a strong, calm, and confident leader (e.g., *Izvestiia*, 4 June). Personality plays an important role in diplomacy, one observed, and there were a number of "firsts," including the absence of "ideological struggle." He reported that faces of Washingtonians brightened when Gorbachev stepped out of his car and talked to people; then "we realized that the Soviet president is dear to them as a contributor to lasting peace." (*Pravda*, 9 June.) For American readers the scene was one of smiling presidents, a new hope for a better future, and, despite problems, "trust" as the key to better relations (*Soviet Life*, July). In his report to the USSR Supreme Soviet (12 June), Gorbachev said: "You could see on television how we were received in America. We fully felt the interest and sympathy and even solidarity" (*Speech by Mikhail Gorbachev* [Novosti, 1990], p. 27).

Following Iraq's invasion of Kuwait, the two presidents met in Helsinki, Finland, on 9 September. Their joint statement declared: "We are united in the belief that Iraq's aggression must not be tolerated." In his 11 September address before a joint session of the U.S. Congress, President Bush said that his meeting with Gorbachev had been "very productive" and that the leaders "are working together to build a new relationship." (Address and joint statement in *Dispatch*, 17 September, pp. 91–94.) The presidents maintained contact by telephone, and at the Paris CSCE meeting they had a personal discussion. In addition, dialogue between Baker and Shevardnadze as well as other meetings at various levels continued. All reflected "a new ability to work together constructively on a broader range of issues." (U.S. Department of State, "US-Soviet Relations," *Gist*, 4 December.) Shortly thereafter, the Department of State announced the long-delayed opening of a U.S. consulate in Kiev, to be operational in February 1991.

An important aspect of U.S.-Soviet relations has been exchanges in education, exhibits, performing arts, television, film, sports, science, technology, youth, and citizens. From a modest beginning in 1956 the exchanges have developed, with a few hitches, into a panoply of programs. For Soviet officials, contacts between "ordinary" people contribute to the USSR-U.S. dialogue. The Kremlin's willingness to expand exchanges attests to a belief in their effectiveness. The aim is to influence policymakers, with the stress on achieving peace, friendship, demilitarization, and denuclearization. Among others, the Kremlin promoted the Dartmouth meeting, Chautauqua dialogue, Soviet Peace Committee, Committee of War Veterans, sister-city movements, Friendship Force contacts, Soviet Women's Committee, and youth exchanges including schoolchildren. It was said that more than five hundred organizations in the United States wished to develop contacts with the USSR. (*Soviet-American Relations*.)

Since 1956 the two countries have distributed, on a reciprocal basis, monthly magazines—*Amerika Illustrated* and *Soviet Life*. The Russian-language *Amerika*, published by the USIA, is designed "to create a better understanding of the United States" and is sold in about 80 cities around the USSR through Soyuzpechat'. By 1990, the newsstand and subscription sales of *Amerika* totaled 100,000; in addition, complimentary copies were distributed by the U.S. embassy. (USIA, *Facts about America Illustrated*, January.) During the summit, USIA director Bruce Gelb and Deputy Foreign Minister Aleksei Obukhov signed an agreement providing for 250,000 copies per month of *Amerika* and *Soviet Life*, beginning in 1991; by the end of 1991, ceilings will be eliminated. However, USIA chose to publish only 150,000 copies during 1991. (*USIA World*, August; telephone interview with USIA staffer, 28 December.)

The English-language *Soviet Life* is published by the USSR embassy in Washington and printed by an American firm in Maryland. Material is provided by Novosti. Although *Soviet Life* has become a slick publication, it continued to lag in subscriptions, according to its managing editor, averaging about 55,000 during the year with a print run of 66,000. The Soviet embassy also distributed complimentary copies. Higher numbers are expected following a promotion campaign. (Telephone interview, 31 December.) The publication contains pictorial stories on a range of topics about the Soviet Union and generous coverage of U.S.-USSR topics, especially those with a human interest.

Also at the summit, the governments concluded a "historic agreement" to establish reciprocal cultural and information centers in Washington, D.C., and Moscow. These nondiplomatic centers, which will allow free and unrestricted access to the public, will include libraries, seminars, film showings, language instruction, and student counseling. (*USIA World*, p. 20.)

The year 1990 began with exuberance over Malta and Gorbachev's best wishes to the American people, and denunciations of the United States over Panama. These events exemplified the paradox of Soviet official and mass media commentaries beamed toward the United States. The Gorbachev leadership adapted its reporting about the United States and capitalism, so that the tone was no longer as strident and the content was more balanced, informative, and subtle, resulting in greater effectiveness. Anti-American comments continued, however, concentrating on military objectives, the Central Intelligence Agency, and regional conflicts.

Some officials questioned U.S. foreign policy motives and "global calculations" serving long-term interests. At the end of World War II, the United States differed with the Soviets and considered that the USSR was a geopolitical threat. One Soviet foreign ministry writer cited a White House publication as proof that the current leadership follows that national interest today. (Vadim Udalov, "Balance of Power and Balance of Interests," *International Affairs*, June.) In the same issue, a consultant to the CPSU Central Committee's ID charged that U.S. policy is to impose "Western values," viewing the "transition to social uniformity . . . as a prerequisite for a full end to the Cold War." In the same vein, a *Pravda* (9 August) writer alleged that "neoglobalism" means "strong-arm interference by the U.S. in the world's troubled spots."

Although Defense Secretary Richard Cheney was cited on military cuts (*Pravda*, 26 October; TASS, 17 October), Soviet publicists were skeptical. *Krasnaia zvezda* (1 November) said that the cuts were not "substantial." A *Pravda* (6 November) writer warned that the new NATO doctrine indicated that forces in NATO were intent on reviving the "enemy image" of the USSR. A department head at the USSR Academy of Sciences held that "the threat from the U.S. military machine . . . certainly persists. The arms race is not ended yet." (*International Affairs*, October.)

A TASS (11 October) military analyst charged that NATO general John Galvin had demanded a U.S. military presence in Turkey and the Mediterranean "to build up NATO flank forces in close proximity to Soviet borders," as a "relic of the past cold war." One TASS military observer wrote numerous articles criticizing military exercises, the Strategic Defense Initiative, and nuclear arms as indicators of "defensive" doctrine. "The U.S.," he said, "has pursued qualitative superiority in arms, and this could set the balance in favor of Washington" (e.g., TASS, 3 August, 28 December).

Frequently the Soviet media cited U.S. reports and organizations to make their point. For example, *Rabochaia tribuna* (13 July) referred to "public organizations" in support of Soviet disarmament efforts. The Pentagon's *Soviet Military Power 1990* received scrutiny, with Foreign Ministry spokesman Gerasimov commenting that "images of the Cold War . . . are still alive in some U.S. circles" (TASS, 27 September). A USSR colonel wrote that, although this edition is different from previous ones in "reflecting the positive changes in U.S. public perception of the USSR and its defense policy," it is nevertheless an "instrument of concentrated propaganda" (*Krasnaia zvezda*, 7 October).

Criticism of U.S. involvement in regional conflicts focused on Central America, the Middle East, and Afghanistan. The attacks on the Panama operation continued into 1990. *Pravda* (8 January) headlined it as "recurrence of Imperial Thinking," citing the "Monroe Doctrine," the "big stick," and "gunboat diplomacy" to control Latin America. This theme was reflected in "What Is behind the Invasion of Panama" in *World Marxist Review* (February). Regarding Afghanistan, a TASS (7 March) report on the military coup attempt suggested U.S. complicity. For the summit, the tone softened. The media handout said that "unfortunately," Soviet proposals for an intra-Afghan dialogue and a conference to settle the issue "did not receive a constructive reaction" from the United States (*Soviet-American Relations*). Later, a Radio Moscow program in Farsi charged that continuing arms shipments by Washington "contribute . . . to the war's escalation" (Radio Moscow, 31 October; *FBIS*, 1 November).

In the Middle East, Soviet anti-U.S. rhetoric hit on military aid to Israel and campaigned for a superpower solution to the Arab-Israeli issue. This abated during the coalition war against Iraq, but the large U.S. presence near the USSR border sparked debate not only about Soviet participation but about the ultimate U.S. objective. Other attacks focused on U.S. military bases abroad. A broadcast in Tagalog charged that many Filipinos consider the bases as "symbols of American domination of the country" (Radio Moscow, 5 October; *FBIS*, 10 October).

In Africa, *Izvestiia* (29 November) alleged that "U.S. soldiers are still serving with UNITA" in Angola. A number of programs commented on U.S.-Japanese tensions (e.g., *Izvestiia*, 3 May), and *Pravda* (25 February) said that the two countries "do not exclude the possibility of war" in the Asia-Pacific region, despite Soviet attempts to reduce tensions.

The CIA continued to be a prime target of USSR propaganda. *Sovietskaia Rossiia* (30 December 1989) implicated the CIA in the Panama operation, and *Pravda* (8 January) alleged that when President Bush was director of the agency he had met with Noriega and that therefore the CIA was "favorably disposed toward him." Another *Pravda* (12 April) article rekindled allegations about CIA involvement in experiments during the 1950s and 1960s on Canadians that included "brainwashing," and *Sovietskaia Rossiia* (4 May), citing U.S. newspapers, carried a long piece entitled "License to Kill" on alleged CIA activities. The CPSU publication *Dialogue* (no. 14) published the prologue and first chapter of Stewart Steven's book *Operation Splinter Factor: The Untold Story of America's Most Secret Cold War Intelligence Operations*, with other chapters to follow in subsequent issues.

John J. Karch
Falls Church, Virginia

MIDDLE EAST
AND NORTH AFRICA

Introduction

That part of the Middle East now frequently called Southwest Asia spawned its fourth war of the decade with Iraq's invasion of Kuwait on 2 August. Despite Baghdad's spurious claim that Kuwait was part of Iraq, its conquest in no sense represented a civil war like the one in Afghanistan (with Soviet military occupation) or that in the People's Democratic Republic of South Yemen (PDRY). Nor was this a war between major regional powers such as the long conflict that began in 1980 with Iraq's invasion of Iran and whose origins lay principally in the ideological force of Iran's revolution. Although Saddam Husayn's Ba'athist party's pan-Arabism offered a convenient philosophical justification for conquest, that same Ba'ath party had formally rejected Iraq's claims to Kuwait in 1963; in fact neither Ba'athist doctrine nor "Nasserism" has prescribed Arab unity by force.

The resulting new polarization of the region cut across traditional ideological lines to test whether raw military power was an acceptable instrument of change. Syria and Egypt's presence in the coalition punctured Baghdad's "poor versus rich" propaganda, already contradicted by Iraq's traditional role as a major oil producer. Similarly, King Husayn's cooperation with Iraq undercut Baghdad's "Arab nationalists versus the monarchies" propaganda theme just as Syria's presence in the coalition undercut Saddam's attempt to define the conflict as a battle of the rejectionists (against settlement with Israel) versus the traitors to Arab solidarity.

In assessing these ideological crosscurrents three reminders are germane. First, all four of the region's wars involved states directly and closely associated with the USSR—Afghanistan, the PDRY, and, twice, Iraq. Second, the profound Soviet policy changes associated with *perestroika* were stimulated in part by the Afghanistan disaster.

Third, in each country long and deep Soviet involvement ended in debacle, with the Marxist regimes in both Kabul and Aden nearly consumed by civil strife.

These events, combined with the tumultuous changes in the Eastern bloc during the year, weighed heavily against left parties' in the region finding external support for their programs or competing successfully with rising Islamic groups. In the as yet undetermined realignments that will follow the gulf crisis over Kuwait, the USSR's ability to exert regional influence through its former allies in the Middle East appears evermore problematic. The likely eclipsing of Baghdad's Ba'athist regime could allow Iraq's deeply repressed polity greater freedom. But, in contrast to Lebanon and Jordan where communist groups have at least a fragile base, the Iraqi Communist Party (ICP), according to one of its spokesmen, has only a symbolic presence in Iraq apart from its military wing in the Kurdish north (*Le Monde*, 14–15 October; *FBIS-NES*, 17 October).

Given the severe revenge measures taken against the Kurds by the Baghdad regime following the cease-fire with Iran and the subsequent forced population settlements of Kurds to Arab areas of Iraq, the ICP military posture cannot be robust. In addition to these resettlements thousands of Kurds were reportedly killed, and estimates of those fleeing to Iran and Turkey ranged up to 250,000.

Before the 2 August invasion, Iraqi opposition groups tried to forge a common program only to founder in a confrontation between Islamic groups and secular groups led by the ICP over whether resolutions should be made "in the name of God" (*CSM*, 20 September). But in late 1990, 21 opposition groups agreed on a common effort following several months of meetings in Damascus and Beirut. Like other regimes in the region, Baghdad has utilized Islamic symbols and downplayed its strident secularism to gain mass appeal during its struggles with Iran and the coalition allies. This tension between secularists and religious fundamentalists is reflected by various Iraqi opposition groups' assembling in Saudi Arabia, Syria, and

Iran—in each case influenced by the predominant ethos of the host country. Purportedly, the democratic regime in Baghdad sought by the Damascus group would be pluralist, with an interim steering committee and a secretariat in which the ICP would be represented. (*Middle East International*, 11 January 1991.)

In Afghanistan, which is still ruled by a Marxist party, the Democratic Party of the Afghan Masses (PDPA) changed its name midyear to the Homeland Party (HP) (Radio Kabul, 28 June; *FBIS-NES*, 2 July). Unlike the ICP, which struggles with determined Islamic ideologues in exile, the HP continues futilely trying to draw Islamic and other groups into the national government by attempting to disown its traditional Marxist orthodoxy. The HP, like the ICP, faced the issue of Islamic invocations. In reworking the old party constitution to appeal to noncommunists, the HP substituted an Islamic invocation for the dedication to "support the practical experience of Marxism-Leninism," along with similar changes (*Afghanistan Forum* 18, no. 6 [November]). Apart from its problem of staging a convincing ideological metamorphosis, the HP's most daunting hurdle lies in evidencing independence from Moscow. After the departure of Soviet forces in February 1989, the value of the continuing arms lift from Moscow reportedly has grown from $300 million per month to $400 million. (*CSM*, 16 April.)

With the formation of the new Republic of Yemen (ROY) in May by the merger of the People's Democratic Republic of Yemen (PDRY) with the Yemen Arab Republic (YAR), PDRY's ruling Marxist Yemen Socialist Party (YSP) entered a new phase of sharing power with the YAR's military, tribal, and merchant leaders in a vigorously capitalist economy. Although the YSP holds powerful positions in the new government, its potential for influence is clouded by (1) inherent weakness after the civil war of 1986 when its strongest leaders were killed or exiled and (2) deep conservatism in the YAR, including influential tribes traditionally supported from Saudi Arabia. As yet unclear is the potential political role, if any, of those important surviving YSP leaders who may still be in exile. The equation is complicated by a history of intermittent armed conflict between the YAR and the PDRY. To diffuse the legacy of distrust, the PDRY defense minister announced in January that both armed forces had been removed from sensitive border areas. Plans were also announced to merge the two armies and to disband the security services

of both the YAR and the PDRY. With a YAR population of 8 million to the 2 million of the PDRY, and a considerably more robust agricultural economy in the YAR as well as oil exports, it seems unlikely that the old YSP could gain control of the ROY.

King Husayn's efforts toward democracy, which began with the November 1989 elections, have resulted in unprecedented freedom of action for the Communist Party of Jordan (CPJ). This freedom, however, is strictly limited by the wide successes of Islamic political groups, which overshadow the relatively small following of Jordan's left. In January, Jordan's Anti-Communist Law of 1953 was repealed. Although martial law is merely suspended rather than canceled, Jordanian authorities have allowed moderate levels of political activity. In July the CPJ joined a varied leftist political bloc in Parliament to oppose the Islamic bloc; in August the CPJ joined a large National Front made up of a cross section of Jordanian political groups to protest foreign intervention in the gulf crisis (*Jordan Times*, 20 August; *FBIS-NES*, 29 August). It was doubtless painful for the CPJ to support the Ba'athist regime in Baghdad, which has been notorious for its bloody executions and repression of communists. For King Husayn and for the Western democracies it was ironic that greater political freedom in Jordan had resulted in a severe straining of ties with the West.

Like other communist parties in the Middle East, the CPJ was hurt by its USSR connection as tensions mounted among Palestinians on the West Bank partly because of the continuing large Jewish immigration to Israel. President Hafiz al-Assad of Syria summed up these sentiments in March when he stated that the migration of Jews would force Palestinians from their homeland and that "Israel was the first beneficiary, among all the nations of the world," of the changes sweeping the Eastern bloc (*San Francisco Chronicle*, 9 March). In addition to problems of association with the Eastern bloc, the continuing political upsurge of Islamic groups has kept Marxist parties of the region on the defensive. The Palestine Communist Party (PCP), for instance, which is an affiliate of the Palestine Liberation Organization, has been severely criticized by the Palestinian Islamic Resistance Movement (Hamas) for favoring peace negotiations with Israel. Accused of being against Islamic religion, the PCP has had to make public denials, in themselves an embarrassment (*al Yawm al-Sabi*, 26 April; *FBIS-NES*, 1 March).

In contrast, the militia battles in Lebanon cast the Lebanese Communist Party (LCP), a favorite target of Islamic groups, as a struggling peacemaker between warring Islamic factions in South Lebanon. Undoubtedly sensing that it would be devoured if the wrong mix of factions were to triumph in a partitioned Lebanon, the LCP has pushed for a genuinely reconstituted central government as opposed to continuing anarchy among fighting militias. The LCP, reflecting its need for outside support, has also welcomed *perestroika*. The LCP's deputy general secretary, 'Abd al-Karim Muruwwa, called *perestroika* "a real attempt at liberating socialism from mistakes of the past, basically the wrong interpretation of socialism as it was conceived by . . . Marx and Engels, and Lenin afterward" (*al-Nida'*, 22 July).

Reflecting a defensive posture taken since the 1989 elections when Islamic parties won up to 30 percent of the popular vote in major urban areas, the Tunisian Communist Party (PCT) felt it necessary to support the central government. With a small political role at best, the PCT undoubtedly prefers a pluralist government to an Islamic regime even though the PCT opposes most of the government's economic policies.

The relationship between the gains and losses of the Soviet Union in the area has seldom correlated usefully with the prospects for the Middle East's communist parties. This year saw two positive breakthroughs for Soviet policy in Iran and Saudi Arabia; it is difficult, however, to discern benefits for the affected parties. Despite markedly improved political and economic relations between the USSR and Iran, there was no sign that the Tehran government had moved to de-Satanize the Communist Party of Iran (Tudeh Party). The Tudeh noted its own failings, the crisis caused by *perestroika*, and the serious consequences of government attacks on the party (Radio of the Iranian Toilers, in Persian, 10 October; *FBIS-NES*, 22 October). At the same time, Moscow and Tehran announced the resumption of natural gas exports from Iran to the USSR after a ten-year hiatus, resulting in nineteen Soviet technical and economic projects in Iran to be financed by gas sales. The illegal and presumably exiled Communist Party of Saudi Arabia (CPSA) will serve only as a severe irritant in Saudi-Soviet relations when, in the wake of the gulf crisis, Saudi authorities reflect on events like the CPSA's representation on the *World Marxist Review*'s editorial board and the participation of a CPSA-affiliated organization's delegate to the November Twelfth World Trade Congress in Moscow (*WMR*, January–May/June).

In Saudi Arabia the Soviets benefited from their diplomatic support to the U.S.-led coalition against Iraq by reestablishing diplomatic relations with the kingdom after a lapse of many decades (*NYT*, 5 December). Reports also spoke of a substantial Saudi loan to Moscow. The action reflects long-standing Soviet objectives to diversify from its small group of economically and politically unsuccessful associates in the region. Saddam Husayn's reckless adventurism in Kuwait confirmed the wisdom of these objectives and became the catalyst for the Saudi decision.

James H. Noyes
Hoover Institution

Afghanistan

Population. 15,862,293 as of July (*World Fact Book*)

Party. Formerly the People's Democratic party of Afghanistan (Jamiyat-e-Demokrati Khalq-e-Afghanistan, literally Democratic Party of the Afghan Masses, PDPA) but formally renamed the Hezb-e Watan (Homeland Party, HP) on 28 June (Radio Kabul, 28 June; *FBIS*, 2 July). *Heywad*, the Pushtu word for homeland, is also used for the new party name. Under whatever name, the party still has two basic and mutually antagonistic wings, Parcham (Banner) and Khalq (Masses), though the Khalqis suffered a major defeat in 1990. The party also has numerous smaller factions that have developed since 1986.

Founded. 1 January 1965

Membership. Party membership claims remain contradictory, ranging from a high of 200,000 (Radio Kabul, 29 November; *FBIS*, 3 December) to a detailed low of 173,614 members in 28 provincial or equivalent organizations; 22 city organizations; 173 ward, district, and subdistrict organizations; 4,925 primary organizations; and 14,221 party groups. There were 15,924 women; 114,853 persons had "linked their fate" to the party since the declaration of the national reconciliation policy in January 1987 (Radio Kabul, 27 June; *FBIS*, 3 July). In fact, however, no membership figure claimed by the party has ever been reliable or consistent: for example, the reported surge in membership since 1987 does not jive with the reported totals claimed for that year (185,000) and the total claimed today. For several years, the claimed proportion of party members in the security forces (regular police, secret police, and armed forces) has been about three-fifths of the total membership; the latest available figure was 65.4 percent (Radio Kabul, 31 December 1989; *FBIS*, 4 January).

Chairman. (Chairman, occasionally rendered as "president," replaces the old title of general secretary, presumably discarded because of its communist connotations.) Lieutenant General Najibullah, also known as Dr. Najib, Mohammed Najibullah, Mohammed Najibullah Ahmadzai, and variations, about 45, Pashtun, studied but never practiced medicine (*YICA*, 1987), in 1990 almost always addressed or listed only by his state rank of president. Vice-presidents (no equivalent under the PDPA): Najmuddin Kawiani, about 41, preparty background unknown, in charge of the former Central Committee (CC) International Relations Department, House of Representatives (HR) delegate from Balkh, chief of HR standing committee on international relations; Suleiman Laeq, 61, Pashtun, a PDPA founder, writer, media expert, minister of tribal affairs; Farid Ahmad Mazdak, 32, Tajik, until January chief of the Democratic Youth Organization of Afghanistan (DYOA), HR member from Kabul City; Nazar Mohammed, 52, Pashtun, engineer, founding PDPA member, minister of construction, technocrat, only entered higher party positions in 1989.

Executive Board. (Replaces Politburo.) 15 members: Najibullah; Mahmud Baryalai, 46, founding PDPA member, half brother of ousted PDPA general secretary Babrak Karmal, full-time party apparatchik since 1980, economist by training but specializing in international relations on both party and state lines until fired from the Central Committee in 1987; Kawiani; Sultan Ali Keshtmand, 55, Hazara, intellectual, a PDPA founder, since 1980 more known as an economist/administrator for Kabul regimes than for party affairs; Laeq; Mazdak; Mohammed; Nur Ahmad Nur, 54, Pashtun, earliest claimed PDPA membership, 1963, intellectual, ambassador to the United Na-

tions; Raz Mohammed Paktin, 52, Pashtun, PDPA member since 1966, Khalqi but basically a technocrat who has concentrated on electric power problems until suddenly named minister of interior in March; Gen. Mohammed Rafi, about 45, Pashtun, a state vice-president; Abdul Wakil, 43, economist/teacher, foreign minister, a founding member of the PDPA; Aslam Watanjar, 45, Pashtun, military officer, minister of defense; Lt. Gen. Ghulam Farouq Yaqubi, 52, Pashtun, minister of state security. There are two alternate members: Sayed Akram Paygir, Turkoman, important deputy positions in party, state, and front apparatuses during the 1980s, and Abdul Quddus Ghorbandi, Tajik, started PDPA career as a Parchami but switched to Khalq in 1974, fired and jailed after Soviet invasion, rehabilitated first as a front official (deputy chief of the National Front) in March 1989 then as a party official (Central Committee member) in October 1989. (Radio Kabul, 28 June, *FBIS-NES*, 2 July.)

Supervisory Board or Supervisory Council. (Possibly a substitute for the old PDPA Secretariat, though more than twice as large as that body.) 33 members, most of whose names have not yet been published but who include as vicechairmen Abdul Ahad Wolesi, Pashtun, Khalqi, who had a brief illustrious career in 1978–1979 under the Khalqi leadership of Taraki and Amin, then vanished, only to reappear in January as ambassador to the former German Democratic Republic, and Mohammed Faruq Karmand, joined PDPA in 1967, was CC staff member till 1987, alternate CC member in 1987, state career in foreign relations from 1983 to 1990 (ambassador to Poland and Vietnam). These may have been joined by the following members of the old Secretariat: Najibullah, Kawiani, Keshtmand, Laeq, Mazdak, Nur, Nazar Mohammed, Ahmad Nabi (secretary of the Kandahar province party committee), Mohammed Daoud Razmyar (secretary of the Kabul city party committee and HR delegate), Mohammed Khalil Sepahi (HR representative from Herāt and secretary of the Herāt province party committee), and Mohammed Sharif (governor of Balkh and secretary of the Balkh province party committee).

Central Council. (Formerly Central Committee.) 144 full members and 59 candidates. This represents an expansion of at least 10 full members and 4 candidates over the previous year. The turnover was even greater because 24 Khalqis were purged from this group in March (*San Francisco Chronicle*, 19 March).

Status. Ruling party.

Last Congress. Second, 27–28 June, in Kabul; national conferences: 14–15 March 1982 and 18–19 October 1987. Plenums: 19 March, 6 June, and 26 June; First General Session (possibly the new name for a plenum) of the HP held in October (Bakhtar, 13 October).

Last Election. 1988. A Grand Assembly (Loya Jirga) was convened in May. Unlike the Loya Jirga of 1989, this one had no announced electoral process, and the only members listed by name were the 50 appointed directly by Najib (Bakhtar, 27 May; *FBIS*, 29 May). Others among the 772 delegates included leading party, front, and state officials, leading politicians, and some religious figures (ibid.). In May, Najib appointed an election commission of seven individuals (all known party members) prominent in legal, educational, and religious affairs and laid the ground rules for appointing parallel provincial commissions made up of officials as follows: local chief justice as chairman and chief of the education and training department as deputy chairman.

Auxiliary Organizations. As with party and state apparatuses, there was a turnover in names and apparent functions of several fronts during 1990, and some new ones came into existence. Among the older fronts, the Pioneers (for grade-schoolers) claimed that it had "organized 182,000 children and adults to assist them in . . . sound rearing and education" (Bakhtar, 26 September). In June, a craftsmen's union of "more than 60,000 persons . . . in 16,500 crafts plants . . . and 52 handicraft cooperatives" was announced. Other changes included a possible renaming of the DYOA into the Afghanistan Youth Union. Its longtime chief, Mazdak, was replaced by a hitherto little-known party activist, Mohammed Ibrahim, first secretary. Except for the Central Council of the Union of Peasants' Cooperatives, Faizullah Alberz, chairman, which claimed 36,000 members in various cooperatives in Kabul City alone, no membership figures were given for these or such other traditional fronts as Artists' Association Union, Mohammed Haider Pardis, chairman; Central Council of Trade Unions, Abdus Satar Purdeli, chairman; Coordination Center of Hazara Nationality, Shaikh Ali Ahmed Fakoor, chairman; High Council of the Ulema and Clergy, Ghulam Sarwar Manzur, chairman; All-Afghan Women's Association, Belqis Omar, chairperson

(replacing Masooma Wardak); Association of Lawyers, Professor Ghulam Sakhi Massoon, chairman; Union of Journalists; Writers' Union; the Peace, Solidarity, and Friendship Association, Basir Ranjbar, chairman; and a host of individual friendship societies with various countries. (For earlier claimed membership figures in these groups, see earlier *YICA*s.) New unions included the Union of Weavers and Tailors, the Union of Public Service Employees, a trade and transport union, and a catchall National Union of Employees of Afghanistan (NUEA), made up of 7 vocational unions totaling 300,000 members, with a leadership that was half nonparty and with "primary union units in every productive collective and administrative unit" (Bakhtar, 12 November).

Also qualifying as auxiliary organizations are those rump political parties that formerly belonged to the Union of Left Democratic Parties, an organization that was formally dissolved on 30 September (Bakhtar, 30 September). Like the PDPA itself, the union's other member parties had already undergone a wholesale rechristening, apparently in an effort to shed the stigma of their former names: the Peasants' Justice party became the Peasants' National Alliance, Mohammed Hakim Tawana, chairman; the Afghan Workers' Vanguard Organization became the Unity of Peace and Progress Fighters of Afghanistan, Zaman Gul Dehati, chairman; the Revolutionary Organization of Working People of Afghanistan became the Movement for Democracy, Mabubullah Koshani, chairman. The last-named also changed its Politburo into a Political Office and its Central Committee secretaries into a chairman and vice-chairmen (*Kabul Times*, 6 August). Within the union, only the Organization of Working People of Afghanistan, Hamidullah Gran, chairman; the Islamic party of the People of Afghanistan, Abdul Satar Sirat, chairman; and the Young Workers' Organization of Afghanistan, Abdul Tara Khail, secretary general (replacing Abdul Ghafar Sharifi), clung to their old names. Other political parties less closely associated with the PDPA included the Ansarullah Union, Safar Mohammed Khadem, chairman, and a newly formed Hizb Allah (party of God), Sheikh Ali Wasiqul Islam Wosoqi, chairman. The latter signed a protocol of cooperation with the HP in November (Bakhtar, 21 November).

A national mediatory commission, Kamaluddin Ishaqzai, chairman, was set up in late 1989 to serve as a link between the government and the resistance. It was still in existence in late 1990 (Bakhtar, 27 December).

Perhaps most significantly, the old National Front (founded as the National Fatherland Front in 1981 and renamed in 1987) faded out of the media and in November became merged into a newly formed Peace Front (PF), headed first by Tawana, then by Mohammed Ibrahim Atahi, and finally by Mawlawi Nasrullah Hanafi, an Islamic party deputy chief. As indicated below, the PF has broader responsibilities than both the predecessor organizations put together.

Publications. The third anniversary of *Sabawoon*, a Union of Journalists' monthly magazine, was announced in October, though the magazine had not been acknowledged earlier. The editor in chief was Zahir Taneen, who previously had been deputy editor of *Haqeqate Enqelabe Saur* (now *Payam*), the official party daily (Bakhtar, 11 October). Likewise, *National Gazette* was mentioned for the first time as the organ of the National Front in February, shortly before the National Front itself went into eclipse. Other newly mentioned publications were *Qalam*, the journal of the Writers Union, and the weekly semiofficial *Akhbar-e-Hafta* (Bakhtar, 30 December). Other publications known to be in circulation in 1990 included the dailies *Payam*, *Anis*, *Heywad*, and the English-language *Kabul Times*. Probably also still going are such journals as *Jamhuriat, Sarbaz* (Soldier), *Darafsh-e-Jawanan* (Banner of Youth), *Dehqan* (Peasant), *Storai*, and *Peshahang* (Pioneer). No claims of circulation were made (for previously claimed figures, see earlier *YICA* editions). The Bakhtar news agency and government radio and television stations continued in operation. In September, the first meeting of a Kabul commission presided over by Minister without Portfolio Faqir Mohammed Yaqubi addressed "problems in . . . publication (and) printing apparatuses, both state and independent," and discussed "fixation of the printing right of free press," both probably oblique indications that some nongovernmental publishing will be permitted in the future.

Background. From its inception, the PDPA (now HP) consisted of two basic factions: the Khalqis (almost purely Pashtun, rural intelligentsia, relatively poor, committed to doctrinaire Marxism-Leninism) and the Parchamis (ethnically broader based but still mostly Pashtun, urban, cosmopolitan, pro-Moscow but more astute in concealing their true beliefs from the generally anti-Soviet Afghan population). The two groups were fundamentally hostile to each other and have remained so. From 1967 to 1977 the two factions were separate parties, but on 3 July 1977, under Soviet guidance and pressure, they reunited in preparation for the coup that was to follow in April 1978. By then, the Khalqis were a majority in the party; more important, they controlled most of the guns, having recruited heavily in the military and police forces.

Within six weeks of seizing power, the old Parcham-Khalq hostilities reemerged, and most of the Parchami leaders vanished into foreign exile. Many who remained in Afghanistan were arrested and tortured, and some were executed. The Khalqis then tried to impose their Socialist ideas on the Afghan population, which reacted with a ground swell of resistance that soon threatened to topple the regime.

To prevent this collapse, the USSR intervened with a military invasion in December 1979, returning the Parchamis to power but imposing another Parcham-Khalq reconciliation. The invasion galvanized the Afghan population into massive resistance that continued until the Soviets finally withdrew, the last troops leaving in February 1989.

Since the Soviet invasion, the PDPA technically has not been a communist or even a Socialist party but merely the ruling party in a country undergoing the "national democratic stage of revolution." In 1987, knowing that they would soon no longer enjoy Soviet military protection, regime spokesmen began emphasizing the non-Socialist nature of this regime, and these denials have persisted ever since. Although loyal to Marxism-Leninism as a creed—and by extension to whatever ideology Moscow espouses at any given time—the Afghan communist leaders have been driven to distance themselves ever further from traditional Leninist rhetoric and practices.

Ever since the Soviet withdrawal, there has been an ongoing wholesale renaming of institutions, journals, parties, the nation itself (to the Republic of Afghanistan), and even the leader, who added the religious suffix ullah to his secular name, Najib. Pseudodemocratic institutions have been set up and a program of "national reconciliation" launched.

These ploys have not deterred or fooled the resistance, which has refused to collaborate with the regime. But a combination of massive Soviet military aid (approximately \$350–\$400 million per month during 1989 and 1990) and a rapidly fissioning resistance movement permitted the regime to survive longer than most observers had predicted.

Nevertheless, 1990 was to prove that, for all its reforms and cosmetic arts, the party was still a prisoner of its past and that its long-term prospects for survival were not encouraging.

Party Leadership and Organization. The first, founding congress of the PDPA, consisting of 27 men, was held on 1 January 1965. In the ensuing 25 years, the PDPA's various leaders often promised to hold a second congress but never followed through; the risk of an open break between the evenly balanced Parchami and Khalqi branches of the party was too great. Only after turning back an abortive Khalqi attempt to seize power in early March were the Parchamis strong enough to keep their word. Ironically, the second PDAP congress, consisting of 868 party members (Radio Kabul, 29 June; *FBIS*, 5 July), was also the last one, for the party emerged from it with a new power balance, a new name, a new set of statutes, and, most significantly, a new proclaimed role. Future congresses would presumably maintain the continuity in numbering (this one was called the second congress), but the PDPA as a name had passed into history. Its successor attempted to project quite a different image. Whether the party's true essence had changed remained to be seen; the signals were contradictory.

On the side of business as usual, Najib several times over was "elected unanimously" to represent various party cells at the congress, most significantly by the Ministry of State Security's department V (WAD, the secret police unit responsible for conducting psychological operations against the resistance), by WAD's Health Services Department (presumably in honor of Najib's medical degree), and by the general staff and headquarters of the armed forces (Radio Kabul, 17, 20 June; *FBIS*, 18, 21 June). It was an electoral circus typical of Leninist regimes everywhere.

On the other hand, a definite slimming down of the party apparatus became apparent in September, when a 40 percent reduction in full-time personnel was announced. Those who were cut were promised new positions but were warned not to expect "above-rank posts" (Bakhtar, 19 September).

At the top of the power pyramid, the old deadlock between Parcham and Khalq had been broken and the way lay open for change. Since the Soviet invasion of 1979, the Parchamis had held the political high ground and controlled WAD (the secret police), but the Khalqis had controlled the regular police (Sarandoy), had been more influential in the military, and had retained considerable clout in the

Politburo. After the failed coup, all that changed. The ousted conspirators counted among their number five of the fourteen Politburo members (including the ministers of defense and interior and the Afghan ambassador to Moscow) and five of nineteen members of the Supreme Defense Council, the government's most potent state organ. All were dismissed, but most were able to avoid arrest by fleeing to Pakistan. Within the PDPA's Central Committee, 24 members were expelled for complicity in the plot.

Nevertheless, despite the wholesale purge at the top and the arrest of some 623 people accused of involvement in the plot (Radio Kabul, 2 April; *FBIS*, 3 April), the Khalqis could not be considered a spent force. They still constituted a significant proportion of the entire party, especially in the police and army. Previous Khalqi leaders (Nur Mohammed Taraki, Hafizullah Amin, Assadullah Sarwari, Sayed Mohammed Gulabzoy) had been politically or physically eliminated, but as each had fallen another had risen to take his place. Najib, sensitive to the Khalqi potential for violence, confined the 27 April Revolution Day ceremonies, normally a massive military parade, to a 36-hour early, 20-minute ceremony in a bunker (*NYT*, 29 April). Politically, however, the Parchamis were in firm control, and at the congress and afterward they took steps previously opposed by the Khalqis. One of these was to change the name of the party to the HP. (As indicated in *YICA*, 1990, the intention to apply a new label was not new, but the Khalqi resistance had previously proven too strong.)

A second was to voice support for political pluralism, dialogue with opponents, "the struggle for legality," and the "growth of multi-economy sectors" (i.e., private enterprise), in effect turning their backs on the traditional Marxist-Leninist values so beloved of the Khalqis. These were not new themes, but there was now no longer the excuse of Khalqi intransigence to explain any failure to move forward.

A third was to promise a new set of party rules, which duly appeared a week later. The only complete set of rules previously available was that adopted at the 1965 founding congress, where it was termed a *constitution* (Anthony Arnold, *Afghanistan's Two-Party Communism: Parcham and Khalq*, Stanford: Hoover Institution Press, 1983, app. B). In the interim there had been some minor modifications, including shortening or eliminating the period prospective members had to spend in probationary status. The new rules, termed a *man-*

ifesto, followed almost precisely the same outline as the old party constitution, thus providing indirect confirmation that the older document was genuine, and differed little from its predecessor. Although it opened with an Islamic invocation and proclaimed its devotion to Islam, as opposed to the constitution's pledge to "carry out the practical experience of Marxism-Leninism" (ibid.), and although it avoided using the term *democratic centralism*, though most of the mechanics of that political philosophy were incorporated in it, the most noticeable change was semantic: In addition to the changed terminology already noted at the beginning of this article, the party congress became the *general assembly*; the central committee became the *central council*; and the cell became the *zone*. (*Afghanistan Forum* 18, no. 6, November.)

Among the items that remained constant were the four-year interval between congresses/assemblies (so far honored in the breach—it was 25 years between the First and Second congresses) and the requirement that members have at least two years' party membership before being allowed to serve as local party chiefs or three years before being allowed to serve as provincial party chiefs. Clearly, the party was maintaining a conservative stance and wished to avoid any revolutionary reform by new members.

The manifesto held one obscure paragraph with no parallel in the 1965 party constitution: the duty of the Central Council to conduct relations with other political parties (Article 13), with the implication that other political parties existed coequally with the PDPA. This had already become explicit in the May amendments to the state constitution, wherein all references to the PDPA and its main subordinate arm, the National Front, were excluded from the document. This at last formalized the party's two-year-old proclaimed intention of "abandoning the monopoly of power," a goal that Najib in March frankly admitted had not yet been achieved (Radio Kabul, 18 March; *FBIS-NES*, 19 March). The amendments also barred all members of political parties from appointment as judges or attorneys. This paved the way for a separation of powers, a concept alien to Leninists, but one that Fazl Haq Khaleqyar, Najib's chosen nonparty prime minister, addressed specifically in a 21 May inaugural address (Radio Kabul, 21 May; *FBIS*, 22 May).

Was it the PDPA/HP's desire to become a genuine democratic party in even competition with its rivals? If so, why? Although there was now unquestionably more latitude for voicing opposition than heretofore, the party still kept the levers of power in its own hands. For example, any political party that wished to become active must be approved by the state supreme court, whose top three members were two longtime regime collaborators (Nizamuddin Tahzib and Abdul Wali Hojat) and a rehabilitated Khalqi (Abdul Hakim Sharai Jauzjani). The registration process would involve full disclosure about the founders (a minimum of 30), members (a minimum of 50), finances, and organization, and the court's decision would be final (*Kabul Times*, 10 September). Such revelations would be suicidal for any party in basic disagreement with the regime, as the founders of the National Unity party discovered when they were arrested (*Afghanistan Forum*, May).

As to why the PDPA/HP might wish even partially to democratize itself, Najib himself gave the answer in an April speech to a Kabul party plenum. Referring to the upheavals in Eastern Europe, he noted that "those parties that delayed the introduction of reforms and the discarding of their previous incorrect stands miserably lost their credit and prestige" (Radio Kabul, 22 April; *FBIS-NES*, 23 April) and suggested that the same fate might befall the PDPA. But he also stressed that tactical reforms were necessary to eliminate the gap between the party and the people. In talking of abandoning the construction of socialism, he repeatedly used phrases such as "in the current phase," "at the present moment," and "at this stage" (ibid.), implying that once the party's power was consolidated it might cast aside democratic principles.

If Najib's statements to the party faithful were more or less straightforward, to foreigners he worked hard to downplay any relation between his government and communist thought. In May and June, he blandly assured foreign journalists that "I have repeated many times and repeat again that the PDPA and government . . . of Afghanistan . . . were [not] communists and are not communists" (Bakhtar, 18 May) and that "our party never pursued socialist or communist objectives in the past" (*Profil*, 11 June; *FBIS-NES*, 13 June); at about the same time, the wheel—symbol of the revolution—was dropped from the state seal (AFP, 9 June; *FBIS-NES*, 11 June).

But old beliefs are not easily shed, and in an exhaustive speech at the party congress, Najib came down hard in favor of unity and discipline. Although giving some lip service to innovation, he resolutely ruled out "freedom of factions in the party" and insisted that any questions about the party's draft program conform to "general national and patriotic interests," as defined, presumably, by him (Radio Kabul, 27 June; *FBIS-NES*, 3 July). Regarding his own convictions, he was still addressing USSR president Gorbachev as *comrade* in the summer (*Pravda*, 5 July, *FBIS-NES*, 11 July), a term he also used for the Afghan party faithful, though this would change by year's end.

In September, while reiterating that the party had given up its monopoly of power, Najib acknowledged that it had a "determining share in government posts" and in no way intended to become "simply an observer" (Bakhtar, 19 September). By the end of the month the old term *vanguard*, discredited only weeks before, was resurrected to describe the party's role in Najib's program of national reconciliation (Bakhtar, 29 September).

Domestic Affairs. The biggest news on the Afghan domestic scene in 1990 was the 6 March failed coup attempt by Khalqi minister of defense Shah Nawaz Tanai in consort with Gulbuddin Hekmatyar, the most radically Islamic of the resistance leaders. Although representing the farthest left (Tanai) and farthest right (Hekmatyar) positions on the Afghan political spectrum, the two leaders differed no more in principle than two other unlikely collaborators of the past—Stalin and Hitler.

Rumors and reports of coup attempts by the Khalqis extended back at least to August and December 1989. The government acknowledged in January that there had been 127 arrests, including 11 generals (*FEER*, 25 January), but high-ranking defectors gave figures of up to 250. Tanai, said one, had secured the release of 70 by appealing to the Soviets, and there was widespread speculation that the Soviets were not only aware of the conspirators' plans but approved of them (*Nation*, AFP, 4 January; *FBIS-NES*, 8 January); such interpretations received even wider currency after Tanai's final attempt in March (London, *The Times*, 8 March; *Report on the USSR*, 23 March; San Francisco Chronicle, 28 March).

Whatever the degree of the Soviets' awareness or complicity, they made no move to intervene after Afghan air force planes tried unsuccessfully to bomb the presidential palace. Although the plotters included the chief of air and air defense forces, several other generals, and a number of pilots, Tanai had had to rush his plans, and a key tank attack on Kabul had been rebuffed by Minister of Interior Mohammed Aslam Watanjar's forces, who remained loyal to Najib. Watanjar's reward was appointment as defense minister, the third time he has held that position since 1978.

For two months the situation remained tense. In early April, to demonstrate the success of its national reconciliation policy, the regime flew East European diplomats and Western journalists four hundred miles, from Kabul to Herāt, to witness the voluntary surrender of resistance groups. But the ceremony backfired when those who were turning in their arms used them instead to ambush the government representatives. Among the ten killed were two generals, including the chief of WAD's department V. The presiding chief of the northwest zone, the ostensibly nonparty Fazl Haq Khaleqyar, was badly wounded (*NYT*, 7 April).

By early May, however, Najib could declare an end to the state of emergency that had been imposed since shortly after Soviet troops quit Afghanistan in February 1989. At the same time, the Supreme Defense Council, which had taken over rule of the country, was disbanded, and plans were announced for a Loya Jirga (Grand Assembly) (Bakhtar, 2 May; *FBIS-NES*, 3 May).

Days later, Najib appointed election commissions made up of lawyers, judges, and prosecutors on both the federal and the provincial level and immediately thereafter decreed a constitutional amendment commission with himself as chief, former National Front chief Abdul Rahim Hatef as deputy, and various prominent party and fellow-traveling politicians as spear-carriers (Radio Kabul, 7 May; *FBIS-NES*, 8 May). The first name on the list was Fazl Haq Khaleqyar, prime minister–elect in the government Najib was putting together, who was still recovering from wounds suffered in the Herāt ambush of the previous month. Although most of the constitutional amendments reflected a liberalizing trend, Articles 128 and 129, dealing with the roles of the central and provincial governments, explicitly established centralism as a basic principle and downgraded the provinces' authority (Radio Kabul, 19 May; *FBIS-NES*, 25 May).

The new Khaleqyar government supposedly represented a radical break with the past by emphasizing the role of technocrats and downplaying the influence of the PDPA/HP. Sixteen new ministers were appointed, two of them to new ministries. According to regime propaganda, the cabinet was independent of the PDPA, with only 12 of the 36 members belonging to the party, 23 being allegedly "non-party," and one belonging to the "Democratic Movement" (Bakhtar, 23 May). A review of information about the new ministers, however, reveals that only six of them were totally new faces. The other 30 had records of collaboration with or membership in the PDPA, with at least 1, Deputy Prime Minister Nehmatullah Pazhwak, known to have been a hidden PDPA member since the 1970s or before.

One member of the previous cabinet who lost his post was Minister of Justice Bashir Baghlani, who in April warned that Najib's promise to share power was all a bluff and that the PDPA would retain control by clinging to the key ministries of defense, interior, state security, and foreign affairs (AFP, 13 April; *FBIS-NES*, 13 April), which in fact it did. Baghlani's dismissal showed how little the party would tolerate dissent. Even if there were true technocrats among the newcomers, the power was very limited; key decision-making authority was in the hands of the six deputy prime ministers, all of whom were PDPA members or close collaborators (AFP, 22 May; *FBIS-NES*, 22 May).

The image of the new government also suffered when Mohammed Asghar, chief of the National Salvation Society (NSS, previously suspected of being a PDPA front), scornfully refused to participate, publicly calling Najib a "dictator par excellence" (AFP, 13 May; *FBIS-NES*, 17 May). Najib's efforts to have exiled King Zahir Shah return from Italy and become part of his government also failed, thus removing whatever residual legitimacy the president might have been able to claim and causing him to accuse the king of "encouraging war" (ibid.). Toward the end of the year, Najib returned from a trip to Geneva claiming to have held talks with leaders of two of the more moderate resistance movements (*NYT*, 22 November) and later to "have reached further understandings with them" (Bakhtar, 1 December), but both men denied his claim (*Afghanistan Forum*, January 1991).

Khaleqyar's program was essentially that of the PDPA/HP as outlined at the June party congress: advocacy of the policy of national reconciliation (heavily emphasized), frank admission of faults (an Afghan version of *glasnost'*?), legality, separation of powers, building trust with the people, purging the government of all manner of sinners and bad practices, encouraging private enterprise and foreign investment in the economy, beating down inflation, keeping a strong defense posture (defined as the "focus of the government's attention"), raising the level of social services and culture, and pursuing a "balanced and sensible" foreign policy (Radio Kabul, 21 May; *FBIS-NES*, 23 May). Near the end of his speech Khaleqyar said the government was "making an effort to pave the way for creation of a popular, broad-based coalition government" (ibid.), thus implying that the government he had just formed had none of these attributes. A day later, he stated that the government supported "a free press and free publications" but then added that it would be necessary to set up a "responsible authority" to act on media criticisms (Bakhtar, 22 May), whether to remedy the discovered faults or come down on their discoverers was unclear.

While these political experiments were under way, the nation's economy continued to deteriorate. On a trip to Paris in August, Najib claimed that in 1980 Afghanistan's per capita income had been the lowest in the world, at $187 per year, and that it had since declined another 24 percent (Bakhtar, 9 August). In agriculture alone, the losses were estimated at $10 billion in the course of the war (Bakhtar, 16 October). The official rate of exchange remained 55 afghanis to the dollar, but the free market rate was 500 to the dollar. At the latter rate, a junior civil servant earned $7 to $8 per month and an academician $24 to $30 per month (Afghanistan, *Sitrep*, January 19–February 6). By June the exchange rate had fallen to 550 to the dollar (Bakhtar, 8 June).

As the year wore on, the regime placed more emphasis on the private sector. The May amendments to the constitution removed earlier verbiage that promoted the state sector and added such private incentives as protection of private property, encouragement of (rather than permission for) foreign investment, and permission for local foreign schools to take in Afghan students.

In February, economic guru Keshtmand declared that there were now 367 private "production institutions," compared with 273 such enterprises in 1979. In 1979, he said, the private sector had taken up 80 percent of the gross national product (GNP), compared with 78 percent in 1989; the drop was ascribed to the heavy war damage sustained in agriculture, 99.2 percent of which was in private hands. In other branches of the economy, the private sector accounted for 100 percent of handicrafts, 85 percent of domestic trade, 60 percent of foreign trade, 40 percent of transport, 20 percent of factory industries, and 10 percent of construction. In the same talk Keshtmand stated that about 15 percent of GNP went for security and defense (Radio Kabul, 7 February; *FBIS-NES*, 8 February), but a more realistic figure of 80 percent was given later by Najib (*Kabul Times*, 5 August).

Before September 1988, 47 percent of Afghanistan's national income came from natural gas exported to the USSR. As the Soviet troops prepared to depart, the gas lines were shut down and have not yet been reopened. The imminent resumption of gas production and deliveries have been announced several times, most recently in August, but by year's end there was no indication that it had begun (AFP, 18 August; *FBIS-NES*, 21 August).

A Loya Jirga was convened 28–29 May and gave its dutiful rubber-stamp approval to the Khaleqyar government and to the draft amendments to the constitution (Bakhtar, 5 June; *FBIS-NES*, 6 June). In addressing the Loya Jirga, Najib appealed to well-known Afghan exiles to return home and help rebuild the country. (None is known to have answered his call.) He also laid out his plan for a "cooling period," to be followed by a "transitional period" during which negotiations with the resistance would take place, and finishing with countrywide elections under auspices agreed to by all sides.

In his quest for legitimacy and popularity, Najib carried on with previous policies designed to build his own prestige while tearing down that of his enemies. On Revolution Day he promoted a dozen brigadier generals to major general and 47 colonels to brigadier (Bakhtar, 27 April; *FBIS-NES*, 1 May). As in earlier years, he declared amnesties for draft dodgers and deserters (Radio Kabul, 31 January; *FBIS-NES*, 1 February), and the media faithfully reported his turnover of confiscated private property to its original owners (Bakhtar, 9 September). Great successes in repatriation of refugees and cease-fires with resistance commanders ("70 percent of the commanders [have] stopped war against the government") (Bakhtar, 22 September) were continually broadcast, but in fact the return of refugees was minuscule, and the one resistance surrender ceremony to which foreigners were invited turned into a resistance ambush. He appealed to women by appointing two as cabinet ministers and vowing to increase their representation in the national assembly from their "present ratio of 12 percent" (AFP, 1 May; *FBIS-NES*, 2 May) (the true figure is about 2 percent). Similarly, he tried to curry favor with the Hazaras, a minority (about 10 percent) group that traditionally had been at the bottom of the Afghan racial pecking order. All reports of military action portrayed government forces as victorious and "mopping up." Finally, he portrayed himself and his regime as firmly committed to stamping out illegal drug production and trade.

On the negative side, he kept up a barrage of propaganda against Pakistan's alleged violations of the U.N. accord on Afghanistan (by the end of November the latest protest serial number on this topic was 1,640) and for Islamabad's alleged plan to form a confederation with Afghanistan. The latter message was fortified by what appeared to be a forged letter to Pakistani defense attachés overseas (*Kabul Times*, 8 May). In his propaganda war against the resistance, Najib accused them of slaughtering civilians by indiscriminate rocket fire, engaging in illegal drug trade, and forcibly preventing refugees from returning home. In one of the more unusual accusations, he claimed that the resistance and the British were working together to plunder archaeological digs and carry off precious finds to England.

Front Activities. Most fronts during 1990 seemed preoccupied with name changes and reorganizations, and so far, it is impossible to judge how much of the change and innovation is purely cosmetic and how much represents a genuine effort to democratize Afghan society. At first it seemed that the National Front would retain its name and be headed by Mazdak, a well-known PDPA figure (Bakhtar, 2 May). After some confusion in the Afghan media, which for a time used National Front and Peace Front interchangeably, the former name disappeared and the Peace Front of Afghanistan (PFA) emerged under the aegis of Abdul Hakim Tawana, president of the Peasants' Justice party, one of eight supposedly independent parties "sharing power" with the HP.

According to its charter, however, the PFA is far more than merely an umbrella front, appearing to act as a supragovernmental body for overseeing the union of the existing Kabul regime and various resistance groups into a coalition government (*Kabul Times*, 25 March). It also obligates itself to "struggle for" matters that normally would be regular governmental functions, such as setting prices for surplus agricultural products, democratizing public media, and restoring confiscated property to its original owners (ibid.).

Before he was named to head the PFA, Tawana outlined its underlying philosophy by stating that "no single party, organization . . . or political and military groupings alone (can) . . . succeed in ensuring comprehensive peace in the country" (Bakhtar, 10 May). But the PFA arrogated to itself something of that role when in its draft manifesto it denied being a "state" (i.e., government) but claimed to be "orienting and leading the country" (*Kabul Times*, 15 March). Later, it declared it would "lead the existing political system of the country," "form the interim government," and "lead it subsequently" (Bakhtar, 10 May). If so, it was doing so without the participation of the resistance, which clearly judged it no more to be trusted than the PDPA/HP or any of the other fronts. Nevertheless the PFA announced its intention of entering the next election "as a broad political platform with the determination to win the mandate of the people so that it can form the future government of the country" (ibid., 9 May).

Amendments to the constitution in May undercut traditional fronts to some degree. The earlier document had obliged the state to promote the interests of various traditional fronts, such as organizations for youth, women, and trade unions, and it had specified that both the National Front and the Council of Ulema and Clergy could propose laws. As amended, the constitution says nothing about either of these matters.

The DYOA celebrated the 14th anniversary of its founding on 23 May (Bakhtar, 23 May) yet announced it would hold only its first congress in the near future (Bakhtar, 20 October). The congress promised to introduce changes in the name, action program, and organization of the group (ibid.). A Youth Union of Afghanistan, first noted in August, may herald the new name for the DYOA (Bakhtar, 13 August). In January, Mazdak, the former first secretary of the DYOA, was replaced by Mohammed Ibrahim, a relatively unknown party activist (*Kabul Times*, 29 January). The participation of Secret Police chief Yaqubi in preparatory meetings for the congress and the heavy weight given in his speeches to youth's role in "foiling plots and conspiracies of enemies" did not augur well for a kinder, gentler DYOA (Bakhtar, 20 October). The long-promised congress finally did convene on 4 December (Bakhtar, 4 December), and the later use of the term Afghanistan Youth Union (AYU) may indicate a definitive name change (Bakhtar, 12 December).

September and October saw several unions holding a first or second major meeting, be it a plenum or a congress, often after a hiatus of many years. No important changes in personnel, organization, or philosophy are known to have resulted from these assemblies, however.

International Views, Activities, and Positions. In its efforts to distance itself from traditional Marxism-Leninism, the PDPA/HP found itself somewhat isolated. Its old international comrades had to be avoided if the image of the new, democratic Afghanistan were to be preserved. In May, Najib—in his capacity as president, not party leader—did welcome a Soviet Komsomol (youth group) delegation and put it in touch with the DYOA, but other than that the closest ideological link was an ongoing exchange of parliamentary and friendship society delegations in January, March, June, September, and October.

The PDPA/HP, however, still had a long way to go before most truly democratic parties would find it acceptable. Even India, whose Congress party in previous years had been the only free world, non-Marxist party to recognize the PDPA, confined itself to economic and political discussions on a state-to-state, not party-to-party, basis.

Najib, who earlier in the year had called the USSR's Mikhail Gorbachev "comrade" in a May Day greeting, took the occasion of October Revolution Day to address him as "your esteemed excellency" (Radio Kabul, 3 November; *FBIS*, 6 November), a careful ideological distancing. Nevertheless, with its virtual complete control over the state apparatus, the party still bore responsibility for Afghanistan's foreign relations and problems.

Concerning relations with the USSR, Najib's survival depended on continuation of the massive arms lift (amounting to as much as $400 million per month, up from $300 million a month in 1989) that had been provided since the departure of the last troops in February 1989 (*CSM*, 16 April). At a time when Moscow was cutting its support to other Third World countries and even Eastern Europe, Najib had to ensure that Afghanistan was an exception if his regime were to survive. As a Soviet dependent, he had few cards to play, but he played them adroitly.

Unlike other Soviet dependents, Najib had the advantage of having come to power on Gorbachev's watch in the Kremlin. He was thus to some degree a Gorbachev responsibility. Moreover, as a close collaborator with (and probably agent of) the Soviet State Security Committee (KGB), his reputation was linked to that organization's. Similarly, the Soviet military, which had occupied Afghanistan for nearly ten years, had a stake in his continued survival: the prestige of Soviet arms was at stake. Also, Afghanistan's geographical position on the USSR's southern flank gave the USSR an added incentive to hold a friendly regime in place; if Afghanistan were to be taken over by a truly Islamic regime, it could prove to be a magnet for the already restive Central Asian Soviet republics.

Finally, although Soviet public opinion was strongly against sending foreign aid of any kind to the Third World, there was an emotional popular ground swell to locate and liberate the estimated 80–100 survivors among the 303 Soviet soldiers reported as missing in action (MIA). According to some informed Soviet journalists, Najib deliberately played on this theme, using the MIAs as hostages to guarantee continuation of military and civilian aid from Moscow. Najib did seem to go out of his way to keep the issue in the public eye whenever he was interviewed by Soviet journalists (Bakhtar, 29 October; *FBIS-NES*, 30 October), but there were only two recorded instances of Afghanistan retrieving and handing over a resistance prisoner to the Soviets (Radio Kabul, 10 April; *FBIS-NES*; 11 April; TASS, 16 June, *FBIS-SOV*, 18 June). (The Soviets tried to skirt Najib and deal with the resistance directly but found that the latter were unwilling to deal until all Soviet aid to Najib's regime had ceased [TASS, 28 September; *FBIS-SOV*, 28 September].)

Regarding civilian aid, the Soviet ambassador claimed that economic aid was 120 million rubles in 1990, down from 500 million rubles in 1988. The aid was divided roughly into three sectors: one-third in food (280,000 tons of wheat, 100,000 tons of sugar, rice, tea, grain, flour, etc); one-third in petroleum, oil, and lubricants; and one-third in cement, glass, equipment, and automobiles. But the Soviets also printed all the Afghan banknotes and even manufactured its military decorations, among myriad other products.

Direct cross-border trade with Soviet Central Asia continued as before. Originally calculated to draw Afghanistan closer to the USSR, there was some question whether the attraction might start working in the other direction, especially because the Afghan side intended to emphasize the private sector in such trade.

In a unique operation, Afghanistan was able in part to repay the Soviets by alleviating a serious tobacco shortage that developed in the USSR in August. By Najib's personal order, 1.5 tons of choice cigarettes were flown by special aircraft to Tashkent, where they were transloaded onto aircraft belonging to the border troops and flown directly to Moscow (*Izvestiia*, 31 August; *FBIS-SOV*, 6 September). Not mentioned in this coverage was the

fact that the Soviet border troops belong to the KGB, another indication of Najib's ties to that organization.

A program of hosting Afghan children in the USSR's Central Asian republics for one month of summer rest was begun in 1980, presumably as a means of inculcating them with Soviet values. Over the next decade 12,909 children took part in this program, or more than 1,000 per year. In 1990 the numbers were only 200 for the Uzbek republic and 30 for the Tajik republic, possibly indicating a phasing out of this program (Bakhtar, 24 September).

Relations with Pakistan showed no signs of improvement as the year came to a close, but the Kabul regime did make some headway in relations with Iran. Tehran, worried about possible Saudi influence in Afghanistan should the resistance triumph, exchanged middle-level official and Red Crescent delegations with Kabul (*FEER*, 18 January). Later, the Iranian embassy presented the Afghan Red Crescent Society with a Chevrolet (Bakhtar, 2 April).

The regime also scored something of a diplomatic coup when the French and Italians decided to reopen their embassies. (Although they announced their intention in January, the French were unable to follow through for several months because of a lack of volunteers.)

In June an Iraqi parliamentary delegation visited Kabul for a week of discussions on "strengthening inter-parliamentary relations" (Bakhtar, 7 June). Whether one week was adequate to exchange all the parliamentary experience that both sides had accumulated is unknown; there is no evidence that the visit was linked to the subsequent Iraqi invasion of Kuwait.

During July and August, Najib visited India, the USSR, and France in his first trips abroad since the Tanai coup. Rumors that his family was with him and that he would remain abroad indefinitely proved false. Nevertheless, the most worrisome international problem as seen from Najib's viewpoint was the likelihood of a U.S.-Soviet agreement to bring peace to Afghanistan in a fashion that would involve his own political eclipse. Throughout the year, reports and rumors of an imminent U.S.-Soviet understanding on Afghanistan continued to surface, but by year's end there were no concrete results. The resignation of Soviet foreign minister Eduard Shevardnadze in December, interpreted by some Afghans as partly a result of KGB/military intransigence on Afghanistan, appeared to have set back any such understanding indefinitely.

Anthony Arnold and Ruth Arnold
Novato, California

Algeria

Population. 25,566,507
Party. Socialist Vanguard Party (Parti de l'Avant-Garde Socialiste, PAGS)
Founded. Founding congress of the Algerian Communist party in 1936 (renamed PAGS in 1966)
Membership. Unknown (estimated by French sources at about 15,000)
General Secretary. Sadiq Hadjeres
Status. Officially recognized, September 1989
Last Congress. First legal, 16–17 December (*Pravda*, 18 December)
Publications. *Sawt ash-Sha'ab* (The voice of the people), issued intermittently

Background. The Algerian Communist Party (PCA) emerged originally in 1920 as a branch of the French Communist Party, attaining its independence in 1936 when it became actively involved in the emerging nationalist struggles sweeping Algeria. It subsequently emerged as one of the major participants during the war of independence against colonial France (1954–1962). Despite this active involvement, the PCA was quickly proscribed by the new Ben Bella government in November 1962. Since then its members have clandestinely organized, renaming the PCA the Socialist Vanguard Party in 1966. Because of political constraints, PAGS has held no regular party congresses but has occasionally (most notably in 1969, 1981, and 1988) issued a number of broad programs and pamphlets. Several of the organization's younger members joined the Algerian National Youth Organization (UNJA) in the early and late 1970s; as in other North African countries the student unions at the universities have been an important source of recruitment for the organization. At the same time PAGS militants have taken up positions in the organization and policy-making functions of the coun-

try's single national workers' union, the Union Générale des Travailleurs Algériens (UGTA). Although PAGS was officially tolerated by the Algerian government, its recognition as a political party following the riots in October 1988 brought some of its leaders to sustained national attention for the first time.

Leadership and Party Organization. Although little is known about either the makeup or the organizational structure of PAGS, observers have repeatedly stressed that it is highly organized. Firmly guided by Sadik Hadjeres—with little evidence of other members participating actively in decision making—the party managed to bring out impressive crowds, mainly unemployed youth and students, after the October 1988 riots. PAGS also has dedicated sympathizers inside the trade union and the country's mass organizations. Despite this dedicated core of sympathizers, however, the party has not been able to organize effectively since its recognition in 1989, perhaps more because of the fractious nature of Algerian politics and its citizens' preoccupation with the lingering economic crisis than an antipathy toward its programs.

Domestic Party Affairs. The political liberalization that followed the October 1988 riots in Algeria benefited PAGS as well as a number of newly authorized parties. Recognized as an official party in September 1989, PAGS general secretary Sadiq Hadjeres was received by President Chadli Benjedid in 1988 and again on 10 January. Both men stressed their determination to cooperate to introduce political pluralism and greater economic efficiency to the country. PAGS cooperation on economic matters has been perceived as important by the Algerian political leadership, who have often contended that although PAGS has a weak base of support, it retains an ideological appeal for many younger Algerians who do not identify with the rapidly growing Islamist movement in the country.

PAGS was originally a strong supporter of former President Houari Boumedienne (1965–78) and his state capitalist economic experiment, despite the party's inability to be recognized during his years in office and despite major difficulties over workers' rights. The tightly organized economic system that put the state in charge of virtually all economic enterprises was perceived by PAGS as necessary to development. The arrival of Chadli Benjedid (Boumedienne's successor, appointed in 1979) marked the beginning of less than enthusiastic support for the state's economic policies. Chadli's support for market-oriented reforms and the dismantling of the country's state companies led to acrimony over the role of the state in Algeria's economy. Hadjeres on several occasions argued that Boumedienne's experiment should not have been reversed and ridiculed the notion that the Algerian state was no longer effectively able to manage the country's economy, as Benjedid's supporters argued.

The 1988 riots served to focus PAGS's complaints. Although the party had no part in instigating the riots, it quickly aligned itself with those taking part. Hadjeres repeated that the riots had been the outcome of the disastrous economic policies of the Benjedid government and its favoring of a class of Algerians who lived in luxury while the average citizen barely had enough to eat. In several communiqués during and after the riots, PAGS castigated the Army of National Liberation (ALN) for killing hundreds of young people at the orders of a small elite who profited handsomely from the new economic direction chosen by Benjedid. The steadily deteriorating economic position of workers and the growing number of unemployed young people inside Algeria provided PAGS with ample ammunition for its antigovernment campaign.

The outcome of the riots—highly publicized political reforms that included a new constitution, a free press, and the announcement of a multiparty system—allowed PAGS to state publicly some of its positions. In a number of newspaper and journal articles, and increasingly in public debates, PAGS officials have put forward strong views on the running of the country's economy and the political malaise that has taken place despite the liberalization measures. PAGS continued to insist that the austerity plan under which the country has labored since 1986 was not the result of difficult international economic circumstances but primarily due to nepotism and bad economic management. The removal of a number of the *Front de Libération*'s more notorious leaders deflected some of this criticism, but PAGS argued that this weeding out of corrupt officials should not be the end point of the reforms.

As in 1989, PAGS continued to focus at least part of its criticism on arrangements the government has made with international financial institutions to reform the Algerian economy. Much of this has been popular rhetoric, muted by the knowledge that if the country's multiparty system ever takes shape, PAGS may well belong to a coalition government that would have little choice but to adhere to the agreement signed with the International Monetary Fund.

To some extent the criticism was also a repeat of attempts by PAGS not to be outflanked by the rival Trotskyist Organisation Socialiste de Travailleurs, whose outspokenness attracted sustained media attention in Algeria in 1989 and 1990 and whose criticisms of governmental economic policy have been sustained and detailed.

The year under review was marked by continued criticism of the government's economic and political actions but gradually shifted toward issues surrounding the Iraqi invasion of Kuwait. Following the June municipal elections in Algeria, PAGS found that it had not managed to attract popular support in any of the country's provinces and that it was outdistanced by a rapidly growing Islamist movement it could not support. If PAGS was recognized, as some observers argued, in the hope of helping to contain the Islamist movement, the strategy backfired. PAGS has traditionally attempted to avoid the divide and rule policy of the government, but the June 1990 elections will force PAGS to adopt a clear position and eventually to abandon the unlikely alliance.

The 2 August Iraqi invasion of Kuwait sparked a number of PAGS commentaries, in both the local and the international press. In general the party has closely supported the Algerian government's position: a condemnation of the invasion matched by a demand that all foreign troops leave the gulf area to enable the Arabs to settle the matter among themselves. PAGS has focused on the economic interests the West, and particularly the United States, have in the Gulf, criticizing the United States as hypocritical and ridiculing the local regimes as suddenly converted paragons of Arab solidarity with a new-found generosity that was lacking when many Arab countries—including Algeria—were struggling to make ends meet.

International Views, Positions, and Activities. The position of PAGS on the gulf crisis has provided the most sustained commentary on international politics, much of which dominated the fall issues of *Sawt ash-Sha'ab*. The traditional concerns with the Palestinian *intifada* and the rapidly changing political situation in Eastern Europe and the Soviet Union received sustained attention but noticeably less so toward the end of the year. PAGS has generally supported the changes in Eastern Europe and the Soviet Union, with repeated notes of caution for the destabilizing effect they may have in the region.

Dirk Vandewalle
Dartmouth College

Bahrain

Population. 520,186
Party. National Liberation Front of Bahrain (NLF/B)
Founded. 1955
Membership. Unknown but believed negligible
Chairman. Yusuf al-Hasan al-Ajajai (not noted since 1983)
General Secretary. Saif ben Ali (noted from 1987)
Governing Committee. (List incomplete): Yusuf al-Hasan al-Ajajai (last noted 1983), Saif ben Ali, Abdallah Ali Muhammad al-Rashid, Muhammad Ali, Ali Nagi Abdallah, Badir Malik, Aziz Mahmud (last noted 1983), Yusuf al-Hasan (alternate member only)
Status. Illegal
Auxiliary Organizations. Bahrain Peace and Solidarity Committee (affiliated with the World Peace Council and Afro-Asian People's Solidarity Organization), Democratic Youth League of Bahrain (affiliated with the World Federation of Democratic Youth), National Union of Bahraini Students (affiliated with the International Union of Students), Women's Organization of the NLF/B (affiliated with the Women's International Democratic Federation), Federation of Bahraini Workers (affiliated with the World Federation of Trade Unions)
Publications. *Al Jamahir* (The masses, newspaper; *Al Fajr* (The dawn), theoretical quarterly; *Al Sharara* (The spark), internal news bulletin

The NLF/B is regarded by the Soviets as one of some thirteen "vanguard revolutionary democratic parties," a category of organization falling just short, owing to ideological and disciplinary shortcomings, of a full-fledged communist party (*Problems of Communism*, March–April 1982; Alexander Subbotin, ed., *First-Hand Information* [Prague: Peace and Socialism International Publishers], 1988, pp. 9 and 63). This party has, however, habitually participated in meetings where all other groups had full communist party status (see *YICA*, 1989). The latest example noted was in early August, when the NLF/B was one of eleven "communist organizations" signing a communiqué de-

manding that Iraq withdraw from Kuwait and that the United States get out of the gulf area (the attack on the U.S. presence echoed previous NLF/B statements) (*Morning Star*, 17 August; *YICA*, 1990). (The Bahrain Peace and Solidarity Committee, incidentally, took the same stand [Helsinki, *Peace Courier*, no. 8].) The other activity noted on the part of NLF/B during the year was the attendance of its representative, the aforenoted Abdallah Rashid, at the French Communist Party congress in December (Paris, *L'Humanité*, 19 December).

A 1988 article in the Soviet-edited *First-Hand Information*, as well as one written by NLF/B spokesman Abdallah al-Rashid for the November 1989 *World Marxist Review*, stressed that the immediate domestic goal of the organization is to restore the parliamentary regime and democratic freedoms that the country had until 1975 (Subbotin, *First-Hand Information*, p. 64; *WMR*, November 1989). (The NLF/B sees itself subjected to increasing repression stemming from "fictitious charges" that it is attempting to "overthrow the regime and establish socialism" [ibid.].) Given the present policy of the Soviet Union, its establishment of diplomatic relations with Bahrain in September is not likely to result in any serious pressure for easing restrictions on the NLF/B.

Some forward movement appears to have been made in the NLF/B's policy on alliances, at least during 1988–1989. Whereas in early 1988 it claimed to have been "working to establish cooperation with" the People's and Islamic Fronts for the Liberation of Bahrain, in late 1989 it claimed an alliance with the former and a dialogue with the latter and made a joint statement with both to the Gulf Cooperation Council (*YICA*, 1989; *WMR*, November 1989).

In fact, this emphasis on a "united front from above" contrasted somewhat with the mid-1988 stress in *First-Hand Information* (p. 64) on "mass organizations," in which the NLF/B claimed to be both cooperating with the Popular Front and recruiting its members for itself. Whereas *First-Hand Information* (ibid.) mentioned positive underground activity in all the fields covered by the "auxiliary organizations" listed above, the November article talked only of the party's trade union activity; this information was coupled with a complaint that the government had set up a rival, legal Workers Committee of Bahrain (*WMR*, November 1989). It would appear that the NLF/B's domestic activities in the field of mass organization have not gone well at all.

It appears that the Bahrainis noted as active in international front organizations during 1990 were from among those few previously cited in this context, suggesting that only a limited number are available for such activism. There is little doubt that the Abd-al-Hadi Khalaf and Husayn Musa, who represented the Bahrain Peace and Solidarity Organization at the February Athens World Peace Council meeting, also represented the same organization at the New Delhi Afro-Asian Congress in November 1988 (Session of the WPC, Athens, 6–11 February 1990, *Documents*, p. 97; *YICA*, 1990). It seems quite likely that the Qasim Husayn Abdallah of the Federation of Bahraini Workers, who represented that organization at the November Moscow Twelfth World Trade Union Congress, is identical to the Husayn Abdallah of the same organization who attended the East Berlin Eleventh World Trade Union Congress of September 1986 (Twelfth World Trade Union Congress, *List of Participants*, p. 3; *YICA*, 1987).

Wallace H. Spaulding
McLean, Virginia

Egypt

Population. 54,705,746
Party. Egyptian Communist Party (al-Hizb al-Shuyu'i al-Misri; ECP)
Founded. 1921; revived, 1975
Membership. 500 (estimated)
General Secretary. Farid Mujahid (apparently)
Politburo. Michel Kamil (chief of foreign relations), Najib Kamil, Kamal Muhammad Magdi, Magheed Ibrahim; other names unknown
Central Committee. Farid Mujahid, Yusuf Darwish, Magheed Ibrahim; other names unknown
Status. Proscribed
Last Congress. Second, 1984
Last Election. November; no information on Communist candidates running as independents (if any); total number of seats in the legislature: 454 (including 10 appointed members)
Auxiliary Organizations. Union of Egyptian Peasants; participation in other groups (see below)

Publications. *Al-Intisar* (Victory), main ECP newspaper, published about nine times a year, beginning in 1973; *al-Wa'i* (Consciousness), intraparty issues; *Hayat al-Hizb* (Party life), party work; *Kadaya Fikriya* (Questions of ideology), theoretical journal; *Aurak Ummaliya* (Workers' Gazette). In the recent past, Egyptian Communists in Paris have published *al-Yasar al-Arabi* (The Arab left).

Background. The Egyptian communist movement remains as splintered as ever. Besides the ECP, several groups have surfaced in recent years, including the Revolutionary Current, the Egyptian Community Party-8 January, the Egyptian Communist Workers' Party (*Hizb al-Ummal al-Shuyu'i al-Misri*; ECWP), the Popular Movement, the Armed Communist Organization, the Egyptian Communist Party-Congress Faction, the Revolutionary Communist League (a Trotskyite organization), and the Revolutionary Progressive party. Some of these may be merely descriptive labels given by the government, which leftists sometimes accuse of reporting organizations that do not exist, rather than formal names of organizations, and it is not known whether there is any relationship between these groups and the ECP (or, in most cases, whether they continue to exist).

In May, a few days before his trip to the USSR, President Hosni Mubarak pardoned members of an unnamed communist organization who had been imprisoned "in the case concerning the party's reestablishment and the convening of its general conference in 1981." The prison sentences of one to five years were begun at the end of 1989 following unsuccessful attempts by members of the party to appeal the verdict, and the convicted individuals then asked for amnesty. (London, *al-Sharq al-Awsat*, 9 May; *FBIS*, 10 May.) All evidence points to the relative insignificance of communist groups in comparison with the threat posed to the regime by militant religious movements.

Leadership and Party Organization. Little is known about the ECP's leadership and organization. Few party officials have been mentioned in available publications, and official statements of ECP leaders published abroad are mostly anonymous. The names most often mentioned are two Politburo members, Michel Kamil (the party's chief of foreign relations) and Kamal Muhammad Magdi (the representative to the *World Marxist Review*). All indications point to the typical pattern of "democratic centralism," albeit in a rudimentary form resulting from the group's small membership and clandestine character. Official communist publications in recent years described the ECP as open to the presentation of diverse points of view with decisions then made democratically. More than 30 percent of the members of the party are said to be workers, while more than half of the total membership is made up of people under 30 years of age. Members may recommend others as candidate members for determination by "one of the party organisations." This status lasts for four months in the case of workers, six months for nonworkers, and nine months "for members of non-Marxist political organisations." The party organizes courses throughout Egypt for "educating its members and training its cadres." (*First-Hand Information: Communists and Revolutionary Democrats of the World Presenting Their Parties* [Prague: Peace and Socialism International Publishers, 1988], p. 125.)

Politburo member Muhammad Kamal Magdi spoke of "the general tendency towards decentralisation," which however has not prevented the continuation of divisive tendencies in the communist movement. He added that since the restoration of the ECP in 1975, it had attempted "to find the right combination of centralism and democracy" in the belief that "a *democratic dialogue* is the only way to renew the party's policy line." He explained that the publication *al-Wa'i* is designed to allow diverse positions to be presented within the party "whenever organisational or political differences arise" and that "a series of meetings with the participation of party activists to discuss draft resolutions," as well as "broad discussion," precedes decisions of the Central Committee but that "once a decision has been taken, everyone must submit to majority views." (Toronto, *WMR*, January.)

There is no information on communist candidates' contesting the November general elections. Four communists ran unsuccessfully as independents in 1987 (see *YICA*, 1988).

Auxiliary and Front Organizations. Little information has come to light about auxiliary organizations of the ECP, but it has been closely tied to the Union of Peasants, the Progressive Union of Women, the Democratic Union of Youth, the Egyptian Peace and Disarmament Committee, unions of lawyers and journalists, and the Progressive Union of Youth. The party has sponsored successful candidates in trade union elections in the past. It is also possible that the ECP is involved in the Egyptian Committee for Afro-Asian Solidarity.

More important than the ECP—which recurrently calls for the establishment of an even broader national front—or any other communist organization is the broad, legal leftist opposition front, the National Progressive Unionist Party (NPUP), whose general secretary is longtime Marxist Khalid Muhyi al-Din. (For a biography of Muhyi al-Din, see *YICA*, 1984.) The secretary of the Central Committee is Rif'at Sa'id. Some members of the NPUP are Marxists, including those from the ranks of the ECP. Others are Nasserites or other opponents of the non-Socialist, pro-Western direction of the regime. The NPUP publishes the widely circulated weekly newspaper *al-Ahali*. Having gained only 2.2 percent of the vote in the general elections of 1987, the NPUP did not get any seats in the People's Assembly. Interior Minister General Zaki Badr admitted in 1990, however, that his vote rigging prevented Muhyi al-Din from winning a seat (New York, *Africa Report*, March–April).

The Nineteenth Session of the NPUP Central Committee met in January. It postponed the party's third general conference, setting December as the deadline for the session, and called for mass involvement in the preparations, which "should aim to rebuild" the party. The General Secretariat was instructed to carry out the preparations and to study "the negative phenomena hampering party work and limiting its mass influence." The Central Committee report spoke of "international detente" and the hostility of "international monopolies" to it, "deep crises" in the capitalist world, the "plundering [of] Third World countries" by capitalist countries, and the "calls for democracy and attempts to restore the real human face of socialism" in European Socialist countries. The report affirmed the party's "unshakable belief in political diversity, its upholding of democracy as the path conducive to socialism, its espousal of the pan-Arab cause, its positive view of the role of religion, . . . and its rejection of any preconceived type or mode of socialism." It accused Arab regimes of failing to live up to their resolutions in support of the Palestinian *intifada* and "called for using all effective Arab weapons" to pressure the United States and Israel. It also called on people to pressure the Egyptian government to support the *intifada* and dealt with the dangers posed by Soviet Jewish emigration to Israel, asking Moscow to suspend such immigration until the Palestine question is settled and Cairo to urge that restraints on Jewish immigration to the United States be revoked.

As for domestic affairs, the Central Committee discussed the burdens on "working people and even the middle class groups" that the agreement with the International Monetary Fund and the World Bank will impose. Calls were made for abrogating the emergency laws, passing a new electoral law, releasing detainees, restoring the leading role of the public sector, increasing grain production and concentrating generally on agricultural development, using investments to solve the unemployment problem, and getting the state to make "basic commodities" affordable. (Cairo, *al-Ahali*, 31 January; *FBIS*, 12 February.)

On 8 August, the leaders of all the legal parties, including the NPUP, met with President Mubarak. After hearing the president's account of his attempts to solve the Kuwait crisis within an Arab framework, all opposition party leaders declared their support for the steps he had taken. (Cairo Domestic Service, 8 August; *FBIS*, 10 August.)

A statement issued by the NPUP Committee on Freedoms in 1989 deplored "the appalling prison conditions" and generally "the persecution" of leftists arrested in connection with the strike in Helwan in September of that year (Toronto, *WMR*, December 1989).

After the Supreme Constitutional Court declared unconstitutional the electoral law on which the 1987 general elections were based, voters approved a referendum dissolving the People's Assembly and calling new elections, which were held on 29 November. Three other legal opposition parties (the New Wafd party, the Socialist Labor party, and the Liberal Socialist party) boycotted the elections, but the NPUP did not participate in the boycott. The new electoral law differed from the previous one in doing away with party lists and requiring candidates for the 444 elected seats to run at least technically as independents in two-member districts. Rif'at Sa'id explained that the "legal guarantees" of a truly free vote that the NPUP sought—namely, the use of identification cards and "full observation by judges" to "remove the hand of the Ministry of the Interior"—were not forthcoming (New York, *News from Middle East Watch*, 15 November), but the NPUP General Secretariat rejected the other parties' decision to boycott as implying "that all parties have given up on the possibility of bringing about democratic transformation of society" (*al-Ahali*, 24

October; *FBIS*, 31 October; *News from Middle East Watch*, 15 November). NPUP spokesman Mahir Assal explained that even without the guarantees his and other parties had sought, support for the democratic process as the way to bring about change created an obligation "to participate in all general elections" (Nicosia, *Middle East Times*, 27 November–3 December). Sa'id later complained to the Ministry of Interior and the Office of the President that the governor of Aswan province had threatened all local leaders with dismissal if they failed to prevent the candidates backed by the governing National Democratic party from losing in any district (*News from Middle East Watch*, 15 November); *al-Ahali*'s editor in chief, Philip Gallab, criticized the NDP's monopoly on radio and television and reported that the NPUP was "asking for access to" these media (ibid.). The NDP again won an overwhelming majority; six NPUP candidates were elected (London, *Middle East*, January 1991).

International Views, Positions, and Activities. In August, the ECP joined eleven Arab communist organizations in a statement published in the Lebanese communist newspaper *al-Nida* that condemned "the annexation of Kuwait by Iraq against the wishes of the Kuwait people" and asked for "a peaceful resolution of the crisis between the two countries within the framework of the Arab League." The communiqué called both on Iraq to withdraw from Kuwait and on U.S. forces to leave the Persian Gulf region (London, *Morning Star*, 17 August).

In 1989 (apparently about October), Politburo member Kamal participated in a meeting sponsored by the *World Marxist Review* International Communist Movement and Exchanges of Party Experience on the internal life of communist parties (Toronto, *WMR*, January). He opined that "perestroika in the USSR," far from undermining "the principle of democratic centralism," is designed "*to apply it correctly in concrete circumstances*" (ibid.). A column by Muhammad al-Hayawan on Egypt's past experience with Soviet interference in its domestic affairs, however, pictured Egyptian Communists— without citing any examples—as "obdurate" in refusing to accept change "even if their masters [the Soviets] have" and of "criticizing Gorbachev" and "clinging to the idols of socialism" (Cairo, *al-Jumhuriyah*, 16 May; *FBIS*, 18 May).

Glenn E. Perry
Indiana State University

Iran

Population. 55,647,001 (July)
Party. Communist Party of Iran (Tudeh Party)
Membership. 1,000 to 2,000 hard-core members; 15,000 to 20,000 sympathizers
First Secretary. Ali Khavari
Status. Illegal
Last Congress. 1986, National Conference
Publications. *Rahe Tudeh* (Tudeh path); *Mardom* (People); *Tudeh News* (in English)

Domestic Affairs. For a fleeting moment in 1990 the Tudeh Party of Iran capitalized on apparent opposition to the revolutionary regime to call for a "United Front" to destroy the government, using the "antigovernment" demonstrations of 16 February in the areas surrounding the Amjadieh and Azadi stadiums in Tehran. The demonstrations were actually touched off by the cancellation of a soccer match. Apparently the crowds, disappointed in the failure of the authorities to announce the cancellation in advance, or in response to shooting by Jondollah patrolmen, vented their anger by setting fire to patrol vehicles.

The following day, 17 February, in its official statement on the event, Tudeh urged "politically active people" to transform their autonomous demonstrations into a freedom movement to foil the regime's suppressive activities, to dissuade armed forces personnel from confronting the masses, and to neutralize the efforts of the regime's political police to discover and crush resistance cells (Radio of the Iranian Toilers, in Persian, 18 February; *FBIS-NES*, 20 February). Tudeh seemed to credit the leftist Mojahedin-e Khalq Organization with the antigovernment demonstrations, but its call for united action addressed all "progressive and combative forces and politically active cells."

In 1989 the Tudeh leadership tried to ignore the democratic revolution (see *YICA*, 1990), but in 1990, the party tried to face the reality of the general crisis. According to the party Central Committee, the root causes of the crisis were "greater changes in the Soviet Union and Western Europe and fundamental changes in ideological and political values of leftist movements as well as the conse-

quences of attacks made on the party [by the Iranian regime], and the mistakes, shortcomings and organizational problems of recent years" (Radio of the Iranian Toilers, in Persian, 10 October; *FBIS-NES*, 22 October). Missing in this statement was an acknowledgment of the increasing weakening of the party because of defections over the years. Even when the party Central Committee admitted this fact, it refused to explain it fully: "Dear comrades, all of us know that during recent years a number of the members and supporters of the Tudeh Party have left the party ranks due to many practical and ideological reasons which cannot be elaborated here" (Radio of the Iranian Toilers, in Persian, 16 May; *FBIS-NES*, 18 May).

By the beginning of the Iranian New Year (21 March), the party seemed to be getting together. The plenum of the Central Committee issued a message about holding the Third Congress of the party, more than 40 years after the convening of the Second Congress. The Central Committee message emphasized the importance of convening the new congress in a "democratic" manner, "holding elections in foreign units, attempting to find ways for the participation of party supporters inside the country [Iran] in all aspects of the party life, and formulating the constitution and program of the party through creative and open discussions among its members and supporters" (Radio of the Iranian Toilers, in Persian, 16 May; *FBIS-NES*, 18 May). This was an admission of the need for restructuring the Tudeh party, the most important aspect of which would concern the formulation of a new constitution. This formulation, according to the Central Committee, should "make use of all the former points of strength, while on the other hand one should oppose all nondemocratic and unacceptable principles and ideas."

It took the Tudeh Party about eight months to spell out what these acceptable "principles and ideas" were. Given the party's history of rampant factionalism and infighting, it is important to note that the "unity and solidarity" of the party were given greater weight than the principle of "diversity of opinions." According to one analysis, published in *Mardom*,

Theoretical pluralism and the complete safeguarding of the rights of the minority are among the basic principles of the reconstruction of the party. However, the point at issue is the strengthening of the unity and solidarity of the party in the fields of political and social struggle; namely, the main principles upon which each Tudeh member bases its relations with the party. (Radio of the Iranian Toilers, in Persian, 10 October; *FBIS-NES*, 22 October.)

Foreign Relations. The foundations for new relations between Iran and the Soviet Union, which had been formalized in 1989, were bound to be tested sooner or later (see *YICA*, 1990). As it happened, testing events came in 1990 when the simmering rebellion in Soviet Azerbaijan burst into the open. As will be seen below, the effects of this uprising spilled over into Iranian Azerbaijan, causing brief tensions in the blossoming new relations between Moscow and Tehran. But retrospectively, this challenge to the Soviet-Iranian relationship was met successfully by both sides; hence the improvement in Soviet-Iranian economic relations in 1990 was eventually matched by expanding diplomatic relations.

The single most important development in Soviet-Iranian economic relations since the Iranian revolution in 1979 took place in 1990. After a ten-year break in the export of Iranian natural gas to the Soviet Union, the gas began to flow again on 9 April amid Soviet-Iranian ceremonies in the border town of Astara attended by high-ranking officials. The Iranian national pipeline carries natural gas over 1,160 kilometers, from the refineries of Kangan in Bushehr province and Bid Boland in Khuzestan province to the Astara pipeline. The Soviet-Iranian agreement initially called for the export of 3 billion cubic meters of gas per year. According to the statements of the Iranian officials, the volume of gas exported may increase up to 8 billion cubic meters (London, *Keyhan*, in Persian, 26 April; *FBIS-NES*, 16 May). During the shah's regime, gas exports to the Soviet Union began on 21 March 1970; a total of 70 billion cubic meters of gas was exported between 1970 and 1979 through the pipeline known as Irgat-1, with a 16.5-billion-cubic-meter capacity of output per year.

The resumption of Iranian gas exports to the Soviet Union was even more important economically. Given the revolutionary regime's aversion to foreign loans on the one hand and the imperative of implementing the country's first five-year plan since the revolution on the other, the income from gas exports has become an engine of Iran's postwar reconstruction efforts. According to Iran's minister of finance and economic affairs, Dr. Mohsen Nurbakhsh, "the export of gas to the Soviet Union is the main axis of our bilateral economic cooperation" (Domestic Service, in Persian,

9 April; *FBIS-NES*, 10 April). The landmark visit of Hashemi-Rafsanjani to the Soviet Union 20–23 June 1989 was the occasion during which the new foundations of Soviet-Iranian relations, including the gas relationship, were formalized. On the basis of technical and economic agreements then signed, nineteen projects in Iran were to be undertaken by the Soviet Union, funded from natural gas sales amounting to $6 billion over a ten- or possibly fifteen-year period. The dispute over the price of gas had largely caused the export stoppage in 1980. Ten years later the two governments agreed to calculate prices on a par with international prices.

The opponents of the revolutionary regime criticized it for having failed to explain clearly the base price of gas. Given the projected annual revenues from the sale of natural gas at $300 million, a simple calculation, according to the critics, indicates that the gas will be sold for ten cents per cubic meter. "This seems very exaggerated, since the Soviet Union presently sells its gas in Europe at an average price of six cents per cubic meter. How could the Soviet Union sell natural gas at six cents per cubic meter in Europe, which is a real market for natural gas, and buy the same amount for 10 cents at the Astara border, which is far away from the consumer centers?" (London, *Keyhan*, in Persian, 26 April; *FBIS-NES*, 16 May). The many answers to this question could include the inadequate information on which the criticism is based. Overlooked is the fact that post-Khomeini Iran is trying to reenter the international gas market after ten years of self-imposed isolation. It is also aspiring to exploit its potentials as the world's second-largest (after the Soviet Union) gas-rich nation for economic reconstruction and development. Possessing only one-fourth of Iran's gas resources, Algeria is exporting nearly fourteen times Iran's exports today. The revolutionary leaders realize that they have a lot of catching up to do.

Economic and technical cooperation in 1990 in two other areas deserves consideration. First, it was revealed in June that a group of Iranian and Russian experts jointly dug the first underwater oil well in the Caspian Sea at a depth of 3,267 meters and expected to strike oil at several thousand meters. Extensive exploration and exploitation of the oil and gas reserves in the Caspian Sea were part of the agreement signed by Hashemi-Rafsanjani during his visit to Moscow in 1989 (London, *Keyhan*, in Persian, 14 June, *FBIS-NES*, 18 July).

The second major development concerned rail and air links between Tehran and Moscow. Beginning on 21 March 1991, travelers going to the two cities will be able to make the trip by passenger train; thus the Soviets and Iranians signed an agreement so that Iran could buy two hundred railcars from the Soviet Union. In expanding cooperation in the area of air travel, the Iranian company Homa and the Soviet company Aeroflot reached agreement for flights to Tehran and Moscow every week. Furthermore, Iran expressed interest in leasing Soviet Yak-42 passenger aircraft with a capacity of one hundred passengers; if the quality proved satisfactory Iran would purchase such passenger planes (London, *Keyhan*, in Persian, 26 October; *FBIS-NES*, 9 November).

Implicit in the foregoing description of Soviet-Iranian economic cooperation during 1990 has been the fact that both Moscow and Tehran managed to meet the challenge of the rebellion in Soviet Azerbaijan, but the subject requires explicit discussion because of its importance as the test of the new Soviet-Iranian relationship. The people who live in Soviet and Iranian Azerbaijan today have inhabited the area for thousands of years. Until the immigration of the Oghuz Turks from the Seljuk dynasty (ca. eleventh century), these people spoke Persian, but since then they have spoken a Turkic language that is related to the Turkish spoken in Turkey (see Cedric Maxwell "National Identity in Southern Azerbaijan," *Central Asia and Caucasus Chronicle*, May; *NYT*, 17 January). This linguistic characteristic is part of the Azeri identity as distinguished from the Persian and the Russian identities, but although both the Soviet Azeris and the Iranian Azeris share a common religion with the Persians—Imami Shia Islam—they have no religious affiliation with the Russians.

The territorial division between the Soviet and Iranian Azeris or Azerbaijanis is the result of the defeat of the Persian Empire at the hands of the stronger Russian Empire in the nineteenth century, until which time all the Azeris had lived under the direct control or suzerainty of Iran. Russia then imposed on Iran the humiliating peace treaty of Turkmenchai in 1828, which divided the Azeri people into two groups along the Aras River. What became the Soviet republic of Azerbaijan in 1920, after a brief spell of independence in the wake of World War I, today covers 33,000 square miles inhabited by about 6.7 million people, while Iranian Azerbaijan covers 41,000 square miles with a population of about 4 million. Soviet Azerbaijan includes the Nakhichevan Autonomous Republic, which is separated from the rest of Azerbaijan by

the Armenian republic and which borders on Iran for about 120 miles. It also includes the Nagorno-Karabakh oblast, the main focus of Azerbaijani-Armenian conflict in recent years.

In late 1987, the Christian Armenians, who live in the Nagorno-Karabakh enclave under the administrative control of Shia Muslim Azerbaijanis, demanded unification with Armenia. This demand led, by February 1988, to violent clashes between Armenians and Azerbaijanis during much of the year, resulting in 90 deaths. In retaliation, the Armenians attacked with stones and guns a convoy of buses carrying Azerbaijanis through the Nagorno-Karabakh capital of Stepanakert on 2 January 1990.

This date opened a new chapter in Soviet Transcaucasian violence that directly affected Iran. Thousands of Soviet Azerbaijanis rioted near the Soviet-Iranian border, destroying property, harrassing Soviet and Iranian border guards, and, in some cases, trying to cross illegally into Iran, according to Soviet sources (*WP*, 3 January). The turmoil actually began on the eve of the New Year and had been fiercest about 80 miles from the Iranian border in the Nakhichevan region. In regard to the border turmoil of 2 January, Vagiv Samedoglu, a leader of the Azerbaijani Popular Front political movement, rejected the Soviet charges of rioting and intoxication of the Azerbaijanis as a "monstrous lie and libel" on his people and claimed that they had demonstrated peacefully along the Iranian frontier to demand an open border between the Nakhichevan region of Azerbaijan and the Iranian province of Azerbaijan. He also said, "We are not extremists, as the Soviet media and Moscow bureaucrats call us, but we want to be able to see relatives and have free trade across the border" (ibid.). The Azerbaijanis, reacting to the failure of Soviet authorities to respond to their "ultimatum" of mid-December 1989, demanded that the Soviet authorities dismantle border-crossing blockades by 31 December (*NYT*, 4 January).

Violence continued and spread during the next two weeks. On 5 January, the local communist party chief in Soviet Azerbaijan quit his post because of border violence. While the Soviet Foreign Ministry was saying that restrictions on border crossings would be eased in cooperation with Iran, the Armenian Parliament approved a plan for social and economic development, including development measures for the disputed Nagorno-Karabakh region. In response, several hundred Azerbaijanis blockaded government offices and briefly seized the local radio station in the Caspian port city of Lenkoran on 12 January (*WP*, 13 January).

The next day, violence spread to the Azerbaijani capital city of Baku, where up to half a million people packed the city center to adopt a resolution calling on the local legislature to hold a referendum on the republic's secession from the Soviet Union (*WP*, 14 January). The deaths of at least 25 people were blamed on mobs that broke away from the huge rally demanding the withdrawal of Azerbaijan from the Soviet Union. According to Soviet officials, "gangs" continued to roam the Armenian quarter on 14 January, committing "atrocities and pogroms" (*NYT*, 15 January).

On the night of 15 January, the Soviet Union declared a state of emergency in parts of Azerbaijan, including the Nagorno-Karabakh enclave and border regions in Azerbaijan and Armenia, and ordered army, navy, and Soviet State Security Committee (KGB) forces to help contain what officials called ethnic hostilities verging on civil war. The decision to declare the state of emergency was made at a hastily convened session of the presidium of the Supreme Soviet chaired by President Mikhail Gorbachev. The Kremlin decree said that the situation in several cities had become particularly tense, reaching "the point of murders, robberies, and attempts at armed overthrow of Soviet power and at changing by force the state and social system enshrined in the constitution of the U.S.S.R." (*WP*, 16 January.) Although the Azerbaijani Popular Front blamed the Armenians for the violence, its new Council for National Defense deplored the attacks on Armenians and claimed that the front members had tried to halt them (ibid.).

Early on the morning of 20 January, Soviet troops fired on Azerbaijanis in Baku and pushed through street barricades with tanks toward the center of the republic's capital in an attempt to end the civil insurrection (*NYT*, *WP*, 21 January). According to official and other accounts, somewhere between 60 and 120 people were killed when the army stormed into Baku, destroying barricades erected by Azerbaijanis. Addressing the nation in sorrowful tones, Gorbachev said that the Kremlin had exhausted all peaceful means before ordering the army into Baku. He added, "It is the duty of the state to put an end to illegality and inhumanity, to resolutely cut short criminal actions and the actions of extremists who are ready to sacrifice others for the sake of their personal ambitions and profiteering for power" (*WP*, 21 January). Once in control of the situation in Baku, the Soviet Union sealed its border

with Iran in the Azerbaijan region, allowing Soviet Azerbaijanis who had gone to Iran to return but permitting no further travel across the border by Soviet citizens. Thus ended two weeks of free movement of some 20,000 Azerbaijanis who had crossed to the other side of the Aras into Iran, some swimming across the river.

Speculation about the root causes of the Azerbaijani upheaval is not merely academic, for understanding may help contain not only the conflict between the two Soviet republics but also the spillover effects of the unrest onto Soviet-Iranian relations. Strangely enough, both President Gorbachev and Ayatollah Khamenei, Iran's spiritual leader, seem to single out what Gorbachev calls "Islamic fundamentalism" and Khamenei calls "Islamic zeal" as the cause, although for entirely different reasons (*WP*, 20 January; *NYT*, 21 January). Gorbachev considers anachronistic Islamic fundamentalism as a threat to the security of the Soviet Union, especially because of the high birthrate among Soviet Muslims as compared with the Russians. Khamenei, in contrast, considers the outpouring of "Islamic feelings" of the Azerbaijanis, after 70 years of suppression, as vindicating the correctness of Iran's Islamic ideology. Some academics, such as Richard Pipes, also believe that Azerbaijani-Armenian antagonism is "fundamentally religious" (*NYT*, 17 January).

Other academics, such as Richard G. Hovannisian, seem to attribute the conflict between the two Transcaucasian nations to intercommunal and ethnic differences. These differences surfaced in the form of direct clashes for the first time between 1905 and 1907, when they were referred to as "the Armeno-Tatar conflict" (ibid.). Other academics, such as Firuz Kazemzadeh, emphasize a diversity of factors. The conflict thus reflects a combination of religious, ethnic, and territorial differences between the two people, the territorial factor—the dispute over the status of the Nagorno-Karabakh enclave—being the focus of the Azerbaijani-Armenian conflict in recent years.

Yet the question remains, what one factor would seem to have been at least the proximate, if not the root, cause of the conflict? The answer to this question, in my opinion, lies in Azerbaijan's being the principal scene of the upheaval rather than Armenia. Why? According to most accounts, the core of the uprising was a seething community of Azerbaijani refugees, more than 130,000 of whom had settled in slum and squatter districts in Baku (*NYT*, 18 January). The parallel between the homeless, the jobless, and the uprooted peasants and farmers who changed the character of Baku and those who dwelled in the slums of Tehran just before the eruption of the Iranian revolution is striking. The difference is that the Iranians blamed it all on the shah's regime, while the Azerbaijanis blamed it all on the "atrocities suffered at the hands of the Armenians."

The rebellion in Soviet Azerbaijan in 1990, like the insurrection in Iranian Azerbaijan in 1946, in my opinion, fundamentally stemmed from the miserable social and economic conditions of the poorer classes, which in both instances provided the recruits for the respective political movements. In the case at hand, it was no coincidence that Baku slum dwellers constituted the rank and file of the People's Front of Azerbaijan (PFA). Nor is it a coincidence that the number one principle of the front's manifesto states that the PFA is "a general social movement aiming to improve and democratise all spheres of our lives" (see the text of this document in *Central Asia and Caucasus Chronicle*, August 1989). Just as the Iranian Azerbaijanis did not want to become part of the Soviet Union through a merger with Soviet Azerbaijan in 1946, the Soviet Azerbaijanis did not wish to become part of Iran through unification with Iranian Azerbaijan in 1990. Both movements were essentially triggered by age-old social, economic, and political grievances against the incumbent central governments.

For more than two weeks—between the eve of the year 1990 and the Soviet military crackdown in Baku on 20 January—the border turmoil threatened the new Soviet-Iranian relations. Yet both Moscow and Tehran managed to limit the damage. The Soviet and Iranian governments, in effect, pursued two-track policies, each in its own way. Although the Iranian press and media were allowed to report fully the disturbances in Soviet Azerbaijan, particularly criticizing the Soviet military intervention in Baku, the Iranian government confined itself to expressing "deep regrets" and calling for "restraint." Meanwhile, Iranian officials continued discussions with Soviet authorities aimed at containing the unrest. Although the Soviet government, by intervening militarily in Azerbaijan, deviated from the peaceful approach to domestic turmoil it was practicing in regard to the Baltic states, its Foreign Ministry officials kept talking to the Iranians about easing border tensions through the establishment of a new border regime for the region.

Neither Tehran nor Moscow wanted to scuttle the development of their new relationship for the very reasons that impelled its establishment in 1989 in the first place (see *YICA*, 1990). Although militant factions in Iran clamored to exploit this opportunity to export Islamic revolution to neighboring Soviet Azerbaijan, the Iranian government, dominated by the pragmatists, stuck to the principle of noninterference in internal affairs, one of the fundamental principles on which the two countries had agreed during Hashemi-Rafsanjani's visit to the Soviet Union. Even after the Soviet military crackdown in Baku, Iranian foreign minister Ali Akbar Velayati expressed "hope" in his letter to Soviet foreign minister Eduard Shevardnadze that the Soviets would be able to solve the situation in Azerbaijan "peacefully." More important, he said that Iran was concerned about the well-being of all Muslims throughout the world but emphasized that Tehran was "firmly committed to the principle of noninterference in the internal affairs of other countries" (Tehran, Iran News Agency, in English, 24 January; *FBIS-NES*, 25 January).

The mutual restraint between Tehran and Moscow did more than protect the overall cooperation between the two capitals: it planted the seeds of expanding economic cooperation and regulated freedom of movement between the Soviet and Iranian Azerbaijanis. For example, across the border, travel between Iran's West Azerbaijan province and the Soviet republic of Nakhichevan was scheduled to begin on 22 May, although all border travel and trade were to take place within the framework of economic and cultural protocols signed between Tehran and Moscow. To facilitate border travel, the two sides envisaged the construction of two bridges over the Aras River, one connecting Takdagh of Iran to Nkromeh on the Soviet side and the other linking the Iranian city of Pol Dasht with Soviet Shakhtakhty (Tehran, Iran News Agency, in English, 30 April, *FBIS-NES*, 1 May). Border travel also took place frequently between Iran's East Azerbaijan and Soviet Azerbaijan as in November, when the Soviet Azerbaijanis visited the Industrial Production Exposition in East Azerbaijan and an Iranian economic delegation visited neighboring Soviet Azerbaijan, indicating the prospects of cooperation in the exchange of raw materials for the aluminum production industry, the use of the region's mineral waters, stone-cutting machinery, construction of prefabricated housing units, and so forth (London, *Keyhan*, in Persian, 22 November; *FBIS-NES*, 13 December).

Three other noneconomic issues in Soviet-Iranian relations during 1990 require brief mention. First, Iranian officials spread disinformation about the nature of Soviet "defense aid" to Iran in 1989. Iran's first deputy foreign minister announced unequivocally then that "we have gone into negotiations with various countries except the Soviet Union for the purchase of fighter bombers" (see *YICA*, 1990). Yet on 22 September Tehran media claimed that Iran's air force began flying its first batch of advanced Soviet MiG-29 attack airplanes, an agreement for which was perhaps reached during Hashemi-Rafsanjani's visit to Moscow in June 1989 (*Tehran Times*, in English, 24 September; *FBIS-NES*, 28 September).

The second issue was the problem of Afghanistan. Although Soviet-Iranian relations drew closer on the Afghan problem in 1989, compromises still had to be made by both Tehran and Moscow if their positions were to become compatible in fact and not just in rhetoric (see *YICA*, 1990). Two differences kept the Soviet and Iranian approaches apart in 1990: One was Iran's insistence on excluding the United States from participation in the settlement process. Hashemi-Rafsanjani had said in Moscow in 1989 that Iran, Pakistan, the People's Republic of China, and the Soviet Union should help the Afghan people arrive at a decision on their country's destiny. In 1990 Foreign Minister Ali Akbar Velayati specifically ruled out "any role for Saudi Arabia and the United States," whereas Pakistan and possibly the Soviet Union wished to see the United States play a role (London, BBC World Service, in English, 21 June; *FBIS-NES*, 21 June). The other difference between Moscow and Tehran was the continuing problem of Soviet support for the Kabul government, although Foreign Minister Velayati showed a rather conciliatory attitude when he was asked whether President Najibullah's party could take part in a general election under U.N. supervision. Reportedly, Velayati replied that the party's members could participate as "individuals," presumably indicating Iran's preference for avoiding the intense rivalry among guerrilla parties and between them and President Najibullah's party (ibid.).

The third and the last major issue in Soviet-Iranian noneconomic relations is the Iraq-Iran stalled peace negotiations during most of 1990 and their sudden disappearance from the scene after the Iraqi invasion of Kuwait on 2 August 1990. Although in January the Soviet Union reiterated its previous proposal to play some kind of a mediating role in removing differences between Iran and Iraq—without prejudicing the U.N. role—and Iran accepted the proposal in principle, no progress toward a settlement was made. It fell to Saddam Husayn to give Iran whatever it wanted, including acknowledgment of the validity of the 1975 Algiers agreement, withdrawal of his forces from Iranian territory, and exchange of prisoners of war, all with the snap of a finger on 14 August. He thus freed Iraqi forces from the eastern front for confrontation with the U.S.-led multinational forces in the southern front in Kuwait. At least for the balance of 1990, the inconclusive Iraq-Iran peace negotiation was effectively removed from the concerns of Soviet-Iranian relations. Whether it will stay there remains to be seen.

Yet just as soon as this issue was removed from the concerns of Soviet-Iranian relations, a new one took its place. The deployment of massive U.S. forces in the Persian Gulf alarmed Iranian leaders, with the potential for a continued U.S. military presence in the Persian Gulf region long after the resolution of the gulf crisis. In 1990, as in 1987–1988, Moscow and Tehran found themselves on the same side, opposing the presence of U.S. forces in the region. But in 1990, unlike in 1987–1988, the larger interest of the Soviet Union in cooperating closely with the United States in world politics outweighed Moscow's concern with the temporary U.S. military presence in the gulf region, especially considering that during his Helsinki summit meeting with President Gorbachev on 9 September, President Bush invited the Soviet Union to participate in the Arab-Israeli peace process after thirteen years of Washington's having excluded Moscow.

As one looks back on the domestic politics of the Soviet-Iranian relations at the end of 1990, the Soviet and the Iranian scenes seem quite different. Whereas Gorbachev is facing the specter of political paralysis, Hashemi-Rafsanjani is succeeding in consolidating political power. More ominous for the Soviets, while the Soviet empire faces an epidemic demand for sovereignty, which first began in Soviet Azerbaijan on 23 September 1989 and then spread to every one of the other fourteen republics in 1990, the Iranian state remains unchallenged by its minorities. The nature of Soviet-Iranian relations in 1991 will depend more on the fate of the Soviet, rather than the Iranian, regime and state. Even if the Gorbachev regime survives, the process of "Soviet disunion" may prove to be inevitable.

R. K. Ramazani
University of Virginia

Iraq

Population. 18,781,770
Party. Iraqi Communist Party (ICP)
Founded. 1934
Membership. No data
First Secretary. Aziz Muhammad, 66 (Kurd, worker)
Politburo. (Incomplete): Zaki Khayri, 80 (Arab/ Kurd, journalist); Fakhri Karim; Abd al-Razzaq al-Safi, 60 (Shia Arab, lawyer)
Status. Proscribed
Last Congress. Fourth, 10–15 November 1985
Last Election. 2 April 1989; 250-seat National Assembly, no communists
Publications. *Tariq al-Sha'b* (People's road), clandestine; *Al-Thaqafah al-Jadidah* (New culture), an ideological journal

Background. Two developments greatly affected the ICP during late 1989 and 1990. The first was the collapse of communist regimes in Eastern Europe, which dispersed exiled ICP leaders from their customary sanctuaries there. The second was Iraq's invasion and annexation of Kuwait. Iraqi president Saddam Husayn ordered the action to seize Kuwait's wealth, to use its oil revenue to bail Iraq out of a $5 billion annual balance of payments deficit, and pay for an expensive and ambitious military expansion program (*Le Monde*, 3 August). Saddam's action split the Arab League, brought international condemnation and a U.N. Security Council–mandated boycott and embargo on trade with Iraq, and arrayed a large, U.S.-dominated military force against him. These developments have given exiled Iraqi groups opposed to Saddam—the ICP among them—what they perceive of as new opportunities to prepare themselves in case of the hoped-for demise of the Iraqi leader.

Leadership and Organization. Draconian security measures drove the ICP to move most of its activities to Kurdish areas of northern Iraq years ago (*YICA*, 1983). The Iraqi regime's campaign against the Kurds in late 1988, immediately following the cease-fire with Iran, drove a quarter of a million Kurds into Turkey and Iran. Forced popula-

tion transfers from Iraqi border areas sent an equal number to relocation centers in Arab areas of the country. ICP organization suffered severely in consequence. The party leadership was already abroad, and it has continued to function there. Even before the Kuwait crisis, the ICP Central Committee criticized Saddam's regime in a telegram to the Twenty-eighth Congress of the Communist Party of the Soviet Union (*Pravda*, 12 July; *Soviet Union and the Middle East* 15, no.7:25).

First Secretary Aziz Muhammad spent several months in Damascus. In mid-July he discussed ICP-Ba'ath (Syria) relations with a senior Syrian Ba'athist official (Damascus, *Syrian Arab News Agency*, 10 July; *FBIS-NES*, 11 July). He was in the Syrian capital in September, October, and December, apparently making it his headquarters now that Eastern Europe is no longer hospitable. Syrian president Hafiz al-Asad has long extended hospitality to individuals and organizations opposed to Saddam's regime. Muhammad or his representative participated in a meeting of eleven Arab communist parties that condemned Iraq's "annexation of Kuwait against the wishes of the Kuwait people" and called for a peaceful solution (Beirut, *Morning Star*, 17 August).

A few other ICP leaders have surfaced in exile in the West. Politburo member Fakhri Karim gave an interview in the United Kingdom during the autumn (London, *Al-Sharq al-Awsat*, 22 October; *FBIS-NES*, 26 October). The ICP also has an official spokesman in the British capital, as do many Iraqi opposition groups (*Le Monde*, 14–15 October; *FBIS-NES*, 17 October; London, *Al-Sharq al-Awsat*, 14 December; *FBIS-NES*, 19 December).

Iraqi communists were prominent (in comparison with the previous five years) in the pages of the *World Marxist Review* during its final year. An indirect criticism of the rigid centralism of the ICP under Aziz Muhammad appeared in the report of a *World Marxist Review* commission on the exchanges of party experience.

Rahim Ajina, a Sunni Arab doctor with over three decades of experience in the ICP, said, "A whole generation of Communists raised in the underground have been taught that illegal status and [party] democracy are incompatible, and that centralism is paramount. Both centralism and democracy are essential. Everything possible must be done *to secure the fulfillment of majority decisions*." (*WMR*, January, emphasis in original.) Other contributors took up new trends in communist thinking under the titles "Human Rights and Global Security" (Bilal Samir, July 1989), "The Global Character of Third World Problems" (Kadhim Habib, August 1989), and "Let the South Disarm" (Moules Abid, January). The last advocated reducing tensions and conflict in the southern half of the globe, where problems were blamed on U.S. arms supplies.

Domestic Affairs. Iraq's invasion of Kuwait galvanized groups opposing Saddam's regime from exile into activity. Representatives of the major opposition elements—more than fifteen separate ones —had met in 1989 in an attempt to hammer out a common platform. Islamic groups insisted that any resolutions be issued "in the name of God," whereas secularists, led by the ICP, resisted bitterly. (*CSM*, 20 September.) Nothing came of the meeting. A second attempt to gain agreement in late 1990 has had some success. After more than two months of meetings in Damascus and Beirut, 21 opposition groups announced that they were combining to work against Saddam Husayn. The agreement contains provisions for replacing the current Iraqi regime with a pluralist democratic system. The ICP is represented on the seventeen-man Secretariat along with members from Islamic parties, Kurdish groups, anti-Saddam Ba'athists, and independent nationalists. The five-man steering committee for the alliance also has a communist member; each of the five has a veto. (*Middle East International*, 11 January 1991; *NYT*, 30 December.) The six parties (five Kurdish, plus the ICP), which formed a coalition to fight the Baghdad regime in 1988, are all in the new group (*YICA*, 1989).

The Iraqi regime's internal security apparatus has made it impossible for opposition forces to conduct activities inside the country in recent years. An ICP spokesman in London admitted that the party's presence in Iraq was only symbolic, except for its military wing in Kurdistan. (*Le Monde*, 14–15 October; *FBIS-NES*, 17 October.) The diversity of views among the groups and parties argues against a significant degree of effectiveness by the new coalition. A former Ba'ath party leader now in exile assessed the opposition as not having "even a minimum of agreement on a political program" (*Le Monde*, 14–15 October; *FBIS-NES*, 17 October). Politburo member Fakhri Karim could only cite the opposition representatives' "unified position in condemning the occupation (and annexation) of Kuwait" in reply to a question (London, *Al-Sharq al-Awsat*, 22 October; *FBIS-NES*, 26 October).

International Relations. The ICP is in general agreement with the USSR on the need for Iraq to withdraw from Kuwait. Saddam Husayn's regime, which has had good relations with the USSR during most of the past decade, has been at loggerheads with Moscow over the Kuwait affair. The USSR voted for U.N. Security Council Resolution 660 on 2 August, which condemned the Iraqi invasion, and for the succeeding ten Security Council resolutions condemning annexation, instituting the boycott and embargo on trade, and taking other measures to bolster opposition to Iraq's action in Kuwait. Poland, Czechoslovakia, Bulgaria, Romania, and Hungary also agreed to discontinue arms shipments and support sanctions despite the economic consequences. Iraq owes nearly $4 billion to the five countries, and there are lost economic opportunities as well. (*Report on Eastern Europe*, August 24.)

The Soviet commitment to the international coalition against Iraq has remained firm since the start of the crisis when demonstrators in Moscow protesting the invasion were given coverage in state media (Moscow TV, 9 August; *Izvestiia*, 10 August; *FBIS-SOV*, 10 August). Iraqi foreign minister Tariq Aziz's effort to drive a wedge between the USSR and the rest of the coalition was rebuffed (*NYT*, 7 September). Although Moscow has been cautious about endorsing the use of force against Iraq, Gorbachev has given the continuance of good relations with the U.S. high priority. The Soviet military, however, has long had strong ties with Iraq's armed forces. Several weeks of discussion and negotiation between Washington and Moscow were needed before Moscow agreed to support U.N. Resolution 678, which authorized "all necessary means" to compel Iraq to withdraw from Kuwait if it did not do so voluntarily by 15 January 1991. The ICP differs with the USSR on this point, repeatedly insisting on the need to avoid armed conflict, most recently in an Aziz Muhammad interview (Al-Shariqah, *Al-Khalij*, 16 December; *FBIS-NES*, 20 December).

Iraq has received some support from Cuba and a little from China. Although Cuba supported the U.N. resolutions condemning the Iraqi invasion, annexation, violation of diplomatic installations, and destruction of Kuwaiti civil records, it abstained on five resolutions, including those mandating a trade embargo and means to enforce it. Cuba also voted against the embargo on air traffic to Iraq and against Resolution 678. China voted for ten U.N. resolutions but abstained on the last, which permitted the use of force after mid-January 1991 to eject Iraq.

John F. Devlin
Swarthmore, Pennsylvania

Israel

Population. 4,409,218 (not including territories occupied in 1967, except for 193,000 Jewish settlers)

Party. Communist Party of Israel (CPI) or Israeli Communist Party (Miflaga Kommunistit [or Qomunistit] Isra'elit [MAKI or MAQI]); also called New Communist List (Rashima Kommunistit Hadasha [RAKAH])

Founded. 1922 (a short-lived organization in 1920)

Membership. 2,000 (estimated)

General Secretary. Meir Vilner (71; member of the Knesset [Parliament] until January)

Politburo. 9 members, including Meir Vilner, David ("Uzi") Burnstein, Benjamin Gonen, Wolf Erlich, Emile Habibi, David Khenin, Tawfiq Tubi (deputy general secretary and, until July, member of the Knesset), Tawfiq Zayyad (member of the Knesset until January and mayor of Nazareth); 4 alternates, including Zahi Karkabi and Salim Jubran

Secretariat. 7 members, including Meir Vilner, Salim Jubran, Salibi Khamis, David Khenin, George Tubi (chief of the Central Committee's international section), Tawfiq Tubi, Jamal Musa

Central Committee. 31 members, including Nimr Marcus and L. Zakhavi; 5 candidates (data on organs not necessarily up to date)

Status. Legal

Last Congress. Twenty-first, 21–23 May

Last Election. 1 November 1988; 3.7 percent of the vote, winning 4 seats (with the Democratic Front for Peace and Equality [DFPE]); total number of seats in the legislature: 120

Auxiliary Organizations. Young Communist League, Young Pioneers, Democratic Women's Movement

Publications. *Al-Ittihad* (Tawfiq Tubi, publisher; Salim Jubran, acting editor); *Zo Ha-Derekh* (Meir Vilner, editor); *al-Jadid* (Samih al-Qasim, editor); *Information Bulletin, Communist Party of Israel* (sporadically); *al-Didd*; *al-Darb*; *Arahim*; *Der Weg*

Background. The CPI dates its origin back to 1919 (in 1920, according to other sources), when the partially communist ("proletarian Zionist") Socialist Workers' party was founded. The Palestinian Communist Party was established in 1922 (1921, according to current CPI claims), becoming the Israeli Communist Party after 1948. Following a split in the Israeli communist movement in 1965 largely along ethnic lines, the disappearance of the heavily Jewish Israeli Communist Party (Miflaga Kommunistit Isra'elit; MAKI) left the mainly Arab, pro-Moscow RAKAH—which now also calls itself MAKI—as the undisputed claimant to being the Communist Party of Israel (CPI), as the party is known internationally. With Arab nationalist parties not permitted (although the joint [Arab-Jewish] Progressive List for Peace [PLP] emerged in 1984 to espouse the cause of Palestinian self-determination and thus to compete for the Arab vote), Rukah has served mainly as an outlet for the grievances of the Arab (Palestinian) minority, now numbering almost 800,000, more than 18 percent of the population (Elie Rekhess, "Arabs in a Jewish State: Images vs. Realities, "*Middle East Insight* [Washington, D.C.], January/February). It is estimated that more than 90 percent of the party's vote comes from this sector of the population (Joel Beinin, *Was the Red Flag Flying There? Marxist Politics and the Arab-Israeli Conflict in Egypt and Israel, 1948–1965* [Berkeley: University of California Press, 1990], p. 251). The CPI-dominated DFPE got about 50 percent of the Arab vote in 1977 but failed to get more than 35 percent during the 1980s. Starting in the 1970s, the DFPE dominated most Arab town councils, but victories by Islamists (the Islamic Movement) in council and mayoral elections in 1989 came at their expense in several localities. (For an analysis of the challenge of radical Arab nationalists to Israeli communism, see Elie Rekhess, "The Arab Nationalist Challenge to the Israeli Communist Party (1970–1985)," *Studies in Comparative Communism, Winter 1989.*)

Leadership and Party Organization. The organization of the CPI, typical of communist parties in general, is described by party leaders as based on the principle of "democratic centralism." The congress normally meets at four-year intervals and chooses the members of the Central Committee and the Central Control Commission, while the Presidium, Secretariat, and general secretary are chosen by the Central Committee. There are also regional committees, local branches (90), and cells. Cells are based on both residence and place of work. The CPI is said to be the best organized party in Israel, which gives it an important advantage in its rivalry with the non-Marxist PLP for Arab votes.

About 80 percent of the members of the CPI are Arabs, although the party claims that the two ethnic groups are represented about equally. But Jews predominate in the top party organs, with a slight majority in the Politburo and the Central Committee. In recent years, the Jewish general secretary has been balanced by an Arab deputy general secretary. Similarly, a Jew, Wolf Erlich, heads the Central Control Commission, while the deputy chairman of that body is Ramzi Khouri, an Arab. Despite Muslim representation during the past two decades, Christians (largely Greek Orthodox) predominate among the Arab leaders. Although the party has been noted as a nearly unique arena of Arab-Jewish amity, there are reports of dissatisfaction on the part of Arabs because of their inadequate representation at the top.

Domestic Party Affairs. The CPI continued to champion the cause of the Arab minority, particularly the widely recognized neglect of services in Arab communities. Protesting inadequate aid from the central government, 47 Arab local councils shut down municipal services for twenty days—amid a one-day general strike and demonstrations among the Arab population—before reaching an agreement with banks on rescheduling debt payments in February. Members of the Knesset Interior Committee agreed that funds allocated to Arab councils were far smaller than those to Jewish communities of the same size. Mayor Ibrahim Nimr Husayn of Shafaram, chairman of the National Committee of Arab Local Councils, explained that the Arabs engaged in these protests only because there was no other way to rectify the situation. (*Jerusalem Post*, international edition, 4–10 March.) Arab mayors met with the Egyptian ambassador to discuss their communities' financial distress, while Mayor Shaykh Riyad Salah of Umm al-Fahm spoke of the possibility of taking the problem to the United Nations (*Jerusalem Post*, international edition, 25 February–3 March). Arab communities protested again in March by shutting down services (*Jerusalem Post*, international edition, 1–7 April, 8–15

April). Arab leaders, including members of the Knesset and local council heads, met to call a general strike and rallies on the Day of the Land (30 March), celebrated by Palestinians in Israel and the occupied territories since the 1970s (*Jerusalem Post*, 18–24 March). An aid package presented by Health Minister Ehud Olmert designed to improve living conditions in Arab communities during the following decade was welcomed by Mayor Husayn of Shafaram on behalf of most other council heads (*Jerusalem Post*, international edition, 1–7 July). Municipal employees in Sakhnin went on strike after the town's deficit prevented them from receiving their September salaries (*Arabs in Israel*, 25 November).

The Arab community demonstrated much concern over the rapid influx of Jewish immigrants from the USSR. Authorities in Nazareth announced that the displacement of Arabs in predominantly Jewish Upper Nazareth is expected to create housing shortages, and there were expressions of fear that Arabs would be displaced from their jobs on a large scale. *Al-Ittihad* (20 September) reported that unemployment in various Arab communities is already much higher than official figures show. (Tel Aviv, *Arabs in Israel*, 1 November.) The Joint Public Council for the Advancement of the Arab Community in Jaffa, an umbrella organization of various Arab groups formed after Mayor Shlomo Lahat presented a plan to populate the city with Soviet immigrants, protested against plans to "Judaize" the city and proposed a housing plan to ensure that local people, including Arabs, would not be pushed out (*Jerusalem Post*, 22–28 July).

A rally in Nazareth in April protested what it called racist comments by right-wing Israelis who accused Arab members of the Knesset of taking orders from PLO chairman Yassir Arafat; Arab leaders argued that the charges amounted to proposals for apartheid (*Jerusalem Post*, 29 April–5 May). More than 130 Arabs were arrested in Nazareth in June following riots, and statistics showed a 40 percent increase in incidents of unrest during the past year (*Jerusalem Post*, 10–16 June). Further shutdowns of municipal services in Arab communities on 6 June protested "police provocation," while schoolchildren, in accordance with a call made at a meeting of Arab council heads and elected representatives four days earlier and backed by the National Committee of Arab Mayors, protested against shortages in equipment and staff in their schools (*Jerusalem Post*, 10–16 June). Arab schoolchildren carried out another protest against their inadequate facilities as the school year began (*Jerusalem Post*, international edition, 1 September). CPI deputies introduced a bill in the Knesset banning any party that proposes the deportation of Arab citizens (*Arabs in Israel*, 25 November).

There was renewed discussion during the year of the possibility of autonomy for the Arab population. Arabs speaking against the concept included CPI secretary Salim Jubran and Chairman Husayn of the Committee of Arab Local Council Heads (Sofia Kabaha, "The Motto of Equality Remains the Same," *Haaretz* [Tel Aviv], 10 October; *Arabs in Israel*, 25 November).

There were accusations that Nazareth's mayor, Tawfiq Zayyad, had attacked policemen on the previous New Year's Eve. Zayyad proclaimed such allegations to be lies and spoke of a "provocative and political investigation." (*Jerusalem Post*, international edition, 24 August–1 September.)

On 15 March communist and Arab deputies provided 5 of the 60 votes that forced the dissolution of the government of Prime Minister Yitzhak Shamir (who later headed a new government) because of its rejection of terms suggested by the United States for starting Israeli-Palestinian peace talks. There was a realization that it would be "difficult if not impossible" for the Labor party to form a coalition that would include these five deputies. (*NYT*, 16 March.) CPI deputy general secretary and Knesset member Tawfiq Tubi later denied a statement by Shimon Peres that a Labor party–led coalition would be guaranteed the votes of the DFPE, specifying that "only during negotiations and after an agreement on the path, commitments, and actions of such a government" would the DFPE's position "toward the government Mr. Peres is trying to form . . . be decided" (Jerusalem Domestic Service, *FBIS*, 5 April).

Vilner resigned from the Knesset—in which he had been a deputy since 1948—in January. At the invitation of the speaker, Vilner made a statement as the session started, with almost all the members sitting "in silence to pay their respects." He later said that although his party had always taken the correct positions in the past, it had not always done so publicly and promised that "we shall not keep our decisions secret in the future." (Asher Wallfish, "Meir Wilner Leaves the House," *Jerusalem Post*, international edition, 14–20 January.)

After 41 years in the Knesset, Politburo member Tawfiq Tubi also resigned from that body in July. After Tubi gave his farewell speech, the valedicto-

ries in the Knesset continued for almost one and a half hours and "had no precedent in Knesset history for the warmth and respect they showed the retired parliamentarian." (*Jerusalem Post*, international edition, 15–21 July.)

In March, Shaykh Abdullah Nimr Darwish indicated that the Islamic Movement, of which he is the "spiritual head," would contest the next general elections as a separate party or as part of a joint Arab list (*Jerusalem Post*, international edition, 24 March). If so, this would seem to offer the prospect of reducing the DFPE's role in national politics.

A move to establish a coordinating framework for the Arab movement in Israel led to rumors that formation of a Nasserist party was in the works. *Al-Ittihad* recognized the legitimacy of coordination but expressed the view that existing parties "should remain independently operative." (*Arabs in Israel*, 1 November.) The Jewish-Arab list that included the DFPE won 4 percent of the vote in the elections for the Histadrut national council in November 1989, the same percentage received by the DFPE alone in 1985 (*Jerusalem Post*, international edition, 19–25 November 1989).

Felicia Langer (see her biography in *YICA*, 1984) emigrated to the Federal Republic of Germany during the year because of "her loss of faith in [the Israeli] system" (*The Soviet Union and the Middle East* [Jerusalem], no. 5).

Auxiliary and Front Organizations. The CPI dominates the DFPE, which includes the following noncommunist partners: the Black Panthers, an Afro-Asian or Oriental Jewish group protesting discrimination by Jews of European origin whose leader, Charlie Biton, is a member of the DFPE delegation in the Knesset; the Committee of Arab Local Council Heads, whose candidate, Hashim Mahamid (former mayor of Umm al-Fahm), was number five on the DFPE list in 1988, barely missed getting elected, and indeed took Vilner's seat when the latter retired from the Knesset in January (the committee consists of sixteen members, half of whom are "communists or 'front' activists" and is sometimes labeled "the parliament of the Israeli Arabs" [Elie Rekhess, "Arabs in a Jewish State: Images vs. Realities," *Middle East Insight*, January/February]); and the Nitzotz-Ashara organization, whose newspaper is *Derech Ha Nitzotz* (Way of the spark), with an Arabic counterpart under the title *Tariq al-Sharara*. In addition to its delegation in the Knesset, the DFPE is particularly well organized in Arab towns and villages.

Another leftist group, the Israeli Socialist Left (SHASHI), broke away from the DFPE in 1984 but recommended that its members vote for that list in 1988. SHASHI and some other leftist individuals tried unsuccessfully in 1988 to bring together a broader slate that would have included the DFPE and the PLP and that some say could have won as many as eight seats.

The CPI sponsors the active Young Pioneers and the Young Communist League. At least in the past, it also sponsored or actively participated in the Committee against the War in Lebanon, There Is a Limit (an organization calling on Israeli soldiers to refuse to serve in Lebanon and the other occupied territories), the Nationwide Committee for the Defense of Arab Land, Mothers against the War, Soldiers against Silence, Women for Peace, the Israel-USSR Friendship Society, the Israeli Association of Anti-Fascist Fighters and Victims of Nazism, and Arab student committees, notably CAMPUS. Other groups that official communist publications in recent years have listed as including members of the CPI are the Movement of Democratic Women in Israel, the Initiative Committee for the Improvement of Relations with the Soviet Union, the Israel-Cuba Friendship Committee, the Israel-Bulgaria Friendship Committee, the Israel Peace Committee, the League for Human and Civil Rights in Israel, the Druze Initiative Committee, and the Committee against Racism.

International Views, Positions, and Activities. The CPI calls for peace based on self-determination for the Palestinians, for Israel to withdraw from all the territories occupied in 1967, and for an international peace conference in which the PLO as well as Israel would participate as the road to such a "two states for two peoples" settlement. In his farewell speech to the Knesset in January, Vilner pointed to the alleged fact that a fourth of the chamber's members now support talks with the PLO as the vindication of his own party's call for such talks in 1977 (*Jerusalem Post*, international edition, 14–20 January).

At the beginning of Nazareth's annual international work camp in March (organized by the CPI and the CPI-dominated city government and attended by individuals from Israel and the occupied territories and by delegations from the USSR, East Germany, and twelve other countries), demonstrators called for a two-state solution to the Palestine question, for equality for Israel's Arab population, and for ending the settlement of immigrants in the occupied territories. A "mass rally" ensued at the city's high school. (*Jerusalem Post*, international edition, 29 July–4 August.)

The massacre of Palestinian workers in May evoked demonstrations in most Arab communities (London, *Middle East*, November). The killing of Palestinians at the Haram al-Sharif in October was followed by a general strike by the Arab population in Israel. Speaking at the funeral of an Israeli Arab who was among those killed, Zayyad asked for "the unity of forces operating within the Arab sector, in order to protect Israeli Arabs and aid Palestinians in the territories in their struggle for national liberation." There were mass demonstrations in several communities, and Zayyad and Workers' Council general secretary Muhammad Abu Ahmad headed a delegation from Nazareth that visited al-Aqsa Mosque to express solidarity with the people of the occupied areas. (*Arabs in Israel*, 1 November.) *Al-Ittihad* criticized the Israeli Commission of Inquiry to investigate the incident and called for an independent commission (*Arabs in Israel*, 25 November).

An editorial in *al-Ittihad* (22 October) condemned the retaliatory murder of three Jews in Jerusalem and clarified that the Israeli Arabs were not part of the *intifada*, while Tubi opined that the extension of the uprising to Israel proper would be harmful to the Arab minority there (*Arabs in Israel*, 25 November). Various CPI spokesmen strongly opposed the government's decision to cut off passage of workers from the occupied areas into Israel (*Arabs in Israel*, 25 November).

The CPI Politburo declared that Iraq's occupation of Kuwait must be ended through the United Nations and the Arab League but not through military force. It also warned against any Israeli military action against Iraq and against the use of the situation to justify actions directed at the Palestinians and Jordan. (Jerusalem Domestic Service, 14 August; *FBIS-NES*, 17 August.)

The party's Central Committee called on the presidents of the USSR, China, and France to prevent the Security Council from being a rubber stamp for the war it said the United States was planning. It also accused Israel of planning a war against Iraq. (Jerusalem Domestic Service, 17 November; *FBIS-NES*, 21 November). It was reported that "for the first time ever," the CPI had "launched a blistering attack on the Soviet Union" through a leaflet distributed in Galilee calling Moscow's failure to take a stand against U.S. interventionism in the gulf a form of complicity in a criminal venture.

Pointing to a demonstration in which 1,500 Arabs in Nazareth proclaimed their support for Iraq and burned a U.S. flag and a picture of President Hosni Mubarak of Egypt, one reporter spoke of spreading support for President Saddam Husayn among the Arab population, but there was no specific mention of the CPI role in these developments (Jerusalem Domestic Service, 20 August; *FBIS*, 24 August). Zayyad, however, was quoted as saying he did "not want Iraq to withdraw because of the military threat" (*Arabs in Israel*, 1 November). Politburo member Emile Habibi expressed concern over the extent of popular Palestinian backing for Baghdad, saying he was afraid that "this rash attitude will come near to bankruptcy" and that such Palestinians are "forgetting their tragic experience of 1948 when they waited in vain for a knight in shining armour to come and rescue them" (*Middle East*, November). *Al-Ittihad* (20 September) denied that Arabs in Israel back the invasion and occupation of Kuwait or support the Iraqi regime but said they "justifiably oppose American involvement and the danger of Israel becoming involved in attacking Iraq or the Arab world as a whole" (*Arabs in Israel*, 1 November).

As president of the state of Palestine and chairman of the PLO Executive Committee, Yassir Arafat sent congratulations to Vilner and Tubi following their reelection as general secretary and deputy general secretary, respectively, by the Central Committee. Arafat's cable expressed confidence in the CPI's role in bringing about a just Arab-Israeli peace that would involve the Palestinians' right to return and to self-determination. (Sanaa, Voice of Palestine, 22 July; *FBIS-NES*, 25 July.)

The CPI has always been strongly aligned with Moscow. No available statements demonstrate the continuation of the former uncritical acclaim for the USSR, but contacts continued. A CPI delegation that included Deputy General Secretary Tubi, Politburo member David Burstein, and alternate Politburo member Salim Jubran traveled to Moscow in February and met with the International Department of the CPSU. The two groups emphasized the need for a just settlement of the Arab-Israeli conflict that would balance the concerns of all sides, condemned brutal actions by Israel in the West Bank and the Gaza Strip and the illegal settlement of immigrants from the USSR and elsewhere in Palestinian territories, and expressed their wish that friendly ties between the communist parties of the two countries would continue to develop. (TASS, 17 February; *FBIS*, 13 March.) In May, the CPSU Central Committee sent greetings to the Twenty-first Congress of the CPI, wishing "Israeli Communists success in the struggle for the rights of their country's working people—Jews and Arabs—and for a just settlement of the Near East conflict" and expressing "willingness to continue developing the traditional friendly ties between our parties" (*Pravda*, second edition, 22 May; *FBIS*, 24 May). Mikhail Gorbachev also sent a message of congratulations (undated) to Vilner and Tubi, wishing them "success in your work for the benefit of the Israeli people and in the interests of peace and socialism" (*Pravda*, second edition, 17 June; *FBIS*, 20 June). Gorbachev sent another message of greetings to the Twenty-first Congress of the CPI in May (*Pravda*, 22 May).

Politburo and Secretariat member David Khenin and George Tubi, a secretary and chief of the CPI's international section, were in Warsaw in January. They met with Mieczysław Rakowski, first secretary of the Polish United Workers' party Central Committee. Rakowski informed Khenin and Tubi on developments in Poland, especially on the role of leftists and on preparations for formation of a new leftist party, and stated his party's support for a peaceful settlement of the Arab-Israeli conflict on the basis of Palestinian self-determination and the security of Israel and the other states in the area. The meeting dealt with the scope of cooperation between the two parties, and both sides expressed their willingness to see an expansion of cooperation between the CPI and the new Polish leftist party. (Warsaw, PAP, 16 January; *FBIS*, 17 January.) Makram Makhul, director of *al-Ittihad*'s Tel Aviv–Jaffa office, received the International Reuters Prize for Journalism for his reports on the *intifada* in Gaza (*Arabs in Israel*, 1 November).

Other Marxist Organizations. For background information on the Israeli Socialist Organization (Matzpen) and groups that broke away from it, including the Revolutionary Communist League, see *YICA*, 1982, 1984.

Glenn E. Perry
Indiana State University

PALESTINIAN COMMUNIST PARTY

Population. More than 5 million (estimated) Palestinians, including 1,058,122 in the West Bank,

615,575 in the Gaza Strip, about 800,000 in Israel, and more than 1.5 million in Jordan (estimated)

Party. Palestinian Communist Party (al-Hizb al-Shuyu'i Filastini; PCP)

Founded. 1982

Membership. Accurate estimate not available

General Secretary. Unknown but possibly Bashir al-Barghuti (journalist); Sulayman al-Najjab, deputy general secretary

Politburo. Sulayman al-Najjab (exiled from the Israeli-occupied territories; member of the PLO Executive Committee); Dr. Taysir al-Aruri (physics professor at Bir Zeit University); Na'im Abbas al-Ashhab; Dr. Mahir al-Sharif (editor in chief of *Sawt al-Watan*); others not known

Secretariat. Sulayman al-Najjab; others not known

Central Committee. Dhamin Awdah, Mahir al-Sharif, Sulayman al-Nashhab, Ali Ahmad, Mahmud al-Rawwaq, Na'im Abbas al-Ashhab, Mahmud Abu-Shamas, Dr. Walid Mustafa (member of the Palestine National Council), Mahmud Shuqayr; others not known (names on various lists not necessarily up to date)

Status. Illegal, but tolerated to a large extent in Israeli-occupied areas

Last Congress. First, 1983

Auxiliary Organization. Progressive Workers' Bloc (PWB)

Publications. *Al-Tali'ah* (The vanguard), weekly newspaper, Bashir al-Barghuti, editor; *Sawt al-Watan* (Voice of the homeland), magazine, Dr. Mahir al-Sharif, editor; published in Cyprus; *al-Katib* (The writer), monthly cultural magazine; As'ad al-As'ad, editor

Background. With the approval of the Communist Party of Jordan (PCJ), the PCP was organized in February 1982, although its statements identify it with the pre-1948 Palestinian Communist Party. The new party was to include former members of the West Bank and Gaza Strip Palestinian Communist Organization, previously a section of the JCP, as well as members of the Palestinian Communist Organization in Lebanon and all other Palestinian members of the CPJ except those living in Jordan, that is, the East Bank. (PCP membership does not include Palestinians in Israel.)

Leadership and Party Organization. Relatively little is known about the organization of the PCP. The First (constituent) Congress met in September 1983 and adopted a program and rules

for the party, as well as selecting the members of the Politburo, Secretariat, and Central Committee.

Several non-PCP publications refer to Barghuti as the party's leader (or as its leader in the occupied territories), but there is no evidence that he is necessarily the general secretary. Central Committee member Dr. Walid Mustafa explained that "the secret circumstances of activity inside and outside the areas of occupation" preclude publication of the name of the general secretary (Kuwait, *al-Siyasah*, 2 April; *FBIS-NES*, 5 April). The newspaper *al-Dustur* (Amman, 1 February; *FBIS-NES*, 1 February) referred to Sulayman al-Najjab as the general secretary, presumably a mistake because he has been described as deputy general secretary in the past. Most members of these top party organs, which describe their organization in terms of "democratic centralism," are said to reside in the occupied territories.

Politburo member Sulayman al-Najjab described the party's organization as "based on democracy within the framework of the PCP's central structure, and in a manner which guarantees the unity of will and action and allows the possibility of development in the forms of democracy in view of the changes in the Soviet Union and in response to internal factors" (Amman, *al-Dustur*, *FBIS-NES*, 1 February). Al-Najjab quoted the draft program then being discussed (it is not confirmed that the program was adopted) as stating that the PCP "is based on democracy within the framework of the party's central structure" and cited provisions guaranteeing the right of minorities to express their ideas, "including the use of the party's internal publication," thus making it unnecessary for blocs to form "that may hamper the unity of will and action within the ranks of the party." He explained that membership requires only "acceptance of the broad lines of the party's policy, and not acceptance of [every detail of] the party's policy, as stipulated in the previous bylaws," and that a new higher organ, the Central Council, was being formed that would meet each year and "monitor and investigate the work of the Central Committee." The new rules also require that a third of the members of the Politburo be changed every five years and that the maximum tenure of the general secretary be ten years, "after which he will not occupy any leading position in the party." (Paris, *al-Yawm al-Sabi'*, 26 February; *FBIS-NES*, 1 March.) Central Committee member Dr. Walid Mustafa explained that the program "includes a new concept of the relationship between the Central Committee and democracy in giving more democracy to the cadres and bases" and limiting the Central Committee to prevent it from exercising "sovereignty at the expense of democracy" (*al-Siyasah*, 2 April; *FBIS-NES*, 5 April). Politburo member al-Najjab stressed that the new program makes the PCP a party "for all Palestinians regardless of their social class... not only for the working class" (Amman, *al-Dustur*, 1 February; *FBIS-NES*, 1 February).

A meeting of the PCP Politburo, held in Moscow, was reported in January (Amman, *al-Ra'y*, 31 January; *FBIS-NES*, 1 February). A meeting of the Central Committee (apparently in the occupied territories), which drew up the new draft program designed to replace the one adopted in 1983, was held in February (Kuwait, *al-Siyasah*, 2 April; *FBIS-NES*, 5 April). Otherwise, nothing is known about meetings of party organs during the year.

The Palestinian communists' failure to engage in armed struggle seems to have saved their party structure from dismantlement by the Israelis in the early years of the occupation and thus to enhance their position in the West Bank and Gaza, while weakening their appeal in the Palestinian diaspora. Their "long experience with mass movements" has further given them an advantage during the current uprising. All of this is said to make the PCP the most successful communist party in the Arab world today at a time when communism has reached its nadir elsewhere in the region.

Palestinian Affairs. The PCP has been particularly active in the Israeli-occupied territories. The fact that "most of its cadres operate inside the occupied territory" has been called the party's "most distinctive feature," contrasting it with other groups represented in the Palestine Liberation Organization (PLO) (Kuwait, *al-Siyasah*, 2 April; *FBIS-NES*, 5 April). But its activities extend to the Palestinian diaspora as well, though not to Israel proper. Although the PCP is illegal in the occupied territories, it is in fact generally tolerated. But sometimes there are crackdowns, and people are arrested for possessing communist literature. At least in the past, this toleration has been explained in terms of Israel's wish to limit other groups and not to provoke the Soviet Union, as well as the influence of the Communist Party of Israel (which is doubtful) and the PCP's emphasis on political rather than military struggle. Unlike other organizations affiliated with the PLO, the PCP apparently lacks a military force.

Barghuti, who was once imprisoned by the Jor-

danians and subjected to town arrest by the Israelis during the early 1980s, edits the weekly party newspaper *al-Tali'a* in East Jerusalem. Published since 1976, it has "a high circulation among West Bank intelligentsia and students." The PCP has also published "a monthly literary and political magazine" entitled *al-Katib* since 1980 in addition—sporadically during the past decade—to its underground "official organ," *Sawt al-Watan*.

There are reports of rapid increases in the party's membership during the late 1980s, mainly from among youths involved in the uprising.

There has been much rivalry between the communists and other Palestinian organizations. Intra-Palestinian clashes in one West Bank village in July, according to some accounts, pitted backers of Fatah against people favoring the PCP and the PFLP, while the Islamic Resistance Movement (Hamas) bitterly attacked groups like the PCP and the overall PLO that favor negotiations for peace with Israel (*CSM*, 16 July). There was one report of a "tactical alliance" between the Islamist groups, that is, Hamas and Islamic jihad, and the leftist PFLP in opposition to the moderate position of Fatah, the DFLP, and the PCP (*Jerusalem Post*, international edition, 8–14 April).

Although the uprising in the Israeli-occupied territories began spontaneously in December 1987, a Unified National Leadership of the Uprising (UNLR) soon emerged that included representatives of the PCP along with those of other Palestinian organizations. Along with Fatah, the PFLP, and the DFLP, the PCP is one of the main groups—working "with the Islamic Jihad from time to time" in Gaza—involved in the uprising (Jamal R. Nassar and Roger Heacock, "The Revolutionary Transformation of the Palestinians under Occupation," in Nassar and Heacock, eds. *Intifada: Palestine at the Crossroads* [New York: Praeger Publishers, 1990], p. 191). The UNLR issues manifestos about twice a month directing the uprising (Michael Jubran, "'Not Planned but Not Spontaneous': The Intifada, Its Leadership and the PLO," *Washington Report on Middle East Affairs*, December 1989). The PCP also participates in underground local committees whose composition seems to vary from place to place. These committees (or cells) have five to twenty members each, with the representatives of various groups, including the PCP, typically rotating as leaders on a monthly basis (ibid.). Local "branch commissions" are said to provide assistance in dealing with curfews and in helping to teach methods of food production and craftsmanship aimed at allowing the people to dispense with Israeli-made goods.

The PCP has consistently called for a two-state settlement of the Palestine question, with Israel withdrawing from all the territories it occupied in 1967 and the creation of an independent Palestinian state in the West Bank and the Gaza Strip. This would come about as the result of an international peace conference in which all parties, including the PLO, would participate.

Politburo member al-Najjab expressed his party's "call for the establishment of a democratic Palestinian republic based on a multiparty system, parliamentary neutrality, and equality." He also denied that the PCP had ever "been against religion," despite the hostility of some religiopolitical movements to communists. (*Al-Yawm al-Sabi'*, 26 February; *FBIS-NES*, 1 March.)

Abd al-Rahman Awdullah was the representative of the PCP at a preparatory meeting of Palestinian factions that met in Amman on 7 April to consider "reshaping the Palestine National Council" (Amman, *Jordan Times*, 8 April; *FBIS-NES*, 11 April).

Auxiliary and Front Organizations. The PWB, which is closely tied to the PCP, has long dominated the General Federation of Trade Unions (GFTE) in the occupied areas. Communists have also been involved in student, professional, youth, and women's groups. This is in addition to the organizations created during the uprising (see above). The GFTE in the West Bank announced the formation of a sixteen-member unified executive board that would reorganize the trade union movement and prepare for general elections within a year (Algiers, Voice of Palestine, 3 March; *FBIS-NES*, 5 March); no information was available on the possible role of the PWB or the PCP in such developments.

Various trade unions and professional associations in Gaza held elections early in the year. Except for the victory of Fatah supporters in the physicians' association ballot (Jerusalem Domestic Service, 20 January; *FBIS-NES*, 23 January), no information is available on the success or failure of PCP candidates.

The PLO, which the PCP recognizes as the sole legitimate representative of the Palestinian people, has long been the equivalent of a government in exile, although the formality of declaring a Palestinian state did not come until the end of 1988. The PLO's supporters and its leadership span the political spectrum, and the inclusion of a PCP representative in its Executive Committee, which is analogous to a cabinet, as well as representation in the PNC since 1987, would seem to qualify it as a popular front (or government of national unity) despite the peripheral role of the Communists in the organization. The PCP is said to be "the fourth or fifth largest" faction represented in the PLO (Kuwait, *al-Siyasah*, 2 April; *FBIS-NES*, 5 April).

The PLO's dominant component, Fatah, might itself be called a united front because it avoids ideology in favor of pursuing a national cause. Its members are ideologically diverse, but it is dominated by centrists like Yassir Arafat. Fatah and the communists struggled with each other to control the Palestine National Front, which was formed in 1973 in the occupied areas, and each has blamed the other for its disintegration. The communists have accused Fatah of being dominated by rightists and, at least in the past, of dependence on the support of conservative regimes in the Arab world. Small groups like the Popular Front for the Liberation of Palestine (PFLP) and the Democratic Front for the Liberation of Palestine (DFLP)—both of which are represented in the PLO institutions—are Marxist, but are not considered communist.

The PCP draft program unanimously adopted by the Central Committee in February called for the formation of a "unified leftist Palestinian party," with the DFLP and the PFLP allegedly responding favorably. Central Committee member Dr. Walid Mustafa noted that the fact that "the intifadah and the occupied territories have become the center of Palestinian action" (in contradistinction to the situation when the previous program was drawn up in 1983) and developments in the USSR and Eastern Europe prompted the new plan. Dr. Mustafa made clear that the enlarged party "was not aimed at establishing a bloc against other parties" and affirmed "that the PLO is the organizational framework of national Palestinian action" to which PCP members "adhere and seek to entrench." He reported that the possibility of changing the name of the party had come up in the Central Committee meeting and that it was nearly unanimous that such a change was not called for, but he added that the question would continue to be discussed, with a decision to be reached by the next party congress, the time of whose convening he did not mention. (Kuwait, *al-Siyasah*, 2 April; *FBIS-NES*, 5 April.) Politburo member al-Najjab said that the program "affirms the historical importance of the unity of these [leftist] forces" but stressed that the PCP is willing to cooperate with all forces, regardless of ideology, "that support the objectives of national liberation and independence." He reiterated the PCP's support for the PLO as "the political and organizational framework for the broadest national front" and denied that a leftist "axis" within the PLO was envisaged or that "the party's alliances with other Palestinian nationalist forces" would be undermined. Although proclaiming pride in his party's name and saying that this was not considered to be "an urgent issue," he too expressed the PCP's willingness to discuss the question, which any success in uniting the left would raise. (*Al-Yawm al-Sabi'*, 26 February; *FBIS-NES*, 1 March.)

International Views, Positions, and Activities. The PCP was represented at the meeting of eleven Arab communist organizations that called for an Iraqi withdrawal from Kuwait and for U.S. forces to leave the Persian Gulf region (London, *Morning Star*, 17 August). (For further quotes, see the profile on Egypt in this edition of *YICA*.) An interview with Politburo member al-Najjab was published in the Kuwaiti newspaper *al-Watan* on 10 May (*FBIS-NES*, 22 May).

Although insisting that this was not the only factor, Politburo member al-Najjab admitted that the changes being introduced into party affairs by the draft program were in part a response to "international developments, especially the Soviet perestroyka, the new political thinking it has brought about, and the sweeping changes" in Eastern Europe (*al-Yawm al-Sabi'*, 26 February; *FBIS-NES*, 1 March).

In an interview in *al-Bayan* (Dubai, 16 January; *FBIS-NES*, 19 January), al-Najjab spoke of "discreet talks" then "under way to normalize Syrian-Palestinian ties" in order to facilitate holding an Arab committee meeting to include representatives of Egypt, Syria, Palestine, Jordan, and Lebanon to discuss the convening of an international peace conference. He opined that renewed Syrian-Egyptian diplomatic relations would also help bring such a meeting about. In what he called a "step backward," he complained that "the United States seeks to lower the level of contacts" in the then ongoing Palestinian-U.S. dialogue. He further stated his belief that it was too early to hold an extraordinary meeting of the Palestine National Council to evaluate the peace effort.

In April, al-Najjab announced the PLO's rejection of a resumption of the recent contacts relating to a Palestinian-Israeli dialogue in Cairo, indicating that it would continue to push for an international peace conference and confirming its adherence to the PNC's initiative adopted in 1988. He said that Israeli Labor party leader Shimon Peres "still disregards the Palestinian people's right of self-determination." Al-Najjab welcomed a European role and called for coordination between the PLO and Western Europe, the USSR, and China. He referred to former President Jimmy Carter's recent statements favoring an international peace conference as "recognition that separate solutions are incomplete solutions." (Dubai, *Al-Bayan*, 7 April; *FBIS-NES*, 11 April.)

Al-Najjab responded to the prospect (later realized) that the United States would end its dialogue with the PLO by dismissing the whole process as being designed "to make the PLO accept an alternative leadership to itself," saying that Washington "has not given up on what Israel could not achieve" (*CSM*, 5 June). Central Committee member Mustafa indicated that contacts with the USSR on the issue of Jewish immigration "have led to acceptable steps that we believe will limit this danger" (*al-Siyasah*, 2 April; *FBIS-NES*, 5 April).

Central Committee member Mustafa indicated that—aside from "scattered remarks on numerous issues"—other Arab communist parties had generally reacted positively to the PCP's new program. He noted, somewhat obscurely but apparently in the context of organizational changes (see above) that although some other parties "wish to adhere to the Marxist-Leninist program," the PCP's new program is based "on the dialectic program." He contrasted the PCP's "new . . . concept of popular solidarity" that differs from some of the other Arab communist parties' continuing stress on "the popular proletariat." (*Al-Siyasah*, 2 April; *FBIS-NES*, 5 April.) Apparently further referring to the disagreement with other Arab communist parties, al-Najjab reaffirmed his party's commitment to "dialectal Marxism" but warned of damage that history demonstrates to be caused by turning this into "a rigid doctrine"; he spoke of Lenin as having been "one of the best students of Marx" but stressed the need to consider the Palestinian and broader Arab experience (*al-Yawm al-Sabi'*, 26 February; *FBIS-NES*, 1 March).

Revolutionary Palestinian Communist Party (RPCP). Since 1988 (possibly 1987) a breakaway faction called the RPCP has rejected the PCP's moderate position on the Palestine question. Based in Damascus, the RPCP is a member of the pro-Syrian Palestine National Salvation Front

(PSNF). Its general secretary is Arabi Awwad, who commanded an inactive PCP military arm for a while during the 1970s and later broke away to establish an organization called The Temporary Headquarters (Meron Benvenisti, with Ziad Abu-Zayed and Danny Rubinstein, *The West Bank Handbook: A Political Lexicon* [Boulder, Colo.: Westview Press, distributed by the *Jerusalem Post*, 1986]). The members of its Politburo include Jiryis Qawwas and Abdullah Nimr. Nothing else about the RPCP's organizational structure and leadership is known.

PNSF chairman Khalid al-Fahum indicated at a meeting of the PNSF (apparently in late 1989 or the beginning of 1990) that he had invited all Palestinian groups "to join ranks within the PLO framework to pursue the joint struggle and to support the intifadah" and that the component organizations, including the RPCP, were studying the proposal (Paris, Radio Monte Carlo, 3 January; *FBIS-NES*, 4 January). Al-Najjab responded with an announcement that PLO organs "are always open to all Palestinian factions boycotting the PLO" (Radio Monte Carlo, 3 January; *FBIS-NES*, 4 January).

Glenn E. Perry
Indiana State University

Jordan

Population. 3,064,508 (*World Fact Book*). The West Bank is not included; after 31 July 1988, residents of the West Bank were no longer considered Jordanian citizens, or the West Bank to be part of Jordan.
Party. Communist Party of Jordan (al-Hizb al-Shiyu'i al-Urduni; CPJ)
Founded. 1951
Membership. Accurate estimate not available
General Secretary. Dr. Ya'qub Zayadin
Central Committee. 'Isa Madanat, Amal Naffa', Fa'iq Warrad, Ishaq al-Khatib, 'Awni Fakhir, 'Abd al-'Aziz al-'Ata, Fawwaz al-Zu'bi, Hashim Gharaybah, Ahmad Jaradat (partial list)
Status. Illegal but no longer singled out by special law as proscribed

Last Congress. Second, December 1983
Last Election. November 1989. 'Isa Madanat won a seat in the 80-seat parliament. Percentage of votes that went to other Communist candidates is not available.
Auxiliary Organizations. None but strong presence in organized labor unions
Publications. *Al-Jamahir* (The masses), put out by the Committee for Workers Affairs; *al-'Amil* (The worker), put out by the Central Committee of the CPJ; *Tariquna* (Our path), for students; *al-Ghad* (Tomorrow), for youth; *Sawt al-Mar'ah* (Women's voice), for women; and *al-Haqiqah* (The truth), an ideological and intellectual publication

Background. The origins of communist activity in Transjordan are to be found in labor organizing efforts that culminated in 1932 in the establishment of a two-thousand member-strong Union of Jordanian Workers. Jordan's working class and intelligentsia, however, were small in size, and after a few months the union collapsed. In general, the British-installed amir, 'Abdallah, attempted to neutralize most political parties in Transjordan; the communist party was never recognized, and in May 1948 it was proscribed by the Anti-Communist Law. Across the Jordan River, in British mandate Palestine, in contrast, political parties were regulated by the Ottoman Organizations Law of 1907 and the Communist movement was known as the National Liberation League ('Usbat al-Taharrur al-Watani). For full background, see *YICA*, 1990.

Domestic Attitudes and Activities. The elections held in Jordan in November 1989 set in motion a series of political liberalization measures that have had an important impact on all the parties in Jordan but none so much as the communists. Officially proscribed since 1948, the CPJ was able to come out of hiding just before the elections. Beyond that major victory, however, in mid-January the CPJ celebrated the repeal of the 1953 Anti-Communist Law. Although all political parties remain officially illegal because martial law has been merely suspended, rather than canceled, the CPJ is no longer singled out as illegal. Now, like the other political parties, the CPJ awaits only the official overturning of martial law and the publication of a national charter (a document intended to serve as a new basis for regulating relations between the government and society) before it receives formal sanction for its operation.

The insistence by the government that there be such a national charter evoked resistance and suspicion from a number of political parties, including the communists. The CPJ's position has been that it opposes the concept of such a document; however, it wanted to be a part of the drafting process if for no other reason than to monitor and have a say in it. As part of a series of meetings between the palace and representatives of various political forces in the country, Member of Parliament (MP) 'Isa Madanat (Kerak) and CPJ general secretary Ya'qub Zayadin met twice with the king's political adviser 'Adnan Abu 'Awdah to discuss the charter. The prime minister also had several meetings with representatives from Hashd (Hizb al-Sha'b al-Dimuqrati, the People's Democratic party, an offshoot of the Marxist Democratic Front for the Liberation of Palestine [DFLP]) and the Marxist Popular Front for the Liberation of Palestine (PFLP) in the late winter and early spring.

While the country awaits the formal issuance of the charter, the political parties continue to operate as if they were legal. In the case of the CPJ, the office of its one representative in Parliament, 'Isa Madanat, has become the unofficial party headquarters. The office is open daily and serves not only as a place where citizens meet with MP Madanat but also as a gathering place for party members, various CPJ auxiliary organizations, and as a point of distribution for the party's various publications.

In an atmosphere in which political parties continue to be officially illegal, political blocs have emerged periodically within Parliament. In July, the largest non-Islamic group—the Jordanian Nationalist Arab Democratic Group (JNADG)—announced its establishment. It is a loose leftist-nationalist coalition that appears to have evolved in opposition to the Islamic blocs in Parliament. (Islamic candidates of varying stripes secured 32 out of 80 seats in the 1989 elections.) MP Madanat is a member of this group. Other prominent communists who signed their name to the group's founding statement but who are not MPs were Amal Naffa', Fa'iq Warrad, and Ya'qub Zayadin. Other members from at least nominally Marxist organizations are MPs from Hashd (Bassam Haddadin) and the Jordanian branch of the PFLP.

The JNADG's founding statement promised to work toward protecting and enhancing the democratic process. Efforts were to be directed toward canceling the Defense Law of 1935 and replacing it with a modern defense law that would not conflict with the rights and duties of Jordanians as stipulated in the constitution; efforts were also to be made to overturn the 1967 martial law, the election law of 1986, and any other laws that restrict political freedoms. The bloc stressed the need for economic reform: loosening the grip of the International Monetary Fund (IMF) and the World Bank on national economic policy; protecting and supporting the public sector; supporting the private sector in industry, agriculture, and tourism and ending all bureaucratic obstacles to enhancing productivity in these fields; and funding small industries and businesses throughout the country by financial institutions under the supervision of the Central Bank. The JNADG also called for Arab and national unity to confront the Israeli threat and indicated support for Jordan's national unity, for Palestinian unity, and for the Palestine Liberation Organization (PLO) as the sole, legitimate representative of the Palestinian people.

MP Madanat is a member of a new parliamentary committee, the General (Public) Freedoms Committee. The committee's range of responsibilities includes ridding the country of laws that limit citizens' abilities to exercise their rights; amending certain laws, such as the press law, the defense laws, and the election law; following up on the government's promise to reinstate or find jobs for all those who were dismissed in the past for political reasons and making sure that the security forces are no longer involved in employment decisions or labor union affairs; ensuring that people are no longer imprisoned or prevented from traveling for political reasons; and checking into the condition of political prisoners and demanding a general amnesty.

In addition to his participation in this committee, MP Madanat was the parliamentary deputy charged with chairing the session in November in which the vote for the next president of the Chamber of Deputies was held. It was the first time in the history of the Jordanian Parliament in which a session was chaired by a communist deputy. Ironically, the MP who won the vote was 'Abd al-Latif 'Arabiyyat, the spokesperson for the Muslim Brethren (al-Yawm al-Sabi', 26 November).

The CPJ's position on the most critical national issues was summed up in a July memorandum to the prime minister and the speaker of the House. The eight-point memo called on the government to address rising prices and contended that limited-income groups were bearing the brunt of the ongoing economic restructuring program agreed upon by the government and the IMF early in 1989. The party called for a new taxation policy and for the creation of a wage-price balance. It also called on the government to deal with the problem of unemployment (estimated at more than 20 percent before the additional economic difficulties triggered by the 1990 gulf crisis) by creating jobs, giving priority in employment to Jordanians over foreigners, and increasing investment. The memo demanded that the government speed up its efforts to deal with corruption cases (from the previous regime). It asked for swift measures to assist farmers who had suffered as a result of the drought and called for an end to the security authorities' excesses, especially in the area of employment, where stringent security investigations were used to filter out politically undesirable applicants. The party demanded greater popular participation in the democratization process and a drastic change in the country's information policies so that Jordan could mobilize to deal with the challenges posed by the United States and Israel and so that it could more effectively pursue the struggle for the reestablishment of Palestinian rights (*Jordan Times*, 10 July).

Given the Iraqi Ba'ath party's history of persecuting communists, the CPJ was less enthusiastic regarding Saddam Husayn's invasion of Kuwait than much of the rest of the Jordanian population. On 5 August the party's central committee issued an official position on the gulf crisis that called for all possible efforts to prevent foreign intervention in the area as a prelude to a military invasion. It warned of the explosive situation in the gulf and noted the history of U.S. and imperialist aggression against the independence of Third World peoples. It called for Arab efforts to prevent further escalation and to prevent the internationalization of the problem (*al-Ra'y*, 6 August), In mid-August, however, along with ten other Middle East communist organizations, the CPJ issued a communiqué in the Lebanese Communist Party paper *al-Nida'* demanding Iraqi withdrawal from Kuwait and that U.S. forces get out of the gulf. It also called for "a peaceful resolution of the crisis between the two countries within the framework of the Arab League" (*Morning Star*, 17 August).

On 20 August the formation of a national front was announced. The CPJ, along with various other forces—Islamic, secular, leftist, and nationalist—joined together to confront the challenge to the Arabs posed by the gulf crisis. The purpose, according to MP Madanat, was to form a broad coalition to confront U.S. aggression. Activities were planned, including sponsoring joint rallies against

the U.S. intervention (*Jordan Times*, 20 August; *FBIS*, 29 August).

In late November, the CPJ issued a statement in which it joined other voices in the country criticizing U.S. interference in regional affairs. Specifically, the statement charged the U.S. embassy in Amman of carrying out surveillance and spying in the al-Ruwayshid area (the major crossing point between Iraq and Jordan) in order to monitor the border and ascertain that the U.N. embargo resolutions imposed on Iraq were being implemented (*Sawt al-Sha'b*, 22 November; *FBIS*, 23 November).

Within the labor union movement, in which the CPJ has a strong presence, in 1990 leadership elections, the Union of Bank Workers and the Union of Weavers and Spinners remained in CPJ hands, although the party was shut out of leadership posts in the Dock Workers' Union. In April and May, Communist members of the central council of the General Federation of Jordanian Workers, the country's trade union federation, joined a group within the central council called the Democratic Syndicalist Group to protest the continuing interference by the Jordanian government in the labor union movement. The protesters also charged the government with attempting to prevent the union from effectively addressing labor issues. The formation of the group constituted a serious challenge to the existing union and to governmental control. It appears, however, that by offering the CPJ representation on the central council (something the party had previously been denied), the government was able to woo the party away from the group. Because the communists constituted the largest faction, their defection crippled the protest and shored up the position of the government (author's July interview with labor activist Yusuf Hawrani).

Party Internal Affairs. The CPJ has been plagued by numerous splits since 1970, the most recent of which, in 1987, came in the wake of several organizational measures taken by Zayadin and led a number of members of the Central Committee to form an independent wing of the party. The party did manage to patch over internal disputes before the 1989 elections, although the reunification that took place before the elections has been described by some as superficial. Efforts to achieve real unity have reportedly been ongoing. (*Al-Yawm al-Sagi'*, 29 January.) The most serious challenge facing the party is to define its role in the wake of the demise of the communist parties of

Eastern Europe and in the face of the ongoing crisis in the Soviet Union. Events in the traditional centers of communism have, by admission of CPJ members, affected their ability to attract people to the party (author's July interview with Y. Zayadin). The party's view of the situation in Eastern Europe is that the principles of communism and socialism were good but that they were badly implemented. Like communist parties elsewhere, the CPJ has debated the Stalinist legacy, the future of democratic centralism, and the meaning of *perestroika* beyond the Soviet Union (CPJ member Said Salem in *WMR*, January).

In late January, a delegation from the CPJ spent several weeks in Moscow discussing recent developments in the Soviet Union and Eastern Europe and their ramifications. The CPJ was particularly concerned about the immigration of Soviet Jews to Israel and during its meetings with CPSU officials urged the Soviet Union to halt the emigration until a comprehensive peace settlement on the Palestinian issue could be reached. Previously, MP Madanat had defended the Soviet position during Jordanian parliamentary debate on the grounds that the Soviet Union opposed the settling of Soviet Jews in the occupied territories (the West Bank and Gaza Strip). However, apparently after coming under attack, particularly by Islamists, the CPJ decided to take a firmer stand. The CPJ representatives then argued that allowing this emigration would have dangerous consequences for peace prospects in the area and would tarnish the Soviet image, for people would begin to equate Moscow's stand with that of the United States. The CPJ position on Soviet Jewish immigration marked the CPJ's first public disagreement with Soviet policy (*Jordan Times*, 9 February). Anger with this Soviet policy as well as with their support for the anti-Iraq coalition in the gulf crisis led to the targeting of the Soviet Union, along with the United States, Israel, and Great Britain, in student and other demonstrations throughout the country.

On the domestic front, the CPJ no longer promotes a revolutionary approach to politics in Jordan. Since the beginning of the liberalization, the party has expressed its willingness to work within the system to try to push for greater freedom, democracy, and social justice and for workers' rights, women's rights, improved services, electricity, better housing, and the like. Ideological campaigning, to the extent that the CPJ ever engaged in it, has been abandoned. Indeed, none of the opposition parties of the left is calling for the overthrow of the monarchy. CPJ members argue that there are no other options and that if the king were to be overthrown Israel would invade, the military would assume power, or the fundamentalists would come to power. (Author's July interview with Y. Zayadin.)

International Views, Positions, and Activities. On 27 June the executive program for cultural and scientific cooperation for 1990–1991 was signed between the Jordanian and Soviet governments. The program provides for various forms of student, language, and cultural exchange and the development of cooperation between the Jordanian Red Crescent Society and the Soviet Federation of the Red Cross and Red Crescent societies.

On 22 July a Soviet parliamentary delegation led by Valentin Tetenov, a member of the USSR Supreme Soviet Presidium, arrived in Jordan for three days of meetings with officials and parliamentarians. The visit to Jordan was part of a tour of countries in the region to explain the new Soviet Middle East policy, particularly regarding the immigration of Soviet Jews to Israel. Shortly thereafter Soviet assistant deputy foreign minister for Middle East affairs Gennadii Tarasov made a three-day trip to Amman, departing on 1 August. He met with Deputy Prime Minister and Foreign Minister Marwan al-Qasim and again discussed Jewish immigration, among other issues.

The gulf crisis was the subject of a visit by Soviet Middle East expert Yevgeni Primakov, who arrived on 3 October. During his one-day stay in Amman, Gorbachev's adviser met with King Husayn and PLO chief Yassir Arafat. From Amman, Primakov went directly to Baghdad. As part of international efforts aimed at finding a peaceful solution to the gulf crisis, a number of foreign officials made trips to Jordan. People's Republic of China foreign minister Qian Qichen arrived on 9 November for a two-day visit. He stressed China's independent position and its concern with regional peace and stability. On 15 November Budimir Loncar, Yugoslav federal secretary for foreign affairs, arrived in Amman for several hours of talks. Shortly thereafter, former Nicaraguan president Daniel Ortega met with King Husayn and other Jordanian officials during an 18–20 November visit to the Jordanian capital.

Economic relations were the focus of a meeting of the Jordanian-Soviet joint committee. Led by Deputy Minister of Foreign Economic Relations Vladimir Mordinov, the Soviet delegation arrived in Amman on 24 October. Meetings with Jordan's finance minister, Basil Jardanah, focused on Jordanian problems in servicing its Soviet debt. A protocol concluded in February stipulated that Jordan would export goods amounting to $42 million in one year as part of a repayment on the debt (Amman Domestic Service, in Arabic, 24 October; *FBIS*, 24 October). On 31 October minutes of the meetings were signed at the Ministry of Industry and Trade. The Jordanian side was represented by Ibrahim Badran, the secretary general of the Ministry of Industry and Trade. The minutes discussed two major areas: economic and technical cooperation and trade cooperation and expansion. There was also agreement to increase cooperation in the fields of energy, in the study of desertification, and in the possibility of establishing joint projects, especially in phosphates (Amman Domestic Service, in Arabic, 31 October; *FBIS*, 31 October).

Laurie A. Brand
University of Southern California

Lebanon

Population. 3,339,331 (*World Fact Book*)
Parties. Lebanese Communist Party (al-Hizb al-Shuyu'i al-Lubnani, LCP); Organization of Communist Action in Lebanon (Munazzamat al-'Amal al-Shuyu'i, OCAL)
Founded. LCP: 1924; OCAL: 1970
Membership. LCP: 20,000 (claimed) 2,000–3,000 (estimate, *World Fact Book*); OCAL: 1,500 (see *YICA*, 1990)
General Secretary. LCP: George Hawi; OCAL: Muhsin Ibrahim
Politburo. LCP: 11 members
Central Committee. LCP: 24 members
Status. Legal
Last Congress. LCP: Fifth, February 1987; OCAL: First, 1971
Last Election. 1972
Auxiliary Organizations. LCP: Communist Labor Organization, World Peace Council in Lebanon, and a number of student unions and movements
Publications. LCP: *al-Nida'* (The call) daily, publishers are George Hawi and 'Abd al-Karim

Muruwwa; *al-Akhbar* (The news) weekly; *al-Tariq* (The road) quarterly. OCAL: *al-Hurriya* (Freedom) weekly, publisher is Muhsin Ibrahim.

Background. Violent and bloody intracommunity battles and a return to a shaky status quo characterize 1990 in Lebanon. General Michel 'Awn's "war of liberation" was complemented by a "war of cancellation" (*harb al ilgha'*) of the al-Ta'if agreement (see *YICA*, 1989, 1990). The rebel Christian leader wanted to destroy his rival in the Lebanese forces, Dr. Samir Ja'Ja', and establish his hegemony over the Christian community. By the spring the war between Lebanese Christians resulted in more than 1,000 casualties and the exodus of 400,000 Christian Lebanese to Western Europe, the United States, and Australia. In October, with the tacit consent of Israel and the Bush administration, Syrian troops entered East Beirut for the first time since 1978. Violent battles and bloody massacres were the result of this Syrian intervention. General 'Awn had to escape from the presidential palace and seek refuge in the French embassy where, as of January 1991, he was still hiding.

The second conflict opposed the Shi'ite militias of the Syrian-backed Amal movement and the pro-Iranian Hizb Allah (see *YICA*, 1988, 1989, 1990). This inter-Shi'ite battle for the control of South Lebanon and the Shi'ite community has not been definitely settled, and its resolution hinges on the balance of power that will emerge as a result of the crisis in the Arabian/Persian Gulf.

In 1990 the LCP and its Lebanese and Palestinian allies pursued guerrilla activities against Israel and its proxies in South Lebanon (see *YICA*, 1988, 1989, 1990). Internally, the situation in Lebanon deteriorated further, and the Lebanese pound lost much of its exchange value against the U.S. dollar (800 Lebanese pounds for one U.S. dollar). The year also witnessed the formation of two consecutive governments in Lebanon, one headed by Dr. Salim al-Hoss and the other by Omar Karameh. Meanwhile, the Lebanese Parliament approved the constitutional reforms contained in the al-Ta'if agreement and reelected Hussein al-Husseini as the speaker of the Parliament (see *NYT*, 22 September). Finally, 1990 also had its share of political assassinations. In October, following the intervention of Syrian troops in East Beirut, Danny Sham'un, leader of the National Liberal party (al-'Ahrar), was brutally assassinated in his home along with his wife and children.

Leadership and Organization. The LCP's highest organ is the congress, which convenes every five years and elects the Central Committee. Since 1924, the LCP has held only five congresses, and George Hawi has served as its general secretary since 1979. OCAL, since its foundation in 1970, was and is still led by Muhsin Ibrahim.

Domestic Views and Activities. In January George Hawi, general secretary of the LCP, introduced a seven-point plan for a cease-fire in South Lebanon between Amal and Hizb Allah. The main points of this plan included a call for a total cease-fire, the withdrawal of all forces to their positions before the most recent confrontation, the formation of a "neutral and nationalist" force of interposition, agreement on a plan of resistance against Israeli occupation and aggression, mobilization of the "political, popular, and military forces in the battle against partition as symbolized" by General 'Awn's rebellion, and finding a joint strategy to transform the struggle for South Lebanon and Israeli occupation into a national issue and consolidate the "authority of the legitimate government over all regions"; finally, Hawi suggested that Syrian and Iranian support must be sought to guarantee the implementation of the Damascus accords (see *YICA*, 1989, 1990) between the Shi'ite militias (see *al-Nida'*, 4 January).

In early February the LCP issued a statement related to the violent clashes between the forces loyal to General Michel 'Awn and the militias of the Lebanese forces. In that statement the LCP warned of the dangers ensuing from 'Awn's rebellion and especially his "fascist and dictatorial plan of hegemony" to satisfy his power ambitions. The LCP statement went on to assert that the only alternative was to belong "to the national democratic plan." This plan would preserve Lebanon's unity, freedom, independence, sovereignty, democracy, Arab identity, and true liberation (*al-Nida'*, 8 February). Again the LCP called for the unification of all Lebanese regardless of their party or religious affiliation. The only salvation, according to the LCP, is to support the legitimate government authority, which is bolstered by Arab and international support.

In late March the situation in South Lebanon was again at the center of the LCP's attention. At the end of March William ("Bill") Robinson, a U.S. Christian fundamentalist preacher, was assassinated at his "settlement" in Rashayya al-Fukhaar, a small Lebanese village near the Israeli border. According

to *al-Nida'*, Robinson came to Lebanon in 1978 and established "Middle East Television" and the "Voice of Hope," which were operated by Israel's Christian Lebanese proxies in the self-proclaimed "security zone." Robinson was killed by the Lebanese National Resistance Front, which was created following the Israeli invasion of Lebanon in 1982 and which included Palestinian and Lebanese factions in South Lebanon. The U.S. preacher was accused of illegally purchasing land to establish "Israeli settlements" in South Lebanon. Following this action OCAL issued a statement praising the assassination of Robinson and calling for a serious consideration and resolution of the precarious conditions in South Lebanon (*al-Nida'*, 30 March). In September the Lebanese National Resistance Front celebrated its eighth anniversary. On that occasion Ilyas Atallah, a member of the Politburo, gave a long interview in which he expressed his disappointment at the lack of unity among the various groups and factions operating in South Lebanon (*al-Nida'*, 16 September). Since the Israeli invasion in 1982, the LCP has been trying desperately to reconcile the warring Shi'ite factions in South Lebanon, calling for unity in purpose to resist the Israeli occupation and military actions against both Lebanese and Palestinian civilians. Furthermore, the LCP had to confront the fact that South Lebanon had become an arena of confrontation between regional powers with a major stake in the future of the region, that is, Syria, Israel, Iran, and the Palestine Liberation Organization (PLO).

In the summer of 1990 Arab and international efforts were exerted to end the intra-Christian conflict in Beirut. In July, Lakhdar Ibrahimi, who was appointed by the Arab League to implement the al-Ta'if agreement, visited Lebanon (see *YICA* 1990). The purpose of his visit was to urge General 'Awn and Dr. Samir Ja'Ja' to join the Lebanese government's appeal to normalize the situation in the country. Following a visit to Dr. al-Hoss, the Lebanese prime minister, and Hussein Husseini, the speaker of the Parliament, George Hawi expressed his support to the Lebanese government and called on the population in East Beirut to respond positively to the government's initiative to restore the unity and sovereignty of Lebanon and find immediate remedies to the crumbling economic situation (*al-Nida'*, 18 July). In July the Central Committee of the LCP issued a statement on convening the Sixth Congress of the LCP. A preparatory committee was formed whose agenda included the following items: (1) orientation of party activity in light of Lebanese and Arab developments; (2) activity of the Central Committee in implementing LCP's political plan adopted by past congresses; (3) organizational situation in the party and suggested reforms of its internal status; and (4) election of the LCP's central leadership (*al-Nida'*, 22 July). In this context it is important to mention a significant interview by 'Abd al-Karim Murawwa, deputy secretary general of the LCP.

In that interview, Muruwwa tackled several topics, among them the relationship between Arab nationalism and Marxism and the LCP's attitude toward religion and *perestroika*. On the first issue, Muruwwa stated that the LCP had always followed the correct interpretation of Marx and Engels regarding the relationship between the proletariat and nationalism. According to Muruwwa, Marx and Engels gave "to the national question a class dimension. . . . The nation which is governed by the bourgeoisie is not the proletariat's and the latter has to create its own nation." Muruwwa's clarifications answered criticism from inside the LCP, where he was accused of working to transform the party into an Arab nationalist communist party. On the question of religion, Muruwwa emphasized that the LCP had never stated that membership entailed total adoption of the Marxist philosophy toward religion. The LCP, according to Muruwwa, was hoping to discuss at its Sixth Congress the modalities of opening membership in the LCP to believers and "all those who want change regardless of their philosophical orientation." Muruwwa then dealt with the issue of *perestroika* and its impact on the LCP. Muruwwa stated that it was a "revolution" in that it was a "real attempt at liberating socialism from the mistakes of the past, basically the wrong interpretation of socialism as it was conceived by its founders Marx and Engels and Lenin afterward." Further, Muruwwa stated that what we have to cling to and develop in *perestroika* is freeing "socialism from anti-democratic stands; that is what is against the principle of a democratic research and investigation for innovative ideas and for the consolidation of human rights" (*al-Nida'*, 22 July).

International Views and Contacts. In 1990 the LCP consolidated its ties with the Syrian government and other Arab and international communist parties. In October, the LCP celebrated its 66th anniversary in Moscow. In January, George Hawi dispatched a congratulatory note to Muhammad Ibrahim Nakad, a member of the Sudanese Communist Party, for his release from jail by the military government in Khartoum. Also in January the Politburo sent a letter to the leadership of the Bahraini National Liberation Front on the 35th anniversary of its foundation (*al-Nida'*, 18 February).

The question of the immigration of Soviet Jews to Israel became a fundamental concern of the LCP in its relationship with the Soviet Union. In early February the Politburo issued a statement in which it expressed its "deep concern for the increased immigration of Soviet Jews to Israel" and called on the Soviet Union "to exert all its efforts to make sure that this immigration does not negatively affect the struggle of the Palestinian people and the support the Soviet people had offered to the Palestinian cause and the Arab cause in general" (*al-Nida'*, 7 February). In an editorial entitled "The Immigration of Soviet Jews and the Needed Stand," Mahir al-Shareef, member of the LCP's Politburo, called on the Soviet Union to "cancel definitively all the direct flights between Moscow and Israeli airports and link the immigration of Soviet Jews to the issue of putting an end to Israeli settlements in occupied Palestinian territories." Shareef also wrote that Soviet Jews emigrated for purely economic reasons and suggested that the PLO in coordination with the Arab League could encourage Arab economic investments in areas populated by Jews in the Soviet Union. This plan, according to Shareef, could be complemented by an "intensive campaign among Soviet Jews to illustrate the difficult conditions inside Israel and the dangers they might face in the occupied Palestinian territories" (*al-Nida'*, 9 February).

In March, Nadeem Abdel-Samad, deputy general secretary of the LCP, concluded a visit to France, Algeria, Tunisia, and Morocco. The purpose of the trip was to consolidate the LCP's relationship with the French Communist Party and the progressive forces in North Africa (*al-Nida'*, 23 March). At the international level, the LCP maintained its links and contacts with various parties and countries around the world. In February, an LCP delegation headed by George Hawi visited the People's Republic of China and was welcomed by Jiang Zemin, general secretary of the Chinese Communist Party. Following an hour-long discussion, the Chinese communist leader repeated his country's strong support for the Arab and Palestinian people and reiterated his support for the independence, sovereignty, and unity of Lebanon (*FBIS*, 8 February). Between April 28 and May 3, and at the invitation of the Central Committee of the Cuban Communist Party, a delegation of the LCP headed by George Hawi visited Havana. During its encounter with Fidel Castro and other Cuban leaders the LCP delegation discussed the fifteen years of war in Lebanon and the prospects of peace in the Middle East (*al-Nida'*, 22 May).

The relationship between the LCP and the regime of Saddam Husayn was further strained when the Iraqi army invaded the Emirate of Kuwait on 2 August. In a statement issued by its Central Committee the LCP criticized the United States "for appointing itself as the absolute administrative ruler and policeman of the world" in violation of U.N. Security Council resolutions. The statement went on to state that, regardless of the nature of the regime in Baghdad, "the task of defending Arab territory against US invaders is the basic task today." The LCP also had harsh words on the Iraqi invasion. In fact, the Central Committee stated that the Iraqi action diverted attention from "the Palestinian people's *intifada* and the methods of supporting this *intifada*."

Finally, the LCP's statement called on Iraq to withdraw from Kuwait and "urged seeking an interim Arab settlement under which the Arab people of Kuwait would be given the opportunity to determine their destiny and their country's future on their own" (*FBIS*, 21 August). In early October, at a symposium held in Libya on The Revolutionary Arab Dialogue, George Hawi offered an eight-point plan that contained conditional guarantees for an Iraqi withdrawal from Kuwait. First, there must be a guarantee not to resort to violence and threat of war and an acceptance of a political solution to the crisis. Second, there should be total withdrawal of all military "imperialist" troops from Arab lands. Third, there must be recognition that U.N. resolutions apply equally to the occupied Palestinian territories, Syria, and Lebanon. Fourth, temporary placement of Kuwait under Arab and U.N. supervision, allowing the people of Kuwait to determine freely their own destiny. The fifth point in the Hawi plan included a proposal to place Saudi Arabia and the holy shrines of Islam (Mecca and Medina) under Arab and Islamic forces. The last three points dealt with the right of all Arabs to oil and other resources, lifting the sanctions against Iraq and solidarity with the peoples of the Arabian/Persian Gulf to achieve their minimum civil rights, and, finally, Arab solidarity against Israel and its "Zionist protectors" (*al-Nida'*, 12 October).

The warm relationship between the LCP and the Soviet Union was illustrated by farewell parties for Vasily Kolotusha, the Soviet ambassador in Lebanon, and the welcoming party for Gennadi Illitchev, his successor. In July the LCP organized a farewell banquet to honor Vasily Kolotusha, who had been appointed head of the Near East and North Africa section of the Soviet Foreign Ministry. In the course of that banquet George Hawi launched the idea of creating an Arab investment and development fund to invest Arab capital in the Soviet Union (*al-Nida'*, 20 July). Throughout his tenure in Lebanon, Kolotusha played an active and important role in bringing some kind of normalization to the Lebanese scene (see *YICA*, 1988, 1989, 1990). In December the LCP banquet in East Beirut welcomed the new Soviet ambassador to Lebanon. The significance of this event was the presence among the guests of representatives of the Phalangist party (Hizb al-Kata'ib al-Lubnaniyya) and the Lebanese forces, two of the LCP's major foes during the civil war in Lebanon. In his speech George Hawi called for the convening of a "National Congress for Dialogue and Reconciliation" between the various Lebanese factions (*Arab American News*, 12 December).

Publications. Publications of the LCP include the daily Arabic language *al-Nida'*, the weekly *al-Akhbar*, and the journals *al-Tariq* (The road), *al-Thaqafa al Wataniyya* (National culture), *al-Wakt* (The time), and *Sawt al-Amil* (The worker's voice). The LCP has also a publication in the Armenian language, the weekly *Kanch* (The call). The LCP-operated radio station Sawt al-Shaab (Voice of the People) has been broadcasting since 1987. The station now reaches 80 percent of Lebanon and some areas in the north of Israel, Jordan, Syria, and Cyprus.

Biography. *Artine Madoyan.* In July, Artine Madoyan, one of the LCP founders, passed away. Madoyan, a member of the Central Committee, was born on 10 April 1904 in Adana, Turkey. In 1922, Madoyan joined his family in Lebanon where it had fled in 1921 following the massacres perpetrated against the Armenians in Turkey. In 1924, Madoyan formed the Spartacus party, also known as the Armenian Communist Party, in Lebanon. In 1925, after the establishment of the Lebanese People's Party (LPP), Madoyan amalgamated his group with the LPP to form the Lebanese Communist Party. In December of that year Madoyan was elected as a member of the Central Committee. He was arrested frequently for printing several papers including *Spartak*.

In the early 1930s Madoyan was active in asserting the Arab character of the communist party in Syria and Lebanon. In 1943, he was elected member of the Lebanese National Congress, which included prominent nationalist figures fighting for the independence of Lebanon. Madoyan is the recipient of several honorific awards and medals and the author of many publications and books such as *For the Unity and Progress of the Armenian People* (1937), *Answers to Cardinal Agagianian* (1948), and *Armenian Ideological and National Issues* (1974), all in Armenian, and *Life on the Barricades* (1986), published in both Armenian and Arabic. His daughter Susie is married to George Hawi (*al-Nida'*, 6 July).

George Emile Irani
Franklin College

Morocco

Population. 25,648,241
Party. Progressive Socialist Party (Parti du Progrès et du Socialisme, PPS)
Founded. 1943 (PPS, 1974)
Membership. An estimated 4,000–5,000; the PPS and the *World Marxist Review* claim membership in excess of 50,000.
General Secretary. 'Ali Yata
Politburo. 'Ali Yata, Ismail Alaoui, Muhammad Ben Bella, Abdessalam Bourquia, Muhammad Rifi Chouaib, Abdelmajid Bouieb, Umar al-Fassi, Thami Khyari, Abdallah Layachi, Muhammad Moucharik, Abdelwahab Souhail, Amina Lemrini
Secretariat. Umar al-Fassi, Abdallah Layachi, Muhammad Moucharik, Abdelwahab Souhail
Central Committee. An estimated 65–70 members
Status. Legal
Last Congress. Fourth, 17–19 July 1987, in Casablanca. Meets every four years. Total number of delegates at congress: 1,339.
Last Election. 14 September 1984. The PPS won 2 out of 306 seats in the country's Parliament.
Auxiliary Organization. Moroccan Youth of Progress and Socialism (Jeunesse Marocaine du Progrès et du Socialisme; JMPS)
Publications. *Al-Bayan* (The manifesto), in both Arabic and French; *al-Bayan al-Thaqafi* (The cultural manifesto); *al-Iqtisadi wa al-Mujtama'* (Economy and society), in French and Arabic; *Nisa' al-Maghrib* (Women of Morocco); and *al-Wujud* (Presence)

Background. Like its Tunisian and Algerian counterparts, the Parti Communiste Marocain (PCM) was initially created in 1943 as a branch of its French counterpart. It was subsequently banned by the French government during the protectorate period. Legalized at the country's independence in 1956, it was later banned (in 1959) and subsequently reemerged in 1974 under the new name of Progressive Socialist Party (PPS). Since then the party has participated in all municipal and national elections but has managed to garner only marginal support at the local and regional levels (two seats on the Casablanca city council in 1983; two seats obtained during the national elections of 1984).

Leadership and Party Organization. During its last regularly held elections at the national congress in 1987, the PPS reelected 'Ali Yata as general secretary of the party, as well as retaining most of the old members of the Central Committee. Yata, like many of the country's current party leaders, belongs to the preindependence generation. At the same congress, its members also elected a thirteen-member Politburo, in addition to a number of new adherents that joined the party's Secretariat and its financial commission. As on previous occasions, the election did not produce an infusion of large numbers of new members, an indication that the PPS has not been able to build a strong base of support among younger Moroccans.

Domestic Party Affairs. As in previous years, the PPS has largely reacted to the economic and political initiatives of Hassan II, the country's monarch, whose policies Yata and his fellow PPS members have often obliquely criticized but never confronted outright. There were a few indications in 1990, however, that the party was willing to move toward a greater open criticism of what it has often referred to as "Hassanian democracy"; the PPS also seems to feel that the monarchy's continuous use of the Green March as a source of legitimacy—the so-called Saharan consensus—has reached its limit. The PPS throughout 1990 squarely focused its attention on the country's dire economic straits following an economic downturn of unprecedented dimension in 1989 and the role that internal financial institutions would play in the country's economic future. As several other parties, the PPS has urged the government to proceed carefully with the economic liberalization strategy and to protect the country's low-paid and unemployed when it adopts a new austerity plan. In its publications the PPS has repeatedly targeted some of Hassan II's advisers, particularly Driss Basri, the long-serving interior minister and *homme dur* of the regime, who have argued for rigid implementation of austerity measures to protect the economic gains of the previous five years.

The PPS's unease over the prospect of austerity measures increased when the monarchy decided at the end of 1989 to postpone national elections by means of the often-used mechanism of a popular referendum in which the monarch's decisions are routinely (and massively) adopted. Yata obliquely linked the austerity measures and the political heavy-handedness to the king, who wants no criticism of the fact that large amounts of money have been spent on his new palace in Agadir and for the completion of the mammoth Hassan II mosque in Casablanca. Hassan II, Yata has charged, is intent on imposing the austerity plan without having it approved by a newly elected parliament—a measure that hints at the marginal effectiveness of the country's opposition within the monarchy's formal political institutions.

In an interview in August 1990 Yata indicated his impatience with the continued exclusion of the PPS (and other small parties) from the kingdom's political life. He declared himself willing to join a new, national coalition government, arguing that the one currently in power has outlived its usefulness and can no longer meet—as the referendum issue hinted at—the challenge of devising a new economic plan for the country. Yata strongly supported the no-confidence vote introduced by the opposition parties to bring down the Parliament a few weeks before the referendum. He tried to project an image of agreement among the country's opposition parties, but insiders have noted that several of them, including the Istiqlal party and the Socialist Union of Popular Forces, have little patience with the PPS and therefore refused to join a committee to investigate a number of proposed constitutional amendments.

Yata, along with several other leaders of the country's opposition parties, was received on several occasions by the king in 1990, most recently in mid-August. Hassan II has attempted to project a unified policy on the current Iraq-Kuwait crisis. The PPS has in general followed the king in his condemnation of the Iraqi aggression—arguing that Iraq's behavior mirrors that of Israel—but distanced itself from the monarch's decision to deploy about a thousand crack troops from the Western Sahara battalion to the gulf. At the same time the PPS has been extremely critical of the role of the United States in the current conflict and of the presence of the large number of foreign troops in the region. The U.S. intervention, according to PPS views, is fueled by the need for access to cheap oil and the fact that sudden oil shortages could bring the United States to the brink of a recession and beyond. The party has argued that the current crisis is a purely internal affair, to be settled by Arabs alone. In several editorials in *al-Bayan*, the PPS has above all been angered by the deep divisions and the weakness of the Arab states in the crisis. Decrying the impact of the crisis, particularly on the Arab Maghreb Union, *al-Bayan* has noted that it could well lead to further disagreements within the still weak regional organization.

As opposed to last year, when the Saharan issue prompted extensive commentary from the PPS, the gulf crisis has clearly taken over as the most important issue. As in previous years, however, the current Iraq-Kuwait debacle has once again proved how marginal the PPS remains to the politics of the kingdom, although it has sought to carefully orchestrate its actions with those of other opposition parties within the implicit (and unwritten) rules of political behavior within the monarchy. As in previous years, the PPS introduced a number of amendments and proposals in the country's parliament, to no avail. The more or less formal opposition coalition that had emerged at the end of 1987 floundered on the austerity measures and Hassan II's measures in regard to the gulf. All this has led Yata and his supporters to argue insistently that the king could break the moribund nature of the country's political system but is simply not interested in doing so. The party's commitment to national education—what the government refers to as a "culturally valid" education—has largely been drowned out by more general worries over the economic difficulties that lie ahead. As in 1989 there were a number of strikes and demonstrations throughout the country, but few if any can be linked to the PPS; rather, they seem to take place spontaneously. In general, and contrary to what the PPS has long claimed, there is no clearly articulated feeling of economic disenfranchisement that can be mobilized for political action: the monarchy retains an extraordinary ability and persuasiveness in settling disputes, particularly in the rural areas of the country, where Hassan II's legitimacy remains vigorous and virtually unopposed. Overall the PPS has not yet brought forward a clearly articulated economic plan that could rival some of the stipulations of the austerity measures now being put into place. Although the PPS can correctly point to the fragile bases on which the Moroccan economy rests (see *YICA*, 1989) and to the political disenfranchisement inside the country, the PPS's standing among the population and its limited membership among primarily urban dwellers remain circumscribed. In the multilevel, fragmented, and carefully controlled political system headed by North Africa's last remaining monarch, the PPS has not managed to attract a powerful following despite the growing number of population dislocations. Above all, a possible crisis over generational renewal inside the PPS looms ahead for the party; Yata and most of his advisors are preindependence personalities who have not managed to attract a new political elite to their ranks or to hand over political power and responsibility. In Morocco's variegated political system, this does not augur well for the party's political fortunes.

International Views, Positions, and Activities. As in previous years the Arab Maghrebi Union (AMU) dominated the PPS's concerns this year. Following the meeting of the representatives of the region's communist parties in Casablanca in 1989, the PPS argued for greater cooperation among them within the framework of the AMU. Although the AMU assumed a much lower visibility as the gulf crisis unfolded, the PPS stressed the need for further regional cooperation among mass organizations and professional organizations as a precursor to greater political and economic integration. This "functional approach" has so far only met with limited success, in part because of the region's preoccupation with the Iraq-Kuwait confrontation.

Dirk Vandewalle
Dartmouth College

Saudi Arabia

Population. 17,115,728
Party. Communist Party of Saudi Arabia (CPSA)
Founded. 1975
Membership. Number unknown but believed negligible
General Secretary. Mahdi Habib
Leadership. Abd-al-Rahman Salih, Salim Hamid, Abu Abdallah, Muhsin Abdallah, Hamad al-Mubarak (Politburo member)
Status. Illegal
Last Congress. Third, August 1989
Auxiliary Organizations. Saudi Peace and Solidarity Committee (affiliate of the World Peace Council and Afro-Asian People's Solidarity Organization), Saudi Democratic Youth (affiliate of the World Federation of Democratic Youth), Workers' Federation of Saudi Arabia (associate member of the World Federation of Trade Unions), Democratic Women's League of Saudi Arabia (affiliate of the Women's International Democratic Federation), Committee for the Defense of Human Rights—Saudi Arabia
Publication. *Tariq al-Qadyhin* (The road of the working people)

The CPSA was one of eleven Arab communist organizations that signed a communiqué in early August demanding that Iraq withdraw from Kuwait and that the United States quit the gulf area (*Morning Star*, 17 August). The latter half is certainly consistent with the party's August 1989 call for the elimination of foreign military bases in the Near East (*YICA*, 1990). It is inconsistent, however, with the current Soviet approval of the presence of foreign troops in Saudi Arabia as a result of the Iraq-Kuwait crisis.

Another inconsistency would be the continued persecution of the Saudi communists and their allies following the Saudi-Soviet rapprochement. The reestablishment of diplomatic relations took place in September, and this was followed by Saudi participation in a $3 billion Soviet loan package (*NYT*, 5 December). The USSR has not taken the Saudis up, however, on a virtual invitation to participate in the multilateral force stationed in their country; it is unclear whether the upsurge of Soviet Jewish immigration to Israel at the end of the year will put a damper on the relationship (such activity, apparently on a smaller scale, had evinced a predictably unfavorable reaction by the Saudis early in the year) (Radio Riyadh, 26 January; *FBIS*, 29 January).

In any case, the very existence of the current crisis in the country should be enough to divert the attention of the Saudi government from persecuting local leftists, as long as the latter keep a low profile and do not advertise the extent of their alleged activities as they had during 1988–1989 (*YICA*, 1990). In fact, like the eleven-party statement mentioned above, the other examples of such activity noted this year were international rather than domestic: the continued presence of a CPSA representative on the Prague *World Marxist Review* Editorial Council during the January–May period and the attendance of Workers' Federation of Saudi Arabia International Secretary Adil Ibrahim at the November Twelfth World Trade Union Congress in Moscow (*WMR*, January–May/June; Twelfth World Trade Union Congress, *List of Participants*, p. 30).

Wallace H. Spaulding
McLean, Virginia

Syria

Population. 12,483,440
Party. Syrian Communist Party (al-Hizb al-Shuyu'i al-Suri; SCP)
Founded. 1924 (officially as a separate party in 1944)
Membership. 5,000 (estimated)
General Secretary. Khalid Bakhdash, 78; Yusuf Faysal, 64, deputy general secretary
Politburo. Khalid Bakhdash, Yusuf Faysal, Ibrahim Bahri, Khalid Hammami, Maurice Salibi, Umar Siba'i, Daniel Ni'mah, Zuhayr Abd al-Sammad, Ramu Farkha, Ramu Shaykhu (list of names not necessarily complete or up to date)
Central Committee. Nabih Rushaydat, Muhammad Khabbad, Issa Khuri, R. Kurdi, A.W. Rash-

wani (not necessarily up to date; other names unknown)
Status. Component of the ruling National Progressive Front (NPF)
Last Congress. Sixth, July 1986
Last Election. 22 May
Publication. *Nidal al-Sha'b*

Background. Seemingly no longer a serious threat and following a foreign policy that often paralleled that of the Ba'athist regime, the SCP gained quasi-legal status after 1966 and finally joined the Ba'ath-dominated NPF in 1972.

The Syrian communist movement has undergone several schisms in recent years. Riyad al-Turk, who was chosen general secretary of one breakaway group in 1974, has been imprisoned without trial since 1980 and subjected to beatings and torture. Turk's organization is one example of the "national communist" factions opposing "the pro-Soviet Arab communist conservative leadership" in the region that, by the 1970s, "had significantly eroded the power of traditional Arab communism" (Elie Rekhess, "The Arab Nationalist Challenge to the Israeli Communist Party (1970–1985)," *Studies in Comparative Communism*, Winter 1989). Dozens of members of the proscribed communist party Political Bureau have been imprisoned without trial since the early 1980s, although many others were released in the mid-1980s. Yusuf Murad, a former member of the SCP Central Committee, formed another group, the Base Organization, in 1980. Many members of the Party for Communist Action and others suspected of having ties to that group were imprisoned without charges during the 1980s. Another illegal organization, at least one of whose alleged founders was imprisoned for a while during the 1980s, was called the Union for Communist Struggle. It is not known whether these organizations continue to exist.

Leadership and Party Organization. Little is known about the dynamics of the SCP's leadership except that General Secretary Khalid Bakhdash has long been the dominant figure. There have been some divisions among the top leaders; for example, Politburo member Ni'mah (now a representative of the SCP on the Central Command of the NPF) broke with the party temporarily during the 1970s. There were also some reports of dissent within the party during 1986. No information is available on meetings of party organs during the past four years.

Domestic Party Affairs. In the context of growing discontent, Bakhdash—in a statement published in Kuwait but not in Syria—said that "we want to see the regime reformed out of concern for it rather than enmity toward it." He went on to express his party's "concern over the unforeseen developments," fearing that "reactionary forces [will] ride the wave of frustration." He called for an end to the martial law that has been in effect since 1963 and for "realizing the rule of law in all fields, officially recognizing all parties of the front and enabling them freedom of work." (Alan Cowell, "Trouble in Damascus," *NYT Magazine*, 1 April.)

According to one report, some members of the SCP, along with members of political detainees' families, participated in a demonstration—dispersed by the police after calls for an overthrow of the regime were heard—in Damascus on 5 February calling for a release of these people from prison (Jerusalem, in Arabic, *Arab World*, 2 March; *FBIS*, 5 March). It is possible that this report confused the SCP with a different communist faction. The SCP Central Committee met in August. Otherwise, no information is available on meetings of party organs during the year.

Spokesmen for the SCP in international forums have regularly proclaimed their distaste for the socioeconomic aspects of the Ba'athist regime. No information is available on the SCP's role in the general elections held on 22 May or on the number of seats (if any) the party won in the People's Assembly (newly enlarged to 250 members from the previous 195). A new electoral law increased the number of seats allocated to independents from 22 percent to 40 percent of the total (Damascus Domestic Service, 15 April; *FBIS*, 16 April).

Auxiliary and Front Organizations. Little information (none of it current) is available on auxiliary organizations. According to *First-Hand Information: Communists and Revolutionary Democrats of the World Presenting their Parties* (Prague: Peace and Socialism International Publishers, 1988), the SCP participates in labor unions and in "mass organisations," particularly "youth and women's organisations." The party also presumably participates in such groups as the Arab-Soviet Friendship Society, the Syrian Committee for Solidarity with Asian and African Countries, the National Council of Peace Partisans in Syria, the Syrian-GDR Friendship Society, and the Syrian-Bulgarian Friendship Society (if they still exist).

The present Syrian regime is officially based on the NPF, which includes the SCP (the only Marxist grouping represented), the Arab Socialist party, the Arab Socialist Union, the Nasserist Unionist party, the Islamic party (newly admitted during 1990, in addition to another party, the name of which is not available) (Kuwait, *al-Watan*, 1 March; *FBIS*, 6 March), in addition to the dominant Ba'ath party. A resolution was reportedly being drafted for consideration in the upcoming Ninth General Congress of the Ba'ath party, scheduled for April, urging that the various organizations in the NPF be allowed to open offices in each governate (London, *Sharq al-Awsat*, 2 March; *FBIS*, 6 March). The cabinet includes two members of the SCP, which is also represented in the central leadership of the NPF and in local governmental bodies. This does not mean that the SCP has any significant influence but that it has for the time being more or less abandoned revolution in favor of a largely formal role. The quiet position of the regime's partner also conforms to the wishes of the USSR.

A general congress of the NPF, which was expected to amend the front's charter to allow for the participation of other groupings, was being planned early in the year (Kuwait, *al-Watan*, 1 March; *FBIS*, 6 March); no information on the congress was available at the time of writing.

Adnan Sa'd al-Din, general secretary of the Syrian Muslim Brotherhood and a member of the Political Bureau of the National Front for the Salvation of Syria, accused the NPF of representing "only itself" and of being a "mere decoration that the authorities adorn themselves with and hide behind" (Paris, *al-Yawm al-Sabi*, 5 March; *FBIS*, 8 March).

The Syrian government increasingly showed disillusionment with trends in the USSR. In President Asad's first speech on these developments, he refrained from blaming the Soviets, who had recently indicated that they expect faster payment of the $15 billion debt and that future weapons sales will be less forthcoming than before, but deplored the growing emigration of Soviet Jews in terms of "the freedom of occupying other people's [Palestinians'] territory and expelling them from their land." (*NYT*, 9 March.) There were reports that the Soviets were significantly reducing the number of military advisers in Syria (Kuwait, *al-Ray al-Amm*, 15 January; *FBIS*, 18 January). One Israeli report indicated that the number of Soviet military experts in Syria had dropped "from 4,000 to 2,000 during the past five years" (Jerusalem Domestic Service, 29 January, *FBIS*, 30 January). It was in the context of the decreased reliance on the USSR and the Iraqi invasion of Kuwait that Damascus's relations with Western countries experienced notable improvements.

There were continuing reaffirmations of the strength of Syrian-Soviet relations. Soviet ambassador Aleksandr Zotov described Syria as occupying a remarkable place among the Soviet Union's friends in the region and invoked the Syrian-Soviet treaty of friendship and cooperation as the firm basis of the close relationship (Damascus Domestic Service, 25 July, *FBIS*, 26 July). The Syrian press repeatedly emphasized the solid nature of the country's ties with the USSR (Damascus Domestic Service, 18 January; *FBIS*, 19 January).

President Asad headed a delegation that held talks with President Mikhail Gorbachev in Moscow in May. Syrian officials emphasized the positive contribution of these talks to Syrian-Soviet cooperation. Asad later emphasized that the USSR "understands the Arab concern over Soviet Jewish immigration" and had committed itself to reconsidering the issue "within the context of Arab rights" (Damascus Television Service, 16 May; *FBIS*, 17 May).

There were numerous other contacts between the two countries. Soviet foreign economic relations minister Konstantin F. Katushev headed a delegation to Damascus in December 1989 that engaged in talks culminating in an agreement on trade relations and economic and scientific cooperation (Damascus Domestic Service, 29 December 1989; *FBIS*, 2 January). A USSR-Syria Friendship Society delegation traveled from the USSR to Damascus in March and held meetings with Syrian state and Ba'ath party officials and signed a friendship and cooperation pact with its Syrian counterpart (Damascus Domestic Service, 21 March, 26 March; *FBIS*, 22 March, 27 March). Meetings of the Syrian-Soviet joint committee on oil were held in Damascus in May (Damascus, *Sana*, 2 May; *FBIS*, 3 May), as was the eleventh session of the Permanent Syrian-Soviet Committee for Economic, Scientific, and Technical Cooperation (Damascus Domestic Service, 4 May; *FBIS*, 7 May). Shakir Is'id, chairman of the Arab and Foreign Relations Committee of the Syrian People's Assembly, was a member of an Arab Parliamentary Union delegation that visited the USSR in July (Damascus, *Sana*, 17 July; *FBIS*, 17 July). A delegation from the USSR Congress of People's Deputies visited Damascus later in the same month and met with Syrian vice-president Abd-Halim Khaddam and the Ba'ath party's assistant secretary general, Abdullah al-Ahmar (Damascus Domestic Ser-

vice, 21 July; *FBIS*, 23 July). A Soviet envoy, Mikhail D. Sytenko, was in Damascus for talks on the Persian Gulf crisis during August (Damascus Domestic Service, 16 August; *FBIS*, 16 August). A delegation headed by Colonel General Nikolay Kotlovtsev visited Damascus as guests of the Popular Army in October (Damascus, *Sana*, 15 October; *FBIS*, 16 October). A Soviet economic delegation visited Syria in November (Damascus, *Sana*, 13 November; *FBIS*, 15 November). Aleksandr Belonogov, Soviet deputy foreign minister and special envoy, met with President Asad and other top Syrian leaders in Damascus in November for talks concerning the Persian Gulf crisis (Damascus Syrian Arab Television Network, 18 November; *FBIS*, 19 November).

Contacts with other Socialist countries included a visit from a Chinese delegation headed by Li Lanqing, Chinese vice-minister of foreign economic relations and trade, in August (Damascus Domestic Service, 19 August; *FBIS*, 20 August). A delegation of the Korean Workers' party Politburo met with Syrian leaders, including President Asad, in Damascus in March (Damascus Domestic Service, 30 March; *FBIS*, 2 April). A Syrian Ba'ath party delegation traveled to Pyongyang in October to participate in the celebrations of the 45th anniversary of the founding of the Workers' party of Korea (Pyongyang, Korean News Agency, 12 October; *FBIS*, 16 October).

Ba'ath party assistant general secretary Abdullah al-Ahmar received representatives participating in the meeting of Arab communist parties in August (Damascus Domestic Service, 11 August; *FBIS*, 17 August). He met with Iraqi Communist Party general secretary Aziz Muhammad in July for talks related to relations between the two parties and other developments in the region (Damascus, *Sana*, 10 July; *FBIS*, 11 July).

International Views, Positions, and Activities. There is little available information on the SCP's international activities. It was one of eleven Arab communist organizations that joined in a statement calling on Iraq to withdraw from Kuwait and on the United States to withdraw from the Persian Gulf region (London, *Morning Star*, 17 August). (For further quotes, see the profile on Egypt in this volume of *YICA*.) The SCP Central Committee also "expressed great concern over" both the invasion—described as a violation of the charters of the Arab League and the United Nations and of international law, as damaging Arab solidarity and the struggle for Palestinian rights—and against Jewish immigration and the ensuing Western buildup. This was put in the context of other "previous adventures" by the Iraqi regime, "such as launching a war against the Iranian revolution and against its own people and using chemical weapons against them, its conspiracy against Syria, and the oppression of nationalist and progressive forces in Iraq." The statement described "imperialism and its allies" as having used the situation "to strengthen their presence in the Gulf and their hegemony on the region and its people." (Damascus, *Sana*, 19 August; *FBIS*, 20 August.) A meeting of the NPF Central Command, chaired by President Asad on 19 August, also expressed concern over these developments, stressed that the recent Cairo summit resolutions provide the proper solution to the problem, and endorsed the position taken by Syria.

An SCP statement of 13 March condemned U.S. threats against Libya. Washington was accused of continuing an aggressive "policy of state terrorism," while its opposition to holding an international conference on the Middle East and its continued supply of aid to Israel and "ignoring its nuclear and chemical armament" were cited as evidence of a lack of sincerity in United States' talk about peace in the region (Damascus, *Sana*, 13 March; *FBIS*, 14 March).

SCP Politburo member Daniel Ni'mah, a member of the Central Command of the NPF, was a member of the delegation that accompanied President Asad to Moscow in April (Damascus Domestic Service, 29 April; *FBIS*, 1 May).

Glenn E. Perry
Indiana State University

Tunisia

Population. 8,095,492
Party. Tunisian Communist Party (Parti Communiste Tunisien, PCT)
Founded. 1934
Membership. 2,000 (estimated); the PCT claims 4,000–5,000
General Secretary. Muhammad Harmel

Politburo. 9 members: General Secretary Muhammad Harmel, Muhammad Ennafaa, Hichem Sekik, Abdelhamid Ben Mustapha, Junaidi Abdeljawad, Bujuma Remili, Ahmed Ibrahim, Abdelmajid Triki, Rachid Mcharek
Central Committee 22 members: Ahmed Ben Younes, Junaidi Abdeljawad, Bujuma Remili, Ahmed Ibrahim, Habib Kasdalghli, Rachid Mcharek, Sadik Labidi, Tarak Chaabani, Abdelhamid Larguech, Abdelhamid Ben Mustapha, Abdelmajid Triki, Ali Khmira, Abdelwahab Abassi, Muhammad Ben Della, Muhammad Harmel, Muhammad Ennafaa, Muhammad Lakhdar, Muhammad Kallel, Muhammad Khelifi, Mustapha Ouannen, Noureddine Metoui, Hichem Sekik
Status. Legal
Last Congress. Tenth, June 1989
Last Election. 2 April 1989 (legislative and presidential)
Auxiliary Organization. Tunisian Communist Youth
Publication. *Al-Tariq al-Jadid* (The new path), weekly

Background. Founded like its Algerian counterpart as an offshoot of the French Communist Party, the PCT was formed in 1920 and then established itself as an independent political organization in 1939. Its members were in the vanguard of the struggle for independence from France, but the organization was quickly disbanded after Habib Bourguiba and his Destour (Constitutional) party became the leading—and single—political organization in the new republic after 1956. The PCT was officially disbanded in 1963 and was not resurrected until July 1981, when the Bourguiba regime embarked on a temporary period of political *ouverture*. The PCT then functioned for slightly more than two years (July 1981–November 1983) as the only political opposition party in the country—in itself a clear indication that the Bourguiba regime never considered it a powerful political adversary. (See *YICA*, 1984, for additional details about the creation of political parties in Tunisia.)

Leadership and Organization. Tunisia's Communist Party's local and regional cells are all coordinated from the central headquarters in Tunis. The party, dominated by Muhammad Harmel and an aging leadership, has seemingly attracted few young adherents to reinvigorate its cadres. Overall membership is low, for the country's political life is still largely dominated by the Constitutional Democratic Rally (RCD), headed by president Zine el-Abidine Ben Ali, and a growing number of largely ineffective opposition parties.

Domestic Party Affairs. The virtual standstill in Tunisian politics made 1990 a year of disappointment and frustration for the country's communist party. Many of the political initiatives generated by President Ben Ali in 1988 and 1989 had promised a possibility of greater political pluralism, which Muhammad Harmel defended at the time with enthusiasm (see *YICA*, 1989, for details). The PCT participated in the signing of the November 1988 National Pact, an attempt by the Tunisian president to rally all opposition parties behind his restructuring of the country's political life. In the parliamentary by-elections of January 1988, the PCT had been the only opposition party to field candidates. But by the end of 1988 and throughout 1989, the PCT's comments in local and regional newspapers hinted at growing dissatisfaction with the policies of the Tunisian president. Harmel, in the wake of the 1988 elections, turned increasingly critical of the government's intentions, as did several other opposition leaders who saw their chances at participation annulled by the nature of the country's voting system and by the stranglehold of the Constitutional Democratic Rally inside Tunisia.

The 2 April 1989 presidential and parliamentary elections marked a breaking point between the PCT and the country's single party that has dominated its political life since independence. Harmel, like the other opposition leaders, felt himself caught between what the PCT perceived as little concrete change that could improve its chances at political participation and the need to support the government against a rapidly growing Islamist movement. The outcome of the April 1989 elections—in which the Islamist movement obtained 14 percent of the popular vote and up to 30 percent in the major cities—indicated the growing strength of a (still unrecognized) Islamic movement and brought home to the PCT how little the party means in the country's political system. Harmel repeatedly singled out the electoral procedure as an indication of Ben Ali's inability to reform the political system and stressed that the arrangement assured that the Islamist movement would remain the only viable alternative to the Constitutional Democratic Rally.

Thus throughout 1990 the PCT continued its wavering policy of support for the government, arguing for continued reform of the political and economic system but skeptical that this will ever afford it a chance for active participation. Harmel continued to criticize the government's attempts to incorporate opposition figures in the government, arguing that Ben Ali is "buying out" the opposition rather than structuring a truly pluralist political system in Tunisia. The PCT has consistently seen itself as the only opposition party capable of bringing pressure to bear on the government. Throughout 1990 Harmel and other party leaders responded more cautiously than usual to the government's calls for increased participation by opposition groups. They have vigorously criticized not only the lack of political opportunities but the country's recent economic restructuring legislation, which, they argue, threatens further the already precarious lifestyles of many of the country's poor and workers. Not surprisingly the workers also constitute the socioeconomic group targeted by the Islamists, and the PCT has found itself in competition with the Islamist movement for its traditional supporters, a struggle it seems to be losing.

All these developments caused the PCT, already a weakened player in Tunisia's political life, to lose a substantial amount of ground during 1989 and 1990. It was widely rumored in Tunis that the party at one point could not even muster the 75 votes necessary to register as a political party during a recent local election. The struggle with the Islamic movement has, perhaps temporarily, emerged as a focus of attention for the party. Throughout 1990 Harmel and his collaborators continued to insist that Islam should not be exploited for political purposes—a statement that ironically demonstrated a close affinity to what the government has been arguing for years. Even more ironically, the PCT had long been the defender of the now burgeoning Islamist movement when it was repressed during the Bourguiba regime. The rise of the Islamists and the sagging fortunes of the PCT have seemingly gone hand in hand and do not augur well for the future of the party.

The 2 August Iraqi invasion of Kuwait provided a new focus for the PCT. But here also it found itself having to support the government's statements that ultimately the crisis should be settled by local governments with the help of fellow Arab leaders. The party's newspaper predictably printed a number of anti–United States and anti-Western articles. But events in the gulf, the rapid growth of the Islamist movement, the relative success of the country's economic reforms, and marginal local interest in its political program have made the PCT's future as a viable political party more difficult than ever. Although ritually consulted by the government, who perceives it as a spoiler rather than an active participant, it is clear that the PCT represents little in the country's political life.

International Views, Positions, and Activities. Events in the gulf made up the most consistent focus of the PCT after the 2 August Iraqi invasion. Before August the PCT continued to express hopes that the October 1989 meeting of the Tunisian, Algerian, and Moroccan Communist Party leaderships in Casablanca would produce a unified stance on several issues of regional importance. Hardly surprisingly, the PCT has viewed the Arab Maghreb Union as a possible way of coordinating the policies of the region's parties. So far few of the initiatives discussed in Casablanca have come to fruition, a development that clearly frustrated Harmel. Events in Eastern Europe and the Soviet Union received substantial coverage—mostly editorials arguing that the pace of reforms was to be encouraged, mixed with a precautionary note that local leaders should remain vigilant in pursuing equitable social and economic arrangements.

Dirk Vandewalle
Dartmouth College

Yemen

Population. 9,746,465
Parties. Yemeni Socialist Party (al-Hizb al-Ishtirakiya al-Yamaniya; founded 1978); General People's Congress (al-Mu'tamar al-Sha'bi al-'Am; founded 1982); many other small parties
Chairman of the Presidential Council. (President and head of state): Gen. 'Ali 'Abdullah Salih (elected 22 May)
Deputy Chairman of the Presidential Council. 'Ali Salim al-Bayd
Presidential Council. Al-Qadi 'Abd al-Karim al-'Arashi, Salim Salih Muhammad, 'Abd al-'Aziz 'Abd al-Ghani
Prime Minister. Haydar Abu Bakr al-'Attas

Speaker, House of Representatives. Dr. Yasin Sa'id Nu'man
House of Representatives. Number of members unknown (all appointed by president)
Advisory Council. 45 members (all appointed by president)

On 22 May, following centuries of division, aspirations of Yemeni unity were finally realized. On that date, the Republic of Yemen was formally created by a merger of the Yemen Arab Republic (North Yemen, YAR) and the People's Democratic Republic of Yemen (Democratic Yemen or South Yemen, PDRY). The new Republic of Yemen (ROY) formed the Arabian peninsula's largest state in terms of population and its only nonmonarchy. The two halves of North and South Yemen form a single unit in terms of ethnicity (Arab), language (Arabic), and religion (Islam, divided into the Sunni and Zaydi sects). However, the political orientations of the former governments—the PDRY had been a single-party Marxist state since independence while the North since 1974 had been run by military governments and a laissez-faire economic system—had long posed a severe obstacle to unity.

Background. North Yemen was recognized as an independent state on the departure of the Ottomans at the end of World War I. The traditional monarchy of the imamate was eradicated by a military coup d'état on 26 September 1962. The ensuing civil war between royalist and republican forces did not end until 1970, when the new YAR was assured of permanent status. The civilian government was overthrown in 1974 by a military coup led by Ibrahim al-Hamdi, who wielded increasing authority until his assassination in 1977. Nine months later, his successor was also killed, and 'Ali 'Abdullah Salih, a young and seemingly unqualified junior army officer, took over. After molding his style of governing after Hamdi and surviving several assassination attempts, 'Ali 'Abdullah gradually began to strengthen his control over the army, the government, and the independent-minded tribes of northern North Yemen. The discovery of oil in the mid-1980s and its subsequent export were inadequate, however, to counteract the YAR's growing economic woes, which were caused by falling remittances of Yemeni workers abroad (especially in Saudi Arabia) and declining aid flows.

To the South, violent opposition to the continued British presence in bustling Aden colony and the more traditional Aden protectorates began in the early 1960s. Eventually, after years of armed struggle, the British handed over power to the leftist National Liberation Front (NLF) on 30 November 1967, which formed the first government. Although it had overcome its more moderate rivals before independence, the NLF was riven with factionalism and infighting. Internal power struggles reached climaxes in 1969, 1971, 1978, 1980, and the civil war of January 1986. By 1978, the NLF had gone through several phases of reorganization and had been reborn as the Yemeni Socialist Party (YSP), with several other small legal parties folded into it.

The January 1986 attempt by President 'Ali Nasir Muhammad to eliminate his rivals within the YSP provoked bloody battles and ended in 'Ali Nasir's exile to North Yemen. The Adeni government was then restructured with 'Ali Salim al-Bayd, one of the few remaining party leaders who had fought in the war for independence, as the new YSP secretary general. Salim Salih Muhammad, perhaps the most powerful member of the YSP, was appointed assistant secretary general. The new president was Haydar Abu Bakr al-'Attas, who had been prime minister for only a short period previously. It should be noted that the party had held supremacy over the government apparatus since the bloody confrontation of 1978.

Despite the many years of division under rival colonial powers and the division into separate Yemeni states, nearly all Yemenis continued to desire a single state. The avowed goals of the YAR revolution in 1962 were not only to topple the imamate but also to put an end to British colonialism in the South. Similarly, the revolutionaries in the South espoused the same goals and even used the North as a base for their operations. However, about the time that the South became independent, the YAR government was moving toward reconciliation with its royalist opponents and expelling its leftists. In the South, the next few years saw a series of struggles and purges within the ruling party that left a militant left wing in control. As a consequence, the two Yemeni states grew further apart and fought a brief border war in October 1972. The subsequent agreement to end their differences by merger was never put into effect.

Another cycle of hostilities began in 1978 when a growing rapprochement between the two presidents was aborted by the killing of the northern president in Sanaa, which was followed by the subsequent capture and execution of the southern president. Less than a year later, another border war erupted during which the South penetrated deep into the North before being stopped. A second declaration to merge had the same effect as the first. Then a third period of tension emanated from the civil war in Aden during January 1986. YAR president 'Ali 'Abdullah Salih reportedly considered intervening on 'Ali Nasir Muhammad's behalf but was dissuaded. Nevertheless, the granting of asylum to 'Ali Nasir, along with upwards of 50,000 of his supporters, continued to fray relations.

An additional factor derived from the prospects of oil deposits in the border area between the two countries. A number of clashes occurred between the armies before an agreement, reached in 1985, to declare a neutral zone with a single company to exploit its resources was implemented in 1988.

The March toward Unification. Perhaps the first sign that unification was in fact on the verge of reality came out of the 4 May 1988 meeting between the two Yemeni presidents in Sanaa. In addition to a renewed commitment to the official machinery of unification, this meeting lowered the barriers to the free movement of people and goods between the two halves. Furthermore, the pace of ministry-to-ministry agreements on future cooperation quickened through 1989. The apex was reached in Aden on 30 November 1989 at the twentieth anniversary of South Yemen's independence. The two presidents announced that Yemeni unity would be achieved within a calendar year, following ratification of their accord by existing legislative bodies and popular referenda; they also provided details on the shape of the new state-to-be.

The 30 November announcement brought in its wake a flurry of incremental developments that seemed to indicate that unity indeed would soon be a reality. Most significant of these was the first joint meeting of the two cabinets in Sanaa 20–22 January. This session laid much of the practical groundwork for the new state. The many resultant decisions concerned

1. Instructions to the Economic and Financial Committee to complete standardized laws on tariffs, Central Banks, currencies, and income taxes

2. Instructions to the Education, Culture and Information Committee to complete standardized laws on education and travel procedures for tourists

3. Instructions to the Legislative and Judicial Committee to complete standardized laws

on the judiciary and penal, commercial, and civil codes

4. Instructions to the foreign affairs and diplomatic and consular representation

5. Terms on which ministries, departments, and public corporations were to be merged and a proposed list of new ministerial portfolios

6. Terms for unifying the two civil services and creating a common system of salaries and benefits

7. Directing ministers on the absorption of all employees within the framework of the new ministries

8. Directing ministries without unification committees to meet to discuss their mergers

9. Creating a subcommittee to generalize the civil service and social security

10. Creating a subcommittee to create a draft law for local government

11. Reiterating the emphasis on free movement of citizens between halves

12. Discussing laws on individual rights and liberties and the allocation of responsibilities for devising new laws in this regard

13. A decision to release immediately all political prisoners

14. Stressing that political committees must complete their work before 20 February, including the initiation of dialogue with political organizations and national figures

15. Authorizing the two prime ministers to undertake a comprehensive assessment of the two Yemens' experience in economic, political, cultural, and social areas, and in the field of democratic practice; and

16. Tasking all ministers to continue to work pending completion of all measures relating to mergers.

In other fields, a meeting on cooperation between the Defense Ministries had been held in late December 1989, and the PDRY defense minister announced on 10 January in Kuwait that both armed forces had been withdrawn from the sensitive border areas. He also added that a complete merger of the armed forces would take place before the end of the year. Subsequently, in May, both armies were removed from their respective capitals and detachments were stationed in the other half. A parallel move saw the official disbandment of the South's State Security Organization and Ministry and the North's National Security Organization.

Flights by the national air carriers, Yemenia (North) and al-Yemda (South), were to be regarded as domestic as of March, a first step toward merging the twelve-aircraft fleet. On 4 May, following devaluations, both currencies were declared legal tender in either half, with the Yemeni dinar (South) pegged at 26 Yemeni riyals (North). This too was regarded as an interim step until a single monetary unit could be created. Other measures were taken toward codifying regulations on political parties and on cooperation between the two official parties: the General People's Congress (North) and the YSP (South). In April, Aden released several individuals that had been arrested the previous year for being northern intelligence agents.

Given all these flurries of activity, it was not too surprising when the date of unity was sharply advanced, to 22 May. One reason for shifting the date may have been Islamic opposition to the merger. According to *The Economist* (26 May), some 25 members of the YAR's new Consultative Council (Majlis al-Shura) were reported to have refused to vote for the merger. Equally, it may have been because so much progress had been made on the details that there was no need to delay any longer.

New Government of 22 May 1990. On 22 May, a joint meeting in Aden of the YAR's Consultative Council and the PDRY's Supreme People's Congress unanimously approved the five-person membership of the new Republic of Yemen's Presidential Council. Immediately after taking the constitutional oath, the council held its first meeting at which 'Ali 'Abdullah Salih (formerly the YAR president) was elected council chairman (i.e., head of state) and 'Ali Salim al-Bayd (formerly secretary general of the PDRY's YSP) was elected vice-chairman. (One day before these events, the YAR Consultative Council had promoted 'Ali 'Abdullah Salih from colonel to lieutenant general.) The other members of the council were al-Qadi 'Abd al-Karim al-'Arashi (formerly YAR vice-president), Salim Salih Muhammad (formerly YSP assistant secretary-general), and 'Abd al-'Aziz 'Abd al-Ghani (formerly YAR prime minister). As previously agreed, Sanaa became the political capital of unified Yemen, whereas Aden was named the economic capital; government functions were to be divided between the two cities.

The new president, 'Ali 'Abdullah Salih, immediately issued a multitude of presidential decrees, one of which named Haydar Abu Bakr al-'Attas (formerly the PDRY president) as prime minister and entrusted him with forming a government. The new 39-person cabinet was announced on 24 May. Of the four deputy prime ministers, two were chosen from each former half. Southerners were appointed to such key portfolios as defense, expatriates' affairs, finance, information, oil, planning and development, and state for foreign affairs. Northerners occupied the portfolios of civil service and administrative reform, education, foreign affairs, and interior and security.

Another presidential decree on 24 May reconstituted 'Ali 'Abdullah Salih's Advisory Council, now expanded to include a number of southerners. A third decree directed the new House of Representatives (Majlis al-Nawwab) to meet on 26 May. Elections were scheduled to be held at the end of the 30-month transition period. Dr. Yasin Sa'id Nu'man (formerly the PDRY prime minister) was elected speaker at the first meeting. Subsequently it was announced that the lines between regional governorates would be redrawn, with the likely intention of blurring the former boundaries between North and South and thereby helping to make the process of unity increasingly irreversible.

In many ways, it seems that the merger worked more to the North's advantage, most obviously in the election of 'Ali 'Abdullah Salih as president. This was probably inescapable given the far greater population in the North (8 million to the South's 2 million) and its relatively stronger economy (greater agricultural potential, more expatriates working abroad, and oil exports). It also undoubtedly reflected the years of increasing control and political mastery practiced by 'Ali 'Abdullah Salih. Conversely, it also seemed to reflect the continuing malaise among the southern political elite.

Severely weakened by the civil war of January 1986, southern politicians seemed to be uncertainly balanced between the rival camps of prominently situated pragmatists (who could be well described as technocrats and included the former president and prime minister) and the hard-liners (who included the few remaining leaders from the days of independence as well as a younger generation of ideologically committed party members and mid-level army officers). Although the appointment of a southerner as defense minister (Haytham Qasim Tahir, filling a role that in the PDRY had often meant being a kingmaker) could mean a recognition of the South's formidable military might, it could just as easily represent a subordination of the newly unified armed forces to the government, a significantly new development as far as the North was concerned because the YAR had never had a Defense Ministry.

It is not yet clear what role the two official parties (the General People's Congress [GPC] and the Yemeni Socialist Party [YSP]) will play in the new republic, and it is possible that they will merge. Although the GPC was clearly a manipulative attempt to inculcate grass roots support for the old Sanaa regime, the YSP had been the locus of power in the South, and its demotion, if not its demise, undoubtedly would be viewed by southern ideologues as a betrayal of the revolution. Even before unity, the Aden government had legalized several small opposition parties; after unification, the numbers of recognized parties and political newspapers increased dramatically, especially in the North. Most significantly, no Islamic party was legalized, undoubtedly because the Islamic opposition appears to pose the most serious challenge to the regime. This holds true not only for the more traditional North but also for rural areas of the South. An Islamic demonstration in al-Mukalla in March 1990 turned violent and resulted in the wounding of a policeman; other Islamic demonstrations took place about the same time in Aden.

The Impact of the Gulf Crisis. That the Iraqi invasion of Kuwait on 2 August came so soon after the merger of the Yemens could be seen as particularly bad luck for the southwest corner of Arabia. One primary spur to unity in both halves of Yemen had been severe economic difficulties: a steady and alarming decline in workers' remittances, shrinking financial aid from the gulf states, and disappearing aid from other international sources. Meanwhile, corruption was on the rise in the North; in the South, any benefits to having had Soviet military advisers, East German security advisers, and Cuban economic advisers ended with their recall home in 1989 and 1990. In addition, food shortages and wildcat strikes were becoming endemic in Aden. Thus the prospect of economic integration became tantalizing even more so because Yemen's principal oil fields were located astride the North-South border; full and efficient exploitation could be achieved only through unity.

At the same time, the YAR joined Iraq, Egypt, and Jordan in the Arab Cooperation Council (ACC), a membership subsequently extended to the

ROY. Some observers saw the encirclement of Saudi Arabia as a principal motivation for the ACC because the member states did not seem to have a lot in common either economically or politically. Yemen's membership may also have been based on its growing ties to Baghdad, as evidenced through the YAR's sending troops to Iraq during the Iran-Iraq war and the consequent Iraqi aid to Sanaa.

Although President 'Ali 'Abdullah Salih disassociated himself from the invasion, he nevertheless condemned sending troops to the gulf. Yemeni viewpoints on regional issues received considerable attention and Western displeasure because the ROY occupied the Arab League's seat on the U.N. Security Council at the time. Much as with Jordan, Yemen was perceived by its neighbors and the West as showing a pro-Iraqi bias in its stance on the situation, and Yemeni violations of the U.N. embargo were alleged. Throughout August, pro-Saddam demonstrations were staged outside the U.S. embassy in Sanaa, and some Yemenis allegedly demonstrated in Riyadh and Jidda. Briefly,

in August, the British consul general in Aden was declared persona non grata as a consequence of observing ship movements in Aden harbor.

Although initial hearsay about Iraq sending military aircraft to Yemen for safekeeping seems spurious, Saudi Arabia was so incensed at Yemeni behavior that it took the drastic step in September of expelling 30 ROY diplomats and, in October, of requiring Yemenis resident in Saudi Arabia to find Saudi sponsors and owners of their businesses. In the next few months, anywhere from 400,000 to 800,000 Yemenis returned to Yemen, with a devastating impact on the already reeling Yemeni economy. Yemeni anger against Saudi Arabia was also fueled by allegations of detention and torture of hundreds of Yemenis by Saudi security forces. These allegations were examined by Amnesty International (*NYT*, 2 November). These external developments placed additional, and perhaps fatal, strains on the fragile nature of the unified Yemeni state.

J.E. Peterson
Muscat, Sultanate of Oman

WESTERN EUROPE

Introduction

The dramatic events of the late summer and autumn of 1989 were so overwhelming that a proper assessment of their meaning did not begin to emerge until 1990. The symbolic end of the cold war, illustrated by the opening of the Berlin Wall on 9 November 1989, produced in both parts of Germany the greatest celebration in Europe, referred to by some cynics as *die nationale Besoffenheit* (the national intoxication), since the end of World War II. The celebration of freedom and the power of the free market left the wall a gray relic of communist tyranny.

In the new year, Germany became formally united as one country on 2 December and the governments of Poland, Czechoslovakia, and Hungary struggled to create viable democracies and free markets. In Romania and Bulgaria progress was slower, but the road to democracy was traveled there, too. In all these countries, and especially in the former German Democratic Republic, communism as well as socialism were thoroughly discredited. The effects of the crumbling Soviet empire and the collapse of dictatorial regimes were felt by the communist parties of Western Europe as well but in different ways and by no means uniformly. Speculation abounded that the communist movement in Western Europe was dead. Certainly the decision taken by the parties of Italy and Sweden to change their names, as well as coalitions formed by communist parties with parties of the left, indicated that the majority of Western Europe's communist parties were restructuring, with effects that would not be immediately evident.

Another consideration of tremendous importance in democratic countries was the electoral challenge of the ballot box. The verdict presented by this measure was not yet in by the end of the year. General elections were held only in Austria, Denmark, Greece, and Germany, which meant that the Communist parties of Cyprus, Finland, France, Great Britain, Iceland, Ireland, Italy, Luxembourg, Malta, the Netherlands, Norway, Portugal, Spain, Sweden, Switzerland, and Turkey were not judged by their respective electorates. In those countries where national elections were held, the communist parties fared poorly; this was particularly evident in unified Germany. Of the thirteen parties with legislative representation, that of San Marino held the highest percentage of seats based on votes received (28.7), followed by Cyprus (27.4), Italy (26.6), Finland (13.8, counting both majority and minority faction electoral fronts), Iceland (13.2), France (11.3), Portugal (11.0), Greece (10.28), Spain (9.05), Sweden (5.8), the Netherlands (4.1), Luxembourg (3.6), and Switzerland (0.8). Of these thirteen countries, elections were only held in Greece; thus, the true strength of twelve of the thirteen parties had not yet been measured.

As a member of the Norwegian Communist Party commented in 1990, the communist movement lay in ruins in Europe. But although the movement was uncertain and demoralized, it spent the year in taking stock, as party congresses assessed what role their parties could play in the remaking of Europe. In September 1989 the director of the Center for Strategic Studies at the Free University of Rome drew a conclusion that continued to apply in 1990:

> The majority of Communist leaders in Western Europe now celebrate the marvels of market economy, private entrepreneurship and individual profit, although they know this is the ideological patrimony of their adversaries: liberal, Christian Democratic and—enriched with large doses of social-welfare policies—Social Democratic parties.
>
> Rationally, it seems suicidal for a political party to emphasize the ideological values of its adversaries. The fact is that Communists have learned painful lessons: A modern state cannot be run by central planning; but they also know that without central planning the Communist Party will become irrelevant. . .[the communist parties] in Western European democracies are trying to ride two ponies in opposite directions. Theirs is a fascinating, perilous, exceedingly difficult—and probably hopeless—endeavor.

(Enrico Jacchia, "Western Europe Communists: Being Left without Ideology," *LAT*, 3 September.)

Whereas the communist movement was trying to ride two ponies, the socialist movement, in the words of the president of the Socialist International, Willy Brandt, "has been discredited by the mess created in the so-called 'socialist countries.'" When the Socialist International met in New York in October 1990 for the first time since the fall of the communist dictatorships in Europe and for the first time in more than a century in the United States, the mood vacillated between optimism and pessimism. The former prime minister of France, Pierre Mauroy, concluded that "we are traditionally the third way, in between the totalitarian state and the unregulated free market." His conclusion stood in sharp contrast to that of a former general secretary of the Socialist International, Hans Janitschek, who recognized that "although Europeans do make a distinction between Communism and Social Democracy, the collapse of the first and only socialist experiment in history will have long lasting repercussions on the Socialist movement as a whole." (Frank J. Prial, "Socialists Ponder a Changed World," *NYT*, 11 October.)

Those conclusions were important not because the Socialist International saw the collapse of communism as an historic opportunity for a new start for the left but because the communist parties of Western Europe saw in social democracy an opportunity to restore their image. During the year the communist parties prepared to embrace the rebirth of socialism with a democratic face, seeking to ally themselves with socialist parties. No other alternative, for the time being, was open to them. Indeed, the majority made it clear that restructuring, including changes in name such as that chosen by the Italian Communist Party—Democratic Party of the Left—or by the former Communist Party of East Germany—Party of Democratic Socialism—was aimed at recapturing credibility via usurpation of the image of socialism. Whether this effort would prove successful was not clear at the end of the year. But the majority of Western Europe's communist parties indicated the intention to embrace a communism with socialist colors. In October, Jean-Pierre Cot, a leading French socialist in the European Parliament, concluded as follows: "We said for 70 years that there could be no socialism without democracy. Now we have to prove that what failed is Communism—not Social Democracy." (Ibid.) Cot's observation was, however, also a challenge for the

communist parties and one that would not go unmet. As a consequence, 1991 was virtually guaranteed to be a year of new struggle between the communists and the socialists to win the allegiance of Western European electorates.

Throughout the 1980s the role of the French Communist Party (PCF) in France's political life was among the most interesting of the communist parties of Western Europe. During the decade the party's popularity waxed and waned, as it joined a coalition government with the French socialists in 1981 and then withdrew in the mid-1980s. Party life was affected by internal divisions during 1987, 1988, and 1989, with public demands that PCF general secretary Georges Marchais resign and accusations that the party leadership refused to adjust its policies and programs to reflect fundamental changes in French society.

In 1990 the PCF turned 70, as did Marchais. Both anniversaries, however, were somber milestones for the PCF, which began and ended the year mired in the same misfortunes that have beset it for several years—marginalization in French political life, declining membership, factionalism, reactionary leadership, and a public image of obsolescence. Party membership is estimated at approximately 200,000, and the PCF continues to hold 25 of 577 seats in the French National Assembly, which it won through gaining 11.3 percent of the vote in the 1988 elections.

Under Marchais the PCF leadership experienced a year of severe internal dissent. Accumulating evidence of the party's impotence and plummeting esteem, together with a growing sense of rank and file isolation from the changes that were overtaking the rest of the communist world, helped drive disagreement to a new pitch. The revolt produced a third current of opposition in the already factionridden party, this one led by former Transportation Minister Charles Fiterman (see *YICA*, 1990). This new current, which refers to itself as the *refondateur*, is widely considered to be the pro-Gorbachev faction within the PCF; Fiterman, suggests the noncommunist party press, is Gorbachev's preference for Marchais's successor.

Criticism of Marchais, and mounting pressures from within the party for him to resign, escalated noticeably in the wake of his mid-November 1989 performance on French national television, when he clumsily feigned a lapse of memory concerning the party's 1961 welcoming of the construction of the Berlin Wall. In 1990, with the party's Twenty-seventh Congress scheduled just before Christmas, infighting focused on the leadership's stolid refusal to end its tradition of democratic centralism and permit free discussion of the party's internal problems. Marchais rejected proposals to change the party's name and drop the hammer and sickle emblem. He also successfully forestalled a demand for an extraordinary congress before December to take up the issues of the party's declining prominence in French politics and the leadership's refusal to democratize and modernize the party. Fiterman forced a plenary session of the Central Committee in September to consider a 23-page minority resolution for the party congress that proposed a drastic shake-up of the PCF organization and fundamental democratization of party procedures. Although the resolution was rejected, criticism of Marchais continued. At the beginning of the party congress on 18 December, reformist member Claude Poperen set the tone for much of the pessimism at the congress by declaring that the PCF would be "the last communist party in Europe to refuse change, even after Albania." In response, Marchais pointed to Fiterman's continued membership on the Politburo as proof that the "Communists are using their democratic rules better than ever." (Paris, AFP, 18 December.)

At the congress, Marchais delivered a three-hour keynote address that portrayed French communists as relentlessly high-minded and world communism as on the brink of renaissance; his report was approved by 98.9 percent of the congress delegates. Marchais held out an olive branch to the dissidents, however, by promising to reform the party's statutes at the next congress, set for 1993, but reformers noted that this would be after France's next legislative elections. Marchais suffered another heart attack in late December, virtually ensuring that 1991 would begin on a new wave of speculation about his political longevity and the party's future.

The Communist Party of Italy (PCI) has argued since 1986 "that the old differences between the communist and socialist movements are not sustainable" (*YICA*, 1987). Party membership is claimed to be 1.3 million, and in the last national elections the PCI won 177 of 630 seats in the Italian Parliament. In 1988, under the new leadership of Achille Occhetto, the PCI was charged with "the conquest of the center" in Italian politics. In December 1989 the PCI decided to hold its Nineteenth Congress in March in Bologna. Almost simultaneously, Occhetto introduced a proposal that the congress consider establishing "a new democratic political formation, reformist, open to progressive

lay and Catholic components" and, after months of declining, endorsed the proposal to drop the *communist* label from the Italian Communist Party, as well as to eliminate the hammer and sickle as its symbol. Whereas the PCF considered the Soviet government's policies of *glasnost'* and *perestroika* with antipathy, the PCI welcomed them, for these policies gave the party considerable flexibility on the Italian political stage.

The party congress debated Occhetto's proposed changes, but ratification was postponed to the Twentieth Congress, scheduled for early 1991. The new name, to be approved in the new year, was Democratic Party of the Left. Although Occhetto's proposal had majority support, it was opposed by approximately one-third of the party, who rejected what it considered the "liquidation" of the PCI, which, the opposition pointed out, had long ago taken a highly critical stance toward the discredited communist regimes of Eastern Europe. As the year continued, the opposition, calling itself the No Front, sharply criticized Occhetto's support for a new strategy and theoretical and cultural renewal, a development that threatened to split the party. By midyear, however, indications were that compromise would avoid a serious rift, as Occhetto made clear that the new party's future would not liquidate the old party's past: "The most creative and original part of Italian Communism [will not be] erased, but will live on and generate real new processes and new ideas in a wider context." (*UN*, 27 June.)

As preparations for the Twentieth Congress continued, Occhetto became even more explicit in an effort to assure reconciliation. He thus underscored the conviction "that no one wants to dissolve absolutely anything [and] that the 20th congress is not meant to be and will not be a congress of dissolution, but one of foundation, transformation and rebirth." In a phrase that many members of the opposition would later cite favorably, he concluded that constitution of a new formation could only take place through "the contribution of forces that have equal dignity." Borrowing a phrase of the No Front, he asserted that all members of the PCI should take seriously those who speak in terms of renewal, but he reminded the minority that the majority's project was the creation of a new formation of the left. (*UN*, 24 July.) At year's end the PCI was preparing to shed its communist heritage, at least in name, and, more important, to begin a new role in Italian politics. What was not yet clear was how the Italian electorate would judge the party in 1991.

The Spanish Communist Party (PCE) has operated legally within Spain since 1977 and has an estimated membership of 83,000. In the mid-1980s party strife significantly changed the image the Spanish communist movement presented to its electorate. In 1983 pro-Soviet dissidents withdrew from the PCE to form the Communist Party of the Peoples of Spain (PCPE); it has a claimed membership of 16,500 and is led by Juan Ramos Camarero. Another group was informally constituted in 1982 by Santiago Carrillo following his failure to be reconfirmed as the PCE's general secretary. In 1987, Carrillo formally resigned from the PCE and established the Spanish Workers' Party—Communist Unity (PTE-UC); estimated membership is fourteen thousand. The party's general secretary is Adolfo Pinedo, and Carrillo serves as chairman.

In the last national elections (October 1989), the PCE was able to form an electoral coalition of the United Left with strong support from members of the PCPE and the PTE-UC. The coalition as a result was able to capture 9.05 percent of the vote and win 18 of 350 parliamentary seats (1986: 4.6 percent and 7 seats). This victory brought the PCE into the new year as a credible force after a decade of turmoil and as a party that endorsed the political changes sweeping across Central and Eastern Europe.

In 1990 the PCE, led by Julio Agusta Gonzalez, 50, continued its political activities under the umbrella of the United Left but emphasized that, unlike the Italian Communist Party, it had no intention of changing its name or of abandoning Marxist principles. Indeed, Gonzales considered the United Left not as a political party but as "a crucible in which the blending of the New Left can begin." Consistent with this position he rejected social democracy as synonymous with accepting the capitalist system. In November, Gonzalez was reelected coordinator of the United Left coalition, but the year ended with continued pressure within the PCE to reform the party along the lines taken by the PCI in Italy. How these pressures would affect the PCE will likely dominate the party's activities in 1991.

The Portuguese Communist Party (PCP) claims a membership of 200,000; the country's population is approximately 10.5 million. The party's general secretary is Álvaro Cunhal, who has served in this position since 1941. The last national election in Portugal was held in 1987. At that time members of the PCP, in an electoral alliance of leftist parties called the United People's Alliance Coalition, were elected to 25 of 250 parliamentary seats; other parties in the coalition won an additional 5 seats.

The PCP, the most Stalinist party in Western Europe, has successfully resisted minority demands for a change of the party's name, program, and goals. Cunhal, in an effort to moderate the terms of the debate, supported creating the position of deputy general secretary at a special party congress in May. A moderate, Carlos Carvalhas, was elected to the position and was expected to succeed Cunhal at an undetermined point in the future. This step, an attempt to limit internal party dissension, proved successful for the remainder of the year. In 1991 the PCP would face legislative elections for the first time in four years, and the party's rigid adherence to communist dogma would face its first major challenge since the political upheavals in Europe in 1989.

In San Marino, Malta, Turkey, Cyprus, and Greece, the communist parties do not determine domestic and foreign policy to a major degree. The Communist Party of San Marino (PCS) represents an extension of the Italian Communist Party, just as the country's other political parties reflect the views of their Italian counterparts. General secretary of the PCS is Gilberto Ghiotti, a 38-year-old political scientist, and claimed party membership is 1,100. In the last general election in San Marino (1988), the PCS won 28.71 percent of the vote to hold 18 of 60 parliamentary seats. Like other communist parties in Western Europe, the PCS reappraised its role in San Marino's political life. During the Twelfth Party Congress in April, the PCS changed its name to the Progressive Democratic Party and replaced the hammer and sickle on its masthead with Picasso's dove. Party leaders concluded that they had "mistakenly called ourselves communists. We have always accepted pluralism and capitalism" (*UN*, 23 March). Indeed, the party maintained its highly successful image as a respected participant in San Marino's government, and at year's end there was every indication that this would continue to be the case during 1991. (Of the seven ministers and three secretaries of state in the Congress of State, two secretaries and two ministers are communist party members. In addition, during 1989–1990 two successive captains regent, Gloriana Ranocchini and Adamiro Bartolini, were also party members.)

Established in 1969, the Communist Party of Malta (CPM) has an estimated membership of one hundred and is led by General Secretary Anthony Vassallo, 71. After its dismal performance in the most recent national elections (1987, when it received 0.08 percent of the vote), the party's membership has steadily declined. In 1990 it stopped publishing its monthly journal as well as its newsletter. Anthony Vassallo endorsed the summit meeting between Presidents Bush and Gorbachev in Malta in December 1989, but the party's voice in Maltese politics is powerless. The sweeping changes in Central and Eastern Europe and the fading international image of Marxism-Leninism have taken their toll on the CPM as they have on Western Europe's other communist parties. As a consequence, the party is without political influence, and there is no indication that it will improve its credibility in 1991.

In Turkey the United Communist Party of Turkey (UCPT) was formed in 1988 as the result of a merger of the Communist Party of Turkey (TCP) with the Workers' Party of Turkey (WPT) but, like its predecessors, has remained proscribed. The party's leaders, Haydar Kutlu and Nihat Sargin, who returned to Turkey from self-imposed exile in 1987, were released from prison by the Turkish government in May and immediately became subject to legal proceedings that continued throughout the year. One month after their release the UCPT filed an application for legal status with the Turkish Ministry of the Interior that classified it as a Marxist, revolutionary workers' party based on class struggle; immediately thereafter the Turkish government initiated legal steps to ban the party. By year's end, legal proceedings were still under way and the party had not yet been declared illegal. In November a new political party, the Unity Party of the Socialists (UPS), was formed in Ankara, and its founding congress was attended by representatives of the UCPT. At the beginning of 1991 it was clear that the party's future depended on whether Turkey's constitutional court would grant legal status to the UCPT as well as to the UPS. If the UPS is allowed to operate legally, it will serve as an umbrella organization for the UCPT. For the time being, therefore, the party's legal position as well as its future influence is in abeyance.

In Cyprus the Progressive Party of the Working People (AKEL) continues to be led by General Secretary Dimitris Christofias, 44. The party claims a membership of sixteen thousand (an increase of a thousand over 1989). In the most recent elections, held in 1985, AKEL garnered 27.4 percent of the vote and won 15 of 56 seats in the Cypriot Parliament. In April 1990, however, dissident members led by Pavlos Dinglis and Michael Papapetrou split from AKEL and established the Democratic Socialist Renewal Movement (ADISOK), with a claimed membership of 1,200. Dinglis and Papapetrou, along with three other ADISOK members, held five of AKEL's fifteen parliamentary seats; thus, at year's end AKEL held 10 of 56 parliamentary seats. The issue that split AKEL was support for *perestroika*, with the dissident members of ADISOK declaring themselves in support of "a pluralistic, democratic movement" in Cyprus.

AKEL's response to division within the party was evident during the party's Seventeenth Congress in October under the theme Renewal, Uniqueness, Strength, and Prepared for Struggle. The congress, for the first time open to the public, elected General Secretary Christofias to a four-year term and committed itself to improving its public image before the national elections scheduled for 1991. The party's popular support is drawn primarily from the Greek Cypriot majority, which makes up approximately 80 percent of the island's estimated population of 707,000; Christofias claimed that AKEL would capture more than 30 percent of the vote in the forthcoming elections. Consistent with past positions the party continued to call for reconciling Greek and Turkish Cypriots, as well as for an international conference on the Cyprus issue. Concerning political and economic changes in Europe and the Soviet Union, the AKEL congress endorsed *perestroika* and "the progressive forces of the Soviet Union." The political future of AKEL, like many of Western Europe's communist parties, was closely connected to the degree of credibility it found among the electorate. For this reason the outcome of the parliamentary elections in the new year would provide at least an initial indication of the damage caused by the fall of communist dictatorships in Central and Eastern Europe. AKEL enjoyed not having to consider changing its name because the word *communist* did not appear in the party's title, but the electorate would judge AKEL's views and positions in 1991.

The Communist Party of Greece (KKE) has an estimated membership of 50,000 and in 1989 moved to the forefront of the political stage. At the beginning of 1990, KKE was participating in an "all-party" government under the mantle of the Coalition of Left and Progress, a loosely knit alliance of KKE with the Greek Left (E.AR, the former KKE-Interior; see *YICA*, 1990), which the two parties formed in 1989. The coalition was headed by KKE chairman Kharilaos Florakis, whereas the party was headed by General Secretary Grigoris Farakos. KKE's participation in the Greek government ended in April when the conservative

New Democracy party was able to obtain a majority in the Greek legislature; in parliamentary elections held on 8 April the coalition's candidates were only able to poll 10.28 percent of the vote (1989: 10.97 percent), thus reducing its legislative seats from 21 to 19.

For the remainder of the year the party's attentions were focused internally in preparation for KKE's Thirteenth Congress, scheduled for November. In the summer the liberal wing of the party, led by Farakos, drafted new party theses to be approved at the congress. The theses reflected the effort to reconcile Marxist-Leninist theory with the new realities of European politics following the collapse of the communist dictatorships in Central and Eastern Europe. They therefore emphasized that KKE "is based on Marxist-Leninist theory . . . as a guide to action" as opposed to dogma. The theses rejected the use of the term *dictatorship of the proletariat* as no longer expressing "the goals and the values the party sees in Socialism" and endorsed "free multiparty competition." Although the theses were designed to give the KKE a new image, party Chairman Florakis took a more conservative approach before the Central Committee in June, flatly opposing the abolition of such terms as *dictatorship of the proletariat*, *democratic centralism*, and *proletarian internationalism* and the removal of the hammer and sickle as the party's emblem. As a consequence, a new set of theses was drafted in October and the party congress was postponed to February 1991. Although the revised theses represented a compromise they did contain, for example, the right of dissenting members to air their views in public, limits on the terms of members elected to the Politburo and the Secretariat, and a clause requiring at least 25 percent of the Central Committee to be replaced at future congresses. This compromise, however, assured a heated debate within the party in 1991, and the outcome would determine whether KKE would follow a more conservative or a more liberal course in the future. In turn, the party's credibility among the Greek electorate will be decidedly affected.

Party leaders of the Communist Party of Great Britain (CPGB) are preoccupied with the continuing decline in support. Party membership, which has been steadily dropping since 1980, stood at less than eight thousand in 1990, its lowest point since World War II. The waning fortunes of the party were illustrated in Britain's last general elections (1987), when the party's nineteen candidates polled only 6,078 votes. Even as electoral support for the CPGB plummeted during the Thatcher era, intraparty struggle intensified. The Eurocommunist CPGB fought the Stalinist breakaway groups, who were unstinting in their support of the ideology and policies of the Soviet Union and the East European bloc. In 1990, with communist governments either fallen or in severe crisis, the entire British movement including the reformist CPGB finds itself badly discredited.

At the most recent party congress, in November 1989, longtime Chairman Gordon McLennan supported a new party platform entitled Manifesto for New Times that argued for a new flexibility, a willingness to recast the communist movement as a part of the social democratic tradition and a willingness to work within the pluralistic democratic system. In January a new party leader, Nina Temple, was elected to replace McLennan. At 33, Temple is the youngest person and the first woman to head the CPGB. How the party will develop in the future is uncertain, but Temple argued throughout the year for major changes, including a change of name and a renunciation of the commitment to Marxism-Leninism as well as to democratic centralism. At the end of the year the party approved convening a new congress in November 1991, at which time it is expected to take final decisions on the new direction of the CPGB.

The Communist Party of Ireland (CPI) is a recognized political party but does not exert any influence on Irish political life. It is without representation in Parliament, and the modest support it does enjoy is based primarily in Dublin and Belfast; it has less than five hundred members. During the year the continuing political division of the country, its economic problems, and the upheaval in Eastern Europe and the Soviet Union were the central issues, in addition to continued opposition to the creation of a fully integrated European common market in 1992. Its last party congress, convened in October 1989, was reconvened in May. The CPI emphasized democratic participation within the party, as well as collaboration with "progressive" forces, but recommitted itself, unlike the CPGB, to Marxism-Leninism and democratic centralism as guiding ideological tenets; hence its criticism of the European Community as a mechanism for exploiting the Irish working class. As a consequence its role in Irish politics is certain to remain insignificant.

The communist parties of Belgium, Denmark, Luxembourg, and the Netherlands exercised marginal influence on the political life of their respective countries in 1990. The Communist Party of Luxembourg (CPL) holds one seat in the country's Chamber of Deputies, won in national elections in June 1989, and has an estimated membership of six hundred. The most significant event during the year was the death in October of party Chairman René Urbany, who had headed the party since 1976, when he succeeded the party's founder, his father. The date of Urbany's death also marked the opening of the CPL's Twenty-sixth Congress, held under the motto A Fresh Breeze from the Left. The "fresh breeze" was led by Urbany's successor, Aloyse Bisdorff. Under his leadership the congress approved new party statutes and elected new Executive and Central committees while abolishing the party's Secretariat. At the end of the year the CPL was earnestly seeking a new role in Luxembourg politics. But like so many of its European counterparts, it had a major credibility problem that was unlikely to disappear.

The Communist Party of the Netherlands (CPN) claims a membership of six thousand to seven thousand, and, as a result of an electoral coalition with the Pacifist-Socialists (PSP) and the Radicals (PPE), the three parties won 6 of 150 Dutch Parliament seats in 1989. This grouping styled itself as the Green Left, a name chosen for its electoral appeal. In 1990 the CPN took decisive steps to strengthen the credibility of the coalition by approving, at its extraordinary congress in June, dual membership in its own party and in the Green Left. The future of the CPN, however, as well as that of the Green Left, is far from certain. The CPN is overshadowed by the larger sizes of its partners, and the three parties do not share a common ideological heritage. Thus, the Green Left alliance is unlikely to result in a new party and appears to be living on borrowed time. The three parties have entered into a marriage of convenience; 1991 will determine its longevity.

The minuscule influence of the Union of Communists of Belgium, which consists of two regionally and linguistically distinct parties with a central leadership superstructure, became even less during the past year as its membership dropped 20 percent (from an estimated five thousand in 1989 to four thousand during 1990). The larger, French-speaking Parti Communiste de Belgique (PCB or PC) followed the lead of most other European communist parties in examining, at an extraordinary conference in Charleroi 10 and 11 March, the viability of its goals and membership in the face of the change in communist orientation. The result

was a majority decision (104 of 117) to expand the base of support by cooperating with ecologists and other leftist progressives (*DR*, 13 March). The Flemish-speaking Kommunistische Partij van Belgie (KPB) shared the PCB's interest in collaborating with socially aware progressive leftists and ecologists.

With the exception of Ludo Martens, the leader of the tiny Marxist-Leninist Belgian Labor Party who traveled with his study group to North Korea and praised the success of its communist government (Pyongyang, Korean Central News Agency, 21 June; *FBIS-EAS*, 25 June), and the general rejoicing at the liberation of Nelson Mandela, international activities were at a minimum. Domestic problems of education, abortion, drugs, unemployment, and urban conditions were the major concerns of both regions' parties.

The Communist Party of Denmark suffered three major setbacks: its steadily eroding membership, down to three thousand, more than 50 percent (*Det Fri Aktuelt*, 5–6 January 1991), reinforced its political/governmental inconsequence as revealed by the 12 December elections; financial difficulties shut down its major public organ, *Land og Folk*, at the end of the year; and ideological dissension within the party caused two hundred members, among them former DKP general secretary Poul Emanuel, to resign to form a more rigidly orthodox party, the Communist Forum (KF), and the complete dissolution in May of the party's youth wing, the Young Communists of Denmark (DKU), which had been a major source of party recruitment.

Indications of great upheaval and attempts at damage control were evident in the two congresses held during the year. At the Twenty-ninth Extraordinary Congress 20–21 January, Chairman Ole Sohn ousted the orthodox members and tried to expand party influence by appealing to trade unions that contained a number of former DKP members. However, in light of the tug of war between the Stalinist and the reform-minded camps, the unions decided to look elsewhere for support. The Thirtieth Congress, 14–15 April, which elected Anne-Marie Jørgensen as leader of the Secretariat, attempted to open up and realign the party along democratic principles; with the walkout of the Stalinists, Chairman Sohn was able to win the support of nearly two-thirds (251 of 395) of the members present. The Stalinist KF held its first and founding convention 29–30 September, electing Betty Frydensbjerg Carlsson as chairwoman (*Berlingske Tidende*, 1 October; *FBIS-WEU*, 20 November).

The election on 12 December saw the DKP participate in an electoral front, Unity List, along with the Left Socialists and the Socialists Workers' party; however, the three parties garnered only 1.9 percent of the vote, short of the 2 percent necessary for parliamentary representation.

In the Nordic countries of Iceland, Norway, Sweden, and Finland, the communist parties were active but did not exert a significant impact on political affairs. The People's Alliance of Iceland (PA), founded in 1968, continues to be headed by Olafur Ragnar Grimsson, 47. Iceland's population is approximately 251,000; party membership is estimated at three thousand. In the last national elections, in 1987, the PA received 13.2 percent of the vote and 8 of 63 seats in the Icelandic Parliament; the party's most recent congress was held in November 1989, just after the opening of the Berlin Wall.

The PA began the year as a member of a broad center-left coalition of five parties and held the cabinet posts of finance (occupied by the party's chairman), communications and agriculture, and education and culture. Although formation of the coalition and the PA's role in it represented a major tactical coup for Grimsson, the party's popularity, according to public opinion polls, has declined by almost one-third since 1987. This development and the pressures of governing with four centrist parties contributed to the continued fragmentation of the PA in 1990 between reformist and Marxist wings. Opposition within the party mounted for Grimsson to resign, but resolution of the dispute was postponed until after the national elections, scheduled for April 1991. By year's end, it was clear that the PA would face a major electoral contest in the new year. Indeed, its future participation in the Icelandic government would depend on the outcome.

The Norwegian Communist Party (NKP) has an estimated membership of 1,500 to 2,000 and has been without representation in Norway's Parliament since 1973. On the left the NKP completes with several small parties, especially the Socialist Left Party (SV), established in 1975 by former members of the NKP, as well as with the Workers' Communist Party (AKP). Both are larger than the NKP, with estimated memberships of eleven thousand (SV) and five thousand to seven thousand (AKP).

After the NKP split in 1975 it sought "an alliance of the working-class parties that is able to unite all those who are objective opponents of monopoly capital and imperialism." In 1987, when the last

party congress was held, the NKP adopted a new party program for the first time since 1973. At that time it reaffirmed its commitment to Marxism-Leninism and class struggle and, in a classic example of contrast, took the position that the "Social Democrats are our most important alliance partners on all the major political issues today" (*Friheten*, 30 April 1987). In Norway's national election in 1989, the NKP, in coalition with the AKP, received less than 1 percent of the vote. Thus in 1990 one could have expected the NKP to take steps toward, if not party reform, at least restoring its credibility. A new Central Committee was elected in June, but the party must thoroughly restructure itself if it is to have any future in Norway.

The Left Party Communists (VPK) in Sweden have been represented in the Swedish Parliament throughout the 1980s. Under the leadership of Lars Werner, the party received 5.8 percent of the vote in the last national elections, in 1988, and won 21 out of 349 parliamentary seats. Its claimed membership has remained constant at between seventeen thousand and eighteen thousand, and it held its Twenty-ninth Party Congress in May 1990.

Like Italy's Communist Party, the VPK began analyzing its role as a party of the left following the opening of the Berlin Wall; at the close of 1989 party Chairman Werner addressed the issue: "The question is whether developments in East Europe and the process of democratization do not occasion a change of program" (*Svenska Dagbladet*, 23 November 1989). In 1990 at the party congress the delegates, by a margin of only three votes, approved a resolution to drop the word *communist* from the party's name and adopted the official title The Left Party (V), a name, according to the party's spokesman, "that can be used in connection with elections" (*Dagens Nyheter*, 26 May). The congress also unsuccessfully challenged Werner's position as chairman and decided to postpone adopting a new party program until the next scheduled congress in 1993 (to replace the program approved in 1988). At year's end the future direction of the party was in doubt; although it had a new name, it continued to carry the Marxist burdens of the past.

Eroding support for the scrapping Finnish Communist Party factions, a general climate of change, and the desire to survive motivated the political alliance that emerged this year. A new front, Left Alliance (Vasemmistolitto, VL), which registered as a political party, included Greens and non-communist leftists and managed to unite the long feuding majority and minority factions of the Finnish Communist Party, though not without considerable rancor (*Helsingen Sanomat* [HS], 5 February). The basically separate communist party factions have transferred political power to the VL. The majority Finnish Communist Party (SKP) and the minority faction Finnish Communist Party—Unity (SKP-Y) wrote themselves out of existence on 30 April (SKP) and 9 September (SKP-Y), as did their respective electoral fronts. Formal dissolution—pending a winding down of financial and legal matters supervised by an elected skeleton caretaker staff—will not actually take place until the final congress in 1993 (*Hufvudstadsbladet* [*Hb*], 9 April). VL now has twenty front representatives in the legislature (*HS*, 3, 11 May, 12 September; *Hb*, 3 May). Even the SKD party organ *Kansan Uutiset* was declared to be an independent newspaper.

This new broad alliance was the brainchild of SKD chairman Jarmo Wahlström and of its electoral front chairman, Reijo Käkelä. As evidence of an almost universal softening of Marxist hard lines, Käkelä resigned after the delegates at the planning meeting expressed reluctance to install an old-time authoritarian leadership in the new organization. They defeated his proposal for a closed congress, voting instead for open participation (*HS*, 21 May). A secret ballot, which Wahlström opposed, failed to elect him to any office in the SKP's last Politburo or Central Committee.

At the Twenty-second Congress, 23–25 February, the SKP officially ended its political activity and set into motion the dismantling process. Minority communist party delegates were also present for the first time since 1985. Jarmo Wahlström resigned as party chairman. General Secretary Helja Tammisola was elected chairman and Asko Mäki became general secretary.

On 29 April the founding congress of VL assembled with three thousand delegates and elected Socialist Claes Andersson party chairman; the hundred-member Central Committee elected Matti Viialainen general secretary. The business accomplished at the congress included deleting old terminology (*majority, minority, socialist, communist*) in favor of *leftist* and establishing a party platform calling for labor reforms, sound environmental policies, more public service, and less military spending. It also expressed solidarity with the Baltic republics. By 31 May, VL was registered as a political party and claimed to have distributed 12,500 membership cards.

Although the minority faction was fully represented at the VL congress and although its members held elected offices in the new party (approximately one-fourth to one-third of the elected offices and two minority communists on the fifteen-member executive committee [*HS*, 30 April; *FBIS-WEU*, 30 April]), the SKP-Y chose not to disband. It maintained that it would continue to advocate "red policies for a green and just future" (*HS*, 21 May) and provide a "Marxist forum" for the left (*Tiedonantaja*, 22 May). Despite this declaration by the SKP-Y, the Workers' Communist Party, a splinter of the minority faction, now considers itself to be the only genuine communist party, claiming to have a thousand card-carrying members (*HS*, 27 February).

Minimal roles are played by the Communist Party of Austria (KPÖ) and the Swiss Labor Party (PdAS) in the political arenas of their countries, and this continued to be the case during 1990. The KPÖ, however, underwent major changes during the year. The party's Twenty-seventh Congress was held in January in Vienna with the theme Think New—Act New. The congress replaced longtime chairman Franz Muhri with two cochairmen, Walter Silbermayr, 39, and Susanne Sohn, 47. Burdened by aging party leadership and declining membership, the KPÖ under its new leaders announced a thorough restructuring of the party's apparatus, which included abolishing the Politburo and the Secretariat in February and replacing them with an eight-member committee.

The dilemma of how to react to the systematic breakdown of the communist system in Central and Eastern Europe was thus addressed by the KPÖ with the election of new leadership, but it did not prove sufficient to improve the party's political fortunes. Whether the Austrian electorate judged the efforts at reform to be cosmetic, or whether any serious attention was paid to the KPÖ by the Austrians, was moot. The party suffered its worst election defeat in decades in national elections held in October, despite the announcement in February that an extraordinary party congress would be convened in 1991 to approve a new party program. What this program would contain will undoubtedly have a major effect on the KPÖ's future credibility.

In Switzerland the PdAS continues to occupy an insignificant role in Swiss political life. National elections have not been held in Switzerland since 1987; at that time the PdAS polled 0.8 percent of the vote and won one seat in Switzerland's two-hundred-seat Parliament. Thus, like a number of its counterparts elsewhere in Western Europe, it has not had to face an electoral challenge since the collapse of communist regimes in Central and Eastern Europe. The PdAS held a national party conference, as distinct from a congress, in Geneva in May to discuss its future. By the end of the year its efforts to form a coalition of leftist parties had not succeeded, and although it began to describe itself as the new PdAS in November, its organizational structure remained unchanged. The party faced a dismal future if it failed to adapt its ideological commitment to Marxism-Leninism to the realities of economic and political freedom, and there was no convincing indication that the PdAS intended to do so.

Of all the communist parties in Western Europe, the activities of the German Communist Party (DKP) were the most unusual because Germany was unified in October and held its first national elections as a unified country in December. The collapse of communist power and ideology in the German Democratic Republic (GDR), marked by the emotional opening of the Berlin Wall in November 1989, represented a fatal threat to the DKP. Not only did the party's membership begin to decline dramatically but its financial subsidies, which it depended on, ceased coming from the GDR. East Germany's communist party, the Socialist Unity Party (SED), not only changed its name to the Party of Democratic Socialism (PDS) but completely discredited the communist movement in West Germany. Throughout the year Germany's (and Europe's) attention was focused on the disintegration of the old SED and on the political and economic crimes committed by its members; the DKP was thereby basically erased from the political stage.

The DKP leadership under Chairman Herbert Mies recognized in late 1989 that the movement for unification would challenge the very existence of the party and therefore called for an extraordinary party congress in Dortmund in March 1990. In complete disarray and with its news media either closed or publishing only weekly, the DKP made only cosmetic changes. Its single chairmanship was replaced by a collective leadership of two women and two men, and the party chose not to seek union with its renamed East German counterpart, the PDS. As steps toward unification proceeded, the DKP offered to form an electoral alliance with the PDS. This proposal was refused, and the PDS created its own electoral alliance, the Left List-PDS, that excluded the DKP.

During the summer the PDS opened offices throughout West Germany preparatory to the first free election in unified Germany on 2 December. The DKP fielded no candidates in the elections but did call for support of the Left List-PDS. The PDS won seventeen seats in the new Bundestag, polling 2.4 percent of the vote in Germany as a whole but only 0.3 percent in the former Federal Republic and 11.1 percent in the former GDR. In future elections, however, the PDS will have to capture 5 percent of the vote nationwide to be represented in the German Parliament, an election law that has applied to West Germany since its founding in 1949. There is no question that the PDS, as the heir to the SED, and the DKP, as the SED's former West German counterpart, will find this a heavy burden. The issue, as one former member of the SED put it, is "whether the experiment of renewal of a party shaped by Stalinism will succeed" (Berlin, *Disput*, November).

In 1989 the Socialist Unity Party of West Berlin (SEW), the city's East German counterpart of the SED, claimed a membership of seven thousand. In the election to the West Berlin Parliament of that year, the SEW received 0.6 percent of the vote and held no parliamentary seats. As communism crumbled in the GDR and the Berlin Wall became a relic of tyranny on 9 November 1989, the SEW suffered the same fate as the SED.

In late November the party called for an extraordinary party congress in February 1990. The SEW's chairman, Dieter Ahrens, resigned, and 52 percent of the eight hundred delegates voted to dissolve the party, short of the 66 percent necessary. Half the delegates left the congress, and at a second congress in April the SEW was transformed into a new party, the Socialist Initiative (SI), whose ideological manifesto mirrored that of the successor to the SED in East Germany, the PDS. With a claimed membership of 1,600, the SI did not run candidates in the first election in unified Berlin on 2 December. The PDS received 1.1 percent of the vote in what was formerly West Berlin and 23.6 percent in former East Berlin, which amounted to 9.2 percent for the city as a whole. In the future the SI, like the DKP, will play a marginal role in German politics, and the PDS in Berlin, like in Germany, will struggle with a political heritage the Germans will not soon forget.

Dennis L. Bark
Hoover Institution

Austria

Population. 7,644,275
Party. Communist Party of Austria (Kommunistische Partei Österreichs, KPO)
Founded. 3 November 1918
Membership. 11,000–12,000 (estimate)
Party Chair. Walter Silbermayr (b. 1951), Susanne Sohn (b. 1943)
Politburo. Abolished 8 February. Permanent members of the working committee of the Central Committee (Arbeitsausschuss des Zentralkommittees): Walter Silbermayr, Susanne Sohn, Othmar Grünn (chairman of the Central Committee), Dr. Rosmarie Atzenhofer, Mag. Walter Baier, Eduard Danzinger, Dr. Heinrich Geiszler (Salzburg party secretary). Mag. Julius Mende (art instructor), Veronika Stöckl-Holzknecht. Temporary members: three members of Central Committee, rotating in alphabetical order
Secretariat. Abolished 8 February
Central Committee. 59 members
Status. Legal
Last Congress. Twenty-seventh, 19–21 January, in Vienna
Last Election. Federal, 7 October, 0.55 percent, no representation
Publications. *Volksstimme* (People's voice), Lutz Holzinger, editor, KPÖ daily organ, Vienna (weekly as of 1 February 1991); *Weg und Ziel* (Path and goal), Ernst Wimmer, editor, KPÖ theoretical monthly, Vienna

The year brought new leadership to the party, as well as important organizational changes, though a more thorough restructuring is to take place at an extraordinary congress, planned for late 1991. Reforms have not made the party more popular to date. In fact, its showing in the election of 7 October was its poorest yet in the postwar era. The party's vote share dropped from 0.72 percent (1986) to 0.55 percent. Above-average results came in Vienna (0.85%), Styria (0.72%), Vorarlberg (0.63%), and Tyrol (0.57%), although Tyrol was the only province in which the KPÖ's vote share did not drop. The actual vote was down in all of Austria, from 35,144 (1986) to 24,859 (*Volksstimme*, 9 October).

Municipal elections were held in Lower Austria and Styria on 25 March. The communist vote declined (compared with 1985) in Styria from 1.11 percent to 0.89 percent, in Lower Austria from 0.72 percent to 0.59 percent. *Volksstimme* lists results in 55 municipalities; 9 showed modest gains for the KPÖ (*Volksstimme*, 27 March). In the hard-pressed mining town of Eisenerz, the KPÖ increased its vote from 12.5 percent to 20.3 percent (*Standard*, 26 March).

Leadership and Organization. *Volksstimme* (13 January) contains the report of the Central Committee to the Twenty-seventh Party Congress as presented by Walter Silbermayr ("Think New, Act New"). In view of the events in Eastern Europe, the KPÖ faced either complete self-renewal or a dwindling lack of importance. Only a restructured party can bring about complete self-renewal. Silbermayr criticized the reforms of 1984 and 1987 as insufficient, saying that the party's administrative structures themselves brought on continued administrative centralism and that there must be a dialectic connection between upward democracy and downward responsibility.

Before the party congress, Silbermayr said he expected "criticism, but no assignment of blame" because one wanted to avoid a "collective suicide" (*Presse*, 17 January).

The renewal effort was expressed by a *Volksstimme* headline of 20 January: "Turbulent Beginning of the KPÖ Party Congress in Vienna's Austria Center." Without giving details, the paper then reports that a debate over the order of business delayed Silbermayr's address by two hours. The opening address by Franz Muhri, the outgoing party chairman of 25 years, was mentioned without any indication of its content. The relatively old age of party members can be gleaned from the fact that no fewer than 8 percent of the members had died since the previous triennial congress.

The sessions of 20 January contained long debates over the selection and restructuring of the Central Committee (*Volksstimme*, 21 January). Susanne Sohn presented a comprehensive women's program. *Volksstimme* also noticed at the congress the sale of books by Ernst Fischer, the party's late chief ideologist, who had left the party after the invasion of Czechoslovakia in 1968. Guest delegates came from the Soviet Union, Hungary, Poland, Switzerland, East Germany, France, Czechoslovakia, Bulgaria, Cuba, South Africa, El Salvador, and Palestine.

Late on Saturday night, 20 January, the congress elected the Central Committee. There were 283 voting, and 142 votes were needed for election (*Volksstimme*, 23 January). Fifty-nine of the 60 proposed delegates were elected. The exact number of against votes (141 permitted for election) was also published. The one defeated candidate (154 against) was Otto Podolsky, Vienna party chairman and member of the Politburo. Eight other Politburo members were candidates for the Central Committee; five of them ranked second to sixth in votes against. They were, from second to sixth, Rudolf Slavik (Lower Austria party chairman), Ernst Wimmer (chief ideologist), Michael Graber (*Volksstimme* editor in chief), Willi Gaisch, and Franz Muhri (party chairman, voted against by 99 voters). Of the other Politburo members up for confirmation, Walter Baier ranked 16th in no votes, Susanne Sohn 20th (44 no votes), and Walter Silbermayr 27th (31 no votes). Of others who ended up as nominators or nominees for leadership positions, Veronika Stöckl-Holzknecht was 23d in negative rankings, Eduard Danzinger, 26th, Julius Mende, 37th, Othmar Grünn, 41st, Heinrich Geiszler, 46th, and Rosmarie Atzenhofer and Hans Slamanig were tied at 48th (out of 60).

Between 1:30 and 4:30 A.M. on Sunday, 21 January, the members of the new Central Committee met at party headquarters. Gaisch nominated Silbermayr as party chairman, who in turn nominated Sohn, not as deputy chairperson, but as equal partner. Forty-six of 52 votes were cast for the leadership duo. Silbermayr, Sohn, Grünn, Slamanig, Geiszler, Mende, and Atzenhofer were elected to a commission that would propose the Central Committee candidates for the Politburo and the Secretariat, to be elected in February.

In his final speech, Silbermayr relaunched the KPÖ as a party of Austrian, democratic, left, and Socialist politics, as a party of the street, and as a party of action. Most of Muhri's parting words were omitted by the *Volksstimme* typesetters. Of all the comments on the party congress, the most devastating came from the *Salzburger Nachrichten* (quoted in *Volksstimme*, 23 January): "The KPÖ was always an ideological straggler among the Communist parties of Western Europe. Since its party congress, it also limps behind its East European brother parties."

On 2 February, *Volksstimme* gave a progress report of the Central Committee's commission for party restructuring. The commission, *Volksstimme* reported, would propose the abolition of the Politburo and the Secretariat. An eight-member working committee would take their place. Also, the Central Committee would elect a chairman. The Central Committee would be asked to form a working group to restructure *Volksstimme* and one to re-examine party history, especially regarding the victims of Stalinist terror and the 1968 invasion of Czechoslovakia.

The crucial restructuring meeting of the Central Committee took place in Vienna on 8 February (*Volksstimme*, 10 February). The Central Committee elected Othmar Grünn chairman by a unanimous vote. Elected as the six permanent members of the working committee (in addition to Silbermayr, Sohn, and Grünn) were Atzenhofer, Baier, Danzinger, Geiszler, Mende, and Stöckl-Holzknecht; they were voted against by from one to twelve members. Three members of the Central Committee, rotating in alphabetical order, were to be temporary members of the working committee.

Baier and Stöckl-Holzknecht were designated as coordinators of the 1991 special party congress for a new party program and party statute. Silbermayr was asked to chair the working group to reform *Volksstimme*; Dr. Lutz Holzinger, the working group to develop a media concept; and Drs. Josef Ehner and Winfried Garscha, the working group to revise party history. To demonstrate that the Central Committee, now definitely the leading party body between party congresses, was democratic and transparent, it was seated at a round table.

On 4 April the Central Committee called on all of Austria's leftists, mentioning particularly Green groups, to form an electoral coalition in the federal election of 7 October. Should this coalition not come about, the KPÖ would fight the election by itself (*Volksstimme*, 6 April).

On 7 April, Susanne Sohn said in a radio broadcast that the party did not identify with any Communist government and was skeptical toward *perestroika* (*Wiener Zeitung*, 9 April).

When the Vienna KPÖ met on 23 June, there were seventeen men and fourteen women candidates for the party executive. *Volksstimme* (26 June) reported with some pride that thirteen of the women and only eleven of the men were elected.

On 12 July, Anton Pelinka, probably Austria's ablest political scientist, agreed to engage in a debate with Silbermayr and Sohn on the topic "Is the Renewal Coming Too Late?" (*Volksstimme*, 17 August). Pelinka claimed that the KPÖ renewal had come too late and that there was too little of it. Pelinka stated that the only good era for a KPÖ renewal had been 1968–1969 and that the KPÖ was beginning to think and criticize because the Communist Party of the Soviet Union was now encouraging thinking and criticism. The party, Pelinka said, has an apparatus for a party polling 45–55 percent of the vote and its members are too old. Silbermayr claimed that the KPÖ was moving away from Stalinism; Pelinka, that it needed to move away from Leninism. Pelinka concluded that the question facing the KPÖ was the status quo and thus being on the way to the museum or turning into Social Democrats or left Social Democrats. Sohn and Silbermayr answered with an attack on the Social Democrats and some optimism for the KPÖ.

On 24 August, *Volksstimme* displayed its *perestroika* by publishing an article commemorating the 50th anniversary of the assassination of Leon Trotsky. At the 17 October meeting of the Central Committee, a position paper about the election results and the renewal of the party was defeated by a tie vote (*Volksstimme*, 19 October). Later in October, there was open conflict between the radical reformer Silbermayr and the go-slow renewer Baier (*Volksstimme*, 23, 25 October).

Domestic Affairs. The party's concern with domestic issues lagged behind its structural worries. As usual, the Austrian economy received some attention. *Volksstimme* (11 May) reported that Austrian enterprises had increased their profits in 1989 by 38.4 percent and contrasted this with the lack of agreement on a minimum monthly wage of $1,000. Three weeks later (31 May), *Volksstimme* reported that Vienna's economic growth rate for 1989 was lowest in the provinces, 2.6 percent, well below the Austrian growth rate of 4 percent. On 30 June, *Volksstimme*, quoting two economic institutes, reported an anticipated slowdown of economic growth for 1991, whereas unemployment was predicted to rise slowly and prices somewhat more. Austria was reported to be taxing movable property at a lower rate than most Organization for Economic Cooperation and Development (OECD) countries (*Volksstimme*, 8 August). Unemployment in Austria increased from June to July from 4.9 to 5.2 percent. Unemployment was highest, at 8.2 percent, in Leoben, the largest Styrian steel city (*Volksstimme*, 17 August).

Volksstimme (28–29 January) and Walter Silbermayr congratulated the workers at the nationalized vehicle plant, Steyr-Daimler-Puch, on their successful major strike, which made management give up plans for major dismissals. On 18 September, *Volksstimme* warned that the three large parties were all thinking of further privatization of nationalized enterprises. Earlier, *Volksstimme* (19, 27–28 May) ran a campaign against McDonald's, which it accused of destroying rain forests in Central America for cheap beef production. The campaign used the inelegant slogans Vomit Yourself Free! and Swallow, Gag, Go!

In May, it became obvious that Alois Rechberger, president of the Styrian Chamber of Labor, drew a number of yearly salaries worth close to $400,000 (*Volksstimme*, 13–14 May, 7 June). *Volksstimme* (13 June) called for a thorough democratization of the chambers of labor and trade unions. On 14–15 June, *Volksstimme* attacked the agreement of Austria's governing coalition parties, People's party and Socialists, on a maximum yearly income of about $250,000 for economic politicians with several jobs. On 13 July, *Volksstimme* attacked the raising of chamber of labor president's salaries to a scale of $110,000 to $180,000. When the coalition partners agreed on a partial reform of the chamber of labor, *Volksstimme* (19–20 August) urged that the functionaries, not the useful functions, should be reformed.

The year also brought a KPÖ campaign to abolish Austria's armed forces (*Volksstimme*, 7 March). The party joined a movement for a plebiscite on the issue (*Volksstimme*, 18–19 March) and claimed 20,000 signatures (15 May).

The abolition of Austria's state police was the target of a major KPÖ effort (*Volksstimme*, 27, 28 February). *Volksstimme* (6–7 May) reported that freedom of information actions showed that the state police registered the names of all demonstrators for such matters as peace and women's rights. *Volksstimme* (17 May) claimed that the state police worked for private enterprise and for the United States. Gerd Bacher, who had headed the Austrian broadcasting system ORF twice in the past, was under heavy *Volksstimme* fire (24–25 May, 12, 14 July) as he successfully obtained a third term of office.

On 9 June, the KPÖ passed a strong program of women's issues (*Volksstimme*, 12 June). Women's concerns had been recognized earlier by Susanne Sohn's selection as cochairperson of the party and by *Volksstimme*'s nonsexist usage (e.g., *Kommunisten*, male; *Kommunistinnen*, female; *KommunistInnen*, per *Volksstimme*). Although *Volksstimme* (5 July) welcomed the introduction of two years' maternity leave, it predicted that one-third of all mothers and one-half of all single mothers would not be reemployed after their leaves. *Volksstimme* (16 May) reported that Silbermayr supported the social pastoral letter of Austria's Catholic bishops of the day before.

In matters of democracy, the KPÖ backed the principle of civic initiatives at the Vienna borough level (*Volksstimme*, 22 February) and the vote for foreign workers (*Volksstimme*, 1 March). Throughout the year, *Volksstimme* wrote about various scandals involving the other parties (e.g., 10, 28–29 January). *Volksstimme* warned several times of neo-Nazi attacks on communists (e.g., 3 May, 19 June).

On 6 July, Silbermayr evaluated the governing coalition (*Volksstimme*, 7 July). He criticized it for privatization, rearmament, propagation of joining the European Community, helping the right-wing Freedom party, and high unemployment during prosperity. He gave them credit for failing to reform the electoral system, the railroads, and the pension system.

On 26 July, President Kurt Waldheim opened the prestigious Salzburg festival. Before he became president of Czechoslovakia, Vaclav Havel had agreed to attend the ceremonies. His visible support for Waldheim was severely criticized by *Volksstimme* (20, 21, 24, 27 July).

When Bruno Kreisky, Socialist chancellor, 1970–1983, and possibly Austria's leading statesman since Metternich, died on 29 July, *Volksstimme* devoted front-page stories to him and his funeral on 31 July and 7 and 8 August. Silbermayr's evaluation read (31 July):

Tied to Kreisky are reform politics and the development of a comprehensive understanding of neutrality as basis of an active policy of neutrality and detente. It is part of his personal tragedy that the "struggle against communism," led by him, weakened the forces of left socialism and strengthened those tendencies of right social democracy which today destroy his life's work step by step. It is the task of the left to protect Kreisky's legacy of reform against those who today determine Austria's politics, and to develop it further.

On 21 September, *Volksstimme* featured an article that attempted to demonstrate that the communist putsch of 1950 was not a communist putsch after all. Is this the beginning of the revision of history announced earlier in the year by the KPÖ?

International Views. Austria's status as applicant for membership in the European Community (EC) continued to be an issue for the KPÖ. On 31 March, *Volksstimme* accused Chancellor Vranitsky of intending to give up Austria's sovereignty in joining the EC. In a press conference on 20 September, Silbermayr suggested that the Austrian government withdraw its letter of application to join the EC now that it was developing into a "German Europe" (*Volksstimme*, 21 September).

Developments in Germany were a constant source of worry to the KPÖ in 1990. On 25–26 February (*Volksstimme*), Silbermayr came out for a demilitarized, neutralized, united Germany. Once the German-German treaty was approved by the East Berlin Volkskammer, Gregor Gysi, chairman of the Parteie des Demokratischen Sozialismus, the former Sozialistische Einheitspartei Deutschlands, was supported by *Volksstimme* (22 June) in calling the treaty an *Anschluss* (annexation) in violation of international law. Former Prime Minister of the German Democratic Republic Hans Modrow called the unification of 3 October an *Anschluss* in a *Volksstimme* (30 October) interview. The same issue of the paper protested the hoisting of the German flag from Vienna's city hall.

Although *Volksstimme* denounced Iraq's invasion of Kuwait (3 August), it was equally critical of U.S. troop movements (9 August). In the 12–13 August *Volksstimme*, Michael Graber asks why Saddam Husayn may not do what the United States did in Grenada and Panama. The next day, Graber attacked the Austrian government in *Volksstimme* for giving permission for U.S. overflights under U.N. resolutions. When President Waldheim flew to Baghdad to free the Austrians trapped in Iraq, Susanne Sohn said he should have stopped U.S. overflights instead (*Volksstimme*, 25 August).

The KPÖ throughout made itself the champion of Austria's neutrality. When Roy Huffington, U.S. ambassador to Austria, said that Austria's neutrality did not mean the same as before 1989, he was strongly attacked by Silbermayr, who said he should "go home" (*Volksstimme*, 27 September). *Volksstimme* (16, 25 October) strongly turned against any modification of Austria's neutrality.

Publications. On 21 August, the Central Committee dealt with the financial plight of *Volksstimme* and wondered about its future in view of the planned restructuring of the KPÖ (*Volksstimme*, 27 April). It proposed that, although the paper would remain the property of the party, the circle of publishers be widened to include a broader left spectrum, including all of labor, the peace, women's and environmental movements, and virtually all progressives. On 29 June, the Central Committee voted to turn *Volksstimme* into a "leftist daily" (*Volksstimme*, 1–2 July).

When the 101-year-old Socialist daily *Arbeiter-Zeitung* was temporarily threatened, *Volksstimme* (20 August) thought of possible collaboration. On 18 October, the Central Committee elected, by a vote of nineteen to four, Lutz Holzinger as editor in chief and Ulrich Perzinger as deputy editor in chief of *Volksstimme* (20 October). The paper received a new format on 23 October; instead of being called "central organ of the KPÖ" and "leftist daily," it is now called simply "*Volksstimme*."

Frederick C. Engelmann
University of Alberta

Belgium

Population. 9,909,285 (July)

Party. Union of the Communists of Belgium, organized linguistically into the Parti Communiste de Belgique (PCB or PC) and the Kommunistische Partij van Belgie (KPB).

Founded. 1921

Membership. 4,000

National Leadership. President: Louis Van Geyt, vice-president: Marcel Levaux

National Bureau. Pierre Beauvois, Claude Renard, Robert Dussart, Ludo Loose, Dirk Vonckx

Council General of the Union. 33 members; 5 candidates. Francophone members: Pierre Beauvois, Robert Dussart, Marcel Levaux, Jacques Moins, Jacques Nagels, Claude Renard, Marcel Couteau, Anne Herscovici, Jules Pirlot, Hubert Cambier, Jean-Claude Raillon, Jean-Marie Simon (Liège), Jean-Pierre Michiels, Susa Nudelhole, Jean-Marie Simon (Borinage), Jean-Paul Brilmaker, Maurice G. Magis, Daniel Fedrigo, Robert Houtain. Dutch-speaking members: Ludo Loose, Dirk Vonckx, Jos Gijbels, Willy Minnebo, Louis Van Geyt, Miel Dullaert, Filip Delmotte, Jos Wolles, Luk Dombrecht, Ber-

nard Claeys, Robert Crivit, Roger Broos, Marc De Smet, Michel Vanderborght. Francophone candidates: Jacques Coupez, Marcel Bergen, Michel Godard. Dutch-speaking candidates: Bert Vermeiren, Jos De Geyter.

PCB Leadership. President: Pierre Beauvois; president for Brussels region: Anne Herscovici. Francophone bureau: Pierre Beauvois, Michel Godard, Anne Herscovici, Robert Houtain, Marcel Levaux, Pierre Lisens, Maurice G. Magis, Jean-Pierre Michiels, Jules Pirlot, Jean-Claude Railleo, Claude Renard, Jean-Marie Simon (Borinage).

KPB Leadership. President: Ludo Loose. Dutch-speaking bureau: Bernard Claeys, Jos De Geyter, Filip Delmotte, Hugo De Witte, Miel Dullaert, Jos Gijbels, Ludo Loose, Willy Minnebo, Dirk Vonckx.

Status. Legal

Last Congress. Twenty-sixth National, 18–19 March 1989

Last Election. 13 December 1987, 0.8 percent, no representation

Publications. *Drapeau Rouge*, daily party organ in French, André Gérardin, editor; *Rode Vaan*, Dutch-language weekly, Miel Dullaert, political director; Filip Delmotit, senior editor. The party also publishes a periodical in French of broad theoretical and political commentary, *Cahiers Marxistes*.

The recent history of the Communist Party in Belgium continues to be that of a small party with few members, no parliamentary representation, and the support of less than 1 percent of the Belgian electorate trying to find a formula by which it can survive in Belgian politics. During the past decade, the once unitary party tried to fit itself to the realities of the bilingual, regionalizing Belgian state by dividing itself into two separate parties, one for French-speaking and one for Dutch-speaking Belgium. During the first year of the new decade, the focus was on sculpturing the resultant parties to fit the economic, social, and political realities of their respective political environments inside the Belgian state.

Party Organization and Structure. At the party's Twenty-sixth National Congress, held 18–19 March 1989, the Belgian Communist Party capped a nearly decade-long process of internal reform and party federalization by formally reorganizing itself into a new, highly peripheral federal association between the center and its two distinct, linguistically organized components. Each of these components now possesses its own governing bodies, joined at the center beneath a common president and vice-president, a five-member governing bureau, and a 33-member Counsel General of the Union, which replaced the party's Central Committee. In the resultant reorganization, the national party was renamed the Union of the Communists of Belgium and the center was charged with facilitating the union's international contacts and coordinating its component parts on such system-wide domestic issues as the budget. To the constituent units was left the determination of specific policy positions on local and regional matters. (*YICA*, 1990.)

In 1990 the issue of party structure and strategy thus shifted to the regional level and the efforts of the French- and Dutch-speaking communist parties to reorganize themselves into effective forces in their regions. In this area, the lead was appropriately taken by the Parti Communiste de Belgique—frequently referred to in party literature as the Parti Communiste or PC—as the larger of the two and the party operating in the area traditionally according the strongest support to the Communist Party in Belgium. On 10–11 March a party congress was held at Charleroi to decide the PC's future. Preceding this conference, congresses were held by its locally organized components and an extensive, month-long debate on the future of the party took place almost daily on the pages of the party's newspaper, *Drapeau Rouge (DR)*. The bulk of the correspondence to the paper urged that the party remain united, albeit in a reformed format. Calls for the dissolution of the party and its gradual incorporation into the Socialist party, however, on the reasoning that the historic role of the party is now over, were not unheard of even from party members in the PC's stronghold in Liège. (*DR*, 8 February.) Ultimately, the party's Central Committee prepared two motions for the delegates at the conference. One proposed restructuring the party into "a force for the redynamization of the left in francophone Belgium"; the other called in essence for creating a new party. (*DR*, 9 March.) By a vote of 104 in favor and 4 against, with 9 abstaining, the delegates opted for a modified version of the first option but stressing (1) that the left is not limited to parties and organizations of workers but includes a broad category of progressive Christians, ecologists, and students and (2) that the party needs to open itself to these forces and collaborate with them. (*DR*, 13 March.)

Activities. The idea of reinvigorating Belgium's communist movement by expanding party activities to enfold all dynamic and progressive leftist forces in Belgian society did not find its first articulation at the PC's 1990 conference. The idea had long been stressed by Louis Van Geyt, president of the national party apparatus. (*YICA*, 1989.) Moreover, in a roundtable discussion published in the *World Marxist Review* in late 1989, Jacques Nagel, a member of the union counsel, provided additional arguments for the action on the basis of the realities of decentralized capitalism in general and the fact that "new technologies will further reduce the numerical strength of the industrial working class" in particular (*WMR*, December 1989). Nevertheless, the PC's March decision to reconstruct itself on this principle; its subsequent discussion of party strategy for becoming a force for restructuring the pluralist left in francophone Belgium at an extraordinary congress that the PC held six months later in Charleroi (*DR*, 3–4 November); and—above all—the PC's decision to introduce, in January 1991, a daily party newspaper committed to the concept of pluralism in leftist thought (*DR*, 29–30 September) collectively represented a major effort by the party to give meaning to the idea. Certainly the PC pursuit of the idea dominated communist party activities in Belgium during 1990.

Otherwise, the union and its constituent parties functioned during the year much as they were intended to when the party reorganized in 1989. The union's officers focused on broad domestic issues, for example, the king's decision in April to abdicate for a day rather than violate his personal principles and enact into law the pending legislation to liberalize Belgium's abortion laws. (*DR*, 6 April.) Meanwhile, the regional-linguistic party structures devoted their attention to local issues and alliances with kindred spirits. Thus, both the PC and the KPB stressed ecology, the value of Red-Green forums, and collaborative ventures. (*De Rode Vaan*, 29 June; *DR*, 18 May.) For its part, the PC continued to stress its solidarity with the objectives of the Wallonia Region of Europe movement in Walloon Belgium (see *YICA*, 1990). The PC also joined, as did its provincial and local components, in faculty and student demonstrations throughout Brussels and Walloon Belgium over the government's educational policy, described by the PC as a battle between the country's social and political classes (*DR*, 19–20 May, 3–10 June, 12 October). Finally, in the debate over financial relations between the center, Walloon Belgium, and the francophone community that occurred during the year, the PC was likewise active, at one point accusing the Belgian government of using events in the Persian Gulf to justify further cutbacks in transfers to the Liège region.

In some areas, however, the party was noticeably less active during 1990 than in previous years, reflecting perhaps both the party's altered circumstances at home and the changing environment in neighboring communist states. Union leaders, for example, less visible in party affairs in Belgium, given the 1989 reorganization that left most domestic party activities in the hands of the leadership of the union's constituent parts, and less visible abroad. In past years, visits to communist government and party leaders in neighboring Eastern Europe were common; however, given the turmoil in which the communist parties to the East found themselves during 1990, such trips were noticeably curtailed. Indeed, Ludo Martens, leader of the tiny Marxist-Leninist Belgian Labor party, received most of the attention when he led his party's summer study group to North Korea and paid homage to the successes of the communist government of that country before departing (Pyongyang, KCNA, 21 June; *FBIS-EAS*, 25 June). Meanwhile, in Belgium the *Drapeau Rouge*'s activities, which as late as 1988 had sponsored educational tours to Eastern Europe, shrank in 1990 to running giveaways and selling educational books to its subscribers. Indeed, except for its May Day festivals, party-sponsored social activities were almost nonexistent in 1990 compared with the recent past.

Domestic Policy. Beyond the issues of the abortion bill and the king, education policy, and regional budgetary austerity, the French- and Dutch-speaking party organizations devoted their attention to the domestic issues of primary concern to their respective regions. None stood out for the KPB in the Flemish north, but for the PC, it continued to be the economic problems of Liège, described as the "slow death of a city" that was once the largest in Wallonia and today is primarily distinct for having the country's largest unemployment rate (23 percent, according to the PC). (*DR*, 15 February.)

Elsewhere the topics in the party press stressed its progressive leftist orientation: racism and the problems of foreign immigrants in Belgian life, especially those of Islamic heritage (*DR*, 27–28 January, 14 February); issues involving women (abortion, abuse, and a major series on prostitution)

(*DR*, 23–26 March); the interests and problems of youth (including education and drugs); and issues related to the environment and the interests of Green groups in Belgium and Europe.

Foreign Policy. As in previous years, the developments in the world tended to control the subject matter of the organs of the Belgian parties vis-à-vis international relations. Gorbachev continued to receive strong support on the pages of the *Drapeau Rouge* and the *Rode Vaan*, though perhaps less frequently than in the previous year. Events in Eastern Europe, especially those involving nationality problems in communist Eastern Europe and the Soviet Union, also received extensive coverage, with the *Drapeau Rouge* running a large number of excellent pieces on these topics by its correspondent in Moscow, Hubert Cambier. Similarly, the parties' commentaries continued to castigate apartheid in South Africa (rejoicing in Nelson Mandela's release) and Israel's sidestepping of peacemaking efforts in the Middle East; to stress the need for progress in the direction of disarmament (including Belgium's role in a diminished North Atlantic Treaty Organization), and to emphasize the need for global environmental policies. The crucial stories throughout the year focused on the U.S. intervention in Panama in January, the defeat of the left in the spring election in Nicaragua, and, above all, Iraq's aggression in Kuwait. No friend of Saddam Husayn's to begin with, the party presses that attacked him in March over the issue of Iraq's execution of a journalist ("The Myth of the Good Saddam Hussein," *DR*, 16 March) regularly focused in a highly critical manner on the behavior of this dictator from the time of Iraq's invasion of Kuwait in August to the end of the year.

Joseph R. Rudolph, Jr.
Towson State University

Cyprus

Population. 707,776 (estimated, July) Ethnic divisions: 78 percent Greek, 18 percent Turkish, and 4 percent other
Party. Progressive Party of the Working People (Anorthotikon Komma Ergazomenou Laou, AKEL)

Founded. 1926 as the Communist Party of Cyprus; AKEL, 1941

Membership. 16,000 (official AKEL claim, November. All are from the Greek Cypriot community; 46 percent are under 40 years of age; 24 percent are women; 67 percent are employees in the industrial sector, civil service, or the party structure; and 20 percent are peasants and middle class.

General Secretary. Dimitris Christofias, 44 (first elected in 1988 and reelected in 1990)

Secretariat. 7 members: Dimitris Christofias, Loukas Aletras, Nikos Dimitriadis, Venizelos Zanettou, Andreas Christou, Denis Christofinis, Andonis Chrisostomou

Politburo. 15 members; the 7 Secretariat members plus Theoris Zambas, Lakis Theodoulou, Nikos Katsourides, Yiannakis Kolokasides, Melis Lambrias, Nicodemos Melissos, Andonis Christodoulou, Fanis Christodoulou

Control Commission. 3 members from the Central Committee; current chairman, Michaelis Olympios

Central Committee. 100 members, no alternates. The composition is 39 full-time members of the Central Committee or district committees; 13 full-time trade unionists; 4 full-time members in the women's movement; 3 full-time members in the youth movement; 4 full-time members in the farmers' movement; 19 employed in private companies; 11, self-employed; 7 in the civil service or semigovernmental sector.

Status. Legal

Rival Party. Democratic Socialist Renewal Movement (ADISOK) founded by ex-AKEL members in April. Its leaders are Pavlos Dinglis, president, and Michael Papapetrou, vice-president. Both are members of parliament, along with 3 other ADISOK members: Dinos Constantinou, Andreas Fantis, and Andreas Ziartides. They claim about 1,200 members.

Last Congress. Seventeenth, 3–7 October, scheduled every four years. Last extraordinary congress, 20 December 1987, to endorse George Vassiliou as the successful presidential candidate.

Last Election. 1985, 27.4 percent of the vote, which originally won 15 of 56 seats. After the disaffection of the five ADISOK members, AKEL now controls 10 seats in Parliament. The next elections will be in 1991.

Auxiliary Organizations. Pan-Cyprian Workers' Federation (PEO), 75,000 members, Avram Antoniou, president; United Democratic Youth Organization (EDON), 14,000 members; Confederation of Women's Organizations (POGO); Pan-Cyprian Peace Council; Pan-Cyprian Federation of Students and Young Professionals; Union of Greek Cypriots in England, 1,200 members (considered London branch of AKEL); Pan-Cypriot National Organization of Secondary Students (PEOM); Cypriot Farmers' Union (EKA) (Athens branch founded in 1988).

Publications. *Kharavyi* (Dawn), AKEL daily newspaper; *AKEL News Letter* (in English), periodically; *Neos Democratis*, AKEL monthly theoretical magazine; *Ergatiko Vima* (Workers' stride), PEO weekly; *Neolaia* (Youth), EDON weekly; *Parikiaki* (Ethnic community), AKEL weekly (London); *Kyria* (Mrs.), POGO bimonthly; *Yeni Duzen* (New order), Turkish Cypriot left-wing daily newspaper.

Background. The outbreak of violence in December 1963 between the island's Greek and Turkish populations led to the breakup of the constitutional order that had created the first Republic of Cyprus in 1960. The two communities were further estranged after the Turkish invasion of 1974, which gave the Turkish Cypriots de facto control of more than one-third of the island. Although it may be argued that the island has experienced more than sixteen years of uninterrupted peace, it has come about only through stationing mainland Turkish troops on the island. The removal of the Turkish troops, as well as the thousands of subsequent settlers from the mainland, is an issue that confounds the on-again, off-again intercommunal talks between the president of the republic, George Vassiliou, and the Turkish Cypriot leader, Rauf Denktash. In 1983, Denktash unilaterally declared the independence of the Turkish Republic of North Cyprus, which is recognized only by Turkey. The mainland and island Greeks refuse to recognize a legitimate state north of the "green line" buffer zone, which has been patrolled by a U.N. peacekeeping force for the last 26 years. The Republic of Cyprus has maintained an economic boycott of the occupied northern part of Cyprus, but the Turkish Cypriots have created a functioning state that has enjoyed economic and social progress despite the sanctions.

The leaders of the two communities on the island agreed to resume the stalled negotiations to settle the Cyprus problem in August 1988, but the target date of June 1989 for finding a solution came and passed without any agreement. The U.N.-sponsored talks broke down in July 1989 because Denktash denied the secretary general the right to offer proposals, saying that these should instead come from the principals. The Greek Cypriots rejected that idea as tantamount to the recognition of Denktash and his "pseudo-state." The two men did meet with the U.N. secretary general in 1989 but to no avail. Resolution 649, which called on the two leaders to "pursue their efforts to reach freely a mutually acceptable solution providing for the establishment of a federation that will be bi-communal as regards the constitutional aspects and bizonal as regards the territorial aspects," was passed by the U.N. Security Council on 12 March. Since that time, the intercommunal talks have been on hold.

Although the AKEL is not banned in the Turkish Cypriot community, the party has chosen not to be active in the north because of the difficulty in maintaining contacts across the "green line." There are three left-wing parties among the Turkish Cypriots: the Republican Turkish Party (CTP), the Communal Liberation Party (TKP), and the New Cyprus Party (YKP). The CTP is Socialist and led by Ozker Ozgur; the TKP is social democratic and led by Mustafa Akinci; and the YKP is radically left and led by Alpay Durduran. The CTP was founded in 1970 and is the oldest organized political party in the Turkish community; as a result of polling 22 percent of the vote in the 1985 elections, it is considered the second-largest party. The TKP was formed in 1976 and garnered 15 percent of the vote in 1985. The YKP broke away from the TKP in 1990 and scored only 1 percent of the vote in the elections that year. The percentage of votes polled by the CTP and the TKP in the 1990 elections is not known as they entered the election in alliance with the New Birth Party (YDP), the party of Turkish immigrants from mainland Turkey. The three parties together polled 45 percent of the vote. The three left-wing parties advocate a federal solution of the Cyprus problem and believe in intercommunal rapprochement as a means of achieving it. According to the leader of the CTP, "The three left-wing parties are unique in themselves and none is a copy of any party in the South of Cyprus or any part of the world" (personal communication from Ozker Ozgur, 6 November).

Leadership and Organization. Although the AKEL is reputed to be tightly controlled, a crisis within the party erupted in November 1989. At a public lecture, the general secretary of the left-wing labor union PEO alleged that the AKEL does not support *perestroika* and that it still "bore the stain of supporting the Soviet aggression against Czechoslovakia in 1968" (*AKEL News Letter*, special issue, April). PEO general secretary Pavlos Dinglis "had every opportunity to put into the agenda of the Political Bureau the above issue . . . yet he had chosen to create a scandal by his public attack on AKEL" (ibid.). During a four-day-long plenary meeting of the Central Committee in December 1989, it was revealed that a group of AKEL cadres had been functioning as a faction within the party since January 1986. This followed the AKEL election defeat in December 1985 for which the party leadership took the blame. Rather than expressing regret for their activities against the party, Dinglis and his cohorts demanded the resignation of the new and youthful general secretary, Christofias. After much heated discussion, the plenum ended on 17 December 1989 without taking punitive action against the faction and with a pledge to maintain party unity by stopping public dialogue. But this did not happen. An AKEL member of Parliament, Andreas Fantis, issued a public declaration on 21 January that "constituted a full slander against the Party." The faction continued its public attacks; the climax came on 8 March when five AKEL members of Parliament declared that they no longer belonged to the AKEL party. By this act they set themselves as "openly working to split AKEL" and went on to organize their own splinter party under the name of the Democratic Socialist Renewal Movement (*Ananeotiko Dimocratico Socialistiko Kinima*, ADISOK). The ADISOK officially came into being on 29 April and held its first congress 7–8 July. It calls itself "a pluralist, democratic movement . . . especially in its socialist orientation, irrespective of their theoretical starting points" (from an ADISOK communication dated 18 September).

Despite this upheaval and ensuing damage, the AKEL held its Seventeenth Party Congress 3–7 October. Out of 1,401 elected delegates, a total of 1,280 actually attended the congress as voters. The theme of the congress was "Renewal, Uniqueness, Strength, and Prepared for Struggle." The AKEL banners were displayed over the entire Greek-controlled southern part of the island. For the first time the proceedings were open to the public, with the exception of the actual voting for the Central Committee. Reflecting the new openness, the congress was spiced with spirited debate in the corridors and polite criticism when appropriate in the formal sessions. The congress elected incumbent general secretary Dimitris Christofias without a rival for a full four-year term. The election was made after a secret ballot by the new 100-member Central Committee, which has 20 more members than the previous one and which does not include any of the old members, who voluntarily "abstained from candidature to allow younger members to come forward in line with the Party's new policy of 'rejuvenation'" (*Cyprus Mail*, 7 October). The main focus of the congress was "on improving the party's profile, its renewal and modernization from an ideological and an organizational point of view" (ibid., 4 October). Moreover, Christofias insisted that despite the emergence of ADISOK, the splinter party, AKEL was "strong in the Cyprus political arena," and he predicted that the party would win more than 30 percent of the vote in the 1991 parliamentary elections (*Kharavyi*, 4 October). One advantage that the AKEL leaders had was that the word *communist* did not exist in their title; thus party leaders did not have to suffer the indignity of having to change its name to prove that they had acquired a "new look" in the face of the new internationalism.

Domestic Party Affairs. In his speech to the Seventeenth Party Congress, General Secretary Christofias stressed that AKEL's highest priority is "the struggle for the liberation and reunification of our country and people." Thus, the indispensable prerequisite for the solution of the Cyprus problem is "the rapprochement between the two communities with the aim of cultivating once again mutual trust, mutual respect and friendship." He also pointed out that the solution for the Cyprus problem must include the withdrawal of the Turkish troops and the demilitarization of the island, as well as the withdrawal of the Turkish settlers and the right of the Greek refugees to return to their pre-1974 homes. The AKEL replayed its old theme for the convening of an international conference on the Cyprus issue. Such a conference is needed "to convince the world that only pressure on Ankara and Denktash can insure progress in any intercommunal talks" (ibid., 23 October).

One issue that drew a heated response from the AKEL was the proposal for compulsory conscription of women into the National Guard. Although women are now allowed to enlist on a voluntary basis, the AKEL stance was that the continual reference to a military buildup among the Greek Cypriots gives the world the wrong message (i.e., that a search for a solution outside the peaceful option is being sought). A statement from the party's Central Committee concluded: "Defense preparedness is necessary but on no account should this be taken as preparation for the military option" (*Cyprus Mail*, 10 November). The Republic of Cyprus spends about $1 million a day on defense, and this too has come under criticism from the AKEL leaders.

At a plenary meeting on 3 March, the Central Committee expressed AKEL policy on taxation. Being concerned that the state budgets are "permanently in deficit," the AKEL proposed an immediate decrease of the state's nonproductive expenditure (e.g., the military). The critical financial situation in the republic "cannot be managed with the decrease of state expenditures alone...there also must be an increase of state revenue." To achieve this aim, "reconsideration of the existing tax policy is needed." (*AKEL News Letter*, special issue, March). The new taxation policy must lead to "a fairer distribution of the taxation burdens" and no decrease of "direct taxation for the richer layers of the population and for legal fictions, i.e. companies" (ibid.). The AKEL is firmly against the imposition of a value-added tax (VAT), as that would fall "more heavily upon the already low standard of living of the poorest layers of the population." Instead of imposing the VAT, the AKEL proposed fifteen other measures for raising public revenue. Among these measures, the AKEL wanted to "increase the taxation coefficient for offshore companies; impose taxation on church property; and introduce a tax on the purchase of luxury goods" (ibid.).

International Views, Positions, and Activities. In a document entitled *Our Concept of Socialism*, which was prepared in June for the Seventeenth Party Congress, a section was devoted to "The Position of Cyprus in the Modern World." In it the AKEL noted that the most important characteristics of our times are "the failure to solve a series of universal problems which constitute a danger to human civilization, the interdependence of the world and the coexistence of different socioeconomic systems with their differences." Moreover, "the solution of global problems is impossible without a system of collective military, economic and ecological security." To these ends the United Nations has to play a unique part because "it is universal from the point of view of the activities it embraces." An objective analysis of the strategic and geographical position of Cyprus "at the crossroads of three continents" determines its role in the international system and "will affect the aims and goals of our foreign policy—a policy of non-aligned friendship based upon mutual benefit and cooperation."

Christofias also addressed the restructuring of the Soviet Union and the changes in the countries of Eastern Europe in his speech at the Seventeenth Party Congress. He said that he would "regard with awe the idea of a world without the Soviet Union." Therefore, the AKEL is "unreservedly in favor of Perestroika and . . . justifiably concerned about its fate." The AKEL "is in solidarity with the Communists and the progressive forces of the Soviet Union and of other countries." In Eastern Europe, the "stubborn refusal" of the parties in power to review their methods of operation and exercise of power resulted in the "re-charting of the political map of Europe and the whole planet." The AKEL is "sincerely sorry about the fact that the Communist Parties of these countries had not realized in time the need to renew." In truth, the Cypriot communists are probably unhappy that they will no longer be invited to be state guests of those countries as they had so often been in the past.

Turning to the gulf crisis, Christofias told the party congress that it has "brought to the forefront the complex and contradictory nature of the contemporary world, with the dangers but also all possibilities that are hidden in it." From the beginning, the AKEL "condemned" the Iraqi invasion of Kuwait and "the use of force as a means of settling problems." Christofias claimed that he is faithful to the principles of international law and the United Nations. Therefore, he also had to condemn "the zeal of the USA to exercise the role of international gendarme, dispatching armed forces to the Gulf region before a prior UN resolution." He then denounced "the hypocrisy of the USA and their partners" who acted so swiftly in Kuwait but then conveniently "forgot the Israeli occupation of Arab territories and the Turkish occupation of Cyprus." He concluded that the gulf crisis brought about an "upgrading of Turkey's role" and that this development "constitutes a negative factor in the efforts to settle the Cyprus issue."

In an official document entitled *Theses for the 17th Congress of AKEL*, there was a section devoted to "Cyprus-EEC Relations, European Integration" (Nicosia, draft proposal, 3–7 October). For the past four years, the AKEL has maintained that it would be detrimental for Cyprus to become a member of the European Community (EC) because it would have to give up its nonaligned foreign policy

and become subservient to a union in which "eleven of the EEC [European Community] twelve member-countries are at the same time NATO members" (see the speech of the general secretary to the Seventeenth Party Congress). There may be advantages in some form of association with the EC, but "the best way is to sign a series of agreements with the community and not become members to it" (ibid.). Even before that step is taken, the AKEL insists that a referendum in Cyprus be held "so that the sovereign people can decide." Still the chances for Cyprus becoming an EC member anytime soon are remote. It is unlikely that the EC members would want to turn the "Cyprus problem into a Community problem." Hence, membership "will almost certainly have to wait until the Cypriots sort themselves out" (*The Economist*, 21 July). On 4 July the application was submitted to the EC.

Guest delegations from 20 countries were invited to attend the AKEL's Seventeenth Party Congress. Of the 25 delegations from the 20 countries, only 11 referred to themselves as *communist party*. The majority now prefer to use *Socialist* or *Social Democrat*, which reflects the new thinking in former communist-controlled countries. Trips to these former communist states by AKEL members were severely curtailed in the past year. In fact the only notable official visit made by the general secretary was on the invitation of the Cuban Communist Party. Only two members were in the AKEL delegation, but they did meet with Fidel Castro to discuss their common insular problems. On its way back to Cyprus, the delegation stopped in London, "where Christofias spoke at a mass gathering of the Cypriot community" (*Kharavyi*, 16 November). The Cypriot president, George Vassiliou, did lead a delegation to the People's Republic of China (PRC) in August, where he received assurances of support for his position as well as agreements on "developing trade relations between the PRC and Cyprus" (Nicosia Domestic Service, 30 August).

T. W. Adams
Nicosia, Cyprus

Denmark

Population. 5,145,100 (October)
Party. Communist Party of Denmark (Danmarks Kommunistiske Parti, DKP)
Founded. 1919
Membership. 3,000 (*Det Fri Aktuelt*, 5–6 January 1991)
Chairman. Ole Sohn
General Secretary. Anne-Marie Jørgensen
Executive Committee. Ole Sohn (chairman), Anne-Marie Jørgensen (Secretariat head), Gunnar Jørgensen (secretary), Dan Lundrup, Lars Bjerre, Flemming Bock, Thorbjørn Waagstein, Bernard Jeune, Ole Sørensen
Secretariat. Anne-Marie Jørgensen, Ole Sohn, Gunnar Jørgensen, Ole Sørensen
Central Committee. 35 members
Status. Legal
Last Congress. Twenty-ninth Extraordinary, 20–21 January 1990; Thirtieth, 14–15 April 1990
Last Election. 12 December 1990, 1.9 percent (Unity List, an electoral front including the DKP, Left Socialists, and Socialist Workers' Party), no representation in Parliament
Auxiliary Organization. Communist Youth of Denmark (Danmarks Kommunistiske Ungdom, DKU), dissolved in May 1990.
Publications. *Land og Folk* (Nation and people), daily, circulation, 5,300 weekdays and 10,000 weekends, editor, Frede Jakobsen, folded on 28 December; *Tiden-Verden Rund* (Times around the world), theoretical monthly; *Fremad* (Forward), DKU monthly, folded in May.

In a country renowned for its political fragmentation, the Danish communists are no exception. Denmark's communist movement has increasingly taken on the character of a centrifuge, perhaps a reflection of the trend in the Soviet Union. Even with unparalleled electoral cooperation on the far left in the 12 December national election, the communists were unable to break through the 2 percent threshold for parliamentary representation. The DKP, the flagship of the movement, splintered once again and saw both its youth organization and newspaper disband in 1990. Rumors abounded during the year that the DKP was seeking a merger with the Socialist People's Party (Socialistisk Folkeparti, SF). As a conservative-led, nonsocialist government entered its tenth straight year, Denmark's communists seemed incapable of arresting their steady slide into oblivion.

The DKP's long-term goal continues to be representation in the Folketing, although it appears increasingly resigned to doing so in a broad leftist front. If DKP members were elected to the Folketing, they would probably support a government led by the mainline Social Democratic Party (SDP) and the SF. Having captured only 0.8 percent of the popular vote in the May 1988 Folketing (parliamentary) election, the DKP agreed in 1989 to form a joint slate with two other leftist parties, the Left socialists (Venstresocialisterne, VS), and the Socialist Workers' Party (Socialistisk Arbejderparti, SAP). Under the banner of the Unity List, their common program calls for the removal of the nonsocialist government, an active peace and environmental policy, pension reform, and withdrawal from the European Community (EC). Although they had time to organize before the 12 December election, they were nevertheless unable to secure the necessary 2 percent of the vote to gain representation in the Folketing. In an interview with *Det Fri Aktuelt*, DKP chairman Ole Sohn discussed an initiative to create a broad leftist party with the cooperation of the SF, but thus far the SF has responded coolly to the proposal. (*Det Fri Aktuelt*, 5–6 January 1991; *Land og Folk*, 4 September; *FBIS-WEU*, 20 November.)

With the conservative-led government of Prime Minister Poul Schlüter entering its tenth year, the Danish left continues its longest period in opposition. The SDP, however, has gained steadily in opposition and secured fourteen more seats in the December election. The SDP currently has ten more seats than the conservative-liberal coalition that emerged from the election, a situation that will complicate Prime Minister Poul Schlüter's political maneuvering. Traditional consensus politics, now a matter of practical necessity for the minority coalition, will continue to ensure the SDP a role in policy formation. The SDP's calls for official ties with the Baltic states and a shift in spending from defense to aid for Eastern Europe have also found considerable resonance in Denmark. The SDP's gains, however, have come largely at the expense of other parties on the far left, thus providing no large mandate to challenge the nonsocialist hold on government.

Leadership and Organization. Having survived numerous leadership challenges in 1989, including one that succeeded in removing him temporarily from office, DKP chairman Ole Sohn faced
far less internal opposition in 1990; this year the
opposition simply walked out. The final split had its
impetus in the January extraordinary party congress during which most of the so-called Stalinist
wing of the party was ousted. At the congress's end,
Sohn secured the support of 30 of the 35 new Central Committee members. At the party's Thirtieth
Congress in mid-April, Sohn managed a similar
victory when his proposals for openness and rejuvenation in the party won the support of 251 of the
395 party members present. (*Ritzau's Bureau*, 29
January; *Politiken*, 15 April.)

Sohn's victories were Pyrrhic, however, as he
watched his party's membership drop by more than
half in 1990. Meeting on 28 April the ousted Stalinist wing (about two hundred former DKP members) established the Communist Forum (Kom-
munistisk Forum, KF), which dedicated itself to the
principles of the communists' program of 1976.
Former party Secretary Poul Emanuel and former
Land og Folk chief editor Gunnar Kanstrup joined a
number of small local party organs in switching
affiliation to the KF. The new party took its final
shape in September, when it held its first national
convention, electing former DKP Central Committee representative Betty Frydensbjerg Carlsson
chairwoman by unanimous vote. Although Sohn
could have foreseen his revisionist policies might
alienate much of the orthodox old guard, the DKP
was ill-prepared to deal with numerous defections
to the SDP and SF on its right. By the middle of
1990, Sohn could count barely 4,200 dues-paying
members on the DKP's membership rolls; this
number fell to 3,000 by year's end. (*Land og Folk*, 1
May, 10 August; *FBIS-WEU*, 5 June, 21 September; *Det Fri Aktuelt*, 5–6 January 1991.)

If the loss of party membership to the left and
right was a serious setback for the DKP, the dissolution of its youth arm, the DKU, proved the most
foreboding. Tensions in the past between the DKP
and the DKU were driving a wedge between the two
organizations, but a split seemed inevitable when at
its October 1989 national convention the DKU discussed establishing relations with other leftist parties to parallel those with the DKP. Sohn, who
himself rose through the DKU ranks, fought bitterly against this move. His objections became
moot when, at its Thirty-ninth Congress in May, the
DKU formally dissolved its organization. The

DKU's demise removed a major source of new party
members for the DKP and may have contributed to
Sohn's decision to seek cooperation with other leftist parties. (*Berlingske Tidende*, 14 May.)

Financial problems continued to dog Sohn
throughout 1990. With debts of more than 15 million kroner, losses on the party's day-to-day accounts, and declining readership of its daily newspaper, *Land og Folk*, loans against the DKP's
headquarters at Dronningens Tvaergade finally ran
dry. The party held a flea market and auction in
early April to prepare for the move from their
10,000-square-meter headquarters of 45 years to a
more modest 250 square meters on Norrebrogade.
The 80,000 kroner netted at the event covered the
cost of the move but provided no solution for *Land
og Folk's* worsening liquidity problems. The financial situation was exacerbated by the nonpayment of
party dues by almost a fifth of the membership at
midyear. (*Berlingske Tidende*, 11 April; *FBIS-
WEU*, 9 May.)

Domestic Affairs. After the 1979 Folketing
election in which the DKP lost all seven of its
parliamentary seats, the DKP became an increasingly irrelevant observer and critic of Danish
domestic affairs. In an effort to regain influence on
the political scene, the DKP has focused on three
primary areas of action: electoral campaigns, labor
union activism, and general leftist propaganda.
Elections are the most important venue because
government posts not only confer a direct influence
on policy but also give the party a platform and
resources from which to promote its program.
Moreover, merely participating in electoral campaigns allows a party generous access to radio and
television time (without expense), as long as it appears on the ballot. Given the frequency of Danish
parliamentary campaigns (seven since 1973), the
DKP considers it essential to secure a place on the
ballot. The electoral pact formed with the VS and
the SAP in 1989 and extended through the December 1990 national election was its most recent
but failing effort to break the 2 percent minimum
cutoff for Folketing representation.

Labor activism continues to absorb a large part
of the DKP's attention, although the recent party
split has complicated its efforts. The DKP has had
considerable difficulty establishing a role for itself
in industrial labor relations. Consensus politics has
ensured cooperation between the SDP and the
conservative-led government on labor questions,
and the SDP's size has enabled it to take the leading

role in the protection of labor's interests. The factions of the labor movement the SDP does not control have tended to associate with the SF, which has fifteen seats in the Folketing. The SAP and the VS are also in competition for labor's ear, limiting the DKP's influence to the fringes.

In a move designed in part to win back support from the trade unions, Sohn made a major push to expand DKP-labor ties in 1990. Three of his six new executive committee appointments were trade unionists. He also made a strong pitch after the January extraordinary conference to work more closely with the Trade Union Forum, an organization of approximately 250 communists that has played a large part in labor market actions and demonstrations since the early 1970s. In doing so, however, he found the Communist Forum already active there, particularly his former DKP colleagues and union organizers Harry Osborn and Jorgen Madsen. The leadership of the Trade Union Forum, however, chose to avert this turf battle and elected to pursue broader union ties outside the communist camp. (*Land og Folk*, 1 May.)

The DKP's main propaganda vehicle, *Land og Folk*, published its last edition in December 1990. The paper was forced to withdraw its Prague and East Berlin correspondents in the spring when Czechoslovakia and former East Germany stopped paying their salaries. After the April party congress, the DKP held a month-long fundraiser with a goal of 700,000 kroner just to pay outstanding bills. When that failed, the DKP leadership decided to broaden *Land og Folk*'s audience by diversifying the editorial staff and creating what Editor in Chief Frede Jakobsen termed a "progressive, independent, and critical socialist daily for the entire left wing." SF member of Parliament Pelle Voigt and VS member Poul Petersen were invited to join the staff. With a daily circulation that nevertheless dwindled to below five thousand and ran regular annual deficits of 4–5 million kroner, saving the paper proved impossible, and it printed its last edition on 28 December. It is ironic that in attempting to legitimize itself through greater objectivity in its reporting, *Land og Folk* lost much of its most diehard readership. (*Land og Folk*, 11–12 August; *FBIS-WEU*, 3 October; *Information*, 30 January.)

While struggling to gain representation in the Folketing, the DKP backs in principle a socialist alternative government against the nonsocialist coalition. Although the VS and the SAP have also followed this pragmatic line, it is germane only to the SF, which has the only leftist representation in the Folketing aside from the SDP. Across the board, the leftist parties have criticized the nonsocialists for their austerity program. The DKP supports proposals for shorter working hours (without reductions in wage demands), increased business taxation, restoration of the automatic cost-of-living adjustments, and restrictions on the movement of capital in and out of Denmark. Where the DKP differs from the mainline Social Democrats is in its call for the nationalization of large industrial and financial concerns. The DKP program also calls for sharp cuts in military spending, which even the SDP renounced on reaching a defense budget consensus with the government in 1989. On the whole, the DKP's program shows little change over the past few years. Much of this has to do with its long absence from power and its lack of influence on the SDP. It also reflects the chaos within the party ranks that discouraged long-range planning in 1990.

Foreign Affairs. Under Sohn's leadership, the DKP began to break out of its strict pro-Moscow orientation. On the Danish left, the DKP has traditionally been the only Danish party to follow a policy of uncritical support of the Soviet Union. Sohn continues to visit Moscow regularly, but during a May visit to meet with the Communist Party of the Soviet Union (CPSU) International Department head Valentin Falin, he found little to discuss. Soviet KGB officer and defector Oleg Gordievskij's public revelations that the DKP received as much as one million kroner a year from the Soviet embassy in Copenhagen and was the funnel for instructions to various peace movements most certainly affected both the party's orientation and its public image. (TASS, 25 May; Oleg Gordievskij, *KGB: The Inside Story of Its Foreign Operations from Lenin to Gorbachev*.)

When *Land og Folk* began to take a more objective view of Soviet foreign policy in 1988, the sole remarks on the situation from the DKP leadership concerned the paper's editorial conduct. Sohn and a few others in the Central Committee have recently spoken more openly and positively about liberalization in Eastern Europe, but it took the ghost of Danish communist Arne Munch-Petersen to spark a confrontation with Moscow. A Soviet historian uncovered evidence in 1989 that Munch-Petersen, assigned in 1935 to the Comintern in Moscow, was jailed by Stalin in 1937 and died in a Soviet prison camp three years later. Munch-Petersen's widow immediately called for her husband's exoneration, and Sohn contacted the Soviet embassy in

Copenhagen to demand the facts in the case. World-wide publicity concerning the case of Swedish diplomat Raoul Wallenberg, who apparently died in a Soviet prison shortly after World War II, undoubtedly influenced Sohn's action and prompted him to demand Munch-Petersen's rehabilitation. (*FBIS-WEU*, 4 August 1989.)

Despite these embarrassments, the DKP still maintains a *Land og Folk* correspondent in Moscow whose salary is paid by the CPSU, and its basic foreign and security policy platform remains little changed. The DKP is strongly opposed to the North Atlantic Treaty Organization (NATO) and anti-EC, cooperating with like-minded activists throughout Europe. But almost three-quarters of the Danes support NATO membership, and there is strong business endorsement of the EC; thus the DKP has remained largely on the fringes of these debates. Only its early support for a Nordic nuclear weapons–free zone and other antinuclear positions have gained it significant attention, but the signing of the Conventional Forces Talks in Europe treaty has largely silenced the DKP's bread-and-butter rhetoric. (*Information*, 30 January.)

International Party Contacts. The DKP's internationalism distinguishes it from other Marxist parties in that it identifies closely with the "proletarian internationalism" of the CPSU. But as the CPSU has retreated from its rhetoric and activism of the past, the DKP has become increasingly isolated. Political upheaval in Eastern Europe and the Soviet Union has limited contacts between the DKP and the remaining or reformed communist parties in these countries. In perhaps the only remaining and representative gesture to the DKP's former ideological allies, former party Secretary Ingmar Wagner offered his villa in Denmark to deposed East German ruler Erich Honecker after the latter's release from prison last February.

OTHER MARXIST/LEFTIST GROUPS

The DKP is only one of several left-wing parties active in Danish politics. The elections in May 1988 left only the Socialist People's Party (SF) in the Folketing, a situation that remained unchanged after the December 1990 election. Originally a splinter group from the DKP (in 1958), the SF steadily gained ground despite a decade (from 1968 to 1977) of internal splits and electoral setbacks. Ever since it first gained parliamentary representa-

tion in 1960, the SF has courted the SDP in an effort to pull it leftward. In 1966–1967 and 1971–1973, SF votes kept the Social Democrats in power. The first experiment in formal SF-SDP collaboration, the so-called red cabinet, ended when the SF's left wing broke off to form the VS. The SDP has always been wary of too much collaboration with the Marxist left, particularly after several moderate Social Democrats abandoned the party to form the Center Democrats in 1973. Neither the SF nor the SDP has excluded political collaboration in the future. The SDP's strong showing in the December polls, however, came largely at the expense of the SF, which lost nine seats.

The SF's program may explain at least part of this dramatic loss. Preferring firm ideological stances, it has tended to reject negotiation as a method to influence policy. Its platform positions, rigid and largely unacceptable to the SDP, include a reduction in the work day to seven hours (without wage cuts), compulsory employee profit sharing and codetermination ("economic democracy"), fiscal and monetary policies free from EC control, and the declaration of Denmark as a nuclear-free zone. One instance of the SF's hard-line conviction is its attack on Danish participation in NATO's Nuclear Planning Group, whereas the SDP believes Denmark's presence allows it to influence policy. On the EC, there is some evidence that the SF has moderated its opposition to Danish membership, and some party officials are even planning to use the EC Parliament as a venue to political power. After its stunning losses in the 1990 polls, the party may also seriously embrace environmental issues, which received considerable attention at the May party convention.

The SF is explicitly non-Leninist in its internal governance and attitudes toward Danish parliamentary democracy, a reason perhaps for Sohn's interest in cooperating with it. Its earlier feuds and schisms have largely faded under the leadership of its veteran chairman, Gert Petersen, although its position as an opposition party has allowed it somewhat greater internal pluralism. With just under ten thousand members, nearly a sixth of the parliamentary vote, and a substantial presence in local government and labor unions, it is an attractive alternative to the SDP and other leftists, including the DKP. The SF's generally independent stance, however, did not stop it from opening up direct contact with Moscow in 1988, when Petersen led an SF delegation to the Soviet Union to meet with CPSU, government, and labor officials. (*Ritzau's Bureau*, 27 September 1988.)

Preben Moller Hansen's Common Course Party (Faelles Kurs, FK) disappeared from Parliament in the May 1988 election, having polled a tenth of 1 percent under the required minimum for representation. The FK failed again in last December's polls to break the 2 percent threshold, despite its tactical election cooperation with ousted Progress party chairman Mogens Glistrup. Its program follows the same themes of nationalization and confiscation that characterize the programs of the other leftist parties, especially the DKP, on whose Executive Committee Hansen sat until his feud with the DKP's old guard. Unique to the FK are its anti-immigrant and antirefugee proposals, probably the only commonality with far right Progress party leader Glistrup. Its populist views had provided some entertainment in the normally staid Danish Parliament, but they have done little to help the party's credibility. (*Det Fri Aktuelt*, 19 June; *FBIS-WEU*, 21 June.)

The Left Socialists (VS) have continued their sharp decline in voter support, buoyed last fall only by their participation on the Unity List. In the process of this decline, the party's Leninist faction, under the leadership of Keld Albrechtsen, took over the Executive Committee. Although the decline of its pragmatic leadership has relegated the VS to the fringes of the political scene, its electoral alliance with the DKP and the SAP last December succeeded in netting the three parties a 15 percent increase in total votes over their combined showing in 1988.

Two other small parties inhabit the far left of the political spectrum. The Socialist Workers' Party (SAP), a Trotskyite Marxist party, has no permanent political base. It is the Danish branch of the Trotskyite Fourth International, and its weekly paper *Klassenkampen* (Class struggle) is well informed on Danish leftist politics and the international Trotskyist movement. In the last municipal elections the SAP was able to gather little more than four hundred votes, and in the December Folketing election it participated in the Unity List with the DKP and the VS, where it is by far the junior partner. The Marxist-Leninist Party (Marxistisk-Leninistiske Parti, MLP) models itself after Enver Hoxha's Albanian Communist Party; having last participated in an election in 1987, it is by all accounts now defunct.

Another small radical leftist movement, the Communist Labor Circle (Kommunistiske Arbejderkreis, KAK), entered the news in 1989 not for its politics but for its criminal activities. Created in 1963 by former DKP member and *Land og Folk* journalist Gotfred Appel, KAK espoused sympathies with the Chinese communists after the Sino-Soviet split. KAK and its youth group, the Communist Youth League (KUF), turned their attentions to the Middle East in the late 1960s, first organizing assistance programs and later sending members for terrorist training in radical Palestinian camps. Members of the group were recently convicted in a string of postal and bank robberies in Denmark and for caching weapons stolen from Swedish defense mobilization centers. (*Information*, 13–14 May 1989.)

Neither the DKP nor other Danish far left groups have direct ties to parties in Denmark's autonomous territories: Greenland and the Faeroe Islands. Although the Faeroes have no significant Marxist movement, Greenland's politics have shown a significant left-wing character since the island obtained home rule from Denmark in 1979. A coalition of the pan-Eskimo Inuit Ataqatigiit (IA) and Socialist Simuit parties presided over the withdrawal of Greenland from the EC in 1982. The coalition broke apart in 1988 in part over IA chairman Arqaluk Lynge's strong opposition to Greenland's NATO membership via Denmark. Lynge has also established close ties with the CPSU to promote contacts between the Inuits (Eskimos) in the Soviet Union and those in Greenland, Canada, and Alaska, a move the Soviets capitalized on through their first attendance at the Inuit Circumpolar Conference in July 1989. Lynge participated in a Russian Arctic People's Conference in Moscow in late March and met with Gorbachev while there. (*Berlingske Tidende*, 21 July; *Information*, 7 March.)

Randolph McNeely
Greenbelt, Maryland

Finland

Population. 4,977,325
Parties. Finnish Communist Party (Suomen Kommunistinen Puolue, SKP) contested elections as part of the Finnish People's Democratic League (Suomen Kansan Demokraattinen Litto, SKDL); registered party dissolved 29 April. Finnish Com-

munist Party—Unity (Suomen Kommunistinen Puolue—Yhtenäisyys, SKP-Y) candidates for office appeared on list of an electoral front group, the Democratic Alternative (Demokraattinen Vaihtoehto, DEVA), disbanded 9 September; SKP-Y is registered as a political association claiming to be a legitimate representative of communist movement. Communist Workers' Party (Kommunistinen Tyoekansan Puolue, KTP), "revolutionary" splinter from SKP-Y. Left Alliance (Vasemmistolitto, VL), broad-based party that includes communists as individual members; replaced SKDL in Parliament and on local councils.

Founded. SKP: 1918; SKDL: 1944; SKP-Y/ DEVA: 1986; KTP: 1988; VL: 1990. SKP terminated political activity 1990, to be dissolved 1993. SKDL and DEVA disbanded 1990.

Membership. SKP: 20,000 estimated when disbanded; SKDL: 45,000 when disbanded; SKP-Y: 10,000 estimated; KTP: 1,000 estimated; VL: 12,500 claimed

Chairs. VL: Claes Andersson; vice-chairs, Salme Kandolin and Kari Uotila. SKP: Jarmo Wahlström resigned 30 April; succeeded by Helja Tammisola. SKDL: Reijo Käkelä resigned 2 February; succeeded by vice-chairs Hilkka Aalto and Timo Laaksonen; Ari Parvianen named caretaker chairman 31 March. SKP-Y: Esko-Juhani Tennilä resigned 26 July; succeeded by Yryö Häkanen, 10 September. KTP: Timo Lahdenmaeki.

General Secretaries. VL: Matti Viialainen (party secretary). SKP: Helja Tammisola; succeeded by Asko Mäki as caretaker 30 April. SKDL: Salme Kandolin; office abolished 29 April. SKP-Y: Yryö Häkanen succeeded by Arto Viitaniemi 10 September. KTP: Heikki Mannikko.

Executive Committee. VL: 10 full and 5 alternate members; Jan-Otto Andersson, Tapani Kaakkuriniemi, Marya-Liisa Löyttyjärvi, Asko Mäki, Maija Pietilä, Mikko Raudaskoski, Pirkko Rissanen, Marja-Liisa Romppanen, Leena Ruotsalainen, Esko Seppänen; alternates: Risto Hynynen, Pia Hyötynen, Mikko Kuoppa, Pauliina Murto-Lehtinen, Katja Syvärinen

Central Committee. VL: 100 members. SKP: 30 members

Status. Legal. SKP (inactive) and KTP registered as political parties. SKDL and DEVA were registered as political parties and eligible for public subsidies until disbanded in 1990. SKP-Y and SKDL registered as political associations, SKDL until accounts of former party are closed. VL registered as political party eligible for subsidy following disbanding of SKDL.

Last Congress. SKP: Twenty-second Congress (23–25 February 1990), Helsinki; SKDL: Fifteenth Congress (23–25 May 1988), Helsinki; SKP-Y: First Congress (5–7 June 1987), Espoo; KTP: First Congress (17–18 June 1989), Vantaa; VL: Founding Congress (29 April), Helsinki

Last Election. General election for 200-seat Eduskunta, 15–16 March 1987. SKDL: 9.5 percent of vote, 16 seats (including 11 SKP); DEVA: 4.3 percent of vote, 4 seats; 20 members elected from SKDL and DEVA lists in 1987 sit as VL caucus. Next general election March 1991. Presidential election, 31 January–1 February 1988 (popular election), 15 February 1988 (electoral college); Kalevi Kivistö ("Action 88" candidacy endorsed by SKP/SKDL), 10.5 percent of popular vote, 26 (of 301) seats in electoral college; Jouko Kajanoja (DEVA), 1.4 percent of popular vote, no electoral college seats. Local elections, October 1988; SKDL: 10.3 percent of overall vote; DEVA: 2.5 percent. Most local councillors elected from SKDL and DEVA lists sit as VL delegates.

Auxiliary Organizations. Most auxiliary organizations affiliated with the SKP, including the Finnish Women's Democratic League (SNDL) and communist student groups, were disbanded in 1990 along with the party. The Finnish Democratic Youth League (SDNL) remains active as an independent, party-unaffiliated organization. SKP-Y continues to sponsor parallel organizations. VL does not plan auxiliary organizations directly affiliated with the party.

Publications. The formerly SKP/SKDL-affiliated daily *Kansan Uutiset* (Helsinki, est. circ. 40,000) became an independent newspaper in 1990, supporting but not affiliated with the VL. It is published four times a week, including weekly magazine. Other former SKP newspapers continuing publication as left-oriented independents include *Hämeen Yhteistyo* (Hameenlinna, est. circ. 11,000), *Kansan Tahto* (Oulu, est. circ. 16,000), *Kansan Sana* (Kuopio, circ. under 8,000), *Kansan Ääni* (Vaasa, circ. under 10,000), *Satakunnan Työ* (Pori, est. circ. 10,000), all published three times weekly. *Ny Tid* (Helsinki) is leftist Swedish-language weekly formerly affiliated with SKP. SKP-Y: *Tiedonantaja* (Helsinki, circ. 16,000 claimed, including complimentary distribution) was daily newspaper reorganized in 1990 as weekly journal of Marxist analyses of news and issues.

The SKP was legalized in 1944 following the armistice with the Soviet Union that ended the Continuation War. Communist candidates in local and parliamentary elections stood for office on slates offered by the SKDL, an electoral coalition that included the SKP as well as Socialists and other "progressive" groups committed to a leftist agenda. In 1969, the SKP formally adopted a reformist line promoted by its pragmatic and nationalist majority wing in the face of opposition from a significant dogmatic and Soviet-oriented minority wing. In protest against the majority's "revisionism," the minority excluded the majority from the eight (of nineteen) minority-controlled district organizations. In 1985, a special party congress authorized the SKP central committee to expel those organizations. The SKP subsequently purged party members linked to the minority. The minority refused to accept their expulsion and, in 1986, set up a parallel party apparatus, the SKP-Y, which claimed to be the legitimate SKP. Minority candidates contested elections through a front organization, DEVA, that like the SKDL was registered as a political party. (For historical background and discussion of intraparty and party/front relations, see *YICA*, 1989.)

Finnish communists took stock of their divided movement in wide-ranging end-of-decade debates on ideology, historical interpretation, procedures, and the nature and future of the party itself. SKP chairman Jarmo Wahlström and Reijo Käkelä, the communist chairman of the SKDL, set in motion negotiations for the formation of a completely new party, the VL, that would appeal to communists and noncommunists alike, including the Greens, and replace the SKDL. Supporters of the plan argued that a more broad-based party that stressed issues over ideology would shift the center of gravity in Finnish politics to the left and open the way for the VL's participation in the government.

Sharp divisions in the SKP/SKDL soon became apparent, however, on questions such as group versus individual and open versus qualified membership, terms for accepting minority communists, dual membership in other parties, and whether the SKP should be abolished or continue as a separate cooperating party. Wahlström hammered through Central Committee acceptance of his and Käkelä's scenario according to which the SKP would read itself out of existence if it were to allow majority communists to join the new party as individual members. Individual minority communists would be accepted as members only if they broke with the SKP-Y.

As a result of the debate, Wahlström lost credibility among grass roots communists, who complained that Marxism would be diluted if the SKP was fused into a new party that was largely noncommunist. Although expressing their eagerness to join the new party, minority communists were unwilling to concede the abolition of the SKP-Y. Meanwhile, many noncommunist leftists wondered if the Wahlström-Käkelä plan meant that the VL would become the SKP under a different name, espousing the majority line. The erosion of Käkelä's position in the SKDL by the beginning of 1990 indicated that the scenario for the VL was not developing according to the script he had prepared. (For the debate on the VL, see *YICA*, 1990.)

Sixty representatives of SKDL district and auxiliary organizations met with party executives in early February at Kulttuuritalo (Culture House, the SKDL and SKP headquarters in Helsinki) to plan the transfer of the party's political activities to the VL. DEVA members of Parliament were also invited to participate. Discussion focused on the composition of delegates to the new party's founding congress, scheduled for April. Käkelä and other top-ranked majority communists, including Wahlström and SKP general secretary Helja Tammisola, demanded a closed congress restricted to no more than three hundred representatives of SKDL district organizations. (For reporting of the SKDL conference and commentary, see *Helsingen Sanomat* [*HS*], 30 January, 1, 5, 6, 7, 17 February; *Hufvudstadsbladet* [*Hb*] 6 March, 9 April.)

In response, leaders of the SKDL's socialist caucus argued that many district organizations were controlled by majority communists who would gain a dominating influence at the VL congress if Käkelä's plan were adopted. SKDL general secretary Salme Kandolin and Claes Andersson (see Biographies) offered a counterproposal that would recognize delegates from free constituency organizations, operating outside the SKDL, that could present petitions with at least twenty signatures to the congress on the condition that they also approved the program of the VL. Minority communists from the DEVA parliamentary delegation supported the socialist proposal, although Marja-Liisa Löyttyjärvi, who was also SKP-Y vice-chair, suggested that the number of signatures required be reduced to ten. Representatives of the SDNL (youth organization) went several steps farther, calling for a completely open market square–style meeting that would admit anyone interested in making a contribution to the founding of the new party.

Käkelä warned that an open congress would be orchestrated by whichever group brought in the most supporters, would fragment the new party from the outset, and would probably lead to its domination by a strongman. In the vote on proposals that followed, open participation was approved decisively by a margin of 39 to 22, representing a clear defeat for Käkelä and the SKP leadership by an unlikely coalition of SKDL socialists, minority communists, and SKP reformers. The twenty-signature formula for open participation was subsequently adopted.

Following the vote, Käkelä announced his decision to quit as SKDL chairman. The proximate cause of his sudden and unexpected resignation was the defeat of closed participation, but opposition had been building for some months among SKDL socialists to Käkelä's authoritarian style and had influenced their position during the floor debate as much as the relative merits of closed or open participation at the VL congress. Socialists were also troubled by the increasingly blatant exertion of SKP dominance within the SKDL organization during his tenure, and some expressed foreboding that Käkelä aimed at making the VL a surrogate for the majority communists.

Disputes within the SKP also weighed heavily on Käkelä. Yrjö Rautio, editor of *Kansan Uutiset*, demanded editorially that Käkelä give up his dreams of chairmanship of the VL and provided space in the party newspaper for critics of his policies who were unwilling to accept the liquidation of the SKP. One writer, Pertti Lahtinen, a member of Parliament, advocated preserving the SKP but sending Käkelä to a museum! Lahtinen and other reformers in the so-called Tampere group professed to see in Käkelä's authoritarianism a reflection of Wahlström's methods of running the SKP. Käkelä was reportedly stung by the criticism leveled at him and his project in the pages of a party organ. He was referring to Rautio in his resignation speech when he said that "a free Nordic man [Käkelä] does not have to tolerate everything that is thrown at him. . . . If some person [Rautio] is so poisonous that by his mere existence he keeps the SKP alive, I can no longer participate [in it]." (*HS*, 5 February.)

Käkelä proposed Kari Uotila, a communist trade union official, to succeed him as SKDL/VL chairman (see Biographies). Esko Seppänen, a communist member of Parliament, and socialist Claes Andersson, both of whom had opposed Käkelä, were also offered as candidates. It was determined, however, that until the formation of the VL, the SKDL

chair's duties would be assumed jointly by vice-chairs Timo Laaksonen and Hilkka Aalto. The SKDL's executive board held its final meeting in April on the 45th anniversary of the party's founding; at that meeting it was decided to sponsor the publication of a history of the party. The SNDL was given leave to withdraw from the party as an auxiliary group to work independently in support of the VL. It was agreed, however, that the SKDL would continue as a political association for a four-year period while its finances were put in order and that application would be made to protect its name from being used after that time by another group. Ari Parvianen was later named to chair the caretaker committee that would administer the association. (*Hb*, 9 April.)

Käkelä's fall was greeted with undisguised joy by the SKP-Y. Chairman Esko-Juhani Tennilä announced immediately that a large number of minority communists would attend the VL's founding congress. He directed them to begin collecting names for free constituency organizations to send delegates to the congress. "Only in this way," he wrote, "will we demonstrate that we give our unconditional support to bringing together the VL." Tennilä strenuously denied that his faction was plotting to pack the congress but affirmed that the SKP-Y intended to prevent "old" majority communists from grabbing control of the VL by default. (*Tienonantaja* [*Ta*], 6 February.)

Kansan Uutiset saw Käkelä's resignation as opening up the VL, which an editorial described as "a venture no longer tied to one person," whereas the nonleftist press generally agreed with *Helsingen Sanomat*'s assessment that he was "leaving a sinking ship" (*Kansan Uutiset* [*KU*] and *HS*, 6 February). *Helsingen Sanomat* also pointed out that his abruptness had made him enemies and that his political vision no longer carried weight on the left, conceding that it was likely he would have been defeated for the VL leadership if he had not resigned.

Käkelä explained that he had stepped down to show his confidence in the new party's ability to stand on its own under different leadership but expressed concern about the influence that the minority communists might exert on an open congress. Before leaving with his family for a week's vacation in China, Käkelä, the architect of the VL, said that he would seek no further role in the new party and would not be available to support it. (*HS*, 4, 17 February.)

On 23 February, the SKP opened its three-day Twenty-second Congress under "extraordinary" circumstances to begin dismantling the party. Minority communists were admitted for the first time since 1985. According to an allotment of one delegate per one hundred members, SPK district organizations sent two hundred delegates, the minority, forty-eight. Majority officials, however, questioned the accuracy of SPK-Y district membership rolls.

In his keynote speech, Wahlström accused the Soviet Union of having interfered with the internal operation of the SKP since the party was legalized in 1944. He criticized the stifling effect that the so-called era of foreign policy liturgy had on Finnish-Soviet relations during Urho Kekkonen's presidency (1956–1981) and regretted that signs of the same restraint were still evident. Wahlström also pondered the future of the Soviet Union, where, he said, "an omnipotent state came into being instead of the equal and free society [promised by communism]." (For reporting of the SKP congress and commentary, see *HS*, 20, 23, 26 February.)

Minority delegates might regard the party leaders around Wahlström as "old men" who unlike them did not recognize the potential of the VL's "radical spirit," but their presence had surprisingly little impact on the congress. The biggest challenges to the SKP leadership came from majority reformers. Wahlström's condemnation of Soviet totalitarianism did not prevent his being labeled a Stalinist by members of the Tampere group because of the arbitrary methods he tried to employ within his own party. Esko Seppänen accused him of "Ceauşescu-like" tactics. (Seppänen reminded the congress that Wahlström had sent party Education Secretary Oiva Bjorkbacka to Bucharest as an observer at the Romanian party congress in November 1989 against the objections of many in SKP.) Wahlström defended Aamo Aitamurtu against the "outrageous attack" made on him by Seppänen in the pages of *Kansan Uutiset*, where Seppänen referred to the SPK vice-chairman and others in high positions as mafiosi who had manipulated party finances. Seppänen called for a record of the SKP's property holdings to be made public before the party dissolved itself.

Minority communists argued for preserving a united SKP as a Marxist party, paralleling and participating in the VL, but the majority-dominated congress voted overwhelmingly to transfer political activity to the new party once it had been formally constituted. The Central Committee would be reduced from 50 to 30 members and would remain in office until released by a final party congress in 1993, but a majority of the congress agreed, against minority opposition, that the SKP would no longer exist as a separate party. District organizations and local cells were asked to apply independently for incorporation in the VL. Communists were urged as individuals and as members of local groups to "participate boldly, actively, and without bias" in the VL. Expenses for a slimmed-down party apparatus would be met from an endowment of 6.5 million markkaa administered by the SKP Support Foundation. Remaining assets would eventually be turned over to the VL, a decision that drew complaints from minority delegates.

In a further action, the principal party organ, *Kansan Uutiset*, was declared to be an independent newspaper. Smaller provincial newspapers controlled by the SKP assumed a similar status. Some party assets were transferred to these newspapers, none of which had been self-supporting, but their financial future was uncertain. To cut costs, all subsequently reduced the number of issues published weekly.

The political activity of the SKP having been terminated by a vote of the congress, Wahlström resigned as party chairman. Election of executive officers and members of the Central Committee and Politburo, who would keep the watch during the run down to 1993, was by secret ballot, a victory for the reformers who had pressed the issue against Wahlström's opposition during the debate on voting procedure. Helja Tammisola received the largest number of votes (165) of any candidate for a seat on the Politburo, but otherwise delegates clearly demonstrated their irritation with the old leadership in the selection of the Politburo and Central Committee. Wahlström was left out of both bodies as were his closest allies. Likewise, only two from the minority faction were elected to the Central Committee.

Tammisola was chosen as party chairman (nineteen to seven) by the Central Committee over Pekka Peltona, who had been closely identified with Käkelä in the SKDL. Asko Mäki was unanimously approved as general secretary to succeed Tammisola. Over the next few weeks, all party employees were fired, leaving only the general secretary and a small office staff behind at Kulttuurialto to supervise the sale of property holdings. (*HS*, 21 May.)

Nearly three thousand delegates assembled at Kulttuuritalo on 29 April for the opening of the VL's founding congress. The first order of business was the formal dissolution of the SKDL as a political party; the next was the election of the successor party's officers. Contrary to expectations of some that an open congress would be unmanageable, delegates approved procedures for electing the party leadership without debate or dissent. Choosing from the field of three candidates nominated at the SKDL congress in February, they elected Claes Andersson (1,635 votes) as party chairman over Kari Uotila (618 votes) and Salme Kandolin (537 votes), who were named vice-chairs. A hundred-member Central Committee chosen by district organizations elected Matti Viialainen general secretary. Viialainen narrowly defeated Matti Hokkanen with strong support from minority communists on the committee. (Old personal and political rivalries had emerged in district-level elections for committee members held earlier in the month. Estimates of the percentage of minority communists elected ranged from one-fourth to one-third of committee members. A precise count was not possible because supposedly many minority candidates concealed their allegiance.) However, only two of the fifteen members and alternates that the Central Committee named to the VL's executive committee, which would have functions similar to those of a politburo, could be clearly identified as minority communists. (For reporting on the VL congress and commentary, see *HS*, *FBIS-WEU*, 30 April.)

The new party's platform adopted by the congress was described in the nonleftist press as "woolly pinkish-green." Under the heading "A Viable Option: Sustainable Development," it called for labor reforms and programs to ensure full employment. It defended greater spending for public services coupled with reductions in military expenditures. The environmental plank proposed an energy policy that would freeze energy consumption by the year 2000 and cut thereafter by 10 percent. Among the items dealing with foreign affairs, the VL platform expressed solidarity with the people of the Baltic republics. Mention of Finland's Treaty of Friendship, Cooperation and Mutual Assistance (FCMA) with the Soviet Union was conspicuously absent, while the proposition of European Community (EC) membership for Finland was not formally rejected. (Viialainen was subsequently quoted as saying that he expected to see Finland join the EC by the end of the decade. See *HS*, 5 July.) Again, there was an absence of debate.

As had been the case earlier at the SKP congress, minority communists failed to make an imprint on party policy, despite their disproportionate repre-

sentation. Several resolutions proposed by the minority, including one that affirmed support for the FCMA treaty, were rejected. Some bitterness was expressed, but most minority communists seemed content to be inside Kulttuurialto again. By mutual agreement among delegates, the old designations of *communist*, *majority*, *minority*, *socialist*, and the like were discarded in favor of *leftist*. Journalists covering the congress noted many familiar faces among the delegates, who appeared to be predominantly middle-aged. Attendance on the floor of the congress was sparse; the largest contingents of delegates gravitated toward the bar or relaxed on the terrace. Alexander Dubček declined an invitation to be guest of honor at the VL congress, choosing instead to be present for May Day celebrations in Madrid. Ironically, among the delegates attending was Taisto Sinisalo, who in 1969 led the minority revolt in the SKP to protest the majority's support for Dubček's Prague Spring.

The VL was formally registered with the Ministry of Justice as a political party on 31 May and announced that to that date the party had distributed more than 12,500 membership cards. Viialainen regretted, however, that the old political labels were still being applied to and by new members, implying that some retained a dual allegiance. (*HS*, 22 May, 1 June.)

The Central Committee met in Kuopio to prepare for the party's registration. The VL was described as having a "light" apparatus, much smaller than those of either the SKP or the SKDL. The committee confirmed that hiring for full-time positions on the professional staff would be on a competitive basis, not subject to patronage, and that each party worker's contract would be for a limited duration. Elected party officials were restricted to two three-year terms in office. The VL would be a decentralized party. District and functional organizations associated with the party were considered independent units, each with its own budget, rules and procedures, and structure. The district organizations were based entirely on SKDL and SKP district organizations that had agreed to transfer political activity to the new party. (*HS*, 24 May, 7 June.)

Although minority communists were urged to join VL organizations, the SKP-Y Central Committee announced that the "association" would continue political activities that were "competitive, overlapping, and parallel" with those of the new party, advocating "red policies for a green and just future." Officials also reaffirmed a long-held contention among the minority faction that the SKP-Y was the legitimate communist party in Finland and were reported in *Helsingen Sanomat* as having underscored the SKP-Y's role as providing a "Marxist forum" for the Finnish left. (*HS*, 21 May.)

Tiedonantaja was quick to clarify that the SKP-Y did not intend to form a Marxist faction within the VL and that minority communists joined the new party as individual members. The SKP-Y-as-forum, the party newspaper explained, was not meant to "espouse Marxism" as much as it was intended to offer an "open forum" where Marxists could come together. (*Ta*, 22 May.) The VL leadership was not convinced about the minority's intentions, however, recalling bad experiences in the past with Stalinists that hardly inspired confidence in their trustworthiness. One source joked that minority chairman Tennilä had already "switched sides a hundred times"; although that was an exaggeration, the point was made. Viialainen rebuked the SKP-Y for perpetuating divided loyalties in the new party and went on record several days later as refusing to accept members with dual allegiance. (*HS*, 22, 29 May.)

The debate on dual allegiance focused on the inclusion of DEVA members of Parliament in the VL delegation in the Eduskunta. The sixteen SKDL members became the VL parliamentary delegation of 3 May, Esko Helle continuing as group chairman. Tennilä stated that the DEVA delegation was prepared to merge with the VL group, but the date for the transfer of DEVA's political activity to the VL had already been postponed several times. Wahlström, a member of the VL group, pointed to the incongruity of accepting into the VL delegation Tennilä, Löyttyjärvi, and Ensio Laine, who were simultaneously officials of a competing political party (SKP-Y). Speaking for the VL caucus, he laid down conditions for admitting the DEVA delegation: formal disbanding of DEVA and the transfer of its party subsidy to the VL caucus; the resignation of former DEVA members of Parliament from posts in the SKP-Y, to be followed by dissolution of the party; and shutting down publication of *Tiedonantaja*. (*HS*, 3, 11 May; *Hb*, 3 May.)

Tennilä stepped down as chairman of the SKP-Y, and Löyttyjärvi and Laine resigned from the minority's Politburo in late July. Yrjö Häkanen, who had been general secretary, replaced Tennilä as SKP-Y chairman in September. DEVA disbanded on 9 September, and two days later its four-member delegation was inducted into the VL caucus, which had dropped demands for disbanding the SKP-Y and

closing the party newspaper. Nor were the four required to renounce membership in the SKP-Y. (*HS*, 12 September; *FBIS-WEU*, 10 September.)

The inclusion of Tennilä and the others threatened to provoke a rift between the VL leadership and the parliamentary caucus on the one side and former SKDL activists and majority communists in the new party's district organizations on the other. The latter argued that, although DEVA attracted less than 2 percent support in the polls, minority communists, who had one-fourth or more of the seats on district committees, would be able to pad VL electoral lists with their own candidates at the next general election. Earlier in the year, the Lapland SKP had refused to accept Tennilä as a candidate on the party list in that district. The VL district organization, which had succeeded the SKP organization in Rovaniemi (Lapland), sustained the refusal. Likewise, the VL's Varsinais-Suomi (Turku) district organization excluded Ensio Laine, chairman of the former DEVA caucus, from its list. District party officials appealed to Laine, a 25-year veteran in the Eduskunta from Turku, not to stand in the next election to save himself and the local party embarrassment. After some delay, the two district organizations reluctantly accepted Tennilä and Laine as candidates, apparently responding to pressure from party leaders in Helsinki for whom a unified leftist front on the March 1991 ballot outweighed consideration for local political sensitivities. (*HS*, 3 March, 21, 26, 28, 30 September, 7 October; *Hb*, 1 May.)

Some former majority communists in the Lapland district who were not reconciled to Tennilä's adoption proposed presenting a parallel list of candidates in the party primary from which the former minority leader's name would be deleted. A number in Rovaniemi turned in their recently issued VL membership cards to protest Tennilä's inclusion on the list. One local party officer objected that the VL "pets old Stalinists like an antique porcelain figure and spatters mud in the eyes of its own people." (*HS*, 30 September.)

The decision of the SKP in February to read itself out of existence was proof for members of the KTP that theirs was the only genuinely communist political movement left in Finland. Expressing an attitude typical of the small "revolutionary" party that splintered from the SKP-Y in 1988, party Deputy Chairman Pekka Tiainen advised leftists, "If you want to vote for communists, vote for us." The KTP, which began as a local revolt by minority communists in Helsinki and Uusimaa, counted seven district organizations around the country by early 1990 and claimed about a thousand card-carrying members. (*HS*, 27 February.) Disbanding the SKP and, later, DEVA did, in fact, leave the KTP as the only remaining communist movement that had registered party rights. (The SKP-Y is registered as a "political association" as distinct from a party.)

Although before the SKP congress Jarmo Wahlström had called for a complete and immediate divestiture of the party's assets, many non-communists in the leftist movement were suspicious that majority communists would control the transfer of SKP funds to tether the VL. (*HS, Hb*, 6 February.) Combined assets in accounts, investments, and property were estimated to be in excess of 150 million markkaa, but that figure was considered arbitrary because so much of it was tied up in a depressed real estate market. The SKP congress set a three-year deadline for the disposal of property and investments. Aside from an endowment earmarked for funding the staff responsible for carrying out this assignment, most liquid assets were turned over directly to the VL. Title to separate SKDL holdings transferred automatically to the VL when the former disbanded as a political party. These assets, which were widely dispersed, were brought together by the VL under the Avantisaatio (forward) Foundation, chaired by Salme Kandolin, proceeds from which would be used to fund party-sponsored cultural, educational, and labor activities. (*HS*, 27 July.)

In June, the VL moved its headquarters from Kulttuurialto, where it had inherited the SKDL's office space, to a modest building on Pasilakatu that was owned by a company recently divested by the SKP. Relocation was a cost-saving measure and a rationalization of office requirements for the new party's smaller staff, but, just as important from a political standpoint, the VL was seen to be escaping from reminders of its communist family background. In addition, Kulttuurialto, a building designed by Alvar Aalto, was suffering from the effects of deferred maintenance and needed to be closed for repairs. (*HS*, 28 June.)

Both the SKP and the SKP-Y had tried to take advantage of liberalized financial regulations in place since 1987 to build investment portfolios, and both had lost heavily from their speculations (see *YICA*, 1989). *Helsingen Sanomat* estimated that the SKP had lost 35 million markkaa in bad investments in 1989 alone. The press also inquired into reports that in a three-year period more than 40 million markkaa from unknown sources had been laundered through unidentified middlemen and funneled into secret accounts. Trusted custodians, it was believed, had periodically doled out just enough from these accounts to keep the party's official books balanced for inspection. (*HS*, 31 January.)

One of the party's more-embarrassing bad investments, reported in a popular magazine, was the purchase of a large quantity of condoms in Korea that were intended for sale at bargain prices to members; however, they were of such poor quality that they could not be marketed. The correspondent suggested that by disposing of them an opportunity had been lost to remedy the problem of declining party membership, which might have increased nightly had they been distributed as planned. (*Suomen Kuvalehti*, 19 January.)

Meanwhile, the SKP-Y hovered near bankruptcy because of business failures, the real estate squeeze, and the loss of important Soviet contracts by its Kursiivi printing plant. But SKP-Y officials laid a large part of the blame for the minority faction's dire financial situation on Markus Kainulainen, founder of the KTP. Kainulainen had been the SKP-Y's district chief in Uusimaa, and his district organization had retained title to valuable properties in Espoo and Vantaa when he made it the basis for the splinter party. To the amusement of *Kansan Uutiset*, Kainulainen at one point evicted the SKP-Y from offices where the KTP was the landlord. (*KU*, 9 March, 27 July.)

In the search for additional sources of income, the SKP-Y established a foundation entrusted with assisting potential donors to make out wills leaving the party as beneficiary. Less in jest than as an honest assessment of the situation, one party official was quoted as saying that the SKP-Y had nothing left to contribute to the VL except its debts. (Ibid.)

Citing declining circulation, rising costs, and the loss of subsidies from the Communist Party of the Soviet Union (CPSU), the editors of *Tiedonantaja* announced in September that the newspaper would become a weekly publication focusing on Marxist analysis of issues produced by a smaller staff. The editors reminded readers that, although it would support the program of the VL, the SKP-Y organ was Finland's only remaining communist newspaper. (*Ta*, 11 September.) The continued publication of *Tiedonantaja* by the SKP-Y was regarded by the VL as a serious impediment to the unity of the new party.

Public support for the VL in the polls declined

steadily, from 11.3 percent in June to under 10 percent by the end of the year. This compared to a combined vote of 13.6 percent for the SKDL and DEVA in the 1987 general election and indicated that the VL had not succeeded in attracting all former SKDL voters. Nor had former DEVA voters committed themselves. Many former SKDL organizations and units remained outside the VL as late as September. Ulpi Iivari, Social Democratic Party (SDP) secretary, actively courted one-time prominent SKDL figures, among them Reijo Käkelä and Ele Alenius, a governor of the Bank of Finland and former spokesman for the socialist caucus, who had refrained from joining the VL because of minority communist participation. (*HS*, 6 May.)

Kansan Uutiset explained in an editorial that ideological indecision was a problem: "Everyone wants a room in the VL," the paper concluded, "but nobody knows how to furnish it." It criticized the VL's rush to embrace the market economy. Although admitting that planned economies subject to political control did not work, the former SKP organ advised readers that "reliance on markets did not guarantee economic growth and conservation of the environment." (*KU*, 10 August.)

Exchanges with communist parties abroad dwindled in 1990. Tennilä and Laine visited Moscow as guests of the CPSU in May and again in August shortly before they resigned their SKP-Y posts. On the August trip, they met with Politburo member Genaadiy Yana, who was responsible for Finnish relations in the CPSU's International Department. Representing their respective parties, they agreed to cooperate in "revising the concepts of Marxism and Socialism." The Finns also met with Politburo member Boris Pugo, later named Soviet interior minister. (*Ta*, 25 May, 1 September.) The SKP-Y was on record in support of *perestroika*, "the essence of which is the development of democracy and ethnic self-determination." (*HS*, 21 May.)

Matti Viialainen defined the VL's relationship with the CPSU as "natural" rather than fraternal. He reported in May that exchanges with the CPSU and visits to the Soviet Union were planned but that the VL wanted to expand contacts with nationalist movements in that country and with "new leftist parties" being generated in the Soviet "multiparty system." He emphasized Finland's affinity with Estonia and the other Baltic republics. In July, Viialainen carried out part of his pledge by visiting Boris Yeltsin, president of the Russian Federated Soviet Socialist Republic. (*HS*, 4 July.)

Estonian Communist Party chairman Vaino Valjas came to Finland in January as a guest of the Paasikivi Society. He also met with President Mauno Koivisto during his visit. In a speech to a gathering of the society in Helsinki, Valjas expressed his party's desire for closer ties between Estonia and the Nordic countries. (Helsinki Domestic Service, 15 January; *FBIS-WEU*, 17 January.)

Biographies. *Claes-Johan Rudolf Andersson.* Elected chairman of the VL at the new party's founding congress in May 1990, Andersson, who had been better known as an author and jazz musician than as a politician, challenged SKP Politburo member Reijo Käkelä as dark horse candidate for chairmanship of the SKDL in 1988.

Andersson was born into a middle-class environment in Helsinki in 1937. He studied medicine at the University of Helsinki and subsequently practiced as a psychiatrist in public health facilities, an experience that reportedly was instrumental in shaping his political consciousness. He left medical practice in the early 1970s to devote himself full-time to writing, working initially with a subsidy from the writers' union. Andersson was also one of the rare Swedish-speaking Finns active in the SKDL. In the 1987 general election, he was elected to the Eduskunta, where he joined the SKDL's five-member socialist caucus. The following year, he won a seat on the Espoo city council. Andersson's surprise nomination to oppose Käkelä for the SKDL chairmanship was backed by trade union delegates as well as by many communists, whereas Käkelä had the support of the socialist bloc. Andersson, who won 40 percent of the vote, spoke out during his brief campaign for a more broad-based and open SKDL that was "courageous enough to engage in differences of opinion."

Salme Maria Kandolin. Named vice-chair of the new VL in 1990, Kandolin is a native of Uukuniemi in eastern Finland, where she was born in 1947. She has a degree in public administration from the University of Tampere and studied law at Leipzig in 1973–1974. Kandolin, a civil servant, was employed by the Ministry of Justice (1974–1981) and as a secretary to the parliamentary committee on education (1981–1988). Already an officer of the socialist faction of the SKDL, she was elected to the Eduskunta from the party list in 1987. Her nomination as general secretary of the SKDL in 1988 was unopposed. As Reijo Käkelä's personal choice as the front's noncommunist second in command, she promoted the establishment of the VL as a party open only to individual membership. Kandolin resigned her seat in the Eduskunta following her appointment as vice-chair of the VL.

Kandolin is an effective speaker who is fond of reminding audiences of her humble origins. Critics sometimes note the incongruity between her image as a "woman of the people" and her expensive life-style.

Kari Antero Uotila. Joint vice-chair of the VL with Salme Kandolin, Uotila was born in 1955 in Pertunmaa in Savo. He trained as a shipwright after leaving school and was subsequently employed as a sheet metal worker at the Wartsila shipyards and at the Masa yards. Uotila came to public notice as a high-profile union shop steward in the troubled shipbuilding industry and as an outspoken representative of the younger generation of SKP activists. He challenged SKP chairman Jarmo Wahlström's plans for the party's fusion in a broad-based VL, arguing instead for a loose leftist union of progressive groups that would include a separately constituted SKP and allow participation by reconciled minority communists. He was elected to the Espoo city council in 1988 and remains an official of the Trade Union Federation (SAK).

Although the distinction between socialist and communist tendencies has been formally erased within the VL, Uotila clearly is regarded as the communist counterbalance to Kandolin in the new party's leadership. He is also expected to block attempts by Esko-Juhani Tennilä, a minority communist, to gain greater influence in the VL (see *YICA*, 1990).

Matti Tapani Viialainen. Party secretary of the VL, Viialainen was elected at the founding congress in May 1990. He is also a company director and business consultant and has served as a consultant to the SKDL parliamentary delegation, the parliamentary defense committee, and the Ministry of Foreign Affairs.

Viialainen was born in Leppavirta in 1953. He received a degree with honors in political science and history from the University of Helsinki, where he was an officer in both the SKDL's youth league and the SKDL's student association. Following graduation, he remained active as a party worker and was an organizer in the soldiers' union while doing his military service. Viialainen initially sided with the minority, but he switched his allegiance to the majority faction in time to escape the 1985 "purge" of minority communists from the SKP. Until the party was dissolved, he led an independent SKP cell in Malminkartano. Viialainen's nomination as general secretary of the VL was strongly supported by minority communist participants in the party congress. Viialainen brings with him into the VL leadership experience in public relations and a background in international relations.

Robert Rinehart
Washington, D.C.

France

Population. 56,358,331 (*World Fact Book*); 56,556,000, French census (*Témoignages*, 30 June–1 July)
Party. French Communist Party (Parti Communiste Français, PCF)
Founded. 1920
Membership. 200,000 (claimed, *FBIS-WEU*, 30 January 1989)
General Secretary. Georges Marchais
Politburo. 20 members: Georges Marchais, Charles Fiterman, Claude Billard, Pierre Blotin, Antoine Casanova, Jean-Claude Gayssot, Maxime Gremetz, Guy Hermier, Philippe Herzog, Jackie Hoffmann, André Lajoinie, Francette Lazard, René Le Guen, Roland Leroy, Gisèle Moreau, Jean-Paul Magnon, Pierre Zarka, Alain Bocquet, Robert Hue, Francis Wurtz
Secretariat. 7 members: Jean-Claude Gayssot, Maxime Gremetz, André Lajoinie, Gisèle Moreau, Pierre Blotin, Jean-Paul Magnon, Pierre Zarka
Central Committee. 154 members
Status. Legal
Last Congress. Twenty-seventh, 18–22 December; next congress planned for December 1993
Last Election. 1989, European Parliament, 7.7 percent
Auxiliary Organizations. General Confederation of Labor (CGT); World Peace Council; Movement of Communist Youth of France (MCJF); Committee for the Defense of Freedom in France

and the World; Association of Communist and Republican Representatives

Publications. *l'Humanité*, Paris, Roland Leroy, director, daily national organ; *l'Echo du centre*, Limoges, daily; *Liberté*, Lille, daily; *la Marseillaise*, Marseille, daily; *l'Humanité Dimanche*, Paris, weekly magazine; *la Révolution*, weekly publication of the Central Committee; *la Terre*, weekly; *Cahiers du Communisme*, monthly, theoretical journal; *Europe*, literary journal; *Economie et politique*, economic journal; 5 journals published by the Marxist Research Institute; 4 monthly magazines. Other periodicals on sports, children's themes, and the like and books on political, economic, and social topics are published by Editions sociales, the PCF publishing house in Paris.

The French Communist Party turned 70 in 1990, as did its general secretary, Georges Marchais. Both anniversaries, however, were somber milestones for the PCF, which began and ended its year mired in the same misfortunes that have long beset it—marginalization in French political life, declining membership, internecine factionalism, reactionary leadership, and a public image of shopworn obsolescence. Rebounded from a heart attack that hospitalized him late in 1989, Marchais was forced to spend virtually the entire year dodging accusations of failure and incompetence and defending himself from a hail of increasingly bitter charges, ranging from creeping insanity to recalcitrant Stalinism. Accumulating evidence of the party's impotence and plummeting esteem, together with a growing sense of rank and file isolation from the changes that were overtaking the rest of the communist world, helped drive internal dissent to a new pitch and produced yet a third current of opposition in the already faction-ridden party, this one led by former Transportation Minister Charles Fiterman.

Meanwhile, the run-up to the party's Twenty-seventh Congress in December featured a new round of infighting over the leadership's stolid refusal to end its tradition of democratic centralism and permit a free discussion of the party's staggering internal problems. On the international front, relations with Moscow remained at low ebb, in large part because PCF bosses continued to stonewall acceptance of the democratizing and reformist implications of *perestroika* and *glasnost'*. Domestically, the PCF remained locked in unofficial and painful parliamentary alliance with President Mitterrand's Socialists, but events at year's end showed clearly that the tenuous leftist partnerships, at both the national and the local levels, were becoming badly frayed. More than one pundit noted that, in these circumstances, the party's birthday congress failed to convey the attitude of proud tradition and staying power that the leadership had hoped and instead gave the unwanted impression of ossification and spent vitality. As if to highlight the flickering embers of reaction within the PCF, Marchais suffered yet another heart attack in late December, virtually ensuring that 1991 would begin on a new wave of speculation about his political longevity.

Leadership and Internal Affairs. By early 1990, majority conservatives in the PCF Politburo and the party's increasingly beleaguered leader confronted three as yet vaguely differentiated currents of communist dissidence, one outside and two still within the party. The oldest faction, *renovateur* (renovator), was led by renegade former Politburo spokesman Pierre Juquin. Declared by the leadership to have placed himself outside the party because of his public refusal to accept the line of the Twenty-sixth Congress, Juquin had offered himself as a communist alternative to the PCF's official presidential candidate—André Lajoinie—in the 1988 presidential balloting. The renovators now operate almost entirely as outside critics of the party leadership or on the fringes of the PCF.

The *reconstructeur* (reconstructor) faction, led by former Central Committee dissidents Félix Damette, Claude Poperen, and Marcel Rigout, is distinguished by its early decision to keep arm's length from Juquin and to rebuild communism from within the PCF, largely by replacing its hard-line leadership and introducing democratic debate on the party line. By the end of 1990, however, some members of this faction were reportedly weighing the prospect of gathering expelled dissidents into an alternative French communist party, outside the PCF.

The new *refondateur* (refounder) current is headed by former Transportation Minister Charles Fiterman and includes Politburo member Guy Hermier (former director of the Central Committee's theoretical organ *la Révolution*) and former Minister Anicet Le Pors. The refounders differ little from the reconstructors in their analysis of the party's condition and necessary remedies, but they are apparently more determined to apply only subtle pressure from within. The refounders are widely considered the Gorbachevien faction of the PCF because of their insistence that party leaders embrace *perestroika* more enthusiastically. Not surprisingly, Fiterman is widely touted by the noncommunist press as Gorbachev's preference for Marchais's successor.

As the PCF's year began with Marchais under relentless and almost unprecedented attack, Fiterman had every reason to expect that he would soon become—as one irreverent French daily put it— "the Egon Krenz of French communism." Criticism of Marchais escalated noticeably in the wake of his mid-November 1989 performance on national television, when he clumsily feigned memory lapse as to the party's 1961 position on the Berlin Wall and just as maladroitly confessed to similar forgetfulness when jolted by questions of whether dissident calls within the PCF for admission of "error" concerning PCF support of the Soviet invasion of Afghanistan had been initiated by Soviet foreign minister Shevardnadze. Said one rival in the party leadership, "he has gone off his rocker"; and another insider said that "Georges has gone crazy." Even the leftist press likened Marchais to a "punch drunk boxer" and reported that the PCF delegation in the National Assembly and the faithful at the party's bunkerlike headquarters—Place Colonel-Fabien—were "stunned." (*Libération*, 17 November 1989.) This, together with Marchais's recurrent heart ailment, touched off a wave of analyses, many of which concluded that Marchais was "finished," that he had come to "the end," and that, as one centrist newspaper put it, "one thing is certain, Marchais will go" (le *Quotidien de Paris*, 9 January; "Marchais: La fin," *le Point*, 15 January).

Marchais's agonies more than doubled with the impact in France of the Romanian "Christmas revolution." In the exaggerated French media coverage of events in Bucharest, the noncommunist press spotlighted photos of Marchais enjoying summer vacations with the Ceauşescus in happier years. The galloping perception that Marchais had supported the Ceauşescu dictatorship and had even benefited from it struck a responsive chord among party dissidents, who saw a parallel in the PCF boss's own attachment to democratic centralism and the defunct Romanian regime's struggle to stifle dissent. Particularly embarrassing, Marchais had dispatched a prominent delegation to the November Romanian Communist Party congress, barely one month before the dictator's execution. Said one communist officeholder, "If Georges Marchais had been in Romania, he would have behaved like Ceauşescu." Party reformers immediately released a statement charging that when Marchais visited

Romania in 1984 he "could not ignore the fact that he was the guest of a butcher." Still other critics reminded communists that Marchais and other hard-liners had engineered the expulsion of 1,200 party members in 1985 for proposing a condemnation of the Ceauşescu regime during a party congress. (Paris, AFP, 28 December 1989; *le Point*, 1 January; *CSM*, 11 January.)

Caught flat-footed by the dramatic events in Bucharest, Marchais and party bosses at first refused comment and then came in with their now well-honed reaction that the balance sheet on the collapsing Eastern regime was "globally positive" and that people in the East were "wrong" to trade socialism for social democracy. Official PCF silence on the unfolding Romanian rout of Ceauşescu prompted Petre Roman—the new Romanian prime minister who was then in France—to confess that he had the "impression" that the PCF had "not yet carried out a thorough analysis of its Stalinism." (*NYT*, 9 January.)

The fall of communist regimes throughout Eastern Europe and revelations about the corruption of despots who had been close comrades of PCF bosses gave party dissidents a windfall of opportunities to underscore the spectacular poverty of Marchais's leadership. Former communist minister Marcel Rigout and expelled Central Committeeman Félix Damette—both, with Claude Poperen, movers of the reconstructor faction of the party—tarred Marchais with his failure to criticize the activities of East European regimes and drew the obvious parallels between the disintegrating Eastern bloc dictatorships and the "parodies of democracy" in the PCF. Rigout, meanwhile, played variations on the theme that Marchais's ouster was a "necessary condition" for the party's revival and for the PCF to finally confront "the complete failure of [its] bureaucratic and statist socialism." (*NYT*, 9 January; *le Monde*, 4, 30 January.)

Marchais's suddenly enhanced level of vulnerability gave rise to unprecedented party discussion, even among the leadership, about his succession. The reconstructors declared the issue of Marchais's departure open and moved for an irregular session of the party congress to decide the issue. Jean-Pierre Brard, communist mayor for the red belt Seine-Saint-Denis constituency, implied on national television that Marchais was old enough to retire. Meanwhile, Jacques Isabet, communist mayor of the Paris suburb of Pantin, refused to mince words: "I wish that Georges Marchais would go," he said, "I am for retirement at age 60." (*le*

Point, 15 January, 18 December.) French media speculated that the beleaguered party boss would engineer his own, more graceful departure at the coming party congress, turning over the secretary generalship to a trusted protégé—failed presidential candidate André Lajoinie and Politburo enforcer Jean-Claude Gayssot were most often mentioned—and retire to the éminence grise of an improvised party "presidency" (Libération, 17 November 1989; le Point, 1, 15 January; The Economist, 17 February).

Meanwhile, Fiterman—also recently released from the hospital after recovering from injuries sustained in an automobile accident—largely failed to reinvigorate the attack he had launched against Marchais and entrenched hard-liners the previous fall. Surprisingly, he and other refounders assumed a low profile—le Monde said they bore more of a resemblance to "repenters"—apparently hoping that in the storm of protests and personal invective Marchais would somehow fall prey to the weight of his considerable mistakes and that a "palace revolution" would catapult Fiterman to the party leadership in a bloodless victory (Oliver Biffaud, le Monde, 20 January). Nonetheless, the newly hoisted banners of the refounders reportedly attracted new blood to the ranks of party dissidents, including former Marchais stalwarts who were, like Fiterman and others, determined to remain within the party as voices for reform. In addition to Hermier, the left-wing press connected two other Politburo members with the refounders—longtime party economic guru Philippe Herzog (reportedly eager to mediate between Fiterman and the conservatives) and Antoine Casanova, a recently elected member of the Politburo, the head of PCF's intellectual section, and the editor of the party's venerable intellectual journal la Pensée.

Fiterman's slowness to follow up his fall offensive may have given Marchais just enough room to maneuver. Regardless of circumstances, Marchais and his orthodox allies, including l'Humanité director Roland Leroy and editor Claude Cabanne, launched a vigorous and bitter counterattack against the secretary general's critics. Labeling all such criticisms part of a rightist conspiracy to destroy communism, hard-liners branded party reformers as heretics and lackeys of Socialist president Mitterrand—the latter charge almost certainly a reference to press reports of close relations between the former communist ministers (Fiterman, Rigout, and Le Pors) in Mitterrand's first administration and prominent Socialists, such as former

Prime Minister Pierre Mauroy. (le Point, 19 November.) Marchais blasted dissent within the PCF as "anti-communist." Responding to dissident charges of Marchais's complicity in the Ceauşescu dictatorship, l'Humanité orchestrated a four-page special feature "putting the record straight on relations between French officials and Ceauşescu," whereas Marchais gave numerous renditions on television and radio of a new speech claiming that his relations with the Ceauşescus had permitted him to intervene on behalf of victims of the repression "with some success" (Paris, AFP, 28 December 1989) and that, in any event, he had "never been on particularly good terms" with Romanian communists.

Help for the counteroffensive came from a number of sources but none more robust than from Pravda's Paris correspondent, Vladimir Bolshakov (a confidant of the l'Humanité leadership). Bolshakov eagerly took up the refrain that dark forces, prematurely gleeful at the "collapse of communism" in Eastern Europe, were targeting the PCF and its leaders. According to Bolshakov, "virtually all the mass media" of France were involved in a "carefully coordinated campaign" to persecute French communists. (Pravda, 12 January). Meanwhile, issue after issue of l'Humanité published evidence that directly linked prominent dissenters to long-standing "plots" against Marchais. For example, Pas-de-Calais federation secretary Rémy Auchedé contributed "a reminiscence of 1984" that linked both Fiterman and leading reconstructor Félix Damette to a 1984 plan to stage "a veritable putsch at the center of the party," a plan, according to Auchedé, reminiscent of the way things were done "under Stalin." Still, Marchais took pains to distinguish between Fiterman and the reconstructor but in a way that misrepresented Fiterman's grievances as merely "political disagreements" with a "majority of the Politburo" in contrast to "other comrades [who]. . . want us to stop being communists. . . [and become] a reserve force for the PS." (le Monde, 6 February, reporting a television interview of 4 February; le Point, 15 January.)

More important, Marchais and the conservatives hatched a plan to organize their counteroffensive against "anti-communists" at the federation level. In a telex to federal (department-level) secretaries, later leaked to the noncommunist press, party leaders called for an ideological war against the anti-communist bombardment. A task force, composed of several members of the propaganda group of the Central Committee and 25 members of the party's national propaganda and communications commission, was empowered to direct the campaign at the department level. Getting out the leadership line would be accomplished by quickly produced and disseminated tracts—so-called *riposte rapide*—designed to reach "6 million salaried employees" of private and state-owned enterprises. A key interest of the leadership message was to deny as often as possible the widely circulated and reported story that Marchais intended to use the party's 70th anniversary congress to announce his own elevation to the PCF presidency. (*le Point*, 15 January.) Marchais's constant answer to such suggestions was that "for the time being, I have absolutely no desire to go" (Paris, AFP, 28 December 1989).

The PCF was neither about to change its name nor drop its use of the hammer and sickle, as had other beleaguered communist parties and as was becoming a mainstay among the demands of party dissidents. PCF leaders also stonewalled the more important reform demand for an extraordinary congress—or at least for an early convening of the already scheduled Twenty-seventh Congress—to take up the issues of the PCF's declining prominence in French politics and the leadership's refusal to democratize and modernize the party. The liveliness of Marchais's counterattack notwithstanding, dissenters of the reconstructor faction stepped up their own attacks. Unofficial spokesman Damette claimed early in the new year that "approximately one third, if not more, of the PCF membership" now supported the reform movement, not to mention the "thousands of communists" who had already been "excluded from the party . . . because they did not agree with Georges Marchais's political line" (*le Monde*, 4 January). But the reconstructor challenge was not based solely on the leadership's failure or on the need for democratization. According to Damette, the PCF remained bogged down in "a veritable political culture that emerged from the mold of the Third International." Connecting the PCF's troubles with those in Eastern Europe, it therefore was "part of the same collapse." Damette set the tone for the reconstructor argument by concluding that "it is the essence and very definition of a communist party that must be questioned . . . what is now collapsing is the concept of the communist party as society's vanguard party, society's leadership party" (*le Monde*, 4, 30 January).

Throughout the year the refounder critique remained substantially focused on the failure of leadership and especially the paucity of internal democracy. What Fiterman, Le Pors, and Hermier drew attention to was the continued use of democratic centralism to suffocate dissent and evade the honest exchange of views that, in their reckoning, would be the party's only hope of regeneration. Marchais's committee for the *riposte rapide* and the leadership's ability to select federation officials continued to function in 1990, according to dissident communist historian Philippe Robrieux, as a method for quarantining reformists. Despite this power, however, substantial dissent continued to emanate from several departmental organizations throughout the year, notably from the federations of Doubs, Corse-du-Sud, Val-de-Marne, and Haute-Vienne and, most worrisome to party conservatives, among communist mayors. Fiterman's own Var federation, Hermier's Bouche-du-Rhône, and the red belt stronghold of Seine-Saint-Denis produced nettlesome rumblings from time to time. Leadership problems also continued to plague the troubled PCF-controlled Confederation of Labor (CGT). Reform-minded CGT secretary general Henri Krasucki—long alienated from Marchais and fellow Politburo members—continued to press for less heavy-handed PCF direction of the union. Clearly responding to long-standing signs that the CGT rank and file wanted the union to focus on work-related issues, Krasucki also declared that the CGT would adopt a line that was more *syndicale* and, by implication, less political. But Krasucki's efforts to chart a more unionist course for the CGT were bedeviled throughout the year by Marchais loyalists within the union's leadership, notably Krasucki's own deputies, Louis Viannet and Michel Warocholak—both handpicked by Marchais to thwart Krasucki's reformist tendencies. Viannet also remained the widely reported choice of Politburo conservatives to replace Krasucki, if the opportunity should arise. (*le Point*, 18 December 1989, 15 January; *Libération*, 17 November.) Meanwhile, Fiterman's return to the Central Committee in mid-February from his near-fatal accident was reportedly greeted with silence (*le Point*, 19 February), but his relaunching of the refounder reform effort—however tardy—drew increasingly sharp reactions.

Fiterman's efforts were assisted by accumulating indications that rank and file communists, demoralized by the party's doldrums, were continuing, as in years past, to desert PCF ranks. Although party bosses continued to boast that the PCF could count "over 600,000 members" (Jean-Claude Gayssot, *The French Communist Party*), one authoritative study of the PCF (undisputed even by the party's academics) maintained that current membership could be no more than 330,000 and, if trends since 1987 (the last year for reliable estimates) had continued, probably far fewer. Still other observers put the effective strength of the party much lower, between 100,000 and 150,000, as anecdotal testimony mounted to highlight how party leaders have cooked the books on membership figures over the years. (Thierry Portes, "The PC: Cracks in the Cathedral," *le Figaro*, 13, 15 December 1989; Philippe Button, "Le PCF depuis 1985, une organisation en crise," *Revue 'Communisme'*, nos. 18–19, 1988.)

Moreover, according to academic studies of PCF sociology, the party continued its dramatic shift away from its traditional moorings in the working class and youth movements and toward a more white-collar, lower-middle-class electorate. Reliable studies of the PCF vote in 1988 and 1989 further indicated that the party was losing strength among women, who once constituted just over 50 percent of its members, and young people, who have now fallen from 41 percent to below 25 percent of the rank and file. Meanwhile, factory workers and laborers, who in 1979 accounted for 47 percent of the party militants, now constituted only 30 percent of the faithful, the slack being taken up by a fairly dramatic shift to white-collar employees (from 18 to 29 percent between 1979 and 1989). (*le Figaro*, 15 December 1989.) Corroborating indications from opinion surveys and voting in recent elections, which showed communist vote-getting strength down to around 7 percent nationally, underscored the PCF's spectacular unpopularity, especially that of its leaders. Soundings throughout the year showed Marchais skimming the bottom of lists of politicians to whom French voters were willing to say they felt "close." Only 9 percent felt "close" to the PCF boss in *le Point*'s February "Baromètere tricolore"; he had improved to only 10 percent by December. (*le Point,* 12 February, 10 December.) Similar surveys indicated that only an embarrassing 18 percent of factory workers and manual laborers wishes "to see Georges Marchais play an important role in the coming months and years" (*le Figaro*, 15 December 1989). Moreover, polls that asked French citizens to express confidence or no confidence in political leaders consistently showed that extreme-right National Front leader Jean-Marie Le Pen could best Marchais by a margin of about four percentage points (*Paris Match*, 15 November).

Despite these further indications of slipping support and despite the relentless winter attacks on Marchais, the leadership was able to rebound partly on the strength of off-year elections in which incumbent communist mayors in Colombes, Clichy-sous-Bois, and Pantin managed to hold their offices (*le Point,* 2 April). Meanwhile, as if to celebrate its role in defending Marchais from the attacks of critics and the emerging authority of its director, Roland Leroy, *l'Humanité* announced the conversion of its Sunday edition, *l'Humanité Dimanche*, into a jazzy new magazine. By spring, the leadership was able to announce the "unanimous" support of the Central Committee for holding the Twenty-seventh Congress as scheduled, between 18 and 22 December. (*le Point*, 21 May; Paris, Antenne 2 television, 14 May.)

But indications of restored harmony proved ephemeral, as the Central Committee plenum of mid-May became an insurrection against the leadership line. Critics were galvanized into action by the emergence of the Politburo majority's draft resolution for the coming congress. CGT leader Henri Krasucki and now suspect party economist Philippe Herzog were unexpectedly absent from voting on the draft resolution, which had been drawn up by Marchais protégée Gisèle Moreau. (*le Point*, 21 May; Paris Domestic Service, 16 May.) In an atmosphere described by one observer as "generally quite morose," party reformers blasted the leadership's hallowed cult of unanimity by abstaining on the resolution. Prominent in the present but not voting column stood Fiterman, Hermier, Le Pors, and the PCF's one remaining intellectual of national stature, the philosopher Lucien Seve. Le Pors took the occasion to rub salt in Marchais's wounds by proposing a motion of censure over the publication of the general secretary's new book, *Democracy*. Le Pors's point, which proved a nonstarter in the gloomy Central Committee, was that by coming just six months before the congress, the publication constituted an "irregularity" in preparations for the congress. (Paris Domestic Service, 16 May; Moscow, TASS, 12 September.) The leadership's almost incredible reaction to the hullabaloo at the plenum—delivered to the press by Marchais and Moreau—was that while there were disagreements in the leadership and even in the Politburo, there was "no internal crisis" or "divisions" within the PCF. But the party could not conceal the fact that new faces within the Central Committee had joined Fiterman and Le Pors in opposition, including the historian Roger Martelli, regional secretary of Lorraine, Roland Favaro, and Marcel Trigon, mayor of Arueil in Georges Marchais's home district. (*Le Point*, 21 May.) The specter of new defections from the Central Committee, the prospect that the continuously organizing refounders would present an alternative resolution, and the threat by reconstructors to demonstrate in front of PCF headquarters marred Georges Marchais's birthday celebration (7 June), but the general secretary's birthday message to the dwindling faithful was a defiant one—the PCF would never change its name and, by implication, would never sacrifice its traditions. (Hanoi Domestic Service, 7 June; *FBIS-EAS*, 11 June.) Although Marchais also announced at every opportunity that, despite events in the East, communism was alive and well, the thickening air of gloom that hung over the party's preparations for the coming congress was noticeably augmented by the deaths in early July of Marchais stalwart, Central Committee secretary, and Paris municipal councillor Paul Laurent and Politburo conservative Gustave Ansart. (Paris Domestic Service, 8 July; Antenne 2 television, 9 July; *NYT*, 12 July; *le Monde*, 26 December.)

After the party's summer hiatus, which seemed longer than most, the Central Committee gathering in September—the ritual beginning of the PCF's political year—made clear that reformers did indeed intend to make life difficult for the leadership's well-telegraphed hope of orchestrating an old-style congress, colorless, odorless, tasteless, and totally prepared to accept the new Politburo line. In what was described as an "animated" session, Fiterman forced the September plenum to consider a 23-page minority resolution for the party congress, which proposed a drastic shake-up of the PCF organization and fundamental democratization of party procedures. The three-day session rejected the proposal as an official preparatory text for the congress and adopted the Moreau draft, but Marchais and the party bosses agreed to publish Fiterman's text in *l'Humanité* as a gesture to "party democracy." (Paris, Antenne 2 television, 21 September; Paris Domestic Service, 22 September; Paris, AFP, 23 September; *FBIS*, Hanoi Domestic Service, 1 October.) In an equally transparent effort to marginalize dissent within the Central Committee and the Politburo, Marchais named Fiterman to a special commission, headed by hard-liner André Lajoinie, charged to select rank and file comments on the draft resolution that would be published in the Forum column of *l'Humanité* in the run up to the congress. After less than a month, however, the split

between orthodox and reformers widened substantially, and in early November Fiterman abruptly quit the ad hoc commission in a letter charging that the process for selecting comment on the leadership platform was no more than "censorship." Fiterman particularly complained that the few critical letters that were published were later singled out for harsh rebuttal in *l'Humanité* "but without any right of reply." Fiterman's fellow commission members published a collective reply in the same issue of *l'Humanité*, lambasting the resignation and Fiterman's views as "excessive" and "very severe." (Paris, AFP, 6 November.) After a week of "extreme tensions" at PCF headquarters, however, Marchais made a self-styled "overture" to Fiterman and the reformers. Declaring that the leadership draft was "only a point of departure" but affirming that substituting Fiterman's draft would be "out of the question," Marchais called on his erstwhile Politburo colleague to "resume his place" on the publications commission. Fiterman took this as an offer of negotiation and listed his conditions for "working together": guaranteed pluralistic expression at all levels of the party, a procedure for electing federation and section leadership bodies that would guarantee "incorporating diversity," and leadership guarantees that the congress would be allowed to "rewrite the final resolution." Reformers pressed for a special Central Committee meeting to formalize debate on Fiterman's demands. Party hardliners ignored these demands, and some reportedly began to grumble that Marchais was going too far in making concessions to Fiterman's "social democratic" ambitions. (*Libération*, 14, 17–18 November.)

As the party's Twenty-seventh Congress opened in the chilly and dreary sports complex in the working-class Paris suburb of Saint-Ouen, it was clear to everyone that democratic centralism had once again worked its magic, producing 1,500 delegates who were primed to approve the leadership line. Party leaders were able to announce on 10 December that 92 percent of the delegates already backed the draft; federation meetings were so well choreographed, said one leftist newspaper, that the selection of delegates was merely "housekeeping." (*Libération*, 10 December.) Reconstructor leader Claude Poperen complained to the press that although 20 to 25 percent of the PCF favored reform, the process for selecting delegates had clearly "filtered out" all but 2 or 3 percent. Poperen set the tone for much of the reformist pessimism at the congress by also declaring that the PCF would be "the last communist party in Europe to refuse change, even after Albania." Meanwhile, party bosses like Marchais and Leroy pointed to Fiterman's continued membership on the Politburo as proof that the "Communists are using their democratic rules better than ever." (Paris, AFP, 18 December.)

As snow storms battered France outside the sports palace and delegates shivered within, Marchais delivered a three-hour keynote report on the party that portrayed French communists as relentlessly high-minded and world communism as on the brink of a glorious renaissance. Delegates and congress organizers brushed aside Anicet Le Pors's complaints that Marchais produced the leadership report without asking anyone. As expected, an overwhelming majority of delegates approved the report; just 22 abstained and only 3 voted against. After approving Marchais's report by a margin of 98.9 percent, the handpicked assembly reelected Marchais to yet an eighth term as party general secretary, with Le Pors casting the lone dissenting vote. As in the past, Fiterman and a handful of dissidents later spoke to the clearly hostile audience. The crowd grew abusive after one reform spokesman criticized the party on television, his face and voice electronically disguised. Marchais held out an olive branch, promising to reform the party's statutes at the next congress, set for 1993, but reformers noted that this would be after France's next legislative elections. Fiterman's summary judgment on the congress was that although there had been "a few advances, . . . on essential questions the controlling line remains the same." (Reuters, 21 December; Paris, AFP, 22 December; le Monde, 21, 22 December.) Almost as an afterthought to the congress, the Central Committee voted to retain Fiterman and Hermier on the Politburo but added five new members, all more orthodox Marxists. The new members replaced the three Politburo members (Marchais loyalists Gaston Plissonnier, René Piquet, and Madéleine Vincent) who retired and the two (Gustave Ansart and Paul Laurent) who died in 1990. (Paris, AFP, 22 December; le Monde, 26 December.)

But conservative celebrations of their successful congress were short-lived. Four days after adjournment, Marchais suffered yet another heart attack. After two days in intensive care, Marchais emerged from the hospital claiming that his latest heart attack had been only "a light problem" and protesting that "retirement isn't for me." (Paris Domestic Service, Paris, AFP, 26 December; AP, 28 December.)

Domestic Affairs. In a year that was virtually free of elections, the party's domestic agenda was crowded with an assortment of both emotional and bread-and-butter issues, most revolving around the PCF's souring relations with François Mitterrand's governing Socialists and the party's continuing opposition to the extreme-right National Front. Throughout 1990, the PCF persisted in its informal parliamentary alliance with the government of Prime Minister Michel Rocard but with increasing indications that the party's supportive abstentions gained it no leverage over Socialist policies. Governing with only a minority, Rocard often depended on both independent centrist and communist votes (or abstentions) to pass legislation and to survive a barrage of Gaullist censure motions. Certain that communists would either vote for the left or abstain rather than side with the right, Rocard took communist support for granted and was able to pay almost nothing for the votes of the 26 communist deputies. This position cut two ways for the PCF leadership: On the one hand, they were a de facto part of the governing leftist majority, and therefore the media sought out their views and made a fuss over how communists would vote on any issue. On the other hand, it was a persistent embarrassment to PCF bosses that they got nothing for their support and were even expected to back Rocard in social and fiscal policies that ran counter to PCF constituent views. Moreover, Rocard held over PCF heads the threat of a return to a proportional voting system— like the one enacted by Mitterrand in 1984—which studies showed would eliminate the PCF from the National Assembly. By year's end, however, PCF willingness to preserve the Rocard government had worn thin.

Although communists generally held their collective noses and continued to support or at least abstain from voting on Socialist legislation, PCF spokesmen increasingly served up undiluted vitriol on the theme of Socialist corruption and the conspiracy between Socialists and rightists to subvert justice and destroy the communist party. The first serious test of the PCF's tacit support came in May and concerned a controversial rider to an election reform bill, which effectively granted amnesty to politicians guilty of violating election laws. Having bailed out the Rocard government on numerous censure motions and with 75 percent of public opinion running solidly against the government amnesty, the communists toyed with the notion of a revolt. At first, however, party spokesmen made light of the issue, calling it an "absurd right-wing operation," but Marchais finally realized the seriousness of the problem and called a special Central Committee meeting to consider how the party should cast its 26 votes on the Gaullist motion. When the vote came, communists lined up behind Rocard, who apparently provided the PCF with a figleaf by restricting the scope of the bill's amnesty provisions. (Paris, AFP, 8, 9 May; *Financial Times,* 9 May.)

Most important, however, the party's support for Rocard gained it no leverage at all on the hottest policy issue of the spring—the government's plan to separate the post and telecommunications services of the government monopoly that was heavily organized by the communist-controlled CGT. Division, which would have weakened the CGT's grip on both services, was also opposed by other trade unions and was especially irksome to communists because it came at the very moment the CGT could see Renault slipping from their control through Rocard's plan to denationalize the auto giant. Krasucki made common cause with the noncommunist unions in May, bringing thousands of workers into the Paris streets for an early start to the strike season. Animosity ran so strong that Krasucki refused to participate with Labor Minister Jean-Pierre Soisson and other union leaders in a joint celebration of the centenary of May Day. (*le Point*, 26 March, 7 May; *Financial Times*, 9 May; *Atlantic*, August.)

Although relations were strained at the top of both the PCF and the Socialist party and although there was no question of managing another Union de Gauche (Union of the Left) any time soon, worsening relations now began to put pressure on the local political pacts that had survived the breakup of the Union de Gauche in 1983 and that both leftist parties had preserved in the interest of denying local offices to the right. There were fairly widespread reports, most from Socialist officials, that it was becoming more difficult to bring Socialist voters out to back communist incumbents where election agreements called for them to do so. This was especially the case in mayoral elections in the Parisian suburbs of Pantin and Clichy-sous-Bois, where Socialist activists complained publicly that their militants would not turn out for communists who headed the joint leftist tickets. (*le Point*, 19 February.)

Relations grew measurably worse after mid-November, when communists broke with the Rocard government on a motion of censure. The PCF defection focused on the government's plan to sponsor a 1.1 percent annual tax on salaries and wages (a so-called General Social Contribution [GSC]) in order to hold the line on government spending and yet finance the increasingly burdensome French social security system. Both the PCF and the CGT opposed the tax vehemently, as did a large plurality of the French population. (Reuters, 22 October; *Libération*, 16 November.) Already furious at Rocard's post and telecommunications measures and at the Renault decision to merge part of its operations with Volvo (thereby closing down its communist-ridden flagship factory at Ballincourt) (*Les Echos*, 26 February; *Atlantic*, August), Krasucki determined to launch a major fall labor offensive on the issue of the GSC. Beginning in October, CGT leaders called a series of spot strikes of public service workers, which at one point were timed to coincide with a 24-hour work stoppage by Paris taxi drivers. (Reuters, 22 October.) Finally, in mid-November, the CGT mobilized over 10,000 strikers (not 40,000 as claimed) in an antitax protest, the effect of which was magnified because it came in tandem with a massive demonstration by more than 300,000 high-school students organized in part by the Communist Youth Movement (MJCF) to pressure Rocard for better conditions in schools and more money for education (*le Point*, 12 November; Paris, AFP, 13, 14 November). The issue came to a showdown in late November, when conservatives in the National Assembly moved to censure the GSC. In an unprecedented break with the Socialists, the communists sided with the right, including the National Front, in voting no confidence in Rocard. (Paris, Dow Jones, 19 November.) Although the government survived by garnering a few centrist votes, the episode further embittered PCF relations with the Socialists, some of whom now promised political reprisals against the communists. Much of the press speculation centered on whether this meant that local alliances of the left were endangered by what most Socialists viewed as the PCF treachery.

In a matter of lesser political importance to the PCF, communists joined with parties across most of the French political spectrum in denouncing the apparently escalating acts of racism and intolerance, cast into bold relief by the much-publicized desecration of Jewish graves in a cemetery near Avignon. Communist mayors were in the thick of the burgeoning controversy over the thorny issue of regulating Arab immigration to France. The problem for the PCF was especially acute in Clichy-sous-Bois, where communist mayor Christian Chapuis watched in embarrassment as 30 percent of his constituents bolted to the National Front over swelling numbers of North Africans in their community, and at Vaulx-en-Velin, near Lyons, where communist mayor Maurice Charrier confronted a wild rampage by mostly Arab youths fueled by resentment at what the rioters considered a long-standing pattern of police brutality. (*NYT*, 27 May, 19 October.)

Foreign Policy and Security Issues. The PCF's foreign policy featured the familiar themes of past years: uncompromising appreciation of the "globally positive" accomplishments of Eastern Europe's imploding communist parties, studied coolness toward Soviet reform as a dangerous flirtation with social democracy (or worse), warming relations with equally recalcitrant communist parties around the world—notably in Vietnam, Portugal, and Cuba—and near-universal denunciations of U.S. policies, in particular in Europe and the Third World. In the fall and winter, however, most of these faded to secondary importance, as the PCF's foreign policymakers strained to whip the faithful into a frenzy of hostility to German unification and to the U.S.-European coalition opposing Iraqi aggression in Kuwait.

The party's frigid relations with Moscow remained unthawed in 1990 and may even have hardened a degree or two because of increasingly shrill PCF objections to the Kremlin's sanction of German unification and Moscow's participation in the U.S.-led coalition arrayed against Baghdad. Nonetheless, party officials were clearly angered by persistent stories in the French media that strains in their relations with Moscow were growing, and most lost few opportunities to mouth familiar truths about *perestroika* representing an important step toward "a democratic and humane socialism." But praise for Gorbachev was often unsubtle pressure. For example, amid growing indications of Gorbachev's willingness to sanction a diminished role for the Communist Party of the Soviet Union (CPSU), Jean-Claude Gayssot applauded the Soviet leader's support for "a communist party whose vanguard role is not decreed by the constitution but is realized through a permanent link with the people." (Moscow, *Izvestiia*, 9 February.) Meanwhile, Marchais stressed as often as he could that although both the PCF and Moscow were working to "give socialism a second wind," each party operated "under entirely different conditions" (Moscow, *Pravda*, 5 July). Confronted with the evidence of the failure of communist regimes in the East, Marchais did not

shrink from pleading on national television that his party had been "duped" by Moscow concerning the success of Soviet-style communism (Paris, AFP, 11 April).

Dismal as relations between the PCF and Moscow had become in recent years, they reached a low ebb in September over Moscow's support for the U.S.-led anti-Iraq coalition. The PCF's early criticism of the invasion of Kuwait and its insistence on a return to the status quo ante soon turned to invective against U.S. efforts to mobilize global pressure on Baghdad and to organize a military coalition to protect Saudi Arabia and force an Iraqi retreat from Kuwait. (*l'Humanité*, 3 August.) Mitterrand's early and vocal support for President Bush drew the first volley of sniping from PCF spokesmen, who portrayed French policy as knee-jerk subservience to the U.S. oil monopolists (Moscow, *Sovetskaia Rossiia*, 17 November). But Marchais and other conservatives quickly shifted their fire to Moscow when Gorbachev took a decidedly tough line against Baghdad in his early September meeting with the U.S. president in Helsinki. Said Claude Cabanne in an unusually virulent editorial in *l'Humanité*, "Yesterday we would have hoped that Moscow would... propose loud and clear the means to negotiate the evacuation of Kuwait [by Iraq] and the liberation of hostages. This was not the case, we can only regret it." Party foreign policy chief Maxime Gremetz joined the fray, seconding Cabanne's charge that Gorbachev was guilty of failing to "reverse the logic of war" and echoing communist "disappointment" that "the Soviet position has evolved" toward sanctioning war. (*l'Humanité*, Paris Domestic Service, 10 September; Paris, AFP, 11 September). During a post-Helsinki visit to France, a Soviet delegation headed by CPSU International Department chief V. M. Falin met with Marchais and Gremetz to "synchronize watches... in particular [on] events in the Persian Gulf." But thereafter it did not appear that the PCF was reconciled to Moscow's position on the looming Middle East crisis. (Moscow, TASS, 24 September.)

PCF chiefs organized numerous demonstrations against U.S., French, and European policies in the gulf. Marching under the slogan Down with War, Down with Bush, a Lyons rally drew participation from anarchists, pacifists, conscientious objectors, and Turkish dissidents; nationally the French Greens also supported communist efforts to incite mass protest. (*FBIS-SOV*, 22 October; Moscow, *Sovetskaia Rossiia*, 17 November; *FBIS*, Voice of the PLO, 28 December.) Although communists managed to mobilize leftists who would turn out for just about any demonstration against French or U.S. government policies, the effort to evoke a massive public reaction against the U.S.-led coalition fizzled.

Year-long PCF attempts to excite French fears of a united Germany also failed. Although party spokesmen lambasted Bonn's "annexation" of the GDR and condemned East Germans for wanting to "trade socialism for capitalism," they served up their sharpest rebukes to Gorbachev, who in PCF rhetoric stood self-convicted of allowing the GDR to slip under the *droit de regard* of the North Atlantic Treaty Organization. PCF leaders—notably Lajoinie—warned of a repetition of German history, of a revival of the German "threat," and of the "danger" that would again haunt Europe if Germans were once more permitted a unified state at the crossroads of the continent. At the very least, argued communist leaders, any such united Germany should be "demilitarized." (*l'Humanité*, 22 February; *ND*, 22 February, 20 April; Paris Domestic Service, 13 February; *le Point*, 17 September.)

Soviet leaders, meanwhile, lost no opportunity to demonstrate their increasing diffidence toward the PCF. The Soviet embassy in Paris publicly stepped up its contacts with communist dissidents and reform-minded federations. (*le Point*, 18 December.) Georges Marchais did not visit Moscow during the year (mainly because foreign delegations were not invited to the CPSU congress), and on a one-day visit to France in October to confer with Mitterrand on the gulf crisis, Gorbachev pointedly did not see Marchais, not even for the half hour he had accorded the PCF leader on their last meeting (Paris, AFP, 29 October). As the finale to a year of souring relations, Moscow dispatched only a low-level delegation to the PCF's much-ballyhooed congress (Reuters, 21 December.)

International Activities. The PCF's international initiatives slackened in 1990 partly because familiar allies in Eastern Europe had disappeared and also because of its weakening ties to Moscow. A PCF delegation headed by Roland Leroy journeyed to Moscow early in the year, ostensibly to recement relations between *Pravda* and *l'Humanité* but also presumably to take the temperature in the Kremlin about the beating Marchais and party conservatives were then taking in Paris. *Pravda* director and Politburo member I. T. Frolov returned the visit in September, when he turned up at *l'Humanité*'s annual

Fête de l'Humanité to mouth familiar and soothing aphorisms about the partnership of the two communist parties and their media. (Moscow, *Pravda*, 17, 21, 23 January, 18 September.) Meanwhile, Marchais and PCF leaders entertained a number of newly risen East European "Socialist" (read communist) leaders, notably East German party chairman Gregor Gysi, who helped Marchais underscore the potential horrors of German unification, and Czechoslovak party head Ladislaw Adamec, who pledged continued "cooperation between the two parties in the new conditions" (*FBIS-EEU*, Prague Domestic Service, 8 February; *l'Humanité*, 22 February). Such events were stage-managed by Gremetz in the traditionally stiff but proper manner. Fortunately, they came early in the year; by April Marchais was charging in television interviews that the new breed of communist leaders in Eastern Europe were mostly opportunists who had "become social democrats" for the sake of their careers. (Paris, AFP, 11 April.)

If there was a theme in the party's foreign activity, it was the noticeable effort to bolster relations with like-minded parties around the world, in particular those of Portugal, Cuba, and Vietnam. Marchais loyalists Gaston Plissonnier and Gremetz received a high-level delegation from Vietnam in March, building on strengthened relations that began with two visits the previous year. The proof of the blossoming relationship could be seen throughout the year in the increased media coverage that each communist party gave to the activities of the other. (*FBIS-EAS*, Hanoi, VNA, 22 March; *le Point*, 17 September.) Similarly, a PCF delegation traveled to Lisbon to polish relations with the hardline, that is, anti-*perestroika*, party of Alvaro Cunhal—relations that had also taken a decided turn for the better in 1989 (Lisbon, *Avante!* 26 July; *le Point*, 17 September). Building on Georges Marchais's visit to Havana in January 1989, PCF International Department officials lavished unprecedented attention on relations with the Cuban party. A Cuban delegation headed by CPC Politburo member Jorge Risquet got red-carpet treatment when it visited French comrades in June; the PCF publishing house, Messidor, launched a flattering collection of Castro interviews with Jean-Edern Hallier entitled *Fidel Castro: conversation au clair de lune* to celebrate the new importance of the Cuban relationship; and Maxime Gremetz announced at the Twenty-seventh Congress that France, Europe, and other Mediterranean countries will send a ship loaded with oil to Cuba, presumably to make up the expected shortfall of Soviet oil deliveries. (Havana Tele Rebelde, 28 May, 20 December; *FBIS-LAT*, 8 June, 21 December; *le Point*, 17 September.) Such was the eagerness of PCF leaders to strengthen ties with equally unregenerate communist parties that some of the French media began to speculate about "an anti-gorbachevian axis: Marchais-Cunhal-Castro" in the making (*le Point*, 17 September).

Other PCF international initiatives underscored the party's ever popular anti-imperialist theme. Delegates from 83 countries attended a party seminar on "The Liberation of Mankind," where most speakers reportedly yearned for the "final victory of socialism over capitalism." (*FBIS-EAS*, Hanoi Domestic Service, 12, 24 November). In African affairs, Marchais was able to embrace Winnie Mandela and Nelson Mandela during the ANC leader's June visit to France, and a PCF delegation participated in the Third Congress of the Senegalese Party for Independence and Labor (PIT) (*FBIS-AFR*, Dakar, Pana, 24 March; *FBIS-AFR*, Johannesburg Domestic Service, 7 June; *le Figaro*, 12 June).

Meanwhile, PCF dealings with Beijing remained decidedly off-key, evidence that there were limits to even French communist willingness to court other hard-line parties. A correct but cool visit by Chinese Communist Party (CCP) International Liaison head Zhu Liang failed to clear the air of the PCF's harsh 1989 criticisms of communist repression in the People's Republic of China. Later, continued criticism of Chinese communist brutality in the Tiananmen Square shootings triggered fresh instances of Chinese pique, as when the CCP delegation stormed out of the Twenty-seventh Congress in the wake of further denunciations by Georges Marchais. (Xinhua, 4 April; Paris Domestic Service, Paris, AFP, 18 December; *FBIS-CHI*, *FBIS-WEU*, 19 December.)

Edward A. Allen
Washington, D.C.

Germany
Federal Republic of Germany

Population. 62,168,200 in July, before unification; 82,000,000 (estimated, after German unification 3 October and including ca. 5,000,000 foreigners)

Party. German Communist Party (Deutsche Kommunistische Partei, DKP)

Founded. 1968

Membership. ca. 20,000 claimed; some party delegates estimated membership at only 10,000, of which 7,000 were dues payers.

Chairpersons. Heinz Stehr, Anne Frohnweiler, Helga Rosenberg, Rolf Priemer

Governing Board. 46 members, half women

Status. Legal

Last Congress. Tenth, 26–27 March, in Dortmund

Last Election. DKP fielded no candidates in the December federal elections but supported Left List/Party of Democratic Socialism, which won 2.4 percent of the votes (11.1 percent in former East Germany) and 17 seats in the Bundestag.

Auxiliary Organizations. Socialist German Workers' Youth (Sozialistische Deutsche Arbeiter Jugend, SDAJ); Marxist Student Union-Spartakus (Marxistischer Studentenbund-Spartakus, MSB-Spartakus); Young Pioneers (Junge Pioniere, JP)

Publication. *Unsere Zeit* (Our time), Düsseldorf. Because of party financial crisis, weekly since late 1989.

Introduction. The 1990s find German communists in the throes of crisis. Only the Party of Democratic Socialism (PDS) is a credible electoral and parliamentary political force. However, it is burdened by its own history, being the heir to the Socialist Unity Party of Germany (SED), which misruled the German Democratic Republic (GDR) for 40 years. Its attractiveness is restricted to the eastern parts of reunified Germany and Berlin, and its future in German politics is not bright. The DKP in the western part of Germany remains as irrelevant as ever, and it has been badly battered by the collapse of communism in the GDR, to which it was always uncritically servile. It has suffered great losses in membership and capacity for action; the cutoff of funding from the GDR shattered its party organization, and its leaders no longer have the confidence of the rank and file. It has lost its theoretical bearings. Only the highly diverse collection of Marxist-Leninist, Trotskyite, anarchist, and autonomist sects, which maintained independence from the ruling communist parties in East Berlin and Moscow, remains stable. As always, they are impotent at election time, but they can make their presence known in demonstrations, squatting, and terrorist actions.

History of the DKP. The DKP, which was traditionally unswervingly loyal to Moscow and East Berlin, grew out of the Communist Party of Germany (Kommunistische Partei Deutschlands, KPD). The KPD had been officially founded 31 December 1918 by left-wing Spartakists who had broken away from the Social Democratic Party of Germany (SPD) following the Bolshevik Revolution in Russia a year earlier.

After the war, the KPD was the first party to be legalized (11 June 1945). It toned down its revolutionary rhetoric and advocated the creation of an "anti-fascist democratic order" and a popular front. It sought to merge with the SPD as a unified German workers' party, something that actually happened in the Soviet zone of occupation on 22 April 1946, when the SED was formed. Because of bitter opposition to such a merger by leading Social Democrats in the Western zones, especially Kurt Schumacher, no unification took place in the West. The KPD had 2 representatives (out of 65) on the Parliamentary Council, which existed from September 1948 to May 1949 to produce a Basic Law (constitution) for the Federal Republic of Germany (FRG); in the end, the KPD decided to oppose the Basic Law, which came into effect in 1949.

In the first federal elections in 1949, the KPD won 5.7 percent of the votes and gained fifteen members in the Bundestag (Lower House of Parliament). In the next election, in 1953, its vote plummeted to 2.2 percent, far short of the minimum 5 percent required for seats in the Bundestag. Until 1990 communists never again won seats, and their vote percentage steadily declined. The weakening popular support for the KPD merely increased its dependence on a foreign patron, notably the SED in the GDR. Such dependence contributed to Constitutional Court's outlawing the KPD in August 1956.

By the time the party was renamed the DKP and, as a concession by Chancellor Willy Brandt to the Kremlin, again legalized in 1968 (with new statutes and statements of purpose carefully crafted to be compatible with the Basic Law), two important developments had occurred: first, the party's membership had shrunk to about seven thousand. Second, the tumultuous 1960s had produced in the FRG scores of radical and independent communist or radical leftist groups to compete with the traditional orthodox party. The DKP did not regard itself as having supplanted the KPD, which in theory continued to exist underground. The DKP continued to demand that the decision to ban the KPD be rescinded. The KPD, the Spartakist-Workers' party, and the Independent SPD (USPD) were reborn in the GDR during the closing months of that sinking regime in 1990. They offer Socialist alternatives to the capitalist system, but all proved to be negligible political forces.

Crisis within the party. The year 1989 brought a crisis on the entire DKP from which it will never recover. The collapse of communist power and ideology in the GDR and the Soviet Union's encouragement of reform in Eastern Europe threatened the survival of the DKP, which was always studiously servile to the SED and the Soviet rulers. The DKP's leadership was incapable of responding to these changes, which brought the party to the brink of fragmentation and bankruptcy.

Intraparty tensions had reached explosive proportions several years before the Berlin Wall came tumbling down 9 November 1989. Former leader Herbert Mies admitted in 1988 that "profound changes had taken place" including changes "in the internal development of the party." Therefore, the party leadership drew up for approval by the Ninth Congress a report called "Bundesrepublik 2000" (Federal Republic 2000), which contained suggestions for a "peace oriented and democratic reform alternative for the 1990s." Mies declared that socialism remained the party's goal but that urgent questions could not wait until a fundamental restructuring of society occurred. His party could draw useful conclusions from the *perestroika* process in the Soviet Union, for which the report contained restrained praise, and abandon all that is obsolete. In advance of its approval by the Ninth Congress, that report, which addressed the question of how the party should proceed in the future, was widely discussed within the DKP. Although Mies criticized the attempts made by some party members to turn the DKP into a pluralistic party, he noted that the report was an "offer of discussion to all forces of the working class movement, all leftist forces, the peace movement, and social and solidarity movements." (*ND*, 1 July 1988; *FBIS*, 7 September 1988.) However, as we shall see, the Ninth Congress was so divided that adoption of the report had to be postponed.

In the past, the DKP's total loyalty to both East Berlin and Moscow created few problems for the party except to reduce the DKP's electoral strength in the FRG to practically zero. Like the SED, it had consistently pointed to the Soviet Union as the exalted model of "real socialism" and as the country to be emulated. The Communist Party of the Soviet Union (CPSU) was seen as an unerring party, and the DKP's motto was "To Learn from the Soviet Union Means to Learn to Be Victorious." Both the DKP and the SED had almost always lined up behind the Soviet Union's foreign and defense policy objectives and lent full weight to their accomplishment. However, the emergence in the Soviet Union of a new-generation party leader, Mikhail Gorbachev, who attacks corruption and self-serving privilege within the party and advocates intraparty democracy, openness (*glasnost'*), and general restructuring (*perestroika*), created a serious dilemma for the DKP.

On the one hand, Gorbachev's calls for more democracy were avidly embraced by the DKP's rank and file, who had long been restless over the "lack of possibilities for intra-party influence and participation," to use the words of party author Erasmus Schöfer. Embarking upon a new path has its risks, Schöfer admitted, but "Communists in the FRG have nothing to lose but their lack of success!" (*Spiegel*, 7 September 1987.) Thomas Riecke, a top functionary of the MSB-Spartakus, declared in regard to *glasnost'* that "we must know everything and be able to decide about everything" (*Die Zeit*, 16 October 1987). There were calls for free election of cadres, who are now appointed by the party leadership.

Mies had to admit in a May 1987 interview in *Unsere Zeit* that "there is hardly another topic on which so many party functions and with such a large number of participants have been held over the past several years. . . . The sympathy for the changes in the Soviet Union is unanimous." He recognized that "the attractive power of existing socialism has been growing" under Gorbachev, who, polls continued to

indicate, enjoys enormous popularity in the FRG. An overwhelming percentage of West German respondents consider him to be a "man who can be trusted." In 1988 only 11 percent (down from 71 percent in 1980!) believed that the Soviet Union threatens world peace while the United States does not. Gorbachev's welcome disarmament proposals presented the DKP with "fresh opportunities in, among other things, our united action and alliance policy" and "made it easier for Communists to act as respected and equal partners in the peace movement and other democratic movements. Not least important among the fresh opportunities is the possibility of using the growing sympathy for Soviet policy to spread the influence of the DKP as the party of socialism." (*Unsere Zeit*, 20 May 1987.)

Gorbachev's dramatic announcement at the United Nations on 7 December 1988 that the Soviet Union would unilaterally reduce its manpower and weapons in the USSR and Eastern Europe and the Soviets' declaration in Paris on 7 January 1989 that the USSR would begin unilaterally to destroy its stocks of chemical weapons were the kind of dramatic initiatives on which the DKP hoped to capitalize. Throughout 1988 and at the Ninth Party Congress in 1989, DKP leaders repeatedly praised the Soviet Union's arms reductions proposals and called for nuclear- and chemical-free zones, a "zone of trust and security in Central Europe," conventional force reductions from the Atlantic to the Urals, a Western response to unilateral Soviet withdrawal of some short-range missiles from the GDR and Czechoslovakia, and a rejection of North Atlantic Treaty Organization (NATO) plans to modernize its nuclear forces in Western Europe.

On the other hand, the SED remained cool toward the Gorbachev reforms. In August 1987 Max Schmidt, director of the International Institute for Economics and Politics in East Berlin, told a DKP delegation that "much has yet to reach fruition" and that "much will perhaps be undone." The SED prevented *Unsere Zeit* from publishing a January 1987 speech in which Gorbachev asserted that "we need democracy as air to breathe" and threatened not to distribute any copies via East Berlin to other Socialist countries. (*Spiegel*, 7 September 1987.) The SED's message was "Go slowly, and wait and see!" It did not want to be exposed to the bacillus of *glasnost'* from both West and East. SED chief Erich Honecker knew that Gorbachev desired his downfall, so he ordered the DKP leaders to suppress reformist efforts within the DKP at all costs. (See the following important articles in *Das Parlament*,

9 November: Manfred Wilke, "Die Krise der Deutschen Kommunistischen Partei"; Patrick Moreau, "Krisen und Anpassungsstrategien der kommunistischen Strömungen in der Bundesrepublik Deutschland und der ehemaligen DDR"; and Hans Josef Horchem, "Der Verfall der Roten Armee Fraktion.")

The DKP could not ignore these warnings from East Berlin. Confronted with what the relatively liberal Hamburg DKP organization called "a crisis in the party," the DKP leadership tried to dampen the enthusiasm caused by the "strong impulses" coming from Moscow. In *Unsere Zeit* a cautious Mies warned that in a capitalist country like the FRG "there can be no imitation of the Soviet approach" and that the party must be careful "not to throw the baby out with the bath water." One should not "reduce the splendid history of the Soviet Union . . . to economic and moral problems." DKP members should inform themselves through reports by "fraternal parties," not by "reading tea leaves or using the slanders cooked up by the bourgeois mass media." Although there is much need for

> invigoration of inner-party life, encouragement of inner-party discussions, and broader involvement of the party membership in the decision-making process, it is not a matter of weakening the principles of democratic centralism in the CPSU. . . . Inner-party democracy for us is not a game, not an end in itself. It is designed to mobilize the party's collective knowledge and strength, and to unite it for the purposeful and centralized actions in the fight against the highly-organized class enemy facing us. We need to have a further development of inner-party democracy, while keeping our communist principles intact. (*Unsere Zeit*, 20 May 1987.)

Thus, the party resorted to censorship to try to silence the enthusiasm for the reform impulses from Moscow. When Peter Schütt, the party poet and member of the party executive, wrote a poem in 1987 with the lines "After decades of radio silence, the red star is again sending signals" and "there are comrades who have held their hands in front of their faces for so long that they have unlearned how to understand the new radio code," he was advised by the chief party ideologue, Willi Gerns, not to publish the poem. To Schütt's surprise, the poem was published by the moderately conservative *Frankfurter Allgemeine Zeitung*. The DKP leadership was reportedly embarrassed by this, especially when the editors of the Moscow publication *New Times*

thanked Schütt for supporting *perestroika*. (*Spiegel*, 7 September 1987.) Schütt remained an ardent reformer, saying in March 1989: "We must move away from the old cadre party and become a modern membership party, by shifting the weight of communist activity and decision-making back to the rank and file." (*FBIS*, 15 May 1989.)

In 1988 the DKP faced its most serious crisis in two decades of existence. For the first time in fifteen years, its membership dipped to 38,000 and its members' average age rose. Half those who left the party cited political and ideological reasons. Many comrades who remained were disillusioned or unmotivated, as the party leaders were increasingly reproached for "a tendency toward dogmatism" and for encouraging "conformist behavior and closed, inflexible, and authority-minded thinking." (*FBIS*, 15 September 1988.)

Unheeded by many members were pronouncements such as that made by Mies in November 1987: "It would be irresponsible, precisely in times of radical change, to eliminate something of the Marxist, revolutionary character of our organizational principles. Precisely in such times, . . . not less, but more Marxism, not less, but more Leninism is required" (*Innere Sicherheit*, 30 August 1988.) The party leadership was always proud of having resisted Eurocommunism on the grounds that communist parties that had tolerated some pluralism within their ranks had been weakened or split. Ellen Weber tried in 1988 to argue that the talk of *glasnost'* and *perestroika* was merely "the effort of the bourgeois media and politicians to drive wedges and organize dissension." But Hamburg party chief Wolfgang Gehrke stated forthrightly that "there are fissures which one must work on. Everyone is looking toward Moscow." (*Stern*, July 1988.)

By early 1988 Mies had to admit that, for the first time in the party's history, there were differences of opinion within the party that were extremely difficult to reconcile. In a speech 3–4 September, he acknowledged two directions within the party. Alongside a majority wing of Bewahrer (Maintainers), a minority of Erneuer (Renewers) had formed to call certain party principles in question: "A break with essential principles of democratic centralism is appearing in outlines." (*FBIS*, 15 September 1988.)

The DKP tried to cope with this challenge in two ways: first, it departed from its customary practice by permitting open discussion within the party and allowing the party news organs to report those disagreements. Never before had there been so much frankness in the party's publications or in discussions at party gatherings. At the September 1988 Presidium meeting, two contradictory discussion papers were allowed for the first time: 18 out of 94 members could not agree with the top party leadership, and therefore no agreement could be reached on a common text. At the same time, the DKP tried to place limits on discussions, declaring that they may show a diversity of opinion but "not lead to political confrontation or to splintering of forces." They must always serve "the conscious unity and strengthening of the fighting power of the party." (*Die Welt*, 23 June 1988.) That is, criticism had to remain subordinate to the principles and goals of the party. In Mies's words, it was important to "withstand a trend which would not lead to a renewed, but to a ruined DKP."

The second way of trying to erect a dam against the flood of demands for more "democratization" and a more public party was to discipline those Renewers who crossed the vague line that the top leaders had tried to draw between permissible and impermissible criticism. In March 1988 the DKP issued a warning to Andreas Müller-Goldenstedt, a Hamburg district leader, for demanding that the DKP must primarily operate "for our own country" and that the comrades in the GDR had to be told once and for all that "we don't want this and that here [in the FRG]." Disciplinary action was also taken against Helmut Krebs, former member of the Karlsruhe leadership, for writing a discussion paper entitled "How Should the DKP Proceed" in which he faulted the DKP for underestimating the economic strength of the FRG. The deficiencies of socialism could no longer be denied, he wrote, and the West German working class would tolerate a Socialist order only if it did not bring a reduction in their living standard or a diminution in their freedom and human rights. Therefore, the party should renounce all unconstitutional means of struggle. (*Innere Sicherheit*, 27 May 1988.)

The DKP leadership could have no illusions that the Ninth Party Congress, which took place in Frankfurt am Main 6–9 January 1989, would be like the ones before it. It was attended by approximately seven hundred DKP delegates, along with numerous guests from affiliated and communist-influenced organizations, fraternal communist and workers' parties, "anti-imperialist liberation movements," and Socialist embassies. According to the DKP's own information, almost all of the delegates were trade union members and close to half were women. Most important, however, was that one-third of the delegates were reformers, who came to make things difficult for the conservatives, whom they called "concrete heads." Citing the DKP's political impotence and lack of electoral success, the Renewers also mounted an unprecedented challenge against the leaders and demanded more internal democracy, freedom of debate, and toleration of dissent. They also explicitly invoked the reform spirit of Gorbachev, a point well supported by Alexander Yakovlev, who pleaded with the party "to let the human face of socialism emerge again." The SED's delegate, Hermann Axen, did not even mention *perestroika* and sounded the call to traditional militancy. (*RAD Background Report*, no. 4, 11 January 1989.) Mies admitted to the congress that "the party is beset by hitherto unparalleled inner contradictions" (ibid.) and that he had learned from some of his own mistakes (which he did not specify). He also acknowledged an 18 percent loss in party membership in the past three years. But he insisted that the only way to overcome this drift was to strengthen the unity of the party. Ever the good Leninist, he adamantly rejected the formation of factions within the party.

Under the slogan, For the Renewal of the Federal Republic, bitter and divisive debates took place in a charged atmosphere of personal attacks. Many observers asked what ever happened to comradely solidarity. One delegate described the "personal debate" as "no holds barred." In fact, the election question was so hot that, for the first time ever, it had to be postponed for a week. Also for the first time, 110 candidates ran for only 98 seats. When the leaders were finally selected, Herbert Mies had to settle for only 71.8 percent of the votes; his deputy, Ellen Weber, failed to receive a third of the votes. Nevertheless, the top leadership was able to prevent all but a handful of Renewers from gaining seats in the Presidium and Secretariat. Two of them (youth leaders Birgit Radow and Werner Stuermann) were purged from these bodies in May 1989 because they had participated in the organization of "trend meetings" by DKP Renewers; the leadership wanted any talk of party renewal to take place inside, rather than outside, existing party structures. Also, the conservative majority voted down all the Renewers' motions during the congress. But approval of the two most important documents, "Federal Republic 2000" and "On the DKP's Situation and Future Development," had to be postponed. In an unprecedented move, the congress's concluding session was put off for six weeks. Mies admitted ruefully that the DKP had "possibly come within seconds of a split." (Ibid., no. 14, 27 January 1989.)

Collapse of the GDR and German Unification. The intraparty perils that the DKP faced at its 1989 party congress pale in comparison with those brought on by the political earthquake that hit the party's exalted models—the GDR and the SED—in the second half of 1989. In late summer a human hemorrhaging westward commenced, as East German vacationers began crossing the newly opened border between Hungary and Austria. The next avenue of escape was through Czechoslovakia, from which "freedom trains" took thousands of East Germans through the GDR into the West. The stampede grew when Czechoslovakia opened its western borders. The GDR's media accused the FRG of provoking the crisis, and then Deputy Ellen Weber followed the SED line in true DKP character by publicly deploring West German "interference" in the GDR's internal affairs. (*RAD Background Report*, no. 178, 20 September 1989.) In its first departure from the SED line, in the aftermath of the violent crackdown against demonstrators in China on 4 June, the DKP distanced itself from the SED by declaring that "we condemn the death sentences and executions of people, for reasons of humanity, as well as political reasons" (*FBIS-WEU*, 27 June 1989).

Under enormous stress, the GDR celebrated its 40th anniversary in October. The SED's slogan for the event was Ever Forward—Never Backward! The prediction was accurate, but SED chiefs were badly mistaken about which direction was forward. On 18 October, Honecker was ousted from power. He had reportedly wanted to use force against demonstrators in Leipzig, but he was restrained by subordinates, including Egon Krenz, who took over the reins of power for six weeks. (*Time*, 11 December.) Communist rule without the backing of Soviet troops could not survive anywhere in Germany.

On 9 November the Berlin Wall came tumbling down. It is ironic that a wall that had been constructed in 1961 to keep East Germans in was opened in 1989 for the same reason! The new leadership calculated that people who were free to go would come back. Within minutes millions of East Germans began pouring over the border. In the first two days, one-sixth of GDR's population went West for a visit and almost all of them returned home. Germans who for decades had suppressed displays of national feeling experienced a deeply emotional outpouring. While millions sat in front of their televisions and wept, Berliners danced together on top of the wall, embraced each other on the streets, and chiseled away at the ugly barrier. Suddenly German reunification was back on the agenda, and developments toward it raced faster than any government's ability to react. Demonstrators in the GDR unfurled banners bearing Germany—One Fatherland! while support began to grow in both Germanies for unity of some kind. This was a genuine revolution in the streets, unlike the revolution that the DKP had hoped for.

It was excruciating for the DKP to witness the rapid collapse of communist rule in the GDR because communism was being thoroughly discredited in Germany—the events "shock us!" (*FBIS-WEU*, 21 November 1989). Honecker and many other leading SED figures were not only removed from office but arrested and charged with corruption and enriching themselves while in office. Enraged East German citizens watched television images of the "proletarian" leaders' luxury compound in Wandlitz, estates with as many as 22 staff members, hunting lodges, deer parks, well-stocked wine cellars, and satellite dishes to enhance the reception of Western broadcasts. All were signs of living standards totally removed from the meager, everyday existence of normal GDR citizens long fed on exhortations for austerity. Even worse were revelations of shady financial dealings, totaling millions of marks, involving illegal arms sales to Third World countries and foreign currency maneuvers, the profits of which ended up in Swiss bank accounts. Said one rank and file SED member: "We did not expect this of Communists and their creed of equality." (*Time*, 18 December 1989.)

The entire SED Politburo and Central Committee resigned, and the party decided to abolish these institutions altogether. Honecker's replacement, Egon Krenz, was also forced to step down and was replaced by a peripheral party member, Gregor Gysi. Gysi is a lawyer who made a name for himself by defending East German dissidents and the opposition New Forum and by heading the prosecution of former SED leaders accused of corruption. On accepting the leadership, he admitted that a complete break with Stalinism and a new form of socialism were needed and that the SED was responsible for plunging the GDR into crisis. Feeling betrayed, 700,000 of the 2.3 million members left the party within two months. The party initiated a change in the GDR consitition that eliminated the communists' monopoly on power. Prime Minister

Hans Modrow, former head of the Dresden party and one of the few leading communists untainted by corruption scandals, announced that free elections would be held 18 March. The communists cast off their discredited SED initials, as well as their disgraced former leaders and claims. They renamed themselves the Party of Democratic Socialism (PDS); the term, emphasizing democratic socialism, was bound to make hard-line DKP members cringe. The PDS won only a sixth of the votes, far behind the opposition groupings, especially the conservative Alliance for Germany, which came within a whisker of winning an outright majority. As in 1949, Germans turned to the Christian Democratic Union (CDU) as the party of prosperity and assured democracy. The hated State Security Forces (Stasi), which numbered about 85,000 officers and more than a half million informants, were defanged and ceased being an instrument of fear. They had penetrated every niche of GDR society and maintained files on 6 million persons. Agents were dismissed or reassigned to other duties, and crowds of citizens entered Stasi installations to protect files for later prosecution. The Office of National Security, which directed Stasi, was abolished in December, and the Defense Council resigned, leaving the armed forces under the control of the government, not the SED. The armed militia units (Kampfgruppen) were also disbanded; they were hated by many citizens because they had sometimes been used to put down demonstrations or labor unrest.

Germans must decide what to do with the Stasi files, which had been assembled with a complete disregard for the individual's privacy. They hold many keys to rooting out and punishing those persons who suppressed citizens' freedom, but their misuse could endanger that very freedom. Those files also shed light on the GDR's extensive contacts with terrorist organizations; especially embarrassing to the DKP was the revelation in January that Stasi had trained up to 300 DKP members in secret camps inside the GDR in the use of weapons and explosives so they could serve in a secret military organization within the FRG. Some DKP renewers confirmed the allegations, as did the GDR Defense Ministry in February. This prompted the Federal Office for Criminal Investigations to search DKP members' homes and offices for further evidence. (*Süddeutsche Zeitung*, 30 December 1989; *FBIS-WEU*, 4 January; Wilke, "Krise," p. 37.)

In June nine former Red Army Faction (RAF) killers who had been harbored and given a new identity by the GDR were arrested there (Horchem,

"Verfall," p. 54). Support for such terrorists had reportedly been a pet project of Honecker's. Stasi files can also help Bonn uncover spies who had infiltrated the FRG more thoroughly than had ever been imagined. Revelations were made almost daily. Their biggest catch was Klaus Kuron, a senior West German counterintelligence officer in charge of converting East German spies into double agents. Colonel Joachim Krase, former deputy chief of military intelligence, who died in 1988, had spied for the GDR for at least a decade. Garbriele Gast, who helped prepare a top secret intelligence summary for Chancellor Kohl, had passed copies to East Berlin for six years.

The furor over Stasi touched off an intense debate among literary critics concerning the extent to which authors and other intellectuals had collaborated with the communist regime. In a short novel entitled *Was Bleibt* (What Remains), East German author and SED member Christa Wolf described her life under Stasi surveillance. The book had been written a decade ago, but she waited until the regime had fallen to publish it. In the eyes of critics, this demonstrated cowardice, collaboration, and opportunism on the part of an author who had criticized certain aspects of an authoritarian regime while enjoying its privileges.

When Chancellor Helmut Kohl made a historic visit to Dresden on 19 December, he was greeted by throngs of enthusiastic East Germans, and the leaders of both Germanies announced many new agreements that were to lead to complete unity. The march toward one Germany proceeded in 1990 with dizzying rapidity. On 1 July the West German mark was introduced in the GDR in a large-scale currency reform without precedent. In a stunning diplomatic breakthrough, Kohl went to the Soviet Union 14–16 July to get Gorbachev's assurances that he would not stand in the way of German unity and that a united Germany could decide "freely and by itself if, and in which alliance it desires membership"; in other words Germany would not have to leave NATO in order to be united. Returning to Moscow 12 September, Bonn's leaders joined GDR chancellor Lothar de Maizière (who was forced in December to renounce his cabinet post and vice-chairmanship of the CDU because of alleged earlier cooperation with Stasi) and the foreign ministers of the four Allied powers to sign the "2+4" treaty granting full sovereignty to Germany and suspending the four powers' rights. The Conference on Security and Cooperation in Europe (CSCE) endorsed this agreement in New York on 1 October.

It went into effect at midnight on 2 October when a liberty bell given by the United States sounded Germany's unification in Berlin. Those few Germans who knew the words sang the national anthem pledging "unity, justice and freedom" for the "German fatherland."

DKP Response. It is an understatement to say that the DKP was overwhelmed by unification and the peaceful revolution in the GDR. A few diehards asserted a "betrayal of the working class" and "democracy flim-flam" when the "class enemy" is given free rein to eject communists from power through elections. (*FBIS-WEU*, 21 November 1989.) The minority wing seized the opportunity to convene a Renewal Congress in Frankfurt am Main in October 1989. The central topic was the division within the DKP. The Renewers decided to create their own structures, which would enable them to prepare separately for the DKP's future congresses, including the extraordinary party congress in the spring of 1990. A "break with the traditional socialism and party conceptions of the DKP," the allowance of factions within the party, and the resignation of the entire leadership were demanded as necessary preconditions for the wing's further work within the party. The Renewers further decided to create their own office in Cologne and to publish a monthly information letter. For the first time, the split in the DKP was described in *Neues Deutschland* (*ND*, 24 October 1989). Although they initially decried these demands as an ultimatum, Mies and his deputy Weber conceded that they had to draw conclusions from the "breathtaking" changes in the GDR and the DKP's ruinous internal crisis; they announced that they would step down at the March 1990 congress (*FBIS-WEU*, 3 November 1989; *ND*, 24 November 1989).

Although the Renewers had shaken the DKP at the roots, they were unable to take control because of some serious tactical errors: They were unable to create unity within their own ranks and were therefore unable to agree on a common tactic for steering the party in a new direction. What little glue there was came from their rejection of the leadership style of the party's bosses, who had dominated since the 1950s. They overestimated their strength within the DKP. They therefore remained inside the party and generally accepted the apparatus's rules of the game rather than openly challenging the party leadership. By DKP standards, the Renewers' Frankfurt congress in October 1989 was a daring move, but they adjourned with-

out offering party comrades an organizational alternative to what had existed for decades. Finally, although their numbers within the DKP grew, they were the first ones to leave the party in disgust. Forty percent of all DKP members left the party in the wake of communism's collapse in the GDR, but by the end of 1989, 95 percent of the Renewers had gone, either joining the PDS or other leftist groups or turning their backs on politics altogether. (Moreau, "Krisen," pp. 46–48.) On 28 March *Neues Deutschland* wrote that it had been "one of the most shameful chapters of the entire GDR publishing" that these momentous disputes within the DKP had not been reported because they foreshadowed the bitter debates within the SED after 9 November that had led to its replacement by the PDS.

Disaster struck the DKP in late November: the SED informed it that all foreign currency support (which despite DKP denials amounted to an estimated 50–70 million marks sent annually through conspiratorial channels) would be terminated. SED subsidies had always been essential to financing the high costs of maintaining party headquarters in Düsseldorf, an office in Bonn, more than two hundred local offices, the production and distribution of propaganda materials, mass rallies and election campaigns, and subsidies to DKP-affiliated or -influenced organizations. DKP functionaries were kept on the payrolls of communist firms and travel agencies directed by the SED. The DKP had a few other financial sources, particularly membership dues and income from the sale of party publications. Clandestine subsidies from the SED were about three times higher than the DKP's revenues from within the FRG.

No other Western communist party was so reliant on a foreign party as was the DKP on the SED. The DKP was controlled by the Department of International Politics and Economics (which until 1984 was known as West Department) of the SED's Central Committee. Leaders of both the SED and the DKP had to agree on an annual plan for West German communists, and the DKP leadership regularly reported to the SED. Even the DKP personnel files were kept in East Berlin.

As of the end of 1989 the DKP had to operate completely on its own. No financial help could be expected from the Soviet Union. Contributions by GDR firms operating in the FRG dried up. The split in the party prompted many members to leave or to stop making their contributions. Almost all the party's bloated staff was dismissed, about five hundred persons in all. In February the PDS paid "damages" amounting to 6 million marks to the DKP to alleviate the "social costs" of those functionaries who had lost their jobs. The money, however, was misappropriated by the DKP, which used it to build up a new party apparatus of about 50 persons rather than distributing it among the unemployed comrades. (Moreau, "Krisen.") What few funds remained were in the hands of the apparatus; the Renewers lost everything. The party's publications were severely affected. The daily organ, *Unsere Zeit*, was converted to a weekly, and some other party publications were terminated. The DKP's news agency, Progress Presse-Agentur (PPA), and publishing house, Paul-Rugenstein-Verlag, were shut down. The latter's bankruptcy eliminated the vital prop for the DKP's most important publication aimed at domestic alliance partners: *Volkszeitung*. East German advertising in DKP publications disappeared. (*FBIS-WEU*, 30 November 1989; *Spiegel*, 4 December 1989.)

It was a shattered, demoralized DKP that assembled in Dortmund the end of March for its Tenth Party Congress. Few Renewers remained among the 311 delegates, so the spirit of confrontation was largely absent, although a pluralism of opinions was manifest. Delegates noted that in order for the party to achieve renewal, it had to recognize the reasons for its difficulties, its leaders' false calculations, and the uncritical idealization of conditions in Socialist countries. The orthodox former vice-chairperson, Ellen Weber, spoke of blindness toward the reality of "real existing socialism." In the presence of a visiting delegation from the PDS, a greeting from its chairman, Gregor Gysi, was read in which he apologized in the name of the PDS for the old SED leadership's share in the blame for the DKP's deep crisis. (*ND*, 28 March; *FBIS-SOV*, 30 March.)

There was much talk of renewal, but almost no steps were taken to bring it about. The DKP made a few cosmetic changes. The single chairmanship was replaced by a collective leadership of four spokespersons—Heinz Stehr, Anne Frohnweiler, Helga Rosenberg, Rolf Priemer—all fundamentalists. The party leadership was reduced to 46, half of whom were women; all are orthodox Communists who had opposed the Renewers. The party's statutes were temporarily changed to allow DKP members to criticize the party's leaders or policies internally in lower party echelons, but public criticism remained forbidden. The delegates' most important decision was not to seek union with the PDS. Ellen Weber proclaimed the end of West Ger-

man communists' dependence on East Berlin. This was a great relief for the ambitious PDS, which could only be hurt by being associated with the orthodox DKP; the heir to the SED had enough image problems as it was, and a linkage with the DKP would have been a kiss of death at election time. It was a good electoral tactic to stress its own democratic commitment in contrast to the DKP on its left. The PDS was even more determined to distance itself when the DKP met with Maoist and other active groups in Leverkusen 23–24 June and made a joint offer of an electoral alliance with the PDS, which refused. Instead, the PDS at the end of July created an electoral party of its own called the Left List-PDS, which excluded the DKP. At the same time, the heterogeneous grouping of DKP Renewers ended once and for all. When the PDS opened four regional offices in the West in July, it relied for logistics on former Renewer Wolfgang Gehrke, whose team was almost completely composed of former DKP reformers. A few weeks later it created, in the ten western lands, party organizations whose leaders were former Greens and DKP Renewers. Although the DKP attacked these "PDS revisionists," it had no alternative but to support them in the December elections. In a rare glimpse of realism, it was admitted at the DKP's Executive Committee session in Essen 22–23 September that hopes that the "PDS, the DKP, and other leftist-socialist and communist forces may eventually arrive at a common position . . . will require a long time." (Moreau, "Krisen," pp. 42–49; *ND*, 25 September; *FBIS-WEU*, 2 October.)

Ideological Training and Propaganda. The GDR and the Soviet Union always provided vital educational support for the DKP. Over a third of its members had attended courses in the GDR and the USSR. The DKP also maintained long-established insititutions for this purpose. Founded in 1968, the Institute for Marxist Studies and Research (IMSF) in Frankfurt am Main cooperated closely with the Institutes for Marxism-Leninism of the Central Committees of both the SED and the CPSU. The Marx-Engels Foundation in Wuppertal served as a venue for seminars and conferences. The Marxist Workers' Education (MAB), founded in Frankfurt in 1969 to oversee the FRG courses and lectures, featured instructors from both Germanies for politically active Germans who were not members of the DKP. The DKP annually organized approximately eight thousand educational lectures, seminars, and courses on such subjects as security in the atomic age, communists' roles in economic policies, global affairs and culture, and electoral alliances and strategy.

It also laid great stress on contacts with fraternal parties. Until the democratic revolution, which occurred in most Eastern European countries in the fall of 1989, the DKP maintained close contacts with all ruling parties in Eastern Europe, especially with the Soviet Union and the GDR. It sent high-level delegations to their party congresses and received such delegations to its own. Just days before the January congress Mies sped to Moscow on an image-building trip to see Gorbachev. A DKP delegation led by cochairman Rolf Priemer visited the *Pravda* offices in Moscow on 17 May, and one led by cochairman Heinz Stehr traveled there to meet Politburo member G.I. Yanayev on 18 November. Communist leaders want to know what the DKP is doing, but they place far more value on their contacts with influential noncommunist parties in the West and give them far more coverage in their press.

Party Publications. The DKP is so insignificant in the FRG that it receives little attention in the noncommunist press. East German publications, such as *Neues Deutschland*, give it much broader coverage, but until Honecker was replaced in October 1989, they did not report on disagreements or problems within the DKP or with the SED; nor did they report precisely how little electoral support the DKP receives within the FRG. The DKP produced many publications of its own, including the weekly party organ *Unsere Zeit*. It sometimes publishes special editions with up to 300,000 copies called *Extra Blätter*. The editor claims that the FRG's "ban on occupations" (legal restrictions on members of antidemocratic parties in public service) discourages some potential subscribers; in some cases, this is probably true. *Unsere Zeit* is guided by party decisions and operates in close contact with the party leadership, who appoint the editor in chief and editorial board. It strives to uphold the German communist press tradition begun by *Rote Fahne* (Red banner), founded by Rosa Luxemburg and Karl Liebknecht, and continued by *Freies Volk* (Free people). In response to the turmoil within the DKP, the party leadership permits more open discussions in the party press than ever before. Nevertheless, an internal survey revealed that 94 percent of DKP members do not regularly read *Unsere Zeit* (*Spiegel*, 7 September 1987). Half of all new readers cancel their subscriptions within one year, and

overall circulation is declining (*Innere Sicherheit*, 27 May 1988).

By 1990 all party publications faced financial ruin and extreme future uncertainty. Most are certain to be shut down over time. *Volkszeitung* (earlier *Deutsche Volkszeitung/Die Tat* [German people's newspaper/the deed]) had a circulation of about 30,000. However, it ran out of money by 1990 and faced extinction. The *Illustrierte Volkszeitung* (Illustrated people's newspaper) appeared quarterly. The *DKP Pressedienst* (DKP press service) *Info-dienst* (Info service), which provides print for the party's factory, residential area, and student newspapers, and the *DKP-Landreview* (DKP rural review) appeared at irregular intervals. On a bimonthly basis, the DKP Presidium produced *Praxis—Erfahrungen aus dem Leben und der Arbeit der Partei* (Practice—Experiences from the life and work of the party) with a circulation of 7,500. The *Marxistische Blätter*, published bimonthly with a circulation of 7,300, was the party's theoretical organ. The party also published approximately 340 factory and 450 local newspapers, some of which had a dozen annual editions with as many as 120,000 copies.

Providing these publications with news were two principal news agencies that no longer exist: The PPA, with headquarters in Düsseldorf and offices in Bonn, Mannheim, Munich, and Kiel, had approximately fifteen editors and correspondents and, five times a week, published the *PPA Daily Service*, which featured party activities and selected articles from the noncommunist press. About one-third of the material in DKP publications came from the GDR news agency, Allgemeiner Deutscher Nachrichtendienst (ADN).

Youth Organizations. The largest group is the SDAJ, whose membership had plummeted by late 1989 from approximately fifteen thousand to six thousand; its local groups have declined in number from 1,088 to 674. Its fall continues steadily in 1990: it had 30 groups in factories and 20 in schools, compared with 90 and 140, respectively, in 1988. Its traditional self-image is the "revolutionary young workers' organization" devoted to "the teaching of Marx, Engels and Lenin" and fighting for a "socialist Federal Republic" with a planned, Socialist economy and power being exercised by the workers. Birgit Radow was not only SDAJ chairperson but a member of the DKP Presidium and executive until she was purged in 1989 for supporting the Renewer faction within the DKP. By 1989 many followers and functionaries in the SDAJ were calling for party reform involving the recognition of pluralism of opinion and autonomy from the DKP. However, the orthodox majority retained the upper hand at the SDAJ congress in June 1989. The SDAJ faces extinction. By 1990 it had to close its offices and lay off its paid functionaries.

The group's activities are supposed to support those of the parent party and are aimed particularly at students, apprentices, and soldiers. It seeks contacts with Young Socialists (Jusos), Greens, and various groups within the peace movement. Its two monthlies, *Elan—Das Jugendmagazin* and *Artikeldienst für Betriebs-, Lehrlings, Stadtteil- und Schülerzeitungen* (Article service for plant, apprentice, neighborhood, and pupils' newspapers) as well as *Jugendpolitische Blätter* (Youth political pages), were terminated in 1990 and replaced by a bimonthly, *Treffpunkt Gruppe* (Rendezvous group). The Young Pioneers (JP) is for children and once counted four thousand members. Its functionaries were trained at the Youth Education Center at Burg Wahrburg, which was closed in March, and many belong to the SDAJ and/or DKP. Its executive published a monthly *Pionierleiter Info* (Pioneer leader info), a child's newspaper, *Pionier*, which ceased in 1990, as well as *Diskussionsmaterial für Pionierleiter* (Discussion material for pioneer leaders). It had ties with children's groups in the GDR, including a vacation program with other Socialist countries and with the International Commission of Children's and Adolescents' Movements (CIMEA), an auxiliary of the World Federation of Democratic Youth (WFDY).

Represented at postsecondary institutions was the MSB-Spartakus, which dissolved itself on 23 June. It published the monthly *Rote Blätter* (Red papers), which folded at the beginning of 1990, as well as a newspaper, *Avanti*. MSB-Spartakus was the largest and most powerful left-extremist organization at the university level, despite a severe loss of membership, and it cooperated with all left-wing groups, including the Liberal Students' League (affiliated with but to the left of the Free Democratic Party, FDP) and Jusos. MSB-Spartakus and its permanent alliance partner, the dogmatic Socialist University League (SHB), occupied about a fifth of the seats in student parliaments and had representation in about half such assemblies. The MSB-Spartakus represented the United German Students' Association (Vereinigte Deutsche Studentenschaft, VDS) in diverse coordinating committees for protest and peace movements. Most top MSB-Spartakus lead-

ers were DKP members and regarded "the struggle for peace" as one aspect of the class struggle and as a revolutionary objective. MSB-Spartakus worked feverishly to undercut NATO and the Strategic Defense Initiative (SDI) and to gain support for nuclear-free zones and other objectives that had a high priority for Kremlin leaders. Unlike the DKP, many MSB activists and leaders unreservedly supported Gorbachev's reform course. The DKP considered its well-organized students to be the essential contact point between the intelligentsia and the working class.

The DKP regards the intelligentsia in the FRG as a lucrative reservoir for influence. Former Presidium and Secretariat member Gerd Deumlich wrote that "past and present experience shows that the intelligentsia in the FRG is largely in opposition to the ruling circles" because of the "ignominy of fascism and the guilt of German capital in starting World War II," even though "the views of many intellectuals can hardly be regarded as consistently progressive, and while their thinking is under the influence of bourgeois illusions and anti-communism." He continued: "The FRG is a visual example of the crisis of capitalism permeating and interweaving every aspect of life in the society: economics, politics, ideology, morality and culture." (*WMR*, September 1987.)

Cover Groups and Citizens' Initiatives. For decades the DKP and other communist groups have faced mistrust and rejection on the part of the FRG's general population. For this reason, it has operated through a wide variety of cover groups and has sought to cooperate with protest groups that enjoy greater respectability. The DKP supported by approximately 50 organizations and action groups, which it heavily influences but which attempt outwardly to appear independent; the majority of their members and leaders does not belong to the DKP. Party members are indeed appointed to certain high positions, but the key to these groups' effectiveness is that the DKP's role be as underplayed as possible. In 1989–1990 their dependence on the DKP and SED was made visible by the DKP's financial plight, which caused them either to cease to exist or greatly to curtail their operations. Many of the larger of these cover groups are also affiliated with Moscow-directed front groups, such as the World Peace Council (WPC).

Among the more important DKP front groups is the Association of Victims of the Nazi Regime/ League of Antifascists (VVN/BdA), with fewer than 14,000 members. Its monthly publication, *Antifaschistische Rundschau* (Antifascist review), folded in 1990. Although the VVN/BdA always denied that it depended on the DKP, the latters' financial collapse made it necessary for the VVN/BdA to shut down its central office in Frankfurt and its 50-member apparatus in the FRG. Its leaders admitted that all personnel decisions had been made by the DKP leadership. Only the land organizations of the VVN/BdA will try to continue their work. (*Verfassungsschutzbericht 1989*, hereafter *VSB* [Bonn: Der Bundesminister des Innern, 1990], p. 38.)

The German Peace Union (DFU), with about a thousand members and a monthly publication, *Abrüstungs-Info* (Disarmament-info), which folded in 1990, tried to break down anticommunist sentiments and gain support for the DKP's objectives within bourgeois and Christian circles. It sponsored annual Easter Marches. The central manifestos and accounts for contributions were almost exclusively traceable to functionaries of the DKP and the DFU. The continued decline in the perceived military threat to Western Europe and the greatly improved superpower relations made dramatic arms reduction agreements possible. This fact and another surprise—the GDR completely cut off its funding—threaten to pull the rug entirely out from under the DFU's feet. (*Spiegel*, 4 December 1989.) In November 1989 DFU leader Willi van Ooyen admitted publicly what the DFU had for years claimed was an "intelligence service lie": "Due to the development in the GDR, a decisive financial source has suddenly dried up. . . . The DFU depended on the GDR for 80% of its funds. . . . Criticism is justified that in past years we were nothing but the paid advanced guard of the SED." (*VSB*, p. 39.)

The German Peace Society/United War Resisters (DFG/VK), with about ten thousand members, is the largest DKP front group and has the greatest number of noncommunists, but it is plagued by declining membership and revenues and had to reduce spending for its quarterly publication *Civil Courage* (circulation: twelve thousand). Communist influence within the DGF/VK is uneven; some groups and individuals have repeatedly criticized the DKP's power at the highest level without being able to do anything about it. Other groups are the Union of Democratic Doctors; the Committee for Peace, Disarmament and Cooperation (KFAZ), which published *Friedensjournal* and *Friedens-schnelldienst* (Peace journal and Peace express service); the Democratic Women's Initiative (DFI),

with headquarters in Essen, which publishes the quarterly *Wir Frauen* (We women) and focuses on women's issues on which the DKP has a firm position, such as opposition to military service for women; the Association of Democratic Jurists (VDJ), a section of the Soviet-controlled International Union of Democratic Jurists (IVDJ), is centered in Frankfurt and counts about fifteen hundred members and a quarterly publication, *VDJ-Forum*. The Anti-imperialistic Solidarity Committee for Africa, Asia, and Latin America (ASK), with headquarters in Frankfurt, serves as the framework for joint efforts on behalf of "liberation movements" and in opposition to U.S. military objectives. The ASK publishes about four thousand copies a month of *Dritte Welt-Zeitschrift: Anti-imperialist Information Bulletin*. The Patron Circle of the *Darmstädter Signal* was founded by members of the DKP, SPD, Green parties and Protestant and Catholic clergymen in 1983 to dissuade federal army (Bundeswehr) soldiers from taking part in nuclear warfare. The Federation of Democratic Scholars (BdWi), with its main office in Marburg, counts fifteen hundred members and publishes two quarterlies: *Informationsdienst Wissenschaft und Frieden* (1,500 copies) and *Forum Wissenschaft* (2,500 copies).

Domestic Attitudes and Activities. A party that has never received more than 0.3 percent of the votes in federal elections has a problem, as former DKP boss Mies openly acknowledged. In an interview in the Polish newspaper *Trybuna Ludu* on 20 July 1987 he explained that "the DKP has not been able to win a suitable place among representative bodies; its influence on the working class as a whole does not suit today's needs. The party realizes this . . . and right now it is at a stage of productive unrest, involving the seeking of ways generally to increase our influence on the working class."

The DKP, trying to break out of its isolation by forming electoral alliance, attempts to contribute in some way to parliamentary life. It jumps on the bandwagon of extraparliamentary movements whose momentum stems from dealing with issues of broad concern in the FRG. Looking back over land (state) and local elections in 1990, the party saw nothing but dismal failures and often could not even find candidates to present. It won 0.1 percent of the votes in the Saarland in January; in Bavarian local elections in March it competed in only 10 of 2,051 cities and communities, often in alliances, and managed to get only two of its members elected. In Schleswig-Holstein local elections in

March it ran independently in only Kiel and Wedel, where it won a resounding 108 and 91 votes, respectively. Thus, facing the 2 December Bundestag elections, it decided to spare its members further embarrassment by supporting the Left List/PDS, which won 0.3 percent of the votes in former West Germany and 11.1 percent in former East Germany.

There is little evidence that the DKP made significant contributions to its proclaimed goals of strengthening peace and détente through its policy of alliances with domestic partners, although there are a few instances of cooperation on the local level. Following local elections in Hesse in March 1989, the DKP formed its first governing coalition with the SPD in the city of Langenselbold and entered an SPD-Green-DKP alliance in the village of Dietzenbach. However, both the SPD and the Greens are aware that their electoral performance would be harmed, not helped, by collaboration with the communists and that the DKP's minuscule vote-getting potential would be irrelevant to any electoral outcome. There are indeed discussions within the SPD and Green parties concerning possible alliances, but these discussions revolve around alliances with each other, not with the DKP. Neither the SPD nor the Greens are dealing with security issues because they have been prodded by the DKP; defense and arms control questions are on the political agenda of all parties in the FRG. The Greens and the SPD's youth, student, and women's organizations are not left-radical groups, although some of their members do share some views of the extreme left in an abstract way and although some have been willing to take part in "unity of actions" with leftists and communists. Common ground is most often found in support of the Soviet Union's disarmament campaigns, nuclear- and chemical-free zones in Central Europe, or efforts to reduce the power of the U.S. military, the Bundeswehr, or NATO. The party's leaders have been wary of the potential risks of bringing in new members from extraparliamentary alliances. A 1987 party report pointed out the danger that

the allies' ideological and organizational attitudes also have an influence on the Communists. When working in the alliances, they [Communists] use the tactics of compromise, but often also carry it over to relations within their own party, so ignoring the fundamental distinction between a patchwork association and the Marxist-Leninist vanguard of the working class.

The report also noted that "there is a change in the social make-up of the DKP" because it is recruiting among broader social strata than the working class. Indeed, only 20 percent of communists work in "material large production." For instance, the biggest DKP plant group in North Rhine–Westphalia, the FRG's largest state, was not in the coal and steel industry but in the city hospitals (*Spiegel*, 7 September 1987). Thus, concluded the DKP report, "it is not right to forget that most of the new members lack what the workers acquire in fighting for their rights at enterprises and in the trade unions, namely, the conscious need for organized and collective action" (*WMR*, January 1987).

The DKP tries to appeal to workers, a steadily declining class in the FRG's modern economy, by demanding such measures as a 35-hour workweek without pay cuts, job creation programs, job security, higher real wages, saving the declining steel and shipbuilding industries, protecting the right of participation in managing mining and steel-producing facilities, and an end to mass layoffs and social welfare cuts. But the DKP faces a problem recruiting workers at a time of high unemployment in the FRG. In 1989 *Neues Deutschland* publicized several cases—an elementary teacher in Stuttgart, a postal employee in Giessen, a city administrator in Osnabrück—who were fired on the grounds that their activities with the DKP were not compatible with their "obligation to loyalty" to the state. These were not the first instances of such firings, and a dismissed DKP member has difficulty getting another job. As one such person remarked bitterly, "the alleged black mark of DKP membership is an insurmountable hurdle." (*Spiegel*, 19 October 1987.) Thus, a new recruit must be prepared for possibly sacrificing his livelihood. It is no wonder that the DKP calls for an end to *Berufsverbot*, "bar to occupations" (this term is used by those who oppose the law; the official title is *Radikalenerlass*, "Radicals Decree"). That this law remained on the books even after unification is a source of continued anxiety and uncertainty for German communists. (*ND*, 2 February 1989.)

The party orders its members to take an active role in trade unions, with the goal of persuading trade unionists that workers' interests are only served by class struggle. It places great value on its "educational work," particularly for the union youth organizations; many union instructors are products of the student movement and advocate orthodox Marxism. Even though few DKP members have risen to leading positions in the unions, three--

fourths of them belong to unions, and they exercise influence in some, particularly those of printers, journalists, and mass media. Communists are especially strong in the Mass Media Trade Union, which was set up in 1985 to include the Union of Print Workers, the Union of Journalists, the Union of Writers, the Union of Radio and Television Workers, and the main unions in music, drama, and the figurative arts.

Despite potential dangers, the party works toward forming broad alliances. These can be the "working class unity of actions," namely, DKP cooperation with trade unionists, workers not affiliated with any party, Christian workers, and Social Democrats, as well as with intellectuals and the bourgeoisie. Such "coalitions of reason" can seek broader objectives, and DKP members need not occupy the leading offices and can use "political flexibility" while maintaining "ideological conviction." That is, cooperation should be based on common interests and should not be brought about through compromises with reformist positions. (*Innere Sicherheit*, 12 May 1986.)

The DKP leadership believed it saw the wall breaking down between Social Democrats and communists, a wall which has existed since the foundation of the KPD in 1918 and which was strengthened by the effort of the KPD to absorb the SPD after the Second World War. Serious disagreement continues to exist between the two parties on "the system question": what kind of regime and economic order is best for the FRG. It has long sought to eliminate or lessen *Berührungsängste* (fears of contact), which has made most groups in the FRG disinclined to deal with the DKP. While there are no high-level party-to-party contacts and absolutely no talk within the national SPD of any form of alliance or formal cooperation with the DKP, some Social Democrats serve on governing boards of DKP-influenced organizations, as well as on citizens' initiatives and friendship societies with certain Socialist countries. Speakers from both parties sometimes appear at the same discussions or meetings. Also, some interviews with Social Democrats are printed in *Unsere Zeit*, although such speeches and interviews seldom involve prominent Social Democrats. In 1988 the DKP adopted the slogan Continue on This Path: Toward Social Democrats—For Unity of Action! (*VSB*, p. 87), which led nowhere. The SPD also observes a hands-off policy toward the PDS. At the university level, the predominantly leftist Social Democratic SHB had for years joined in "unity of actions" with the MSB-Spartakus and, unlike the larger SPD, favored an SPD-DKP alliance. (*Innere Sicherheit*, 12 May 1987.)

The DKP also joins broad-based protest efforts that bring it into contact with a wide spectrum of noncommunist groups and, it hopes, widens its appeal. It opposes nuclear power and reprocessing plants and is present at the often bloody protests against such installations as the Wackersdorf nuclear reprocessing plant. The DKP claimed to have helped expose the true purpose of Wackersdorf: "to be a center for the manufacture of Germany's own nuclear weapons." (*WMR*, September 1987.) In fact, no responsible German leader advocates the FRG's acquisition of such weapons. In 1988 the DKP demanded that all atomic plants be completely nationalized and placed under strict democratic control (*ND*, 1 February 1988). The DKP advocated protection of the environment and cleaning up the polluted Rhine River. It joined in the movement against taking a census, reasoning that the information thereby gained would strengthen the FRG's character as an "authoritarian surveillance state," as well as support the FRG's "antidemocratic security laws," and thereby serve ultimately "the preparation for war." (*Innere Sicherheit*, 15 May 1987.)

Perhaps most important in the party's efforts to reach out to other groups was its participation in the peace movement. Kurt Schacht, a member of the DKP executive, maintained that

> the participation of DKP members in the peace forums has unquestionably given the party valuable experience and...has had a positive effect on the peace movement itself. Cooperation between the Communists, Social Democrats, and Greens has been fostered by the considerable concurrence of their views on questions of war and peace. (*WMR*, March 1987.)

Operating within the peace movement was particularly comfortable for the DKP because it was thereby able to devote its energies to supporting Soviet and GDR security objectives. In the aftermath of the intermediate-range nuclear forces (INF) treaty, the DKP demanded in 1988 that all trials of participants picketing for peace at U.S. missile bases be stopped and that all convicted peace activists be given an amnesty on the grounds that the legitimacy of their efforts had been confirmed by the treaty. (*FBIS*, 18 February 1988.) Throughout 1989 the party also attacked tentative NATO plans to modernize short-range nuclear weapons in Europe, but these plans were quietly forgotten in a year of dramatically improved super-power relations and promising arms reduction.

Neither the DKP nor the many communist splinter parties (K-Groups) are the initiators or string-pullers of the peace movement, within which they remain a small minority. For a while, their active role was willingly accepted by the non-communist majority, which in the early 1980s rallied behind such proclamations as the largely communist-inspired Krefeld Appeal. However, by spring 1982 tensions between communists and non-communists within the movement were obvious. Robert Steigerwald, a DKP leader, scorned ecological and religious elements as "upper-level salaried employees and intellectuals" because they demanded, in the words of Petra Kelly, a "peace movement which thinks and acts in a bloc-free manner." Heinrich Böll commented that "inasmuch as the Communists are controlled from Moscow, their orders are to destroy what is meaningful in these movements by taking part in them and indeed by forcing their way into them." The noncommunist elements within the peace movement did not reject logistic support, which was the communists' greatest contribution to the movement; the DKP and its affiliated organizations had a disproportionately large representation in many of the movement's operational coordinating committees. For example, DKP delegates regularly attended meetings of the Coordinating Committee of the Peace Movement (KA), although the DKP did not formally belong. Nevertheless, the Greens and other noncommunist activists in the peace movement intensified their efforts to distance themselves from communists. Clearly, the peace movement in the 1980s was far too large and heterogeneous to be controlled by outside powers or the DKP. The party failed to capitalize on its support of the peace effort; five thousand newly won members from the movement left the DKP within two years. (*Armed Forces and Society*, Spring 1984; Moreau, "Krisen," p. 47.)

Communists have no reason to be happy about their attempts to work together with the badly divided Greens, whose decline was underscored by the fact that West German Greens failed to win 5 percent in the 1990 federal elections and were therefore ejected from the Bundestag. Although there are former communists within the Greens, they are from the militant communist splinter parties, which tend to be hostile or uncooperative toward the DKP.

The Greens never discussed coalitions with the communists, even though the DKP agreed with the fundamentalist Greens' position on violence in demonstrations: that there should be an end to the state's "monopoly on the use of force." (*CSM*, 24 November 1987.) Responding to a government statement by Chancellor Kohl, the DKP Presidium declared that "Kohl's stinging attack on those who allegedly resort to 'violence' during demonstrations disguises the intention to curtail still more the right to meetings and demonstrations" (*Innere Sicherheit*, June 1987). Few if any of the several hundred militant demonstrators who travel throughout the FRG to turn every demonstration into a violent conflict with the police, however, are following orders from the DKP. Such *Chaoten* (chaotics) are not suited for the kind of disciplined party that the DKP tries to be.

An obviously exasperated Robert Steigerwald noted that the DKP is

"working hard to secure a political alliance with its representatives while criticizing the erroneous and sometimes reactionary views of the latter. . . . Most of the Greens keep aloof from the working class, asserting that it is unable to bring about a revolutionary transformation of society. Marxism is dismissed as a nineteenth-century theory; political economy is replaced with ecology. Marxists and those who worship economic development are equally presented as prisoners of an obsession with economic growth and consumption. (*WMR*, November 1986.)

The DKP's hope of gaining an advantage by riding the extraparliamentary protest wave and participating in the peace movement were bound to be disappointed because the momentum and drive of the movement had largely vanished by 1990. There are several reasons for this. The most important is the INF agreement, signed in December 1987 between the Soviet and American leaders, that called for the removal from Europe of all U.S. and Soviet medium- and short-range missiles. This agreement was made possible by Gorbachev's implicit admission that Soviet missiles were not purely defensive in nature and are part of the problem. This undercut the DKP's persistent efforts to show that the United States and its president were the sole obstacles to disarmament. Also, in contrast with the early 1980s, the peace movement's demands were incorporated in the SPD and Green manifestos. Thus, the former extraparliamentary opposition against the arms race had been brought directly into Parliament, eliminating much of the raison d'être of the extraparliamentary peace movement. (*FAZ*, 27 May 1987.) Gorbachev's dramatic announcement of unilateral conventional arms cuts at the United Nations on 7 December 1988 was seen by NATO foreign ministers who were meeting in Brussels as "among the most promising developments" and a basis for further negotiations aiming at a military balance at a much lower level of armaments. In 1990, the Conventional Forces Talks in Europe (CFE) culminated in a dramatic agreement. The 34 CSCE states pledged to refrain from using or even threatening force against each other. Reiterating an earlier NATO announcement that the Soviet Union was not an enemy, they declared that "they are no longer adversaries, will build new partnerships and extend to each the hand of friendship." They agreed to destroy a quarter of a million conventional arms in what *The Economist* called "the biggest scrap-metal deal in history." Because the Warsaw Pact had an overwhelming quantitative advantage, it will have to make more than 90 percent of the reductions.

Other Leftist Groups. In addition to the DKP, there are many active left-extremist small groups and parties, initiatives, and new left revolutionary organizations. All renounced the DKP's earlier pro-Soviet/SED policies, which is why they, compared with the DKP and its satellite organizations, survived the collapse of communism in the GDR. They remain ideologically deeply divided, even though most are willing to cooperate in action alliances. More than thirty groups were active in 1990. About three thousand persons belonged to a variety of Marxist-Leninist groups, about eight hundred, to Trotskyist ones, and more than five thousand were members of other revolutionary Marxist organizations (*VSB*, pp. 53–54). Together they produce about two hundred publications with a total circulation of almost seven million. They also operate a few pirate radio stations (*VSB*; *FAZ*, 27 May 1988; *Innere Sicherheit*, 24 July 1987).

The new left, composed of Marxist-Leninists, Trotskyites, anarchists, autonomists, and antidogmatic revolutionaries, preaches class struggle. It identifies the proletariat as the essential revolutionary force leading the fight to tarnish the image of the FRG's political order in the eyes of its citizens and to overthrow the bourgeois state and capitalist system. Most advocate establishing a dictatorship of the proletariat culminating in a Socialist and ultimately communist order. The autonomous anarchist groups advocate the eradication of the state, to be superseded by a "free" society. Most new leftists unabashedly advocate using violence to achieve their aims.

Dogmatic new left. There are a variety of Marxist-Leninist groups, or K-Groups, the strongest of which is the Marxist-Leninist Party of Germany (Marxistisch-Leninistische Partei Deutschlands, MLPD), which has about 1,400 members, has its headquarters in Essen, and is organized in sixteen districts and aproximately 100 local units. It regards itself as the only Marxist-Leninist party in the FRG. Its official organ is *Rote Fahne* (Red banner), whose weekly circulation is about seven thousand; it also publishes a monthly, *Lernen und Kämpfen* (Learn and fight), with a circulation of 1,500. It participated in the 1987 Bundestag election, winning 13,821 second votes. Receiving virtually 0 percent of the total vote indicated how little electoral hope there is for the K-Groups and persuaded the MLPD to sit out the 1990 vote. Party spokesman Klaus Vowe argued that the party would have gotten more votes were it not for the "falsification" of the party's arguments by the bourgeois media. After German unification, which the party opposed, the MLPD raised its sword against European unity, which it claims serves the cause of imperialism. (*Innere Sicherheit*, 3 April 1987; *VSB*, pp. 55–56.)

The MLPD has three ineffective affiliated organizations with about four hundred members. They are the Marxist-Leninist Workers' Youth Association (AJV/ML) with a press organ, *Rebell*, and a children's group, Rotfüchse (Red foxes); Marxist-Leninist Pupils' and Students' Association, whose organ is *Roter Pfeil* (Red arrow); and an active Marxist-Leninist League of Intellectuals.

The United Socialist Party (Vereinigte Sozialistische Partei, VSP) was born from the 1986 merger of the Communist Party of Germany-Marxist Leninist (KPD, earlier known as KPD-ML) and the Trotskyist Group International Marxists (GIM). The VSP, with about four hundred members, has its headquarters in Cologne. Its biweekly publication, *Sozialistische Zeitung* (Socialist newspaper, circulation: 2,500), in 1986 replaced the KPD's earlier *Roter Morgen* (Red morning) and the GIM's *Was Tun* (What to do). Its youth group is the Autonomous Socialist Youth Group (ASJG). It opposed German unity, and after the collapse of the GDR, the VSP asserted that socialism remains "a real utopia," even though it exists nowhere. (*VSB*, pp. 57–58.)

The League of West German Communists (Bund Westdeutscher Kommunisten, BWK), which emerged in 1980 from a split in the now defunct Communist League of West Germany (KBW), has its headquarters in Cologne and counts approximately three hundred members organized in groups in eight lands. Its efforts to recruit more members failed. It publishes the biweekly *Politische Berichte* (Political reports), with a circulation of about 1,200 copies. The BWK is the dominant member of the People's Front, whose business office is in the BWK's main office in Cologne. The People's Front, with about six hundred members and a biweekly, *Antifaschistische Nachrichten* (Antifascist news, circulation: 600), is an instrument for an alliance of left extremists. The BWK is willing to cooperate with the DKP and its affiliated or influenced organizations. It condemned the internal movements against communist regimes in Eastern Europe as "counterrevolution." (*VSB*, pp. 56–57.)

The Communist League (Kommunistischer Bund, KB) has its headquarters in Hamburg, where about half of its four hundred followers live. Demanding "confrontation with the state" and abolition of the "capitalist republic," it has considerable influence within the Green-Alternative List (GAL). The KB publishes a monthly, *Arbeiterkampf* (Worker struggle), which has a circulation of about five thousand. Group Z split from the KB in 1979 and joined the Greens, with many of its members rising to top positions in the Greens' federal and state organizations. The KB militantly opposed German unity, claiming that Germany had no right to self-determination and that unity was an attempt to establish Germany as a major power which threatens other countries.

About fifteen Trotskyist groups and circles, some only in certain regions, grew by 1990 to a total of about eight hundred members. Advocating "permanent revolution" and the "dictatorship of the proletariat," they decry "real existing socialism" in communist-ruled countries as "bureaucratic" or "revisionist decadence" and saw the collapse of communist regimes as confirmation of their ideology. Unlike most other Marxist groups, they interpreted the opening of the Berlin Wall as a good opportunity to establish the "unity of the German working class" and a "red council republic in Germany." To this end, some of them expanded their activities into the eastern part of Germany. The League of Socialist Workers (BSA), with headquarters in Essen, is the German section of the International Committee of the Fourth International in London. Together with its Socialist Youth League, it counts fewer than 100 members, and its weekly organ, *Neue Arbeiterpresse* (New workers' press), has advocated a general strike for overthrow of the government. The

smaller Trotskyite groups, such as the Trotskyist League of Germany (TLD), which publishes the weekly *Spartakist*; the International Socialist Workers' Organization (ISA), which is centered in Cologne and publishes the monthly *Sozialistische Arbeiterzeitung* and *Internationale Tribüne*; the International Communist Movement; the Socialist Workers' Group (SAG), headquartered in Hanover and publisher of the monthly *Klassenkampf*; and the Posadistic Communist Party, protest against animosity directed toward foreign workers in the FRG and for revolutionary struggles in the Third World.

The Marxist Group (MG) is a Marxist-Leninist cadre party with a rigidly hierarchical structure, severe discipline, intensive indoctrination, and secrecy. Most of its five thousand members do not publicly acknowledge their affiliation. They and several thousand sympathizers are mainly students and academics, and the focus of their efforts is Bavaria. Their numbers are growing, and members are expected to live together in communes and largely cut off contact with outsiders. The MG is convinced that trained agitators must spark a class-conscious proletariat to engage in class struggle. It advocates "thoroughly destructive criticism of all existing conditions." (*VSB*, pp. 60–62.) It communicates through its bimonthly *MSZ-Marxistische Streit und Zeitschrift-Gegen die Kosten der Freiheit* (Marxist controversy and magazine against the costs of freedom, twelve thousand copies), its *Marxistische Arbeiterzeitung* (Marxist workers' newspaper, *MAZ*, which appears irregularly and has a circulation of about ten thousand), its *Marxistische Schulzeitung* (Marxist school newspaper, about seven issues yearly with almost seven thousand copies), and its *Marxistische Hochschulzeitung* (Marxist university newspaper, weekly during the semesters with a circulation of about fourteen thousand). The MG has expanded to the point where it now has more members than did the K-Groups in their zenith in the 1970s; its publications have a wider distribution than all other groups in the new left put together. It actively sponsored more than four hundred events in 1989 and normally spurns cooperation with other leftist groups. It scorns Gorbachev's policy of *perestroika* and blames the SED for failing to establish a workable planned economy and for creating anticommunists. MG rejects any attempt to give socialism a human face and criticized the SED for trying to compete with the West to realize "antiquated humanist ideals of the French Revolution."

In its view, the SED got what it deserved. (*VSB*, pp. 61–62; *Innere Sichereit*, 30 May 1989.)

Autonomous anarchist groups of the undogmatic left. These groups renounce strict organizational structures and are extremely divided over aims and whether to use violent or nonviolent action to change society. Their numbers grew in the last years of the 1980s. They maintain Info-Stores and Libertarian Centers in more than 50 cities. They were generally skeptical of the collapse of the GDR and of communism in Eastern Europe, seeing in it a "capitalist reunification" and a capitulation to the blackmail of multinational corporations. (*VSB*, pp. 67–68.)

The Free Workers' Union (FAU), which has two hundred members in twenty local groups and a headquarters in Cologne, is a member of the anarcho-syndicalist International Workers' Association (IAA) and publishes a bimonthly *Direkt Aktion* in Dieburg. It founded Schwarze Hilfe (Black Help) to assist imprisoned anarcho-syndicalists, anarchists, and autonomists. It also maintains contact with the international coordinating office of the anarchist Black Cross in London. The principles espoused by anarcho-syndicalists can be summarized as antistate, antiparliamentary, and antimilitary. FAU adherents oppose both Western capitalism and the "state capitalism" practiced in communist countries. They see as their supreme task revolutionary work in factories to create collective resistance against capitalism. They dream of a society characterized by decentralization and self-administration. There are some independent opposition FAU organizations that wish to work outside the factory arena. These include the FAU Anarchist Party (FAU/AP) in Heidelberg, which occasionally publishes *Fanal*, and the FAU Council Communists (FAU/R) in Hamburg.

A Federation of Violence-free Actions Groups—Grass-Roots (FÖGA) counts about five hundred followers in about 80 groups and collectives. Its monthly *Graswurzelrevolution* (Grass roots revolution), with a circulation of three thousand, advocates a nonviolent revolution and the creation of a decentralized society based on anarchy and self-administration to replace present state power. Their aims are primarily antimilitarism, peace, and "social defense." Environmental protection, especially against nuclear power and reprocessing plants, is also important. They maintain an information and coordination center in Cologne.

The diverse autonomous anarchist groupings within the undogmatic new left tend to be tiny, loosely organized, short-lived, and prone to violence. They attract several thousand predominantly young people, who engage in "solidarity actions" to support Third World liberation movements. But their contacts with like-minded left-extremist groups outside the FRG were sporadic and generally limited to specific actions.

The FRG has many foreign extremist organizations that operate within the country and whose numbers are growing as the FRG becomes a haven for more refugees from the Third World. The presence of so many visibly alien people creates domestic political tensions and provides a convenient scapegoat and target for right-wing German extremist circles. The BfV estimates that by 1990 about 54,300 foreigners belonged to Marxist extremist organizations (more than twice the number of those belonging to corresponding right-wing extremist groups). The most active and violence-oriented is the orthodox Communist Workers' Party of Kurdistan (PKK). The Liberation Tigers of Tamil Ealam (LTTE) makes its presence felt, as do violent Irish, Palestinian, Iranian, Turkish, and Yugoslavian groups. (*VSB*, pp. 148–50.)

Hard-core terrorist groups. Deadly and destructive terrorist actions continue, although their numbers continued to decline into the 1990s. The hard-core Kommandobereich (command level) of the Rote Armee Faktion (Red Army Faction, RAF) is still composed of about twenty underground killers, approximately the same number as in the mid-1970s. They engage in political assassinations and dramatic bombings. On 30 November 1989, RAF assassins killed Deutsche Bank chairman Alfred Herrhausen by a remote-controlled bomb. The RAF, which has murdered more than twenty West German business and political leaders since the early 1970s, claimed that changes in Europe require a "new chapter" for the "revolutionary movement." (*WP*, 6 December 1989.) Closely supporting the RAF terrorists is a second echelon of RAF militants, numbering approximately 250 persons. Recruited from anti-imperialist resistance circles, they handle logistics for the Kommandobereich such as documents, vehicles, weapons, explosives, and secret housing. These militants reportedly engage in violent actions against material targets but not against human beings. A further echelon is composed of RAF sympathizers, who number around two thousand. They engage in propaganda and public relations for the terrorists and assist those who are in prison. (*Innere Sicherheit*, 24 July 1987; *VSB*, pp. 75–91.) Herrhausen's murder was, according to an RAF letter, partly to support a 1989 hunger strike by faction members in prison who demanded an end of isolation and the right to be housed together. That strike had also been supported by Italian Red Brigades. (*FBIS-WEU*, 29 March 1989.) As was proven in 1987, when French police captured four leaders of Action Directe in a farm near Orleans, the RAF maintains close political collaboration with like-minded foreign terrorist groups such as Action Directe in France, the Fighting Communist Cells in Belgium, the Red Brigades in Italy, and GRAPO in Spain, despite serious setbacks in 1987. The RAF failed to mobilize a Western European guerrilla movement and therefore reportedly shifted from a strategy of shattering the "military-industrial complex" to one directed against the "European world power." This call also failed to elicit a response, as large-scale operations with other terrorist organizations failed to materialize. (Horchem, "Verfall," pp. 54–61.)

The Rote Zellen (Red Cells, RZ), their female affiliate Rote Zora, and various "autonomist groups" also launch terrorist attacks. The RZ find themselves in basic ideological agreement with the RAF's "socialist revolutionary and anti-imperialist" aims. The various other groupings and individuals lumped together as "autonomists" also chose their victims in the same basic way as the RAF and RZ and apply the same rationales for their attacks as are expressed in the "letters taking responsibility" sent by the RAF and RZ. The common characteristics of these groups are hatred of the political, social, and economic systems of the FRG and a rigorous readiness to use violence, no matter what the cost in life and limb.

The Party of Democratic Socialism (PDS). The only communist party or grouping in Germany of any relevance in electoral and parliamentary politics is the PDS. As its performance in the 2 December 1990 federal and Berlin state elections indicated, the PDS is a political force only in Berlin and the former territory of the GDR. As the senior partner of a Left List/PDS electoral alliance, it garnered 0.3 percent of the votes in the former West Germany and 11.1 percent in the East for a total of 2.4 percent nationwide and seventeen seats in the Bundestag. Party leader Gysi won a directly elected seat in East Berlin's Hellersdorf-Marzahn, an unusual feat for a candidate from a small party. In future Bundestag elections the PDS will have to capture the usual 5 percent of the votes nationwide to win seats. In Berlin state elections, the PDS captured 1.1 percent of the votes in the western sector and 23.6 percent in the eastern sector, where former SED functionaries and intellectuals are concentrated, for a total of 9.2 percent and 23 seats in the legislature.

The PDS casts itself as a party that has purged itself of Stalinism but not of socialism. In the electoral campaign it advocated a middle road between the discredited "real socialism" in the East and capitalism in the West.

We are against the fact that all socialist ideas and reflections of a basic social emancipation are declared null and void concurrently with the justified complaint of human rights violations that were committed in the name of socialism. . . . Many of us gained our leftist identity in opposition to "real socialism"; others tolerated and supported this system too long. Together we stand before the rubble of a failed policy. (*ND*, 5 September; *FBIS-WEU*, 3 October.)

Its slogan was *Lust auf Links*, and Gregor Gysi, its leader, was its only media star in a mixed bag of socialists. Gysi, a witty, brilliant lawyer, asserted: "I was already defending political victims when your Kohls and Strausses gave Honecker billions in credits!" He tried to give the party a modern, with-it image, and his followers wore buttons reading, in English, Take It Easy Gysi! The noticeably well-funded party ran an extremely professional campaign. Gysi filled halls whenever he appeared in the West; the attendees were predominantly young people who liked his unconventional and open style and refusal to speak in "functionary's-Chinese." ("Ein Alleinunterhalter und die Last der Vergangenheit," *Das Parlament*, 27 November.)

The PDS's burdens make it unlikely that it will be able to maintain and enlarge its role in the FRG regime. One burden is its overreliance on the popular Gysi, without whom the party's visibility and attractiveness would fall rapidly. The other burden is its history, as the heir to the discredited SED. Its response to scandals that were uncovered and publicized by the press, not by the party's leadership—the Modrow government's attempts to protect the security services, the abuse of the party's temporary monopoly over news media press houses, and, above all, the attempts to cling to the sizable property and bank account holdings—showed that the PDS has dealt with its history too selectively.

Dr. Heinrich Bortfeldt, former researcher for the Academy of Social Sciences in East Berlin and SED party member, spoke for many disappointed intellectuals when he wrote that many PDS members never adjusted to their new role in the opposition, never put aside their SED-shaped way of thinking, and never threw their opinion of capitalism overboard, all of which blocked their openness to what was new in Germany and prevented them from seeing anything progressive in German unity. "The PDS remained fixated on the GDR." Many members accepted the FRG's Basic Law (constitution) only out of tactical calculation and refused to accept it as a matter of principle. Renewal within the party was sought only half-heartedly. He concluded: "Whether the experiment of renewal of a party shaped by Stalinism will succeed remains more open than ever." (Heinrich Bortfeldt, "Hat die SED die PDS eingeholt?" *Disput* [Berlin] 2 November.)

Wayne C. Thompson
Virginia Military Institute

BERLIN

Population. 3.5 million

Party. Socialist Initiative (SI), heir since 1990 to Socialist Unity Party of West Berlin (Sozialistische Einheitspartei Westberlins, SEW). (The Party of Democratic Socialism, PDS, is the heir to the Socialist Unity Party of Germany, SED, and is the dominant communist party in both the eastern and the western parts of unified Berlin.)

Membership. 1,600 (fewer than 1,000 dues payers)

Politburo and Secretariat. Collectively resigned November 1989

Status. Legal

Last Congress. Founding congress, 28–29 April

Last Elections. 1989, 0.6 percent and no representation; SI did not compete in first all-Berlin elections 2 December.

Auxiliary Organizations. About 200 persons belong to Socialist Youth League Karl Liebknecht (Sozialistischer Jugendverband Karl Liebknecht, SJ Karl Liebknecht); Young Pioneers (Junge Pioniere-JP); SI university groups

Publication. *Konsequent* (Consistent), a quarterly magazine, circulation: 2,500

Background. After 1945 West Berlin was under formal Allied occupation by the armed forces of the United States, the United Kingdom, and France,

which maintained about ten thousand troops there. The 1971 Quadripartite Agreement, signed by the above three powers and the Soviet Union, confirmed Berlin's special status in that West Berlin was not a part of the Federal Republic of Germany (FRG) but had links with it. On 3 October 1990 Germany regained full sovereignty, and the city of Berlin became unified.

Membership and Organization. Since April 1990 Socialist Initiative (SI) has been the battered heir to the SEW, which was broken down into twelve suborganizations and had a number of affiliated organizations: communist youth organized in the SJ Karl Liebknecht, which had a monthly journal, *Signal*; the Young Pioneers (JP); the SEW-influenced Action Group of Democrats and Socialists (ADS-West Berlin), which published the biweekly *Ads-Info*; the Democratic Women's League Berlin (DFB), which produced the monthly *Im Blickpunkt der Berlinerin* (In the perspective of the Berlin woman); the German-Soviet Friendship Society—Berlin; the West Berlin organization of the Victims of the Nazi Regime/League of Antifascists (VVN/BdA), which published a quarterly antifascist magazine, *Der Mahnruf* (The warning). The SEW exercised considerable influence over the Berliner Mietergemeinschaft (Berlin Renters' Community), whose eight thousand members oppose the elimination of rent controls. It publishes a bimonthly *Mieterecho* (Renters' echo) with a circulation of eight thousand. (*VSB.*) The SEW published its own newspaper, *Neue Zeitung* (formerly *Die Wahrheit*), which folded at the end of 1989.

Traditional Policy Stance. In defense, the defunct SEW totally backed Soviet and GDR demands, something about which former party chairman Horst Schmitt made no bones: "We—the Communists of West Berlin—support with all our strength the peace policy of the Soviet Union, the GDR and the other socialist states." It favored all disarmament proposals made by the Soviet Union, asserting that "this is ever more necessary because the most aggressive quarters in the U.S. and Western Europe bound up with the military-industrial complex are concocting ever more pretexts to frustrate disarmament moves." (*ND*, 17 May 1987; *IB*, September 1987.) In foreign affairs it was an unfailing spokesman for the SED's policies, especially with regard to the status of West Berlin. It stated that it is time to end the backward-looking "myth of a metropolis"—of one Berlin. "West Berlin is not 'part' of a whole city; it is a large city developed in nearly 40 years under the special conditions of an occupied territory." The SEW called on West Berlin's and Bonn's governments to recognize the GDR and "stop interfering in the internal affairs of the GDR." It also agreed entirely with the SED's rationale for the Berlin Wall, which it called "the secured state border of the GDR vis-a-vis West Berlin: it led to stability in the area and will remain in place until the reasons for which it was erected in the first place disappear" (i.e., Western meddling). (*ND*, 16–17 May 1987; *IB*, September 1987; ADN, 25 May 1987.)

Like the DKP in the FRG, the SEW was open to "unity of action" with Social Democrats, the Alternative List (AL—a leftist grouping in which Berlin Greens participate), and trade unions, especially in the "fight for peace." It joined in the opposition to the census, invoking the "right of resistance" on the grounds that it violates "basic constitutional rights." It joined many other groups in a demonstration protesting against "police terror and for democratic rights" on the occasion of President Ronald Reagan's visit to West Berlin 12 June 1987, when he demanded that the wall be torn down. (*ND*, 29, 30 June 1987.) It opposed unemployment, "poverty caused by social dismantling," "hopelessness," denial of renters' rights, capitalist application of education and technology that harms workers, destruction of the environment, especially the "continuing liquidation of small gardens, fields and forests for the profit-oriented housing development policy," relegation of thousands of artists to a minimal standard of living, and discrimination against women and foreigners. "Our party takes the view that the foreign workers are part of the working class and that we have a common enemy: monopoly capital" (*ND*, 16–17 May 1987; *Innere Sicherheit*, 15 May 1987). Despite its efforts to become a part of a broad front of "progressive" groups, the SEW's collaboration was never sought by the SPD-AL coalition, which ruled in West Berlin from January 1989 to December 1990.

Search for a New Policy Direction. The year 1989 brought the SEW so many bitter shocks and setbacks that its only alternatives were to attempt to either reform itself or perish. Campaigning under the banner of the right to work and to live in peace and democracy, the SEW's performance in the 29 January 1989 elections was dismal: 0.6 percent of the votes. The party's public claims that it had made an important contribution to the defeat of the CDU-FDP coalition were not credible, given the SEW's extremely low vote count. More and more SEW activists realized that such poor electoral performances were likely to continue as long as the SEW retained its character as an unswervingly pro-SED and pro-Moscow party, tightly organized along standard Marxist-Leninist lines, financially dependent on East Berlin, and internally divided over *glasnost'* and *perestroika*. West Berlin voters had not forgotten the message that former SED Politburo member Alfred Neumann brought from the SED to the SEW's party congress in May 1987: "The SED and the SEW are linked not only by common roots, traditions, and the same goals and class interests but also by the socialist world view and the Communists' confidence in victory" (ADN, 16 May 1987).

In January 1989 the SEW's official organ reported heated discussions within the party concerning its future direction. Unlike the DKP majority, which was rejecting the applicability of Gorbachev's *perestroika* in Germany and voting down the reformist faction within the party, the majority within the SEW concluded that "*glasnost'* and *perestroika* must be recognized as principles of socialism" and that "new thinking over the SEW's relationship with the SED must be developed." The SEW began a process of shifting its ideological loyalties from the GDR to the Soviet Union. (DPA, 23 January 1989; *RAD Background Report*, no. 14, 27 January 1989.) Like the DKP, the SEW departed from the SED line for the first time in June by expressing the "shock and opposition" of West Berlin communists toward the Chinese communist leadership for its brutal suppression of demonstrators in Beijing: "We belong to a party that is characterized by profound humanism, the broadest democracy, and a firm class position." SEW members were annoyed and angered by the SED's pressure to make the SEW change this position. (*FBIS-WEU*, 22 June, 12 July, 14 August 1989.)

The dramatic changes that occurred in the GDR and the rest of Europe (see the preceding chapter on FRG) in the fall of 1989 surprised and overwhelmed the SEW, which had historically been totally servile to and dependent on the discredited SED. On 15 October 1989, the SEW changed the name of its newspaper from *Die Wahrheit* (The truth) to *Neue Zeitung* (New newspaper). The first issue under the new name asserted that "the times today call for new thinking, new acting—nothing remains as it is." SEW communists hoped that the *Neue Zeitung* would appeal to readers outside their tiny circle and would serve "the growing need of the leftist, democratic, trade union spectrum for a dialogue toward a common new orientation." The new paper folded almost immediately after its birth. (*FAZ*, 16 October.)

In the wake of the political hurricane that blew down the Berlin Wall on 9 November, 40 percent of SEW's members stormed out of the party and the entire Politburo and Secretariat resigned to prevent "unjustified tensions from emerging within the party." (*ND*, 15 November 1989). In November 1989 the SED decided to dissolve the SEW, but the PDS's new leader, Gregor Gysi, opted in December to try to stabilize the SEW, which had been purged of most of its Stalinist members. An SEW resolution acknowledged that the massive pressure of the GDR's population had forced a change toward a renewal of socialism, but it pointed to risks that the momentous events could be misused by "class enemies" bent on creating a reunified Germany in a capitalist image. The nationalist outburst could wipe away "progressive positions" that had been achieved in West Berlin. (*ND*, 21 November 1989.)

Nevertheless, Klaus-Dieter Heiser, an SEW leader, emphasized that "the process of renewal within the SEW was accelerated by the development in the GDR" and that there would be a personal, programmatic, and political renewal of the SEW. He admitted that, in the past, the SEW had idealized the achievements and situation in the GDR and had therefore been blind to or had not wanted to see the growing alienation between the people and the leaders of the SED and the state. "We had believed that the collective human rights developed in socialism were to be valued above the individual human rights, such as freedom of movement, which had been fought for in the bourgeois revolution." What is astounding about Heiser's admissions is not only their self-critical openness but that these were reported in *Neues Deutschland*! (*ND*, 28 November 1989.)

The SEW had to struggle to survive in a city that became very different after 9 November 1989. At the beginning of its extraordinary party congress on 17–18 February, Dieter Ahrens resigned as chairman: "I thus take responsibility for the production of wrong political models." His deputy, Inge Kopp, also stepped down, as had the entire party executive at the end of January. (Hamburg, DPA, 16 February; *FBIS-WEU*, 20 February.) All eight hundred delegates knew that the party's iron link with the SED had been harmful, but they had varying opinions about the way out of the crisis. In a tense atmosphere 52 percent of the delegates voted to dissolve the party. Because this was short of the 66 percent necessary to terminate the party's existence, half the representatives stormed out in disgust.

Under chaotic circumstances those who remained could only agree on a second congress 28–29 April, which sealed the fate of the SEW. The 250 elected or self-appointed delegates, representing no more than 1,600 total party members, transformed the SEW into the Socialist Initiative (SI), whose ideological manifesto parroted that of the PDS. However, the SI was unable to establish a durable alliance with the PDS, which decided to expand its own organization into West Berlin and the rest of the FRG in order to enhance its prospects for electoral success. (Moreau, "Krisen"; *VSB*, pp. 29–32.) The SI was unable to field its own candidates in the first all-Berlin elections on 2 December, and it was equally unable to help enlarge the vote of the PDS in the western part of Berlin. There the PDS won only 1.1 percent of the votes, which together with the 23.6 percent it won in the eastern part of the city, where thousands of former SED functionaries reside, amounted to 9.2 percent for the PDS in all of Berlin. Faced with massive disillusionment with the way the SED had ruled the GDR for 40 years and with further embarrassing revelations at the end of the year about large-scale financial chicanery, the long-term future of the PDS is bleak. Nevertheless, the PDS will be the major communist political force in Berlin and the rest of the FRG for several years into the 1990s. The SI will remain irrelevant.

Wayne C. Thompson
Virginia Military Institute

Great Britain

Population. 57,365,665 (July)
Party. Communist Party of Great Britain (CPGB)
Founded. 1920
Membership. 6,000 (*Morning Star*, 10 December)
Secretary. Nina Temple
Cochairs. Marian Darke, Asquith Gibbes, Mhairi Stewart, Arthur Adlen

Political Committee. Trevor Carter, Doug Chalmers, Marian Darke, Asquith Gibbes, Judith Gradwell, Bill Innes, Martin Jacques, Ian McKay, Ann Pocock, Gerry Pocock, Dave Richards, Nina Temple, Terry Wilde (*7 Days*, 20 January)

Executive Committee. 35 members; for list see *Morning Star*, 10 December.

Status. Legal

Last Congress. Forty-second, Special, 9 December 1990

Last Election. June 1987, 0.1 percent, no representation

Auxiliary Organizations. Young Communist League (YCL), Liaison Committee for the Defense of Trade Unions (LCDTU)

Publications. *Morning Star, Marxism Today, Communist Focus, Challenge Spark, Our History Journal, Economic Bulletin, Medicine in Society, Education Today and Tomorrow, The New Worker, 7 Days* (ceased publication 26 May)

The CPGB is a recognized political party and contests both local and national elections. It does not, however, operate in Northern Ireland, which it does not recognize as British territory. The party has had no members in the House of Commons since 1950, but has one member, Lord Milford, in the nonelected House of Lords.

Leadership and Party Organization. The CPGB is divided into four divisions: the National Congress, the Executive Committee and its departments, districts, and local and factory branches. Constitutionally, the biennial National Congress is the party's supreme authority and, during most of its history—but not in recent years—rubber-stamped the decisions of the Political Committee. Responsibility for overseeing the party's activities rests with the 45-member Executive Committee, which is elected by the National Congress and meets every two months. The Executive Committee is made up of members of special committees, full-time departmental heads, and the sixteen members of the Political Committee, the party's innermost controlling conclave.

Party leaders are deeply preoccupied with the continuing decline in support. Electorally, the party is so battered that it no longer contests as many seats in the House of Commons as it once did. Membership, at fewer than 7,000 (only some 50 percent of whom have actually paid their fees) is at its lowest point since World War II. The decline in electoral support was most graphically illustrated in Britain's last general election (1987) when the party's nineteen candidates polled a mere 6,078 votes.

This poor showing of the CPGB at the polls belies, however, the party's still important strength in the trade union movement and in influencing opinion. Although it does not directly control any individual trade union, the party is represented on a number of union executive committees and has played a major role in most government-union confrontations of recent years. The CPGB's and other communist influence is partly attributable to low turnouts in most union elections, to the fact that it is the only party seeking to control the outcome of these elections, and to its close interest in industrial affairs, which ensures support from workers who might not support other aspects of the party's program.

Domestic Affairs. The collapse of communism in Eastern Europe and the turmoil in the Soviet Union have profoundly affected the CPGB, as well as the entire communist movement in Britain. These enormous events humiliated the movement and led to a quickening decline in membership. The liberal and reform-minded CPGB has taken some solace in finding itself more in the mainstream of events than any of its competitor organizations. But this comfort is slight because it is also witnessing the collapse of its own organization and the prospects for the future.

Recent events are damaging, for they come as yet another blow against a movement that has suffered serious internecine warfare for many years. Even as electoral support for the communists plummeted during the Thatcher era, the intraparty struggle intensified. The Eurocommunist CPGB fought hard against the Stalinist breakaway groups who were unstinting in their support of the ideology and policies of the Soviet Union and the East European bloc. Now that communist governments have fallen or are in crisis, the entire British movement, including the reformist CPGB, finds itself badly discredited.

The CPGB began to react strongly to the events in Eastern Europe and the Soviet Union during 1989, as it became clear that change was rushing faster and further than anyone in the movement had anticipated. The key event for CPGB was its regular Forty-first Party Congress at the end of the year. At that meeting Gordon McLennan, the then general secretary, welcomed the changes taking place and, along with many speakers, congratulated his party for its long and consistent criticism—however mild

—of many Soviet policies. He and others also reassured the party that it had taken the correct approach in embracing Eurocommunism as compared to the hard-line breakaway rivals, the Communist Party of Britain and the New Communist Party.

McLennan's positive words did not hide, however, the reality that the party faced an uncertain future in which it would need to find a new attractiveness. The leadership's immediate answer was to offer a fresh political approach. Martin Jacques, its ideologue and editor of the party monthly, *Marxism Today*, presented his own and the Executive Committee's draft of a *Manifesto for New Times*.

Quite simply, *Manifesto for New Times* declares that the communist system, as it has been defined during this century, is finished:

This is the end of the road for the communist system as we have known it: the central plan, the authoritarian state, the single-party system, the subjugated civil society. Stalinism is dead and Leninism—its theory of the state, its concept of the party, the absence of civil society, its notion of revolution—has also had its day.

In presenting this draft to the congress, Jacques added that the international communist movement was also at an end, a victim of its own inflexibility and isolation from a democratic mandate. In place of the old ways, the *Manifesto* argued for a new flexibility, a willingness to recast the communist movement as a part of the social democratic tradition and, therefore, a willingness to work within a pluralistic democratic system.

The congress not only adopted this new *Manifesto*, it installed an entirely new reformist leadership of young people who were pledged to carry out change that would go as far as necessary to restore the party's appeal.

In 1990, the CPGB proceeded with these changes at an accelerating pace. Nina Temple became the new party leader, holding the title of secretary rather than the previous and more familiar communist party title of general secretary. She was joined by a new Executive and Political Committee of much younger people.

Temple is the first woman and the youngest person ever to serve as party leader in the 70-year history of the CPGB. She took office committed to go further than the *Manifesto for New Times*. In a series of interviews with British and American journalists in January, Temple made it clear that she would press for drastic change. She immediately launched a month-long debate in the party's weekly newspaper, *7 Days*, about the party's future direction. But she loaded the debate by indicating that her own view was that the party should seriously consider abandoning its ideological rootings as well as its way of doing business. She even went so far as to suggest that "it's going to be such a thorough overhaul that we might not be the Communist Party anymore." In addition, she told the *New York Times* that the changes should probably include a renunciation of the commitment to Marxism-Leninism, as well as to democratic centralism. Thus, she added, there should probably be a new constitution and organizational structure and an end to the name, *communist party*. In fact, the party should explore, she said, the possibility of becoming part of a federation of left organizations within British politics. (Later in the year, Temple astonished an interviewer by asserting that she has never regarded herself as a Marxist-Leninist.)

Although the debate within the CPGB raged on for months about these issues, the direction that Nina Temple set in January dominated the agenda throughout the year. In September, the party's Executive Committee endorsed this approach and set the stage for a special congress in December. All the while, of course, events seemed to force the party to move even faster, so that by the time the congress met in December, Temple's proposals, appearing rather revolutionary at the beginning of the year, were seen as rather less dramatic and even imitative of what other communist parties in Europe were already doing. The special party congress did not approve the proposals, and there is now a commitment to produce a new consitition in 1991. Another party congress is slated to convene during November 1991 to consider the new document and other radical changes, including the possibility of a new party name, which is expected to be *Radical Socialist Federation*.

Competing communist organizations in Britain were contemptuous of the CPGB reforms. Because virtually all of them hold a much harder and more orthodox view of communist ideology than the CPGB, they accused the CPGB of essentially abandoning the communist movement.

The largest and most vocal opposition is the Communist Party of Britain and its newspaper, the *Morning Star*. Almost gleefully, the *Morning Star* reminded its readers that it had been warning for years that the CPGB was a traitorous organization whose Eurocommunism was a mask for its abandonment of the movement. Now, it said, the mask was off and all pretense of CPGB commitment to communism had fallen away.

This reaction was not very different from the years of warfare between the two sides. The Communist Party of Britain had been organized in 1988 as a competing party to the CPGB, but the main force of the disagreement has been the struggle between the CPGB's Executive Committee and the breakaway *Morning Star*, owned by the People's Press Printing Society (PPPS). Despite long-running efforts by the CPGB to retake control of the PPPS, the paper has continued to be in the hands of what the CPGB Executive Committee has described as a Stalinist majority. The substantive disagreements between both sides have focused primarily on Stalinist objections to CPGB criticisms of Soviet policies and leadership in emphasizing Eurocommunism.

The string of serious defeats for the left in Britain during the years of the Thatcher government greatly sharpened these arguments. Most important of these have been the miners' strike of 1984–1985, together with the years of unsuccessful struggle with the Thatcher government on a whole range of issues. As a result, the already fractured communist movement drifted into an even sharper debate within itself. Who was to blame for these defeats? How should they proceed to bolster the party's position, along with the position of the left? Should the party adopt a more cooperative relationship with the Labour party and even parties to the right? How should it deal with the British union movement?

The CPGB has tended, and now more so, to answer these questions by advocating broad alliances with less ideological leftist parties and groups. This has infuriated the harder left, including the Communist Party of Britain and its *Morning Star*, as well as the other breakaway, the New Communist Party. To be sure, there have been fractious problems within this opposition, but there is general agreement that the CPGB leadership is guilty of soft-headed thinking that has caused the movement to lose its leadership of the working class.

Over the last few years, a pattern of vicious attacks from each side against the other, including CPGB expulsion of rebel hard-line members, almost completely dominated the time of all the participants and further hurt the appeal of the party. The 1987 election results graphically showed how extensive the damage had become. Whereas the party fielded 35 candidates and won more than 11,000 votes in 1983, it only offered 19 candidates

and won fewer than 7,000 votes in 1987—a small fraction of 1 percent of the entire British electorate.

The events in Eastern Europe and the Soviet Union have thus had a devastating impact on an already bad situation for the British communist movement. It is interesting to note that even while attacking the CPGB for its alleged abandonment of communism, the *Morning Star* has gone some distance toward acknowledging the crisis and calling for significant reform. It is careful to defend the historical record of socialism in the Soviet Union and to call for the defense of the ideology. But even while doing so, it admits serious failures needing the most urgent changes:

> Whatever difficulties exist today, whatever mistakes and crimes were committed in the past, particularly under Stalin, these enormous positive achievements of Socialism cannot be dismissed out of hand.
>
> To cope with the challenge presented to it, the Socialist revolution opted early on for the path of rapid industrialisation. The centralised administrative command structure facilitated this, but instead of being seen as temporary, it became entrenched, assisting the limitation of democratic involvement which took place, and ultimately choking economic and technological development.
>
> It is this administrative command structure which is dead, but as yet it has not been replaced by the more flexible regulated Socialist market needed to release the popular initiative that can exploit the potential for increased productivity inherent in modern science and technology.

In domestic affairs, the CPGB continued its long drumbeat campaign against what it describes as the "uncaring," "oppressive" Tory government. One of the party's few pleasurable moments in 1990 came when Mrs. Thatcher resigned. She had been a special target for many years, and her demise was greeted with joy. Although the CPGB supports the notion of a Labour victory and return to office at the next general election, it is somewhat suspicious of Labour party leader Neil Kinnock. The party frequently wonders out loud about Kinnock's leadership abilities as well as his "opportunistic" nature.

The CPGB has been especially interested in the issues of the poll tax and the state of the National Health Service. The party was active during the spring of 1990 when there were riots in London against the poll tax and pleased with the publicity Mrs. Thatcher provided for its efforts by her denunciation of the turmoil that occurred.

In May, the party lost its major platform for direct public communication when its newspaper, *7 Days*, ceased publication because of lack of funding. Its more popular but less campaigning publication, *Marxism Today*, is also in financial difficulty. The CPGB's only solace in this situation is that its rival newspaper, the larger *Morning Star*, is also in difficulty and has been forced to decrease the size of its issues.

Auxiliary Organizations. In industry, CPGB activity centers on its approximately 200 workplace branches. Its umbrella organization is the LCDTU. Although the CPGB is riven by internal disputes, its trade union structure can still command considerable support from prominent trade union leaders. The YCL, the youth wing of the party with only about 500 members, ceased (*Morning Star*, 10 December).

The party retains a number of financial interests, including Central Books, Lawrence and Wishart Publishers, Farleigh Press, London Caledonian Printers, Rodell Properties, the Labour Research Department, and the Marx Memorial Library.

International Views and Activities. The CPGB has vocally supported the upheavals in the Soviet Union and Eastern Europe. It argues in favor of multiparty systems, free elections, adherence to human rights guarantees, and an end to the secret police institutions as well as a broader European integration. The party has also adopted a pro–European Community stance, reversing years of opposition. The CPGB supports antigovernment activity in South Africa and condemns the apartheid policy.

The CPGB has supported the British government position against Iraq's invasion of Kuwait and accepts its insistence that Iraq withdraw its occupation. The party, however, has been much more hesitant about the use of force to resolve the issue. It has, instead, supported sanctions and insisted that every effort be made to make negotiations work.

Other Marxist Groups. Besides the CPGB, several small, mainly Trotskyist groups are also active. Although some of these groups grew swiftly in the 1970s, their memberships are now waning.

The most important of the Trotskyist groups is Militant Tendency, which derives its name from its paper of the same name. Militant Tendency claims to be merely a loose tendency of opinion within the Labour party, but there is no doubt that it possesses its own distinctive organization and that for some years it has been pursuing a policy of "entryism" (the tactic of penetrating the larger, more moderate Labour party). Militant Tendency controls about 50 Labour party constituencies, but has been in decline recently.

The other significant Trotskyist organizations are the Socialist Workers' Party (SWP) and the Workers' Revolutionary Party (WRP). The SWP has been particularly active in single-issue campaigns, notably the antiunemployment campaign. It gave active support to striking miners' families but, in fact, enjoys little support in the coal mining industry. The WRP's activities are more secretive but are known to center in the engineering, mining, theater, and auto industries. It focuses its attention on the young and has set up six youth training centers, which are primarily concerned with recruitment.

Gerald A. Dorfman
Hoover Institution

Greece

Population. 10,028,171
Party. Communist Party of Greece (Kommunistikon Komma Ellados, KKE)
Founded. 1921
Membership. 50,000 (estimated)
General Secretary. Grigoris Farakos, 66, Greek, electrical engineer, former editor of *Rizospastis*
Politburo. Kharilaos Florakis, chairman; Grigoris Farakos; Nikos Kaloudis, 72; Loula Logara, 62; Kostas Tsolakis, 62; Orestis Kolozov, 57; Dimitris Gondikas, 49; Aleka Papariga, 44; Takis Mamatsis, 64; candidate members: Dimitris Kostopoulos, 50; Spyros Khalvatzis, 44; Dimitris Androulakis, 38; Dimitris Karagoules, 38; P. Lafazanis; G. Dragasakis; Thanasis Karteros, 45
Secretariat. Yiannis Mavrakis, 37; Kostas Voulgaropoulos, 50
Chairman. Kharilaos Florakis
Status. Legal
Last Congress. Twelfth, 12–16 May 1987, Athens
Last Election. 8 April 1990, 10.28 percent (as part

of the Coalition of the Left and Progress) 19 of 300 seats

Auxiliary Organization. Communist Youth of Greece (KNE)

Publications. *Rizospastis* (daily); *Kommunistiki Epitheorisi* (Communist review, *KOMEP*) monthly theoretical review

The beginning of 1990 found the KKE participating in an all-party government under veteran banker Xenofon Zolotas. The other participants in the government were the conservative New Democracy party, which had won a plurality but not a majority of seats in the legislature in November, and the Panhellenic Socialist Movement (PASOK), which had been in office between October 1981 and 18 June 1989, when it lost its parliamentary majority in the election.

KKE participated in the government under the mantle of the Coalition of Left and Progress, a loosely knit alliance of KKE with the Greek Left (E.AR) (the former KKE-Interior), which the two parties formed in February 1989.

In the voting in the legislature in April for the election of a new president of the republic to replace outgoing President Khristos Sartzetakis, the Coalition of the Left supported Sartzetakis as its candidate whereas PASOK supported Yiannis Alevras, the former president of the legislature. The New Democracy wanted to support K. Karamanlis, who had served as president of the republic between 1980 and 1985, but Karamanlis refused, knowing that he could not muster the 180 parliamentary votes needed for election. Eventually K. Karamanlis was elected after the new parliamentary election of 8 April, when under the Constitution only 151 votes were required.

The 8 April election gave the New Democracy a working majority (151) in the legislature and ended KKE's participation in government. The attention of the party, at least as far as the electoral process was concerned, turned to the municipal elections scheduled for October. But the major problem facing the party was its internal cohesion. The collapse of the communist regimes in Eastern Europe inevitably caused confusion and uncertainty in KKE's ranks. The Greek communists cannot claim, unlike their East European counterparts, that communism was imposed on them from the outside. They embraced Marxism-Leninism on their own and find it much harder to give it up; it is their reason for being. KKE has been traditionally an orthodox communist party. In 1968 it split into two factions—KKE-

Exterior and KKE-Interior—because the KKE leadership remained dogmatic in its outlook. Eventually, KKE-Interior became E.AR and moved away from Marxist-Leninist ideology and the traditional emblems and trappings of communist parties. KKE remained the guardian and standard-bearer of Marxism-Leninism.

In the closing days of 1989, Grigoris Farakos, KKE's general secretary, made an effort to veer away from the party's Marxist-Leninist dogmas. He explained away the collapse of the communist regimes in Eastern Europe by saying that "certain Communist parties had been cut off from the people" and that "this disassociation from the people is now being punished, and in a way this is a positive [development]." Throughout his political career in KKE, Farakos has not been known for his liberal or innovative views. He was elected to the post of general secretary in July 1989 when then General Secretary Kharilaos Florakis moved to the post of chairman—a post created by the Twelfth Party Congress in 1987 but left vacant. Florakis thus relinquished the post of KKE's general secretary to become the chairman of the Coalition of the Left and Progress. Farakos, who was initially considered to be an interim appointment to the post of general secretary, moved to consolidate his position by assuming the leadership of the renovators within the party hierarchy. Florakis, for his part, tried to play a balancing role between the hard-liners and the renovators, not always with much success.

In the summer of 1990 the renovators, led by Farakos, drafted the new party theses to be submitted for approval by the party's Thirteenth Congress, at that time projected for November. The authors of the theses and the accompanying programmatic declaration acknowledged that the theories of Marxism-Leninism were identified with the systems in Eastern Europe that had collapsed, but attributed the collapse to the distortions committed by the "dogmatists." KKE, the theses emphasized, "is based on Marxist-Leninist theory," which "is not a dogma but a guide to action." Another key point was the assertion that "the conquest of power by the forces of Socialism and the exercise of power by them will take place in conditions of free multiparty competition, with full safeguards for human rights, and by ruling out the identification of a governing party with the state." The theses embraced "a multiplicity of forms of ownership" and "the full utilization of the market and of its planned direction" and added that "the historical-theoretical term of the dictatorship of the proletariat . . . can no longer express the goals and the values the party sees in Socialism."

The theses revealed a painful effort to reconcile Marxist-Leninist theory with the new realities. In a way, it was a half-hearted and tortured attempt to move to an almost "social-democratic" framework. The problem with this approach is that this moderately Marxist form of socialism has already been preempted by E.AR and even more so by PASOK. KKE's credentials to spearhead such a movement are suspect and tarnished to say the least. Moreover, many among the KKE rank and file became party members out of a conviction that Marxism-Leninism was the wave of the future and that social democracy was either a joke or a betrayal of socialism.

On 2 June, the KKE Politburo, dominated by General Secretary Farakos, approved, after a two-day meeting, presenting the draft theses and programmatic declaration to a broad plenum of the Central Committee. In the broad plenum, which met two weeks later, Kharilaos Florakis sided with the hard-liners, declaring that he opposes the abolition of such terms as the "dictatorship of the proletariat," "democratic centralism," and "proletarian internationalism," and the removal of the "hammer and sickle" as the party's emblem. Farakos openly disagreed with Florakis and asked the broad plenum to approve the drafts for presentation to the congress. Dimitris Androulakis, a candidate member of the Politburo and one of the leading innovators, asked Florakis to come back with specific proposals for changing the draft theses. Florakis responded with a mild, vague speech, but through a clever parliamentary maneuver the hard-liners pushed a majority vote in favor of drafting a new set of theses for the party congress.

The debates within the party continued, and finally, on 24 October, a Central Committee plenum approved the new draft theses, the programmatic declaration, and a new party charter for presentation to the party congress, which was postponed and rescheduled for the second week of February 1991. The new draft charter establishes the post of associate general secretary and retains the principle of democratic centralism except that the views of the minority will now be recorded and made known to the membership. Moreover, the dissenting members will have the right to publicize and defend their views through the party media. Until changed, however, the decisions of the party organs will be binding in keeping with the principle of democratic centralism. The new draft charter provided that the members of the Politburo and the Secretariat cannot be elected to more than two consecutive terms (a total of approximately eight years). Finally, there is a requirement that each party congress will replace at least 25 percent of the Central Committee membership with new members. It is not difficult to predict that in the Thirteenth Party Congress in February (unless postponed again) the struggle between hard-liners and renovators will be fierce. The outcome, however, cannot be predicted. A resurgence of the hard-liners in the Soviet Union will likely embolden the KKE hard-liners and weaken the renovators.

In the closing days of 1990, the party rank and file were shocked to learn that Nikos Zakhariadis, who had been appointed by Stalin as general secretary of the KKE in 1931 and had served in that post for 25 years, had died in 1973 by his own hand in his place of exile, despondent over the deteriorating conditions of his life and the treatment he had received from the Soviet authorities after his removal from the party leadership in 1956.

During the year, KKE faced problems within the Coalition of the Left and Progress. The main issue was whether to cooperate with PASOK in the October municipal elections. Several KKE and E.AR leaders within the coalition objected to such cooperation because PASOK had been accused of economic scandals. Others favored such cooperation, which would lead to the election of many left-leaning mayors. Under the electoral system only candidates receiving more than 50 percent of the votes could be elected in the first round. In municipalities where no mayor was elected in the first round, the two candidates with the largest block of votes would compete for a majority in a runoff election. Considering that PASOK and the coalition together attract more than 50 percent of the popular vote, their joint support assured a candidate's election. In the end, PASOK and the coalition ran separate candidates in the first round in most municipalities. The New Democracy candidates scored several important successes during that first round, capturing posts in Athens and Thessaloniki. The coalition candidate was elected in Pireaus. During the second round, however, the left-leaning candidates received the support of PASOK and coalition voters, and many were elected.

The disagreements between KKE and E.AR, however, go beyond the issues of the municipal elections. Many in E.AR favor an ideological framework that is almost social democratic in character. A shift of KKE toward a more dogmatic, hard-line approach in the Thirteenth Congress will shake the coalition to its foundations and may lead to its breakup. The prospects for the left in Greece are not overly bright. In the 8 April parliamentary election, the coalition candidates received 10.28 percent of the total vote, even less than what KKE and E.AR candidates running separately normally received in the past.

The left, however, is also represented by PASOK, which still draws the support of almost 39 percent of the voting public. Despite New Democracy's strong showing in the April election (46.88 percent), a leftist mentality remains strong among ordinary people.

Strange as it may seem, the revolutionary banner is now hoisted mostly by terrorist organizations, with 17 November at the forefront. Its proclamations—issued after every terrorist attack and published in full by several newspapers—employ the full arsenal of revolutionary rhetoric together with a theoretical analysis of Greek society, economy, and politics. Its avowed aspirations notwithstanding, this terrorist organization cannot play the role of a political party because of the secrecy that surrounds its leaders, its cadres, and its operations. Other small parties, which operate in the open and which favor revolutionary changes, have minimal support; candidates of such parties together received less than 1 percent in the April election. Evidently, the revolutionary left (both terrorist and political) has minimal support in the country.

Leadership and Organization. Until now the KKE has continued to maintain the basic organizational structure it adopted in the days when it operated illegally, except now it practices less secrecy, at least about the identity of members and cadres. Many internal disputes also reach the public because of leaks to the press or open discussions in the Central Committee and the party congress. The party members are organized in *pirines* (cells) in factories, workplaces, schools, and neighborhoods. Party *fraxies* (factions) are organized by party members who are also members of trade unions, professional organizations, and cooperatives in the countryside. The major cities have city committees headed by secretaries who are also members of the Central Committee. The party has also committees in every prefecture and regional committees supervising the party work in the major regions in the country—Crete, the Peloponnesus, Thessaly, Epirus, Macedonia, Thrace—each headed by a regional secretary. One may have to

wait until the forthcoming Thirteenth Party Congress in February to see if this structure will change in any substantial way.

In E.AR the major change came with the election of respected attorney Fotis Kouvelis, a moderate, renovating thinker, to the post of secretary, previously held by Leonidas Kirkos. Kirkos became chairman.

Views and Positions. In 1990, KKE, the major partner in the Coalition of the Left and Progress, muted the strong criticism it had leveled in 1989 against PASOK, its leader Andreas Papandreou, and the economic scandals allegedly perpetrated by his party while in office. PASOK's participation in the all-party government between November 1989 and March 1990 blunted the issue of the scandals, although the judicial prosecution continues. Many in KKE, led by Kharilaos Florakis, felt that it was in the interest of the party to cooperate with PASOK in the April parliamentary election, primarily to prevent New Democracy from winning a working majority and forming a government, which would deprive KKE of its balancing role. Although cooperation remained limited to the four single-seat electoral districts, the KKE's criticism of PASOK virtually disappeared.

For KKE the main ideological problem has been the collapse of the communist regimes in Eastern Europe. The party's views are confused and uncertain, vacillating between hard-liners and renovators. In the absence of a clear vision, the party mechanically reiterated its opposition to the North Atlantic Treaty Organization (NATO), the European Community (EC), and the presence of U.S. bases in Greece. This last issue has lost much of its urgency because the Americans voluntarily removed two bases near Athens and because Athens and Washington signed a new agreement that allows the remaining bases to stay. Even KKE's anti-NATO and anti-EC rhetoric has lost much of its virulence. That virulent rhetoric is now being used primarily by the terrorist organization 17 November and the like.

The relatively more moderate views of the party, compared with the past, are not being shared by many in the rank and file, especially the young members of the Communist Youth Organization (KNE), although it is also confused and vacillating.

Domestic Activities. Most of the party's domestic activities revolved around the parliamentary election of 8 April, the municipal elections of October, and the preparations for the Thirteenth Party Congress. Details are given in the preceding pages.

International Contacts. International contacts were limited in 1990. Many of the parties that had extended invitations in the past were no longer in power. The most notable meeting with foreign delegations took place in early September (6–8) at the invitation of KKE. The delegations represented communist and workers' parties from countries in the eastern Mediterranean, the Middle East, and the Red Sea. Florakis denounced the invasion of Kuwait and the holding of hostages, but he also expressed the party's opposition to the massive U.S. troop presence in the area.

G. I. Yanayev (now vice-president of the USSR) was present at the Second Party Congress of PASOK in Athens, 22–22 September.

Other Marxist-Leninist Organizations. Several such groups exist, but they are marginal in terms of their influence and following. Their fielding of candidates in recent elections showed that all of them together do not represent even 1 percent of the voting public. Their members are mostly young unemployed university graduates, unemployed laborers, university students, and some young workers. Of these fringe organizations we may mention for the record the KKE-Interior/Renovating, the Greek International Union-Trotskyists, the Revolutionary Communist Party of Greece (EKKE), the Communist Party of Marxist-Leninists (KK-ML), the Organization of Marxist-Leninists of Greece (OMLE), the Socialist Revolutionary Union (ESE), the Greek Leninist Revolutionary Movement (ELEM), the Organization of Communists—People's Power (OK-LE), the Organization of Communist Internationalists of Greece (OKDE), and the Revolutionary Communist Party—Greek Section of the Fourth International, another Trotskyist organization. Most of these groups make their existence known through an occasional pamphlet or wall posters, usually in the center of Athens in the old university area. They also participate with banners in street demonstrations called by political parties or trade unions. As mentioned earlier, several terrorist groups such as 17 November, 1st of May, ELA, Revolutionary Solidarity, and the like have picked up the revolutionary banner and have added the clout of bombs and bullets to theoretical arguments.

D. G. Kousoulas
Howard University

Iceland

Population. 251,000 (November)
Party. People's Alliance (Althydubandalag, PA)
Founded. 1968
Membership. 3,000 (estimated)
Chairman. Olafur Ragnar Grimsson
Executive Committee. 14 members: Olafur Ragnar Grimsson, 47, finance minister and professor of political science; Steingrimur Sigfusson, 35, minister of communications and agriculture and deputy party chairman; Svavar Gestsson, 46, minister of education and former party chairman; Svanfridur Jonasdottir, 41, former deputy party chairman; Bjorn Sveinsson, 41, PA party secretary; Bjargey Einarsdottir, 40, PA treasurer; Alfheidur Ingadottir, 42, managing director of a salmon farm; Sigurjon Petursson, 53, Reykjavik city council member; Gudrun Agustdottir, 43, special assistant to the minister of education and Reykjavik city council member; Ottar Proppe, 42, civil servant, Hafnarfjordur Port Authority; Asmundur Stefansson, 45, economist and president of the Icelandic Federation of Labor; Armann Magnusson, 41, Icelandic Federation of Labor official; Stephania Traustadottir, 41, Office of Equal Rights Council; Kristin Olafsdottir, 42, Reykjavik City Council member, folksinger, and actress
Party Secretary. Bjorn Sveinsson
Central Committee. 70 members, 20 deputies
Status. Legal
Last Congress. 16–20 November 1989
Last Election. 1987, 13 percent, 8 of 63 seats
Auxiliary Organization. Organization of Base Opponents (OBO); organizer of peace demonstrations against the U.S.–North Atlantic Treaty Organization bases
Publications. *Thyodviljinn* (daily), Reykjavik; *Verkamadhurinn* (weekly), Akureyri; *Mjolnir* (weekly), Siglufjordhur

Iceland is a land of fire and ice, and its politics are known for their mixture of extremes. Not since the eleventh century, when the world's first Parliament (the Althing, established in 930) voted unanimously to embrace Christianity, have Icelanders practiced the consensus politics of their Nordic brethren. In fact, few of the rules of European politics apply on this remote island, where personality plays a larger role in government than parties or institutions. Iceland is the only West European country to have a party with recent communist origins in government, but the PA fits few traditional communist molds and has largely discarded Marxist-Leninist rhetoric. It is currently in a broad center-left coalition of five parties and holds three cabinet portfolios.

The PA occupies the left flank of Icelandic politics. It is the successor to a long line of leftist parties dating back to 1930, when the Icelandic Communist Party (Kommunistaflokkur Islands) was formed out of a left-wing splinter group of the Social Democratic Party (Althyduflokkur, SDP). In 1938, the SDP split again, and one faction joined with the communists to create the United People's Party–Socialist Party (Sameingingar flokkur althydu–Sosialista flokkurinn, UPP-SP). In character with Iceland's tradition of setting its own course in history, this new amalgamation broke early with the Comintern, etablishing the precedent of independent radical socialism without foreign ties. Still another faction from the SDP merged with the UPP-SP in 1956. The PA emerged in its present incarnation from the ashes of the then Socialist Unity party in December 1968. Before its inclusion in the current government, the PA last participated in a governing coalition with the PP from 1980 to 1983. That government dissolved after the April 1983 parliamentary elections, in which the PA netted little more than 17 percent of the vote. (RFE *Research Report*, 12 January 1970.)

The PA's decline continued through the April 1987 elections, when it polled 13 percent and received only 8 seats in the 63-seat Althing. For the first time, the reformist SDP, which received 15.2 percent of the vote and ten seats, outpolled the PA. SDP chairman and current Foreign Minister Jon Baldvin Hannibalsson outflanked the PA with his strong stump speaking and effective, if ideosyncratic, leadership. But the PA lost votes to more than the SDP. An unconventional radical feminist party, the Women's List (Samtok um Kvinnalista or Kvennalisti, WL), also continued to surge in the polls at the expense of the PA. (*JPRS-WEU*, 29 September 1988)

When the center-right coalition government led by the Independence Party (Sjalfstaedisflokkur, IP) collapsed in September 1988, the PA entered a four-party coalition with the agrarian Progressive Party (Framsoknarflokkur, PP), the reformist SDP, and a splinter parliamentarian group from the Progressives elected under the banner Association for Equality and Justice. With an even split in the lower house of the Althing and only a one-vote majority overall, the coalition was weak from the start. Hamstrung by deadlocked legislation, the government was forced in September 1989 to invite the moderate Citizen's Party (Borgaraflokkur, CP) into the coalition. Meanwhile, the economic downturn in the late 1980s that undermined the previous government bottomed out in 1990, but forecasts of improved economic performance seem to have done little to boost the coalition's popularity. (*Morgunbladid*, 13 October.)

The coalition formed by PP chairman and current Prime Minister Steingrimur Hermannsson was a major tactical coup for both him and PA leader Olafur Ragnar Grimsson. Hermannsson, whose party commanded only 13 of 63 seats in the Althing, was able to knit together a broad platform that all five current parties could accept. Grimsson, who failed to win a parliamentary seat, desperately wanted a cabinet ministry; this not only would allow him to speak and present bills in the Althing (though not vote) but also would give him a leading role in Icelandic politics. He fought strong opposition within the PA to bring the party into the coalition and secured the strategic Finance Ministry for himself. He also landed two other portfolios for the PA, which the party has exploited to pursue its objectives. Steingrimur Sigfusson became the minister of communications and agriculture, from which he has pushed for an air traffic agreement with the Soviet Union. Svavar Gestsson received the Ministry of Education and Culture at a time of concern that taking part in the European integration process would threaten Icelandic customs and traditions.

One Icelandic tradition that appears to be holding on strong is the fall in popularity of whatever parties are in power. The current government is, however, breaking all records. After two years, the government coalition as a whole has the support of less than a quarter of the public. The PA's popularity itself sank to between 8 and 10 percent in various polls taken during the fall, a drop of approximately 4 percent from the 1987 election. These figures led SDP foreign minister Hannibalsson to comment that governing was not a popularity contest. Elections, however, are, and few believe that the coalition will survive the national elections of April 1991.

Leadership and Organization. The broad composition of the PA's Central Committee and its history of factionalism have worked to maintain an open, democratic character within a party apparatus that has never followed a strict Leninist organizational model. The intense infighting following the 1987 election, Grimsson's election as party chairman, and the decision to join the coalition in 1988 continue that open character at the local and national level. By negotiating the culture and education portfolio for former party chairman Gestsson, Grimsson temporarily coopted his strongest rival. Gudrun Agustsdottir, a member of the Reykjavik town council and vocal opponent of the PA's participation in the government, became Gestsson's special assistant. Other major PA figures who opposed the coalition, like Asmundur Stefansson, president of the Icelandic Federation of Labor, have distanced themselves from the PA rather than speak out publicly against it.

Declining popularity and the pressures of governing with four centrist parties contributed to the continued fragmentation of the PA in 1990. The May 1989 split of the Reykjavik PA Society into a traditionalist group and a pro-Grimsson Birting Society remained unresolved at the end of 1990. In addition, the SDP's offer to form common election slates with the PA in the May municipal elections created a new cleavage. A number of PA officials ran on a slate with the SDP called the New Area (Nyr Vettvangur, NA) that, with the support of Birting, managed to steal two of the PA's three seats in the Reykjavik city council. The PA was undoubtedly also hurt by Grimsson's refusal to lend his support to either the official party slate or the breakaway NA-Birting grouping. In the May municipal elections across Iceland, the PA lost four council seats and gained none, a strong indication of problems to come. (*Morgunbladid*, 22 April.)

The poor results put additional pressure on Grimsson to resign. Minister of Communications and Agriculture Steingrimur Sigfusson and Education Minister Svavar Gestsson commented publicly that the party was coming apart and that a change of leadership was essential to restore the party's unity and image. Both lobbied the PA Executive Council to replace Grimsson, but few in the party hierarchy wanted to face such a divisive question so close to the national election. (*Morgunbladid*, 21 and 22 April.)

With the next general election due in April 1991 according to the constitution, the PA has been holding primaries around the country to select candidates. Brimsson, currently only an alternate member of the Althing, has secured the first position in the PA's party slate in the southwest district of Reykjanes. Despite his unpopularity in this area for opposing the siting of a new aluminum plant there, Grimsson looks certain to shore up his political position by gaining an Althing seat. The PA's slate in the rural northeast will be headed by Sigfusson, who as agriculture minister is expected to use his post to boost the PA's popularity in the area. (*Morgunbladid*, 1, 2, 3 December; *Thjodviljinn*, 1, 2, 3 December.)

Rumors that the participation of the PA and SDP in the government coalition would lead to the renewal of a leftist front and election cooperation in 1991 also fell victim to the PA's fragmentation. Joint speaking tours planned for Grimsson and SDP chairman Hannibalsson never materialized. The failure of the New Area slate to gain its goal of three seats in the Reykjavik city council was a further setback. As 1990 came to a close, the idea of a joint slate in the national election appeared only a remote possibility.

The recent struggles within the PA are essentially rooted in continued friction between its academic and labor wings. Grimsson is a professor of political science and has been trying to reform the party under more social democratic lines. His deputy, Sigfusson, is a hard-line Marxist with a strong labor background. Atlantic Trade Union Federation head Gudmundur Gudmundsson actually resigned his seat in the Althing to protest the PA's white-collar orientation and openly proposed that a labor-oriented party splinter off from the PA. Particularly troublesome for labor during the debate over PA's participation in a coalition government was a May 1988 provisional law suspending the right to collective bargain and strike. The PA had to accept this law as a condition for entering government. Furthermore, it was forced to support a temporary wage and price freeze and sales taxes on food, measures that the PA had earlier opposed on the grounds that they were regressive. By making these concessions, the PA further alienated its labor constituency, which accounts for the lion's share of its voting support.

Leadership challenges at the top have also gained momentum as women in the PA have taken on a more assertive role. The political challenge of the Women's List focused attention on the all-male composition of the PA's ministerial appointments. Party rules call for at least 40 percent of all posts to go to women. Gudrun Helgadottir, a leader of the reform faction, felt particularly slighted in not being chosen for one of the three cabinet positions and was only partially assuaged when she was elected the first female speaker of the united Althing in October 1988. Jonasdottir's defeat as deputy party chairman in November also prompted criticism of the PA as an all-male club. If the WL continues to steal votes from the PA, the PA will have to address this issue of female representation in party and government posts. (*Thjodviljinn*, 22 November 1989; *Nordisk Kontakt*, no. 14–15, 1988.)

Domestic Affairs. The recent upswing in the economy and indications that the government's austerity program has curbed inflation have done little to bolster either the coalition's or the PA's showing in the polls. Economic forecasts show Iceland's gross domestic product will post a 1.5 percent growth rate in 1991, the first positive figure in three years. Inflation is also expected to moderate to below 15 percent for 1990. Higher fish prices internationally contributed to this turnabout, and Iceland is expected to post its second straight trade surplus in 1990. (*News from Iceland*, November/December.)

Despite the success of the coalition's economic policies, the PA's main constituency, workers, bore the brunt of the sacrifice to establish a degree of price stability. The government's embrace of wage controls, even for a short time period, succeeded in reducing inflation, but Finance Minister Grimsson has proven unable to convince traditional PA voters of inflation's dangers. His 1989 crackdown on businesses that did not pay sales taxes was widely cheered at the time but netted little additional revenue, and the move may have contributed to the recession and unemployment. With the PA's future tied to Grimsson's coattails, his two years as finance minister have endeared him to few. (*News from Iceland*, August 1989.)

Grimsson joined the coalition knowing that Iceland faced some difficult choices, but it was his intent (and the focus of his arguments to the PA membership) that only in power could the PA affect where budget cuts would fall. He has successfully fended off some austerity measures that would fall more heavily on labor and pushed forward a new, more progressive tax revenue package that raised personal income tax to 38 percent and corporate tax to 50 percent. He also secured greater individual tax exemptions and increases for old-age and disability pensions.

Despite what can objectively be considered a successful administration, the coalition is poised to fare miserably in the 1991 national election. The PA appears likely to lose three to five percentage points and possibly two seats in the next Parliament. More important, the conservative Independence party is set to post large gains and may seek a reunion with the SDP in a new center-right coalition. This would negate any role for the PA in the next administration, either as participant or as ally. In opposition, many of the centrifugal pressures on the party will disappear, but few expect the Birting society or New Area separatists to return quickly to the fold.

Foreign Affairs. The once central issue in Icelandic foreign policy and one the PA has kept center stage, East-West relations, has been swept away by the end of the cold war. The PA has, however, begun to focus on arms control. As memories of the various Soviet submarine accidents off northern Norway in 1989 faded, the signing of the Conventional Forces Talks in Europe (CFE) agreement in Paris last fall added new impetus to calls for naval arms control. The PA has encouraged Prime Minister Hermannsson, the most vocal proponent of naval arms control, and drowned out Foreign Minister Hannibalsson's more cautious advice. The PA remained a strong voice for Iceland's withdrawal from the North Atlantic Treaty Organization (NATO) and for the removal of all armed forces from the island. The PA has used the Organization of Base Opponents (OBO) and its control of the Communications Ministry to keep pressure on Keflavik. In Central Committee meetings, the PA continues to pass resolutions for an eventual Nordic nuclear weapons–free zone.

The PA's relationship with Moscow chilled further in 1990 over nuclear testing, the Soviet treatment of the Baltic states, and the failure of a proposed Aeroflot air traffic agreement. In November, Grimsson, leading a delegation from Parliamentarians for Global Action, presented Soviet president Gorbachev with a petition to end nuclear testing. The PA also supported Nordic Council initiatives to seek ties with the Baltic republics and to deplore Soviet aggression against their newly elected governments. Only the party newspaper, *Thjodviljinn*, took a more cautious stand by arguing the danger of "Lebanonization" in the Soviet Union. Foreign Minister Hannibalsson's strong stand against an air traffic agreement with Aeroflot, pursued by Communications Minister Sigfusson, removed one of the last Soviet initiatives from the PA's agenda. (*Morgunbladid, Thjodviljinn*, 16 May.)

As economic integration in Europe has accelerated with the approach of 1992, Iceland focused increased attention on maintaining access to European markets for its fish products. Iceland has remained outside of the European Community (EC) primarily because of the EC requirement that Iceland open up its fishing grounds in exchange for the benefits of a single market. The PA has fought EC membership and is concerned about the current negotiations between the EC and the European Free Trade Association (EFTA), of which Iceland is a member. In October, PA parliamentarian Hjorleifur Guttormsson strongly criticized Foreign Minister Hannibalsson for the emphasis he was placing on completing an EC-EFTA agreement. The PA feels that the single-market requirements of free movement of labor and capital would allow foreign ownership of Icelandic companies and otherwise change the country's cultural identity. (*Thjodviljinn*, 1 November; *Morgunbladid*, 21 November.)

International Party Contacts. The PA and its predecessors have always remained aloof from international communist movements. As the first to disassociate itself from Stalin's Comintern and denounce Soviet intervention in Eastern Europe, the PA maintains the Icelandic tradition of self-reliance and political independence from Europe. What little contact does exist is mainly with radical Socialist parties in the other Nordic countries, namely Norway's Socialist Left and Denmark's Socialist People's party.

Other Marxist and Leftist Groups. The PA's internal pluralism has discouraged the formation of independent parties with competing Marxist ideologies. In so doing, it has often been described as more an organized argument than a political party. Although there were brief flurries of interest in the 1970s, Maoism and Trotskyism are not represented in Iceland by organizational structures. The PA remains a heavily divided party, but its ability to maintain some degree of party discipline in parliamentary votes shows that it combines flexibility with ideology, a mixture that has in recent history discouraged the formation of permanent breakaway parties.

The Women's List (WL) is a phenomenon peculiar to Iceland. Women continue to be prominent in Icelandic politics and public life, as symbolized by the republic's president and most popular politician, Vigdis Finnbogadottir (whose powers are largely ceremonial, but not irrelevant in a cabinet crisis).

The WL is a radical feminist group, but its pragmatic domestic program attracts wide support in this highly egalitarian society. Given its electoral gains in the 1987 election and strong continued popularity, more than 10 percent in November polls, the WL will probably hold onto its six seats in the 1991 election. It is unlikely, however, that the WL would play a role in the formation of a new government under the IP. (*Morgunbladid*, 13 November.)

All the other parties accord the WL's parliamentary leaders considerable respect. Nevertheless, given the requirements for economic austerity that faced the new government, the WL's demands for massive wage increases for low-paid employees, the majority of whom are women, would have made it a problematic coalition partner in this time of austerity. The WL's general line emphasizes redistributional and social welfare policies over economic growth and investment. On foreign affairs, its position is strongly pacifistic and opposed to Icelandic commitments to NATO. The party's internal organization is very loose, with annual rotation of top positions. The WL has clearly attracted many voters who may otherwise have been inclined to support the PA. (*JPRS-WEU*, 4 October 1988.)

Randolph McNeely
Greenbelt, Maryland

Ireland

Population. 3,500,212 (July)
Party. Communist Party of Ireland (CPI)
Founded. 1933 (date of record)
Membership. Under 500 (*World Fact Book*)
General Secretary. James Stewart
Executive Committee. Includes Michael O'Riordan (chairman), Andrew Barr, Sean Nolan, Tom Redmond, Edwina Stewart, Eddie Glackin
Status. Legal
Last Congress. Twentieth, 28–29 October 1989; 26–27 May 1990
Last Election. June 1989, no representation
Auxiliary Organization. Connelly Youth Movement

Publications. *Unity, Irish Socialist, Irish Workers' Voice, Irish Bulletin*

The CPI was founded in 1921 when the Socialist party of Ireland expelled moderates and decided to join the Comintern. During the civil war, the party became largely irrelevant and virtually disappeared, although small communist cells remained intact. The CPI was refounded in June 1933, the date the communists now adopt as the founding date of their party.

The party organization was badly disrupted during World War II because of the neutrality of the South and the belligerent status of the North. In 1948, the communists in the South founded the Irish Workers' party and those in the North, the Communist Party of Northern Ireland. At a specially convened "unity congress" in Belfast on 15 March 1970, the two groups reunited.

The CPI is a recognized political party on both sides of the border and contests both local and national elections. It has, however, no significant support and no elected representatives.

Leadership and Organization. The CPI is divided into two geographical branches, North and South, corresponding to the political division of the country. In theory, the congress is the supreme constitutional authority of the party, but in practice it tends to serve as a rubber stamp for the national executive. The innermost controlling conclave is the National Political Committee. Such little support as the CPI enjoys tends to be based in Dublin and Belfast.

Domestic Affairs. The continuing political division of the country, Ireland's economic problems, and the upheaval in Eastern Europe and the Soviet Union were the main issues for the party in 1990. The CPI views the United Kingdom as an imperialist power that gains economically from holding Ireland in a subordinate position. Although continuing to advocate the creation of a single, united Socialist Ireland, the party remains opposed to the use of violence and denounces the use of force by armed gangs on either side of the communal divide.

The party believes Irish unification can be achieved only by promoting working-class solidarity and thus overcoming the communal divide between Protestants and Catholics. Executive Committee member Morrissey put the CPI view succinctly: "As long as the working class is divided along religious or other lines, the exploiting classes will dominate the political stage and Ireland will remain subordinate to imperialism."

The Twentieth Congress of the CPI met in late October 1989. The main political resolution agreed on by the delegates reaffirmed the party's condemnation of the Anglo-Irish agreement. The CPI continued to deplore the agreement as a form of British imperialism that allows a continued British presence in Ireland without consequent violence. The congress also reconfirmed its long-standing opposition to Irish membership in the European Community (EC) and warned of the further dangers posed by the creation of a fully integrated common market by 1992.

Addressing the upheaval in the international communist movement, the congress decided to reconvene in 1990 to discuss the ideological implications of unfolding events in Eastern Europe and the Soviet Union.

The Twentieth Congress reconvened at the end of May 1990. In the months between the end of the previous session in November 1989 and the new session, a number of committees examined every aspect of the party's ideology, structure, and activities. The resumed congress accepted the recommendations of these committees.

Overall, there were few changes in the party's traditional views. What changed was the emphasis on democratic participation within the party, as well as its willingness to collaborate with other "progressive" forces. The party recommitted itself—unlike the Communist Party of Great Britain—to Marxism-Leninism and democratic centralism as well as the full range of traditional views about international affairs and Irish unity and neutrality.

International Views and Activities. The CPI historically has remained staunchly pro-Soviet and outside the Eurocommunist movement. As events in Eastern Europe and the Soviet Union unfolded, the CPI reluctantly and hesitantly followed President Gorbachev's leadership toward reformist policies. It was clear, however, that the CPI was not enthusiastic about these changes. In the important relationship with its British comrades, the CPI feels much closer to the views of the breakaway Communist Party of Britain (CPB) than to the mainstream and much larger, but Eurocommunist, Communist Party of Great Britain (CPGB).

The CPI remains strongly anti-American and denounces U.S. policy in Central America, the Middle East, and elsewhere. It favors arms reduction talks in Europe and opposes the deployment of missiles and former President Reagan's Strategic Defense Initiative.

The CPI is staunchly against Irish membership in the EC. It recognizes that chances are poor that the Irish government will follow its views but insists that the EC is a mechanism for the exploitation of the Irish working class.

Gerald Dorfman
Hoover Institution

Italy

Population. 57,664,405
Party. Italian Communist Party (Partito Comunista Italiano, PCI)
Founded. 1921
Membership. 1,431,000 at Nineteenth Congress; "over 1.3 million" claimed at the end of 1990.
Chairman. Alessandro Natta, 72
General Secretary. Achille Occhetto, 54
Secretariat. Occhetto; Antonio Bassolino, 43, program coordinator; Massimo D'Alema, 41, coordinator of the Secretariat; Claudio Petruccioli, 48, special tasks; Livia Turco, 35, women's commission
Directorate. 52 members
Central Committee. 357 members
Guarantees Commission. 84 members
Status. Legal
Last Congress. Nineteenth: 8–12 March 1990, in Bologna
Last Election. 1987: 26.6 percent, 177 of 630 seats, in the Chamber of Deputies and 28.3 percent, 100 of 315 seats, in the Senate (1983: 29.9 percent, 198 seats, in the Chamber and 30.8 percent, 107 seats, in the Senate)
Auxiliary Organizations. Italian Communist Youth Federation (FGCI), Italian General Confederation of Labor (CGIL), National League of Cooperatives
Publications. *l'Unitá*, daily, Renzo Foa, editor; *Rinascita*, weekly, Alberto Asor Rosa, editor; *Critica marxista*, bimonthly theoretical journal, Aldo Zanardo, editor; numerous specialized journals and a publishing house, Editori Riuniti

Historical Summary. The PCI was founded in 1921 when a heterogeneous grouping of radical elements seceded from the Italian Socialist Party (PSI) and joined the Comintern. The party was led by Amadeo Bordiga, who was purged by the Comintern in 1926 and replaced by Antonio Gramsci. In the same year, the Fascist dictatorship outlawed the PCI; the organization was forced underground, party headquarters were moved to France, and Gramsci was imprisoned. He was replaced by Palmiro Togliatti, who then led the party until his death in 1964 and who, more than anyone else, was responsible for many of the PCI's most unique features.

Relentlessly persecuted under fascism, the party organization had been reduced to, at most, five thousand members by 1943. The collapse of the regime, followed by the Resistance (in which communists played an important role) provided the PCI with broad legitimacy by war's end. In coalitions with the Socialists, the PCI regularly received the majority of the vote in the red belt of north central Italy and was initially strong in the industrial northwest as well. The PCI participated in governments of National Unity from 1944 to 1947, until it was expelled from the coalition (along with the PSI, with which it was to maintain strong links until 1956). Togliatti ignored strict Leninist principles and insisted on building up a mass party, present everywhere in society. By the time the PCI was expelled from the government, it claimed more than 2 million members. Membership would gradually decline from the mid-1950s onward, but the party still had more than 1.5 million members at the start of the 1970s. The total rose to 1.8 million in the late 1970s but has declined steadily since then.

Under the leadership of Togliatti and a younger generation of renovators, the middle and upper reaches of the party organization were de-Stalinized in the latter half of the 1950s. The late 1950s and 1960s also saw an increasing tolerance of internal dissent and a fairly loose form of democratic centralism, even after Togliatti died and the helm passed to Luigi Longo. By the 1960s, a general consensus had emerged throughout the leadership and in much of the rank and file around the Togliattian Italian Road to Socialism. Some ambiguities about the party's complete commitment to Western democratic values and institutions persisted into the 1970s, when they were dispelled under Longo's successor, Enrico Berlinguer, who became general secretary in 1972 and led the party until 1984.

Although Togliatti always remained close to Moscow, he staked out increasingly autonomous positions in the 1950s and 1960s. He criticized the limits of de-Stalinization in the USSR and called the communist movement polycentric. He deplored the Sino-Soviet rift and refused to join in condemnations of the Chinese. The highly competitive Italian political arena, with numerous forces laying claim to left-wing credentials, accelerated the PCI's evolution in the 1960s. By 1968, Longo was able to condemn the invasion of Czechoslovakia in far stronger terms than almost any other non-ruling communist party. By the end of the 1970s, stimulated domestically by the desire for democratic legitimacy and externally by Brezhnev's repressiveness and adventurism, Berlinguer had staked out extremely critical positions. Following the imposition of martial law in Poland in 1981, Berlinguer declared that the October Revolution had lost its propulsive energy and no longer had anything to offer progressive Western forces. He also denied the notion of an international communist movement as distinct from other forces on the left. Following these pronouncements, relations with the Soviets reached the point of a *strappo* (tear or break).

Relations with the USSR improved in the post-Brezhnev era; by the end of the 1980s the Soviets admitted that Berlinguer's earlier criticisms had been well-founded. Throughout this period, the PCI jealously guarded its complete autonomy and independence. The most reform-minded elements in the ruling parties of the Eastern bloc countries all acknowledged their debt to the PCI in the late 1980s.

Electorally, the PCI obtained 19 percent of the vote in the first postwar elections in 1946, compared with 21 percent for the PSI and 35 percent for the Christian Democrats (DC). By 1948, after the Socialists lost their right wing, the communists became the largest party on the left, growing to 27 percent by the end of the 1960s. By then the PSI had been reduced to roughly 10 percent and was floundering between the PCI and the DC. During the 1970s, the PCI effectively wrote off the PSI and proposed a "historic compromise" with the DC; when the communist vote reached 34.4 percent in 1976, the PCI, already in power in Italy's largest cities, became part of the governmental majority but was denied cabinet posts. By the end of the 1970s, the PSI indicated its willingness to form majorities without the PCI; this act relegated the communists back to the opposition, where they have

remained since 1979. In 1980, they definitively dropped the historic compromise and called for an alternative to the DC's generations-long domination of Italian politics.

In the three general elections since 1979, the PCI's share of the vote fell steadily; with just under 27 percent in 1987, it was where it had been at the end of the 1960s. The party's local vote also declined steadily through the 1980s, although its immense strength in its strongholds kept it in power in most of the red belt. The only exception to the party's steady downward electoral slide has been in the elections to the European Parliament. In 1984, the PCI's total jumped to a third of all votes cast, surpassing the DC for the only time in postwar Italian history; this turned out to have been a sympathy vote for Berlinguer, who had died in the midst of the campaign. In 1989, the communists obtained nearly 28 percent of the vote, which seemed at the time to arrest the decline and validate Occhetto's bold initiatives. But this, too, turned out to be a fleeting upturn in the party's fortunes.

Since the 1980s, a politically isolated PCI has been threatened by new formations like the Greens on the one hand and by an increasingly assertive PSI on the other. Relations between the PCI and PSI have been strained as the Socialists, now with nearly 15 percent of the vote, appear willing to countenance an eventual alliance with the communists only if the PCI is reduced to the status of junior partner. In the course of the 1980s, the PCI increasingly championed a united European left that would transcend the historical division between communists and Socialists (or Social Democrats). Lingering Eurocommunist ambitions or claims to be seeking a "third way" (i.e., between Eastern state socialism and Western social democracy) were dropped by the late 1980s as well, along with almost all vestiges of a communist model of party organization. The collapse of the Soviet-style regimes in Eastern Europe provided party Secretary Achille Occhetto with the excuse to push the complete overhaul of the PCI's identity to its logical limits: late in 1989, he announced that the party's name and symbol would be changed in an extraordinary congress to be held early in 1990. As 1989 ended, a badly divided PCI was preparing for the Nineteenth Congress in Bologna.

Domestic Politics and the PCI. Local elections were scheduled in most of the country for May 1990, and there was speculation that the communists might at least halt their long decline at the polls. They had done surprisingly well in the nationwide vote for the European Parliament only a year earlier, and although the recently concluded Nineteenth Congress had revealed deep divisions within the party, it had also shown that the leadership was resolute in its commitment to carrying out the PCI's change of identity. Members of the majority that emerged victorious from the congress hoped that votes from noncommunists sympathetic to the PCI's new course would offset the expected disengagement of disgruntled militants.

The results were deeply disappointing to the leadership. In both provincial and regional voting, the PCI was barely able to garner 24 percent, compared with about 30 percent in the previous local elections in 1985, and just under 27 percent in the 1987 general elections. Those results demoralized Occhetto and those around him; not only had the communists' showing been poor, but local Regional Leagues with a strong antisouthern and anti-immigrant appeal had done exceptionally well in Italy's most advanced northern regions. Many communist leaders considered that the Regional Leagues were symptomatic of a broader crisis in Italian politics, which made all the more urgent the PCI's need to end its destructive internal squabbling and play a more decisive role on the national stage. (*UN*, 26 May.)

Internal divisions unquestionably contributed to the party's poor showing. Rumors in the aftermath of the vote spoke of a passive campaign by exponents of the internal opposition, who hoped the poor result would embarrass Occhetto. There were reports of postelectoral celebrations in PCI sections that had opposed Occhetto's initiative. (*L'Europeo*, 26 May.) Occhetto himself openly criticized the "degenerations" that had taken place when the PCI's electoral lists were drawn up when he addressed the May plenum of the Central Committee in the aftermath of the elections (*UN*, 16 May). Immediately after the elections, Massimo D'Alema, the number two person in the party, acknowledged that the fierce internal divisions carried over from the Nineteenth Congress had caused some supporters to stay at home (*La Repubblica*, 9 May).

Toward the end of 1990, a strange sequence of events generated one of the more serious political crises of recent years in Italy, raising questions about the entrenchment of democratic institutions and reopening painful memories of the 1960s and 1970s. Renovations on an apartment that had been a Red Brigade (BR) hideout in the 1970s brought to light a supply of arms, money, and photocopies of Aldo Moro's writings, composed when the Christian Democratic leader was a prisoner of the BR for 55 days before he was murdered by them in 1978. Some writings were unknown or had not previously been released to the public. One document referred to a shadowy organization with links to both the Defense Ministry and the secret services of Italy and the North Atlantic Treaty Organization (NATO), with the apparent aim of forming the core of an armed resistance within Italy in the event of the country's occupation by hostile forces.

These revelations eventually produced high-level acknowledgments, inside and outside of Italy, that such structures had indeed existed since the 1950s—even in countries that were not NATO members (*NYT*, 16 November). Information about the Italian structure—code-named *Gladio*—was politically explosive for several reasons. Testimony by some experts formerly associated with *Gladio* suggested that some participants viewed it not only as a force to resist outside intervention but also as a potential counter to the PCI. A dozen caches of arms and explosives ostensibly buried by *gladiatori* for possible future use turned out to be missing, and the missing munitions were of the same type used in many of the terrorist attacks that Italy suffered throughout the 1970s. Perhaps most ominously, declassified information about an abortive 1964 coup (led by renegade elements in the secret services and national police, or *carabinieri*) showed that the plotters had intended to put *Gladio* infrastructure to use in their seizure of power. Many leading politicians turned out to have been well-informed about *Gladio*, and at least some appeared to be implicated in a few of the shadier episodes.

Some of the more compromised figures included Prime Minister Giulio Andreotti and President Francesco Cossiga, both of the DC. Former Socialist prime minister Bettino Craxi was badly embarrassed when he had to admit that he had been informed about *Gladio* in such a matter-of-fact way that he had not considered the issue particularly significant. Giovanni Spadolini, a Republican who had also been prime minister, angrily denounced the fact that, despite his office, he had never been informed of the organization. This of course raised serious questions about the constitutionality of the arrangement. The debate became acrimonious even among members of the five-party governing coalition, with President Cossiga making uncharacteristic—and institutionally questionable—political charges and comments.

The PCI had clearly been the prime target of the renegade forces in Italy's secret apparatuses, and it used the *Gladio* affair to raise questions about the extent to which the security services had been involved in some of the darkest episodes of recent Italian history. The communists also called attention to what they characterized as Italy's limited sovereignty in light of *Gladio*'s bypassing Italian legislation that had supposedly reformed the secret services in the late 1970s. Finally, the PCI used the occasion to wring concessions from the government. Pressured by its own left wing, the PCI threatened to absent itself from Parliament's January vote on the budget unless Andreotti promised to bring all material relevant to *Gladio* before the appropriate parliamentary committees. Andreotti finally acceded to this demand. That was still not sufficient to appease the PCI's left wing, which announced that it would not present itself for the vote. (*La Repubblica*, 22 December.)

The *Gladio* affair is only one of the many events in recent years that has cast Italian politics in a less than flattering light; in a similar vein, the strong showing by the Leagues in May was widely viewed as a profound protest against the country's established institutions. Since its relegation to the opposition in 1979, the PCI has been aware of extensive areas of dissatisfaction with the status quo but frustrated by its inability to capitalize on them. As the year wore on, the party announced its adherence to a referendum campaign that would modify Italy's nearly pure system of proportional representation, which is widely viewed as at least partly responsible for the fragmentation and proliferation of parties in the country. Because the communists generally are not supportive of Italy's abrogative referendum and because the smaller parties could be hurt by a change in the existing rules, many observers assumed that the PCI's position had some sort of anti-PSI objective. In his address to the July plenum of the Central Committee, Occhetto argued that this was not the case. The PCI simply wanted to do everything it could to unblock the paralyzed political system, he insisted (*UN*, 24 July).

As this last point shows, relations with the PSI continue to be a central consideration in all the PCI's domestic calculations. Communist-Socialist cooperation is essential for the eventual creation of an alternative to the DC, and both parties know it. At the same time, Socialist support is essential to the present five-party coalition, which gives Craxi a lot of leverage with the DC. Relations between the two major parties of the left thus tend to fluctuate considerably, depending on short- or medium-term calculations.

In 1990, as usual, these relations seesawed, with pronouncements by the Socialists before the PCI's Nineteenth Congress casting doubt on the communists' willingness to change. This was followed by a warming of relations during and immediately after the congress that got considerable attention in both the party and the national press. Once the congress showed that the party was indeed committed to redefining itself, the Socialist leader, after a much-publicized meeting with top PCI officials, argued that Occhetto should stop his foot-dragging (*UN*, 24 March). Craxi also made clear on numerous occasions that he felt the communists should adopt a name with Socialist in the title.

Shortly before Occhetto was scheduled to announce the proposed new name of the party—which would have to be ratified formally at the Twentieth Congress in 1991—Craxi pulled a maneuver that illustrates the ambivalent nature of PSI-PCI relations. After a meeting of the Socialist leadership in which nothing of the sort had been on the original agenda, he announced that the PSI had changed its name (*La Repubblica*, 5 October). This not only stole some of the headlines from Occhetto but underscored the speed and agility of decision making for which Craxi is noted. Moreover, the audacious choice of the name Socialist Unity suggested that Craxi's hegemonic ambitions for the left remained in place. Finally, it was generally agreed that Craxi's maneuvers had caused the most damage to those in the PCI who are the most committed to an agreement with the PSI at all costs: not only had Craxi's action guaranteed that Socialist would not appear in the PCI's new name, but his seemingly cynical calculations put his aspiring allies on the defensive.

A development with great significance for the Italian labor movement took place in the autumn of 1990 as a direct consequence of the changes under way in the PCI. In September, Bruno Trentin, the communist general secretary of the CGIL, the PCI-dominated General Confederation of Labor, announced that the party's actions obviously made redundant the continued existence of a formally organized communist component within the union. A gradual dissolution of the group was thus set in motion. (*La Repubblica*, 21 September.)

Party Leadership, Organization, and Debates. Two extraordinary congresses—the only ones in the PCI's postwar history—dominated the party's affairs in 1990. The Nineteenth Congress was called in the wake of Occhetto's dramatic announcement in November of 1989 that communism had run its course as an historical movement. His announced intention was creating a new formation of the Italian left, one that would no longer carry the PCI's name and symbol; this new party would move as rapidly as possible to join the Socialist International. (See *YICA*, 1989, for details.) When unexpectedly strong opposition to Occhetto's policies surfaced, he was forced to slow the pace of change: the congress was pushed back to March 1990, and it would no longer give rise to a new political force. The Nineteenth Congress would, however, pass judgment on Occhetto's proposal; if that proposal were successful, the party would then proceed to lay the groundwork for *another* constituent congress that would, after debating competing alternatives, ratify the changes supported by a majority of delegates. By the end of the year, Occhetto, victorious in the Nineteenth Congress, presented the majority's proposal for ratification by the Twentieth Congress, scheduled for the end of January 1991. The new party would be called the Partito Democratico della Sinistra (PDS) or the Democratic Party of the Left (*UN*, 11 October).

The Nineteenth Congress and its aftermath. The 1989 Eighteenth Congress had already put an effective end to "democratic centralism" in the PCI, but fierce opposition to Occhetto's proposal forced the party to depart even further from old practices and work out procedures to guarantee equal time (and space in the party press) to all contending motions. Gender quotas, recently adopted for top leadership positions, were now mandated for lower levels of the party and for delegates to the national congress. For example, at least one-fifth of the leadership of the party's nearly fourteen thousand sections and a third of the directing committee of each provincial federation must now be women. Delegations to party congresses must have a ratio of female members that corresponds to the female presence in each federation (the national average is just under 30 percent), and when a decision is taken to elect leaders by secret ballot, separate male and female lists must be presented to guarantee the women's ratio. (*UN*, 22 December, 1989.) Finally, the Central Committee's female component, which had risen to 30 percent in 1989, jumped to 40 percent after the Nineteenth Congress. It did so by using the same mechanism employed in 1989: expanding the body from an already large 300 to nearly 360.

It was clear from the beginning that Occhetto's proposal had majority support, but this was a very heterogeneous majority. Similarly, the opposition—just over a third—was larger than many observers had expected and was equally heterogeneous. The No Front, as the opposition became known, was dominated by a disparate bloc headed by some of the party's elder statesmen but including a large number of its more radical intellectuals; the remainder consisted of a smaller group gathered around Armando Cossutta. A traditionalist, Cossutta had refused to condemn the USSR's invasion of Afghanistan and never accepted the PCI's break with the Soviets in the early 1980s. His group presented a separate motion in the debates leading up to the Nineteenth Congress. (For details on the opposition, see *YICA*, 1989.)

In that debate, which ran from late 1989 through February of 1990, the PCI's lower-level organizations held congresses that voted on three contending motions: Occhetto's, that of the largest opposition grouping, and Cossutta's. Roughly 30 percent of the PCI's membership, or just over 400,000 members, eventually cast their vote. The outcome of the national congress was therefore known well in advance; as the national congress approached the only questions were the exact strength of the combined opposition and whether the differences that had emerged in an increasingly acrimonious debate would lead to a split in the party.

The forces grouped around Occhetto eventually came to the congress with two-thirds of all delegates committed to their motion. The major opposition motion was also committed to profound changes but rejected what it considered the "liquidation" of the PCI, which had long ago taken a highly critical stance toward the discredited communist regimes of the East. The chief sponsors of the principal opposition motion were Alessandro Natta, 72, party chairman; Pietro Ingrao, 75, the extremely popular historic leader of the PCI's left wing; and former *l'Unità* editor Aldo Tortorella. Their motion garnered the support of 31 percent of the delegates to the Nineteenth Congress, obtaining a majority in several provinces where radical tendencies had always been strong (e.g., the Tusco-Ligurian coast). This motion also did quite well in Rome. (*UN*, 13, 27 February.) Cossutta's motion obtained just over 3 percent, which is roughly the proportion of support his positions had obtained in party congresses throughout the 1980s. Although it did not win in a single federation, Cossutta's motion did manage to collect nearly 40 percent of the delegates' votes in the small Piedmontese province of Asti, which has long had a strong pro-Soviet tradition.

Knowing that two-thirds of the delegates were committed to Occhetto, the No Front attempted to thwart what had become a fait accompli by shifting final decision-making power outside the Nineteenth Congress. They proposed a motion that would require a two-thirds majority of the Central Committee on all "important questions." When this failed, they submitted a motion stipulating that any changes to the party's name or nature would require assent from an absolute majority of all PCI members—fewer than half of whom had voted in the congressional debate in 1990. The congress also rejected this proposal (*La Repubblica*, 13 March.)

Scrupulously applying the proportionality principle adopted when serious divisions appeared in 1989, the congress elected a Central Committee of 357 members. Occhetto's majority could claim 236 members, the Natta-Ingrao motion 105, and Cossutta's followers 12 (4 members were appointed ex officio). The same proportions obtained in the National Guarantees Commission (Rome, ANSA, 12 March; *FBIS-WEU*, 13 March). Observers after the congress noted that even with the enlargement of the party's top organs to accommodate more female leaders, many top communists were not reelected (*La Repubblica*, 13 March).

In an effort to reconstruct the party's battered unity, the presidency of the Central Committee was given to one of the most prominent leaders of the opposition—Aldo Tortorella. The Central Committee then elected a directorate according to the proportionality principle, but after rumors to the contrary chose a "politically homogeneous" Secretariat, that is, one consisting entirely of Occhetto supporters. (*UN*, 31 March.) In a long-expected move, shortly after the congress, Renzo Foa was named managing editor of *l'Unità*, the party daily. This appointment is significant because Foa is the first person to hold this position who is a journalist by profession, not a party operative. This is a trend in all the party's cultural enterprises and represents a further guarantee of evenhandedness in providing space to all opinions within the organization.

This most conflictual congress in the PCI's history ended on an emotional and unifying note: Ingrao embraced Occhetto in the closing moments, and, amid extended applause, the party secretary then put his head down and wept openly. But the conflict had been intense, and the apparent rapprochement between Occhetto and Craxi during the

proceedings fueled the opposition's fear of a headlong rush to jettison the party's past. As noted above, the PCI's poor showing in the local elections that followed the congress by less than two months also aggravated internal tensions.

From the May to the July plenums of the Central Committee. The period following the May elections witnessed the sharpest conflict within the party and the strongest rumors that a split had become all but inevitable. This period saw Cossutta announce that he would henceforth make common cause with the rest of the opposition, and preparations were begun for gathering all components of the No Front with the aim of presenting a single motion at the Twentieth Congress in 1991.

The May plenum of the Central Committee, which was to examine the electoral results, was thus filled with tension. Occhetto underscored how the party's paralysis in the face of internal divisions was particularly harmful at a time of great political uncertainty. Pointing out that an entire cycle of political life had come to a close in Italy and elsewhere, he said that the left had been surprised by all the changes around it. For these reasons, the PCI had to find a new strategy and continue down the road to the theoretical and cultural renewal it had agreed to undertake in its 1989 congress—with a large majority including the present No Front. Occhetto also denounced the aberrations on *all* sides that had taken place during the electoral campaign and that, in his view, had seriously weakened the PCI's public image. (*UN*, 16 May.)

Despite his forceful tone, in the days following the May plenum, Occhetto talked openly about avoiding a split in the party that no one really wanted and also pleaded for an end to "reciprocal name-calling" (*La Repubblica*, 26 May). In fact, the party appeared by June to have weathered its most serious internal crisis. A number of leading figures from the majority and the opposition began to make conciliatory gestures. Then, on 18 June, the No Front met and declared that it was less concerned about the party's name and symbol than it was about the contents and program of any new formation, although the opposition reiterated its belief that the old PCI had a glorious heritage that ought not to be rejected (*l'Espresso*, 24 June). It was now clear that there was not going to be a split of any serious dimensions and that there might even be some flexibility or fluidity in the previously rigid postcongressional alignments.

In a meeting of the directorate late in June, Occhetto was able to report that the atmosphere within the party had substantially improved in the wake of the No Front's June meeting. Using conciliatory language, he made it clear that the new party's future would not liquidate the old party's past: "the most creative and original part of Italian Communism [will not be] erased, but will live on and generate real new processes and new ideas in a wider context." Referring to recent painful divisions, he stressed that the party was committed to go beyond democratic centralism but wanted to avoid "frozen currents." A new mechanism had to be found that would permit tendencies to group together around specific issues but then "disperse once a decision on these issues has been democratically made." (*UN*, 27 June.)

At the end of July, a plenum of the Central Committee and Guarantees Commission was the scene of more extensive reconciliation. Occhetto's address underscored the entire party's conviction "that no one wants to dissolve absolutely anything [and] that the 20th Congress is not meant to be and will not be a congress of dissolution, but one of foundation, transformation and rebirth." He went on to say that all groups in the PCI needed one another to avoid the dispersal of the party's original heritage and asked everyone to commit themselves to lowering the level of argument. In a phrase that many members of the opposition would later cite favorably, he concluded with the observation that the constitution of a new formation could only occur through "the contribution of forces that have equal dignity." Borrowing a phrase of the No Front, he asserted that everyone should take seriously those who speak in terms of refoundation, but he reminded the minority that the majority's project was the creation of a new formation of the left. (*UN*, 24 July.)

In his much-anticipated comments, Pietro Ingrao repeated the minority's points of differentiation from the majority, but he also echoed many of Occhetto's phrases and emphasized the need to avoid "a dissolution of the party's patrimony." Numerous other members of the minority, in their interventions or in postplenum comments, applauded the new atmosphere in the party and spoke hopefully—as did some members of the majority—of future agreements on programmatic and organizational questions. Occhetto's conclusions maintained the same open tone; significantly, the only strong criticism he voiced was of Armando Cossutta, who was clearly not in the mainstream of the opposition. (*UN*, 25 July.)

That the summer's events had led to a broad reconciliation of the party's major elements at the expense of its fringes was evident from the dissatisfaction of the most moderate wing of the PCI. This group, known as the *miglioristi* (meliorists), is committed to a radical break with the past, a rapid rapprochement with the Socialists, and the party's assumption of a governing role in Italy. Led by the highly respected "shadow foreign minister" of the PCI, Giorgio Napolitano, the *miglioristi* lost no time in voicing concern that the reconciliation between majority and opposition might delay or sidetrack the dramatic changes that had to be undertaken. Luciano Lama, former general secretary of the CGIL, in the wake of some of Occhetto's terminology, felt compelled to recall that the last congress had committed itself to the foundation of a *new* political formation, not to the refounding of the PCI. (*La Repubblica*, 25 July.) In an interview a few weeks after the July plenum, Napolitano expressed anger at the course of events since the Nineteenth Congress; in his view, Occhetto had been altogether too solicitous of the minority in that period. His group did not want to reject the PCI's entire past, but it did think that a great deal would have to be abandoned for the new formation to be effective. (*Epoca*, 8 August.) Judging from these and many other reactions, the *miglioristi* obviously do not view the loss of much of the party's left wing with the same alarm as the rest of their comrades in the majority.

Toward the Twentieth Congress and the birth of the PDS. Long awaited and temporarily upstaged by Craxi's coup de main a week earlier, the party's new name and symbol were finally presented to the public early in October. The choice of a symbol for the new Democratic Party of the Left reflected the conciliatory gestures already apparent in June and July: the new logo was dominated by an oak tree, but the PCI's old hammer and sickle symbol and even the letters PCI were clearly visible at the base of the tree, albeit much reduced in size. The presentation was accompanied by the majority's Declaration of Intent in which its rationale for change was spelled out yet again. There was little in Occhetto's presentation, aside from the symbols, that was new, but he spent a considerable amount of time sketching a vision of an extremely open, flexible, and democratic party that had little in common with communism's traditional forms and practices.

(*UN*, 11 November.) The stage was now set for the new round of local congresses that would culminate in the Twentieth (and last) National Congress of the PCI; shortly thereafter, a brief meeting of the Central Committee established that the congress would begin in Rimini on 29 January 1991 (*UN*, 25 October).

There were a few interesting developments in internal party debates during the fall. Antonio Bassolino, a longtime follower of Ingrao who had nevertheless remained in the Secretariat, announced in October that he would be presenting his own motion to the congress, one that would go "beyond a simple yes or no." It had, in fact, been clear as early as June—when polarization was still high in the PCI—that a group around Bassolino felt there was a potentially "soft" area in both the majority and the minority that might be attracted by a fresh initiative. A number of prominent party intellectuals from the minority, committed to the renovation of the party but concerned that the new party not abandon its commitment to deep social change, were the most visible group to adhere to this new motion. Local congresses soon made clear that Bassolino was largely drawing his support from the No Front, not from the majority around Occhetto.

By the end of 1990, the majority's support was slightly greater than it had been a year earlier: it went into 1991 with roughly 70 percent of the delegates, compared with 66 percent for the previous congress. The old minority—in a combined motion—had the support of about a quarter of the party, while Bassolino's motion obtained roughly 5 percent.

The debate was by no means free of conflict, however. Late in the year, both Bassolino and representatives of the old minority complained that blatant manipulations of PCI membership and recruitment figures were taking place in some southern federations, with the goal of inflating the number of delegates destined for Rimini. This practice has a long history in the South, but the PCI had previously seemed immune to it. The head of the party organization, Piero Fassino, minimized the extent of the "degeneration" but acknowledged that there was some substance to the charge and that an investigation was under way. He argued that isolated incidents should not present a distorted picture of an organization with more than 1.3 million members. (*UN*, 6 June.)

International Views and Contacts. After the tumultuous events of 1989, the international dimensions of the PCI's formal statements and activities were relatively subdued in 1990. The most important issues for the party tended to be those with strong domestic political implications or those that became contentious issues in debates between the majority and minority. These included Italy's role in the Atlantic alliance, the question of German unification (which also had implications for NATO), and the situation in the Persian Gulf following Iraq's invasion and occupation of Kuwait.

The PCI's position on NATO had evolved to one of grudging acceptance by the mid-1970s. Abandoning its earlier outright hostility to the alliance (and calls for unilateral withdrawal), the party argued that although it eventually wanted to see all military blocs disappear from Europe, this would have to take place through negotiations. With the events of 1989 effectively removing the Warsaw Pact's threat to Western Europe, the PCI argued that the time had come to think in terms of redefining NATO's role and, more broadly, of undertaking serious disarmament in Europe. It took a dim view of what it considered the persistence of old ways of thinking about NATO, arguing, among other things, that the perpetuation of NATO tended to isolate the USSR and undermine many changes taking place there precisely at a time when such changes should be encouraged. (*UN*, 24 July.)

This attitude was evident when, in the face of the rapid process of unification under way in Germany, the Italian Parliament met to debate the issue. Although over the years the PCI has increasingly joined a broad foreign policy consensus in Italy, on this occasion its dissent was marked. The communists voted against a passage in the government's foreign policy motion that explicitly mentioned the inclusion of a united Germany in NATO. They abstained on the rest of the motion, which included references to speeding European integration and the creation of a monetary union. (*La Repubblica*, 22 March.)

The same broad issue arose in more limited form with respect to what the PCI considers Italy's subordination to the United States within the framework of NATO. After Spain announced, late in the 1980s, the closing of a U.S. air base, Italy quickly agreed to accept the displaced F-16 fighter bombers in the early 1990s. The PCI opposed this gesture and stepped up its opposition in 1990. Early in the year, the party led protests against the transfer (*UN*, 14 January); it even called for unilateral Italian action to refuse the planes (*UN*, 2 February).

Given the deep divisions that marked the PCI, it was evident that NATO would become a key issue of contention in internal party debates. Early in the year, the secretary of the Youth Federation (FGCI), Gianni Cuperlo, announced the FGCI's opposition to NATO. It was immediately evident not only that this position had the support of the No Front but that it appealed to sectors of the majority as well. (*UN*, 7 January.) In fact, at the Nineteenth Congress, the FGCI presented a motion calling for Italy's unilateral exit from NATO, and Occhetto had to intervene in the ensuing debate to guarantee that the motion was rejected. The vote was 353 in favor, 498 opposed, and 53 abstentions. (*La Repubblica*, 11–12 March.)

That NATO would continue to be a topical issue was guaranteed late in the year by the revelations (see above) concerning *Gladio* and the possible linkages of this organization to earlier coup attempts and to the general climate of destabilizing tension that had characterized Italy throughout the 1970s. As already noted, *Gladio*'s linkage to NATO led to communist accusations that Italy's subordination to the Western alliance had limited its sovereignty and violated legality. In the heated national debate that took place during the autumn and winter of 1990, the communists were not alone in voicing such concerns.

We have seen how the *Gladio* affair led the No Front to announce at the end of the year that it would not join the rest of the PCI in the parliamentary vote on the budget early in January 1991. This was the second such breach of discipline by the minority in four months. The first no-show exercise occurred in August, when Parliament voted its support of the U.S.-led confrontation with Saddam Husayn in the Persian Gulf. Although the PCI opposed Italy's sending warplanes to the gulf, its opposition did not go far enough in the eyes of the minority within the party. Party leaders continued to speak out against the more aggressive elements within the Italian government through the fall (*UN*, 23 September), but the public display of such serious internal divisions clearly undermined the PCI's effectiveness on this issue.

Two other aspects of the PCI's international initiatives in 1990 are worthy of mention for the way in which they underline the party's long-standing efforts to assert its independence and redefine its identity. These are (1) the PCI's desire to forge links with European Socialist parties and eventually to gain admittance to the Socialist International and (2) its continued support of Gorbachev's reform efforts while emphasizing the exhaustion of the international communist movement.

On the first point, the PCI's overtures toward and contacts with Socialist leaders was far less marked in 1990 than had been the case in 1989. One reason for the diminished attention was the fierce internal debate that consumed so much of the leadership's time in 1990—and that also made the leaders leery of appearing to be overly willing to liquidate the PCI's heritage, as the minority charged. But another reason was the continued resistance to rapprochement on the part of Bettino Craxi and the PSI. Committed to an eventual realignment of the Italian left, which sees the PSI in the dominant position, and always suspicious of being outmaneuvered by the communists, the Socialists under Craxi have consistently tried to thwart, or at least delay, the forging of close ties between the PCI and the larger European Socialist parties. Thus, after pressuring the PCI to change its name for years, Craxi abruptly shifted gears when it appeared that the change was about to take place. In a meeting of the Socialist International in Geneva at the end of 1989, he emphasized that if the PCI continued to attack the PSI, a change of name would be meaningless. As is his custom, he put himself on center stage, admonishing his comrades that "it is with me, and not with you, that the Italian Communists must settle accounts." (*La Repubblica*, 24 November 1989.)

For its part, the PCI tried to keep up the pressure on the PSI. In an interview that laid out the PCI's goals for 1990, Occhetto put great emphasis on Italian communism's affinities with the largest Socialist parties of Europe, with which it had long had close and friendly ties. The PCI secretary noted that his party was particularly close to the French Socialist party, to Neil Kinnock of the British Labour party, to the German Social Democratic party, and to the late Olaf Palme's positions in the Swedish Socialist party (*La Repubblica*, 17–18 December 1989.) Occhetto's New Year's editorial in the party paper put the PCI's transformation within the context of the hope for a new "Euroleft," a favorite theme of the communists for the past decade. He spoke of a Euroleft "that will in the future breathe life into the ideals of socialism and democracy, transcending the communist tradition and that of social democracy." (*UN*, 31 December 1989.)

In an interview shortly after the Nineteenth Congress, Massimo D'Alema, coordinator of the PCI Secretariat and less favorably inclined toward Craxi and the PSI than most of his top-ranked colleagues, reiterated the party's main criticisms of the Socialists. Drawing attention to PSI's anomalous situation compared to other Socialist parties, D'Alema pointed out that this was the only Socialist party in Europe in a coalition dominated by conservatives. He also noted that the PSI regularly took positions, in the European Parliament and at home, that diverged from the Socialist mainstream on matters ranging from broadcast policy to NATO. (*La Repubblica*, 31 March.)

The most notable contact with European Socialists took place in March at a formal gathering of European Socialist and communist parties that met to discuss "The Socialism of the Future." The gathering was important enough to attract Occhetto, as well as various prominent Socialist leaders like Michel Rocard of France and Felipe Gonzales of Spain.

The PCI continued to exercise its prestige and initiative among the reform forces of East European communism—a prestige that had been evident in 1989 if one takes the praise heaped on the Italians by the East Europeans as evidence (see *YICA*, 1989). In 1990, there was much less activity of this nature on the party's agenda as communist parties shrank from prominence almost everywhere in the East. An indicative encounter was held in September that included Occhetto and leaders of the Slovenian communists. Discussions centered on cooperation with the Socialist International and both parties' commitment to democracy. Also in September, at the PCI's annual Festival of *l'Unità*, the PCI sponsored a roundtable on "Ideas of Freedom and Social Progress after the Revolutionary Transformations of 1989" that featured Soviet and East European participants (*UN*, 23 September).

The PCI's relations with the USSR have flourished under Gorbachev after reaching a nadir in the early 1980s. Although it fully supports Gorbachev's reforms, the PCI has prominently and consistently discussed the difficulties and delays faced by the Soviet leader. The Italians have also continuously referred to their complete break with the traditions of the communist movement and to the damage they think that movement, dominated by a repressive USSR, wrought on the left throughout the world. Thus, although applauding Soviet reforms, Occhetto made the point that "an ideological, political, and institutional shell that froze democratic and socialist potentialities has been dissolved" (*UN*, 24 July). In the course of presenting the PDS and its new symbol, Occhetto recalled how the USSR's lack of democracy and "bureaucratic collectivism" had "damaged the forces of progress and dissipated an ideological heritage." The actions of the Soviets had contradicted and obfuscated the prospects for human liberation originally embodied in the ideals of communism, thereby undermining the left throughout the entire world. (*UN*, 11 October.)

In November, Occhetto was invited to Moscow by Gorbachev for a personal meeting. The encounter took place 14–15 November, and the subject matter was wide-ranging, emphasizing the crisis in the Persian Gulf and general trends in the Soviet Union. Gorbachev claimed that there is still a strong attachment to Socialist ideals in the USSR but that socialism cannot be the "barracks, administrative-command socialism" that was a residue of Stalinism. Occhetto reconfirmed the PCI's support of Gorbachev's reforms and expressed his solidarity with the Soviet president. (Moscow, TASS, 15 November; *FBIS-SOV*, 16 November.)

Stephen Hellman
York University

Luxembourg

Population. 383,813 (July)
Party. Communist Party of Luxembourg (Parti Communiste Luxembourgeois, CPL)
Founded. 1921
Membership. More than 500
President. Aloyse Bisdorff
Executive Committee. 11 members
Secretariat. Canceled, according to the new statutes
Central Committee. 45 full
Status. Legal
Last Congress. Twenty-sixth, 10–11 November 1990, in Bettemburg
Last Election. 1989, under 4 percent, 1 of 64 seats
Auxiliary Organizations. Jeunesse Communiste Luxembourgeoise; Union des Femmes Luxembourgeoises
Publication. *Zeitung vum Letzebürger Vollek* (Newspaper of the Luxembourgian people), daily, 1,500–2,000 copies (CPL still claims up to 20,000)

It sounded pathetic when the CPL's own daily party newspaper on 12 June 1990 proudly featured a major front-page story on the communists' at least second place in the election in Czechoslovakia or when even Andre Hoffmann, the new representative of the tiny CPL in the Luxembourg Parliament, at the Twenty-sixth Party Congress, stubbornly announced that "the communists still will continue to refer to Marx and Marxism" (*Zeitung vum Letzebürger Vollek*, 13 November).

Because of the country's size, which barely equals the area of Rhode Island, and because its government is a constitutional monarchy (Luxembourg has been an independent Grand Duchy since 1868), the CPL plays no significant role in the European communist movement and only a modest domestic political role. In the last federal election to the Chamber of Deputies (June 1989) the communist voting strength was reduced to one seat.

Leadership and Organization. Probably the most remarkable events in 1990 for the CPL were Rene Urbany's death, on 10 October, and the Twenty-sixth Congress. Urbany had been party president since 1976, and the CPL almost seemed to be a family operation as the political as well as the theoretical leadership of this active party were dominated by the Urbany family. The chairman's father, Dominique Urbany, was one of the party's founders and led it until 1977. He remained in the CPL as honorary chairman until his death in October 1986 (*ND*, 27 October 1986). Some key positions within the party and its auxiliaries are still occupied by members of this family. Serge Urbany is a member of the new Central Committee and the new Executive Committee. Jaqueline Urbany was a member of the important Finance and Control Commission. The Twenty-sixth Congress clearly served to de-Stalinize the CPL and make it a more attractive new leftist party. The result was a new statute and newly elected and rejuvenated Central and Executive committees. Rather pathetically, the congress also passed a new leftist fundamental platform that is open for future cooperation with "all progressive forces." There are still members of the party who believe that the Socialist idea had not failed but only the "real existing socialism." The CPL's publishing company COPE continues to print and distribute not only its own daily newspaper but also the French edition of the *World Marxist Review*. Since October 1990 Andre Hoffmann has held the one seat in the Luxembourg Parliament. Although the party's positions were somewhat strengthened in the capital and

in some municipalities of the industrialized South, its political influence has been in a decline since 1968.

Domestic Affairs. An important event of 1990 for the PCL was its Twenty-sixth Congress in Bettemburg, which was held under the vague motto Fresche Wand vu Lenks (a fresh breeze from the left). The main points discussed were a new statute, new voting procedures, and a new, more open fundamental platform—a desperate move to attract a new segment of the population. Luxembourg's rapid deindustrialization, major shifts in the social structure, and a fashionable concern for global environmental problems were the major economic issues. In his opening remarks Aloyse Bisdorff lamented that the party had arrived at a turning point. The collapse of the "real existing socialism" and the disappearance of the Soviet Union as a persuasive role model had caused disappointment among many potential followers and apparently dissuaded them from joining the CPL. François Hoffmann and Andre Hoffmann tried to make people believe that there are new challenges and important tasks for communists. Social issues (whatever the term means) also played an important role in the discussions. Because more than 20 percent of the workers in Luxembourg earn less than 35,000 francs, the party announced a vague initiative to foster "social justice," rent control, money for children, and guaranteed jobs for the first two years, among other issues (*Zeitung vum Letzebürger Vollek*, 14 November). According to the newspaper the CPL offered a whole array of environmental measures to ensure "more responsible" production, to cut down on individual car traffic, and to encourage alternative energy. The party's platform renewed its long-standing offer to work with the Socialist Worker's Party (POSL) and all other left-wing forces. The POSL forms a coalition of 40 seats with the People's Christian Social party. Athough it was repeatedly denied last year, the CPL, the Greens, and the POSL already cooperated in three regions.

Because most citizens use television as their main information source, the party tried to give its newspaper a more attractive format. The *Zeitung vum Letzebürger Vollek* continues to emphasize commentaries, ideology, and interpretation to balance the alleged bourgeois information given over television.

International Affairs. There were no major international contacts or visits by party officials. In the beginning of April, Jiang Zemin, general secretary of the Chinese Communist Party Central Committee met with a delegation of the Luxembourg-China Friendship Association. This small and obscure association is presided over by Adolphe Franck, who is 97 years old and has visited Beijing 56 times. *Pravda*, on 12 October, reported "comrade" Rene Urbany's death on page 3 and described him as a true friend of the working class (*Pravda*, 12 October). In January 1989 the CPL had warmly received an official Socialist Unity party of Germany delegation under the leadership of Werner Eberlein, a member of the Central Committee. As usual in those days, topics of mutual interest such as international solidarity, disarmament, and peace were on the agenda (*ND*, 26, 27, 28 January 1989). Even the party's traditional Pressefest in September apparently took place only in obscurity.

Kurt R. Leube
California State University at Hayward

Malta

Population. 354,679 (September, Malta Central Office of Statistics)
Party. Communist Party of Malta (Partit Komunista Malti, CPM)
Founded. 1969
Membership. 100 (estimated)
General Secretary. Anthony Vassallo, 71
Central Committee. 12 members, C. Zammit, president; A. Vassallo, general secretary; V. Degiovanni, Central Committee and international secretary; R.J. Mifsud, propaganda secretary; D. Mallia, organizational secretary; J. Attard; L. Attard-Bezzina; J.M. Cachia; A. Caruana; A. Cordina; K. Gerada; M. Mifsud
Status. Legal
Last Congress. Fourth, 15–17 July 1988
Last Election. 9 May 1987
Auxiliary Organizations. Malta-USSR Friendship and Cultural Society, Malta-Korean Friendship and Cultural Society, Young Communist League (Ghaqda Zghazagh Komunisti), Union of Progressive Youth, Peace and Solidarity Council of Malta, Women for Peace, Malta-China Friendship Committee
Publication. *Bridge of Friendship and Culture*, quarterly journal of the Malta-USSR Friendship and Cultural Society

The CPM almost ceased operating in the open during 1990. Following its steady decline after its sorry performance at the 1987 elections, it has seemingly been left to its devices, and to all appearances its sources of finance have dried up completely. It has ceased publication of its glossy monthly tabloid *Zminijietna*, whose last issue appeared in November 1989. The Young Communist League has likewise vanished into thin air and discontinued the publication of its newsletter *Bandiera Hamra* (Red flag).

Some CPM activists are known to have wandered into the ranks of the Maltese Socialist party. The CPM Central Committee has not held any activity noted by the Maltese media except three press releases: the first was issued on Women's Day and congratulated the women of Malta for the advances they had achieved (*Orizzont*, 10 March); the second was a formal message to the workers of Malta in anticipation of May Day (Malta, *The Times*, 23 April), and the third registered the CPM's protest to the broadcasting authorities of discrimination in the allocation of broadcasting time to discuss proposed amendments to the electoral law (Malta, *The Times*, 15 June).

During the year, General Secretary Anthony Vassallo indicated that he was still around. In the February issue of *World Marxist Review*, reflecting on the Bush-Gorbachev Malta summit, he observed that this marked the first occasion that "formidable-looking Soviet and U.S. warships met in this area for the sake of greater mutual trust, not mutual intimidation."

Although the Maltese government and Maltese public opinion displayed immense satisfaction at the outcome of the summit, the CPM general secretary expressed reservations, saying that

the two leading superpowers which personify two rival and even mutually opposed ideological and political systems have made another step towards each other. What does this mean? Is it a move to free intergovernmental relations from ideology? If it is, it hardly involves a renunciation by either side of its distinctive interests or its identity.

Vassallo was also observed abroad when he headed "a delegation" from the CPM, which had participated in the "World Conference for a Re-unified Korea by Founding the Democratic Con-federal Republic of Korea," had talks in Paris on 21 October with a delegation of the Workers' Party of Korea (WPK). The Korean communist delegation was headed by the Central Committee secretary of the WPK, Kim Yong-sun (Pyongyang, KCNA, 13 October; *FBIS-EAS*, 30 October).

The former prime minister and leader of the Malta Labour party, Dom Mintoff, was invited to attend this conference in his capacity of honorary president of the organizing committee. Mintoff could not take up the invitation but expressed his moral support (*Orizzont*, 21 October).

It may be significant that the CPM general secre-tary was in Paris when the official responsible for the Malta Desk of the International Department of the Communist Party of the Soviet Union, Leonid Popov, was visiting Malta and was reported to have met with a delegation from the Malta Labour party.

Popov was received by the MLP deputy leader for parliamentary affairs, Dr. Joe Brincat, and the international secretary, Leo Brincat. In a terse re-port it was stated that the talks concentrated on interparty relations, the situation in the Mediterra-nean, and the latest developments in the Arab gulf (*Orizzont*, 19 October).

Although the CPM has not been seen to function as an active party and has ceased publishing its own media, the Soviet embassy has filled the vacuum. In this, it was assisted by the Malta-USSR Friendship and Cultural Society. The sweeping changes in Cen-tral and Eastern Europe, the fading international image of Marxism-Leninism, and the economic difficulties now being experienced by the USSR have severely reduced the effectiveness of the Soviet effort in Malta. Nevertheless, Moscow has con-ducted a systematic program to sustain its political and other investments in the island. In this respect, the Soviet embassy has had to work single-handedly following the defection of the Kremlin's East Euro-pean satellites. The Bulgarian embassy in Malta closed down (*Nazzjon Taghna*, 27 July), and the Czech embassy started to concentrate on trade rather than politics.

The major initiative was the inauguration of the Soviet Cultural Centre, which was opened with pomp and circumstance (Malta, *The Times*, 9 No-vember) by Oleg Yu. Ivanitsky, first vice-president of the Presidium of Soviet Friendship Societies. The center is in a sixteenth-century building, once the residence of Sir Oliver Starkey, the only British knight among the defenders in the great siege of Malta in 1565.

The inauguration was a highly orchestrated show business event that drew the attention of the Maltese media for the best part of three weeks. To give the event a touch of solemnity, the Soviets brought an Orthodox priest to Malta to bless the new premises. A rare masterpiece by the French painter Antoine Favray, depicting the interior of Saint John's Cathedral, the conventual church of the Order of Saint John, was transported to Malta for the occasion from the Hermitage in Leningrad. A three-week festival of Russian culture, a number of seminars, and many press conferences kept Maltese ministers, high officials, members of the intelli-gentsia, and journalists busily occupied. Although the center is one of 60 said to be operated in differ-ent countries by the Union of Soviet Friendship Societies, its first director is the first secretary for cultural affairs at the Soviet embassy, Anatoli Masko (*The Times*, 25 October).

During the same week, the Russian Soviet Fede-rated Socialist Republic (RSFSR) minister of trade, Victor Voreshenko, signed a special trade protocol with the Malta government, the first of its kind contracted by the RFSU (Malta, *The Times*, 3 No-vember). This is distinct from the troublesome Malta-USSR trade protocol. A countertrade agree-ment in terms of the RSFSR protocol provides for the barter of 60,000 tons of coal for Maltese prod-ucts needed in the RSFSR consumer market (*Nazz-jon Taghna*, 6 November).

Throughout the year, the Soviet embassy orga-nized cultural and other exchanges at regular inter-vals. Thirteen football coaches were invited to a two-week training camp in Leningrad (*Nazzjon Taghna*, 5 January). Professor Lev Karpov, head of the Economic Research Institute of the USSR Acad-emy of Science, was brought over to lecture on changes taking place in the Soviet economy (Malta, *The Times*, 30 January), and exchange program for youth and journalists were arranged with the lead-ership of the Nationalist (ruling) party. Two officials from the Committee of Soviet Women came to Malta to meet with Maltese women's organizations. Twenty-five Maltese Boy Scouts were invited for an extended visit to the USSR after which a Komsomol group returned the visit (Malta, *The Times*, 5 July). A group of 25 children from the Chernobyl area were invited by the Maltese government for a Malta holiday, staying in Maltese homes (*Orizzont*, 30 August).

A Maltese trade unionist was invited to attend the Twelfth Congress of the World Federation of Trade Unions (Malta, *The Times*, 18 November), and the Soviet ambassador held a press conference to announce the launching of *Vestnik*, a new publication of the Soviet Ministry of Foreign Affairs (Malta, *The Times*, 1 June).

The above were supported by visits from theatrical groups, art experts, sports personalities, and other sponsored specialists to give maximum visibility to the Soviet image. Less ostentatious but of greater intensity was the dissemination of Soviet literature to the media corps and to key officials in trade union, political, youth, student, and social organizations. Literature comes by Aeroflot, which flies through Malta seven days a week and includes all the latest *Novosti* publications.

Auxiliary Organizations. The Malta-USSR Friendship and Cultural Society was the auxiliary organization that kept a high profile during 1990. All other auxiliary organizations were dormant and achieved the status of sleeping partners.

The Malta-USSR Friendship and Cultural Society, which celebrated its fifteenth anniversary, outlined its program of activities for the year after electing its committee for 1990–1991 (*Orizzont*, 20 March). It organized group visits to the USSR, offered bursaries and scholarships in the Soviet Union, maintained its program of Russian-language courses, held a number of public forums and exhibitions, and sponsored the programs of many Soviet personalities who visited Malta under its auspices. These included theatrical and folk dancing groups, academics, and others. Early in the year, the society established a branch in the sister Island of Gozo, and this is now run by its own committee (*Torca*, 21 January).

Policies of the Malta Government. The Malta government maintained its relations with the Soviet Union on a nonideological basis. These relations mellowed on the diplomatic plane particularly after Mikhail Gorbachev's visit a year ago and the formal end of the cold war. These advances, however, were flawed by mounting difficulties in bilateral trade relations.

Maltese exporters to the USSR began experiencing delays in payments for their orders. Bound by formal contracts, they were obliged to maintain their deliveries to their USSR clients or risk penalties they could ill afford. These complaints were brought to the attention of the Parliamentary secretary for industry, John Dalli, who undertook a number of initiatives to maintain the flow of trade. (*Nazzjon Taghna*, 9 June.) Dalli reported that a new trade protocol was expected to be signed in the near future that would replace the 1985–1990 trade protocol. By year's end, however, this agreement had not materialized. No explanation was forthcoming as to why the accord, described as "imminent" by Dalli in June, was not consummated. The Maltese side likewise failed to meet important Soviet expectations in terms of the protocol.

The preceding Socialist administration had set up a shipyard—known as the Marsa Shipyard—which accepted a Soviet order for the construction of eight timber carriers on 13 December 1984 (*Malta Government Economic Survey 1985*). Once construction work was begun, however, there were various delays arising from design modifications and delivery of on-board equipment.

The delays continued, and the first ship was delivered to the Soviets in June 1989. According to the 1989 *Economic Survey*, the Marsa Shipyard incurred a 10 percent penalty in terms of the contract. The Maltese shipyard was relieved of this penalty after the personal intervention of Mikhail Gorbachev.

The second timber carrier of seven thousand tons was belatedly delivered on 11 April (*Orizzont*, 12 April). There is no firm knowledge about when the remaining six ships are to be delivered. Parliamentary Secretary John Dalli stated publicly that "the ships being built for the Soviet Union will cost Lm 40 million, but these will be sold for only Lm 12 million [in terms of the 1984 contract]. This will involve substantial losses since every ship will be sold at one third of its cost." (*Nazzjon Taghna*, 7 May.) Speaking during the budget debate, Prime Minister Edward Fenech Adami declared that the Marsa Shipyard was in a parlous situation, which he qualified as "disastrous." He went on to state that the decision to set up the yard was "a mistake." (*Mument*, 15 December.)

The above-mentioned factors threaten to undo efforts to build up an ongoing and businesslike trade relationship between the two countries, with resultant dislocations in the Maltese work force engaged in meeting Soviet orders. The government-sponsored Malta Export Trade Corporation organized an exhibition of Maltese goods in Moscow in September, whereas the Soviets had their own stand at the Malta International Fair in midyear. Both endeavors failed to generate much in the way of new business.

On the political plane, a high-level Maltese delegation visited Moscow in July to discuss current international problems and the role of neutral and nonaligned countries in the Conference on Security and Cooperation in Europe process with particular reference to the issue of peace in the Mediterranean. The Soviet spokesman was Deputy Foreign Minister Yuliy Kvitinsky, who also discussed the general run of Maltese-Soviet relations (Moscow, TASS, 24 July; *FBIS-SOV*, 25 July).

In reply to a parliamentary question, the Maltese government stated its position on the declaration of independence by the Lithuanian Parliament in April. The prime minister went on record with the statement that "the Government of Malta believes in the right of every people to choose how it should be governed on the principle of self-determination. In this respect, the Government of Malta acknowledges the validity of the declaration of the Lithuanian Parliament on Independence as that of the people of Lithuania" (Malta, *The Times*, 6 April).

The government party took another public position when it issued a statement condemning "the aggression of the Government of Romania," which had reacted to popular protests by urging miners to enter Bucharest and assail their own brethren in the most barbaric manner (*Nazzjon Taghna*, 21 June). In the same statement, an appeal was made to the Maltese government to use its good offices to urge the Romanian administration to respect human rights.

Various other efforts were made by the Malta government to establish new relationships with East European countries that had taken the road to democracy during the year.

After a visit by the deputy prime minister of Czechoslovakia, Jiří Dienstbier, Malta and Czechoslovakia lifted visa requirements for nationals traveling from one country to the other (Malta, *The Times*, 4 August). The same decision was taken in respect to visas between the German Democratic Republic and Malta for stays up to three months starting in August (East Berlin, *Der Morgen*, 7 August; *FBIS-EEU*, 9 August). With the unification of Germany, all visa requirements were abolished.

The Chinese minister of communications, Cian Yong Chang, visited Malta to assess the possibility of using the Malta freeport for the transshipment of Maltese goods (Malta, *The Times*, 1 June). A proposal was made to the Chinese minister for the two countries to sign a shipping agreement (*Democrat*, 2 June). Malta thus became the first European country with Chinese ships on its shipping register; the initial registration of ten ships belonged to a subsidiary of the China Ocean Shipping Company (*Nazzjon Taghna*, 21 December).

The North Korean deputy foreign minister, Song Ho-Gyong, visited Malta for talks with his counterpart and other ministers (*Orizzont*, 6 September). At the end of his visit, he said at an airport conference that his talks were "successful" and that he had no objection to the establishment of diplomatic relations between Malta and the Republic of (South) Korea. His object was to discuss the issue of Korean unification and bilateral relations in education, culture, and economic affairs (Malta, *The Times*, 13 September).

J. G. E. Hugh
Valletta, Malta

The Netherlands

Population. 14,936,032
Party. Communist Party of the Netherlands (Communistische Partij van Nederland, CPN). Allied since 1989 with the Radicals (PPR) and the Pacifist-Socialists (PSP) in the Green Left (Groen Links).
Founded. 1909
Membership. 6,000–7,000
Chairman. Henk Hoekstra
Central Committee. Truus Divendal-Klok, chair
Status. Legal
Last Congress. Extraordinary congress, 10 June 1990, Amsterdam
Last Election. 1989: Green Left won 4.1 percent of the vote and 6 of the 150 seats in the Second Chamber (lower house). In 1987, the CPN won 1 of the 75 seats in the less powerful First Chamber (upper house).
Auxiliary Organizations. CPN Women, General Organization of Dutch Youth (ANJV), Stop the Bomb/Stop the Nuclear Arms Race, CPN Youth Platform, Schooling and Education, Women Against Nuclear Weapons
Publications. *De Waarheid* (The truth), official CPN daily newspaper, circulation about 10,000;

CPN-leden krant (bulletin for party members); *Politiek en cultuur* (theoretical journal published ten times per year); *Komma* (quarterly journal published by CPN's Institute for Political and Social Research); Pegasus Publishers (owned by CPN)

In 1989, the leadership of the CPN federated with two other small left parties, the PSP and PPR, in an electoral alliance meant to reverse the parliamentary extinction that the party had suffered in 1986. The strategy worked insofar as the federation, Green Left, won six seats. In a sense, the Green Left may be seen as the latest in a series of efforts over the last generation to make the CPN more appealing by associating it with the popular causes of the mainstream left. The Green Left is so internally diverse, however, that it is unlikely to be a long-term solution to the problems of the CPN, at least in the form that it has existed in since 1909.

As a Stalinist party of international Socialist solidarity, the CPN was never able to take root in Dutch society. Evidence of control from the Kremlin always caused severe erosion of party support, as in the 1925 election campaign when a directive from Moscow removed the party's two sitting parliamentarians from the candidate list, leading to a halving of electoral support.

The CPN's links to the Soviet Union and its record of resistance to the Nazi occupation briefly won the party popularity in the postwar years. In the 1946 elections, the CPN won 10 percent of the vote and 10 of the 100 seats in the Second Chamber. One less-noted reason for that result is that the CPN newspaper, *De Waarheid*, was one of the few dailies not closed down in 1946 for collaborationist practices during the Nazi occupation. *De Waarheid's* temporary surge in readership translated into an all-time high watermark in the CPN's vote share. Over the next decade, however, the advantages of wartime resistance faded and the disadvantages of the Soviet connection grew in the wake of the suppression of the Hungarian uprising. In the 1956 Dutch elections, the CPN fell back to its typical level of 2 percent of the vote.

The party's response to its electoral decline through the 1950s was to begin a series of efforts to widen its base of support. In the 1960s, the CPN began to distance itself from Moscow. The party had been silent on the 1956 invasion of Hungary, for example, but in 1968 it denounced the invasion of Czechoslovakia. As the student movement grew in the late 1960s, the CPN made efforts to reach out to the noncommunist left. They were aided in this by their longtime (1956 to 1986) parliamentary representative Marcus Bakker, who greatly enlivened parliamentary debates and who was frequently able to get the better of representatives of other left parties, at least in applause and in humor.

With Bakker as the party's public face and with the party's antiwar and anticolonial stances enjoying new relevance in the Vietnam era, the CPN increased in membership and votes in the late 1960s and the 1970s. The new recruits shifted the social base of the party from one centered on workers (with some highly visible participation by intellectuals) to include the students, teachers, and social service providers that David Gress called "the classic core groups of the '1968 generation'" (*YICA*, 1990).

The electoral success of this strategy depended in part on the fortunes of the mainstream left Labor Party (PvdA), for the CPN was always able to attract more protest votes when the left was in power. But there were true successes as well, and the political and social influence of the CPN expanded greatly in the 1970s. The high point of this development came in 1977–1978 with the success of the Stop the Neutron Bomb organization. Between September 1977 and April 1978, Stop the Neutron Bomb gathered 1.2 million signatures on a petition to the Dutch government to prevent introduction of the neutron bomb into the North Atlantic Treaty Organization (NATO) arsenal.

The success of the campaign against the neutron bomb brought an end to the struggle between older party activists with a working class orientation and a Stalinist organizational philosophy and younger activists who would take the party in new directions. The new pacifist, feminist, and environmentalist wing of the party was able to take control at the 1982 party congress. In 1984, that wing abolished democratic centralism, declared support for parliamentary democracy, and adopted a party platform of "Marxism-feminism." The revamped party took part in the wave of protest against the modernization of NATO's intermediate nuclear forces (INF) between 1980 and 1985. This massive movement put nearly a half million marchers into the Amsterdam streets in November 1981; even more people, more than 4 percent of the Dutch population, marched on The Hague in October 1983. Although the CPN participated in this movement with its organization Stop the Bomb/Stop the Nuclear Arms Race, it was overshadowed by the Interchurch Peace Council (IKV), a massive antinuclear organization rooted in the Dutch churches, as well as by the much smaller but extremely radical anarchist group Weeds (*Onkruit*). The ultimate failure of the CPN's strategy of recruiting among the new middle class is indicated by the fact that the party lost its parliamentary representation in the 1986 elections, the height of the antinuclear protest movement. Sixty-eight years of continuous representation in the Dutch Parliament came to an end in the midst of the greatest mass mobilization in Dutch history.

The problem for the CPN was that the antinuclear, environmental, and feminist movements of the 1970s and 1980s led to the creation of a wide variety of party and movement organizations. Virtually all these groups, whether Christian, Social Democratic, or anarchist in persuasion, were better equipped to meet the demands of the new activists for participatory, grass roots activism than was the CPN, with its Stalinist history and its continuing pattern of organizational centralization despite the reforms. The traditional Marxian model of building a base among the working class had failed consistently in the 50 years (1917–67) that it was tried; the replacement strategy of tapping into the new left activism of the middle class also failed to develop a large base for the party. The decision in 1989 to ally with two other small left parties was both an admission of defeat and an extension of the strategy of seeking support among the middle-class left.

Conclusion. The Green Left has had its successes: by winning six parliamentary seats in 1989, it doubled the number of seats held by the Radicals and the Pacifist-Socialists from 1986 to 1989. The CPN has shown its determination to move ahead with the federation by approving at its 1990 congress dual membership in the CPN and the Green Left (*ND*, 11 June).

But the future of the CPN within the Green Left will not be an easy one. It is overshadowed in size by both of its partners. Moreover, the three parties do not share a common ideological heritage. The Pacifist Socialist party was founded in the late 1950s with the goal of revitalizing socialism by breaking decisively with the image of the Soviet Union as the model Socialist state. The Radicals split off from the Catholic People's party in 1971, advocating income redistribution and environmentalism from an ideological background that continues to bear traces of the social gospel that first inspired the party. All this suggests that the Green Left alliance is unlikely to lead to a full merger of its constituent parties, following the model of the highly successful Christian Democratic Appeal (CDA), which fused one Catholic party and two Protestant parties in 1980. The three parties within the Green Left are simply too diverse for that to happen.

The federation between these three parties, then, is clearly a marriage of convenience. The very name, *Green Left*, was chosen for its electoral appeal and conceals considerable differences in origins, organization, and program from the other Green parties of Europe. The 1989 election showed that there is still room on the Dutch left for small parties of principled opposition, particularly when the social democratic Labor Party (PvdA) is in power and thereby handicapped in its ability to co-opt emerging issues. The history of the fissiparous left in Dutch political life suggests two likely developments. One is that the far left will not remain united in a single parliamentary party; the other is that the communists will not be important players among those left groups that do survive.

Thomas Rochon
Claremont Graduate School

Norway

Population. 4,252,806 (*World Fact Book*)
Parties. Norwegian Communist Party (Norges Kommunistiske Parti, NKP); Socialist Left Party (Sosialistisk Venstreparti, SV); Workers' Communist Party (Marxist-Leninist) (Arbeidernes Kommunistiske Parti [Marxist-Leninistene], AKP [M-L]). In the most recent parliamentary election, the NKP and the AKP ran jointly as the County Slates for the Environment and Solidarity (Fylkeslistene for Miljø og Solidaritet).
Founded. NKP: 1923, SV: 1975, AKP: 1973
Membership. NKP: 1,500–2,000 (estimated); SV: 11,000 dues-paying members (official figure); AKP: 5,000–7,000 (estimated)
Chairs. NKP: Kåre André Nilsen, journalist; SV: Erik Solheim; AKP: Siri Jensen, bookbinder
Central Committees. NKP: 8 full members: Kåre André Nilsen; Maria Hansen, deputy chair; Bjørnhild Stokvik, deputy chair; Svein Johnny Ballo; Paul Midtlyng; Svend Haakon Jacobsen;

Bernt Haugen; 2 alternate members: Else Sollund, Reidar Aarsand. SV: 4 members: Erik Solheim, Kjellbjørg Lunde, deputy chair, Per Eggum Maurseth, deputy chair; Hilde Vogt, party secretary. AKP: 17 full members: Siri Jensen, 41; Aksel Nærstad, 37, deputy chair for political affairs; Arne Lauritzen, 41, deputy chair for organizational affairs; Eli Aaby, 34, leader for women's affairs; Frode Bygdnes, 37, leader for labor affairs; Sigurd Allern, 43, editor in chief, *Klassekampen*; Kjersti Ericsson, 45; Pål Steigan, 39; Tellef Hansen, 41; Vidar Våde, 46; Marion Palmer, 36; Torild Nustad, 36; Torstein Dahle, 41; Solveig Aamdal, 42; Geir Johnsen, 40; Tone Anne Ødegaard, 45; Bente Moseng, 39.

Status. Legal

Last Congress. NKP: Nineteenth, 23–26 April 1987, in Oslo; SV: April 1989, in Skien; AKP: December 1988, "somewhere in Norway" (*Klassekampen*, 13 December 1988)

Last Election. 1989: SV: 10.08 percent, 17 out of 165 representatives; joint lists of NKP and AKP: 0.84 percent, no representation

Auxiliary Organizations. NKP: Norwegian Communist Youth League (NKU), SV: Socialist Youth League, Socialist Information League, AKP: Norwegian Communist Student League (NKS).

Publications. NKP: *Friheten* (Freedom), semiweekly, Arne Jørgensen, editor. SV: *Ny Tid* (New times), weekly. AKP: *Klassekampen* (Class struggle), daily, Sigurd Allern, editor.

The Norwegian Labor Party (Det Norske Arbeiderparti, DNA)—a moderate, generally pro-Western social democratic reform movement—controlled the Norwegian government continuously from 1935 to 1963. Through most of this period the Labor party could count on parliamentary majorities. However, in 1961 the Labor party lost its parliamentary majority, which it has never managed to regain. In 1963 the Labor government was defeated by a coalition of non-Socialist parties and the Socialist People's party; since then the Norwegian government has alternated between Labor party minority governments and various coalitions of non-Socialist parties. None of the parties to the left of the Labor party has ever been in government.

In the 1981 election the Labor party was ousted from power by a center-right coalition headed by Conservative party leader Kåre Willoch. Willoch served as prime minister until May 1986, when his government lost a vote to increase gasoline taxes to cope with the fiscal crisis caused by declining oil revenues. The Labor party leader, Gro Harlem Brundtland, replaced Willoch as prime minister. Brundtland, then, in 1981 became the first Norwegian woman prime minister and was able to steer her second minority government through the remainder of the 1985–1989 parliamentary term thanks to the support of the SV and the unwillingness of the agrarian Center party to defeat her government. The general election of 11 September 1989, however, resulted in stunning setbacks for Brundtland's Labor party, as well as for its main adversary, the Conservatives. The Labor party received only 34.3 percent of the popular vote, its worst result since 1930, whereas the Conservatives declined from 30.4 percent to 22.2 percent. The big winners of the election were the right-wing libertarian Progress party, which won 22 seats in Parliament (against 2 previously) and the Socialist Left party, which increased its representation from 6 to 17. Despite the electoral setback of its dominant party, a non-Socialist coalition government headed by Conservative leader Jan P. Syse took office in October 1989. This government had no legislative majority and relied on the support of the Progress party for its 1990 budget. Syse's government lasted just over a year, collapsing in October 1990 because of disagreements between the Conservatives and the Center party over Norwegian membership in the European Community. On 3 November 1990, Brundtland assumed the prime ministership for the third time, presiding over a government supported by only 63 of the 165 members of the Storting.

The Norwegian Communist Party. The NKP began as the minority faction of the DNA, when the majority of the latter party decided in 1923 to sever its ties with Moscow. The NKP gained 6.1 percent of the vote and six representatives in the general election of 1924 but later fell into decline and could not elect a single member of Parliament during the 1930s. During World War II, NKP support for the war effort against Nazi Germany and the Soviet liberation of northern Norway boosted the party's popularity, giving it 11 seats out of 150 in the first postwar Parliament. During these early postwar years, the NKP had as many as 35,000 members, according to official sources. However, the party's fortunes fell quickly with the onset of the cold war. Since 1945 the NKP's vote share has declined in every single general election. In 1985, the most recent election the party has contested under its own name, the NKP received no more than 4,245 votes.

Thus the party remains one of the weakest communist parties in Western Europe. It has elected no member of Parliament since 1973, when it ran as part of the Socialist Electoral Alliance and elected its chairman, Reidar Larsen, to the national assembly. In 1989 the party ran jointly with the AKP and other left-wing groups as the County Slates for the Environment and Solidarity (Fylkeslistene for Miljø og Solidaritet). The election results represented a modest gain for these parties collectively, but even jointly their candidates were not in serious contention for representation in any district. Owing to its extremism and electoral weakness, the NKP has had virtually no impact on Norwegian political debate.

The weakness of the NKP was exacerbated in 1975 when the party split over whether to participate in the formation of the Socialist Left Party (SV). Under the leadership of Martin Gunnar Knutsen, the majority faction decided to withdraw from the SV and remain a staunchly pro-Soviet, Stalinist party. However, Chairman Larsen and several other party leaders abandoned the NKP and joined the SV. The gulf between the NKP and the SV has remained wide. A party congress of the NKP in April 1988 advocated a "red-green" alliance consisting of "forces in the union movement, the peace movement, the environmental movement, the women's movement, the solidarity movement, and the progressive women's movement" (*Friheten*, 13 April 1988). Such an alliance materialized in the formation of the County Slates for the Environment and Solidarity (see above).

A national party conference in Oslo 23 April 1989 decided by a sweeping majority to rehabilitate former NKP leader Peter Furubotn and 170 other former members who were expelled by the party after its defeat in the election of 1949. Furubotn and the other expelled members were at that time accused of factionalism, Titoism, Trotskyism, and various right-wing deviations.

At its Nineteenth Congress in 1987, the NKP adopted a new party program ("Program of Principle"), which replaced its 1973 program. In its new program, the NKP reaffirms its commitment to Marxism-Leninism, scientific socialism, and class struggle. However, the new program puts greater emphasis on international peace, "the most important issue of all." The NKP sees the threat of war as a consequence of imperialism and the boundless greed for profit and power in monopoly capitalism. The deterioration of the international situation since the mid-1970s is ascribed by the NKP to the United

States and its military-industrial complex. In the main resolution adopted at the congress, the NKP advocated forcing the United States to accept a nuclear test ban treaty, preventing the implementation of the Strategic Defense Initiative, and creating a Nordic nuclear-free zone. The communists also rejected Norwegian membership in the European Community (EC). Domestically, the NKP favors restrictions on finance capital, the expansion of public credit institutions, and subsidies for moderate-income housing. The 1987 party congress also elected Kåre André Nilsen the new party chair. Nilsen, a veteran journalist for *Friheten* and a former manual worker, has been associated with the Knutsen/Jørgensen faction (against Kleven) in the NKP. However, Nilsen seems mainly concerned to unite the party. His main political interests are international and security affairs.

A new Central Committee was elected at a meeting of the NKP national committee in Oslo 9–10 June. Opposition to EC membership, further endeavors to promote red-green cooperation, program work, and an effort to safeguard the continued existence of the newspaper *Friheten* will be major tasks for the new party leadership. *Friheten* will celebrate its 50th anniversary in 1991, and a financial campaign has been launched with a goal of raising 500,000 krones for the newspaper (*Friheten*, 15 June).

In September, former party leader Martin Gunnar Knutsen announced his defection from the NKP after more than 50 years as a member. He discusses this decision in his book *Bitter Reckoning*, which was published by Tiden Norsk Forlag in the fall of 1990. "The doubt has been there for a long time," he says. "But in the last five years, the disclosures have come thick and fast, and left all I believed in, in ruins." (*Aftenposten*, 4 September.)

The NKP maintains international contacts primarily with the communist parties of the Soviet Union and Eastern Europe. However, the party also has ties to orthodox communist parties in Western Europe.

The Socialist Left Party. The SV is the strongest party left of the Labor party. Although the party includes Marxist elements, it does not define itself as a communist party, and the current program of principle is more moderate and pragmatic than the previous version. The SV was the result of a merger of the previous Socialist People's Party (Sosialistisk Folkeparti, SF); the Democratic Socialists (Demokratiske Sosialister, DS-AIK), an anti-EC splinter group of former members of the DNA; and segments of the NKP. These three parties had previously run jointly in the 1973 general election. The electoral support of the SV has increased steadily in the 1980s. In the September 1989 general election the party won 10.1 percent of the national vote and became the fourth largest Norwegian party, trailing Labor, the Conservatives, and the Progress party. The party won seventeen seats in Parliament, an increase of eleven since 1985.

In Parliament the SV has tended to support Labor minority governments such as the ones led by Gro Harlem Brundtland (1981, 1986–89, and 1990–). However, the party has never held cabinet office. Although the SV has frequently criticized the Brundtland governments, it has made no attempt to oust the Labor party, presumably because the only alternative would be a more conservative government. In recent years, relationships between the SV and the Labor party have become more cordial.

A leadership struggle in the SV became apparent when party chairman Erik Solheim challenged parliamentary leader and former chair Theo Koritzinsky for the party's safe Oslo seat for the 1989 general election. Solheim was eventually persuaded to withdraw his candidacy and let himself be nominated elsewhere. At the 1989 party congress Arent M. Henriksen, a member of Parliament and a prominent figure in the party's right wing, criticized the election of Kåre Syltebø as leader for labor affairs. According to Henriksen, Syltebø had undesirable ties to the Workers' Communist Party (AKP).

According to party reports, the SV currently has a membership of about eleven thousand dues payers, whereas the official rolls stand at approximately fourteen thousand members. The party has particular strengths among people 35 to 40 years old, women, the well-educated, and urban voters. More than half of all SV supporters work in the public sector, whereas one-third are industrial workers. The SV platform for the 1989–1993 parliamentary term was adopted at its party congress in Skien in April 1989. The program stresses environmental issues such as large additional taxes on fossil fuels, restrictions on the use of automobiles in urban areas, and expansion of public transportation. The party wants to combat unemployment through public sector expansion (especially in the area of health care and welfare), increased taxation of high incomes and property, and public funds for industrial development. The SV further favors better care for children and the elderly and extension of the national maternity leave. Internationally, the SV anticipates renewed discussion of Norwegian membership in the EC, which it opposes. The SV is also the only Norwegian parliamentary party opposed to North Atlantic Treaty Organization membership. The party has in the past criticized U.S. naval strategy in the North Atlantic and called for disarmament and the creation of a nuclear-free zone in the Nordic area. The party wants no foreign bases or arms depots on Norwegian soil and favors banning entry to Norwegian ports of any ship not certifiably free of nuclear weapons.

The SV maintains international contacts with a variety of Socialist and Marxist parties but has particularly close ties to such Nordic parties as the Swedish Communists (VPK) and the Danish Socialist People's Party (SF).

The Workers' Communist Party. The AKP was born in the late 1960s as a splinter group from the youth movement of the Socialist People's Party (SF). The founders were generally Maoist and revolutionary in orientation and dissatisfied with the moderate course of the SF. The AKP emerged as a formal organization in 1973 but has generally contested elections as the Red Electoral Alliance (RV). The RV has not fared well in elections, never reaching 1 percent of the national vote in general elections or electing a single member of Parliament. However, the party has had greater success in local elections in some of the larger cities (particularly Tromsø) and has representation on several city councils.

The AKP has recruited its members mainly among students and other youth and is not a genuine working-class party. However, the party has adopted a policy of proletarianization of its cadres and now draws a disproportionate share of votes from individuals between the ages of 35 and 45, mainly former student radicals. The party has until recently been highly secretive and sectarian. Although the AKP has maintained an estimated five thousand to seven thousand voters, its support among Norwegian students and intellectuals has declined precipitously since its heyday in the 1970s. The AKP currently stresses its opposition to the austerity policies of the Labor government, especially wage controls. The party also opposes Norwegian membership in the EC and favors an open immigration policy and efforts to improve the condition of women.

The Fifth Congress of the AKP took place somewhere in Norway in the first half of December

1988. Contrary to previous practice, the party subsequently held simultaneous press conferences in Oslo, Tromsø, and Bodø and released the names of all members of the newly elected Central Committee. Out of seventeen members, nine are women, eight are workers, and three are from northern Norway. With one exception, all were between the ages of 35 and 45 at the time of their election. The congress decided that henceforth congresses should take place every two years, as opposed to every four years. During the press conferences party leaders stressed the economic crisis in northern Norway, a national plan for public sector employment, higher corporate taxes, women's issues, and support for refugees and immigrants. Party leaders declined to take a more critical position on Stalin than in the past. There was considerable discussion of the proper evaluation of Stalin during the party congress, which narrowly decided to retain him among the "classics of socialism" (*Klassekampen*, 13 December 1988).

In September, former AKP activist Harald Skjønsberg published an insider's history of the party under the title *In a Party with Stalin?* Skjønsberg, a secondary school teacher from suburban Oslo, today regrets his past as a self-described "fellow traveler," claiming that it would have been a catastrophe if the AKP had had any influence. According to reviewers, Skjønsberg's book contains valuable historical material that should be preserved (*Aftenposten*, 28 September).

County Slates for the Environment and Solidarity. In the 1989 parliamentary election the AKP joined forces with the NKP and other Socialists in the County Slates for the Environment and Solidarity (see above). For electoral results, see above under AKP.

Kaare Strom
University of Minnesota at Minneapolis

Portugal

Population. 10,354,497 (July, *World Fact Book*)
Party. Portuguese Communist Party (Partido Comunista Português, PCP)
Founded. 1921
Membership. About 200,000 (claimed April 1990)
General Secretary. Alvaro Cunhal (since 1941)
Deputy General Secretary. Carlos Carvalhas (*Expresso*, 26 May; *FBIS*, 10 July)
Secretariat. 11 full members: Alvaro Cunhal, 76; Carlos Carvalhas, 48; Domingos Abrantes; Luísa Araújo; Henrique de Sousa; Francisco Lópes; Albano Núnes; Octávio Pato; José Soeiro; Blanqui Teixeira; Vidal Pinto (ibid.)
Political Commission. 14 full members: Alvaro Cunhal, Carlos Carvalhas, Domingos Abrantes, Jorge Araújo, Carlos Brito, José Casanova, Edgar Maciel Correia, Vítor Dias, Agostinho Lópes, Francisco Lópes, Luís Sá, José Soeiro, Octávio Teixeira, Angelo Veloso (ibid.)
National Executive Commission. 33 members (ibid.)
Central Commission on Control and Cadres. 17 members
Central Committee. 175 members
Status. Legal
Last Congress. Twelfth, 1–4 December 1988, in Oporto; Thirteenth, Special, 18–20 May
Last Election. 1987, United Democratic Coalition (CDU, Communist coalition), 11 percent, 30 of 250 seats
Auxiliary Organization. General Confederation of Portuguese Workers (Confederação Geral de Trabalhadores Portugueses—Intersindical Nacional, CGTP), which, with 1.6 million members (*WMR*, April 1988), represents more than half of Portugal's 2.5 million unionized labor force out of a work force of 4.58 million (*World Fact Book*, 1989).
Publications. *Avante*, weekly newspaper, António Dias Lorenço, editor; *O Militante*, theoretical journal; *O Diário*, semiofficial daily newspaper until it closed down in mid-1990, Jorge Araújo, editor (all published in Lisbon)

The PCP, which remains the most Stalinist party in Western Europe, dominates the Portuguese communist movement and most of the unionized labor force. It continues to adhere rigorously to traditional Marxist-Leninist dogma and to squelch demands by party "renewalists" for internal reform. Communist clout is limited to the industrial belt, Lisbon, and the southern Alentejo farm region, though the party's political strength and its control over cooperatives are in decline.

Organization and Leadership. Dissident PCP factions coalesced sufficiently in early 1990 to launch the Institute of Social Studies (Instituto des Estudos Sociais, INES), a "forum for debate" on party matters (*Expresso*, 6 January; *FBIS*, 9 February). Some party hard-liners called for purges and "selective disciplinary measures" against members of this "splinter group," though Cunhal counseled caution. He did warn that "honest critics" in INES were being exploited by those engaged in "organizing discord." (*Semanário*, 23 December 1989; *Expresso*, 27 January, 7 April; *FBIS*, 1 February, 25 May.)

One of the harshest critics, Zita Seabra, who had been dismissed from the Political Commission and the Central Committee in 1988 (see *YICA*, 1989), was expelled from the party in January after she called for the resignation of the entire party leadership and a change in the party's name, program, and aims. Some INES backers supported her expulsion because the changes she demanded were "so extensive that they wind up being foolish." (*Semanário*, 6 January; *FBIS*, 9 January.)

Dissidents were partially placated at the PCP's Thirteenth Special Congress in May, when moderate Carlos Carvalhas was designated deputy general secretary. This position was created to groom him to succeed Cunhal. Associated with a young and "discreetly reformist" wing of the party, Carvalhas was nonetheless loyal to the orthodox party line. Conservative Domingos Abrantes was originally thought to be Cunhal's preferred candidate when he was endorsed by the 1988 party congress as "second in command" (see *YICA*, 1990), but he had a poor public image and was increasingly unpopular among the reformists. According to some sources, Cunhall accepted Carvalhas only after determining that the latter was the leader generating the greatest consensus within the Secretariat (*Expresso*, 13 April, 26 May; *FBIS*, 24 May, 10 July).

The congress made additional changes in the structure of the executive by assigning most power

to the Political Commission (*Expresso*, 26 May; *FBIS*, 10 July). Influence in that body was reportedly evenly balanced between moderates and conservatives, though it remained to be seen how stable the balance would be once Cunhal was no longer there to smooth over conflicts and to make major decisions (*Expresso*, 25 August; *FBIS*, 3 October). Carvalhas was said to lack the strong personality necessary to replace Cunhal effectively (*Expresso*, 26 May; *FBIS*, 10 July). Conservative Angelo Veloso was reportedly Cunhal's second choice, but Veloso's prolonged illness in 1990 took him out of the running (*Semanario*, 17 March; *FBIS*, 1 May).

Meanwhile, the PCP platform remained unchanged on such fundamental issues as Marxism-Leninism and democratic centralism (Lisbon Domestic Service, 20 May; *FBIS*, 21 May). Cunhal closed the congress with a call for unity, warning critics that they must abandon their campaign against the party (*Diário de Notícias*, 15 July; *FBIS*, 30 August).

Most reformists reportedly said in May that they were prepared to "respect party discipline" and "hibernate for a while." One did express his "deep disappointment" in the party leadership by resigning his post as chairman of the Lisbon Municipal Assembly; another resigned from the party. (*Expresso*, 17 March, 25 August; *O Jornal*, 12 April; *FBIS*, 1 May, 15 June, 3 October.)

Domestic Affairs. Cunhal announced that the PCP was prepared to go "halfway or even further" to reach agreement with the Socialists for a convergence in the next legislative elections to oust the right from the government. However, Socialist leader Jorge Sampaio emphatically ruled out any coalition or commitment. Buoyed by polls that showed the Socialists gaining in popular support, Sampaio said that the strategy developed for the Lisbon City Council (see *YICA*, 1990) was not an arrangement that could be reproduced in legislative elections. (*Diário de Notícias*, 4, 15 July; *FBIS*, 13 July, 30 August.) He did hedge that convergence could only be a "last resort" (*Expresso*, 21 April; *FBIS*, 17 May).

Even though it was a foregone conclusion that Mário Soares would be reelected in the January 1991 presidential election, the PCP decided to put Carlos Carvalhas in the race as a symbolic candidate. Cunhal saw this as training for the legislative race and as a chance to use the airwaves to convey the communist message. (*O Independente*, 17 September; *FBIS*, 16 October.) The party's critical sectors called the decision "buffoonery"; Caralhas himself was said to be uncomfortable, doubting that his candidacy would benefit the party. The PCP old guard reportedly hoped this would "box" him in, causing him to emerge from the race with decreased prestige. (*Tempo*, 26 July, 30 August; *FBIS*, 12 September, 16 October.)

Auxiliary Organizations. The popular labor leader José Luís Judas continued to be the preferred candidate of party renewalists for the future leadership of the PCP (see *YICA*, 1990). It is thought that the political importance of the CGTP, in which he enjoys great prestige, will tend to increase as the PCP crisis grows worse. Observers consider that he has been very skillful in avoiding an open break with party leaders despite his public criticism. In a document he presented in April that criticized the theses to be presented at the May congress, he emphasized the "constructive sense" of his analysis and denied any thought of radical confrontation with the party. All the same, the document was rejected. (*Expresso*, 21 April; *FBIS*, 15 June.)

Carvalho da Silva, coordinating secretary of the CGTP, decided in January to stop attending the plenary meetings of the PCP's Central Committee. He was the only trade union leader with observer status, a position that gave him all the rights enjoyed by the other elected members except that of voting. He reportedly made his decision following a dispute with Cunhal over proposals by party renewalists for the upcoming party congress. (*Expresso*, 17 February; *FBIS*, 4 April.)

A growing openness to the noncommunist labor movement led the CGTP in April to apply for membership in the European Trade Union Confederation (CES) that had been affiliated with the Soviet-backed World Federation of Trade Unions (WFTU). (*Expresso*, 21 April; *FBIS*, 15 June.) A proposal to merge the CGTP with the Socialist General Workers' Union (UGT) divided CGTP leaders and was opposed by most UGT leaders, who adopted a "reserved" attitude. (*O Jornal*, 12 April; *FBIS*, 15 June.)

Of the 550 communist-controlled cooperatives with 72,000 members operating in Portugal in 1975, reportedly only 210 cooperatives with less than 12,000 members remain (*NYT*, 17 May).

International Views and Activities. The major thrust of the theses presented to the PCP's May congress was to absolve communism from the serious "errors and deviations" that had brought down communist governments abroad. The principal shortcomings were seen to have been an excessively centralized, despotic economic organization, an overgrown bureaucratic apparatus, and the removal of workers from the management of the state. The PCP insisted that the mistakes of others did not justify abandoning Marxism-Leninism and democratic centralism, the "backbone" of the party's identity and operations. (*Expresso*, 10 March, 26 May; *FBIS*, 24 April, 10 July.)

The PCP expressed its support for reform efforts in the Soviet Union but was wary of "opportunistic objectives being pursued under the cover of perestroika" (*Expresso*, 27 January; *FBIS*, 12 March). Cunhal also criticized parties that had recently "thrown out the baby with the bathwater" by renouncing communist goals and ideals (*Pravda*, 21 May; *FBIS*, 24 May).

Cunhal assured his comrades that if the party had been aware of the abuses in other communist countries, "we would have denounced" them (*Expresso*, 27 January; *FBIS*, 12 March). To the suggestion that the Chinese and North Korean Communist parties should be criticized for recent excesses, however, Cunhal countered that the situation was not propitious for the public expression of such differences (*Expresso*, 10 May; *FBIS*, 24 April). Carvalhas explained that it was a matter of principle to criticize other communist governments privately—across the negotiating table—but never publicly (*Semanário Revista*, 12 May; *FBIS*, 28 June). Cunhal acknowledged that the cult of personality in China and North Korea had been raised to a level that "to us seems very strange," but he said that there is no reason to criticize the "positive role" those countries play in the world (*Expresso*, 7 April; *FBIS*, 25 May).

At a meeting in Lisbon with the Angolan minister of foreign relations, Cunhal reaffirmed the PCP's "active solidarity" with the Angolans in consolidating the independence and sovereignty of their country (Lisbon Domestic Service, 30 April; *FBIS*, 1 May).

Biography. *Carlos Carvalhas.* The PCE's deputy general secretary and heir apparent to succeed Cunhal is said to be an amiable but lackluster politician who "plugs along with many successes." Politically active at the age of fifteen, he took part in Humberto Delgado's campaign for the presidency of Portugal. Following the 1974 revolution, he served in five provisional governments and was elected in 1976 to the Assembly as a communist deputy. Heading the PCP slate in a Lisbon Municipal Council election, he received the highest vote, 28.5 percent, ever earned by the communists. In 1979, he was elected to the European Parliament on the PCP slate.

Carvalhas was born to a wealthy family. He joined the PCP in 1969 and became an alternate member of the Central Committee in 1976 and an active member in 1983. In 1988, he was elected to the Political Commission. (*Expresso*, 13 April, 19, 26 May, 2 June; *FBIS*, 24 May, 28 June, 6, 10 July.)

H. Leslie Robinson
University of the Pacific

San Marino

Population. 23,123 (0.6 percent birthrate; *World Fact Book*)

Party. Communist Party of San Marino (PCS) until 29 April 1990; changed to Progressive Democratic Party of San Marino (Partito Progressista Democratico Sammarinese, PPDS) at Twelfth Party Congress.

Founded. 1921; renamed 1990.

Membership. 1,100 registered members in 10 cells, 3 of which are in Italy (*L'Unità*, 23 March; *FBIS-WEU*, 10 May)

General Secretary. Gilberto Ghiotti, 38, political scientist

Honorary Chairman. Gilberto Gasperoni, 84

Secretariat. Alberto Mino; others unknown

Last Congress. Twelfth, 27–29 April 1990

Last Election. 29 May 1988; 28.71 percent of the vote; 18 of 60 seats

Publication. *La Scintilla*, publisher, Giuseppe Morganti. After the congress it was renamed *Progresso*, publisher, Enzo Colombini. In 1990, *La Scintilla* had two issues in April (nos. 1 and 2); *Progresso* seems to have had only issue so far (no. 0).

The Communist Party of San Marino is no more. The massive changes that swept Eastern Europe radiated southwest and moved the tiny republic government's communist coalition partner to follow suit; its parent, the Italian Communist Party, had foreshadowed a similar action at its Nineteenth Congress in March.

Instead of the hammer and the sickle, Picasso's dove now graces the masthead of the newly named Progressive Democratic party's paper *Progresso*. Only the general color scheme, red and white, remains. Even the editor is new, though Giuseppe Morganti, *La Scintilla*'s editor, writes in a new paper on the importance and responsibility of San Marino's soon-to-be independent radio and TV station to the republic's culture. In the first issue of *Progresso*, General Secretary Gilberto Ghiotti bridges the old and the new by reflecting "on our way of existence, our method of work and comparison" (*Progresso*, no. 0). The new editor, Enzo Colombini, in his inaugural editorial, nostalgically subtitled "Addio...*Scintilla*...Addio," hopes that the paper will be not only the organ of a political party but a source of information for all progressive, cultural, and ecological views (ibid.).

As detailed a description as *La Scintilla* gave of the work of the committees preparing the business of the congress, going so far as to list the names and districts of all 135 representatives to the congress (*La Scintilla*, no. 2, April), in the postcongress issues of the paper there has been no mention of other officers besides the general secretary and no indication of the governing body or the number of members of the Politburo, Secretariat, and so forth. The names known come from scattered references.

The anguished deliberations on change began last year but took on concrete form with the meeting of the Central Committee and the Control Commission 9, 12, and 13 March, when the date of the Sixth Congress was fixed and the new name and symbol for the party were proposed (*La Scintilla*, no. 1, April). General Secretary Ghiotti, quoted in *L'Unità*, mused that "the problem is not with the party, but rather who will run it." Ghiotti maintains that there has always been a split between those whose inclinations were democratic and pragmatic, realizing that a successful party has to have a wide base of support, and those who wanted to hold on to the old power structure. (*L'Unità*, 23 March; *FBIS-WEU*, 10 May.) But it seems that former General Secretaries Gildo Gasperoni, 84, and Umberto Barulli, 69, also wholeheartedly supported the new direction; they wanted a genuine act of change supported by all the people but especially the youth of the republic, not just a perfunctory, cosmetic transformation (ibid.).

Gilberto Ghiotti, who remained the general secretary of the newly launched Progressive Democratic Party, sees the change as a natural evolution of the ideological trend that began in 1968 (ibid.) and became crystallized when the PCS established a governing coalition with the Christian Democratic Party (PDCS) in 1986. Alberto Mino, a member of the Secretariat, echoed this sentiment in a *L'Unità* interview when he said that "we mistakenly called ourselves communists. We have always accepted pluralism and capitalism" and fought for it as far back as 1945. The events in Tiananmen Square and Ceauşescu's actions reinforced this trend toward formal change. After the March Central Committee meeting, Mino wrote in *La Scintilla* that the party had always followed democratic and independent thought including condemning the 1968 Warsaw Pact invasion of Czechoslovakia to crush Dubcek's Prague Spring (ibid.; *La Scintilla*, no. 1, April).

As if to support this change, Italian president Cossiga visited San Marino some time after the congress (*Progresso* does not provide dates either for the paper's masthead or for the visit; it does not even number the pages, which were counted by the reader), declaring that both Italy and San Marino have "reacquired" the fundamental elements of development. The two captains regent as well as most of the Congress of the State, with Secretary of State for Foreign Affairs Gabriele Gatti in the lead, were the hosts of this visit. The discussions with the prime minister touched on subjects important to San Marino: the beginning, by 1992, of San Marino's own radio and television broadcasts, which have not existed for fifteen years; the establishment of the Rimini–San Marino express train line; and the internationalization—presumably the expansion—of the Miramare airport, to be called the Rimini–San Marino International Airport.

Of the seven ministers and three secretaries of state in the Congress of State, two secretaries and two ministers are PPDS members (*Europa World Yearbook 1990*, p. 2202), as are two successive captains regents: Gloriana Ranocchini from September 1989 to April 1990 and Adalmiro Bartolini from April to October 1991. The captains regent are elected in April and September by and from the 60-member unicameral legislature, the Great and General Council. The Congress of State wields the executive power, and the captains regent act as heads of state.

Progressisti in Festa (progressives on holiday) took place in Falciano on 4–5 August. The festival is a successor to the *La Scintilla* festival, which had usually been a cheerleading occasion for the party. This one, however, was decidedly nonpolitical; the theme was good nutrition with natural foods and concern for global ecology (*Progresso*, no. 0).

The mood of the party is upbeat; the leftist part of the coalition looks forward to a better, sounder government with the PDCS and a generally new beginning. Harmony is already indicated by an agreement reached on 28 June on health and social security matters, as detailed by Alberto Mino (ibid.), who considers the agreement a direct result of the Twelfth Congress and a turning point.

International Views and Concerns. Benny Nato, an African National Congress representative, visited San Marino on 19 March and was received by General Secretary Ghiotti. With the agreement of the council and the mandate of the government, a human rights foundation has been established, dedicated to Nelson Mandela (*La Scintilla*, April 1990, no. 1).

The Soviet Union Communist Party's Central Committee sent the Twelfth Congress congratulations, wishing it success and assuring "developing relations between our parties in the interest of strengthening peace world-wide and asserting humane socialist values" (Moscow, TASS, 26 April; *FBIS-SOV*, 27 April). A Soviet Communist Party delegation including Central Committee first deputy department head V. Mikhailov and International Department executive L. Popov participated in the Twelfth Congress of what on 27 April was still the Communist Party of San Marino.

The stormy Twenty-eighth Congress of the USSR led Alberto Mino to write in an article entitled "The 28th Congress of the USSR: Perestroika Has Not Stopped" that the Soviet congress only confirmed the principle of socialism within democracy and the enhancement of human rights "whose principles and objectives our 12th Congress has fully assumed" (*Progresso*, no. 0).

Margit N. Grigory
Hoover Institution

Spain

Population. 39,268,715 (July, *World Fact Book*)
Parties. Spanish Communist Party (Partido Comunista de España, PCE); Communist Party of the Peoples of Spain (Partido Comunista de los Pueblos de España, PCPE); Spanish Workers' Party—Communist Unity (Partido de los Trabajadores de España—Unidad Comunista, PTE-UC)
Founded. PCE: 1920; PCPE: 1984; PTE-UC: 1987
Membership. PCE: more than 83,000 (claimed 1989); PCPE: 16,000–17,000 (claimed); PTE-UC: 14,000
General Secretary. PCE: Julio Anguita González, 49; PCPE: Juan Ramos Camerero; PTE-UC: Adolfo Pinedo
Chairman. PTE-EC: Santiago Carrillo, 75
Secretariat. PCE: 9 members: Julio Anguita González, Juan José Azcona, Juan Berga, José María Coronas, Francisco Frutos, Lucía García, Salvador Jové, Josep Palau, Francisco Palero. PCPE: 9 members: Juan Ramos Camarero, Leopoldo Alcaraz Redondo, Jaime Ballesteros Pulido, Quim Boix Lluch, Josep Cónsola, José Antonio García Rubio, Carmen Morente, Mariá Pere Lizandara, Margarita Sanz Alonso
Executive Committee. PCPE: 22 members: Juan Ramos Camarero, Leopoldo Alcaraz Redondo, Jaime Ballesteros Pulido, Quim Boix Lluch, Estéban Cerdán Francés, José Miguel Céspedes, Josep Cónsola, Leopoldo del Prado, Juan Luis García Córdoba, José Antonio García Rubio, Guillermo Gil Vázquez, Manuel Guerra Lobo, Carlos Gutiérrez Garcia-Alix, M. Angels Martinez Castells, Carmen Morente, Juan Muñiz Acedo, Vicente Peragón Herranz, Mariá Pere Lizandara, Miguel Roselló del Rosal, Nicasio Sancho González, Margarita Sanz Alonso, Francisco Trives Mesequer
Political Commission. PCE: 28 members
Central Committee. PCE: 101 members; PCPE: 72 full members, 23 alternate members
Status. All legal

Last Congress. PCE: Twelfth, 19–21 February 1988, in Madrid; PCPE: Third (extraordinary) March 1989; PTE-UC: First, 8 February 1987
Last Election. 1989, United Left (PCE electoral front), 9.05 percent, 18 of 350 seats; PCPE, PTE-UC, no seats
Auxiliary Organization. Workers' Commissions (Comisiones Obreras; CC OO), claimed membership of about 1 million, almost a third of Spain's unionized workers, Antonio Gutiérrez, chairman. (The CC OO is considered an auxiliary organization of the PCE, but all three Spanish communist parties have direct influence in it; 90 to 95 percent of CC OO officials are said to be PCE members.)
Publications. PCE: *Mundo Obrero* (Labor world), weekly, Juan B. Berga, editor; *Nuestra Bandera* (Our flag), bimonthly ideological journal, Pedro Marset, editor (both published in Madrid). PCPE: *Nuevo Rumbo* (New direction), biweekly, José Antonio García Rubio, editor; *Revista Teórica* (Theoretical journal), Carmen Morente, editor; PTE-UC: *Ahora* (Now), weekly, Santiago Carillo, editor

Most Spanish communists are active in the rejuvenated PCE, which dramatically improved its political strength in the 1989 elections. It carries out political activities increasingly through the United Left, a coalition—which it dominates—of communists and renegade Socialists.

The PCPE was formed by dissidents who protested the PCE's Eurocommunism, but no activity by that party was reported during 1990. It was weakened when much of its membership returned to the PCE. The PTE-UC was founded by Santiago Carrillo, who left the PCE in 1986 after having been removed as general secretary.

Occasional acts of terrorism continue to be carried out by a Marxist guerrilla group called Basque Homeland and Liberty (Euzkadi ta Askatasuna, ETA) and by the October First Antifascist Resistance Group (Grupo de Resistencia Antifascista Primero de Octubre, GRAPO). ETA demands Spanish recognition of Basque independence. Little is known about GRAPO; its name commemorates the killing of four policemen in Madrid on 1 October 1975.

Organization and Leadership. The PCE general secretary sought to dispel any notion that his party would, following the example of the Italian Communist Party, change its name or abandon

Marxism. At the party's Sixth National Conference in April, he gave assurances that there would be no communist "hara-kiri" any time soon that would risk the party's becoming "diluted" in the United Left coalition. (*Expresso*, 7 April; *Pravda*, 15 January; *FBIS-SOV*, 22 January; *FBIS-WEU*, 22 May.) He saw the United Left not as another political party but as a "strategy—a crucible in which the blending of the new left can begin." Meanwhile, there were reports that in areas where communism is weakest, hammer and sickles were being replaced by newly painted United Left emblems (*Cambio 16*, 18 December 1989; *Ya*, 7 April; *FBIS-WEU*, 12 March, 22 May).

Angered by the PCE's "lack of receptiveness toward issues such as military service and conscientious objection," the Spanish Communist Youth Union withdrew from the party's leadership organs (*El Independiente*, 30 December 1989; *FBIS-WEU*, 16 February).

Domestic Affairs. Most Spanish communists were said to agree that, following the collapse of the iron curtain, the gap that has separated communists and Socialists since the 1920s has begun to close while the prestige of social democracy among the left has grown (*Cambio 16*, 18 December 1989; *FBIS-WEU*, 12 March). Anguita dismissed such a conclusion as ludicrous. To practice social democracy, Anguita said, simply means to accept the capitalist system. Spanish communists would certainly not move closer to Socialists if that meant accepting the economic and social policies—"which have nothing to do with socialism"—of Prime Minister Felipe González. (American Broadcasting Company, 12 March; *Expresso*, Lisbon, 7 April; *FBIS-WEU*, 3, 22 May.) Anguita said that he did not rule out a convergence with the Socialists but that he thought agreement with the top echelon of that party was not possible (Madrid Domestic Service, 30 January; *Diario 16*, 13 March; *FBIS-WEU*, 31 January, 27 April). One observer noted that Anguita does not really want agreement because the only chance for the United Left to keep on growing is at the expense of the Socialists (*Cambio 16*, 9 April; *FBIS-WEU*, 18 May).

Spanish communists and Socialists were said to be working together amicably at various lower levels, such as the Madrid and Catalan city halls, labor unions, and the European parliament. The former Catalan Communist Party was reportedly transforming itself into a new Socialist force. (Ibid.)

In November, Julio Anguita was reelected coordinator of the United Left coalition. The leadership includes ten PCE members, five from the Party of Socialist Action, four independents, and two from the Republic Left. (Madrid Domestic Service, 26 November; *FBIS-WEU*, 27 November.)

Communists who spent long years in prison for resisting the Franco dictatorship blame the Socialist government's "anti-communism" for its reluctance to meet their recent demands for compensation and recognition for their sacrifices (*NYT*, 20 June).

Auxiliary Organizations. The Socialist General Workers' Union (UGT) lifted its veto to help the CC OO join the European Trade Union Confederation (CES) in 1990. Previously, the CES had only accepted social democratic unions. (*Cambio 16*, 9 April; *FBIS-WEU*, 18 May.) The new UGT-CC OO rapport appeared to be jeopardized, however, by a conflict in July over the manner of holding union elections. At stake was a CC OO effort to erase the gap between its own representation in the unions and that of the UGT. (Barcelona, *La Vanguardia*, 14 July; *FBIS-WEU*, 24 August.)

Asserting that he found "very positive" the changes the Italian communists had made in their party, CC OO leader Antonio Gutiérrez said that the revamping of PCE "must go farther and faster" (*Cambio 16*, 9 April; *FBIS-WEU*, 18 May).

International Views and Activities. Following discussions in October with Mikhail Gorbachev, who was in Madrid on a state visit, Anguita stressed the "notable coincidences" between current Soviet thinking on *perestroika* and the policy defended by the PCE and the United Left (Madrid Domestic Service, 26 October; *FBIS-WEU*, 29 October). The prevailing view of PCE officials was that not communism but its evolution since World War II was being challenged. The word *communist* had been "usurped" to justify governments that had turned their backs to society and the communist ideal. (*Cambio 16*, 18 December 1989; *Mundo Obrero*, 20–26 December 1989; *FBIS-WEU*, 8 February, 12 March.) Anguita insisted that the 1917 revolution in Russia was necessary and that substantial social advances had been made (*Pravda*, 15 January; *Expresso*, Lisbon, 7 April; *FBIS-WEU*, 22 January, 22 May). A United Left delegation visited the Soviet Union in May to study that country's experience with *perestroika* and the development of democratic processes (*Pravda*, 19 May; *FBIS-SOV*, 24 May).

To suggestions that the PCE follow the path of the Italian Communist Party in making changes, Anguita countered that what the Italians were attempting had been accomplished by the PCE some time ago with the integration of Socialist sectors in the United Left (*Diario 16*, 13 March; *El Independiente*, 24 March; *FBIS-WEU*, 27 April, 3 May). At the same time, Anguita opposed the notion, advanced by some comrades, of having the PCE affiliate with the Socialist International; he stressed that the PCE and the United Left would never join it so long as he was general secretary (*Expresso*, Lisbon, 7 April; *FBIS-WEU*, 22 May).

The PCE and the United Left condemned Saddam Husayn's aggression in Kuwait but opposed the Spanish government's decision to send three Spanish warships to the gulf. Complaining that Spain was bending to U.S. pressure, the United Left forced Parliament into a special session to require Prime Minister González to explain the Spanish role in the military buildup. (*NYT*, 21 September; Havana, *Granma*, 30 September.)

A heated diplomatic clash between Spain and Cuba followed Spain's granting of asylum to some Cuban dissidents in July. The latter were allowed to leave the Spanish embassy in Havana in September in exchange for promises that they would not be punished. A United Left and PCE official visiting Havana tried to smooth over the affair, calling it a "negative page" in the history of the two countries in which there was now a "more constructive view" of a period of "excessive zeal." (*NYT*, 11 September; Havana, *Granma*, 30 September.)

Anguita expressed admiration for the "model way" in which the Portuguese Communist Party is organized as well as for the party's "perfect integration" in Portuguese society (Lisbon, *Expresso*, 7 April; *FBIS-WEU*, 22 May). He also told a visiting official of the Chinese Communist Party that he hoped for increased contacts between that party and the PCE (Beijing, *Xinhua*, 28 September; *FBIS-CHI*, 28 September).

Rival Communist Parties. Saying that "our knuckles are sore from knocking on the PCE's door," Santiago Carrillo concluded in March that a merger of all Spanish communists was impossible. He compared the PCE's present leadership with the Soviet Union's most inflexible, hard-line sectors. Carrillo's party then decided to seek a rapprochement with the Socialist party because the ideological differences between Socialists and communists "have become dissolved." He said he opposed the United Left because he did not think that there was political space for a government alternative to the left of the Socialist party. In fact, he said he thought Socialist policy had taken a definite turn to the left. (*Cambio 16*, 18 December 1989; *Diario 16*, 5 March; *FBIS-WEU*, 12 March, 27 April.)

Anguita seemed to dismiss Carrillo as a pathetic figure who "does not exist" as a problem for the PCE. He referred to the aging leader as a "great personality" who would "go down in history" but wondered whether he would be able to bring his political life to an end "with dignity." (*Ya*, 7 April; *Tiempo*, 23 April; *FBIS-WEU*, 22 May.)

Left-Wing Terrorist Groups. Police hailed the arrest of a band of French terrorist suspects near Seville as one of the most important strikes ever against ETA. Never before thought to be participating directly in terrorism in Spain, the French Basques reportedly had carried out at least 33 killings over the last twelve years on behalf of ETA. (*NYT*, 11 April.) With the arrest of four ETA suspects in southern France, police learned that the group planned attacks on Olympic targets in Barcelona. ETA claimed it had carried out at least eighteen killings during 1990. (*AP*, 9 December.) GRAPO claimed responsibility for two murders in northeastern Spain during 1990 (Madrid Domestic Service, 5 April, 18 May; *FBIS-WEU*, 6 April, 21 May).

H. Leslie Robinson
University of the Pacific

Sweden

Population. 8,526,452 (July), growth rate, 0.5 percent

Party. Left Party (Vänsterpartiet, V). The party changed its name in May from Left Party Communists (Vänsterpartiet Kommunisterna, VPK.)

Founded. 1921 (VPK: 1967, V: 1990)

Membership. Ca. 17,800, principally in the far north, Stockholm, and Göteborg

Chairman. Lars Werner

Managing Committee. Lars Werner; Lennart Beijer, deputy party chairman; Gudrun Schyman, deputy party chairman; Kenneth Kvist, party secretary and Left Youth chairman; Gunnar Agren; Karin Nilsson; Lena Ohlsson

Executive Committee. Berra Ahnberg, Kaj Andersson, Maj-Lis Andersson, Brittis Bonzler, Bitte Engzell

Party Board. 25 members

Status. Legal

Last Congress. Twenty-ninth, 23–26 May 1990

Last Election. September 1988, 314,031 votes, 5.8 percent, 21 out of 349 seats

Auxiliary Organization. Left Youth (VU)

Publications. *Ny Dag* (New day), a semiweekly, suspended publication on 30 August 1990. The party had published *Volkvillan* (People's will), a weekly, and *Socialistick Debatt* (Socialist debate), a monthly theoretical journal; there was no information as to whether they were still being published.

The ancestor of the Party of the Left was Sweden's Communist Party (Sveriges Kommunistiska Partiet), which was established in 1921. Its greatest moment came right after World War II, when it obtained 11.2 percent of the vote in local elections, largely due to the popularity of the Soviet Union at the end of the war. Since that time the communist party (later the VPK until 1990) usually won between 4 and 6 percent of the vote. The party, which has never made a major contribution to communist history, has had marginal influence in Swedish politics. Its most important role has been to allow the Social Democrats to govern during much of Sweden's recent history. During the past half century, the Swedish Social Democrats have been Europe's most dominant social democratic party, having governed Sweden for 51 of the last 58 years. During many of their years in power, they have relied on a combined majority with the communists in the Riksdag (parliament). The communists, however, have never been part of the government. In Sweden, a party has to clear a 4 percent threshold in order to be represented in the Riksdag; after the bitter reaction to the Soviet invasion of Czechoslovakia in 1968, the VPK fell beneath 4 percent and was not represented. In the 1970 and 1976 elections, it received 4.8 percent, and in 1979 and 1982, 5.6 percent of the vote. The VPK dropped to 5.4 percent of the vote in 1985 and went up to 5.8 percent in 1988.

The communists changed both the name and the direction of the party during the party congress in 1967. Blue-collar workers had constituted the majority of the communist electorate in previous years, but during the 1970 elections the VPK increasingly attracted white-collar and younger voters. In the 1979 elections, 56 percent of the voters were under the age of 30, and 36 percent of the voters were in the white-collar class. In the 1982 elections, those under 30 years of age slipped to 45 percent, but those from the white-collar class rose from 36 to 41 percent. Over the years, the VPK has projected a Marxist image, even though it has been regarded as one of the more moderate West European communist parties.

The history of the VPK had been characterized by stormy internal fighting, and the internecine battling in 1987 was worse than usual. The arguments focused on policy and personnel decisions that were made by the Twenty-eighth Party Congress in May of that year. Much of the dispute centered around the chairman, Lars Werner, who by 1987 had served twelve years as party leader, longer than any other leader in the history of the VPK. (His predecessor, C. H. Hermansson, served eleven years.) Werner came under increasing criticism from members of the party's inner circle, who felt that he should take a tougher line against the Social Democrats in Parliament. Some wanted to oust Werner at the Twenty-eighth Party Congress, but it voted to retain him and to remove three of Werner's opponents from the Executive Committee. Another major opponent of Werner resigned as vice-chairman of the Executive Committee in 1988. Even though some of Werner's opponents remained on the Executive Committee, he seemed to be in a stronger position in relation to his VPK opponents at the end of 1988 than he had been two years previously.

The dominant political event in Sweden in 1988 was the September election. On the basis of polls taken early in 1988, there were predictions that the communists might not surmount the 4 percent barrier and so might not be represented in the Riksdag. A poll in February 1988 indicated that the VPK would get only 2.8 percent of the vote. It therefore surprised many observers when the VPK received 5.8 percent in the election. Speculation was that part of the VPK vote came from Social Democrats who wanted the communists to be represented in Parliament, thereby helping the Social Democrats to form the government. Much of the Swedish voters' attention in 1988 was focused on environmental issues, and indeed the Green party won 5.5

percent of the vote and was, for the first time, represented in the Riksdag.

Party Name Change. During 1989 and 1990, the VPK, like most of the world, focused on the seismic events in the Soviet Union and Eastern Europe. During a wide-ranging interview with *Svenska Dagbladet* in late November 1989, Werner indicated that the events in Eastern Europe had prompted soul-searching within the VPK and that the party was rethinking its policies and even considering changing its name. The name change came to pass during the Twenty-ninth Party Congress of 23–26 May. Much of the delegates' time and energy was devoted to the highly controversial matter of the name change. In the end, the decision to exclude the "communist" label from the party passed by only three votes—136 to 133. (*Dagens Nyheter*, 25 May.) The congress voted to have a committee decide what the party name should be. The six names considered were the Left party, the Socialist Left, the Left Socialists, the Socialist Left party, the Left Party of Socialists, and, simply, the Left. Werner favored the Socialist Left party, although he quipped that the National Rescue Front might be more appropriate. In the end, there was a unanimous vote by the committee for the Left party. Herman Schmid, the spokesman for the committee, said that the "Left party" is a name "that can be used in connection with elections and as a party name without complications." (*Dagens Nyheter*, 26 May.)

Other Party Internal Affairs. One dramatic event of the Twenty-ninth Congress was a challenge to Werner's leadership. Gudrun Schyman, deputy chairman of the party, received a respectable 99 votes for chairman; 161 delegates voted to retain Werner. There were 13 blank ballots. According to Ake Ekdahl, writing in *Dagens Nyheter* (25 May),

> Criticism of Lars Werner's leadership has grown stronger during recent years. The debate about his consumption of alcohol, his inclination to use dictatorial methods in controlling the party, and, now, most recently, his great indecision regarding the party's regeneration and change of name have been brought forward as weighty arguments against him.

Schyman said that she was not really challenging Werner: "I am doing this so that the congress will get a chance to choose the chairman." (*Dagens Nyheter*, 25 May.) There was a lengthy and arduous debate in the congress that seemed at first to favor Schyman but then swung over to Werner.

There were wholesale changes in personnel in the party executive body. The number of members of the executive body was reduced from 35 to 25, and 17 of the members were new. Further, only four or five persons who wanted to keep "communist" in the party name were in the new executive body, which seemed more friendly to Werner's policies than the previous one. Most of Werner's strongest critics are no longer in leadership positions. (*Dagens Nyheter*, 26 May.) Bertil Mabrink who, as deputy party chairman, was Werner's highest-ranking critic, resigned his party position in June (*Dagens Nyheter*, 2 June).

Another notable change was the decision by former party leader C.H. Hermansson, 72, to step down from the party's executive body after having been on it for 44 years (*Dagens Nyheter*, 25 May). Journalist Ake Ekdahl described Herman Schmid as "Lars Werner's new strong man on the party's top level." Schmid, who is now considered to be the party's foremost interpreter of Marxism, received the highest number of votes to be on the Vänsterpartiet's new executive body—247 out of 275 delegates. (*Dagens Nyheter*, 26 May.)

An editorial in *Dagens Nyheter* said that the "Communist Left Party is in wild and disorderly flight from its past." Indeed, there seemed to be considerable confusion at the congress regarding the party's future direction. Because of the extraordinary changes in Eastern Europe, party members did not want to commit themselves to a party program. The delegates decided to drop the party program that was adopted just three years ago and not put forward a new party program until the next congress in 1993. (*Dagens Nyheter*, 26 May.) The party delegates did, however, pass a vague interim measure of "program points" that suggested that "a radicalized workers' movement, a well-informed environmental movement, and a purposeful women's movement, together, can turn developments in our country around—and offer hope for a better world, free of oppression and impoverishment." (*Dagens Nyheter*, 27 May.)

There were increasing indications throughout the year that the combined Social Democrat–VPK parliamentary majority of the past may not be part of the future political picture in Sweden. For one thing, the VPK voted on 15 February with the conservatives and other opposition parties on an economic rescue bill that resulted in the government resigning. (*NYT*, 16 February.) The Social Democrats later formed another government. In late September, Werner told his parliamentary group that the Vänsterpartiet may no longer be part of the Social Democrats' political strategy. He said that "the government does not trust us. They think that we have been too independent. We can see that the Social Democrats have moved to the right." Werner went on to surmise that Prime Minister Ingvar Carlsson was considering a deal with the Liberal party on the European Community issue and the nuclear issue. There were increasing suggestions from the Vänsterpartiet that the V (the new initial of the party) desired common electoral strategy with other leftists and the Green party. (*Dagens Nyheter*, 27 September.)

Paper ceases publication. Another party event that caused tremors was the party paper *Ny Dag*'s ceasing publication in August. Ever since 1930, *Ny Dag* had been the printed voice of the VPK. The paper had a circulation of 20,000 ten years ago but had dropped to 7,000 by 1990. Thus, a 60-year era ended when the Vänsterpartiet decided that *Ny Dag* was too expensive to subsidize. (Stockholm International Service, 31 August; *Dagens Nyheter*, 23, 29 August.)

Foreign Relations. Because of the upheaval in the communist world, there were no reports of Vänsterpartiet visits to communist parties in other countries. Party secretary Kenneth Kvist said that "we have now discontinued all our relations with our former fraternal parties in East Europe and we have even passed an Executive Committee resolution that we no longer have fraternal parties." In brief, the Vänsterpartiet decided to bide its time and put all of its international relations in a holding pattern. (*Dagens Nyheter*, 6 July.)

Rival Party Groups. The minuscule Communist Workers' Party (APK) continued to be an orthodox communist party and kept its contacts with Eastern European communist parties. The APK split off from the VPK in the 1970s because it thought the latter to be too far to the right. Rolf Hagel, the head of the APK, was quoted as saying, "The upheaval in Eastern Europe and the reevaluation in the Soviet Union are a temporary defeat for the Communist movement. But I will never give up the Communist idea." (*Dagens Nyheter*, 26 September). The APK lost its party newspaper, *Norrskensflamman*. The newspaper's editor, Alf Lovenborg, left the APK because of conflict over

the party's policies. Hagel accused the newspaper's executive board of a political coup and said, "We must have *Norrskensflamman* back. Otherwise it will die. A newspaper must have a party to back it." (*Dagens Nyheter*, 26 September.)

Peter Grothe
Monterey Institute of International Studies

Switzerland

Population. 6,742,461 (July)
Party. Swiss Labor Party (Partei der Arbeit der Schweiz/Parti suisse du travail/Partito Svizzero del Lavoro, PdAS)
Founded. 1921; outlawed 1940; reestablished 15 October 1944
Membership. 4,500 (estimated)
General Secretary. Jean Spielmann
Politburo. 14 members
Secretariat. 5 members
Central Committee. 50 members
Status. Legal
Last Congress. Thirteenth, 27 February–1 March 1987; national party conference, Geneva, 19–20 May 1990
Last Election. 18 October 1987, 0.8 percent; 1 seat in the National Council, the lower chamber of the national Parliament; 8.72 percent of the vote in Geneva canton and in addition represented in the Parliaments of the Vaud, Neuchatel, and Jura cantons. In March 1990 left-wing and Green parties, although not formally united in a coalition, have secured an absolute majority in the city council of Zurich
Auxiliary Organizations. Communist Youth League of Switzerland (KVJS), Marxist Student League, Swiss Women's Organization for Peace and Progress, Swiss Peace Movement, Swiss-Soviet Union Society, Swiss-Cuban Society, Central Sanitaire Swiss
Publications. *Voix Ouvriere* (Geneva), weekly, circulation ca. 8,000; *Vorwaerts* (Basel), weekly, circulation ca. 6,000; *Il Lavatore*, Italian-language edition; *Zunder*, KVJS organ

Switzerland still has three organizations of some political significance that can be labeled communist parties. The by far largest and oldest of these three groups is the Partei der Arbeit der Schweiz/Swiss Party of Labor (PdAS/SPL), which is the only communist organization officially recognized by the Soviet Communist Party. The two others are the Sozialistische Gruen Alternative (SGA, the former SAP) and the Progressive Organization of Basel (POB), the former POCH.

The collapse of communist regimes in the Eastern bloc forced almost all of these organizations to cease emphasizing their old ideological positions and shift their political efforts more toward human rights issues, environmental problems, Swiss militarism, and moral problems connected with the Third World. Despite the dramatic collapse of Marxism and socialism of all stripes throughout Central and Eastern Europe, Switzerland's leftist organizations as a whole gained somewhat in influence, though none of them publicly addressed the apparent failure of the so-called Real-Sozialismus.

The SAP, a group founded by young Trotskyists in 1969 who left the PdAS, dissolved itself and reemerged as the SGA (Socialist Green Alternative). The SGA operates mainly in larger cities, and because it was organized as a cadre party, its membership after the restructuring slightly increased. This new party or group exercises some influence among the younger students at major universities. The ideas of central economic planning and the nationalization of the means of production, which played such a major role in its program, have been replaced by environmental slogans. Since 1989, under the name Revolutionary Socialist Youth (RSJ), the SGA has been active in centers of production and supported the antinuclear power movement. Its main weekly publication still appears in four languages. (*Bresche, La Breche, Rosso,* and *Roia*).

On 25 August POCH ceased to exist only to reemerge as POB (Progressive Organization Basel). POCH was founded in 1972 in Basel by students disappointed with the sterile politics of the PdAS. Under Georg Degen this organization replaced old-fashioned, doctrinaire Marxism with the more attractive ideological concepts of the Greens' movement and featured itself as the "voice of conscience" (*WMR,* June 1989). A POCH subsidiary, the Organization for Women's Affairs, was the most important women's group in Switzerland and is still quite active among German-speaking students. POCH published the weekly *POCH-Zeitung* with

an estimated circulation of six thousand copies. After the reorganization the membership is reported to be decreasing, making it the third-largest party in Basel.

Several other leftist organizations, with some support by the above-mentioned groups, gained some influence during 1989, and left-extremist SPS members gained strength within the party's leadership. The large Social Democratic Party of Switzerland (SPS), with Helmut Hubacher as its influential chairman and with some radical wings, is still the only major party not to oppose the call for the abolition of the army. The SPS, with 18 percent of the votes in the election three years ago, accepted the help of the former SAP-connected Gruppe Schweiz ohne Armee (Group for a Switzerland without Military, GSoA). This small but active group is now supported by the PdAS and collected the signatures that led to the antimilitary referendum on 26 November 1989, which was supported by 35.6 percent of the vote (*NYT,* 6 December 1989).

Another radical Socialist splinter organization is the Autonomous Socialist Party (PSA), under the leadership of Werner Carrobbio. Because the Swiss proletariat is made up more and more by foreign workers from southern European countries, the PSA operates exclusively in the Italian part of Switzerland. The estimated membership is about one thousand. This active party is the result of a split within the SPS in 1960. The Communist Party of Switzerland/Marxist-Leninist (KPS/ML) must also be mentioned. The two major Swiss peace groups—the Schweizerische Friedensbewegung (Swiss Section of the World Peace Council, SFB) and the International Women's League for Peace and Freedom (IFFF)—are controlled by the PdAS. There are indications that all the leftist organizations contributed to the success of the antiarmy referendum. The political bureau of the PdAS continued to propose to POCH, SAP, and the Green alliance that they form a single left opposition in Parliament.

In addition there were two separate Green parties in Switzerland: the first group, the Swiss Ecologist party, is known as a *cucumber* because it is all green; the second organization, the Green Socialist Alternative, is called a *watermelon* and is tied to the SGA. The Green movement in Switzerland rests entirely at the left side of the political spectrum.

Leadership and Organization. Although the center of Swiss political and economic power lies in the German-speaking part of the country, the PdAS strongholds are located in the French-speaking areas. After Jean-Philippe Becker organized the first international Socialist congress in Geneva in 1866, that city has developed a tradition of being open and progressive. That almost half its population is foreigners certainly plays a role. It is therefore not surprising that the old Socialist ideas are more attractive in the country's western part and Basel, whereas the newly organized environmental-oriented approaches have more followers among intellectuals in the German-speaking urban areas. Probably owing to a lack of active support, however, the Central Committee of the PdAS in 1989 voted to dissolve the Basel section of the party (*WMR*, 1989).

Despite continuing efforts, the party has no groups in small rural and conservative cantons. Its organization is still territorial and follows the historically developed regions.

The main organizational change (and one of the most notable aspects of recent years) was rejuvenating the party's leading bodies. In 1987, eleven members of the Central Committee were replaced with younger delegates. But the party is still haunted by the dominance of the politically stubborn party establishment. The bitter defeat in the last federal election reflects the party's failure to adjust to sociological changes.

Domestic Affairs. To gain appeal the PdSA continued to emphasize its fresh ideas and importance. After 15 November, *Vorwaerts*, its weekly organ, began to call the party the New PdAS. During 19–20 May there was a national party conference in Geneva to discuss the party's future. Radical options were proposed, such as completely banning arms exports, which would hurt the Swiss economy badly, reducing military spending, lifting the banking secrecy, or calling for a working week of 35 hours with full pay. According to *Vorwaerts*, General Secretary Jean Spielmann addressed a "large crowd with enlightening new proposals" (*Vorwaerts*, 22 May). Elsewhere, the same event was described as a "somewhat diffuse, lyrical and pathetic struggle of an ideology to adapt to the reality." Nevertheless, the de-Stalinization apparently went well, and the PdAS issued a document underlining the party's continued efforts to fight for concrete disarmament, social solidarity, and "Radio Freedom," a radio station for the African National Congress (ANC). *Vorwaerts*, the party's German newspaper, has traditionally called for the forma-

tion of a leftist coalition, which seems to have generated some political success. The weekly paper nevertheless seems to be in serious financial trouble and kept appealing to its faithful readers. It remains a mystery how this poorly funded and small party can finance its multilanguage press and its various other activities. The old rumor persists that the PdAS is aided financially by the Kremlin.

International Affairs. There were only two noteworthy highlights of 1990. On 9 June Jean Spielmann officially met with Nelson Mandela in Geneva and gave him a "solidarity check" to establish a radio station in South Africa that will be operated by the ANC. The other event was the visit of the secretary general to Moscow on 19 December, where he was received by V. A. Ivashko, a member of the Presidium.

On 27 October Spielmann sponsored an event organized by Vereinigung fuer Marx Studien in Zurich. The most intense relationships with foreign party organizations were maintained with what is left of the hard-line Socialist establishment of the former German Democratic Republic. The party's main international resolutions of its 1987 congress seem still to be in place. This "peace-advancing economy" approach aims at five areas: the repudiation of the arms race; gearing and controlling the economy to solve important problems; balancing scientific and technological progress to protect the environment; massive support of the Third World and radical changes in the political ties with less-developed countries; and peaceful coexistence.

General Activities. The national party conference, which was not a party congress, made it clear that the Swiss left is still remarkably active but focused almost exclusively on problems of disarmament, environmental issues, and solidarity with the Third World. The most significant political activities were restructuring, reorganization, and the successful reemergence of SAP as SGA and of POCH as POB. The left seems to be shifting from the western part of Switzerland to the more affluent eastern part.

Kurt R. Leube
California State University at Hayward

Turkey

Population. 57,163,085 (July)

Parties. United Communist Party of Turkey (Türkiye Birleşik Komünist Partisi, TBKP), established through merger of the Communist Party of Turkey (Türkiye Komünist Partisi, TKP) and the Workers' Party of Turkey (Türkiye İşçi Partisi, TİP). Socialist Party (Sosyalist Parti, SP; People's Labor Party (Halkın Emek Partisi, HEP); Unity Party of the Socialists (Sosyalistlerin Birleşik Partisi, SBP).

Founded. TKP: 1920; TİP: 1961; TBKP: 1988; SP: 1990; HEP: 1990; SBP: in progress

Membership. Negligible

Party Leadership. TBKP: Nabi Yağcı (aka Haydar Kutlu), general secretary; Nihat Sargın, chairman; Mehmet Karaca, deputy general secretary; Osman Sakalsız, deputy chairman. SP: Ferit İlsever, president; Osman Bilge Kuruca, deputy president. HEP: Fehmi Işıklar, president.

Status. TBKP, quasi-legal; other parties legal

Last Congress. TBKP: October 1988. The party held various district-level congresses in Turkey during 1990. The first such meeting was the Bakirköy District Congress on 28 October. TKP: November 1983; SBP: 24–28 November 1990 (preestablishment congress).

Publications. The following publications were listed in the indictment of the TBKP/TKP general secretary and attributed to Kutlu's own testimony in *Atılım*. Domestic: *Adımlar* (Steps); *Alınteri* (Toil); *Görüş* (Viewpoint); foreign: *Atılım* (Progress); *Sol Birlik* (Left union); *Türkiye Postası* (Mail of Turkey); *Yol ve Amaç* (Means and goals); *Yeni Çağ* (New age); *Gerçeğin Sesi* (The voice of truth); *Proleter İstanbul* (Proletarian Istanbul); *İleri* (Forward). Other leftist publications: domestic: *2000'e Doğru* (To the year 2000); foreign: *Hedef* (Target); *Mücadele Bayrağı* (Banner of struggle); *Komun* (Commune); *Orak-Çekiç* (Sickle-Hammer); *Devrimin-Sesi* (Voice of revolution); *Ocak* (January); *Emeğin Bayrağı* (The banner of toil); *Yeni Demokrasi* (New democracy); *Mücadele* (Struggle); *Devrimci-İşçi* (Revolutionary worker); *Toplumsal Kurtuluş* (Communal liberation).

Unlike the previous year, 1990 has been an eventful one for the TBKP and various organizations on the extreme left. Three political parties of the extreme left emerged on the political scene, and leftist terrorist organizations accelerated their activities against the state. The jailed leaders of the TBKP, Haydar Kutlu and Nihat Sargın, were released by the state security court, and important developments occurred in Turkey's relations with the Soviet Union.

Perhaps the most important event was the release of Kutlu and Sargın in May after they had spent nine hundred days in prison following their return to Turkey on 16 November 1987 from self-imposed exile in Europe. The trial of Kutlu and Sargın will continue, and the court has barred them from traveling abroad during this time. If convicted, they risk a prison term of fifteen years. At the time of their arrest, Kutlu and Sargın's aim was to establish a legal TBKP despite the fact that Articles 141 and 142 of Turkish Penal Code and the Turkish Constitution ban communist parties and communist activities in the country. After their imprisonment, widely publicized domestic and external campaigns protested the detention of Kutlu and Sargın. These campaigns included calls for their release by international human rights organizations and the European Community. Despite such pressures and a hunger strike by Kutlu and Sargın, however, Turkish officials refused to release them until May 1990. During the period leading up to the release of Kutlu and Sargın, numerous administrators and members of the TBKP were placed under house arrest by the police as they attempted to hold illegal meetings. The breakdown of these arrests is 29 detained, of which 5 were later arrested, in Izmir and 30 arrested in Zonguldak (*Cumhuriyet*, 11 January); 38 members, including the provincial leader, placed under house arrest in Ankara (*Cumhuriyet*, 14 January); wife of Haydar Kutlu, Ayse Çiçek Yağcı, was arrested after returning to Turkey on 6 January (*Cumhuriyet*, 15 January); and 94 persons associated with *Adımlar* were also detained (*Cumhuriyet*, 18 February). The restraint and arrest of the largest number of TBKP members occurred in Istanbul on 10 February, when some one hundred individuals were placed under house arrest by the police (Istanbul, *Cumhuriyet*, 12 February; *FBIS-WEU*, 21 February). Thus, between January and March, about four hundred TBKP members were confined.

On their release, Kutlu and Sargın submitted the TBKP's official foundation documents to the Interior Ministry on 3 June, thus ending the party's (including the TKP) 70 years of illegal and underground existence (Ankara, Anatolia, 4 June; *FBIS-WEU*, 7 June). In these documents, TBKP's charter states that it is a Marxist, revolutionary workers' party based on class struggle. However, because the present Turkish constitution and legal code prohibit the formation of Marxist or religious parties, it is debatable to what extent the TBKP has gained legal status. In fact, Ankara's chief prosecutor began legal action with the constitutional court seeking the closure of TBKP (Ankara, Anatolia, 14 June; *FBIS-WEU*, 15 June).

While these legal proceedings continued, the TBKP began its district-level congresses in Turkey. The law of political parties requires completion of most district-level congresses before a political party can hold its national congress. The first district-level congress of the TBKP took place in Bakırköy (Istanbul province) on 28 October (*Cumhuriyet*, 29 October). On this day, the TBKP members placed a wreath at Atatürk's statue for the first time in 70 years and announced that deliberations of the Constitutional Court did not negate the legality of the party. Furthermore, TBKP leaders called for unity among their party and other leftist political parties—particularly HEP and SBP.

Eleven leftist members of the Social Democratic Populist Party (SHP) who resigned after four members of the party were expelled for attending a meeting in Paris on the Kurdish question and 66 other individuals formed the People's Labor Party (HEP) on 7 June (Ankara, Anatolia, 4 June; *FBIS-WEU*, 7 June). This political party views itself as an umbrella organization for individuals with Socialist, Social Democratic, progressive, Marxist, leftist liberal, and democratic views. However, its appeal to a large number of individuals has been lacking. Its membership is small but includes such prominent leftist political figures as Abdullah Baştürk (chairman of the Revolutionary Labor Unions Confederation, DISK), Fehmi Işıklar (former member of the Republican People's Party, CHP), Ahmet Türk, Cüneyt Canver, and İlhami Binici.

The Unity Party of the Socialists (SBP) is one step up in integration from HEP; that is, once it is established, HEP and other small leftist parties will join the SBP. The founding congress of SBP took place in Ankara during 24–28 November (*Cumhuriyet, Milliyet*, 25–29 November). Representatives of HEP, TBKP, SHP, leftist organizations, intellectuals and writers, and members of the dissolved Socialist Workers' Party of Turkey (TSIP)

attended the meeting. At this gathering, the participants decided to submit the necessary document for establishing the SBP to the Interior Ministry by 15 January. Furthermore, the participants accepted a joint declaration (*Cumhuriyet*, 28 November) calling for

1. Removing Articles 141, 142, and 163 from the Turkish Penal Code and liquidating bureaucratic controls over individual civil and political rights
2. Recognizing TBKP as a legal political party
3. Ending state pressures and bans on Kurdish language and culture and officially recognizing the existence of the Kurdish minority in Turkey
4. Ending state intervention in collective bargaining and recognizing strike rights of trade unions
5. Complete equality between the sexes in every aspect of social life
6. Recognizing the freedom of religion and belief
7. Extending economic, cultural, and political support for Turkish citizens abroad

The communist parties ended their illegal activities and emerged as legal organizations in 1990, but other leftist terrorist groups continued their campaign against the Turkish state. According to a study by the Internal Security Directorate of the Internal Ministry, there are seventeen leftist terrorist groups that are currently active in 31 of Turkey's 70 provinces (*Milliyet*, 29 November). These leftist groups are the Revolutionary Left (DEV-SOL), the Revolutionary Path (DEV-YOL), the Kurdish Labor Party (PKK), the Communist Party of Turkey/Unity—Armed People Unites (TKP/B-SHB), the Revolutionary Communist Party/Armed People Unit (DKP/SHB), the Revolutionary Communist Party of Turkey (TDKP), the Marxist-Leninist Armed Propaganda Unit (MLSPB), the Communist Labor Party of Turkey (TKEP), the Revolutionary Communist Party of Turkey (TİKP), the June 16 Movement, People's Liberation Party of Turkey/Front—Urgent (THKP/C-Acilciler), the Liberation Organization of Northern Kurdistan (TKKKÖ), the Action Union, the Communist Party of Turkey/Marxist-Leninist Movement (TKP/ML-Hareketi), the Communist Party of Turkey/Marxist-Leninist Partizan (TKP/ML-Partizan), the People's Liberation Party of Turkey/Front—The Revolutionary Vanguards of the People (THKP/C-Halkin Devrimci Öncüleri), the Communist Party of Turkey/Marxist-Leninist—The

Liberation Army of Peasants and Laborers of Turkey (TKP/ML-TİKKO).

The most significant development in this regard is that all these organizations accepted the PKK's call for unity to fight the Turkish state. Terrorists train in camps in Greece, Iran, Iraq, Lebanon, and Syria and then enter Turkey secretly to carry out terrorist actions. All these groups are active in Istanbul province, and their operations extend to all corners of Turkey. Other provinces where terrorist activity currently occurs are Adana, Ankara, Antalya, Artvin, Batman, Bingöl, Bursa, Diyarbakır, Edirne, Erzincan, Eskişehir, Gaziantep, Hakkari, Hatay, İzmir, İzmit, Kars, Kayseri, Malatya, Mardin, Mersin, Samsun, Şanlıurfa, Siirt, Şirnak, Sivas, Tekirdağ, Tokat, Tunceli, and Van. The breakdown of these operations by provinces is

1. *Istanbul*: All terrorist groups
2. *Ankara*: DEV-SOL, DEV-YOL, TKP/ML-TİKKO, TKP/B-SHB, PKK, TİKB, TDKP, Action Union
3. *Black Sea provinces*: DEV-SOL, DEV-YOL, TKP/ML-TİKKO, TDKP
4. *Izmir region*: DEV-SOL, DEV-YOL, PKK, TDKP, Action Union, TKP/ML-Hareketi
5. *Adana-Hatay-Kayseri triangle*: DEV-SOL, DEV-YOL, TİKB, PKK, TKP/B-SHB, DKP/SHB, June 16 Movement, THKP/C-Acilciler, TKP/ML-Hareketi
6. *Southeastern provinces*: PKK, TKP/ML-TİKKO, TKKKÖ, TDKP

Despite this long list of leftist terrorist organizations, the Internal Security Directorate (MİT) announced on 28 October that these groups do not present a serious threat to Turkey. The director of MİT stated that these groups, with few exceptions, were barely keeping themselves alive and that the real threat was coming from the Kurdish organizations, the PKK, the Islamic Party of Kurdistan (PIK), and other Islamic terrorist groups (*Cumhuriyet*, 29 October). In fact, Islamic terrorist groups carried out several assassinations of influential Kemalist intellectuals, writers, and journalists during 1990. With regard to Kurdish organizations, Turkish intelligence agencies established that new terrorist groups emerged to execute a separatist campaign against the state. These organizations are as follows (*Günaydın*, 2 April):

1. The Kurdistan Vanguard Workers' Party (Kürdistan Öncü İşçi Partisi, KVWP). This organization

was associated with the Revolutionary Democratic Masses Association until the 12 September 1980 coup. It is headed by M. Ali Çılgın, code name Serhat Dicle, who lives in Switzerland. The KVWP has two publications, *Pesenk* and *Armanc*.

2. The Socialist Party of Kurdistan-Turkey (Türkiye Kürdistan Sosyalist Partisi, SPKT). This party is headed by Kemal Burkay, who lives in Switzerland. Medhi Zana, former mayor of Diyarbakır, is among the founding members of SPKT. This organization published a monthly known as *Özgürlük Yolu* before 1980 and currently publishes *Komkar Roja* (Unity and a new day).

3. The National Liberation Fighters of Kurdistan (Kürdistan Ulusal Kurtuluşçuları, NLFK). This is the extension of the National Liberation Fighters of Kurdistan, which had been crushed by the security forces after the September 1980 coup. The current leader of the NLFK is not known. Its current publication is *KUK-SE*.

4. Rizgari. This organization is headed by a lawyer, İbrahim Gülcü, who received a thirteen-year prison sentence during the 1980–1983 military rule. He was released from prison in 1984 as a result of an amnesty.

For its part, the PKK has continued its attacks on Turkish security forces, officials, and villagers throughout the year. A report compiled by the Turkish Armed Forces High Command stated that the PKK has numerous offices in foreign countries: 32 in Germany, 3 in the Netherlands, 1 in France (*Cumhuriyet*, 20 March). Furthermore, Syria serves as bridge between the PKK's forces in Turkey and other units in Greece, France, Bulgaria, and Germany. The report also points out that Syria provides the largest assistance to PKK and that Syrian officials endorse the training of Kurdish guerrillas in their country. Finally, the report identified 32 PKK camps in northern Iraq, where the presence of the Iraqi army is negligible.

During 4–13 May, the PKK held its second national conference, as reported in the June edition of *Cologne Serxwebun*. Although the venue of the conference was not provided, the report included speeches delivered by PKK general secretary Abdullah Öcalan at the conference (Cologne, *Serxwebun*, June; *FBIS-WEU*, 31 July). At this meeting, the PKK reaffirmed its commitment to fight against the Turkish state and to join forces with all leftist groups that oppose the Turkish regime. According to Turkish Interior Ministry sources, there have been 1,883 PKK-related operations in Turkey since the state of emergency governor was established in the southeastern region three years ago. In these operations, 9,969 suspects were arrested, 606 PKK terrorists were killed, 46 terrorists were wounded and captured, and 192 terrorists surrendered. The casualties of Turkish security forces were 344 killed and 602 wounded. In addition, 529 civilians died and 318 were wounded in these operations (Anatolia Press release, 28 November). More than two thousand people have died in terrorist-related incidents in southeast Turkey since 1984, when the PKK launched a campaign of violence.

As PKK activities intensified during this year, Turkish officials broadened the scope of the security forces operations in the southeastern provinces. The expanded measures include evacuating villages and farming settlements to interior regions and doubling the size of special operation teams in the Hakkari-Siirt-Mardin area. The present size of these forces, including civilians known as *korucu*, is half a million men. Furthermore, the government has plans to deploy aircraft and helicopters with infrared cameras in the region to discover PKK camps (*Günaydın*, 2 April). Also, the government granted new powers to the state of emergency governor by authorizing him to reassign and deport from the area not only government personnel but also military personnel, judges, and prosecutors whenever he sees fit (*Hürriyet*, 15 May). It should be noted, however, that, since the beginning of the gulf crisis, the number of PKK activities in southeastern Turkey has decreased. One major reason for this decline is the mobilization of 100,000 additional Turkish troops, supported with tanks, helicopters, aircraft, and artillery batteries, on the border with Iraq.

In other domestic developments, 1 May (May Day) was again a scene of clashes between demonstrators and state security forces. May Day celebrations are banned in Turkey, yet every year thousands gather in city centers in defiance of the government. This year, 40 civilians and 7 policemen were hurt in hostilities between the two groups, and the security forces detained about 2,500 persons (almost 90 percent of them in Istanbul) for violation of the government decree banning May Day celebrations. Most of these individuals were later released.

During 1990, the Turkish government also began to restrict press coverage of PKK activities and official policies in southeastern provinces. Among the publications affected by these new restrictions is *2000'e Doğru*, a left-wing weekly magazine published by the well-known Maoist Doğu Perinçek.

When Perinçek ignored the bans and continued to print articles criticizing the security forces' campaigns against the Kurds, the officials confiscated the magazine's press run and brought a lawsuit against him. Perinçek has been in hiding since July and is facing a possible six-year prison term on charges of "promoting regional and ethnic separatism." (*NYT*, 29 July.)

With regard to foreign affairs, Turkey's relations with the Soviet Union were strained by events in Caucasia. When Soviet troops entered Azerbaijan's capital, Baku, killing at least 1,500 people, thousands of Turkish citizens and Azerbaijanis living in Turkey demonstrated against the Kremlin's actions (reported by all Turkish dailies, 20–27 January). The Nakhichevan People's Front board called the Azerbaijanis' Turk Solidarity Association chairman, Nihat Çetinkaya, on 21 January to confirm the declaration of independence of Nakhichevan and to inform him that the Azerbaijanis intended to ask for military aid from Turkey under the Kars agreement of 1921 (Ankara, Anatolia, 20 January; *FBIS-WEU*, 22 January). However, the Turkish government did not want to get involved in Soviet internal affairs and simply raised concerns about the matter with Soviet officials.

Nevertheless, as soon as the crisis in Azerbaijan subsided, Turkish and Soviet officials began to carry out a series of negotiations aimed at increasing trade relations between the two countries. On 4 August Turkish and Soviet representatives signed a trade protocol in Ankara (Ankara Domestic Service, 4 August; *FBIS-WEU*, 7 August). Under this protocol, the two countries will increase the volume of their mutual trade to $4 billion and develop cooperation in the fields of industry, medicine, communications, all metals except iron, coal, transportation, and border and coastal trade. Furthermore, they agreed to exchange students, teachers, and scientists. Finally, the first deputy chairman of the USSR Council of Ministers, Lev Voronin, said that the USSR maintains a favorable view of the Black Sea Economic Union, which the countries of the region plan to establish.

These positive economic developments with the USSR also extended to Turkey's relations with other countries in Eastern Europe. Relations with Bulgaria have improved since the fall of the Jikov regime and the reinstatement of the Turkish minority's rights in that country. Interestingly enough, even Soviet Armenia, declaring "independence" from Moscow, approached Turkey to establish trade links between the two countries. Perhaps such rapprochement might help end decades of animosity between the Turks and the Armenians.

The above developments show important changes in communist affairs in Turkey. Whether the communist and Socialist leaders can gain support from the people will depend on how well they can join forces to form a single party and address the needs of the masses and whether the constitutional court will permit the TBKP's establishment. If the court closes the TBKP, it is highly probable that officials will seek similar decisions for the HEP and SBP. As for terrorism, Turkish authorities have acknowledged that the threat from the extreme left is not as serious as in previous years; however, the threat posed by the PKK is as strong as ever. It is likely that the Kurdish separatists (especially the communist PKK) will continue their armed struggle against the Turkish state. In this regard, some of Turkey's neighbors are guilty of contributing to PKK activities. Nevertheless, relations with the Soviet Union and Bulgaria have improved.

Birol A. Yeşilada
University of Missouri at Columbia

Select Bibliography, 1989–1991

GENERAL

Albright, David E. *Vanguard Parties and Revolutionary Change in the Third World*. Berkeley, Calif.: Institute of International Studies, 1990. 126 pp.

Bertsch, Gary K., et al. *After the Revolution: East-West Trade and Technology Transfer in the 1990s*. Boulder, Colo.: Westview Press, 1991. 227 pp.

Brzezinski, Zbigniew. *The Grand Failure: The Birth and Death of Communism in the Twentieth Century*. New York: Charles Scribner's Sons, 1989. 278 pp.

Bugajski, Janusz. *Fourth World Conflicts: Communism and Rural Societies*. Boulder, Colo.: Westview Press, 1990. 308 pp.

Bukowski, Charles, and J. Richard Walsh, eds. *Glasnost, Perestroika and the Socialist Community*. New York: Praeger, 1990. 187 pp.

Chang, Gordon H. *Friend and Enemies: The United States, China and the Soviet Union*. Stanford, Calif.: Stanford University Press, 1990. 383 pp.

Commission on Security and Cooperation in Europe. *Implementation of the Helsinki Accords: Paris Human Dimension Meeting* (Hearing, 18 July 1990, Washington). Washington, D.C., Government Printing Office, 1990. 173 pp.

Corm, Georges. *L'Europe et l'Orient: de la balkanisation à la libanisation*. Paris: Editions de la Découverte, 1989. 383 pp.

Duncan, W. Raymond, and Carolyn McGiffert Ekedahl. *Moscow and the Third World under Gorbachev*. Boulder, Colo.: Westview Press, 1990. 260 pp.

Fritsch-Bournazel, Renate. *Europa und die deutsche Einheit*. Bonn: Verlag Vonn Aktuell, 1990. 280 pp.

Gilberg, Trond, ed. *Coalition Strategies of Marxist Parties*. Durham, N.C.: Duke University Press, 1989. 323 pp.

Goldstone, Jack A., et al., eds. *Revolutions of the Late Twentieth Century*. Boulder, Colo.: Westview Press, 1990. 352 pp.

Hill, Ronald J. *Communist Politics under the Knife: Surgery or Autopsy?* London: Pinter, 1990. 224 pp.

Katz, Mark N., ed. *The USSR and the Marxist Revolutions in the Third World*. New York: Cambridge University Press, 1990. 150 pp.

Keddie, Nikki R., and Mark Gasiorowski, eds. *Neither East nor West: Iran, the Soviet Union and the United States*. New Haven, Conn.: Yale University Press, 1990. 295 pp.

Longmire, R. A. *Soviet Relations with South East Asia*. New York: Routledge, 1989. 280 pp.

Łoś, Maria, ed. *The Second Economy in Marxist States*. New York: St. Martin's, 1990. 240 pp.

Lustig, Michael M. *Trotsky and Djilas: Critics of Communist Bureaucracy*. Westport, Conn.: Greenwood Press, 1989. 184 pp.

Nation, R. Craig. *War on War: Lenin, the Zimmerwald Left, and the Origins of Communist Internationalism*. Durham, N.C.: Duke University Press, 1990. 313 pp.

Ramet, Pedro, ed. *Catholicism and Politics in Communist Countries*. Durham, N.C.: Duke University Press, 1990. 449 pp.

Staar, Richard F., ed. *Yearbook on International Communist Affairs, 1990*. Stanford: Hoover Institution Press, 1990. 766 pp.

Taras, Raymond, ed. *Leadership Change in Communist States*. Boston: Unwin Hyman, 1989. 210 pp.

Vacca, Giuseppe. *Gorbacev e las sinistra europea*. Rome: Editori Riuniti, 1989. 217 pp.

Voslensky, Michael S. *Sterbliche Götter: Die Lehrmeister der Nomenklatura*. Vienna: Straube, 1989. 527 pp.

Wessell, Nils H., ed. *The New Europe: Revolution in East-West Relations*. New York: Academy of Political Science, 1991. 214 pp.

AFRICA

Alexiev, Alex. *Marxism and Resistance in the Third World: Cause and Effect*. Santa Monica, Calif.: Rand Corporation, 1989. 53 pp.

Christie, Iain. *Samora Machel: A Biography*. London: Zed Books, 1989. 175 pp.

Collelo, Thomas, ed. *Angola: A Country Study*. 3d ed. Washington, D.C.: Government Printing Office, 1991. 318 pp.

Cook, Chris, and David Killingray. *African Political Facts since 1945*. London: Macmillan, 1991. 280 pp.

Costa, António Augusto da. *A guerrilha e o caos militar*. Pontinha, Portugal: Arquimédia, 1989. 164 pp.

Davidson, Basil. *Modern Africa: A Social and Political History*. 2d ed. New York: Longman, 1989. 289 pp.

Decalo, Samuel. *Coups and Army Rule in Africa: Motivations and Constraints*. 2d ed. New Haven, Conn.: Yale University Press, 1990. 366 pp.

De Waal, Victor. *The Politics of Reconciliation: Zimbabwe's First Decade*. Trenton, N.J.: Africa World Press, 1990. 146 pp.

Diaz-Briquets, Sergio, ed. *Cuban Internationalism in Sub-Saharan Africa*. Pittsburgh, Pa.: Duquesne University Press, 1989. 211 pp.

Gann, Lewis H., and Peter Duignan. *Hope for South Africa?* Stanford: Hoover Institution Press, 1991. 223 pp.

Herbst, Jeffrey. *State Politics in Zimbabwe*. Berkeley: University of California Press, 1990. 283 pp.

Holland, Heidi. *The Struggle: A History of the African National Congress*. London: Grafton, 1989. 252 pp.

Human Rights Watch. *Angola: Violation of the Laws of War by Both Sides*. New York: George Braziller, 1990. 252 pp.

Johns, Sheridan, and R. Hunt Davis, Jr., eds. *Mandela, Tambo, and the African National Congress*. New York: Oxford University Press, 1991. 353 pp.

Khalid, Mansur. *The Government They Deserve: The Role of the Elite in Sudan's Political Evolution*. London: Kegan Paul International, 1990. 480 pp.

Magubane, Bernard. *The Political Economy of Race and Class in South Africa*. Rev. ed. New York: Monthly Review Press, 1990. 396 pp.

Meer, Fatima. *Higher than Hope: The Biography of Nelson Mandela*. New York: Harper and Row, 1990. 464 pp.

Mungaze, Dickson A. *Education and Government Control in Zimbabwe*. New York: Praeger, 1990. 133 pp.

Norwal, Morgan. *Inside the ANC: The Evolution of a Terrorist Organization*. Washington, D.C.: Selous Foundation, 1991. 356 pp.

Patman, Robert G. *The Soviet Union in the Horn of Africa: The Diplomacy of Intervention and Disengagement*. New York: Cambridge University Press, 1990. 250 pp.

Ray, Donald Ian. *Dictionary of the African Left: Parties, Movements and Groups*. Aldershot, Hants., Eng.: Dartmouth, 1989. 273 pp.

Sachs, Albie. *Running to Maputo*. New York: Harper, Collins, 1990. 215 pp.

South African Communist Party. *The Path to Power: Programme of the South African Communist Party* (as adopted at the Seventh Congress, 1989). Johannesburg: SACP, 1990. 69 pp.

Torp, Jens Erik. *Mozambique, Economics and Society: Fifth Congress Supplement*. London: Pinter, 1990. 15 pp.

Vanneman, Peter. *Soviet Strategy in Southern Africa: Gorbachev's Pragmatic Approach*. Stanford: Hoover Institution Press, 1990. 142 pp.

Villa-Vicencio, Charles. *Civil Disobedience and Beyond: Law, Resistance and Religion in South Africa*. Cape Town: D. Philip, 1990. 165 pp.

Wiseman, John A. *Democracy in Black Africa*. New York: Paragon, 1990. 228 pp.

Wunsch, James S., and Dele Olowu, eds. *The Failure of the Centralized State: Institutions and Self-Governance in Africa*. Boulder, Colo.: Westview Press, 1990. 334 pp.

AMERICAS

Alexander, Robert J. *Venezuela's Voice for Democracy: Conversations and Correspondence with Romulo Betancourt*. Westport, Conn.: Praeger, 1990. 172 pp.

Bugajski, Janusz. *Sandinista Communism and Rural Nicaragua*. New York: Praeger, 1990. 146 pp.

Castro, Fidel. *In Defense of Socialism*. New York: Pathfinder, 1989. 274 pp.

Cavallo, Ascanio, et al. *La historia del regimen militar: Chile, 1973–1988*. Santiago: Editorial Antartica, 1989. 172 pp.

Colburn, Forest D. *Managing the Commanding Heights: Nicaragua's State Enterprises*. Berkeley: University of California Press, 1990. 151 pp.

Edmisten, Patricia Taylor. *Nicaragua Divided: La Prensa and the Chamorro Legacy*. Gainesville: University of Florida Press, 1990. 142 pp.

Fast, Howard. *Being Red*. Boston: Houghton Mifflin, 1990. 370 pp.

Fitzgerald, Frank T. *Managing Socialism: From Old Cadres to New Professionals in Revolutionary Cuba*. New York: Praeger, 1990. 161 pp.

Geyer, Georgie Anne. *Guerrilla Prince: The Untold Story of Fidel Castro*. Boston: Little, Brown, 1990. 445 pp.

Glotzer, Albert. *Trotsky: Memoir and Critique*. Buffalo, N.Y.: Prometheus, 1989. 343 pp.

Halebsky, Sandor, et al., eds. *Transformation and Struggle: Cuba Faces the 1990s*. Westport, Conn.: Praeger, 1990. 320 pp.

Hanratty, Dennis M., and Sandra W. Meditz, eds. *Paraguay: A Country Study*. 2d ed. Washington, D.C.: Government Printing Office, 1990. 288 pp.

Healy, Dorothy. *Dorothy Healy Remembers: A Life in the American Communist Party*. New York: Oxford University Press, 1990. 263 pp.

Jonas, Suzanne. *The Battle for Guatemala: Rebels, Death Squads and U.S. Power*. Boulder, Colo.: Westview Press, 1991. 271 pp.

———, and Nancy Stein, eds. *Democracy in Latin America: Visions and Realities*. New York: Bergin and Garvey, 1990. 232 pp.

Kolasky, John, ed. *Prophets and Proletarians: Documents on the History of the Rise and Decline of Ukrainian Communism in Canada*. Edmonton: Canadian Institute of Ukrainian Studies Press, 1990. 481 pp.

Lewy, Guenter. *The Cause That Failed: Communism in American Political Life*. New York: Oxford University Press, 1990. 359 pp.

McCormick, Gordon H. *The Shining Path and the Future of Peru*. Santa Monica, Calif.: Rand Corporation, 1990. 58 pp.

Montaner, Carlos Alberto. *Fidel Castro and the Cuban Revolution*. New Brunswick, N.J.: Transaction, 1989. 214 pp.

Munroe, Trevor. *Jamaican Politics: A Marxist Perspective in Transition*. Boulder, Colo.: Lynne Rienner, 1990. 350 pp.

Needler, Martin C. *Mexican Politics: The Containment of Conflict*. 2d ed. Westport, Conn.: Praeger, 1990. 168 pp.

Prisk, Courtney E., ed. *The Commandante Speaks: Memoirs of an El Salvadoran Guerrilla Leader*. Boulder, Colo.: Westview Press, 1991. 145 pp.

Prizel, Ilya. *Latin America through Soviet Eyes: The Evolution of Soviet Perceptions during the Brezhnev Era, 1964–1982*. New York: Cambridge University Press, 1990. 288 pp.

Radu, Michael, and Vladimir Tismaneanu. *Latin American Revolutionaries: Groups, Goals, Methods*. Washington, D.C.: Pergamon-Brassey's, 1990. 386 pp.

Sand, Gregory W. *Soviet Aims in Central America: The Case of Nicaragua*. Westport, Conn.: Praeger, 1989. 138 pp.

Stubbs, Jean. *Cuba: The Test of Time*. London: Latin American Bureau, 1989. 141 pp.

Tablada, Carlos. *Che Guevara: Economics and Politics in the Transition to Socialism*. Sydney: Pathfinder, 1989. 286 pp.

Tarazona-Sevillano, Gabriela, with John B. Reuter. *Sendero Luminoso and the Threat of Narcoterrorism*. Westport, Conn.: Praeger, 1990. 168 pp.

Timerman, Jacobo. *Cuba: A Journey*. New York: A. Knopf, 1990. 125 pp.

Torres Rivas, Edelberto. *Repression and Resistance: The Struggle for Democracy in Central America*. Boulder, Colo.: Westview Press, 1989. 165 pp.

United States Congress. House Committee on Foreign Affairs. *Cuba and the United States: Thirty Years of Hostility and Beyond*. Hearings. Washington, D.C.: Government Printing Office, 1990. 436 pp.

———. *From Duarte to Christiani: Where Is El Salvador Headed?* Hearings. Washington, D.C.: Government Printing Office, 1989. 122 pp.

Walker, Thomas W., ed. *Revolution and Counterrevolution in Nicaragua: The First Decade*. Boulder, Colo.: Westview Press, 1991. 400 pp.

ASIA AND THE PACIFIC

Bark, Dennis L., and Owen Harries, eds. *The Red Orchestra: The Case of the Southwest Pacific*. Stanford: Hoover Institution Press, 1989. 280 pp.

Chang King-yuh, ed. *Mainland China after the Thirteenth Party Congress*. Boulder, Colo.: Westview Press, 1990. 550 pp.

Cheng Chu-yuan. *Behind the Tiananmen Massacre: Social, Political and Economic Ferment in China*. Boulder, Colo.: Westview Press, 1990. 256 pp.

Dirlik, Arif. *The Origins of Chinese Communism*. New York: Oxford University Press, 1989. 315 pp.

Evans, Grant. *Lao Peasants under Socialism*. New Haven, Conn.: Yale University Press, 1990. 268 pp.

Foreign Language Press. Editorial Board, comp. *Who's Who in China: Current Leaders*. Beijing: Foreign Language Press, 1990. 1,226 pp.

Gunn, Geoffrey C. *Rebellion in Laos: Peasants and Politics in a Colonial Backwater*. Boulder, Colo.: Westview Press, 1990. 240 pp.

Hamrin, Carol Lee. *China and the Challenge of the Future*. Boulder, Colo.: Westview Press, 1990. 257 pp.

Heberer, Thomas. *China and Its National Minorities: Autonomy and Assimilation*. Armonk, N.Y.: M.E. Sharpe, 1990. 131 pp.

Hicks, George, ed. *The Broken Mirror: China after Tiananmen*. Harlow, Eng.: Longman, 1990. 500 pp.

Kleinberg, Robert. *China's "Opening" to the Outside World*. Boulder, Colo.: Westview Press, 1990. 277 pp.

Lee, Chin-Chuan. *Voices of China: Interplay of Politics and Journalism*. New York: Guilford Press, 1990. 353 pp.

Lee, Chong-Sik, ed. *Korea Briefing, 1990*. Boulder, Colo.: Westview Press, 1990. 176 pp.

Lee, Feigon. *China Rising: The Meaning of Tiananmen*. Chicago: Ivan R. Dee, 1990. 269 pp.

Lintner, Bertil. *The Rise and Fall of the Communist Party of Burma*. Ithaca, N.Y.: Cornell University, Southeast Asia Program, 1990. 237 pp.

Liu, Binyan. *A Higher Kind of Loyalty*. New York: Pantheon, 1990. 294 pp.

Lord, Bette Bao. *Legacies: A Chinese Mosaic*. New York: A. Knopf, 1990. 245 pp.

Luo, Zi-Ping. *A Generation Lost: China under the Cultural Revolution*. New York: Henry Holt, 1990. 342 pp.

Macdonald, Donald Stone. *The Koreans: Contemporary Politics and Society*. Boulder, Colo.: Westview Press, 1990. 336 pp.

Michael, Franz, et al. *China and the Crisis in Marxism-Leninism*. Boulder, Colo.: Westview Press, 1990. 255 pp.

Miller, Joseph T. *The Politics of Chinese Trotskyism*. Boulder, Colo.: Westview Press, 1990. 210 pp.

Milne, R. S., and Diana K. Mauzy. *Singapore: The Legacy of Lee Kuan Yew*. Boulder, Colo.: Westview Press, 1990. 214 pp.

Mosher, Steven. *China Misperceived: American Illusion and Chinese Reality*. New York: Basic Books, 1990. 260 pp.

Robie, David. *Blood on Their Banner: Nationalist Struggles in the South Pacific*. London: Zed Books, 1989. 313 pp.

Ross, Russell R., ed. *Cambodia: A Country Study*. Washington, D.C.: Government Printing Office, 1990. 362 pp.

Shapiro, Michael. *A Korean Year of Love and Sorrow*. New York: Atlantic Monthly Press, 1990. 240 pp.

Shrestha, Nanda R. *Landlessness and Migration in Nepal*. Boulder, Colo.: Westview Press, 1990. 200 pp.

Smith, Christopher J. *People and Places in the Land of One Billion*. Boulder, Colo.: Westview Press, 1990. 355 pp.

Spence, Jonathan D. *The Search for Modern China*. New York: W. W. Norton, 1990. 876 pp.

Steinberg, David I. *The Future of Burma: Crisis and Choice in Myanmar*. New York and Lanham, Md.: University Press of America, 1990. 100 pp.

Steinberg, David Joel. *The Philippines: A Singular and a Plural Place*. 2d rev. ed. Boulder, Colo.: Westview Press, 1990. 218 pp.

United States Congress. House of Representatives. Committee on Foreign Affairs. *The Crackdown in Burma: Suppression of the Democracy Movement and Violations of Human Rights*. Hearings and Markup. Washington, D.C.: Government Printing Office, 1990. 103 pp.

Voronin, A. S., and E. V. Kobolev, comps. *Kho Shi Min: izbrannoe vospominaniia*. Moscow: Politizdat, 1990. 464 pp.

Yang, Benjamin. *From Revolution to Politics: Chinese Communists on the Long March*. Boulder, Colo.: Westview Press, 1990. 248 pp.

Yi, Mu, and Mark V. Thompson. *Crisis at Tiananmen: Reform and Reality in Modern China*. San Francisco: China Books, 1990. 283 pp.

EASTERN EUROPE

Abel, Elie. *The Shattered Bloc: Behind the Upheaval in Eastern Europe*. New York: Houghton Mifflin, 1990. 278 pp.

Adler, Hans Gerd. *Wir sprengen unsere Ketten: die friedliche Revolution in Eichsfeld*. Leipzig: Thomas Verlag, 1990. 196 pp.

Altmann, Franz-Lothar. *Albanien im Umbruch: Eine Bestandsaufnahme*. Munich, Oldenbourg Verlag, 1990. 292 pp.

Arnold, Karl-Heinz. *Die erste hundert Tage des Hans Modrow*. Berlin: Dietz Verlag, 1990. 112 pp.

Bähr, Vera-Maria. *Wir denken erst seit Gorbatschow: Protokolle von Jugendlichen aus der DDR*. Recklingshausen: Bitter Verlag, 1990. 160 pp.

Bahrmann, Hannes. *Wir sind das Volk: die DDR im Aufbruch—eine Chronik*. Berlin: Aufbau, 1990. 226 pp.

Beckmann-Petey, Monika. *Der jugoslawische Föderalismus*. Munich: R. Oldenbourg Verlag, 1990. 376 pp.

Belwe, Katharina, and Ute Reuter, eds. *Dokumentation zur Entwicklung der Blockparteien der DDR von Ende September bis Anfang Dezember 1989*. Bonn: Gesamtdeutsches Institut Bundesanstalt, 1990. 198 pp.

Berend, Ivan. *The Hungarian Economic Reforms, 1953–1988*. New York: Cambridge University Press, 1990. 352 pp.

Biberaj, Elez. *Albania: A Socialist Maverick*. Boulder, Colo.: Westview Press, 1990. 157 pp.

Biedenkopf, Kurt H. *Offene Grenze, offener Markt: Voraussetzungen für die Erneuerung der DDR-Volkswirtschaft*. Wiesbaden: Gabler, 1990. 98 pp.

Bohley, Bärbel, et al. *40 Jahre DDR . . . und die Bürger melden sich zum Wort*. Hanser: Büchergilde Gutenberg, 1989. 196 pp.

Brogan, Patrick. *Eastern Europe, 1939–1989: The Fifty Years War*. London: Bloomsbury, 1990. 281 pp.

Burton, Gaida C. *USA-DDR: Politische, kulturelle und wirtschaftliche Beziehungen seit 1974*. Bochum: Studienverlag Dr. Brockmeyer, 1989. 496 pp.

Champseix, Elisabeth, and Jean Paul. *57 Boulevard Staline: Chroniques albanaises*. Paris: Éditions la Découverte, 1990. 311 pp.

Csepeli, György. *Structures and Contents of Hungarian National Identity*. Frankfurt am Main: Verlag Peter Lang, 1989. 129 pp.

Cullen, Michael S. *Das Brandenburger Tor: Geschichte eines deutschen Symbols*. Berlin: Aragon Verlag, 1990. 130 pp.

Curry, Jane L. *Poland's Journalists: Professionalism and Politics*. New York: Cambridge University Press, 1990. 306 pp.

Decker, Peter, and Karl Held, eds. *DDR kaputt—Deutschland ganz: eine Abrechnung mit dem "realen Sozialismus" und dem Imperialismus deutscher Nation*. Munich: Resultate Verlag, 1989. 335 pp.

Djilas, Aleksa. *The Contested Country: Yugoslav Unity and Communist Revolution, 1919–1953*. Cambridge, Mass.: Harvard University Press, 1990. 259 pp.

Doehler, Edgar. *Militärische Traditionen der DDR und der NVA*. East Berlin: Militärverlag der DDR, 1989. 448 pp.

Dohnanyi, Klaus von. *Briefe an die Deutsche Demokratische Revolutionäre*. Munich: Knauer, 1990, 215 pp.

Dyker, David A. *Yugoslavia: Socialism, Development and Debt*. New York: Routledge, 1990. 201 pp.

Echikson, William. *Lighting the Night: Revolution in Eastern Europe*. New York: Morrow, 1990. 295 pp.

Eyal, Jonathan, ed. *The Warsaw Pact and the Balkans: Moscow's Southern Flank*. New York: St. Martin's, 1989. 246 pp.

Felkay, Andrew. *Hungary and the USSR, 1956–1988: Kádár's Political Leadership*. Westport, Conn.: Greenwood Press, 1989. 343 pp.

Fieber, Hans-Joachim, and Michael Preussler. *Deutsche Orientierung: deutschlandpolitische Dokumente und Materialen seit Oktober 1989*. East Berlin: Militärverlag der DDR, 1990. 96 pp.

Fodor, Neil. *The Warsaw Treaty Organization: A Political and Organizational Analysis*. London: Macmillan, 1990. 235 pp.

Frenzel, Paul. *Die rote Mark: Perestroika für die DDR*. Herford, W. Germany: Verlag Busse-Seewald, 1989. 197 pp.

Gabert, Josef, and Lutz Priess. *SED und Stalinismus: Dokumente aus dem Jahre 1956*. East Berlin: Dietz Verlag, 1990. 160 pp.

Garton Ash, Timothy. *The Magic Lantern: The Revolution of '89 Witnessed in Warsaw, Budapest, Berlin and Prague*. New York: Random House, 1990. 156 pp.

———. *The Uses of Adversity: Essays on the Fate of Central Europe*. New York: Random House, 1989. 335 pp.

Gati, Charles. *The Bloc That Failed: Soviet-East European Relations in Transition*. Bloomington: Indiana University Press, 1990. 236 pp.

Gatow, Hanns-Heinz. *Vertuschte SED-Verbrechen: eine Spur von Blut und Tränen*. Berg: Türmer Verlag, 1990. 280 pp.

German Democratic Republic. *Die Aktuelle Programmatik von Parteien und politischen Vereinigungen in der DDR: Dokumentation*. East Berlin: Zentrum für politikwissenschaftliche Information und Dokumentation, 1990. 276 pp.

———. *Jugendbewegung in der DDR*. East Berlin: Staatsverlag, 1990. 96 pp.

———. *Politische Bewegungen der DDR, über sich selbst: Handbuch.* East Berlin: Staatsverlag, 1990. 96 pp.

Gerritts, André W. M. *The Failure of Authoritarian Change: Reform, Opposition and Geo-politics in Poland in the 1980s.* Aldershot, Hants., Eng.: Dartmouth, 1990. 260 pp.

Gilberg, Trond. *Nationalism and Communism in Romania: The Rise and Fall of Ceauşescu's Personal Dictatorship.* Boulder, Colo.: Westview Press, 1990. 320 pp.

Glässner, Gert Joachim. *Die andere deutsche Republik: Gesellschaft und Politik in der DDR.* Opladen, W. Germany: Westdeutscher Verlag, 1989. 350 pp.

Goetz, Hans Herbert. *Honecker und was dann: 40 Jahre DDR.* Herford, W. Germany: Verlag Busse-Seewald, 1990. 256 pp.

Gonnermann, Bernhard, ed. *DDR ohne Waffen: Sicherheitspolitische Dokumente.* Berlin: Brandenburger Verlag, 1990. 96 pp.

Goodwyn, Lawrence. *Breaking the Barrier: The Rise of Solidarity in Poland.* New York: Oxford University Press, 1991. 466 pp.

Graubard, Stephen R., ed. *Eastern Europe . . . Central Europe . . . Europe.* Boulder, Colo.: Westview Press, 1991. 354 pp.

Grémion, Pierre, and Pierre Hassner, eds. *Vents d'est: Vers l'Europe des états de droit?* Paris: Presses Universitaires de France, 1990. 141 pp.

Grothausen, Klaus-Detlev, ed. *Bulgaria.* Göttingen: Vandehoeck & Ruprecht, 1990. 815 pp.

Gruhler, Wolfram, et al., eds. *Wirtschaftliche und soziale Perspektiven der deutschen Einheit.* Cologne: Institut der deutschen Wirtschaft, 1990. 271 pp.

Gysi, Gregor. *Wir brauchen einen dritten Weg: Selbstverständnis und Program der PDS.* East Berlin: Konkret Literatur Verlag, 1990. 220 pp.

Havel, Václav. *Disturbing the Peace: A Conversation with Karel Hvizdala.* New York: A. Knopf, 1990. 228 pp.

Hedeler, Wladislaw. *Stalins Erbe: Stalinismus und deutsche Arbeiterbewegung.* East Berlin: Militärverlag, 1990. 64 pp.

Herles, Helmut, and Ewald Rose. *Parlaments-Szenen einer deutschen Revolution: Bundestag und Volkskammer im November 1989.* Bonn: Bouvier Verlag, 1990. 223 pp.

Heuer, Uwe-James. *Marxismus und Demokratie.* East Berlin: Staatsverlag, 1989. 448 pp.

Hoffman, Jürgen, ed. *Es ging um Deutschland: Vorschläge der DDR zur Konföderation zwischen beiden deutschen Staaten.* East Berlin: Dietz Verlag, 1990. 130 pp.

Hoppert, Leo. *Egon reiss die Mauer ein . . . Leipziger Demo-Sprüche.* Münster: Coppenrather Verlag, 1990. 96 pp.

Jasiński, Jerzy, ed. *Problems of Social Maladjustment and Crime in Poland.* Warsaw: Wydawnictwo Polskiej Akademii Nauk, 1989. 294 pp.

Johnson, Paul M. *Redesigning the Communist Economy: The Politics of Economic Reform in Eastern Europe.* Boulder, Colo.: East European Monographs (distributed by Columbia University Press), 1989. 281 pp.

Kennedy, Michael D. *Professionals, Power and Solidarity in Poland: A Critical Sociology of Soviet-type Society.* New York: Cambridge University Press, 1990. 520 pp.

Klein, Fritz. *The Reason behind the Crisis of the SED and the PDS.* East Berlin: Panorama DDR, 1990. 12 leaves.

Klier, Freya. *Lüg Vaterland.* Munich: Kindler Verlag, 1990. 189 pp.

Knabe, Hubertus, ed. *Aufbruch in eine andere DDR: Reformer und Oppositionelle zur Zukunft ihres Landes.* Reinbek bei Hamburg: Rowohlt, 1989. 318 pp.

Kornai, János. *The Road to a Free Economy: Shifting from a Socialist System, the Example of Hungary.* New York: W. W. Norton: 1990. 224 pp.

Kott, Jan, ed. *Four Decades of Polish Essays.* Evanston, Ill.: Northwestern University Press, 1990. 403 pp.

Krenz, Egon. *Wenn Mauern fallen.* Vienna: Paul Neff Verlag, 1990. 245 pp.

Kurz, Robert. *Auf der Suche nach dem verlorenen sozialistischen Ziel.* Erlangen: Verlag Marxistische Kritik, 1989. 97 pp.

Laba, Roman. *The Roots of Solidarity.* Princeton, N.J.: Princeton University Press, 1991. 247 pp.

Land, Rainer. *Das Umbaupapier (DDR): Argumente gegen die Wiedervereinigung.* Berlin: Rotbuch Verlag, 1990. 189 pp.

Langguth, Gerd. *Berlin and the "German Question": The Berlin Policy of the German Democratic Republic.* Boulder, Colo.: Westview Press, 1990. 150 pp.

Lees, Michael. *The Rape of Serbia: The British Role in Tito's Grab for Power, 1943–1944.* New York: Harcourt Brace Jovanovich, 1990. 348 pp.

Loew, Konrad, ed. *Beharrung und Wandel: die DDR und die Reformen des Mikhail Gorbatschow*. Stuttgart: F. Steiner Verlag, 1990. 387 pp.

Lühr, Hans Peter, et al., comps. *Wir sind das Volk: Aufbruch 89*. Leipzig: Mitteldeutscher Verlag, 1989. 95 pp.

Martin, David. *The Web of Disinformation: Churchill's Yugoslav Blunder*. San Diego, Calif.: Harcourt Brace Jovanovich, 1990. 425 pp.

Menge, Marlies. *"Ohne uns läuft nichts mehr": die Revolution in der DDR*. Stuttgart: DVA, 1990. 256 pp.

Michel, Robert. *Feuer Wasserland: DDR, das letzte Jahr*. Berlin: Tacheles Verlag, 1990. 183 pp.

Michta, Andrew A. *Red Eagle: The Army in Polish Politics, 1944–1988*. Stanford: Hoover Institution Press, 1990. 280 pp.

Molnár, Miklós. *From Béla Kun to János Kádár: Seventy Years of Hungarian Communism*. New York: Berg, 1990. 281 pp.

Myant, Martin. *The Czechoslovak Economy, 1948–1988: The Battle for Economic Reform*. Cambridge, Eng.: Cambridge University Press, 1989. 316 pp.

Myritz, Reinhard. *18. März 1990; die Parteien in der DDR und Ihre Programme*. Cologne: Institut der Deutschen Wirtschaft, 1990. 136 pp.

Nelson, Daniel N. *Balkan Imbroglio: Politics and Security in Southeastern Europe*. Boulder, Colo.: Westview Press, 1991. 128 pp.

Neues Forum. *Wirtschaftsreform der DDR*. Berlin: Nicolaische Verlagsbuchhandlung, 1990. 125 pp.

Partei des Demokratischen Sozialismus. *Eine neue Partei? Erneuerungskonferenz der PDS, Berlin, 8./9. September 1990*. East Berlin: PDS, 1990. 135 pp.

———. *Linke PDS Liste, für eine starke Linke Opposition: Gesamtdeutscher Wahlkongress der Linken Liste/PDS, Berlin, 15/16 September 1990*. East Berlin: PDS, 1990. 78 pp.

———. *Programm und Status*. East Berlin: Dietz Verlag, 1990. 64 pp.

———. *Wahlparteitag*. East Berlin: Dietz Verlag, 1990. 158 pp.

Prins, Gwyn. *Spring in the Winter: The 1989 Revolutions*. Manchester, Eng.: Manchester University Press, 1990. 252 pp.

Rachwald, Arthur R. *In Search of Poland: The Superpowers' Response to Solidarity, 1982–1989*. Stanford: Hoover Institution Press, 1990. 148 pp.

Rein, Gerhard, ed. *Die Opposition in der DDR: Entwürfe für einen anderen Sozialismus*. Berlin: Wichern Verlag, 1989. 223 pp.

Reuter, Ute, ed. *Dokumentation zur Entwicklung in der DDR vom 7. Oktober–19 November, 1989*. Bonn: Gesamtdeutsches Institut Bundesanstalt, 1990. 205 pp.

———, et al., eds. *Dokumentation zu den Volkskammerwahlen in der DDR am 18.3.1990*. Bonn: Gesamtdeutsches Institut Bundesanstalt, 1990. 60 pp.

Révész, Gábor. *Perestroika in Eastern Europe: Hungary's Economic Transformation, 1945–1988*. Boulder, Colo.: Westview Press, 1989. 182 pp.

Richet, Xavier. *The Hungarian Model*. New York: Cambridge University Press, 1989. 211 pp.

Rohnstock, Katrin. *Frauen in die Offensive: Texte und Materialen zu neuen Frauenbewegung in der DDR*. East Berlin: Dietz Verlag, 1990. 80 pp.

Rother, Karl-Heinz. *Parteiverfahren für Marx: hier irrten Kurt Hager und andere*. East Berlin: Dietz Verlag, 1990. 130 pp.

Runge, Irene. *Gregor Gysi: "Ich bin Opposition": Zwei Gespräche mit Gregor Gysi*. East Berlin: Dietz Verlag, 1990. 127 pp.

Rupnik, Jacques. *The Other Europe: The Rise and Fall of Communism in East-Central Europe*. New York: Schocken Books, 1990. 291 pp.

Scherzer, Landolf. *Der Erste: eine Reportage aus der DDR*. Cologne: Kiepenhauer und Witsch, 1989. 211 pp.

Schlosser, Horst Dieter. *Die deutsche Sprache in der DDR: zwischen Stalinismus und Demokratie*. Cologne: Verlag Wissenschaft und Politik, 1990. 232 pp.

Schumann, Frank, ed. *100 Tage die die DDR erschütteten*. East Berlin: Neues Leben; West Berlin: Elefanten Press, 1990. 191 pp.

Shoup, Paul S., ed. *Problems of Balkan Security: Southeastern Europe in the 1990s*. Washington, D.C.: Wilson Center Press, 1990. 286 pp.

Sobell, Vladimir. *The CMEA in Crisis: Toward a New European Order*. New York: Center for Strategic and International Studies/Praeger, 1990. 118 pp.

Sodaro, Michael J. *Moscow, Germany and the West from Khrushchev to Gorbachev*. Ithaca, N.Y.: Cornell University Press, 1991. 424 pp.

Spittmann, Ilse, and Gisela Helwig, eds. *Chronik der Ereignisse in der DDR*. Cologne: Edition Deutschland Archiv, 1990. 96 pp.

———. *Von der SBZ zur DDR, 1945–1949.* Cologne: Verlag Wissenschaft und Politik, 1989. 288 pp.

Staar, Richard F., ed. *East-Central Europe and the USSR.* New York: St. Martin's Press; London: Macmillan, 1991. ca. 220 pp.

Stokes, Gale, ed. *From Stalinism to Pluralism: A Documentary History of Eastern Europe since 1945.* New York: Oxford University Press, 1991. 267 pp.

Swoboda, Jörg, ed. *Revolution der Kerzen: Christen in den Umwälzungen der DDR.* Wuppertal: Oncken, Verlag, 1990. 320 pp.

Tieding, Wilfried, comp. *Ein Volk im Aufbruch: die DDR im Herbst 89.* Berlin: Panorama DDR, 1990. 46 pp.

Tomaszewski, Jerzy. *The Socialist Regimes of East Central Europe: Their Establishment and Consolidation, 1944–1967.* New York: Routledge, 1989. 305 pp.

Venohr, Wolfgang. *Die roten Preussen: vom wundersamen Aufstieg der DDR in Deutschland.* Erlangen: Straube, 1990. 360 pp.

Weber, Christian. *Alltage einer friedlichen Revolution: Notizen aus der DDR.* Stuttgart: Quell, 1990. 120 pp.

Weichhardt, Reiner, ed. *The Central and East European Economies in the 1990s: Prospects and Constraints.* Brussels: NATO Economic Directorate, 1990. 221 pp.

Winkel, Gabriele. *Konservatismusforschung in der DDR, 1971–1990.* Jena, E. Germany: Universitätsbibliothek, 1990. 246 pp.

Wroblewsky, Clement, ed. *"Da wachste eines Morgens auf und hast 'nen Bundeskanzler": wie der DDR-Bürger über ihre Zukunft denken.* Hamburg: Rasch und Röhring Verlag, 1990. 238 pp.

USSR

Adzhubei, Aleksei. *Te desiat'let.* Moscow: Sovetskaia Rossiia, 1989. 333 pp.

Alexander, Edward. *The Serpent and the Bees: A KGB Chronicle.* Lanham, Md.: University Press of America, 1990. 279 pp.

Alexeyeva, Ludmilla, and Paul Goldberg. *The Thaw Generation: Coming of Age in the Post-Stalin Era.* Boston: Little, Brown, 1990. 339 pp.

Armstrong, John A. *Ukrainian Nationalism.* Englewood, Colo.: Ukrainian Academic Press, 1990. 271 pp.

Balzer, Harley D., ed. *Five Years That Shook the World: Gorbachev's Perestroika.* Boulder, Colo.: Westview Press, 1991. 268 pp.

Benn, David W. *Persuasion and Soviet Politics.* Oxford, Eng.: Basil Blackwell, 1989. 243 pp.

Black, J. L., and Norman Hillmer, eds. *Nearly Neighbors: From Cold War to Détente and Beyond.* Kingston, Ontario: Carleton Series in Soviet and East European Studies, 1989. 174 pp.

Bon, Alexander, and Robert Van Vren, eds. *Nationalism in the USSR: Problems of Nationalities.* Amsterdam: Second World Center, 1989. 131 pp.

Borovik, Artyom. *The Hidden War: A Russian Journalist's Account of the Soviet War in Afghanistan.* New York: Atlantic Monthly Press, 1990. 288 pp.

Braun, Aurel, ed. *The Soviet-East European Relationship: The Prospects for Adaptation.* Boulder, Colo.: Westview Press, 1990. 200 pp.

Breslauer, George W., et al. *Soviet Strategy in the Middle East.* Boston: Unwin Hyman, 1990. 320 pp.

Brown, Archie, ed. *Political Leadership in the Soviet Union.* Bloomington: Indiana University Press, 1989. 245 pp.

Brumberg, Abraham. *Chronicle of a Revolution: A Western-Soviet Inquiry into Perestroika.* New York: Pantheon, 1990. 266 pp.

Cimbala, Stephen J., ed. *The Soviet Challenge in the 1990s.* Westport, Conn.: Greenwood Press, 1989. 325 pp.

Clark, William A. *Soviet Regional Elite Mobility after Khrushchev.* New York: Praeger, 1989. 206 pp.

Clemens, Walter C., Jr. *Can Russia Change?* Boston: Unwin Hyman, 1990. 384 pp.

Cohen, Stephen F., and Katrina van den Heuvel. *Voices of Glasnost: Interviews with Gorbachev's Reformers.* New York: Norton, 1989. 339 pp.

Colton, Timothy J., and Thane Gustafson, eds. *Soldiers and the Soviet State: Civil-Military Relations from Brezhnev to Gorbachev.* Princeton, N.J.: Princeton University Press, 1990. 370 pp.

Crummey, Robert O., ed. *Reform in Russia and the USSR: Past and Prospects.* Urbana: University of Illinois Press, 1989. 318 pp.

Davies, R. W. *Soviet History in the Gorbachev Revolution.* Bloomington: Indiana University Press, 1989. 232 pp.

Doder, Dusko, and Louise Branson. *Gorbachev: A Heretic in the Kremlin.* New York: Viking, 1990. 450 pp.

Eklof, Ben. *Soviet Briefing: Gorbachev and the Reform Period*. Boulder, Colo.: Westview, 1989. 195 pp.

Fehér, Ferenc, and Andrew Arato, eds. *Gorbachev: The Debate*. Atlantic Highlands, N.J.: Humanities Press, 1989. 234 pp.

Figatner, Iu. Iu. ed. *Deiateli SSSR i revoliutsionnogo dvizheniia Rossii*. Moscow: Sovetskaia entsiklopediia, 1989. 831 pp.

Ford, Robert A. D. *Our Man in Moscow: Diplomat's Reflections on the Soviet Union*. Toronto: University of Toronto Press, 1989. 356 pp.

Garrard, John, and Carol Garrard. *Inside the Soviet Writers' Union*. New York: Free Press, 1990. 303 pp.

Gleason, Gregory. *Federalism and Nationalism: The Struggle for Republican Rights in the USSR*. Boulder, Colo.: Westview Press, 1990. 170 pp.

Glotzer, Albert. *Trotsky: Memoir and Critique*. Buffalo, N.Y.: Prometheus Books, 1989. 343 pp.

Golan, Galia. *Soviet Policies in the Middle East from World War Two to Gorbachev*. New York: Cambridge University Press, 1990. 319 pp.

Gottstein, Klaus, ed. *Western Perceptions of Soviet Goals*. Boulder, Colo.: Westview Press, 1990. 440 pp.

Gray, Francine du Plessix. *Soviet Women: Walking the Tightrope*. New York: Doubleday, 1990. 213 pp.

Gromyko, Andrei. *Memoirs*. New York: Doubleday, 1990. 414 pp.

Hajda, Lubomyr, and Mark Beissinger, eds. *Nationalities Factor in Soviet Politics and Society*. Boulder, Colo.: Westview Press, 1990. 331 pp.

Hazan, Baruch A. *Gorbachev and His Enemies: The Struggle for Perestroika*. Boulder, Colo.: Westview Press, 1990. 320 pp.

———. *Gorbachev's Gamble: The 19th All-Union Party Conference*. Boulder, Colo.: Westview Press, 1990. 485 pp.

Heldmann, Henri. *Les fils du peuple de Staline à Gorbatchev*. Paris: Henri Heldmann, 1989. 420 pp.

Helf, Gavin. *A Biographical Directory of Soviet Regional Party Leaders, 1990*. Boulder, Colo.: Westview Press, 1990. 250 pp.

Heller, Agnes, and Ferenc Fehér. *From Yalta to Glasnost: The Dismantling of Stalin's Empire*. New York: Basil Blackwell, 1990. 228 pp.

Herspring, Dale R. *The Soviet High Command: Personalities and Politics*. Princeton, N.J.: Princeton University Press, 1990. 322 pp.

Hill, Ronald J., and Jan Ake Dellenbrant, eds. *Gorbachev and Perestroika: Towards a New Socialism?* Aldershot, Hants., Eng.: Elgar for the International Library of Studies in Communism, 1989. 234 pp.

International Institute for Strategic Studies. *The Military Balance, 1990–1991*. London: IISS, Autumn 1990. 245 pp.

Jackson, George, ed. *Dictionary of the Russian Revolution*. New York: Greenwood Press, 1989. 704 pp.

Jones, Anthony, et al., eds. *Soviet Social Problems*. Boulder, Colo.: Westview Press, 1991. 337 pp.

———, ed. *Soviet Update, 1989–1990*. Boulder, Colo.: Westview Press, 1991, 276 pp.

Jones, Robert A. *The Soviet Concept of "Limited Sovereignty" from Lenin to Gorbachev*. New York: St. Martin's Press, 1990. 337 pp.

Kagarlitsky, Boris. *The Dialectic of Change*. New York: Verso, 1990. 393 pp.

Kaiser, Robert G. *Why Gorbachev Happened: His Triumphs and His Failures*. New York: Simon and Schuster, 1990. 476 pp.

Kamenetsky, Ihor, ed. *The Tragedy of Vinnytsa: Materials on Stalin's Policy of Extermination in Ukraine during the Great Purge, 1936–1938*. Toronto: Ukrainian Historical Association, 1989. 265 pp.

Khobo, Kh., ed. *Osmyslit' kul't Stalina: Perestroika—glasnost', demokratiia*. Moscow: Progress, 1989. 650 pp.

Khrushchev, Sergei. *Khrushchev on Khrushchev: An Inside Account of the Man and His Era by His Son*. Boston: Little, Brown, 1990. 423 pp.

———. *Materialy k biografii*. Moscow: Politizdat, 1989. 366 pp.

Kokeyev, Mikhail, and Andrei Androsov. *Verification: The Soviet Stance*. New York: United Nations, 1990. 125 pp.

Laird, Robbin F., and Susan L. Clark, eds. *The USSR and the Western Alliance*. Boston: Unwin Hyman, 1990. 269 pp.

Lapidus, Gail W. *State and Society in the Soviet Union*. Boulder, Colo.: Westview Press, 1990. 300 pp.

Likhachev, Dmitrii S. *Reflections on Russia*. Boulder, Colo.: Westview Press, 1990. 150 pp.

Macgregor, Douglas A. *The Soviet-East German Military Alliance*. New York: Cambridge University Press, 1989. 186 pp.

Mammarella, Giuseppe. *Da Yalta alla perestrojka*. Bari, Italy: Laterza, 1990. 153 pp.

Mann, Dawn, et al. *The Supreme Soviet: A Biographical Directory*. Washington, D.C.: Center for Strategic and International Studies, 1989. 168 pp.

Marchenko, Anatoly. *To Live Like Everyone*. New York: Henry Holt, 1989. 227 pp.

Matthews, Mervyn. *Patterns of Deprivation in the Soviet Union under Brezhnev and Gorbachev*. Stanford: Hoover Institution Press, 1989. 158 pp.

Medvedev, Roy, and Giulietto Chiesa. *Time of Change. An Insider's View of Russia's Transformation*. New York: Pantheon Books, 1989. 346 pp.

Melville, Andrei, and Gail W. Lapidus, eds. *The Glasnost' Papers: Voices on Reform from Moscow*. Boulder, Colo.: Westview Press, 1990. 350 pp.

Mlynar, Zdenek. *Can Gorbachev Change the Soviet Union?* Boulder, Colo.: Westview Press, 1990. 194 pp.

Nahaylo, Bohdan, and Victor Swoboda. *Soviet Disunion*. New York: Free Press, 1990. 432 pp.

Paul, Ellen Frankel, ed. *Totalitarianism at the Crossroads*. New Brunswick, N.J.: Transaction Books, 1990. 217 pp.

Petro, Nicolai N., ed. *Christianity and Russian Culture in Soviet Society*. Boulder, Colo.: Westview Press, 1990. 244 pp.

Pomper, Philip. *Lenin, Trotsky, and Stalin: The Intelligentsia and Power*. New York: Columbia University Press, 1990. 446 pp.

Pozner, Vladimir. *Parting with Illusions*. New York: Atlantic Monthly Press, 1990. 324 pp.

Priimak, N. I., ed. *Partiinye konferentsii: ikh mesto i rol' v deiatel'nosti KPSS*. Leningrad: Izdatel'stvo leningradskogo universiteta, 1990. 169 pp.

Rahr, Alexander, comp. *A Biographical Directory of 100 Leading Soviet Officials*. Boulder, Colo.: Westview Press, 1990. 210 pp.

Raleigh, Donald J., ed. *Soviet Historians and Perestroika: The First Phase*. Armonk, N.Y.: M. E. Sharpe, 1989. 289 pp.

Ramet, Pedro. *The Soviet-Syrian Relationship since 1955*. Boulder, Colo.: Westview Press, 1990. 276 pp.

Saivetz, Carol R., ed. *The Soviet Union in the Third World*. Boulder, Colo.: Westview Press, 1989. 230 pp.

Sakharov, Andrei. *Memoirs*. New York: Knopf, 1990. 773 pp.

Sand, Gregory William. *Soviet Aims in Central America: The Case of Nicaragua*. New York: Praeger, 1989. 138 pp.

Simon, Gerhard. *Nationalism and Policy toward Nationalities in the Soviet Union*. Boulder, Colo.: Westview Press, 1990. 467 pp.

Smith, Hedrick. *The New Russians*. New York: Random House, 1990. 621 pp.

Soviet Union. S'ezd narodnykh deputatov. *Congress of the People's Deputies of the USSR: Documents and Materials, May 25–June 29, 1989*. Moscow, Novosti Press, 1989. 111 pp.

Staar, Richard F. *Foreign Policies of the Soviet Union*. Stanford: Hoover Institution Press, 1991. 352 pp.

Taylor, S. J. *Stalin's Apologist, Walter Duranty: The New York Times's Man in Moscow*. New York: Oxford University Press, 1990. 404 pp.

Thom, Françoise. *The Gorbachev Phenomenon: A History of Perestroika*. London: J. Spiers, 1989. 141 pp.

Thompson, Terry L. *Ideology and Policy: The Political Uses of Doctrine in the Soviet Union*. Boulder, Colo.: Westview Press, 1989. 220 pp.

Tolz, Vera. *The USSR's Emerging Multiparty System*. New York: Praeger, 1990. 122 pp.

Urban, Michael E. *An Algebra of Soviet Power: Elite Circulation in the Belorussian Republic, 1966–86*. New York: Cambridge University Press, 1989. 183 pp.

Van Tuyll, Hubert P. *Feeding the Bear: American Aid to the Soviet Union, 1941–1945*. Westport, Conn.: Greenwood Press, 1989. 212 pp.

Van Voren, Robert, ed. *Soviet Psychiatric Abuse in the Gorbachev Era*. Amsterdam: International Association on the Political Use of Psychiatry, 1989. 112 pp.

Weichhardt, Reiner, ed. *Les Réformes économiques en URSS: la mise en oeuvre*. Brussels, NATO, 1989. 289 pp.

Yeltsin, Boris. *Against the Grain: An Autobiography*. New York: Summit Books, 1990. 263 pp.

White, Stephen. *Gorbachev in Power*. Cambridge, Eng.: Cambridge University Press, 1990. 268 pp.

Woodby, Sylvia, et al., eds. *Restructuring Soviet Ideology*. Boulder, Colo.: Westview Press, 1990. 226 pp.

MIDDLE EAST

Aronson, Geoffrey. *Israel, Palestine and the Intifada: Creating Facts on the West Bank*. London and New York: Kegan Paul International, 1990. 376 pp.

Aruri, Nasser H., ed. *Occupation: Israel over Palestine*. 2d ed. Belmont, Mass.: Association of Arab-American University Graduates, 1989. 467 pp.

Beinin, Joel. *Was the Red Flag Flying There? Marxist Politics and the Arab-Israeli Conflict in Egypt and Israel, 1948–1965*. Berkeley: University of California Press, 1990. 251 pp.

Bocharov, Gennady. *Russian Roulette: Afghanistan through Russian Eyes*. New York: Harper Collins, 1990. 187 pp.

Borovik, Artyom. *The Hidden War: A Russian Journalist's Account of the Soviet War in Afghanistan*. New York: Atlantic Monthly Press, 1990. 288 pp.

Entelis, John P. *Culture and Counterculture in Moroccan Politics*. Boulder, Colo.: Westview Press, 1989. 131 pp.

Fisk, Robert. *Pity the Nation: The Abduction of Lebanon*. New York: Atheneum, 1990. 678 pp.

Freedman, Robert O. *Moscow and the Middle East: Soviet Policy since the Invasion of Afghanistan*. New York: Cambridge University Press, 1991. 432 pp.

Gause, F. Gregory, III. *Saudi-Yemeni Relations: Domestic Structures and Foreign Influence*. New York: Columbia University Press, 1990. 233 pp.

Gowers, Andrew, and Tony Walker. *Behind the Myth: Yasser Arafat and the Palestinian Revolution*. London: W. H. Allen, 1990. 356 pp.

Al-Haj, Majid, and Henry Rosenfeld. *Arab Local Government in Israel*. Boulder, Colo.: Westview Press, 1990. 211 pp.

Halliday, Fred. *Revolution and Foreign Policy: The Case of South Yemen, 1967–1987*. New York: Cambridge University Press, 1989. 327 pp.

Hinnebusch, Raymond A. *Authoritarian Power and State Formation in Ba'thist Syria: Army, Party, and Peasant*. Boulder, Colo.: Westview Press, 1990. 352 pp.

Ismael, Tareq Y., and Rifa'at El-Sa'id. *The Communist Movement in Egypt, 1920–1988*. Syracuse, N.Y.: Syracuse University Press, 1990. 218 pp.

Kostiner, Joseph. *South Yemen's Revolutionary Strategy, 1970–1985*. Boulder, Colo.: Westview Press, 1990. 110 pp.

Livingstone, Neil C., and David Halevy. *Inside the PLO*. New York: William Morrow, 1990. 336 pp.

McDowall, David. *Palestine and Israel: The Uprising and Beyond*. Berkeley: University of California Press, 1989. 322 pp.

Nassar, Jamal R., and Roger Heacock, eds. *Intifada: Palestine at the Crossroads*. New York: Praeger, 1990. 191 pp.

Peretz, Don. *Intifada: The Palestinian Uprising*. Boulder, Colo.: Westview Press, 1990. 246 pp.

Reich, Bernard, ed. *Political Leaders of the Contemporary Middle East and North Africa: A Biographical Dictionary*. New York: Greenwood Press, 1990. 557 pp.

Rezun, Miron, ed. *Iran at the Crossroads: Global Relations in a Turbulent Decade*. Boulder, Colo.: Westview Press, 1990. 250 pp.

Richards, Alan, and John Waterbury. *The Political Economy of the Middle East: State, Class and Economic Development*. Boulder, Colo.: Westview Press, 1990. 510 pp.

Sabagh, Georges. *The Modern Economic and Social History of the Middle East in Its World Context*. New York: Cambridge University Press, 1990. 161 pp.

Shaked, Haim, and Ami Ayalon, eds. *Middle East Contemporary Survey*. Boulder, Colo.: Westview Press, 1990. 809 pp.

Wenner, Manfred W. *The Yemen Arab Republic*. Boulder, Colo.: Westview Press, 1990. 128 pp.

WESTERN EUROPE

Ashdown, Paddy. *Citizen's Britain: A Radical Agenda for the 1990's*. London: Fourth Estate, 1989. 159 pp.

Austria, Communist Party of. *Frauen der KPÖ: Gespräche und Porträte*. Vienna: Globus Verlag, 1989. 74 pp.

Baker, John A. *Italian Communism*. Washington, D.C.: National Defense University Press, 1989. 282 pp.

Bark, Dennis L., and David Gress. *A History of Germany*. Oxford: Basil Blackwell, 1989. 2 vols.

Belorgy, Jean-Michel. *La Gauche et les pauvres*. Paris: Syros, 1989. 223 pp.

Benson, John. *The Working Class in Great Britain, 1850–1939*. Harlow, Eng.: Longman, 1989. 219 pp.

Berger, Denis. *Le Spectre défait. La fin du communisme?* Arles, France: Coutaz, 1990. 156 pp.

Bew, Paul. *The Dynamics of Irish Politics*. London: Lawrence Wishart, 1989. 178 pp.

Braunthal, Gerard. *Political Loyalty and Public Service in West Germany: The 1972 Decree against*

Radicals and Its Consequences. Amherst: University of Massachusetts Press, 1990. 249 pp.

Brandt, Willy. *Erinnerungen.* Frankfurt/M: Propylaen, 1989. 512 pp.

Breen, Richard. *Understanding Contemporary Ireland: State, Class and Development in the Republic of Ireland.* London: Gill and Macmillan, 1989. 248 pp.

Brocci, Giancarlo. *Ridatemi il PCI: la grande crisi del partito nell'analisi e nell'elaborazione di un communista professionista.* Montepulciano, Italy: Editori del Grifo, 1989. 125 pp.

Bundesministerium für innerdeutsche Beziehungen, ed. *Bürger und Staat: Eine vergleichende Untersuchung zu Praxis und Recht der BRD und der DDR.* Cologne: Verlag Wissenschaft und Politik, 1990. 330 pp.

Canfora, Luciano. *La crisi del Este e il PCI.* Bari, Italy: Edizioni Dedalo, 1990. 123 pp.

Chambaz, Jacques. *Réalités et stratégie: le Parti Communiste Français, une démarche nouvelle.* Paris: Messidor, 1990. 160 pp.

Cohen, Yolande. *Les Jeunes, le socialisme et la guerre.* Paris: L'Harmattan, 1989. 253 pp.

Colajanni, Napoleone. *La resistibile ascesa di Achille Occhetto.* Florence: Ponte alle Grazie, 1989. 222 pp.

Communist Party of Great Britain. *The Anti-Fascist People's Front in the Armed Forces: The Communist Contribution, 1939–1946.* London: Communist Party History Group, 1990. 39 pp.

––––––. *Labour-Communist Relations, 1920–1951. Part I: 1920–1935.* London: Communist Party History Group, 1990. 72 pp.

Curi, Umberto. *Lo scudo di Achille: il PCI nella grande crisi.* Milan: Angeli, 1990. 115 pp.

Dalmasso, Sergio. *Il caso "Manifesto" e il PCI degli anni '60.* Torino, Italy: Cric, 1989. 162 pp.

De Giorgi, Fulvio. *La storiografia di tendenza marxista e la storia locale in Italia nel dopoguerra.* Milan: Via e pensiero, 1989. 180 pp.

De Giovanni, Biagoio. *La nottola di Minerva: PCI e nuovo reformismo.* Rome: Editori Riuniti, 1989. 130 pp.

Denver, David. *Elections and Voting Behavior in Britain.* Oxford, Eng.: P. Allan, 1989. 155 pp.

Dreyfus, Michel. *PCF: crises et dissidence de 1920 à nos jours.* Brussels: Complexe, 1989. 285 pp.

Fabien, Jean. *Les Nouveaux secrets des communistes.* Paris: Albin Michel, 1990. 198 pp.

Fay, Victor. *La Flamme et la cindre: histoire d'une vie militante.* Vincennes: Presses Universitaires, 1990. 274 pp.

Field, Frank. *Losing Out: The Emergence of Britain's Underclass.* Oxford, Eng.: Basil Blackwell, 1989. 199 pp.

Flores d'Arcais, Paolo. *Oltre il PCI: per un partito libertario e reformista.* Genoa, Italy: Marietti, 1990. 143 pp.

Galante, Severino. *Alla ricerca della potenza perduta: la politica internazionale della DC e del PCI negli anni Cinquanta.* Manduria, Italy: Lacaita, 1990. 147 pp.

Gallo, Max. *La Gauche est morte. Vive la Gauche!* Paris: Odile Jacob, 1990. 233 pp.

Gandillot, Thierry, and Thomas Kamm, eds. *Mille jours pour réussir l'Europe? Vingt patrons vous donnent les clés de 1993.* Paris: J. C. Lattes, 1990. 257 pp.

Gayssot, Jean-Claude, *Le Parti communiste français.* Paris: Messidor/Editions Sociales, 1989. 102 pp.

Gerard-Libois, Jules. *Elections et électeurs en Belgique.* Brussels: CRISP, 1989. 223 pp.

Gianmanco, Rosanna Mulazzi. *The Catholic-Communist Dialogue in Italy: 1944 to the Present.* New York: Praeger, 1989. 171 pp.

Giraud, Henri Christian. *De Gaulle et les communistes.* Vol. 2. Paris: Albin Michel, 1989. 485 pp.

Guidici, Marco. *Dopo il PCI: cronica di una svolte annunciata.* Rome: Cinque Lune, 1990. 139 pp.

Grass, Günter. *Two States, One Nation?* New York: Harcourt Brace Jovanovich, 1990. 123 pp.

Groux, Guy, and René Mauriaux. *La CFDT: La vie politique.* Paris: Economica, 316 pp.

Hughes, Colin. *Labour Rebuilt: The New Model Party.* London: Fourth Estate, 1990. 217 pp.

Italy, Communist Party of. *Viaggio nel cuore del PCI: inchiesta sugli orientamenti e sugli umori del popolo comunista.* Rome: Rinascita, 1990. 76 pp.

Judick, Günter, et al., eds. *KPD, 1945–1968: Dokumente.* Neuss, W. Germany: Marxistische Blätter, 1989. 2 vols.

Juquin, Pierre, et al. *Pour une alternative verte en Europe.* Paris: Editions de la Découverte, 1990. 128 pp.

Koch, Karl. *West Germany Today.* London: Routledge, 1989. 169 pp.

Kraus, Elisabeth. *Ministerien für das ganze Deutschland? Der alliierte Kontrollrat und die Frage gesamtdeutscher Zentralverwaltungen.* Munich: Verlag R. Oldenbourg, 1990. 375 pp.

Margolies, David, and Linden Peach, eds. *Christo pher Caudwell: Marxism and Culture*. London: .11London University Press, 1989. 110 pp.

Meade, Robert C. *The Red Brigades: The Story of Italian Terrorism*. New York: St. Martin's, 1990. 301 pp.

Mensing, Wilhelm. *Nehmen oder Annehmen: die verbotene KPD auf der Suche nach politischer Teilhabe*. Zurich: Ed Interform, 1989. 113 pp.

Moltedo, Guido. *PCI, la grande svolta: Il nome, il simbolo, il nuovo partito*. Rome: Edizioni Associate, 1989. 175 pp.

Moreira, Vital. *Reflexões sobre o PCP*. Lisbon: Editorial Inquerito, 1990. 165 pp.

Moss, David. *The Politics of Left-wing Violence in Italy, 1959-1975*. London: Columbus Press, 1990. 423 pp.

Nanetti, Raffaella Y., and Raimondo Catanzaro, eds. *Italian Politics: A Review*. Vol. 4. London: Pinter Publishers, 1990. 220 pp.

Ott, Matthias. *Deutschland—eine Ausreisemärchen: die dokumentarische Geschichte einer Übersiedlung aus der DDR*. Koblenz, Germany: Verlag Friedrich Bublies, 1990. 180 pp.

Pistillo, Michele. *Gramsci come Moro?* Manduria, Italy: Lacaita, 1989. 322 pp.

Portugal. Partido Comunista Português. *Programa e estatutos do PCP*. Lisbon: Ediçiões Avante, 1989. 143 pp.

Pudal, Bernard. *Prendre parti: pour une sociologie historique du PCF*. Paris: Presses de la Fondation Nationale des Sciences Politiques, 1989. 329 pp.

Puete, Isaac. *Le Communisme libertaire*. Paris: Le Groupe Fresnes-Antony de la Fédération Anarchiste, 1989. 45 pp.

Rubbi, Antonio. *Incontri con Gorbaciov*. Rome: Editori Riuniti, 1990. 307 pp.

Russo, Emilio. *Antonio Gramsci*. Rimini, Italy: Luise, 1990. 195 pp.

Schöneburg, Volkmar. *Kriminalwissenschaftliches Erbe der KPD, 1919-1933*. East Berlin: Staatsverlag der DDR, 1989. 103 pp.

Schulz, Eberhard. *Die deutsche Frage und die Nachbarn im Osten*. Munich: Oldenbourg Verlag, 1989. 169 pp.

Schwarz, Anne. *Reform und Revolution: Neue strategische Überlegungen in kommunistischen Parteien Westeuropas*. Berlin: Akademie für Gesellschaftswissenschaften, 1990. 235 pp.

Schweissfurth, Theodor. *Fahrplan für ein neues Deutschland*. Erlangen, Germany: Straube, 1990. 217 pp.

Seiffert, Wolfgang. *Die Deutschen und Gorbatschow: Chance für einen Interessenausgleich*. Erlangen, Germany: Straube, 1990. 250 pp.

———. *Das ganze Deutschland: Perspektiven der Wiedervereinigung*. Munich: Piper, 1989. 189 pp.

Seve, Lucien. *Communisme, quel second souffle?* Paris: Messidor, 1990. 284 pp.

Smith, Gordon, William E. Paterson, and Peter H. Merkl, eds. *Developments in West German Politics*. Durham, N.C.: Duke University Press, 1990. 400 pp.

Soziale oder sozialistische Demokratie? Beiträge zur Geschichte der Linken in der Bundesrepublik. Marburg, Germany: SP-Verlag Norbert Schüren, 1989. 302 pp.

Spadolini, Giovanni. *San Marino: l'idea della Repubblica: con documenti inediti dell'Archivo di Pascale Villari*. Florence: Le Monnier, 1989. 129 pp.

Stavrakis, Peter J. *Moscow and Greek Communism, 1944-1949*. Ithaca, N.Y.: Cornell University Press, 1989. 243 pp.

Steinberg, Rolf, et al. *Berlin in November*. Berlin: Nicolaische Verlagsbuchhandlung, 1989. 128 pp.

Stovall, Tyler Edward. *The Rise of the Paris Red Belt*. Berkeley: University of California Press, 1990. 249 pp.

Streiter, Rudolf. *Österreichs kommunistische Gewerkschafter in der 2. Republik*. Vienna: Österreichische Gewerkschaft, 1989. 267 pp.

Thies, Jochen, and Wolfgang Werner. *Das Ende der Teilung: Der Wandel in Deutschland und Osteuropa*. Bonn: Verlag für Internationale Politik, 1990. 340 pp.

Valentini, Chiara. *Il nome e la cosa: Viaggio nel PCI che cambia*. Milan: Feltrinelli, 1990. 187 pp.

Weber, Hermann. *"Weisse Flecken" in der Geschichte: die KPD-Opfer der stalinistischen Säuberungen und ihre Rehabilitierung*. Frankfurt/M: ISP Verlag, 1989. 168 pp.

Wyden, Peter. *The Wall: The Inside Story of Divided Berlin*. New York: Simon and Schuster, 1989. 762 pp.

Cumulative Index of Biographies

Index of Names

Index of Subjects